FISHERMAN'S FRIEND

Stephen Reynolds 1910 (*see page 373*)

Fisherman's Friend

A LIFE OF STEPHEN REYNOLDS

CHRISTOPHER SCOBLE

HALSGROVE

First published in Great Britain in 2000

British Library Cataloguing-in-Publication Data
A CIP record for this title is available from the British Library

ISBN 1 84114 092 9

HALSGROVE
PUBLISHING, MEDIA AND DISTRIBUTION

Halsgrove House
Lower Moor Way
Tiverton, Devon EX16 6SS
Tel: 01884 243242
Fax: 01884 243325
website: www.halsgrove.com

Printed and bound by The Cromwell Press Ltd, Trowbridge

For my mother
who introduced me
to S R

Contents

Illustrations

SECTION TWO

MAPS

drawn by John Gilkes

Acknowledgements

My first thanks must go to the current members of the firm of Woolley and Reynolds who have helped me in so many ways with papers, photographs and family anecdote: Stephen Wiltshire, grandson of Reynolds' sister, Dot; Frances Woodward, granddaughter of Bob and Mam, and daughter of Semaphore; Roger Elliott, grandson of Tom and Nellie; and Nigel Chanter, grandson of Bobby. I am equally grateful to Margaret Wallace, the daughter of Harold Wright, especially for her permission to quote from the unpublished writing of Stephen Reynolds.

For access to papers and use of copyright material, I have particularly to thank Annie Allen, Richard Garnett, Margaret Gibson Phillips, John Handford and Robert Machesney of Macmillan Archive, Ann E. Hardham, Duff Hart-Davis, Rosalinde Jenkins, Peter Nockles and staff of the John Rylands University Library, University of Manchester, Sheila Lindlar, Shaw McCloghry and Bloxham School, Grizelda Maurice, Anthony Mildmay-White, Christopher Sinclair-Stevenson, and Myfanwy Thomas. For other copyright permissions I am grateful to the Estate of Joseph Conrad and Cambridge University Press, John Johnson (Authors' Agent) Ltd., David Higham Associates, the Library Association, Random House Archive and Library, the Society of Authors in its own right and as literary representative of the Granville Barker and John Masefield Estates, the *Spectator*, and University of Sussex Library. If any untraced copyright holders would care to come forward, I should be happy to engage with them.

I owe a debt to the staff of a number of archives and libraries and for permission to quote from their collections. For their tireless assistance, I must single out in particular Cliff Farrington of the Humanities Research Center, University of Texas, and Ellen Howe and Russell Maylone of Northwestern University Library. But my thanks go also to Stephen Crook of the Berg Collection, New York Public Library; Philippa Bassett and University of Birmingham Library; Bodleian Library; Elizabeth James and staff of the British Library; British Library of Political and Economic Science; Cornell University Library; Devon Record Office, Exeter; Marie-Noëlle Maisonneuve and the Bibliothèque de l'École des Mines de Paris; Edinburgh University Library; Michael Meredith and Eton College Library; Forbes Magazine Collection; House of Lords Record Office; Huntington Library, San Marino, California; Library of the International Council for the Exploration of the Sea, Copenhagen; University of Illinois Library at Urbana-Champaign; Keele University Library; Lancashire Record Office, Preston; Manchester Central Library; Manchester City Council; Departmental Records, Ministry of

Agriculture, Fisheries and Food; Departmental Records, Ministry of Defence; National Library of Scotland; National Library of Wales; Clive Powell and the Trustees of the National Maritime Museum, Greenwich; George Orwell Archive, University of London; Polish Library, Hammersmith; Public Record Office; Punjab University Library; Queen's University Archives, Kingston, Ontario; Michael Bott and University of Reading Library; Central Library, Royal Military Academy, Sandhurst; RSPB Library, Sandy; City Librarian, Sheffield Libraries, Archives and Information Services; Rosalind Whitfield of Sid Vale Heritage Centre, Sidmouth Museum; Sue Tattersall and staff of Sturminster Newton Library; Pamela Colman and Lorna Haycock of the Wiltshire Archaeological and Natural History Society Library, Devizes Museum; Westcountry Studies Library, Exeter; Wiltshire Record Offce, Trowbridge. And my warmest personal thanks to my neighbours in the next village – Gerard Casey for allowing me to quote from his collection of papers of Philippa Powys, and Louise de Bruin for her patience in arranging access and fielding my questions.

I continue to be amazed by the kindness and enthusiasm of those whom I have approached for help in this enterprise. My thanks go also to Ron Appleton, Alan Bennett, Chuck and Diane Barbaz, Anthony Carew, Peter Daniels, Jane Deverell, John and Hilary Drew, Peter Foss, David Garforth-Bles, Robert Garforth-Bles, David Garnett, Kate Harrison, Gordon Jones, Reginald Lane, Rosemary Lauder, Tim Laycock, Kevin McCulloch, Campbell McMurray, Margaret Mead, Peter Melchett, Jeffrey Meyers, Zdzislaw Najder, Mary Paynter, Alan Pearsall, Henrietta Phipps, Anne Scott-James, Andrew Sewell, Judith Stinton, R. George Thomas, and Oliver Wilkinson.

I am grateful to John Osborne, the pioneer of Reynolds' research in the 1970s, for reading my manuscript and for help with photographs and papers. Finally, my special thanks to Theresa Tenbusch, who carried out two pieces of research for me at the University of Texas, to John Gilkes for the maps, and to Sara Hannant for the photographs.

CLS
Sturminster Newton
16 May 2000

Prologue
15 August 1906

Three o'clock on a Wednesday afternoon in late summer. It is warm and sunny, as it has been since morning. A cool breeze from the south-west gently freshens the air all around.

A young man is standing on the brow of the hill looking down the narrow green valley into the town whose houses cluster on either side of the steep slopes. He can see past the cornfields and pastures of the heather-capped hills out into the bay and the rippled waters of the English Channel. Little white houses are dotted among the trees near the sea. The sun shines on a window as if a star were resting on earth. A dog barks in the distance and a slight murmur rises up the valley.

He is short and sturdy, robust looking and yet at the same time strangely frail. His dark hair is parted neatly in the centre above a wide intelligent brow. There is a nervous tightness about his narrow mouth belied by the humorous lights that dance in his grey eyes beneath the little round wire-framed spectacles. A massive brindled Great Dane sits at his side, gazing too towards the town and the sea. You see her before you notice him. Both man and dog are hot and weary. They have walked a hundred dusty miles since Saturday. This at last is their destination.

He stares on down the valley as towards the lost domain. It is a moment suspended in time....

Meanwhile the world grinds on, revolving slowly on its axis, oblivious of him. Dr Grace is batting beautifully for the MCC at Lords as if the days of Queen Victoria had never ended. The King is on a motor tour of Homburg, the Kaiser seated at his side – the most unlikely picnic party in Europe. Gustav Mahler has spent the morning in his cabin among the trees at Maiernigg scoring his Symphony of a Thousand, regardless of expense. Marcel Proust is asleep in his suite at Versailles, dreaming of future Albertines.

The young man has no Albertine, neither past nor yet in prospect. Apart from the dog, he is utterly alone in the world. His family has cast him off. When his writing failed three years ago he had a breakdown and nearly died. Now he is on the road to recovery. This year's walk, and that last year, is indelible proof. So is his writing. The week before last he finished his first novel after two years' work. For the first time, he inhabits that strange no-man's-land between completing a book and starting the revision. He has no means of knowing whether it is very good or very bad.

He has earned himself a holiday. He has not been in this seaside town, where his breakdown occurred, for two years now. He plans to stay just a couple of days before marching on to Dartmoor. Just time to look up old friends, the fishermen......

The dog walks forward a few yards, stops, looks round and waits. In her look there is something very forbearing. She wants to move on.

In less than a quarter of an hour, they are on the esplanade that divides the town from the sea. It is packed with fashionable tourists taking their after-lunch stroll. Man and dog stand together on the sea wall gazing down on the activity on the beach below where fishermen are pushing off with boat loads of trippers – their summer catches.

The young man has located the entrance to the little square where he is to stay for the first time with the fisherman he met here three years ago. It is on the sea-front, just over the shore road, a narrow opening between a large hotel and a row of lodging houses.

The dog at his side, he crunches down the shingle path in hope of a bath, a cup of tea, a long-needed rest. He is on the brink of an encounter that will change his life – and, who knows, perhaps ours too.

He's only 28 and if his health does not give out
we may yet have some comfort from that baby.
Joseph Conrad to John Galsworthy 10 December 1909

As to my being a good friend to fishermen, as you say. . . .
They've been better friends to me, and when I first
went to live with them I needed it more than they do.
Stephen Reynolds to Francis Mildmay 21 October 1914

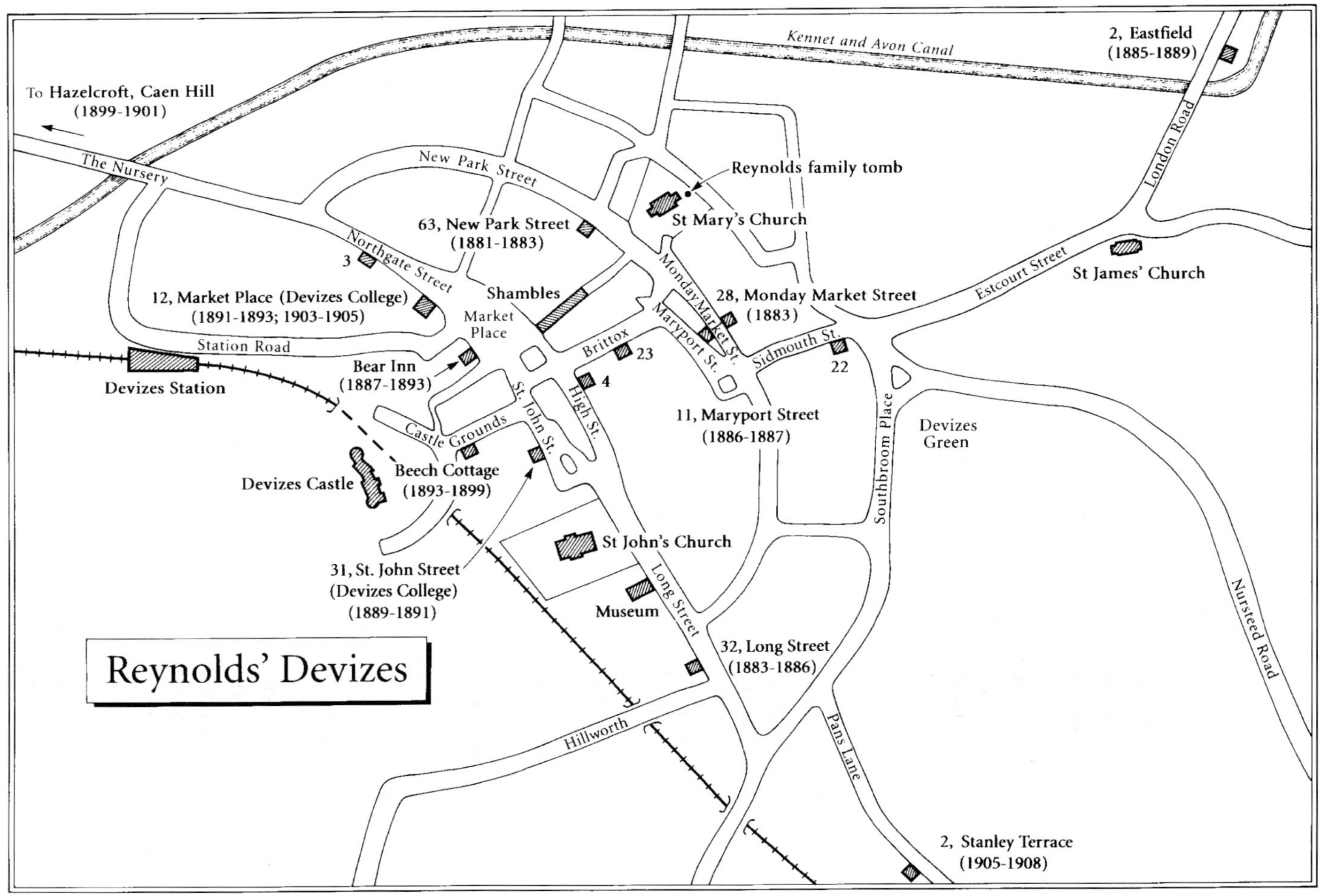
Reynolds' Devizes
Kennet and Avon Canal
To Hazelcroft, Caen Hill
(1899-1901)
The Nursery
New Park Street
63, New Park Street
(1881-1883)
Reynolds family tomb
St Mary's Church
2, Eastfield
(1885-1889)
London Road
Estcourt Street
St James' Church
Northgate Street
3
12, Market Place (Devizes College)
(1891-1893; 1903-1905)
Shambles
Market
Place
Monday Market St.
28, Monday Market Street
(1883)
Maryport St.
Sidmouth St.
22
Brittox
23
4
Station Road
Devizes Station
Bear Inn
(1887-1893)
St. John St.
High St.
11, Maryport Street
(1886-1887)
Southbroom Place
Devizes
Green
Castle Grounds
Beech Cottage
(1893-1899)
Devizes Castle
St John's Church
31, St. John Street
(Devizes College)
(1889-1891)
Long Street
Museum
32, Long Street
(1883-1886)
Nursteed Road
Hillworth
Pans Lane
2, Stanley Terrace
(1905-1908)

ONE

Trowbury 1881–92

He would lie awake the long hot summer evenings in the little night nursery, his young sister asleep at his side, and listen to the stamping of the horses in the stables below, the odd arrival of a coach sweeping in from the Station Road (a rare event now since the railways had come) and the constant murmur of the voices from the public bar, rising and falling as conversation and argument achieved its natural crescendo on the warm air, the drinkers spilling out on to the paved yard at the back with the tall dark columns of the old Assembly Rooms towering high above them. When he was older, he would go down and peer in at the long dark smoke-filled bar, with its yellowing ceilings and round black pillars, and wonder at the milling swarm of grown-ups, his father at the centre, engaged in rituals the purpose of which no child could come close to fathom.

In the morning he would waken to the sound of the empty barrels being rolled across the yard and new ones drawn up from the cellars beneath the house to ensure that the rituals could continue for at least one further day. His sister Dorothy (Dot to the family), whose protector he was and whose courage he admired in the face of her constant illnesses, would chatter from her bed. And then the arrival of his closest friend. Peter, the young black cat with white shirt-front, round white shoes and no tip to his tail because he *would* sit underneath the nursery fire, would cry at the door to be let in. He leapt for their beds and bade them "Good morning" with his regulation purr.[1]

Looking out from the back of the house in the still summer morning, he could see across the side garden with its gravelled paths, across the stables and back garden beyond, out over the railway tunnel to the broad green mound with its pretend castle of nineteenth century Norman towers and Victorian crenellations. He would wander to the front of the house and peer through the large bay windows across the market place, packed with farmers for the Thursday market held here every week since the thirteenth century, to the market cross where a hundred years ago the legendary Ruth Pierce had called upon God to strike her dead – and He had.[2]

The Bear Inn had stood since Tudor times adding a little elegance to the south-west corner of the market place in Devizes, the small old market town shaped like the segment of a circle on a slope of the Wiltshire Downs, with bare windy hills above it and good fat grazing lands below.[3] Not much of the L–shaped Tudor building with its timber frames had survived the nineteenth century improvements. The young Sydney Reynolds (Sydney to distinguish him from his grandfather – another Stephen) never saw the elegant greystone Tudor fireplace, the present pride of the small front bar, which was not uncovered until 1931.[4] The alterations were needed as the development of turnpike roads in the early eighteenth century brought a new coaching trade to the town. By the 1750s Devizes had become a principal staging-post on the route from London to Bath and the Bear began to inscribe its list of famous names who stopped on their way through for refreshment or to change the horses: in 1786 the Archduke and Duchess of Austria; in 1789 George III and Queen Charlotte; in 1817 Queen Charlotte again, alone this time, her husband forcibly detained in Windsor Castle; and finally in 1830 the future Queen Victoria with her mother, the Duchess of Kent, on their way to visit Stonehenge.[5] There was one more royal guest to come, but not until Reynolds himself was twelve and about to be packed off to boarding school.

But the Bear had artistic as well as royal connections, of a slightly longer duration than the hour or two required to change horses. In 1773 Thomas Lawrence arrived from Bristol to take over the running of the Bear and soon built a reputation on the road as "the only innkeeper for warm rooms, soft beds and reading Milton."[6] He brought with him his four-year-old son, another Thomas Lawrence, the future President of the Royal Academy and leading portrait painter of his age. Like Sydney Reynolds, he was to spend the whole of his formative childhood there, finally leaving Devizes for London at the age of eleven.

When Fanny Burney in April 1780 stayed the night at the Bear on a journey to Bath with Mr and Mrs Thrale, the young Thomas Lawrence was proudly brought before her, "a most lovely boy of ten years of age, who seems to be not merely the wonder of their family, but of the times for his astonishing skill in drawing. They protest that he has never had any instruction, yet showed us some of his productions which were really beautiful. Those that were copies were delightful, those of his own compositions amazing...... This house was full of books as well as paintings, drawing and music."[7]

Life had changed at the Bear in the intervening century. In his guide to Devizes, written in 1906, Reynolds could not resist a slight dig at the business failure of the Lawrences and their early departure for London: "The culture of the Bear Inn must have been too much for Devizes."[8]

Life inside the Bear was not ideal for a growing child of seven or eight. Though the family lived in the imposing eighteenth century extension to the south of the Tudor inn and partly separated from it, it was no normal domestic environment. There was no escape from the daily routine of hotel management and neither parent had much time to spare for their son.

Frank, his father, when not caught up in the work of the inn, was actively engaged in Council business, local sporting activities, judging livestock at local shows. He was a lively, gregarious, if rather shallow, man, not the ideal companion for a sensitive, intelligent and introspective small boy.[9] He had a violent and unpredictable temper which, more often than not, was taken out on the rest of the family. It created a black cloud over family life. The young Sydney was forever looking over his shoulder for fear he might have done something wrong, a neurotic attitude he was to carry with him into adult life.

In later life, Reynolds spoke rarely of his mother, Clara, but there is little doubt of the strength of his love for her; nor of his inability to express it to her face. In good Victorian style, the open show of emotion, Frank's temper apart, was frowned upon in the Reynolds family. Clara's own maternal failings were beyond her powers to overcome. She had a weak constitution, inherently tubercular, which had not been helped by two difficult confinements. The tuberculosis, which she bequeathed to her son, became a reality in the 1880s. She was constantly ill and gradually grew into a permanent invalid, with her own professionally qualified nurse to look after her day and night. As Reynolds grew older, the atmosphere of the sick-room pervaded the house.

When the family had meals together, they were rather strict affairs. The children were forced to eat frugally – a piece of bread and a potato for each slice of meat; and the combination of jam and butter together was never permitted except on Sundays and birthdays.[10]

Like most middle-class children deserted by their parents, the young Sydney and his sister Dot turned to the nearest servant for the love and attention they lacked. Polly Oakford was a local girl, born in Devizes and just 22 when they came to the Bear in 1887. As their nurse, she was to see both of them safely through childhood and adolescence to adult life. Fifteen years later, she was still writing to Master Sydney at university with all the family news. She was young enough to play with them and act the substitute elder sister as well as substitute parent. She read to the children, seated round her on the nursery floor. He later recalled how one Christmas (he never liked Christmas) she had read aloud to them from one of his presents, Mrs Walton's *A Peep Behind the Scenes*, and on hearing the sentimental story of the cruelly treated circus child, she had dissolved into tears, with both children weeping at her side.[11]

Though he tended to prefer books to people, there was at the Bear a strange kind of extended family which could make up for the deficiencies of the nuclear one. There were the permanent hotel guests, retired refugees of Empire: Mr Anderson, the ex-Captain of Infantry from South Africa; old Mr Mason, the retired timber broker, born in St Kitts, with his two unmarried daughters on the lookout for unwary males. For an imaginative small boy, here were fireside tales for the telling. And there was a whole bevy of servants to keep the inn running, eight living in, in addition to Polly and Clara Reynolds' nurse, Lena: the cook, hotel assistants, chambermaids, waitresses, kitchen maids, gardeners, stable boys, even (strangest of professions) a billiard marker – a wealth of potential friends.[12] Love of the natural world forged a common link. He struck up a friendship with one of the men and they started to keep pigeons together.

One member of staff in particular at the Bear was to have an impact on his life arguably even greater than his mother or his nurse, in that it lasted right up to his death. Lizzie Powney, a butcher's daughter like Reynolds' mother, had been born in Bath in 1863. She had come to the Bear to work as assistant to Frank Reynolds alongside Ellen Blencowe, two years her senior, who soon became a close friend. She was a lively, ambitious woman, determined to make her way in the world, and soon came to take a protective interest in her master's small son.

But despite the noise and people all around him, he was a quiet introverted child, showing glimpses of the repressed nature that was to follow him through life, both his power and his weakness. At the age of seven he would spend hours every day alone with his books in the nursery, reading up to half a dozen every week.[13] For like all lonely children, potential writers, books were the currency of life. They could work powerfully on his sensitive imagination. "After reading about earthquakes, I used to cry myself to sleep for fear of a volcano which I expected to rise up in a certain field by the London road" – the first subconscious glimmerings, perhaps, of the subject of his first novel, *The Holy Mountain*.[14]

His early reading skills were held up as an object lesson to his younger sisters. Aunt Jane Reynolds, his father's elder sister and another of a long line of surrogate mothers, presented him at the age of six with a copy of Charles Kingsley's *The Water Babies*. She seems to have had something of a fixation on Kingsley, in her view one of the greatest English writers of all time. The gift was intended to be put by till little Sydney was older but, to the astonishment of the family, he devoured it on the spot and could remember many passages by heart.[15]

Apart from the children's classics and usual adventure stories, he was particularly fond of books on animals and the natural world, read with a more adult eye to the science of the subject. At about the age of eight, he developed a passion for the books of Frank Buckland on natural history and on fisheries, and read all he could find from the local library. Buckland was Inspector of Salmon Fisheries at the Home Office and wrote in his spare time, often on the interminable train journeys required to cover his 38 fishery districts. He was a slightly eccentric figure who has gone down in Home Office mythology for beaching the carcase of a whale in one of the quadrangles of the Whitehall building, until the mounting putrefaction eventually ground the department to a halt. It was not until much later that Reynolds remembered the past obsession with this writer-cum-fishery inspector, an unconscious inspiration for his own career.[16]

Indoors too, he came to love music, listening to his mother as she played on the piano, and starting to learn to play himself. In adolescence music was his first love – he dreamed of becoming a concert pianist long before he decided to become a writer. One of the greatest deprivations of his working class existence was the loss of music any more sophisticated than the traditional sea shanties in the evening round the fire. Later he would walk any distance to find a piano to play on.

If books and music were one escape, so was the natural world that lay on his doorstep. The open spaces and curves of the Wiltshire Downs were to him like musical notes themselves. He loved them with an intensity rivalled only by his later passion for the sea and red cliffs around Sidmouth. He knew every step of every walk on the downs round Devizes: through Hartmoor to Potterne in the south; via Roundway to Rowde in the north-west, where Aunt Jane later lived; through Coate to Bishops Cannings in the north-east, where Dot was to go on her marriage; and his favourite walk of all, out to Tan Hill in the east, the second highest point in Wiltshire. There, up on the wildest and most open of the Devizes downs, he revelled in the glorious views over the Kennet Valley, Silbury Hill, Roundway, Pewsey Vale, Salisbury Plain and the breathtaking curve of the Wansdyke sweeping down from the back of Milk Hill and across to Morgan's Hill in the west.[17]

A country child, he rambled alone and untamed. It was a chance to let off some of the steam that had been building up inside at home. Writing in 1905 on those early forays into nature, he could not resist the temptation to shock just a little.

> Short and accurate catapults to pull back to the eye; long, strong and swift catapults to pull back behind the ear; catapult-guns, air-guns and rook rifles have I had. I have worked the hedges of many a country lane, have brought down tom-tits with shouts of joy and hen robins with mixed feelings. I have peppered dogs (an air-gun is excellent for dogs, because the light bullets almost penetrate their hides and cause them to yap pleasantly, like automatic bulls-eyes); I have heard slates rattle down, broken from a roof – crouching a little lower – have smashed the windows of political opponents, and paid for some of them; I have done much evil with many unlicensed arms, and am not very sorry. Yet I cannot remember 'potting at' or willingly hurting a cat, even on the most irresponsible of my days.[18]

The self-denying ordinance was not destined to last for long. Revising this rather raw text for book publication seven years later, the last sentence became: "Yet I never potted at cats – never, that is, till they kept me awake at night."[19]

An element of suppressed violence lay just below the surface throughout his life. It emerged in moments of crisis in physical blows to animals and even more violent verbal blows to human beings. In some of his earliest sketches he wrote about it, as if to exorcise the ghost; most of all when picturing those animals that had been his first love – cats. In the beginning was a tortoiseshell tom. "One day he walked into the room where illness had kept me for a month, and stood hesitating between the foot of the bed and a table from which the smell of whiting bones, no doubt, was wafted to him. Being bored, and therefore scientifically inclined, I set his back on fire to see how it would burn, and when I had put it out, he retired, unhurt, from me and my memory too."[20]

When at the age of six he moved from the family business in Maryport Street to the unknown wonders of the Bear, he was forced to leave his cats behind. "Picture a small cat-lover's disappointment when his family, accompanied by all its furniture but none of its cats, removed into a rambling old house with long passages, dark nooks and corners, an acreage of roofs, and whole suites of attics. Picture again his revived enthusiasm on learning that there were three cats native to the place – a sandy Manx cat, a tabby and – above all things wonderful! – a wild cat." He stalked her patiently and one day found her in an outhouse sleeping on a pile of turnips and carried her off in triumph to the nursery. "On promising that she should neither get into the larder, nor prowl about the attics and passages, nor caterwaul in the garden, on promising, recklessly, that she should be a bad cat never any more, he was allowed to keep her; and she settled down sullenly in a dark corner beside the wardrobe. He petted her, fed her, stroked her under the chin and roughed her chaps. She stayed on his knee at last and purred, and then – she disappeared."[21] They told him that someone across the road had poisoned her; a month later the other two cats went the same way. "Thus it was that a small boy first learned to suspect his elders of lying, and realised after a few days' pondering that he had done what no one else had been able to do – had caught the wild cat for killing."[22]

Then a family of cats, Ma, Pa and Baby appeared before the nursery fire. Ma was the favourite that "taught me much about life and death".[23] On his pillow one morning she gave birth to seven kittens. They too disappeared. He was told she had eaten them. There followed a strange episode in which he found himself for the first time the arbiter of life and death. One of the homing pigeons that he kept together with the servant at the Bear went missing. They thought it had merely flown away until one morning he found one of the fantails half-sitting, half-lying in a flower-bed with its feathers dishevelled, a broken wing and an eye out. The man told him that Ma had done it; he had seen her following the pigeons. As he picked the bird up and cradled it in his arms, he cried out "I wish Ma was dead". And within the hour, he found the beautiful tiger-tabby form laid out on the same flower bed. He cursed the man and ran away in tears to his room. It is a story of the final loss of innocence: "I knew then and thenceforward that *dead* meant *dead*, and wept."[24] This and the other incidents left him with childish feelings of guilt, the external symbol perhaps of others less easily articulated, which gave rise to a succession of stories and sketches about the drowning of kittens, a macabre and otherwise inexplicable feature of his early writing.

His black and white emotions, the fierce temper he shared with his father, his long memory for personal slights, all these Reynolds put down to his ancestry, particularly the Italian blood. Just a week before the outbreak of war in 1914, he told Edward Carpenter

> My own family was originally Italian, and I felt curiously at home when I was there. In fact, in some ways, I seem to have cast back to my Italian ancestors. I'm rather given to vendettas, and I have no understanding of such things as the 'laws of civilized warfare.' Seems to me that if one hates people enough to make war on 'em, one may just as well exterminate them and theirs by any means possible – poisoned streams or ort else. Can't see why not. Civilized warfare, warfare between armies who don't personally hate each other, but, as in the South African war, play cards over the lines at night, seems to me the supreme atrocity.[25]

From where this Italian blood was supposed to have sprung is a puzzle best left to the genealogist. Certainly the most distant ancestor of which we have sure knowledge was very English. He was William Reynolds, born in Badminton in 1700, and a traditional English farmer. He worked the Badminton Home Farm as a tenant of the 3rd Duke of Beaufort. In the one recorded event of his life, a source of much pride to later generations, the Duke presented him with a clock which, passed down from father to son, was still in the possession of Aunt Jane when she died in 1938.[26] William had two sons – Robert, who worked as a tanner at Luckington in Wiltshire, and his brother Edward, born in 1738, who at the age of 13 was apprenticed to the currier John Lea of Corsham and thus laid the foundation for a move up in the world. Tanning with its all-pervasive smells was an unsavoury trade, pushed to the edges of inhabited areas. By contrast, a currier, converting the tanned skins to suitable hides for shoe and harness makers, could readily be welcomed into the social and business world of a small country town. Edward Reynolds grew rich in trade and great in local politics. He died on Christmas Eve 1804 as Bailiff of Corsham, the local term for mayor, and was fittingly buried in a substantial tomb in the north-west corner of the churchyard.

He bequeathed to his two sons, William and Robert, and the succeeding generations of the family, both his penchant for local politics and his professional skills as a currier. William stayed in Corsham to continue the family business. Robert, the younger son, in the latter years of the eighteenth century moved to Devizes, just far enough away to exercise a genuine independence, and with accumulated savings and no doubt some paternal help set up a thriving currier's business there.[27] In 1800, his economic base established, he married the twenty-three-year-old Jane Kifft of Sutton Benger and they settled down at 11 Maryport Street which was to remain the family home for the next 87 years. Jane made her expected contribution to the business, producing over the next 18 years a family of eleven children, eight boys and three girls. All were tall, fair-skinned and red-haired, except for the fifth child, Henry, who was short, sturdy and dark. The boys all made good in the commercial world. William, the eldest, carried on with his father's business in Maryport Street. The next two sons started currier firms elsewhere – Robert in

Swindon and Edward in Andover – which were to thrive for several generations more. Three other brothers took part in this general dispersal, establishing businesses in Newbury, Gloucester and Essex. The youngest brother, Charles, who never married, remained in Devizes and ran a butcher's shop round the corner in Sidmouth Street.

On leaving school and before they spread their wings, the boys all helped in the family firm in Maryport Street. That fate befell the sixth son, Stephen, born in 1813, grandfather of the young Sydney Reynolds. By the time he came of age, it was clear that the eldest brother, William, was unlikely to marry – and all the other brothers had left home. Nothing more natural then that Stephen should join the business on a permanent footing and, if he were to marry, assist its transfer to the next generation.

The business premises owned by Robert Reynolds were substantial. The family lived over the main shop at 11 and 12 Maryport Street, once The Leg of Mutton public house.[28] The shop reached back to the business entrance in Monday Market Street, over the road from which the real work was carried on, in the van house, paddock, workshop, drying sheds and garden. Across the road too were seven cottages, that could be used to house either family or staff. It was an exciting empire for a small boy to inherit, with dark attics, long winding passages, vast underground cellars. At five Stephen was sent to the dame school run by Miss Smart in Monday Market Street and Reynolds' Aunt Jane in later years was the proud purveyor of a string of stories about her father's daring and misbehaviour at school, for which he was suitably punished. In 1820 at the age of seven, he was sent away to complete his education at a boarding school run by a Mr Tanner at Lyneham where, in spite of the usual boyish scrapes, he enjoyed his time and won a special place in the affections of the Tanner family. He had a good retentive memory and Mrs Tanner would call upon him to recite to her guests at her frequent evening parties.

Like most newly arrived entrepreneurs, Robert Reynolds had set out to make a solid contribution to the social, religious and political life of Devizes. He was for years a staunch worshipper at St Mary's Church and held many official posts in the parish. He loved the church so much that he organised a collection to buy up cottages in New Park Street, pulling them down to open up the present western entrance. In 1847 he was presented by his fellow parishioners and townsmen with a silver vase and a scroll in red and black lettering thanking him for his services to the parish and for "his honest, manly and independent conduct during a residence of nearly half a century in the town of Devizes." It was the first of many such addresses to be made to future generations of Reynolds there.

In 1849 Jane and Robert Reynolds died a few months apart and were buried in the family vault, below the east window of St Mary's Church, under the box tomb which stands forlornly there today. Stephen was promoted co-partner with William in the family business. On the strength of his new status, he brought back to Maryport Street in 1851 a young bride, Harriet Green from Trowbridge. They had three children: Jane, "Aunt Jane", in 1852; Frank, Reynolds' father, in 1855; and in 1856, Alice, "Aunt Allie", an invalid for most of her life, whom her father called "Nell" because like many Victorians he could never put out of his mind the death of Little Nell.

Where Robert Reynolds had been a newcomer to Devizes, eager to please, Stephen was soon an established pillar of the community, so much so that he sometimes forgot he was only second generation. At the Mayor's Banquet in 1873, he spoke of himself as "a member of one of the oldest families in Devizes", though it was less than a century since his father had first arrived. He stood as councillor for the South Ward of the borough, which he represented for many years, often topping the poll. He served as a magistrate, winning a reputation for balance, fairness and integrity.

In 1873, at the age of 60, he was elected mayor, the pinnacle of municipal achievement. He had been approached to stand many times before, but had stood back, in part because of the demands of the business which took him regularly away from the town, and in part through a natural reticence and humility. When he did finally agree to stand, he was a truly popular choice, not just for the burgesses but among the ordinary people of the town as well.

He was a tall man, with a broad-jowled face, white beard and rather gentle dreamy eyes – in looks a typical Victorian paterfamilias but with none of the traditional severity. His speech at the inaugural banquet was of the "ordinary fellow" kind, expressing genuine surprise at the response to his elevation: "The kindness he had received quite unnerved him, and he really did not know how to thank them enough. An amount of kindness and confidence had been shown to him by all classes for which he could in no way account; he really did not know what he had done to deserve it."[29]

Frank Reynolds had rather less of this humble integrity, and was later to rebel against his father and the business just as his son was to rebel against him. But in the beginning, to all appearances, he followed very much in father's footsteps, taking his schooling locally, joining the now well-established currier business in Maryport Street, and entering into local politics at a very early age. He became a town councillor at 22 and, apart from one break in 1890 when his wife was seriously ill, continued as council member until his departure from Devizes early in the new century. In 1899 he was elected alderman, an honour conferred on his father 17 years before. He too was a magistrate and for three years served on the Wiltshire County Council. The only office he did not attain was that of mayor; but this distinction was to be conferred on him in 1904, as it were honorifically, by his son in his novel *The Holy Mountain*.

This background in local politics spanning the previous four generations was a crucial formative influence on the life and outlook of the young Sydney Reynolds, growing up in Devizes, and of Stephen Reynolds, the mature writer, building his reputation in Sidmouth and London. Most immediately, it furnished him with living material for his novel in which he satirized the narrowness and presumption of parish pump politics, and its potential for corruption. But more generally, it gave him a natural affinity to politics and public life, an understanding of where the springs of power lay and how individual and social wrongs could be righted. If you saw injustice on your doorstep, you wrote to the local paper; but you demanded a meeting with the Council as well. Reynolds' career was not a fortuitous drift from writing into local and national politics, a diversion from the natural path; nor even more a deliberate switch to *political* action because the power of the pen had failed. Politics and bureaucratic manipulation were in his marrow. This was something that Edward Garnett and the others who lamented the loss of early promise as a writer were never fully to understand.

The two fixed points in Stephen Reynolds' writing life were Devizes and Sidmouth. Strangely, the connection between the two towns had been forged many years earlier in the person of Henry Addington, Prime Minister in the shadow of the Younger Pitt and then as Home Secretary the hated Sidmouth of the Six Acts. Addington had represented Devizes from 1784 and his choice of Sidmouth as his title when elevated to the peerage in 1805 left a small mark on the Wiltshire town.[30] In 1826, in honour of their former MP, the Corporation changed the name of Leg of Mutton Street, wholly appropriate for a street with so many butchers shops, to the more mundane Sidmouth Street.[31] And it was at 22 Sidmouth Street, over one of those butchers shops, that Reynolds mother, Clara, was born in March 1858. Her father, George Cox, master butcher, had established a highly successful business, with his own small abbatoir next door, and just before his death in 1873 he preserved the future of the company by forming a partnership with another butcher, John Rose. The firm of Rose & Sons is still operating on the site today.

Quite possibly Frank Reynolds had known the young Clara Cox for some years before he asked her to marry him. In a town as small as Devizes the major tradesmen's families were all well known to one another and Clara lived just a stone's throw away. Frank's uncle Charles had, after all, also run a butcher's shop in Sidmouth Street. Both Frank and Clara had been born and brought up on business premises – he among hides of leather, she among sides of beef. It was the perfect rural match.

They were married at St John's Church on 29 March 1880 and went to live, with their housemaid Mary Woodroffe, across the town at 63, New Park Street, a little square box of a house built in the 1840s of red brick with tall, distinctive Georgian-style windows. Stephen Reynolds senior owned property in New Park Street and the house may conceivably have belonged to him.

It was here on 16 May 1881 that Stephen Reynolds junior was born. It may well have been a difficult birth, like that of Alec Trotman, Reynolds' rather colourless *alter ego* in *The Holy Mountain*.[32] Clara had a weak constitution and may already have shown signs of the onset of tuberculosis that was to kill her.

And the new baby was not baptised until 30 November, a long delay for a mother and child both perfectly well.[33]

He was christened Stephen Sydney – Stephen after his grandfather and Sydney after his father's cousin, a midshipman who had been drowned 13 years before doing another sailor's work in a storm at sea.[34] The two christian names were a resource exploited to the full. In Devizes and within the family circle, he was known throughout his life as Sydney, initially to distinguish him from his grandfather. In London and in literary circles, he was called Stephen. In Sidmouth and to all his fishermen friends, he was simply Steve. In this way he was able to maintain distinct and separate identities in the three very different worlds which formed the core of his life.

On his marriage, Frank Reynolds became a formal partner in the business in Maryport Street, now Reynolds & Son, curriers. The young couple and their small baby lived happily in the little house with its elegant central staircase running down to the spacious basement where the housemaid cooked the meals on the kitchen range. In 1883 Clara was sufficiently well for them to think of a second child, but the house in New Park Street was too small for an expanding family. Thus when Sydney was two, they moved to 32 Long Street, an older stone-built terraced house, with impressive label moulds over the ground floor windows and a narrow rounded arch above the front door.[35] It had a larger garden at the back in which a small boy could run and explore. There in September 1884 his sister Dorothy was born, another child destined to inherit the physical weaknesses of their mother.

In the following year an event occurred which was to change the lives of all the Reynolds in Devizes. In July, Stephen Reynolds senior, head of the extended family and fount of its wealth, died at the age of 72, simple but stout-hearted to the end. The rector visited him a few days before his death and had not heard "a more child-like, simple, rugged and evangelical expression of faith." He was buried in the family vault beneath the east window. The funeral was attended by the Mayor and town council, leading citizens and a large contingent of the ordinary people of the town. The loss was general. Blinds were drawn and shutters closed in the town for the greater part of the day.[36]

But the loss was greater for his widow and her two maiden daughters, Aunt Jane and Aunt Allie. They moved out of Maryport Street, the family home since the start of the century, to make way for Frank and his family, the new head of the firm; and found a temporary home at 3 Northgate Street, just down from the Market Place.[37] At the end of 1885, the young Sydney Reynolds, now aged four, moved once again with his family to the old house in Maryport Street.[38] But it was not to be for long. Under the will of Stephen senior, his property was to be divided equally between the three children. Whether Frank was unable or unwilling to buy out his sisters, he decided in 1887 to sell up the business in Maryport Street and moved as landlord to take charge of the Bear Inn in the Market Place.

With their share of the proceeds of the sale, Aunt Jane and Aunt Allie, with their widowed mother, moved out to Prospect Rise, an imposing square-built house in the nearby village of Rowde, where they were to remain for the rest of their lives.[39] By this time, the future of both daughters had been settled. Aunt Allie had once been engaged to be married but was struck down by rheumatoid arthritis and all the plans had to be abandoned. Aunt Jane had been in love with a local clergyman but, in a sacrifice typical of the time, gave up in her turn all thoughts of marriage to look after her stricken sister.[40] Throughout his life, Prospect Rise became a safe haven for Reynolds, his main link with the family past, where Aunt Jane entertained his literary friends from London and his fishermen friends from Devon, dispensing food, wisdom and familial love.

Reynolds was just four when his grandfather died and had only the vaguest memories of him. But the old man had a great interest in the child, the only male heir in his branch of the family. He was keen that the young Sydney should begin his education with Mary Harrison and her sister who had opened a school at No.2 Eastfield in London Road, and arrangements were made to meet the dead man's wishes. Reynolds seems to have enjoyed his time at Eastfield in a world so different from that at home. As Aunt Jane said later, no one was Miss Mary's equal in his eyes.[41] The feeling must have been mutual for Miss Harrison could not have had a more eager and able pupil to whom to teach the rudiments of reading and her old-fashioned pointed Italian writing.[42] It was no doubt the stimulus of this school which produced the precocious early reader of Charles Kingsley.

His next scholastic move and his next teacher were to have the greatest impact on his life and outlook on the world. In 1886, at the age of 24, Ada Bennett had come to Devizes together with her elder sister Sarah and their close friend, Clara Cole. Sarah and Clara opened a school in Potterne Road, eventually to become the Girls High School in the Castle Grounds, while Ada set up another at 19 Long Street. Ada had been brought up in Dover of a middle class family and she and her sister had all the financial backing to establish their own business. In 1888 she moved her school to 31 St John Street, just up the road from the Bear, and named it The Academy. It was there that Reynolds joined it at the age of eight.

The following year, she changed the name to Devizes College (Sarah's and Clara's school formed a separate Girls' Branch in the Castle Grounds) and in 1891 moved to 12 Market Place, a tall four-storey Georgian building, the other side of the Bear, from where she continued to run it for the next 23 years.[43] It was organised on public school lines, with a core curriculum that included English, Mathematics, Book-keeping, Latin, French and Drill, and with Greek, German, Shorthand, Piano and Drawing offered as optional extras. It also laid emphasis on games and recreation, including the teaching of swimming – the only physical recreation that Reynolds could stomach.

When he was old enough, he joined the school as a weekly boarder, just a few doors down from his home. This was some recognition by his parents of the unsuitable environment for a young boy afforded by an inn where his mother was dying. But such was the influence of Miss Bennett upon him, it may have been Reynolds' own demand to go and live with this new substitute mother.

Ada Bennett was by all accounts a gifted teacher, strong (she could wield the cane) but open minded, with wide horizons and a highly liberal view of the world, so different from the narrow shuttered outlook of the late nineteenth century country town, with its strict divisions of class, sex and religion. Reynolds paid his best testimonial to her and the school in his Devizes guide of 1906.

> Of many excellent schools, the most interesting is perhaps the College, where Miss Ada Bennett carries on a successful experiment in partial co-education – boys' school, girls' school and kindergarten, each with its own class-rooms and its own head master or mistress, chosen for many qualifications besides mere academic distinction. Development of individual character and of reasoning powers, rather than cram; fitness for the brunt of life rather than for the examination room; unforced play, health, no evening work, handicrafts for boys and household management for girls, are the primary aims of this rather original school, which does not attempt to suit everybody's educational notions; and it says much for the College, as well as for the religious feeling of the town, that, though the principal is distinctively a Churchwoman, there are yet in the school as many children of Nonconformists as of Churchpeople.[44]

This experience at the College of an "alternative" education was the seedbed for his later strongly pronounced views on the inadequacies of traditional education, particularly in its efforts to turn working-class children into pale imitations of their middle class counterparts – views which were to get him into much hot water with the educational establishment. And ironically, it was while he was acting as an occasional teacher at the College itself in 1904 that he became convinced of the barrenness of middle class education, the forcing of children with all their natural instincts into conformist "gentlemen".

In the early 1890s, however, Miss Bennett and the College were his whole world. In later life, he would refer to her only in superlatives: "She is a great woman, an educational genius, and runs a splendid school. I got all the best of my education there."[45]

It was there that he received his first glimpses of the wider world of late Victorian England, the rapid social and political changes, the new philosophical ideas which sprang from the expansion of science, the writers that were to have the greatest influence on his own style and philosophical thought.

New forces were springing up in the English society of the 1880s. The Forster Education Act of 1870 had created a revolution which was now producing the first mass literacy the country had known, building the cohort of *Daily Mail* readers of the next decade. It had also spawned large numbers of female teachers, other Ada Bennetts, to cope with the expansion in schools – the growth of a female professional class that was to add weight to the issues of female emancipation in the period before the First World War.

With the move to universal male suffrage in the Acts of 1867 and 1884, succeeding governments had to take increasing account of the working-class voice in politics; but the voice they chose to listen to was not, as Reynolds was to spend his life pointing out, the authentic voice of real working people but rather one they had concocted for themselves to fit more conveniently the existing party structure. The new franchise brought working-class politics gradually to centre stage at a time when the old centres of power associated with the landed aristocracy were assailed by forces they could neither understand nor control. Round Devizes in the 1880s, and all through rural England, agricultural rents fell disastrously as cheap American grain, speeded by steamships, flooded into the domestic market. The agricultural depression was to mark the extinction of the economic base of the English aristocracy, though its pretensions to political power were to survive one generation more.

The world of ideas was also in turmoil. Darwin in 1859 had dealt a punishing blow to the security of religious belief and, as the momentum of scientific discovery gathered pace, had spread throughout the thinking classes the fashionable crisis of doubt. By the end of the century, aided in part by the growing literacy, the language of science and, in particular, the Darwinian jargon had come into popular currency. It became common to talk of the development of society in terms of natural selection; and newspapers began to fret about the genetical inheritance of the mass of Englishmen and their physical capacity to survive. Reynolds, with his intellectual bent towards the practical, was intrigued by these issues – "I revelled in the mid-Victorian controversy between the Darwinian agnostics and the theologians" – and equally by the new science, though it was hard to find a school at this time that actually taught it.[46]

But the debates of science and religion were to lead him on to wider philosophical speculation and into serious literature. Like most young writers at the beginning of the twentieth century, he looked to Flaubert as the great model and it must have been at least in his early teens that he first devoured *Madame Bovary* and *L'Education Sentimentale*. And it was around this period too that the three great formative influences on his writing and thinking were in the flood-tide of their careers. Friedrich Nietzsche completed *Zarathustra* in 1885 and his final collapse came four years later. In 1889 too, the young Henri Bergson wrote his first philosophical treatise on time and consciousness, *Essai sur les données immédiates de la conscience*. And in 1882, the year after Reynolds was born, Walt Whitman published his ninth edition of *Leaves of Grass* and planted a kiss on Oscar Wilde.

The decline of Victorian values and certainties, like all such declines, took time to register. The 1880s marked also the growth of Imperialism, a switching of focus from economic supremacy at home to territorial supremacy abroad. It was Imperial fervour that invested what was to all Victorians looking back the highpoint of the period – the Golden Jubilee of 1887. This fevered celebration of the certainties of a world that was fast losing all certainty came also to Devizes but, nothing if not original, six days late. While most of England celebrated on 22 June, Devizes waited till the 28th.

The planning for the day got off to a bad start. The committee set up to oversee the celebrations was far too unwieldy, and decisions painfully taken were then rapidly unpicked. Food for the masses turned out a success. An ox was roasted on the Green and distributed in the afternoon to all-comers. The public dinner for the more select was set up in the Shambles and quickly developed into one. Many more tickets were issued than places available and hundreds were turned away angry and empty.

For children like the six-year-old Reynolds, the arrangements for the great event were carefully designed to stick in the memory for ever. In mid afternoon the children of the town, some 2000 in all, assembled at their respective schools and marched with their teachers on the Market Place, each child wearing round its neck a shiny medal, bearing the Queen's profile on one side and the Devizes Borough Arms on the other. Once gathered together, they sang the national anthem by sections, many too eager for the impending party to give much attention to the singing. Then they marched off, school by school, each with its distinctive banner and accompanied by musical bands, passing up the Brittox and Park Road to Roundway Park, the very young children, like Reynolds' two-year-old sister, travelling at the front in waggons trimmed with evergreens.

Arriving in the park, each child was sat down on the grass, Jubilee mug in hand, and plied with tea, bread and butter, and cake. The final act of the children's day in the park was the athletic sports, with Frank Reynolds much to the fore as official starter and one of the chief organisers. This was not an entertainment designed to appeal to the young Sydney Reynolds who throughout his life loathed organised sports of all kinds. He could not have been amused by the last event, a pick-a-back tournament for grown-ups in which his uncle on one side beat his father on the other.

At dusk the park was cleared, and as the children walked home, tired but happy, through the illuminated streets, a brilliant firework display was starting up on the Green.[47] For most of the children of Devizes, celebrating that day the longevity of the Great Queen, this was their first brush with royal ceremony. Not many years were to pass, however, before they had their first glimpse of royalty in the flesh.

In April 1893 came news that the Prince of Wales would visit Devizes the following month to celebrate the centenary of the Wiltshire Volunteers. The local paper noted: "The day will undoubtedly be one of the most noteworthy in the annals of our ancient and Royal borough.... It is an honour which towns of far greater importance than our own vainly covet."[48] It was an important, not to say anxious, day for Frank Reynolds too, since much of the festivities were to centre on the Bear. Great care was taken with the decorations. Rows of little coloured lights were hung all across the house front and along the eaves, together with drapes in red, white and blue. Masses of greenhouse plants and flowers were set up in the windows and over the portico. Over the Reynolds' private entrance was an illuminated plume of feathers with the princely motto in crystal, and a crown surmounting a floral device. Reynolds' own school, Devizes College, was not to be outdone. Across its imposing front two mottoes were emblazoned "God Save the Queen" and "God Bless our Prince".

When the great day dawned on 24 May, special trains brought crowds from all over Wiltshire until the Market Place was bursting at the seams. The Prince arrived at Devizes Station from Paddington at midday and drove by carriage to the Bear. When he passed the Assize Courts, a choir of 1000 children, Reynolds no doubt among them, sang "God Bless the Prince of Wales". On the Prince's arrival, the Town Council lined up on the pavement in front of the Bear while the Mayor presented the Prince with a public address. Then to the most important business of the day – the official lunch.

At about this time, Reynolds had composed a poem on the culinary prowess of the Bear. It was in doggerel, in the time-honoured style of Thomas Hood or Charles Barham, and like much of Reynolds' poetry did not scan. It is one of the few childhood pieces that remain.

> In the year eighty three in the town of Devizes,
> That can boast of its Sessions as well as Assizes,
> About 30 hungry fellows sat down to a dinner,
> All table linen and plate "as I am a sinner".
> Two poor little Pheasants, 1 cock and 1 hen,
> Was thought a good blow out for 30 good men.
> The rest was all done in that niggardly style
> Which raises a man's dander and stirs up his bile.
> And I hope the Committee will take very good care
> Never again to dine at the .... .[49]

We may take it that there had been some improvements at the Bear since 1883. For the Prince on this day there were four opening courses of olives farcis, caviare on toast, clear turtle soup and fillets of sole. The main dishes were substantial, but with none of your London sophistication: hashed venison, lamb cutlets and peas, hind quarter of lamb, mayonnaise of salmon, roast chicken, Wiltshire hams, ox tongues, forequarters of lamb, galantine of veal, timbales of chicken, lobster salad and prawns in aspic. The feast was rounded off with maraschino and orange jellies, vanilla and Queen Mab's creams, grapes and strawberries. Cook had done her stuff.

When the Prince emerged from the Bear at two o'clock smoking a cigarette, a great cheer went up. He was then whisked off to Roundway Down for the formal inspection of the troops, the ostensible reason for his visit. Returning once more to the Bear for refreshment, he signed the visitors' book, asking all those in his entourage to do the same, and then, beaming with smiles, he set off back to London. There was a grand carnival in the town that evening with fireworks in Southbroom Park.[50] The Reynolds family, relaxing in the Bear, had good reason to celebrate a difficult job well done. What had stuck most forcefully in Reynolds' mind was that lusty singing of "God Bless the Prince of Wales".

One member of the family had not seen the Prince that day. In the late 1880s, Clara Reynolds' tuberculosis grew worse by the month and the prognosis was poor. She had to stay for longer periods in bed attended by her nurse and saw less and less of her children. In the autumn of 1890, her liver began to break down. In March of the following year she developed dropsy and the end was not far off. In the afternoon of 24 June, a day of summer thunderstorms throughout Wiltshire, in her private bedroom at the Bear with her husband at her side, she finally gave up the struggle. She was just 33.[51]

From her own small inheritance, she left her son an annual income of about £30 and a capital sum of £300 when he reached the age of 21.[52] This was to have a more than symbolic significance for his ambitions as a writer. But the emotional bequest to the ten-year-old boy must have been so much the greater. To a child of his sensitivity, with a propensity to turn his feelings in on himself, the impact was immeasurable. Her death sent shock waves through him, rippling outwards for the rest of his life.

In later days, he rarely mentioned his mother and even more rarely her death, a significant sign how deep the wound had gone. He got some of it out in his writing. There is at least one early story in which a mother dies in desperate pain: "In her pain she called so for her husband that, towards the end, he sat by day, and slept or watched by night, in a chair by her bed." And the tragedy of the husband, like that of Reynolds himself, is that he cannot tell her to her face that he loves her.[53]

He dropped the odd clue to how much he felt. When 23 years later he built his own house, he couldn't hide his excitement at the thought of having around him once more his mother's pictures and china that had been left at the Bear for safe keeping. Her death may have left him with a large residue of guilt; and an unresolved anger at being thus abandoned. It may have had much to contribute to his general neuroticism and the turbulence of his sexual life.

All this is speculation. The only hard evidence we have from this period is the earliest remaining photograph of him. He is standing with his sister on either side of his grandmother, Harriet Reynolds, probably in the garden at

Prospect Rise, dressed in his summer Sunday best, grey well-tailored suit, a broad light-patterned tie and white shoes. He stands stiffly, a slim willowy figure, his legs crossed, shoulders hunched, leaning on the back of the chair. His lips are tight, his eyes half-shuttered. His sister stares into the camera, in her eyes the look of an adult that has suffered more than her share of pain. At all times Reynolds hated being photographed, and there may be some of that short-lived anxiety here. But this looks to go deeper. There is a still poignancy about this picture which betokens great loss.

The death of Clara Reynolds marks the beginning of the emotional break-up of the family. Now Reynolds was fully exposed to the increasingly unwelcome governance of his father and began to gravitate towards others. Lizzie Powney, the assistant at the Bear, stepped in to take over the place that his mother had vacated. Of all his surrogate mothers, she was the one closest to him, both physically and emotionally, at the time he needed a mother most. He never forgot it.

But there was a future yet unwritten which was to provide the real fulfilment he sought so desperately over the next 15 years. As Clara lay on her death-bed at the Bear, a hundred miles away in a poor man's house in Western Town, Sidmouth, a third son was being born to a twenty-six-year-old fisherman, Robert Woolley, and his young wife Annie. For Sydney Reynolds the childhood family was breaking up. For Stephen Reynolds a new one was already waiting in the wings.

TWO

Bloxham 1893–8

On a Monday morning in the autumn of 1859, two young curates from the village of Deddington in Oxfordshire took a walk into Banbury, three miles away, to see the vicar there...... and on the way back one of them founded a school.

It happened through a chance but crucial circumstance. Instead of walking back through Adderbury the way they had come, they decided to alter their route and return via Bloxham, a village which stands on the hilly banks of a brook about three miles south-west of Banbury, its brown stone farms and cottages clustered round the tall slender spire of its fourteenth-century parish church. As they reached the bottom of the hill where the Banbury road swings round to enter the village, they saw on the corner for the first time the imposing central building of a Church of England school which had been started by a Mr Hewett, but which now stood derelict and abandoned. They learned it was to be sold by auction in three days time. Forty years later one of them recalled the events of that day.

> We went to the Vicar of Bloxham and obtained the keys of the building, and went over it – lamenting that it had been abandoned and the work given up, the more so as there was talk of its falling into the hands of those who were opposed to the Church. The idea of re-starting the School was suggested to me by my friend and rejected promptly by myself, as I said that it was the very last thing in the world that I should think of, to become a schoolmaster. However, as we walked back to Deddington the matter was discussed again and again, and as I had then no immediate plans for the future, I at last began to think that it would be a work to which I might devote my life and do some good in.[1]

The young curate with a mission was Reginald Egerton, and the school he founded All Saints' School, Bloxham. Egerton saw what had happened that Monday morning as nothing less than a call from God and devoted the rest of his life to the success of the school, his own personal contribution to the revival of the Church of England led by the Oxford Movement.

The moving spirit behind the school was that of Nathaniel Woodard, who had been at Oxford in the 1830s, a disciple of Keble, Newman and Pusey, and who believed firmly in Thomas Arnold's idea of the Christian state and the duty of the church towards education. It was his special aim to bring church education to the middle classes, particularly the lower middle class in whom an interest in religion was seen to be sadly lacking. In 1848 he had founded the Society of St Nicolas College, Shoreham, composed of seventeen men all in holy orders, whose aim was to plant at least one middle-class school in every diocese in the country.

One of those seventeen members of the Society was John William Hewett, who was appointed curate at Bloxham and determined to start a school there on Woodard principles. He had the advantage of the great Victorian architect G.E. Street, fortuitously diocesan architect for Oxford, as designer of the school, whose main building of 1855 still confers an aura of distinction on the site today. He had the disadvantage of no money and a rather cavalier administrative style – and the new school went bust in just four years.

It was left to Egerton, educated at Oxford and a firm Anglo-Catholic, to pick up the pieces. One of his first acts was to consult Nathaniel Woodard and to spend three weeks at Hurstpierpoint to gain first-hand experience of the Woodard system. Woodard withheld his personal support from Egerton's enterprise, believing the site at Bloxham was too confined to lead to success. So, while following the Woodard principles, Bloxham was left outside the formal pale of the Woodard Corporation for another forty years despite repeated requests for admission.

The new foundation throve under Egerton. The school was opened in January 1860 "as a Grammar School, for the Education of the Sons of Tradesmen, Farmers, Clerks, and others of the Middle Classes."[2] It was to provide a public school type of education for middle class boys, who would normally go straight into business on leaving. It was no part of the aim to prepare boys for university. Through the 1860s and 70s it expanded in numbers of pupils, in income and in new building. It reached a high point of almost 200 boys in 1876, but then began a gradual decline, as the agricultural depression affected the ability of farmers and market town businessmen to pay the fees, and competition emerged from the developing education system created by the 1870 Act.

In 1886 Egerton retired as headmaster and handed over to a former pupil, Frederick Boissier, a brilliant mathematician who had been teaching at the school for seven years. Boissier was an able administrator with less of Egerton's panache and his feet more solidly planted on the ground. The challenges he faced were severe. The school was in decline and in 1889 began to run at a loss. When Reynolds first arrived, it was only just over half full. Boissier determined to improve the academic standards and to advertise more forcefully. The school prospectus now had a slightly different emphasis. It was "intended to give a sound general education in the distinctive principles of the English Church, in a manly and liberal spirit, to boys going direct to the Universities or the business of life."[3]

Frank Reynolds, the ex-currier and landlord of the Bear, a small businessman in a small market town, was just the kind of parent to whom this prospectus was designed to appeal. He had always been Anglo-Catholic by inclination, and had a deep respect for the Catholic church. He was friendly with a local catholic priest who was a regular visitor to the house.[4] The Woodard approach was the right education for his son. Furthermore, the school laid claim to value for money with its aim "to furnish a good general education at the lowest possible price compatible with real efficiency" and the fairly modest fees of 43 guineas a year were well within reach of the salary of £250 a year, small by middle-class standards, which in the early 1890s he was earning out of the Bear.[5] Thus it was that in the summer of 1893 he decided that his son, now aged twelve, should go to Bloxham.

The move to the new school marked a major change in Stephen Reynolds' life. Although he had been a weekly boarder at Devizes College, that was so close to the family home as not really to count. Now, it seemed, he was *really* leaving home. So it was with some trepidation that he arrived at Banbury Station for the opening of term on 12 September, resplendent in his new blue cap and with his trouser pockets tightly sewn up. This was one of the more idiosyncratic rules at Bloxham, designed in part to prevent the carriage of contraband, but primarily to promote the sound posture that went with no hands in pockets. At the end of term, by the time the horse and brake had reached Banbury Station again on the return journey, all boys pockets had become, miraculously, unstitched.

In the welcoming service on the first Sunday of term, the Archdeacon of Oxford, an honoured guest, delivered an upbeat sermon on youthful energy and its uses:

> Youth is the time of energy, before grey hairs bring feebleness of mind or body, before experience of evil brings distrust of others, before experience of danger brings timidity, before experience of failure dries up the springs of hope...... Boyhood is a special time of energy, though not the only time. If there is one thing more than another which stamps a character on school life, it is energy.[6]

One new boy took the Venerable Archdeacon at his word and, showing an unexpected superfluity of energy, decamped on the third day of term back to his home in Gloucestershire. Two days later he was returned dejectedly to school by his elder sister and Boissier, the headmaster, noted reprovingly in his log book, in which he kept a running record of events: "He is a very backward and 'spoilt' boy of the farmer class."[7]

The 1675th pupil to enter the school (Bloxham was always hot on statistics), though perhaps sorely tempted, was less inclined to make a run for his home in Devizes.[8] Waking up in his dormitory in the main school building was quite a different experience from the old familiar Bear. Fourteen beds ran down each side of the great black-and-white room with its angular overarching beams, and down the centre on narrow wooden trestles stood a long line of washhand basins, beside each a mug without a handle. At half past six every morning a member of staff would ring the big brass bell outside the Schoolroom door and the boys would leap out of bed with a shudder to strip to the waist and face the ice cold water before them, poured from jugs which in winter literally froze over. All boys would assemble by seven o'clock in the Great Schoolroom with its long thin desks and wooden forms, and then march up the stairs to the Chapel for the early morning service which on good days would last only twenty minutes.[9]

Breakfast, a relatively free and easy meal, took place at eight in the dining hall, arranged on similar lines to the dormitories with two long tables running the full length of the room, a shorter table in the centre for the prefects, and at the far end the high table for the masters, the centre place reserved for the headmaster at dinner time. The tables were covered with a white cloth, on which at various intervals were placed large urns of tea with a tap on either side and round them a cluster of handle-less mugs like the ones in the dormitories. Breakfast was a spartan meal of tea and bread and scrape – margarine just scraped across the bread to leave a thin film of grease. It was a few years after Reynolds left before porridge and eggs were introduced, and then only for the boys who could pay.

First school was from nine to eleven, followed by a quarter of an hour break; next school from 11.15 to 12.15, and then three-quarters of an hour of free time when boys lounged around, played soccer in the playground or, the more energetic ones, worked in the carpentry shop. Sharp at one o'clock, the bolt on the dining hall door would fly back and the boys would surge in for the main meal of the day. They stood at their places while Mr Wilson, the senior master of the school, would make a stately entrance down the centre aisle, reach the end, turn round, fold his hands and recite a long grace, too long for the more famished of the boys: "The eyes of all wait upon thee, O Lord" and the boys would chant in unison "And thou that givest them meat in due season."

The meat, in fact, followed a very regular season. Sunday was roast beef, two enormous mounds of which came up in the lift and were put on the tables by village boys dressed in little blue-and-white striped coats. This was the culinary high point of the week; it was all downhill from then on. Monday was Monday hash – the remains of the beef put into some thick brownish gravy; Tuesday – roast mutton; Wednesday – Wednesday pie, the remains of the cold mutton put into a pie with a pastry crust, palatable though a little on the greasy side; Thursday was roast beef, a repeat of Sunday.

Friday meat was the cold beef salted – hard, tough and *very* salty. On Fridays, they always scrubbed the wooden floors of the dining hall, and the smell of damp wood was fixed in most boys memories with the taste of Friday meat. On Fridays too rice pudding was served, a sea of milk with a few grains floating about in it which most boys politely declined. It was thought that the milk was strained off and served with the afternoon tea. On Saturday the remains of the salt beef were hashed up into cottage pie or a similar concoction. Then back to Sunday and the repeat of the cycle with never a change, summer, winter, year in, year out. During the meal the headmaster would come in and take his place at the centre of the masters' table. Sometimes if he had an announcement to make, he hammered on a little bell, whereupon each boy put down his knife and fork and turned halfway round to listen to the words of wisdom.

After dinner, the boys had half an hour to change for football in the winter and cricket in the summer. On days when it was too wet for either, they went for a cross-country run, the Four Mile Grind, to be completed in three-quarters of an hour, two prefects running round the opposite way and checking off each boy as he passed. School began again at four o'clock and continued until six with just one five minute break. Tea at six was a repeat of breakfast – tea and bread and scrape.

All boys were at their desks in the Schoolroom by seven for prep, supervised from the dais in complete silence by the duty master. For the new boys in the Lower School, prep was interrupted on Mondays for bath night. There was one bathroom for the whole school, a room with a cement floor and kerbstone running down the middle. On the left-hand side as you entered were four galvanised iron tubs with handles at either end.

The prefect in charge would remove his shoes and stockings and roll up his trousers to the knees; his job, apart from keeping order, was to fill the baths with hot water and keep a pail of cold water beside them. Four boys went up at a time, stripped off their clothes, got in and soaped themselves from head to foot. By the time they were washed, the next four boys had arrived, and the Prefect called "Out". Any boy not out in a few seconds would receive a full bucket of cold water. The newly clean boys would dress and make their way back down to prep.

At 8.15 the duty master in the Schoolroom would call "Fall in the Choir" and the boys would march out to the Chapel for evening service. At the bottom of the Chapel stairs a prefect was posted to observe law and order, another one just inside the Chapel door and yet another at the far end with his back to the altar watching to see that each boy knelt down reverently in his pew. A quick supper was taken in the dining hall after Chapel, and then the tired boys would be led back to the Schoolroom for the final ceremony of the day. The headmaster would enter formally and shake each boy by the hand, wishing good night to each one separately – a touching ritual started by Egerton and followed devoutly by his successors. Then up the stairs to the dormitory, with no talking, whispering or laughing, and Reynolds, like all the other boys, would kneel in silence beside his bed to say his final prayers of the day. A bell would ring and, once in bed, you could talk for ten or fifteen minutes. Then a second bell and lights out.

The school was primitive by modern standards. There was no electricity or telephone. It was lit by flaring gas jets supplied from the village gasworks. Cows would occasionally wander off the Banbury road on to the playground to the fury of the boys who had to dodge the cowpats as they played their own brand of tennis-ball soccer. The outside lavatories were ordinary earth closets with no bolts or locks on the doors. When a new boy arrived and modestly closed the door behind him, it was immediately kicked open by the first boy passing. Water was drawn from wells on the site which posed a dual problem: germs could easily get into the system, and the capacity was never quite sufficient for the school's needs. In Reynolds' first term, water proved very short in the main school well and the elaborate ritual of the weekly bath had to take place in the isolation hospital where the nearby well provided a better supply.[10]

Reynolds' time at Bloxham coincided with its period of sharpest decline. When he joined in 1893 along with ten other new boys, the number of pupils was 107, a fall of three on the previous year. When he left in 1898, the total had fallen steeply to 62 and the school was only a third occupied.[11] It was the unfortunate lot of Frederick Boissier throughout his headmastership to struggle against this downward spiral. Falling intake meant falling revenues, and even greater expenditure cuts to a régime that was already fairly spartan.

As with all schools, disease was an ever-present threat and, apart from the problem of the water supply, largely beyond the control of any human agency. At the end of Reynolds' first term, a dozen boys developed influenza and seven had to remain in school when the boys went home on 16 December for the Christmas holidays. The following term there was an outbreak of scarlatina, the first for 20 years, and by the end of March 30 boys had succumbed. When Easter fell early in the year, school term was extended to take in the Easter and Holy Week services, but in 1894 medical precaution triumphed over religion and all boys were sent home before Easter while the school was disinfected. When it reopened on 7 May for the cold and miserable summer of that year, 25 boys were still at home recovering from the disease.[12]

In July of the following year, a boy was found to have typhoid but, fortunately, this was successfully isolated. In July 1896, 20 boys went down with mumps. When school brokc up for Christmas that year, Boissier noted in his log book: "There have been during the term 25 cases of chicken pox and 26 of Measles, some boys having both."[13]

This was not the best medical environment for a boy like Reynolds, a potential consumptive who had been plagued with illness for much of his young life; but parents faced the same lottery at every school. So it was surprising that during his time at Bloxham he actually recovered much of his health.[14] The spartan physical régime had something to be said for it after all.

One medical condition did not improve. It was probably about the time of his entry to Bloxham that short sight was first diagnosed and he took to wearing the little round wire-framed spectacles that became, in later years, as much his trademark as the fisherman's garb. He took care they should not appear in formal publicity photographs and it is only rarely we catch a glimpse of him with them on.

In the face of growing competition from other schools, Boissier concentrated on improving the academic standing of Bloxham. The basic course of instruction included English, Latin, French, Mathematics, History, Geography, Writing, Drawing and Vocal Music. Like many other schools of the period, science subjects were notable by their absence. In the Upper School, boys could choose one additional subject from Greek, German or Chemistry. Reynolds, who had already studied some natural science, chose Chemistry.[15]

Below Boissier, there was in Reynolds' time a core of about half-a-dozen assistant masters, nearly all Oxbridge graduates, who taught to a high standard. Foremost among them was the remarkable C.J. Wilson, known to the boys as "Pym", whose career was in itself a complete history of Bloxham. He joined as one of the first two boarders when the school opened in 1860 and remained there for the next 76 years as pupil, master, bursar, and finally resident secretary of the Old Bloxhamist Society, even obtaining his Oxford degree without resigning his mastership. He left in 1936 because he could no longer get up the stairs, and died three years later. He was a short man with a drooping moustache and with, even as a child, a doleful countenance which grew gradually more doleful as the years progressed. He taught Reynolds the love of French that was to take him to Paris and form an important thread below the surface of his literary life.[16]

Wilson's appearance was deceptive. He had a great sense of humour and used to teach the language with tremendous force and verve, feeding the younger boys simple dodges for memorising arcane points of grammar or vocabulary. One was only too relevant to Reynolds' future career – the distinction between the feminines of *pêcheur/pécheur, pêcheuse* (fisherwoman) and *pécheresse* (female sinner): "the fisher is an honest man and he pays for his shoes". Ten years later in Boulogne, Reynolds was still struggling to distinguish the sinner from the fisher.[17]

Every Sunday, after lunch, Wilson would go for a walk and anyone from the school could join in and listen to him teaching as he went. After tea he would read to any boys who cared to come up to his room, and would hand round a bag of striped bullseyes. Though he was well able to keep order, he was kindly, generous and much loved by the boys.

Another formative influence on Reynolds was J.F. Turner, a Cambridge graduate, who taught him maths and a little science until his last two years. He was a tall, boyish-looking man, a very good teacher but with a reputation as a stern disciplinarian. He would correct the arithmetic books of the weaker boys with remarks in red ink such as "Rubbish", "Nonsense", "Rot", and those who failed to add up correctly would, after two warnings, get two cuts with the cane.[18]

This was seldom a problem for Reynolds who loved maths and science as much as English and French, and was good at all four.

Bloxham had been a centre for the Cambridge Local Examinations since 1865 and all boys were prepared for these exams annually, remaining candidates until they obtained a First Class Junior or were too old. The examination, taken each December, became a fixed and recognised focus of academic achievement, up to which the year's work led and by which it was regulated. When the results came through in the middle of the Easter term, excitement filled the school.[19]

Reynolds performed well in these examinations throughout his time at Bloxham. In December 1894, then aged 13, he passed in the preliminary examination, Religious Knowledge and English, but failed in Euclid. The following year he passed in six subjects, adding Mathematics, French and Natural Science to the list, and was awarded a Second Class Certificate. In 1896, Latin was added to a list of seven passes and the following year he obtained a Third Class Senior Certificate with a distinction in Religious Knowledge, on the strength of which the school was granted a half-holiday.[20]

In the annual school prize-giving in July, he was awarded an examination prize every year from 1894 to 1898, together with a history prize in 1895 and two Bloxham prizes in his final two years. In August 1898, at the end of his final term, he became only the second boy from the school to be entered for the Oxford and Cambridge Local Board Examination, which he passed in French, Elementary and Additional Mathematics, Scripture Knowledge and, his new love, Chemistry. Interestingly for a man destined to become a writer, he had now dropped English as an examination subject.[21]

If Reynolds excelled in the academic work which was now the primary objective of the school, he was not backward either in the religious study and observance which had been the *raison d'être* at the school's foundation. Religion played an all-pervasive part in the daily school routine. On rising in the morning the boys said their prayers at their bedside or, if there were time, went up to the Chapel to say them while the Chaplain celebrated Communion. All boys took part in Matins in Chapel before breakfast and Evensong at night after prep. Originally, it had been full Matins and full Evensong every day, but now the full services were reserved for Sundays only, when the Chaplain would preach at Matins and the Headmaster at Evensong. In the early 1890s, the Upper School was still spending more time on Divinity than any subject other than Mathematics and Euclid. Boissier did his best to try and reduce this emphasis which he recognised was impairing Bloxham's ability to compete academically with the much-improved education offered by the board schools and high schools and, with the growing prejudice against High Church practices, was turning off many parents who might otherwise have sent their sons there.[22]

Divinity in Reynolds' day was taught by the Rev. H. Wigan, the first chaplain at Bloxham who was not a dormitory master with disciplinary powers. He was not a man to be drawn into the finer points of theological argument. When faced with an awkward query, he was known to reply "That is a question of metaphysics into which I cannot enter here".[23]

It is clear, nevertheless, that Reynolds took to religious studies not just in a conformist mood but with some personal enthusiasm. He had worshipped regularly as a child at St Mary's in Devizes and Julia Jepp in *The Holy Mountain* gives perhaps some insight into both his ambivalence of approach and his love of the forms and social ambience of religion:

> When a girl she had not liked church any better than most children; but to-day St Thomas's, which reminded her of quiet childish hours and of one or two childish attempts to talk to God like real holy people, calmed her magically...... And afterwards, to come out from the dim porch into the brilliant July sunlight, among the chattering people, greeting one another heartily; to walk back in the sunshine with the only good dinner of the week awaiting her....[24]

Given the loss of his mother and sense of separation from his crumbling childhood family, it is not surprising that as an adolescent he should take some consolation from religion – "in my younger days, of course, I went through a religious phase".[25] On Palm Sunday 1895, just five weeks before his fourteenth birthday, Reynolds was confirmed by the Bishop of Reading along with 37 other boys.[26] It may have meant more to him than many of the others. Certainly he took to Divinity as a subject with some avidity. He knew his Bible well and passed in Religious Knowledge in the local examinations every year, in his last achieving a distinction. At the end of his first summer term, he took with the other boys an examination made up of questions on Staley's *Catholic Religion*. Even at this age, his performance was good enough to win one of the Old Boys' Divinity Prizes and he was presented with a volume of *Heroes of Hebrew History*. In addition to the other academic prizes, he won a divinity prize every year for the next three, culminating in 1897 in a presentation of Blunt's *Annotated Common Prayer*.[27]

How much did this intensive routine of religious observance and instruction impact on Reynolds' approach to life and outlook on the world? In February 1909 he told a journalist: "I went to a Church of England public school, where I got so many prizes for divinity and learnt so much about church services that I've only been to weddings and funerals since."[28] At the height of his celebrity, he was keen to brandish his rejection of formal religion as a part of his general rejection of middle-class life and standards. He talked of religion, like all other systems of thought, in precisely the way his working-class friends would have done, with a strong dose of anti-clericalism thrown in for good measure.

But privately, the religion of his childhood and the years at Bloxham had a deep and lasting impact on his thought. They formed the backcloth to the intensely mystical response he was to make to his breakdown in 1903, and were the reason behind his continuing recourse to the Bible to explain the feelings and happenings of everyday life. In 1913, as a Christmas splash, the *Christian Commonwealth* invited 84 "representative people" to make personal confessions under the title "The Faith I Live By". Characteristically, in the course of his essentially agnostic response, Reynolds betrays the lasting legacy of those divinity lessons at Bloxham.

> I don't in the least know what faith I live by. Don't want to know. I suppose Wordsworth's *Lines Written above Tintern Abbey*, 88-111, come somewhere near, though it seems to me that a faith which can be put into words isn't a faith, but merely a belief. If there's another life, well and good. If there isn't, well and good again. That's how 'twill be, whether 'tis or not. I shall know somewhen, or cease knowing altogether. Meanwhile, there's a lot else to do; life to be lived as much and as well as possible. The Bible, as a supernatural revelation of fact – I don't believe a word of it. But I notice that when one has thought and felt much about anything, it is always a phrase from the Bible that leaps up to embody one's conclusion. Hence, it seems to me that the Bible, while worthless as factual knowledge, is beyond price – and beyond argument – as a depository of ancient human wisdom. But it seems to me, too, that in this so-called scientific age, knowledge and facts are absurdly exalted at the expense of wisdom.[29]

Of the public school trinity of academic learning, religion and sport, Reynolds excelled at the first two, but failed abysmally in the third. In his own CV, written for a friend in 1909, he wrote "Detest competitive games of every sort" – and he meant it.[30] Although Bloxham was perhaps not so fanatical about sport and exercise as some other schools (some of the fanaticism was reserved for prayer), the authorities were always proud to cite "the good effect which systematic physical exercise, coupled with the wholesome rule of 'no trouser pockets' has had upon the general build of boys. A regular 'sloucher' is rarely seen here in these days."[31]

Cricket was the most important school game, with the masters taking part alongside the boys in competitive matches because of the relative dearth of pupils. In football, before the formal development of Rugby and Association rules, every school played to its own set. At Bloxham, because Egerton was a Wykehamist, they played 15-a-side soccer, with an emphasis on dribbling and individual play rather than combination and passing, under rules rather eloquently described as "founded on Winchester and common sense".[32]

For Reynolds, most of this was purgatory. But one physical exercise he *did* enjoy and was very good at – and that was swimming. In his day, there was no swimming pool at Bloxham and generations of boys were taught by W.J. Bridger, the master in charge of the junior school, in the Sor Brook about a mile down the Banbury Road. Novices were taught in the mud shallows, known as the "pea soup", where boys went in white and came out covered in mud from head to foot which they subsequently washed off under the weir. Once they could swim the pea soup, they were allowed into the "deep water", about 25 yards long and seven feet deep, and full of bright clear water.[33]

Swimming in the summer was an afternoon out. On the cycle ride back to school, boys would stop at the mill house to buy a penny slice of cake out of their sixpence a week pocket money. Bridger may have helped Reynolds improve his swimming in the summer of 1894, before leaving the school later in the year. After this, swimming was taken by the Drill Instructor. In the summer of 1898, Sergeant Millard gave lessons to non-swimmers on Saturdays and Reynolds himself took on that responsibility on other days of the week.[34] Swimming was always a sensual experience for him. Some ten years later, he discovered the pleasure of bathing naked on the little beach beyond Jacob's Ladder at Sidmouth, both improving his health and causing a little local scandal into the bargain.

As a country school, Bloxham inevitably gave scope for childish country pursuits, not always officially approved, such as birds nesting, rat hunting by Sor Brook, shooting with air guns – occupations which Reynolds learnt to pursue both at school and at home.[35] But the interest in wildlife also took a more academic and responsible form. In November 1895, Reynolds was instrumental in setting up the new Natural History Society when the remains of the old School Museum were dusted off and moved to the old Library, which had been replaced by the Egerton Memorial Library, the one prestige building project of Reynolds' time. *The Bloxhamist* reported

> Thanks to the energy and perseverance of Reynolds and Massey such specimens as have survived their long neglect have emerged from their state of chaos and have been once more duly classified, arranged and numbered. Under these circumstances it was thought that, as an incentive to greater interest in the Museum, and with a view of stimulating boys to improve and extend the collection which we have inherited, it would be a good thing to start a Natural History Society. With this object in view a preliminary meeting was held in the Liddon Room on Sunday, November 17th, which was attended by a large number of boys, some of whom were attracted by the curiosity which anything new always seems to excite in a certain class of mind while others showed a genuine interest in Natural History. The former class were relentlessly weeded out, as the inclusion of a number of indifferent members would have been fatal to the success of the Society.

At a further meeting the following Sunday, the Headmaster was elected President of the Society and the Chaplain, Curator of the Museum. Reynolds was among the thirteen founder members who qualified under Rule 1: "No boy to be eligible for membership who is not a bona fide collector of objects approved by the Society." The meeting ended with a hearty vote of thanks to Reynolds and Massey "for their valuable services in the arduous task of arranging, numbering and cataloguing the varied assortment of curios and specimens already belonging to the School."[36] Further donations were badly needed, and to this end Reynolds contributed a piece of quartz and some butterflies.

At the beginning of the summer term the following year, the Society agreed that special efforts should be made to form a really good local collection of butterflies, eggs, fossils, flowers and other exhibits. It was a busy summer. By the autumn, Reynolds and three others had put together some prize collections of butterflies and moths, pressed flowers, birds' eggs and fossils, all almost entirely of local origin. He remained an active member, taking part in meetings and organised rambles, right up to his final term.[37]

Cycling and photography were the most popular free time activities through the 1890s and Reynolds joined the school Photographic Society, the high standard of which is fully attested by the quality of the photos passed down to us today.[38] This early experience of camera work and composition was fully applied to his own creative work. In later years he took a more than professional interest in the quality of the photographs included in such books as *Alongshore*.

Apart from the odd poems he wrote at home, Reynolds does not appear to have been deeply involved, or perhaps much interested, in the literary endeavours of the school. In December 1897 the senior form decided to found a Literary Society "for the purpose of producing attractive and healthy fiction during the idle hour known as 'Prep'".[39] This has the authentic Reynolds' ring about it, but the new society was an idea that never got off the ground. Throughout his time at Bloxham the school magazine, *The Bloxhamist*, was thriving but he does not seem to have taken a particularly active part. In the autumn of 1896 he joined the editorial staff, along with three other boys, because of a surprise clear-out of the existing school members, but a year later he had left.[40] This first experience was to prove typical of his later chequered career in editorial work. He could never survive in one job, taking orders from someone else, for more than a matter of weeks. Most of the articles, stories and poems in *The Bloxhamist* of the period are unsigned but there is nothing which clearly stands out as from Reynolds' pen.

Music was a far more engrossing activity than writing. For an extra 30 shillings a term, boys were given two piano lessons a week, but this was only recommended for boys "who have a very decided turn for Music and are willing to make some sacrifice of play hours for this object."[41] S.S. Reynolds was patently such a boy. J.G. Clarke was organist and music master for much of the 90s, but Reynolds also profited from the presence of H.M. Hain, the German master from Bavaria, who was an outstanding musician with a high reputation outside Bloxham and who brought a new impetus to the musical life of the school, starting in his early years a flourishing string band among the boys.[42] Clarke arranged concerts from time to time, and there was always one on prize day at the end of July before the presentations. Reynolds was soon good enough to take part in these public performances. In July 1896 he performed a duet, "Spanish Dance", with another boy as the first item in the concert; and at his last prize day in 1898 he and the new music master, W.H. Nixon, opened with another duet "The Overture to Zampa" by Hérold. Reynolds played later in the programme a solo piece, "First Valse" by Durand. It was the success of these public performances that gave him a new ambition – to become a professional concert pianist.[43]

He began to blossom too in other performing arts. There had been no history of putting on plays at Bloxham, a consequence perhaps of the high religious tone of the school; but J.H.T. Goodwin, the English master, was keen to fill this gap. In 1897 he decided to put on a play at Founderstide, All Saints Day, and in the summer began rehearsals of *Julius Caesar* before reluctantly deciding that Shakespeare was too ambitious for an untried company. Goodwin then hit upon a standard Victorian comedy by William Suter, *A Test of Truth*, in which a wealthy eighteenth-century gentleman decides to test the characters of his two nephews by pretending to die, leaving all his possessions to the wicked one and nothing to the good. Predictably, the wicked nephew fails the test by exhibiting only greed for the inheritance while the good nephew manifests genuine sorrow for his uncle's death.

With no track record of acting in the school, a committee was set up to choose "a number of boys whose faces or figures or general bearing 'looked like acting'".[44] Reynolds was chosen to play Major Freeheart, a pivotal character and friend of the good nephew, who persuades the uncle to carry out the test. His few interventions call for a good Victorian melodramatic style, with such resonant lines as "Avaricious wretch, ere long you will yourself need pity".[45]

A large stage with a handsome curtain was erected at the southern end of the Schoolroom and an audience of some 150 assembled there on the afternoon of 1 November with keen anticipation. Just before the performance, a photograph of the distinguished cast was taken in the corner of the quadrangle where all formal school photographs took place. They all look nervous, but none so much as the sixteen-year-old Reynolds, a squat sturdy figure, tight lipped as usual, but the only one of the company with *two* clenched fists. He is dressed in the full regalia of Major Freeheart, hired from a costumier in Covent Garden: scarlet coat with yellow facings, white kerseymere breeches, silk stockings, cocked hat, powdered wig with queue, and dress sword.

They had no need to be nervous of the impending performance. There were glowing notices in the *Banbury Guardian* and *Banbury Advertiser*. The latter thought "S.S. Reynolds was exceedingly good as the retired officer" and on the short farce that followed the main play, in which Reynolds played a short-sighted patron of the arts, commented "S.S. Reynolds had evidently bestowed much care upon the preparation of his difficult role, and that he was thoroughly successful there could be no shadow of doubt."[46] It was the first dramatic performance the school had ever put on. Boissier noted in his log book, perhaps with some relief: "In the afternoon *the boys gave a play* in the School Room. About 160 tickets were sold and all passed off successfully."[47]

This was not the end of Reynolds as Thespian. In February the following year, the school put on an "entertainment" in aid of the Universities' Mission to Central Africa. A concert was followed by a performance of the farce *The Area Belle* in which Reynolds played a local Bloxham Volunteer. *The Bloxhamist* was a little more harsh with its criticism than the average local newspaper: "In thus criticizing the performance we are performing a thankless task, but it is far better to point out where matters may be improved than to apply the oleo-margarinic process, and make it appear that all those, who are kind enough to amuse us, are heaven-born singers or actors, and have only to apply to Sir Henry Irving or the Handel Festival Authorities to be welcomed with open arms." Against this severe yardstick, Reynolds came off rather well. He "made a very fair 'Bloxham Volunteer'; a little more life would have been requisite had he undertaken the part, as originally written, of a Guardsman".[48]

It seems from both his dramatic and musical performances that in his later years at Bloxham the social side of Reynolds' nature had overtaken the more reclusive literary one. He was clearly enjoying the externals of school life and playing a full part. Internally, growing up in the monastic atmosphere of a boys boarding school, he must have had his fair share of adolescent turmoil. No such school at this or any other period could avoid the usual undercurrents of homosexuality, though Bloxham was small enough to be able to keep this and other "anti-social" tendencies under some control.

At the beginning of Reynolds' second year, two separate scandals swept the school. In December 1894 a boy was caught stealing stamps and postal orders from masters' rooms, was publicly birched before the whole school and expelled. More significant, a month before, a long-serving master was forced to resign, as Boissier delicately put it, "in consequence of immoral relations between him and some of the smaller boys."[49] How close Reynolds came to this incident we can only surmise. Certain it was that, from his place in the junior school, he would have been close enough to know all the details.

This was a significant time. 1894 was the last year in which homosexuals in England could live full lives with any degree of confidence. Six months after the episode at Bloxham came the Oscar Wilde trial and for the next seventy years the pattern of persecution forced most homosexual activity underground. Adolescent boys of the 1890s were fully conversant with the Wilde scandal, none more than Reynolds whose literary tastes were fast moving towards the Yellow Book. On subsequent evidence it seems likely that at Bloxham he kept his own sexual feelings and behaviour well under control. But many have discovered their homosexuality in English boarding schools and it would be surprising if, in this particular life story, Bloxham did not play its part.

Though relatively happy at Bloxham, Reynolds like all boys was reluctant to go back after the holidays. Years later, when leaving Sidmouth to go back to work in Devizes, he recalled the anxious feeling: "Curiously, I felt, the first time for years, as if I were leaving home for boarding school – the warmth behind, the chill in front. I smelt again the rank soft-soap in the great bare schoolrooms".[50] And he was always glad at the end of term to arrive back home, where Peter, the cat with the white shirt front, would be there to greet him, holding off a moment, sniffing, recognising, rubbing against his ankles, purring with delight.[51]

Major domestic changes had been going on in Devizes while he was away. In June 1893, just before Reynolds was packed off to school, his father had married again. His new wife, Leonie Christian, a miller's daughter from Hertfordshire, was the same age as Clara had been when she died. It may be because of the lingering presence of Clara that the new couple decided not to live in the Bear. On return from their wedding in London, they moved into Beech Cottage (now The Beeches) just round the corner from the Bear and on the edge of the Castle Grounds. Frank Reynolds continued as innkeeper but no longer had the worry of a family on the premises. Three years later, Leonie gave birth to Reynolds' stepsister, Frances.

Reynolds' relationship with his new stepmother did not follow the lines of the traditional fairy story. They seem in fact to have got on rather well. In an early short story published in 1906, Reynolds describes the effects on three children of a widowed father remarrying, in this case through the lonely hearts columns, an unlikely refuge for Frank Reynolds. The children react at first with trepidation and hostility but are soon won over by the homely warmth of their new mother.[52] From the picture we have of her playing with the young children in the garden, Leonie Reynolds too was a warm person with a sympathetic humorous face. Like her predecessor she was a good pianist and gave full support to Reynolds in his musical ambitions.

One other thing she gave him was beyond price – an introduction to the little seaside town of Sidmouth in South Devon. The Christians owned a holiday house there and it was their traditional summer haunt. It was a habit immediately taken up by the Reynolds family too, and that vast expanse of sea and sky, the gorse-covered hills and red cliffs, the fishermen mending their nets below the Bedford steps, soon became a familiar part of the summer holidays from Bloxham.

He felt comfortable enough even to write one of his doggerel verses about her. Although the record of a rather strange confrontation between mother and stepson, it has in it all the elements of a strong affection:

Last Saturday night when I came in,
There rang in my ears a most terrible din,
For there stood the missus and maid in a stew,
And of buckets and mops a most terrible crew.

They both seemed determined for that night at least,
Not a soul in the house should have any peace.
I ventured a word by way of remonstrance,
Mrs R. cut me short declaring 'twas nonsense,
Told me to mind my own business, not meddle with hers,
And get out of the house while I'd a safe pair of ears.
I took the hint quickly, nor made a reply,
Said I'd look in again, when the kitchen was dry.[53]

Back in Wiltshire he still kept up with his string of surrogate mothers – Ada Bennett at Devizes College, and Lizzie Powney who, since he had gone off to Bloxham, had made her own career move. Frank Reynolds had now lost both his assistants at the hotel. In 1895, together with her friend Ellen Blencowe, Lizzie had left the Bear for Salisbury where the two now ran the popular Angel Hotel in Fisherton Street.

In November 1897 she married George Tanner, then working as a brewer, in a Salisbury wedding which Frank Reynolds attended as a witness. George had been born in Devizes in October 1873, the son of Joel Tanner, a boot and shoe-maker at 23 Brittox, and a solid customer, no doubt, of the currier firm of Reynolds. His father had died when he was just a child and he had been brought up on his own by his widowed mother who continued to run the shop. Perhaps not surprising, therefore, that he should have chosen a wife ten years older than himself whom he may well have met when Lizzie was working at the Bear.[54] Now as her husband, he joined her in the hotel trade. Reynolds kept in touch with them both in his school holidays and was soon just as close a friend of George, who was almost his own generation. He became the new couple's adopted child.

He was also a favourite of his mother's elder sister, another Lizzie, who together with her husband, Thomas O'Reilly, ran a drapery store at No.4 High Street and a family of six children.[55] At Christmas 1894, she gave him a copy of *The Tennyson Birthday Book* and he wrote proudly on the fly-leaf "Stephen S. Reynolds from Auntie Lizzie Xmas 1894". It had been published in 1891 by the firm of Macmillan & Co. and printed by R. & R. Clark of Edinburgh, names to become all too familiar before long....[56]

Reynolds' formal successes at Bloxham in academic work and his knowledge and example in religion were rewarded with status and responsibility. In September 1896, at the age of 15, he was appointed a sub-prefect and at the beginning of the following term a full prefect in joint disciplinary charge of Dormitory III.[57] In the summer of 1898, he was appointed Senior Prefect, the Bloxham term for Captain of the School. This was normally conferred on those with both sporting and academic prowess, and it was some recognition of his impact on the school that he was made Senior Prefect despite his total lack of interest in sport. Indeed, the honour put him in the embarrassing position of *ex officio* member of the Committee of Games, organising the cricket fixtures for the summer. It must have been one of the few committees he ever sat on on which he played a less than active part.[58]

But in other contexts, the proposals of the Senior Prefect had to be considered seriously. In June 1898 he had his second brush with the Prince of Wales, who was due to pay a visit to Lord and Lady Algernon Gordon Lennox at nearby Broughton Castle. Remembering Devizes five years earlier, the new Senior Prefect made the patriotic suggestion that the whole school should attend to welcome the Prince with a chorus of "God Bless the Prince of Wales". The proposal was put to Lord Algernon who tactfully suggested that, since the visit was to be a private one, the Prince might not wish for quite this degree of scholastic fervour. In the event the school turned out in force at Banbury to give the Prince a good cheer; and Dr Hain and the school band were invited to play to the Prince at Broughton. Dr Hain was formally presented and the Prince, in fluent German, said what a charming orchestra it was and what very pretty pieces had been selected.[59]

Reynolds left Bloxham after prize-giving at the end of July 1898 with the Oxford and Cambridge examinations before him but little else in terms of plans or direction. He knew that on his future there would be battles in plenty to fight at home.

For the headmaster, Boissier, this was also the end of the line. After the years of struggle against sickness and water shortage, declining numbers and expanding losses, he finally advised Egerton to reopen negotiations with the reluctant Woodard Corporation where he believed the only safe future lay for the school. The Corporation, which had financial worries of its own, eventually agreed to take it over and the formal transfer was made in August 1896. With the Corporation behind it, the school was now able to raise money and provide a new start with enlargement of the wells, new bathrooms, installation of central heating in Schoolroom and Chapel and, irony for Reynolds, the opening of a science laboratory the term after his departure.[60]

Having managed the transition, Boissier decided to resign to make way for a new headmaster appointed by the Corporation. Bloxham had been his whole life and he went with some reluctance. Three days before Christmas 1898, when the boys had gone down and the school was empty, he made the final entry in his log book.

> December 14
> The boys presented Rev.F.S.Boissier (Headmaster) with a handsome chiming clock as a mark of their respect and esteem on the occasion of his resigning his work.
> Mr Boissier was a boy in All Saints' School from 1865 to 1871; – Second Master 1878–86. Head Master 1886–98. He is succeeded by Rev. G.H. Ward, Scholar of Hertford College, Oxford and Assistant Master at St

> Paul's School, Kensington, London.
> So ends my official connection with Bloxham.[61]

But not quite the end of his connection with Reynolds. After Reynolds' death, his friend and literary executor, Harold Wright, wrote to Boissier, then vicar of Denby in Derbyshire, for the final word on his five years at Bloxham: "During the whole of that time [he] bore an excellent character, and was head of the School when he left". Reynolds, who equated good conduct with colourless conduct, would have summed up the experience in rather different words.[62]

THREE

Manchester 1899-1902

Frank Reynolds was growing tired of the Bear. After ten years of unremitting labour and pretty meagre financial returns, even the privilege of being at the centre of the social and political web of the town was beginning to lose its compensatory quality. The fabric of the old building was crumbling, and costing him money too. The stone tiles in the roof were sinking and letting in the rain, wreaking havoc among the decorations in the hotel bedrooms which he had to put right out of his own pocket. Any new painting organised by the landlords was botched; and the paving in the yard at the back was uneven and in dire need of attention. At the beginning of 1897 he took the problems up with his landlords, the Bear Hotel Company, and started a legal dispute over the relative obligations under the lease which ended in a spate of surveying and counter-surveying and a loss of good will on either side.[1] From this moment he began to look round for a new occupation.

He did not have to look far. Towards the end of the year plans were afoot to establish a new bacon factory in the town and Councillor Reynolds soon got caught up in them. When in the following August a formal application came before the Council to establish a slaughterhouse on the site of the new factory in the Bath Road, it was Frank Reynolds who took the initiative in proposing approval of the plans after a swift submission to the Medical Officer.[2] When the Central Wiltshire Bacon Company was finally established in 1899, it came as little surprise to the town that the first managing director should be Councillor Reynolds who had helped pull all the appropriate strings.

He gave up the Bear and his house by the Castle and moved to Caen Hill in the west of the town to be close to the factory. The Bear remained, however, in the best of hands. By private arrangement, George and Lizzie Tanner moved from Salisbury to take over the lease. For Lizzie it was a return to run the hotel in which she had learnt the rudiments of the trade. For Stephen Reynolds it brought his good friends back closer again and gave him the run of his childhood home whenever he chose.

While Frank Reynolds was thus rearranging his life, the career plans of his only son were in no less a state of flux. When he came back home in August 1898, after sitting the Oxford and Cambridge examination, he had no clear idea of his future. One thing he knew for certain, he would not fulfil his father's wishes and go straight into business. His only tangible ambition was the dream that one day he might be a concert pianist. The tussle over Reynolds' future at this period was the beginning of the long drawn-out conflict between father and son which was finally to confirm for Reynolds what he had felt for the past three years – that he had no longer a family nor a home.

On the surface it was an argument between the secure well-paid job and the more risky fulfilment of creative ambitions. But deep down it was a conflict of personality between a rigid temperament which looked little further beyond money and social status and a youthful mind open to new ideas and experience and longing for creative expression.[3]

Mutual disparagement made matters worse. In *The Holy Mountain* Reynolds describes his father's outlook on life in the person of the mayor of Trowbury, James Trotman: "His greatest practical ambitions were, to get on in life – to make money that is, – and to be a local celebrity as cheaply and with as much advertisement to his business as possible". And James Trotman's attitude to his son: "I've spent pounds more than I ought to on his education...... I've kept him on at the technical school to learn to be a practical man, and he's neither business-like or a scholar...... He might have been an accountant, or an auctioneer and estate agent, by now if he'd stuck to it."[4] Harsher things were said to each other's face in the privacy of the Reynolds' family home.

In the row over his future, the budding concert pianist won the first round. Supported by his stepmother, it was agreed that his pianistic skills should be put to the test. Frank Reynolds may have seen it as the only way of killing this fanciful ambition once and for all. It was arranged for Reynolds, accompanied by his father, to go up to London to play before Sir Hubert Parry with a view to entering the Royal College of Music of which Parry was then Director. Parry was complimentary about Reynolds' playing and recognised in him a genuine talent, but warned strongly about the hazards of making a living in music against the fierce competition. On sober reflection, it was decided that the idea of a musical career should be dropped.[5]

If not the Royal College, then a university place – if only to stave off the evil day when a firm decision would have to be taken on a career. Reynolds made an application to Owens College in Manchester, but there were further arguments as to what he might study. He himself was keen to read English, or languages, or even music. His father was determined on a science degree which would be of more value to a business career. His father won.[6]

Reynolds travelled up to Owens in June 1899 to take the preliminary examination *in situ*. He was among the 130 odd candidates to satisfy the examiners that summer and gain a university place, but his marks were well below the best.[7] Returning to Bloxham for the last time to attend prize-giving that July, he could face his old masters with the pride of a potential undergraduate.[8]

When he finally went up to Manchester in October 1899, it was Reynolds' first experience of living in a big city. He loathed the damp, foggy climate and its effect on his increasingly tubercular chest, and the hopeless feeling of grime and squalor in most parts of the city. He found comfortable enough lodgings in a small, tree-lined, crescent-shaped street, Swinbourne Grove, in the relatively salubrious suburb of Withington, just a couple of miles out from college.[9] There at No.5 was a welcoming Scots landlady, Annie Laurie, who had kept house for many years for her schoolmaster brother and two or three lodgers, mostly teachers.[10] Since her brother had gone back to Scotland, she ran the place alone. He had one fellow-lodger "a large, gaunt old lady, dragged to failure after a life of work, who had seen her friends die off, and now was ending her days on a meagre pension dealt her grudgingly by some benevolent society". Her cat was her one remaining link to life, and if it stayed out longer than usual "she would rise from her big chair and throw up the window that looked out on a row of poplars and a sad suburban sky. There was the echo of a life's tragedy to be heard in the sound of her broken, failing old voice when she called, 'Kitty, Kitty, where are you? Kitty! Come to me'".[11] The rambling, three-storey Victorian houses on Reynolds' side of the street were all torn down in the 1970s but the row of poplars and the sad suburban sky are very much there today.

On 5 October Reynolds went into college and signed on.[12] Like all students, he was given a small blue pocket book, handed out by the Christian Union, which provided a potted history of Owens College, an introduction to the facilities of the Union and a rundown of the various clubs and societies for freshmen to join. The Union building opposite the college on the corner of Dover Street and Oxford Road soon became a familiar haunt. The Reading Room boasted a fairly comprehensive supply of newspapers and magazines, and doubled in the evenings as the meeting place for the various societies. For those who wanted to do more than lounge and read, there was a Billiard Room, a Chess Room, a Writing Room and a Committee Room. Food was supplied in the refectory on the ground floor. As a prospective chemistry student, he joined the Chemical Society which met at 6 pm on alternate Tuesdays to hear a paper on some aspect of chemical science followed by discussion. He also joined the Literary Society, meeting on alternate Fridays, at which essays were read on literary topics, followed by discussion, and occasionally the reading of a play. Although he was still a keen musician, there was as yet no musical society for him to join.[13]

Owens College had been founded through the will of the Manchester businessman, John Owens, who had died in 1846. It had started in a small way in a private house in Deansgate in 1851, but became the nascent university when the new complex of buildings was opened on the Oxford Road site in 1873. Its ethos was quite the reverse of Bloxham. Owens had wanted an unsectarian college and one condition of its university status was that there should be no testing of religious opinions. As the Principal of the College in Reynolds' day succinctly described the founder's intentions: "The 'atmosphere' he desired to create was one in which all could breathe freely and do their work unshackled, but with the due regard for the feelings of others which courtesy and kindness would impose. He was not anxious to give a special flavour to science, or ensure the teaching of Presbyterian Physics, Anglican Anatomy, or Methodist

Mathematics".[14] The change from the cloistered theology of Bloxham came to Reynolds like a breath of fresh air.

Owens also had a social conscience. The College looked outwards to the wider needs of the city and provided evening classes for both working men and men of business. The student élite were made to see that they were not the only ones in the world. It was the kind of climate in which Reynolds' stirring feelings of rebellion against middle-class life could develop and mature. And even in its very short life, Owens could boast at least one important literary connection. George Gissing had begun a promising academic career at Owens which had been cut short in 1876 by his imprisonment for stealing from his fellow students to support his prostitute lover. It was a symbolic episode for an institution anxious to uphold the rights of the downtrodden.

Owens had had a thriving Chemistry Department since the days of Henry Roscoe in the late 1850s. The new buildings of 1872, comprising a private laboratory, two large teaching laboratories, two lecture theatres and more than 20 research laboratories and staff rooms, were among the best facilities in the country. More up-to-date laboratories were built in the 1890s – the Schorlemmer, Frankland and Dalton laboratories for undergraduates and the Perkin laboratory for organic research. Reynolds' time as an undergraduate coincided with a flowering of chemical excellence at Manchester – the Dixon–Perkin period.

H.B. Dixon succeeded Roscoe as Professor of Chemistry and Metallurgy in 1886 and six years later W.H. Perkin became Professor of Organic Chemistry. They both had an unflagging interest in experimental research, their students and their teaching, and during their period of collaboration they attracted and inspired a remarkable band of enthusiastic staff, research workers and students. As one later commented: "work went on busily day and night during term time and vacation, throughout the year in never-ceasing activity".[15]

Both men had great strength of mind and physique, but otherwise differed widely in temperament, upbringing and outlook. Dixon, a tall, thin man with receding hair and a drooping white moustache, had originally read classics at Oxford and switched to chemistry in mid course. This showed in his lectures on inorganic chemistry which combined an historical approach – vivid and critical accounts of the development of chemical thought and the making of discoveries – with a leavening of spectacular experimental demonstrations. His principal research interest was that of combustion chemistry. Perkin, a younger, dapper man with dark beard and moustache, apparently more concerned with the present and the future, made organic chemistry seem simple with his clear logical expositions. There shone through his lectures the powerful and penetrating intellect of the master of a rapidly developing subject. At Manchester he had begun his experimental work on the synthesis of small carbon rings, but had developed into one of the leading authorities in the difficult field of camphor chemistry.

Inevitably, the interests of both men centred in the research laboratories and the lecture theatre. The conduct of the undergraduate laboratories where Reynolds worked most mornings was delegated to the more junior members of staff. One of these assistant lecturers was Philip Hartog, trained at London University and the Sorbonne, who had come to Owens in 1891 and been promoted senior assistant lecturer in 1895. He was a leading light of the Chemical Society and often presided over its meetings.

He had long been concerned about the inability of science students to express themselves effectively in writing and after his Manchester days became a prominent advocate of a more creative approach to the teaching of English in schools. But already he was a published author, having contributed almost half the biographies of chemists to the *Dictionary of National Biography*. He was also a good pianist and very interested in music. No doubt it was these artistic accomplishments that drew Reynolds to him. Hartog was still a regular visitor to Paris, where his sister lived; and was a friend of Bergson. Paris and Bergson now became new centres of interest for Reynolds too.[16]

The chemistry course was a heavy one for most students and Reynolds found himself fully occupied in his first year with the daily routine. In addition to the experimental work in the laboratories on at least three days a week, there were about forty chemistry lectures to attend each term. What is more, the modules had been expanded just before Reynolds' arrival, requiring in addition a course in Pure or Applied Mathematics (Reynolds chose Pure) and a course in Physics in the first year and one further course in the first or second year to be chosen from a number of options. The maths and physics alone added another fifty lectures and classes to the burden each term.[17]

He completed his first year in a dispirited mood. True, a new life had opened up to him, he had made new friends, there was plenty of intellectual stimulation. But he was depressed by the atmosphere of the gloomy and unending Manchester streets, so far in feeling from his beloved Wiltshire Downs. And he had lost the focus of his life. In his latter days at school, music had been the ambition on which his hopes for the future had rested. Now the idea of a musical career had gone, there was nothing to take its place. Certainly not Chemistry. He had thrown himself fully into his academic work – as he did throughout his life into all forms of work – but this was the compulsive endeavour of the neurotic, not the absorption of fulfilment. There was interest and stimulus in chemistry, but it did not speak to his heart.

Then came the accident that was not only to illumine both Manchester and his second year, but to shape the rest of his life.

In Reynolds' day there was no Chair of English at Owens College. The English Department was a small one presided over by the Rev. H.C. Beeching. In 1900, Oliver Elton, who had been lecturer in English Literature since 1890, was appointed Professor of English at Liverpool. At the close of the same year, Beeching himself was elected to the Chair of Pastoral Theology at King's

College, London and, to fill the gap left by Elton, planned to double this new responsibility with English lectures at Manchester.[18] The plans soon came unstuck. Beeching's new job proved too heavy, and the Council of Owens College found itself at the beginning of the Lent Term of 1901 with no one to lecture to its English students. To fill the urgent gap, it took the risk of appointing a man with good credentials in English studies and criticism, but absolutely no teaching experience. And thus Thomas Seccombe walked into Reynolds' life.[19]

Seccombe was 34, the son of a country doctor in Norfolk and grandson of Sir Thomas Seccombe, an eminent India Office civil servant. He had taken a first in history at Oxford and in 1891 was selected by Sidney Lee, the newly appointed editor of the *Dictionary of National Biography*, to be his assistant editor on the project. Over the next nine years, Seccombe contributed more than 700 biographies to the Dictionary, mainly of eighteenth century writers but also some sportsmen and athletes. On the strength of this work, he had just published *The Age of Johnson*, a volume in a new series on periods in English Literature, edited by Professor Hales, and was preparing a second on *The Age of Shakespeare*.

Seccombe was a tall, burly figure but with a gentle manner. In his work on the *DNB* he had built a reputation for patience, kindliness and courtesy which had made him a favourite among the contributors and assisted materially the general success of the venture through the 1890s.[20] The work had made him many contacts among eminent writers and scholars. He was particularly close to the highly respected Richard Garnett, Keeper of Printed Books at the British Museum, whose breadth of literary and bibliographical knowledge was legendary. Garnett was a contributor in his own right to the Dictionary, but Seccombe often consulted him informally in the course of his editorial work to obtain a volume or track down a reference.[21]

By the end of 1900, the main work on the Dictionary started by Leslie Stephen was now complete and on 31 December Sidney Lee disbanded the editorial staff. Seccombe, with a wife and young family to support, was without a job, and with no clear prospects. It may well have been through Hartog, who had also worked on the Dictionary, that he learnt of the dilemma in the English Department at Manchester. He was welcomed there with open arms in the second week of January. The English students could not have had a more erudite scratch lecturer, particularly on his chosen field of the eighteenth century.

Reynolds, in what spare moments he had from Chemistry, was now immersed in the English poets, from Spenser and Shakespeare, through his great love Blake, to Keats and Shelley. There is no record of his having attended any English lectures at this time, but he may have sneaked in to one or two. It was probably through Hartog that he made Seccombe's acquaintance informally, but it was certainly through the Literary Society that he became formally acquainted with Seccombe's enthusiasm for English Literature and his powers as a lecturer. On 15 February 1901 the new Lecturer in English was invited to attend his first meeting of the Literary Society and was given a hearty welcome. At the next meeting a fortnight later, he stood in at short notice for the scheduled speaker and read a paper on *Romany Rye* which was heard with rapt attention.[22]

Throughout his life Reynolds always made a strong first impression on new acquaintances, particularly once he got over his shyness and started to talk. Seccombe was among the first to be captivated by the young man's clarity of intellect and observation, and by the force with which he expressed his at times unorthodox ideas. For his part, Reynolds was excited to have at close hand someone to whom literature was a living experience, who had published books and come straight from the heart of the London literary scene. Some latent ambitions began to stir at the back of his mind.

Right from Seccombe's arrival, the two men enjoyed each other's company. Seccombe had taken lodgings a few streets away from Reynolds at 39 Egerton Road in Withington and there must have been many evenings that spring and summer when they walked home down the Wilmslow Road together. Though bred to the rigours of London, Seccombe shared Reynolds' feelings about the gloom of Manchester. Returning there in April 1901 to start the Easter term, he wrote to a friend of "the hurly burly of removal back from Hades to Gehenna, in other words from Ealing to Manchester. From the Brent to the Medlock, who can tell which is the more evil as regards odour".[23]

But both men had the sweet smell of English literature to share. And the presence of Seccombe both encouraged and inspired Reynolds to write. He seems occasionally to have tried his hand before at writing for the College Magazine (an anonymous article on Spenser from May 1900 appears to be his) but from February 1901 there begins a whole stream of literary articles, part criticism, part biography, of a kind that might well have gone into the *DNB*: on Keats, the elegies of Milton, Shelley, Arnold and Tennyson, on Izaak Walton and (not forgetting his music) on the funeral marches of Handel, Chopin and Beethoven.[24] They are juvenile pieces, but ones into which a lot of research and effort has gone in typical Reynolds fashion, and which show glimpses of the sharp intellect of his later writing. He is not afraid either, in a slightly whimsical way, to take issue with the immortals. He quotes a passage from *Endymion*

O Moon! . . . . . . the nested wren
Has thy fair face beneath its tranquil ken,
And from beneath a sheltering ivy leaf
Takes glimpses of thee; thou art a relief
To the poor patient oyster, where it sleeps
Within its pearly house. – The mighty deeps,
The monstrous sea is thine – the myriad sea!
O Moon! far-spooming Ocean bows to thee,
And Tellus feels his forehead's cumbrous load.

and comments: "The wren under its ivy leaf makes a pretty little scene...... and the last passage has a sea-like largeness; but what possible relief can the Moon be supposed to afford a *poor patient* oyster?"[25]

He also began to contribute some poems, with a nostalgic look back to Wiltshire, like the one entitled *From Caen Hill*, watching from his father's house the sun set over the Wiltshire Downs.[26] For some of these early contributions, he adopted the pseudonym "Moonraker", the affectionate name for Wiltshiremen drawn from the famous legend of the smugglers and the Excise men. But these longer effusions on sunsets, piano music and on the love he had not yet perhaps experienced were rather less effective than his more ironic pieces on matters that he had experienced, such as this little poem on student poverty published at the end of 1901 and inspired by Austin Dobson's *The Paradox of Time*.

Pecunia Fugit

"Alas, Time stays, – we go!"
......
Time flies apace, the preachers say, –
Don't you believe it!
If Austin Dobson have his way,
'Tis we who leave it.
But that's not all -
'Tis money flies and goes astray, -
Don't you believe it?
Our flight of time good death will stay:
The flight of cash stops ne'er a day, -
What can relieve it?
Why, none at all![27]

Seccombe stayed just two terms. On 3 July the College Council passed a formal vote of thanks to him for coming so ably to their rescue. The previous month, as part of the Jubilee celebrations, it had at long last founded a Chair of English and advertised for its first incumbent.[28] Seccombe was unqualified for an academic post of this importance but he did, at the suggestion of the Owens authorities, apply in August for the Chair at Aberystwyth, but without success. He spent the summer in Hove and then graduated back to London, where he established an advisory role to the publisher Constable and in 1902 started work for the *Bookman* on another mammoth task, an illustrated history of English literature.[29]

Reynolds kept in close touch with him after his departure and the relationship was to thrive for many years more. Seccombe had changed his world. He knew now that he must be a writer, and he had been given the confidence to believe that he could be one. This gift of belief in himself was in a sense more important even than the entrée Seccombe was later to give him into the London literary world. Reynolds was never to forget the debt he owed to "my earliest literary friend" and was quick to identify any attack upon the older writer as one upon himself.[30] When in 1907 Edward Garnett, in some withering comments on Reynolds' first draft of a preface to *A Poor Man's House*, incautiously drew in some slighting reference to Seccombe, he found himself on the receiving end of a deeply emotional confession of faith:

> I would like to ask you not to use Seccombe in driving home any truths about me or my work. You don't know what I really think about Seccombe; I don't know myself; don't care to analyse it; and I'm very sure I couldn't explain, if I tried. If, speaking carelessly about him, I spoke wrongly; editorially, so to speak; then consciously or unconsciously, I must have lied, for I wouldn't be disloyal to him for the world, not knowingly. Seccombe may be an object of deluded hero-worship on my part, but if so, it's an illusion I won't have broken if I can help it. Forgive my saying this. I'm not forgetting your kindness in criticising the draft. But had you been aware of quite the wounding-power of that remark about Seccombe, I'm pretty sure you'd have done anything but write it, and I know, being aware, you wouldn't repeat it.[31]

The first term that Seccombe spent at Manchester was the start of a year of celebrations to mark the Jubilee of the opening of Owens College. It ended on 12 March 1902, fifty-one years to the day, when the Prince and Princess of Wales attended to open the newly built Whitworth Hall – Reynolds' last brush with the heir to the throne, though on this occasion it was a new one. In the evening there was the College's traditional Conversazione in which all departments displayed their latest achievements. On the following day a special degree ceremony took place in the new hall and congratulatory messages were read out from academic institutions all over the country and the world. The students had their own celebrations, including a procession in bizarre dress around the city. The College magazine reported: "One has often heard it said that 'Students are no gentlemen', and to prove this a number came disguised as tramps".[32]

Among the summer celebrations of the previous year was a special smoking concert in May and a garden party at the end of June, in which C.P. Scott made his own garden over to the College for the day. In the evening there was an open air theatrical performance of scenes from *Twelfth Night* in which Seccombe played Malvolio and Hartog Fabian. A photograph of the performance shows the burly figure of Seccombe holding forth, with a rather timorous looking Hartog peering out from behind his back. As the magazine reported in its Jubilee issue, Seccombe became rather carried away with the performance: "His rendering of the part of the pompous steward was forcible and consistent; the impression he gave of dignity and self-love was good and well sustained.

In his great chance, the garden scene in which he finds the letter, Mr Seccombe improved his opportunity to the full. There is always a danger in a case like this of an actor enjoying his chance so much as to forget the audience, and unduly prolong his part. Mr Seccombe did not entirely escape this danger, and lingered over his soliloquy with much apparent relish."[33]

The legacy of Seccombe's influence was now to turn Reynolds for the first time towards fiction. In the summer of 1901, probably at home in Devizes, he wrote his first short story, *Turned Out*, a slight but highly charged piece about a pregnant servant girl, abandoned by her seducer, the son of the house, and left to die of exposure with her baby out on the Wiltshire Downs. The inspiration of *Tess* is clearly evident, but it is more an emotional evocation of Reynolds' own personal plight, abandoned by his family and abused by his father. It is a new departure for the writer of many, and better, short stories to come.[34]

With Seccombe gone, Reynolds returned in his final year to the depressed state of his early months in Manchester. Through the winter of 1901–2 he was suffering from the beginnings of the tubercular condition that had killed his mother and which was to dog him for the next few years, ever a potential threat to life.[35] This was not helped by the Manchester climate and his constant worry over the final examinations that loomed just ahead. With the rise of his literary ambitions, he had lost even the little interest he had felt for chemistry, and the work had become a heavy physical and psychological burden.

He kept up his writing for the College magazine, mainly in the form of long, rather ill-disciplined, satirical pieces that were to pave the way for his first novel, *The Holy Mountain*. One of them, *The Career and Opinions of Doctor Ahazuerus Tims*, is a pastiche of Carlyle out of *Tristram Shandy* which mockingly heralds science as the new religion.[36] In another, *The Narratives of a Laboratory Liar*, there is a rather laboured account of a Frankenstein figure engaged in the task of building living matter by artificial means, of which perhaps the only barely amusing touch is the author's chemical pseudonym of "H.G. Smells". There is, however, in this latter piece, in the form of a street conversation between two schoolboys, a sign that Reynolds was coming to grips with the working-class dialogue which was to be one of the strengths of his later writing. He was taking full advantage of his position in the suburban streets of south Manchester to observe the tongues of the working-class housewives at work, observation he was to use to some effect in his later Manchester story *Mrs Tripp's Flutter*.[37]

He was also obtaining a practical literary apprenticeship in other ways. He had joined the staff of the College magazine and was contributing small pieces to the editorial columns and gaining his first direct experience of publishers' ways in liaising with the Manchester firm of Sherratt & Hughes who brought out the magazine.[38] He also struck up a close friendship with the joint editor, Arthur Skemp, an English student a year his junior who later went on to become Professor of English at Bristol University and was killed in France in the final fortnight of the First World War. Skemp was to act, with Seccombe, over the next few years as literary mentor, until Reynolds fell into the more distinguished hands of Edward Garnett.

He had not entirely forgotten music either. Though Reynolds spoke on occasion of having "studied" music at Manchester, this seems to have been a slight exaggeration, perhaps to disguise his relative academic failure in chemistry. He was, however, a founder member of the College Musical Society and was elected to its Committee at the first general meeting in February 1902.[39] One of the two secretaries of the Committee was the artist Henry Lamb, son of the Professor of Mathematics at Owens, Sir Horace Lamb, and at this time a somewhat reluctant pupil of the University Medical School. His friendship with Reynolds dates from this time and was maintained up to the early days of Lamb's painting career in London.

In his last winter at Manchester, when Reynolds himself was constantly ill and wracked with worry over the approaching exams, his kindly landlady, Annie Laurie, to whom he seems to have been quite close, became herself seriously ill with chronic bronchitis. In reaction he suddenly moved out of Swinbourne Grove and across the Wilmslow Road to take up new lodgings with the Wilde family at 76 Davenport Avenue, a long and gloomy street of tiny terraced houses.[40] He may have anticipated the speedy break-up of his old lodgings and the disruption to his studies. But having lived through his mother's illness and death, he may not have felt equal to living in a house where someone to whom he was close was conceivably about to die. His landlady eventually moved back to Edinburgh where she died two years later at the age of 69.[41]

This unfriendly decision to escape the sick woman's house clearly left Reynolds with a residue of guilt which was to give rise to probably the best of his Manchester stories, because based on actual life – *Her Immortality*. In it a gentleman lodger gives notice immediately he learns that his landlady is dying of cancer; and soon after she hears that he is leaving, she dies. We catch our first glimpse of Reynolds' fastidious obsession with dirt which he was to turn on its head in one of the celebrated "lectures" in *A Poor Man's House*. The lodger, Mr Russell, comes down late to find the maid struggling unsuccessfully to light the fire and sends her off to the kitchen to fetch his breakfast:

> "Soon the girl brought in the customary breakfast, with hands that showed traces of a long struggle with the fire. The bacon was set before the lodger; but he regarded it with an expression of nausea. The truth was, he felt neither well in body, nor agreeable in temper. Looking at the servant, he pointed to some black marks on the edge of the plate.
> 'Look there! Beastly! Just when I wanted it nicer than usual. Take it away.'"[42]

He was already in training for the frying pan out of the coal cupboard in Bob Woolley's back kitchen.

But it was a miserable winter. "At a time when I was overclouded by an approaching examination, ill and unable to work properly" a letter arrived from his nurse, Polly Oakford, telling him that Peter, the cat of his childhood, had died in fits the previous day. It was the last link to that untroubled time before his mother's death. "I went out into the murky Manchester streets and wandered about, wet-eyed, and drank two twopenny whiskies to your memory and to keep my spirits up."[43]

When the final examinations arrived in early June he was still seriously unwell and, through inability to revise as he would normally have done, conscious of his ill-preparedness. He faced five three-hour papers in all; on organic, inorganic and physical chemistry, on the history of chemistry and of chemical philosophy, and one selected from a range of subjects. In addition, there was a gruelling practical examination in the laboratory extending over three days. When the results were announced on 1 July, his fate was a foregone conclusion. In the honours school of Chemistry, there were 15 firsts and 14 seconds. Two candidates fell into the third class – and one of those was Stephen Reynolds.[44]

Manchester and the meeting with Seccombe there was the launch of Reynolds' literary career. But the chemistry course, though ending in such disappointment, was to leave an indelible mark on the content of his writing and his literary style. Not only did it give him the telling scientific image, which he learned to handle more adeptly with experience; more important, it introduced to his work a pervading element of objective inquiry, an ability to observe and then stand back to analyse those observations, at times with a rigorous force. It contributed more than anything to his work that Orwellian gift of observing neutrally even the most fraught of emotional situations, and drawing from them persuasive conclusions set out in cool, clinical prose.

He was always deeply conscious of this debt to his scientific training. "The best thing science has done for me is to make me more patient, or at all events to see the necessity for being so."[45] He was also equally conscious of the price he had paid for his degree, and dismissive of its value. To the journalist in 1909 he recalled his Manchester days: "Was ill with cramming, but just got an Honours B.Sc. Don't forget the Honours – they're as useless as the B.Sc."[46] But at times he still paused to wonder whether the degree might not give a boost to his sales. He wrote to Pinker, his agent, in 1904: "If in any connection my B.Sc. can be of any use, all right. Otherwise, I don't love it; it cost me too much."[47]

FOUR

Paris 1902–3

Reynolds returned home from Manchester in June exhausted by the work and nervous tension of recent months and still plagued by the bad tubercular cough. His first words were not designed to please his expectant father. He announced with a firm decision that whatever else he did in life he would never enter a chemistry laboratory again.[1]

"Home" was no longer Devizes. After little more than two years, Frank Reynolds had abandoned his job at the Bacon Company, though he still maintained his interest in it and was to return later to work the rest of his career there.[2] He had been tempted away by the chance to purchase a new hotel, the Belle Vue at Cheltenham, which had lately become run down and was suffering a dubious reputation in the town. He installed himself as landlord, and with his business drive and outgoing personality, had turned the place round in the space of a year and a half. At the end of March 1902, the citizens of Devizes had said goodbye to him in a ceremony at the Bear in which he was presented with a set of candelabra and the usual eulogies.[3]

Living once more in the neutral environment of an hotel gave Stephen Reynolds some welcome distance from his father and family recriminations. Although unwell, he was mentally buoyant for he knew he was to become a writer. And in his final days at Manchester he had met a new friend with whom he was planning a new escape.

Arthur Bles, a small, dynamic man with a strong sense of humour, was then aged 25 and had already a lifetime's experience behind him. His grandfather, one of those immigrant Jews whose enterprise had added lustre to the new industrial Manchester, had come to the city from the Hague in the 1830s to set up the flourishing merchant and shipping company of S.D. Bles & Sons. He instilled into his numerous sons, all engaged in the business, the love of work that made the company thrive. Arthur, as third generation, was not so enamoured of the business and his tough old Dutch uncles with their worship of the sixty-hour week. At 16 he left school to go to sea, to escape both the business and his mother, who greatly favoured her two daughters and was very hard on her two sons. He sailed from Waterloo Dock bound for Portland, Oregon with a trunkful of books provided for his mental improvement by one of the kindlier of the uncles.[4]

He spent the next years sailing the world, but mostly in the region of the Americas. Life was tough. "The mate of the first ship on which I served as apprentice used to amuse himself by spitting tobacco juice between my toes if I was refractory in repeating the language dictated to me as being the only language fitted to the profession of a sailor. Needless to say I repeated the blasphemies rather than submit to the tobacco juice torture against which it was practically useless to protest."[5] But life was also surprisingly scholastic. "On our barque we had old whalemen, ruined captains, broken down boarding-house keepers, deserters from the Navy, every imaginable variety of sailor-man, but all of them without an exception spent their watch below, all through the passage, reading not Dick Donovan or "Bill Cody's Adventures", but Dickens, Thackeray, George Eliot, even Shakespeare, Dryden, and Milton, borrowing my books...... "[6]

It was in this stark environment that Bles too completed his literary education, and finally returned from sea in 1899, the year Reynolds arrived at Manchester.[7] The Bles family, as befitting Manchester businessmen, had a close relationship with Owens College. Arthur's cousin Charles had taken a degree in engineering there in 1889, and another cousin, Edward, was studying zoology at the same time as Reynolds. So it was most probably through Edward Bles that Reynolds came to know the Bles family, and Arthur in particular.[8]

It was predictable that he and Reynolds should establish a close relationship. Both were deeply interested in literature, music and science; and both had ambitions to write. But Bles was a doer not a dreamer, always on the move with new schemes. When he met Reynolds he was planning to go to Paris to establish an arts magazine, dealing with books, music, painting and sculpture, and published both in English and French. This was to be a unique venture, taking full advantage of the growing *entente cordiale* to bring to both countries a better understanding of their artistic viewpoint and achievements.

For all budding young writers of this period Paris, with its background of 1890s decadence, was where one had to start. Reynolds had been there in the Christmas holidays of 1901, perhaps with Hartog who was an old Paris hand. The images of that Christmas in France had stuck in his memory, particularly the midnight mass in St Eustache with its renowned music when, after a particularly fine rendering of *Noel*, one lone member of the congregation had clapped with great enthusiasm. He was sorely tempted by the idea of joining Bles in Paris where he might keep himself alive by contributing to his friend's journal, and use the rest of the time to write for himself.[9]

But for the sake of the family he needed a cover story; and that summer, perhaps again on Hartog's advice, he signed up with the *École des Mines*, the senior engineering school in France, as one of the small annual intake of external students, the *auditeurs libres*. It may be that Reynolds had genuine intentions of pursuing a practical course at the *École* with real interest, but there is no doubt that the lure of living in Paris and starting his writing career there was uppermost in his mind.

The academic year at the *École* did not start until early November, but he used his four months of freedom to good effect in furthering his writing career. He kept in close touch with London and with Thomas Seccombe, whose main preoccupation at this time, in addition to his work for Constable and the *Bookman*, was a collaboration with William Robertson Nicoll on the *Bookman*

Illustrated History of English Literature which was to last for the next four years. Recalling Reynolds' critical and biographical studies for the Owens College magazine, Seccombe signed him up to make some contributions to this new venture as "the ghost of a ghost". He wrote the chapters on Keats and William Blake which appeared in 1905 and also a fragment on De Quincey, all of which were well received by the editors.[10]

In the chapter on Blake, one of the first of his literary loves, we begin to see the emergence of the clear analytical prose, with its touch of iconoclasm, which was to mark the mature Reynolds style.

> There has been much discussion as to whether Blake was, or was not, wholly sane, in the ordinary sense of the word. Seeing that an accurate definition of what exactly constitutes sanity has yet to be found, the discussion appears to be a little indefinite, not to say futile. Blake saw visions. For many that will be enough. ......According to the rules and regulations of *common* sense, he was certainly crazed. An examination of his work and philosophical dicta proves him to have been something more. Super-sanity is not insanity, neither will it trot between sanity and common sense. And super-sanity, inspiration, intuition – whatever it may be called – was certainly his. In his work he expressed his visions and intuitions; and his best work possesses to so extraordinary a degree the quality of artistic truth and beauty, appeals so powerfully to the inner self, and is, in short, so marked with genius, that, whether he was or not "crazed" or "insane", in the ordinary sense of the words, hardly matters.[11]

These commissions produced a little much needed money, but also gave some equally needed credibility to his long term writing ambitions. He continued through the summer to write short stories to add to the portfolio started in Manchester. And he could not shake off entirely the hankering for journalism stimulated by the editorial work on the college magazine. He got to know the editor of one of the local papers, the *Cheltenham Examiner*, and persuaded him into the offer of a new commission.

Since Edward Spender had invented the "London Letter" for the *Western Morning News* in the middle of the previous century, most major provincial papers carried a similar weekly feature of all-round comment on life and politics as seen from the capital.[12] The *Examiner* had developed its own variation on the theme with "A Lady's London Letter", which dealt rather more with social fashion than with politics, and threw in the occasional feminist remark for good measure. Reynolds suggested that he should try his hand at "A Letter from Paris" to run alongside the London letter at about fortnightly intervals. Perhaps to Reynolds' surprise, the editor agreed to give it a try.

Though busy enough with his writing and his preparations for Paris, the summer of 1902 was also a chance to recuperate from the grind of that final year at Manchester and regain a little of his health. Despite the friction with his father, it seems likely that he went off in August for the usual family holiday in Sidmouth to renew himself once more with the fishing and sailing and walks across the red cliffs.

In late October he at last set off for Paris, suffering on the way his usual stormy channel crossing.[13] He found (or more likely Arthur Bles found for him) an attic room *au sixième* at No 36 rue Bonaparte – one time home of Auguste Comte and today the Hotel St Germain des Prés – just a couple of streets away from the hotel d'Alsace where the body of Oscar Wilde had exploded in death two years before.[14] Reynolds, Bles and the hotel garçon mounted the five flights to the little room that had stood empty for some weeks. Reynolds' eyes swept round the walls of his new, but none too clean, home and one thought sprang straight to his mind: "I hope there are no bugs." "I shouldn't think so," Bles replied, "at any rate they won't bite in the winter."[15] The two friends went off to dine together on the grands boulevards.

Reynolds returned by bus at two the next morning for his first night's rest. He spent a good deal of the night searching every nook and cranny, looking behind every piece of wallpaper, even passing his candle flame over the cracks in the ceiling, in the quest for bugs. He was not to be disappointed. Bugs there were in abundance; but he could not wring an admission out of the *concierge* and, having paid a month's rent in advance, was forced to stay and face them. He wrote a little story, *Pauvre Punaise,* for the Owens College magazine which gives us an ironical bug's eye view of his new abode.

> If it were not for a somewhat too obtrusive cleanliness – the garçon brushes the floor occasionally, and dusts the furniture at least once a week – our room would be one of the most comfortable habitations in Paris. The bed stands in a recess. It is old and of a complicated, cracked construction. The walls in the recess are made of well cracked boarding, whereon is nailed and pasted some ragged wall-paper. Forty-nine of my friends and relations live behind this wall-paper, and find it as comfortable as may be. Moreover, on the other side of the boarding there is a dark, warm cupboard which forms an excellent hybernatorium or winter quarters. Some of my friends also inhabit the numerous cracks and fissures which testify to the antiquity of the ceiling. Long, rich, unshaken curtains made the most admirable of roads from the ceiling to the floor. Hélas, there is insecticide amongst the mattresses![16]

Once more, we have the emotional obsession with cleanliness which Reynolds was later to attack as the hallmark of the middle-class fear of life. He soon made his escape from all the bugs and decamped up the road to another attic room in No 66.[17]

Each morning, he would walk up the rue Bonaparte, past St Sulpice and across the Luxembourg Gardens, to his lectures at the *École des Mines*. The *École* had been started by the chemist, Sage, in 1783 and, after a period in Savoie, had been reconstituted in the hotel Vendôme in the south-east corner of the Luxembourg Gardens in 1816. It had a double goal – to prepare engineers to form the *Corps national des mines* and to train young students for the diploma of civil engineer of mines conferred by the *École*. It ran a range of courses besides mining and machine engineering – metallurgy, industrial chemistry, mineralogy and geology, palaeontology, electrical engineering, railway engineering, agricultural drainage and irrigation, industrial economy and topography.[18]

In addition to the students proper were the *auditeurs libres*, some of whom were foreign students, who could study at the *École* without any entrance test and without taking any final examinations. Instead of the diploma, they were given at the end of their time a simple certificate of studies. There is a break in the records of *auditeurs libres* at the beginning of the twentieth century, so we do not know what course Reynolds tried to follow.[19] Since *auditeurs libres* could dabble in bits of several courses, he may have taken this option. Conceivably, in the short time there, he may have learnt a little of the workings of the internal combustion engine which gave him the skills with which to mend the Tanners' car, and later his own; and more important, an apparently professional ease in handling the motors he campaigned to introduce into fishing boats.

He was one of 52 pupils (perhaps ten of whom were external students like himself) who joined the *École* that November.[20] In the morning, he would attend the two sessions of lectures at 8.30 and 10.15; and in the afternoon from 1.30 to 5 or 6 he would be caught up with practical work in the laboratories.[21] The lunch hours he would spend looking at pictures in the warmth of the Palais du Luxembourg, and often longing for home. "There's a picture in the Luxembourg – by Pointelin, I think. It's called 'Le fond d'un vallon', or 'Le fond du vallon', and is simply a scrubby tree on a hillside. I used to go at once to that picture, and return again to it time after time, though it made me ache to be home. All the wind-swept hillsides I ever knew or longed for were in that picture for me."[22]

In the evenings he and Bles would go and eat in a little restaurant on the outskirts of the Latin Quarter, and would pay one franc (about ninepence three farthings) for a dinner of four courses plus wine. It was in this way that Reynolds was able to live strictly on one and sixpence a day.[23] Although Bles yearned to eat properly on the Boulevard St Michel or on the other side of the river where he worked, Reynolds was caught by the atmosphere of the place and the tall, stout old woman who ran it.

> The spells of initiation are strong in Paris; it is a city of conscious habits. This was my first Parisian restaurant. I felt at home, *chez moi*, under its dingy lights, at its marble-topped tables, with their coarse and soiled cotton cloths; within earshot of the culinary frizzling that went on ceaselessly behind the matchboard partition; in the composite grey smell of

> the place, and under the watchful eye of the Old Woman. We called her *our* Old Woman because for several months we belonged to her. She welcomed us, rain or fine, late or perhaps early, with a slightly grim smile. She asked after Monsieur's cough – "But it would have been worse in the fogs of England, *n'est-ce pas?*" – and prescribed for it herb-tea.[24]

She also kept his French up to scratch. "As a teacher she was stern. Unhappy the day when I asked her for *un cuiller*! Never afterwards did I ask her for a spoon but she waggled it before my nose, enunciating *"Une cuillère! une cuillère!"* until I arrived at the pronunciation, and resolved never to forget that in gender, at all events, a spoon is female."[25]

Occasionally they would go for a drink after dinner and taste the night life in a little café in the Latin quarter. There he made friends with an artist's model, a delicate pale Alsacienne, who dressed like a pre-Raphaelite and, despite his poverty, always persuaded him to stand her glasses of beer and cigarettes – *"Un bock pour moi, mon cher!"* She wanted to go on the stage, and sometimes performed in *cafés chantants*.

> One evening she sang a whole part from *Carmen* into my left ear.
> *"Belle, mon cher, n'est-ce pas?"* she said.
> *"Tu es belle?"*
> *"Non! Ma voix, cochon!"*
> I had heard it very well, although the piano and fiddles were playing Wagner, billiard balls were clicking, white-aproned waiters were shouting, and a couple of hundred voices were going twenty to the dozen. It was the last I saw of her, her costume *à l'art nouveau*. Perhaps she was not highly respectable. I don't know. I never did. She is a *fleur du mal,* crystallised in my memory, and still a little fragrant. Her name was Margot.[26]

It was a name to remember.

In the first few weeks, while Reynolds was working with a degree of commitment at the *École des Mines*, Bles was fully preoccupied with planning the first number of his new periodical, the *Weekly Critical Review*, due out in January. In what spare time was left to him, mostly in the middle of the night when he could not sleep, Reynolds worked away in his attic on his short stories for which Bles had promised some space in the magazine. He also set to work for the *Cheltenham Examiner*. His first *Letter from Paris* was published in the edition of 19 November and, like all the early ones, was a rather lazy *pot-pourri* of snippets from the Parisian press – famous court cases, recent murders, industrial unrest, local controversies – with no real actuality reporting at all. He even translated a French report of the Lord Mayor's Show: "This year's ceremony was unusual in character, because the newly-elected Lord Mayor is an Israelite. At his express desire, the procession passed through that quarter of the city familiarly called the Gehetto, where several thousands of wealthy Jewish families reside. [!]"[27]

But the novelty seems to have gone down well with the editor and Cheltenham readers. The first letter was signed "A Cheltonian", but for the second and subsequent ones he was promoted to "Our Own Correspondent". And as he gained in confidence, a little direct reporting creeps in. He reported the very sharp cold spell at the end of November which, with his bad tuberculous cough, must have hit him hard in his attic lodgings: "Snow fell, and for two or three days the thermometer remained almost steady between 20° and 25°F. Ice covered the water in the basins of the fountains, and snow covered the ice. The sculptured ladies around the fountain in the Place de la Concorde had venerable long white beards of ice, and the poor little naked cupids around the fountain in the Luxembourg Gardens wore sparkling robes of icicles."[28]

By December he was beginning to tire of that morning walk past the fountain with its little cupids to his lectures at the *École des Mines*. It may have been that he was reminded too closely of the last year's grind at Manchester, that he had had just as much as he could take of higher education. Or it may simply have been that up most nights writing his stories and his piece for the *Examiner*, helping out Bles when he could at the magazine's offices in the rue St Honoré, and a full day at the *École*, something had to give – and it was his studies that were the most easily expendable. It was therefore with some relief that he faced the Christmas break.

Throughout his life Christmas was an annual nightmare, reminding him of his isolation from the families celebrating all around him. He went into it in a state of depression and emerged even worse. The Christmas of 1902, his second on the trot in Paris, seems to have been rather different. He had the close companionship of Arthur Bles, and also of his Cheltenham readers, for whom he reported the celebrations with something almost touching enthusiasm.

> Christmas in the French capital has been a busy time for the shopkeepers, and, though New Year's day is the greater fête, yet "Noel" has not been neglected, especially by the children, to whom the shops, full of wonderful toys, must seem like fairyland. For weeks past it has been almost impossible to get inside the Louvre or the Bon Marché in the afternoon...... It is not "hanging up the stocking" which causes excitement in the nurseries in France, but putting the largest slipper to be found in the chimney. Christmas trees are very much *à la mode* this year. Every grocer has a small forest of them outside his shop windows, and inside, he shows one or two already dressed in glittering array. The great thing lacking about Christmas day in France seems to me to be the good old Christmas wish, "A Merry Christmas." It cannot be translated into French...... Christmas Eve, when everyone in Paris keeps *réveillon,* was fine and not too cold. The boulevards and cafés were thronged with merrymakers, for *réveillon* means something quite different from mid-

> night mass to the ordinary Parisian. It was impossible to get a supper table in any of the best known cafés, unless the precaution to reserve one during the day had been taken...... Midnight mass was sung in the churches, the favourite ones being the Madeleine and St Eustache. The latter is a fine old church, hidden behind the market halls, and is well known to have the finest music in Paris. The class of people who attend this service is not that of the café frequenters. The *bon bourgeois* takes his family, and the devout Catholic lady is escorted by her maid, and one and all are clad in rather sombre garments.[29]

Already he was beginning to observe with a natural eye the complex differentiations of class.

It was probably after the Christmas break that Reynolds decided after all not to go back to his studies at the *École*. The time for the launch of the magazine was approaching and Bles found himself in need of a further and permanent pair of hands. He offered Reynolds a paid post as sub-editor which was eagerly snapped up. It was an experiment that benefited both equally. Bles gained a totally committed colleague who had already had some useful editorial experience on his school and college magazines. For Reynolds there was the opportunity to pick up more experience from a properly professional undertaking and, with a small but assured salary, the freedom to use his spare time to write.

The *Weekly Critical Review* was a bold venture to undertake with a limited staff and fragile financial base. Its remit – to bring together England and France in the worlds of literature, music and the fine arts – was a challenging one; and its format, with articles in both English and French, a difficult one to sell. More than one similar venture had been started before in Paris and had folded within weeks. But if nothing else, Bles was a buccaneering character with an *élan* that swept all before it. There was a grandiloquent vein in his mentality which empowered him to accost the leading figures of the day for endorsement and contributions. The list of contributors was highly respectable: on the English side, Ernest Newman, W.B. Yeats, Arthur Symons, Laurence Housman, Morley Roberts, Aleister Crowley, Havelock and Edith Ellis; on the French, Rémy de Gourmont and J.K. Huysmans. One weekly feature was a full-sized autographed photo portrait of one of the leading artists, composers, writers or opera singers of the day. This was clearly achieved in most cases by writing obsequious fan letters, but when the innocent reader saw the portrait of Richard Strauss, dedicated to Arthur Bles, he could be forgiven for believing that this icon was both a close friend of the editor and a devotee of the magazine.

The first number emerged as planned on 22 January 1903 under cover of a eulogistic letter to the editor from Louis de Fourcaud: "You are starting a paper with the object of bringing together intellectually two great nations which were made to understand each other, each having a rich heritage of works and ideas. Your generous initiative is well calculated to bring in contact their minds and languages, their conceptions, their arts, the highest expressions of their lives, so that they may know one another as it were fundamentally, and no longer merely with a prejudiced superficiality." To this number Reynolds contributed a rather rudimentary review of one of the celebrated Colonne Concerts under his old Manchester pseudonym of Stephen Sydney.

For the next few weeks he was busy contributing to the short book reviews and editorial columns, and helping with the general office business. The two stories he wrote for the magazine did not appear until the early summer, some weeks after he had left Paris. One is a rather weak attempt at a love story, *A Piano and an Omnibus*, about an American in Paris, Godfrey Leland, who woos his girlfriend by means of his prowess on the piano. It offers an eloquent account of the power of music over Reynolds at this time: "If it is that music cannot communicate definite thoughts and emotions – rather influencing that subconscious emotion which pervades and, as it were, envelops the more delimited feelings – it has, nevertheless, a potency to revivify banished longings and to open the doors behind which civilized people, for decency and safety's sake, are wont to keep their passions. Music seems peculiarly akin to that something in us, that fundamental emotion, of which we are most cognizant on awaking from sleep, before our livelier consciousness has covered it up, as a gust of wind will cover still, deep, waters with ripples that hide their mysterious depths."[30]

But the most interesting aspect of this story is a rare attempt by Reynolds to write about himself, to probe the physical contrast between his sturdy physique and the more delicate, feminine aspects of his body, and the psychological contrast between his apparent power and control and the potential storm inside him which could burst out at any moment and go smash. Godfrey before the piano in his elegant Montmartre flat is the same man as Reynolds hunched up in bed over his pen and paper in the little attic room on the left bank.

> It happens more often than not that a face strongly lighted from above or from the side is much more interesting than the same face surrounded by broad daylight. Thus it was by the light of the one piano-lamp in Godfrey Leland's room. In allowing his less marked features to lose themselves in shadow, the light only brought out more strongly the main characteristics of his face. And it was interesting; for though, with the heavy shadows playing around, his face was vigorous and not unhandsome, it contrasted almost absurdly with the small, delicate and, in a word, finical hands that hopped and twisted gracefully about the keyboard. A large nose and a small mouth also went ill together. Very carefully clipped and brushed hair, neither long nor short, above such a face as his, tended to look like a wig. From the too studied negligence of his clothes, even, it would not have been difficult to conclude rightly that he was, so far as concerned his inner self, an earnestly serious, somewhat egoistic, personage. As his appearance was seemingly a hotch-

> potch of two, so his nature was composed of two antagonistic parts which, cunningly trained to run together as unanimously as a pair of carriage-horses, did, on occasion, indulge in somewhat furious fights. A certain amount of atavism – that partial 'casting back' of the human breed which, more than culture, produces strong men – had gifted Godfrey Leland with considerable power over his fellows, and had, at the same time, left him with comparatively little control over himself, or, at all events, made him difficultly self-controllable. This is why the elegant exterior of his person and mind was sometimes rudely pushed up and scattered, in the same way as the surface of the ground is forced to bulge, and finally pushed aside, by the living thrust of a potentially forceful seedling.
>
> It was hardly Godfrey Leland's fault when this happened. Perhaps, if he and the Parcae had allowed it to continue, a fair tree might have grown up upon the site.... But the best part of him was compelled to stay in the potentially forceful state. Except for a few outbursts, as alarming at the time as a smash of chinaware, he continued until full middle age to be a veritably elegant young man.[31]

He wrote another heterosexual story, *The Conjugal Segregation Experiment,* in the small hours when he was too afraid of the bugs to go to bed and at a time when he was "full of words".[32] Too many words, in fact. A radically slimmed down version, renamed *The Blue-Stocking,* was published three years later. It is a story of a domineering feminist who forces her husband to agree to live one month together and one month apart so that they can continue their intellectual work when separated, but who crumbles when the husband carries off their first baby on their month apart. Despite some inevitably juvenile touches, it is well conceived and executed, with some amusing writing. It has a Jane Austen start: "There are in these latter days independent strenuous women who, devoting themselves to knowledge, instead of men, succeed in embracing the skeletons of all arts, philosophies, and sciences."[33] And some neat mysogyny: ".....after marriage men and women cease to gain in individuality. And – worse still – a woman becomes a baby-washing, small-talking phonographic machine. With a man, things go in at one ear and out at the other: with a woman, they go in at two ears and rush out at the mouth."[34]

We have in this early story the first glimmerings of a mature and confident style, shown perhaps at its best in the episode when Ralph, the separated husband, determines to try and put the baby to bed himself.

> He took it to his own room, lighted the fire and got the bath ready. After tearing one or two upper garments, he turned the child round and round until he had taken out all the safety-pins he could feel; whereby the process of undressing was much facilitated. Then he bathed it as tenderly as if it had been old china, wondering the while how womenfolk

> can pull babies this way and that, turn them up and turn them down, and hold them up by their feet. His little son cried, of course. Men have a curious notion that when babies cry they have something to cry for. Ralph decided that it was a matter of nutriment. He made a bottle of food according to the directions on the tin, with as much care as he would have used in a chemical experiment. This did quiet the baby, but no sooner was it finished than the cries began again. It might be good to imitate the women further.... He waved his hand above his son's infinitesimal nose, then suddenly gave it a timid dig in the ribs. The end was vocal. He patted it on the chest; it squalled the more. He grasped its night-dress, and, by alternately pulling and relaxing, he made it rock nicely on its rotund little back. What followed was horrible to hear and see – ear-piercing shrieks, furious clawings of the air, extreme redness of the face.
>
> But they sing to babies.... Ralph could not sing. But he was desperate. He made a dash for it. There was only the child to hear.
>
> He sang....
>
> "Oh, sir!" It was the nursemaid with the cradle.
>
> "See to him," said Ralph, retreating, "and tell me when he's asleep."
>
> He went down to his study thoroughly exhausted, and meditated on the infrequency of infanticide.[35]

Reynolds himself was always wary of babies. "Their possibilities in life frighten me – squashy little things".[36]

His writing for the *Cheltenham Examiner* was improving too, going out on the streets for Mardi Gras and other springtime celebrations, reporting direct the views of kiosk holders on the latest newspaper war. He was becoming a journalist and enjoying it.[37]

But despite the progress with his writing, it was not overall a happy spring. His tuberculosis grew worse, aggravated by the cold and the poor nutrition that was all his 1/6 a day allowed, and he fell seriously ill. For a fortnight he abandoned the Old Woman and her little restaurant to eat more wholesomely elsewhere at a franc and a half. "Consequently I was never able to go there afterwards. The illness broke the habit: I dared not break the absence. I knew how the Old Woman would look."[38]

The homesickness he had felt in the Luxembourg in the early weeks now grew more intense. He wrote a story, *Self-Exiled*, which Bles later published, about an Englishman stranded in Paris for years on end, and longing for letters from his family back home. In the man's plight, there is a lot of Reynolds at this time. "I was very lonely, and always expecting a letter. My *concierge* must have known my face; I used to peer through her window every time I went out and in. There was never a letter, and it always made the five flights of stairs seem dreadfully high. The heart and feet aren't so very far apart. When home is gone, one seems to be floating in chaos. I made no friends in Paris. ....No place like Paris for making no friends – good God, there isn't! Even the dogs are exclusive, stand-offish."[39]

But one correspondent did not fail him – and that was the indefatigable Aunt Jane. A letter he wrote her in April confirms in real life the mood of isolation that was setting in.

> It's most miserably cold here.
> For one reason I like it. It allows one to go to bed in the night. I told you that I sometimes find bugs, – caught one biting me. It gave me such a scare that if I go to bed I don't sleep, so now I read or work from 10 or 11 p.m. till 5 a.m. when it is light, and get up at midday. It has another advantage of saving something on food, because I cannot get anything to eat in the night whether I am hungry or not.
> I see the dawns, am getting quite a specialist in dawns, in fact. It is the only time when the courtyard and roof view from my window is worth looking at. The said window faces my bed and occupies nearly half the wall; so I open it wide and lie in bed smoking watching the cruel morning light on the roofs. When I am tired of that I can shut my eyes and listen to the interesting things the voices, which I nearly always hear at night, are saying round me. Or I concoct stories and articles, but the awkward part of this is that, although I am quite sure that I think of some fine things, I've always forgotten them by the next morning. In this way I am able to go to bed feeling it is a happy lazy place and not the abode of man-eating insects.
> If you want to read some fine novels and stories get Joseph Conrad's *Youth* and *Lord Jim*. He is magnificent and comes, I think, up to Meredith and Hardy, with Theodore Watts-Dunton, whose Aylwin I believe you have read. If not, you have something in store.
> ......It's silly to call bombs infernal machines; the name should be kept for typewriters, which give one worse headaches than anything I know, except people one does not like and railway trains......
> Please write fairly soon. I am not favoured with many letters from the family; which is perhaps as well...... they have their own concerns, into which it is true I have often precipitated myself like a bull in a china shop, breaking not a few culinary and pretty ornaments.
> But at times I do feel inclined to feel that some officious angel or devil has cut my line and left me drifting derelict.[40]

The lament about typewriters was a signal that the editorial work in the little office in the rue St Honoré was beginning to get him down. And not just the typewriters either. His relationship with the domineering Bles was heading for a breakdown. In April, Bles had found another protégé, a young man who was prepared to learn the mysteries of high-class journalism for nothing. With the magazine ever in a rocky financial position, Reynolds felt himself under pressure to give up his salary if he were not to be usurped by the newcomer. He took it as a matter of principle – and resigned.[41]

The vehemence with which he reacted to the incident gives us the first hint that this was not just the break up of a professional partnership, but that his relationship with Bles may possibly have been something rather closer than friendship. He wrote to Aunt Jane

> You will be pleased to hear that I have at last taken measures to publish my book of stories. I have not heard from the agent yet, but I suppose some publisher or other will take them. If they hurry up, they should be out in August. I daresay their Frenchiness will be objected to; but I can't help that; the French are miles ahead of us in fiction. They haven't got a Marie Corelli who writes idiocy and sells by hundreds and thousands. The review is over, and I am glad. The amount of bunkum was too much. The more one sees of journalism, the less honest one finds it. I listened to some editors talking yesterday. Beasts! They were ready openly to avow their methods of cheating chance contributors. Of course, that doesn't apply to all, but you'd be astonished what a lot of that sort there are.[42]

Within days, he had said a thankful goodbye to the *concierge* and headed for the coast to take the next boat home. He planned on a few weeks' holiday just to marshal his resources.[43] He would return again to continue his apprenticeship in writing.

For once in his life, he had missed a royal visit. Just a month later Edward VII made his fêted entrance into Paris to ratify the new *Entente Cordiale*. Never one to miss an opportunity, Bles sent the monarch the latest copy of his *Review* and received a complimentary letter in reply. From then on it carried on its masthead the influential message "Approuvée par Sa Majesté Le Roi Édouard VII".[44]

The *Weekly Critical Review* was to survive for a further year, the photographs growing glossier and the text thinner and thinner by the week. Most worrying for a magazine published in Paris the French content was overwhelmed by the English until Bles was forced to the expensive device of a supplement of translation. With the edition of 25 March 1904 he announced the doubling of the English price to sixpence and a smaller increase in the French price to 50 centimes. With that, it folded on the spot.

Bles continued with his swashbuckling career, becoming more and more extravagant as the years advanced. He married a French woman, dabbled in translations of German books on music, and claimed to have discovered a process for manufacturing mercury, styling himself "Le Roi de Mécure". At the beginning of the First World War he formed and trained off his own bat a squadron of English volunteers in Paris, "Bles' Roughriders", with the intention of joining the British Expeditionary Force. He fought the War in the Royal

Welsh Fusiliers, ending up as Major Arthur *de* Bles, Town Major of Cologne.

In October 1919 he went to the United States to continue the series of lectures he had been giving in Europe on the strategy of the War. He settled in New York, publishing several books on English furniture and one upon "Saints in Art". He established the "International Order of British and Allied Officers of the World War" with himself as "International Commander" and included among a bevy of Honorary Patrons Lloyd George, Poincaré, Joffre and Pétain. He moved to San Francisco in 1933, where he married an American woman and now styled himself *Count* Arthur de Bles. He died in Los Angeles in 1935 while staying at the Hollywood Roosevelt Hotel and was accorded a Municipal funeral by the authorities in San Francisco. The bill for a genuine oak coffin with brass handles was sent to his brother in England, who was not amused.[45]

Reynolds back in England kept in touch with him for a few weeks more, but purely as a business contact while his two stories were published in the *Review* that summer. He also carried back with him a book of Yeats to review, positively his last piece of work for the magazine. For Aunt Jane and Aunt Allie he brought back a framed photograph of Balastries Beethoven which hung proudly in Prospect Rise until their deaths.[46] For himself he carried home a copy of Pierre Louÿs' *Aphrodite*, that delicately wrought story of orgies and female crucifixion, a symbol of the decadent world from which he had just emerged.[47]

But he returned home a consumptive, defeated by illness and by the loneliness of living isolated in a great foreign city. And perhaps also by the loss of love. All that he had left in the world was the £300 he had just inherited from his mother – and his talent. He made a vow to invest the money in himself and live on it till he could earn his living by writing.[48] It was an investment fraught with peril.

FIVE

Into the Abyss 1903–4

Beside the meandering country road from the ancient hill fort of Clovelly Dykes to the village of Hartland in North Devon stands a formal stone gateway which, though built to impress, leads nowhere but into an open farmer's field. It was erected to celebrate the coronation of Edward VII in 1902 and carries a plaque, scarcely decipherable today, which bears patriotic witness to that fact. This strange memorial was startlingly new and its message easily readable when Stephen Reynolds first walked past in the spring of 1903.

Just a quarter of a mile further on lies the little hamlet of Velly, or Felye as it was called in the Middle Ages because the semi-circular ridge on which it stands reminded the ancient Devonians of the "felly", or ridge, of a cartwheel.[1] A track leads off the road between high hedges, filled with ferns and foxglove spikes in summer, past Higher Velly Farm, takes a sharp right hand turn down to a small group of trees and a stone gatepost which marks the entrance to Nether Velly, the only other habitation. The entrance drive, once quite grand, swings down to the left between clumps of oak and hazel, and a sheltering belt of pine, and opens out on to a wide clearing in which stands the old farmhouse, built in local stone with round-headed, churchlike windows, and (in 1903 but not today) an ornamental conservatory at the southern end, built for Queen Victoria's Jubilee, with a touch of the Taj Mahal about it.

There had been a dwelling on the site since the twelfth century but the present house is seventeenth century in origin. It looks out upon a broad expanse of lawn with fields to either side, whose fences still today are seemingly never strong enough to prevent the farm animals from trespassing on to the human domain. The lawn ends at a flight of steps, guarded by two raised ornamental urns, which lead down through an iron gate to a pond at the second level. From there, the ground slopes gently away to a small stream where woods run along the bottom of the valley. The bedrooms look out across the lawn to the wooded valley at the bottom of the garden and over the hills beyond to the sea just a mile away. Reynolds' stepsister Frances, who lived at Nether Velly for 83 years, used to call it "the best view in the world".[2]

It was here that Frank Reynolds, restless as ever, decided in 1903 to establish himself in a new role as farmer, landowner and country gentleman. In March he said goodbye to the Belle Vue at Cheltenham at yet another farewell dinner, in which he was presented with a silver spirit flask by the eighty diners who all bemoaned his departure and with whom he left a final message that "it was time that Cheltenham 'bucked up'".[3] It was to Nether Velly the following month that the prodigal son returned from Paris.

Inclined to personal vanity, he was sporting a small French beard as the mark of his foreign adventure, which caused some consternation and amusement in the family. It was quickly shaved off. He was ill, depressed and weak from malnutrition, but soon took strength from the sea air and the beauty all around the new family home. He could give a hand with the farm animals, find new country walks and delight his six-year-old stepsister with tales of the wonders of Paris. Always cheered by the company of children, he would take Frances for tramps in the woods down in the valley, sometimes in the late evening when he would point out the stars to her.[4] But, however idyllic this place and however much he enjoyed the company of stepmother and sister, he could not stay long under the same roof as his father.

To escape from that presence and take positive steps to restore his health he made for Sidmouth for a fortnight's holiday, for the first time on his own. He still harboured thoughts of a return to Paris when the holiday was over and resume once more the unequal struggle to become a writer. He was practically penniless and may well have walked all the way down from Velly, sleeping rough.

He could not afford lodgings in the town without breaking into his mother's money, and he seems to have spent his first nights in Sidmouth in the shelter on the front by the Bedford steps. Certainly it was there that he was first spotted in the early morning by two fishermen, the brothers Bob and Tom Woolley – a lone figure on the skyline, staring out to sea, watching for the mackerel boats to come safely home.

After a few of these early morning encounters, when the fishermen realised he was sick and practically destitute, they took pity on him. Tom Woolley invited him back to his little terraced house by the River Sid to stay for free in the downstairs front room which was let to holidaymakers in the summer months.[5] In a very few days he became part of the fishermen's circle on the beach and began, with a writer's eye, to trace their very distinctive personalities.

Bob Woolley was then 38 and had been a fisherman for over 20 years.[6] It showed in his red, weather-beaten face, his close-cropped hair just beginning to turn grey, and in his body which, though iron strong, was bent from rheumatic fever suffered as a child, from too much exertion and too many nights at sea in an open boat. He had clearly been attractive as a younger man and the strength of his personality still shone through in his blue eyes and in his puckish sense of humour, at its liveliest when young women were around.

Tom was a contrast in every way. Nine years younger, he was still at the height of his strength and more conventional good looks. He had a powerful handsome face, with a high forehead, and a wiry muscular body of which, from his carriage, one could tell he was highly proud. Where Bob was open and simple in outlook, there was a brooding reticence about Tom and a stern independence – he would ingratiate himself with nobody. Where Bob had accepted his fate as a poor fisherman who would never get "no for'arder", Tom still had ambition and a hankering after middle-class betterment. Moreover, he had a public reputation away from the beach as an outstanding rugby forward for Sidmouth, Plymouth Albion and for Devon. There were few in Sidmouth who could pick a fight with Tom and come out on top.

Out on the beach too Reynolds came close to the previous generation of Woolleys – Bob and Tom's father, George Woolley, known as "Punch" perhaps because he looked like one, and his younger brother Uncle Sam, then aged 57, the popular hero of *A Poor Man's House*. Bob and George Woolley lived close to the seafront "down the Gut" in Bedford Square, at the back of the Bedford Hotel, while Uncle Sam was just round the corner in a little cottage in West Lane which he ran himself because his wife was a failure as housekeeper.[7] Uncle Sam was small and wiry, like Tom, with much the same shaped face, the piercing Woolley blue eyes and a small white fringe beard which gave him the authentic look of ancient mariner. He had given up regular fishing to earn his living independently from inshore work, catching lobsters and crabs, winkle-gathering and eking out his simple economy with the flotsam he found and stored under the cliffs. He lived on a diet of tea, sugar, bread and onions, but could still row farther and faster than a man half his age. He was a walking repository of all the known lore of weather, tides, the handling of boats and the finding of fish and other seafood. Few dared ignore his advice and put out in a boat if warned it "wasn't fitty".

The unexpected encounter with these new friends – his sudden admission into their strange exclusive world – completely changed every aspect of Sidmouth for Reynolds. It was no longer just the town of childhood holiday memories. On his own in the place for the first time, and with recollections of Manchester and Paris so close, he began to see with new eyes the peace and beauty of it all. His favourite walks across Peak Hill and High Peak to Ladram Bay, and over Salcombe Hill in the other direction, took on a novel freshness.

He was working on his last book review for Arthur Bles – of Yeats' *Ideas of Good and Evil* – and could not hold back a reference to his surroundings.

> I have read *Ideas of Good and Evil* in a part of England where meretricious beauty in a book would quickly be put out of mind by the beauty all around, and I have thought about it in sight of the sea by day and by night, on high red cliffs, on bracken-grown hills and on scented rabbit-run fir woods.[8]

The draw of his new friends and of this new perspective on the town was too much for him. All thoughts of Paris flew out of the window. He decided to stay on and start his writing life here.

But although he had paid some part of his way by helping out with jobs on the beach, he could not live off Tom and his wife Nellie for very much longer. The holiday season would be starting soon and they had a family – including their 18-month-old son, Chip – to support. So he at last broke into his mother's money and took a couple of rooms at out-of-season rates in Jubilee

Terrace, the imposing row of 18 houses built on the southern side of All Saints Road to mark the Golden Jubilee of Queen Victoria. This was the "Egremont Villas" of *A Poor Man's House* – one back bedroom and a frippered sitting-room, furnished in true middle-class Edwardian style with aspidistras and antimacassars.[9]

On days when he was not writing in his lodgings, he would gravitate down to the sea-front and sit chatting with the fishermen, lounging by the Bedford steps, mending their nets, recovering from the last hard night at sea and preparing for the next. The mackerel fishing was unpredictable that spring – on some nights as much as a thousand good fish, on many nights nothing.[10] Bob and Tom took him out on pleasure trips in their boat, the mainstay of fishermen in the holiday season when the catches were poor. They were his boatmen and he, for a short time at least, was their "fright", a term which Reynolds himself is well qualified to explain.

> Frights are two-legged fish. When a lady who is walking down to a boat with the intention of hiring it hears one fisherman call out to another: 'Dick, there's a fright for thee there!' she is apt to look a little startled. It has to be explained to her that *fright* is a way of pronouncing *freight*. But I don't think most ladies like it, after that.[11]

Reynolds, with his scientific curiosity and his practical bent, could not remain a passive pleasure tripper for long. He persuaded Bob and Tom to take him out on the occasional fishing trip as a third pair of hands. When communal activity was needed on the beach, he would join in to haul up the boats out of reach of high tide or struggle with the others on the end of the seine net. One Sunday night, he joined a seining team led by Uncle Sam hauling for sole two miles up the beach from Sidmouth under the eastern cliff. He wrote proudly to Aunt Jane

> Last Sunday night we went up the coast and shot the seine net four times. It was a fine sight – the sea just heaving, the broken red cliffs behind, and eight of us disposed symmetrically along the beach, hauling the grass rope for all our worth. Over all the most brilliant moonlight.[12]

He wrote it up in more lyrical vein six years later, and doubled the number of hauls.

> We worked all night, the eight of us, four on each arm of the seine – shooting, long-hauling, boating the net, boxing the fish, shifting further east, and shooting again. Eight hauls we made. The harvest moon rose red above the horizon; climbed the sky; bathed sea and cliffs in a silvery shimmer. Before us was the limitless water and a moonglade that stretched to the end of sight; above us the cliffs seemed to reach right up

> to the tranquil star-splashed heavens; and underneath, on a narrow strip of shingle, netting a little strip of sea, we laboured till dawn was heralded by a change in the colour of the moonlight. Thereupon, with aching backs and stiff sore hands, keeping as close as possible to the water's edge for fear any cliff should fall upon us, we tramped along a couple of miles of shingle home.[13]

But for the trips to sea he was entirely dependent on the goodwill and availability of Bob and Tom. To gain more freedom, he dug a little further into his capital and bought a small sailing boat, the *Ivy*, which was to become in his book the famous *Moondaisy*. It was a purchase which symbolised the decision to stay on in Sidmouth and it filled him with a "too excessive joy".[14]

He quickly assembled his own little crew of teenage boys who jumped at the chance to go out with him sailing and fishing. There was Bob's eldest son, Bill Woolley, almost 16, and just waiting for the day when he could join the Navy; and Bill's 15-year-old friend, Alf McLeod, the son of Fido McLeod, a plumber who lived in Bedford Square. He was to figure in *A Poor Man's House* as "Looby Smith", the land boy who thought of nothing else but of going to sea, and was to end up in the Navy alongside Bill.[15]

And finally there was Freddie Ware, with his pale, small sharp face, at 17 a little older than the others, though you would not have known it from his build. He had been born and brought up in Chapel Street where his father, Fred senior, belonged to a long-established fishing family. But the family past had cost him dear. He had been born with congenital syphilis which, untreated as in most poor homes, had reached by the age of four its tertiary stage. His spine had grown bulbous and his movements gangling and uncoordinated. He was fit enough to form a full member of the crew, but that spring of 1903 his heart was beginning to give out and everyone knew that he was not long for this world. Reynolds dubbed him in real life his "little admiral", and in his book "the hunchbacked Little Commodore".[16]

They would row out, all four, at sunset in search of conger eels.

> Ah! those were the days...... the fights with the conger in the dark or by the light of matches or of an old lantern that blew out when it was most wanted; the absurd way the crew turned up their noses at my nice tomato sandwiches and gobbled down stringy corned beef; their quiet slumber round the stern seats and my solitary watch amidships over all the lines, and at the sea-fire trailing in the flood-tide; their crustiness when I awoke them to shift our mark and their jubilation when a whopper was to be gaffed; the utter peacefulness of the night after they had gone to sleep again; our merry row home and hearty beaching of the boat; the cup of hot tea.... [17]

They would sometimes go out in the daytime as a nautical picnic party. On one such day in the middle of the summer they rowed and sailed out past Chit Rocks to one of the little bays to the west of Sidmouth in search of cakes and clotted cream. "We ate the cake and cream lying in a circle round a teapot, on a beach so sunny that the heat of the pebbles struck through jerseys and shirts to our elbows."[18] On the way home the boys began to grow yellow in the face – "not with sea-sickness exactly, so much as with what one might call sea-cream-sickness". They got caught in a fog bank which suddenly appeared out of the blue. "Soon the warm light of the sun was polluted by a cold whiteness. The sun itself, for a passing moment a shining round thing in the heavens, disappeared altogether. The fog was upon us, thickening. In an instant the great high red cliffs to landward were snuffed out as if they had been a shuttered light. The fog got down our throats, putting us in mind of suffocation nightmares. We were curiously alone; no land, no sun, no clouds, no sky; hardly any sea; not even darkness visible!"[19] They rowed for a time in some trepidation, unsure that they were not in fact rowing out to sea. When the fog partially lifted, they were astonished to find themselves no more than two hundred yards from land!

But these idylls on the water were not the whole story of that summer. While Reynolds was steering his little boat safely out of fogs, his literary career was fast heading for the rocks. Though determinedly grinding out stories and articles from his lodgings in Sidmouth, it was London and their reception there which alone mattered. The prospect he had glimpsed in Paris of a book of short stories, and the agent who was to make it a reality, both failed him. What was worse, he found he could not place even single stories or articles in any of the London periodicals; real writing life was proving more testing than his experience in Manchester and Paris where he had had his own tame outlet for whatever he produced.

As the summer wore on, rejection slip followed rejection slip, most usually without a word of explanation, comment or encouragement. G.R. Halkett of the *Pall Mall Magazine* was the only editor who took the trouble to enclose a kindly letter.[20] While Seccombe was able to offer bits and pieces of work on the *Illustrated History of English Literature* in which he was still fully engaged, his influence did not extend to making unsaleable work saleable, even with the *Bookman* for which he wrote most. Towards the end of the summer, Seccombe took his holiday in the West Country and joined Reynolds for a time in Sidmouth.[21] He offered what encouragement he could, and gave him some ideas for new subjects, but could not fail to notice that his friend was gradually succumbing to his usual depression.

The visit may well have reminded Reynolds only too painfully of the high hopes of the spring of 1901 when the two men had first met and talked positively of a future life of writing. Since then he had twice come close to collapse, in that dismal last year of over-strain at Manchester and with the break-up of his literary world in Paris. He had now been working exclusively at his writing for half a year and had even less to show than when it had been merely a part-time occupation. In his personal life, the outlook was equally bleak. Rejected by his family, which since the death of his mother was no longer his family, he felt now more than ever that someone had cut his line and he was indeed "drifting derelict". He was 22 and had no close intimate relationship in the world. True, at Sidmouth he could make friends easily enough with 16-year-old fisher boys, but he was too keenly aware of the dangerous waters into which his sexual feelings might carry him to be able to relax. There was a secret in his life that had to be suppressed, and suppression was something he was good at. He kept his equilibrium by furious spasms of physical and intellectual work. When that work too turned out a failure, there was nothing left to stop him from toppling over the edge.

Through that summer he had had one or two lone experiences which heightened his mystical awareness but showed too that he was moving perceptibly away from the unequal struggle with practical life. He would drift of an evening down to the sea-front, as if drawn back to the destitute feelings of those first spring nights he had passed in the shelter there. Often late at night he would stand transfixed on the Parade, just gazing out to sea. On one such night he had an overwhelming feeling that some one was invisibly with him. On another night he sat through the hours of darkness on the shore and, quite uncannily, a wandering retriever came and sat beside him, and the close presence of the dog made the beauty of the sea strike him almost with violence. These were the prelude to irrational fears that came from beyond himself and with which he tried, unwisely and ultimately unsuccessfully, to wrestle. On the verge of breaking down, he had a panic attack each time he was about to set foot in the boat to go to sea and he forced himself pretty savagely to overcome them.[22] Firm exercise of the will was always his way out of situations when his nerves were threatening to let him down. In normal times it was a strategy that worked. For a man on the edge of breakdown, it was the most dire reaction conceivable. The pressure overwhelmed him and he suffered a total collapse.

A hundred years ago nervous breakdown was a commonplace of literary life. Most of Reynolds' literary friends, even the most eminent, suffered them from time to time. The combination of the traumas of creation, lack of critical recognition and the anxieties of perpetual poverty had a lethal effect on solitary, hypersensitive authors. Today, the feelings are no different but there are psychoanalysts and drugs to maintain some stability of living. In Reynolds' day, doctors could do no more than attach the comforting label "neurasthenia" and advocate rest.

For years Reynolds had suffered from the usual symptoms of the neurotic: insomnia, depression, elation, severe headaches, panic attacks, heightened senses, especially of smell, a general hypochondria; but he had never experienced anything quite like this. One of the most vivid descriptions of what it was like comes from a young contemporary author, Grant Watson, who had his own personal breakdown some years later in 1914.

> I could not sleep, I imagined I was going out of my mind, and was like one who found himself in a pit with the vaguest sort of bottom, and one from which I could see no means of escape. Escape I did by a series of accidents, as by accidents I seemed to have fallen in.[23]

Practically, he could not cope with an illness of this severity from the bedroom of his lodgings with no one to look after him. He could not look either to Nether Velly for comfort; to return "home" in this state would be the ultimate admission of defeat. The only option was Devizes where he could count upon friends who would sympathise and strengthen him. In a rare moment of remission, and relying on the iron will, he managed to clear his effects in Sidmouth and make tracks for his birthplace a hundred miles away. Among his last acts, he made a present of the *Ivy* to his two fishermen friends, Bob and Tom Woolley.[24] He never thought to survive to see Sidmouth again.

He arrived a total wreck at the front door of Devizes College in the Market Place and Ada Bennett, his old schoolmistress, took him in. He had lost the will to live and was closer to death than he had ever been before.

For some days it was touch and go. But Miss Bennett was the woman who had had most influence over his life and, by a combination of careful nursing and strong personality, she slowly revived in him the will to climb back out of the bottomless pit into the light. In later days, he openly acknowledged to friends that she had saved his life.[25] He was treated professionally by Dr Thomas Savill of Harley Street, a leading expert on neurasthenia who had lectured on the subject. For wider public consumption, he assigned his cure, somewhat disingenuously, to the hapless Savill: "Finally, when the doctor said I should never do anything again, I began to recover."[26]

But once the immediate crisis was over, it was a long haul back towards complete recovery. The autumn and winter of 1903 saw a slow process of revival towards something approaching normality, but with frequent setbacks along the way. Ada Bennett knew that it was vital to rekindle his interest in writing and give him hope that there was still a centre to his life. He said later that she "nursed me back to playing about with pens and paper";[27] but the reality may have been rather more stark than that. There is a tradition in the Powys family, passed down from Katie with whom he had good cause to share the secrets of his breakdown, that when he tried to put pen to paper again, he found he could not form the letters. Under Miss Bennett's tutelage, he had to relearn from scratch the entire English alphabet.[28] For the rest of his life he was an unreconstructed bad speller, peppering his texts with schoolboy howlers of the "i before e" variety.

Given the pent-up emotions that he had carried fast inside him throughout 1903, the breakdown with its relaxation of the grip can be seen in retrospect as a life-saving necessity. Once he began to feel a little better, however, the control mechanisms, backed by the iron will, took over once more. He outlined the recipe for combatting depression to a young friend, Will Goodchild, a few years later.

> Don't imagine you are very ill. Nerves are *most curable* things, especially if the nervous one determines to help the physic-bottle, and practises the art of not allowing himself to feel depressed. It's a hard art to learn – hardish, say – but it can be done. Finding pleasant quiet occupation for all the time is a great thing. I used to invent all sorts of mind-resters, nerve-resters rather. But then I was a good deal worse than you – and now am exuberant...... It is perfectly possible to make oneself vastly better simply by determining to be so, imagining one is so.[29]

It was a philosophy of control that ensured Reynolds' survival in the short term, but made certain that he could never escape the potential explosion of nerves and suppressed feelings that was cooking up inside. For the rest of his life, the second breakdown was lying in wait just around the corner.

He saw his breakdown as a creative experience, but not because it gave him a long-needed release from the control. To him, on the contrary, its value lay in teaching him how to reinforce that control: "My own illness was an experience which I have never for a moment regretted; it made me better in body, mind and, I think, character than I should otherwise have been by driving me to many measures of self-discipline".[30] For his writing, it was a turning-point. He could not work properly for almost two years, but when he started again he was far better able to express his feelings, especially his sexual feelings; and he began to see the world in a clearer, more relaxed, light which gave a new depth to his natural mysticism. Without the breakdown, the revelation of 1906 at Sidmouth might never have occurred nor found itself so arrestingly in print.

By the start of 1904, Reynolds was beginning to emerge back into the light. Devizes College, with its elegant grey-stone facade, was a small town house of four stories. It could accommodate only a handful of pupils in dormitories that were really only small private bedrooms sleeping two or three boys to a room. Though it boasted a library and museum, a carpenter's shop and a gymnasium in the attic, the teaching space was limited and the main schoolroom little more than a private living room.[31] It provided a homely, cocoon-like atmosphere for a patient who needed above all quiet and rest. Apart from Miss Bennett, there was William Brimicombe, a teacher who lodged on the second floor and with whom Reynolds quickly became close friends.[32]

And there were other friends all around. Next door at No.11 was the corn-dealers shop of Reynolds' 'uncle', Fred Drew, who had married Frank Reynolds' cousin Fanny from Andover – the uncle who had raced Frank Reynolds in the pick-a-back competition at the Jubilee celebrations so many years before. Uncle Fred took a close interest in his nephew and his recovery, and in later years was to play a crucial role in helping to finance the first Reynolds' motorboat. On the other side, the little two storey building at No.13 housed the offices of the *Devizes Gazette and Wiltshire Telegraph* and the Simpson family who ran it.[33] George Simpson, then 49, had been for some years the proprietor of the *Gazette*, founded by his grandfather in 1816. When he was better, Reynolds would wander into the newspaper office of a morning to discuss the latest news and politics and see the current edition being put to bed.[34] It kept him in touch with the atmosphere of journalism and with a world in which writing still offered a means to a living. Emily Simpson, even more than her husband, took Reynolds' under the family wing. She gave her piano over to him to practise, one of the little "nerve-resters" that kept him from depression. Three years later, when he was still struggling and impoverished, she wrote offering to send him a blank cheque to fill in whenever he ran short.[35]

A few doors up the Market Place, George and Lizzie Tanner were still running the Bear and as welcoming as ever. He could relax nostalgically in his old childhood environment, still graced by his mother's pictures, without the weight of parental reproof hanging over him. It was about this time that he developed the habit of hot grog – a tot of whisky and hot water – as a nightcap and cure for his rampant insomnia. What more natural than to drop into the Bear at the end of a day to take his medicine.

When the strength had come back into his body, he was able to make the two-mile walk over to Prospect Rise to report to Aunt Jane on the progress of his recovery and on his plans for the future; and commiserate with the invalid Aunt Allie, surrounded by her black spaniel, Toby, and her two sedate long-legged cats. But socialising was still a major strain on his nerves. Some days when out for a meal, he would stop half-way through and just have to get up and go home.[36]

He was to remain as a guest at the College for a further thirteen months until he was almost on his feet again and no longer in need of the sheltered environment. He did something to pay his way by teaching and generally helping out in both the boys and girls schools, and by taking the pupils out on nature rambles along the downland paths that had been his joy when he too had been at school there. But he was depressed by the ethos of turning young boys away from the natural springs of life and into young gentlemen, which was what the school now seemed to him to be all about. The pupils fell far short of the spontaneity and warmth of the fisher children who overwhelmed him in Sidmouth with their love.

> A few years ago, when I had so much to do with the boys and girls of a high school, they liked me pretty well, I think, and trusted me, but they did not take to me, nor I very greatly to them. They went about their business, and I about mine. If I invited them for a walk, they came gladly, not because it was a walk with me, but because I knew of interesting muddy places, and where to find strange things. Their manners to me were always good: good manners smoothed our intercourse. But in no ways were our lives interwoven. We were side-shows, the one to the other. I was content that it should be so, and they were too.[37]

He was beginning to formulate, perhaps subconsciously still, his unease with the soulless quality of middle-class existence.

By February 1904 he was fit enough to travel and continue his recuperation at Nether Velly. He knew his family had been worried and wanted too to see his stepmother and sister again. Above all, the peace of Velly, the walks and the sea air were certain to revive him further. He settled down to a quiet routine, helping out with the farm animals when the opportunity arose. This short interlude was later to come in handy in boosting his credentials as a "country" writer when he could genuinely claim to have actually worked on a farm.

One constant hazard of Nether Velly then, and today, was the ease with which the animals could break the fences and make their way onto the perfect sweep of lawn at the front of the house with threats of untold damage. He wrote to a friend about one such episode that February in a strangely juvenile tone which harks back to the sardonic doggerel poems he had used to write in Devizes some years before. It is a letter which betrays both an affection for the family, even perhaps his father struggling to evade the domestic clamour, but also a fundamental unease which forces him to an ironic distance. Most of all, in creating a dramatic narrative out of nothing, it shows him beginning to flex his muscles as a writer once again.

> This morning we had a final uproar. The shire mare was in the garden and the sheep and the mare both made for the lawn. Now my mater loves much the fair greensward. "Father! father! the mare's out. Put her in! We can't have her on the lawn. Father! father, the sheep are on the lawn! Father, father!" He put them in the fields just round. Then hearing a noise of guns in the woods adjoining his, he went right down to the bottom to see – and stayed.
> Then the child came in successively, a Mercuria of evil tiding.
> "Mother, oh! the sheep are in the lower orchard!"
> "Mother, they are coming to the lawn!"
> "Mother, the shire mare is ON the lawn."
> They went on. "Oh you old devil"; they addressed this lady like a badge of pedigree. They drove her into the further yard.... where the sows run.

> "Mother, the sheep are in the garden – they are on the lawn – now they have gone to the top orchard!"
> Frantic were the cussful cries. "They'll get blown in that lush grass" said I; "and no one here knows how to stap a blown sheep."
> "Mother, the sows are in the garden."
> Then my mater, lawn lover, lost her head. She went round to all the out buildings; "Oh! you devel, Oh you devel!" she said, not specifying the shire mare, the sows, my pater, or the sheep. The mare I took by the fore-lock and walked to the field. But she looked lovingly on the lawn and having no halter I could not make her pass so fair a place. Politely I patted and exhorted, ditto she looked toward the lawn.
> But they pursued her, so well bred a mare, with sticks and stones and unkind tongues, as if they made mouths at Elijah. She went. More sows and sheep being got out, my mater called "Father!" She went to an out building where roosting fowls have been this long time as if he would take his pipe and his siesta there. Like a tragedy-queen, great-aunt to the lawn, she called "Father!" I chased the pigs till I was giddy, tied the gates of the orchard (with the sheep in it) and all was quiet. Ho! for the life of a farmer.

He ended this uproarious letter on a note which expressed more faithfully his continuing struggle against the relapse into depression.

> It's uncomfortable to see far into the futility of things.[38]

He stayed at Velly long enough to see in the spring blossom and the leaves. In May he set out for London and Thomas Seccombe to do what he could to start up his writing life again. The contrast with the peace of North Devon confirmed him in his lifelong loathing of the capital. He wrote to Aunt Jane

> Aunt Allie should make great efforts to get down to Velly. The place is lovely, now all the trees are out; I can hardly imagine a more beautiful. London appears to me more dreadfully dull than ever. One hears its noise all the time. I called at the Academy this morning. There were the usual horrors of pictures, with some truly remarkable portraits with pink and blue faces. Also there were some pictures of the sea and fishermen; but these made me feel so miserable for boats and the sea that I got no pleasure from them, and then left the place. I cannot and will not live in London.[39]

From talking to Seccombe he knew only too well the dilemma he faced in attempting to launch a literary career from the provinces. He needed to be in London to exploit openings and cement contacts; but he could not live in London, let alone write there. The only solution was to find a proxy who could make the contacts and place the material for him. It was no doubt Seccombe who suggested he should get in touch with J.B. Pinker.

By 1904 the literary agent was a relatively new phenomenon, but was beginning to be seen as essential to most serious authors by offering a specialist knowledge to match that of the publisher and thus redress the balance of power. Pinker, then 40, had been a foreign correspondent and magazine editor before starting up his agency in 1896, with H.G. Wells as one of his first clients. He was to add to his list for a brief period Oscar Wilde and Bernard Shaw, and then as permanent clients such names as Henry James, Joseph Conrad, Arnold Bennett, George Gissing, Ford Hueffer, Rudyard Kipling, Hugh Walpole and countless others. Despite the competition from A.P. Watt and Curtis Brown, he could well lay claim to be the foremost agent of the early twentieth century.

He was a short, compact Scotsman with a round rosy face and close-cropped greying hair, who spoke in a distinct but hoarse voice that came close to a whisper. In Frank Swinnerton's telling description of his professional skills "he knew the monetary secrets of authors and the weaknesses of publishers, terrified some of these last and was refused admittance by others, dominated editors, and of course enjoyed much power."[40] He had a shrewd understanding of the current public taste which was invaluable to his authors, and when contracting business his sense of humour and flow of anecdote was such that the unfortunate publisher found himself agreeing to terms that ten minutes before he would have rejected out of hand.[41] His client care went far beyond the strict letter of the ten per cent contract. He nurtured promising young authors, helping them with both advice and money. He acted as welfare agent-cum-banker to Conrad for most of the latter's writing life, lending sum after sum with little certain hope of repayment.

Reynolds called in upon Pinker's manager at the offices in Arundel Street off the Strand and agreed to come up again on 21 May armed with specimens of his work. But it was not to be. Returning to Devizes, he found that the brief stay in London had so knocked up his head that he could not travel up again so soon. So he wrote direct to Pinker enclosing a number of short stories, together with detailed plans for a book entitled "Back on the Land", inspired perhaps by the stay at Nether Velly, and for a translation of Baudelaire's *Paradis Artificiels*. He did not disguise his urgent need for help: "I beg you to give the matter of handling my work as favourable consideration as may be possible. Bad health which prevents me from living in town – on the spot – and ignorance of the literary market make me doubly helpless by myself".[42]

He waited anxiously for the reply which came a fortnight later. Pinker wrote a friendly letter, returning the manuscripts and regretting that none were suitable for his use, but adding that he might be able to handle other work. Reynolds jumped at this opening: "If, after what you have seen of the MSS. sent, you would be so kind as to give some hint as to the nature of the 'something else' that you *would* handle, I should be very grateful. For a man – an embodied headache rather – who can't live in Town and who is too ignorant of this sort of thing (the disposal of MSS.) to work successfully from the country, is sadly in need of the expert help literary agents afford...... "[43]

Pinker invited him up to discuss it and an afternoon appointment was fixed on 15 June.[44] From the moment he walked into Pinker's office, the die was cast. They talked at length about Reynolds' past, his writing, the breakdown and his plans for the future. The tough-minded businessman who could twist publishers round his little finger was overcome by the resilience of this young man, the sharp intelligence, the earnestness with which he described his current writing projects. He agreed there and then to take him on.

Two weeks later a draft contract arrived and Reynolds, who much enjoyed the detail of legal documents, went straight into negotiating mode, offering some tentative amendments, including the suggestion of fixing a time-limit: "You will understand – will you not? – that I don't want to be contentious or mistrustful etc. But I do want to have all contingencies included, so as not to leave room for any discussions or possible unpleasantness after signature."[45] By 12 July the detail was settled and Reynolds was apologetically grateful: "the short agreement exactly as it stood was like getting married! with no provision for equitable divorce, or a latch-key!"[46] Pinker had suggested a cancellation clause instead of a time-limit and Reynolds accepted with a disclaimer "I was not very keen on a time-limit so long as there was provision for cancellation. Without that I know I should have been like a bluebottle in a closed room, whether I wanted to or not."[47] Pinker had also agreed to Reynolds' proposal of a clause freeing him to undertake his own negotiations direct with publishers when occasion offered – "it seems to me that I should wish to use it seldom enough, but that it might be advantageous to me, and indirectly so to you, sometimes to send an MS. to an editor through a common friend."[48] He was probably thinking of Seccombe and the value of his contacts, but eventually the clause was to prove vital in finding a home for Reynolds' first book.

Now signed up with the foremost literary agent of the day, his hopes took a lift. He sent Pinker his portfolio of nineteen manuscripts, mostly short stories, of which at least six were eventually to find their way to print.[49] The most recently written was a little story, *A Kitten: That's All*, which was his first to be published in a professional London periodical – and it is one of his best, both in feeling and in execution.

That summer George and Lizzie Tanner, after almost five years at the Bear, had handed over to a new landlord, William Sudweeks, and gone to farm in the village of Ford on the outskirts of Salisbury. They moved into a small seventeenth-century farmhouse, built on the crossroads in the centre of the village – originally Castleford Farm House, but now called simply Ford House. It was set on a meandering bend of the River Bourne, with cows grazing in the pastures all around, from where you could look up or down the beautiful valley enclosed by the gently rolling wooded downs. Its most striking feature was its old walled garden of weathered red bricks enclosing a wealth of flowerbeds, vegetable plots and well-tended lawns – a place in which time had stood still for 250 years.[50]

For the next few years Ford House was to prove another of Reynolds' safe havens, to which he could make his escape when, either through illness or worry, life in Devizes was threatening to collapse on him. Though much of *A Poor Man's House* was in reality written in Devizes, it was the house at Ford that gave Reynolds the Salisbury location for those parts of the fictional journal in the book that were supposed to have been written away from Seacombe.

He fell in love with the Tanners' cat, Minnie (formerly Mimi-Meaow), a short-haired tabby with a broad soft ruff inherited from her Persian father. Whenever he arrived there, she would come pattering along the corridors to greet him. She would travel downstairs in the morning on his shoulders; and would sit on his shoulders again at dinner, competing for tit-bits with an outstretched paw.[51] She was one of his favourites in a lifetime of cats. The story is about the killing that June of one of her kittens.

It opens with a tense discussion with Lizzie Tanner over which kitten to kill.

> Two kittens were hidden in her fur, and her fore leg lay protectingly across the third. She looked at us with still soft yellow eyes, and purred.
> "We must not keep them all."
> "How many?" I asked.
> "And she must have one for her health's sake."
> "Then we must kill two."
> "No. Let her have two. They play so prettily together."
> "Very well."
> "We will have the two prettiest. Let us look at them."
> I detached the kittens from Mimi-Meaow and placed them on the table. Mimi-Meaow stood up in her basket, and looked at us, and looked at her kittens, and looked at us again – and purred. Tabby kittens they were. Two of them were sturdy, but the other was not. Its legs were barer of fur, its neck was thinner, its blind eyes bulged further from its head. Its cry was weaker and more plaintive. It rolled helplessly upon its side and back.
> "That is the one."
> "Yes," I said.
> The weakling was chosen for death.

And then the execution, stark in its Orwellian detail.

> I found a bucket in the scullery, and I found a piece of string, and I picked up a hollow stone. I filled the bucket with water, and I took the weakling kitten (how soft it was!), and I tied one end of the string around the kitten's waist (being thin, it had a waist), and I made fast the other end to the stone.

> While I did it the kitten clung to the stone with its weakly leg and soft claws. (Why was the stone like a rock and the kitten like a man cleaving to it?)
> The kitten cried with a tiny voice; but Mimi-Meaow was purring on somebody's lap, under somebody's caresses.
> Very gently I dropped the kitten into the bucket. The scullery was dank and dark, the water darker. As I looked to see that all was well, I saw the kitten sprawl down into the blackness of the water, as if into a dark eternity.

And finally the psychological aftermath.

> It was sadly I went back and took it out. (How wet and limp it was!) I tried not to touch it, and I cut the string, and I dropped it into a little paper bag.
> With a broken spade I dug a grave for it behind a dying laurel bush; and covered it in, and stamped upon it.
> And I went away, thinking to walk about the garden and to smell the roses and lavender and to look down the valley that is between the garden and the plain.
> But I saw the kitten, flickering on the blue haze wherewith the trees in the valley were wrapped about, the kitten ever sprawling into blackness, and I could not by any means or any thought put the shadow of it from me. The kitten going suddenly to death, the dark water; where I looked they were there – impalpable like the blue haze.
> I wondered when the sight of it would go from me.
> I took three sprays of cluster-roses and wove them into a wreath. I laid them on the kitten's grave, and in the centre I placed a red rose and a white, and I left them on the ground.
> I don't know why I desired to lay flowers there, nor why roses, three clusters of roses, a red rose and a white.[52]

It is the outcast in himself, still weakened by his own recent wrestling match with death, who weaves this subtle contrast between the beauties of the garden and the ugliness of the killing. When he got within the emotional skin of his subject, he could not help but write well.

The two months it took to settle the agreement with Pinker was a worrying anxious time for Reynolds. He wrote polite letters of enquiry when a week passed without news from Pinker's office. No surprise then that when the deal was finally struck in the middle of July he should suffer a new and severe relapse which put him to bed for three weeks. When he surfaced again at the beginning of August, he wrote to Pinker: "After another illness, I am only just beginning to look after affairs again. Doctor says, as much idleness as possible; specialist, that I may be better in a year if I don't do more with anything than play about. But I hope to have sent you a good deal before that...." In opposition to the medical opinion, he could see clearly the restorative value of getting down to writing. He sought Pinker's advice on whether, in default of tackling harder work, he should start the Baudelaire translation and continue with the "Back on the Land" book: "It is so far sketched out that I think I might try to get on with it and escape making myself ill again."[53] Pinker responded with some kindly and positive encouragement which, typically enough, induced in Reynolds a certain feeling of guilt: "I feel more than a *bit* of a fraud, knocking up like this just when I ought not to do so. However, I will get on with "Back on the Land" as soon as my head's a little less irritable, and some short things I have in mind as well. But I don't think I shall start the Baudelaire translation without a destination in view."[54]

He had been planning since early July to continue the habit of previous years and spend some weeks in August by the sea in Sidmouth.[55] This year the holiday was needed more than most. But the sudden relapse had set back his plans and it was not until September that he felt sufficiently well to make the journey. There was a bitter-sweet feeling about the venture. He loved the freedom of the place – the sea air, the sailing, the walks – but at the same time he had the fear that this first return since the breakdown would reawaken memories of those desperate feelings of the previous autumn just before he went under.

He signed in at his old lodgings in Jubilee Terrace, unpacked his few belongings and wandered down to the shore road to look for signs of life. To his horror, the first thing he ran across was his old boat, the *Ivy*, lying derelict and abandoned in the gutter above the sea wall – and all the memories of the previous summer, and a lost innocence, came flooding back. It is the opening of *A Poor Man's House*, heavy with a nostalgic foreboding.

> The sea is merely grinding against the shingle. The *Moondaisy* lies above the sea-wall, in the gutter, with her bottom-boards out and a puddle of greenish water covering her garboard strake. Her hunchbacked Little Commodore is dead. The other two of her old crew, George Widger and Looby Smith are nowhere to be seen: they must be nearly grown up by now. The fishermen themselves appear less picturesque and salty than they used to do. It is slack time after a bad herring season. They are dispirited and lazy, and very likely hungry.
> These old lodgings of mine, with their smug curtains, aspidestria plant, china vases and wobbly tables and chairs....
> But I can hear the sea-gulls screaming, even here.[56]

On 21 September he saw Bill Woolley, the fictional George Widger, parading along the front with two of his mates in the unaccustomed garb of a creased blue suit. He learned from Bob, the fictional Tony, that he was off that day to Plymouth to join the Navy.[57] In the evening after dark, he met Bob again standing outside a brilliantly lighted grocer's shop, crying his heart out at what his son might be feeling on his first night launched on a cruel and lonely world. Reynolds immediately took charge.

> "Come along down to the Shore Road, Tony."
> It seemed wrong, hardly decent, to let his grief spend itself in the lighted-up street. The Front was deserted and dark, for there was rain in the wind, and the sound of the surf had a quick savage chop in it. Away, over the sea, was a great misty blackness.
> As we walked up and down, Tony talked between tears and anger – tears for himself and George, anger at the cussedness of things. He looked straight before him, to where the row of lamps divided the lesser from the greater darkness, the town noises from the chafing surf; it is the only time I have ever seen a fisherman walk along shore without a constant eye on the sea.[58]

After Reynolds had gradually calmed him down a little, he took him off for a touch of hot grog, his own curative draught for dispersing misery and bringing sleep, and saw him safely home down the Gut. Next day was like the morning after the start of a love affair.

> This morning, when I saw Tony on the Front, he was more than a little awkward; looked shyly at me from under his peaked cap, as if to read in my face what I thought of him. He had slept after all, and spoke of the hot grog as a powerful, strange invention, new to him as a sleeping draught.[59]

It was an episode that had opened both men to each other – the beginning of an intimate relationship which was to change both their lives.

It was only a brief holiday stay, and he then made tracks northwards for Nether Velly. There he followed the relaxed pattern of the spring, walks into Clovelly and along the coast, helping out on the farm, writing in his bedroom looking out over that exquisite view. He was fascinated by the discovery of Mouth Mill, the "weird opening" in the cliffs just west of Clovelly where a stream tumbles down between the rugged tree-covered hills into the sea, and where boats from South Wales loaded with limestone landed on the rocky open beach to feed the little lime kiln there which served the country all around with cheap lime fertiliser.[60] The mouth of the cove is guarded by the towering pinnacle of Blackchurch Rock which stirred him to write a short mystical fable, *A Legend*, full of his own plight and yearnings for love.

> Back in those days there was a man who could find no foothold in life. Therefore he took his wife to the grey cottage in the combe of the Black Abbey Rock, at the western edge of the land, hoping always to find peace and something that his soul might hold to and have. Twice in a day and night the sea came up to the house, and twice in a day and night the waters went back and left a wilderness of great stones, in the midst of which uprose the Black Abbey.
> ...... The man loved the body of his wife, who was beautiful, as a lily is beautiful on an altar in a dim church. Yet he hated her too, for her soul was vast and empty, so that the four winds of heaven could not have filled it, and in her eyes was nothing. She feared the sea that he loved, and that was more beautiful than she was. She stayed always in the grey cottage, or wandered, and was like light, in the day-long dusk under the pine-trees which were as thick as giant moss upon the slopes of the combe. When he hated her he was sorry, and when he loved her, sorrow was the end of it. Two sorrows he took to the sea.[61]

There is enough material here to keep a conference of psychoanalysts busy for a fortnight. The hero riven by his sexual conflicts is captured, body and soul, by the Rock-Woman, an embodiment of the sea, at once both alluring and signifying death. With the killing of his children, he goes through a symbolical breakdown.

Escaped from his own private nightmare, Reynolds knew now, if not before, that the sea had captured him too.

> Afterwards the man forsook the cottage in the combe of the Black Abbey, and returned among mankind, hoping to find forgetfulness and something that his soul might hold to and have; but always he yearned for the sea...... [62]

SIX

The Holy Mountain 1904–6

One day in 1903 Thomas Seccombe was walking from Westerham in Kent to the Cearne, Edward Garnett's home in the High Chart, when he had an idea – a startling idea of some literary promise.[1]

It was a walk he had taken several times before. He had come to know Edward, now a reader with the publishing firm of Duckworth and building a reputation as literary critic and discoverer of writing talent, through his father, Richard Garnett, who had helped Seccombe so selflessly with his work on the *Dictionary of National Biography*. Edward Garnett had little time for what he called the academic critics, who he thought "boiled the old bones of the great departed, but could not recognise a living genius."[2] But he made an exception in the case of Seccombe, a fellow toiler for the house of Constable who also looked out for young authors whose careers were in need of help.

The route took him on his left past the distinctly *un*mountainous eminence of Crockham Hill – when suddenly out of the blue his imagination took wing and spirited away that poor unsuspecting hill to arise again in the heart of the London metropolis. For the next few hundred yards of his woodland walk he was left pondering the enormous consequences of this strange miracle – political, social and financial. He was prone to such vibrant imaginings, but lacked the creative spirit that might turn them into books. He put the matter out of mind.

Later that summer when his holiday had taken him to Sidmouth and he was strolling with Reynolds along the red cliffs, he suddenly looked up at High Peak, which *was* a hill to be reckoned with, and said: "Suppose a hill like that were suddenly to arise in London, what a disgusting scramble there would be for it, to make money out of it. Think of the newspapers and financial syndicates...."[3] With that he bequeathed the germ of an idea that Reynolds was to build into a book. It was a double-edged bequest: a powerful image but, unless carefully handled, bordering on the preposterous.

It struck a chord in Reynolds' mind, but no more. He was on the edge of breakdown and in no mood to plan novels just then. But a year later, walking over High Peak again in the autumn of 1904, the idea filtered back through his memory and he took it home with him on return to Devizes at the beginning of November. From there, as he went for his usual country walks, High Peak became transmuted into his beloved Wiltshire Downs – it was a Roundway Hill, a Tan Hill, that was now winging its way to London in his mind. The idea began to gather all sorts of details round it and a cast of characters, a new fictional population for Devizes, who began to take charge of themselves and talk to him in the darkness of his bedroom at the College as he struggled to get to sleep.[4]

As the idea grew inside him, it became the vehicle for all the resentment he felt for the closed world of his home town which had bred the sickening attitudes of his father and which now regarded him, ill though he was, as a waster who would not shake off his hare-brained writing schemes, working through his capital rather than do a proper job. Outside his small circle of friends, he was conscious in a half paranoid way of eyes watching him. "Even the nicely-tailored young clerks in the bank used to look over their ledgers, as if to say: 'Here's that bad egg wants more money. Why doesn't he do something? He's living on his capital. We shall soon close *his* account – no assets.'"[5] This active feeling of resentment gave an energy to the book, though one that was always in danger of running away with itself. But giving vent to a little spleen had a curative effect also upon his health, so that the book, whatever people thought of it and whatever its objective quality, came to symbolise for him the passage back from the hell he had been through to the relative comforts of normal life. That is why he defended it bitterly against all criticism and stuck grimly by it despite the countless vicissitudes through which it was destined to pass.

For the last weeks of 1904 and the first of 1905 there was more thinking and planning than writing. A novel was an expensive undertaking for a new writer with a declining bank balance. Priority had to go to the ephemeral – the story or article that would butter the bread in the short term. At the beginning of November, Halkett of the *Pall Mall Magazine* expressed some interest in *The Conjugal Segregation Experiment*, the story he had written in Paris, but told Pinker: "It is excellent in some respects but much too long for us. I would like to see some short stories of under 5000 words from him. The present one ought to have been kept to this length."[6] Reynolds groaned internally – "fancy asking an author to cut out 74% of his valuable words!" – but was flattered by the first positive request he had received for work. On 13 November he went up to London to see Savill about his still troublesome head, but missed Pinker who was himself sick and away from the office. He left some specimen outline essays on which he set his hopes over the next few weeks for capturing the interest of the periodicals and establishing a steady run of work.[7]

By early December he had managed to cut *The Conjugal Segregation Experiment* by two-thirds and meet the requirements laid down by Halkett.[8] On Christmas Eve he received from Pinker's office a puzzling package – the return of another of his early stories, *A Love's Hunger*, with a compliments slip but no explanation of why it had been sent. He made a tentative enquiry of Pinker: "Perhaps something got left out in the fog and the hurry of before Xmas".[9] He was pleased to learn that Halkett was keen to take this story as well, but with considerable alteration, which Reynolds duly completed on New Year's Day – "I was relieved to know that 'A Love's Hunger' was not meant as an ironic Christmas Card."[10]

The prospect of publication spurred him on to renewed activity. In addition to some initial work on *The Holy Mountain*, he completed in January 1905 a sketch *In Praise of Cats*, later *A Citizenry of Cats*, a running record of all the cats in his life from Peter at the Bear to the Tanners' Mimi-Meaow at Ford. A year of recuperation at Devizes was bringing back nostalgic memories of childhood and he was beginning once again to feel sufficiently good about himself to indulge in "egotistical essays" of this kind.[11]

At the end of January he moved out of the College to take private lodgings in the town. He was now no longer an invalid, and space for Miss Bennett in her little school was as always at a premium. He celebrated his move by going down immediately with influenza and for the next few days was confined to his room, unable to crawl out of bed. But he was cheered to receive from Pinker a cheque for twelve shillings and twopence for *A Kitten: That's All*, which had appeared in the *Week's Survey* for early December. It was the first money he had received for his writing since Paris two years before. He asked in puzzlement "Whatever is the *Week's Survey*?" and could not restrain his mirth at the reply: "I am still smiling over the sale of 'A Kitten' to the *Week's Survey* – a journal devoted to Colonial and American topics!"[12] On 6 March the *Pall Mall Magazine* offered to take *A Love's Hunger* for three guineas.[13]

With these little boosts to confidence, he could feel at last that his career was on the move. So much so that when the opportunity of a strange holiday came to him in the late spring, he did not hesitate to put aside his stories and sketches, and the very slow work on the *Mountain*, to embark for a month on a Mediterranean cruise. It was not a cruise as most people would recognise it. He was to travel on a Welsh cargo steamer, the S.S. *Coranian*, a small steel-built ship of well under two thousand tons and owned by the Cardiff firm of Owen, Watkins Williams, carrying out Welsh coal to Italian ports and returning laden with general cargoes – onions, hides, bark-extract for tanning and oranges.[14] It was a chance to put the final seal on the recovery from his two-year illness and to pick up some colourful copy into the bargain.

On 16 May he met Captain Jones at the offices in Swansea – a jolly little red-faced man, rounder than he was long, who had risen rapidly from ship's cook to his present command. He was a friendly, approachable man but frustrated by the inexorable tie of the sea. He would light one pipe after another and always repeat dismally "More nails in the coffin!"[15] They went together with Teddy, the younger of the two ship's boys, to the Board of Trade office where Reynolds was signed on for a shilling a month as "purser", an honorary role to escape passenger regulations. He joined the *Coranian* in the Prince of Wales dock at midday and was introduced to the officers over a surprisingly good lunch of soup "better than Bloxham, though not unlike", mutton and an excellent pudding. All five officers were Welsh-speaking Welshmen and, with the coal coming on board, all but the captain were as black as chimney sweeps.[16] There was a motley crew of two Greeks, two English boys, steward, cook, and seven Spaniards, not one of whom could speak much English nor could steer – they had to have the course pointed to them on the compass-card.[17]

They had a problem in setting off because the owners had been putting pressure on the captain to overload, and the ship's loadline was too low and her keel out of trim. With some adjustments she was finally given clearance to sail and by the evening was making good progress down the Bristol Channel. The first day was a fine one and crew and officers spent most of the time cleaning the coal dust off themselves and the ship. With coal dust everywhere, Reynolds had to abandon his usual fastidiousness. Keeping clean was a problem because of the state of the bathroom in the officers' quarters, and he soon settled down to his own routine of a Turkish bath in the engine room at night and a hose down in the morning when the men were washing the decks.[18]

He would spend the day pacing the bridge with the captain and was eventually allowed to take watches himself; or squatting hunched up in a mackintosh on the coal bunker behind the wheel-house scribbling in his journal. He soon gravitated to the least frequented part of the ship – "I go there too much, but it is so interesting" – the engine room which held the dual fascination of throbbing engines and muscular men stripped to the waist.[19] "Look down into the engine-room when the ship is under way – down two flights of iron steps, through two floors of iron grating. You can see the engineer on watch pacing up and down before his engines. He watches them tenderly and keenly, as wild animals at the Zoo watch succulent children."[20] Down there in the bowels of the ship, he would chat for hours with the chief engineer against the noise of the engines – "our quiet little talk was in reality a quiet little shout".[21] They talked about promotion, pay, work ashore, marriages, children.... and the chief even told him of one Atlantic crossing when he had blackmailed a pretty Irish girl into giving him a kiss by threatening to turn a valve and blow up the engines in the middle of the night. Before long he was actively helping to look after the engines and crawling with the engineer through the tunnel that housed the propellor shaft to sort out a problem there.[22]

Three days out they had passed Finisterre and the conditions were improving. "The sea has become very beautiful, a much brighter blue with more wave and less roll. Still there's much too much roll to attempt shaving. A pretty set of pirates we look."[23] But by 21 May the wind and sea had increased, and he was kept awake at nights by the drumming of the empty wine casks for Bastia against the sides of the hold beneath his cabin. As they came through the straits the following day, he found to his disappointment that Gibraltar was not the high bold cliff of his imagination but merely a hill with a low foreshore between it and the sea.

"Most people, I think, have an idea that the Mediterranean is a placid sort of place. I thought so."[24] But they met higher and higher seas. One immense wave broke over the bridge, flooding the steward's pantry and cabin and injuring the stores. To his dismay, the officers had discovered that he was a writer, with a rather distorted version of his status. "It leaks out – bother it, for it's awkward – that the owners told the ship's officers that I was a very considerable writer – a big author, as they put it – with hair like a Welsh bard for their amusement. When they expect bread for their amusement and get – editors being kindly – a little stone or two – 'twill be awkward. My strong truth against the matter is taken for modesty. Modesty! Lord!"[25]

The officers soon put him to the test. The last passenger they had carried had brought them storms throughout the voyage, so they asked for a fair weather rhyme from Reynolds to ward off a repeat performance. The first two stanzas of his *Ballad on Fair Weather* did nothing to impair his reputation.

'Tis nothing this! the Captain said,
When a big sea took the boat
And the Steward's pots and sacks and stores
And the Steward himself by his pantry doors
Were more or less afloat.

"We crossed the Bay with scarce a roll –
What more do you want than that?"
With sunshine bright and moonshine light
Blue seas by day and no fog by night,
From the Wolf to the Cape de Gat.[26]

Reynolds was surprised to find that all the officers talked disparagingly of the sea life and longingly of their desire to settle down on land. As they passed Cape Corso on 26 May, Captain Jones "jerked his pipe irritably towards the blue Corsican mountains and the green fields that slope down to the sea. 'If only I had a hundred a year, I'd settle down in one of those places and take things easy. A little farm, labour cheap – you can live like a shipowner there for a hundred a year.'" The malaise spread right down to the little ship's boy: "Gettin' used to it.... Not me! I'm not never comin' to sea any more. Not if I knows it! Land's the place!"[27]

On 27 May they made land at Leghorn and unloaded some of their cargo. By the evening they were ready to sail. "We were in Leghorn Harbour, on the point of sailing, of course, and except for the racket aboard ship the place was very calm. The light of an opal sunset was dying away on the red walls of a tattered old house by the southern quay. The short Italian twilight was rapidly gathering in."[28] Reynolds as ever was down in the engine room with the chief engineer and the Greek donkey-engine man. He thrilled with a writer's eye to the start of the engines.

> The Chief placed himself near the reversing wheel and valves. He gave the wheel a turn, started the small reversing engine. Slowly, very slowly, the links above tumbled ahead and astern, and the eccentrics shifted. Six masses of forged steel, the cranks, rocked in their pits, half a turn towards

> us, half a turn away. Fifteen tons of metal swayed backwards and forwards, up and down....
> Do you know how a cat sways just before she springs? It was like that; like some monstrous beast of prey whose limbs and claws were pistons, crossheads, rods, and cranks....
> Cocks are turned, valves opened. Steam rushes from boiler to cylinders with a hollow gurgling hiss. The cranks make half a turn, a whole turn. She is under way.

And then catastrophe.

> There is a sudden loud report, followed by a long, savage, deafening hiss. Almost instantly the engine-room is filled with a stinking fog of hot oily steam, driving upwards through the gratings, but thickening, nevertheless.
> It was the high-pressure steam-joint.
> Lighted on the one side by a hundred candle-power burner and on the other by the smoky coffee-pot lamp, the Chief and Donkey stayed by the reversing wheel. Their faces were still turned towards the cocks and valves, but their eyes had shifted to the steam-joint overhead. Muscles taut and swollen – magnified, as it were, by the brilliant light and the deep, hard-cut shadows – they were like a group by some painter of heroes, like tormented forms peering in at the Gate of Hell.
> It was only for a moment. One's first thought was to race up the iron steps to the open air; one's second, to face it out, as the engineers had to face it out; one's third, to realise that the steam would be more scalding above than below.[29]

He stayed with them and took his share of wrestling to repair the steam-joint and, in turns, watching anxiously to see how the packing around it held through the night as the little craft sped on to Genoa over the silent moonlit sea.

They were delayed longer than expected at Genoa by the stupidity of agents and late deliveries of cargo. On 2 June he took a tram after breakfast out to the Campo Santo to admire the old graves and statuary there; and wandered the town in the evening, taking an ice in the gardens by a big piazza and an egg and some chianti in the Via Carlo Felice. The packing of the steam-joint had held more or less when the engines were started again, so he climbed to the upper bridge as they made their departure to watch the harbour lights blue in the water and the lights on the mountains, so high and so close, adding a multitude of new stars to the sky.[30]

They docked the next day at Bastia which Reynolds found much more to his liking than the Italian ports. In the afternoon he strolled down to the old town with the chief engineer to watch the boat-building there in the cellar-like shops under the houses. "The little town is built round the harbour, and just behind it are high, dark green, partially cloud-covered mountains. The sun nearly strikes one to the ground. In the gardens, aloes, yuccas and cacti grow to immense sizes. There are olive-groves along the shore-road." That Saturday evening, he went ashore again with the second engineer to wander admiringly round the gardens and consume a little too much cognac.[31]

On the Monday morning, he accompanied the captain and steward in the official role of interpreter to the market in the old town to buy potatoes, cherries and eggs for the onward journey. Neither the stallholders nor his shipmates could understand what he said to the other party and he drove some good bargains by making out the captain as a mountain of obstinacy. "You ought to have seen us buying eggs in Bastia market. The steward, in Welsh, told the skipper what was wanted; who told me in English; who told the old egg-woman's daughter in French; who told the old woman herself in the Corsican dialect of French and Italian mixed. She wanted to sell us nineteen eggs for twenty, because, she said, they were big ones, and the steward wouldn't have it. For half an hour or so we haggled, backwards and forwards along the line, and, by the time we compromised on something else, I was sweating all over."[32]

In the afternoon he was out once again, buying insecticide for the bug he had found in his cabin the day before and more than a pound of excellent Corsican tobacco for the bargain price of two shillings. He was sitting that evening outside a café sipping a crème de menthe when suddenly he heard the *Coranian*'s hooter down below in the harbour and made it just in time as the boat set sail.[33]

He was seasick in a heavy storm as they crossed the Gulf of Lyons, but was becoming more stoical about the bugs and fleas in his cabin. "I have been certain for some time that though it is a fine thing to be constantly clean, it is finer to be able to be unclean if necessary. My voice! The prospect of a flea disturbs me but little, and if I am really tired I don't inspect my cabin for bugs. And of course I don't get bitten any the more for getting used to it."[34] The cleanliness philosophy of *A Poor Man's House* was beginning to stir in his mind.

They reached Valencia on 8 June and the following day he went up to the town in the evening with the captain. "When we got there the theatres were just going in and the streets crowded with people and carriages. Not many signs of poverty, I thought. Certainly the mantillas set off the beauty of the Spanish women, such as it is – pale, pasty, nothing much. The youngest begin to look old, the fat old frumps they will become."[35] They found a restaurant where they had to draw poached eggs on the back of the menu to make their order understood. Back on the ship, they were joined in the galley by the second mate and had a long argument about the current Welsh religious revival, one of the subjects for which Reynolds was planning a satirical treatment in *The Holy Mountain*. "For about an hour and a half they tried to convince me that the Welsh revival is other than an evil press-vamped thing. All the old narrow-minded arguments – men soberer and debt paying etc. – trotted out with eloquence."[36]

They sailed in the early morning for the nearby port of Burriana to take on a cargo of oranges. "We are back off Burriana, a little flat place, brilliant in the sunshine, surrounded by bold reddish mountains, with cloud shadows resting on some of the flanks and spurs. The crops appear to grow right down to the sea-shore. Two of our winches are going, and high-prowed boats, stacked with oranges, keep coming off from the little pier opposite the central street. The shore looks almost like that of Sidmouth. I can fancy Tom Woolley and Uncle Sam leaning against one of the boats drawn up on the little beach."[37]

Later that morning Reynolds and the captain went ashore for more provisions for the homeward journey – fresh meat, in particular, to give some relief from the salt beef. "We took the butcher (a villainous black-looking man) in tow and went to inspect his live-meat shop, hopping over the ponds and puddles left by yesterday's heavy rains. The butcher's place was a filthy yard, littered with grasses, rotten vegetation, palm-branches and dung. It contained several litters of cats (eaten here), many rabbits of various sizes, some small fowls and two skinny sheep. While they were diving about catching samples, the yard was a whirl of sheep, cats, kittens, fowl, dogs and rabbits. The result of our bargaining was a sheep, four live rabbits (now alive in a cage aboard), vegetables and eggs." They met their agent in Burriana town and lunched in a long cool room behind a hotel off sweet tender meat, red wine, fish, olives and peaches. They missed the train and had to walk back to the harbour, got caught in a thunder-storm rowing out to the ship and arrived on board soaking wet. They found that the oranges that had been taken on were all bad, but they were being shipped to England for tenpence a box nonetheless.[38]

At eight o'clock that evening they upped anchor and set a homeward course for Liverpool. Reynolds saw nothing of this final departure, being stretched out on his bunk with a wet handkerchief around his head and the worst of headaches, the effect of the long walk in the hot sun. They were plagued with illness on the return journey. Most of the crew collapsed with terrible stomach cramps because of bad water they had taken on at Bastia. Reynolds, who took his water boiled, escaped unharmed. One day out on 11 June, the cook went down with suspected diphtheria, diagnosed by Reynolds who had now taken on the further honorary role of ship's doctor. The next day he appeared better, however, and they all breathed a sigh of relief at the thought of escaping quarantine at Liverpool.[39] They had another rough passage up the Portuguese coast and across the Bay of Biscay – Reynolds exhausted by the rolling which disturbed his head and prevented sleep. Nearing home on 18 June, he enjoyed a quiet Sunday with not much work to do. "The seamen wash themselves most of the morning. It is an astonishing and very fine sight when they peel off their dirty rags and discover a fair clean man underneath – a sort of metamorphosis – a sort of emergence from a chrysalis."[40]

As they approached the South Wales coast and he saw his first gull, his spirits revived at the feel of home waters. "Somehow or other, the high seas, the historic Mediterranean even, have something lacking without the birds, and do not mean so much, nor even seem so sea-like as the cries of the gulls. The romance of the sea, and the beauty of it too, I think, are most intense where sea and land meet."[41] Just after one o'clock on 20 June they berthed at the Herculanean Dock in Liverpool and Reynolds was relieved to smuggle his Corsican tobacco through customs unsearched.

He planned to go on to Manchester for a few days to see his old friends.[42] He also visited Henry Lamb, now embarking on his artistic career in London, whose home in Cheyne Walk was a more convenient place to stay than with Seccombe out at Acton. It was probably there that Lamb made the brilliant line-drawing of a robust-looking Reynolds, complete with pince-nez, the only portrait of him from this period.[43] He arranged for Lamb to take his drawings to Pinker with book illustration in mind, but made it clear to Pinker he had no doubts about their quality: "You'll judge for yourself. He doesn't appear to me to need my bolstering."[44]

The trip had opened his mind to new countries and new experiences, improved his sea-legs and his knowledge of shipboard engines. But more than that, the tough open-air regime had relaxed him mentally and restored his health. Back in Devizes on 29 June he wrote to Pinker: "I am returned from the voyage very much improved in health." He had done little writing while away, except the sea journal, and was anxious for news of the skeleton essays which he hoped might buy him the time to get down to his novel with a revived will. "Are any of those Essays going off? I wish they would, and so keep the pot boiling while I get on with the 'Holy Mountain'".[45]

The *Coranian* trip marked another new beginning. He had at last found lodgings where he felt comfortable to write. On his return, he moved in to a little two-up, two-down terraced house – 2, Stanley Terrace – in Pans Lane on the southern outskirts of the town. The terrace had been built in the early 1890s, perhaps originally intended for workers in the new North Wilts Dairy Company plant nearby, but No.2 was now occupied by Harry Wyer, a 31-year-old commercial clerk and his wife, Phoebe who, like most landladies, took at once to the young author. He was given the furnished bedroom at the front of the house, just 13 foot by 12, with a curved alcove opposite the door.[46] His writing desk was placed before the little front window, cut in two by a stone mullion, from where he could see out to the right the puff of smoke from trains chugging up the cutting to the castle tunnel, and straight ahead over rough common land to the western rim of the Salisbury Plain. It was here over the next two-and-a-half years that he was to write *The Holy Mountain* and much of *A Poor Man's House*.

He shared the Wyers' table in the little back kitchen, taking his breakfast there alone, a book always open beside his plate.[47] Phoebe Wyer looked after him with a special diet whenever he was ill.[48] She did not object either when he told her he was planning to buy a dog, although she could not then have guessed what she was letting herself in for. Two years before, in the summer of his breakdown, at a dog show in Devon his eye had lighted on a brindle Great Dane which had won a very highly commended. "Being very lonely, I watched with envious eyes how it jumped upon its keeper, placed its forepaws on his shoulder, fondled him, licked his face, and whimpered with delight. And I thought to myself, 'Some day I will have a dog like that.'"[49]

That July he took the train for London armed with a copy of *Exchange & Mart*. He was looking for a Great Dane for about two guineas, gentle but strong enough to tramp twenty miles a day with him in the West Country. He found a stuffy little back shop just north of Whitechapel where they had Great Danes for sale. "They took me through a dismal North London square, where empty tins and pickle pots grew instead of grass on the central plot, through a dingy house where a woman held a baby to her bare breast with one hand and washed dirty clothes with the other; and we entered a high iron cage inside of which eight huge dogs, barking and growling, made one feel like Daniel in the lions' den. ......They opened a ramshackle little wooden kennel. A three-quarter-grown pup rushed out, sniffed at me, sprang on me, and had my best clothes dirtied all over in an instant. ....You were mine – mine from that moment. I didn't choose you; you chose me."[50] She was seven months old and he called her Margot after the Pre-Raphaelite girl who had sung to him in the café in Paris. For the next eight years she was to fill the role of the intimate companion he had not yet found and to share with him his triumphs and disasters.[51]

When he got her back to Pans Lane the Wyers, thankfully, were on holiday at the seaside. "You tore up one mat, demolished a slipper, bit my new sea-going rug into holes (that was put down to keep you off the cold stones between the kitchen and the scullery doors), and you took a flying leap upon the breakfast table. Strange to say, you only smashed a plate, a jug, the jam-jar and the lid of the best tea-pot."[52] He feared that he would not be able to keep her and went to bed every night trembling with fatigue at this new responsibility, only to be dragged out again to stop her howling. But it was worth the strain to have this new, almost human, companionship. "But I've seen you laugh, Margot. I recollect your face...... when, on those lovely mornings, the sun lit up Salisbury Plain and we rushed out of the house together."[53]

He had bought her with his summer holiday in the west particularly in mind. On 9 August they set off on an ambitious tramp to Cornwall – as he told Pinker "'Holy Mountain' in the mornings, ambling in the afternoons, and wayside pubs in the evening."[54] They made for Nether Velly, through Wells, Glastonbury and Bridgwater, and then right along the north Devon coast through Minehead, Brendon and Lynmouth to Clovelly. For Reynolds, the accompaniment of this strangely massive animal, as tall as himself and almost as heavy, gave him a new slightly bohemian identity which he relished. In later days she was to become, even in London, as much his trademark as the fisherman's jersey. And at the same time, wherever they went, she became the first talking point and focus of attention which took some of the social pressure off himself.

This first walking holiday was the start of their love affair. "It was then that we learnt the jog-trot of our life together. Everywhere they said, 'Shouldn't like to meet he in the dead o' night, Mister.' In stableyards they stood round watching while I washed your feet and groomed you with a borrowed dandy-brush. 'Jest like a bloomin' hoss,' they said. You opened the conversation at the inns where your master had his bread and cheese and beer, and you your pint of milk. Because you looked ferocious, they fed and patted you the more when they found you gentle."[55]

There was plenty of incident along the way. At Wells she was put on a bed of damp peat-moss in a mouldy tower and kept half the town awake by howling all night. At Bridgwater, while Reynolds was having a well-earned bath, she escaped from the hotel skittle alley in an attempt to find him. Half-clothed he raced round the town until they found each other in the market place and she almost knocked him down for joy. In a coffee-room at Clovelly she was stung by two wasps and dashed wildly over the crockery and cold joints.

There were the down times too. "Keeping you is not all meaty bones. Sometimes it is mere dry dog biscuit." In the Lyn valley, he thrashed her for eating garbage, and again at Nether Velly for stealing a pound of fresh butter. These beatings taught him more about himself and the explosive Reynolds temper. "Would that one never had to beat you. Yet I think you prefer hot anger to cold justice. Uncalculating love, a fit of muddy fury boiling up from the atavistic depths of one, a struggle, curses, and quick repentance.... You understand such people; you have a fellow-feeling with them, and love them better than those cool, prudent, proper, respectable citizens, swaddled in civilisation, who seldom act without good reason and never repent or abase themselves. You dogs keep one in touch with one's own primeval nature. You are the companions of joy and sorrow, not of a stagnant temperateness in all things. But I do wish you would not cry out under the strap. It stirs too much the brute in one."[56]

When they reached the farm at Nether Velly, his stepsister Frances was overwhelmed by Margot. They played together endlessly "head-over-heels, somersault, roly-poly, batter pat, jump, flop!" For a seven-month-old puppy, Margot had done well. They had walked a hundred and twenty miles in the height of summer, though there had been times, like the thundery afternoon on the North Devon moors, when they had both been dead-beat. The planned long trek through Cornwall seems to have been wisely put aside, though they did manage a special pilgrimage to the border and Parson Hawker's church at Morwenstow where Margot showed her piety by jumping the altar rails.[57] Not many pages of *The Holy Mountain* could have been completed on this boisterous journey, but the rather calmer days at Nether Velly gave him more time to catch up on his writing.

Back at Pans Lane in October, he got down to more concerted work on the *Mountain* and by the beginning of December had completed the first half, which he posted off joyfully to Skemp at Berlin University for some professional academic advice.[58] He was still writing stories and sketches to keep the dribble of money flowing, and in the middle of December completed *Twinses*, published in the *Speaker* the following summer, the first of his stories about working-class poverty and resilience and the condescension of middle-class charity.[59] The publication of *A Love's Hunger*, proof-read by Brimicombe while he was away on the *Coranian*, was still hanging fire but he got a promise from the *Pall Mall Magazine* of a slot in the spring. More important, Halkett had agreed to take *The Conjugal Segregation Experiment*, published the following April as *The Blue-Stocking*, for the princely sum of twelve guineas, the most he had yet been paid for a single item of work.[60]

In October his autobiographical essay on cats had been published in a new magazine, the *English Review*, which went bankrupt before Pinker could lay hands on the payment.[61] Its title was to be borrowed three years later by a more illustrious successor. He had also entered the book review market, with a short article on Blake in the *Speaker* in May, and from November some continuous bread and butter reviewing for the *Bookman*, behind which must be seen the hidden hand of Seccombe. Pinker was also helping out by giving him clients' manuscripts to report on at two guineas a time.[62] Though it was nose to the grindstone work, he could at last see the prospect of a regular flow of ephemeral work which would buy him the time for the more serious business of writing novels.

He spent Christmas alone in the house – the Wyers had gone off to visit relatives – and he buried himself in his books to hide from the merciless feelings of loneliness that always assailed him at that time of year. He wrote up that Christmas and those feelings in a sketch which no one would publish until a further five years had gone by.[63]

1906, his *annus mirabilis*, started unpromisingly. His sister, Dot, fell dangerously ill, but to everyone's relief just as quickly recovered. Margot, one day in a fit of joyful exuberance, jumped up on him and knocked him down, spraining his right arm and hand. He gave her the heaviest beating yet, followed by the usual remorse.[64] At the same time he developed a touch of influenza which was later diagnosed as tonsillitis. The middle of January found him in a sorry state, confined to his bed, typing letters to Pinker with his left hand and signing them off with a childlike scrawl: "The influenza has turned out to be tonsillitis, but I'm as merry as may be with an arm in splints and a throat painted with caustic twice a day. After all, it's nothing compared to what my head was. Hadn't you better turn theatrical agent too and put me amongst Barnum's Freaks as the Husky Curser or the Lightning Left-hand typist."[65]

By early February he was better and went up to London, still buzzing with the Liberal landslide in the January election.[66] There he met for the first time

Edward Garnett, probably at the Mont Blanc restaurant in the company of Seccombe. Garnett was a central figure of the London literary scene, as literary critic and publisher's reader for Duckworth. Even more significant was his informal role as author's reader and spotter and nurturer of young talent. He had "discovered" Joseph Conrad and W.H. Hudson just as he was later to discover D.H. Lawrence and Henry Green. With his sharp insights, his tough talking when his protégés strayed from the paths of honest writing, his enthusiastic encouragement, his generous and tireless guidance, he inspired young writers to write their best for him. As Conrad put it when writing of Garnett as a character in a novel: "For many years I had been writing quite as much to satisfy him as to satisfy myself."[67] His emphasis above all was on writing from experience and maintaining a truth to life. He was a voracious consumer of manuscripts, most of which he would read at home at the Cearne, the house he had had built ten years before on simple mediaeval lines, "encearned" or encircled by the woods of the High Chart on the Kent and Sussex border.

He developed a regular routine of working in London on Tuesdays and Wednesdays, and of presiding over the Tuesday lunch in a small upper room of the Mont Blanc at the western end of Gerrard Street. These celebrated lunches date from the day in September 1901 when Garnett first met Hudson at Heinemann's offices to discuss Hudson's latest book and they adjourned to the Mont Blanc for lunch.[68] The two men formed the habit of lunching there together at 1.30 on Tuesdays, and slowly the habit spread to other of Garnett's literary acquaintances – in 1903, Galsworthy, Seccombe, Belloc and Chesterton (though only Seccombe was a regular); in 1905 Edward Thomas and Perceval Gibbon; from 1906 Ford Hueffer and March Phillipps; in 1907 W.H. Davies, John Masefield, R.A. Scott-James, Archibald Marshall, Muirhead Bone and Joseph Conrad (a rare visitor); in 1908 Frederic Chapman; in 1911 Norman Douglas and in 1912 Richard Curle. The lunches flourished with this shifting clientele right up until the First World War. By 1915 they were tailing off; Garnett still lunched there most Tuesdays, but often just with Edward Thomas for company.[69] He was still lunching there regularly in the 1920s, but the habit had changed to 1.45 on Fridays.[70]

R.H.Mottram was taken there by Galsworthy in October 1904 and has left us with a lasting impression.

> I was led through a rather dim ground floor full of the market porters of whom Albert Chevalier was then singing, to the first floor, where, between walls painted with romantic Swiss landscapes, a long table was set, in true continental style, with piles of plates and carafes of rough red wine, on a coarse table-cloth. Here sat, at the head, Edward Garnett, something clerical in his garb belied by the fact that he was eating with his fork, holding a book which he was presumably scanning for review in the other hand, and controlling the conversation with a full mouth. On his left was Hilaire Belloc, bowler-hatted like myself, talking like a

> machine-gun between draughts of wine, Thomas Seccombe and Jack [*Galsworthy*] being opposite. Hudson, if present, made no impression.[71]

Ford Hueffer, who later quarrelled with most of his literary friends, described the gatherings in somewhat less deferential terms. The Mont Blanc was a place where "the elect of the city's intelligentsia lunched and discussed with grave sobriety the social problems of the day...... under the presidency of Mr. Edward Garnett who has for so long been London's literary – if Nonconformist – Pope".[72]

Though the talk inevitably was of books, publishers and the literary world in general, the Mont Blanc groups did not form anything of a literary coterie with articulated aims. Rather the lunches made their informal contribution to English writing by bringing together authors who otherwise might never have met and in some cases establishing long-lasting and productive friendships. Above all, they introduced the young aspiring authors to the old established hands with illuminating benefits to either side. Garnett took to Reynolds at once and, as always with a new acquaintance, showed a particular interest to see his work. Reynolds invited him down to Devizes for a long weekend to talk about work and to show him the Downs.

Reynolds came home from London in a buoyant mood, feeling now more sure than ever that his literary career was on the launch pad. The *Pall Mall Magazine* had rejected *Twinses* and he responded vehemently to Pinker: "Mr. Morley wrote that 'Twinses' is a 'little coarse from their point of view'. I'm afraid I shall never understand the suburban-drawing-room line between coarseness and t'other thing. Seems to me they were very indecent to be born. And as for their pre-natal affairs.... Lord, Lord!"[73] He was busier than ever. In addition to three lectures on literature he had agreed to give locally for free, the meeting with Garnett had decided him to dust off some of the old stories and rewrite. It also had given him a renewed resolve to pick up his novel which had hung fire during his illness. On 18 February he told Pinker: "'The Holy Mountain' is on the slow move (as becomes a mountain) again..."[74]

Three weeks later Edward Garnett came down on the Wednesday evening to stay in the little house in Pans Lane for the promised long weekend. They went out walking on the Downs by day – Reynolds always took new visitors on his favourite walk over Tan Hill – and in the evenings after dinner talked, read and wrote letters. Garnett had brought all his manuscripts with him and on the Thursday wrote a long letter to Galsworthy with his views on *The Silver Box*. There was another Galsworthy manuscript to tackle: "I'll bring up the MS. of *Dance* on Tuesday. I shall be walking about here, most of the time – but will read it in between whiles."[75] On the Friday evening they walked out to Prospect Rise and had dinner with Aunt Jane.[76]

These five days were to cement a strong relationship that, with some hiccups, was to remain solid for the next five years. Garnett looked over some of Reynolds' manuscripts, including no doubt the half finished novel, and saw promise there. From that moment Reynolds joined the distinguished list of Garnett protégés. It was no doubt Garnett who in early April persuaded the *Speaker*, to which he was a regular contributor, to publish *Twinses* and to give Reynolds some reviewing work. And who probably gave him the introduction he took to the *Tribune* which published that summer *Dear Papa's Love Story*. From now on, when Reynolds wanted advice and encouragement, his manuscripts and outline ideas went first to Garnett rather than to Seccombe, Pinker or Skemp.

The close attention from Garnett concentrated his mind on finishing the first draft of the *Mountain*. He was tied up that May with an urgent local commission, but from June onwards the writing began to flow. Six years later he recalled how well things had gone that summer in the little bedroom in Pans Lane: "Some writers gain facility with practice, and some don't. I don't, worse luck! And in these laborious days, when one short newspaper article often means a heavy week's work, I look back with envy at the way the *Mountain* swung along, mostly between four in the morning and breakfast time, at a little window overlooking the wide western edge of Salisbury Plain."[77]

On 3 July he wrote to Pinker, buoyed up by the latest publication of two of his stories: "We move apparently. Even the 'Holy Mountain' (I know you'll be surprised to hear it) has got beyond its third book and 70,000th word."[78] A month later, it was finished. He told Pinker on 10 August "Did I tell you that the Holy Mountain was successfully removed to Wiltshire a week ago with the dead Alec and his Julia thereupon. 'Tis done! Long life in heaven to 'em!"[79] But the moment of completion left him with an acute sense of loss. "After it was finished, I remember walking to the Plain, very miserable, as if a door had been slammed on friends I should never see any more. So I started and wrote the book all over again."[80]

It was almost two years since the book had started to grow in his mind, and three since Seccombe had produced the seminal idea of the mountain that moved. In that time he had developed that simple plot into a swingeing satirical attack on his home town and its political chicanery, on the religious revival movement, and on the popular press as epitomized by Northcliffe.

Perhaps the best succinct description of the plot, though slightly pejorative in tone, comes from the pen of Perceval Gibbon.

> The story concerns a miracle. ....From the neighbourhood of Trowbury, in Wiltshire, an effort of faith removes Ramshorn Hill, and sets it down at Acton, near London. The mover of the Mountain is Alexander Trotman, son of the mayor of the town. He has set his watery affections on Miss Julia Jepp, of Clinch's Emporium, "who was flat-footed, and walked badly," and it was while they sat together on the Downs that he, mourning over his impending departure to London, performed the miracle. It was as though he had opened a door to the whole vulgarity of the time. From London, on the heels of the reporters, comes Sir Pushcott

> Bingley, proprietor of the *Halfpenny Press*, owner of the controlling interest in the *Times*, cynic, financier, and monologist. He is not slow to see the value of a manageable young man who can perform miracles, and forthwith adds a controlling interest in the Mountain-mover to his other possessions, subsequently leasing him to a party of revivalists at the Crystal Palace and later to a music-hall. But the cream of the thing is in the new freehold created at Acton by the presence there of Ramshorn Hill – the Holy Mountain, as it has come to be called. While Alexander undergoes vicissitudes of love and ulcerated stomach, Sir Pushcott Bingley proceeds to turn the hill into dividends. ......the reader may learn from the book how a temple was built on the crown of the mountain, how the religious bodies of this country misbehaved themselves there, how the temple was converted into a People's Pleasure Ground, and how finally Alexander Trotman moved the hill back to the Downs and perished in the moving.[81]

The book is set in the future, sometime after 1912, but the early chapters draw their inspiration from the Devizes of his childhood in the 1880s and 90s with the Bear at the centre of social and political intrigue. Some of the better descriptions are of that little world that he knew so intimately, as with the children peering down the passage into the public bar, which he himself had done so often before.

> Children passing the porch of the Blue Boar Hotel, look down the hospitable passage, into the hall and at the pillars thereof, as reverently as a yokel takes his first peep into the Houses of Parliament. If they are sent there on an errand, to order the bus, to buy brandy or a bottle of wine, they creep along the passage with timid steps and wait on one foot just inside the swing-doors until that great lady the barmaid calls them up to the long bow-windowed bar. Then they advance shyly to the side, and deliver their messages in wee small voices, so that the great gentlemen who lounge at the front window shall not be able to hear. If they are kept waiting, which is more than probable, they steal glances at the white, red and green glasses, at the crystal spirit-kegs and decanters, at the hanging tankards and piled-up cigar boxes inside the windows; or else they open their eyes at the larder on the other side of the hall, with its old bull's eye panes of glass, its Stilton cheeses and its mighty joints of beef. They wonder into what mysterious and sacred regions the wide staircase leads, and what is on the other side of the broader spring-doors which are covered with highly tinted paper transparencies of saints, and which, if they should open, reveal the spacious, cavernous, cook-smelly and fly-blown Blue Boar kitchen. They shift out of the way of waitresses scurrying by with laden trays. They jump when an electric bell goes off above their heads. They look down at the ground respectfully if the

> awful dignity of the proprietor approacheth. When one of the great gentlemen saith a great big *damn* it hath an auguster sound than father's *damns* at home. It is something like church to them, the low-ceiled, vault-like, pillared hall, with its artificial light browbeating the daylight, its brightnesses, and its dark and dingy shadows.[82]

His tone is less sure in trying to capture the beauty and mystery of the Downs all around. The London journalist who has come to scoop the story of the moving mountain cycles out onto the Downs to locate the site of Ramshorn Hill, and stops in the dusk to contemplate the magic of his surroundings. In a Reynolds' autobiographical touch, he conjures up the face of his dead mother and tears come to his eyes.[83] But a combination of hyperbole and the odd slack expression contrive to nullify the feeling of these downland scenes which never quite come off.

One criticism of the book among early readers was that it did not contain a single attractive character. It would be fairer to say that it did not contain one character at all. Reynolds, in some respects again like Orwell, did not have the creative imagination to draw characters with an ounce of flesh and blood about them. Alec Trotman, the hero and Reynolds figure, at war with his father, is flat and colourless. The women, Julia Jepp and Edith Starkey, are cardboard cut-outs with no emotional depth. Even the more robust figures, James Trotman, the father of Alec, and Sir Pushcott Bingley, the Northcliffe parody, are primarily vehicles for the opinions on which the satire of the book is based.

Reynolds' best writing comes in the set pieces, where the interplay of crowd and action creates a vivid atmosphere without the need for any depth of character portrayal. He was himself conscious that these were the strongest parts of the book: "I couldn't better the descriptions of the Crystal Palace Empire Revival Mission and the Church and Empire Ballet – no, I'm hanged if I could!"[84] In the Ballet at the Neapolitan Music Hall, crammed with the latest technology in magic lanterns, cinematographs and dissolving view apparatuses, a phalanx of missionaries, churchmen, soldiers, engineers and merchants march across the British Empire, picking up the natives as they go, from Canada to Africa, Australia to India, from stirring theatrical scene to stirring theatrical scene. Here is Africa.

> Through the succeeding darkness there came a monotonous throbbing and jarring that made the more sensitive among the audience shudder. The sound, the horrible beating sound, gradually developed into a savage and voluptuous music, made up of rhythmic discords. When the stage lightened a little, so that black figures could just be distinguished, flitting about in the darkness, the rattling wail of the music became as furious as a tropical storm. The scene was a small clearing between the tree-trunks and tendrils of a swampy West African forest – one of those orgies to which from time to time frenzied negroes abandon themselves.

> A dim fire in the centre of the clearing threw strange streaks of light on the dancers around it, who were apparently naked; on the foliage and tree-trunks and on the slimy ground; but it illuminated nothing. The music alone, beating ever and ever more fiercely, suggested the weird depravity of the dance; the dancers themselves remained always more than half invisible, black against blackness, a shadowed rhythm on the darkness, dancing wildly to a mysterious music, rising, falling, whirling, jarring....
>
> Fiercer grew the mad orgy – awakening a latent savagery, visions of unimagined lustfulness, in the audience, till many ached and twitched to join the negroes. Suddenly at the side of the stage appeared the Church and Empire Procession, rifles and crosses uplifted; and the dancers, screaming, rushed to the back and there crouched down in a fearful heap.
>
> For a moment, darkness: then the music changed to a fresh, cool gladness, while the missionaries and privates, the colporteurs and engineers, the red-cross nurses and sisters of medical missions, the clergymen and merchants, the dignitaries and officers, the field-marshal and bishop, filed past the desolate scene of the orgy, accompanied by regenerate negroes now clad respectably in white duck trousers.[85]

And later the scene shifts to pre-Christian Alexandria, drawing heavily upon Pierre Louÿs' *Aphrodite*, the scandalous book brought back from Paris three years before.

> The limelight sun went down and rose again over the Garden of Aphrodite in ancient Alexandria. Somewhat unhistorically it was arranged that the pyramids and the Sphinx overlooked the luxuriant place, its palms and large-leaved plants, its fountains and its columns festooned with flowering creepers. Courtesans, long since dead and gone, walked in the garden with voluptuous step, their garments the tall thin draperies of the Greeks. To one among them, the most beautiful, was brought ceremoniously the philtre of love and death. She drank: and to the long-drawn music of the orchestra, to its spiral convolutions of sweet sound, ever rising higher, ever becoming richer and faster, they danced the Dance of Love, which ends in death, in the Garden of Aphrodite, beneath the pyramids and the Sphinx. They danced till the Garden was a melody of twirling feet and floating filmy draperies and glimmering colours. She who had drunk of the philtre whirled in a sheen of light, adored by all the others; the incarnation of a love and rapture beyond human reach, the symbol of love's uttermost frenzy; until it seemed to the hard-breathing audience that the ballet could no longer go on without becoming really too indecent for the English stage.
>
> Then it was that the Church and Empire Procession appeared, crosses

> and rifles uplifted; and the ancient courtesans, stricken with a new shame, fled like ripples on a lake.[86]

The combination of sensuality and irony in these descriptions shows a sureness of touch of which any 25-year-old author might well feel proud.

He could achieve the same effect once in a while closer to home in the Trowbury scenes. His satirical account of the Mayor's banquet, as reported in the local press, page after page of it, bears a not very distant resemblance to his own grandfather's inauguration. Once the formal proceedings are over, decorum is thrown to the four winds in true Dickensian manner.

> The most characteristic, the most Trowburian, part of the feast did not find its way into print in the *Trowbury Guardian.* After the Chairman had left, the lights of the room became dim with smoke, so that it seemed as if the tobacco was burning itself up a second time in the gas flames. Complaints, ever becoming louder, were heard against the price and quality of the caterer's whiskey, and many of the guests both amused and revenged themselves by throwing empty bottles at one another's legs underneath the table. Roars of laughter shook the Town Hall, attracting the attention of people outside. Merriment and horse-play were in command. The waiters, refusing to wait, retired to the cloak-room with a dozen bottles of champagne, and soon could not have waited even had they been willing. In order to prevent the destruction of all the glass and crockery (hired for the evening) the caterer was obliged to turn off the gas at the main, and to hide himself at the foot of the Assembly Room stairs, behind a bust of the Prince Consort.[87]

The book as a whole, however, has an air of Wells rather than Dickens about it, a point which Reynolds himself noted rather ruefully: "I know they're going to chuck Wells at my head because there's a non-natural happening in it".[88] Characters such as Pushcott Bingley have a Wellsian bravado about them and the studied melancholy of the climax has also distinct Wellsian overtones.

But it is not Wells. The book contains many uncertain notes, forgiveable in a young writer, but surprisingly not weeded out in the two rewrites he undertook after completing the first draft. There are some weak juvenile expressions, straight from *Boys Own Paper,* some creaking dialogue, a few failures of continuity and on occasion a very pedestrian unravelling of the narrative.[89] But the main problem, apart from the failure to draw characters, is that the supernatural event itself sits uneasily with the realistic action of the rest of the book. The miracle of the mountain has no philosophical or motivational grounding to inform the rest of the action. It deserves no suspension of disbelief from the reader, who finds his basic incredulity transferred to other parts of the narrative. Thomas Seccombe's gift to Reynolds of the key to the plot was a dangerous one, as Seccombe himself came to recognise when he read the finished text.

All this said, the satire itself, whether directed at the worthy councillors of Devizes, at the Church, at Imperialism, or at the Northcliffe press, stands up very well at a distance of almost a century. Here the keen Reynolds' observation of institutional behaviour comes into its own. On journalism, for instance.

> He was, though few knew it, the unworthy local correspondent of the *Halfpenny Press*; unworthy, because he could never learn the second of the local correspondent's two commandments:
> 1. Thou shalt send no news to any paper but ours.
> 2. Thou shalt send the news at once and find out afterwards whether it is true or not.
> He could never get into his head that time equals circulation and that the possibility is greater than the reality – things axiomatic to the born journalist.[90]

And his analysis of the relationship between press and politics has a rather modern ring about it.

> "I can remember," said the Mayor, rolling a banded cigar between his lips, "when the Press was very different to what it is now. In my young days we had newspapers for every shade of opinion, but nowadays they all seem to be on one side. At least, all the go-ahead newspapers do."
> "Yes," replied Sir Pushcott. "All on the side of the angels. Eh? As a matter of fact there are no real parties. Liberalism and Conservatism are obsolete. There is the party in, and the party out; and not a pin's difference between them, except in their names and election cries. Of course, there is the Labour Party, but in trying to manage Labour they have succeeded in representing anything except labourers; nothing except themselves; they are negligible. The Press is party. First the Press puts one side in and then the other side. Parties have become simply the machinery – and a deuced clumsy one at that – by which the Press rules the country. The electorate, it is true, decides upon some quibble or other which party shall go in next; but it is the Press that invents the quibble. In point of fact, I, as Director of the *Halfpenny Press, I* am the true, free, independent and democratic voter. I am the real ruler. I am like the trusty butler of an old and fussy dowager. She does the fussing and I rule."[91]

And there are memorable satirical scenes, as when the Archbishop of All the Empire, egged on by his clerical supporters like a latterday King Canute, goes out to try and move Silbury Hill, as an Anglican counter-attraction to the Holy Mountain, and succumbs to a heart attack.[92]

Reynolds' literary friends were sharply divided about the ultimate quality of the book. W.H. Hudson thought it "a ghastly thing", while Edward Garnett called it "the strongest and most pungent satire that I have met for many years".[93] The reason for this divergence lay in the word "satire". Those who read it as an ordinary novel found a badly crippled work of imagination, in which the weakness of character portrayal itself weakened any element of humour or of satire. Those who saw it as a work of satire were delighted by the acuteness of observation and the pungent barbs, and were not the least affected by its imaginative failings.

Reynolds himself was deeply conscious of its shortcomings. "The real failing of the book is that it was written in a mood of bitter resentment against a little local world which had put me down for a waster.... "[94] But this made him even more determined to protect its reputation. It was the first lengthy piece of work by which he might justly claim the name of writer; and through it he had emerged back into the world from the desolation of his breakdown. It had a symbolic importance for him far beyond the words on the sheets of paper. "Going back through one's own work, into its bygone moods, is like living backwards. To me *The Holy Mountain* is the most readable of my own stuff; it's the most distant; the most, as it were, some one else's. It represents a nightmare passed."[95]

But in the long struggle for publication, there were plenty more nightmares to come.

SEVEN

Revelation at Seacombe 1906–7

At the beginning of May 1906 Reynolds broke off from the final two months of work on the *Mountain* to take up a commission from the Devizes Town Council, which was to embroil him in a vitriolic little local squabble of just the kind he was attempting to satirize in his novel. He himself was to emerge more or less unscathed and with his bank balance eleven guineas to the good.

The unfortunate victim of this episode was Russell Gillman, who since 1894 had been proprietor and editor, in succession to his father, of the *Devizes and Wiltshire Advertiser* operating out of Maryport Street. Reynolds was not so close to Gillman as to George Simpson, the editor of the rival *Gazette*, but knew him as a cultured man who had edited books on Addison and Lamb, and published translations from French and German. His family had links to the mighty, his great uncle being the Dr Gillman of Highgate who had taken personal charge of Coleridge in the 1820s.

Russell Gillman had been active in town politics alongside Reynolds' father, becoming both alderman and Mayor in 1898.[1] But he was a Liberal in a predominantly Conservative borough and was culturally speaking more than a cut above his fellow councillors, whom he frequently castigated from the editorial columns of his newspaper. He had retired from the Council in 1905 and the subsequent débâcle over the Devizes guide may well have been seen by his Conservative opponents as a heaven-sent opportunity to cut him down to size.

Early in 1906 the Town Council had passed a resolution approving an application from the Bournemouth firm of W. Mate & Sons to commission Gillman to write an official guide to the borough to take its place in the then popular series of Mate's Guides which covered most of the south of England.[2] Gillman was the obvious choice – writer, journalist, local politician and an authority on the local history of the town. It was the depth of his historical knowledge that was to be his undoing. The Council set up a Committee, under William Butcher, to superintend the production of the guide and at their initial meeting with Gillman gave instruction not to embark on a formal historical work full of technical detail, but rather a bright, readable and entertaining narrative, touching only lightly on technical matters, and giving full range to the attractions of the neighbourhood and recent developments in the town.[3]

For some weeks Gillman worked steadily away at his commission. Then, in the second half of March, he was approached by Mates in a deadline panic with a demand for the copy by the end of that month, compressed to 10,000 words. He managed the final draft by 7 April, whereupon it was printed up and circulated to members of the Committee in time for their meeting on the 20th. They were not pleased with what they found. Instead of the breezy narrative of modern developments, the bulk of the text was a detailed history of the borough from the middle ages to the nineteenth century, with only one final chapter headed "The Surrounding Districts" covering the modern local attractions so dear to their hearts. The Chairman wrote to the publishers with some feeling: "The Committee regret that Mr. Gillman does not appear to have grasped the fact that a popular and not a mere history of the town is what the Council instructed the Committee to obtain and what is required...... The Committee feel that they have a duty to perform not only to the General Public, but also to the Advertisers and to your firm in making the Guide as readable, bright, and up to date as possible."[4]

The Committee compounded these slights from their Chairman by passing a formal resolution which, while accepting with some amendments the passages on the early history of the town, specifically directed Gillman to abandon the rest of the material and substitute short paragraphs on the churches, chapels and public buildings of the town and the walks and drives of the surrounding neighbourhood. Councillor Butcher passed on these instructions to the publishers, and included his own demonstration paragraph on the local sewage works as an example of what was desired. When Gillman saw the sample paragraph, he printed it with unconcealed glee in the next edition of the *Advertiser.*

> THE SEWAGE WORKS, DEVIZES
> The Devizes Sewage Works are situated to the South West of the Town, and are now supposed to be among the best and most efficient works of the Country. They have been recently reconstructed under the direction and upon the principle designed by Mr. Dibden, Victoria Street, London. The Principle adopted is that of Bacteria beds consisting of eight coarse beds of slate debris, and eight fine beds of fine screened coke breeze, as well as two stone beds, which come into use during heavy rains. By this process the Sewage is first treated in the coarse beds, and exposed to bacterial action, the effluent afterwards passing over the land, or if not so required is passed into a brook hard by. The works have now been in operation since September 1905, and the results have so far proved very satisfactory.[5]

Throughout his life Reynolds could never resist stirring up local controversies that were just coming nicely to the boil in the press. He did so frequently in both Devizes and Sidmouth, most often by joining the lists with an anonymous letter in ironical vein, the irony of which was regularly lost on the local populace. His eye was now caught by Gillman's pained attack in the *Advertiser* on the censoring Committee and its resolution "as offensive as it is uncalled for".[6] When he saw the specimen paragraph on the sewage works, he knew that here was a chance to have some fun.

Consequently, the *Advertiser* of 3 May, no doubt with the knowing connivance of Gillman, carried a letter from "A Resident" purporting to give support to the harassed Committee.

> Sir, – The sub-committee are quite right, although the spelling and grammar in their letter is somewhat peculiar. We don't want a lot of sentimental rubbish about the Norman Castle and the Civil Wars, and things like that; what we want is present day facts. Who will be attracted to visit Devizes, or to live here, because we happen to have a history of well-nigh a thousand years? Give us facts, not sentiment. The model paragraph about the Sewage Works was very neatly put; my only complaint is that it is too meagre. The description does not even give the cubic capacity of each tank, nor the average daily flow, nor yet the cost. I hope the committee will arrange to have two or three views and a plan of the works. Why, sir, deputations have already visited the works from various towns and cities, from the War Office, and even from abroad. The town ought to make a good thing from our Sewage Works, if they are properly boomed. During the summer months we may expect to see G.W.R. bills in big type, "Cheap Excursion to the Devizes Sewage Works".[7]

The author of *The Holy Mountain* was taking time off from his sweated satirical labours only to indulge himself in a veritable busman's holiday.

The letter went on to recommend that the Committee leave out descriptions of the local churches, the battle of Roundway and the chapter on mediaeval Devizes to make room for the refuse destruction works, the water and gas works and the asylum; and ended on an upbeat note: "There are many other attractions that should not be overlooked, such as the Prison, the Cemetery, the Barracks, with its septic-tank system of sewage, the Workhouse (they talk of having a modern wash-house built I am told), our grand new Infectious Hospital, and I don't know what besides. All this could easily be squeezed inside of 10,000 words, provided the Committee don't waste too much room on other things."[8]

Before the publication of this seminal correspondence, it appeared as if the Committee had at last made peace with Russell Gillman. On 1 May the "Committee of Taste", as Gillman now insisted on calling it, met for the first time with all its members and in an atmosphere of recrimination. Many of them knew nothing of the critical letter that Butcher had written to the publishers, some disavowed it openly and others called for Gillman to attend to help them out of their difficulty. The matter then degenerated into a fictional farce that Reynolds himself could not have bettered, as a house-to-house search was put in hand to locate the dissident author. He was finally discovered at the house of a friend and, to show there was no ill feeling, reluctantly agreed to wait on the Committee. In the hour and a half's negotiation that then ensued, Gillman refused the Committee's request to delete the whole of the eighteenth century chapter and radically amend the one on the nineteenth century, but did agree to reduce both chapters and to provide a fuller descriptive account of the local churches. Finally, the Committee went through the manuscript word by word and, as Gillman understood, accepted it subject to the agreed additions and some minor alterations. The storm seemed over.[9]

But some of the councillors, no doubt including the Chairman, had been sorely offended by Gillman's public references to them as the "Committee of Taste" and were actively looking round for an excuse to ditch him.[10] It came two days later with the publication of Reynolds' anonymous letter. Whether they were attracted by the style in which "A Resident" had written to the press, or by the robustness of his approach, or by his apparent knowledge of the town, it is difficult to say. It is not beyond the bounds of possibility that some took him at face value and welcomed the new champion of the sewage works. It may in the end have been a case of "he's so clever, let *him* try".

Whatever the reason, Reynolds received the next day an approach from Mates to write the Official Guide to Devizes from scratch – 10,000 words in three weeks for the sum of ten guineas. As always, he drove a hard bargain. Three days later, on 7 May, the Council Committee put the final seal on an agreement whereby the author would be paid in addition his out-of-pocket expenses, or else be allowed to put in an extra thousand words for an extra guinea.[11] Gillman took a generous approach to this last minute substitution by his friend, referring in public to Reynolds' qualifications for the task as "excellent".[12] But in retaliation he immediately published his own version of the guide, "written by R.D. Gillman FRGS and rejected by the Committee of Taste of the Corporation of Devizes", at the knockdown price of one penny so that the wide circulation would show the councillors up for the uncultivated philistines they were.

The week in which Reynolds had been drawn into this sorry affair had proved difficult for other reasons. The work on his novel and his bread-and-butter reviewing was interrupted on 3 May by the wedding at St James' Church of his sister Dot to a local farmer from Bishops Cannings, Robert Harraway. She was a few weeks pregnant at the time which seems to have caused the predictable family upheaval, with Frank Reynolds washing his hands of the whole business. As a result, the burden of the arrangements fell upon Reynolds himself and his long-suffering landlords, the Wyers. With his duties finally accomplished, he beat a hurried retreat to the peace of the Tanners' at Ford House, from where they were planning to take a short motoring holiday down to Dartmoor. He wrote to Pinker with a sense of relief: "After this absurd quarrelsome Box-and-Cox affair of the Guide, tremendous family bedevilments and rows, and my sister's wedding from my place, with me as father, mother, brother, chargé d'affaires and bridesmaid, I'm about done for, but my head having stood well I'll soon buck the rest of me up on Dartmoor."[13]

The Guide was a fairly formidable assignment to complete in just three weeks; in normal circumstances, it would have taken more time than that to collect and assimilate the materials. Fortunately, the Guide Committee had its own background materials which it made available to him. He spent a week with the Tanners at Rowe's Duchy Hotel at Princetown, getting up very early to work on the Guide and spending the rest of the day out on the moors, revelling in the glorious wildness of the country. Despite the pressures of time, he wrote confidently to Pinker: "They are almost bound to take my work when it's done, because there has been such a violent storm in a tea-cup over the rejection of the last man's, and they want to publish without delay. 'Twill pay for my holiday which was much needed."[14] After 17 May when he got back to Devizes, the pressure began to mount and his tone turned to one of panic: "I'm being rushed to death over the Guide with haste and local intriguers. Had to call in a typist's help to get it done in time. Wish I hadn't undertaken it, ************ it!"[15]

He met his deadline nonetheless. On 28 May, exactly three weeks to the day since receiving the commission, he posted off the Devizes section of the Guide to the publishers, with the promise of the "Roundabout" section in a matter of days. He was 3000 words over the 10,000 limit, but assured Mate & Sons that they would not wish to cut it down. He was determined not to suffer the fate of his predecessor and laid down a firm stipulation: "This MSS. is submitted to you on the sole condition that you use it as it stands in its entirety, your acceptance of all or any part of it to be considered as your admission of that condition. If Members of the Committee want things altered, you can tell them you have no power to do it and refer them to me. After all the Guide needs no official imprimatur, by way of advertisement. They must take it, or leave it, as a whole."[16]

In the end, they did, but Reynolds spent much of the second half of June locked in negotiation with the Committee, no doubt over some of the more waspish asides in the text which were designed deliberately to twist their tails. When the text was finally settled, he wrote to Pinker in early July: "I am expecting 'Devizes and Roundabout' out daily. You shall be sent an early copy. We had no end of a time getting it passed by the Guide Committee here, and I'm anticipating delightful ructions when it does appear."[17]

The Guide was published in the first week of July 1906 and was Reynolds' first freestanding book to make it into print. It is a workmanlike performance given the pressures of time, with the history and topography well researched and laid out. But it is not the usual dryasdust concern a reader would expect from a local guide. The prose throughout has a literary quality and at times sparkles with the author's ironic love-hate relationship with the town and his purer, unqualified love for the Downs in which it nestles. He sets out his stall clearly enough in the preface.

> Towns about whose history there is nothing doubtful, have as a rule no history at all worth talking about. This little work makes no pretence to original historical research...... I have done no more than choose between authorities often at variance...... About the section on Walks

> and Drives, which stand, surely, among the greatest of the attractions of Devizes, I feel a little less humble, and write from a fair amount of research, Ordnance Survey in hand. Bearing in mind that this is a guide, I have sought to give guidance rather than description; actuality rather than history: in short, to present less an appreciation of Devizes and Roundabout, than a basis whereon people may the more easily rear their own appreciations for themselves...... Should this guide initiate anyone into the very real charm of Devizes, and above all of the Downs, it will have done something not altogether valueless.[18]

And the first paragraph of the introductory chapter, in which Reynolds leads off with his French credentials, warns the reader that this will be different from normal guide writing.

> It was in a French railway train that our ears were greeted with: "Ah, Devizes – vous connaissez Devizes, monsieur? – cette jolie petite ville en Viltshire! And indeed most people do seem to know at least something of 'that pretty little town'; to have been through it *somewhen*, as a Wiltshireman would say.[19]

The text is peppered with sufficient idiosyncratic asides to keep the Guide Committee in almost perpetual session. On modern attitudes "It is easy in Devizes to live the modern life or the 'simple'; to keep in touch with progress so-called or to escape it." On class "So far Devizes Fair has withstood the onslaught of those refined persons who, possessing 361 days of the year in tranquility, would yet prevent the so-called common herd from enjoying the other four days after their own picturesque and jolly, if rather noisy, fashion." On municipal reform "...the Devizes Fire Brigade, which has recently submitted to efficiency and reform, if not economy... ". On the Corn Exchange and local gullibility "In the front are four Corinthian columns, supporting a carven cornice, and a statue of Ceres, somewhat characterless perhaps for its elevation, and supposed by children (and others also, maybe) to be a public memorial of Ruth Pierce." On the pretensions of the Castle "The public may go as far as the bogus portcullis at the lodge, but no further, without special permission." On the Town Hall "The whole building has lately been repaired and re-decorated at a cost which staggered humanity (in Devizes)!" And on one of his pet hates, Christmas "Those who like rows upon rows of dead flesh should take a look at the butchers' shops before Christmas – the time of peace on earth, good-will towards men, and death to fat animals."[20]

It was not for nothing that he had insisted that the Council should take the whole text or none of it. He knew that they were under pressure of time and could not afford another full-scale row outside the doors of the Council chamber. But some barbs were aimed closer to home even than the Council. His new brother-in-law cannot have been thrilled by the depiction of his home village.

> Cannings people are celebrated in Wiltshire for their superior originality and imaginativeness. It is now some years since a Cannings farmer bought a most convenient gas-stove in Devizes, and took, or sent, it home. Unfortunately, there is no gas-supply in the village! And lately, we understand, a man of Cannings planted some "Bile Beans" in a flower-pot, tended them carefully, and 'didn' think much o' they beans vor zeed!'[21]

And he could not forget the sewage works, at the core of his remit, dismissing it with a light but studied irony.

> The Sewage Works situated at some distance to the west of the town. The process adopted after much experiment and expense is a combination of open bacteria beds with passage of the effluent overland. Though this effluent is not yet so drinkable as one enthusiastic councillor predicted it would be, the Sewage Works may now be considered quite satisfactory.[22]

The most original aspect of the Guide is the second half, entitled "Roundabout", in which Reynolds describes in detail thirty walks and eleven drives in the vicinity. All are identified on a copy of the Ordnance Survey by Reynolds' own cartographical system of letters and numbers, and there are some very personal tips on how to cope with orienteering difficulties: "The bit of road, c4, is now overgrown; walk in the field alongside";[23] and "From d4 to the field-farm, pathway is lost. Aim at the tall poplars by the field-farm, and again aim at more poplars by Rowde Field".[24] On the most famous landmarks of the area, such as Stonehenge, the personal instructions, compiled from long experience of the Tanners' motor trips, take on even more Reynoldsian colour.

> In hot weather drive to Stonehenge by Charlton, Netheravon, the river villages and Amesbury; returning over the Downs by Shrewton, Tilshead, the Robber's Stone and West Lavington. When, however, the Downs are cold, and the evening flies along the river less troublesome, the reverse way is better...... Borrow's *Lavengro* and Hardy's *Tess* contain fine descriptions of the ancient place, so dwarfed by the Downs, yet so weird and commanding. Now that it has been found necessary to add to it a wire railing, a wooden hut and a British policeman, the best view is obtainable perhaps from the edge of the wood a little further from Amesbury on the Devizes road. From there the policeman etc. appear insignificant, and nothing clashes with the mysterious, still sacred, beauty of Stonehenge.[25]

Reynolds concluded this section on drives and walks with some general advice on how to comport oneself in the country, intended as public information in traditional style, but because of the author's radical views on such matters as private property in land, it was to cause some consternation locally.

> In advising our readers not to be dismayed by trespassing notices – which it is the amusement of some landlords to place by the rights of way – we also beg them never to break hedges, nor tread down mowing-grass or standing corn, nor let their dogs chase farmstock or game. (For city people, mowing-grass may be defined as Spring grass with no cows on it.) Unlike the cottagers in overrun Devon, Wiltshire people usually provide tea etc. rather as a favour than as a matter of business; and therefore asking for it as a favour may prevent disappointment. Nevertheless, at the few inns where they refuse to serve non-alcoholic refreshments, a hint of the next Brewster sessions, and of the instability of licences, will soon make the kettle boil.[26]

When the Guide appeared, Gillman, from the editorial desk of the *Advertiser*, was suitably reticent, determining not to entangle his friend in the continuing private quarrel with the Council. But he could not resist jumping on the first Appendix, a list of places with their road distances from Devizes, which contained some startling misprints of the relevant mileages. In a passage which appears, almost telepathically, to foreshadow the contents of the yet unfinished *Holy Mountain*, he noted that a recent map-guide had put Silbury Hill in the wrong position: "But it is not only Silbury Hill which has been moved, but Southampton and Worton have been moved as well. My authority is not the map-guide referred to above, but the brand new official guide to Devizes. As this guide is vouched for by the Devizes Town Council, it is of course correct. Our Town Council never makes mistakes. Worton, which used to be close at hand, is now 41 miles distant. We are sorry to lose Worton, but the loss is more than compensated for by the bringing nearer of Southampton, which is now distant 15 miles only. This moving must have been a bigger job even than the removal of Silbury Hill."[27]

The curator of the Devizes Museum rushed forward to correct some minor errors and to point out emphatically that the guide was mistaken in advising in its bibliography that books on Wiltshire could be consulted in the Museum library, since the collection was not open to the public and could only be consulted under special circumstances.[28] These pin-pricks irritated Reynolds a little, but were nothing to the full review of the Guide which appeared in the *Gazette* on 19 July. On the whole, the review was commendatory: "The writer of this Guide deserves credit for what everyone may not perceive – his self-denial, or self-restraint. Several passages prove that he has the gift of a pleasant literary style, which is moreover a style of its own, and not too artificial...... Taking the publication as a whole, we like it; it is informing, suggestive, and crisp, the kind of Guide a visitor would like...... "

But the reviewer deplored one aspect of the style. "It is sometimes flippant, which an Official Guide should not be, especially when the writer uses that means of expressing personal views on matters of local controversy." The reference to trespassing notices was a grievous error: "......he is unwise to invite, as practically he does invite, visitors to the town to commit acts of trespass wholesale." The reviewer also noted that the Guide "mentions one hotel out of several, and one school out of five. Anyone can guess the reason." The hotel just happened to be the Bear and the school Devizes College.

The review went on to compile an exhaustive list of minor factual errors, becoming more pedantic as it progressed.[29] On the origins of the town, Reynolds had jocularly remarked: "When was Devizes not Devizes? That is what one asks after reading the efforts of antiquarians to extend antiquity".[30] The reviewer took him up on it. "Personally, we strongly object to the perpetuation of the error of calling antiquaries 'antiquarians'."[31]

Much of this clearly got under Reynolds' skin, but the journalist in him saw the opportunity of stirring up a little more publicity, and he prepared a suitable riposte, of which he gleefully told Pinker: "I am having great game with local critics, and have appearing next Thursday a series of epigrams 'How to Write an Official Guide and How to Review It' – which will doubtless cause some commotion hereabout".[32]

His hints for the writer begin

> * The creation of a little Guide is a work of great guile.
> * Don't be flippant. You will raise a laugh before your critic has time to speak, and he will surely take revenge when he does hold forth.
> * Have no opinions of your own. It is most conceited to hold opinions not bought for a halfpenny from the jingo press.
> * If so be you do have opinions of your own, avoid expressing them. You might make your guide more readable, but you would be sure to offend somebody.
> * Don't call an antiquary an antiquarian. According to good dictionaries, an antiquarian is "one devoted to the study of antiquity", while an antiquary is "one devoted to the study of ancient times through their relics"....
>
> "With sharpened sight pale antiquaries pore
> The inscription value, but the rust adore."
>
> The antiquarian, you see, is the less grubby sort of person, and the more scientific. He is the greater and contains the less. That is why some honest students of antiquity prefer to be called antiquaries, and not antiquarians.
> * Sooner disturb a dog in his manger than an antiquary in his library.
> * "To err is human" say the copybooks. But remember that little details please little minds, and so do little errors.

The hints for the reviewer illustrate even more clearly Reynolds' lifelong facility for getting his own back, but the irony here shades into a touch of bitterness which shows he had been genuinely riled.

> * To write decent English, it is essential to know what you mean.
> * You will, of course, have reason to find fault; but if you cannot find fault enough, you can always pervert the author's meaning, and fill up space by criticising your own perversions.
> * If you are tempted to praise anything, beware. To patronise is more dignified.[33]

The episode of the Guide had given him good practice in undertaking a complex piece of work under severe time pressures; it had brought him a little more local notoriety as a writer with some firm opinions, preparing the ground for the local uproar that was to follow the publication of the *Mountain*; and best of all, it had brought him in eleven guineas. But how to collect? On 10 July, he made a tentative approach to Mate & Sons, and received an ominous sounding reply: "Regarding your enquiry re cheque, unfortunately, our Manager left for his holidays yesterday and this will necessitate a little delay...."[34]

With the Guide published and out of the way, Reynolds was free to take up a return invitation from Edward Garnett to a long weekend at the Cearne. On 18 July he joined Garnett at the end of his two-day stint in London and that Wednesday evening they caught the train down to his house in the Kent countryside.[35] There he met for the first time Edward's wife, Constance, who delighted in showing new visitors round her beloved garden. Most of Edward's literary protégés, from W.H. Hudson through Edward Thomas and D.H. Lawrence to H.E. Bates, were steeped in the countryside and had an encyclopaedic knowledge of wild flowers and plants. Reynolds was yet another who found as much pleasure in touring the garden with Constance as discussing politics on the verandah with Edward.

Apart from flowers, Constance's other obsession was Russian literature. In the early 1890s, inspired by the family's Russian revolutionary friends, she had taught herself the language armed only with a Russian text, grammar and Russian-English dictionary.[36] At that time, English acquaintance with the great Russian authors was confined to French translations and it was Constance who almost single-handedly brought to the English reading public a knowledge of Turgenev and Tolstoy, Chekhov and later Dostoyevsky. On summer afternoons, the most common sight in the garden at the Cearne was the slender frail figure, scribbling furiously her verbatim translations, without pause or hesitation, and tossing each completed page in a pile on the lawn beside her, until by the end of the day the pile was almost higher than the chair she was sitting in.[37]

This was Reynolds' first introduction to the Russian authors too, and he took away from the weekend a new interest in Turgenev and Tolstoy which was to form the basis of his holiday reading over the coming weeks. When a few weeks later, Constance mislaid the copy of her translation of *Smoke*, he paid her, through Edward, the best compliment for which any translator could wish: "D'you know, when you said in your letter that Mrs. Garnett had lost her corrected copy, it struck me for the first time that I had been reading Turgenev in translation and not as 'twas written".[38] Some time later he wrote: "Please remember me to Mrs. Garnett. Her gentle bearing and revolutionary sentiments have astonishingly stuck in my gills."[39]

It was on this occasion or on one of his subsequent visits to the Cearne that Reynolds first met Garnett's fourteen-year-old son David, then at University College School in London. They were to meet later in London too, at the Mont Blanc and when Reynolds was living with Ford Hueffer in Holland Park. David Garnett remembered his first impression of him as "a short sturdy man with thick, neatly parted hair". Always good with children, particularly on country walks, he took David off for rambles in the woods of the High Chart all around, where David found him the most delightful of companions.[40] He always connected David with those walks. When the following year David went down with mumps, he commiserated with his father and added: "It's improper for a woodland boy like David to be ill".[41]

This second marathon "weekend" with Edward Garnett, from Wednesday evening to Monday morning, brought the two men even closer together. Garnett as ever was working on his manuscripts, but in the evenings after dinner he would lie stretched out on the couch, a bottle of red wine at his side, on the little verandah that ran along the side of the house and the two men would talk politics and literature into the early hours. They talked about social and economic reform, and Reynolds, whose nostalgic conservatism was already beginning to gather shape, taxed Garnett and the band of liberal reformers with being too impatient, too materialist, of trying to push ahead too fast: "If one considers that the only real advance must be spiritual, and tries to decide the precedence of qualities of character, it appears (to me anyhow) that forced reform is rather grossly material".[42]

They talked of the farce, *Super Author*, that Reynolds had been working on, no doubt under the influence of Garnett's own creative efforts for the stage. And with the *Mountain* only a week from completion, of Reynolds' next major project, the *Ex Profundis* book, (Wilde's *De Profundis* had appeared the previous year) which would trace his breakdown from its physical onset in Sidmouth to the convalescence and spiritual recovery in Devizes. For the rest of that summer and autumn Reynolds was to wrestle with his ideas for this the most personal and ambitious of his writing projects to date, and in particular with the literary form that it should take. Garnett as ever sat patiently by, listening to the outpourings of the young man and offering the occasional word of cool advice.

To embark upon another major work of this kind he needed above all the security of regular periodical writing that would not take up too much of his time or emotions but would pay rather better than book-reviewing. Pinker had offered to try to find him the most cherished of young writer's dreams – a regular *causerie* slot in a well-established periodical. Back home in Devizes, he worked away on a specimen *causerie* on Marie Corelli, which he fired off to Pinker but without any conviction: "Here is the specimen causerie – tub-thump. Couldn't get the thing to go, just because it was an opportunity I've been wanting. If the specimen is no good for the purpose, tear it up. But if you do send it in, perhaps it would be well to say that I am (or ought to be) capable of varying the discourse with scientific topics treated in a – a highly authoritative manner!!"[43]

But the first draft of the *Mountain* was now written and mid-August was holiday time – he could afford a few weeks' respite from the toils of a writing career. He left in Pinker's capable hands the capture of the *causerie* and the equally strenuous task of securing payment for the Devizes Guide: "I hear from a man who ought to know that the firm of Mate does not pay up if it can help it. Would you be kind enough to collect the money. ......It seems I'm always handing you on little bits of dirty work."[44]

Reynolds had been so taken by his week on Dartmoor with the Tanners that May that he decided to repeat the holiday, this time avoiding motor travel – "not so nice to my mind as Shanks's pony" – by tramping down with Margot, staying at pubs as they had done the previous year.[45] Their eventual aim was North Devon where Margot was to go into kennels to mate – not so much for the money the puppies would fetch as to give her a little bit of natural life. Now that Margot was older he planned an even brisker itinerary to keep pace with the onset of her "marriage-time" – Devizes to Princetown in about eight days with a stopover for one or two nights in Sidmouth to recover breath.[46]

He had not been to Sidmouth for almost two years, not since that dismal autumn of 1904 when he had been ill and morose and yet had given comfort to Bob Woolley on the night he had lost his eldest son to the Navy. It was during that visit that Bob had caught wind of his distaste for his fussy, middle-class lodgings in the town and had offered him a bed on his next visit at his own house at the back of the Bedford Hotel: "Yu let us know when yu be coming thees way again; that is, if yu don' mind coming wi' the likes o' us."[47]

He wrote to Bob in July in the hope of a bed for a couple of nights and received back a prompt postcard, reproduced with perhaps not much refining in *A Poor Man's House*.

> A card from Tony Widger:
> Dear Sir in reply to your letter I have let to the hotel which is full for the 28th july until the 6th Aus, but I have one little room to the back but you did not say about the time it would take you to walk down also John [*Tom Woolley*] to Saltmeadow [*Riverside*] have let so you can have that room if you can manage or you can see when you come down their are a lot of People in Seacombe or you write and let me know and I will see

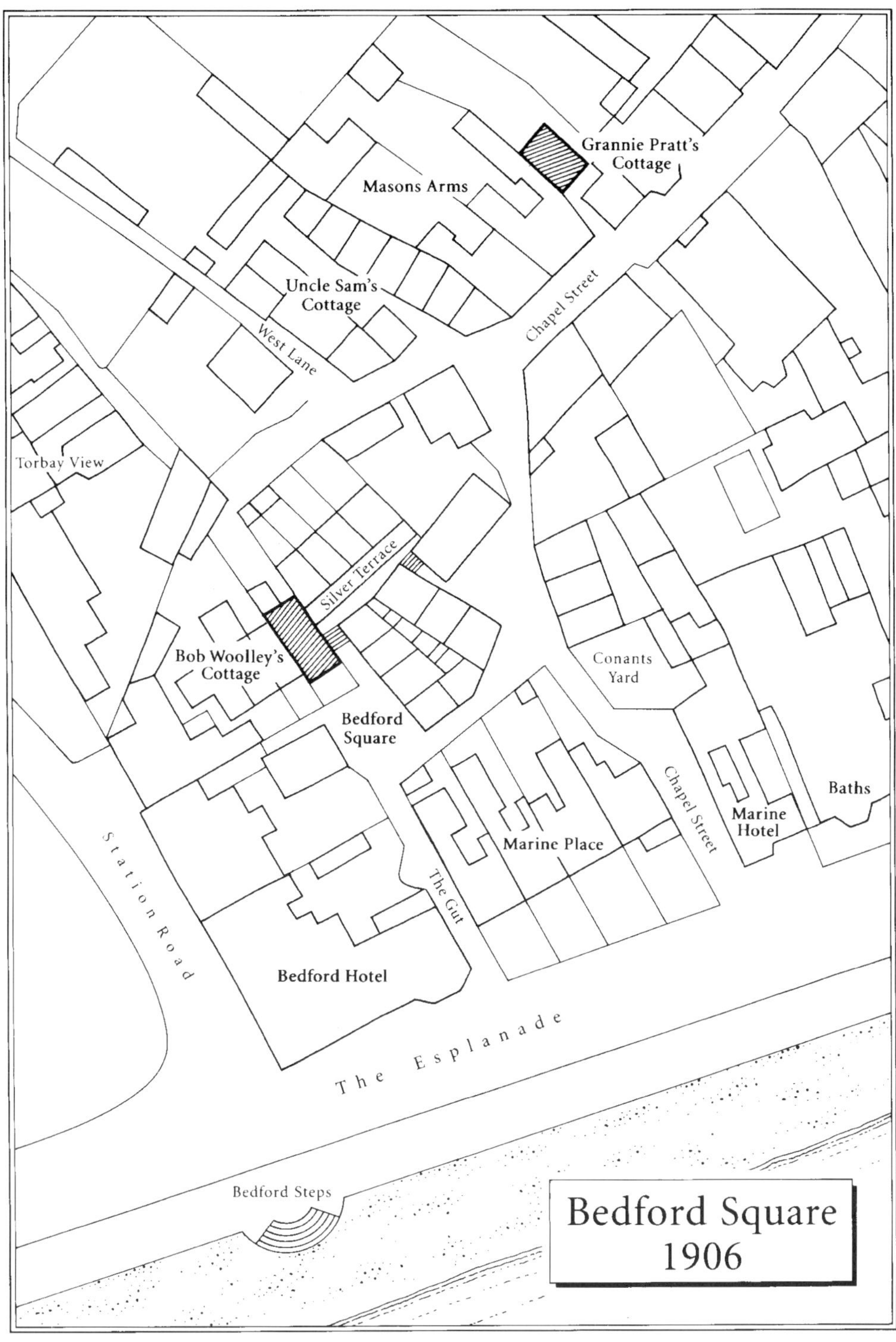
Grannie Pratt's Cottage
Masons Arms
Uncle Sam's Cottage
West Lane
Chapel Street
Torbay View
Silver Terrace
Bob Woolley's Cottage
Bedford Square
Conants Yard
Chapel Street
Baths
Marine Hotel
Marine Place
Station Road
The Gut
Bedford Hotel
The Esplanade
Bedford Steps
Bedford Square 1906

> if I can get rooms for you if you tell me about the time you will be hear from yours Truly Anthony Widger.

No room at the inn, but the stable stood waiting.

> Risky; but never mind. There is always the sea. It is something to have the certainty of a bed at the end of a long day's tramp. Besides, I want to see Tony, and George too, if by chance he is at home. And there may be a little fishing. And -
>
> And stepping westward seems to be
> A kind of *heavenly* destiny.
>
> That's the real feeling at the back of my mind. I want to go west, towards the sunset; over Dartmoor, towards Land's End, where the departing ships go down into the sea.[48]

He had planned on two nights. He stayed a lifetime.

Stephen Reynolds set off with Margot from Pans Lane early on the Saturday morning of the 10th of August. By tea-time the following Wednesday they had completed their hundred miles of dusty road and stood at the entrance to the Gut, the narrow shingle-paved alleyway that ran between the Bedford Hotel on the seafront at Sidmouth and Marine Place, then a row of tall lodging houses and now the Hotel Riviera. Emerging from the northern end of the Gut into Bedford Square, they found themselves in another world. To the right was a row of thatched cottages two storeys high, projecting out from the northern side of the square almost to the back of Marine Place. Further to the right, another row of thatched cottages ran along the eastern side of the square. On the north-east side, a small flight of steps ran up to a further row of cottages whose relative height above the ground gave them a degree of protection from the constant flooding that ravaged the square in winter.

Blinking into the sunlight of the little square, Reynolds' first impression was of "an incredible number of recesses and sub-corners, so to speak, with many more doors in them than one can discover houses belonging to the doors. Two cottages, I am told, have no ground floors at all. Cats sun themselves on walls or squat about gnawing fish bones. A houdan cockerel with bedraggled speckly plumage and a ragged crest hanging over one eye struts from doorstep to doorstep." The children, at the sight of the stranger and his formidable companion, ran like rabbits in a warren to their respective doors, stood there and stared.[49]

Straight opposite the northern end of the Gut ran a small row of cottages, on the corner of which, hard by the flight of steps, stood the most distinctive cottage of them all. It was tall and thin, three stories high, built of red brick with tiles in place of its neighbours' thatch, "straight up and down like an overgrown doll's house". Its distinctive size and shape reflected the fact that a lawyer, Henry Pinn, had lived there for thirty years in the middle of the nineteenth century.[50] Reynolds borrowed his family name for Bob's fictional mother-in-law. At the front of the house was a small cat-trodden garden, enclosed by a three foot wall, in which only wallflowers and some box edging had survived. Over the front door was a broken trellis-work porch, and the masts and spars that propped up the front wall announced to the world that the lawyer had long since been replaced by occupants of a more nautical persuasion.[51]

He threaded his way through the children and cats to the open door he guessed to be Bob Woolley's.

> A pleasant looking old woman – short, stout, charwoman-shaped – came out of the passage just as I raised my hand to knock the open door. "Are you Mrs Widger?" said I. "Lor' bless 'ee. I ben't Mrs Widger. Here, Annie! Here's a gen'leman to see 'ee."
>
> Mrs Widger, the afternoon Mrs Widger, is a quite slim woman who – strangely enough for a working-man's wife – looks a good deal younger than she is. She has rather beautiful light brown hair and dresses tastefully. I am afraid she will not feel complimented if the old woman tells her of my mistake.
>
> Her manner of receiving me indicated plainly a suspended judgment, inclined perhaps towards the favourable. I was shown my room, a little long back room, with ragged wall-paper, and almost filled up by a huge, very flat, squashy bed. After a wash-over (I did not ask for a bath for fear of exposing the lack of one) I went down to tea.[52]

That afternoon in the little back kitchen, as he balanced politely in the courting chair with its broken arm and watched the children come in from play and Bob from the beach to devour their fried mackerel with eager, dirty hands, his life was changed from dust to fire. For the first time he was in the presence of real people, battling with the essence of existence, people whose lives were beyond his experience or his imagination. Their directness hit him in the face. No pilgrim to Damascus could have seen a more blinding light.

But as with all religious conversions, there was one more formal test to overcome before the supplicant could cross the threshold into the promised land. It happened the next morning when he came down to breakfast.

> This morning, when I arrived downstairs, the kitchen was all of a caddle. Children were bolting their breakfast, seated and afoot; were washing themselves and being washed; were getting ready and being got ready for school. Mrs Widger looked up from stitching the seat of a small boy's breeches *in situ*. "I've a-laid your breakfast in the front room."
>
> Thither I went with a book and no uncertain feeling of disappointment. The front room looks out upon Alexandra Square. It is, at once, parlour,

lumber room, sail and rope store, portrait gallery of relatives and ships, and larder. It is a veritable museum of the household treasures not in constant use, and represents pretty accurately, I imagine, the extent to which Mrs Widger's house-pride is able to indulge itself. But I have had enough at Salisbury of eating my meals among best furniture and in the (printed) company of great minds. The noise in the kitchen sounded jolly. Now or never, I thought. So after breakfast, I returned to the kitchen and asked for what bad behaviour I was banished to the front room.
"Lor'! If yu don't mind this. On'y 'tis all up an' down here...."[53]

He spent the next four days, twice as long as he had intended, in a heaven of new delights – out early in the morning to go sailing with Bob, playing with the children in the Square, sitting chatting in the evenings in the little back kitchen with the buzz of the family all around. The sea had been either too rough or too calm for successful fishing, but Bob suggested he come back in September when the mackerel hooking would be in full swing.[54]

He had booked a room in Princetown for the night of 21 August, and on the Monday morning he knew reluctantly that he must move on.[55] At 6 a.m., while the others were out to sea, he grabbed a moment to write to Garnett about the new happiness that had come flooding into his life.

It's not often a wonderful bit of one's life bears reconstruction after breakage, and I feel in the thankful sort of mood one has when the sun comes out after two or three days' rain. I've been living the last week with one of my fishermen – one of the nicest of them, who – which ain't so common – has a nice wife and the jolliest little brown children with sea-blue eyes, who don't make an atom of difference in their pranks for me being in the house. Certainly at first one gets a bit squeamish when they pull a tooth out during breakfast or grab at all the grub within reach, but one soon gets used to that, and indeed, I'm getting quite a connoisseur in the methods of devouring fried mackerel without knives or forks. They wanted to 'make me welcome', i.e. take no pay for my room, and as it is they want me to come down and spend Christmas with them. They've almost left off calling me 'sir' or 'the gen'leman'. And the welcome I got when I came here.... I don't think even a book out could make me half so proud or pleased.
You are a student of the whims of heredity.... How is it I get on better with seafaring people than with any other class? Why should they like me better, or put up with me more easily than any other set of people? And they've had me here two years ago when I was ill and morose.... Do they feel intuitively how I, so to speak, reach out to them? my almost reverence for their seafaring? my desire to know all about the sea that they've been reared on? I know what I say is right from a curious

physical fact: borrowing other peoples clothes revolts my dog-like sense of smell, yet I can borrow these fishermen's jerseys and things and no more notice them than my own duds.[56]

Despite Bob's offer to "make him welcome", he settled on a sum with the always more down to earth Mrs Woolley. The parting was even worse for Bob's six-year-old son, Bobby (the fictional Jimmy), who had been captivated by this strange gentleman guest.

As I was setting out, Jimmy said to his mother: "Don't 'ee let Mister Ronals go, Mam 'Idger." He followed me to the end of the Gut; would have come farther had I not sent him back. That, and Tony's desire to make me welcome, brightened the bright South Devon sunshine. I kept within sight of the sea as long as possible. The little sailing boats on it looked so nimble. I have a leaning to go back, a sort of hunger.... [57]

He tramped on that morning with Margot, making for Dartmoor, his head still buzzing with the experiences of the last few days. Arriving at Princetown, they settled in for a short stay at Rowe's Duchy Hotel where they could enjoy the peace and beauty of the moor around them. But try as he might, he could not recapture the feeling of the spring holiday there with the Tanners when he had worked all morning on the Guide and roamed the moors freely for the rest of the day. Something had changed. The proximity of middle-class people and middle-class values had now become unbearably oppressive.

I don't think I can remain here...... The Moor is as splendid as ever, but this hotel life, following so soon on the life of Under Town.... Though the good, well-cooked food, neither so greasy nor so starchy as Mrs Widger's, is an agreeable change, I sit at the table d'hôte and rage within. I am compelled to hear a conversation that irritates me almost beyond amusement at it. These people here are on holiday. Most of them, by their talk, were never on anything else. They chirp in lively or bored fashion, as the case may be, of the things that don't matter, of the ornamentations, the superfluities and the relaxations of life. At Tony Widger's they discuss – and much more merrily – the things that do matter; the means of life itself. Here, they say: "Is the table d'hôte as good as it might be? Is the society what it might be? Is it not a pity that there is no char-a-banc or a motor service to Cranmere Pool or Yes Tor?" There, the equivalent question is: "Shall us hae money to go through the winter? Shall us hae bread and scrape to eat?"...... Here, comfort is at stake: there, existence. Coming here is like passing from a birth and death chamber into a theatre, where, if the actors have lives of their own, apart from mummery, it is their business not to show them. It is like

> watching a game from the grand stand, instead of playing it; betting on a race instead of running it.[58]

The subconscious class feeling that had run as undercurrent through his childhood in Devizes, his schooldays at Bloxham and his university life in Manchester now at last had a voice.

Man and dog moved hurriedly on north to Nether Velly – Margot bound for her mating, Reynolds to relax for the rest of his holiday, write a little, take stock of the past week's experiences. He was in a musing, mystical mood. Reading Wordsworth in bed in the old farmhouse surrounded by pine-trees, he jotted down in his notebook some disjointed, melancholy thoughts.

> This is the place to read Wordsworth in bed (that apotheosis of Charles Lamb's reading by candle-light) when the wind is roaring through the pine-belt, and all else is quiet. Then I see the Solitary Reaper in her vale profound, and the still floating clouds beyond the hills; I hear her melancholy strain, and seem to see many dull sorrows. Below all, yet dominant, is the wind in the pines; – 'tis as if, while I read of others, I hear my own life.[59]

The days had been long and hot, but with the arrival of September a thick sea fog spread each morning across the rolling fields around the farm. He was reading Tolstoy for the first time, his *Essays* and *Resurrection*, and confided his mixed reactions to Garnett: "He's very huge, but he seems to me impatient, and too little appreciative of those who aren't on the way to his ideals...... He seems to me to fall short of nearly all your critical standards; except the main ones, perhaps, of frankness and determination to stomach the conclusions he comes to."[60]

He was too disturbed in mind and emotions to work properly. After more than a week's stay, he had written one short story, "Mother of the Woman", which he parcelled off to Pinker as a possible contribution to the *Pall Mall Magazine*.[61] He was worrying about the next big book, the ideas for which had been thrown into even more turmoil by the Sidmouth revelation. He confessed to Garnett: "Have been doing next to no work – one silly short story, that's all. Seem absolutely run out of wits. But have browsed a good deal on the *Ex Profundis* book idea. Shall have to see you somewhen before I start it. The thing doesn't crystallise. Can't decide on the main point of view, nor precisely how deep to try and go." He could sense that the novel experience of life in the fisherman's house was calling up a new political perspective, which was perhaps the point of view he was now after. "My own politics are boiling in the pot, and don't seem in a hurry to get cooked; and God knows what will come out in the end. Yet it seems to me that some definite idea – right or wrong, but definite – is necessary before one can tackle men and things – an idea not necessarily to be expressed but to lend steadiness to one's exploring – ballast for the boat."[62]

But he was also beginning to recognise that the view from the fisherman's window would have to find expression in words. On his last day in Bedford Square, it had been at the forefront of his mind: "I could satirize them, but to write down the rest of it is beyond me; it would be poetry, and I ain't a poet, even a minor."[63] After a week or so away from the source of the new stimulus in his life, the desire to write was more compelling and the sense of his own incapacity even more forbidding. He confided to his notebook in the same emotionally disjointed prose

> I have seen things of which a work of genius, that would draw all men to it, might be made. And just because I doubt my power to recreate these things into the work of genius, so do I now put them down, and *say* that I have seen them. I cannot make all the world see them too, but if I say I have seen them perhaps some will believe them, and know that they are there, even though I have not proved it to them.[64]

The draw of Sidmouth was becoming too strong for him. He cut short his stay at Velly and on 6 September set off back down south, leaving Margot to the charms of her first husband. In two days he was on Dartmoor again, this time studiously avoiding Princetown and its vacuous middle-class tourists for a friendly bed-and-breakfast in Widdecombe-in-the-Moor. All the way he had been pondering the great book he was to write about his breakdown and at Widdecombe an anonymous stranger walked into his life at just the right moment to clear up some of the more difficult puzzles with which he was grappling. This strange encounter was for him another semi-mystical experience and he wrote of it to Garnett in awed tones as if he were recounting an angelic visitation out of the Bible.

> When I got to Widdecombe-in-the-Moor, the landlady said there was a vegetarian young man staying in the house. Taking by mistake some of his special bread over supper, I made his acquaintance. A tall, fair, long-haired man about my age, pince-nez, and evidently accustomed to pretty wealthy surroundings. A writer certainly, though possibly an architect by profession. Remarks on vegetarianism, and then he said it had cured him of bad neurasthenia. I made a remark which must have showed that I had been in the same box – sundry remarks – and then he spent the whole evening unfolding before me his analysis of the subject. It was a queerly impersonal uncanny sort of conversation, and some of the things he said were very subtle. We discussed the state as if it were a metaphysical question, not as something which had apparently very nearly upturned the pair of us. Neither of us enquired the other's name; neither knew it. Next day he accompanied me some miles over the moor, took lunch with me on a boulder, and disappeared; a help to me to clear several disorderly and muzzy ideas, used, and dropped by the way.[65]

He tramped on along the coast and arrived at Sidmouth in the late afternoon of 10 September to the by now traditional welcome.[66] Bobby came to greet him three-quarters of a mile up the road from his home. "So anxious was he to take me in house that he scarcely allowed me time to go down to the Front and look at the sea and at the boats lying among a litter of nets and gear the length of the sunny beach."[67] Back home in the little kitchen Mam Woolley had the kettle on in a flash and had brought out the mainstay of the Woolley table, the big familiar blue enamelled teapot.

He planned to stay for at least ten days. But by 17 September, he had decided to stay on until the 22nd; and by the 23rd he was planning a further week.[68] In all, this second visit was to last 23 days. He was put in the front bedroom this time which overlooked the Square and gave him, up through the Gut, a narrow view of the sea. But it had its drawbacks. At ten o'clock on that Monday night of his arrival, Bob's sister Alice, who lived almost next door, gave birth to a daughter, Winifred, a sister for Vera and Laura. He could hear from his bed the Square in uproar until well gone midnight. "If it were not that the window of the back bedroom is over the scullery, the ash-heap and the main drain, I would ask to move back there."[69]

He soon settled down to the regular daily routine which was to form the rhythm of *A Poor Man's House*. He was up first in the morning at half past four, would light the fire in the back kitchen, call Bob and have the tea waiting for him when he came down. Before first light the two of them were pushing off from the beach, headed for the mackerel grounds. "By the time the sun rises, south of Beer Head, he's worked himself into a temper over the lines, and I've laughed him out of it, and we are fishing, grimly and silently, cutting baits from live fish, if they're biting hard; hauling them in and throwing them off the hooks with a jerk; or singing blatant songs, laughing with a sea-loudness and talking, if the fish are not keenly on the feed; or concocting fifteen or twenty reasons for it, if they won't bite at all. There we are – ourselves, the sea and the dawn – the sea heaving up to us and ourselves forever heaving higher, up and over it. It exalts us, so that we hardly need words to talk with. We are in the more immediate presence of each other. About eight we sail off home, haggle on the beach for our price, stooping over a glittering heap of mackerel; and then after a wash, we breakfast on mackerel, well-contented, in a kitchen which is more than half a lavatory because the children are being sent off to school. Quite prosaic, you see; not overclean; yet needing the touch of a Maeterlinck to bring out the mysterious wonderfulness of it and light up the door where the soul-house opened."[70]

This new experience of sea air and regular fishing gave him a physical boost. He told Garnett: "I find the rowing etc. has exercised a wonderful curative action on my groggy inside, and it might help my design to be a perfectly healthy man before I'm thirty".[71] He was in an even bouncier mood with Pinker: "I shall babble on if I'm not careful – being full of a happy confusion. Next week I'll go home and unravel my brains and get soft hands and a pasty face...... "[72]

Though the physical side was important, the emotional, mystical element went far deeper. Steeped as he was in the Bible, the religious imagery of fish and fishermen hovered round his mind. It was to form the unspoken sub-text that ran below all he wrote on fishermen and the sea, adding to his message a distinctive Messianic quality.[73]

But the immediate questions were more down to earth. The short Sidmouth mackerel season was a poor one that autumn of 1906. On 11 September, his first day back, they caught 18 dozen; the next day 6; on the 22nd, 17½...... and so on.[74] With winter approaching, Reynolds felt for the first time the chilling sensation of a household facing the threat of real deprivation – and perhaps starvation.

The rest of the day was spent sailing, out on the beach mending nets and lines, writing in the little bedroom which doubled as his study. After tea, there was talk round the kitchen table, Bob recounting the trials of his first childhood job at Trumps, the local grocer or, when Mam had gone off to the Dutch auction held most evenings at the Market House, letting go with memories of his first wife and the children he had lost.[75]

When Reynolds first appeared down the Gut, there were four Woolley children at home: the fair-haired Bobby, aged 6; little Reggie, with the glasses and squint, aged 5; and the two youngest daughters from Bob's first marriage – Gertie aged 12 and Ethel 9. The two elder children were working away – Bill, now 19, in the Navy and Florence (Lulu to the family – her second name was Louisa), aged 14, just started in service.[76] But the family past was more complex, as Reynolds learnt in those autumn evenings in the little back kitchen alone with Bob.

Bob's two marriages had been only too typical of a working-class family at the end of the nineteenth century – little money, dangerously unhealthy accommodation, and the ever-present reality of death. He had had his fair share of "graveyard luck".

In December 1886, at the age of 21, he had married Annie Driver, a fisherman's daughter from Beer, two years his junior – Reynolds borrowed her christian name for the fictional second Mrs Widger. They set up house in Portland Cottage in Sidmouth where Bill was born the following July. Bob's next three sons all perished as babies. Albert, born in November 1888, died of measles in June 1891 after the family had moved to another house in Western Town. There Ernest had been born in March 1891, only to die four years later in May 1895 of leukaemia and noma, a cancerous condition of the mouth associated with sickly children from the slums. By 1892 the family had moved to Chapel Street where the fourth son Henry was born in October 1895.[77] He died of teething convulsions the following June. Little wonder that Bob was so inordinately proud of Bill, the only son to survive.

By contrast, the three girls all lived – Lulu, born July 1892, Gertie July 1894, and Ethel December 1896. But having given birth to seven children in less than ten years, Annie herself became the next victim. In 1897 the landlord of the cottage in Chapel Street took up the drains and left them open the whole of that long hot summer. Both Bob and his wife fell ill.[78] On 26 August, after five days of acute diarrhoea, Annie died at the age of 30. Bob, who had nearly died himself, was out of his mind; but he had four young children that had to be cared for. A year later, on Christmas Eve 1898, he married Mary Jane Pratt, a farm labourer's daughter from West Hill, and brought her home for Christmas to Chapel Street and the four children that awaited her: "'twer queer, like, wi' the childern asleep upstairs what were to be mine, an' wasn't. I did wonder to meself what I wer starting on".[79]

Her own children arrived soon enough – Bobby at Chapel Street in October 1899 and Reggie in December 1900, the first to be born in the tall house in Bedford Square to which the family had removed that year. But then the ill fortune struck her too. In 1905 she gave birth to twin boys – "what nobody didn' know nort about" – who did not survive, and she was very ill for weeks after.[80] And even worse was the fate that befell the little fair-haired girl, Lilian Clarice, born on 26 January 1904. In late November, at the age of ten months, she went down with whooping cough. On 23 December it developed into pneumonia and she died that Christmas Eve because their family doctor, Dr Pullin, was away and the other doctor approached refused to come out at night to attend her.[81] Lilian was her only daughter, and Mary Woolley was inconsolable. For months after, she walked every evening after tea the mile up to the cemetery to watch by her grave, a ritual which only ended after the twins were born when she became too ill. When Reynolds arrived, she was still walking up every Sunday.[82]

He was introduced to Lilian (the fictional Rosie) on this September visit.

> For the last two or three days there has been a large flat brown-paper parcel standing against the wall on the far side of my bed. I have wondered what it was.
>
> This evening, after we had all finished tea, while Tony was puffing gingerly at a cigarette (he is nothing of a smoker) with his chair tilted back and a stockinged foot in Mrs Widger's lap, Jimmy said, as Jimmy usually says: "Gie us another caake, Mam 'Idger." He laid a very grubby hand on the cakelets.
>
> "Yu li'l devil!" shouted his mother. "Take yer hands off or I'll gie 'ee such a one.... Yu'd eat an eat till yu busted, I believe; an yu'm that cawdy [finical] over what yu has gie'd 'ee...."
>
> Tony took up the poker and made a feint at Jimmy, who jumped into the corner laughing loudly. With an amazing contrast in tone, Mrs Widger said quietly: "Wait a minute an' see what I got to show 'ee, if yu'm gude."
>
> She went upstairs with that peculiar tread of hers – as if the feet were very tired but the rest of the body invincibly energetic, – and returned with the flat parcel. She undid the string, the children watching with greedy curiosity. She placed on the best-lighted chair an enlargement of a baby's

photograph, in a cheap frame, all complete. "There!" she said.
"What is ut?" asked Tony. "Why, 'tis li'l Rosie!"
"Wer did 'ee get 'en?" he continued more softly. "Yu an't had 'en give'd 'ee?"
"Give'd me? No! Thic cheap-jack.... But 'tisn' bad, is it?"
"What cheap-jack?"
"Why, thic man to the market-house – wer I got the cruet."
"O-oh! I didn' never see he.... What did 'ee pay 'en for thic then?"
"Never yu mind. 'Twasn't none o' yours what I paid. What do 'ee think o' it?"
"'Tisn' bad – very nice," remarked Tony, bending before the picture, examining it in all lights. "Iss; 'tisn' bad by no means.
Come yer, Jimmy an' Tommy. Do 'ee know who that ther is?"
"Rosie!" whispered Jimmy.
"What was took up to cementry," added Tommy in a brighter voice.
"Iss, 'tis our li'l Rosie to the life (mustn' touch), jest like her was."
A moment's tension; then, "A surprise for 'ee, en' it?" Mrs Widger enquired.
"My ol' geyser!"
The children's riot began again. "Our Rosie. . . ." they were saying. Mam 'Idger, slipping out of Tony's grasp, carried the picture off to the front room. She was sometime gone.
Wordsworth's *We are Seven* came into my mind:
"But they are dead; those two are dead!
Their spirits are in heaven!"
    'Twas throwing words away; for still
    The little maid would have her will,
And said, "Nay, we are seven!"
I knew, of course, intellectually, that the poem records more than a child's mere fancy; but never before have I felt its truth, have I been caught up, so to speak, into the atmosphere of the wise, simple souls who are able to rob death of the worst of its sting by refusing to let the dead die altogether, even on earth. Rosie is dead and buried. I perceive also – I perceived, while Tony and the children stood round that picture – that Rosie is still here, in this house, hallowing it a little. The one statement is as much a fact as the other; but how much more delicately intangible, and perhaps how much truer, the second.[83]

In the summer of 1999, the picture of "Rosie" made its second appearance. It was found, grey with dust, leaning up against the water tank in the loft of the Sidmouth house of Bob's youngest daughter, where it had stood undisturbed for almost fifty years. It had the answer to Tony's question. When the dust was all blown away, there emerged on the back in a pencilled hand: "Mrs Wooley. Bedford Square. 1/6."

There were other emotional moments on those September days and evenings. He heard from Fred Ware in Chapel Street how Freddie, the "little admiral", had finally died before his eyes back in May 1904, just six weeks after his eighteenth birthday. "The other day, too, they told me how my little hunch-backed 'admiral' (whom I used to take to sea with me) died. As near as possible it was like this: 'He was in to house one mornin', an' I thought 'e was sleepin', an' I said, "Freddie, will 'ee 'ave a cup o' tay, you'm been sleepin'"; an' he says "No, I 'aven't, but I been sort o' dreamin'", an' 'e said as 'e'd see'd a green valley wi' a stream o' water like runnin' down the centre o' it, an' he thought 'e see'd granfer there (that we losted jest before 'en). 'E sat on's mother's lap, an' 'e jest died suddint like, went away, an' we buried 'en up to the cemetery to Landpart."[84]

Reynolds, who had sensed the almost Shakespearean quality of these lives, wrote this into his book, with very little change, as though it were the death of Falstaff.[85] He was beginning to learn that here, unlike Devizes, death was entwined with the very warp of life.

On another evening, with Mam again down at the Market House, Bob began to talk of Annie. "Then the yarn shifted to his first wife. He loved her very much. He's that sort of man. It is very beautiful to see him playing with the present wife with what the novelists call love-light in his eyes. I looked at her photo, also at a dreadful, pathetic memorial card framed on the wall. He was a bit wet in the eyes; I was rather worked up; for I knew before most about it, and how he nearly went off his head, and besides two years ago, the day his son went to sea, I had him with me all the evening until he was fit to go to bed. The untidy little kitchen, with dark shadows and white clothes drying, was oppressive with his first wife. And he concluded that yarn with: 'Yes, her was a nice woman; a nice woman; I 'adn't no complaint to make against she.' Whether it was because I knew the feeling behind the expression, or whether it lay in the imperfection of it even, I was simply hit flat by the wonderfulness and beauty of it. In the one sentence he hit all his sorrow into me, so to speak, in a single blow. I wish I could picture it for you properly, for it seems to me that I suddenly had the luck to see something very sacred."[86]

This was the emotional turning point. If he did not know it before, he knew it now. He had fallen in love with Bob. In the letters to Garnett there now began to appear those physical descriptions which were to give to *A Poor Man's House* its homosexual undercurrent which few readers spotted and from which those who did carefully averted their eyes. As when, soon after his return, he went out fishing with both Bob and Bobby: "I rowed all the time with the finest sight before my eyes.... You ought to have seen it – I wished you there at the time. They were so perfect in colour and position; – the father in navy blue, his face a beautiful tan red, china-blue eyes excited with fishing, and his strong body slightly gnarled and bent with the rheumatics; the kiddie standing sturdily and straight as a die on his brown legs and feet, and hauling in his line with an alert cat-like movement; a delicate replica of his father, coloured less strongly. The similarity and difference were exquisite, like the semi-duplication of a two-part fugue in motion instead of sound. If I could have painted.... I've never felt so strongly, so pitifully almost, the age I've left behind me, and the age that's got to come – an old platitude newly quickened."[87]

If it were a physical relationship, it was one of complete sexual innocence, as when later that winter they cuddled up together under the mainsail of the drifter to keep out the cold of the night as they waited for the nets to fill.[88] Or when every evening, after taking their last look at the sea, they would march together arm-in-arm down the Gut home to their hot grog and bed.[89] His love for Bob, perhaps through fear of his own homosexuality, became transmuted to an equally deep love of the family, of Mam Woolley, the children, especially Bobby, of Bob's brother Tom (which at times would spell trouble), of Uncle Sam; and wider, to the house, the Square, the beach, the cliffs and, above all, the sea. The place was the people and the people the place. For the first time in his life, he found himself accepted for what he was – with trust and love. He had found a home.

The experience was too overwhelming for him to sit back, there and then, and write about it in cold blood. But from the front bedroom, looking out over the Square and up the Gut to the sea and the horizon beyond, there flowed a stream of excited letters to Edward Garnett by which the jumble of thoughts and emotions could find their way into words. He was fully conscious of the purpose that these letters were serving. In the first week he wrote to Garnett

> Have I been overwhelming you with letters lately? 'Tisn't to be helped. I'm collecting ideas – or rather impressions to grow into ideas – at such a rate, that I must spout them to and share them with somebody; and no one but you that I know is likely to see what I'm getting at. Indeed, one or two of your remarks, and various political considerations, have had more than summat to do wi' 't. My astonishment at, and zest in, these people's lives has suddenly started me on a most determined effort to find the exact differences between their lives and ours.... [90]

And a week later

> Still here, and shall be till next Monday. And like me, this almost journal letter continueth. I know the craze to scribble will come, but at present I couldn't, even if I did go home. I'm living much too much to turn round and regard anything fixedly enough for literary purposes. It's queer how at times the world takes on a new lease of wonderfulness, and Saint Prosaic receives a new batch of haloes from the heavenly tailors. Fishing, sailing, and pigging it in a cottage – that's all 'tis outwardly. Yet inwardly it's something which, like great music, sanctifies things for one;

> makes one thankful and in a sense humble; incapable of appropriate words and incapable of silence.[91]

And three days later still

> If, as you say, these snippets from my tangle give you pleasure, I'll go on; for they give me more than pleasure to write. I can't do any work any more than I can look at the sun and examine the mountains in it, and at least, by scribbling letters, I can clear my mind a bit.[92]

Garnett could see with clarity the artistic potential which was gathering around this experience and these letters. He was in his element when coaxing books out of young authors – no one could do it better. He suggested to Reynolds that he should "feel the working-man's life and interpret it back to me", but the explicit nature of the invitation made Reynolds distinctly uneasy: "Your exhortation.... is pleasant in reading, but.... I don't know, of course; things happen so rapidly; but I don't think I can. I'm not single-hearted enough. My Jekyll and Hyde, enthusiast and laugher and critic, have such a rude habit of speaking at once. The spirit's willing, but the pen damn'd weak. Only one thing I'm sure of: if the subject compels me to write about it, I shall; and if it doesn't, I shall do no good by compelling myself."[93]

But despite the reluctant disclaimer, over these three September weeks he was to put together, in experience and in the letters, at least half the content of what was eventually to become *A Poor Man's House* – the meals in the back kitchen, the father and son at sea, Bob's childhood and first wife, the death of Rosie and the "Little Commodore", the daughter home from service; the political arguments over thrift, and between self reliance and economic improvement; the image of the two high walls dividing the classes; the lectures on cleanliness and pluck *versus* courage; the Whitmanesque verse. It was forming in his mind whether he liked it or not; and he had to get most of it down in words.

He had neither time nor emotional space to give much thought to his writing proper, but when he did so, it was the shape and form of the *Ex Profundis* book with which he was still trying to grapple. It was looming large in his mind at the beginning of the three week stay when he asked directly for Garnett's help.

> The *Ex Profundis* book doesn't clear itself yet, though I've meditated a lot.... Keep me up to it please: your interest will do a lot to make me worry the subject persistently. I can't decide on the central theme, and on that depends entirely the plane it will have to be written on. The fundamental thing is, I think, that I have come out of the illness with a sort of religion, so intangible I can't explain it in the least. A sort of large security in things, a sense of being an integral part of the universe, and

> as such unharmable in the long run, has substituted itself for a shattered sense of security among men and things. And at the same time it has made me feel as if all disputations about gods and the hereafter simply don't concern me, except as other people's feelings interesting to examine. The question to me is: shall I go for that, be my mystical self, and risk shipwreck on the high seas; or shall I try to do a better work on a lower plane; the laughing, scientific, twisty self that talks to you sometimes? For though you may think I've pretty well spit up my heart before you, I haven't, and couldn't, even to so good a listener as yourself.[94]

On his first week in Sidmouth, however, he was able to advance at least one small facet of his literary business – the problem of the payment for the Guide. He wrote to Pinker with some glee: "Last week Messrs. Mate's guide-book representative had the ill-luck to stumble across me before several gossiping Sidmouthians with whom he hopes to do business this week. Whip being so provided, I whipped him up gently and effectively. Usual lies about the firm's manager going on holiday with the keys of the firm's safe in his pocket! Next day, he told me he'd written for the money to be paid at once."[95] A cheque did indeed emerge from this encounter, but crossed with a letter from Pinker's solicitors demanding payment. Mate's solicitors wrote back in high dudgeon: "We have already sent this cheque to Mr Pinker some days ago and when same is presented at Bank it will be met. We do not usually pay our accounts twice."[96] Not surprisingly, the cheque bounced. It took another month for Pinker finally to secure the eleven guineas.[97]

As the end of that wonderful September drew nearer, Reynolds saw that he could not postpone the return to Devizes any longer, but must get back there to work hard through the winter and rake in some money. But amidst the melancholy recognition of these final days that the dream was coming to an end, there came too a determination not to let it slip from his grasp. He began to plan how Sidmouth could now be integrated permanently into his life. He knew he could not throw up everything to go and live there for good. As he told Garnett: "Your question, why I don't live by the sea has often occurred to me. But you see, Sidmouth is too relaxing for me to stay very long in, and I've no wish to go anywhere else; I make new friends so slowly, and am so fond of those I have here. Besides, I can't leave the Downs for long; they are essential for my general wellbeing; I'm rooted there so to speak, wherever else I may blossom out. I love Devizes and loathe it. The sea calls one, but the Downs lie waiting; and the waiting wins." The compromise would be to share the two: "As soon as I'm earning a bit more money, I shall be much up and down...."[98]

He was also beginning to formulate more concrete plans of going into business with Bob during the fishing season. "Bob's fishing and boating has got beyond him single-handed, and yet is not enough for him to employ a man to whom he'd have to give a continuous living wage. So it's possible I shall come down next mackerel season and help him. 'Twill be a great game if I do."[99]

The last weekend of September George and Lizzie Tanner were planning another short motoring holiday, but Reynolds refused the invitation to go with them.[100] He was clinging on to a few more days in Bedford Square. On the morning of 2 October, after a stormy night, he went down to the front to watch his last dawn come up and then back to the house to write his last letter to Edward Garnett, just as he had done on the last day of his first visit in August.[101]

As he sat in the train at Sidmouth station waiting for the off, his mood was as melancholy as the weather, as if he were going back to boarding school once more: "Rain spattered against the carriage windows. Dead leaves scurried by. I wanted to get out, to go back. I wanted to know whether Tony was at sea".[102] The Tanners must have met him at Salisbury, for they whisked him straight off with them to Ford, planning to spend a day or two in the Hampshire countryside.[103]

When he woke up in Ford House the next morning, he was still in the same nostalgic mood for Sidmouth, intertwined with guilt at his subdued reaction to the company of the Tanners – his friends who had done so much to give him practical help and comfort, in Lizzie's case as far back as the death of his mother, but who could never fill the emotional gulf now left by the absence of Bob. Ever awake to Biblical allusion, he thought at once of the story of Martha and Mary. He continued his letter to Garnett in an oddly lyrical tone.

> This morning, a French window, red geraniums and moon-daisies in the foreground, out-branching apple-trees and willows, and behind them rounded elm tops, stretching away to a lovely line of Down under the orange clouds of dawn. A cow mooing and birds instead of the sea's chafing on the beach. Friends who have been good to me and stood by me since my mother died. So that I feel rather ashamed of myself for having the surf and Bob's out-of-tune songs in my ears all the time, and the sea in my mind's eye; and for wishing that I were having tea in my damp sea-rig in the cockroachey little kitchen.
>
> That tale of Martha and Mary in the Bible has a wider application than religion. One's friends are Marthas and Marys. The Marthas are good to one, well-tried and immovably faithful, yet the Marys by simply being and doing nothing – by allowing oneself to react on them – seem to possess a straight road to the deeper strata of one's soul. In dirty weather one flies to the Marthas; on one's beam ends one requires only the presence of the Marys, and expects them to do nothing but be. I used not to realise that, and when those to whom I was a Martha, showed me I was not a Mary, as I flattered myself to be, I used to get bitter. And probably shall again, not realising quickly enough that these matters are governed by the uncontrollable or semi-controllable sub-conscious part of people.[104]

There was more dirty weather ahead which was soon to find him fleeing once again into the arms of the Tanners and their Martha-like support.

He went fishing with them to Fordingbridge that day and was back in Devizes the next to give the first of a series of evening lectures on English Literature for which he had been signed up the week before by the Devizes Education Committee for the princely sum of four shillings a time.[105] To his chagrin, the lecture had been postponed for a fortnight and he realised it had cost him a few extra days in Sidmouth.[106] He was also planning a move out of Pans Lane at the end of the following week, a decision taken while still at Sidmouth and probably through his own general restlessness rather than any desire on the part of the Wyers.[107]

The following week he was up in London shadowing Garnett's usual Tuesday and Wednesday in town, and called in on Pinker to discuss the problem of Mate's late payment which then had still not been resolved.[108] Discussion at the Mont Blanc that Tuesday was full of the Sidmouth experience, but there was a more general interest in the future of the *Speaker* which had changed management that summer and left regular contributors like Garnett and Reynolds waiting to see what their fate would be. Reynolds himself, who had a number of contributions in the pipeline, had been cheered by the publication that Saturday of a thoughtful article written earlier in the year entitled *Autobiografiction*, which claimed to identify a new literary genre at "the point where fiction, autobiography, and the essay meet".[109]

In the article he drew attention to simple works like Gissing's *Ryecroft* and A.C. Benson's *The House of Quiet* which gave readers the refreshment of an uplifting spiritual experience, whose power would be totally lost in the narrative tangles of fiction. Reynolds may have been the first to articulate the development of this genre in such clear terms, but the essay is essentially an attempt to rationalise his own personal dilemma over the *Ex Profundis* book. He had written one mediocre novel and knew that, for him at least, the fictional form was insufficient to express the major spiritual experience of his breakdown.

The article is typical of most of Reynolds' literary or philosophical theorising in that it is a direct extension of his own experience, an attempt to talk through his own personal problem.

> So the genesis of autobiografiction may be imagined thus. A man, usually of an introspective nature, has accumulated a large body of spiritual experiences. He feels that he must out with it; *cacoethes loquendi* is upon him. What is he to do? Fiction is impracticable. He does not wish, or is not able, to invent such a complicated apparatus for self-expression. Besides, the story's the thing in fiction. To use that medium would be to scatter and sink precisely the spiritual experience which he wants to record. Formal autobiography would present much the same difficulty – the introduction of a large amount of (for his purpose) extraneous matter – for a man's life and the events of it, chronological sequence and completeness, are the aim in autobiography. Essays, again, would be too disconnected and would scarcely admit of an attitude frankly egotistical

> enough. How, then, are the pitfalls of spiritual experience in bulk to be avoided? He invents a certain amount of biographical detail, or (which comes to much the same) he selects from his life the requisite amount of autobiographical material, adding perhaps a quantity of pure fiction, and on that he builds the spiritual experience, with that he dilutes it, and makes it coherent and readable. The result is autobiografiction, a literary form more direct and intimate probably than any to be found outside poetry.[110]

This is perhaps the best description we have of the technique that was eventually to go into *A Poor Man's House*, which owes its power not to imitation of the models of Gissing or Benson but to having been worked out so carefully and painfully for himself.

Those two days in London he discussed his current autobiografiction with Garnett. "That *Ex Profundis* book is getting serious. It ought to be as clear as a pikestaff before starting it, and it isn't by any means. You say you have a clear idea. Please tell me yours if you have time. Probably I sha'n't tumble to it, but it will clear up mine."[111] And so it proved. Unlike some other authors, Reynolds was always keen to show his independence of Garnett by not swallowing wholesale his detailed advice. But Garnett's good sense had often a catalytic effect. Returning to Devizes, Reynolds at last hit upon the right form: "The *Ex Profundis* book has cleared itself up – prologue – irregular journal undated – epilogue. Where to begin – the question now."[112]

On 12 October he carried out the planned move of lodgings. He went to live with Mary Harrison, his first schoolmistress, now aged 63, at No.2 Eastfield in the London Road. But he was no longer the admiring pupil of the 1880s and he sensed immediately he had made a mistake. Wherever he went, he now seemed unable to escape the oppression of middle-class surroundings. "The move is accomplished. Seems queer. My landlady is a little gentlewoman (emphasis on the 'gentle') who used to be my first schoolmistress – and of the unworldliest. The bath in my bedroom is the one my mother used to bathe me in when I was a baby. Everything very pretty and dainty – but God! for the roughnesses of Sidmouth and the fried fish and the brats."[113]

There followed a miserable week in which he was wracked by money worries, anxiety about the first lecture, dismal weather, tension with his relations, and above all inability to settle in his new digs which heightened the longing for Sidmouth and for Bob. Throughout his life Reynolds could never keep a journal; the few tentative starts he made never lasted more than a matter of days. The process of writing up the events of the day last thing at night so stirred his emotions that sleep then became impossible.[114] His insomnia demanded a soporific in the shape of the nightly tot of whisky, not a stimulant of this kind. But just as the departure from Sidmouth in August had led to the jottings in his notebook at Nether Velly, so now the loss of Sidmouth once more led to a depth of introspection which could not be shared easily with friends like Garnett, but only with his diary.

The first three days in the new lodgings had sent him into a depression, and by the Tuesday a letter from Bob had reopened the deep wound of nostalgia for Sidmouth. That night he wrote to himself: "Somehow, everything remindful of Sidmouth nearly makes me weep. I am as if I were in love; filled with an intense longing to be there, and a fear that fate may intervene to prevent me getting there. It is love; not a sensual sort of love; but the old one – mine – purified. Yet I long to be in the same room; to look out late at night to see if the boats be right, and return to Western Town, arm in arm; have a grog together, and then to bed and sleep. I've not been so depressed to-day – working too hard for it, and sleeping out the interval – but I had a wretchedly neurasthenic head in the morning – fuzzy and ear-blown."[115]

His painfully-won recovery from the desolation of breakdown into the security of his own special brand of mystical belief had brought him peace. But he now began to recognise the human love flooding into his life as a new resolution of his predicament, usurping the old one of religious belief – both finer and yet at the same time more unsettling. "My House of Happiness that I builded for myself has begun to tumble down. I thought it was only temporary – till love came. And so it's proved. It's not that I don't know that what I call God is still there. He is. But he's more hidden. For days I have hardly been able to get on the plane where everything is peaceful. I feel that the next thing to do, is fight, mix up with men."

In working on the rewrite of the *Mountain* he had come across a quotation in a reference book "There is in man a Higher than Love of Happiness; he can do without Happiness, and instead thereof find blessedness!" It struck an immediate chord. "It's true. The Sidmouth revelation has not made me happier – but blesseder. I seem to be better in myself, to have been made naturally *gooder*. Will it last? I don't know."

He had been pondering for days the big question. "To go, or not to go, and live and fish at Sidmouth is deciding itself for me. I think I must. Miss Ada thinks so too, likewise Garnett...... Good God, I must go. Besides, there's health there, and strength. I don't think I've a greater ambition than to be a man, instead of an intellect and an emotional register stuck in a groggy body."[116]

But amidst all this emotional turmoil which was to keep him from sleep, there was always the safe haven of his writing. "If I hadn't written this I should have done a letter to Garnett. Perhaps this diary will spare my friends when I am bubbling over. Queer – I'm writing this with an idea in the bottom of my mind of someone seeing it, eventually. Is it the practice of writing to be read – or in hope of it? Does anybody or thing amuse me so much as myself? – I doubt that too...... What I ought to do with this diary is to take the essence of the day and develop that. If I write carefully here, it will improve my style. – Always my scribbling at the end! – my final cause."[117]

In the mornings he was hard at work on the second draft of the *Mountain* and rejoicing as he approached the end of the first and longest of its four books: "Thank goodness. I be zick o't."[118] In the afternoons he went for his usual downland walks and, despite the stormy autumnal weather, responded to them in his lyrical mystical mood. On the Wednesday he walked to Urchfont through Potterne and Easterton and noted "The edge of Salisbury Plain was like a glorious clean-topped wave, with the ricks etc. standing out most beautifully. At sunset the elms of Urchfont had that wonderful, serious, almost menacing, yet restful, dark green. They were like a threat indefinitely suspended over perfect repose."[119]

Next day was that of the first lecture and he woke with a bad head and painful liver to look out on the pouring rain. He took the shorter walk to Roundway, daydreaming most of the way on Sidmouth and the future. His plans were now becoming sharper – he would take two of Mrs Woolley's rooms, buy a drifter and work it with Bob.[120] This was one of his favourite walks and whenever he took it he gloried in the nature all around. "I saw a magnificent sunset over the dark trees, many of them pines, round the top end of Roundway Park. First one's eyes travelled over the arable fields with the sun glint in them, then stopped at the broad gloomy belt of trees and above them, shining behind and into them, was the glorious yellow sun. I always feel that the other world must be where the sun goes down – the melancholy, beautiful other world."[121]

He had prepared carefully his course of lectures on English Literature which began at the newly built Secondary Schools that evening. As an introduction and with carefully selected examples, he demonstrated the growth of poetry, the subtle differences between rhyme that isn't poetry, poetry that does not rhyme, and prose which is practically poetry. He proposed to develop the subject from its early period, studying an individual poet each week. To give himself some respite, each lecture would end with half an hour for comment and debate.[122] The audience was impressed this first evening but, as always on public occasions, he was unhappy with his own performance and blamed it on his neurasthenic head. As time went by, he found his weekly four shillings increasingly hard to earn and his audience – "my old maids" – increasingly opaque.[123]

The following morning, 19 October, at the end of a dismal week of see-sawing depression and elation, now on an upswing with the lecture over, he sent Garnett a list of his sufferings.

> Necessity of realising an investment.
> Neurasthenic head (mild), liver, and numb leg, all come back, to say nothing of pretty constant pain from that sprain.
> *Speaker* in nubibus.
> Annoyance extreme from relations.
> Dismal weather.
> Desire, beyond bounds, to be at Sidmouth.

> Failure of first lecture, owing to a bad head putting me in a dreamy incoherent state.
> Guide-book people not paid up yet, and bank balance £+/-0.
> Total failure of new digs from the point of mental comfort, and therefore ability to do decent work.[124]

If he stayed there much longer, another breakdown was imminent. As ever, the Tanners with their Martha-like devotion, came to his rescue. That afternoon they rushed over in their car and whisked him off to Ford House, from where, as he recuperated in the beauty and peace of the garden, he was able to negotiate with the Wyers a return to Pans Lane and security at the end of the following week.[125]

But there were two other developments to revive his spirits. On 23 October a much pregnant Margot came home to her master after their six weeks' parting. He met her at Salisbury station where she "delighted the porters by knocking off my spectacles, scratching my face all down and then licking the place to make it well. She's a dear thing".[126] Once she had given birth, he would be tied to Devizes and the puppies for a time, so he determined that he would make it to Sidmouth before then for a few days to work out his future. His spirits immediately rose. On the first Sunday evening back in the comfort of Pans Lane, his thoughts turned automatically to Bob and the life to come.

> Last night I wrote to Skemp, and told him I was going to Sidmouth to live with my fisherfolk. I find myself thinking of them very constantly. At times, when I'm very comfortable, I don't exactly look forward to the roughing it there, but I know I shall like the roughing it when it comes. I long to sit opposite Bob, chat to him, and admire him like a fine piece of art. Nothing attracts me so much as a strong man. I often feel I'd give up my intellect to be a fine animal with unsophisticated emotions. Indeed, it's they who give me the feeling of humility, and not my intellectual superiors. To be strong, to eat and to sleep, and to have the dependent affection there is among working families.... Yet perhaps it wouldn't be the same without my cultivated ability to make so much of all my experiences...... I wonder how much loneliness has to do with the love I, so to speak, cast about me.... How I yearn for a return of it! But perhaps everybody is the same. We are eternally alone, as G. de Maupassant says in *La Solitude.* But I have such a fighting desire to break through it. It is the basis of the artist, that. If I fight on.... Good work, if not assuagement, will follow, I believe.[127]

And the artist in him had been given a further fillip by a new suggestion from Pinker, ever on the look-out for fresh ports of call for his young client. In 1906 the publishing world had been riven by the setting up of the *Times* Book Club which sold used circulating library books at a fifth of the retail price. Northcliffe, with his eye on a takeover of *The Times*, thought the controversy might weaken sales of the Literary Supplement and that autumn decided to establish a rival supplement with the *Daily Mail*, soon to become known as "Books". He appointed the veteran Edmund Gosse as editor which proved a bad mistake. Gosse's literary interests were on altogether too exalted a plane for the humble readers of the *Mail* and he regarded the enterprise from the outset as somewhat *infra dig* and his £400 a year, almost half his House of Lords salary, as immoral earnings. After five months in the job he wrote to a friend: "......the labour of bringing out "Books" every week has been a very trying one, largely because I am an old dog to be set at a new trick...... I don't know how long I shall be able to keep it up. The dilemma is one which I heard put by a perfectly awful old woman, years ago, who was describing with horror the exposure of her person which some maiden had to make at a music-hall. 'What an awful position for a chaste young girl! Of course – she is generously paid to do it.' That is exactly my prostituted case."[128] This was not the attitude that had made the Northcliffe millions and Gosse was quietly retired that spring with a golden pay-off.

He was succeeded by Archibald Marshall who had been assistant editor since the beginning and had done most of the bread-and-butter work in getting the new enterprise off the ground. Marshall was a writer and journalist who had been a founding director of the publishing firm of Alston Rivers, which published Hueffer among others. Despite an at times sparkling, terse prose style, he never really made it as a novelist, though many children in the late 1920s were to be delighted by his sophisticated stories which ran A.A. Milne close.[129]

On 17 October Pinker drew Reynolds' attention to this new journalistic opportunity and advised him to send off some specimens post-haste to Marshall.[130] Marshall was pleased and sent Reynolds at once a copy of Dewar's *Faery Year* to review, a task he accomplished during the week's recuperation at Ford, though not without his usual first-night nerves: "His demand for 'a high standard of critical reviewing' rather gave me pen-fright, but I'm hopeful the thing will do".[131] In the event it did, and for the next few weeks Reynolds' spirits were constantly raised by the exciting thud of more books to review falling through his letterbox. As befitted a Northcliffe enterprise, "Books" paid well at three to four guineas a column and this reviewing was to be the mainstay of Reynolds' income until the supplement folded in the summer of 1907.[132]

Reynolds got on well with both Marshall and Gosse, and on his mid-week visits to London would often look in on the little office, lent by Northcliffe himself, which they shared together in Sackville Street. Marshall has left us with a small vignette of Reynolds as he popped into the office in the early months of 1907.

> He would come up to London sometimes, and I can see his stocky figure, in his blue serge suit which he kept for best, coming into the office now,

> his face beaming behind his round spectacles; and he would write me long letters, with lots of Devonshire in them.[133]

Though his reviewing and the planning of the *Ex Profundis* book were at the forefront of his mind, throughout that autumn and winter Reynolds plugged on with the rewrite of the *Mountain*. On 30 October he completed the first book, by the end of November had passed 60,000 words, on 18 December was reaching the end of the third book, and on 30 January 1907 he finally put down his pen.[134] On 30 October he sent the first book with some trepidation to Pinker to get an initial view. He felt the need to make a half apology for one of the weakest characters and to spell out the plot to come: "Miss Starkey, who seems rather a loose end in this book, has a great deal to do with bringing about the crisis at the end. Book II has Alec lionised in London at revivals, etc., and the Imperial Temple on the Holy Mtn. a fiasco; Book III shows Alec made mayor of Trowbury, the banquet etc,; and in Book IV, Miss Starkey confesses, finds out what Sir Pushcott Bingley is really up to, and Alec and Julia are married and the Mtn. moved back again."[135]

Pinker's response was lukewarm in the extreme. He was "much amused by it, but frankly I do not see where you are going with it. I think there are some passages where wayward fancy has developed into license, but I expect you will correct these before you finally hand over the book...... I shall be most curious to see the complete thing." This was more than Reynolds had bargained for and caught him on his rawest of nerves. He blasted off to Garnett

> Oh, be damn'd to him. Three years work. "Wayward fancy." "I shall correct." Compromise, slime over, like a Russian editor. I shall never understand what's license, and what's not. And compromise I won't, shan't, can't.
>
> It makes one think that the thing really has some originality. And you know, if I do that Ex Profundis book, I shall again tread on their beastly be-corned patent-leathered toes.
>
> My "wayward fancy". Why the devil do they say all effort to look straight at things is wayward fancy? It's just the same here when I tell 'em Margot's expecting to have pups, a simple, natural, beautiful thing to do. They look, and I hear 'em saying to themselves, "It's Sydney Reynolds – he can't help it – a wayward fellow". I suppose everyone will say, "Yes, I *am* amused; I should enjoy it; but it's so, so wayward." Oh, cuss 'em. But I'm not cussing very heartily, for I'm so much amused. I never thought so well of the *Holy Mountain* before. My satisfaction mounts to the point when the unsaleability of it appears a flea-bite. My dear Garnett, I'm sure the thing's worth reading; a point I was getting very doubtful on before. And if nobody'll have it, it shall become head among my penates.[136]

By the time he wrote to Pinker, he had calmed down a little and was keen to talk over the practical issue of whether further work on the rewrite would be justified in terms of time and money: "Thank you very much for your letter, your bolt in blue! My poor 'wayward fancy'!...... I want badly a clear notion of the odds; for I don't mind standing to lose, but I won't stake work on a three card trick. Besides, I can't put decent work just at present into a thing foredoomed."[137] At midday on 6 November he called into Pinker's office in Arundel Street and they had a quiet chat over the prospects. Pinker managed to persuade him that it was indeed worthwhile to go on with the rewrite and that the problems with Book 1 were not terminal. He left in an altogether more confident mood about the book. But this had been only a foretaste of the trials and tribulations both it and he had still to face.

He walked over to Gerrard Street for lunch with a sympathetic Garnett at the Mont Blanc. There he met, probably for the first time, Ford Hueffer whose most recent book, *The Heart of the Country*, Reynolds had reviewed in the *Speaker* in August, sympathetically but without adulation: "Mr. Hueffer has, from a new standpoint, made a valuable and most interesting contribution to country literature, but he has, it seems to me, just missed the quality of permanence."[138] Hueffer at this time was very active on behalf of his publishers, Alston Rivers, in and out of their office, advising, recommending books, acting in general as though he were on the board. At this time, he was looking for a new reader for the firm, and Garnett had suggested Reynolds to him. Hueffer, who did his own sponsoring of young literary talent, was immediately taken by Reynolds and tentatively offered the reading, subject to confirmation.[139] Reynolds, always suspicious of extravagant manners, was rather less taken with Hueffer, but came away from the lunch with the impression that the new appointment was almost in the bag.

A week later, he found that Pinker had organised for him an appointment to the advisory committee of a Literary Correspondence College which promised another tranche of regular and profitable work.[140] He spent a few anxious days wondering if the two opportunities might clash, but in the event neither of them came to anything. It was not, however, a propitious start to his relationship with Hueffer; the older man had made more than a half-promise but had failed to deliver. Reynolds, with good cause as it turned out, was never really to trust him again.

On 16 November he set off to Sidmouth for the planned week's stay. He arrived with a raging toothache and had two teeth out on the first day. It was a dull season and they didn't get out on the water once. He found Bob had not earned as much as a couple of pounds since his last visit and was growing fat with nothing to do but eat and sleep. But he made two new acquaintances who were to feature as secondary characters in *A Poor Man's House*. At the weekend he walked over to Budleigh Salterton to talk with the coastguard Battershall (the fictional Ned Luscombe) about the iniquity of the wholesale closing down of coastguard stations. And in the little back kitchen he came across Bob's mother-in-law, Grannie Pratt, the "dry old stick" with whom he had his own joking relationship, as though she were *his* mother-in-law too.

No matter how low the money or prospects for fishing, the excitement of his welcome back to the heart of the family was not any the less. "But it is good to be back in this little kitchen again and hold high disorder at one end of the table with Bobby, and jabber, and drink tea, and tease Bob's mother-in-law. There's no fishing, worse luck. The sprats and herrings haven't come in the bay yet. What a pleasure, though, there is in being well welcomed. I purr like a cat under it."[141]

He had come, however, with a special purpose in mind – to settle once and for all the future plans that had been buzzing through his brain for the past month. It was agreed that Bobby, who idolized him, should make the planned trip to Devizes to spend Christmas there. For the longer term, they had come to an amicable business arrangement. He would spend half the following year in Sidmouth, and was already in negotiation with Uncle Sam, now getting too old for fishing proper, to buy his drifter off him. He would go into partnership with Bob and Tom, taking half the proceeds for himself and the boat, leaving them with a quarter each where Uncle Sam had left only a third between them.[142]

On 22 November he had reluctantly to abandon the Woolleys and rush back to Devizes to deliver his next lecture – this time on Keats. His old maids were in typical good form. Full of the emotion of leaving Sidmouth once more, he must have waxed more than usually eloquent when he came to the account of how Keats' passion for Fanny Brawne had hastened the poet's death, prompting one lady to pipe up from the back of the hall "Are you speaking from your own experience, Mr. Reynolds?"[143]

The weekend brought a new trial for his nerves. His sister Dot, who now lived with her husband four miles away on their farm at Easton, near Bishops Cannings, was shortly to give birth. Ever since childhood his protective feelings for her had been strong and no pregnant father could have been more worried when the time came. He wrote to Garnett after the birth in a state of nervous exhaustion. "We have had a terrible time. In the week my sister became ill, and on Saturday her child decided to arrive. Things got no forrader by Sunday evening; it was evident they never would naturally; and a couple of doctors drove out (she lives near Tan Hill) with their surgical paraphernalia – and we waited – God, how we waited. Under chloroform the child was born, and so I'm constituted uncle of a niece. Both are alive, strange to say. We did not expect it. Comically enough, I stayed in here seeing and hearing the whole procedure with infernal imaginative power – not knowing that the worst of it took place under chloroform. Miss Bennett was there all night, calming poor Dot, guarding the door and chattering to the husband who had had no sleep for days and was showing signs of going off his head. But the child was brave: she always is when she's badly ill."[144] She was to die in childbirth eight years later.

He was in any case in a fragile, superstitious mood just then. Two weeks before, he had been reviewing Locke's *Beloved Vagabond* for the *Bookman* when suddenly he was confronted with a miserable episode from his past. "One of those curious little coincidences which give one such a shock, happened to-night. – You know bugs were my bane in Paris? Well, just as I was reading about The Beloved Vagabond's appartement au cinquième in the rue des Saladiers, there, on p.137, was a squashed dead bug! Strange, wasn't it?"[145] It was followed by an even more sinister experience. On the morning of his niece's birth, one of the most popular and cheerful of the Devizes postmen, Walter Stone, died of consumption, then a common occupational hazard of all postal workers, as mailbags carried in the sputum off the streets. That Sunday evening, while waiting for news of his sister, he saw the dead postman walking through the town.[146]

He was becoming overworked and heading for trouble. Each day he ground out the *Mountain* before breakfast, followed by five books a week to review for the *Mail*, still a regular supply for the *Speaker* and the odd bundle from the *Bookman*.[147] A week into December and he collapsed under the strain. After a few days in bed, he wrote to Pinker in the usual apologetic mood that followed his collapses: "I'm sorry, and ashamed, to say that I've been more or less ill, with an article requested by the Mail itself and a lot of work on hand for the Speaker – none being done. The Bookman sent me 19(!) beastly educational books to review in one week, and that coupled with the reaction from great anxiety and a lot of rows.... Isn't it like me to go wrong in the middle of a good literary flutter? I wonder your patience doesn't give out with these eternal forced holidays of mine."[148]

It was not just the strain of overwork and reaction to his sister's illness, but also the desperate feeling of loneliness that came upon him each year in the run up to Christmas. The only saving grace this year was the visit of Bobby from Sidmouth: "A small fisher boy is coming up for Christmas. We are going to imitate a family circle and dine in state on a bunny rabbit."[149]

To Garnett he was even more open about his feelings. "Bobby is coming up on Saturday. That will be very good. I'm not high and dry enough to do without the material evidences of affection. We English admire a dignified reserve, but God! the price we pay for it; and then we can't chuck it off when we would. You'll smile wisely behind your gig-lamps and say, Reserve, indeed – Reynolds! But, you know, the nearest I get to the opposite is to take my silly self and diagnose it and exhibit the result like a zoological dissected rabbit. My sort of reserve is a quickset hedge round the real garden that I wish to God some one could break through, only no one can. And ten to one I'd prosecute them for trespass." And he ended on a plaintive note: "Prithee write a Christmas epistle that shall make one feel less like a worm that has strayed into a puddle."[150]

The call did not go unheard. Just before Christmas there came from the Cearne a cheering, friendly letter covering a volume of Nietzsche. Three days before Christmas he met an excited Bobby at Salisbury station and took him back to Pans Lane. It was a strenuous few days chasing after a little boy perpetually on the move and finally in the evening tucking him up in bed in the small front bedroom where he did his writing. And despite the keen feelings of rejection by the world which Christmas always brought on, he was given on Christmas day one of the best presents he would ever receive: "Christmas morning, Bobby paid me the sweetest compliment I've ever had. The night before I quite convinced him about Santa Claus, and he remains so convinced. In the morning, however, before it was light, he called across the room from his little bed in the corner: 'You'm like Father Christmas, Misser Reynels, 'cause you'm kind'. Isn't that sweetly thought out and put?"[151] He wrote it into the fictional Christmas with the Widgers in *A Poor Man's House*, and added the conclusive rider "Jimmy doesn't know how kind he is to me. And I don't suppose it would do him any good to tell him".[152]

He took Bobby back to Sidmouth on Boxing Day to the usual welcome. "Yesterday we came down here – came home, as I feel it. This little kitchen has become as homelike as the propinquity of my bookcase. And a welcome.... Isn't a good welcome a good thing? Small kids, calling out and laughing, grimy paws to shake, chattering womenfolk, and some people calling in to see me and take up the old lines of teasing. By God, it's good!"[153]

The day after Boxing Day he went walking in the afternoon on High Peak and was startled by a charge of shot whistling round his ears and spattering into the ground all about. "Pleasant feeling. Sole impulse – say Damn! and turn my back, which I did."[154] In the evening he wrote to Garnett, resting on the kitchen table. "Bob has gone out to sea. I wanted to, but thought better of it on so cold a night for the first time this visit. A queer scene is going on here. Mrs. Bob one side of the fire with a ricked back, little maid with toothache in the courting chair, and two others of the girls scattered round. And they are holding a trial of all the pieces of mischief they've committed during the day. 'I didn't!' says the defendant. 'You lie!' says the jury; and then one of the jury is hauled out for trial on some other piece of mischief".[155]

He was still smarting in a prickly way from his Christmas, and the long lament he wrote to Garnett that evening stands for the hurt feelings of all Christmases, those past and still to come. And as in all such laments to his friends, he punctuated the asperity of the self-pity with a call to look on the bright side which never carried quite the same conviction.

> "I wrote to you Xmas evening to thank you for your letter and the Nietzsche; but as I had the hump Xmas day, I stuck the letter in the fire next morning. In fact, I was rather hurt in spirit. I gave several people presents – because I wanted to, of course, and had the pleasure in the giving of 'em, – and ran myself in, like a fool, for about seven pounds. Anyhow, a good many people accepted things, and thanked me, most of

'em, quite sincerely. But it didn't occur to anybody at all, except Bob and you, to send me any little token, present, or Christmas letter. If it had occurred to them, they'd have done it, I know; but it didn't occur. 'Twasn't that I wanted the things, but I should have liked the notion to have occurred to a few people; and it made me feel devilishly out of the running – intensely like the spectator I am mostly, and don't like being. Beastly lonely. 'Twasn't until after I had written the now cremated letter, I realised how much in the way of kindness I'd had during the year, and what a thing it was for Dad and Mam Woolley to send Bobby all the way up to Wiltshire and trust him with me; and for Bobby, aged seven, to come, right up to Salisbury by himself. I realise now that I've had much more than mere presents, but it took the day to do it in. And now I don't yet see why it didn't occur to a few people that one or two twopenny-ha'penny things would have pleased me beyond measure. Why didn't it occur? What notion of me do I give them? – There, I believe, I'm still a little sore – feeling aloof. I want everything, I suppose."[156]

But the herring season was in full swing and the excitement and physical exertion soon put paid to the Christmas blues. That night and the following one Bob and Tom, in Uncle Sam's drifter, caught next to nothing, but on 29 December they took Reynolds out with them, despite the cold, and had the catch of the season – 22,000 herring brought safely to land. They had only been able to carry the contents of five-and-a-half of their seven nets, and even then staggered home with the boat less than a foot above the water line. They came back to land for a heroes' welcome: "Then we walked up beach, heroes of the largest catch, so to speak, calling on townsfolk (who had come to the beach) as of right, to help us wind the boat up. The delight of feeling we'd done good work, and had a right to expect help! I came in house, yelled the catch upstairs to 'thic Mam Woolley', cleaned herrings and cooked them for Bob's and my second (1.30 A.M.) supper – and, with the frying pan in one hand (but I didn't realise the comicalness of it at the moment), I started reviewing "Five Italian Shrines" for the *D.M.* with t'other. There's a situation for you, inadvertently concocted!"[157] The review of Waters' book duly appeared in the *Daily Mail* three weeks later, with some pungent criticisms that showed few traces of its unlikely genesis.[158] But the story of the frying pan review was to regale the author's new friends for many years to come.

The immensity of the catch and the relative poverty of the remuneration for it brought Reynolds up for the first time against the iniquities of the fishery markets which over the next few years he was to do so much to change. They sold the herrings locally for 18 shillings a thousand, but by the time they reached Exmouth they were selling on for 29 shillings, and the next day they were up to 48. Reynolds immediately sized up the situation. "These Sidmouth men do not make use of wire or telephone. They have no London agent. They go on selling to the cheating local buyers, ' 'cause that's what us has always done.' At the same time they know they could make much higher prices if they only set to work, and laid out a little in communicating with the big markets, instead of letting the middlemen and buyers do it. If Uncle Sam sells me the drifter, I shall use every means of learning prices, and bargain by telephone, and if possible start a London agent similar to a literary agent. And we'll see if that little remnant of business in me, that you so despise, can't make Sidmouth fish fetch proper prices."[159]

Two days later, still buoyed up by the catch, the Woolley family and its new member celebrated the best New Year he had ever had. With Bob and Mam, he sat up late drinking execrable port and ginger wine and sang the year in with sea songs – "sad things, but vigour infusing".[160] They went out into the little back garden and looked across the roofs to Saint Nicholas' Church to hear the clock strike midnight. It is the highly charged emotional ending to *A Poor Man's House* with the sharp little anti-German sting in its tail.

> At a minute or two before twelve by the clock, the three of us went out to the back door. When the cats had scuttled away, the narrow walled-in garden was very still. By the light of the stars, shining like points in the deep winter heavens, I could see the beansticks, the balks of wood and the old masts and oars. I could also smell the drain. Tony, in his stockinged feet, leant on his wife's shoulder while he raised first one foot from the cold stones, and then the other. We were a little hushed, with more than expectancy. So we waited; to hear the church clock strike and to welcome in the New Year.
>
> And we waited until Tony said that his feet were too cold to stay there any longer. The church clock struck – *ting-tang, ting-tang* – in the frosty air.... A quarter past! The New Year had been with us all the while. It was our German-made kitchen clock had stopped.[161]

Some of the same mood of peace and thankfulness for the wonders the past year had brought was still with him when early on 2 January he went down to the front to see if the sea were still there. "This morning I was out at 6 to see such a spectacle – the ghostly dead-looking town under the misty moon, with the breakers rushing against it. One never seems to weary of watching the rollers. Each one gathers itself chiefly at one spot, for its most furious hurlment. I thought I had never seen such a symbol of death and life, as the dead-asleep town, hardly real, standing quite still in front of the madly-living breakers. They seemed to typify also the way one hurls one's own self against things and eternity – the feeling one has very really, that being part of things one can never really be beaten any more than a wave can be obliterated."[162]

And typically, he punctures the spell with the simplest of personal admissions: "By which you'll perceive that having hauled that up out of the subconscious, I must be much better again. And so I am, and ought to be. It's here one has not so much to be perpetually fighting to preserve one's own identity. Therefore one is rested most, and is exceedingly happy...... This wandering, scratching cat has found a fireside where it can lie down and purr."[163]

At last the power of the Sidmouth experience, reinforced by the new excitement and emotion of herring drifting on this latest visit, was beginning to filter through into the writing cells of his brain. Throughout the autumn he had been wrestling with the content and form of the *Ex Profundis* book. He had now decided on the form – intermittent journal – and on much of the content – the episodes leading up to his breakdown, the mystical images summoned up from the bottom of the pit, and the slow quasi-religious recovery. As early as October he had realised that the book must now end with the Sidmouth revelation, but he was not thinking, or daring to think, of the Sidmouth experience as a book in itself.[164]

The catalyst was Archibald Marshall supported by Gosse. Much impressed by Reynolds' first reviews for "Books", Marshall had asked him in early December for an article which in all the traumas of that month he struggled to deliver.[165] The *Mail* kept up the pressure. "Marshall has written me a most decent letter, saying he and Gosse like my stuff, and asking me if I mind going on doing *short* articles for them; and saying he hopes it will lead to something better. It's the second time he's said that, and I'm agog to know what it means."[166]

Now the buoyancy of Reynolds' post-Christmas letters from Sidmouth had led to a new, and more explicit, commission. "The *Daily Mail* has asked me through Marshall to let them have some sketches of fishing from the inside point of view. *Voilà de la chance*! Marshall's suggestion to them – I asked him if any other of his reviewers cooked herrings with one hand and reviewed books on Italian sculpture with the other. He's been exceedingly kind. It appears I satisfy Gosse, and am the only man Marshall has recommended to him".[167]

He asked Garnett to let him borrow back his two latest long letters describing in detail the recent herring trips. He was excited but perplexed as to how to set about it. "Well, I'm hopelessly stumped as to what form to do the things in. My so enormous mass of material is not nearly digested – my thoughts and impressions are not yet ready to haul out of the (to most people) unintelligible dialect in which I think them. If I take them out prematurely they lose their savour. At present, I'm doing a humorous sketch (from life) – "The Shooting Star goes Herring Drifting" – in which only the circumstances, setting forth, absence, and return are dealt with – not the drifting itself. Then, probably, an article informing how herring and mackerel drifting is done – material details etc. – in 20–25 ft. open boats. Then a sketch of an ordinary night like last night; then "The Catch of the Season". To produce the atmosphere and at the same time, without spoiling the atmosphere, to work in enough information to make the process understandable, is the difficulty. What form to use? I am inclined to put it down as a sort of hourly diary, supposed to be jotted down throughout the night."[168]

A week later, he was none the clearer. "I'm in a vile fix with the articles – to find the precise narrative form I want. My pride in being a useful member of a drifter's crew won't let me write like a journalist, an outsider, a novice, experiencing the thing. No, I'm damn'd if I will!"[169]

By 13 January, four days before he was to return to Devizes, the planned articles had developed a new dimension.

> "I have a good idea for a successor to the neurasthenia book – *Letters from a Poor Man's House – esquisses de la vie intime.* 'Twould be no wise considered a breach of hospitality here; that I know. Approached from a non-philanthropic, non-patronising attitude, it should be interesting. It's the last place anyone would expect a me-like person to find most homelike. But I do. I suspect that in the essentials of life they have much the advantage of me – for all my this, that and t'other. – Don't you think there's something good in the idea – treated with a quite scientific tentativeness?"[170]

The seed had been sown. His big book was on the move.

EIGHT

Marketing the Mountain 1907

For Stephen Reynolds 1907 was a year of transition – between two homes and between two books. He divided his time almost precisely between Devizes and Sidmouth in keeping with his plan to share both the sea and the Downs. He spent a month in the spring with the Woolley family and stayed with them again for the whole of a long summer (mid May to mid October) taking just a few days breather in Devizes in July. Inevitably, much of the ecstatic emotion of 1906 had worn off as he settled down to the routine of life in Bedford Square. He discovered he could feel lonely and out of sorts even there.

Devizes was still for him the place to which he could retreat for spells of concerted writing, free from the distractions of sea and beach, the wild and friendly children, and the noise of Bedford Square; but by the middle of the year, as his income from ephemeral writing began to dry up once more, he had to face the practical reality that someone with his bank balance could not continue to maintain two establishments forever. In planning a long-term life in Sidmouth, he had always hoped to earn just enough from writing to buy him the freedom to sail and fish, and thereby regain his health. But by midsummer, these plans had turned on their heads. It was the meagre income from fishing and boating that kept him alive and able to press on with his books. Since he could not fish in Devizes, Devizes would have to go.

In his writing life, he found his attention torn between the book he had just completed and the one he was struggling to begin. Throughout the year he fought a new emotional battle – to get *The Holy Mountain* into print. But as he lurched from one publisher's rejection to the next, he was all the time steadily working away at the book that was to make his name. And as the year went on he found, much to his surprise, that he could write, and write well, in that first floor front room overlooking the noisy and bustling square, with the salt spray in his nostrils and in his ears the constant grind of surf on shingle.

He had packed so much, both physically and emotionally, into the two week New Year's stay at Sidmouth, it was a major wrench when on 17 January he went home to Devizes "to spout on English Fiction to my old maids".[1] He had spent the last few days of the holiday writing furiously the four fishery sketches requested by the *Daily Mail*, and had in the process almost knocked himself up once again.[2] There was a dismal welcome for him back at Pans Lane – the first of the sketches had already been rejected for what appeared the most trivial of reasons. "It was done for the Mail, but now they say they can't do with sketches containing dialect. Disappointing. I've got to hack about the other things I've done no end, and as I always speak dialect myself on fishing boats it's most difficult to keep it out of fishing sketches".[3]

And within a very few days he was feeling homesick again for Sidmouth. He wrote to Garnett: "Back these three days and far from well pleased. A feeling that the savour of life is very much wanting. Cans't thou explain, O Seer? What is it that pours contentment into one's subconscious self down there? I believe it is being among people fond of one – which quickly translates itself through the consciousness to the physical."[4]

With his usual discipline, however, he got straight down to work and spent the next two weeks hammering out the rewrite of the final chapters of the *Mountain*. It was with a massive sense of relief, as of a major milestone passed, that he told Pinker on 30 January "You may really believe it: The 'Holy Mountain' is done; every word of it rewritten. Unbelievable! after having the thing on one's mind for 2½ years."[5] The following week he was up to London for two days, lunching with Garnett at the Mont Blanc and calling in on Pinker to take stock of the position now that the *Mountain* was finished and the new book was boiling in his mind. He pressed Pinker to redouble his efforts to find the long-desired *causerie* which would give him the space to write his new book.

Alone in Pans Lane once more, he was suddenly assailed by feelings of guilt which tended to sweep over him whenever he put pressure on others for help. Always in his mind there lurked the fear of retribution that had been instilled by long years of dealings with his father. He remembered all too painfully that when his finances had been at their lowest ebb the previous year, Pinker with his usual generosity had offered for the time being to waive his commissions. Had he now overstepped the mark, had he pressed him *too* hard? He wrote a letter of contrition which was also a confession of dependence, emotional as much as economic.

> Since seeing you I've been uncomfortably aware that my jogging you, as I did, over the much-desired causerie was very ungraceful and inopportune, coming so soon after your getting me the Mail Supplement job, which has been a godsend, and after your kindness over the commissions, which really meant ever so much more to me than simply the money-value of it. Not that I don't want to get hold of a causerie – I do, because I think 'twould be a congenial stand-by; but please believe I'm not so ungrateful as I must have given you cause to think.
>
> I suppose when I've got my finger properly into the literary pie, I shall be able to look back and say, Yes, 'twas the devil of a struggle. But I doubt many struggles have had such good friends to help them through. When I first came to you, I was resolved on having purely businesslike relations – no commendation or encouragement for kindness' sake, but market-value topmost. You've broken my resolution for me and I don't know how to thank you. Perhaps you don't quite realise what all these things

> mean to a depressionable fool living a long distance away from the centre where his luck is being decided.[6]

Pinker gave a lifetime of such kindnesses to impoverished authors, and in return received more brickbats than bouquets. Perhaps Reynolds himself did not quite realise what such a letter might mean to the "Pink Spider" at the centre of his London web. It was a typical Reynolds exchange, which tied the two men more closely together in bonds they were certainly to need for the trials that lay ahead.

With the *Mountain* in typing and temporarily out of mind, Reynolds spent much of February in Pans Lane wrestling with the format of his new book on the Sidmouth experience. He wrote an explanatory preface and sent two versions of it off to Garnett in the hope of an official blessing on the launch of the enterprise. He was dismayed to receive, almost by return, a startling castigation of the kind Garnett saved only for his friends. He did not mince his words. The preface was packed with juvenile egotism of the worst kind and simply would not do.

Reynolds was in a quandary about the book. He hadn't really thought it through and knew, deep down, that the unhappy preface was merely a blind attempt to get the thing moving. Rather shaken, he went straight on to the defensive: "You hit hardish. But you're quite right. Why I sent you *two* versions of the Preface and my notes, I don't know. Must have been very fuddled. Anyhow, almost as soon as sent, I didn't like the thing, and decided it was wrong and superfluous; only it was too far gone to recall and destroy, and I was expecting to hear from you. It was knocked on the head, and now it's buried. Indeed, you have, so to speak, put a capper to my own rather damnable meditations."[7]

It was an inauspicious start. He was still undecided as to form, and the sting of Garnett's words had made him half inclined to throw the whole thing up. "Whether letter or diary form, I don't know. It would be more sporting to stick to the letters and *grind* 'em into something decent. Or whether to go on with the book at all.... I don't know, and for the moment don't much want to. In any case, you shall see the thing when it's done, and if it isn't right it shall be torn up. The material is too good to use less than well." And a chance reference by Garnett to him as "patron and discoverer of the fisherfolk life" had put him very much on the alert. "Now *discoverer*, very well; but if there's any *patronage* in the finished thing, in the total effect, promise please to tell me, because I shall have failed in expression, and put down what I don't want to say, and won't appear to say, not if it were the only thing wrong in an otherwise decent book. When I say that on the whole I believe their lives and themselves to be better than the lives of the likes of me, I mean what I say precisely, and the Lord preserve me from believing what I believe in that direction because, in one or two respects, I have the advantage of them, or for the sake of a book. So help me avoid it please."[8]

Though Garnett's words had hurt, and despite the setback with the *Mail* fishing sketches, all four of which had now been rejected, he was still in a determined mood: "I believe I've hopped lightly into a losing fight; tried to fly and flopped into a dunghill; laid my odds on a crock diseased – but that's no reason for giving in, is it?"[9]

When two days later the completed typescript of the *Mountain* came back from London, he hesitated for a moment before sending it to Garnett. "Do you care for me to send it as we arranged? Perhaps you've had enough of my stuff lately?"[10] With Garnett in this mood, he naturally feared the worst. On 8 March, very much to his surprise, there came from his friend a letter full of praise for the strength of the satire, the facility of the writing and with only one minor reservation – a passing reference to the coarseness of the physical detail which Garnett thought might harm the prospects of the book. Garnett knew Reynolds had already arranged that Seccombe, the initial progenitor, should try it on Constable, for whom he worked as reader. But failing that, he was keen to get in on the action himself: "If Constables don't take it I should like to advise Duckworth, strongly, to take it up – but I daresay you can do better."[11]

Garnett's reaction was more than Reynolds had ever dared to expect – "too good to be true, it seems to me" – and he wrote back with a genuine sense of surprise and relief: "How can I thank you for your generous praise of the Mountain? I don't think any success it may possibly have will give me nearly the pleasure your letter has just done. In fact, I know it won't." But as if to compensate for this unexpected praise of the book, he let slip a little of his own private misgivings about it, lamenting the facility with which he could write up his hates in contrast to his loves, the dilemma he now faced with the Sidmouth experience he was battling to turn into words. "The real defect of the book, I believe, is that the motive power is hatred and irritation – West Country hatred, which you mayn't understand or credit, for it's a sort of thing that tracks its object t'other side of death, never relents and has wonderful patience to bide its time. That is the galling miserable thing to me – that I can express my hatred of what I hate, and picture it, but I can't express my love of things and mankind and I can't picture what I love. The beast in me bellows finely but the damn'd angel can hardly twitter. At the back of my mind I sort of hate the *Holy Mountain*, because, really, it's the success and expression of failure – a sort of lie."[12]

Yet he had been stirred sufficiently by Garnett's praise to look upon the final step of publication as almost a foregone conclusion. "Constable's have the promise of refusal, and if they don't take it, I should much like to send it to Duckworth's with your backing. My own impression is that for the £.s.d. part of the matter, Alston Rivers would be the people to give it the right sort of rather noisy splash, but Constable or Duckworth more satisfying in other ways and probably, in the end, all round."[13] It was a show of confidence that the real world was soon to shatter.

On 12 March he went up to London for the usual Mont Blanc lunch and to look round for the chance of more work. In the morning he called on H.W. Massingham, the newly appointed editor of the revamped *Speaker*, now retitled the *Nation*, to discuss two pieces of work accepted by the old management but recently returned, and the general prospects for future contributions.[14] Massingham, like other editors before him, fell for the eager intelligence of the young man and promised some reviewing work. A week later he sent Reynolds a volume of Maeterlinck to review which produced once again the usual first-night nerves: "he gave me a bad attack of literary stage fright by writing and exhorting me to do it carefully."[15] The review was never printed, causing Reynolds considerable irritation for some weeks, and for the time being he and the *Nation* gradually drifted apart.[16]

In the afternoon he called in on Pinker for a round-up discussion of his current work, including the prospects for the *Mountain* about to be placed before Constable. He was planning to return shortly to Sidmouth and this would be the last opportunity for some time for a face-to-face with his agent.[17]

There was much talk of the *Mountain* at the Mont Blanc that day. Garnett had brought along the typescript to return by hand and was loud in its praise. Ford Hueffer was there to join in the congratulation, but sadly Thomas Seccombe, the original progenitor, had had to cancel at the last minute.[18] But there was a new face at the table in the upstairs room. Reynolds saw for the first time a tall, slim figure, loose-limbed and athletic looking, with fair hair worn long, a sensitive mouth and large grey, dreamy eyes – at once melancholy, yet fearless and steady. He had all the appearance of the young poet. He was a poet – but no one knew it as yet. It was Edward Thomas.

For the past two years, Thomas had been a fairly frequent attender at the Mont Blanc. Until recently, he had lived with Helen, his wife, and their two children in an old farmhouse in Kent within easy walking distance of the Garnetts at the Cearne, and the two families had got to know each other well. The previous December he had moved from Kent to Berryfield Cottage at Ashford near Petersfield, close to Bedales where his seven-year-old son, Merfyn, was at school.

He was then just 29, three years older than Reynolds, and although it was ten years since he had published his first book, their writing careers had reached a very similar stage. Thomas kept himself and his family alive on a constant diet of book reviews and journalism, interspersed with the editing of anthologies and similar works. He was a perfectionist in his writing as in his daily life, often spending days more on reviews than the meagre payments justified; but as a result had built for himself a reputation of some distinction as a literary critic.

Though in many respects more unworldly than Reynolds, he shared with him the constant anxiety of where the next meal was to come from, heightened by a sense of guilt that he was not providing adequately for wife and children. The Thomases had had many desperate moments in their early marriage. Both men shared too a propensity to depression, though rather different in kind. Reynolds could fight through his with hard work and strong discipline. Thomas's were deeper and hung constantly over him. They could only be exorcised by going off alone into the country, accompanied frequently by thoughts of suicide.

This commonality of feeling and sensitivity must have communicated itself early on at this first meeting. Both were good walkers and talkers. They made plans to meet again. Thomas was to spend the following weekend with a friend in Chepstow, walking round Tintern and the ruins of Chepstow Castle. Reynolds invited him to drop in on Pans Lane for a few days on his way back. Thomas had spent many blissful childhood holidays at his grandmother's in Swindon and shared strongly with Reynolds a love for Wiltshire and the Downs. Though they had met for only an hour, he immediately agreed.

At midday on 18 March Thomas arrived in Devizes and Reynolds whisked him straight off for his favourite fifteen-mile walk, west to east across the rolling heights of Tan Hill, where the strong March winds bit through them, down to All Cannings at the foot, and back through Coate along the beautiful open trackway that emerges by Devizes Green. It was the first of many downland walks together. The next day they walked twice as far, the wind still bursting about their ears, through Savernake Forest to Marlborough and back, Thomas in his usual manner consulting the Ordnance Survey at every turn of trackway and congratulating himself that they never once missed their path. They got on well together. Thomas made a cryptic note in his diary: "Reynolds good company".[19]

On the final day, they took a gentle stroll through Urchfont, Ridgeway and Easterton. The wind had finally dropped, and after dinner on a very calm evening, they wrote letters together in Reynolds' bed-sitting room and talked into the night in a mystical vein of joy and life, of Methodism and the immanence of God.[20] The three days of shared walking and talking had brought them very close. When Reynolds on the Thursday morning saw Thomas off on the London train, he knew this was the start of another important friendship.

It was to remain strong for the next three years, finally tapering off as Reynolds grew more distant from Garnett and made only rare appearances at the Mont Blanc. But in those first three years they were constant correspondents, Thomas faithfully recording in his diary the flow of incoming and outgoing letters. Sadly, none of them has survived to give us an inside view of their friendship. All of Reynolds' letters went up in smoke in Thomas's back garden in July 1916 as he cleared the decks in preparation for the Western Front. All of Thomas's to Reynolds were allowed to moulder away in an attic in the 1930s. We shall never know their quality.

Reynolds was still longing to be back in Sidmouth and on 27 March, with considerable joy, he set off for a three-week break with Bob and his family. There was an expectant reception party waiting for him at the little station on the outskirts of the town. "Whilst the train was drawing up at the platform, I noticed the people moving and looking downwards as if dogs were running wild amongst them. Then I saw two whitish heads bobbing about in the crowd. It was Jimmy [*Bobby*] and another boy come to meet me."[21] They had come, as he told Garnett, with concrete expectations: "These children have a delightful combination of naivety and artfulness. There was a bevy of them to meet me at the station – some there under the impression I was going to charter a cab – or an omnibus – to ride down!"[22] But it was not to be. As they walked with him down the long hill towards the sea front in a rather sulky silence, he realised how great had been their disappointment and vowed to make it up to them next time.

He was soon back in the familiar kitchen, picking up exactly where he had left off in January. He made a new friend – the children's little cousin, Vera Channing, the five-year-old daughter of Bob's sister Alice who had given birth in the Square the night of his arrival the previous September. He gave her the nickname Straighty, to distinguish her from her curly-headed sister, the two-year-old Laura. She was tongue-tied to begin with, but soon had him in her thrall.

> Midway through tea, Straighty crept into the kitchen. "What do yu want?" shouted Grannie Pinn. "Bain't there enough kids yer now?" Straighty stood in the centre of the kitchen, sucking three fingers and looking shyly at me from beneath her tousled tow-coloured hair.
> "You've not forgotten me, Straighty?" I asked. "You're not frightened of me, are you?"
> "Go an' speak to 'en proper," commanded Grannie Pinn. "Wer's yer manners, Dora?"
> "*Yu* didn' speak to me proper, Grannie Pinn! Wer's yours?"
> "Aw, my dear soul! Now do 'ee shut up wi' yer chake!"
> Straighty remained sucking her fingers in the middle of the kitchen. She seemed about to cry. Quite suddenly, her eyes brightened. She glided over to me, put her wet fingers round my neck ("Dora!" from Mrs Widger), and gave me a big kiss on the chin. Then she told me all about everything, sitting with her head on my shoulder in the old courting chair.
> A tiny little episode, I grant; but very sweet.
> "That's your mark?" Grannie Pinn shouted. "You'll hae to wait for she!"
> Straighty is established as my mark, and takes her duties, as she has learnt to conceive them, with amusing seriousness. She will not let me go out through the Square without being told where I am off to, nor let me return in house until I tell her where I have been. At the beginning

> of every meal we hear her creeping up the passage; see her yellow hair against the door-post. By the end of the meal she has summoned up courage to claim a kiss. "Now be off tu your mother!" says Mrs Widger.[23]

He told Garnett somewhat wrily: "I'm coming in for a good deal of chaff over my "mark" whom Gran Pratt, Mrs W's mother, has been saying for a long time she was going to find. They don't understand how a fellow my age can be not in love with some girl or other".[24]

Now that he had started the book, each new experience became a competitor for inclusion in it. Two weeks after his arrival back, Henrietta Cordey, Mam Woolley's home help from Bedford Square, began preparations for her confinement – a daughter, Violet, born on 18 April. The plight of this woman, with a lazy and unreliable husband, who did not know how her children would survive while she was "up over", stirred Reynolds deeply, and he wrote her courage into the book in the guise of Mrs Yarty.

But despite the abundance of material all around him, still the writing would not flow. "'The Poor Man's House' is going again – more out of cussedness than anything else. It's damnably difficult. The material is so overwhelming and unsorted – and the way of putting it an utterly unsolved problem. So I'm going to drive ahead, let all so-called artistic considerations go to the devil, and trust to luck. Then perhaps a chunk o' summat'll produce itself. Damn art! There, I've said it. Cast me into outer darkness if you like. Art, isolated, conscious, *per se*, is an impertinence to life."[25]

After a week of sunny weather, with the distractions of fishing and sailing, he was still in despairing mood about the book.

> We've an end of the weather. The sea has got rough again, so there's neither fishing nor sailing. The sudden summer knocked me up and gave me a fine dose of neuralgia which wasn't much helped by hopeless grovellings over the Poor Man's House book. I *can't* get the damn'd thing to go; can't get any spring into it. It's horribly stodgy and disconnected. I seem to be putting down such ordinary every-day sort of stuff, and hardly dare hope that what seems ordinary to me, now, won't seem so much so to other people. I've run through my first wind, and haven't got second wind yet; – know too much for a first swift impression, and haven't made the thing cohere into a deeper second impression. The 6000, or so, words I've ground out seem dreadfully inadequate.[26]

But there was something else preying on his mind which was disturbing the fluency of his writing. In addition to the neurasthenic symptoms, which came and went, he had throughout his life battled against physical weaknesses which belied his outwardly strong and sturdy frame – bad digestion, a troublesome liver, weak lungs that had just survived tubercular infection, varicose veins in his legs, and piles. It was the latter that were now giving him most trouble, and he was due to go to London to repeat an operation he had had on them some years before.

He was now beginning to fret about the ordeal he would face in a fortnight's time. "I know that being compulsorily in London with Spring outside will madden me. Indeed, that, and what I may dream under the anaesthetic – I always do dream horrors that leave a stain for days afterwards – are the two things that bother me. The last time I had nitrous oxide I went through this very operation with such vividness that I can remember every detail at the present moment. 'Tisn't nice to dream like that".[27] It was only the second time he had written to Garnett from Sidmouth in a self-pitying mood: "Write when you have time. Things seem rather adrift".[28]

The problem was more, however, than just fear of the surgeon's knife. All his life, Reynolds was anxious to be in control – both of situations and, more importantly, himself. He knew how dangerous an out of control Reynolds could be. He had recovered from the breakdown of 1903 by a firm exercise of his will; but controlling psychiatric symptoms was relatively easy. For his physical symptoms he had set himself a rigid plan – to become a whole man by the age of 30. The tough outdoor régime of fishing and sailing at Sidmouth was a crucial part. What frustrated him most of all, however, was that so often the physical symptoms could be neither regimented nor explained.

As he waited for his appointment in London, new varicose veins started to appear in his legs, which seemed to make the limited operation he was facing even more pointless. Garnett sent him a comforting letter and suggested bandaging his legs to give the veins support. Reynolds was in more buoyant mood when he came to reply, but still deeply frustrated by the perplexing behaviour of his body. "As for the veins and bandages – confound bandages! I'm quite enough medically supported as it is. It's not the veins or any pain that worry me, but the fact of having them; the falling short of health, not the ill-health. I see the causes and conditions of neurasthenia, and rub on quite hopefully, and successfully too; but I can't find out what controls the tendency to varicosity. If I could, I should set about remedying it and be quite satisfied. It's so disappointing at the end of a long successful struggle, just as I was saying: 'In two years you'll be a whole man, S.R.'. Perhaps the operation will mend things a bit. But what weakness, to depend on knives, anaesthetics and bandages. I'm bitterly ashamed of the necessity."[29]

His lifelong hypochondria was not fear of death, but rather the identification of illness with moral inadequacy, perhaps the legacy of a childhood dominated by a healthy, outgoing father who would not tolerate weaklings.

One sign that he was now in a more resilient mood was his relaxed reaction to news of the reception of the *Mountain* at Constable. "Seccombe says one of their partners has read the *H.M.* 'and laughed over it, but thought the satire rather too full-blooded – timid folk, publishers.' I almost hope they don't take it. I don't want timorous folk at the back of the book, nor an apologetic attitude. If it's not boldly marketed, it will bounce back and hit me."[30]

It was not a good omen, but he could afford to be more detached about the *Mountain* because now the *Poor Man's House* was fully engaging his time and his emotions. He had written a further 4000 words in the preceding week and was beginning to feel sufficiently comfortable with it to seek an urgent first reaction from Garnett.

> I'm going to send you, as soon as I've done a little more, the first ten or twelve thousand words of the Poor Man's House. You'll see I've adopted the journal form. Also I'm doing it by what I call the cumulative method – trying to picture the book as one whole, into which the scattered details shall ultimately fall. So, a good deal in the first 12000 words is written with a view to what's to come, and in its place is more or less irrelevant. But if I succeed in clinching the book, it will ultimately fall into place all right. As you'll see, the diary part is a lot more objective than *Ryecroft*. I propose to write a very short prologue and an epilogue to contain one or two final conclusions out of place in the diary part – stating for one thing, my firm belief that on the whole, in the widest sense, the poor make a better thing of life, and are evolved in a more balanced manner, than the other classes. Whether I'm wrong or not, don't so much matter. I want to advance that view, and two good books published lately, *The Next Street but One* and Lady Bell's *At the Works* rather support the opinion. The two Salisbury entries, I'm prepared to cut out. They're left in at present in order to make the Poor Man's House stand out more clearly, by, as it were, killing off the life behind it.
> What I'm going to send has to be all rewritten. Only please tell me if it's interesting, and picture-suggesting. I hope there's not now a morsel of egotism in it which doesn't throw light on the P.M'sH.[31]

He sent off the manuscript three days later with the defensive rider "I think some of this will have to be both chastened and elaborated".[32] He was fretting about his baby. Two days later he wrote again: "I am very anxious to hear whether you still consider the thing rather hopeless".[33] He need not have worried. On 19 April the message came back from Garnett: it was good.

This was the turning point. From now on all doubts were banished and the writing went from strength to strength. "I *am* glad you like the thing; for I feel that if it is to be any good it won't be because of the literary work I put into it, but because what I write most easily will be good, whether I know it or not. Isn't it true that all good work already exists in one long before one begins to write? I should like to do this book well, above all things."[34]

They had done no serious fishing on this visit because the drifter was lying up at Exmouth being re-keeled. On 11 April he set off with Uncle Sam and Bob to fetch it back, walking the four miles to East Budleigh station in the midst of a thunderstorm, the others cursing all the while. At Exmouth they had to wait around for the tide but, as they were packing the boat, Reynolds noted with pleasure that he was being watched. The role of fisherman was still sufficiently new to bring out the exhibitionist in him. "Bob and I had to put all the gear, even the bottom boards, into the boat, and the men at the yard wondered most obviously and amusingly who the devil I was, obeying skipper's rather cuss-full orders; for I always obey the skipper for the time being as implicitly as I expect anybody to obey me when I'm doing skipper aboard a boat. Indeed, discipline at sea seems different to any other. Certainly it's the only kind I've ever felt inclined to knuckle under to." They had to row with the giant oars, or sweeps, the eleven miles home through a glorious multi-coloured sunset and he found to his delight that he had weathered the physical brunt even better than his hardened companion. "When we got home we were both more or less done, but to my great glee, Bob was stiff next day and I wasn't, and I don't think he had rowed twice as far as I had. Shall get level with 'em yet."[35]

The long row had also had a surprising effect upon his medical condition which awakened in him the outside possibility that he might evade the dreaded operation after all. "It's a most curious thing, and whether due to some hard rowing or not, I don't know – the veins which were to be extirpated have got decidedly better. The other evening when it came on rough, I hauled my best at not less than 20 boats. Certainly, I felt some pain, but it didn't continue till next day, whereas last year it would have knocked me up for a week, and necessitated iodine and belladonna and the deuce of a fuss. And rowing back from Exmouth the sweeps didn't knock me up a bit. I have a wild glimmering hope that with continually improving *general* health and the rowing, some improvement may have come about and might be got to go on. But I shall come up to London and see the surgeon just the same, next Tuesday, and entirely follow his advice in the matter."[36]

As the day of the operation grew nearer, however, so did the fears increase. He forced himself, as usual, to face them head on. But though he could accept the possibility of death, he was in the middle of writing his best book and would not give up life that easily.

> It's never any use my trying to run away from unpleasant things, or not thinking about them, so I have been facing that operation out beforehand – daring it, so to speak. And I find, somewhat to my surprise and satisfaction, that there isn't in me any fear of death itself. I seem to have a pretty complete faith, beyond reason, that it could only mean, at the worst, an absorption into the spirit of things; more perfect union with what one is always reaching out towards; an improvement in attitude. But on the other hand, though I don't find in myself much but a pleasant calm looking forward to what might come, I do find an infinite unreadiness to give up what is, to change this good state for a better of

> any sort; a determined disinclination to go on to any future, leaving the possibilities of the present so unexhausted.

And then, as usual, he laughed it all off.

> Now don't 'ee go thinking I be getting morbid, and be spitting the mud of my mind at you. On the contrary, I am most pleasant-minded and merry. We have been having no end of a time the last few days, teasing Bob's mother-in-law, Grannie Pratt, a very spry, humorous young-old peasant. I've succeeded in laughing her out of half a night's sleep even. New role for me – mountebank.[37]

On 23 April he was lunching once again with Garnett at the Mont Blanc and rejoicing in good news.[38] The surgeon, on a fresh examination of the now much-revived patient, had decided the operation was no longer needed. Instead of spending the next weekend languishing in a nursing home, he took advantage of the unexpected freedom to pick up an invitation from Edward Thomas and go down to Petersfield for a few days. In the late afternoon of 25 April he found his way to Berryfield Cottage, the little grey house about a mile from the village of Ashford, standing at the bottom of a fir-capped juniper-dotted hillside and reached by a dark, deep winding lane covered by overhanging trees.[39] The Thomases had been there only four months but were still delighting in the peace and beauty of the garden and the surrounding nature. Only a few days after their arrival, Thomas had written to a friend: "It is the most beautiful place we have ever lived in. We are now become people of whom passers-by stop to think: How fortunate are they within those walls. I know it. I have thought the same as I came to the house and forgot it was my own."[40]

Reynolds received a warm welcome from Thomas's wife Helen, with her dark hair and striking looks, the rock behind her gifted, mood-laden husband, whose prose writing she was later to equal – some might say surpass. The afternoon of the arrival of a special visitor was always given up to baking, the traditional country welcome. Reynolds, who always responded first to children, must have been taken too by the lively, country-wild Merfyn and Bronwen – closer in spirit, despite their middle class, to the natural instinctive children he loved so well in Sidmouth. The grown-ups talked on after dinner in an atmosphere as warm as the little back kitchen he had left behind at home, but with the added spice of cultivated conversation. They did not turn in until just before midnight.

He stayed for the next four days, up at seven most mornings, rambling the countryside most of the day and eating and talking late into the night. On the Saturday they walked north to Selborne and Woolmer to visit the shrine of Gilbert White; on the Monday south through Ramsdean to Butser, across War Down to Buriton and home.[41] While Reynolds talked in the evenings of his hopes for the *Mountain* and the *Poor Man's House*, Thomas had been up in

London the previous week negotiating with Roger Ingpen, Hutchinson's reader to whom he had first written from Pans Lane in March, for a biography of Richard Jefferies, the Wiltshire nature-writer and mystic, dear to both young writers' hearts.[42] Though the Jefferies' commission had not yet been clinched, Thomas was about to embark on an unremitting four-year stint in which he was never without a book, mostly commissions, on his hands and sometimes two or three together. But as with Reynolds, work never seemed to turn the tide of poverty and bare subsistence.

It was a stay of both stimulation and relaxation, and it was with some reluctance on 30 April that Reynolds was up at six and off to London, leaving Thomas to catch up on a day's reading and letter writing.[43] He was in town for the usual Mont Blanc lunch and consultation with Pinker, but on the following day took lunch with Edmund Gosse and Archibald Marshall – "the Mail Supplementarians" – mainly to make sure that his reviewing work for the Supplement was still secure.[44] Reynolds had made something of a hit with Gosse when they had met for the first time earlier that spring, finding common ground in Gosse's Devon childhood and his detailed knowledge of Sidmouth and of Western Town.[45] He took advantage of the lunch to float with Marshall the idea that the reviews of country books in the *Mail* might be concentrated into a periodic *causerie*, written by Reynolds, and thus take advantage of the "back to nature" bandwagon that was gathering momentum in literary circles. Marshall agreed a week later to commission a monthly column on the lines proposed. Reynolds wrote to Pinker: "I've got a causerie – hardly *the*".[46] It was a step towards the long-held ambition, but not the weekly slot that would have given him security; and unfortunately it was tied to a frail journalistic vessel that was on the point of capsizing.

On the same day, he called on Anderson Graham, the editor of *Country Life*, to see if there were any openings for articles or sketches. Graham "knew my name, but didn't know how; nor did I". He agreed to look at Reynolds' work.[47]

At home once more in Pans Lane, he was soon itching to get back to Sidmouth for the first full summer in Bob's house. But Margot had picked up some poison while he had been away at Petersfield and, though recovered, was not yet in a fit state to travel.[48]

The third week of May began with a body blow. Since his new book had started to pick up pace, he had largely forgotten the fate of the *Mountain*. Now Seccombe brought news that, after ten weeks of havering, Constable had finally decided on rejection. The decision had clearly been taken only after long internal wrangling within the firm and had left Seccombe personally in an invidious position, caught between his colleagues on the one hand and his young protégé on the other. Six weeks later he was to comment, partly in self-exculpation, that the book had become "a reproach and byword chez la grande maison Constable!"[49]

Reynolds rushed up to town to see Garnett in his office at Duckworths, who were to have the next bite of the now slightly tarnished cherry. They had a long talk about the strategy. Garnett still stood four square behind the book and reassured his young friend that he would press all the buttons he could on its behalf. He went on to explain at length how he would push the book once it were taken, a conversation which, as Reynolds admitted later, curiously chilled him as he sensed the incompatibility of commerce and friendship.[50]

The rejection had been a blow, but he left Henrietta Street with full confidence in Garnett's advocacy and powers of persuasion. He called in on *Country Life* to hear the reaction to the samples of work he had sent in. "Anderson Graham was pleased to tell me that my MSS. were very unequal. I knew that, and was pleased on my part to hear that he had chosen the very worst one for publication and left the ones that ought to get somewhere else with luck."[51]

Margot was now fit again and he travelled down with some relief to Sidmouth, bent on making his home there for the whole of the summer. He had not forgotten the disappointment of his last arrival and this time laid out a hard won couple of shillings on hiring one of the small landaus that plied between the station and the town. The four children, Bobby, Reggie and a friend, and Reynolds' special girl friend, "Straighty", were in seventh heaven as they raced down the hill and along the sea front. "I wonder where else the two shillings I paid for the drosky would have purchased so much delight. Or rather, the delight was in ourselves, in the children; the two shillings served only to unlock it."[52]

It was the first time that Margot had been in Sidmouth since the miraculous few days of the first visit the previous August, and her presence gave an extra edge to the children's excitement. "Coming down from the station I had a most comic drosky-full. Six pieces of luggage, three grubby boys and one small girl who had come up to meet me, Margot and myself. We made quite an excite coming through the town – the kiddies yelling for joy and Margot jumping up and down. It's remarkable how they take to Margot here. She's really just at present the central figure of the town and of great use in making acquaintance for me with all sorts of people I should never get to know otherwise, from whom I get a deal that is interesting. And she tries so pathetically hard to be good."[53]

The first few days he spent slaving away on a difficult parcel of books for the first *Mail causerie*. He was still waiting anxiously for news from Duckworths of the *Mountain*, which had been assigned, so Garnett told him, to the dullest of their readers, Stuart Reid: "Have you heard what the 'dull person' made of the *Holy Mountain*?"[54] On 25 May came news that Reid had put in a not very approving report which, taken with Garnett's enthusiasm, brought the attitudes within the firm to something of a balance. Garnett thought that they would, nevertheless, make an offer for the book and suggested Pinker should bring matters to a head by asking for a definite decision one way or the other.[55]

Garnett now found himself approaching the same awkward predicament that Seccombe had just been in, at odds with his publishing colleagues for what looked like personal favouritism and at the same time about to let down his young friend to whom he had promised so much. He gave the news of Reid's report in an apologetic manner to which Reynolds reacted strongly: "You don't need to tell me you've done your best to get them to take the *Hy.Mtn.* That's never for a moment in doubt. But damn all haverers! Strikes me that if people were to spend as much trouble pushing on as they do over prudence, they'd do a lot better in the end. I'll write to Pinker to-morrow, if I don't hear before then. I take it that if they do accept the book, they will, with you behind them, work it without vacillation. I hope Duckworth's do publish it, because I doubt Alston Rivers being suitable for *The Poor Man's House* and one or two other books I have in view. I'm rewriting the portion of the *P.M's H.* that you saw (about 1/6 of the whole), partly to get better into the swing of it before going on. Now I am so used to the life here, it has become rather difficult to divine the points and pictures which would interest strangers to it. But no doubt 'twill be all the better for not taking much thought of that."[56]

Pinker's pressure had the desired effect, producing an immediate decision. Duckworth put together some conciliatory words about Reynolds' great promise, but could not see his way to take the book.[57] Over lunch at the Mont Blanc on 28 May Garnett was in a desolate mood about the whole affair. He asked Hueffer if he could count on him to support the book now it was to go on to Alston Rivers, the next port of call. Hueffer, with the usual sense of his own importance, thought it would carry more weight within the firm if he were to appear to discover the manuscript himself.

Garnett wrote sorrowfully from his office that afternoon to break the bad news. He assured his young friend that the book was hitting these barriers as a result of its sheer originality; and suggested he contact Pinker immediately to have the manuscript sent on direct to Hueffer. It was news that Reynolds had been half expecting, and his first reaction was to try and relieve his friend of his despondency. "I can't thank you appropriately for your efforts on behalf of the damn'd book. Strikes me I'd better resign myself to the notion of its falling to bits in the hands of the London publishers. 'Tisn't much use to try and be original when one's belly wants looking after, though your saying that the thing is so soothes one's mind."[58]

He was not wholly convinced by the strategy of employing Hueffer as agent. He was not in a trusting mood with the Hueffers just then. By the same post as Garnett's letter came a cheque from Oliver Hueffer, Ford's even more maverick brother, for reading work Reynolds had done for his literary agency the previous month. It had been dishonoured by the bank. "Curse the fellow. Why didn't he tell me honestly instead of sending along worthless paper? I'd have done the work for nothing for him, if he wanted a leg over, but I won't work for deferred payments and bad cheques."[59]

Nonetheless, he could not in the circumstances second-guess Garnett's judgement and he sent off a telegram to Pinker with an urgent request to send the manuscript direct to Hueffer at the National Liberal Club.[60] He followed it up with a short explanatory letter that could not hide his general irritation. "Garnett wrote hastily saying it (the MS.) had better be sent direct to F.M. Hueffer, because then he can appear to discover it, or some tommy-rot, the more irritating because, apparently, it had better not be neglected. Oliver Hueffer's cheque, for work done in April, has been dishonoured. I suppose I'd better not press hard while t'other one has to do with the MS...... The devil knows when I'm going to be a profitable going concern to you."[61]

Pinker was equally put out that he was to be by-passed for Hueffer, in whom he too had little confidence, but did as his client had requested and rang up Hueffer who was in his usual lively, lordly mood. For once, Reynolds had to send Pinker a placatory note: "I should have greatly preferred not interfering with you over the sending of the MS. (and indeed sha'n't do so again) but that Garnett was very chagrined over Duckworth's refusal and so I didn't like to ignore his advice for fear he would think me piqued with him, which is far from the case. Your talk with Ford Hueffer must have been very comic. Somehow he always excites my laughter, and, worse luck! he knows it."[62]

Although it was strictly Reynolds who was the injured party, he had to continue the consoling job on Garnett too. "I'm afraid I wrote rather irritably last time – and don't feel much less so this. I followed your – or rather Hueffer's – suggestion to send the MS. direct to him very reluctantly. To be 'found' by you or Seccombe is one thing – but to be 'found' by a rabbit-man like Hueffer is quite another – to my mind anyhow. Duckworth was good enough to tell Pinker that I have 'great promise' – damn him. These patronising non-committal phrases don't go down after your probably too generous praise of the book. But don't 'ee be chagrined because it isn't taken. 'Twill come out someday right enough, unless I go under meantime. I may be only half-satisfactory, as you once said, but I know I've got, like most Wiltshiremen, a talent for biding my time without forgetting or relaxing."[63]

The episode of the Duckworth rejection and the Hueffer commission was no more than a minor storm in a tea-cup, but the flurry of letters with Pinker and Garnett – bad news, ill temper, soothing of hurt feelings – had set all three men's teeth on edge. The fate of the "damn'd book" was now deep buried in each subconscious, wrapped round with personal slights, misgivings and feelings of guilt. The ground was well prepared for the real atomic explosion that was just two months away.

The episode had been made worse for Reynolds by a simultaneous source of personal irritation much closer to home. Now the holiday season was under way, the back room he had inhabited the previous August was being used as normal to catch the summer overspill from the Bedford Hotel. It had been taken by a Scotsman who, to Reynolds' disgust, dominated the whole house and the family meal times, "quoting Burns by the yard".[64] He went off in a sulk. "There's some villainous northcountryman taken the back room here, and grubs with us. Can't endure him, the boom-burr of his voice, so am practically confined to my bedroom when in house. One of us will have to go."[65]

But Mrs Woolley, who could manage her playful, feckless husband with consummate ease, was more than a match for a spoilt child who had to be coaxed out of his moods; for which Reynolds himself was ultimately grateful. Three days later he wrote to Garnett: "The northcountryman is still here. My bellicose intentions have come to nought. His wife – who has worked as cook near by till she's nearly fifty – looked so happy that one couldn't risk damping her even indirectly. I've been worsted all round and I'm glad o' it. The way that clever woman, Mam Woolley, managed me was a sight for the gods. Marvellous."[66] Nonetheless, as soon as the lodger disappeared, Reynolds snapped up the backroom for himself and took the whole of the first floor from then on.[67]

Meanwhile, goaded on by his failure with Duckworth, Garnett had been racing round in London to put pressure on Alston Rivers; and had got an assurance that they were looking seriously at the book with a view to taking it. Reynolds was delighted, but still felt the need to comfort his friend with the thought that the Duckworth rejection had been all for the best after all. "What good news in your letter! If your advocacy didn't get Duckworth's to take the book, I think it was you that made Rivers bite at it. I know – your faithfulness to literature itself has made the *immediate* commercial value of your opinion sink even at times to a minus value; I knew it perfectly well when Duckworth's had the MS, and discounted my chances privately on that account. Ye cannot serve God and Mammon, again – and Mammon distrusts you. I believe I'm better at that job than you are. And in a way, at the very back of my mind, I'm half glad that your representations chez Mammon on my behalf didn't succeed. Primarily, the book had to be published and me fed and bedded; but secondarily, the less I have of commercial relations with you the better, for in commercial relations I know myself to be rather cynical and a grasper of main chances. I'm ready to bluff and fool Hueffer, if need be, because, frankly, he's antipathetic to me. I couldn't have done that with you. At least, I hope I shouldn't. Your little talk in your sanctum about what you'd do to push the book if it were taken, curiously chilled me. I didn't like it."[68]

Typical of Reynolds, over the next two weeks when he didn't hear from his friend he began to worry that he had been too outspoken, particularly about Hueffer who was himself an old friend of Garnett. When the letter was long out of Garnett's mind, he wrote to him in a mood of apology. "My last letter to you has been rather on my mind. I'm afraid I spoke rhetorically, instead of as subtly as I ought to have done, especially about Hueffer. When I said I'd feel able to bluff and fool him if need be, I meant really that I'd feel able to resort to the ordinary means of commercial negotiations, i.e. not showing my hand before the moment, and keeping all the advantage possible; whereas, with a friend like you, I should feel a pig if I didn't tell you what was in my mind before putting it into action. I'm not yet so commercial but all bargaining appears to me as a sort of fight in which one produces one's artillery at the right moment for ambush; therefore to bargain with friends is a horrid process, as bad as borrowing money from them."[69]

But he remembered in time that it had been only three months since he had rebuked Garnett for some highly unsympathetic remarks about Seccombe: "But I am afraid, very much, that I often speak to other people of *their* friends in a way I shouldn't for a moment allow them to use in speaking about my friends to me. If I play that trick on you, 'twill be lack of thought; you must consider the nature of the beast."[70]

Despite the disappointing progress of the *Mountain* through the London publishing houses, he managed throughout June to put the book and its consideration by Rivers out of his mind, and battle on with the *Poor Man's House* which had been set aside during the distractions of his first two weeks back in Sidmouth. "The P.M's H. is going again. I do trust 'twill be good. I've hopes – in fact, I feel a better grip over my material and seem to have a clearer sight of what I'm aiming at than I've ever had with any other work."[71] The better grip had come from taking time out to organise the material in a conscious and disciplined way. "I've been doing a labour of Hercules – getting about 300 note-headings into the right order for the Poor Man's House – scheming the whole book in detail, in fact, down to the appropriate spots for bits of conversation. Do you plan books right out? I didn't do the Mountain, and had no idea what a labour it was, especially when there's not much narrative or chronology to decide the order of things for one. This little job, however, will make the writing of the remainder of the book very much easier."[72]

After two weeks' further writing, he was approaching 18,000 words and his optimism about the book was growing apace. He wrote to Garnett in the middle of June: "The Poor Man's House has got to p.70 of this paper. It's going to save me from being a one-book man, I do believe. That synopsis was a splendid idea – saves one no end of worry about what's to come next, and where this and that is to go, and leaves one all one's attention for what one is at. Frankly – though I says it as shouldn't – I'm sure the book's going to be far better than any of my other attempts. It gives me a comfortable feeling that I'm doing it as well as in me is. Which is strange and pleasant."[73] And at the same time he confided to Pinker: "I have a feeling that it is a lot better than anything I have managed to do before, and 'tisn't so far as I know like anything by anybody else."[74]

In the next ten days he completed a further 7000, including the celebrated lecture on cleanliness, about which he felt proud but also a little defensive, as if sensing even at this early stage the struggle he might have to keep it in the book. He was keen for Garnett to take a look. "The *P.M's H.* is up to its hundredth of my big 250 word pages. When you are less busy I'd like you to see the remainder, though I'm afraid the thing's too taut in my mind for me to benefit by anybody's advice much. Has it ever struck you how intimately English snobbery is bound up with cleanliness? I've written a pretty vigorous, very scientific chapter on it which is going to stand whether it's liked or not, for without tackling the subject and plunging at the absurd cant of cleanliness which burkes fleas and puts up with houseflies, sniffs at slums and keeps decayed teeth in its mouth, the *P.M's H.* and *P.M.'s* life *cannot* be properly appreciated. There is, I believe, nothing which so strongly separates classes as a difference in conventional cleanliness. Yet from the point of view of ideal cleanliness we are all, tramp and daily bather, so dirty that there's almost nothing to choose between us. And the need of cleanliness is a weakness, whether or no the practice of it is a strength. I suppose my romanticalness will repel the scientific, and my science the romantic-minded...."[75]

On 29 June he sent off the whole of the manuscript so far. "It's awfully good of you to spend time again over the P.M's H. I send the lot (you'll see I've altered the Salisbury chapter) and also some fishing sketches to be incorporated later, and possibly enlarged a little – they were cut 75% for the *Mail.* The stuff you haven't seen anything of begins on p.47, but I think the preceding chapter is improved somewhat. XIX on cleanliness and snobbery is to my mind a very important chapter, but in rewriting I must try to put it better. And I must also try and put several things less first-personally, and squash out an occasional tone of preachiness. I hope to do a good deal in the revision, but there's the matter o' it."[76]

He wanted Garnett to come down for his holiday and see the place for himself. But the process of writing so intensively about life with the Woolleys was making him more self-conscious in the day-to-day routine of living and suspicious of their reaction to him. It was all quite different from the trusting acceptance of one another of the previous year. The very fact of writing it was changing his perception of the experience and making him begin to question its reality, at least as far as the human relationships were concerned. "I wish you could come down here with me somewhen. Have you the faculty of plunging out of one mode of life and thought into another? I haven't really, I'm afraid; there's always a *me* that sits outside and observes; but I pay so much attention to cultivating the faculty that in the end I hope for success. Still, they feel the presence of the outside critic; they know intuitively that one is thinking more than one says; and that keeps alive a lingering distrust, and a certain amount, however little, of ill-grounded respect. How hard it is to live another man's life with him! Can one, d'you think, ever quite succeed? – other than in imagination?"[77]

This was deeper than he knew. The next ten years was to teach him the true limitations on success. But for the moment, when the writing was put aside, he found himself as closely caught up in the emotions of family life as ever before. He followed that summer the daily routine he had adopted the previous September, up first in the morning to light the fire and make the tea to carry up to Bob and Mam at the top of the house. In addition to this early morning kitchenmaid role, dictated primarily by his insomnia, he now occasionally took over from Mam Woolley the task of putting the boys to bed. "Bob's out to sea. I've just enticed Bobby and Reggie in to bed with shoe nuts. We made a fearful commotion on the promenade this evening. When Margot is out the kids all cling round her, giving her not a moment's rest from their caresses, and if another dog comes along they set to and clout its head, quite regardless of the fact that t'other dog may not be so amiable. You can imagine the looks of the many grown-ups who funk Margot when they see the kids round her."[78]

And he still knew in his heart that he had at last found a real home to which he could make his own contribution. "The fishing's a total failure. It gives me a certain amount of pleasure to know that my being here stays the household somewhat. And they are so good – I've got a beastly attack of gastric catarrh from eating a boughten fish – constant toothachy pain in my inside which, most luckily, don't affect my head like ordinary indigestion – and Mam Woolley is looking after me no end, she and Bob much distressed it's thinning me a bit. Her invalid diet is not so extraordinarily good as Mrs. Wyer's, but it's a greater departure from the usual. Really I don't know why I've been so lucky in my pro-homes, and been so well looked after. My father used to say that every sensible person detested me and wouldn't live with me on any account."[79]

Since the fishing was so poor, he only went out on occasion when the feeling took him. As on the evening of 23 June when he went mackerel-drifting with Bob and Tom with his own private ambition of seeing in the Midsummer dawn.[80] It was a dangerous night. The seas were high, there was rain in the wind, and they feared that if the wind backed they would have to make a run for it. When the wind did back a little, he had a momentary anxiety that they might never make it home, and thought instantly of the book that might never be completed – the sole reason for his existence. "One minute I wished myself home, thought with a deep regret that *The Poor Man's House* might be left unfinished. (It's curious that when I'm in a fix I find myself thinking of nobody and nothing except my work; but it is so, and was so when I was ill.)"[81] In *A Poor Man's House* itself he kept from the reader the knowledge that the lamented unfinished work was the book that he or she was now reading: "One minute I wished myself home, safe in bed, and thought with grotesque grief of some unfinished work."[82]

The mood passed and the sea danger became more exhilarating than frightening – "the grey, slightly sheeny boil of the water round was wonderful."[83] They made it safely home – but at two o'clock, too early for the dawn. "Afterwards I went out with Margot to see the sun rise, but as it was only a gradual whitening, and Margot didn't like it, I came in and read myself to sleep with Chesterton on Dickens." The emotions of that night had knocked up his nerves and taught him the painful truth that he would never become a proper fisherman like his friends. "Do you know, I think I could do everything to fishing except stand the racket of my own thoughts night after night. The beauty of it tears one to bits. I slept nearly all the next day – so dead asleep that they couldn't wake me for meals. It was only my own emotions which had knocked me up. Had I had to go out next night.... I couldn't have. I slept again, and didn't wake even to light the fire to make tea."[84]

A rather different, though equally tense, emotion was to await him the last week of June when for the first time he went out prawning with Uncle Sam. From the breathless account he retailed to Garnett, it was clear he knew he was on to even better copy for his book.

> Two nights and one day this week I have been prawning with Uncle Sam. It's weird work among the rocks by a stormy moon, with the surf roaring just outside one. Half the time one walks on ridges that are *underneath* the water, feeling one's foothold with a bamboo pole, and dropping one's baited net by a string in the deep places into which a false step will drop oneself also. When other people follow Uncle Sam to the places he knows so well, he simply decoys them into deep pools so that they have to swim for it and go home. We even go secretly out of the town by back ways, our cat-smelly sacks and poles over our shoulders. He wades up to the waist – an old man nearly 70 – tripping about on submerged rock ridges yards out to sea. Nobody here can prawn like Uncle Sam. Then he most expands, and my going with him at that work has warmed the cockles of his heart towards me more than they were before, so that he's showed me places and tricks most of the fishermen don't know. The rocks look so different at night – so menacing. Wednesday I found myself to an awful place – Hospital Rock by name, near Danger Gutter (such names they have) – a huge black rock, the top at mean level, but arched underneath with downhanging oar-weed, and at the bottom of all a deep black weed-fringed pool running right under the arch, and far below the sea-level outside at the bottom of the pool. As I found afterwards, Uncle Sam was watching me from outside to see if Hospital Rock was going to put me off prawning as, it appears, it has done several people. Luckily, I did prawn there, but I had to lie on the weed to get my net down, and the sound of the surf – air-borne and rock-borne together – was like an orchestra of the mad damn'd. One would never think that out to Chit Rocks there was one place with such a powerful sinister individuality. Uncle Sam is about on the rocks under the high cliffs most nights. Once he has brought home on his shoulder a dead smashed woman who had fallen over the cliff, and another time a drowned nigger. Fancy walking between the grey sea and black cliffs with a drowned nigger on one's back! In the dead of night! The nigger's drown'd-man's eyes![85]

At the end of June, much to Reynolds' delight, Garnett agreed to come down in August. "You will be very very welcome in August. July would be a much better month – town less full, more fishing and less pleasure-boating – but if August is better for you, then August."[86] And he was hoping to entice Garnett *into* the water as well as on it. "Margot and I had a glorious bathe this morning – one can simply run out from here in a vest and shorts – and so many people collected that we are thinking of giving a daily performance and sending Bob round with the hat! When you come to Sidmouth you'll be a distinguished person – not Edward Garnett – oh, no – but an intimate of Margot's! I'm not myself. But merely Margot's owner."[87]

It was in the summer of 1907 too that Reynolds received his first blooding in politics – over what became known as the problem of the shingle, which was to exercise him on and off for the whole of his time at Sidmouth.

For centuries the exposed nature of the beach at Sidmouth had been a major handicap for the longshore fishermen there. Certain winds and tides would sweep tons of shingle away, so eroding the beach that landing fishing boats on it became even more hazardous than usual. Attempts to build piers and breakwaters to create something of a protective harbour had in the past come to nought – in fact it is only in the 1990s that engineering works have finally introduced some stability to the Sidmouth beach, though many doubt it will last for long.

The problem had been made worse by local townsmen, including the Lord of the Manor, Colonel Balfour, who claimed ownership of the foreshore, carrying away further tons of shingle for building works. When challenged by the fishermen, they claimed that their exploitation of this resource was too small to contribute to the natural erosion of the beach; indeed, they disputed that there was any long-term erosion at all, claiming that as much shingle as was swept away was returned by contrary winds and tides.

In the 1880s the coastguard at Sidmouth had drawn the problem to the attention of the Board of Trade which, in addition to its responsibilities for harbours throughout the country, had recently established a separate Fisheries Department and was now responsible for the fishing industry in the country as a whole. In 1888 the matter came to a head with the proposed removal of substantial amounts of shingle to build a reservoir in the town. Colonel Balfour claimed his rights to the foreshore stemmed from a 1611 grant by James I to the Lord of the Manor. The Board asserted in response that the foreshore was vested in the Crown, but privately decided to put the whole tangled legal web before the Law Officers. With an excess of caution, the Board decided in 1896 that it would not challenge any removals of shingle in the future.

The matter was resurrected in 1906 by Godfrey Jobson, a fishing boat owner in the town in dispute with the Manor which had banned the machinery he had built for hauling his motor launch up the beach. When challenging the Manor's claims to ownership of the foreshore, Jobson protested that the shingle was now four feet below the seawall whereas formerly it had been only one.

The burden of dragging boats up over the wall to save them from being swept away was something that even Reynolds had experienced that summer. In August 1906, officials of the Board decided at last to consider the making of an order prohibiting further removal of shingle, and passed the papers to the Solicitor, who promptly sat on them for a further year.[88]

It was towards the end of his short stay in November 1906 that Reynolds decided to become involved himself and sought help from Garnett. "The townsfolk here are taking away the beach in large quantities for building, so that the tide comes nearly up to the wall, and greatly hinders the fishing industry here. It's illegal, but no one's duty to put a stop to it. I want to make representations 'in a proper place' and get it stopped. Can you suggest any high body I can get at, and how to get at him?"[89]

His sudden return to Devizes put the affair on hold but he returned to the charge the following spring. On 12 April he went into Exeter to seek the support of the Clerk to the Devon Sea Fisheries Committee, who referred him to the Board of Trade with the assurance that they would most certainly stop it. With usual Reynolds care to prepare his ground, he asked Garnett to find him a contact in the Harbours Department. "We shall have to send up a petition probably, but I want to see someone at the Board of Trade first, as it's going to be no joke to fight the all-powerful manor, and I don't want to fight at all unless I can see success pretty clear, else, in case of failure, seven devils will carry away beach where one does now."[90]

A week later he made his *démarche* at the Board in person and managed to prise even the Solicitor's Department up off its bottom.[91] As the summer progressed, he became more and more immersed. By mid June he began to despair of the task of steering conservative fishermen towards political action but, in spite of the weary disclaimers, he was revelling in the complex legal battle. This was much more fun than arguing minor contractual points with agents or publishers.

> The beach question has assumed appalling proportions and complexity. I've got the Harbours' Act down to-day, and written to the Bd. of Trade for their interpretation of a clause [*sic*] which simply damns our case unless we can screw out of it on the rather subtle ground that the Manor's possession of the foreshore does not give the Manor a right to destroy that which it possesses, and on which other people have prescriptive rights of use. They have an idea here that the Bd. of Trade and a signed paper are almighty; can't understand that the Bd. of Trade can only work within various Acts of Parliament and is itself subject to the law as it stands; and then people who've never gone into the matter come along the beach and tell them they ought to sign a petition and all would be well; the less those good folk know the more airily they speak; and the more airily they speak, the more the fishermen believe them – and it's trying to the temper when one is up to the ears in legalities and

> responsible for any mistake in tactics and harm that may accrue. It's unfortunately the power of the Bd. of Trade itself that is in question. I don't want thanks and palaver, but I do want more confidence in my slow proceedings and less in the obiter dicta of irresponsible people talking through the top of their head. Nobody's to be relied upon. A benevolent old gentleman (to whom a deal of the Manor is mortgaged) who has always been saying he'd like the beach removal stopped, and to whom they have been trying to get me to go, sent his gardener down yesterday for six loads of shingle for his damn'd drive![92]

At the end of June he breathed a sigh of relief when the Sidmouth Council at last became involved. "The Sidmouth Council is taking over the beach question at last for the sake of its sea-wall. I'm profoundly glad to be relieved of a job in which there is so much work and so many more kicks than ha'pence. They are going to brief counsel. If I'd had money.... 'Twould have been done by now."[93] It was by no means the end of his involvement in the affair, but it was the beginning of his long apprenticeship as politician and civil servant.

It was also in the summer of 1907 that he made a new friendship that was to introduce him to Cambridge and the academic approach to politics, and was to last for the rest of his life. Harold Wright, then just 23 and three years younger than Reynolds, had been a regular holiday visitor to Sidmouth since 1901. He had been out sailing in Bob Woolley's boats and had stayed with Tom Woolley at his cottage by the river Sid. He was a sensitive man with a gentle nature – frail-looking, with a round face, thinning black hair and a full moustache. Though gifted with a sharp intelligence, he had lost out on education, having spent most of his childhood as an invalid with a bone disease which had involved countless operations on his legs and had affected his heart.

In 1905 he had been given a boat, the *Cockbird*, as a coming-of-age present and when each year he came down from Surrey for his summer holidays he could regularly be seen out on the water, with Florence Easton, his future wife. One evening the couple were pushing their boat down the beach to go out pollacking, when a stranger appeared and gave them a hand. Wright asked him to join them and Reynolds, delighted by the invitation, rushed off to change out of his best clothes. It was an important trip for both Wright and Reynolds. They caught one squid; but they also caught each other.[94]

In the second week of July Reynolds had arranged to visit Wright's home at Sutton where he lived with his parents. But it turned out a hectic three days because of a new eruption of the *Mountain*. Throughout June he had remained quietly confident. Alston Rivers, egged on by Garnett and by Hueffer, were obviously biting and had been discussing with Pinker the question of royalties. In the middle of June he heard from Edward Thomas that it was on the way to being taken. On Garnett's advice, he told Pinker to waive the advance if that would further the negotiations.[95]

But as the matter dragged on into July, he was becoming distinctly nervous. He had earned only a couple of guineas in June and found he could not continue easily with bit work alongside the serious writing of the *Poor Man's House*.[96] He needed either a serialisation of his new book as he wrote it, or an injection of money from even so unlikely a source as the *Mountain*.

On 9 July he went up to London for the usual Mont Blanc lunch and ostensibly to put pressure on Pinker to bring matters to a head with Alston Rivers. At lunch he was introduced to a tall, dark figure, with bushy beard, beak-like nose and eyes that flashed like an eagle's. It was his first encounter with the co-founder of these lunches, W.H. Hudson, who had been back three weeks from the west of Cornwall, where he had been, on and off for the past 18 months, working on the book that was to become *The Lands End*.[97] Both the Wiltshire Downs and Salisbury Plain were close to Hudson's heart and Reynolds had long admired the simple humanity of the old novelist-cum-naturalist. Despite the difference in age, the two men immediately found much to share in each other's views and experience. It was the start of a relationship which lasted to the end of Reynolds' life. The two men met infrequently, but kept up a regular correspondence – Hudson with his inexhaustible curiosity using Reynolds, like all his friends, as a source of local information on both people and wildlife, which eventually found its way into his books.

The following day Reynolds stayed overnight at the Wrights' house in Surrey and quickly took to the free intellectual atmosphere there – to Harold's father Charles, a marine insurance broker and salvage expert, and most of all to Rose, his friend's mother, with whom he was soon engaged in friendly intellectual argument. He sent her a typical thank you letter. "For the most delightful rest-time in the three days I have to thank you; and for what most chiefly you'd not guess. Please tell Mr. Wright that if the Education Act of 1870 could produce more Mrs. Wrights tending (being able to tend) their flowers and canaries after breakfast, it would be a better argument for it than all his appallingly formidable batteries and wire entanglements; and I'd forgive the said Act for producing 1,000,000 readers for the *Daily Mail*. I'm not trying to pay a clumsy compliment. I'm grateful for more than being bedded, dined, and given a fine word-battle, and I don't see why I shouldn't say so, though I'm well aware that it's not quite proper to say pleasant things unless with obvious insincerity to discount them."[98]

On the third day in town, the bubble burst. He called in early on Pinker to learn that Alston Rivers had finally rejected the *Mountain* "with some damnable compliment or other".[99] Reynolds was furious that after six whole weeks of deliberation this should be the outcome. He now wanted instant decisions. Pinker was in some difficulty as to who to turn to next, but decided, with Reynolds' assent, on an approach to Grant Richards. He rang Richards straight away, assuring him of at least one good opinion he had had of the book, and the publisher agreed to take a look. Reynolds, anxious as ever, looked in again a little later to confirm the position and offered to take the manuscript over in person, with a polite covering note from Pinker reminding Richards of his promise to give the book a prompt reading.[100] "With my manuscript under my arm, in the ancient approved fashion for young authors, I hastened down the Strand to another publisher's. The London pavements weren't made of gold; they stank with heat that morning."[101]

In his office that morning Pinker, who had never met Garnett, suggested Reynolds might ask his friend to jot down a recommendation of the book for him to use at the right moment. Reynolds recounted the exchange for Garnett's benefit.

> *Pinker* That might be a great help.
> *S.R.* With the literary ones. I don't think Garnett's good word would be an advantage with the purely commercial-minded ones. They'd say, 'twouldn't pay, because Garnett has praised so many badly paying books.
> *Pinker* (emphatically) If a publisher were to take Garnett's advice entirely, it *would* pay. The reason why it doesn't pay is because they only half take it, and try to compromise.
> That warmed the cockles of my heart.[102]

But with the newspapers gossipping about a Northcliffe nervous breakdown, and the press baron having fled the country to avoid giving evidence in the disastrous Lever libel suit, Reynolds was now anxious that the main object of his satire might be long dead and buried before the book saw the light of day: "The matter is rather urgent, because once Harmsworth begins publicly dying, the book, unless published before that, may as well be put in the fire; but, if published before that, should receive a famous impetus."[103]

He got back to Pans Lane on the evening of 11 July for a few days break and went straight over to the College for a nostalgic dinner with Ada Bennett. It was seven weeks since he had been in Devizes and, after the talk with Hudson in Gerrard Street, the beauty of the Downs seemed more potent than ever. But his current lack of earnings, combined with the fresh burden of two rooms to pay for at Sidmouth, faced him with a new and heart-rending dilemma – he could not for long afford to maintain two homes. "The Downs are so lovely to look at – nothing in Devon touches them except the sea – nothing. If only I could hit off the marvellous impression of the downland curves.... But no comparison except a musical note seems adequate. I've been thinking of transferring my goods to Sidmouth – the expense of keeping up two places being considerable, but I can't anyhow reconcile myself to being without a pied à terre near the Downs. Lord, lord! tis like the chap as loved two maidens!"[104]

His most immediate need now was to get a serialisation agreement for the *Poor Man's House* to pay the way for its completion, and he had set his sights on the *Albany Review* and its editor Charles Roden Buxton. He looked for Garnett's help. "Oh.... I wonder do you know enough of Charles Buxton, or he know enough of you, for you to give him a recommend to the P.M's H. – when you're not quite so harassed? I don't know how to tell him about it myself – to make plain what it's going to be from what it is – its point of view. He might think I was mazed. I bother you frankly, you see. If you like you may sit on me in your best ironical yokel-crushing manner."[105]

Still smarting from the Duckworth refusal of six weeks before, Garnett was only too happy to write the recommendation for Pinker on the one book and broach the other with Buxton. Back in Sidmouth once more, Reynolds was a little embarrassed by his eagerness to help. "It's awfully good of you, being pressed, to take so much trouble over my damn'd affairs. Pinker will, I know, be very pleased. It's quite evident that he values your opinion very much. Don't hurry overmuch with the P.M's H. I have a good deal of other work to do this week. My hope is that, when you are less pressed, you'll give me a little introduction to Buxton, pointing out where the P.M's H. is more or less unique on account of unique opportunity having gone to the making of it – and, an it so please you, on account of certain objectionable but, for the purpose, useful qualities of the writer thereof. You see, I can't rewrite at the present stage, unless a *probable* serial destination makes the loss of time worthwhile, nor for the same reason, can I afford to have it typewritten."[106]

He took the same pragmatic approach to the problem of the two homes. He was becoming more and more convinced that, despite the best efforts of Pinker and his London friends, his present predicament with publishers was in part due to his own absence from the fray. He needed to be around at least some of the time to rub the literary noses into his manuscripts. He would henceforth specialise on seaboard subjects which made Devizes redundant. "I'm thinking of throwing up Devizes; making Sidmouth my headquarters and counterbalancing the increased distance from London by taking a furnished chambre à garçon in Town, for a month, twice a year. There are more people writing decently on inland subjects than on such subjects as one has at hand here; and I don't know nearly so much about farming as I do about fishing. Hence I may as well try to specialize on longshore work."[107]

On 16 July Garnett wrote the promised recommendation of *The Holy Mountain*. Although prepared with a commercial purpose, it did not in any way distort his genuine view of the quality of the satire, for he was not one to bend his opinion to the pressures of the market. It is the nearest thing we have to a Garnett reader's report on Reynolds' work – a cool piece of Garnett prose which subtly puts pressure on the prospective publisher by appealing to his courage and maturity.

The Holy Mountain
By Stephen Reynolds

It is often said that *Satire* is dead, but Mr. Reynolds' remarkable novel

demonstrates the contrary. It is the strongest and most pungent satire that I have met for many years. The literary workmanship is remarkably clever: the whole picture has the intimacy and the force of actual life.
The publisher to whom I recommended the book was a little afraid of it. But I think that some other publisher will prove him in error. The one question that we ask about Satire is – *Is this deserved?* and I think there cannot be a question that in attacking certain developments of sensational journalism Mr. Reynolds scores very heavily. The study of provincial burgess life in a small country town in the South West of England, though *satirical*, is very convincing; and the exposure of many aspects of modern humbug (in the religious world for example) is carried through with a deftness of touch that is just remarkable.
Of course a great many people who dislike plain speaking will not like *The Holy Mountain.* That goes without saying. But the novel, in the hands of an enterprising publisher, should attract much attention. It provides excellent 'copy' for the reviewers. It is an extremely *original* work, and one that makes for clear thinking. It will probably be attacked in various quarters, and this will help to increase its circulation. It should be handled vigorously, and boldly advertised as a *Satire,* and I repeat that its justification is that the aspects and elements in public life that the author is 'showing up' richly merit the severe handling they receive.[108]

Garnett at this stage had not registered the fact that Pinker had already gone to Grant Richards with the book. He himself had been in favour of an approach to Heinemann, because he had worked for the firm for four years at the turn of the century and still had a good relationship with Sydney Pawling there. By a quirk of fate, Pinker was then *persona non grata* with Heinemann, who was at war in general with literary agents, and Garnett was not on speaking terms with Richards. Garnett sent on his recommendation to Pinker with a word of caution. "Our friend Stephen Reynolds tells me that a 'recommendation' from me of his *Holy Mountain* might be useful to you. I therefore enclose it. I think myself that Heinemann ought to take it. I will go and speak to Pawling if you give me the word. If you go to Grant Richards, do not put *my name* to the enclosed, as he has reason to dislike me."[109]

The recommendation, however, came too late for Richards who had kept his word and dealt with the manuscript over the weekend. He wrote to Pinker: "I quite agree with the previous opinion you have had about 'The Holy Mountain': it is extremely clever. I very much doubt its being successful, however, so I am sending it back to you."[110] A bomb exploded in south Devon. "Confound Richards! These publishers' abortive testimonials are becoming an insult."[111]

In the space of two months, the book that was dearest to his heart and symbolised his emergence from the traumas of his youth had been rejected by four London publishers, despite the efforts of his friends to utilise the last ounce of their personal influence. And still, the odd outburst apart, he maintained his general composure and his humour. But the hurt of rejection had gone deep and it would not take much to bring the full emotion to the surface. What broke the dam was not a further rejection of the book, but a quite peripheral matter – the refusal of a few publishers to countenance the relatively new breed of literary agents.

When the bad news came from Grant Richards, Pinker at last determined that there was nothing for it but to go to John Lane. Lane, the farmer's son from Devon, had come late to publishing through his private passion for book-collecting. With Elkin Matthews he had established from nothing the most influential and avant-garde publishing house of the 1890s, the Bodley Head, whose Yellow Book had created its own artistic movement. Despite the break with Matthews, Lane still had a high reputation for taking risks with new authors. Arguably, Pinker would have gone to him long before with Reynolds' work had it not been for one very awkward fact – Lane, like Heinemann, was one of those publishers who simply execrated the literary agent and his impertinent invasion of the cosy familial relationship between publisher and author. He refused point blank to have dealings with them.

Pinker suggested Reynolds should carry the manuscript round in person to Lane but conceal the fact that he had an agent. It was a ruse that Reynolds could not stomach on any account. For one thing, he was friends with Reginald Page, one of Lane's readers who knew of the connection with Pinker, and was thus certain the concealed news would soon get out. But more than that, honest dealings, even in business, were a matter of principle with him. He told Pinker straight: "I will come up and see Lane, or anybody else, next Tuesday, if you think it advisable. But I shall tell him I'm one of your people, in any case, and he can ride the high horse (as you may think I am now doing) if he likes. But, not the possibilities, the probabilities, are too unpleasant. One of his readers knows perfectly well that you are my agent; and in fact he was saying one day that he thought it a pity Lane would have nothing to do with agents; so detection of the ruse would be certain, and subsequent remarks unpleasant, no doubt. If you think I have any chance by being frank with Lane, I'll come up. I want to catch the editor of the Albany. If you don't think it any good, please send the MS. anywhere you think it may get put forth quickly. But bustle 'em."[112]

It was a pity that Pinker was not prepared to let Reynolds go openly to Lane as he had proposed. It would have saved a further five months of worry and heartache. But he feared his young friend might receive such a snub as would have turned his whole world upside down. He took Reynolds' reaction quite calmly and fell back on Plan B – Garnett's suggestion that he himself should take the manuscript to Heinemann, whose objections to literary agents in general, and to Pinker in particular, were every bit as strong as Lane's.

Reynolds was now becoming obsessed with the idea that the book must be got out quickly before the Lever libel case drove Northcliffe from the public stage and killed it stone dead. He reacted ironically to the new plan: "I daresay Heinemann will find the book strong in parts but inopportune owing to the price of strawberries. Anyhow, I hope he knows he's got to hurry up one way or t'other. If the time ain't vitty for thic book, t'won't never be – after Morgan-Browne and Lever. I don't think nearly so well as Garnett of the thing, but its possibilities, properly worked, are all right, especially now."[113]

He made it clear, however, that he would be as open with Heinemann as he had planned to be with Lane, though by now he was becoming a little defensive about this principled stand. "As you like to do about Heinemann.... I've been always rather vain of being one of your clients, and I don't intend to hide it, certainly not for a problematical advantage. But I'm really very sorry one of my cussednesses should have turned uppermost at the present moment."[114] He felt a need too to justify to Garnett his attitude over Lane: "It was most awkward just when Pinker is taking so much trouble, but if the ruse had been successful, I should not have been able to look my publisher straight. And when he found out, as he would have, and if he had been decent meantime.... I daresay I do a lot of things Pinker wouldn't, but I couldn't stomach that. The fortunate thing is that Pinker and I haven't in the least fallen out over it. I like Pinker well."[115]

But Garnett, who had just gone to the trouble of carrying round the manuscript in person to Pawling at Heinemanns, was rather less patient with his protégé. He told Reynolds straight that he would have to conceal the Pinker connection and deal with Heinemann direct since, given the history of the manuscript, now was not the time to raise a question of principle. Reynolds was close to the edge of his patience and this friendly lecture was just too much.

> It's awfully good of you to take the MS. to Heinemann's yourself. I'm afraid I'm constitutionally incapable of distinguishing between the times when 'principle' may be raised and the times it mayn't. And I don't intend to try. I shall not go out of my way to tell Heinemann I'm a Pinkerite, and I shall not go out of my way to hide it. I'll have the MS. back first, burn it, and pay Pinker an estimated commission.
> If you object to this direct expression of what I mean, and want to throw me over for a blockheaded fool, I shall be sorry, very, but you must do it. I haven't so many scrupulosities that I can afford to throw one away – especially one that comes fairly easy – in return for any amount of help and kindness whatever. I believe that you wrote in a hurry, not exactly what you mean; for I don't believe that you stow your principles when the stake's important and the position awkward, and I shan't stow mine. Your anxiety for the welfare of me and my MS. has led you to ask me to do what I shan't believe you'd do yourself. I refuse absolutely to take any action steps towards playing a trick on any publisher to make him take my MS.[116]

He felt that Pinker deserved an explanation, but the row had so stirred up his nerves that he could not help but vent his feelings on him too.

> I have received a letter from Garnett telling me that he has taken the MS. to Heinemann without your label because you and H. have a feud; that I "will" deal direct with H., and that "the present is not the time to raise a question of principle". I have told him the same as I told you over Lane. I sha'n't stow what principle I have when the stake is important and the position awkward. I will not go out of my way to tell H. you are my agent, and I won't go out of my way to hide it. I had rather burn the MS. and offer you an estimated commission.
> It isn't that I think my own code of straightness any better than anybody else's. I don't. Your generosity to me has been worth ten of my stand in this. But, knowing this goes against my particular code of straightness, I do not think you will ask me to act so, or claim it in return for your many kindnesses. I'm the sort of man who must be very sober, or very drunken; harshly straight, pig-headedly so, or very crooked. Suppose Heinemann took the book after I had actively pretended you weren't at the back of me; suppose he were rather decent.... How could I meet him? People have hated me, but they have always *trusted me* absolutely and I should collapse without it now. The whole affair: that two men to whom I owe so much should apparently expect me to act as I (being myself) can't and won't, has made me very sick and miserable, and indeed, ill. Think what you like, but for God's sake don't land me into any more of these turmoils out of solicitude for my welfare. My health will be smashed again long before my determination will give out.[117]

It seemed perhaps too easy to shelter behind his health, but he was now genuinely on the point of a new collapse. The first euphoria of life at Sidmouth had worn off and his earnings from writing were tailing off too. The old feeling of destitution was fast approaching. His anger over this question of principle had become blown up out of all proportion – and he knew it. After a further night without sleep, he felt only remorse at the way he had treated his friends and a desire to wash his hands of the whole wretched business. Against all these feelings, the ultimate fate of the book itself paled into insignificance.

On 26 July he wrote two letters. First to Pinker. "Sorry to trouble you. Please don't tell me anything more about the MS. till I enquire or it's sold. You can have a power of attorney if you like. I'm practically collapsed – hardly any sleep for three days and appalling dreams in the little I have had. Shall probably go away for a change if I can't sleep to-night. If a publisher takes it, he is not to have hidden from him the fact I have an agent. Apart from that, I don't care anything for the present, till I've staved off these infernal neurasthenic symptoms."[118]

Then to Garnett. "Please don't refer to the MS. when you write. That and one or two other bothers have smashed me up – only get snatches of sleep and those full of ghastly dreams. Shall probably go away for a change. Daren't bother further. Have offered Pinker a Power of Attorney, so that I shan't hear anything more about it. But I *will not* have the MS. published by a publisher kept in ignorance of the facts. If you want to cap your kindness, inform Heinemann, from me, that Pinker is my agent. Tell him I'm a damn'd fool – anything you like – but inform him."[119]

He had, at the same time, been having a less vociferous dispute with Garnett over the cleanliness chapter in *A Poor Man's House* which Garnett wanted excised ostensibly on grounds of taste, but more probably because he recognised it did not fit well in the context of the book as a whole. Reynolds felt the need to make a clear statement of his artistic purpose but his response could not conceal the tetchy mood he now found himself in. "I explained to you very carefully that the Cleanliness chapter is to be very greatly revised, its present form being merely to get the facts in order. But I am determined not to leave it out, for the simple reason that it is vitally important, in my thinking, to the book. I can't too plainly say that I'm writing this thing not to produce an artistic work (primarily) but to say what I have to say. These people have opened their lives to me; they have given me a sort of home and are my friends. It seems to me that my knowledge of them is a sort of trust, which I ought not to garble for any artistic purpose whatever. You desiderate sincerity in literature. In the P.M's. H. you have it, to my utmost capacity to exercise it; and if it carries objectionable things in its wake, you (i.e. the reader) must put up wi' 'em. I mean to try and make the book artistic, so far as that, in my view, doesn't interfere with the truthfulness of it, and not a bit further. No doubt I shall fail in both points, but it shan't be for lack of trying. Good Lord, man, can't you see that I'm trying hard to put down some of the very essence of the best things I've seen in my life, and that I no more dare to trifle with it for literary purposes than a deeply religious man dares trifle with what he holds sacred. Please make allowance for my point of view."

Then he sensed he might have gone too far. "And above all, don't think I undervalue your advice and encouragement. I don't. It's very great. But as you know, when one is pretty deeply stirred, one has to go one's own way, which nobody else can quite see for one. 'Tisn't that I don't want your advice: don't think that. All I want to make plain is the reason why I imagine myself bound to drive off my own way on a good many occasions, rather than take the advice of people who know better than I do."[120]

After the Heinemann row, Reynolds did as he had promised and escaped to Wiltshire, most probably to the safety and sympathy of the Tanners at Ford. Back in Sidmouth in early August, he was much recovered and writing cheerfully to Pinker of the holiday cottage he had been looking out for him both in

Wiltshire and Devon. But Garnett had taken him at his word when he asked not to write about the manuscript, and had not written at all. Pinker was anxious that Garnett was now the badly wounded party. He was relieved on 11 August by the briefest message from his young client: "Have heard from Garnett. All right."[121]

Two weeks later, Reynolds challenged Garnett once more on the criticism that parts of his new book lacked taste. "Very, very glad to get your letter, because I wanted very badly to make my standpoint plain – make plain, I mean, how and why a youngster like me should sometimes take up a definite opposition stand to a critic like you...... A scientific training makes one very obtuse over *nuances* of taste. I don't pretend to any at all. Taste is like duty, a poor substitute for right feeling. So, when you talk about taste, I don't agree mostly, but I do find out what the strangers, who form the majority, think about it. Most English work is not coarse, but exceedingly vulgar. Mine's not very vulgar, but it's coarse, and will be, and that's why it don't go down: they miss the vulgarity and resent the coarseness. You'd have it neither. Impossible – for me. If I can be told when I'm passing the limit – very good. I can then decide whether I wish to pass it or not, once I am informed where the limit lies."[122]

Following on their first meeting, he had started an altogether gentler correspondence with W.H. Hudson where the only intellectual controversy concerned the nesting sites of birds or the history of local eccentrics. On 20 July, on one of their night expeditions, Uncle Sam had shown him a raven's nest among the Sidmouth cliffs. He wrote off to Hudson in some excitement, pointing out that ravens were supposed to be extinct in the south of England.[123]

Hudson wrote back a friendly letter with a string of queries, about the Wiltshire Downs and about a Miss Hayward, an amateur naturalist who had lived in Sidmouth. He also asked after an article by Reynolds, *Field Club Devastation*, published in the *Daily Mail* that January, which he had not seen but was causing him some trouble. In it Reynolds had advocated the use of the camera rather than the gun for collecting specimens of wild life, and had quoted at length from *Birds and Man*, giving the impression that Hudson was in support and putting him at the mercy of the shooting and stuffing brigade.[124] Reynolds was duly contrite: "I'm so sorry I landed you into a controversy. Doubtless you came out uppermost. May I enclose the offending article (not my title). You will see how much it draws on you – Hudson adapted to the vulgar, I'm afraid."[125] Reynolds, who had long admired Hudson from both a scientific and literary perspective, was greatly flattered by the old man's attentions, and this was a relationship bound to last with unwavering respect on either side. It would not be long before Hudson was down in Sidmouth to see those ravens for himself.

By the middle of August Reynolds was in a sufficiently philosophic mood to take the next, scarcely unexpected, blow – a rejection by Heinemann. On 14 August Pawling wrote to Garnett in more than ordinarily forthright publisher rejection-speak: "As regards *The Holy Mountain* MS., I took it home to read, but

I cannot agree with your view about it, as the taste of it seems to me execrable, and what cleverness there is in it is quite misspent. I will return it to you in due course."[126]

Reynolds was now thinking he would have to face the inevitable and go below the first-line publishers. Edward Thomas suggested, with tongue in cheek, that he should try the controversial *Times* Book Club, selling at knock down prices.[127] Five years later, Reynolds recalled the despair of that time: "Most publishers had the trouble of rejecting it, some with patronage, some in a kindly manner, and a few with sarcasm or gratuitous advice never to print it. The typescript lost its bloom. It had longer spells in my agent's pigeon-holes. Thomas Seccombe, who himself acted as reader for a publishing firm, was jocularly scared by the plant which had grown from his seedling. But I meant it to be published, no matter how long it took."[128]

He waited for Pinker's return from holiday before plotting the next move. "You are probably home by now – after an enjoyable trip, I hope. Also you have probably heard from Garnett that Heinemann's rejected the MS. with execration. I think you'll be reduced to trying a lower-down publisher – Greenings and the like. The thing is not genteel enough for the British Public – too coarse and not vulgar enough for 'em. Which is good in all respects except the cash."[129] They finally agreed to make their next approach, possibly the last at this level, to the house of Methuen.

The long drawn out failures of the *Mountain*, taken so personally, had completely obscured in his mind the quality of the book he was now engaged on – and had brought his current writing to a despairing halt. Prospects for journalistic work were bleak. The *Mail* Supplement had published his first *causerie* on 6 July but was suspended shortly after as the money ran out.[130] Though it came back early in September, it was not to survive to the end of the year. Northcliffe, then plotting the capture of *The Times* and its more distinguished supplement, had no further use for it. As a substitute, Garnett promised to have a word with R.A. Scott-James, the literary editor of the *Daily News* and soon to become a Mont Blanc regular.[131] It proved a successful switch and the *News* was to provide a regular standby income, from both sketches and reviews, through 1908 and 1909.

Reynolds aim, as he told Garnett, was "£150 a year out of literature, and I'll forego all the surplus to get that as I like", by which he meant writing his own books, with time for fishing and the Sidmouth life, rather than be devoured by hack journalism. But he was falling well short of the target; for the first seven months of 1907, his income had averaged no more than 33 shillings a week.[132]

As the summer wore on, he discovered that the small amounts he could earn from the fishing were beginning to provide a regular supplementary income which could help sustain life. But there was something much more important than the money. The disastrous progress of the *Mountain* and the nature of the rebuffs from publishers had dealt a devastating blow to his pride. His self-confidence, beneath the buoyant exterior, was plummetting fast down to the days of his youth. Greater than the money that he took from fishing was the knowledge that he could pay his own way at the Woolleys and make his own way on the beach. His pride was being restored from an unexpected source. "Last week, I earned 8/- and 4½d at fishing. Having an inkling that I'm rather cashless and finding me more use than beach-combers, picked up in a hurry, the good fellows call me out to the hauls (at 2 a.m. sometimes) and insist on my taking my share, which I do do, very proudly."[133]

He wrote to Garnett on 25 August with a frank statement of his new attitude of resignation. "At present, I'm doing no work. Furor scribendi is rather quenched by the adventures of the *Mountain*. My present feeling is that I've done at any rate well-intentioned work, and they don't like it; therefore to hell with 'em. Why should I care? The opinion of a few who know is all I want that way. Certainly I become poorer daily; but also healthier and more independent of literature. There's no reason why one should knuckle under to literary conditions any more than to any other conditions. I want very much to get some literary success, but if I can't get it my own way I can keep myself otherwise, and miss but very little happiness, and, I think, make other people happier in other ways. Writing well about life is very splendid; and living it fully, as you say, is better still. The arts are man's very fine efforts to counteract defects in his equipment. With further evolution the arts, as we conceive 'em, should be gradually superseded. So, it seems to me, one may be either artist-counteractor, or a conscious portion of that evolutionary process. And which is it ultimately more desirable to have been? I don't know: but to be either is good, I imagine. Anyhow, I don't think the notion is all rot, even if it has its origin in exasperated defiance – or irritated egoism, if you like that better."[134]

In the middle of August he had spent five days covering for Mam Woolley while she took her holiday, doing the cooking and running the house for the whole family. It was to become an annual arrangement. The Woolleys knew their young lodger was both depressed with his writing and short of cash, and hastened to assure him there would always be a home for him in Bedford Square. "Last night, I had an extraordinarily frank talk with him [*Bob*] and Mam Woolley. She admits, what I know, that work and accommodation aside, having me brings 15/- into the family pocket, and says she'd have taken me for a good deal less than I pay if I had beaten her down. I said that I have my full guinea's worth, but someday might have to draw in and go back to the one backroom. Says Mam W. and Bob, 'If you couldn' pay it, us wouldn' take it; an if you had nort at all to pay, us 'ould never see 'ee go out of this house till you had.' It means this: that from a lodger, I become a contributor to the family purse, and throw, potentially, all I've got or can earn into it. They share my fortune; I theirs. Next summer I shall probably be on the beach with Bob, and, with each supplementing the knowledge and abilities of t'other, I think neither will be the loser."[135]

The offer from the Woolleys touched him so deeply that he wrote it with some emotion and emphasis into the final scene of his book.[136] He was equally proud of his increasing standing on the beach. "Yesterday, I spent all day rigging our new boat. It's Bob's, but called 'ours', because I ordered it, made out the specification and originated the improvements. In such ways, I *can* be of help. Nearly all the fishing-lines come to me now to be made up. Altogether, I feel pretty confident that I'm worth my standing on the beach, as they, indeed, generously say. 'Tisn't that I'm blowing my own trumpet. It's merely that my training and knowledge supplement Bob's and that his business is increased so far beyond a one man job, that it pays him or would pay him to retain that supplement at its worth. The beachcomber who has been helping out there this season is not honest, and can't be trusted to sail a boat, or even to beach one in a lop. It's for those, and other reasons, that I feel myself at liberty to pop into the niche waiting for me. And, you know, I'm no end proud of being able to get there."[137]

Many of Reynolds' literary friends, and most of his readers, were deeply puzzled when, at the height of his celebrity as a writer, he slowly withdrew into fishery politics and administration. For some it was clear proof that he was not a born writer. That was far from the truth – writing and the urge to write was in his blood to his death. In part, the change was purely economic; ironically, public fame did not improve his sales nor secure him from starvation. But its origins can clearly be traced back to these dog days of the summer of 1907. The literary world of the London publishing houses had dealt him such a blow that he was never to trust it again. By contrast, the fishermen had opened their arms to him just when he needed them most. They gave him a tithe of economic security, but it was the emotional security they offered that was the real prize. Little wonder then that he should determine to repay them in full – even with his life.

He sensed the significance of this change in attitude and its impact on his writing career. He felt a need to explain frankly to Pinker his short term withdrawal from writing, but in that explanation was a hint of what might come in the longer term too. He wrote to his long-suffering agent on 28 August in a clear confident tone, with none of the tentativeness of his letter to Garnett three days before – perhaps with an element of bravado, but underneath an undeniable indication that he had cleared his mind.

> I've been having an extraordinarily varied experience for the last few weeks. For five days, while Mrs. Woolley was away, I did all the housekeeping and cooking. Then, being in an unusually bad temper with scribbling, and very flat-brained with disappointment, I said I'd throw up writing till the end of the summer, turn fisherman and boatman altogether for the time, and pick up what money I could in odd coppers and little bits of silver. At any rate, by picking wrinkles all the morning I can earn a couple of shillings which is far from so certain out of a morning's

> Swan-driving. Just at present, pleasure boating being the main thing I'm out on the beach, blue guernsey, ragged trousers and all, hiring out and hauling boats in all respects as a fisherman, getting an immense amount of amusement out of it, some small coin, and much health.
> You see, I'm laying in a stock of health. I'm not quite certain that all this is fair to you, but my brain, without much literary hope in it, is very dead for the time, till it gathers fresh bounce, and in the future, if you have to chuck me overboard, you will be able to do it without much compunction, or feeling that I shall starve; confident that I shall sink quite comfortably into the working class, where, in fact, at present, I'm by far the happiest and most at home.
> Bob Woolley and I, both our existences being precarious in the extreme, have practically thrown in together. He and his wife say so long as they've got 'ort, I shouldn't want grub, and I say that so long as I have any, if he trips up, I keep the house going, and he shares my luck if I have any.
> You see, Pinker, I've been adopted into a family and after 12 years' wandering, quarrelling and hating, have got a home. And really most things else don't matter.
> Perceive also, that your literary big-bugs that rake in the shekels, with their genteel excrescential emotions, don't know life like this; they stultified their poverty by clinging to gentility. Think what poor Gissing missed.[138]

It was at the end of August, during this period of alienation from the London literary world, that the *Daily Mail* published one of his best sketches of this period, *A Yokel's Impression of London*. Ironically, it was not until the cheque came in two months later that he found out it had been printed at all.[139] It reflects a long-standing preoccupation – his intense love-hate relationship for the metropolis, reaching out far beyond the literary cliques who inhabited the place.

He grabs his audience with a boisterous opening.

> Live in London? Not for the world! But there is no place like London to visit. One is glad to go there now and then; glad of a plunge into the middle of things; and very glad to come away again. Thus the visit is good from beginning to end, particularly at the end. What a steady-hearted air of the country lingers about Paddington Station! How pleasant it is to sit in a Western express and to watch the last traces of town, the last haze of smokiness, the last stucco villas, die away some thirty or forty miles down the line.

In an arresting image, he compares his attitude to that of a nervy horse stranded in the traffic.

> The other day from the top of an Oxford-street omnibus I saw a hansom cab stockstill, on tip-toe as it were, right in the middle of the traffic. The horse, a gawky young chestnut, thin and badly clipped, was sweating and trembling and mouthing its bit, but it could not move. For some reason or other it had utterly lost its nerve. It was powerless to do more than stay where it was. Its joints twitched in and out. The traffic roared and clattered around. Two men caught hold of the spokes of each wheel and tried to turn them. Two men pushed behind the cab. The driver lashed with his whip. At last the frightened chestnut tottered up the street, and the fools on the pavement laughed aloud as if it had been a joke. We soon overtook that cab. Once more the horse stood helpless and trembling. Once more there was a turning of wheels and a pushing, a lashing, and laughter.
>
> Poor creature! I thought of the horses in the home field, looking peacefully over the gate and rubbing their necks on the top bar perhaps, far from that pandemonium which is London. If men build cities for themselves, they have no right to take horses into them. The nature of that chestnut will be maimed for life. I should not like to drive it now, for nervelessness in a horse is worse than vice. Why could they not have coaxed and cossetted it a little? Why could they not have given it a little time to regain its nerve? But no; they could not do that. I see they could not. The almighty, unnecessary push of London was behind it. It had to move on, and move quickly.
>
> It is that almighty push that I hate. Were I caught in London, I know I should kick, shy, jib, rear, buckjump, and bite, and I know also that London would push me on, and quite overwhelm me and crush me. I should be worse off than the frightened chestnut horse. London would never let me stay my own man. That is why I hate it, almightily pushing, insensate London!

He has harsh words for the suavity of London social manners, all form and no real feeling, which he had seen above all among his literary contacts.

> Londoners are like sardines. They have been pressed together, and have partly taken one another's shape, and doubtless they are bathed in the oil of suavity in order to lessen the friction of contact. Fishy oil, very nice with something solid, but horridly nasty by itself! Perhaps it is that which sends me away from London parties in a dull rage and desirous of a midnight train into the plain-spoken countryside, where they say, "I shan't, I tell 'ee, and there's an end o' it!"

There is an elegiac note in his description of the beauty of London.

> It is, of course, absurd to deny that London is wonderfully beautiful. It is a great but morbid beauty. It depresses rather than strengthens, leads to unrest rather than tranquillity. It is a beauty born of blackness and smoke, dirt-mist, grim force, and ponderousness. To look on the flowers and trees of London is to pity them for being there. The sunshine itself seems to knock at the door and say, "May I come in?" I have watched sunsets over the outskirts of London – fanfares of smoke and flame, skies inexpressibly beautiful. The sunsets of the country are peaceful assurances before darkness that
>
> "God's in his heaven -
> All's right with the world!"
>
> But the sunsets of London are things of sadness and wrath. They excite; they exhaust. They push one's thoughts towards melancholy and death. I have never seen dawn in London, and I do not want to. Its cold fingers would take too terrible a grip. It is dreadful to lie awake in the city and to picture the miles upon miles of houses that are between one's bed and the green fields and fresh air and wide, open spaces.

And he ends a remarkable piece on a note of superiority, as he comes out of the National Gallery and looks down on the hapless bands of civil servants as they trek back along Whitehall to their gloomy offices.

> One thing above all in London I do like, and that is to stand by the balustrade (do they call it?) at the top of Trafalgar-square and to look down on those puny, petty men who hustle from Charing Cross-road down to Whitehall, from Cockspur-street into the Strand. Look down on them, I say; for I am sure that, though they live in the middle of things, it is nevertheless we yokels who by looking on see most of the game. We are nearer to mother earth than those pavement trotters; we are more in her confidence – earth that is mother of the country and stepmother to the towns.[140]

Unbeknownst to him then, he was to spend the following year two months in the centre of London, the longest ever consecutive period there. The sketch was written at the time of *A Poor Man's House* and shows all the confidence of style and certainty of atmosphere that was to go into his best book.

Garnett's flurry of activity on behalf of the *Mountain* that summer was all the more praiseworthy because he was in the midst of a little local difficulty of his own. He had just completed a play, *The Breaking Point,* exploring the emotions of a young woman who falls in love with a married man whose wife has left him. Her father and her lover quarrel for control of her, while she, fearing she is pregnant, cannot stand the strain and commits suicide. The essence of the work is an exposé of male egotism but the apparent projection of fornication and suicide as honest action was too much for the examiner of plays, G.A. Redford, who banned it from performance. Edward Thomas remarked to Reynolds that this was almost fortunate since it would spur Garnett on to an inspired preface to the printed play – which it did.[141]

When, shortly after, Granville Barker's play *Waste* was also censored, the literary world was up in arms. John Galsworthy, J.M. Barrie and Gilbert Murray set up a committee to campaign for the abolition of the censorship, and organised a petition signed by 71 authors and a march on Downing Street by all the notable dramatists of the day as precursor to a meeting with the Prime Minister. The march and the meeting planned for November had to be successively postponed with the onset of the series of heart attacks that was eventually to remove Campbell-Bannerman from the premiership the following spring.

Finally a meeting was fixed in February 1908 with the lacklustre Home Secretary, Herbert Gladstone, whom Asquith was to sack two years later. Vaughan Nash, then junior private secretary to the Prime Minister but later to play an important role in Reynolds' life, wrote from No.10 to Arthur Ponsonby, the Principal Private Secretary: "The censorship deputation has been chucked to Gladstone as they didn't want to wait indefinitely. The King has chipped in and says he won't hear of the abolition of the censor. Your cousin, the Lord Chamberlain, comes hopping in here like an agitated bird, but he is quite delightful about it all."[142]

The meeting when finally arranged proved the archetype of Ministerial deputations, both before and since, where persons of eminence, a little over-awed before the majesty of power but fully anticipating dialogue and decision, confront Ministers woefully ignorant of the deeper issues and under instruction to listen, say nothing at length and promise only further consideration. When Granville Barker gave Ponsonby an account of it a week later he could not hide just a little disillusion: "It came off as well as could be expected. We were an imposing array and I think Gladstone was really terrified. Barrie was very Scotch and very humorous. Pinero did the 'never in the whole course of my professional experience' sort of thing very well, and Gilbert [*Murray*] was appropriately disagreeable. Gladstone then said nothing at all for almost seven minutes, whereupon Murray got up to thank him and succeeded in about fifty words in lifting the subject to a plane from which even Cabinet Ministers look insects. So we departed and now nothing will be done I suppose unless we can stir things up some more."[143]

Further action was indeed needed. A private members Bill was introduced into the Commons, and duly swept by the Government into a Committee of both Houses, which reported a year later. The result – no action, but in practice a more cautious policy from the Lord Chamberlain's office in the years to come.

The issue was thus to engage much of Garnett's emotional energy for the next two years. It was a personal one which attacked the seat of his artistic integrity and he was irritated, and later aggrieved, by the apparently laid-back attitude of Reynolds who saw the application of censorship in practice as more of a joke than a threat. It was a background source of dissension between the two men at a time when they were coming to recognise their intellectual differences over even more important issues.

As a result of work and the furore in London, Garnett was forced to postpone his planned August visit to Sidmouth but went down for a long weekend in the middle of September to stay in the house in Bedford Square. Reynolds proudly introduced the Woolleys, and they took to him immediately. Garnett abandoned his manuscripts for a while to relax in the sun and some deep-sea bathing. Much to the consternation of Constance who wrote anxiously from London: "I suppose you are enjoying Sidmouth as you don't write. It must be lovely by the sea in this hot weather. Do be careful about swimming so far out. It makes me shudder to think of you".[144]

Reynolds himself had quite recovered from the blues of August with vigorous mental and physical activity, which he kept up even while Garnett was there. As he told Pinker: "Have been working furiously, reviews and boats. 12 mile row last Saturday, and 10 miles last Monday against headwind and tide. How's that for an ex-invalid? Never been busier and never better."[145] He showed Garnett his story, *The Prawner*, about a night under the cliffs with Uncle Sam, which Anderson Graham at *Country Life* had just rejected. Garnett thought it about the best thing he had done, as did a few thousand readers when *A Poor Man's House* came out.[146] They talked endlessly about his prospects as a writer and Garnett was adamant that he should hang on, despite all disappointments, and develop the unique voice he had found with his Sidmouth material "He's very keen on my staying to work the mine (doesn't seem to be a gold mine) properly".[147]

They talked inevitably too of Garnett's play and the censorship controversy. When he got back to London, Garnett sent Reynolds a copy of it which the latter praised highly. But like many others, he was shocked by the starkness of the final scene where the father and the lover discuss the heroine while she is off-stage in the act of committing suicide. He raised it to a discussion of taste and, despite protestations to the contrary, was getting a little of his own back for Garnett's criticism of the *Poor Man's House*. "But (this is not mere retaliation) some of the play offends my taste grievously – as brutally as any of my stuff offends yours. Of course, I don't mean on the score of impropriety – it's the pink of that. But that the characters of Ellwood and Sherrington should be allowed to exfoliate for the benefit of showing anything at all to anybody at all, while the poor creature is gone to kill herself; that they should discuss her condition.... Brutal. Did the audience really fully realise the girl's state of mind they could *not* stand it. It would be all right on a lower plane, but on the high plane to which you have raised the action it is ghastly."

And on the censorship question he twisted Garnett's tail not a little. "If it came to the vote the B[*ritish*] P[*ublic*] had rather have the nice protective censor than you; and you're a democrat, aren't you? You're capable of infecting a town with the vice of thinking. Whether from the B.P.'s point of view you are better or worse than a criminal I ain't sure; but a mental criminal you are, and so am I. Like the criminals we don't recognise the sanctity of *what is.* Your plea that people can stay away isn't sound. God knows whom you may infect with your anti-what-is notions."[148]

It was typical of Reynolds to treat the subject of censorship in a slightly ironic vein. When asked in 1913 for an *ex cathedra* statement on the censorship of books, he made clear his view that in practice he had never suffered and hinted that the righteous indignation of the victims was something of a luxury. "I think all censorship, of any books whatsoever, extremely stupid, though, if there is to be a censorship, I should certainly recommend making a start on those books which whitewash the so-called facts of life with a muddy religiosity. If the public can't take care of itself, and parents of their female young, without the intervention of Meyers and such-like morality-mongers, then it deserves all the evil its prudery may enable it to extract from books. To my mind, the solemn-serious treatment of 'delicate problems' is ten times worse than the Rabelaisian. Laughter's an antiseptic; tears and heroics aren't. No doubt Mr Hall Caine is quite right – in his attack on censorship, I mean. I can't myself complain, nor pretend to the indignation that arises only from personal injury, for so far I haven't been troubled, though I'm much more apt to call a spade a damn'd spade than a divine horticultural implement. On the contrary, I have to thank people for giving me a good deal of rope. I almost fancy, indeed, that plain speaking is as permissible as ever it was, provided it really is open plain speaking, unmixed with whitewash and that highly immoral thing, a high moral purpose."[149]

It was little surprise that Garnett, to whom the issue was serious and deep, should feel let down by this cavalier kind of attitude. But he felt more badly let down still by Reynolds' somewhat ambivalent reaction to the campaign and reluctance to join it with unqualified support. When the agitation began in earnest that October, he wrote to Garnett: "Of course you may depend on me to help fight, and that with gusto. But must expect a bit of a splutter – a certain amount of by-product also – *within* the precincts of our own camp. 'Tis the nature of the beast to hit all the harder for sympathizing with the enemy a little bit."[150]

As summer turned to autumn, Reynolds himself began to turn back to his writing again, but with half a glance over his shoulder to the fate of the *Mountain* which Methuen had now been considering for some weeks. On 24 September he wrote to Pinker: "If you have any news of a stimulating nature, please send it along. Now the boating is nearly over, I am getting to work again, but it's difficult to write stuff for such consistent rejection. The Mail hasn't sent me any books either, and I suppose Methuen has fired out the Holy Mountain.... I shouldn't care much but for the damping effect it has on one's wits."[151]

The next day he received confirmation of his worst fears – news of Methuen's rejection. With it, Pinker had enclosed a reasoned letter from E.V. Lucas, which predictably tried to soften the blow by proclaiming that Reynolds was destined to do remarkable things in the future. Now inured to this kind of message, his first reaction was to take it in his stride: "Same tale. Very kind, I'm sure. But thank you very much for your efforts in the matter. It must be as exasperating for you as it is damnable for me. Nous arriverons quelque beau-jour! Et puis alors...."[152]

But as he mulled over Lucas' letter, he was stung by the remark that the main failing of the book was that it had been written out of pique – something he had acknowledged himself more than once, but was not prepared to hear from other lips. He wrote again to Pinker: "I'm very much obliged for having had a look at Mr. Lucas's letter, which is certainly good in parts, me lord! But I resent strongly the notion that I have used the tale to pay off private grudges – apparently the result of my having made the characters individual as well as typical. Beyond two very minor characters, one comic and the other very complimentary, the persons of the book are, as I said in the note, imagined and not copied directly from life. Nobody seems to see, though I have tried to make it plain, that underneath the satire, lies the adage: Tout savoir c'est tout pardonner. Hence the necessity of showing their squalid environment, which I shall not cut out. I shall not make gentlemanly uncharitable wish-wash of the book."[153]

The *Mountain* had now been rejected by six of the leading London publishing houses in the space of just four months. Wherever it now went, its notoriety would march before it. Pinker counselled wisely that it should be taken out of circulation for a while, and Reynolds was forced to agree. "If you think the MSS. had better be put away, please do so – so long as you act on your own judgement *exclusively*. I do value your advice to act on it, whereas I don't care two pins for the praise or blame of these literary people. Saying I ought to do remarkable things will neither make me do, or not do, them, nor pay for them when they're done."[154]

On 12 October he went back to Devizes to settle in for an autumn of concentrated work rewriting the first half of *A Poor Man's House*.[155] On the 14th, he went up to town in the late morning and was closeted with Pinker that Monday afternoon.[156] The following day, there was another surprise awaiting him when the Mont Blanc party assembled at half past one. Garnett, Hudson and Edward Thomas were there as expected, but among them was a slight, dark figure, with pointed beard and piercing eyes, who greeted him with almost oriental courtesy. It was Joseph Conrad, his principal living literary hero, since the days in 1903 when he had read him late into the night in the cold of his Paris attic.[157]

Conrad had been out of England for the first eight months of 1907, in Montpellier and Champel in Switzerland – a nightmare "holiday" in which his eldest son, Borys, had been seriously ill throughout and he himself had been wracked by financial and creative worries. In September he had moved to Someries, a large farmhouse close to Luton, which was only forty minutes by train to St Pancras and made regular visits to London, and to the Mont Blanc, more feasible than from his old house in the wilds of Kent. For much of his writing life a country recluse, Conrad for these months was to be seen more frequently in London than he ever would be again. It was just a month since publication of *The Secret Agent* to good reviews and fairly buoyant sales, but none of this seemed to lift his general mood of weariness. He was currently labouring on with *Chance* – the book that, ironically, was to make his reputation – but without any realistic prospect of an early completion.

Conrad was just entering on that period of his life when he began to surround himself with young writers, to whom he gave encouragement and wise advice in exchange for vitality and hope, two commodities of which he was fast running out. Reynolds was one of the first. They had, after all, the sea in common. At this first meeting, they discussed Reynolds' work and Conrad asked him for some samples to see. Although in a depressed mood that morning, feeling "damnably done up", Conrad was nevertheless awakened immediately by the force of this young man and his ideas.[158] He straightway invited him down to Someries for the following weekend. It was the start of a close friendship that was to last for the next five years until the end of Reynolds' writing career.

At the lunch, Garnett unloaded on Reynolds and Thomas two tickets for a performance of Galsworthy's new play, *Joy*, now at the end of its third week. That evening the two friends hurried off to the Savoy and very much enjoyed the performance, in stark contrast to the scathing reviews it had received in the press. Garnett reported back to Galsworthy with a note of reassurance: "As I was too busy on Tuesday I gave your tickets for Joy to Reynolds and Thomas who were *delighted* with 'Joy' – and thought Joy herself admirably acted but Mrs Gwyn *very poor and stiff*. They said the audience was very *pleased*".[159]

The following day Reynolds had lunch alone with Edward Thomas.[160] They talked of their current work. Thomas had spent much of the summer in Wiltshire collecting material for his commissioned biography of Richard Jefferies, and was planning to leave home in the New Year to start on the writing. Reynolds regaled him with the joys of the *Poor Man's House* and the sorrows of the *Mountain*. They had both been invited to the Cearne for a day, and went down the next morning with Edward Garnett. The three men spent the whole day talking and talking and talking – and did not finally turn in until half past midnight.[161]

Reynolds and Thomas were up at eight that Friday morning and lunched together again on their way through London, the one heading for Luton and the other for Petersfield.[162] At Someries Reynolds met for the first time Conrad's wife, Jessie, the nine-year-old Borys and two-year-old John. As usual, he got on extremely well with both children and was deeply impressed by the novel experience of spending a night under the roof of a great author. And he was not the only one to be impressed. Conrad told Pinker straight after: "I had Reynolds here. I decidedly think there is a lot in that young man. I also like him for certain qualities he has, which are not on the surface it is true, but which are there all the same".[163]

Reynolds spent the next two weeks hard at work in his little cell in Pans Lane, seeing no one all day except for a couple of hours in the evening.[164] He was reviewing as furiously as ever for the *Bookman* and plunging on with the revision of the *Poor Man's House*. On the visit to London he had also touched base with John Buchan at Nelsons, who had offered him some reviewing work for the *Scottish Review*, the cheaper Scottish version of the popular English religious weeklies, which Buchan had been editing since February. Despite Buchan's radical overhaul of the paper and injection of literary and social features, Reynolds was wary of its uneasy mixture of the ecclesiastical and the secular and wondered how long it would pay its way and, more important, pay *him*.[165] He had hopes, however, that his new friendship with Buchan might lead to more productive work from Nelsons itself.

This new period of concentrated work threatened to knock him up again, but he was buoyed up physically by the effects of the summer at Sidmouth, and mentally by his first, and typically complimentary, letter from Conrad. He wrote proudly to Pinker on 8 November: "The major part of the *Poor Man's House* is written and re-written. I've been working very hard – much harder than I could have worked before and without feeling it much except liverishly. Conrad would see some of my stuff, so I sent him a few little MSS. I had by me, and he replied with a letter that.... I think I should like you to see it. I'm very proud of it. What a fascinating man he is: so ardent and at the same time giving one a sense of detached very calm wisdom behind."[166]

Since the close of the summer, he had been planning with Bob for a major event. "Bob Woolley and myself are coming up for our great week in town next Monday; which will be interesting as well as enjoyable. Reckon he'll be mazed by the end o' it; know I shall."[167] They arrived on 11 November and Reynolds spent a fascinating time, showing Bob the sights and charting his reactions, and proudly showing him off to his literary and other friends. The following day he took him to lunch at the Mont Blanc to meet Garnett, Hueffer and Edward Thomas. It was the first time, but not the last, that a simple fisherman had sat down there among the *glitterati*. Though Bob was never one to be overawed, it was perhaps fortunate on this first occasion that Hudson was also present to lend some sensitive support – Hudson who was always most at home chatting with the ancient rustic and the simple cottager.[168]

The two friends did their holidays in style and stayed this time at a fairly expensive hotel, where Bob was equal to all occasions and did not in the least disgrace himself. Reynolds sensed that here was more good copy for *A Poor Man's House* and used it to illustrate the inbuilt courtesy and natural good manners of the working class, so different from the *learnt* manners of the middle class which collapsed under the pressure of strange surroundings.

> It might have been expected, on the other hand, when Tony and myself went on holiday up-country, stayed at a largish much-upholstered hotel, and dined out several times as he had never done before, that he would have been like a fish out of water, very awkward, and would have committed a number of bad *faux pas*. Nothing of the sort. He was nervous, certainly, and the numerous knives, forks and glasses somewhat confused him at first. But Tony's good manners are not codified. He is sensitive, kindly, desirous of pleasing, quick to observe. On that basis, he invented for himself, according to the occasion, the manners he had not been taught. At the same time he remained himself. And he was a complete success. Nobody had any reason to blush on Tony's behalf. Except once; when he remarked to some ladies after dinner that he found Londoners very nice and free-like; that a pretty young lady had stopped him in the Strand the evening before, and had called him Percy; that he hadn't had time to tell her she'd made a mistake, and that, in fact, he might have knowed her tu Seacombe, only he didn't recollect.
>
> There was a bad pause.
>
> Tony doesn't think ill of anybody without cause. *Honi soit qui mal y pense* might very well be *his* motto.[169]

This was the start of an annual series of early autumn holidays that was to take them, good manners and bad, to Boulogne, Paris and as far afield as Marseille.

London had been full of unexpected surprises that autumn – the meetings with Conrad and Buchan, the lionising of Bob – he was almost getting to *like* the place! But there was one more yet in store. He went up the first week in December and had a long discussion with Pinker in his office. Pinker, as ever, struggled to pull him out of his literary depression and persuade him that all was not lost. "I was more grateful than appeared for the trouble you took to jaw me into a properer frame of mind. The worst o' it is unreasonable beings are so unamenable to reasoning."[170] On the Tuesday he had the usual Mont Blanc lunch with Garnett and Edward Thomas. He stayed up all week because Thomas had arranged to go down with him on Friday evening for another Devizes weekend.[171]

He had time to kill and decided on a piece of private enterprise. Pinker had been sitting on the manuscript of the *Mountain* for a full ten weeks. It had now completed its penance and could rightfully be dusted off once more. On Friday 6 December he decided to revert to the rejected plan of July and go alone to beard John Lane in his den in Vigo Street off Piccadilly.

He had no appointment but managed, much to his surprise, to burst through the underlings in the outer office and make his way to the great man. Not knowing Lane was himself a Devonian, he mentioned Sidmouth in his introduction as a matter of course. The ice could not have been more expertly broken. Lane was delighted to discover that the young author's father lived at Nether Velly, just two miles away from Fostelle Farm, Hartland where he had grown up from the age of three.

From then on the interview went swimmingly with Reynolds pulling all the right strings. Even the sensitive issue of Pinker was turned to his advantage. He told Lane that an agent had been working the *Mountain* for him round the London houses, had achieved a few good readers' comments but nothing else, apart from a tentative nibble from Alston Rivers. So he had taken the manuscript on himself. This was honey to Lane's ears. He told the young author "My advice is have nothing more to do with agents." Reynolds told him that he had brought the manuscript to him because he had heard he was capable of a "go to the devil" attitude, in contrast to the fainthearts that had refused the book.

Then he played the trump card. He mentioned *A Poor Man's House* and described its very Devon subject matter. Though only half complete, Roden Buxton was seriously considering it for serialisation. If Lane would take the risky manuscript, the less risky one would be thrown in with it.

The fish began to bite. Lane asked him who his agent was; and told him to call in again when he was next in town. Reynolds took care to mention the Lane books he had recently reviewed, and his friendship with Edward Garnett, who had just passed on a manuscript with which Lane was well pleased. The confidence had been built. As Reynolds stood up to go, he heard Lane's parting words with disbelief: "You know I couldn't afford to give you anything for it till I had sold some copies."[172] They took time to sink in. Money was nothing to him now; publication everything. His friend of five minutes was talking of publication. He was actually thinking of publishing!

He ran back to Pinker's office in a flurry of excitement, found him out, and scribbled a hurried note. With Lane's parting words ringing in his ears, he knew in his bones he had caught his publisher. He just made the five o'clock train at Paddington with Edward Thomas.[173] Both friends were equally excited by the news. Though neither yet knew it for certain, the *Mountain*, after all its weary wanderings, had finally found a home.

NINE

A Poor Man's House 1907–8

The two young friends travelled down to the country that Friday evening in an undisguised haze of delight. As Reynolds watched the smoke from the engine stream past his window, dancing with black smuts and crimson sparks, he saw a lifetime of rejection slips fly burning past his head. The words kept echoing through his brain "You know I couldn't afford...... to give you anything for it...... till I had sold some copies."

By half past seven they were walking up Long Street, past the Museum where he had researched his Guide, past the house in which he had taken his first firm steps as a child, to the corner of Pans Lane from where they could see the welcoming lights of the little terrace which had been his lonely *Werkstatt* for much of the past two years. The Wyers were there to greet them and share in the good news. But the welcome was tinged with the slightest touch of melancholy. He knew there would not be many more homecomings to Devizes like this. At the back of his mind, he had decided to throw up these old lodgings and put his life in the hands of the fishermen of Sidmouth for good. It might be sooner rather than later; Phoebe Wyer was now seven months pregnant with her first child. Come February she would be needing the front bedroom for her confinement.

For this third weekend together that year the two young writers followed the now accustomed pattern – walking and talking the Downs by day, eating and talking late into each evening. On Saturday they took the traditional first walk to Tan Hill, out through Coate and Horton and back through All Cannings and Coate again in the fading December twilight. That evening they walked through the market place of Devizes, already shimmering with the Christmas lights, and climbed the steep staircase of the College for dinner with Ada Bennett and William Brimicombe.[1] He proudly told his old schoolmistress of the success of his week in London. The book she had so persistently encouraged him to write might soon, after all, be in the shop windows of the little market town it so lovingly derided.

In Reynolds' mind, he had two books, not one, on the point of publication. At the end of July, he had sent half the first draft of *A Poor Man's House* to the editor of the *Albany*, Charles Roden Buxton, who had promised to look at it on return from his holiday in September.[2] The aim that summer had been to secure the serial publication that would subsidise the writing of the second half. But now it was midwinter, he had heard nothing more from Buxton, and life had moved on. In the mad flurry of activity from mid-October to early November, he had written much of the second half of the book and rewritten the first draft.[3] All that remained was to shoehorn the rejected *Daily Mail* sketches into the final chapters and write the explanatory epilogue.[4] The book was as good as written; he was now on the look-out for new ideas for the next.

That Sunday morning, as they took a gentler walk through the meadows to Drew's Pond and Potterne, Edward Thomas outlined to him the story of a commission that had failed to get off the ground, but might just possibly be resurrected.[5] In early September Grant Richards, who had so peremptorily dismissed the *Mountain* six weeks before, had had an idea for a book and called Thomas up to town to discuss it.[6] He wanted to cash in on the "Back to the Land" movement with a lively account of why so many townsmen were moving to the country, and what opportunities they found there for jobs and leisure – what was to become, in Reynolds' shorthand, the *Urban Exodus* book.[7] Thomas was tempted by the offer of 100 guineas to do the work, but he had doubts whether he could meet the precise Richards requirement. "If you have glanced here and there at 'The Heart of England' I think you will probably conclude that I could hardly do the cheerful book you would like and ought to have on the subject. At the same time I have been thinking it over and I do see a way out by means of a series of chapters dealing with an imaginary character who migrates."[8] He was doubtful, however, whether the didactic messages that Richards wanted would not become obscured by the subjective descriptions and reflections that were the hallmark of a Thomas book.

By October Thomas had drawn up a number of schemes for the book and rejected them all. He had plenty of material but could not decide the right form in which to cast it. He had little time to worry with it further since he was coming to the end of his research for the Jefferies biography and would be fully preoccupied in the New Year when the writing phase began. In the circumstances, Richards agreed that they should put the subject on ice and come back to it later the following year.[9] Thomas had by no means discarded the idea and it was, therefore, a strong signal both of his generosity and of his close regard for his friend that he now offered it to Reynolds. The latter jumped at the opportunity. Though he now saw his future as a specialist longshore writer, that was no reason to reject the chance to polish up his old image as a "country" writer. There was also the little matter of the hundred guineas....

That evening in Pans Lane, Edward Thomas wrote seven letters. One of them was to Grant Richards.

> I have lately seen a good deal of a man who would do very well the book you suggested to me a few months ago. As a writer he has done reviewing, signed and unsigned, for 'Speaker' and 'Bookman'; he did the country books for the 'Daily Mail' supplement: and he has written fiction by which (it is still in M.S.) he is likely to make a very great hit in a year or two – so Joseph Conrad and several critics think. Personally, I think that he is brilliant and that the book you wanted me to do would give him ample scope. He is a country man himself, has worked on a farm and is a fisherman. But he

> knows London, Paris and Manchester, and he is an Honours man in science.[10]

It was a letter to bring a blush to Reynolds' cheek – had he seen it. But if he had, he might surely have asked Thomas to tone down the reference to the "fiction" which Richards had just had the honour of rejecting in person. It was a generous act on the part of Edward Thomas and gave Reynolds a new focus for the next six months. It was not, however, destined to bear fruit.

Thomas went off on his own that Monday walking to Marlborough through the Savernake Forest just as the two friends had done the previous spring. They sat up talking late into the night, for Thomas was off to London and the Mont Blanc the following day, leaving Reynolds to tackle with renewed energy the final chapters of the *Poor Man's House*.[11] Reynolds was still glowing from the success of his approach to Lane but was quick to reassure Pinker that he was only making use of the direct access clause they had negotiated together in the summer of 1904. "I am rather pleased at having succeeded in planting the MS. there and at the same time letting them know the adventures of it. In effect, I take advantage of our now-almost-forgotten-by-me agreement, which specifically allows me to place my own MSS. if I do want to. I think both Lane and Chapman, his reader, are favourably predisposed, else Lane would hardly have asked me to call whenever I am in town and have told me there and then that he couldn't afford to give much for it!"[12] But if Lane did decide to take the books, Reynolds would have to act as his own agent in all future negotiations. He had no clue as to what he might be letting himself in for.

The run-up to Christmas this year was quite different from the usual pattern of mounting depression. His optimism over the book he was completing was quiet but assured: "The Poor Man's House ought to get somewhere; it's in no sense secondhand, and the beggars say they want firsthand stuff, though I take partic'lar notice they ain't pleased when they get it."[13] What made this December so different, however, was a quite unexpected invitation to go down to Someries to spend Christmas with Conrad and his family. He could not disguise his surprise and delight. "I'm dividing my festivities: Xmas week, Conrad's, and New Year, Bob's. Wasn't it a kind notion of Conrad's to ask me? I feel all sorts of things, all good, about it."[14]

He was also contemplating rather ruefully the fact that he would be without a home the following spring. Phoebe Wyer was not the only person who was expecting. "I'm in such a comic predicament for February.... both my landlady here and Mam 'Oolley are going in for offspring, an I an't got nowhere to go to! Hard on a harmless bachelor, that!"[15] He was soon thinking, however, of turning the situation to his advantage with a longer than usual working holiday in London: "If the Richards book should come off, I think I shall spend the infantation season raking material at the British Museum."[16]

He had a fine Christmas at Someries with Conrad, Jessie and the boys. Borys, in particular, had found a new friend. Conrad told Pinker: "Reynolds was good company both to me and Borys. There's a lot in that young man".[17] He told Reynolds that he had heard from Buxton that "Reynolds is all right" – a statement which gave the young author renewed hopes for *A Poor Man's House* since that was all Buxton had seen.[18] They talked about the *Mountain* and Conrad asked if he could see a copy.[19]

The short visit seems to have lifted Conrad too, at that time struggling with "Razumov", the short story that was to become *Under Western Eyes*. A week later he told H.G. Wells: "A young man called Reynolds (Stephen) has been here for a day or two. We talked – or rather I let him talk – of you. It was intelligent talk. You put your impress on the minds of the younger generation. An enviable achievement. That youth can write a bit too".[20]

On Boxing Day Conrad went down with a bad attack of gout which was to lead to a severe attack of New Year depression over money and work.[21] The following day Reynolds beat a judicious retreat and, on his way home, had a cheering post-Christmas lunch in a deserted London with Hudson and Edward Thomas.[22]

On 31 December he took the train down to Sidmouth to be in time to see the New Year in and take stock of the past one.[23] In spite of the emotional trials he had been through, 1907 had ended on a note of high optimism with the possibility of publication for both his books. In some ways more important, the year had brought him a whole host of new literary friends to help with support and advice – Joseph Conrad, Edward Thomas, W.H. Hudson, John Buchan and John Galsworthy. Galsworthy was a close friend of both Garnett and Conrad, and Reynolds appears to have met him that year, as he had most of the others, through the lunches at the Mont Blanc. Galsworthy had done his own share of observing the poor at first hand and had too, in an intellectual sense, kicked out against the sterility of middle-class life. He had considerable admiration for the young man who had actually lived this experience as well as written about it. Galsworthy's country retreat was at Manaton on Dartmoor, well within the Reynolds walking range from Sidmouth. He loved the Devon country and saw himself, from the squire's perspective, as much observer of the Devon rustic as Reynolds was of the Devon fisherman.[24]

In Sidmouth on 2 January Reynolds did up his accounts for the year. His total income had come to £86-1-3$^1/_2$, which included three months' work for the *Daily Mail*, two small dividends from the last of the shares of his mother's bequest, which he had been forced to sell in the course of the year, and a few pounds of fishing money. Allowing for his literary expenses, mainly the cost of nine journeys to town, his net proceeds for the year were in the region of £65 – little more than the bare survival income of the average labourer.[25]

Would the new year be any better? The earning potential of his current review work gave no grounds for optimism. John Buchan's friendly offer of work on the *Scottish Review* had been baulked by only too predictable Scottish parsimony. He wrote to Pinker with resignation: "I'm distressed to say that my prophecy about the Scottish Review was a better one than yours. For two-and-

-a-fifth columns in November (a column of review-article and the rest of book notices) Nelsons have sent me two postal orders amounting to the grand total of 14/6. I've changed the blessed orders because I wanted the cash, and have sent them a receipt 'under protest'. What is one to do with people like that? They surely can't pay their Scotch professors so for their ex cathedra pulpitarian book bebabblements. Will you remark that this ass wants more than thistles, or shall I?"[26]

If he were to remain solvent for 1908, much would depend on what he could get for his two books. He determined to use the January in Sidmouth to get along as fast as possible with the second half of *A Poor Man's House*. He kept well to his resolution and by 26 January it was three-quarters done.[27] He made sure also to keep up the pressure on Lane. On 14 January he went up to town and saw Grant Richards at midday to discuss the requirement for the *Urban Exodus* book. Richards was impressed by his ideas and asked him to sketch out a synopsis for him to consider. They also discussed the possibility of Richards taking a new look at the *Mountain*.[28]

After lunch at the Mont Blanc, he called in on Lane. He was shown the readers' reports on the *Mountain* which, perhaps to Reynolds' surprise, turned out to be very good. Lane spoke of making an offer for the *Mountain* and *Poor Man's House* together, if he happened to like the latter. But the publisher was still in a cautious mood. He showed Reynolds the successful outcome of one of his most recent advertising campaigns, but doubted whether he could manage to do the same for the *Mountain*, even in Devizes. Despite the readers' reports, he also wondered whether publication of the *Mountain*, with its strong satirical content, might not prejudice the chances of Reynolds' future work.[29]

Reynolds had had almost a year of havering publishers, and was determined to bring the matter to a head. Back in Sidmouth, he wrote to Lane and asked straight out for a contract for the two books. In typical blackmailing fashion, he hinted that he might throw in the *Mountain* with the *Urban Exodus* book. "I am very anxious to get something more or less settled, first because the present state of unsettlement bothers me into bad nights and worse work, and secondly because I may be able advantageously to throw in the 'Mountain' with another book to be commissioned. I'd rather you were the publisher of it; but, for the sake of my work, if for nothing else, I am prepared to exchange a good deal of probability for a little certainty." He had an answer too for Lane's worries about the effect of the *Mountain* on his career. "As to its publication spoiling the chances of my future work – I had rather the 'Poor Man's House' were published under a pseudonym. It should then be easy to determine which name to go on with, or how far to let the two be identified. As I told you, I very particularly wish not to have the 'Mountain' *follow* the 'Poor Man's House'. It would destroy completely the sequence of the books I have in mind" As a parting influential shot, he asked Lane to send the *Mountain* manuscript direct to Conrad because he was very anxious to read it.[30]

He was now the master of his own negotiations, and reported regularly back to Pinker, forced to stand on the sidelines in deference to Lane's views on agents. But the extra responsibility was beginning to take its toll. "I'm in the middle of some rather gingerly negotiations with Lane...... trying to squeeze a contract out of him. However, if something don't happen soon, I shall throw up the thing. I enjoy these niggling negotiations, but they stop me sleeping and I've been rather ill, until I turned to and rowed till I was dead beat. You see, I can't do without you. No good pretending my strength's good enough for the writing and business too. 'Tisn't".[31]

On 1 February 1908 Reynolds gave over his two rooms in the poor man's house to make space for the now heavily pregnant Mam Woolley and headed for London where he was to spend the next ten weeks.[32] He had arranged to stay with Ford Hueffer at 84 Holland Park Avenue, the maisonette in which Hueffer had been living for a year as part of the long drawn-out process of separation from his wife, and which, as the later office of the *English Review*, was to become one of the most prestigious literary addresses in Edwardian London. Reynolds took the top flat in this accommodation which was on three floors above a poulterer's and (heavenly coincidence) fishmonger's shop. Douglas Goldring remembered his own introduction to it later in the year: "You reached it by a side door which gave on to a dark flight of stairs. I have an impression of almost pushing my way through the suspended carcases of rabbits, fowls and game birds to get to the door, and of standing on a mixture of blood and sawdust as I rang the bell."[33] Though middle-class literary London might turn up its nose at such a venue, for Reynolds these were the smells of home.

Although he was suspicious of the more extravagant behaviour of Hueffer, he was nevertheless grateful to have a roof over his head in a location close to the centre of literary life. It seems that Hueffer, despite his own dwindling finances, had decided to allow Reynolds his lodgings for free. This was certainly a significant concession to Reynolds' poverty for when he left and the flat was taken over that summer by R.A. Scott-James, the literary editor of the *Daily News*, a proper rental was charged.[34] But the question of the free rent was to lead eventually to one of the bitterest quarrels in Reynolds' life.

For the time being, however, and despite the differences in temperament, both men seem to have got on well. A daily woman came in each morning to prepare their breakfast, and most evenings they would dine together there or in a restaurant, perhaps going on to the Shepherd's Bush Empire, one of Hueffer's favourite haunts. In Hueffer's sitting room was a piano, a creature comfort Reynolds had not seen since his days at Devizes College. One thing they shared in common was strong personality and unwillingness to be worsted in argument; their life together became a constant, but affectionate, squabble. Hueffer took a genuine interest in Reynolds' work and thought highly of it. He soon came to realise that his friend's latest book was going to be even bigger than the *Mountain*.

Reynolds spent much of those ten weeks working on the final chapters of *A Poor Man's House*. He had prepared a synopsis of his next planned work, the *Urban Exodus* book, but Grant Richards, owing to a combination of overwork and illness, duly sat on it for three months.[35] There was, therefore, little incentive to do detailed research for it at the British Museum as Reynolds had originally intended. On Tuesdays he went regularly with Hueffer to lunch at the Mont Blanc, where most talk centred on the anti-censorship campaign which had become an obsession with Garnett.[36] The two-year-old relationship between Reynolds and Garnett, which had grown so emotionally close in those first days in Sidmouth in the autumn of 1906, was beginning to falter. Garnett was hurt by Reynolds' lack of interest in the censorship campaign and by his own bruising over the *Mountain* the previous year. Reynolds, for purely practical reasons, was now sheltering under Hueffer's wing and more inclined to acquiesce in the cooling of the old flame.

Some weekends he went down with Hueffer to Hurst Cottage at Aldington in Kent, owned by Elsie Hueffer who moved in permanently at the beginning of March.[37] On others he travelled to Burgh Heath to visit his friend, Harold Wright, and they would go out on the Sunday for "a tramp and a jaw"; or Harold would come up to take tea with him at Holland Park.[38] At the end of his second week in town, he went down to Someries again to spend a night with the Conrads and to receive a little (faint Conradian) praise for the *Mountain*. Conrad was working, but still ill and the visit seems to have cheered him a little. He wrote to Galsworthy: "Young Reynolds has been here also for a night. We talked of you – becomingly. He's excited at the thought of your Devon novel."[39]

His main objective throughout the London stay was finally to close with Lane on the publication of the two books. He was determined not to go back to Sidmouth until he had clinched the deal. To his frustration, Lane was out of the country for part of February, but in the third week he received a cheering letter from Buxton, full of enthusiasm for the *Poor Man's House* and offering to serialise it in the *Albany* that spring. Hueffer was also lining up Alston Rivers once more if the Lane proposal should founder. Though Rivers had already rejected the *Mountain* the previous year, Hueffer had persuaded them to consider, like Lane, the two book package, based on the prospective sales of the *Poor Man's House*. But Byles, the managing director, was in Japan and no formal decision could be taken till his return.[40]

When Lane came back to England, Reynolds was able to use the threatened competition to put renewed pressure on him, whilst all the time assuring him of his disinclination to go elsewhere. "I need hardly repeat how anxious I am to get the affair settled, for I'm doing no work, and can't while this is on hand. It is for that reason that I have not accepted the offer of serialization next spring, nor the request to wait till Mr. Byles returns from Japan."[41]

Reynolds' friendship with Page provided him with useful intelligence of what was going on in Lane's office. The very first reader's report on the *Poor*

Man's House had been glowing: "Mr Stephen Reynolds has produced a book to which it would be difficult to find any adequate parallel, and it is difficult to discover any terms of praise which are not open to the suspicion of exaggeration. 'A Poor Man's House' ought to make Mr Reynolds a famous man in one bound".[42]

By the beginning of March, Lane had also received from his principal reader, Frederic Chapman, a formal report on the manuscript, now complete as a first draft apart from the final few pages. Chapman was a grave and studious man, with a prodigious knowledge of English literature, both in the mainstream and in countless specialist fields. Lane had discovered him in 1892 working in a Leicester bookshop as manager of a circulating library and had hired him on the spot. After sixteen years working together, he trusted his judgement implicitly.

Chapman's report was favourable, but extremely superficial. He seems to have regarded the book as a semi-touristic account of Devon fishing life, designed to appeal to those who loved sailing and the West Country. True, he immediately spotted the power of character portrayal as a central strength of the book and, like many future readers, took objection to the socio-political lectures. But he seems to have missed almost entirely what gives the book its emotive force today – the psychological journey of the narrator as he moves from personal despair to a reawakening to the joy of life through close proximity to the lives of real people.

It is the only full reader's report we have on any of Reynolds' books and stands as an interesting document in its own right – the first independent assessment of the book that was to make his reputation.

> POOR MAN'S HOUSE
> BY
> STEPHEN REYNOLDS
>
> The worst thing about this book is its title. At sight of it I felt certain I was let in for a disquisition on Urban Housing, or The Life of the Poor as seen from Toynbee Hall. Somehow one doesn't think of sturdy Devon fisherfolk as *poor*, and the book is mainly about these, their boats, their mackerel-fishing, regattas and prawn catching.
>
> It is the diary of TONY WIDGER, a delightful 'old salt' of Seacombe, as written by his lodger, Mr. Imber, as he calls himself. The relations between the Widger family, (Granfer, John, Mam Widger, and other offshoots,) and their lodger are happily described:-
>
> "Mackerel hooking has raised me from the position of a mere lodger, a household excrescence. It has given me a niche of my own, at sea the mate on a mackerel hooker, on shore a loafer ready to lend a hand, and in the house a sort of male Cinderella...... I am neither a sky pilot, nor a district visitor, nor a reformer, nor a philanthropist, nor any sort of

worker, useful or impertinent, but simply a sponge to absorb and an understander to sympathize."
These sketches of fisher life are quite admirable in their way and the character drawing is very good. Tony himself, for instance, his wife, his brother, and such stray people as Mrs. Yardly [*sic*], "who works better for others than she works for herself", are really alive.
But the pity of it is that he has set these sketches in an economic milieu, i.e. his real interest is not the fisher life for its own sake but a sociological comparison of the life of the rich with the life of the poor, and he has therefore chosen for his title "Poor Man's House". If Mr. Reynolds were not content merely to delineate a charming picture of a fisher family, he might somehow have interwoven with it a thread of plot and thus come into line with the ordinary novel. Certainly readers who are attracted by the breezy Devonian atmosphere of the book will resent this invasion of Sociology.
The sentiments of Tony were worth inserting but there is no excuse for the prolonged dissertations (ex cathedra as it were) on education, hospitals, servants, Christ and the Superman, the difference between pluck and courage, vulgarity and coarseness, and other subjects better left to Club-bores.
The book ends with a syllogism which sums up the author's spasmodic reflections. "Harmoniousness is more to be valued than mere rapidity of progress. The Poor Man's House contains more of this harmony than any other house. *Therefore* the poor man's house is the best to live in."
If Mr. Reynolds would prune his soliloquies, his work would appeal all the more both to lovers of sailing and sea faring and to West Countrymen who will appreciate Mr. Reynolds' observation:- "'Yew dang'd ol' fule!' can mean so much. Here it appears to be an expression of almost limitless confidence. I have not met the like before."
There is a good seasoning of nautical songs and some happy bits of poetry, and the whole is adorned by stout Devonshire dialect."[43]

Chapman can perhaps be forgiven for seeing the book essentially as "a charming picture of a fisher family" since it was his task to make an audience assessment and no doubt the average Edwardian reader might be thought to see no more in the book than this. But while a judgement on the level of "picturesque Devon" must have driven Reynolds wild, it was certain to appeal to the nostalgic, sentimental side of Lane. The question that, therefore, loomed large that March was not whether the two books were publishable; but whether publisher and author, acting for himself, could agree on a price.

The negotiations were fiercely fought as only a Reynolds could fight them. The main sticking point was purchase of the copyright. Lane wanted an outright purchase (still a fairly common practice in the days before the royalty deal became universal), while Reynolds stuck out for reversion of copyright to him after ten years. Finally, at their last encounter on 27 March, Lane gave way, conceding even better terms than Reynolds had initially asked. His decision may have been hastened by competitive pressures that Reynolds was a past master at exploiting. That morning the author had received an offer from L.J. Bathurst, the co-founder of Alston Rivers, agreeing to take both books on the terms initially asked of Lane. Reynolds had no intention of signing up with Rivers, who were still apparently demanding deletion of the chapter on cleanliness, which had been for Reynolds a *sine qua non* for more than a year. But after all the trials with the *Mountain*, the irony of receiving firm offers from two publishers on the same day was not lost on him.[44]

Under the deal with Lane, he was to receive that year £120 for the copyrights of the two books, which would then revert to him after ten years. He would be tied to Lane for his next two books, for which he would receive royalties of 15% and 20%. It was an extremely generous package for a new author and clearly betrayed Lane's affection for him and confidence in his promise – "the old chap has really been very nice".[45]

Though Reynolds had been relatively optimistic about placing the two books, ever since the first meeting with Lane in December, it had taken almost four months to reach the point of certainty. His feelings were of both relief and delayed elation. On arriving back at Holland Park Avenue from the meeting with Lane, his first spontaneous thought was to write to Garnett whom, despite the cooling of their relationship of late, he still regarded as the "onlie begetter" of the *Poor Man's House*.

> I do believe if we haven't been and gone and done it.... Can't say how I feel. The relief so great as to be hardly realizable yet. Nor will I try and thank you for your big part in the thing. You can be sure, anyhow, that I haven't shut it out of my mind – à la your own prophecies. And you'll let me dedicate the *P. M's H.* (which is after all to come out first – a point I conceded) to you and "Tony", jointly.
> I'll be frank.... You've seemed sometimes lately to sit on me unnecessarily much. I suppose it's partly due to disappointment to a certain degree in finding that on so many intellectual points I don't – and shan't – agree with you. I know I'm a heretic in the matter of the opportuneness of the censorship agitation, for instance. I think the whole thing was inadvisable at the moment – and hope it wasn't. But, you see, I'm very happy and relieved beyond telling – filled with a sort of first day of spring feeling, and I know quite well how great your part has been in the happiness, whether or no you were in at the death, so to speak; and don't let any damn'd intellectual differences interfere with that, which is much better.[46]

It was typical of Reynolds' honesty and generosity of spirit that he should use the excitement of success to try and heal the wounds that were opening up in the relationship. Though he was capable of vendettas, that was only once a state of war had been reached. He could not pursue petty-minded stand-offs with those to whom he was really close, and was always the first to swallow his pride and place the issue of contention four-square on the table. In part it may have been his own insecurity that led him to such action; but mainly it was bigness of heart. The two friends agreed to meet again the following week.

On 30 March there was a further, even more joyous, reconciliation.[47] For the two months he had spent in London, he had had neither sight nor sound of Margot. In January, she had given birth to two pups – one dead and the other died shortly after; he had been forced to leave her back in Sidmouth to recuperate.[48] Now, whilst he was planning his return to Devon, she came up to town to share the last fortnight with him. Wherever she went, Margot created a sensation and this brief two weeks in London stuck in people's memories as if she had stayed for two years.

David Garnett, then a schoolboy in London and a regular visitor to Holland Park Avenue, remembered rather more of Margot than of Stephen. Even allowing for the added colour of his descriptive writing, Margot was clearly a tough responsibility when let loose in the London streets.

> One of Ford's protégés whom I first met at Holland Park Avenue was a rather short, thick-set man called Stephen Reynolds. He lived in the flat above and kept a Great Dane, a glorious aloof beast, brindled almost like a tabby cat. She terrorised the neighbouring butchers, entering their shops, helping herself to prime sirloins or legs of mutton and making off for home. Often a butcher followed on her heels and presented a bill which Reynolds could ill afford to pay.[49]

She provided too a great boost to Ford Hueffer's vanity, the perfect accessory to his morning walk across Kensington Gardens, down Rotten Row and across Green Park to his club in Pall Mall. "Every morning about eleven you would see me issue from the door of my apartment. I should be wearing a very long morning coat, a perfectly immaculate high hat, lavender trousers, a near-Gladstone collar and a black satin stock. As often as not, at one period, I should be followed by a Great Dane. The dog actually belonged to Stephen Reynolds but he disliked exercising it in London because he was nervous at crossings. But a policeman will always stop the traffic for a Great Dane to cross."[50]

On 13 April Reynolds' old rooms in Sidmouth became free at last and he and Margot returned home with some relief.[51] In his absence on 16 February, Bob Woolley's thirteenth child was born in the first floor front room where Reynolds used to write, in the large flat white bed "usually piled up with brain-babies in the shape of books". Mam Woolley told him that she had never had a baby in such a draughty room – "and I can quite believe it, especially when the wind is blowing half a gale from the sou'west and salty drops ooze through the rotten old window frame. The sound of the sea fills the room like the scent of flowers; a scent that flows and ebbs with each wave outside."[52] It was a room that had already given birth to one remarkable book; now it gave birth to a remarkable baby.

She was christened Doris May but that was never her proper name. Her real name was conferred by Reynolds himself on that first day home.

> When I returned from the exile into which her coming drove me, my kitchen corner, that used to contain boots and guernseys and socks for darning, was occupied by a cradle and a squeak. Over the cradle, which rocked in bumps on the uneven stone floor, was hung a line of tiny many-coloured garments. At intervals, being hungry, the squeak squeaked. A crazy patch-work quilt heaved feebly. (The heave is less gentle nowadays.) Two tiny red arms waved themselves about; jerked and waved. 'Twas like a semaphore – with a foghorn attached. 'What a semaphore of a baby!' I remarked. 'Semifore! Semifore!' cried the elder children.[53]

So Semaphore she became.

Because she had been the source of his exile, and because he had witnessed the beginning of her life and christened her, Semaphore took a very special place in his affections. As with "Straighty", his pretend girl-friend, he used her, his pretend daughter, to tease his readers and himself about the relationship and in a way expiate some of the burden of his homosexuality. "I don't know why one wants to kiss babies. One does. I did; but, being a bachelor, failed to attain to the full deed. Semaphore and I touched noses merely. She was delighted."[54] And once she could talk, her language and *her* naming of *him* was a source of delighted amusement. In October that year he wrote to Garnett: "Bob has got Semaphore out on the promenade. She is a bonnie kid – calls her father Bob and me Dad! Lucky I'm trusted auprès les femmes."[55]

On 9 February, back in Devizes, Phoebe Wyer also gave birth, but to her first child – a baby boy they christened Philip Henry. The little house in Pans Lane was too small and too middle-classy to accommodate both a new baby and the old lodger. The arrival of Philip resolved the dilemma that Reynolds had been wrestling with for over a year – whether or not to continue to divide his life between Devizes and Sidmouth. On 12 June he wrote to Pinker from Western Town, Sidmouth: "Please ask all your departments to alter my address to the above, and delete Pans Lane altogether".[56] It was his final break with the Wiltshire Downs. Apart from the occasional visit, he was never to live in Devizes again.

Through the spring of 1908, Reynolds' relationship with Lane began slowly to develop, nervously on Reynolds' part and with his usual fear when making new contacts of offending them. It was crucial that it should develop well, for he had chosen a publisher who would brook no intermediary with his authors; and the business side of his present and future books would have to be negotiated direct. On signing the agreement with Lane, he had asked for a stamped copy and, on not hearing further from him, began to wonder whether he had caused some grave offence. Typically, he wrote straight away to put the issue on the table. "I have a most uncomfortable impression that I have, somehow or other, caused you to put down my insistence on a stamped copy of our agreement to a deep personal mistrust. It's not so."

In setting out his explanation, he was also putting Lane on warning that he might have a difficult author to deal with in future. "My reasons for wanting a copy (one can't set them forth in the bustle of your office) are really a little mixed and muddled. I am faddy to have such things done with *formal* shipshapeness, and my stubbornness, when I've set my mind on anything, is a byeword amongst my friends. Also I want to fling the thing at my bank, whose superciliousness I've had to put up with longer than I liked. And lastly, that agreement is likely to be in force when you have retired from active business, and, as I told you, I do view all companies with a certain amount of suspicion. ......please don't draw hard and fast conclusions about the nature o' the beast till you know it well enough to discount its cussedness."[57]

He also wanted to assure Lane that, although he had leased the copyright in the two books and did not stand to gain anything from the sales, he would play his part in pushing them. "If I can do anything to help make the books a success, I will gladly do my best, and will not say that, as you have practically bought the books, it's no business of mine to help. Nor if, by good fortune, you should happen to do well with them, will you hear of my complaining that you gave me too little, etc., etc. I think your terms have been very generous, and the better you can do with the books the better I shall be pleased, quite apart from any reputation it might make for me. I'm not without gratitude for your taking the books at all, after so many rejections. You have given me my luck with them, and now, believe me, I genuinely wish you yours."[58]

He need not have worried that Lane's silence denoted mistrust. In the course of time he was to come to learn that Lane's failure to answer correspondence was more to do with bureaucratic inadequacy than any hidden personal motive. Lane wrote him a reassuring letter, insisting that, from his standpoint, their business relation had been nothing but pleasant.[59] This was no formal reassurance either; Lane's feelings towards the young author were genuinely warm. For the office record, he annotated one of Reynolds' letters at this time: "I have accepted two very remarkable books, both as yet unfinished, from this man chiefly on the reports of Joseph Conrad but backed by Chapman and Page. I had thought of asking him to call in June. He is a very nice fellow. His father oddly enough lives at Velly, Hartland."[60]

Conrad, despite his patchy health, had been delighted by the news of Reynolds' success with Lane. He wrote to his young friend in early May: "I was glad to hear of the vast range and the great success of your activities." He had been re-reading the *Holy Mountain* and made supportive noises, but it is clear from the subdued tone that he was somewhat less than impressed. "Send me Lane's exact address so that I may forward him the MS. of *Mountain*. I've just finished re-reading the whole. My impression – which you know of – is generally strengthened. The book stands looking into very well, very well indeed."[61]

The main change for Reynolds as he returned to life in Sidmouth was the unaccustomed experience of money in his pocket. He had received from Lane a part payment of the £120, the rest to come at the beginning of the following year.[62] "I'm hardly got used yet to the queer sensation of having enough cash to get along with."[63] Though he was now reviewing regularly for the *Daily News* and Scott-James, whom he had got to know well during the stay in London, and a little still for the *Bookman*, he was no longer dependent on this hack work, nor even for the odd scraps of money from fishing. He was determined, however, to keep his hand in with both for fear of harsher times ahead.

He had planned in mid April a little country jaunt with John Masefield, another new acquaintance from his stay in London and currently on holiday in Lyme Regis. Both men had the sea and youthful breakdowns in common and got on well. The meeting was cancelled, however, as Masefield had to return unexpectedly to London as the result of an accident to his wife.[64] Reynolds spent the last few days of April instead collaborating with Ford Hueffer on an advertising puff for the *Poor Man's House*, which he sent off with mock embarrassment to Lane: "I blush exceedingly, but here you are – Reynolds chaffed by Hueffer, Hueffer revengefully revised by Reynolds – great thoughts on a great subject – the game played!!"[65]

By early May he had only one more chapter of the book and the postscript yet to write. He was anxious to get on with revising the whole but the manuscript was held up in Lane's office and he could not start work on it until 20 May.[66] He was also feeling a little anxious over Chapman's remarks that the title was more suitable for a tract on urban housing. On 7 May he wrote to Lane: "Do you think that "*From* a Poor Man's House" would be a more suitable title; less open to misapprehension?"[67] Getting no reply and fearing that Lane's pre-publication list would soon close, he took the decision into his own hands and wrote to the office: "If not too late, please alter title of "A Poor Man's House" in your book-list to "From a Poor Man's House."[68] But it was indeed too late. As we have Lane's love of Devon to thank for publication of the book, so we have his in-built dilatoriness to thank for the shorter, and better, title.

Reynolds completed his final revision of the book in just a matter of days and sent it off for typing. He went up to London on 26 May and lunched with Hudson and Thomas at the Mont Blanc and with Thomas alone the following day. He called in on Lane to discuss the last loose ends before the publication process was put in train.[69] The final typescript was waiting for him when he arrived back at Sidmouth and he posted it off at once to Chapman. The latter was delighted with the completed text and wrote to Lane: "I have really nothing to add to what I have already said about the manuscript. The thing is finished off naturally and skilfully with a chapter which he calls a postscript, explaining his position and his attitude towards the class of folk whose daily life the book describes. I have the greatest hopes of its success."[70]

Reynolds was casting round for his next book which he now had both time and money to write. In June the *Urban Exodus* project came to a predictably sorry conclusion. He had met Grant Richards on 14 January in his London office to discuss the book, and shortly after had provided him with a synopsis. But it was not until 11 April that Richards resurfaced, having read the scheme and asking to discuss it further.[71] By this time, Reynolds was thinking of purchasing the idea from Richards and using it for one of the two new books for which he was contracted with Lane: "I want the subject because I think I can do a noticeable book on it."[72] It was not until his London visit of 26 May that Reynolds met Richards again to discuss it. They reached an agreement on the content, but the publisher would not name his price in spite of much pressure from Reynolds to do so. Richards was, however, taken aback by the follow-up letter from Pinker suggesting a hundred pounds for the book, the broad price Thomas had said he had been offered the previous year.

Richards took the slippery course of writing to Pinker and Reynolds separately, pretending to each he was refusing the other man's demand. On 4 June to Pinker: "I return herewith Mr Stephen Reynolds's scheme for the proposed book on the Urban Exodus. The terms he asks makes it altogether out of the question that I should go further in the matter."[73] On 11 June to Reynolds: "I am sorry to say that the terms Mr Pinker asks on your behalf are such that I must give up the idea of your Urban Exodus book."[74] If this had happened a year before, the volcano would have erupted. It was a sign of how relaxed the young author now was about writing and money that when Pinker asked him whether he should negotiate, the response was one of amused resignation: "Dear me! Do as you think. If concessions, in the royalty direction, not in the advance. He offered £100 originally when he talked about the job to Thomas. Rub it into the heller that he could have got it at pretty near any price if he'd exercised ordinary courtesy in the first place. He's written to me also this morning – less emphatically than to you. S.R. pressure on J.P. to make J.P. abate claim for S.R. Very nice. Mumphead: he must think me – us in fact."[75]

When challenged with the £100, Richards responded in his sniffiest tone: "I have no recollection of anything having been said about an advance of £100 on the book which it was proposed that Mr Reynolds should write. I am sorry to say that I have no belief at all in the book on such terms."[76] At that, the matter was allowed to drop – a lost opportunity for both Reynolds and his future readers. The frustration of the episode lingered in Reynolds' mind a few weeks more. He wrote to Conrad a fortnight later: "The Richards Urban Exodus book is off. He wouldn't rise to my terms, and I told him what a good subject it is, and what a pity it was he did not trouble to come to the point when I asked him to do so, and should have been glad to accept almost any terms."[77]

The completion of work on the *Poor Man's House* and the loss of the *Urban Exodus* book found him, uncharacteristically, by the middle of June without any clear ideas for future work. "Work isn't going over-well. I'm in that horrid slough between two books and can't decide finally which subject I'll take up. But I think a comedy novel."[78] He had sent the outline of such a book to Chapman a couple of weeks before, but it never developed into more than a few lines in a letter.[79] Other ideas for novels, both comic and serious, were to stir him in the next two years but something, perhaps the memory of the *Mountain*, was always to hold him back.

He had a more solid, if bread and butter, commission on the stocks to keep him from complete redundancy. When he had broken with the *Scottish Review* over its frugality, John Buchan suggested that he write the guide to Wiltshire that was now planned for the successful series of Nelson Guides. It was in part a recognition of the originality of the Devizes Guide of two years before, but even more of the depth of his knowledge and love of Wiltshire. He was flattered by the offer and very keen to take on such work for a "serious" publisher, but had to suffer the consequence of waiting around until Nelsons told him he could start. At first it appeared that the project could not go ahead till 1909, but he got word from Buchan at the end of June that it was now set for the autumn.[80] As he told Conrad, he was planning to research the book with Margot: "Poor Margot has been crippled with rheumatism, but is now better, and I'm hoping to have her quite well by the autumn, for the Wilts guide is to be done this year, so I want her to tramp the downs with me".[81]

The work vacuum had him also toying with a more high-flown project – a philosophical work on "Art as Communication" – which had been circulating in his brain for eighteen months or more. It was a different side of Reynolds from the satirist and social observer, but basic to the very intellectual nature of his character. As the earnest lectures in *A Poor Man's House* had shown, he tended to approach social and philosophical issues as a scientific investigation, assembling his instinctive and random ideas and trying to knock them together into some intellectually coherent form. All such endeavours, including his later work on "psycho-economics" – the last of his intellectual obsessions – were simply Reynolds trying to explain Reynolds to himself.

In this particular case, he was grappling with the phenomenon of his isolation from the world – the failure of Reynolds as social and sexual being set against the success of Reynolds as communicator of the written word. It was, of course, the puzzle facing all artists in all ages, but the naive eagerness with which Reynolds approached such issues always gave them a semblance of new ideas, a fresh analysis. In December 1906, he had set out his stall to Garnett with his usual openness.

According to my aesthetic theory – whereby art, religion, love and

> society are all nothing but varied manifestations of the human being's desire to escape its eternal solitude, all at the bottom motived by a desire to communicate and share the incommunicable – if one intends to manifest on the art side, one must be content to be deficient in the others – and lump it. I take it we create an art out of an amusement when we make it subserve the purpose of communication.
>
> I should like to discuss the matter with you, for my theory brings art, religion, love and society into line, defines and places into its proper relation each art, and explains many connections which have been noted but not understood. For instance: Literature becomes the art of putting verbal communications into such an atmosphere that they can best be realised as existent, and understood, (1) by the writer himself, and (2) by the recipient. Style is the means whereby the atmosphere is created. Poetry is the preponderance of atmosphere over statement, because the statement being subtle, the atmosphere must receive proportionate attention. A typical artist's plunges into religion are the outward sign that he despairs of his art, and having failed, as he thinks, at any rate, to break down the wall between himself and his fellows, he proceeds to attack the less solid-looking walls between himself and God. Or, perhaps, religion stands out, and art, love and society are attempts to extend religion and the so-called "love of God" to one's fellow-creatures. A nice point.
>
> But has all this been said before? At present my theory is a bit chaotic, but I believe there's a good deal in it. Since it occurred to me, I've been astonished at the way it works out. What I want is to be asked a lot of awkward questions about it and to read up collateral subjects. Then.... If it *is* new, at all....[82]

By July 1908 he was still wrestling with the same ideas, but now they seemed more focussed on sexuality, and indeed his own homosexuality, than on the creative instinct. He was keen to get hold of Havelock Ellis' great opus on homosexuality, as much, one feels, to throw light on himself as to underpin the ideas for the book. "The Havelock Ellis on the Sex Instinct I shall have to get a look at too by hook or by crook. For my purpose, Sexual Inversion is very important. My book on Art as Communication has very much enlarged its scope, and becomes hardly a treatise, but a suggestive work on Art, Sex and Religion – rather à la Nietzsche, Religion and Art being considered as deriving their force largely by a diversion of the same instinct-towards-unity-with-some-one-else which has so much to do with sex. And, as in so many scientific questions, the abnormal offers a better exhibition of certain emotions and instincts than does the normal. It exhibits them, as it were, more isolated for scientific handling. Very big subject, and I'm rather at sea with the literature of it, though I have the main lines of my argument fairly well weighed up."[83] The ideas did not, in the event, develop into a book; but they show us a Reynolds now beginning to come to terms with his sexuality, more open and more comfortable in his new life with Bob, some of the secrecy exorcised by the writing of *A Poor Man's House*.

What is more, he had found a new girl-friend – a more dangerous rival for Straighty and Semaphore. On 11 June he had gone into Exeter, armed with a letter of introduction from John Lane, to meet another Bodley Head writer – the novelist, M.P. Willcocks.[84] Mary Willcocks was then 39 and had been writing for Lane since 1905, rather dense, meandering Hardyesque novels with a west country setting, their length often sadly in inverse proportion to the strength of their content. She was a dark-haired woman of schoolmistress appearance, with glasses and a severe, rather masculine face, and not a little of Reynolds' own neuroticism. She was a strong personality and both authors soon discovered they were more than a match for each other.

Reynolds had sought the introduction following his recent review of her latest book, *A Man of Genius*, a rather shameless rewriting of *Jude the Obscure*. The book had caught his particular attention because it was set on the Hartland peninsula and its hero, who has returned there to his parents' farm (echoes for Willcocks of Lane rather than Reynolds), rejoices in the name of Velly. He gave Mary Willcocks her due: "In her descriptive passages she has caught the atmosphere of the wild Hartland corner of Devon with its pitiless sea and cliffs, its beautiful hedgerows and combes, and its wide outlines." But he had also included some rather waspish male chauvinism: "The fault which needs mentioning is one very generally to be found in novels by women, namely, the intrusion in the author's comments of what might be called the university extension tone – the intrusion, that is, of great thoughts which the author, though she understands them well enough in the abstract, seems hardly to have made her own. The greatness of a great occasion is better shown in the manner of describing it than by referring to the 'altar of the Unknown Loveliness,' 'a Pisgah vision,' and so forth. Moreover, the strength and the delicacy of Miss Willcocks' direct narrative, and the clearness of her insight, render such aids to impressiveness in her case quite unnecessary."[85]

Much to Reynolds' chagrin, these rather patronising remarks appeared in the *Daily News* just on the day of his visit, and the rest of the review had been so cut about as to give them an unintended prominence. He bemoaned his misfortune to Lane: "Very awkwardly, that horrible review of mine of 'A Man of Genius' came out in the *Daily News* yesterday. They cut out altogether one of the most important paragraphs, so that my one carp, which was a small thing in the original review, bulked largely in the wretched printed muddle. I feel very angry about it. I took considerable trouble over that review, and am not such a youngster at the job that I should be hacked about like that."[86]

But they seem to have got over this unfortunate introduction and established fairly quickly the rather argumentative, joking relationship that was the staple of Reynolds' friendships with those women who could not establish a mother-substitute role over him. His report of the visit to Lane was brisk and cheerful. "I went over to Exeter yesterday to see Miss Willcocks – had tea there, and chattered nineteen to the dozen. She seemed rather nervy, and promptly jumped to the absurd conclusion that I was a deed-dyed pessimist! Whereat, metaphorically, we fought on the spot. I hope she will run up here, but she says she's going up to Town doctors next week, and is afraid of being treated as a 'damn'd visitor' at Sidmouth!"[87]

On 30 June she finally made good the invitation and went down to see Reynolds at Sidmouth, the first of many such visits over the next few years. Uniquely, she has left us with the only detailed account of life in the Poor Man's House and of Reynolds' role in it other than that of Reynolds himself. Her novel *The Eyes of the Blind*, published in 1917, has as its hero a Dr. Daniel Rudd – "a swarthy, beardless man, apparently about thirty. In his fisherman's jersey and blue trousers he seemed sailor rather than professional man".[88] In addition to his medical practice, Rudd lives and works with Sam Cornish, a fisherman "tanned and wrinkled by sun and wind, but the merry blue eyes were full of a childish boldness".[89] His wife, Mam Cornish, "had fair hair, beautifully arranged and shining, a large mouth, capable hands, and a confident smile".[90]

In the early pages of the novel, Rudd takes a male friend home to have supper with the Cornishes, and we have a picture of the Woolleys' kitchen as it appeared to Mary Willcocks on that first June visit in 1908, transposed among memories of many later visits. Mam Woolley is tending the four-month-old Semaphore who, with fictional licence, has turned into a male baby.

> The door into the house was open and Dr. Rudd walked in, shouting down the passage as he went:
> "Mam Cornish, where are you? What have 'ee got for supper?"
> In the light of the fire a woman sat putting a dark-headed baby to sleep. She had just given him his bath and the high fender was hung with baby clothes and coarse knitted men's socks. Opposite the laden dresser a low window looked out into the darkness. The back door was screened off by a clothes-horse laden with shirts and children's clothes. The table under the window was laid with a cloth and littered with tea things which had been used, but not cleared away."[91]

The two men sit down to a supper of whiting straight from the frying pan, and Willcocks notices how well Reynolds makes up for the jam deprivation of his childhood home: "The doctor finished his meal with chunks of bread piled up with plum jam from a two-pound jar with the label of the C.W.S. on it". The meal over, the doctor in relaxed mood "flinging out his feet towards the fender, began to tap a cigarette on the palm of his hand", and begins to lecture his guest on the sins of artificial refinement as compared to the simple acceptance by working people of the facts of coarse living.[92] The description has a convincing ring about it.

There is a sense of distaste in the Willcocks' reaction to Reynolds' proprietorial tone towards the family – a distaste which pervades the book, as if

Reynolds is using the Woolleys for his own personal vanity. But, as Rudd shows the guest around the house, we get a privileged glimpse of the Woolley children, piled in together at the top of the house, and of Reynolds' own cluttered bedroom-cum-study.

> In short, the Cornishes were on show. If Mrs. Cornish felt it, she made no sign, not even when Dr Rudd insisted on going three stories up in the long narrow house to show the back bedroom packed with sleeping children. They slept three in a big bed, with others in improvised cots.
> "Do be careful, Dan. Don't wake 'em up," whispered Mrs. Cornish at the bottom of the steep stairs.
> "One hundred pounds apiece wrenched out of poor old Sam's arms to bring up every one of 'em," said Dr Rudd, when they had returned to his own rooms on the second story.
> "Then why so many?" asked Jemmy, taking a chair by the dusty fire in the old-fashioned grate. In one corner of the room stood an old flock bed, with books scattered about on its bumpy surface. There were books on the untidy shelves, books piled on the table, and in front of the window a typewriter with a litter of papers.[93]

The pejorative tone of many of the descriptions of Dr Rudd stems from a time when Willcocks and Reynolds had become distant and wary of each other. On this first meeting at Sidmouth, however, they seem to have got on well, to have recognised the homosexual element in each other which turned the world's reaction to their relationship into a joke rather than a threat. Reynolds, in particular, delighted in any action designed to *épater les bourgeois* and in the especial irony of becoming the subject of heterosexual scandal. On this occasion, they went for a walk up Peak Hill and there occurred an incident which seemed to cement and typify this strange new relationship. It was with relish he recounted it to Pinker the next day.

> Deuce of a funny thing yesterday. Miss Willcocks came over, and to show her the town I took her up to the top of the cliff. There we flopped, chattering and watching the fish on the rocks beneath. Motor stopped, unable to climb further with its cargo in, on the road about six yards away. Highly respectable people got out. Collected wraps and stowed 'em. I got up. Miss W. got up. They looked. "Oh, how do you do, Miss Willcocks?" They congratulated her on her last book. Then: "And have you been in Sidmouth *long*, Miss Willcocks?" – "No, it's the first time I've been here." I suffered severely from squashed laughter. Off they went to Exeter. They are her most respectable gossipy acquaintances there. Pretty ol' cuffer they'll spin up. I was in very salty guernsey and trousers!
> "Hadn't been in Sidmouth a day before she picked up with some common fisherman. Lying with him on the top of the cliffs. I thought I

> noticed it in her books, my dear!" There's a character gone to smithereens in an ancient cathedral city. Imagine Bob's glee, and Miss W.'s too for that matter.[94]

It was a story he dined off for some weeks to come. He included it in a skit he wrote for the *Bodleian, Miss Willcocks at Large*, purporting to come from the pen of Tony Widger and giving an alternative account of her first visit "down the Gut" that June day.

> Fust time her come'd up here – I can mind it very well 'cause I'd been trying to put away half-an-hour in the armchair – there was my ol' woman, an' my sister, an' another married person all in my kitchen admiring of each other's babies an' thinking their own was ten times better. Howsbeever, the babies was quiet enough – a sight quieter'n their mothers, till Miss Willcocks rushes in.
>
> "Good afternoon," her says. "Oh, the pretty dears! Do let me take one of them."
>
> So her takes my youngest out o' the missis's arms, an' kisses 'en, an' he starts squalling.
>
> Then her takes my sister's baby, an' kisses he, an' he starts squalling.
>
> An' then her takes t'other baby, an' kisses he, an' he starts squalling too. They was all squalling together. Pretty buzz o' it 'twas! Miss Willcocks, her looks a bit awk'ard, an' her says: "Oh, I do love cats, don't you?"
>
> Which my missis didn' think a very fitty thing to say, just at the time like.
>
> Afterwards, while they was a-quietening they chil'ern, I offers to take her to sea 'long wi' me; but her was afraid o' being seasick; an' her gets my mate to show her the way up over cliff for to see the view. Losted me earning a couple o' bob that did, not haeing he on the beach thic a'ternoon. I told 'en he was too rough for to take ladies out, in his fishing rig an' all; – hadn't shaved for three days, to my recollection. Well, they gets to the top of the cliff, just by the road, an' lays down on the edge looking over at the fish swimming in the sea below. Motor-car full o' people stops on the road just by 'em, an' they gets out o' it also for to admire the view. Miss Willcocks, being observed, rises up.
>
> "Oh, how do you do, Miss Willcocks?" says they. 'Twas some o' her gentry-friends to Exeter.
>
> 'Stead o' introducing my mate to 'em – like the likes o' they sort o' people does it – her leaves my mate standing like a blue poop on the edge o' the cliff, until they puts on their fur-lined coats, gets into their motor, an' smeeches on.
>
> Can't say I wants they people to Exeter to think her comes out here simply for to traipse about wi' common low fishermen, as they calls us. 'Twas told me afterwards how they'd been preaching against her from

> the pulpit in to Exeter Cathedral. W'er 'twas on account o' thic cliff turn-out, or w'er 'twas on account o' her books not suiting o'em, that they was blowing their hooters, I couldn't rightly make out; but, anyhow, her an't got much savvey, seems so, not in situations like that.[95]

In between the pranks and the book reviewing, Reynolds had started in once again for this his second full summer at Sidmouth with the routine of boating and fishing. He wrote to Lane on 12 June: "We have started fishing and boating: I've ricked my back and barked my kneecap towards it! But otherwise flourish exceedingly...."[96] The mackerel were a failure for much of June but picked up during the heat wave at the end of the month.[97] He wrote to Conrad on 3 July: "You must be luxuriating in this hot weather; that is, if you haven't the gout, and I hope you haven't. It's hot here with a tremendous heat, but I am getting up at such unearthly hours for the mackerel that I earn the right to go to bedroom in the afternoons".[98]

He was also becoming more closely bound up in Sidmouth fishery politics as the natural spokesman of the fishermen. The long awaited public hearing of the Board of Trade inquiry into the removal of shingle, which he had done so much to stimulate the previous year, was finally held at the Drill Hall in Sidmouth on 24 April. Colonel Balfour and the Manor party were represented by a professional barrister who made a strong case for the unpredictability of the beach which over many years had lost and regained shingle quite independently of any human agency. The Council, represented by the Town Clerk, spoke strongly in favour of a Government prohibition order. It was left to Reynolds to shoulder the novel burden of formal representation of the fishermen, for whom the star expert witness was none other than Uncle Sam. As Reynolds took him through his evidence, he argued cogently from long experience that there had been a quite exceptional shrinkage of the beach in recent years – more shingle came back in two tides years ago than in eighty tides today – which now put both fishermen and boats in extreme peril. Summing up the case for the fishermen, Reynolds made a simple but compelling plea for a safe beach and a good landing place as essential if longshore fishing were to continue as a significant part of the town's economy.

The hearing lasted for a full day and Reynolds was publicly thanked for his contribution by Commander Frederick, the Inspector in charge of the hearing.[99] He was nervously exhausted by the end, but rather proud to have got through it. It was his first taste of real political action and he was beginning to feel it would not be his last. He wrote to Lane: "The Board of Trade Inquiry at which I represented the fishermen turned out a ter'ble gert affair. Opposition had a barrister who insisted on strict law-court procedure. Had to examine and cross-examine, and at the end of 7 empty-stomached hours make a speech – and for days was so haunted by what I forgot to say that work went God knows where. Ghastly experience; useful someday perhaps".[100]

It was to be another eight months before the Harbours Department stirred itself to reach a Board of Trade decision. Meantime, he was taking up another fisherman's battle, this time against the Sidmouth Council who had returned to the old charge of threatening prosecution for cluttering up the Esplanade with capstans which the fishermen argued were absolutely necessary on a bad beach. The affair involved an immense amount of bureacratic work which he had to squeeze in among his usual fishing and writing. On 8 July, though he had risen first at 2 a.m. to haul in a drifter and spend three hours picking mackerel out of the nets, he spent most of the morning in an interview with Philip Michelmore, the deputy town clerk, half the afternoon in follow-up interviews with various fishermen and the rest of the day composing a long formal statement for the Council. Once again, he could not conceal from Garnett his pride in these bureaucratic efforts: "It's lucky, as it happens, that I have got a bit of the business man in me. I think the fishermen are pretty well prepared to follow my lead now, which gives me great satisfaction. Certainly I don't think they'd find anyone to try harder though they might easily get someone more skilful. But I learn; and it's good training for literature that is in contact with life."[101]

His memorandum had instant results when the Council called an urgent meeting for 10 July. "They are calling a special meeting of the Council to meet me tomorrow night. Shall have to go and talk my head off. But it's good, isn't it? that we can make 'em so attend to us".[102] The meeting turned out well, with Reynolds arguing for the fishermen's prescriptive rights and successfully persuading the Council to stay its hand and seek Counsel's opinion.[103] "My negotiations between the fishermen and the Council have come to a successful interim conclusion. Also, if I hear aright, the town generally approves of my letter to the Council and the line I took at the Council Meeting. The fishermen back me well. In time this buffer-work ought to teach me something about the management of men. It's certainly a furiously exciting game. But if I come a cropper.... Lord save us!"[104]

The Counsel's opinion that arrived towards the end of August supported most of Reynolds' arguments, so much so that Michelmore confessed it looked as if Reynolds had been briefing the man.[105] The two sides reached a compromise agreement under which three capstans were removed, leaving a further three to remain on the front. "The row we were having with the Council, over boats and gear up over, has turned out beautifully for us. I induced the Council to defer prosecution, and they submitted a case for Counsel's opinion. We were to be taken definitely in hand, and shown once and for all what we could not do except of the Council's kindness. But Counsel gave us every single point I had claimed on behalf of the fishermen!"[106]

These two affairs – of the shingle and the capstans – began to build for Reynolds that summer of 1908 a new and public reputation. There was even talk of him, at the age of 27, being put on the Devon Fisheries Committee.[107] He was in training for his second career, and clearly enjoying the excitement and novelty of it all. But it was genuine sympathy for the fishermen, not egotism, that drove him on – a part payment for all that Bob and his family had done for him over the past two years.

It also had its downside; he was beginning to experience the backbiting and jealousy that run hand in hand with political action and public reputation. Most disturbing of all, the affairs had created a rift with Bob's brother,Tom, whom Reynolds both strongly admired and slightly feared. In that sense, it went rather deeper than routine political resentments, down to a personal and emotional level. The tensions in the relationship between Reynolds and Tom, which was to blow hot and cold over the succeeding years, seem grounded essentially on sexual sensitivities. Reynolds admiration for Tom was as much physical as spiritual, something that Tom himself must have sensed and been wary of. Little wonder, then, that he should have shown some resentment at the closeness of Reynolds' relationship with Bob – perhaps both jealousy and a degree of distaste. Though the differences between the two men were often overtly about money, beneath the surface lurked the spectre of Reynolds' homosexuality.

Certainly, from Reynolds' description of it, the fall-out on this occasion seems less of political wrangle, and more of lover's tiff. "I am meeting with the usual difficulties of any one who does more or less public work. A lot of lying gossip, mainly engineered by a man I caught stealing our ballast bags, is going round. They are jealous of Bob's 'having a gen'leman behind him', Tom Woolley especially, though I help him a good deal. Last I hear is that I am suspected of sundry 'bloody aims', and have only helped beach against town and manor because it was profitable to me. I don't exactly blame them, though I am rather sick over Tom, for 'gentry people' seldom do help workers without making them pay pretty heavily. Also Tom has great aspirations towards middle-classiness and it is Bob whom the 'gen'lemen' take up with. And I'm supposed to be backing him with money! You see, the Devonshireman is so secretive about all his money affairs, that my frankness over 'em is bound to be misunderstood and put down as lies. My cue is, I think, to take no notice, go on working as usual so long as I'm allowed to, and let the thing wear itself out. They'll come round when they are landed in their next difficulty, I expect. But Tom's black looks depress me; for I like him, and would wish all straight between us. Bob has always been a but for slurs; it is only now that they use me as material. I trust I shall succeed in not having my back put up."[108]

He had also to walk other social tightropes between the middle class from which he sprang and the working fishermen with whom he lived. The visitors whom he took out pleasure-boating soon realised, through accent and conversation, that this young man was no ordinary fisherman. Those who found out he was also a writer, with a book to come out in the autumn, were deeply intrigued. Many of them inevitably invited him home for dinner, invitations he invariably refused to save Bob's feelings, except for one rich American lady, who offered the dual attractions of piano and champagne – and the spice of a little more heterosexual scandal. "Some of my 'frights' have invited me to their places to dinner and so forth, but I have made a rule not to visit in Sidmouth where they are not prepared to ask Bob too. For one thing he doesn't like it: it makes him feel, I think, that as regards a good deal of my doings, he's out o' it; that there's only a bit of me he's got grip of which isn't so, really. The one place I do go, therefore, is to whom we call 'The Merry Widow'. She has invited Bob; she has a Steinway grand piano – a beauty, – and she gives me phizz for supper, which is pleasant, as a change. Devil of a talk over my going there. But the Merry Widow don't mind, and I'm sure I don't".[109]

Much of his literary work that summer was given up to the final preparation of *A Poor Man's House* for publication – photographs and publicity material, final revisions, proof reading. But in June he wrote what he thought his best short story, *Silly Saltie*, about an idiot in a Devon village who steals money from the church box, not to spend but to offer up to his own hidden deity on a rock on the cliff's edge. It was not his best story by a long chalk, as swift rejections from the *Pall Mall Magazine* and *Blackwood's* soon showed.[110] Above all, there is not enough poetry in the prose to create the magical, mystical element he was seeking.

But the story is interesting because it shows Reynolds consciously striving to improve his writing and to tackle a dimension beyond realism. He sent it to Conrad for the master's corrections: "May I send you 'Silly Salty' [*sic*] to look at? I want your opinion, because I have tried very hard in it to avoid my worst faults and I can't tell for the life of me whether I have succeeded, though I'm hopeful. ......Please tell me what you think, if you have time. It's not that this story is of any intrinsic importance; it's a sort of trot match with the cussedness of words and form. I want to learn to get weirdness, to express the uncanny sides of human beings' relation with each other and things without violence of method; and if you can't help me.... Well, I suppose I shan't."[111] Conrad, as ever, was rather more kind than helpful. The episode is revealing in showing both the degree of thought that Reynolds was still giving to his technique, which gives the lie to those who might regard him as a part-time writer, and the extent of his imaginative deficit in execution. *Sillie Saltie* did not in fact find a home until 1911 and then only in the last-minute scramble to achieve magazine publication before his volume of collected short stories came out.

Reynolds had sent the final typescript of *A Poor Man's House* to Frederic Chapman at the end of May 1908. Earlier that month, Charles Buxton fulfilled his undertaking and published excerpts of the unamended text in the *Albany Review*. It was a disappointing taster, consisting of the lectures on class, working class semantics and cleanliness, and thus gave little feel for the real nature of the book. The second instalment in July was a different (and literal) kettle of fish. Reynolds kept Conrad up to the mark with his reading: "Two descriptive chapters (Mackerel hooking and herring drifting) from the Poor Man's House are out in this month's Albany. I think they are better than those of the first instalment."[112] The third tranche in August witnessed a return to the cerebral – the dissertations on class, working-class resilience and wisdom, and the final epilogue. It was not the best choice of extracts to whet the appetite, from a book whose human narrative material was all eminently extractable. Few readers can have placed their orders on the strength of the *Albany* showing.

Lane decided early on that the book, with its picturesque record of that England from which the *Mayflower* had set sail, was ripe for the American market, whose sophisticated advertising would require photographs. "Lane has sent for photographs of me for American consumption this morning. Margot shall be in it. Don't see why I shouldn't take advertizing advantage of her good looks! So Bob, Margot, Semaphore (the baby) and myself are going to have a big photographing to-day. – Not all at once, of course."[113]

The photographs were taken out on the beach on 2 July, probably by the local photographer, Melville Mackay, a friend of Reynolds whose pictures were to adorn the most lyrical of his books, *Alongshore*. One of the best to survive from that day's session shows the firm of Woolley and Reynolds lined up against the drifter – Punch and Uncle Sam, Bob and Tom with Chip, and a very youthful Reynolds, leaning nonchalantly back against the boat with Margot at his feet like a beached whale, not making the most of those good looks. Bobby stands in the background on the Esplanade in his Sunday-best knickerbockers, guarding Semaphore in her pram. Reynolds, a photographic expert from his days at Bloxham, was well pleased with the results when they came through in mid July.[114]

He received the slip proofs in mid August and went through them with Harold Wright, down for his usual summer holiday staying with Tom and Nellie.[115] He was not too unhappy with the final result and wrote to Pinker on the 23rd: "Have just sent back the first proofs of the *Poor Man's House*. They weren't over good, but I don't think I've exceeded my quantum of corrections. Short of being able to write the whole thing over again, I'm pretty well satisfied."[116]

At the beginning of September, he sent the duplicate slip proof to Garnett for a pre-publication view, with the hint of an apology for the more didactic passages. "You won't like all of it, but I hope you'll think it justifies its existence. It is pretty well what I meant it to be: I think I told you that I can't help thinking that, nowadays at any rate, the projection of a life ought to include the thoughts to which it gives rise."[117] He told Garnett of his plan to dedicate the book to him and Bob – "to Bob the inspirer of the book and you the encourager; Bob the fuel and you the governor on the engine."[118]

Garnett went through the motions of a modest disclaimer, suggesting it should on merits be to Bob alone. He was met with an emotional rejoinder, the first whisper for months of the old relationship. "The dedication.... Why, of course to you along with Bob. Most of the thing came to you in letters and but for you I shouldn't probably have started on the thing; and but for disagreeing with you I should have had no clear idea of what I was getting at; whereas I have a pretty clear idea – whether good or bad, the best or not, how am I to know? Besides, I *wanted* your name there – and that's the main thing. And 'tis an honour to have it there. Credit me with believing that for all my pig-headedness. And Bob is pleased it's there too. For they preserve, I think, a better recollection of you than of any of my friends."[119]

But even at this moment, with memories of the shared endeavour of two years before so close, there was a hint of the new distance between them. "It is borne in upon me, as the ranters say, sometimes with a considerable shock, what an incalculable amount I owe to what a number of people. Makes even an individualist realize how mentally gregarious we human beings are. I feel sometimes as if I ought to make a week's tour, simply going round and giving thanks to people, and to you as much as to anybody, though at the back of your mind you don't approve of me. Or is it at the front?"[120]

It was, of course, the usual Reynolds teasing, for when serious he could not disguise the genuine sense of debt. He wrote again to Garnett on the eve of publication: "Anyhow, the P.M's H. has the best of me in it. Shan't do anything else up to it. Believe I'm genuinely grateful to you for your appreciation of that and you can think me as charmless, tactless, ungracious, and all the rest o' it, as you damn well like. I know it."[121]

He made only a few minor grammatical adjustments to the page proofs which by 1 September he had sent back to London, complete with the running heads on the rectos which he had composed and written in himself. He now had only to wait for the fixing of the October publication date.[122] Rather nervously, he broke the news to the Woolley family that he had been writing about them, and was reassured by their reaction. "Have told Bob, and Mrs. Bob and Uncle Sam about the book. They take to the idea very kindly-fashion, though I don't suppose they'll like everything in it."[123] He was keeping the more difficult revelation to Tom very much in reserve until he had worked out the right tactical approach.

He needed to keep close to London, both to oversee the final arrangements for the book and to press the Board of Trade on the shingle issue which was now coming to a head. On 22 September he was in town for the usual Mont Blanc lunch with Hudson, Seccombe, Hueffer and Edward Thomas. The following Tuesday he was there again with Hudson, Hueffer and Thomas, and with John Burns, President of the Local Government Board whom he had been lobbying over the shingle question and who was becoming something of a friend. The next day, Garnett had returned to the Mont Blanc, fresh from a holiday at the Galsworthys' in Devon, and most of Reynolds' friends were there together once more – Seccombe, Hueffer, Thomas and Frederic Chapman.[124] On this visit he had the singular honour of an invitation to dinner at Lane's Lancaster Gate house at which they agreed the list of Reynolds' friends to whom early copies of the book should go – Seccombe, Garnett, Hueffer and

John Buchan.[125] All four could be relied upon for good reviews. Reynolds would send a copy to Conrad himself. It was not a wholly tranquil encounter – they had a snapping argument over Pinker, with Reynolds springing to the defence, and leaving with the feeling that he had rather offended his host.[126]

Before returning to Sidmouth, he stopped off for a few days at Devizes to find that his friend George Simpson had given him an extensive pre-publication puff in the local paper, quoting the Lane announcement that the book was likely to make him famous "in one bound". He feigned embarrassment, but was actually rather pleased. "The Gazette, at Devizes, put in a very funny paragraph, and I landed at Devizes right in the midst o' it."[127]

A week later Lane decided that publication should take place on Wednesday 21 October. The day after, the author's copies arrived in Sidmouth. He took down the first one from the pile and wrote in the fly-leaf "Bob and Mam Woolley, affectionately from Steve Reynolds Oct 22/08".[128]

A Poor Man's House was constructed according to the principles Reynolds had set out in *Autobiografiction* in October 1906; that is, a selected episode of autobiography, slightly rearranged in time and space, written to communicate a deep-felt spiritual experience. It is the journal of an anonymous narrator (the Mr Imber of the first draft had been dropped) which stretches from April in Year 1 to December in Year 2. Within that frame (or more precisely from July Year 1 to December Year 2) Reynolds crams all the major incidents of his six visits to Sidmouth between August 1906 and October 1907.

The chronology of the ten chapters follows pretty closely that of the real events, with a slight manipulation at the beginning and the end. The April episode of the first chapter stands, by way of prologue, well outside the time frame, recording as it does the visit of September 1904 and the first emotional contact with Bob. The next three equally short chapters encompass the decision to revisit taken in July 1906, the first five-day visit in August (here recorded as July–August), and the tramp to North Devon via Princetown.

The core of the book is Chapters 5 and 7 which coincide chronologically with the three week visit of September 1906 and the ten day visit in November. Almost all of Chapter 5 is chronologically accurate – the discussions in the kitchen, the early morning routine of mackerel-fishing, the meditation on cleanliness and pluck *versus* courage, all took place that September. Only the final pages, the winkling trip with Uncle Sam, the midsummer storm and the Regatta are borrowed from the following summer. By contrast, Chapter 7 contains little of the November visit; it is a sort of sweeping up of events from before and after, mostly after since it was written in the spring and summer of 1907. It begins with the arrival by train of March 1907 and most of the material – the meeting with "Straighty", the prawning trips with Uncle Sam, Bill's leave from the Navy, occurred after. The return of Lulu from service is the key event of this chapter which is drawn from the September before.

The two short Salisbury chapters, 6 and 8, mark the returns to Devizes of October 1906 and January 1907 and are used by Reynolds impersonally – the first as a lyrical, philosophical account of fishermen and the sea, a forerunner of *Alongshore*, and the second as a sociological discussion of class, the resilience of the working class, and the role of law and politics in relation to them. They are, in short, reflections at a geographical and psychological distance.

The last substantive chapter, Chapter 9, is set in December a year later and marks the New Year's Eve visit of 1906. Only the hiring of the drosky down from the station (which comes from May 1907) is a chronological distortion. All the rest, the long night at sea for no catch, the catch of the season, the New Year celebration, spring from that visit.

In all, the actual events of 14 months are set in a fictional 17 months and the sequence of visits, if not always of events, is followed very closely. There are only minor adjustments in chronological time. Indeed, the average reader might be forgiven for assuming that the book runs from April to December of the same year; only the word "January" at the head of Chapter 8 gives the lie to that. In some ways, the book compressed in this way would have had a tighter dramatic unity, but it is evident that Reynolds felt that credulity would have been stretched too far if everything, emotional reactions as much as events, were crammed into the space of six months.

Reynolds followed the autobiografiction form also in the slight distortion of space. For Devizes, he chose Salisbury – inspired by his "second" home with the Tanners at Ford. For Sidmouth, he chose Seacombe. The choice of a real name for the one and a fictional for the other is deliberate. Salisbury stands for the routine real world, Seacombe for the lost domain. He had also a strong urge to disguise Sidmouth in order to protect the Woolleys and, rather naively, believed he could do so by fictionalising all the place names and by minor distortions of geography, such as the narrator's arrival by road from Salisbury at the start of Chapter 3 by crossing the bight of the Exe.

The early pages of the book are the sombre days of his *physical* emergence from breakdown. The remainder, from the first arrival down the Gut in Chapter 3, is the account of his *emotional* recovery through the agency of people and place. In that respect, it serves the purposes of the *Ex Profundis* book he never wrote – but much more. The hero is the people and the place rather than the observing narrator. At the core of the narrative there is the contrast between the warm womb of the Woolleys' back kitchen, where the small human dramas of family are played out, and outside the threatening, all-pervading sea where man wrestles for his livelihood with the elements. The two worlds constantly interact. At home, they listen out for the changes in the sea that call them to action; at sea, they dream of the warmth and safety of home. Subtly behind it all is the still voice of the narrator, striving for a foothold in both these strange worlds, who finds redemption through the reality of lives that constantly confront death – by drowning, disease and starvation.

The core material of the book, which gave it its widest appeal, is the personal portraits – Bob slopping round the kitchen in his wet socks and chucking his wife under the chin; Mam Woolley rushing the children off to school with her barrage of mock threats; the children themselves with their cheek and constant laughter, grabbing for every food in sight; Grannie Pratt (Mrs Pinn in the book) with her dry peasant humour, eyeing the whisky bottle on the top shelf. And above all Uncle Sam, the popular hero of the book, with his wisdom of sea and weather, his fierce independence and scorn for soft-living modern man, picking his way through the rock pools like some mythological sprite.

Here is Reynolds' foremost gift – his power of observation – operating at its highest level. It is there in the dialogue – whether of the Woolley family at table, the quarrels of Bob and Tom at sea, town women gossiping among themselves. It is there in the individual touches of descriptive movement – Mam Woolley walking upstairs: "She went upstairs with that peculiar tread of hers – as if the feet were very tired but the rest of the body invincibly energetic".[129] It is there in the sudden switches of mood, from light to dark and back again – the melancholy recollection of the dead children and then the present laughter of man and wife.

Most readers remember Uncle Sam under the dark cliffs jumping from rock to rock, out in his element after winkles or prawns; but the most telling of all the scenes is Uncle Sam back on dry land resting in the little back kitchen, the fish out of water who suddenly takes on his age. Here Reynolds, reaching for the man behind the mask, finds him in his poverty – and without sentimentality – in his overwhelming love of life.

> When at last it was over, I brought Uncle Jake in house and made him a cup of cocoa. We had been nine hours' rowing. Though he could have done the same again, without food or rest, he looked a little haggard. It seemed impossible to believe that the grey old man with disordered hair and beard, clothed in rags and patches, sipping cocoa in a windsor chair, was that same alert shadow who had been reckoning up life, so humorously and wisely, in the darkness under the cliffs. He referred again to the winter's pinch. It must mean that he has not enough money put by from summer for the days coming, when even he will not be able to find some odd job. Yet, as I know very well, when the pinch does come he will go short and say nothing whatever to anybody. He will be merely a shade more sarcastic. One of the children may come home saying that 'thic Uncle Jake a'nt had half a pound of butter all this week,' or that he has been in one of his passions with Aunt Jake for taking in a loaf of bread without paying cash for it. He will bring out a ha'penny from a little screw of newspaper to buy milk for his cats, and he will take some crumbs to leave on dry rocks under the cliffs for the robins that flutter after him there. "Poor things!" he'll say. And to people he will still be saying what he thinks, fair or foul, gentle or hard. To understand his sternness and his kindness, it needs to go with him wrinkling in the

> sunshine and prawning in the dark. He is become very like his beloved rocks and cliffs. He is, as one might say, a voice for them, and his words and deeds are what one would expect their words and deeds to be, did they not stand there, warm, sunny and graciously coloured, or dark and stern, fronting the sea immovably, as Uncle Jake fronts life. "Du *I* want to die?" he says when asked his age. "Why, I'd like to live a thousand years!"[130]

Interspersed with the powerful portraits are the set-piece lectures, the sociological comment which caused so much difficulty for Frederic Chapman and for the many other readers that followed in his wake. Those in the Salisbury chapters (Chapters 6 and 8) seem logically and appropriately placed, if a little dry in content. Indeed, Chapter 8 and the postscript provide the essential message of the book – that the working class, with its courage to live, is naturally superior to the middle class with its insipid utilitarian virtues; and middle class social reformers have no moral justification for legislative interference with working-class lives.

It is the postscript that contains the best known and most often quoted statement of this position: "I am often asked why I have forsaken the society of educated people, and have made my home among 'rough uneducated' people, in a poor man's house. The briefest answer is, that it is good to live among those who, on the whole, are one's superiors".[131]

But the lectures in Chapter 5 – on class, language, and his two especial current obsessions, cleanliness and pluck *versus* courage – have seemed to many readers then and since as an unwarranted intrusion, breaking the spell of the very human narrative. It is the coldness of scientific analysis breaking in on the warmth of human poetry.

There is much to be said for this view, but ultimately it is merely a matter of taste. On a first reading of the book, these lectures may seem a minor irritant; but on subsequent readings they can be seen to serve a wider artistic purpose, providing a much-needed dramatic relief from the personal narrative. As such, they create a light and shade which sets off that narrative more pointedly. Whether Reynolds intended such an artistic effect or not, it is difficult to see the scientific observer and analyst in him eschewing comment of this kind. Given the author, it is difficult to see the book being written in any other way. It is in fact all Reynolds.

And much of it is so well written – strong intellect, clear prose. The lecture on cleanliness, for example, may be over-long for some tastes but it contains some fine writing and conscious variation of style. In the following passage, the first half is pure 1840s Carlyle, the second half pure 1930s Orwell.

> Cleanliness is our greatest class-symbol. In living with people who have been brought up to different ways of life, a consideration of cleanliness is forced upon one; for nothing else rouses so instantaneously and

violently the latent snobbery that one would fain be rid of. Religiously, politically, we are men and brothers all. Yet still – there *are* men we simply cannot treat as brothers. By what term of contempt (in order to justify our unbrotherliness) can we call them? Not *poor men*; for we have *Poor but honest* too firmly fixed in our minds, and we would all like a colonial rich rough diamond of an uncle to appear suddenly in our family circle. Hardly *men of no family*; for men of no family are received at court. Not *workmen*; for behold the Carlylese and Smilesian dignity of labour! Not *the masses*; for the masses are supposed to be our rulers. What then can we call these people with whom we really cannot associate on equal terms? Why, call them THE GREAT UNWASHED. O felicitous phrase! O salve of the conscience! That is the unpardonable social sin. At the bottom of our social ladder is a dirty shirt; at the top is fixed not laurels, but a tub! The bathroom is the inmost, the strongest fortress of our English snobbery.

Cleanliness as a subject of discussion is, curiously enough, considered rather more improper than disease. Yet it has to be faced, and that resolutely, if we would approach, and approaching, understand, the majority of our fellow-creatures.

Chemically all dirt is clean. Just as the foods and drinks of a good dinner, if mixed up together on a dish, would produce a filthy mess, so conversely, if we could separate any form of dirt into the pure solid, liquid and volatile chemical compounds of which it is composed, into pretty crystals, liquids and gases, exhibited in the scientific manner on spotless watch-glasses and in thrice-washed test-tubes, – we might indeed say that some of these chemicals had an evil odour, but we could not pronounce them unclean. Prepared in a laboratory, the sulphuretted hydrogen gas which makes the addled egg our national political weapon, is a quite cleanly preparation. Dirt is merely an unhappy mixture of clean substances. The housewife is nearest a scientific view of the matter when she distinguishes between 'clean dirt' and 'dirty dirt', and does not mind handling coal, for instance, because, being clean dirt, it will not harm her. Cleanliness is a process by which we keep noxious microbes and certain poisons outside our systems or in their proper places within. (It has been shown that we cannot live without microbes, and that there exist normally in some parts of the body substances which are powerfully poisonous to other parts.) Rational cleanliness makes for health, for survival. It is, ultimately, an expression of the Will to Live.

Far, however, from being rational, our notions on cleanliness are in the highest degree superficial. We make a great fuss over a flea; hardly mention it in polite company; but we tolerate the dirty housefly on all our food. We eat high game which our cook's more natural taste calls muck. We are only just beginning to realise the indescribable filthiness of carious teeth, than which anything more unclean, a few diseases excepted,

> can scarcely be found in slums. Even in this great age of pseudo-scientific enlightenment, we do not have a carious tooth extracted until it aches, though we have a front tooth cleaned and stopped on the first appearance of decay. What the eye doth not see.... Yet we presume to judge men by their deviation from our conventional standards of cleanliness.[132]

Given Edwardian susceptibilities, it was perhaps not surprising that Alston Rivers should want to exclude such passages from the final text, nor that this reaction should redouble Reynolds' obsession with the subject and make him leap to the defence of such "coarseness". There was a touch of irony behind it all for those who knew Reynolds intimately as one of the most fastidious of members of the middle class. For him, perhaps the greatest trial of his new life in Bob Woolley's home was coping with the dirt and the table manners, the running noses and the mackerel eaten with the fingers. He had, after all, a neurotic's sense of smell. But this was an emotional distaste which his intellect told him was wrong; and it was the battle of intellect over emotions that produced the obsession and the lecture. It is not so much Reynolds preaching to the average squeamish middle-class woman, but Reynolds preaching to his squeamish self.

Beside the human narrative and the sociological lectures, there is a third strand which makes up the book – what one might call the poetic interludes. These are deliberate and carefully located; some come off and some don't. The prose poetry in Chapter 5, *The Fisher Father and Child,* is one that doesn't. It stems from the period at the end of September 1906 when he was experimenting with Whitmanesque verse, but it has neither the power nor conviction of the immediate experience as set out in prose in his letter to Garnett of 12 September (see page 130 above). The little vignettes of the lacemaker (Chapter 5) and the timeless moment in the Alexandra bar inspired by the music outside (Chapter 7) – "It was as if, for the moment, we had all been very intimate; as if we had all gone an adventure together and had peeped over the edge of the world" – are happier.[133] Both work well in creating the right mood at just the right point in the narrative.

So does the poetry prose of the ode to the generic servant girl in Chapter 7 – a typical Reynolds *tour de force.* He is honest homosexual enough in the previous section when Jenny comes back from service to confess his irritation with adolescent women, particularly of that type – but then his precise observation, both physical and spiritual, takes over and inspires him to a broader, more human perspective.

> Poor brave small servant girls, earning your living while you are yet but children! I see your faces at the doors, rosy from the country or yellowish-white from anaemia and strong tea; see how your young breasts hardly fill out your clinging bodices, all askew, and how your hips are not yet grown to support your skirts properly – draggle-tails! I see you taking the

morning's milk from the hearty milkman, or going an errand in your apron and a coat too small for you, or in your mistress's or mother's cast-off jacket, out at the seams, puffy-sleeved, years behind the fashion and awry at the shoulders because it is too big. I see your floppety hat which you cannot pin down tightly to your hair, because there isn't enough of it; – your courageous attempts to be prettier than you are, or else your carelessness from overmuch drudgery; your coquettish and ugly gestures mixed.

I picture your life. Are you thinking of your work, or are you dreaming of the finery you will buy with your month's wages; the ribbons, the lace, or the lovely grown-up hat? Are you thinking of what he said, and she said, and you said, you answered, you did? Are you dreaming of *your* young man? Are you building queer castles in the air? Are you lonely in your dingy kitchen? Have you time and leisure to be lonely?

I follow you into your kitchen, with its faint odour of burnt grease (your carelessness) and of cockroaches, and its whiffs from the scullery sink, and a love-story that scents your life, hidden away in a drawer. I hear your mistress's bell jingle under the stairs. You must go to bed, and sleep, and be up early, before it is either light or warm, to work for her; you must be kept in good condition like a cart horse or a donkey; you must earn, earn well, your so many silver pounds a year.

In mind, I follow you also into your little bedroom under the roof, with its cracked water-jug that matches neither the basin or the soap-dish, and its boards with a ragged scrap of carpet on them, and your tin box in the corner; and the light of the moon or street lamp coming in at the window and casting shadows on the sloping whitewashed ceiling; and your guttered candle. What will you try on to-night? A hat, or a dress, or the two-and-eleven-three-farthing blouse? Shift the candle. Show yourself to the looking-glass. A poke here and a pull there – and now put everything away carefully in the box under the bed, and go to sleep.

Though I say that I follow you up to your attic, and watch you and see you go to sleep, you need not blush or giggle or snap. I would not do you any harm; your eyes would plague me. And besides, I do not entirely fancy you. You are not fresh. You are boxed up too much. But I trust that some lusty careless fellow, regardless of consequences, looking not too far ahead, and following the will of his race – I trust that he will get hold of you and whirl you heavenwards, and will fill your being full to the brim; and will kiss you and surround you with himself, and will make you forget yourself and your mistress and all the world, the leaves and birds of the Lover's Lane, the shadowy cattle munching in the field and the footsteps approaching.

I wish you luck – that your young man may stick to you. It is after all a glimpse of God I wish you, perhaps your only one. You've got a longish time before you.[134]

Here, as in many other parts of the book, Reynolds treads that narrow and dangerous borderline between true feeling and sentimentality. Today, the false sophistication of our modern age has given us a lower tolerance threshold for sentimentality than our grandfathers would have had a hundred years ago. But even allowing for that, Reynolds safely escapes the hazards of the sentimental, both by the realism of the physical detail and by the odd inspired touch – here "I do not entirely fancy you. You are not fresh." – which brings the high-flown feelings plummetting down to earth.

Behind all these strands of the book is the hovering presence of the narrator – neither intrusive nor egoistic (as Garnett had warned), but quietly authoritative, stitching the narrative together with the pointed subjective comment and dropping here and there little pearls of personal revelation, just enough to create the mystery that invites the reader to ask – who is this man and where does he come from? We are introduced to the Reynolds' neuroticism: "....what I call pluck did not form a great part of my birthright. I find myself too apprehensive by nature; imagine horrid possibilities too keenly; and indeed would far rather hurt myself than think about doing so. I suppose I have a certain amount of courage, for I am usually successful in making myself do what I funk; but I like doing it none the better for that. And up to the present, I have not failed badly in tight corners. On the contrary, I find (like most nervy people) that actual danger, once arrived, is curiously exhilarating; that it makes one cooler and sharper, even happy. One has faced the worst in imagination, and the reality is play beside it."[135] We have a glimpse of the famous Reynolds' temper: "The poor man's bark is appalling; I often used to think there was murder in the air when I heard some quite ordinary discussion; there would have been murder in the air had I myself been worked up to speak so furiously."[136]

But he also uses the personal reminiscence freely to an artistic end. He gives us, for example, a summary autobiography as he draws on his life in Manchester, Paris, Devizes and Nether Velly to point up the perfection of life in Bedford Square.

> Up-country, next week, I shall greatly miss my window overlooking Alexandra Square. I have lived (rebelliously) in suburban streets where only clattering feet, tradesmen's carts and pitiful street singers broke the monotony; in a Paris *chambre à garçon, au sixième*, where the view was roofs and the noise of the city was attenuated to a murmur; in country houses which looked out on sweeps of hill, down, vale and sea, so changeable and lovely that they were dreamlike and as a dream abide in the memory.... Here I have quick human life just below my window, and – up the Gut – a view of the sea unbroken hence to the horizon; a patch of water framed on three sides by straight walls and on the fourth by the sky-line; a miniature ocean across which the drifters sail to the western offing, and the little boats curvet to and fro, and

> The stately ships go on
> To their haven under the hill.
>
> There is always, here, a sound of the sea. When, at night, the Square is still, it seems to advance, to come nearer, to be claiming one for its own.[137]

And there is the intimate Reynolds, laying himself naked before the world, revealing the most fundamental of his innermost problems. The examples are few, but enough to justify the assertion that this is not a book about class, fishing, the simple life, the Woolley family even – but a personal testimony of the author's own grappling with life. As when, for instance, in describing his delight in the fisher children and their response to him, the emotion becomes so strong that he cannot conceal the great void in his life – the impossibility of giving a love which in the past he has never received.

> Here, on the other hand, my difficulty is to get rid of the children when I wish to go out by myself. They follow me out to the Front, and meet me there when I return, running towards me with shouting and arms upraised, tumbling over their own toes, and taking me home as if I were a huge pet dog of theirs. ....I cross the Square, and some child, lolling over the board across a doorway, laughs to me shrilly and waves its arms. If by taking thought, I could send such a glow to the hearts of those I love, as that child, without thinking, sends to mine.... But I cannot. I can only wave a hand back to the child, and be thankful and full-hearted.
>
> It is not that I buy the children bananas or give them an infrequent ha'penny. When bananas and ha'pence are scarce, their love is no less. It is not that I am always good-tempered and jolly. Sometimes I snap unmercifully, so that they look at me with scared, inquiring eyes. It is not that they are always well-behaved. Frequently they are very naughty indeed. The causes of our sympathy lie deeper.
>
> They are more naive than the children who are in process of being well-educated; more independent and also more dependent. ....They make more mistakes and retrieve them better. Affection with them more rapidly and frankly translates itself into action. They laugh quickly, cry quickly, swear quickly. "Yu'm a fule!" they rap out without a moment's hesitation; and I suppose I am, else they wouldn't want to say so. Perhaps I overvalue the physical manifestations of love, but if a child will take my hand, or climb upon my knee, or kiss me unawares, then to certainty of its affection is added a greater contentment and a deeper faith. The peace of a child that sleeps upon one's shoulder, is given also to oneself. The appurtenances of love mean much to me; nearness, warmth, caresses. But I cannot make the advances; I was bred in a different school where, though frankness was encouraged, *naiveté* was repressed; and I am

the more grateful to these children for taking me in hand – for being able to do so.[138]

A Poor Man's House was built primarily on the intensive spate of letters Reynolds wrote to Edward Garnett from Sidmouth in the autumn and winter of 1906 and the spring and summer of 1907. Some three-quarters of all the episodes and character drawing can be traced to one letter or another. In most cases, he expanded and improved the original text, though still using phrases, sometimes whole sentences, almost verbatim. It might be thought an unspontaneous and unwieldy proceeding for a work of art, almost akin to the writing up of research notes. But on the contrary, his direct access to the letters written some months before, and lent back to him by Garnett, gave to the work a freshness and immediacy that could not have been achieved from memory alone. Above all, the stark emotional tone of the letters enabled Reynolds to recapture the original feelings of the Sidmouth revelation at a time when the first entrancing spark of life with the Woolleys was already wearing off.

Some of the letters, as we have seen, were turned at the time (January 1907) into full-blown sketches for the *Daily Mail* and a utilitarian Reynolds felt obliged to shoehorn them into Chapter 9 at the end of the book. Some – *The Catch of the Season*, for example – fulfil their artistic purpose well, in this case by providing the action climax of the work. Others, like *The Shooting Star Goes Herring Drifting*, appear out of place, mere make-weights holding up the narrative.

Leaving aside the debate as to whether the social and political comment destroys the artistic integrity, the book is not entirely without flaws. There are the occasional *longueurs* that add little to character or narrative – Tony Widger's attempt to run away to sea in Chapter 6 is arguably one – and the final postscript is a disaster. Starting well enough, it degenerates into a pseudo-scientific schoolbook discussion of "differential evolution" which completely destroys the powerful feelings generated by the close of the previous chapter. It is almost as if Reynolds were deliberately thumbing his nose at the concept of a "work of art". But for the most part, these are youthful errors – perhaps most of all in strictness of revision. They do not detract in any major way from the undoubted strength of the work as a whole.

The use of language in *A Poor Man's House* is a reflection of Reynolds' very strong views on the subject. Living and working with the Woolleys, he had quickly taken up the Devon dialect for everyday use, partly unconsciously since it was the only language he heard around him, but in part deliberately because Bob, who was a little deaf, heard it better and responded to it more fluently.[139] He treated language, like everything else, as a subject for observation and analysis; one of the most subtle arguments in the book is his analysis in Chapter 5 of the use of the word "like" as an essential element in the working man's efforts to express himself in language. In this context, he approached the Devon dialect as if it were just another foreign language, and reproduced its sounds and its rhythms as closely as possible.

Interestingly, he followed the same procedure in his stories and sketches with a French setting, limiting the direct use of the language to the minimum the English public (and English publisher) would stand, but translating the French dialogue almost literally with the same grammar, rhythms and intonation. In one of his best sketches of this *genre, A Third-Class Journey*, we have the following remarkable dialogue

> "Monsieur," she said to me one day, and there was a bitterness underlying her jest, "Monsieur, I see you are *homme sérieux*.... Will you marry me and take me back to England with you. I am very weary here."
> "But, Madame," I replied as bluntly, "I am a young man – not serious enough, perhaps."
> "You have reason," she said. "I must stay with madame. Perhaps she will have need...."
> A knife-handle tapped on the table impatiently. "Yes, yes, Monsieur. At once! I come. What is it that it is that you want?"[140]

The use of the precise literal translation is a daring move, but it entirely comes off. Far from being stilted or absurd, the rhythm alone of the language carries an authenticity which could not be achieved in any other way.

The Devon dialect in *A Poor Man's House* is used in the same way to achieve authenticity, but also, and much more important, to achieve a fuller range of expression than standard English could provide. Reynolds was proud of his ability to use the dialect both spontaneously and accurately: "I have.... managed to preserve the ability to speak dialect in spite of all the efforts of my pastors and masters to make me talk the stereotyped, comparatively inexpressive compromise which goes by the name of King's English."[141] He had a deeply held view that standard middle-class language was as impoverished as the standard middle-class life and feeling it was designed to express. The use of working-class speech was a release from these restrictions. Above all, it was the best vehicle for expressing that most important ingredient of a real life – the commonplace. This gave a didactic purpose not only to the content of his writing, but also to its mode of expression. He explained it fully to a journalist in 1913: "an attempt has to be made to bring literary language nearer to the language of the common people; it is now too much a dialect of educated people and has become emasculated and flaccid and insipid. It needs to be revitalised by an infusion of the common speech.... "[142]

The widespread use of dialect throughout the book was, nevertheless, a bold venture. The *Daily Mail* had already rejected his fishing sketches because of it, and he was only too well aware that the mere sight of it could put off the average reader and provide the hostile reviewer with a sure source of ridicule. Roy Hattersley, in his generally sympathetic introduction to the 1982 edition of the book, is notably grudging about this aspect: "Attempts to reproduce regional dialects rarely succeed and perhaps the best that can be said for Stephen Reynolds's efforts is that they cause no more embarrassment than the parallel failures of more illustrious writers."[143]

But this is entirely to lose the plot. The dialect in *A Poor Man's House* is not a passing attempt to achieve cheap authenticity, but one of the most carefully crafted ingredients of the book, worked over by a writer who spoke, and was currently speaking, it as a native. The authenticity of written Devon dialect cannot be tested from the silent words on the page, least of all when read internally in a southern counties or even a Yorkshire accent. The phonetical approximations have to be read out loud in a Devon accent and with a Devon lilt. Reynolds, as only to be expected, passes such a test with flying colours. And although the average reader might have no precise knowledge of the sounds and rhythms of Devon speech, they could, as with Reynolds' translations from French, sense the authenticity for themselves. No contemporary voice was raised against the use of dialect in the book. On the contrary, most commentators, from Frederic Chapman on, saw it as a definite source of strength.

One final stylistic point. In *A Poor Man's House* Reynolds introduced a highly expressive ploy of punctuation that had always appeared in his letters – the use of four (and only four) *points de suspension* to complete a sentence and thereby give it a neatly equivocal air. It is there in the second paragraph of the book and reappears countless times – at the end of the first chapter, for example.

> Tony Widger lives, I believe, somewhere down the Gut, in Under Town, a place they call the Seacombe slum. You can see a horde of children pouring in and out of the Gut all day long, and in the evening the wives stand at the seaward end of it, to gossip and await their husbands. Noisy place.... [144]

However much he used it, he took care that it never lost its potency. It became the hallmark of Reynolds' prose style.

A Poor Man's House is a book about the awakening of love – sexual love as much as Christian. Reynolds, who had spent so much of his youth in a homosexual wilderness, could not on any account have kept that element out of his first true book. It was many years before he was openly to admit to it, and then only to Edward Carpenter, the first of his homosexual friends who was open about his sexuality and who, in a very real sense, brought Reynolds "out". It was Havelock Ellis who started the process by introducing Reynolds to Carpenter through the agency of the book. In his first letter to Carpenter in May 1913 Reynolds wrote: "I was glad when Havelock Ellis wrote to me that you were reading my book and intended to write; and delighted when I got your letter. Havelock Ellis remarked that he had given you no hint of what he calls 'the inwardness' of the book, but I daresay you detected the homogenic basis of it. For most people it is by the frankness of its expression that it is hidden."[145]

It is certainly true that Reynolds did not go out of his way to disguise it and possibly true that most readers regarded, for example, the heightened emotional reactions to Bob and all his activities as the natural admiration of one man for another. No contemporary critics even hinted at the possibility of a homosexual element, and only one modern commentator has seriously raised the issue, and then only tentatively. Writing in *The Times* in June 1976, Paul Barker commented of the book: "There is something refreshing about his *pleasure* at being among working people. (Something obscurely sexual, even homosexual, about it, too)".[146]

Yet right from the very first page, with the meeting at night with Tony Widger weeping in the streets for his lost son, there is a subtle undercurrent of emotion that is far stronger than what is going on on the surface. It comes to the surface in the physical description of Tony sailing with his son, in the cold nights at sea where they cuddle up together under the sail for warmth, and pervades the whole book. The minute observation of every detail of action, of speech, of feeling betrays the lover looking upon the beloved.

And there is a homosexual tone to aspects of the work other than the central relationship. It is there in the odd cutting misogynist remark, as when Reynolds, firelighter extraordinary to the Woolley household, comments on the younger daughter's domestic incapacity: "After all, how many women in any station of life, have precision and forethought enough to lay a fire so that it will burn up at once?"[147] It is there in the lovingly detailed description of George Widger home from the Navy: "He used to be so like a cat on a sunny wall; used to lie along the stern seat of the *Moondaisy* so lazy and content that only his ever-watchful eyes held any expression. He was deeply sunburnt: scraggy in the neck; strong and lissome, but not very smart. He is returned home no less strong and lissome, and exceedingly smart. The sunburn is gone; indeed there's many a maiden would envy his complexion; and his long stout neck, with the broadening bands of muscle, would delight a sculptor. The alert expression, that used to be more or less limited to his eyes, has spread, so to speak, over all his face, over the whole of him and into all his movements. He is organised; unified".[148]

And it is seen at its most spectacular in the long eulogy of Tom, physically the finest of the Woolleys: "John is the youngest, handsomest and most powerfully built of the Widgers; the most independent, most brutal-tongued and most logical, though not, I fancy, the most perceptive. The inborn toughness, the family tendency to health and strength, which made fine men of the elder Widgers in spite of their youthful exposure and privations, has, in the case of John who underwent fewer hardships, resulted in the development, unimpeded, of a wonderful physique.... Fair-haired, blue-eyed, his clean-shaven face deeply and clearly coloured; a combination of the Saxon bulldog type with the seafaring man's alertness; his heavy yet lissome frame admirably half-revealed by the simplicity of navy-blue guernsey and trousers, – it is one of the sights of Seacombe to see him walk the length of the Front with his two small boys".[149] In a sense, Reynolds could never have written the book without the homosexual element. It was a book above all that was made by honesty – of purpose, feeling and expression.

A Poor Man's House was certain to have a wide appeal among Edwardian readers. It appealed to the "back to the land" school, to young men in sterile London offices who dreamed of "the simple life" – a phrase and a concept that Reynolds detested with all his being. It appealed to middle-class socialists in Fabian and other groups, who had never in their lives approached a working man as a fellow human being, but who were now given that pleasure vicariously and painlessly. It stirred emotion among liberals and those on the left, and sparked political debate about the "Condition of England" question and the resolution of the working class "problem". But most of all it appealed for its very special qualities, irrespective of social or political debate – its humanity, its intimacy, its commonplaces, its humour, its immediacy, its fullness of life.

For the reader of 1908, the anonymity of its narrator, so near yet tantalisingly so far, led to a widespread search for the author and his background. Taking the book at random down from the shelf today, the modern reader (though benefiting from a modicum of biographical information in recent editions) is faced with the same puzzle. Here is a lively and intriguing, but also quirky and perplexing book – where is its author, how did he come here? It is a book crying out for a context and needs, to unlock its full quality, some knowledge and understanding of Reynolds' life, and of the physical backdrop of Edwardian Sidmouth.

Writing in the *New Age* in 1909, Arnold Bennett said of *Memoirs of a Surrey Labourer* by George Bourne (the writer George Sturt with whom Reynolds was soon bracketed in literary circles) "I shall be surprised if this book does not continue to sell for about a hundred years. ....But the book had no boom such as Mr John Lane recently contrived to enjoy with another very good and not dissimilar book, Mr Stephen Reynolds's 'A Poor Man's House'. Mr Stephen Reynolds was more chattered about by literary London in two months than Mr George Bourne has been in the eight years which have passed since he published his first book about Frederick Bettesworth, the Surrey labourer in question. Mr Bourne will owe his popularity in 2009 to the intrinsic excellence of his work...."[150]

If Bennett intended by this that Sturt would outlast Reynolds, it was a prediction that has not come true. Sturt's book has gone through four editions while Reynolds' has had seven – three new editions since his death, two of them in the 1980s. There will be more in the century just beginning. The reader of 2009 will continue to be struck above all by the timelessness of the human portraits in the book, by the sense, the ultimate accolade for any writer, that Bob and Tom, Mam and Uncle Sam, the children and the Devon kitchen, are with us this very moment – real people, alive and full of life, here, now, always.

Reynolds was the first reader to sense it. In a written, and rather nervously defensive, apologia for the book just after it was published, he told Tom: "We writing people mayn't be much use, but one thing we can do: we can give people a sort of second life in print that lasts longer than their own. I don't know whether it has ever occurred to you that the great dead men who are remembered, even Christ, are remembered only because someone wrote about them. Without that, however great, they would have been quite forgotten. Most people like to think they will not be forgotten after they are dead, and two things I can be certain of: one is that the people in my book will be alive there long after they are dead and forgotten hereabout. And the other is, that those who read the book will get from it nothing but the same admiration for the people in it that caused me to write the book. For the admiration I feel, I can make my readers feel".[151]

Ninety years later, we know it to be true.

TEN

The English Review 1908–9

On 21 October 1908 *A Poor Man's House* burst forth upon an unsuspecting world. It was a day – the publication of his first real book – that Reynolds had been dreaming of ever since his first meeting with Seccombe in Manchester almost eight years before. Now the time had come, he could disguise neither the sense of anti-climax nor his private apprehensions about the world's reaction. He wrote to Garnett a week before publication: "It is to be published on the 21st. Can't say I feel very excited about it. Lane has been advertising that it ought 'to make me famous in one bound', and I'm in fear of a damnable slump."[1]

He was equally apprehensive, but for different reasons, of the reaction of the Woolleys. He used one of his proof copies to try and square Bob, and was initially relieved at the result. "Bob has seen a good deal of it, and is not unpleased I think. The point that appeals to him, I think, is that somebody 'has told off the likes o' they' – i.e. the middle class; has told them what he had in his own mind, but could neither express nor force them to listen to." But he was still anxious about the local reaction that Bob might face and sought Garnett's aid. "If you think I have succeeded at all at that part of the job, and cared to write, or still better to typewrite [*no one could read Garnett's hand*], a congratulation to him, you might be doing me a big service, for which I should be very grateful. It's rather unfortunate that the thing should be published at the time of year when his toxins mount and make him more suspicious than a Devonian always is: I can't forecast with any accuracy the effect of any slurs which may be thrown out at him."[2]

The source of Reynolds' anxiety was the emotional intimacy of his relationship with Bob as portrayed in the book; but in the event it was the intimacy of the physical descriptions of domesticity that caused the main problem for Bob and Mam – ironically, a typical middle-class reaction to the invasion of their privacy. Four weeks after publication, the issue was still creating tensions. He wrote to his friend Scott-James, the literary editor of the *Daily News*, with a pressing plea: "You haven't done the *Poor Man's House* yet.... I wonder if you'd mind my asking you to keep out of your review anything the subjects of the book could take as reflecting on themselves – anything concrete and definite, rather than abstract; – and to give 'em a pat on the back if possible. There's nothing of a row over the book, but I'm so mixed up in local beach v. town politics, that the situation is a bit delicate, if I am not to lose my power of working for the fishing. The things they are inclined to resent are such harmless homely details as my taking tea up to Bob and Mrs. Bob when they are in bed, and so forth. If you'd help me keep the pot upright I should be very grateful...."[3]

In his review the following week, Scott-James came up trumps with a solid pat on the back for both author and his subjects, and the stigmatisation of any potential critics as vulgar and mealy-mouthed.

> An inspiringly real and outspoken book is "A Poor Man's House", with something of the largeness and salty sting of the sea in it.... The author has many qualities underlying his strong literary gift. He has a keen eye for character, a racy sense of humour, a broadly hearty enjoyment of human nature. But it is his intellectual sincerity, strongly marked, that gives his picture of life balance and fairness, and reinforces his artistic talents. All the fisherfolk in the book, and delightful people most of them are, are drawn with the sharp, exact touch of a born observer of men. Only vulgar or mealy-mouthed people would find anything to repel them in the delightful human picture of the life of the "Widger" family, drawn with such sympathy and zest and feeling for its lights and shades. The portraiture of this delightful family is one of the best we have had in literature of the kind since George Eliot's "Mrs. Poyser".[4]

Reynolds was even more deeply anxious about the reaction of Tom. Although their minor quarrel of two months earlier, caused by Tom's jealousy over Reynolds' support for Bob, was now well in the past, the book might threaten to re-open the same wounds. He did not dare to confront Tom in person, but sent him a copy under cover of a carefully crafted letter. As always when writing to the Woolley brothers, he spoke in simplified English, at times a little too *de haut en bas*, but now he remained cautiously defensive throughout, anxious to explain his motivation, to excuse the quality of the product, and generally to appease. It was, above all, a simple confession of faith.

> I honestly believe that, on the whole, the lives of you people are better than the lives of the sort of people I was brought up among. And I believe that the future is in the hands of those who are called "the poor", because they have no capital, and who are wrongly looked down upon and insulted in all sorts of ways by the middle-class. That is why I like to live among you – because I think you make a better man of me. And that is why I have written the book – to prove that the lives of the so-called ignorant are better than the lives of the so-called educated. Most of those who have read the book before publication seem to think I have pretty well proved my case. Anyhow, I've tried my best.
>
> I don't suppose you'll like everything in the book. Nobody likes everything in any book. I can find faults in it myself now I see it in print. One can't paint high lights without painting in some of the shadows, either in word painting or in painting with paints; but there's nothing at all in the book set down in malice. I set out to praise a life, and did it in the best way I knew how. The portrait of John Widger you won't find bad;

> at least, you won't have any reason to; for 'tis a fine figure of a strong man in that chapter, and it makes a good impression.
> You will see the precautions I have taken to put people off the scent of where "Seacombe" is – making out it's near the Eddystone Lighthouse. The book will hardly be heard of in Sidmouth: I have given orders that the sale of it is not to be pushed here; for I know that, owing to my taking the part of the fishing, there are several people here who'd take the least opportunity, good or bad, of making mischief between me and the fishermen, thinking that then the fishermen would lose their amateur lawyer.
> One kindness you can do me if you will – I'd do the same for you if occasion arose. Don't bring the book into your little arguments with Bob. There's nothing in it about you that he told me, and almost nothing about anyone else, himself excepted. I don't mind your arguing about me, or wonder at it; but about the book I am rather tender; for, after all, I have given myself away in it ten times more than any one else, and it is a witness, in print, that you are all a good deal more to me than one cares to say in conversation. Nobody has ever written such a defence of you people. Nobody could write such a defence unless they were more than a little fond of the people written about; and so far as I am concerned, I shall never write another book on the same subject. I don't think I shall ever write another book half so good. So approve the merits you may see in this one, and forgive its shortcomings.
> When my satirical novel about middle-class Wiltshire people, who were not kind to me and whom I dislike, comes out next year, I'll send you that too, if I may. You'll see the difference then. I'm writing this, which isn't meant for anybody but you, because, being a writer, I can make my meaning so much plainer in writing than in talk.[5]

There was no explosion from Tom. His vanity was touched not a little by his own portrayal in the book. But the long-term impact was only to increase further his latent suspicion of the gentleman behind Bob. Whenever Reynolds attempted to offer him help too, it was met as often as not with sulks and a grudging refusal. And for Reynolds a whole heap of bewildered frustration.

Squaring the Woolleys was not his only anxiety on the eve of publication. He was beginning to lose confidence in Lane's lauded ability to push the book, and particularly in the sensitivity of his approach to advertising. He was embarrassed as much by the senseless hyperbole that threatened to oversell the book as by Lane's chosen image of the starving author who had felt the full privations of working class life. Reynolds had no experience of marketing or how to grab the public attention but, like many authors before and since, felt he could do a better job than his publisher and was not backward in telling him so. He was irritated by the triviality of advertising postures and always took the more serious line. He wanted his books to be linked positively to current social or political concerns – the *Mountain* to the overweening power of Northcliffe, the *Poor Man's House* to the problem of the working class and the Condition of England question.

He sensed difficulties ahead as early as August with the pre-publicity in the United States. "Old Lane has had a par. in the *Times* and an awful thing in the *N.Y. Times Sat. Rev.* in which I am described as a 'person of great eccentricity' and 'so Socialistic as to be almost revolutionary'."[6] In England, Lane had been running a little advertisement with a selective quotation from the preface which gave to Reynolds' mind quite the wrong tone to the book:

> A Poor Man's House by Stephen Reynolds.
> This is a true intimate picture of a poor fisherman's life – such as has never before been attempted; imaginative on its synthetic side, just as history is imaginative. MR STEPHEN REYNOLDS records his experiences as an inmate of "a poor man's house". As he says: "I have felt something of the pinch and hardship of the life, as well as enjoyed the picturesqueness...... I have worked in [*sic*] the boats sometimes fifteen hours a day, not as an amateur, but for hard and badly needed coin."[7]

It was a lazy piece of work by someone without the energy to read further than the preface for his inspiration.

On publication day, the thoughtful Frederic Chapman sent Reynolds a kindly letter of congratulation – and received a rocket for his pains.

> Very nice to receive your – as it were – birthday letter – the only one.
> For God's sake get Lane to dry up that asinine little quote in his advertisements about having felt something of the pinch and hardship of the job. That's not the note of the book, and its being so produced is exceedingly offensive to me. Where on earth is his advertising genius? Where the connection of the book with Socialism and Education, which everybody is interesting themselves in? Where, in short, some indication of the contents of the book instead of bloody twaddle about one being an inmate etc., as if the place was an asylum? Where the indication that there is something about fishing in it – a thing romantic to most town-dwellers? Is he mazed? Or penny foolish again?
> There – I don't know why I should fling this anger at your kindly head; but I can't trust myself to write to him direct.[8]

He changed his mind, however, the following day and wrote to thank Lane for the design of the book, copies of which had now arrived. Reynolds always took an obsessive interest in the minutiae of the production of his books and an almost schoolboy delight in the finished artefact: "I cannot too much thank you for producing the book so *chastely*, as we should have said at college. The get-up is exactly what I wished." But this was only the polite preliminary to the real meat of his letter. "I'm going to say, however, that I don't like my impecuniosity being blazed in your advertisements. Too many ink-splashers make a virtue of that necessity. I'm not a reformed tramp – nothing so sensible as a tramp, and nothing so idiotic as a reformed one."[9]

Lane, in the process of recovering from a sharp attack of flu, wrote apologetically to say he had not realised the advertisement might cause trouble. Reynolds took the opportunity to rub the point home and issue a warning for the future: "The impecuniosity advertisement did worry me. It's not so true of *this* year – thanks to you; that is to say, I don't anticipate starvation before next April. Please see that nothing is put in the advertisements – no quote – likely to tread on the corns of the people contained in the book. I'm having a hardish time making them see the thing in the right – i.e. my – light as 'tis."[10]

He was not in a good mood. The first public review of the book came out in the *Daily Telegraph* on the Friday, two days after publication. It was an inauspicious start. The reviewer, while praising the Woolleys to the skies – "nothing could be more direct or unaffected than the home which he describes...... a wonderful embodiment of untidy comfort", seemed determined on picking a quarrel with the author, without whom there would have been no Woolleys.

> Mr Stephen Reynolds has one foible which accords but ill with his subject and his ambition: he is inveterately affected. It is probable that no man was ever more anxious to be unaffected than he...... Nevertheless the reader never gets away from a sense of superiority in the writer, as of a showman displaying his wares. His phrase, too, is apt to be tortured...... his manner is artificial, and that is a pity...... The thing is excellently done, as a picture of genre; nothing spoils it but the occasional intrusive complacency of the author. He cannot forget that he has set out with a purpose: to show us, in fact, that the life of the poor has its own compensations, and cannot be properly estimated by uninstructed benevolence. It is a worthy purpose, and a sensible; but it might have been better kept in the background. For Mr. Reynolds has sounder gifts of description and of character-drawing than he has of philosophy and the art of moralising."[11]

There was, of course, a case to be made for this latter criticism, but Reynolds was furious with the patronising tone, indicative of the class-base of the paper. "Wasn't that *D. Telegraph* note damnable. But there! the book couldn't be expected to please the poops of the Old Maids' Advertisement Budget."[12] When better reviews came in, he suggested that Lane might use this bad one as a foil: "As for the *D.T.* – why not pick out the worst the old lady says and print it side by side with something good from papers of more literary standing? Always have hated the *D.T.*"[13]

But while on the Saturday evening he was ruefully ruminating this first notice as the possible shape of things to come, down at Someries at the end of another gruelling working week his distinguished patron had picked up the book and fallen immediately under its spell. He dashed off a letter to the young author – "I have had a fine letter from Conrad".[14]

Conrad was such a master of courtesy (some might say false courtesy) that one has to look twice at any praise from his pen; but there are ample clues in this letter to show that the feelings were genuine. When Conrad was excited by a book or a letter, he often went to the lengths of describing the precise situation and posture in which he had read it; and false praise from him very rarely contained a note of criticism.[15] In this letter, he feels sufficiently confident to broach the "didactic" nature of the book. And it was written straightaway – late at night after a long week.

> There are books one seems to have read before, and books that one doesn't want to read, books that one reads with annoyance, pleasure, exasperation or wonder but this, your P M's H, is a book for which one seems to have waited all the time, without knowing it exactly; not a revelation but the satisfaction of an intimate need of which one becomes aware after it has been satisfied at last. I am not a critic, as you know, nor a man to utter pretty, beautiful, or deep things about a book. I keep no store of pregnant phrases. The usual civilities I could write to a young author, I dare say if I tried very hard, but since I don't mean to insult you this is not to be thought of. I will tell you instead what has happened. I walked into my room, came up to the table you know, took up your book and opened it at the first page of the text (not of the preface). When I came to myself with a queer sense of unutterable fatigue I was still standing and I had reached p 62 [*the first distracting footnote – on fishing lines*] – not glancing through, mind you, but giving each phrase, each word, each image its full value as I went.
>
> Compact, harmonious, without a single – I won't say false – but uncertain note, true in aim, sentiment and expression, precise and imaginative, never precious but containing here and there an absolutely priceless phrase – that is what I think of your piece of prose. It is, no doubt, also a good action because the aim is worthy and the sentiment is human – if a little didactic. Searching my heart with some care I feel convinced that any difference there may be between us must be merely verbal. If I didn't think you true I would want you to be.
>
> If I were sufficiently saintly or patriarchal enough I would give my solemn blessing to those pages where your great talent speaks to the world in a cause altogether just and in an admirable manner. But I am neither a saint nor a patriarch – I am not even a good man. And a blessing is a serious thing. Unless the hand is worthy evil may ensue. So I hold my hand but I rejoice with you in the accomplished beginning. The thing now is to keep that torch burning bright and to hold it high.[16]

It was a remarkable testimonial from the leading English stylist of the day. Interspersed with the Conradian charm, Reynolds could distinguish the genuine sense of excitement. It was a turning point in his own view of himself as a writer. He had known during the writing that the book was good, probably the best he would ever accomplish; but it needed the confirmation of such a voice to make him really believe it. Henceforth he would face the literary world with a sureness and a confidence that had been entirely lacking in the past – a new self-confidence that some were to categorise as a new arrogance.

For Conrad also it was a change of view. He had had considerable faith in his young protégé, based on his talk and his manner. But the writing he had seen so far, though full of promise, was seriously uneven. Now, from the first sight of this book, he began to build hopes of Reynolds as a major novelist, at the head of the next generation of writers. This was no fantasy; for the next few years it became one of his most personal ambitions. The exhortation to hold the torch high was no empty image.

Reynolds had to wait another three months for the next commendation from a heavyweight friend. That autumn Galsworthy had been working furiously away at Wingstone, his country house in Devon, on the rewriting of *Fraternity*, and on its completion had disappeared for a month abroad over Christmas and the New Year. It was not until February that he at last got down to the reading of *A Poor Man's House*. By then the world had given its considered judgement, and Galsworthy's was no different.

> Fresh from the reading of 'A Poor Man's House' I want to record my enthusiasm. It's a splendid book, with the real thing in it. Both Ada and myself have had delight from the reading of nearly every page; and I don't a bit quarrel with your deductions as I thought I possibly might. The whole thing's so salt and good; and there's true beauty in it. Excellentissime! You have made us know all your friends and love them. The Devon heart of me did not want much persuasion to that I guess, still you so easily might have spoiled them for me; and you've done just the other thing.[17]

The *Daily Telegraph* review with its sniffy tone turned out to be more or less unique. It was followed quickly by a notice in the *Mail* bursting with praise for the character portrayal: "His picture of the great, wise, foolish child of a father, the rough-spoken, tender-hearted, courageous mother, and the horde of rackety, undisciplined, affectionate children is brought out little by little, with an art that hides itself, it is all so simple and unstrained. At the end it is stamped indelibly upon the mind. Its clear and naked truth is the best thing about it...... a remarkable book, and we hope it will receive the attention it deserves."[18]

Despite this, the book was rather slow in getting under way, both for sales and for reviews. The latter did not come on full stream until the middle of November, but the outcome was never in doubt. In the previous two years

Reynolds had built up such a firm phalanx of literary friends that most reviews were not confined just to the text, but had the inestimable advantage of insider knowledge. Thomas Seccombe in the *Readers' Review* waxed loud in its praise: "......a very vivid and powerfully written book which has a strong and original flavour of its own. ......As a first serious attempt at the description of a hitherto unexplored country it strikes me as a remarkable achievement".[19]

Reynolds saw Mary Willcocks, another potential reviewer, twice in the three days following publication. "Bob and myself, being in Exeter Friday, hauled Miss Willcocks down to the city to tea; and yesterday she and a friend walked over from Otterton station and partook of dogs, babies and fried bloaters – with enjoyment apparently."[20] When she came to write her piece in the *Literary World*, she did not let her new friend down. If she went just a little over the top in comparing him to Constance Garnett's Russian immortals, she had nevertheless a significant point to make about the artless flowing structure of the book.

> Three supreme artists there have been who have painted the life of poverty by the intense insight that genius alone can give: Tourgeneff, Tolstoy and Doistoievsky, though they differ in all else, agree in one point – that their "poor folk" are as vividly alive to the joy and pain of life as their richer fellow-travellers along the roadway of existence. ......In this respect, Mr Reynolds's work resembles that of the three Russian artists, for the fisher people of the Devonshire village where he has set his book and his life are intensely alive. Moreover, in the manner of the writing, *A Poor Man's House* resembles Russian rather than English work, for we cannot discern the exact root idea from which the story rose, nor follow the method by which it is woven together. ......Here they are, these folk, we hear their hearts beat, though their coming to us is as strange as birth itself, and their going away stranger still. It is this peculiar quality that gives the book its shapeless yet epic effect...... [21]

Edward Garnett had been squeezed out of a planned review in the *Nation* by Charles Masterman, but he passed his copy on to the sixteen-year-old David, who read it avidly. He told his father: "I have just begun to read Reynold's [*sic*] book and like it very much. Tony is Bob, I suppose".[22]

Edward Thomas was up in London on publication day and started reading the book that evening. He must have had much the same experience as Conrad for it was 1.30 the next morning before he finally put it down and made tracks for bed.[23] He continued reading avidly over the following weekend at Berryfield Cottage and finished it on the Sunday evening.[24] Two weeks later on the morning of 8 November, having lunched with Reynolds at the Mont Blanc that Tuesday, he wrote his review for the December edition of the *Bookman*.[25] It was a typical Thomas review, complimentary and authoritative, but somewhat restrained. He praised the Reynolds power of observation – "It is all genuinely observed and thought out, and its truth, especially as it happens to be expressed in English of equal coarseness and strength, makes for culture in the best sense"; and the archetypal nature of the portrayal of the Woolleys – "people whom you could dump down in any century with a certainty that they would at once begin to be happy, to work, to have a hard time, to breed, and to endure...... "[26]

Reynolds was particularly pleased by the thoughtful piece from John Buchan in the *Westminster Gazette* which was full of quite ravishing compliments. Buchan saw the author as the first middle-class person to succeed in writing about the poor without patronage, and went on: "He has a remarkable literary gift, but none of the false impressionism which too often accompanies it. He does not go out to seek impressions; they come gladly to seek him. Above all, he has a sympathy which is a kind of genius". Buchan had clearly read the book closely and was quick to grasp its salient strengths. He was not short of flattering comparisons: "Of the many scenes which the author gives us, for romance and truth combined it would be hard to beat the story of the great catch of herrings in the last chapter – a passage which Mr. Conrad might have been proud to own".[27]

But Reynolds was most cheered by Buchan's sensitive understanding of the political philosophy behind the book. Almost alone, he put his finger on the main conclusion – that the "courage to live" of the working class was in danger of being destroyed by unthinking social reform.

> The cardinal point to remember is that the life of the poor has its own valuable code, and that if we destroy this we cannot easily replace it by that of another class. ......We have no space to quote at length Mr. Reynolds's acute criticism of so-called democratic policies framed in the interest of the poor; but we would recommend these chapters to our readers as a most apposite tract for the times. ......To those who are weary of the fustian of doctrinaire social reformers, and who believe that the average middle-class mind, judging for itself, cannot estimate either the amount of happiness or of civic value in the lives of the poor, Mr. Reynolds's conclusions will be welcome.[28]

Some months later, Reynolds confessed to Alfred Spender, the editor of the *Westminster*: "It pointed out what I was trying to get at better, I think, than any other notice of the many that appeared".[29]

This was all gratifying stuff for a young author with his first book. Finally, the icing was put upon the cake by another heavyweight intervention from a *future* friend – Arnold Bennett in his Jacob Tonson column in the *New Age*. He saluted Reynolds as "a new authentic talent":

> Already he has strong individuality, a finished style, a notable power of accurate observation, and a quick sympathy which is most pleasingly

> free from sentimentality. His pages on mackerel-fishing, cleanliness, religion, children, night-thoughts, are memorable. In the whole book nothing charmed me more than the extraordinarily fine excursus (pp. 86-87) on the vulgar use of the word "like" at the end of a sentence, – "Tony's getting obsolete, like".[30]

But it was not all unadulterated applause. Some of his friends, like Chapman before them, felt that too much philosophising might have upset the balance of the book. Even Edward Thomas was moved tentatively to suggest "Mr Reynolds's power of putting down what he sees is such that he could almost have done without reflection and argument altogether".[31]

Mary Willcocks took the same view: "Artistically, his book would have been finer without the philosophy, which requires scientific treatment to elucidate it".[32]

But, like some others, she was inclined to question the philosophy itself. Reynolds had reiterated over and over again that the solution to working class poverty was a degree of economic assistance from Government, but not legislative or other interference with lifestyle which would sap the working man's independence and resilience, the vital force in his life – the courage to live. But could this view be taken of all working men? The Woolleys were exceptional members of the class, not industrial workers but small capitalist entrepreneurs – the peasant proprietors of the sea. Mary Willcocks was explicit: "the weakness of his argument is shown here in the fact that he draws his conclusions from a small section of the working-man class, from the fisherman, whereas it is the town artisan who is the typical working-man of to-day".[33] The theme was taken up also by the *Spectator* in an otherwise friendly review: "The result is an extremely interesting and valuable book, though it is open to the objection that in the family selected by Mr Reynolds the quality of self-reliance is developed to an exceptional degree."[34]

In an exchange of letters the following spring, Galsworthy identified the same weakness: "....as a student of faces, and manners I would impress on you the terrible difference between the poor of the towns (the poor such as I am writing of – not perhaps the ordinary workman – and certainly not the artizan) and the poor of the country. Of the latter you write with absolute justice that they are living more than their superiors (!); of the former, I think it is not true; for nothing is more impressive in a miserable way than the gone to seed, don't-care, hang dog looks of the great majority of the underdogs of Town life. You mustn't forget that you are thrown with a special class – a class who by virtue of the peculiar nature of their life and natural surroundings are full-blooded, and vital, and self-respecting, and *hardy*."[35]

In writing to congratulate Reynolds on the power of the book, Harold Wright's father was equally sceptical about the philosophy as an adequate basis for his attack on the collectivist policies of Socialism. "You are, I daresay justly, discouraging to the social reformer. Is it not possible that the life of the seafarer may have elements which redeem it from degradation in a manner not possible to the worker in a crowded town? And yet the legislature can hardly discriminate between them without doing injustice and giving offence."[36]

Reynolds was, of course, wholly aware that there was a spectrum of working class lifestyles, influenced most strongly by geography and working environment, but he had *experienced* the resilience of the Woolleys in the teeth of hardship – it was at base a matter of feeling – and he sensed that this attitude was common to all working people. If people were worse off than the Woolleys, then the force behind their survival must be all the more remarkable. He gave no ground in his response to Charles Wright.

> I wish I *could* discourage "social reformers", or rather, compel them to take fresh bearings and judge social well-being by less materialistic standards. They seem to me to compel exchange of positive virtues for negative virtues by playing on funk. They appear to me like gardeners who prefer an absence of weeds to a profusion of flowers, and prune the trees till the fruit can't grow. But there, they make me so angry, because I'm fond of the people they patronise, that I'd better shut up. Only, it does strike me that to support their horrible circumstances comparatively as well, and certainly on the whole with such cheerfulness, the apparently degraded people of towns must possess a spirit as fine, if not so beautiful, as that of the seafarers. How they do it, I can't think.[37]

Charles Masterman, the junior minister at the Local Government Board, who had made his reputation as writer and social philosopher and had done his own stint of social work among the London poor, in his review of the book in the *Nation* hit precisely the right description of this underlying attitude of Reynolds: "It is the emotional, indeed, against the intellectual: to one point of view, life in an incomplete condition of development; to another, life lived nearer to its central heart."[38] Masterman was sympathetic to the Reynolds critique and cited *A Poor Man's House* extensively in *The Condition of England*, his seminal work on poverty and class, the following year.

Though consummate politician, Masterman had an abstract, at times almost mystical, political philosophy, fully in keeping with his slightly eccentric, unworldly lifestyle. About this time he established his country retreat in a disused railway carriage on Selsey beach, and he was always entirely careless of his clothes. Hueffer, a close friend, has left us with a typical portrait of him a few years later, waiting one summer evening at the foot of the main stairs in the old Home Office building for a telegram to come down from his Private Office. "Masterman stood leering at me in that hall, his queer long nose very much to one side, his top hat extraordinarily ruffled and the invariable rag of satin hanging from the skirt of his governmental frock coat."[39]

He has come to symbolise to some modern commentators, like Samuel Hynes, the failure of the Liberal Government of 1906 (People's Budget notwithstanding) to tackle the problem of working-class poverty which so troubled its conscience. There was over-indulgence in emotional angst to the detriment of clear thinking and firm action: "He shared with other Edwardians the vague, anxious mood of the time – a mood of nostalgia for the past, regret for the present, and apprehension for the future."[40]

Certainly, the collapse of Masterman's promising political career has something of the death-wish about it, but it is a little unfair to tar Reynolds with the same brush as those writers "who regretted the most characteristic features of the present and shared nostalgic feelings for unattainable past simplicities, writers of the kind of social criticism that moves in the wake of the time, deploring faded injustices and admiring archaic virtues." Hynes sees *A Poor Man's House* as "a romanticized version of the working class, close to nature and far from cities, and, whatever its literary virtues, it has little to do with the realities of Edwardian working-class problems".[41]

This is an incomplete understanding of both the author and the book. Despite the didacticism and the philosophising, *A Poor Man's House* was not written as a social tract. It is the record of a psychological experience and should be judged first and foremost as a piece of literature. In so far as it has a social message, it is not bent on drawing up a blue-print of political action for adoption by the Liberal Government – a sort of counter to the Webbs' Minority Report. Rather it is concerned to send a general message to those involved in political action – that materialism is not enough and they abandon the spiritual dimension of life at their peril. It may be a conservative stance, directed towards the preservation of current values; but it is by no means backward-looking. Reynolds was as concerned as anyone to improve the material lot of working people (he knew poverty from the inside) in a programme of economic reform, but he was searching for a formula that would at the same time preserve the best spiritual aspects of working class life – the resilience, the cheerfulness in adversity, the solidarity between neighbours. It is in essence a quite simple view, similar to that expressed in modern times, for example, in contrasting life in the old London slums and life in the tower blocks that replaced them – the critique of a system which gives material security at the expense of social role.

The view of critics like Hynes that he was a romantic conservative, concerned above all to freeze society in its existing postures, is wide of the true mark. In social contexts that he knew well – the small fisheries, for example – he was very clear what economic reform meant. He spent the second half of his public life, scientific pragmatist that he was, putting it into action – motor engines into small fishing boats, promoting fishermen's co-operation, reorganising markets to squeeze out the middleman. This was a forward-looking programme, harnessing modern technology and theories of organisation to improve the routine lot of working people.

Where he was, perhaps, naive was in believing that there was a clear-cut distinction at all between economic and social reform. What appeared to be purely economic action brought with it inevitably social consequences. Just as the abolition of the slums gave rise to the social sterility of the tower block, so did the adoption of motors in fishing boats so improve the productivity of the larger boats that the smaller fishermen were pushed to the wall.

And yet, to be fair to Reynolds, he did not present the conflict between material and spiritual values as susceptible to cut and dried solutions, but rather as a problem to be faced.

> My belief grows stronger that the poor have kept essentially what a schoolboy calls the better end of the stick; not because their circumstances are better – materially their lives are often terrible enough – but because they know better how to make the most of what material circumstances they have. If they could improve their material circumstances and continue making the most of them – that is the problem.[42]

These social and political arguments were more implied than fully developed in *A Poor Man's House* as it appeared in October 1908. They were to be drawn out in more detail in Reynolds' later books, most notably *Seems So!*, and in countless newspaper articles. In that they led to a topical debate about the nature of the 'poor' and the credibility of socialism they kept the book in the public eye and helped to boost sales. Reynolds, of course, made no direct financial gain from the sales of the book, but he kept a close eye on its progress nevertheless. It was slow for the first few weeks, and then raced ahead as discussion of its themes became widespread in the public prints.

But for a much talked about book the sales were not spectacular, and it was almost a year before the first edition was sold out. In September 1909, Reynolds told Lane: "Have had many complaints that booksellers, above all Smith's, say P. M.'s H. isn't procurable. Ought to be remedied.... ?"[43] Lane took the hint and a new English edition (there had been a first American one) was brought out that year. By then sales had fallen off sharply and by the middle of 1910 Lane still had 590 copies of the book on his hands.[44] But like all books of quality, it continued with steady sales over time, sufficient to justify a new cheap edition three years after first publication. Even the cautious editions of the late twentieth century were soon to sell out.

The critical reception and commercial success of *A Poor Man's House* was not the most pressing issue at the front of Reynolds' mind in the autumn of 1908. He had already spent a good portion of the proceeds from that book and its successor, and was beginning to wonder where the next book, and the next meal, was to come from. A week before publication, Bob had hit his traditional end-of-summer blues and Reynolds was feeling as depressed as ever by the sterile weight of book reviewing. He posted off a lament to Garnett.

> There is not much doing here now. The mackerel have gone off the feed. Bob is pretty well physically, but in his autumn mood, though not so badly as last year. I'm afraid I'm not always patient enough: But it's rather difficult sometimes when everything one does produces no satisfaction. And I've been beastly unwell myself with over-much reading of novels for review. I don't seem to make any advance at all in ability to stick at reading. It nauseates me body, brain and soul. God! the pile I've waded through. And they nearly all mean a good deal of trouble taken by somebody or other; a good deal of effort to earn bread and cheese.[45]

He looked to Pinker for the obvious solution. "Please keep your weather-eye open for that long-desired *Causerie*. I want something I can give a day a week to and then banish altogether in favour of other work. This writing short and shortly paid notes on long – Lord, how long! – novels that I've been doing lately knocks me up to a degree that not even getting to sea every day can counteract. An awful pile of novels from the *News* gave me a vile bad bout last week. It's not the writing the reviews; it's the reading the books. It unfits one for tackling any proper work – addles one altogether. Which isn't a complaint; but a snort, and a savage one."[46]

Meanwhile he was struggling to write a short story about a fishery inspection which was to become *Benjie and the Bogey Man* and, as he predicted, would take a long time to sell.[47] In spite of his worries about dearth of inspiration, he had hit upon a vague theme for the next book, harking back to his preoccupation of two years before with the Martha and Mary story. As usual, he tried it out first on Garnett. "I have a fine idea for a novel to be called 'Charm'. The person who has charm, got Lord knows how, who in virtue of it captures the affections of people from others who have slaved and denied themselves to gain and hold them. I think I could exhibit two sorts of charm in operation – that which results from freehanded use of worldly advantages – money, leisure, manners and so on – and that which is inborn and captures in spite of its defects and without extrinsic aid. How does the idea strike you? I think charm results from some kind of extra-moral superiority, not easy to see."[48]

Garnett was sympathetic and encouraged him to worry the subject a little further. What is clear is that he was principally pondering once more the Martha-like qualities in himself: "People seem to me more and more divided up into those who are good by nature and those who achieve some goodness by effort – a division parallel to that I make in the P. M's H. between pluck and courage. Which is better, which represents the further point in evolution, I can't at present make out. Spontaneity attracts me too much: the work of effort I know too well. Perhaps I'll hold the balance the better for it."[49] Like most of his philosophical ideas for books, this one never quite got off the ground, but was drowned beneath a flood of unavoidable short-term work.

To ward off the autumn blues, he and Bob had been saving up to repeat their holiday of the previous year in London and, perhaps, make Paris for a few days to revisit his student haunts. Reynolds went up on 28 October and stayed with Hueffer in Holland Park Avenue.[50] He was suffering a problem with his kidneys and went to see Dr Savill in Harley Street: "Kidneys wrong; not much probably; but as my mother died of 'em at about thirty, I s'pose I'd better look sharp in time."[51] Bob followed him up on 2 November and on the following day they both had lunch once more at the Mont Blanc where Reynolds took the plaudits for his new book from the core of his literary friends – Garnett, Hueffer, Seccombe, Edward Thomas, Frederic Chapman and – a relatively new face – Perceval Gibbon.[52]

That week he had an important piece of Sidmouth business to negotiate. Knowing that Charles Masterman was reviewing his book for the *Nation*, he determined to try and exploit Masterman's position as junior minister to John Burns at the Local Government Board to get some movement out of the Board of Trade on the shingle question. He would use the presence of Bob to press home the point that there were real live people at stake. Masterman agreed to see them both at his room in the House of Commons. He has left us with an all too life-like picture of that fishermen's assault on the corridors of power.

> One evening there were ushered into my room at the House of Commons two strange figures. They were not only fishermen in the accepted term. They were (in appearance) fishermen aggressive: like the fishermen in a play or in "David Copperfield". With their blue jerseys and caps they had invaded London and stalked through the Lobby rather like the Arabian chiefs or native rulers of West Africa who occasionally visit Parliament. Stephen Reynolds had always a strong sense of the dramatic, and one felt that he was thoroughly conscious of the attention of the spectators. He and "Tony" had come on a deputation from their little seaside town. The landlord, or Lord of the Manor, or someone professing authority, was carting away their beach: and the carting away of their beach meant ruin to the fishermen. They had come to London to seek redress from "Government". The thoughts of Mr. "Tony" remained for the most part conjectural. He appeared overawed completely by the "splendor" of the High Court of Parliament. Reynolds put his case well. He appeared to me then, as he appeared ever afterwards, a literary man disguised as a fisherman, and greatly enjoying the adventure.[53]

Masterman was impressed by the case and promised to do everything he could to put matters right. Though something of a dreamer in his political philosophy, he was adept at pulling the strings of Government and achieving political results; he was the one minister in the Liberal Government with the stamina and grasp of detail to pilot single-handed through the Commons the contentious Insurance Act of 1911. He was more than a match for the sluggards of the Harbours Department of the Board of Trade.

Just six weeks later, in the middle of December, Reynolds was presented with the best Christmas present of his life. It was a small piece of paper which read as follows

> SHORES OR BANKS OF THE SEA AT SIDMOUTH
> Removal of Materials Prohibited
> Whereas the Board of Trade, acting in pursuance of the Harbours Act, 1814, as amended by the Harbours Transfer Act, 1862, find it necessary for the protection of the Port of Exeter, to prohibit the taking or removing of any shingle or ballast from the shores or banks of the sea between points situate respectively about 266 yards east and 1870 yards west of the seaward end of Fore-street, Sidmouth, being within the said port.
> Now the Board of Trade do hereby, by this Order, prohibit the taking or removing of any shingle or ballast from the shores or banks of the sea between the points above mentioned
> (Signed) H. LLEWELLYN SMITH
> Secretary to the Board of Trade
> Dated the 17th day of December, 1908.[54]

They had dug up a little-known and little-used provision in an Act almost a hundred years old; but it was Masterman who had provided the impetus to use it. Reynolds was jubilant – not just for the material consequences of the Order, but because all his efforts over the previous eighteen months, in the face of much criticism and scepticism, had at last been vindicated. Scarcely drawing breath, he wrote straight off to Masterman

> What news! Better even than all my good reviews. You must really succeed in getting to Sidmouth to receive in person your great share of the thanks. A sounder sort of thing than merely political gratitude, which hath its base in beer, instead of the solid but eatable-away earth. The devils have been taking more than a hundred tons a week lately, filling up a sandpit and yards and all sorts of things, in their fear of the "Radical Government's wheels!" Well, we will bless and magnify thy name for ever! Which is to say, we are more grateful than we can well express in formal serious language.[55]

Masterman was surprised by the strength of the local fishermen's reaction. But for him too the episode was a vindication of one of his most cherished political beliefs – the power of working-class action, if only the poor could be brought to have faith in themselves. "The gratitude of the fishermen was unbounded: expressed by the offerings of many 'fishy' gifts. Far greater than their gratitude was their astonishment. For them 'Government' always meant something hostile to them. The policemen, the more hated Inspector, the laws that cramped their activities and limited their freedom everywhere, gave them evidence that 'Government' was against the poor man. The idea that 'Mr. Reynolds' and 'Tony' could go up to London, interview 'Government' and that 'Government' would intervene on their side, seemed to them an idea out of fairyland."[56]

At the time of the interview with Masterman that November, it seems that Reynolds and Bob made a fleeting visit to Conrad, who was much taken by the *genuine* Devon fisherman.[57] They then passed a few days strolling round London, a little uncertain whether their money would stretch to the planned trip to Paris. They came across a railway poster advertising cheap weekend tickets to Boulogne, and decided to take the plunge. They set off that Saturday morning. Bob was nearly seasick on the crossing after an unaccustomed evening of cigars and red wine the day before.[58]

They booked in at a good hotel – they were on holiday after all – but Reynolds was perplexed as to how they should describe themselves on the immigration forms they were asked to fill in. He had forgotten the dodge his French master had taught at Bloxham so many years before for distinguishing the sinners from the fishers. "At the moment I could not remember whether *pêcheur* meant a fisherman and *pécheur* a sinner, or the other way round; and besides, I thought, if the Boulonnais look down on fishermen as Devon tradespeople do, we may – as common, low fishermen – be requested to move on. Also there were my wretched spectacles. Not one fisherman in a thousand wears spectacles. But how else describe ourselves? I had had some experience in Paris of the suspiciousness of the French police. There was no knowing what scrapes we might get into. The newspapers at that time were very full of a spy scare, and Boulogne is a garrison town with an arsenal. We could not deny that we were a rather extraordinary pair."[59]

Fortunately, an old piece of paper from three years before came to his rescue. "I remembered that I had upon me my certificate of discharge from the ss. *Coranian*, on which my character for conduct and character for ability were both stamped 'Very good'. So I presented Jim [*Bob*] to the police, and incidentally to the hotel-keepers, simply as *marin* – leaving them to decide whether he was Monsieur le Capitaine or a mere A.B. Myself I put down as *marin* (seafaring man) *et homme de lettres* (wearing spectacles)."[60]

They managed to make it to Paris after all, and Reynolds showed Bob around his student haunts on the left bank which he himself had not seen for more than five years.[61] But it was the three happy days in Boulogne they remembered best, watching the fishery activities in the bustling harbour, and making friends in the fishermen's quarter of the town, most of all in the restaurant of Madame Bonne which was to become their habitual haunt on this and future visits. Bob, as ever, quickly adjusted to the strange environment and was soon chatting up the young women, despite the frustrations of language. He was impressed by the fact that the women worked with their husbands out on the quay. "When I gets back I shall tell the ol' 'oman her'll hae to help me – come down to the boats an' work instead o' biding in house".[62] If he mentioned it to Mam Woolley when they got home the following weekend, history does not record her answer.

While Reynolds was tied up with his French holiday, he missed out on a strange occasion that took place at Someries, Conrad's farmhouse just outside Luton. One evening Ford Hueffer, together with his colleague, Douglas Goldring, and his secretary, Miss Thomas, descended on the homestead armed with reams of tangled papers. Much to the consternation of Jessie, since they devoured a week's groceries in a very short space of time, they had come to work all night. Much later Conrad remembered the event in a nostalgic letter to Ford: "You arrived one evening with your amiable myrmidons and parcels of copy. I shall never forget the cold of that night, the black grates, the guttering candles, the dimmed lamps – and the desperate stillness of that house, where women and children were innocently sleeping, when you sought me out at 2 a.m. in my dismal study to make me concentrate suddenly on a two-page notice of the *Ile des Pingouins*. A marvellously successful instance of the editorial tyranny!"[63] They were putting to bed the first number of the *English Review*.

When Reynolds was staying with Hueffer that February and March, his host talked endlessly of his plans to establish a new literary magazine which would support the best writers and put to shame the rest of the literary world where mediocrity that sold well had a much higher priority than good writing. As he put it at the time, he wanted to create a journal "with the definite design of giving imaginative literature a chance in England".[64] The idea grew originally out of discussions with H.G. Wells when both writers agreed to put up the necessary joint capital and share the editorial duties. Conrad, Edward Garnett and the rest of the Mont Blanc mafia were soon drawn in to the plans.

In a very short time Wells, perhaps already mistrusting the stability of a venture run by the volatility of a Hueffer, drew back from so close an involvement, and Hueffer recruited in his place Arthur Marwood, a close friend who lived near him in Kent. Marwood was the son of an ancient Yorkshire county family with a strong sense of social duty. He had been a brilliant mathematician at Cambridge but, like Harold Wright, had been unable to pursue a career because of constant, unremitting illness. He lived a quiet life as a semi-invalid in the country with his wife who had formerly been his nurse. Apart from being Hueffer's friend, he had two main qualifications for participation in the new venture. He was extraordinarily widely read, with an encyclopaedic memory and a deep and sensitive appreciation of English literature – he helped Conrad, for example, in coaching young authors. And he had money.

Reynolds watched from the sidelines as the plans for the new review built up that summer of 1908. Hueffer recruited his friends to write for the first number and get it off to an explosive start. He hired a young writer, Douglas Goldring, as sub-editor to concentrate on the routine editorial duties, while he sought out subscribers, advertisers and money. Significant sums were involved

– Hueffer claimed later that over the course of the project he had put up £2,800 and Marwood £2,200, small fortunes for Edwardian England.[65] But this was not a money venture. Hueffer's emphasis was on high quality of contribution, not on sales or commercial success – and this was his undoing. He regarded it as essentially an idealistic enterprise based on collectivist principles, proposing to contributors that they should not receive standard payments for their work but share the risks of the editor by taking a proportion of the profits in line with the size of their contributions. He thought that for most writers the true reward would be participation in a venture that shored up the future of English literature, and was surprised, and not a little hurt, when he found they wanted money as well.

He employed that other Mont Blanc stalwart, Reynolds' old friend Thomas Seccombe, to draft the prospectus for the review. Seccombe put up a paragraph that neatly encapsulated the journal's new philosophy, friendly to writers, tough on the reader.

> The Editors of the "English Review" are inviting a number of the best writers of our time to contribute articles on subjects nearest to their hearts and dearest to their imaginations. Such contributors will not be needlessly hampered by considerations of length, conformity to editorial, or other, prejudice, or superficial crispness of presentation. No work will be mutilated; that is a first condition of the new review, the motto of which is to be "without prejudice, and without surgery". Originality of thought – the direct force of expression that comes from conviction – these will be the surest *open sesame* to our pages. ......One word of warning! The "English Review" will hesitate before treating its readers as tired or spoiled children are treated, whose tedium vitae has to be relieved at the shortest possible intervals by ingenious toys, round games, and picture alphabets. Its novelty will take the form of the best treatment, by the best writer, of the burning topic; the notoriety of the obvious, and the "clamor ingens" of placard and hoarding will be, as far as possible, quietly disregarded.[66]

This rather lively draft was melted down into rather less compelling Huefferese.[67]

When he got back from Boulogne that November, Reynolds offered to give Hueffer a helping hand in the last hectic days before the first number came out. He wrote to Herbert Jenkins at Lane's: "I shall probably be running up to Town early next week in order to help Hueffer shove off his new Review. He's given me no end of a puff in his editorial there."[68] On 24 November, the usual Mont Blanc lunch – Garnett, Hudson, Hueffer, Thomas, Chapman, Seccombe and Reynolds – was reverberating to the excitement of the new adventure.[69]

On that visit, Hueffer took Reynolds aside. He was growing tired of the business side of the venture – the balancing of the accounts, the endless search for advertisers – none of which was his forte. He asked Reynolds if he would like to take it on as assistant editor; it could be fitted in fairly easily with his Sidmouth life – just a week a month up in London. And in time, who knows, he might take over the review from Hueffer himself. It was typical of Hueffer that he should recruit a friend rather than a professional business manager; but friends might come cheaper and be more pliable; and he knew of Reynolds' editorial experience in Paris and much admired his intelligence and business sense, however untrained.

Reynolds was wary at first and inclined to refuse. Though they now got on well, he was not a whole-hearted believer in Hueffer and his methods. He was worried about Sidmouth and losing his hard-won position on the beach; but above all he knew he was not cut out for the employee's role, could never knuckle down to the contrived authority of a boss. Hueffer waved all this away and told him to talk it over with Marwood who would explain the job in more detail. The idea of employing Reynolds had been Hueffer's alone, but Marwood was equally confident of his capacity to do the job. He used his best persuasive talents and Reynolds, rather flattered by the offer and the trust of someone of such obvious integrity, capitulated.[70]

Once the decision was taken, all doubt was thrown to the winds. He told Pinker and Thomas proudly of the offer at lunch on 25 November.[71] He wrote to Garnett: "Hueffer has asked me to take on the Assistant Editorship of the Review – not in the place of Goldring, who remains sub-editor, but to look after the business part, advertizing especially, and the initial stages of the literary part. As it means only a week a month up, and gives one a standing, and as, of course, I'm very anxious to see the review succeed, I've taken it on for a while, though not without calling myself a damn fool for not sticking better to my last."[72] He had recently been having some heated exchanges with St John Adcock, sub-editor of the *Bookman*, over a long article on Baudelaire that he had been waiting for months to see published. Adcock had pleaded for some understanding of the editor's lot, and Reynolds now recalled their exchange as something of a sign: "You were weirdly prophetic when you said: 'If you were an editor....' Within a week I was; for I've taken on the assistant-editorship of the *English Review*! But I'm sure I felt all along for you."[73]

Hueffer's admiration for Reynolds at that time did not extend merely to an offer of paid employment. In early September he had offered to serialise the *Mountain* in the new review, following on from Wells' *Tono-Bungay*, but Reynolds, as he told Garnett, had some doubts about whether it would really come to fruition: "He offers to serialize the *Holy Mountain* in his English review if I'll wait to see whether it goes on after its fourth month. So I'm in rather a hole if the P. M.'s H. does well enough to make some certainty nibble at the *Mountain*. I should like it to appear in Hueffer's magazine, but can hardly afford to neglect birds in the hand, even though my (for me) fine income this year gives me a splendid sense of being able to please myself."[74]

By the end of the year, with no further bids to serialise the *Mountain*, he was beginning to look more positively on inclusion in the new review, particularly after the first number had demonstrated what glorious company he would be keeping. It came out in early December with stunning contributions from all the leading writers of the day: a poem from Thomas Hardy, short stories from Henry James, John Galsworthy and Tolstoy (translated for the first time by Constance Garnett), a sketch on Stonehenge by W.H. Hudson, and the first episodes of Joseph Conrad's reminiscences and H.G. Wells' *Tono-Bungay*.

Most flattering to Reynolds, Hueffer had given over the largest part of his first editorial to a loud shout in praise of *A Poor Man's House*.

> But of knowledge of the lives and aspirations of the poor man how little we have. We are barred off from him by the invisible barriers: we have no records of his views in literature. It is astonishing how little literature has to show of the life of the poor.
> ......A serious attempt has now been made to fill in this lacuna and since the principal aim of the ENGLISH REVIEW is by means of the literature which it prints and the literature to which it calls attention to ascertain where we stand and to aid in the comprehension of one kind of mind by another, we feel no hesitation in seriously commending this book to our readers. It is called "A Poor Man's House", and is written by Mr. Stephen Reynolds. Mr Reynolds, we understand, was in his earlier days a science student of some distinction, but circumstances forced him to abandon a career which, if any career could do it, ought to train the young men in the habit of mind to *constater* – to register, that is – not to theorise along Utopian lines. Owing apparently to some freak of his character, or to some social malaise, Mr Reynolds seems to have abandoned suddenly his contacts with what he calls contemptuously "The cultured classes", and to have taken up his quarters in the cottage of a Devonshire fisherman. Here it seems that he has definitely supported himself for several years by acting as mate to the fisherman in question, and by rowing summer visitors for hire. Such a career, if it do not argue a disposition more romantic than that of any other boy who runs away to sea, should at least suffice to prove that Mr Reynolds' nature is no ordinary one.
> His attitude, since he writes for that very cultured world he so despises, is one of unreasonable and jaunty aggression. He flings, as it were, his cap into his reader's face at the very outset; being a scientist he utters his theory with a dogmatism that is a little distressing to ears used to a finer note, but his attitude is no doubt due to youth – though we are uncertain as to the author's age; his dogmatism is due to his scientific training, to his consciousness that he knows his subject.
> ......Mr Reynolds writes of the poor man with a comprehension that is all the more valuable because it is inspired with a great tenderness.[75]

Despite the inevitable Hueffer hyperbole and cavalier approach to the facts, this was the first significant attempt to give a little biography to Reynolds' public. It aroused a trumpet of jealousy from a curious quarter. H.G. Wells was not in a good mood with Hueffer. As publication day of the first number approached, he began to realise that *Tono-Bungay* was probably the best novel he would ever write and that the review was not perhaps the most reliable vehicle for its serialisation. They had a row over the possibility that copies of the review might be remaindered cheaply before book publication could fully exploit its market; but beneath this, Wells was beginning to have serious doubts about the review's viability and whether he would get any money at all.

Hueffer took his usual high-handed attitude, pretending he was doing Wells a favour in serialising his novel. Wells had another grievance. He had been smitten by his friend Arnold Bennett's new novel, *The Old Wives' Tale,* and had been badgering Hueffer to review it in the second number. Hueffer demurred on the grounds he was giving the remaining space to a long letter from Reynolds. When Wells leafed through the first number, he was furious to find how much space had already been given over to the puff on this unknown author and, forgetting Conrad's recommendation of Reynolds a year earlier, he blasted off to Bennett in France: "I have you very much on my conscience...... I've talked about *The Old Wives' Tale* to all sorts of people but I've not written a line anywhere. I'd have liked to. Everyone is reading it and everyone praises it except that old fool Colvin who detects French models and says it's dreadfully heartless (not like dear R.L.S.). That fool Hueffer too isn't doing a shout about it in the *English Review.* I did all I could (short of writing it myself) to get the book done for number 2, but he's got a discovery of his own, a man named Reynolds of about Edwin Pugh's calibre and apparently he's giving up the famed *Review* to him".[76]

The sneering comparison with Pugh, the worthy if uninspired novelist of the London poor, was a little disingenuous. When Wells was a neighbour of Pugh's in Worcester Park ten years before he had pressed the merits of Pugh's books on all his friends, including Bennett.[77] Bennett commiserated with Wells' efforts on his own behalf but nevertheless made clear where he stood on Reynolds: "I think enough has been said about Reynolds for some time to come. But I put him very much higher than Edwin Pugh, and I have a great admiration for him. I don't know yet about Hueffer, but I'm sure the *English Review* won't last unless he alters it considerably."[78]

The business success of the review was now, to some extent, in Reynolds' own hands. He spent the first week of December at 84 Holland Park Avenue working on the second number, taking a break on the Tuesday for lunch at the Mont Blanc with Garnett, Hudson, Seccombe, Thomas and Gibbon.[79] His main task was to obtain advertising for the second number before it went to press on 17 December and secure for future editions a regular flow. Hueffer had picked up advertisements for the first number piecemeal and Reynolds saw that it would be hopelessly inefficient with such a small staff to continue the operation in-house. He therefore obtained Hueffer's consent to approach Pinker to act for them in securing a firm of advertising agents to whom they could farm out the task.

It was a strange reversal of roles with Reynolds now in a bureaucratic position of authority putting business Pinker's way. The current advertising rates offered by the review were 12 guineas a page, rising to 16 guineas for a page opposite reading matter.[80] On that basis Pinker thought he could find an advertising agent to secure a regular monthly £100 of advertising, though not in time for the December deadline. Fortunately, late on the Friday night, Reynolds got wind of an individual advertising man who was keen to do business, and interviewed him the next day. He was commissioned to seek a minimum of £60 worth of advertising for the January issue.[81]

Reynolds was planning to spend £150 to advertise the January number, and £100 on subsequent issues, 80 per cent of which he was prepared to farm out to the agent selected. In early December the outlook was buoyant. He had a list of 78 distinguished subscribers, including such influential names as the Marquis of Bath, Count Metternich, Lady Elcho and Lady Desborough. He estimated the circulation on the first number as 3000 up to 3 December.[82] Either these were over-optimistic estimates or they were Hueffer's figures. When calculations were made much later, the first two numbers added together were found to have reached a circulation of only 2000, and the total advertising revenue for the first four brought in only £140, well below the target figure.[83]

When Reynolds first discussed the advertising commission with Pinker, the latter inevitably raised the question of Hueffer's personal financial viability. Much to Pinker's surprise, he received in the post a bank-book that turned out to be Hueffer's. Reynolds was quick to head off the natural assumption: "Hueffer tells me that he has sent his bank-book to you to show you 'that your mistrust of him is unfounded'. Your natural deduction will probably be that I've been repeating your conversation with me. That's not so. He's got wind that somebody with a considerable knowledge of his affairs has been round putting them in the worst light." But Reynolds had also heard similar gossip about Pinker and sprang to offer his help: "Also – if I may mention it – I hear rumours that you have a great deal of money tied up and are shortish of untied-up cash. I trust it isn't so – I don't want to know – I much prefer to conclude that rumour is wrong; – but, Pinker, please understand that if at any time the small sum I owe you would be any convenience to you, I will furbush round and stump up, and will *not* publish the reason of my getting my own outstanding cash together."[84]

In addition to the business end, he was also involved in the initial consideration of contributions for the review, putting him in the even more unaccustomed position of deciding the fate of some of Pinker's clients. One was Gilbert Cannan, whose *Birth* had been submitted for publication. Reynolds was enthusiastic. "I like it. It's got grip and vision and, generally, the qualities that can't be learnt. ....I'm going to send it on to Hueffer with the suggestion that I should ask the author to revise it, if he can and will, and that then we might print it." In the event, it wasn't taken, but Hueffer agreed to look at further work.[85]

Forced to stay up in London on the Saturday to interview the advertising recruit, Reynolds' weekend plans had gone awry. He had been tentatively hoping to go down to stay with Conrad, who on the Monday wrote rather ruefully to Hueffer: "I rather expected Reynolds to turn up here. Is he still with you? Greet him from us both and *both* boys, because Jackson [*John Conrad*] mentions him constantly".[86]

But Reynolds was too exhausted to make it to Someries. At the end of his first working week, he breathed a deep sigh of relief and headed down that Saturday evening for a couple of days in the safety of Devizes. The tensions of the new job, the pressure of the December deadline, the office atmosphere – it was all too much for his nerves. He collapsed on the Saturday night and spent most of Sunday in bed.[87] It was a bad omen.

Home once more in Sidmouth, there were still some loose ends to tie up and the added irritation of calming local susceptibilities about his book, which was still giving trouble. He wrote to Lane: "Have been run off my head with work and explaining away one or two details that gave offence in 'A Poor Man's House'."[88] He spent the run-up to Christmas working on the final revision of the *Mountain*, due for spring serialisation in the review and book publication in the autumn. He told Pinker: "Am getting on with the *Mountain* pretty fast, and, I think, improving it. In fact, had I read it again before settling for its rewriting, I should probably have rewritten it at any price!"[89]

Like the previous year, it was a more cheerful Advent than usual. In addition to the jubilant news of the shingle Order, came a touching Christmas invitation from Conrad, a little too late for him to act on it. "It is only the fear of being indiscreet that prevented us asking you for Xmas. But only the other day we were saying how nice it would have been to have you with us. To which Borys made the remark "No such luck I suppose". Well we don't ask in so many words now, since you are at present with older and, surely, more valuable friends. We only say that the door stands open wide enough to let in the Holy Mountain too. Comprenez-vous? And it would be appropriate for you to arrive here all in readiness for the day when your Asst-Editorial duties begin. Drop us a line to fix the day of arrival either before, during or directly after the holidays." He had not forgotten the meeting with Bob the previous month and added a postscript "Remember me in real friendly terms to Bob".[90] Reynolds agreed to go down to Someries from London the first weekend of the new year. He spent Christmas with the Woolleys and travelled up in the snow on 29 December to start his second week on the review.[91]

The few weeks following the November spate of notices of *A Poor Man's House* marked another major turning-point in Stephen Reynolds' life. Before, he was an unknown author struggling unsuccessfully to get his work into print; after, he was a national public figure. It was not merely the quality of the book that made this sudden public reputation, though that was influential enough. It was also the power of the image. He was chattered about in London that winter as the only middle-class writer who knew the poor from the inside. There had, of course, been journalists and social scientists who had spent weeks or months alongside the poor; there had been working class writers who had been born into poverty; but never a writer who had thrown his entire lot, physically, emotionally, and in perpetuity, in with the working class. Overnight he became, in the words of one modern commentary, "a cult figure".[92] Certainly, had this sudden shoot to fame occurred a century later, he would soon have been on every arts programme and chat show you might name.

He got his first shock of new celebrity at the end of November when he went up to Cambridge to spend the weekend with Harold Wright. "Came along here for the weekend yesterday to attend a dinner got up by Harold Wright. Rather interesting. They're making such a fuss over the P. M's H., and it really seems to be sinking in a good deal. Last week one of the societies had a paper read on it, and last night there was a debate on 'The Spiritual Squalor of the Middle Classes'. The motion to deplore it got rather heavily beaten, but they say it was an exceptionally fine debate."[93]

For someone as solitary and touchy as Reynolds, this sudden change of situation was to cause more than ordinary problems. In the main, they were problems of ambivalence. Despite his claimed hatred of the limelight, he had more than his share of vanity, particularly of the physical kind. Though shy of the camera, he was always delighted by good photographs of himself. His insistence on walking about London in only one garb – blue serge trousers, fisherman's guernsey and boots – further fuelled the fascination of the public image. We catch a trace of it in John Squire's account after his death.

> He was a short, sturdy man who looked stronger than he was: fair, spectacled, bronzed, moustached. He used to come to London in a peaked cap, reefer coat, a jersey and waterside boots, and his concentration on fishermen's interests was so great that if one had lunch with him, it had to be in an all-fish restaurant.[94]

It was all carefully co-ordinated. He had a Sunday best version of the same clothes; when others dressed for dinner, he slipped into his best fisherman's gear. On one celebrated occasion he turned up at the House of Commons in oilskins and a sou'wester.[95] Like the insistence on taking his friends to fish restaurants, he claimed that his dress was to promote the fisherman's cause. But there was a more personal motive as well. He relished the confused reaction to his appearance and his status, the sense of appearing to be something he was not.

But this was not the whole story. Another part of him was genuinely shy, hated the superficiality of middle-class attention, hated both London and its social round. And he was genuinely in love with the so different world of the Woolleys. A few days of cocktail parties in London found him longing for the very different noise and bustle of Bedford Square. And while he was living with Hueffer, there were parties in abundance – both thrown by Hueffer at Holland Park Avenue and thrown by others where he tagged along in Hueffer's wake, ever conscious of the winks and nudges behind his back. Ten years later, when he had given up all literary ambition, he recalled dismissively the feelings of those days of constant public recognition.

> Position is only useful for dealing with fools; it is personality counts with wise men, and what one stands for, especially in the long run. My literary ambitions have gone fut, though I still hope to finish my psycho-economics, because it wants saying. I had my whack of *succès d'estime*. I shall be well content if, when I crock, croak, or otherwise dispose of myself, I have left my print on the fisheries. It is more to me to be welcomed in a fishing port, than to hear behind my back in London: "That's Stephen Reynolds!" as I used to do. A warmer air to the soul, so to speak.[96]

His own ambivalence was mirrored in that of those whom he now met for the first time. They did not know how to approach him. Was he a middle-class intellectual to be lionised, with rather eccentric tastes and habits to be quietly ignored; or an intelligent working man, to be coaxed and patronised? He did not give them any help. Sometimes the results gave even him amusement.

> I shall not forget the look of a lady at a literary luncheon, who asked me if I did not find the habit of 'week-ending' greatly interfere with Society, and to whom I replied that I hardly knew, because in working for a fisherman it was my duty most of the summer to take people out in boats for two shillings an hour, and sometimes tips. Working for a fisherman? Yes; most interesting and healthy. Work with the hands is no longer shameful. But tips! Tips! (Let me add, however, that the lady made a good recovery from the shock.)[97]

As he spent more time in London, the contrast between this superficial world and the reality of his friends' struggle for existence back in Sidmouth began to depress him. Even the Mont Blanc lunches came to lose their lustre and his literary friends their earlier fascination. For their part, his London friends could not understand his total preoccupation with Sidmouth and the longshore fisheries. If it were obsession, it was a particularly narrow and unhealthy one. They saw its effect upon the range of his conversation, and feared it would affect the range of his writing also. These tensions were soon to become startlingly overt in his relationship with Edward Garnett.

Like anyone who achieves instant fame at a young age – he was still only 27 – he had to face his share of backbiting and jealousy. But even for his middle-class friends and others who were well disposed to him, there was one major question: was this fishing thing merely acting up to gain attention? Was it, in short, all a pose? Mary Willcocks clearly came to think so and wrote him up as such a poseur in her novel about him ten years later. But this was after the two had rather fallen out and allowances must be made for that.

Others outside his most intimate circle were rather overawed by him and fell prey to the same attitudes. Commander Harry Pursey, the popular writer and broadcaster on naval subjects, and later Labour MP, was born in Sidmouth and, as a young able seaman, fell under Reynolds' spell there. After Reynolds' death, he started his own writing career by attempting to imitate, very unsuccessfully, his mentor's fishing stories and sketches.[98] As an old man in the late 1970s, he was toying with the idea of a monograph on Reynolds and the potted biography he noted down at that time speaks volumes for how he had come to regard his former friend.

> Précis. S.R. was a mystery/enigma during last two decades of his career.
> Age 18-38. He never really settled down or knew what he was going to do next.
> Took wrong course at university – father's idea – B.Sc instead of B.A.
> Went to Paris, spent what little money he had, starved in a garret and returned to England a neurasthenic.
> Some success in literature (describe) but insufficient income.
> Conceived idea fisherman and author. Impossible for him.
> Failed realise essential regular weekly article and income. Not have shortage money and worry.
> Having refused, in youth, to take salary job: at 32?, had to admit defeat and take C.S. post as Inspector of Fisheries......
> P.S. Was a poser. Fisherman's jersey in London. Great Dane. Food, money more useful in his pocket. Pig-headed. Ideas often wrong. Date? Dealt with his doctor at Richmond. By letter! Always short of money.[99]

As the final submission for the prosecution, this tells us much more than all the comfortable obituaries put together. Despite the superficiality of some of the judgements, it provides with great clarity *one* view of the man from a point on the outer circle of his acquaintance. A few, and just a few, on the inner circle came to share the same doubts. Edward Garnett may well have been one.

Reynolds himself never claimed to be a genuine fisherman or fully paid-up member of the working class. As we have seen, his struggles to win acceptance on the beach had taught him that that was impossible. In the preface to *A Poor Man's House* he had strongly rebutted any presumption that he was fully integrated into the life of his working class friends: "For myself, I can only claim – I only want to claim – that I have lived among poor people without preconceived notions or *parti pris...... So far as is possible to a man of middle-class breeding,* I have lived their life, have shared their interests, and have found among them some of my closest and wisest friends." [*my italics*].[100] It was not his overt claims, but what others read into his attitudes that gave rise to the charges of posturing.

We know from the complex nature of the man that he was capable of pose and of utter sincerity, both at the same time. What anyone meeting him took from this told a lot more about the observer than the observed. Charles Masterman has given us the most balanced, and therefore most persuasive, summing up:

> I have said that Stephen Reynolds always appeared as a "literary gent" masquerading as a long-shore fisherman. He dressed the part. He went down with the others to the sea in ships, sharing the dangers and enjoyments. He divided the spoil with the others. He lived in a fisherman's home and made great friends with many of them: although I have heard that the publication of their sayings and the description of their lives in his books caused in the past at least a partial estrangement. In the summer seasons he would lie in wait for "frights" with the others, but I doubt if any of the summer visitors he beguiled into an hour's cruise ever mistook him for the real article for more than five minutes. This partially self-conscious literary instinct appears in all his books. They are written about the life of the fisherman. They are written by one who knows the fisherman's condition. They attempt, and in many cases with success, to get within the mind of the fisherman, and to interpret his mind to the world. But no one could ever mistake them for the work of a fisherman......
>
> I am afraid Reynolds would have been annoyed if he had been told that the literary man and the "gentleman" still persisted, after he had adopted the calling of the fisherman. With most of us who have tried the experiment, he was indignant if it were regarded as an experiment. With most of us also, he was more indignant if accused of trying to "do good" to the poor amongst whom he lived. He always believed that those poor could rather do good to the comfortable classes: and in the "Poor Man's House" loudly and defiantly challenged comparison. But none of us, I think, identified ourselves so completely as Reynolds with the life of those amongst whom he lived. He had suffered a serious break-down in health. I think also he had gone through a phase of mental disturbance; perhaps a religious crisis, perhaps perplexity at the extraordinary and unintelligible complexities of modern life.
>
> He went down to live with his fishermen in order to fling himself out of these complexities. He did not go down to write about them. He did not go down expecting after a time to return. He was always trying to convince us that he had chosen this course for his whole life; that henceforth he was one of the "working classes". He was never going to return to other "classes" again. There may have been something of "pose" in

> this, although I think the pose was unconscious. It was the same pose which was symbolically expressed in his clinging to the fisherman's jersey when invited to dinners or London parties. The jersey proclaimed – to his immense satisfaction – "You may admire my books: you may be interested in my social ideas; but here am I – a fisherman – and like the fishermen – half-tolerant, half-indignant, wholly contemptuous of the softness and luxury of you all".[101]

For the average Edwardian reader, in gloomy London office or anti-maccassared surburban sitting room, as they pored over *A Poor Man's House* that winter of 1908–9, the question of authorial pose never entered in. The sincerity of thought and feeling in this new absorbing book spoke entirely for itself.

For Reynolds, the only saving grace of all this fuss and publicity was the chance to get his own views across to that average reader. His private personality soon became public property, even down to the notorious Reynolds temper. A journalist from Lane's new in-house magazine, the *Bodleian*, went down to Sidmouth to interview him in February 1909 – and with a certain trepidation.

> "If you are going down to interview Stephen Reynolds", said a friend of his in London, "you had better be careful. He has got a dog big enough to eat you and a score of fishermen to back him in a row, and he's not very tractable himself. You'll see." It was not, therefore, without some misgivings that I made inquiries in the little town as to where Stephen Reynolds lived. A fisherman told me: "Why, to Tony Widger's in Under Town, behind the Alexandra Hotel, sure 'nuff!" he said. "But very likely you'll find him on the beach, sir, along there where they'm mending nets."
>
> At the spot to which I was directed, two jersey-clad men were at work on a large net, standing one at either end and talking across to each other in a dialect so broad that I could catch little of it except the swear-words. I decided, before seeking further the object of my visit, to go for a row, to try and identify some of the places mentioned in "A Poor Man's House", and possibly to glean some information from the boatman. I approached the nearer man.
>
> He was unable to take me. "Sorry, sir, I'm going to sea herring drifting in an hour or so. Maybe my mate'll take 'ee, sir. Yer, Steve," he called, turning to the other man, "Will 'ee take the gen'leman for a row?"
>
> "All right," replied the one called Steve with no trace of dialect in his voice. I noticed then that he wore spectacles, and that in spite of his jersey and stained blue trousers and stout build there was something about the face that suggested the brain-worker as well as the fisherman pure and simple. "I must take Dane in house," he added.

> At the sound of its name a huge grey dog bounced, as it were, out of the grey shingle, reared up on its hind legs and licked my face. I started back. "He won't hurt you unless he knocks you down accidentally," said Stephen Reynolds coolly.

Once pushed off from the land, the journalist takes his life into his hands.

> "You are Mr. Stephen Reynolds, aren't you?"
> "Yes."
> "Well, will you show me some of the rocks and cliffs that are mentioned in 'A Poor Man's House', where you went prawning with Uncle Jake and so on?"
> "No, I shan't! What's the good of re-naming them all if I'm to give them away to the first fright that comes along?"

With this difficult start out of the way, the interview proceeded smoothly, Reynolds taking the journalist home to the little back kitchen for a cup of tea.

> It seemed to me, when I was placed in the old courting chair in Tony Widger's kitchen, as if a vivid dream had come true. By the way the children talked to Stephen Reynolds in the intervals of demanding "jam zide plaate"; by the way the baby – a new arrival since the book was written – insisted on his nursing her, I could see that it was indeed his home; and I understood, I think, how it is that his book gives one such an extraordinary impression of reality, of something that is being really lived. He has found what is to him the best thing in the world, and he has written it down with all the skill he was able, because, as he says, it was such a revelation that he couldn't keep quiet about it.

For Reynolds the most important question came late in the interview.

> "And now your book has had so much success, " I asked, "I suppose you will give up fishing and boating as a regular thing and be in London more?"
> "What on earth for? D'you think what I said in my book was all lies? This is my home, and, having found it after some trouble, I'm going to stick to it. London's all right for a change, but I can't write there and I can't fish there, and I'm at least as anxious to be a good fisherman as a good writer. Besides, I've become a sort of unofficial representative of the fishermen in their controversies, and I've set my mind on seeing the fishing flourish again some day."[102]

He wrote to Lane to thank him for this opportunity. "I'm also very grateful for having had the chance in the *Bodleian* of contradicting the evil ones who spread a report that having got a book out of Sidmouth I was going to chuck fishing."[103] It was not just an *image* he was struggling to protect.

Despite the odd snapping, at the time of this interview he was feeling considerably more relaxed than he had been for some weeks. For he had broken with Hueffer and the *Review*. He worked through his second full week, from 30 December to 6 January, in a dark, snowy and shivering London. On the surface, all seemed well. He worked with the usual Reynolds frenetic application, and maintained his joshing, argumentative relationship with the editor. Goldring recalls their continued good-natured bantering at this time: "Stephen Reynolds.... was a likeable, ungainly, single-hearted man. ....Ford had a great admiration for him and the two used to squabble, affectionately, by the hour together. I once managed to save the situation, when Reynolds was reduced to speechless rage and could not think up a retort, by saying, 'Well, it won't be an impromptu *now*, Reynolds.' The roars of laughter which followed showed how fond the two were of one another".[104]

But with Reynolds this fondness went little more than skin deep. A fastidious organiser, he was appalled by the chaotic working methods that concealed Hueffer's editorial genius, best illustrated by the weekly ritual when Hueffer took Goldring plus manuscripts down to the Shepherd's Bush Empire where during the duller turns he decided who was in and who was out.[105] Reynolds was anxious about the financial future of the *Review*, which it was his job to sustain, and strongly resented Hueffer's failure to get to grips with the business side or keep him properly informed. Most of all, he loathed London, even for one week a month, and longed for Sidmouth where his hard-won place on the beach might be at risk if he stayed away too long.

When he made his escape to Someries for the weekend of 2/3 January, he was exhausted once more with the office pressures, which heightened his growing depression about the continuing failure of his ephemeral work despite the success of *A Poor Man's House*.[106] He longed to give up the job, even after such a short period of trial, and sought Conrad's support.

Conrad was sympathetic, but firm. Of course he should give up this useless job and all the journalism too. He should be concentrating all his energy on the next *Poor Man's House* – and the next, and the next.... Having put the still gloomy Reynolds back on the train for London, Conrad wondered whether he had perhaps been a little too hard. He wrote to Pinker: "I've been preaching a little to R. The man has a distinct value and I feel that he ought to concentrate his young powers upon production, production and again production. That was my text – and I suppose you understand what I had in mind. His artistic energy ought to be kept concentrated upon the only work which will in the years to come give him satisfaction without alloy. Let him write and not scatter himself upon all sorts of enterprises – distinctly inferior to what his literary gift can do. As I know from him that he has a great liking and regard for you a hint in that direction from you may do good. It would be a pity if he were to turn into a mere workman of letters".[107]

Reynolds went back to Holland Park Avenue with these words ringing in his ears. He knew deep down that an office job in a subordinate capacity was hopeless for his nerves. He worked furiously and fretted about outcomes over which he found he had ultimately no control. As in December, by the end of the week's work he was close to a state of both mental and physical collapse. He went to Hueffer and told him he could no more. Hueffer, not the best of man managers, passed him on to the more sympathetic Marwood, but even *his* attempts at persuasion came to naught.

On 5 January, Reynolds took Harold Wright to lunch at the Mont Blanc with Hudson and Seccombe, and then back to Holland Park Avenue where Wright kept visitors at bay while he and Hueffer got on with the work. He was suffering from an appalling stomach ache which he feared might be appendicitis.[108] The following day, he took the train down to Sidmouth determined that the job was at an end.

After two days complete rest, and a night out "lame-duck hunting" with Uncle Sam, he felt strong enough to write a semi-apologetic letter to Hueffer. "Marwood and I had a long discussion over the assistant editorship, and at the risk of seeming damnably ungrateful, I adhered to my decision. My mistake was in allowing the flattery (to me) of the offer to obscure from me the fact that I cannot do it all. I've knocked up both times, and that is no good either to me or to you. If I can help you irregularly, let me try; you know I'll be willing; but a definite salaried position I'm not fit morally or physically to have. At your orders I should end by hating you, however much against my will. The work I was doing can be done by plenty of men, and unlike you I cannot chop from one kind of work to another in a day, nor yet in three." But the sea and the fishing was his most potent excuse: "They had a big catch while I was away. I ought to have been there".[109]

With Pinker he was a little more open. "Got back; heartily glad; and gladder every day that I've given up that assistant-editorship. I can't think what caused me not to see the situation when I was offered the job, unless it was the flattery (to me) of being offered it. I'm always on the scrape for influence for my fishery jobs, but no amount of that is any good if it means getting out of touch with the fishing. The reversion of the editorship, provided the *E.R.* lives, isn't bad, but being a decent fisher of fish, instead of contributors and advertizers, is ten times better to my mind." But now, with time for contemplation, his natural paranoia had come to the fore and he began to see the whole episode as a gigantic plot. "I fancy that the *E.R.* job was at the bottom an attempt, kindly meant, like most evil attempts, to entice me out of this place now I am supposed to have got what I can out of it. At any rate, several things I have heard point that way, and Bob and I have had a good chuckle over the failure of it."[110] It was little wonder that he was so keen to impress upon journalists that there was no chance he would be lured away.

He was up in London on 20 January to fulfil his final "official" week at the *Review*'s offices.[111] Hueffer was upset at having been abandoned at a moment's notice for what he regarded as wholly trivial and imaginary concerns. He assumed a detached and rather lofty view of the whole affair. Years later he dismissed it with a typically distorted wave of the hand: "I had engaged him as sub-editor before the review started, but he did not last long. He knew nothing about sub-editing, was of too independent a nature and became afraid of London".[112]

Marwood, on the other hand, with his own physical problems and greater personal sensitivity, had been wholly understanding and supportive throughout. Reynolds wrote him a friendly letter to thank him and assure him of his confidence in his successor to the job, a man called Sissons. Marwood was grateful and fully sized up the problem of Hueffer. "I am glad you think well of Sissons. No doubt he will do our job. I wish it had been you but you know your business best, and I should have seen that sooner when you told me at the first why you were unwilling to take on the job. It is all my fault for persuading you against your will. I fear Sissons' solid greed will be less amusing than your sporting spirit. And as I am convinced that the lark is all we shall ever get out of the *E.R.* the difference is serious. To the editor I still am optimistic, indeed that is my function. Or part of it, the other part being to keep him in sight of reality. And he is so splendidly unreal that these duties are in conflict."[113]

The generosity of this letter and the implied sympathy of the criticism of Hueffer touched something in Reynolds and he let all his guilt and the pent-up feelings of the past few weeks come tumbling out.

> Your patient letter has been the pleasantest part of an episode very unpleasant all round. Hueffer is, I'm afraid, almost more than raw with me; and I can't say that the feeling of having been to a certain extent managed leaves me without a trace of bitterness. You say 'twas your fault. That, it was not. The implied flattery of the offer prevented me from seeing at once the situation was not possible. Neither was it good for the review. There is, I know, an opinion in London that London is my proper place. But all my heart is here, and I am primitive enough for that to be my main consideration. As it is, I have missed two large catches of herrings, one each visit to London, when, to preserve my rather hardly-won place as a fisherman here, I ought to have been at sea. And I have not H's facility for doing more than one sort of work at a time, or for working in London.
>
> ....There's that beastly health of mine and at the bottom there is the difficulty of my character; that, whether I wish it or not, I develop an enmity of a non volitional sort against anybody at whose disposal I am for pay.
>
> Superficially I feel I have been a bit of a pig; but still there is this: that all the great deal Hueffer has done for me did not involve an essential alteration of *his* life and aims, whereas becoming a semi-Londoner and losing

> my position in Sidmouth did involve a profound alteration in *my* life. As I say I ought to have seen that at once. After many years troubled by events and illness and loneliness and my own capacity for being miserable, I have found here something, as I said in my book, that is more to me than myself, the *best* I shall probably meet with in life. I can't give it up. It is indeed at the base of the forcefulness which appears to have struck you.

And with his parting shot, and despite the alleged lack of editorial experience, the ex sub-editor took heart from Marwood's doubts about the future of the review to offer a recipe of his own.

> It was a feature of my asst-editorship that, except by you, I was never told how the thing really stood. Hueffer says it is paying its way and that's all I know. At all events I have been hastening on with the *Holy Mountain* and have sent in 30,000 of it in the assurance that it will see daylight. If I were in a position to give advice to Hueffer as regards the Review's policy, I should say "Sacrifice a few niceties of taste for the sake of being able to publish your literary choice at all." Not to make the literature go down by means of diplomatic scoops seems to me a mazed way of going on. The thing is, I take it, to keep the Review alive, whether by drugs or food doesn't much matter till it is thoroughly alive.[114]

After Reynolds' New Year weekend at Conrad's lamenting the Hueffer connection, the older author was waiting for news of the fallout of events at the *Review*. At the end of January, still suffering from his own bout of neurasthenia, he wrote to tell Reynolds of his move from Someries back to Kent and to ask how he had fared in London: "I've had an awful time but at any rate we are going away from here...... My nerves are gone to pieces; otherwise everything here is as usual. How did you get on? In the midst of my sordid (and befogged) worries I spared a thought now and then for the burly form of *one* who pervades the west country nursing the dreams of great deeds and cruel books for the discomfiture of the horrid bourgeois".[115]

Reynolds' nerves too had been shot to pieces over his resignation from the *Review*, and by the end of January he had collapsed under a serious bout of influenza, which first affected his eyes so he could hardly see, and then his taste buds.[116] After ten days of it, he wrote to Pinker: "I'm in the very deep depths. The day after I came home, expecting to sail ahead after the London botherations, I had to go to bed with influenza, and it has knocked me all to bits, physically and mentally; the worst of it being that it has perverted my sense of taste so that everything tastes damnable, even tobacco, and I can't feed back to strength on the infernal muck food is, or appears to be. All my carefully built fabric of health shattered, seems so. And Bob is ill too; half his time to sea out of cussedness, and the other half rolling about in agony in bed; and

I can't take his place on the drifter and give him a rest in. Hanged if I know which of us is wusser; the house is a hospital."[117]

The depression generated by the flu centred, as usual, upon his work. Despite the euphoric reviews of his book, he found to his surprise that public reputation had in no way affected the selling power of his ephemeral work. Stories and sketches, even those on fishing subjects, were still being rejected as though nothing had happened at all. He bemoaned his situation to Garnett: "Work – damn work! I haven't sold a single short story as the result of that blessed book coming out, and I've no inclination to go on writing for the honour of being rejected by editors who are three times more pig-headed than the public they chatter about. 'The Holy Mountain' isn't getting on, naturally, though I suppose I shall start rewriting when I feel up to it."[118]

The rejection that hurt most had come from McClure, the American publisher to whom Conrad had been promoting Reynolds the previous year.[119] He told Pinker: "McClure has sent back 'Silly Saltie' and 'Benjie and the Bogey Man' with some more facile praise of the P. M's H. Here they are. Please foist 'em on some fool of an editor. All my other contributing arrangements have fallen to bits, and I can't write anything, and don't want to except for the means of existing."

This continuous comparison of his rejected ephemeral work with his hugely successful book bit deeply into him. How could he ever write anything better? "I'm awful tired, and the influenza came on the top of a growing uneasiness that I had written the best I had it in me to do; and now I can see nothing in front but tearing a livelihood out of an unwilling brain for a period of years with increasing difficulty".[120]

He sent off the bad McClure news to Conrad who had been his close adviser in the writing of "Silly Saltie". He told the same tale. His book had been praised to the skies, but still no one would take his stuff. Perhaps the meteoric rise was only to show he was a one-book man after all. He had written the best that was in him; there was little point in going on. Conrad was predictably scathing about McClure. "Sorry for the McClure episode. Beastly – wasn't it? And so useless – eh? I assure you and I believe I've told you before that no man has been the better for any connection with McClure. I mean no man of *any value* or any man with a soul slightly bigger than a chicken's."[121]

But he recognised at once the post-depression symptoms of early and unexpected public success, something he had never had the opportunity to suffer himself. His young friend was in need of sympathy and support, and he gave both unstintingly.

> You are too young to give way to the hopeless mood, known, I should say, to all writers at one time or another. I regret that you should know it already. It is not a good symptom to have at 26 or even 28 (I don't know your age exactly) with, say, 4 volumes written and one published. I imagine, I fancy I've observed, that you think a little too much of what

> you've done. The merits of our achievement (I am speaking of *artists*) should not be dwelt upon mentally too much. Contemplated with persistence they cease to be inspiring. The best would be if they could be forgotten completely for long stretches of time and only now and then recalled. For to reject utterly the help of proper pride would be foolish. Remember that a man is never 'done' till he drops; and an artist should be a man and a half. All the others may be anything in the way of a fraction up to 9 tenths and be still quite adequate for their work. For the rest you may take it from me that you are not meteoric – neither so brilliant nor so shortlived. Much could be written on the subject of a writer's hopeless mood but it's a beastly morbid subject. And don't think I am callous. I quite understand that your suffering is tremendously real and your difficulty in arranging your life quite serious enough.[122]

What little energy remained to him in those few weeks of depression had gone into close supervision of a publicity pamphlet for *A Poor Man's House*, containing the four best reviews, which Lane brought out at the end of February. No detail of content or design was too small for him, least of all the photograph of himself which particularly touched his vanity: "Can they make my spectacles look a little less as if they were Chinese instruments with tortoiseshell rims?"[123] He had also fallen into the arms of two new editors, Alfred Spender of the *Westminster Gazette* and St Loe Strachey of the *Spectator*, who over the next three years were to provide him with a regular home for his articles and sketches and were, as yet unbeknown to him, to supply the vehicle for his next two books.

As for his next *planned* book – the Wiltshire Guide commissioned by Nelsons – he was already starting to have cold feet, mainly because it would take him away from Sidmouth and his place on the beach. He told Pinker: "The *Guide* can't be started till the *Mountain* is re-written, and to be frank, I'm rather misliking the doing of it, because I'm afraid that while I am away some beachcomber will slip into my place on the beach and in the boats, that I've been so long getting and have at last pretty well established. I'd rather anything short of starvation than lose that. It's the mooring buoy for this cranky craft."

Despite Conrad's cool advice about not dwelling on the successes of the past, he continued to belabour his long-suffering agent with his despair for the long-term future of his writing. "The combination of circumstances which made me write that book don't happen to a man twice; don't want 'em to; and I don't think I can ever better it; and having had a success beyond my expectations, and found out what 'twas like, I haven't any desire for any more of it, and that incentive to write is clean gone. Apart from wanting the cash to live in my own way, I don't want to write anything any more, and at the same time I know I've got to in order to get peace of mind."[124]

1 Stephen Reynolds senior, Mayor of Devizes 1873.

2 11, Maryport Street, Devizes, home of the Reynolds' currier firm from 1800 to 1887.

Photo: Sara Hannant.

3 The Reynolds family tomb in St Mary's churchyard.

Photo: Sara Hannant.

4 22, Sidmouth Street, Devizes, birthplace of Reynolds' mother, Clara.
"Those who like rows upon rows of dead flesh should take a look at the butchers' shops before Christmas - the time of peace on earth, good-will towards men, and death to fat animals."

5 Frank Reynolds, the writer's father.

6 63, New Park Street, Devizes where Reynolds was born on 16 May 1881.
Photo: Sara Hannant.

7 Reynolds' sister, Dot (1884-1914).

8 Aunt Jane about 1932, with Gerald Wiltshire and the young Stephen Wiltshire, Dot's grandson.

9 Prospect Rise, Rowde in July 1929, where Aunt Jane lived from 1887 to 1938.

10 The Bear Inn, Devizes, Reynolds' home from 1887 to 1893.
Photo: Sara Hannant.

11 The rear courtyard at the Bear.

12 The Prince of Wales arrives at the Bear, 24 May 1893.

13 Stephen and Dot with their widowed grandmother, Harriet Reynolds, in the early 1890s (*see page 21*).

14 The teaching staff of Bloxham in 1896. *Back row, left to right* J.G. Clarke (Music), C.J. Wilson (French), J.F.Turner (Maths), F.J. Winterton, J.H.T. Goodwin (English). *Front row* Rev. F.S. Boissier (Headmaster), Rev. P.R. Egerton (Warden), Rev.H.Wigan (Chaplain).

15 A dormitory at Bloxham in Reynolds' day.

16 1 November 1897. The nervous cast of *The Test of Truth* await their call. Reynolds, as Major Freeheart, is seated left (*see page 35*).

17 A chemistry laboratory at Owens College, Manchester.

18 Swinbourne Grove, Withington in 1972. Reynolds lodged at No 5, two doors down from the fire escape on the right hand side.

19 June 1901 - the Jubilee performance of scenes from *Twelfth Night*. Philip Hartog (*second right*) as a retiring Fabian dwarfed by the burly figure of Thomas Seccombe, an over-exuberant Malvolio (*see page 49*).

20 36 rue Bonaparte, now the Hotel St Germain des Prés, where Reynolds shared his attic with the friendly family of bugs.

21 The *École des Mines* on the Boulevard St Michel.

22 Nether Velly in the early 1900s.

23 The distaff side of the Reynolds family in skittish mood at Nether Velly. *Left to right* Frances (Reynolds' stepsister), Leonie (his stepmother) and Dot.

24 3, Cecil Terrace, Sidmouth where Tom Woolley lived from 1898 to 1953. Reynolds lodged in the downstairs front room in the spring of 1903.
Photo: Sara Hannant.

25 Jubilee Terrace, Sidmouth – the "Egremont Villas" of *A Poor Man's House* – where Reynolds stayed in 1903 and 1904.

26 A pride of male Woolleys in the 1890s. *Front* Bob Woolley. *Seated left to right* George Woolley (father), George Woolley (elder brother). *Standing left to right* Jack Collier (brother-in-law), Harry Woolley (younger brother), Tom Woolley (youngest brother).

27 Devizes College, where Reynolds was taught (1891-93) and recovered from his breakdown (1903-5).
Photo: Sara Hannant.

28 J.B. Pinker, the literary agent, with whom Reynolds signed up in July 1904.

29 Russell Gillman, the censored author of the first Devizes Guide.

30 George Simpson, editor of the *Wiltshire Gazette*.

31 Devizes College in the late 1890s. The boys' school room.

32 (*below*) The school room of the kindergarten.

33 A cramped dormitory.

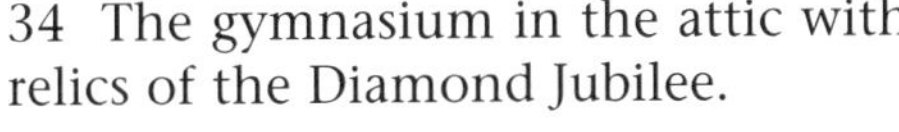

34 The gymnasium in the attic with relics of the Diamond Jubilee.

35 The portrait by Henry Lamb, June 1905 (*see page 94*).

36 Stanley Terrace, Pans Lane as Reynolds knew it. From the upstairs window (*fourth from right*) he wrote *The Holy Mountain* and much of *A Poor Man's House*.

37 2 Stanley Terrace today.
Photo: Sara Hannant.

38 Edward Garnett, a portrait he sent to Edward Thomas when they swapped photographs in December 1907.

39 Ford House, near Salisbury in 1978 – the home of George and Lizzie Tanner. The left hand gable section and the conservatory were added after Reynolds' day.

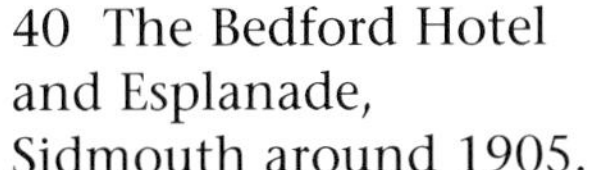

40 The Bedford Hotel and Esplanade, Sidmouth around 1905.

41 Annie Woolley, Bob's first wife, who died in August 1897, age 30. "Yes, her was a nice woman; a nice woman; I 'adn't no complaint to make against she."

42 Companions in arms, the earliest picture of Steve and Bob.

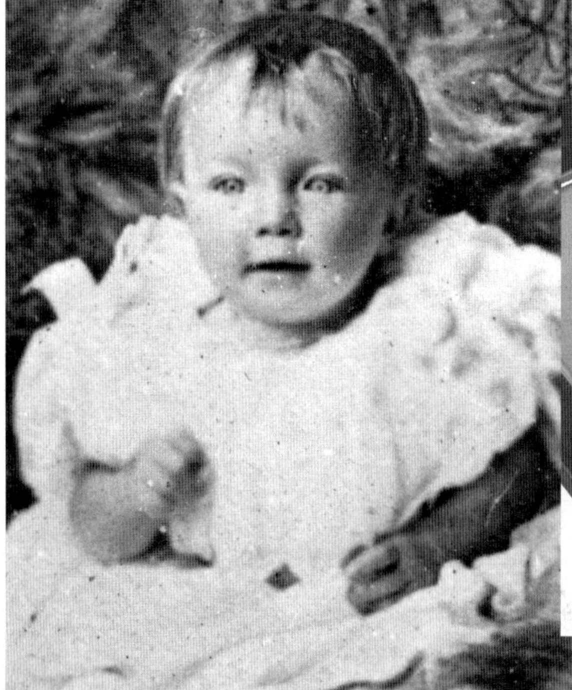

43 Lilian Woolley, born 26 January, died 24 December, 1904.

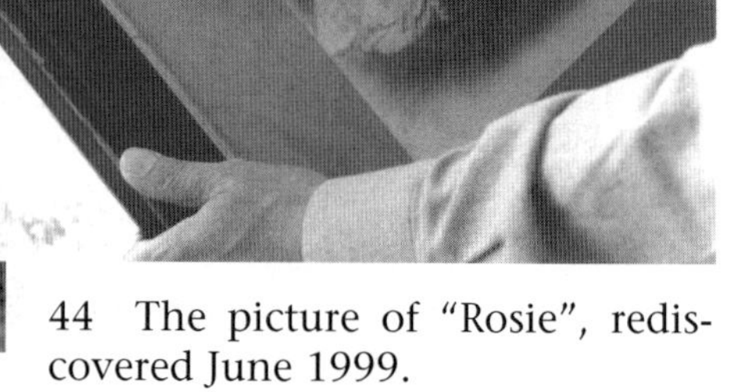

44 The picture of "Rosie", rediscovered June 1999.

Photo: Sara Hannant.

Three views of the Poor Man's House.

45 (*left*) From a water-colour by Norman Keen about 1907, with Bob and Bobby out front and Mam lolling in the doorway. Reynolds' writing window is on the first floor.

46 (*below left*) By Katie Powys, looking down the Gut in the late 1920s.

47 (*below*) In August 1937, a year before it was pulled down.

48 Uncle Sam, the hero by popular acclaim of *A Poor Man's House*.

49 Tom Woolley, the dashing forward for Sidmouth, Plymouth Albion and Devon – face on to the camera in the middle of a line-out for Sidmouth.

50 The handsome young fisherman in more familiar guise.

Pinker had been impressively patient and sympathetic over the previous weeks, absorbing all the laments about the review job, the influenza, the rejection of his stories and sketches. Reynolds was well aware of the burden he was imposing and strove to be reassuring. "Good to get your letter. Don't worry about me, not overmuch. I suppose my botherations are an essential part of my being any good as a writer, and must be put up with. I shall always be in a state of greater or lesser unrest for causes from which there is no escape, and which, therefore, had better be faced; only tolerate my complaining sometimes when my liver's bad and I don't see that living hard and fast is precisely what I should choose, the condition of my getting along at all. After all, I've had much more luck and happiness than anyone could have predicted for me, and I'm quite content though I can't always succeed in bearing it in mind".

He was keen, nevertheless, to keep Pinker's eye on the main ball – the maintenance of a steady income from routine writing. "What we have immediately to face is that for some reason – you know I don't put it down to failure on your part – you can't sell my short stuff. I was in hopes you'd be able to, after the book made its noise". He then produced a long list of suggested editors and magazines that might be good to push. Many an agent would have taken umbrage at this open attempt to teach them their job, but this writer had an uncanny capacity to disarm just at the moment of peak irritation: "All that's tentative suggestion merely, on the principle that a mouse may help a lion. Don't imagine me trying to sit in the centre of the Pink Spider's web!"[125]

From the middle of February, the effects of the influenza were abating: "The influenza got cured by going herring drifting to Seaton Bay in a N.E. wind! and the doctor is trying to get my stupid liver in order with some success".[126] And he was now making good progress with the final rewrite of the *Mountain*. "The *Holy Mountain* is half rewritten and Hueffer, I hear, still declares his intention of publishing it; also he seems to be saying things which cause people to write and ask me: 'Have you quarrelled with Hueffer?' Ludicrous! I haven't, but apparently he considers he has with me. Lord! what a fool I was ever to be persuaded into trying that job!"[127]

In spite of the row over the job, Reynolds' reputation as a writer was still high at the *Review* and, as Wells had complained, with Hueffer personally. Some years later, the latter still remembered Reynolds' special status: "I think the only work of an unpublished author that we had secured before going to press for the first time was *The Mountain* by Stephen Reynolds".[128] In addition to the praise of *A Poor Man's House* in the first number, the second contained a long letter from Reynolds entitled "The Marketing of Small Produce", which set out very cogently the problems of the small fisherman in the face of the larger fish markets and the middlemen who creamed off most of his potential profit. He had already thought out the solution – the organisation of a system of co-operation by fishermen, in the first instance run by businessmen prepared to compete with the traditional buyers on their own ground. In the wake of the sympathy aroused by his book, it was a letter that was quickly noticed and carried some influence. In his column in the *New Age*, Arnold Bennett was particularly complimentary. The second number of the *Review* "comes as near to the ideal as any magazine of pure letters is likely to get...... and perhaps the finest sheer prose is Mr Stephen Reynolds' letter to the editor on getting fish to market in small quantities!"[129]

On 17 February Reynolds went off for a few days break in Devizes, ostensibly to attend the funeral of Ada Bennett's mother.[130] On his return to Sidmouth, he learnt that Hueffer had definitely agreed to start the serialisation of the *Mountain* in the April number of the *Review*.[131] With this his spirits revived, aided by a typically effusive letter from Conrad: "What is good is to hear that you are better in health and therefore looking up in spirit. Write! Write. Write. This is one time to haul on your nets with all your might and make your way home (understand? – *home!*) on the *rising tide*...... Am impatient to see the mountain-top peep above the horizon of publicity."[132]

The first proofs of the serialised *Mountain* arrived at the beginning of March and, after so many years of waiting, the publishing process was finally under way. He read them over to Bob to see how they sounded and was pleased with the result.[133] He told Pinker with a new elation: "They may say what they like about that blessed book: it looks all right in print and it reads *aloud* smoothly; and it's *mine*; more mine, in the sense of being different from anybody else's, than t'other book....."[134] Conrad joined in the encouragement: "I prophesy some noises (of falling brickbats and cheers) about the *Holy Mountain* and are [*sic*] very impatient for the row to begin. There is but little I have to live for but I want that little quick".[135]

The row, when it came, was to be of quite a different kind than Conrad had foreseen. The April edition of the *English Review*, with the first quarter of the *Holy Mountain* on board, came out on 31 March.[136] Douglas Goldring, remembering Reynolds after his death, also remembered the book: "He was a very lovable man, but I have rarely detested any book as much as I detested his novel *The Holy Mountain*, of which it was my duty to read the proofs. My hatred of this story became a standing joke. It has persisted to this day".[137]

Reynolds' other friends were polite but not ecstatic. Galsworthy wrote on 13 April: "I do like the start of 'The Holy Mountain', it has zest, and go, and vim; though the subject does not do you the justice of 'A Poor Man's House'. The scene on the Downs is really fine."[138] Conrad, who had already read the manuscript twice, wrote the following day: "I suppose there is no chance of seeing you here moderately soon. Apart from the sentimental satisfaction there are things (good many of them) that are easier talked over than written about. So I will only tell you that the 1st inst of the novel is brilliantly effective". But there was a warning of potential rocks ahead. "You have made a first rate start but don't be astonished...... should some of the angels turn into devils by and bye and try to gore you."[139] Conrad was thinking of the critics, not the editor of the magazine in which the "brilliantly effective" novel was being published. But a new, and more serious, outbreak of hostilities with Hueffer was just around the corner.

As a result of Conrad's influence, Reynolds had that winter changed doctors, from the long-suffering Dr Savill of Harley Street who had looked after him during his breakdown five years before to Dr Robert Mackintosh of Barnes, Conrad's own doctor.[140] The long drawn out bout of influenza had reawakened the old problem of his veins and the possibility of having to go through after all with the long-feared operation postponed two years before. He wrote to Garnett at the end of March: "I can't get rid of the liver the influenza left me with and probably owing to the interference with circulation that cursed strain of mine is rather bad. If it gets bad enough to interfere with fishing I shall go in for that operation after all."[141]

On Mackintosh's advice, the operation took place three weeks later and was an unqualified success. But it was expensive, and the last week in April found Reynolds on his back at a nursing home in Mortlake pondering the need to realise all his assets. For some weeks he had been counting on the hundred pounds for serialisation of the *Mountain* to pay off his current debts. He had told Pinker the previous month: "As the *Mountain* is really appearing, I shall be able to pay off all my little owings to everybody on getting the cash for that. Blessed relief!"[142]

He now wrote to Hueffer seeking payment for the first half of the book. Hueffer wrote back on 28 April to say that Reynolds had agreed to be paid only if the *Review* made a profit, and it had not. He went on to stress that his personal responsibilities to his partners prevented him paying anything on behalf of the *Review*; if Reynolds still demanded payment, Hueffer would pay him out of his own pocket. Still queasy from the operation, Reynolds was shocked and incensed. He had entered into no such deal and refused to make the absurd distinction between Hueffer as person and Hueffer as editor.[143]

He replied the next day with a straight business reiteration of the request. "Thanks for your letter of yesterday. I cant, and wont, re-enter into such personal matters as the relations between you and your partners, nor do I consider myself less entitled to payment than any others of the contributors. With the instalment of the *Holy Mountain* in the number of the Review now appearing, half the £100 for the pre-publication serial rights of the novel, namely £50, becomes due to me, and I shall be very glad to have it."[144] Hueffer's response was equally terse: he would pay himself when it was convenient, and just then it was inconvenient. Reynolds wrote again demanding payment, Hueffer replied in the same vein. It was a head on collision.[145]

Back in Sidmouth, he put aside for a moment all money worries, and set off to celebrate the success of his operation. He went with Bob down to Devonport barracks to spend a lively weekend with Harry, Bob's petty officer brother, and his naval friends there. "Bob and I have just had a weekend with the petty officers we know at Devonport, preliminary to being tied here for the summer by boating. Rare time. I worked furiously all last week, and then forgot every literary botheration I've got for two whole days, which does one no end of good even including the slight element of bust about it!"[146] Henceforth Devonport was to become the usual venue for long-needed weekends "on the bust".

On the way back, they tried, but failed, to make contact with Mary Willcocks, and Reynolds sent a teasing account to Lane: "This morning we telegraphed to Miss Willcocks to meet us at Exeter, on our way home from Devonport, and lunch at the British Workman (antidote for Rougemont!), but she didn't turn up. Hope you aren't arranging for more of your authors and authoresses to make disappearances. Thought of communicating with the Harmsworth press. 'Noted authoress denounced by the Exeter clergy and disappeared. Is it.... What?"[147]

But the money problem was never far from the surface of his mind. As he explained to Strachey, the aborted payment for the novel would have to be made up somehow: "It looks like getting up before daylight all through the summer to work and make up a loss there somehow, and I'm not blessing it."[148] Having drawn a blank with Hueffer, he was keen to put the matter into Pinker's reliable hands before the *Review* went bust, as everybody was predicting. "It doesn't appear that I'm much of a hand at getting my cash, anyhow. I replied to that letter of Hueffer's I showed you and received another from him in the same strain. To that also I replied on the 4th., and since then have heard nothing. I have written to-night saying I shall be glad of a reply by return. If there is not one, may I send the debt on to you for collection. If you object I won't ask you to do it. This to find out. I don't fancy there will be anything to be got if the matter hangs fire too long, and I don't see why I shouldn't steal a march on the other creditors if I can. I've been put into the position of a creditor who needn't be paid, evidently, for some at any rate of the others have been. You can call me a shillyshallying unsatisfactory sort of a brute if you like, and I'll take it prone, but I think you'll see I am only pursuing the even tenour of my wibbleywobbley way."[149]

On 11 May he went up to London for the day to discuss affairs with Pinker, and for an interview with Willa Cather, McClure's reader, who was in Europe on the look out for material for *McClure's Magazine*.[150] Despite McClure's rejection of his stories in February, he was determined to try again. He was nervous of turning up at the Mont Blanc for fear of meeting Hueffer and was in a sullen mood when he got there, made worse by the fact that Garnett did not greet him as usual.[151] They did not speak throughout the lunch and Reynolds now felt sure that the war with Hueffer was starting to erode this much older and more important relationship. When he got home to Sidmouth that evening, he wrote a long newsy letter to Garnett to try and break the ice, with only the briefest mention of the day's stand-off – "I saw you in Town and yet I didn't".[152]

Garnett wrote back promptly in an attempt to defuse the Mont Blanc incident. He nevertheless pressed Reynolds a little on his own responsibility for what had happened: couldn't he take the hint that there were many at the

Mont Blanc keen to see him turn up there, but who wanted him at the same time to take a full part in the general interchange, not sulk in a corner? It gave Reynolds pause for thought. He began for the first time to ponder why he was now growing more and more cut off from his London friends.

> Your hint about turning up at the Mont Blanc (hint, good Lord!) is neither very deserved nor very unwelcome. I want to see you and one or two others, but some that come there I'd walk a mile to escape, if it wasn't for the ones I do want to see. And I like the room at the Mont Blanc because, eat-wise, I'm used to it. When you came in last time we met there, you omitted to greet me, who had come up from the country, alone of all the table-full. D'you suppose that facilitates gracious conversation? I don't. I thought you were offended over this damnable trouble with Hueffer.
>
> But there! I don't want to indulge in *tu quoque*. Why the devil should I? I know I'm glum and concentrated; more amused to watch people than to talk about subjects that don't much interest me. When I used to spread myself abroad, I was taken to task for not concentrating, and now I do concentrate, that don't suit people – nor me either. The truth of the matter is, I am bending every nerve to earn my own living and get the money for my schemes here, without writing down to money; I become less and less fitted for ordinary "interchange" as you call it; and I have driven my life up to such a pace in the atmosphere of affection which surrounds me here, and which, alone, makes it possible, that directly I go out of that atmosphere, I go flop. And I cannot steady down. If you can't put up with me, I must keep clear. That's all.[153]

This was friendlier than it sounded. Garnett took it all in good part and, writing back, hoped that his friend had not thought he was being huffy. "I didn't think you were huffy; didn't think whether you were or not. I've been so harassed and bothered lately by the *English Review*'s cheating me out of my *Hy. Mtn.* money and the consequent necessity of doing worse than one's best work at double pressure; while at the same time I have had to be out to beach whether there was anything doing or not, on account of two or three men loafing about and trying to slip into my place, that, to be frank, the huffiness of anybody whatever anywhere hasn't been a question to think about."[154] The temporary misunderstanding was patched up, though beneath it all the growing difference of outlook was drawing them inexorably apart.

Meanwhile, the dispute with Hueffer had gone from bad to worse. Hearing nothing more, Reynolds drew Marwood in, sending him an account of all that had happened and asking him where on earth the money was to come from? Hueffer was going through emotional traumas of his own: his marriage was breaking up, he had quarrelled violently with Conrad and with others, the *Review*'s finances were collapsing around his ears, and Reynolds was not the only contributor pursuing him for payment. He had lost patience with the stream of Reynolds' letters and wrote to Pinker with the ultimate threat: "Will you kindly let me know what Reynolds proposes to do, by return of post, since, if he gives me any more trouble I am quite determined to drop *the Holy Mountain*, and this must be decided on tomorrow?"[155]

The ever-patient Marwood too had been surprised by Reynolds' tone, and may have thought that he was seeking the money from *him*. His rather strained reply to Reynolds was taken by the latter as an implied demand for an apology. Reynolds was now no longer capable of distinguishing Marwood from Hueffer and stormed back: "If you have been expecting me to join in your merrygoround of absurdity by apologising for my query in my last letter, you've got the human factors of your calculation wrong...... though I'm sorry for the atmosphere of trouble in which you have been lately. I don't see that any good is to be done by squatting in it myself: and I don't intend to do it."[156] When the letter was gone, he knew he had once more overstepped the mark. He told Pinker the same day he was "a bit afraid what Conrad in his Kentish wild may be induced to believe".[157]

As always when worked up to the point of explosion, Reynolds now subsided into physical collapse and wanted nothing more than to wash his hands of the whole thing. When Pinker suggested he should pass the matter over to the solicitors, Reynolds reacted tersely: "No; I'll not ask you to put the affair into Withers' hands. Please tell Hueffer that, while in no sense whatever giving up my claim that the Review owes me £100 for the English serial rights of the 'Holy Mountain', I shall not pursue the claim further, unless and until the Review changes hands financially. Money isn't worth grubbing up when it's buried in dung-heaps. I'm cheated, and I'll stay cheated. The job is repugnant to you too, I can see. The chief thing I promised myself with that money was to get clear with you. Wait a bit longer. I'll work to get it somehow else, and perhaps I shall work the better for being clear of that set. They were fouling me, and my work too."[158]

Even Pinker, at the centre of the web which tangled Hueffer and Conrad as well, was beginning to lose patience: "I have no repugnance to the job of making them pay, but I am bound to say I feel a little cross with the whole lot of you".[159] Reynolds responded. "I don't wonder. But suppose I had definitely asked you to employ a solicitor on my behalf, and payment from Hueffer were evaded or not forthcoming. I should have been in your debt for the costs – further in your debt than I am already, and that's more than I ought to be. Having to work to make up money that one ought to have been paid is uphill work enough. Working to pay the costs of failing to get paid is a veritable House that Jack Built of toil. And as usual, when I'm particularly worried, I've knocked up into a slack morose muddy-faced beast and there I am! I only wish the debt were saleable to jew or gentile. Your plugging away on your own account, after being so miz-mazed about, is.... Well, hang it! thank you".[160]

Though having decided not to pursue Hueffer any further, Reynolds kept a close eye on the text of the *Mountain* as it continued in the *Review* that summer. He was astounded to see in the later instalments it had been marked 'Copyright in the U.S.A.' and asked Herbert Jenkins at Lane's to call Hueffer to account: "My suspicion, increased by the adding afterwards of the copyright notice, is that Hueffer may have sold the serial rights to some Wild West journal. If so, the proceeds are due to me, not him."[161] He was not in a mood even for bouquets about the *Mountain*. When Jenkins said how much he liked the book, he got an impolite response: "Glad you like the Mountain. Send the roses to Trowbury if you like, but for ....'s sake not here."[162]

It may have been this sense of another Hueffer plot, as well as the possibility of the *Review* changing hands, that persuaded him six weeks later to get Pinker after all to agitate on his behalf with the editor.[163] Hueffer told Pinker to take the matter up with his solicitors, who adopted the sniffiest of tones: "Mr Hueffer tells us that he referred you to us because he is of opinion that if Mr. Reynolds desires to press his claim, he had better issue a Writ. Of course we will accept service. We may say that if Mr. Reynolds considers that he is entitled to be paid because the Review has made a profit, we can easily convince him that he is in error."[164] On that, Reynolds decided to go back to the original plan and wait until the *Review* had definitely been taken over by people with money to pay.

The most damaging aspect of this crisis of May 1909 was, as Reynolds had feared, its effect on his relationship with Conrad. Reynolds took the initiative and wrote to explain his attempts to get hold of the money. He also enquired, rather nervously, whether Marwood had said anything about him. Conrad, who had had his own altercation with Hueffer and now wanted to hear no more of his affairs, was blunt: "I've heard nothing except, some time ago, some expressions of real good will towards you from Marwood. There's nothing more common in life than misunderstandings in the plainest matters. – And since you've mentioned the man's name I'll confess to you that your contemptuous manner towards M'wood has shocked both Jessie and myself. For we two being plain people could not see any reason for it...... On the action you say you've taken I express of course no opinion. But I cannot help feeling that it will fail in its main object. I believe there is still a chance of a sale but I imagine that any sort of complication would be fatal to it. It seems to me that a little more patience on your part would have served your turn better. But it's the *merest impression* as I really *have no idea* of what is going on. I have no communication with the quarter in question and I am rather anxious to keep out of it as much as possible."[165]

Reynolds was stung by Conrad's tone, and wrote a long letter exculpating himself in a rather hectoring manner. For two months he heard nothing from Conrad. The silence got to him – he could never cope with stand-offs, particularly from his closest friends. At the end of July he wrote Conrad a mournful, half-apologetic letter, assuming he was now in his friend's black books. Conrad was brisk and to the point: "I am *not* the man to keep either white or black books. You know on what point our correspondence got suspended. I wrote to you frankly on a matter of good feeling. You answered me by a sort of lecture – and I remained silent on a disagreeable impression."[166]

It was now time for a real apology. He had never meant to lecture Conrad, he said; but it was fate, he supposed, that he should always behave in this way. Now Conrad would have a lasting impression of him which he would never be able to undo. He had been going to send Jessie a copy of the *Mountain*, but perhaps now he had better not. Conrad in turn was moved to offer a genuine olive branch.

> When you have knocked about a little longer you'll discover that impressions *do* wear out, wear off – at any rate with people who are not mere bundle of nerves. It's deeper things, sentiments, judgements that remain. I trust we shall meet as friendly as ever, notwithstanding my outspokenness when my feelings were touched. I never supposed you *wished* to lecture me in this special case tho' I don't see why you should not if occasion offered. I kept quiet for a while; but in that I followed only the traditional wisdom of mankind.
>
> I hope you will send Jessie a copy of your book, and in the very same spirit of good will and friendliness as when you formed the intention. Nothing will please me more.
>
> You are right. Things will be what they must be with our life and work. These things are "written" if not exactly on our foreheads for the fools to scoff at, then deep down somewhere on the bed-rock of our nature. All the same one may be anxious and form wishes – and speak idle words.

And he ended the letter with a phrase that hadn't been seen since the previous March – "All our loves to you".[167]

The affair of the hapless *Mountain* and the *English Review* was put to bed for the time being – it was to be shaken viciously to life once more, but that was two years away. It had blasted for good the relationship with Hueffer, but that had never meant much to Reynolds in any case. The tremulous relationship with Garnett had just survived it. But the relationship with Conrad had, if anything, been strengthened. Down in the wilds of Kent the torch was still burning bright.

The frighting season at Sidmouth started early that summer and by the middle of May Reynolds was already rushed off his feet.[168] For some reason there were more people around seeking trips out with the young stocky figure on Western beach – and many of them were women. No longer were they surprised to discover the man on the oars was a writer; they had already read the book.

On 18 June a small party of tourists arrived from the village of Montacute in Somerset.[169] It consisted of the vicar, the Reverend Charles Francis Powys, his wife and three of their daughters, Marian (May), Lucy, and Philippa – known to the family as Katie. Altogether, there were ten surviving children in the family of whom the greatest noise was to be made in the world by the distinguished literary triumvirate – John Cowper, Theodore and Llewelyn. For Katie too writing was an essential of everyday life. She was to publish a novel, and write several others, but her sensitive and expressive nature made her above all a poet – as Theodore once said "the only poet of our family".[170]

Of the daughters she had the most marked of the Powys physical characteristics – large-boned with rather heavy features, intense eyes and a generous smile. She was a handsome, awkward girl, impetuous, strong-willed with an adventurous mind thirsting for knowledge. The last child but two, she was now 23 and had lived for most of her life in the enclosed atmosphere of the West Country vicarage, dreaming of the world and of becoming a writer. Though surrounded by such a large family, she was introspective, nervous, mystical. In adolescence she grew closest to her younger sister Lucy, a shy and gentle child, to whom she acted as guide and protector. The two girls planned when they were older to run a farm together.

They had discovered Sidmouth on a holiday in February of the previous year when Reynolds was living with Hueffer in London – and it had proved a revelation. Even in the wintry weather, they had climbed the cliffs around the town, explored the woods on High Peak, delighted in the little esplanade and the closeness of the sea.[171] It was for both their first escape into a wider world, and the chance to meet new people. They determined to come back. This second holiday in June 1909 was to change the whole course of Katie's life. She met Reynolds and fell instantly in love, a love that was to survive unblemished until her death as an old woman more than fifty years later.

On this summer visit they spent more time on the beach, swimming, watching the fishing activity all around, going for the occasional row with Katie at the oars. They met Bob and Tom. In the evenings after dinner they would walk the Esplanade, watching the sea and the other summer visitors. The previous year they had come in contact with Melville Mackay, the Sidmouth photographer who had helped with the publicity for *A Poor Man's House* and was to contribute the photographs for *Alongshore*. On this occasion he lent Katie a copy of the book that all Sidmouth was talking about, which she devoured avidly in her bed in the half-light of the summer mornings.[172] It had a powerful effect. "The more I read, the more I became aware of a new self...... It sang to me of the beauty of form and of colour, of the mystery of thought and of emotion."[173]

And then she bumped into Reynolds himself – or rather into Margot, the usual source of all Reynolds' first introductions. As someone who wanted herself so badly to write, she was knocked out by this meeting with a real live author and by watching the book and its characters unfolding before her eyes. At the beginning of July she confided to her diary: "It does attract me to read a book whose characters move and speak separate from the book in front of me. It gives me also a keen pleasure to have to do with the writer though Lucy spoke first to him before we knew we were in trouble with his dog".[174]

When she met him on the beach below the Bedford steps, she was breathless and embarrassed. "I came to give him praise. I came to give him thanks. But in my nervousness my words tumbled forth and my expressions were of the foolish." She invested this first meeting with a deep emotional power. "Together upon the shore we stood; indifferent to the people passing above, as souls banished, but now joined, we stood. Singly, but together, with an understanding and a sympathy more mysterious than the laying on of hands; more occult than the crossing of stars. The falling of the water was forgotten, the powerful burning of the sun was unheeded. I was affrighted; I turned and I fled. As a stranger I had sought him and he had not rebuked me. I had spoken and he had heard. Up the steps I hurried. From the welcome of the others I hid my head, so fervent was the meaning of my secret, so significant the crowning of my love."[175]

By the last week of their holiday, Katie and Lucy were spending more and more time on the beach – "We walk but little now, the characters are too interesting".[176] They gave nicknames to some of the new friends they met, but Katie had a special private one for Reynolds in her diary – Olaf – after the sea-battling King of Norway, celebrated in the works of Elgar and Longfellow. The diary entries were taking on an intimacy of their own: "He must forgive me for calling him by that name but as he assumes a character I must put an assumed name to him. With that I can speak of him more freely".[177]

As she fell for the first time deeply in love, he was her release. "Here was one who broke all paltry conventions. In contemplating his book and perceiving his ways, I unearthed his codes and they incited me. They were of the infinite and of the groundswell...... Below the steps of the sea-wall, below the passing to and fro of the indifferent, I questioned him, and he answered. There, at the slow turning of the day, he disclosed to me the purport of literature. I remembered his words and garnered them in the recesses of my heart. Close by his side, upon the pebbles we talked, and my love for him shivered and blossomed."[178]

On 9 July, the last full day of their holiday, Katie went out for a row with Tom and surprisingly broke through the usual barrier of reserve. "The sea broke our shyness and I felt as I talked with him we might have known each other as Father and I do now...." That evening a blustering rain came on and she gave Reynolds a hand in dragging the boats up the beach above high water mark. He was becoming used to the admiration of lady frights, but by now he must have known that this was no ordinary summer visitor. That evening, as a parting gesture, he signed his name in both Katie's and Lucy's birthday books. And Katie wrote in her diary a farewell phrase that could have come straight from Reynolds' pen "We go tomorrow. The sea wails...."[179] She was already beginning to sink her identity in his.

The departure from Sidmouth that Saturday morning was made easier because Reynolds was himself going up to London, armed with the proofs of the *Mountain* to read on the way, to meet Jewett, Lane's American manager, and discuss publication of his books in the States.[180] He offered to accompany the two sisters by train as far as Yeovil. After lunch that day Katie carried the precious copy of *A Poor Man's House* down to where Mackay lived but, finding him out, followed on down the Gut to Bob's cottage and left it with him to return. There she met Reynolds himself and had a brief chat, wishing all the time that she might stay longer. He went with them as promised the first leg of the journey and the parting for Katie was especially poignant: "my last word and last look was on the platform of the Junction and he disappeared entirely at Yeovil with his proofs".[181]

The picture was to remain in her mind and he in her thoughts continuously throughout the coming weeks, growing stronger as reality faded into fantasy. A week later, on return from an evening excursion to Weston super Mare, he was still at the forefront of her mind: "Coming back so late at night was something quite new. I wished for an apparition of Olaf but Sidmouth or Devizes successfully hid him....."[182] It was an image and a longing that was not going to go away. For someone so romantic and impressionable, from a wholly sheltered background, there was nothing for it but surrender to this first overwhelming experience of love. But she had made for any woman a fatal mistake – fallen in love with a homosexual man without the least suspicion of the barrier that stood between them. It could only end in disaster.

When Reynolds said goodbye to Katie Powys on the platform at Yeovil Junction that July morning, he was much too absorbed in his own concerns to notice very closely her reaction. He had not been looking forward to his next visit to London; as he told Garnett, the meeting to discuss American publication was an unwelcome chore: "Have to come up to meet Lane's American Manager – damn him. What a curse it is – having to meet people one doesn't want to, as part of earning one's bread and cheese." He was also worried about the chance of bumping into Hueffer. "You'll be at the Mont Blanc, I suppose; and equally I suppose I shall call in there. As I said before, one goes to meet certain friends one wants to see, and has to meet with them people one would tramp a couple of miles to avoid, so I can't guarantee I shan't be glum. You must remember that I am not occupied in exchanging ideas, but in trying to live on them."[183]

In the event, it turned out a happy and productive five day visit. Lane entertained him regally at his Lancaster Gate home, and Jewett, the American manager, was both sympathetic and extremely interested in Reynolds' books. They discussed in detail the publication of the *Mountain* in the States and that of the future books he was contracted to write for Lane. On the train journey home, he completed the reading of the initial proofs and returned them to Lane with gratitude: "Got back. They say I look over-fed. Diable! that's you! I don't mean the diable, but the over-feeding me! ......I am glad to have met Mr. Jewett. I liked him. Many thanks for arranging it."[184]

Since the end of May, Reynolds had been fussing with Herbert Jenkins (Lane was not the person to worry about such matters) over the detailed design of *The Holy Mountain*, only three months away from publication. He was inspired to do so by some rather strange criticism of the design quality of *A Poor Man's House* given by Arnold Bennett in the *New Age* – strange only because it was unusual for reviewers to give space to such issues.

> As Mr John Lane is one of the few publishers who take pride in the bodies of their books, and as the unusual salience of the chapter initials shows that original thought has been bestowed on the format of Mr Reynolds's book, I may permit myself a few remarks on the format. The design of the page is bad. The size of type has been unwisely chosen; it is too small. Mr Lane ought to remonstrate with those celebrated printers, Messrs. Turnbull and Spears, about their spacing between words, which is lax and far too generous. The essence of a good page is strict economy of spacing. Further, the lower margin is too narrow. And the "rules" above and below the running-title are inexcusable. Someone has evidently tried to produce a beautiful book and someone has failed. I honour the attempt."[185]

Reynolds left Jenkins in no doubt about the changes required for the new book. "I don't like those lines across the top of the page, especially for a novel, and, if I had my way, should like the type a bit larger (not much) and absolutely as plain and unaesthetic as possible."[186] They agreed a specimen in larger print, but a week later Jenkins sent him some samples in a different typeface. "Don't think I'm merely cussed or anxious to be contrary when I say that I prefer the specimen page you and I chose in the first place rather than this one you send. For this reason: the 'H.M.' is the sort of book, I think, in which the reader should be able to grasp a whole sentence at once with the eye; epigrammatic rather than atmospheric. The specimen page we chose last week fulfils that condition splendidly, besides being large, plain to read, and handsome."[187] He had tried it out on his own guinea pig. "Mam 'Oolley, who wants spectacles for reading, says that she can read this page easier than the other, because its letters, though smaller, don't run into one another and dazzle the eye so much."[188]

He had decided to dedicate the book to Ada Bennett who had so steadfastly encouraged him to go on with the writing back in 1904. In the middle of June he prepared a page-long dedicatory letter and sent it in to Jenkins for setting up.[189] To his surprise, Miss Bennett took strong exception to it, and particularly a passage in which he mentioned being caned by her – something which did not perhaps fit her liberal public image. She demanded its complete removal with the comment "It's a pity I didn't cane you a good deal more!"[190] It was replaced by a simple, colourless dedication: " To the Author's former schoolmistress and present friend, Miss Ada Bennett, to whose generous care he owes, among many other things, his life." For Reynolds, the row over the dedication was just further confirmation of the predestined ill fortune of the book.

By early August he had completed work on the page-proofs and was fretting for a publication date. He was delighted to find that the literary world was treating him with an unaccustomed respect: "About when is the book timed to come out? Yesterday I received a letter from the editor of one periodical asking me if the reviewer he designs for the book is to my liking, and if not, offering me any reviewer I care to choose!!"[191]

He was keen to capitalise on the reputation he had made with his previous book and sent appropriate directions to Jenkins. "You will, I suppose, be sending out soon a shoal of puffs-prelim., on the principle that if you herald me as a big-bug a lot of newspapers will be blarnied into doing the same!"[192] And to aid the process, he concocted his own blurb – "a page of infernal bluff" – to be worked into the advertisements:

> "The Holy Mountain" is described by its author as "A Satire on Tendencies". It is both a satire and a novel. The comical and pathetic love-story of Alexander Trotman, mover of the Holy Mountain, and his Julia, of the Trowbury Emporium, is combined with relentless satire and banter at the expense of humbugs in religion and state, press and theatre, trade and municipality. Beneath its comedy and realism and apparent profanity lies an intensely serious and penetrating criticism of modern life. Incontestably, "The Holy Mountain" is one of the most powerfully satirical stories that has appeared since "Gulliver's Travels".
>
> In his novel, "The Holy Mountain", Mr. Stephen Reynolds has shown that he can describe a Crystal Palace Empire Mission Revival Meeting, a Church and Empire Ballet and a Mayoral Dinner as brilliantly as he has pictured, in the "Poor Man's House", a haul of fish, longshore life, or the aspects of the sea.
>
> The Yellow Press is a topic of the hour. In "The Holy Mountain" will be found the most sweeping attack on, and the best defence of, the "Halfpenny Press" that have yet appeared.
>
> A book totally different from "A Poor Man's House", Mr. Reynolds's success of last year, and likely to give rise to considerable partisanship among admirers of his work. A novel that many will delight in and some will hate. A book to laugh over, to wince at, and to think about – to drop a tear on, perhaps.[193]

He sent Lane a new list of recipients for early copies, which now included Arnold Bennett, whom he had met the previous spring, Willa Cather, Charles Masterman and John Burns. He was keen to instruct his publisher on the timing of release. "Should I not stand a better chance of some first-day reviews if you could get the review copies (especially the Daily News) off to-morrow, in time for the weekend?"[194] And a week after publication, he was quick to apportion blame: "The Mountain seems a bit slow in getting under way – like the other book. The first-day review was unhappily bungled: it would have been better, I think, if the reviewers could have had their copies for the week-end before publication."[195]

He was also keeping a weather eye open on the local shops and bookstalls to see what effect the publicity for the new book would have upon sales of the old. He was appalled to find that W.H. Smith were effectively remaindering it and wrote to Lane for help. "Smiths have been collecting copies of the *P. M's H.* from their branch libraries and selling them by the dozen at Sidmouth station for 1/6. I have protested strongly to the bookstall clerk; for it simply means that when the *Holy Mountain* causes a renewed demand, they will not have it in stock and their subscribers will be told the usual 'not procurable', or out of print, or something of the sort; and unless they are very persistent will not get it. So, by trading on my local reputation, not gained by writing, they will lose me readers. ....Might you not also protest at headquarters."[196]

In the middle of August, he had Mackay take a new publicity photograph for the book. It shows a relaxed, half-smiling author, cigarette in hand, white floppy sun-hat on head, lounging against the cliff face, his full-sleeved white shirt shining in the summer sun. He had prudently removed the little round spectacles. It appealed to his vanity. He sent a copy proudly off to Pinker: "A better photograph of me is enclosed. 'Twas taken for the 'Bookman'. It's 'frighting' rig. Observe the sunburn!"[197] It now adorns the front cover of the 1982 edition of *A Poor Man's House*.

Publication day was finally set for 16 September. As it approached, he started to gain in hope. He told Pinker "The *Holy Mountain* comes out next Thursday, and apparently Lane intends to drop it into the waters of oblivion with a splash".[198] To Lane himself, he confided his hopes for a controversial send-off, with a little domestic analogy. "Everybody is telling me that the Mountain is going to go. I only hope it is. A lot, I feel, depends on the initial splash being a brave one and arousing a bit of controversy. Our baby, Semaphore, the other day, because the suckling did not go to her satisfaction, lifted her head from her mother's breast, and exclaimed, 'Damn!' If you were a woman-publisher, I'd wish the public might lift its head from yours, and say the same, provided they said it well enough."[199]

He received his author's copies on 15 September and, as before, inscribed the first one to Bob and Mam – this time in a more relaxed vein since the book was not about them: "To Bob and Mam 'Oolley, affectionately from Steve. This tale of the likes o' they."[200]

The book had already had its first, if limited, public airing that summer in the pages of the *English Review*. From the response, he knew of at least one literary figure, in addition to Garnett, who was certain to bless it with elaborate bouquets. It was another admiring female fright, though older and rather more ebullient than Katie Powys. Elizabeth von Arnim, then 43, was the Australian-born wife of a Prussian count who in 1898 had achieved overnight success with her own little piece of autobiografiction, *Elizabeth and her German Garden.* The book was an account of her life as a young English wife on the Prussian estate of Nassenheide, whose garden had become the foremost love of her life. It swiftly became a best-seller, passing through 21 editions in the first year, mainly on account of its touching combination of humour, human perception, romantic rural description, tips on gardening, and its author's ironic and outspoken feminism – symbolised by her affectionately satirical nomenclature of her bemused husband as the Man of Wrath.

Elizabeth, as she called herself *tout court*, was in the habit of adopting young, and not so young, authors for her sexual and other purposes. In the previous five years, both E.M. Forster and Hugh Walpole had worked at Nassenheide as tutor to her children. She seems to have been adept at spotting homosexuals, and had teased the latter unmercifully during his stay there. It is not so clear that she had divined Reynolds' sexual affiliations; despite puzzlement at his reticence with women, she seems to have fallen unequivocally under his spell.

In 1908 the von Arnims had been forced to sell up the Prussian estate and had bought for their country home a house near Broadclyst, just a few miles from Sidmouth. Elizabeth had been overwhelmed by the serialisation of the *Mountain* and at the beginning of August 1909 had descended on Sidmouth in search of the author. By chance she went out to sea with Bob, discovered Reynolds was his mate and "has been to sea with us every and pretty well all day since, to the considerable profit of our boats".[201] He used her enthusiasm to try and stir up Lane to more activity on behalf of the book. "I have been taking out a good deal in one of our boats Countess von Arnim (Elizabeth of the German Garden) and she is tremendously keen on the Mountain – much keener than on the other book – and goodness knows how many people she has caused to go to the local bookshop asking for it, in vain as yet. She had read it in the English Review. Judging from what she says, and what several other people have said, I think that, given a good dose of the real John Lane flair – or rather flare – in the production of the book, you have a good chance of making it go well".[202]

Reynolds did not always take easily to women with bubbling, volatile personalities, and his initial reaction to all her exuberance was somewhat withdrawn. Back in her Devon home, there was a tentative note in her follow-up letter: "It was a real pleasure making friends with you. I hope it *was* friends we made, and not that vague cool thing acquaintance?" She was, however, determined to cement the relationship: "Perhaps some afternoon you'll walk or bicycle over here – it is only about 9 miles I think – well within the powers of a sturdy young man...... Anyhow, bless you, boy of hope and glory!"[203]

He put her on his personal list of people to whom Lane would send copies of the *Mountain*, hoping she might review it somewhere.[204] Two days after publication, she sent him back her free copy with a long eulogy in her typical style, no less sincerely felt for all its overblown quality.

> I send you the Lane copy of the book, because I will not batten on you in such a way, and am ordering what I want to send to intelligent friends. I finished it again last night. I am confirmed and strengthened in my opinion of it. It is a glorious book, and you are a youth of the very greatest promise. That being so, pray bear yourself proudly – much as Mary must have done in those pre-natal days when no doubt criticisms abounded, but she could well afford to let people talk, for was that not within her the son of God? Do not, I beg of you, waste your strength describing meritorious fishermen. They, on your showing, are already in a state of grace, compared to which we others are the merest vulgar seethers in sin. Go for the follies and wretchednesses. Six months in the purlieus of London, and then a book about them and the London County Council and the bishops and the philanthropists! Well, I feel it impertinent to suggest, but not to every one is given your clear and fearless way of looking at life and the power at the same time to tell what you see. The Crystal Palace Revival meeting is absolutely perfect; and so is the Church and Empire Ballet. Those two stand out as the wonderful things in the book. *"And they were eating fruits"*. What can't and won't be done with such a heavenly sense of humour.

It was perhaps not surprising that someone of her spiritedness should be bowled over by the quirks and pace of the *Mountain*. But even she had a word of warning about its reception in the real world.

> But you can't expect very good reviews, I think, except from the most inhumanly large minded and enlightened of press men. Don't suppose that none of the book is young and scrappy, because some of it is – the short study habit (a bad one) breaking it up into spurts, if spurts can be broken, which I doubt.[205]

It does not appear that Reynolds took any of this too seriously, and he may have been not a little nervous of the domineering way she threatened to sweep him up into her skirts. Anyway, he did not pursue *her* with the same enthusiasm and she quickly lost interest. A year later she had battened on H.G. Wells and was writing to him in identical terms about *The New Macchiavelli*, the prelude to a much more sexually promising liaison.

Conrad wrote to him the day after publication, having just dipped back into the book which he had read twice in manuscript earlier in the year. It was a letter which signalled how close, despite the recent quarrel, their relationship had become. To mere acquaintances (like Galsworthy in the 1890s) Conrad was fully capable of covering his dislike for a book in a barrage of transparently superficial praise. Now he went out of his way to spell out to his young friend the faults of this book, but in a gently constructive way that could not possibly give offence.

> You are all right – that's clear, rather more clear to me than it was before. It is (apart from more substantial qualities) a very fine charge à fond, in cavalryman's language. And that means dash, brilliancy, courage – and good riding. I use this image because the language for talking about books has grown abominably stale to my senses; it – not to put (in the words of the immortal Snagsby) too fine a point on it – stinks in my nostrils – so much about the book in *se*, its outward spirit, its open declaration. Now for its inside, its art, the indissolubly joined intention and expression. As to that, one's appreciation can be only expressed critically. Anything else can be only verbiage. From that point of view it seems to me that the tempo of the whole is too fast. An effect of skimming is perceptible. I have to defend myself from the absurd notion that the whole thing has been dashed off in an hour and a half. Swiftness is a great quality; but remember my dear boy that twenty lightning blows produce not so great an effect than a deliberately delivered stab – and for all the rapidity displayed they take more time. There is more than one kind of swiftness. Your effect is not enhanced because all your blows (with a most admirable exactitude) land on the nose of your subject. The skill (or the instinct for straight hitting) is wonderful. The reader is amused – but when the tale is told he is not silenced, as he should be, into some emotional state or other. No. He mutters: Dam' clever that! You will get both praise and abuse. I am giving you the truth which is in me. I don't suppose you will take it for disparagement. I show my regard, my high regard, in the best way I know. If you could get a clear idea how I hate writing, you would understand what these few pages mean for me. These pages which you are at liberty to toss aside with the remark that I obviously don't understand what the book is. But as a matter of fact I have said to myself: – do not let us forget that this is Satyre! Well – even with that in my mind I must let my words stand.[206]

Conrad was right in his prediction that there would be abuse. The *Athenaeum*, in particular, upset Reynolds with the uncompromising tone of its criticism.

> One of the strangest things about this disappointing story is that the author of 'A Poor Man's House' should have written it. A main point in that book was its human sympathy. In this extravagant mixture of the supernatural and the realistic there is little but mocking laughter...... Mr Reynolds tries, with more industry than ingenuity, to fit his miraculous event into a framework of realism; but an attempt to put real furniture into a castle in the air could scarcely be more futile.[207]

But Conrad was also right about the praise. As expected, there was a glowing review from Garnett in the *Nation* which stressed the *vraisemblance* of the Trowbury scenes and, by contrast, the brilliant handling of the miraculous plot.

> It is a typical slice from the provincial loaf, one to be met with in every middling-sized town throughout the South of England, and the dull, coarse, peddling ways of the Trowbury burgesses...... are satirised by Mr. Reynolds with a savage harshness that recalls Swift, especially by the stress laid on unpleasant physical details. Fastidious readers may, indeed, be repelled by the earthiness of this picture of Trowbury, which is evidently the fruit of intimate familiarity; but they will be entertained by the audacity of the leading idea and the cleverness with which Mr. Reynolds handles the artistic machinery.[208]

Reynolds was more than grateful: "many thanks for the review. I wish the people who'll be utterly baffled by the book might read it".[209]

But Garnett's was a lone voice. As always, it was possible for Lane in compiling his advertisements to pick out the odd flattering phrase: the *Standard* called it "a very striking book", and the *Observer* "a wild and wonderful tale". But the countervailing view, which Reynolds insisted should go into the advertisement of his books, reflected the more objective appraisals: "*Morning Leader*. – 'Weak and uninspired.'".[210]

The more thoughtful reviews attacked the book more in sorrow than in anger. The *Times Literary Supplement* thought it "all too rancorous, too heady and near-sighted...... Satire flourishes only in an atmosphere of calm; it is scorn remembered with equanimity. Else it simply perishes of its own violence."[211] John Buchan in the *Westminster* regretted "that Mr. Reynolds should have descended into this arena. His talent is for the delicate and truthful depiction of reality without heat or ill-will, and it has no sure footing when it attempts a burlesque...... There are some brilliant passages and many shrewd hits, but on the whole it leaves the sense of hitting rather wildly and blindly. We miss the rallying point for sanity and sobriety which is necessary to make the thing human."[212]

It was left for his friend George Simpson in the local Devizes paper to put his finger on the wider issue of Reynolds' vulnerability as a novelist.

> Mr. Reynolds has the gift of close observation; he has also the power to set down what he observes with realistic fidelity. We saw this in "A Poor Man's House"....... His descriptive work is photographic. That is, he sees things as they are and reproduces them so as to bring to your attention features you had not observed even though you saw them. That, however, is the craft of the descriptive journalist rather than the art of the literary man; the one differs from the other as the work of the

> photographer differs from the work of the artist with the brush. The artist more or less idealises. There is no idealising in this book, and nothing artistic about it. It shows some inventiveness but no imagination.[213]

Other of his friends tried to soften the blow with more positive appreciations of his general skills. Scott-James in the *Daily News* thought the author was well out of his depth in the political and social satire, but attempted to cover his traces in a smoke-screen of generalised hyperbole.

> Mr Reynolds is a vivacious, energetic writer, full of ideas, audacious in asserting them, and never at a loss for words. I think it may be postulated that on whatever subject he writes, whether it is a subject which he does or he does not understand, his writing will be sure to reflect the impetuosity, the keenness, the naiveté, and buoyant vigour which characterise him. He plunges into his subject with a fine "now or never" air; he is himself intensely interested in the matter before him; he gives the impression of being always in a hurry to "get on", and carry you on with him; he uses any words or similes which present themselves to his mind – the jargon of literary criticism, the slang of the gutter, and the King's English are all one to him – and he pours them forth with profusion. He is careless, but vigorous; picturesque, but to the point; opinionative, but ingenuous. He is excellently informed on some subjects, ill-informed on others; but he makes no distinction between them; on all of them he writes with the same attractive earnestness and assurance.[214]

Reynolds saw through this transparent ploy, and wrote to A.G. Gardiner, the reviewer's editor, with a wry amusement: "Scott James' notion that I write carelessly with all the vocabularies of heaven above and hell beneath abundantly at my disposal is a delusion the Irish Fairies stuck into his head".[215]

He could take such effusions in good part; and even the widespread criticism so long as it were serious and informed. One constant misconception that really got under his skin, however, was the assumption that this was his second book, the sequel to *A Poor Man's House,* and that the quality of his work was going backwards. He kicked himself for not sticking to his guns in his first negotiations with Lane when he had insisted that the *Mountain*, the less mature work, should come out first.

A hint of the dangers to come had been given in Arnold Bennett's review of *A Poor Man's House* the previous year when the reviewer looked forward to the possibility of creative fiction from the same pen: "Doubtless we shall have an opportunity, later, of judging Mr Reynolds as a novelist. If he possesses the constructive gift he should assuredly be a novelist of mark."[216]

After reading *A Poor Man's House,* Bennett had been keen to meet the author and an opportunity had arisen in the spring of 1909. On 8 April, a planned lunch between Bennett and John Lane had been cancelled when the latter went down with 'flu, and Frederic Chapman took him out instead.[217] Over lunch they talked of Reynolds and the current serialisation of the *Mountain*, and Bennett expressed a wish to meet him.

So it came about on 20 April that Chapman took Bennett along to the Mont Blanc to meet Reynolds, just arrived in London for his operation. Though Bennett was later to dine, without enthusiasm, at the Mont Blanc, this is the only recorded occasion on which he took part in one of the celebrated lunches there.[218] Both Garnett and Hudson were present, but it was Reynolds he had especially come to see, and a firm friendship was cemented.[219] Henceforth, Bennett's reviews of Reynolds' work took on an even more enthusiastic tone.

It may have been at this first lunch that Reynolds made sure to head Bennett off from any assumption that the *Mountain* was his second book. Discreetly, Bennett did not attempt a review of the new book, but soon after publication made a short disclaimer in the *New Age* on its behalf. " I think it ought to be stated that Mr Stephen Reynolds's new book, 'The Holy Mountain', was written before 'A Poor Man's House'. It has, I believe, been partially re-written, but it remains a less mature work than 'A Poor Man's House'. One may say that 'A Poor Man's House' fulfils the promise of 'The Holy Mountain', rather than vice versa."[220] Delicately put.

But the penny had not dropped with all Reynolds' friends. He had for more than a year been a constant friend and correspondent of Perceval Gibbon, the handsome young novelist, two years older than Reynolds, who had worked for some time in the merchant navy before taking up journalism. He had become a new regular at the Mont Blanc and, like Reynolds, a protégé of Conrad. Their relationship had been affected by the coolness between Reynolds and Conrad that summer – "Gibbon doesn't write. I suppose he's ratty too."[221]

Gibbon's review in the *Bookman* was more than just ratty. It adopted a supercilious tone, laying stress on the immaturity of both content and expression, and made the fatal mistake of placing the writing of the two books in the wrong order. "From the author of 'A Poor Man's House' comes a novel, described in its sub-title as 'a satire on tendencies'. Mr. Reynolds's second book is in his second manner; he has laid aside his gifts of sympathy and tolerance which made his first book a document of outstanding value, to write a tale whose salient character is its vivid and unrelieved ugliness. ......There is a stage of mental development which is marked by the decay of scorn. One ceases to see a humorous aspect in pain and poverty; one loses zest for exhibitions of incomplete humanity. 'The Holy Mountain' carries no evidence that it's author has yet attained that charitable maturity."[222]

Reynolds was incensed. His resentment at the string of bad reviews had been slowly building up and this was the final straw. Before the quarrel with Conrad, Gibbon had praised the serialisation of the *Mountain*. Reynolds now wrote accusing him of trying to work out their recent personal differences under cover of the review. Gibbon responded by pleading genuine ignorance of the order in which the two books had been written, and in turn accused Reynolds of overreacting – he was becoming rather wearing as a friend. Reynolds accepted the plea of ignorance and held out an olive branch; but typically at the same time went to great lengths to justify his own behaviour.

> If you didn't know *The Holy Mountain* was written before the *Poor Man's House*, you didn't, and there's an end of that. It seems almost incredible, seeing how much I chatter about my work, but naturally I accept your word without reserve.
>
> Your review, as a hostile review of my book, doesn't trouble me a bit as I told you. But I think, if you look at it, you will acknowledge that you have pretty well mixed me myself up with your hostility towards the book. One doesn't expect oneself to be criticised unfavourably in print by one's friends under cover of a book.
>
> And if you'll refer to my letter, you'll find it takes the form of a query. Look at the thing the other way round and suppose:
>
> (1) That I saw an early work of yours in serial form, and expressed for it an enthusiasm which you knew to be excessive
>
> (2) That for several months I did not reply to any letter of yours
>
> (3) That I wrote to a paper and asked to have the book for review;
>
> (4) That I produced a review of it containing not only unfavourable criticisms of the book, but extremely unfavourable criticism of you yourself, founded on a mistake which you thought it impossible for me to make – the assumption, namely, that the book was not an early work of yours, but the latest.
>
> Suppose all that, which is precisely a parallel. I fancy you wouldn't do less, if you didn't do more, than ask if the obvious conclusions were the right ones.
>
> I asked you similarly if the obvious conclusions were the right ones. You tell me they are not. Need I say I'm glad of it? To tell you the truth I thought it likely that you were rather more the victim of some lie or other about me, than myself.
>
> Except as an isolated example of a certain type of work carried to an extreme – work done in a certain mood, induced by certain perfectly definite causes – I don't suppose that you object to *The Holy Mountain* half as much as I do. I know perfectly well that in many respects it's a hateful book, only I think that even hateful books have occasionally their place.
>
> As to my being rather wearing as a close acquaintance. ...That's what the turnip said to the rabbit. Forgive me for being a little gleeful on hearing you of all men speaking even for a moment, and for the purpose of a dig at me, as if you were one of the turnips.

> Is there any chance of your being in London the first week in November?[223]

The book had failed to separate them – they were friends once more. Nor did the bad reviews of the *Mountain* do any lasting damage to his literary reputation – the quality of *A Poor Man's House* stood firmly in the way of that. But there was lasting damage in a quarter where he had long since forgotten to expect it.

The anger and frustration with the small complacent world of Devizes which had been the driving force of the *Mountain* was now five years or more in the past. It had been slowly dissipated to a distant memory by his new life in Sidmouth. But for the targets of the local satire who had not yet read the book the experience was only too alive and present. Just a couple of weeks before publication, it suddenly occurred to Reynolds that there might be some ground to prepare, as there had been in Sidmouth the year before. He wrote to his Uncle, Fred Drew, still living next door to Miss Bennett in the market square: "My next book, *The Holy Mountain*, comes out soon. I'm afraid you won't like it much. I wrote it, before *A Poor Man's House*, at a time when those family botherations had made me feel very bitter; and in it I have poked fun at, and satirised, many things that are respected. But if you read the book carefully, I think you will see that it is only the bad sides of them that I have satirised; commercialised religion, for example, and tin-pot Patriotism. Genuine religion and genuine patriotism I respect as much as anybody, though I don't make any great professions either way. It is only the vulgarised, advertised, tin-trumpeted varieties of them that I have fallen foul of in my novel".[224]

When the book was published, it had a devastating effect on the sleepy market town. George Simpson in the local paper was quite relaxed about the Trowbury satire – "some of the characteristics of local life are limned for us not unjustly, though the limner may have hurt our local vanity".[225] But those who found, or thought, themselves pilloried in the book for greed, corruption, hypocrisy and sexual malpractice took a rather different view. Frank Reynolds was appalled by his own portrayal, as were most of the other members of the family. He decided to wash his hands entirely of his errant son. From this time on, Reynolds was a rare visitor to his old home town, and whenever he did visit he had to tread warily. The family never forgave him. Only the indefatigable Aunt Jane stood firm in her undivided loyalty. She declared to her brother and the others that she at least would never abandon her nephew – she would be the bridge.[226] And so she remained for the next thirty years, in his life and to his memory.

The ill fate attaching to the *Mountain* stretched out its tentacles long after the book had by most people been summarily read and then forgotten. The book contained eight sets of press headlines, including a crucial one on the final page which provided the dénouement.

APPALLING CATASTROPHE
HOLY MOUNTAIN GONE
TROTMAN'S TREACHERY
TROTMAN'S END
PERISHES WITH NEWLY WED WIFE
UNPARALLELED OCCURRENCE
INTERVIEW WITH SORROWING FATHER
THE MOTHER'S SANITY
LEADING OPINIONS
THE NEWS AT THE STOCK EXCHANGE[227]

Reynolds took great pains at the production stage to ensure that the headlines remained intact on a single page. "As regards the fresh pages for each chapter, as well as for each 'Book', I don't mind which. But there is this to take into account: Some of the chapters are exceedingly short, and if they begin each of them on a new page, they won't be able so easily to shift the type about in order to get the newspaper headlines always on one single page. All the blocks of headlines ought to be got each on a single page, and not be carried over from one page to another."[228] In all this concern, he never thought to lose a block of headlines altogether.

In July 1912, when writing an article on *My First Book* for *T.P.'s Weekly* in its series *How I Began*, he opened up his new copy of the *Mountain* and was given a shock. He wrote to George Macmillan, his new publisher: "On looking at your rebound edition of it, in the copy you kindly sent me, I find that the last page (p.309, with the newspaper placard) is missing altogether. Not that it matters much. But does the whole of the edition, bound by your binders, end up on the last page but one (p.308)? If so, it's the last stroke on that unlucky book or so I'm going to jocularly make out!"[229]

To start with George Macmillan was equally puzzled. "When I got your letter I sent for a copy of 'The Holy Mountain' from stock and behold it ended, as your copy does, at p.308 with no newspaper placard to explain what really happened to Trotman and his wife. I then had all the copies on our shelves (over 100) but the missing leaf was in them all, so I send a perfect copy herewith. The trouble is that p.309 does not form an integral part of the book but is a separate leaf pasted in. There is therefore always the risk of its being dropped or overlooked when copies are bound up."[230]

The book that had taken years of illness and exertion to complete, that had brought him close to blows with many of his friends, that had taken the whole of that desperate 1907 in the search for a publisher, that had earned him brickbats and no money for serialisation, and that had finally ostracised him from his family, had dealt its final blow. There was no way of knowing how many people had bought it and read it without ever seeing its final page.

ELEVEN

Alongshore 1909–10

The legal agreement of 1908 with John Lane – contracted, as Reynolds was now ruefully wont to point out, on All Fools' Day – obliged the author to supply to the publisher a further two books in addition to *A Poor Man's House* and *The Holy Mountain*.[1] On the day it was signed, Reynolds had just put the finishing touches to the *Poor Man's House* and was free to look round for his next major work.

His hopes were pinned on the *Urban Exodus* book bequeathed by Edward Thomas but these exploded in June 1908 when Grant Richards refused to come up with an acceptable price. Such was the acrimony attaching to that refusal that Reynolds abandoned the alternative of purchasing the idea from Richards and doing the book for Lane. He now found himself in "that horrid slough between two books".[2] The following month he revived his 1906 thoughts of a philosophical work on *Art as Communication* but some desultory preliminary reading soon convinced him of the depth of the muddy waters into which that would sink him. One thing he could *not* afford was to get sucked down into a work taking several years to complete. In October he devised the novel called *Charm*, but just as quickly abandoned it.

Throughout this period he still had a potboiler up his sleeve in the shape of the Nelson guide to Wiltshire. In early July he made plans to start tramping the Downs with Margot in the autumn, but by October was still postponing his visit to London to start the research phase.[3] His appointment to the *English Review* provided a concrete excuse for further procrastination but also a new fear – the loss of his position "out to beach". In February 1909 he wrote to Pinker: "That guide will have to be started soon. It's quite silly probably, but, you know, I'm simply dreading it; the probability of having to be up-country when there are things doing here, and so losing the place on the beach that I've really worked very hard for."[4] It was to prove the clinching argument for withdrawing from the project altogether.

Lane wanted a novel, which would sell rather better than further works of philosophical or impressionistic non-fiction. And despite the tribulations of the *Mountain*, Reynolds had not entirely turned his back on fiction either. Indeed, *A Poor Man's House* had originally been intended as a novel but, as he pointed out in the preface, fiction proved not to be the right medium: "I was unwilling to cut about the material, to modify the characters, in order to meet the exigencies of plot, form and so on. I felt that the life and the people were so much better than anything I could invent".[5]

But even as he started work on *A Poor Man's House*, he was still thinking of a follow-up novel set in a small fishing community with class as its theme. As he told Garnett in April 1907, it was to be "a study of a fisherman's wife's efforts to rise from the working into the lower middle class...... The tale I have in mind is rather a good one in skeleton, with a grimly ironic 'happy ending' – collapse (temporary) of the wife's struggle to rise; collapse (final) of the fisherman's more primitive instincts in their fight against the pin-pricks and lastly the police courts of civilization."[6] It was to be the obverse of the *Poor Man's House* coin – the destruction of working class resilience by the false attractions of middle class betterment.

Two years later this idea had long disappeared into the dust and the beginning of 1909 found him still without inspiration for the next major book. That spring he put together in his mind a new Devizes novel, again with class at its base, to be called *Yesterday and Tomorrow*. It dealt with a middle class Fabian girl who falls in love with a working man, whose theft of property, rather à la Galsworthy, acts as the catalyst in opening up political and philosophical attitudes. The inspiration for the setting is Prospect Rise, where Aunt Jane and Aunt Allie are fussing over Frank Reynolds and his shameful bacon factory, with Reynolds himself as the young Nietzschian hero.

In May 1909, Edward Garnett was given the bare bones of the plot.

> I've got a fine idea for my next novel – the one about the old maids in the country who are afraid of its becoming known that their brother is a butcher. I'm going to make the young man have come under the influence of scientific Nietzschianism and the girl have sentimentalized Slade School fabianism; then let the girl fall in love with the gardener's son whom she is painting; the gardener's son steal in order to deck himself out; and the young man nietzschian detect him and tax him with it. Over the little crime against property, I want the attitude of each party – girl, fellow, old maids and gardener's son – to flash out – and collapse emotionally. All the points of view to be absolutely implicit, as in Tourgueneff. Fine openings for ironical treatment there, aren't there. I should like to push the girl to intimate relations with the gardener's son, and let her *not* have a baby; which would be a novelty in fiction; but I don't see how it can be done without that episode too much overshadowing more important episodes in readers' minds. The end of it all is that the girl and the fellow, after all their emotional and intellectual flutters, simply and contentedly fall into line with the racial and social tendency to get married and have kids, and consider themselves justified. Whether they are or no, I shall leave open.[7]

The following month he was borrowing volumes of Nietzsche from Garnett to bone up on the texts and by the end of the summer had produced a full synopsis and persuaded the John Lane Company in the States to promise publication there.[8] But the situation was complicated by competitors for his pen. His problem now was too many ideas for books, as he told Pinker in September 1909: "I've three blessed novels in my head ready for writing and no time to start on one of 'em".[9]

One of them may have been the comic novel he had proposed to Lane as far back as the spring of 1908, of which no details have survived.[10] The more serious contender was another comedy novel set in Sidmouth – *A Sea-Change: or Mr. Burridge and Mrs. The Bathing-Woman* – which he offered to William Blackwood in March 1910 in hopes of serialisation in *Blackwood's Magazine*.

> Briefly, Mr. Burridge is a very precautionary prudential bachelor who retires to a small seaside place with his she-precise sister. But a seagoing instinct latent in him wakes up, and he comes to depend a good deal on talking with the rather broadly jolly bathing-woman. In the end, much to his own improvement, he becomes so devil-may-care that he even marries the bathing-woman. The plot is mainly concerned with his sister's inquiries into the bathing-woman's not conventionally perfect character, and her efforts to detach her brother from the bathing-woman. Underlying it is a study of the two types of character and life: the prudential and the jolly, the foreseeing plus sour plus dutiful and the happy-go-lucky character whose charm can't be discounted in spite of its very plain defects. All through the book runs the varying influence of the sea on various people.[11]

It was the Martha and Mary story again – perhaps a development of his earlier ideas for *Charm* some eighteen months before. In the character of Mr Burridge was held out the promise of some comic irony directed towards Reynolds himself and the change that Sidmouth and the sea had wrought in his own life.

In December 1909, in a gap in his serial writing, he determined to tackle the comic novel first as a far easier option than the Nietzschian. "I'm not going to do 'Yesterday and To-Morrow' next, but a more humorous thing to be called 'A Sea-Change' or 'Mr. Burridge and Mrs. The-Bathing-Woman'. That won't require so much brain-work and may perchance charm the asses who subscribe to censored libraries."[12] But a year later, in November 1910, he was still prevaricating: "I dread the starting, and haven't yet succeeded in serializing it; which would supply the necessary stimulus."[13]

The financial hurdles were indeed high. A novel, though entirely worked out in his head, would take two years to write well – "And how am I to live meantime? It practically means that to get books published I must throw up writing books, and do only newspaper work."[14] Blackwood expressed some interest in *A Sea-Change* but in May 1910 refused to serialise it without the possibility of book publication after.[15] And under the 1908 contract it had to be offered first to Lane. Conrad, who was eagerly awaiting a new novel from his protégé, could not contain his disbelief at such a dilemma: "But what the devil has Lane to do with your writing books – novels...... Am I to understand that such a tolerably acute person as yourself has delivered himself into his hands to the extent of not being able to negotiate with another publisher?"[16] In the autumn of 1910 Reynolds approached *The Times*, for whom he was writing a series of articles on *Labour v Brainwork*, in the hope of a serialisation but the negotiations came to nothing.[17]

These obstacles were certainly serious and provide the overt reason for his eclipse as a writer of novels. But his reluctance even to make a start on the ideas that were bubbling in his head in these years, at a time he was enjoying the relative financial security afforded by the payment for his first two books, implies a more deep-seated psychological obstacle. He knew from the experience of the *Mountain* the toll exacted by a long and sustained piece of purely creative writing. However boldly he stood up to the harsh reviews of that novel, he could nevertheless compare in his own mind its quality with that of *A Poor Man's House*; and in particular the character portrayal. Put Uncle Jake next to Sir Pushcott Bingley, Tony Widger to Alec Trotman – even a blind man could see the difference. There was no lack of creative instinct. Since the earliest days he had pressed on with a regular stream of short stories. But his best ones, like *An Unofficial Divorce* written in May 1909, were always based on true events, which he had experienced or of which he had heard.

Like most writers, he spent more time worrying about his weaknesses than rejoicing in his strengths. Better than any critic, he had cause and opportunity to reflect on the power of his creative imagination. At the back of his mind, he must have had his doubts about it. Although he never spoke openly of them, he nevertheless voted with his feet. After 1910 the novels written in his mind became swamped by the pressures of serial writing. After the publication of the *Mountain*, his next three books were to be compilations, the first two of articles written for the press. His first novel, *The Holy Mountain*, was also to be his last.

His third book, *Alongshore*, had a long gestation. It had sprung from the same creative impulse that had given birth to *A Poor Man's House* – the fishing sketches commissioned by the *Daily Mail* which he wrote in Sidmouth in January 1907. Those had been rejected by the *Mail* because of the perceived difficulty of the dialect in them, but most had eventually found their way into *A Poor Man's House*. He had not, however, entirely abandoned the idea of a newspaper series.

On his return to Sidmouth at the end of March 1907, the sight of the sea once more revived the inspiration. He told Garnett: "I've got an idea of offering some papers periodic 'Longshore Chronicles' (?) dealing with the sea and shore much as the nature writers deal with their woods etc. The sea has so many more distinct moods than I think most people are aware of, and the fishing and the cliffs are always changing and interesting".[18] It was above all the interface between the land and the sea which had captured his imagination, recalling his feelings on return to home waters in the *Coranian* in June 1905: "The romance of the sea, and the beauty of it too, I think, are most intense where sea and land meet".[19]

That spring he had written a few more sea sketches in the spare moments between fishing and work on his book, and had offered them to Anderson Graham at *Country Life*, who had taken for publication what the author considered the worst.[20] In July 1907 Reynolds had taken the formal decision to specialise as a longshore writer and continue with the sketches. His best one, *The Prawner*, the brilliant account of his night under the cliffs with Uncle Sam, was unaccountably rejected by Graham in September but later incorporated into *A Poor Man's House*, much to the advantage of the book.[21]

For the next year the completion and publication of his book took priority. Anderson Graham took two sea sketches in the spring of 1908, but it was September before a further one, *Squalls*, appeared in *Country Life*.[22] At the same time, Graham commissioned a new article, *Fishermen's Houses*, to go with some photographs he had on his hands.[23] These two latter sketches were to find a place in *Alongshore*, but they had been written piecemeal and the relationship with Graham was entirely haphazard. Reynolds had no confidence in him or his editorial judgement. There was nowhere here the makings of a book.

The turning point seems to have come on the evening of 9 January 1909, when on returning to Sidmouth after resigning from the *English Review*, he set off to the west with Uncle Sam on a lame duck hunt – picking up the overflow catches for which the drifters had no room on board. He told Hueffer next day: "Last night Uncle Sam and I sailed off down to the west-ard of Budleigh Salterton lame duck hunting – *i.e.* to see if any of the fleet down there had more in the nets than they could take in. They hadn't, but we found several nets fouled and saw to them, and boarded several craft and had a glorious sail with a great moon rainbow hanging over Exmouth".[24]

He planned to turn the events of that night into a new sketch, *Lame Duck Hunting*, but the severe bout of flu which accompanied his release from London intervened to prevent it. Five weeks later he was well enough to write it up, but uncertain where to send it since, as he told Pinker, "all my other contributing arrangements have fallen to bits".[25] On 23 February, he sent the sketch off to the editor of the *Spectator*, St Loe Strachey, for whom he had just started to write a series of political articles and who had also expressed interest in taking a series of longshore sketches. In the event, Strachey was too full up for a long way ahead to make any promises.[26]

It was then that John Buchan, who reviewed for the *Westminster Gazette*, suggested that Reynolds approach its editor, Alfred Spender, whom he knew had been much impressed by *A Poor Man's House*. The *Westminster*, with its distinctive sea-green newsprint, had been established in 1892, with Spender as assistant editor, to assume the mantle of London's Liberal evening newspaper in place of the *Pall Mall*, which had defected to the Conservative interest. Spender had taken over as editor in 1896 at the age of just 33 and was to remain for another 26 years. By 1909 the combination of his journalistic skill and the arrival of the Liberal government three years before had made him into one of the most influential editors in the country. Unlike most editors, he was a quiet, humble man with a common touch – altogether a nice person to work for.

On 11 March 1909 Reynolds made his introduction to Spender. "Mr. John Buchan tells me that you have been interested in my book, 'A Poor Man's House', and would not be unwilling to consider some of my stuff. May I send you the enclosed sketch, 'Lame Duck Hunting'? It belongs to a book of 'Longshore Sketches' that I want to do – an effort to hit off the relation of the sea to longshore people like us; but at present, I have no where to print the things serially."[27]

Three days later he received a businesslike but friendly reply. "For the next three or four weeks there are certain serials running, and I am afraid I should not be able to publish any stories or sketches other than I have already in type. But if you do not mind waiting for this period I should very much like to publish Lame Duck Hunting, the sketch you send me to-day."[28]

Reynolds wrote off hurriedly to Pinker – "Here's an opening apparently" – for advice as to whether to write the longshore articles exclusively for Spender, or share them with Strachey and take up the implied offer in Spender's letter that he would look at short stories as well.[29] Pinker favoured the idea of specialising with Spender on the sketches and gave some general advice "to work the men who are interested in you and your achievements".[30]

It was just what Reynolds had wanted to hear. "Many thanks for your advice, which I'm going to take. (Pat yourself on the back three times and send up to heaven two burnt [tobacco] offerings.) That is, I'll stick with Spender to sketches and character sketches that don't arrive at short stories, and he shan't have the last unless he asks for 'em. Probably 'twould be well to try and 'establish personal relations'. I seem myself to make more impression than my work – which proves their asininity."[31]

But he did make his number personally with Spender who turned out to be far from an ass. It was to prove a highly productive relationship for the next three years, with respect and friendship on both sides. Spender agreed to publish *Lame Duck Hunting* (it came out on 5 June) and follow it that summer with the series of *Longshore Sketches* that would form the nucleus of the next book. Ironically, on the same day that Reynolds agreed with Pinker to serialise *Alongshore* in this way, he wrote to Strachey at the *Spectator* to suggest turning his political sketches into a book. Thus on 14 March 1909 the die was cast for his next *two* books.[32]

From 19 June to 2 October 1909 fourteen of the longshore sketches appeared in the Saturday *Westminster*, the distinguished literary offshoot of the evening paper, most at weekly intervals. Together with the two he had already written for *Country Life* and the letter on the marketing of small produce published in the January *English Review* (now named *Longshore Fisheries*), these were to form the first three sections of *Alongshore*.

Reynolds was always keen to rebut any criticism that the book was merely a convenient compilation of existing articles. It was certainly true that the broad idea for the book had been there long before serialisation – it was Conrad who had encouraged him to pick it up again in the spring of 1909 – but if it were mapped out in May of that year, it can only have been in the very broadest terms.[33] The sketches were not by any means pre-written together but were composed "piecemeal and in leisurely intervals" that summer, often picking up contemporaneous incidents on the beach and often written to tight deadlines.[34]

It was something of a tribute to Reynolds' stamina that he was able to keep up the flow that summer when he was putting the *Mountain* to bed, writing a stream of political articles for Strachey and others, reviewing for the *Daily News* and *Bookman*, working flat out at fishing and frighting and, above all, coping with the nervous exhaustion brought on by his emotional battle with Hueffer and the *English Review*. Though he may have sought sympathy from friends for his failure to get on with his two planned novels, he was in actuality coping with far more than an average writer's workload.

He wrote the first sketch, *The Longshore*, at the beginning of June in an enforced break from fishing – "At the present moment I sit here at a table writing this, not simply because I want to, and have been wanting for some days, but over and above all because I am given the opportunity by a fresh north-easter that is turning up the sea feather-white, and is driving in upon the beach a surf which our small craft cannot face".[35] This was the pattern throughout the summer, breaks in the weather enabling him to keep just one step ahead of the clock. On 8 August he reported to Pinker: "I have my Westminster articles written up to the third week in September, and must hope for two or three days bad weather between now and then to let me write another".[36]

In the middle of August, he heard from Spender that the nine sketches published so far had been a great success with the readers, and was surprised to receive the princely sum of four guineas each.[37] After 15 weeks, the series came to an end on 2 October with his final article, *They There Kids*, which took him an unaccustomed ten days to write, competing with a sudden burst of boating business in the spell of fine weather that graced the end of that September.[38] He still had a further seven articles up his sleeve which the *Westminster* enthusiastically agreed to print the next year in a follow-up series with the title of *Beachcombings*.[39]

This gap between the two series meant inevitably that publication of the book would be delayed and by the end of 1909 he had agreed with Lane that it should come out the following June.[40] Conrad, still keeping a fatherly eye on proceedings, approved of the chosen title, *Alongshore*, but commiserated over the delay: "The title of forthcoming vol is really good. Beastly to have to wait for it so long".[41]

With the *Mountain* published and the first *Westminster* series complete, Reynolds took ten days off in the middle of November to make what was now to become the annual pilgrimage to Boulogne with Bob. On 9 November Bob had his usual Mont Blanc lunch with Garnett and Edward Thomas – he was now a permanent fixture of the November London literary scene – and three days later they set off for France.[42] After a few days revisiting their old friends in the fishing quarter, they had planned to work their way along the coast to Brest and from there return home *via* Plymouth and a final couple of days "on the bust". But running short of money, they decided instead to take a trip on one of the largest steam drifters working out of Boulogne to see at first hand how herrings were caught with the most up-to-date French technology. They took the risk of thereby mortgaging three or four days of their holiday if poor catches or bad weather were to keep them to sea; but in the event they were only one night away.[43] Reynolds wrote up this educative adventure in an article published in *Blackwood's Magazine* the following May and squeezed it in as the final chapter of *Alongshore*.[44]

He returned from holiday that November to a slowly deteriorating relationship with John Lane. They had had a small misunderstanding in September over the elaborate arrangements Reynolds was making for the photographs to go into *Alongshore*. He had commissioned Melville Mackay to produce eight photographs, including a superb portrait of Uncle Sam, purchasing the copyright himself so they could not be exploited locally as picture postcards as had happened with the publicity photos for *A Poor Man's House*. He proposed to sell the copyright to Lane for exploitation in the book for eight guineas, a proceeding which Lane, already concerned with the apparent losses he was making on Reynolds' first two books, was quick to question. Reynolds was able eventually to convince his publisher that it was not Lane himself who was being exploited.[45]

But another, more serious, source of friction developed soon after on the issue of American rights. The John Lane Company in the States had accepted *Alongshore* and the projected novel, *Yesterday and Tomorrow*, for independent publication.[46] Lane was annoyed when he heard of it. He had been under the impression that *he* owned the American rights and told Reynolds frankly that the question had been left out of their 1908 agreement quite unintentionally. Always quick to spot an opportunity for negotiation, Reynolds pointed out in his turn that the agreement had also failed to make any mention of advances on royalties. He was prepared to consider a new clause on American rights, but for him the issue was one of attitude rather than money: "The question of the additional clause depends very largely from my point of view on whether there is to be a publisher *cum* author, or a publisher *versus* author, attitude over the books. The former plus the clause is what I should prefer, even with a somewhat smaller cash result".[47]

They discussed the matter in London while Reynolds was waiting to set off with Bob for Boulogne.[48] Immediately after, he sent Lane a draft outline of his terms for the joint English and American rights of the next four books, which now included a planned volume of his short stories.

On the Longshore book £150 advance and 10% royalty in America.
On the Short Stories no advance and 10% in America.
On *Yesterday and To-morrow* £200 advance and 15% in America.
On the fourth book £200 advance and 15% in America.

This was some increase on the payment of £120 he had received jointly for the leased copyright of his first two books, but was not extravagantly ambitious for someone who had been given such media attention over the previous year. In addition he asked to buy back for £25 the cheap book rights of *A Poor Man's House* for him to exploit himself.[49]

He met Lane again on the day he was off to France, having first discussed tactics with Pinker who advised him in the event of difficulty to offer to release Lane from the contract altogether. "I saw Lane again the last day I was in town. Those terms appear to have frightened him horribly. He says he has lost 'nearly £200' on my two books, and will lose on those to come. So I took your tip, and said with humility: 'Shunt me! Break your contract!' 'That,' saith he, 'is a thing I never have done and never will do!' I'm going to tell him to do it again. He begged me solemnly to withdraw my books from the John Lane Co. in America, but I think that was irritation; for he lost his temper and I didn't. (If that isn't acting on your good advice, what is?) The bother is: he says that my Longshore book (which he hasn't read!) is bound to be a failure and that it ought not to be published before a novel...... He was really very offensive, telling me, in effect, that my work is hopeless, but so far my 'personality' (which I have always understood was rather objectionable) has fooled the critics into praising it."[50]

This was not the sort of discussion between publisher and author to promise a fruitful cohabitation for very much longer. Pinker, however, was optimistic that Lane would come round and thought Reynolds was "at a stage that is common and almost inevitable in relations with publishers".[51] But the signs were not promising. Lane at first appeared willing to sell back the cheap edition rights of *A Poor Man's House* but then decided firmly against.[52] Reynolds responded with ironic irritation: "I am relieved to hear that *A Poor Man's House* is a more valuable property than I had been led to understand".[53] He again suggested the cancellation of the contract but Lane refused on the grounds that the publisher needed to be "something of a sportsman".[54]

The row with Lane, combined with a burst of writing on return from the French holiday, had laid him low once more, the inevitable prelude to the run-up to Christmas. He sought commiseration from Pinker: "About a week after I came home, on the top of a hardish burst of work and a collection of worries, I got damnably ill – liver at the bottom of it, I believe – and I'm still so unwell that work is a Conradian weariness (he's better, thank goodness!) and what I am doing seems to me deplorably lacking in verve and spirits. I suppose it will pass off. It has done so before. But the worst of a rotten liver is that it creeps so quickly into one's work in spite of the most strenuous exercising".[55] Sympathy came readily from Galsworthy: "I'm sorry you've overdone it. Spurts are *bad* things for us literary critters. Beware of them".[56]

To Conrad he bemoaned not just his illness but the cul-de-sac down which he believed his career was now stranded. He received the most patient and understanding of assurances: "I sympathise and feel with you to the fullest extent. But you must stand up to it. Life is still before you. Your talent is undeniable – and something more than that too. Try to believe what I say – and perhaps the trust, I have the right to demand, in my sincerity may help you to regain a firmer belief in yourself".[57]

But Reynolds had not altogether lost his sense of humour. He was having an argument with Lane over the cover for *Alongshore* – he wanted the same blue as *A Poor Man's House* while Lane wanted a new colour to distinguish the two books on the booksellers shelves. Reynolds was swift to point out the true realities of life: "I believe that the idea of books of the same colour becoming confused on the booksellers' shelves is another of those kindly imaginations which publishers have about the public. As I said, your books repose on the booksellers' shelves almost invariably in their yaller wrappers. Why not try cerulean wrappers? I still bark for the beautiful chastity of the Poor Man's House's outside, with the gull as a seal, or not, as you like it. If the inside's damn bad, the cover should be good. An author progressively arriving in the colours of the rainbow would be chic, only it might land booksellers' assistants into examinations for colour-blindness".[58]

But in reality he was almost at the end of his patience with Lane. He had consulted Dr Mackintosh by letter about his "wretched liver" and the latter had diagnosed an infected gall-bladder, prescribing a mustard poultice to the abdomen and an acid mixture before meals.[59] Still struggling in the run-up to Christmas with the final articles for *Alongshore*, Reynolds was quick to turn this diagnosis against Lane himself: "You will be pleased to hear that I have developed an impediment in my gall-duct. It would therefore be as well, since I have a book to finish, and the gall is apt to mount into my brain, to communicate with me as little as possible".[60]

It was the predictable dismal Christmas. He sent Garnett a plaintive little card just before: "Best wishes. Hope you are flourishing. Don't seem to have heard anything of anybody for a long time. The Wrights are down here and we're all well except me".[61]

And for Pinker a more extensive assessment on the eve of 1910. "Work has come to an end for the present. Lane's botherations started the ball rolling, and now I'm damn'd utterly with the worst attack of head, sleeplessness and hump that I've had for years – simply can't work – and can't afford to get to sea and be better. It's two chairs to sit between with a vengeance – a bout of work makes me bad, as much now as ever, and a bout of sea-going makes me stony. And I don't in the least see where the cash-in-hand is coming from to enable me to write a novel without interrupting and spoiling it by the continual need to write for bread and cheese at the same time. Can't write two sorts of stuff at once. It takes all one's got in one to write one sort. God! what an infernal trade 'tis you pull the strings of".[62]

He made it up to London to lunch at the Mont Blanc on 11 January with Garnett and Edward Thomas, and again in the middle of February when he called in on Lane but, perhaps with some relief, found him out; but the first two months of the year were a write-off so far as work was concerned.[63] He told Lane at the end of February: "Your book for June still wants three chapters, and I don't know when they'll get done, for I've been able to do no work since Christmas except one short article, and I haven't the least idea when I shall be able to start work properly again. The worries attendant on writing have broken my literary back, seems so. At any rate, I find myself entirely without any desire to write or satisfaction in doing so; and, as it is, I have lost all my writing part of the year".[64]

By March, however, the pressure of newspaper deadlines had drawn him back to work on the last three sketches for the book, and the final seven articles in the *Beachcombings* series duly appeared on time in the *Westminster* from 16 April to 4 June. His interest had also revived in the planned novels and he was keen to use the advance on *Alongshore* – not discussed with Lane since the *impasse* before Christmas – to get on with *A Sea-Change*. In April he decided to break the silence and broached the question directly with Lane: "I should be very glad to know what advance on royalties you intend to give me; for my two months' enforced idleness at the beginning of this year have naturally not improved my finances, and it would be rather a good thing to get along with a novel instead of spending all one's time on pot-boiling".[65]

Lane came back the next day with his reply. He could offer £25 as an advance on *Alongshore and* the next book still to be written. Reynolds was incensed, as much by the slight to his forthcoming book as by the poverty of the offer itself. He told Pinker: "As for Lane's letter, you'll see the damnable artfulness of it; and of course I shan't have his £25 on those terms. If he can't make more than that for me on the book, it seems hardly worth troubling further over it...... I've a good mind to break the contract...... and let him get out of me what he can prove he has dropped on the three books. His publishing is getting worse and worse. He doesn't attend to it and leaves it in the hands of that poop, Jenkins. Moreover, he is skimping expenses all round with a view of turning the concern into a company soon, and making up good accounts for that purpose."[66]

There was an additional source of irritation to underscore the incompetence in Lane's office. In January the preliminary notice of *Alongshore* had pointed up the theme of "where sea and land meet" with a little rhyme.

> The longshoreman has always been looked upon as an amphibian;
> "A kind of giddy harumphrodite,
> Seaman and landsman too."

Reynolds had taken strong exception to this dumbing down and understood the rhyme would be dropped. It had now appeared once more in a further newspaper notice.[67]

In rejecting Lane's proposal, Reynolds was short and to the point. "The terms you kindly suggest for an advance on royalties of £25 involve payment for, or on the security of, unwritten work. It is a rule of mine not to mortgage unwritten work, and I don't propose to break that rule so long as I can rub along by turning my attention to pot-boiling for the periodicals. You have told me before, I think, that I am a very bad bargain to you, and I have offered before to release you from that bargain. I offer again."

But he had not forgotten either the irritating little poem. "That tasteless rhyme about the giddy harumphrodite which was interpolated into the preliminary notice of 'Alongshore' has, I see, been reproduced by the *Daily Chronicle*. I protested against it last January, in ample time to prevent its going to the daily press. I wish to protest again in the strongest manner possible. My book has no connexion with 'Comic Cuts'".[68]

As a counter, Lane suggested rather naively that as an alternative the proposed advance on *Alongshore* might be shared with the advance on the first two books since they at least were already written; but Reynolds was quick to point out that that payment had been for lease of copyright and not an advance on royalties at all. This ill-informed suggestion raised his anger even more: "Advances on royalties of 5% – diable! If you can't publish *Alongshore* to bring me in something more than £25 in royalties.... Well, there 'tis. Why on earth should one trouble to write books?"[69]

He heard nothing further and there followed a silent stand-off lasting some weeks, for part of which Lane was away in America. He sensed it was deliberate on Lane's part and told Garnett at the end of May that *Alongshore* "ought to be out by the end of June, but I have had such trouble with Lane that I am withholding the MS. and don't know when I shall send it in. Lucky I kept on my periodical work; so long as I have that Lane can't very well wear me down, as he is trying to do".[70] He was more trenchant with Pinker. "Haven't yet started 'A Sea-Change', nor have I yet sent in the MS. of 'Alongshore' to Lane. He refuses an advance except on money-lender's terms, so I thought he might as well wait. Soon I am going to write and ask his proposals for efficient publication. The puff-prelim bout he did was feeble in the extreme. His manager is, I'm afraid, an ass, and Lane himself neglects his business to hang on the tails of Society".[71]

The same day, 2 June, he sent in his ultimatum to the publisher he had embraced with such excitement only two years before. "If you wish to reject 'Alongshore' I should be glad to hear it. If, on the other hand, you propose to publish it, otherwise than as a bad egg foredoomed, that also I should be glad to hear; what your proposals are with regard to date and so forth. The efforts at preliminary puffing which took place a month or six weeks ago, were ludicrously feeble – a couple of London papers, and a few provincial copyists! With no advance to make and a royalty of only 12% to pay, I should imagine the book was worth publishing thoroughly well. And as I said before, if you think there's no profit in me you had better get rid of me. I should have imagined that a publisher of your experience would know that the way to get the best, and the most profitable, out of writers is not in the direction of botherations, and reproaches unacted upon, and efforts to wear them down into submission.... As to the terms you offered me before you went abroad.... Diable! The least said soonest mended. I can hardly suppose you made them without understanding them".[72]

Lane did not treat this as pure paranoia but responded patiently with "a touching letter", attempting to justify his actions but at the same time offering at last to release Reynolds from the contract if suitable reimbursement could be agreed.[73] It was with some relief that Reynolds passed the news on to Pinker – "I'm so devilishly tired of prod-prod-prod to keep Lane up to scratch."[74] He told Lane he would come up and talk it over in person rather than consign anything to paper.[75]

The decision to break the relationship was frankly inevitable and ultimately good for both parties. It had been the rather relaxed, incautious attitude of Lane, his willingness to take risks, which had given Reynolds the essential big break two years before. Now Lane, planning a change in the status of his business and with his eye fixed firmly on the bottom line, was beginning to regret that earlier lack of caution and to doubt Reynolds' selling power in the longer term. Now he was safely launched, what Reynolds needed was stability in a publisher, a firm which had full confidence in his long term future and was prepared to back him through the uncertainties of the shorter term.

The most exciting immediate prospect was the chance of a new and more efficient publisher. "I fancy now's the chance to get properly rigged up, if one catches the tide, so to speak...... What I object to about the Bodley Head is that it is being run more and more by an inefficient manager, and that it is running itself cheap preparatory to being made into a company under the same manager...... I'm not so keen about the largeness of advances as about honesty and energy in publishing". He suggested to Pinker the possibility of John Buchan at Nelsons, or Blackwoods – "It seems to me that for a writer of my sort, not very prolific, a publisher with a good magazine is very desirable".[76]

Another welcome side effect of change would be the chance to find a publisher who could tolerate agents and thus allow Pinker to go back to performing his proper job while his client concentrated on his writing. "One thing that pleases me is the chance of regularizing our own relations. I feel that I have taken advantage of your kindness for too long."[77] This made Pinker's choice of whom to approach the paramount one, and by the end of the following week, probably with Pinker's connivance, an interview had been arranged for Reynolds with one of the most prestigious London firms – the house of Macmillan.

Reynolds was up in London on Monday 20 June. That evening, perhaps at the instigation of Elizabeth von Arnim who, as a Macmillan author herself, may also have had a hand in the introduction to his new publisher, he went to the Court Theatre to see the first London performance by the acclaimed Abbey Theatre Company of S.L. Robinson's *The Cross Roads*. He sat next to a young up-and-coming novelist, Hugh Walpole, who interested him rather more than the play with its brutal ending and the two supporting comedies, which both men thought only moderately good. Though the overt homosexual strain in Walpole was not exactly Reynolds' cup of tea, the two chatted amicably enough and the seal was soon set on a new friendship. Sensing, perhaps, a slight diffidence in his new acquaintance, Walpole left it to Reynolds to make the next contact.[78] But he was sure of his own feelings and wrote in his diary that night: "Sat most with Stephen Reynolds who is nice and simple and would interest me if I saw more of him".[79]

The following day Reynolds was planning to call in on Lane and break the relationship for good; but when it came to the point he just could not face it. Instead he wrote to him on 22 June from Pinker's office. "I was thinking of coming round yesterday to tell you one or two things which, as I said in my letter, I don't intend to put on paper. But in the present rather heated state of affairs, I don't think I shall, because what I have to say means more disputation. And besides, I have to go down home. I'm going to adopt your suggestion, and break the connexion between us."

But despite the self-denying ordinance, he could not resist one final sword-thrust. "When things have cooled down, I'll tell you what I intended to say, if you so desire. All I've got to say at present is that I'd rather publish no books at all, than publish with botherations which prevent me writing not only books, but for the periodicals. When I get bothered, I can bother pretty successfully, and it doesn't do either side any good; so I propose on my side to retire from our contract peaceably".[80]

But all the time he had another card up his sleeve. It was during this visit that he had the first interview with Frederick Macmillan, the chairman of the publishing company, at its headquarters in St Martin's Street just off Leicester Square. The offices – now the Pastoria Hotel opposite the Central Reference Library – had been purpose built for the company in 1897 and had the singular advantage of giving on to three roads – St Martin's Street, Blue Cross Street and Whitcomb Street – so that vans could enter the building along a covered way, load from hydraulic lifts, and go out in a continuous stream. In the front of the building on the ground and first floors were the directors' rooms looking out over the area, then a barracks, behind the National Gallery. For the next three years, St Martin's Street was to become for Reynolds the equivalent of a London club – a place he could always drop into for a friendly chat and be sure of a warm welcome.

Frederick Macmillan, then 58 and son of one of the two founding fathers, had been working for the firm for more than forty years. Time and routine had done nothing to dull his enthusiasm for books and especial delight in the fiction, poetry and general literature in which he specialised. He was more open and extrovertly friendly than his cousin and co-director, George Macmillan, four years his junior, who ran the business with him and specialised in music and academic works, was profoundly serious and had a rather austere, even severe, reputation with the staff. As time went on, it was George who took over the handling of Reynolds' work and the two of them, psychologically very much on the same wave-length, became firm friends.

All first interviews went well for Reynolds – the "objectionable" personality was kept well out of sight until much later. In the friendly atmosphere of the Macmillan office, however, it was never to make even a token appearance. Frederick Macmillan was charmed by the author and interested in his new book on the verge of publication. Reynolds himself, with his reputation expanding over the past eighteen months, was not an inconsiderable literary property. He was swiftly signed up.

The move was a highly advantageous one for Reynolds – from an atmosphere of penny-pinching and suspicion to one of generosity and perfect trust. The Macmillans had a remarkable way of keeping the economic concerns of publishing at a distance from their authors so that they could get on peaceably with the job of writing. Conrad, who was later to use Reynolds to sound out the possibility of switching to Macmillan himself, was delighted by the news: "I am, on no very explainable grounds, glad to hear you have changed publishers. I have no reason to think Macmillans to be better than other publishers as far as common decency goes. They are obscene birds one and all. Yet I am glad. I would not reckon too much on their admiration tho'. I have had handfuls of almost fulsome letters from that brood, which as far as any friendliness goes were worth just nothing".[81]

What astonished Reynolds in the first few days was the efficiency of the Macmillan operation. They immediately picked up and ran with the publishing arrangements for *Alongshore*. His letters were invariably answered by return of post, by someone else in the office if the principal were away; and almost invariably the answer was "yes". It was the publisher of his dreams. As he told Frederick Macmillan at the end of their first week together: "For myself, I have been feeling so reposeful about publishing since I tumbled into your office, that I haven't felt so inclined to write for a long time".[82]

One further reason for this new and unaccustomed peace of mind was some momentous developments out on the beach at Sidmouth. Through most of 1909 Reynolds had been worrying away with plans to introduce a small motorboat into the local fishing and boating economy. He had been the first to recognise that motorisation was one key to combatting the decline in the small fisheries, which could not compete with the steam-driven vessels from the larger ports. There were two main obstacles: the conservative attitude of the fishermen to new technology, and the technical problems of designing such a small boat, with an engine both light enough to haul up the beach and fitted high enough to avoid smashing on the shingle. When the proposal was first broached in the summer of 1909, both Bob and Tom were strongly opposed to any such venture.[83] He felt sure that if only one such boat could be introduced as an experiment, its practical and economic success would soon win all the fishermen round.

No immediate decision could be taken but he at least got Bob and Tom to agree to send him off on a roving commission to track down a marine engine that might be suitable. "My qualifications were these: first, that I had been pretty well trained in handling scientific apparatus and boats on a lee shore; second, that in the early days of motor-cars [*his trips with the Tanners*] I had spent some hours grovelling underneath broken-down engines in sweet sylvan spots; third and best, that I had to carry the job through."[84]

In his travels, he finally found his way to the little firm of Smart & Brown out on the marshes at Erith in Kent. "Finally, on the off-chance, mainly because I had a few hours to spare, I took the slowest of slow trains to Erith, and lost myself on the over-built marsh thereabout. And in a black wooden shed – guarded by a hammering and a clanking and a rattle of explosions from the exhausts of internal combustion engines – I found an old engineer who came out blinking, and handled his bits of engines as if he loved them. We tried his motor-boat upon the swirling muddy river. She had life in her on the water. He advised us frankly, if we could not afford an engine powerful enough for our work, to wait until we could. That was our own feeling. I knew where we should buy our engine – if we did."[85]

That autumn, Reynolds negotiated a loan of £70 from his faithful uncle, Fred Drew, in Devizes and they commissioned the firm of W. J. Hodge of Dartmouth to build a new prototype, meeting all the technical requirements of the Sidmouth beach, around a Smart & Brown engine.[86] In the winter and spring of 1910, letters flew fast between Sidmouth and Erith and there were a number of journeys on foot between Sidmouth and Dartmouth. There were numerous arguments among the three partners over design of both engine and boat, but by April the *Puffin* was ready – 17 ft. 6 in. long, by 5 ft. 6 in. beam, by 3 ft. deep, clinker built of elm, with a single cylinder engine developing 4–5 brake horsepower but weighing well under two hundredweight.[87] In the middle of May, Reynolds and Tom brought her home in a fog on her maiden voyage from Dartmouth. Despite some minor trouble with a dirty plug, they astonished each other by covering the 36 miles in just five hours.[88]

The boat quickly built her reputation on the Sidmouth beach towing drifters out to the fishing grounds. She proved much faster than anyone expected, reaching speeds of eight miles an hour.[89] But Reynolds was keen to set an example beyond Sidmouth. He wrote up the story of the building of the boat and her passage from Dartmouth in a sketch, *Puffin Home*, published in

Blackwood's Magazine that autumn and a shorter, more technical, article – *Fisherman and Motorboat* – for the *Daily News*.[90] He sent the latter article off to Morrison Bell, the local MP for Honiton.[91] The era of political proselytising had begun.

The advent of the *Puffin* marked not only the renewal of his political life. It signalled a major change in his working life as well. To accommodate the new investment and the means of paying for it, he managed to persuade Bob and Tom to amalgamate – the first example of co-operation which henceforth was to be his political war-cry to all fishermen throughout the land – and the fishing and boating firm of Woolley & Reynolds was finally born.

It was a complicated undertaking, built on a tangled web of contributions of both property and labour, as Reynolds explained in a letter to *The Times* two years later in the context of the new Insurance Act.

> The nucleus of the "firm" consists of my friends Bob and Tom Woolley, who own jointly (1) a seine boat and net; (2) a sailing boat used for fishing or "frighting" (pleasure boat); (3) small pleasure boats. They also each own separately (1) a couple of sailing boats and some punts, used for fishing or "frighting"; and (2) some more pleasure boats. Their uncle, Samuel Woolley, owns a mackerel and herring drifter with her fleet of nets, and also a sailing boat. Their father, "Granf" Woolley, owns some bathing machines and a fleet of prawn nets. Bob and Tom and myself jointly own a motor boat for general purposes. Tom and Uncle Sam and myself own a punt useful for prawning. Bob owns a fleet of prawn nets and a pollack net. Tom owns a fleet of prawn nets. I own a trawl and a trammel. We all of us jointly or separately own a lot of miscellaneous gear. Sundry brothers at sundry times, and a sister and a fisherman named Cordey, who are not owners, complete the group, except that in specially busy times, and for hauling and seining, we take on any extra hands we can find.
>
> In actual working Bob and Tom work Uncle Sam's drifter, with any others of us as third hand or stop-gap, and sometimes Uncle Sam works for them in picking fish out of his own nets. Bob and Tom work for each other in each other's boats or their joint boats. We all of us go seine-hauling, or take out "frights" in the variously owned pleasure boats. Uncle Sam, with any mate he can get, works Granf's prawn nets. The sister helps with the bathing machines. I run the motor-boat for Bob and Tom and me jointly, with Cordey as motor-boat's puntsman. Bob's mate for mackerel hooking is myself, except that when we go hooking in the motor-boat he is my mate. For working the rest of the gear we pick up mates, or are picked up as mates, according to the occasion, and in every conceivable combination of owner and skipper, or owner-skipper, and mate. The owner is the employer, except when the skipper is.

> Every one of us, in short, works for every other one, separately or jointly, and the non-owners for any or all; and every one of us is paid exclusively by share, except in the case of hauling boats, which is paid for in fish for breakfast or pints of beer.[92]

With the arrival of the *Puffin*, Reynolds worked out an equally complicated scheme for sharing the profits from the new boat. For passenger work, from which he would opt out, 20% would go to running costs and the rest would be divided between Bob, Tom and the fleet of boats. When he used the boat for fishing, all profits would go to him – but in fact he planned to plough them back, together with some writing money, to pay off the debt, which they hoped to extinguish within three years.[93]

The major taste of independence that the boat gave him was the freedom to choose his time for fishing, which he enjoyed, and abandon altogether the frighting, which he loathed. "With fishing one goes out, comes in, and knows one's times; but with boating, for every hour one is to sea, one slops about ten, waiting for the people to turn up."[94] Now life was quite different. "I have taken to the motor boat almost entirely, which gives me a good deal more time, besides making me a skipper on my own account; for all the time I give to the engine does not amount to half the time I used to spend simply waiting about for frights."[95]

But there were some frights even he could not avoid. On Saturday 28 May, soon after the *Puffin* came home, Katie Powys arrived once more at Sidmouth station – for just a day trip this year, again with her younger sister Lucy. Her life was about to change for Lucy had started to court a husband and the old plans of working a farm together were quietly disintegrating. Much of the excitement of the previous holiday had burnt off in the ensuing twelve months, but she knew whom she was looking out for. "As we went down the front we felt sad for there seemed nothing but strangers till I saw Tom Woolley on the beach and better still Olaf sitting on the edge of a boat. He recognized us and after dinner I ventured to speak to Tom. Then I asked Bob to let me go for a row, they settled on Olaf to take me, so Bob launched us on the sea...... "[96]

They were alone together once more. The sea was a little rough, but she did not notice. They talked. She asked him what he thought of Walt Whitman, her favourite poet, and they both agreed he was a fine writer. They talked about Socialism and much to her disappointment he told her of his ambivalence: "I wish he was an entire one but he says he favours them where he can't stand the Conservatives and Liberals".[97] For Katie, this was the first man outside the family circle to whom she could speak freely of politics, religion and literature and who, though hired with the boat, would listen to her views with genuine attention and treat her as an equal. These few minutes out to sea now entirely rekindled the urgent feelings of the previous summer. "It was over too quick but it gave Sidmouth its old delightful appearance. The leaving was cruel."[98]

Reynolds, highly sensitive to sexual situations, could have been in little doubt about the nature of her feelings. When confronted with vulnerability, his kindliest instincts were aroused. Yet, at the same time, he hid his embarrassment behind an urgent smoke-screen of friendly gestures. Once again he was at his most courteous, helped the girls sort out their return train and gave Katie the postcard of a yacht taken by Melville Mackay, who, he told her, had also provided some splendid photos for his new book (she caught the title as "Along the Shore") which was coming out that autumn.[99] Katie, who could not guess at his dark secret, took these friendly attentions at face value. They meant a lot. She travelled back to Montacute that evening, clutching the postcard, recalling every word he had spoken on the boat, and thinking of the book that was to come. Here at least was some consolation for the desertion of Lucy.

There were other visitors that summer. Edward Garnett came down for the last week in September and first in October – his second visit to the Woolleys. As always he brought his manuscripts with him; he was in the midst of a detailed, at times vociferous, argument with Galsworthy over *The Patrician*, which had already been going on for two weeks.[100] Reynolds took him out in the new motor boat and the two men went out walking together just like the old days. One day they tramped the six miles eastwards to Beer along the cliffs, the beauty of which stuck firmly in Garnett's mind when he got back to London.[101]

In fact, it was one of those holidays to make one despair of routine working life and long to throw the whole thing up. Six weeks later, in a most un-Garnett-like letter to Galsworthy, he lamented the very second-hand nature of a life spent criticising the work of others, and was still looking back to the freedom of Bedford Square. "I get very low sometimes as to the second-hand sort of existence that is implied in the game and its sequelae – even when I turn out by accident from an old box a testimony etc., etc. – as I did the other day with a foreign letter of yours in 1905. How long ago it seems! We have both aged a good deal in those five years. However, a truce to these melancholy reflections. I'm tired of books and MSS. – very tired – and I look forward in a few years to living on the seashore, with a little boat and a whitewashed cottage, on a pound or so a week."[102] Reynolds would have been delighted by this conversion but he knew that for most who worked in London there was a massive gulf between the dream and the reality.

But there were others he could not entice down under any circumstances. For some years, he had been working on Pinker and, with the success of Garnett's stay, he redoubled his efforts. He invited him down for 22 October but, rather ambitiously, gave only two days' notice. "Sidmouth is very nice and fresh now along. Come down this week-end. I shall probably be on my way up-country the next. Though I cannot offer to put you up in house, I can easily get you digs on the Front close by, and we should like to see you in here for as many meals as you found yourself able to put up with our racket and grub. Besides which, at this time of year I should have the leisure to show you round a bit. So come down 'right away' if you can, while the winds are northerly. There are good through trains, and I've been wanting you to look down this way and see our turn-out for a long time."[103]

But it was not to be. No Pinker, but in his place a less than welcome Pinker client. A stern mock missive was fired off to London that Sunday evening. "You're a horrid man all the same, and I should like to swear at you hard, only you will protect yourself from such justice with a lady secretary. You, whom I did want very much to run down, didn't do so, and I spent most of Saturday wondering if you would turn up in the wake of a telegram. And a client of yours, one Maurice Drake [*the Exeter novelist of shipboard romances*], did turn up, and exasperated me to a jelly with volleys of questions, and invited himself for a longer period next time. But I'll be hanged if there is going to be a next time. An entirely estimable man, no doubt, but in Bob's words, 'one o' they there sort'. It's a confounded come-down, you know, when one had been anticipating you to have a question-asking heller, as we call 'em."[104]

His close confinement to Sidmouth for the summer months made him more dependent on visitors for stimulation than at any other time. For the same reason, he always took advantage of cultural gatherings when they came down west. In September the Library Association held its three-day annual meeting at Exeter. It may have been at the suggestion of Mary Willcocks, who delivered a technically learned address to the delegates that week on an analytic system of cataloguing for public libraries, that Reynolds was invited as one of the speakers at the final conference dinner at the Rougemont Hotel on 8 September.

He was not a great lover of the library system, which had greatly depressed the sale of his books, and this was a heaven-sent opportunity. Following a number of anodyne and self-congratulatory speeches, he delighted as always in sounding a controversial note – this time on the policy for selecting books. His speech was reported in the conference proceedings in predictably flat tones. "He did not think that, as the libraries chose their books at present, they would get hold of the people at all. He said it quite seriously. They were told that public libraries were, among other things, a great educational force. So he believed they were. But – he could not show more respect to them than by telling the truth so far as he knew it – the chief people they educated were the prigs. If they could devise some way not of educating people, who, perhaps, had to work fifteen hours a day, nor informing or improving them, but of amusing them, he believed they would do a very considerable thing. Libraries had touched the heart of people who were able to buy books, but not of those who could only just read."[105]

He was very pleased with his evening's work. The next weekend he told Frederick Macmillan: "Last Thursday I rather shocked the Librarians Association at their dinner at Exeter by telling them what I really thought of the relation of libraries to 'the masses'. The West-country papers mostly suppressed me, but I don't fancy the librarians will forget me, and the *Times* man was very congratulatory next morning".[106]

Reynolds sent in the final copy of *Alongshore* to Macmillan on 27 June, as soon as he got back from London. A week later the first proofs were in his hands.[107] All his detailed requests about the presentation of the book – typeface, covers, photographs (on which he took the closest care) – were met without demur. He was not used to this.

It took a little longer to sort out Lane. He still had on his hands 590 copies of *A Poor Man's House* (second edition) and 915 copies of *The Holy Mountain*.[108] Assuming a print run of 2000 in each case, it appears that by the middle of 1910 the first book had sold 3,400 and the second just over 1000. Macmillan was willing to pay £190 for the remaining stock, but Lane was demanding a further 15% on sales for "working expenses", a common publisher's ploy at this period.[109] This finally confirmed Reynolds in his low opinion of Lane: "He said re-imburse him what he was out of pocket, didn't he? not re-imburse him for the upkeep of his establishment".[110] Macmillans stood their ground and Pinker was able finally to beat Lane down – "That must have been a fine bit of negotiation, to get Lane to take off the 15%. He has always stuck like grim death to that".[111]

The final contract with Macmillan was signed on 24 August 1910 and, compared with Lane's terms, was generous in the extreme. The royalty on all three books was to be one sixth, with a ten per cent royalty on the American edition and on any future cheap (shilling) editions. The advance on *Alongshore* was to be £100 where Lane, under duress, had offered £25 and with strings.[112] Macmillans had valued the stock purchased from Lane at 1/10 a copy which left a shortfall of £52 on the amount they had paid. This was not to be deducted from the advance on *Alongshore* but to stand against the future royalties on the first two books – a generous concession which meant that the publishers would have to fund the deficit for perhaps some time to come.[113]

Reynolds was delighted not only by the content but by the form of the agreement. "I like the absence, in it, on the publishers' part, of efforts to pick up small mean sums all over the place."[114] He told Frederick Macmillan as much. "It seems to me very good. It's pleasant indeed not to have to wrangle over every silly detail, and I'm correspondingly grateful."[115] And unlike the contract with Lane, there was no stipulation as to future books: "As they won't be binding me for future work, I probably shan't want to get free of them".[116] And so it proved.

Frederick Macmillan recognised early the importance that Reynolds attached to the photographs for the new book, and straightway agreed to a more expensive process, in sepia ink, than that which Lane had been contemplating.[117] Reynolds was grateful and keen that Macmillan should understand their economic significance. "I hope the photographs please you. I think they will have the effect of causing people who know Sidmouth to buy instead of borrow the book. The booksellers here reckon that at least two thousand people here have read a score of copies of the Poor Man's House! They bought so few copies that at times they had twenty or thirty people waiting for the book. Which is all very well from their point of view...."[118] And in recognition of his gratitude he made a gesture he would never have contemplated with Lane. "Will you accept either the Moonglade photograph, or the 'Broad Ebb' (the originals, I mean) as a small memento, so to speak, of my coming along to you?"[119]

And unlike Lane, Macmillan was always relaxed, always willing to explain a decision, giving the impression that everything was under control. This had a much needed calming effect on his new author. In early August Reynolds, impatient as ever, was pressing for publication of *Alongshore*. "When are you thinking of publishing? If it could be done without inconvenience, it would be as well to catch some, at any rate, of the Sidmouth season. The book is being a good deal inquired about here, and visitors returning home up-country act as excellent advertising media."[120] Macmillan was calm and to the point. "We will publish 'Alongshore' early in the season but I think it would be a mistake to bring it out before the end of September even if we could get it ready, for books that appear during the holiday months are apt to be overlooked and neglected by the Reviewers who are themselves taking vacations."[121]

But when he could meet a request, he was generous to a fault. On publication, Reynolds needed twelve copies of the new book: "I don't know how many author's copies it is your custom to send. I shall have to have a dozen, and pay for the surplus, if that is above your number...... Most of my friends, you know, are not book-buyers. Their hair would stand on end at the idea of giving five shillings for a mere book. But they have to have one just the same – and there 'tis". Next day a dozen free copies were in the post.[122]

It was only three months since Reynolds had "tumbled" into the Macmillan office but it was already clear that this, like his relationship with Pinker, was not just about business. A week before publication he sent a parcel of prawns to Frederick Macmillan who, as a devotee of *A Poor Man's House*, asked whether they had been captured by Uncle Jake. "I'm afraid those weren't Uncle Jake's. He's getting oldish now for the job and doesn't go so much, contenting himself with the most fantastic excuses rather than admit the truth. A night's prawning is very hard, cold and eye-straining work. We got them down to Longo, however."[123]

Macmillan, who had celebrated his 59th birthday on 5 October, was understanding. "I can sympathise with Uncle Jake's disinclination to admit that it is his age which prevents him from going after prawns. I entered my sixtieth year last week and I am constantly being annoyed by realising that I had better not undertake things that I could do easily thirty years ago!"[124] Reynolds could never pass up a reflection on age or his unhappy adolescence. "Had no idea you had come to years when you might be allowed to shirk a night down to Longo! As for feeling old.... though I'm not yet thirty, I reluct savagely at the passing of every month, let alone years. But I didn't begin to live till I was twenty-two, or -three."[125]

Alongshore was published on 14 October 1910. It comes from a period when Reynolds was at the height of his powers as a writer, so although it lacks in comparison to *A Poor Man's House* the force of a consecutive narrative, it makes up for it in the maturity and more finished quality of its prose.

At its core, the first four sections, are the two series of sketches he had written for the *Westminster Gazette*. The incidents in the sketches come from a range of periods. Some are historical – *Fogs* and *Seining*, for example, are taken from his visit to Sidmouth in the summer of 1903 – while others are contemporary with their writing, like *A Glut of Mackerel* which records an incident from September 1909.[126] To them he had added a fifth section comprising the accounts of his two holidays in Boulogne with Bob the two previous Novembers, to provide "by way of contrast" accounts of fishing on a large scale from a French port.[127]

As with the postscript to *A Poor Man's House*, he was entirely heedless of the impression given by the final pages. In July he had persuaded Frederick Macmillan to print as an appendix to the book his didactic *Daily News* article advocating the use of motors in small fishing craft and giving a detailed technical description of the *Puffin*'s engine. Now as ever, life came before art: "It ought not to go in the book itself, because it's propaganda rather than literature; but I am keen on not missing the smallest opportunity of furthering my small fishery work."[128]

The core of the book is about life on the longshore, in the words of its subtitle "where man and the sea face one another". He explained its inspiration in the dedicatory letter to Uncle Sam: "For the longshore is powerful to mould men, because, to make a living there, they must fit their whole lives to it, not merely their working hours, but their sleeping and waking and eating, their aims and watchfulness. We wait long and often there: the sea and the fish wait never...... It was about those conditions, in the broadest sense of the word, that I wanted to write a book; not about certain men, women, and children this time, but about the sea and the beach and your rocks; the tides and eddies, both of water and humanity, that set alongshore...... In *A Poor Man's House* the sea was a background for people; here people are in the background; are a part, so to speak, of the scenery".[129]

He knew that such an objective would call for the very best from his expressive and lyrical powers. In September 1909 he had toyed with the idea of rewriting it completely with money from a hoped for American serialisation: "I shall, I think, spend the money in giving myself time to re-write the whole of it from print, tightening it up and making the chapters more continuous, improving its form and style. A book of that sort, I take it, ought to have its style absolutely as perfect as I can make it; and I think I am at last getting some real command over my English...... "[130]

And indeed he was. The book, published without further revision, abounds in natural description whose beauty derives not just from its sensuous prose but from an understanding of the environment which makes comprehensible both its workaday reality and its hidden mystery. Reynolds uses his inside knowledge to give us a novel insider's perspective. Here, for example, is the beach from the viewpoint of idle observer and of user.

> Now that I have worked and watched upon the beach by day and night, I cannot see it any more with the eyes of a seaside visitor. Everything about it means too much. It has undergone the change from an acquaintance, whom one likes, into a friend whom one loves, yet hates for a moment sometimes. Only some chance sound, or peculiarly radiant light, or salty whiff of seaweed, recalls the old feeling, when the beach was simply a sunny bank of shingle, pleasant to lounge upon and interesting to watch; when boats, belonging to I did not know whom, lay along it, and fishermen, whose nicknames and names I had not learnt, mended their nets or stood about with their hands in their pockets, for ever idle, as it seemed, and picturesque, because the toilsome part of their work was seldom seen. Great waves were then a glory; so they are now; but it is also a question of what body of water they contain and how far they will run up the beach among the boats. Mishaps, wettings in beaching and shoving off, provided then a fine entertainment; now they provide shame if they are my mishaps and anxiety if they are somebody else's......
>
> To fishermen who are compelled by lack of harbourage to keep their boats and gear upon a lee shore, the beach is almost more than home itself. From it they shove off, saying, 'Just fitty for mackerel, this,' or 'Us ought to hae a catch o' herrings this here logie [calm, dull] night.' To it they return, sometimes hardly caring whether they have caught anything or not, half perished with cold, and almost too tired to climb the crunching gravel on their way to bed. Upon it they are fleeced by fishbuyers who have spent their night snug.[131]

Reynolds is always good at seeing the world from an imaginative new angle. In the third section of the book which deals with the technical details of methods of fishing and the relevant gear, and always with interest, we have a description of a fleet of nets from the perspective of the fish, which recalls the technique of the bug's-eye view of his Paris attic written six years before.

> A fish's eye view of a fleet of nets, could one take it, would be a strangely impressive sight. One would see – looking up through water growing

> rapidly a darker green in the twilight – the keel and bottom-strakes of a small boat. In clear water one might also see her foresail hauled down, leaving only the mizzen up in order to keep her head to the wind. Then, with that peculiar soft plash which netting makes, fathom after fathom of it would be shot overboard in heaps, and would float away, straightening itself out until there extended from the boat – itself a mere black bubble on the water – an immense brown curtain more than half-a-mile long, and five or six fathoms deep. For mackerel it would hang from the surface downwards, but for herrings it would be sunk in the depth of the water, supported by buoys and lanyards, so that its foot was just free of the bottom – an improvement in fishing discovered not so very many years ago. The motion of the death-curtain, hanging free and unleaded from its headrope, would be inconceivably graceful; for not the finest fabric floating in air, nor the most accomplished dancer, nor even smoke, can vie in delicacy and softness and exquisite suspense with the waving of net in water. So, throughout the night, it would be just visible, drifting in the flood and the ebb tides, and curling back on itself during slack water. And towards dawn the two men in charge of it would be seen to peep out over the gunwale, the boat and nets would draw towards each other, and finally the whole curtain, that had stretched far out of sight, would return to the unknown land whence it had come, snugly piled up between two thwarts of the drifter. To a fish of some intelligence, yet without enough to distinguish between human limbs and the apparently animate nets they shoot out, there would be something terrible in the long arm of fishermen; something as mysterious and as darkly uncanny as the interference of spirits in the familiar life of mankind; something beautiful with the fascination that always accompanies destruction.[132]

And he manages to sustain this sense of the numinous through all the natural descriptions of the book. This on the mystery of wind and waves.

> That, indeed, is what the winds and waves do for us all. Therein lies their strange kinship with mankind. They minister to our wildness which, after all these centuries of civilisation, we still feel to be the best part of us. And if they kill us.... Is not every passion a dangerous thing? Is not man's soul itself an explosive within him – the explosive which drives him, like a projectile, across time? Invalids near the sea have been known to grow madly excited with a rising gale, so much so that they had to be calmed with drugs, and, when the gale had blown itself out, were as if they lacked life. But it is good to see how the eyes of sturdy men, though bloodshot and half bunged-up with salt spray, will kindle in a storm. They will show embarrassment sometimes on finding themselves observed, as they might if you had suddenly come across them hugging their maid in a quiet corner.[133]

And there is as well the odd dream-like sequence which gives the book an other-worldly quality, as when the little fishing crew encounter a Navy ship before sunrise.

> One day before breakfast we were out mackerel hooking roundabout a cruiser that was anchored in the bay. Very bulky, black and lifeless she lay on the calm sea in the early morning haze. Suddenly the guard-call sounded brazenly. Men ran about the decks. The guard fell in across the quarter-deck. Eight bells struck and the bugle sounded *Attention!* Whereupon, while the guard presented arms, and the crew saluted or stood at attention facing aft, according to their rank, the white ensign fluttered out from its staff astern. The ship had awakened. The wide sea was awakened. It was the hour of official sunrise – a comic notion. But it seemed out there, beneath the great ironclad, that the sun by some vast power had been stayed in his course till then.[134]

But despite the undoubted power of the descriptive writing and the objective of keeping the sea firmly in the foreground, it is, as with most Reynolds' books, the people that soon take over once more. The human link running through most chapters is the perennial Uncle Sam, resurrected by popular demand under the pseudonym of Benjie. Reynolds knew his public, and this is what they wanted most. We see Uncle Sam back in top form as he scorns the soft livers and their curiosity to know the contents of the old sack perpetually swung across his shoulder.

> 'Ah! nobody don' know what I got in my bag o' mysteries. But they want to. Back t'other day one o' they papern-collared poops stops me up over cliff: "Hi, ol' fellah! what have you got in your sack?"
> '"Hullo, young 'un!" says I, "what have you got in your pockets? When you turns out they, I'll turn out my bag, an' not afore. If you'd gone where I been, 'long wi' me, you'd know. But you can't go where I goes. You'd tire o' it, the likes o' you would. You'd get your feet wet."
> '"No offence, me man," says he.
> '"Then don't you go out o' your way to give it for the future," says I. "My sack's my pocket – remember that. T'others have got holes in 'em. I wishes you good afternoon."
> 'Lord! they sort couldn't go where I goes. They an't got it in 'em, not to go twice, an' day after day, if they goes once just for curiosity. 'Tis funny how they hates to see the likes o' me carrying a bag they can't look into, they four-meal-a-day soft-sleepers.'[135]

And as in *A Poor Man's House*, we have Uncle Sam in his element, out under the cliff scavenging for flotsam, contrasted with the more vulnerable figure, back in his house yet a little at sea among the gentler arts.

> There seemed to be something ghoulish about Benjie too, as he picked his way along, throwing above high-water mark everything that could possibly be of value to him. Behind Dog's Tooth Point the sun dipped. A chill shadow overspread the Cove. Benjie shouted, holding aloft what turned out to be a yellowed and water-worn tallow dip. 'Poor fellows! Poor fellows, where this come'd from. Shipwrack, that's what that is, unless some fool throwed 'em overboard. Here's another. Lookse! An' another too.' Fourteen or fifteen of them he picked up and put carefully in his pocket; for he still reads in the old-fashioned way, the book, like a folio, spread flat on the table in front of him, and by his side a candle which he snuffs between forefinger and thumb each time his long-sighted eyes begin to smart.[136]

The odd homosexual touches are even more forthright than in his previous book. In *A Sort of a Kind of Wreck* some fishermen from Ware are cast up on the Sidmouth beach in a storm in the middle of the night, rescued and taken into the Woolley house to strip off their wet clothes and dry out.

> So we brought the Waremen in house, found some food, made tea once more, and for a change of clothes we routed out old sweaters, patched trousers, and darned guernseys. The kitchen was choked up with the remains of three suppers and with wet garments lying in heaps on the floor. They stripped and dried themselves where they sat. One of them had the chest and belly muscles grandly clean-cut – developed to perfection by a life spent at the oars. Yet even while I was wishing that some great sculptor would carve his likeness before labour wore him out (knowing very well all the time that no stone statue in a gallery could equal the play of the lamplight upon the living body in a fellow-fisherman's little kitchen) the man jumped up suddenly, and, with a tightened face, staring before him at nothing, he pressed his chest hard against the corner of the table. It was as if, without warning, he had indeed been changed to stone. Straightening himself up slowly, he took our hands and placed them against his chest. The muscles which had been so lissom were knotted and strung to the hardness of wood. ''Tis the cramp,' he said. 'I gets it cruel – gets it to sea sometimes. It passes away.'[137]

But it is with the children that once more Reynolds signals his greatest delight. There is the brilliant little sketch of *Semaphore,* the new baby for whom he was exiled to London in the spring of 1908. As we know, one feature of *A Poor Man's House* which had annoyed the Woolleys was the brief reference to them in bed in the morning. Here, as if to exorcise the complaint, he indulges in an even more detailed and intimate description. It is as if he is trying to prove their initial sensitivities entirely misplaced. One of Semaphore's superior gifts is that she always wakes up smiling.

> If she is left smiling too long, then certainly she smiles no longer; but she has awakened smiling, anyhow. Should I be first down and take upstairs the morning cup o' tay, it is Semaphore receives me, smiling up from betwixt her parents, blithely awake some seconds before her mother has finished yawning and digging the Ol' Man in the ribs. Be the window-blind up or down, she catches one's eye before anything else in the room – before her father's weathered red face, or her mother's hair streaming across the pillow, or the bag of family biscuits on the bedside table. There is something peculiarly proper and beautiful in the sight of a little child snuggled in bed between its father and mother, the fruit of their union still hanging, as it were, with its bloom upon it, to the parent tree, and not unaffected for good, perhaps, in after-life, by the longer proximity. As for the risk of over-laying, shall not those who gave life sometimes also crush it away? We are too squeamish over death, too neglectful of life. Separations come all too soon.[138]

In this sketch, as in most of his sketches and short stories, Reynolds shows himself the master of the perfect ending. This one sums up even better than some of the lyrical passages in *A Poor Man's House* his sense of the sacred nature of the bonds of the Woolley household and the knowledge that, though he is tied by them too, he is yet ultimately an outsider, looking on.

> One understands why pictures of the Holy Family have such a hold upon the imagination of mankind when Semaphore is on her mother's lap and her father comes in, all wet from sea, and kisses her, and licks her face like a great dog, and she laughs aloud and drags him to her by the hair. The mother is so full of patience and the consciousness of power, the father of eagerness and the exercise of power, and the child contains in small so much of God knows what, that every attitude, every movement of the three is at once graceful, cosy and world-wide; delicate and strong. 'Where's Joe?' some one asks. Semaphore looks towards the fender where the cat sleeps. 'Where's Jim?' She turns round to her father. 'Where's Dad?' She smiles across at me! Were it not that her eyes are sea-blue, like her father's, instead of muddy grey, like mine, and all her gestures echoes of his, gossips would no doubt be saying that she was mine. I wish she were.[139]

At the other end of the spectrum of childhood come the rumbustious six year olds as they descend *en masse* on the sea front to wreak havoc on the beach. In this passage the words come cascading after them, Reynolds delighting in equal measure as much in the words as in the children.

> At the beginning of August, when the boats are lying along the beach, new-varnished for the holiday-season and washed out for a busy day, with the oars lying neatly together in them, and all the ropes and sails in order, down come the kids. Down they come to the Front in a chattering swarm, more regular than any shoals of fish, most like a flock of birds collecting for a migration: tousled, joyous, and turbulent; boys on the look-out for a chance of getting to sea; small girls in charge of little ones, little ones dragging babies. We try to get rid of them tactfully. 'Git home,' we say, 'an' tell thee mother to wash thee face!' Poor woman, she has probably done it once or twice already, since they got up, and wants to hurry on with her housework. The kids look, taking our measure. But they don't go. They mean to get down to the beach, they and their babies, and bundles, and perambulators, and go-carts, and slices of bread-and-butter, and penny bottles of raspberry champagne.[140]

They leave behind them a trail of disaster, but what lies beneath it all – the magnetic draw of the beach – is that most mysterious of mysteries which none can evade – the call of the sea.

> Paint and varnish is scratched with hob-nail boots, sails sat upon, gear trampled over. Rowlocks, lines, footing-sticks, all sorts of things are scattered abroad. What a festival it is! The kids don't care; and, indeed, why should they? Long before they came into the world the boats were on the beach. They found them there, a resource to be made use of, a means of amusement waiting for them; just as they found the sea and the land, daylight to play in, and darkness to sleep away. Boats which they neither made nor bought are to them simply so much material for enterprise, like goldfields, or fisheries, or untilled soil to men. And if they do damage.... Do not we grown-up children trample down something beautiful and valuable with every step forward in our own belauded enterprises?
>
> Meanwhile, in some of their mysterious young minds, so clear yet so obscure, like spring water standing in shadow, a process is beginning which will end only with their lives. The sea is laying hold of them, tightening her grip, asserting her authority over seafaring blood. She is picking and choosing among those happy-go-lucky kids; and whom she chooses she never really lets go. If she cannot have their service afloat she still can wreck with cross-purposes their lives ashore. Their imaginations will for ever be running away to sea if they themselves don't.[141]

Probably the best sustained piece of writing among all these sketches is *Frights*. Here, in this typical piece of social and cultural analysis, Reynolds is at his most Orwellian. What Orwell has done for Donald MacGill and the comic postcard,

Reynolds does here for their purchaser – the seaside visitor. He starts on dangerous ground – with the clergy.

> The movements of visitors are so mysterious, and yet so regular, that were they not human beings, more or less accountable for their actions, we should certainly say that their comings and goings were as purely a matter of instinct as the migrations of birds and fish. Once we had an archbishop staying here. He used to come out and take the sea-air about noon. Straightway, it seemed, from every side-street and almost every house, would appear a clergyman, and as the archbishop promenaded so they would promenade too, passing and repassing under the august eye, until you might have thought that the earth was a heaven-bound ship, and our little Front the bridge of it, crowded with sky-pilots. An observer from another world, who knew not our civilisation, might well have imagined them to have been under the sway of some irresistible instinct; and perhaps they were. Or had he been scientific, he would have made a note somewhat to this effect. '*Human Migrations*. Movements of the clergy. Curates attracted by archbishops. *Query*: Does the attraction reside in his face, his gait, or his gaiters?'[142]

Four years later he was to rein in this anti-clerical mood as he found himself entertaining no less a body than the Archbishop of Canterbury himself in Bob Woolley's back kitchen.

But there is yet a certain affection for the visitors in general as they arrive on a Saturday, with an air of vulnerability.

> Shortly afterwards they come out and walk along the front, still rather townish in clothes and manner and complexion, greeting acquaintances if they are old visitors, asking the funniest questions if they are new-comers, and all of them worrying about the weather. Sometimes, when we tell them it is likely to be foul, they appear to be offended with *us*. As if we could help it! They have been let loose from their cities for so short a time that indeed we rather pity them. We like to see them getting sunburnt.
>
> As with visitors in general, so with frights – but more so. I sometimes think of them as spray thrown at us haphazard by a seething sea of humanity in the interior of the country. Fine days they neglect. Foul days, when they are sure to be wet and sea-sick, they want to go out, and often have to be told that 'tisn't fit. ......it is not so easy to explain why certain men should be chosen by omnibus parties, nor why some frights should prefer a talkative, amusing man, some a young man, others an outspoken old man who orders them about; some a man who can do the sea-going flunkey well, and some few a man who can tell them silly scientific stuff about weather systems and the sea, when their holiday-mak-

> ing, or rather holiday-attempting, minds would be far better occupied with the beauty and joy of it all, and only a poet could tell them what they ought to want to know.[143]

Which leads him on to a discussion of the philosophy of frighting and of the essential, but ugly, role of servility in the workplace.

> Frights have this advantage over fish: their greater regularity. Fishing, bad though it has become, is still as good as frighting, and probably better if keenly followed up; but fish may fail altogether for a season or two, whereas the shoals of visitors always arrive at their usual time; and that is a consideration not to be overlooked by men who have families to house, feed, and clothe, and no reserves of money to stay them through the bad seasons. They can hardly be blamed for refusing to face the greater gamble, for adopting the safe, the middling course. And thus the fish have their revenge on fishermen – an insidious long-armed revenge; for boating seldom breeds the men that fishing does. Here, however, fishing is still kept up – by some men right into the frighting season – until the toil of fishing by night and boating by day compels them to leave off one or the other; and, if they possess several pleasure boats, it is the fishing has to go. We are proud of the fact that we have no boatmen on the beach; only fishermen who do boating. We do not tout for frights, or run after people along the Front, badgering them to go to sea, as they do in some towns that we could name. We wait to be hired, like barristers and physicians. Frighting is the fisherman's form of pot-boiling.
>
> It is, of course, a comparatively non-productive kind of labour. Money changes hands just as it does in fishing, but no wealth, in the shape of fish-food from the sea, is at the same time added to the resources of the country. (Yet only a shallow economy reckons as labour in vain the production of pleasure and health.) And it cannot be pretended that frighting is so independent and worthy a job as fishing. There are more misunderstandings over a week's frighting than over a whole season's fishing. At its best, even with those who may be called personal friends aboard, one has to a certain extent to do the flunkey. One holds one's tongue for no better reason than because one has to earn one's pay. My own first fright has amused me ever since. It was a young man from up-country, of the smart, cute, commercial sort; a decent enough fellow in his way, no doubt; but he didn't know how to treat a hired man. Therefore I sat on him severely, with my best brand of dignity, and before we came ashore the unfortunate young man was calling me *sir*. 'Good night, sir,' he said, handing over his couple of shillings.... But that sort of thing doesn't do. I've had to learn better since. In a boat, sometimes, a sudden gust of hilarity strikes me, on realising that, like those horrid

> children who no longer exist outside old people's recollections, I have to be seen and not heard, and wait to speak until I am spoken to. I burst out laughing at myself. The frights think I am grinning at them. And the fat's in the fire again.
> To do the flunkey really well is a work of art and artfulness, worthy of respect; for how else should authors, painters, and musicians be respected, who, except they ignore their public altogether, are brain-flunkeys. Indeed, we are all of us flunkeys in one fashion or another. Flunkeyism does not lie in the non-productiveness of the labour, or in service, or in menial attendance; there is no shame in acting lackey to those we love, because we love them. Flunkeyism is a suppression of personality for pay. It is a negation of living, a slap in the face of life – a slap we have most of us to give in order to live at all. It cannot come to an end till each man works for love of his labour and his fellowmen, and loves his neighbour as himself.[144]

In this final sentence, we have the first statement of the philosophy of work which Reynolds was just beginning to formulate and which would become the obsessive interest of his later years – the greatest regret of his writing life, the *magnum opus* that never quite managed to get itself written.

There is one further strand in *Alongshore* that merits one final quotation. Despite his vanity and pride and his at times cantankerous nature – or perhaps as a reflection of all these facets of character – Reynolds had all his life been on the side of the underdog, the waifs and strays of this world. He had written about them in some of his short stories; they appear on the fringes of *A Poor Man's House* in the shape of the Yarty family, close to destitution. He writes of them from the vantage point of an outsider himself from early youth.

Some writers who had had to struggle as much as he had would, on achieving major public recognition, have abandoned such themes, or rather those themes would have abandoned them. What is remarkable about Reynolds is that from this period of first fame these concerns become stronger and stronger. It is as if the new embrace of a public he half despised had brought him to feel more of an outsider than ever before. From 1909 onwards these vulnerable figures appear more regularly in his writing and in his life. Those who crossed his path, rejected by society and broken in spirit – tramps, the mentally ill, homosexuals, unmarried mothers – were always the first to receive attention, practical help and indeed love. It was the love he had found himself unable to give to those much closer to him.

In the sketch *Beautiful Onionhead* we have the first really powerful portrait of this type – a vagrant on the edge of destitution who helps out with odd jobs on the beach until the fishermen too reject him. Reynolds finds him on the beach one spring morning when all hope of human support has gone. In this portrait there is an empathy no successful, self-satisfied writer could ever have achieved.

> His existence thenceforward – unemployed, untrusted, unhelped – became the puzzle it is; yet he did not seem to live a life of misery. One sunny spring morning – the first in the year when the air was soft and the sea really sparkled – I found him lying on the beach, like a piece of old rain-soaked sacking with human limbs protruding from it, and passed the time of day with him. He looked up luxuriously. 'Beautiful morning, isn't it? Beautiful, very beautiful!' I am sure he meant it, and have wondered ever since how he could find it in him to do so. On another occasion I saw him putting up decorations, holly berries, and cotton-wool snowflakes in a public bar as merrily as if he had a home and Christmas of his own. He did it well, too, and tastefully; and shouted cheerily with a jolly oath or two. It was his presence there among the outward signs of Christmas that shocked one on his behalf.[145]

Self-identification with a vengeance! Just the mention of Christmas says it all.

Alongshore is in every sense a worthy successor to *A Poor Man's House*. It fully meets its objective of capturing the mood and feeling of onshore life. If anything, the writing is more even and secure than its predecessor; and like the earlier book it is bursting with life. What it lacks is perhaps the immediacy and freshness of the 1906 experience, and it is probably that, together with the lack of a clear narrative framework, that has left it sidelined by posterity.

The book, with its brilliant photographs, was an instant hit in Sidmouth. "They seem very well pleased with the book down here, though I hear one of the fishbuyers has fitted on the cap about fleecing fishermen, and wants to scalp me. From what I can hear, Tom and Bob, my partners, gave him a tremendous dressing down yesterday afternoon. The beggar won't blow his hooter when I'm about!"[146]

Reynolds was still revelling in the strange luxury of a publishing house which dispelled all anxiety and carried great weight in the market. He told Frederick Macmillan: "It seemed very curious to be down here, concerning oneself with the usual things, whether the boats were all right and so forth, and to hear in the distance, as it were, mainly through one's news-cuttings, the deep-toned buzz your house makes with a new book – that book being one's own". But he was still a little nervous of the public reaction. "No reviews yet.... I expect one or two of the people whose apple-carts I've upset, will have their fling against the book".[147]

He need not have worried. From the start it received rapturous reviews. Arnold Bennett in the *New Age* was at his most fulsome. "I am in no sort of doubt about this book. There is only one adjective for it – it is a ripping book. It is a book which has my enthusiasm and my almost unqualified regard. I read it with acute pleasure. Here you have youth, vitality, humaneness, courage, independence, insolence, a terrific zest for life: the whole disciplined by a really extraordinary sense of style. Only a born master could handle the English language with the freshness, the freedom, and the rich careless power that mark the best pages of this admirable work...... 'Alongshore' amply fulfils the promise of 'A Poor Man's House'. It is alive, and let there be no mistake about it! Read 'A Herring Haul in a French Steam Drifter', and learn what descriptive writing can be."[148]

Scott-James in the *Daily News* had the temerity to compare it with Conrad's *The Mirror of the Sea*. "Mr Reynolds has none of Mr Conrad's deep, full style; he has not that sort of imagination which can wring the last drop of effect out of facts or feelings. But he has this great advantage – he is writing in the very midst of still continuing experience; his book seems to come, as it were, salt and dripping from the breakers, and as we turn the page we seem to drip again. It is so fresh and zestful, not full of lingering, cherished memories, but bristling audaciously with the very facts which are happening and will happen again when his pen is put away."[149]

Strachey in the *Spectator*, whom Reynolds could now also count as a personal friend, thought that the picture was not so arresting and original as the earlier book because the revelation had been made before. But he noted perceptively that, despite the declared intention to make the sea the leading character in the book, in fact the people had taken over once more. "Although there is even more of the magic and mystery of the sea in this book than in *A Poor Man's House*, Mr Reynolds' great talent lies in the painting of human beings. The figures of the fishermen and longshoremen stand out vividly from his pages, and the reader, who has an uneasy consciousness that were he to visit Mr Reynolds's beach he would become merely a 'fright' – i.e., freight – feels that he will never again go sailing in a pleasure-boat without approaching the boatman in a most humbly conciliatory mood."[150]

For Edward Garnett in the *Nation* it was a book that met entirely his scrupulously high standard for a work of literature. In nostalgic mood from his own recent holiday in Sidmouth, he noted with relief the disappearance of the philosophising which had prevented *A Poor Man's House* from reaching the status of a work of art. Remembering the long battles with Reynolds of 1907, he at last felt vindicated.

> In "Alongshore" Mr Stephen Reynolds has written a very good book. Good books are rare: they come, not by planning, but by the propitious circumstance of favoring wind and weather. In "A Poor Man's House" Mr Reynolds described how he took possession of the promised land of "Undertown", the fishermen's quarters in Seacombe, and how life appeared when seen through the eyes of Uncle Jake, of Mam Widger, and the brothers Tony and John. It was an inspiring book, full of bracing seawind, but the author had not quite settled down to full enjoyment of the life, and it was part of his plan to debate the subject of class differences

> and show that middle-class generalisations on the poor are mostly wide of the mark. Now, we are suffered to forget the pretences to superior virtue of the rich and their exploitation of the poor man's necessities, and, artistically, it is a great gain that all argument should have faded out of the picture. We are face to face with the thing itself, which we see solely in relation to men's daily practice against the background of sea and sky. By a happy instinct, and perhaps a little by luck, the twenty-six sketches which compose the book blend as nicely as the flowers in a cottage-woman's posy, the sea-scapes and weather-pieces showing off the character-sketches and life-stories to admiration. It is so natural in style that the reader has the sensation of breathing in the shore atmosphere and of taking pot-luck along with the characters. The naturalness of the writing, of course, comes from an intimate enjoyment of the flavor of the original and a very keen eye for detail.[151]

Reynolds was delighted with the review, but even more by the covering letter with which Garnett sent him it. "I'd rather have your word that you enjoyed the book than the best critical judgements." He was grateful above all for the image of the cottage woman's posy. "It's funny, by the way, how few reviewers seem able to swallow the fact that *Alongshore* is *one* book, not a collection of papers, although it was miscellaneously serialized. With the exception of about a quarter of it, the book was sketched out as one whole before writing it. Naturally, therefore, it fits together pretty well."[152]

With an astute eye for the main chance, he had copies of the book sent to those who might be of political advantage to him in the future. John Burns, the one working-class Cabinet minister, received a small parcel of prawns. "Will you accept some prawns from my fishermen partners and myself – not many, it's true, but a little tribute, sent with good will? You were good enough to show an interest in my first book.... I asked Macmillans to send you a copy of the last one (on the same subject) the other day, and I hope you got it all right. Consider the prawns as a new sort of appendix!" There came a most friendly response. "Many thanks for the prawns. If the book which I am about to read has the same freshness and the quality of the prawns it will be as appetising."[153]

He sent both books to Colonel Balfour, the Lord of the Manor and ogre of the shingle battle two years before. Balfour was flattered by the gesture and asked him to sign them. They both reflected his own deep love of the town. Reynolds thought it politic to follow with a little more judicious sucking up. "Certainly, if you wish, I will put my name in the books with pleasure. I can well understand your being more than fond of Sidmouth. In a comparatively short time it has become so much a part of my life that I am, as it were, only half alive elsewhere. And I think, if I may say so, that we are all (though we don't all know it) greatly indebted to you for your efforts to preserve the distinctive individuality of the place."[154] When Balfour died in 1952 he left the books to the Sidmouth Museum where they lie today in mint condition in the one display case given over to Reynolds and his works.

In general Reynolds could not suppress his pleasure at so many good reviews but, a month after publication, was still worrying as to whether they would translate into sales. He wrote to Frederick Macmillan: "I hope you are satisfied with them. My own impression is that if the circulation would only come up to the review, the book would do. Still, I trust it is going pretty well. 'A Poor Man's House' didn't move at all till a couple of months after publication. I think, provided people are kept fairly well aware of it, that my stuff is more inclined to ooze into circulation, so to speak, than to bust forth!"[155]

Macmillan, in his usual relaxed manner, was relatively confident. Sensitive as ever, he took the hint about keeping the book in the public eye. "The sale of 'Alongshore' was rather disappointing at first but it began to pick up last week and now that some good reviews have appeared I hope it will go on all right. We are now going to do some special advertizing with extracts from the notices."[156]

Hugh Walpole, the latest friend, was another strong supporter of the book: "I like 'Alongshore' immensely and am reviewing it next week".[157] In his notice in the *Standard*, he emphasised the poetic quality of Reynolds' writing and looked forward to the novel which would make the best use of such material: "a great opportunity is before him to write about these people a series of novels that shall endure both as human documents and as literature; meanwhile one must regard this book as a gathering together of material, and extremely interesting material it is."[158]

It was a theme taken up by Conrad who had been looking for a novel from his protégé for some time. Reynolds wrote to him to apologise for Scott-James' presumption and lack of discrimination in comparing Reynolds to Conrad. Conrad in response was at his most bluff and dismissive: "The critics are mostly fools anyway. You write twenty times better than I ever did and to compare the work of a strong individuality like yours with that of any other man proves not so much lack of discrimination as poverty of ideas. However we must suffer fools – gladly if we can – but we must suffer them." On the book itself: "It's first rate! I expected a good deal but nothing quite so fine as that. There isn't a single page which doesn't toe the mark. It's a magnificent transcript of a very fine reality. I won't mention special passages – I'll leave that to, say, Scott James – because I accept and absorb the thing as a whole, with all the charm of its actuality and its insistent force like the sea on the beach."[159]

But, like Walpole, Conrad could see that the form of the book was a long way from the best use of such powerful material. What he feared most now was a succession of books that took the easy way out, stitching together a string of newspaper sketches. Reynolds' prose promised better than that.

> I am convinced that you know how to take care of yourself (I don't mean the mere mortal envelope) in every way. But onlookers are proverbially

> able to see more aspects of the game. And if we were talking now, under the very strong impression of your latest achievement, I would take up the position that I don't see how you can go further, do better – and even greater – in that direction. I would say: don't specialize (it's so easy!) – I don't mean in the subject but in the form. The great question for me now, when I look forward, is how you are to go further – do greater? Which is the way? I think the way is to be found by giving rein and spurring your imagination. At moments I am haunted by a lofty (but elusive I own) shape of a great seaboard novel by you with the whole of our civilisation, social and political for a background and with all your ideas and feelings presented to the populace, living, palpitating in a dramatic form. For that you'll have to invent – to come out of yourself in a measure. But all great men have been inventors.
>
> This suggestion'll appear to you crude – but any mere suggestion must be that. The first conception of every great enterprise is a raw thing to get hold of. It's about time for a great creative prose work to come out, a fine ringing imaginative utterance drowning the thin, petty babble of fiction. A great *island* novel, with all its life in the setting of the sea and the men nearest to the sea in the foreground – eh? – the foreground of a really inspiring tale. England, the predestined ground of such comedy-drama may yet produce it; and I can't honour you more, in my own eyes at least, than by confessing the thought that you might be the man.[160]

In a sense he was right. Reynolds, with his experience and his distinctive voice, *could* have been the man. But could he invent? Could he come out of himself in a measure? Did he have the imaginative strength and the will to force the issue? At the end of the letter, Conrad added "But these, I dare say, are mere reveries" – and, sadly, in a sense he was right again.

In December 1912 when Garnett was tinkering with the manuscript of *Sons and Lovers*, he sent D.H. Lawrence, relaxing with Frieda on the shores of Lake Garda, the first shock of their elopement behind them, a copy of *Alongshore*. As a born and bred member of the working class who had graduated into the literary middle class, Lawrence can be forgiven a small sneer at the sight of a fellow writer travelling ostentatiously in the opposite direction. And yet his instinctively perceptive assessment of Reynolds' strengths as a writer supply the perfect answer to Conrad's wishful dreams. Lawrence wrote to Garnett: "Thanks for the Stephen Reynolds. *Alongshore* is very interesting indeed. The only thing I find fault with in Reynolds is that he swanks his acquaintance with the Longshoremen so hugely. He writes 'de haut en bas' like any old salt talking to a clerk from London – except that he's the clerk himself, carefully got up as the salt. I like his strong intelligence best – better than his imagination – which runs to journalese."[161]

It is a painful admission, but one which Reynolds had made secretly to himself many moons before.

TWELVE

Seems So! 1909–11

The late Edwardian period, that slice of time so conveniently structured by historians to embrace the first four years of George V, was not the Indian summer of popular imagination – long dresses trailing the turf at Ascot, milk and honey on the lawns of Grantchester, delicate parasols shading the sun through one eternal garden party – the image crafted nostalgically in the shaky world of the 1930s by writers with especially selective memories. Real life was not like that, even for the upper classes. The certainties of pre-1914 England could not have been less certain.

The tectonic plates were shifting. Society was pressing up against its fault-lines, subconsciously praying for the war that would release the pent up flow of lava just beneath the surface. In 1912 forty-one million man days were lost in an incomparable wave of bitter industrial unrest, twenty to thirty times the average at the turn of the century. Two years earlier the Welsh miners strike had erupted in rioting and the troops were called out. The Conservative Party, in a constant rush of blood to the head, took action that went far beyond the accepted tenets of constitutional opposition – in the Lords challenging the right of a Government with a landslide majority to make financial provision; in Ireland attempting to suborn the Army to turn its guns on elected authority. Suffragettes broke windows in Oxford Street, chained themselves to the railings of Buckingham Palace and suffered the ignominies of forcible feeding. Violence was in the air and many feared that the old spectre of the nineteenth century, bloody revolution, was just around the corner.

1909, the year of the People's Budget and Lloyd George's violent invective against the House of Lords, found Joseph Conrad pondering the fate of the artist when the red revolution arrived: "After they have given everybody the 'right to work' and strung up all the horrid Lords to lanterns up and down Pall Mall, Piccadilly and all around Buckingham Palace, the writing of novels shall no doubt become (like maternity) a 'municipal function' with an eight hour day and a living wage; and then perhaps I shall be offered the chance along with the crowd of becoming a government employé – the worthy fate and the only refuge of all sorts of failures under the new dispensation which dawns over our heads."[1]

But Conrad was not a Socialist. Nor, as Katie Powys had perceptively observed, was Stephen Reynolds. He was highly political but a supporter of no political party. For him, the tragedy of political life was that none of the parties came close to reflecting the hopes and aspirations of the mass of the people. The Tories and the Liberals were both essentially aristocratic parties whose social conscience and concern over poverty were ill-informed and no more than skin deep. The ideals of the Socialists were more to the point but the political reality fell a long way short: "As a rule, there is no one so out of sympathy with working-class life as the man who has just climbed above it; there are certainly no such sharks in their dealings with working people. The devotion of the Labour Members to their own idea of working-class welfare, and the divorce of most of them from working-class feeling, is one of the most disheartening spectacles in modern politics."[2]

His own political education had begun in Devizes and at Bloxham, with his rejection of organised religion and middle class values, but the true finishing school was the little back kitchen in Sidmouth after 1906. Such was his identification with the life and feeling all around him that he quickly assumed from his working-class friends the stern streak of political agnosticism and the practical conservatism (with a small 'c') which, if at times it carried with it a whiff of nostalgia, nevertheless best met the needs of lives that were forever on the brink of potential disaster.

For beneath the social anxiety and upheaval of the years before 1914 lay a new and general awareness of two indisputable facts – that there existed an enormous gulf, both of circumstance and of interest, between the classes (aristocrats and middle class) and the masses; and that the mass poverty generated by an advanced industrial economy, now made transparent for the first time, could not be tolerated for very much longer. The work of Booth in London and Seebohm Rowntree in York had demonstrated that some 25 to 30 per cent of the urban population of the country were living in poverty and misery. Conservative elements in society had been shocked by the numbers of volunteers for service in the Boer War who had been rejected as unfit; malnutrition was putting the defence of Empire at risk. More radical elements, including some Liberals, were neither shocked nor surprised by such revelations, but felt unsure of the answer. Socialists of all persuasions thought they knew the answer but were unsure of the power to implement it.

A Poor Man's House and *The Holy Mountain* were both political works, the first more powerfully convincing than the second. In it, Reynolds had outlined the beginnings of a political philosophy for dealing with the problem of poverty – the provision of economic support which would sustain a reasonable standard of life and yet at the same time allow working-class society to develop in its own way, maintaining its natural vibrancy, without pressurising it into a clone of the middle class.

He had been constrained by the structure of the book, and his artistic battles with Garnett, to play down the political philosophising more than he might have wished. Now, as a follow-up to its success, he determined to develop his deeply held ideas about working-class needs within a more transparent and positive framework. He wanted to make a clear political statement but in a format as appealing and readable as *A Poor Man's House*.

One eminent Conservative editor had been moved by the book and found himself, though approaching from a different angle, much in sympathy with its political views. St Loe Strachey, the younger son of a landed Somerset family with a long history, had come to the editorship of the *Spectator*, rather like Spender to the *Westminster*, somewhat by chance and at a surprisingly young age. By acute political writing he had won his way in the 1890s to the assistant editorship, under the protective eye of Townsend and Hutton who had run the paper for a generation. When Hutton died in 1897, Strachey became overnight proprietor and editor, though still only in his mid 30s.

He was an able journalist and sensitive prose writer with a stern moral probity, who had done much to restore the reputation of the *Spectator* by his emphasis on political and social issues. It was, of course, unloved of those on the left – Strachey launched a blistering attack on Wells and *Ann Veronica* in 1910 – but had nevertheless a reputation for straight talking and straight dealing. Even an old cynic like Conrad could admit to falling a little bit under its spell.

It was the publication of *A Poor Man's House* that brought Reynolds into direct contact with Strachey for the first time. The *Spectator* reviewed the book with a splash in the middle of November 1908 and, among a number of compliments, spoke of it as "a study remarkable for its sympathy and poetry as well as its minute observation."[3] Reynolds and Strachey discussed how the political and social themes of the book could be developed further and the latter suggested the young author might tackle a detailed account of working class views on various topical political themes. The two first that came to mind were military conscription, in which Strachey took a special interest, and the women's suffrage movement.

Towards the end of December, Reynolds sent Strachey two sample manuscripts, to give him some feel for his occasional writing while he himself got on with the first of the political articles they had discussed – one on the suffragettes. Immediately, he hit problems with the new article: "I have been working a week at that without getting it to my mind."[4] He was in the usual predicament when starting a new area of writing – knowing what he wanted to say without being quite sure how to say it. He was searching for a format which would give authority to working-class opinions, while avoiding the criticism that they were merely the regurgitation of his own personal views. "How to strike the right tone and attitude with the political articles, how far to write them off my own bat, so to speak, has curdled my brains, but I think I'm getting there. At all events they are going to be a much harder, longer piece of work than I anticipated. The difficulty is how to hit on a form not anti-climax to the book; a form capable of being kept up and at the same time capable of dealing with a variety of questions, on some of which the 'poor man's' point of view includes no details whatever, but only a general atmospheric opinion, as it were; a form self-explanatory too. However, it's for me to worry the thing out, and when I have I will submit the result."[5]

Strachey promised to take the sample manuscripts down to Somerset to read over the Christmas break, but sounded a note of caution against too high expectations of them: "I am sure I shall be very much interested even if I should not think the papers, for one reason or another, suitable to the 'Spectator'".[6]

Reynolds was up in London for the first week of 1909 (the week of his resignation from the *English Review*) and delivered the suffragette article into Strachey's hands. After some discussion, he agreed to restructure it a little and Strachey was pleased to take it in the revised form for the sum of £4, a little more than his standard payment.[7] He was far from happy, however, with the next article on conscription which Reynolds sent him in mid January: "To speak frankly I am rather disappointed in the Compulsory Military Service paper. It is much more of a leading article than the kind of thing I wanted".[8] Just as significant, however, its strong opposition to conscription did not fit in with Strachey's deeply held views on the subject. Although he could not agree to take it, he very generously sent the author a cheque for three pounds for having commissioned it, which Reynolds with equal gratitude and courtesy felt bound to return.[9] Reynolds soon found a home for the conscription article with Massingham at the *Nation*, with whom he was now on better terms, and it was published there in the middle of February, the first of the *Seems So!* articles to achieve print.[10]

The first to be written, the suffrage article, was published in the *Spectator* a week later on 20 February. In the opening paragraph, Reynolds introduces his public to the concept of "Seems so".

> In London the suffragettes have held up public business. Here, in a working man's household a hundred and fifty miles from town, their agitation scarcely stirs us. We are lookers-on; and whether or no we see most of the game, we are not, like the players, under an obligation to take sides. We do not imagine that we know the facts of the woman suffrage question, or of any other political question, either completely or accurately. Who does? All we can say is, 'Seems so to us.' But according to that 'Seems so' we shall vote, though for which party at the next election we haven't the slightest idea...... [11]

Much later, in his introduction to the book of collected articles, he was to explain it more fully.

> Devonshire-men are great at phrase-making: they possess for the purpose, and still use, a splendidly flexible, humorous dialect, only the bare bones of which can be got into writing. When they wish to make a statement which they are ready to grant is after all a matter of opinion or point of view, they first of all make the statement as emphatically as possible, and then admit the possibility of doubt by adding *Seems so!* or

> *Looks so!* Somewhat in the same way a public speaker *ventures to think* his convictions. And hence the title of this book. We have aimed at expressing a point of view – the working-man's. Especially have we tried to express the working-man's *feeling* about things, because we recognize, as Herbert Spencer pointed out so long ago, that it is a man's feelings rather than his opinions, his emotions rather than his intellectual ideas, which make him what he is, and ultimately govern his actions...... [12]

The articles were notionally written jointly by Reynolds and Bob and Tom Woolley, though the early ones were a straight collaboration with Bob alone. In the suffrage article he had found the format that would serve him throughout the series – discussion paragraphs in the collective "we", interspersed with dialogue primarily featuring Bob in his new guise as Dave Perring, joined later by Tom as his brother, Ted. In *The Suffragettes* appropriately enough it is Mrs Perring (Mam Woolley) who has the most say; and as in most of the "Seems So"s the feelings are essentially ones of class division. Suffragettes are seen primarily as upper and middle class women with too much time on their hands.

> Mrs. Perring does not wish for a vote, and she does not believe that most working women do. She says she has no time to waste on politics, as men have. In England there is a vast number of women who, needing neither to struggle nor to work, never come to handgrips with life, and never can learn what a working woman has to contend with; and Mrs. Perring resents any system under which the women who are fully occupied with living would have to depend politically on the busybodies who do not know what life really is. 'I should have to follow the lead', she says, 'of the Miss Penley-Joneses, what puts on us enough as 'tis. Her's got time 'cause her an't never learnt to look after nothing – that I do know – while me that has had to learn experience, I an't got time to be troubled wi' it, an' never shan't have. I reckon they suffragettes wants half-a-dozen kids like this yer squad o' mine. That'd steady 'em.'[13]

It is much the same critique of the women's suffrage movement as Sylvia Pankhurst was later to develop in her organisation of the working women of the East End of London; and was no doubt a typical view of working women elsewhere.

In historical perspective, we now clearly see that the suffrage movement reflected not so much the repression of women as their growing social and economic freedom in an age which had seen more middle-class women than ever before – teachers, secretaries, clerks – flooding onto the labour market. As with all revolutions, it was the loosening of the chains that created the momentum. In this context, the vote was only a symbol of a more general frustration which, except among a minority of socialist suffragettes, had not yet resolved itself into a precise programme of political action. Which is why a desire for the vote was incomprehensible to many working men as end in itself. Here, through the mouth of Dave Perring, Reynolds neatly encapsulates this incredulity and adds to it another chauvinist strand which still survives today as one attitude to feminism – that their real problem was not the vote, but sexual frustration.

> Dave Perring wished to know their aim. On learning that they claim votes, first, because they pay rates and taxes, and secondly, because they say they will do a lot of good when they get them, he was much surprised. 'They'm not kicking up all thic buzz for that?'
> 'They say they are.'
> 'What do 'em propose to do 'xactly?'
> 'That they don't say.'
> 'Then if they don' know what they want, what do 'em want it for?
> I tell thee what, 'tis sweethearts they wants. There's nort like it for a girl as is kicking up a buzz. I've a-proved it.'[14]

This was not the kind of cocksure remark likely to endear either Reynolds or Bob to the local adherents of the women's movement, as they were soon to find out.

The only positive thing to be said in favour of the movement was its entertainment value.

> As for the suffragettes' pranks and bad behaviour, we do not approve, but we thank them for the sport provided. We are glad to see Governments that harass us with school inspectors, medical officers, policemen, so-called temperance reforms, and such-like, harassed in their turn.[15]

But the reaction of Government was another prime example of class inequality.

> To our mind, the most shameful thing about the suffragettes' agitation is their special treatment in prison. If Mrs. Perring, who objects, both maternally and on principle, against having her children hit by anybody else, especially by schoolmasters, were to go and brawl in the town schools on that account, she would probably be sent to prison in the ordinary way, and would feel the separation from her husband and household, and from the children whose welfare prompted her to brawl, at least as much as the 'cultured lady' suffragettes feel their separation from the friends and books that egged them on. There has always been, in practice, one law for the rich and another for the poor; and now apparently there is a third for ladies who assert loudly enough that their bad behaviour was due to good intentions.[16]

For middle class readers, of both left and right, the *Nation* and the *Spectator*, this was a new and intriguing way of looking at the world and its day to day controversies. It was a new voice – albeit purporting to represent the vast majority of voices – couched in a simple and convincing prose.

In this first article, Reynolds makes a short compelling statement of the underlying attitude that was to run through the whole series – the essential conservatism of working class feeling, bred of insecurity.

> We do not see any very grave reason why the suffragettes should not have the vote, except their tendency to revert to the methods of the hustings. Still less can we see why they should. And we certainly do not think that a sweeping alteration in the government of the country ought to be made without very grave reason indeed. England is not precisely a pleasant place to live in for those who have no money and no property, and changes seem mainly for the worse in that respect; but we do know at present what we have to contend with, and, mistrusting small changes much, we mistrust great changes more. People whose weekly income barely feeds and houses them cannot afford to experiment in changes.[17]

And he touches on another pervasive theme, still as much alive today – basic mistrust of politicians, and a sense of disenfranchisement equally as strong as that of the protesting women.

> We are well assured that any party we help to put in power will work for its own ends, not ours, until it wants us to help it into power a second time. If we had a suffragette Cabinet or a suffragette House of Lords, we should expect nothing of them except an attempt to make us act as they think proper, instead of their acting as we think proper. No doubt women will get the vote some day, when it is to the tactical advantage of one or other of the great parties to give it to them.[18]

And he ends by dismissing this minor political issue with a nicely pointed fishy metaphor.

> But the herrings have come into the bay, and herrings here are more important than suffragettes; and when the herrings come into the political bay, they will, we fancy, be found more important there too.[19]

This *Spectator* article was widely read and, to Reynolds' undisguised delight, caused no end of fluttering in the feminist dovecotes. Three days after publication, he wrote to Strachey: "A suffragette attacked us on the beach this morning. We went on mending our nets. 'What we women want to do,' she said 'is to make things better for you men.' 'Might du it now pretty often,' said Bob. Collapse of the suffragette!"[20] Life was imitating art with unnerving accuracy. Two weeks later, the reaction was still as bitter and Reynolds extended a protective arm towards his editor in London: "Suffragettes here, and apparently elsewhere, very angry with us. Trust they haven't torn you in pieces."[21]

Given Strachey's liberal brand of paternalistic Conservatism, this partnership with the mouthpiece of working-class opinion was not so unlikely as it might at first have seemed. Though there were some articles, like that on conscription, that were by implication too left-wing for the columns of the *Spectator*, Reynolds could always find a home for them in the *Nation* or *New Age*, and he firmly trusted Strachey's general support for his critique of public attitudes to working-class life and opinion.

With the publication in February 1909 of the long-awaited report of the Royal Commission on the Poor Law, he found a new but equally controversial theme. Predictably, the Woolley household turned its guns most heavily on the Webbs' Minority Report. "We have been studying the accounts of the Poor Law Commission's Report pretty carefully, and should rather like to do a 'Seems So' on that. I do not think that, effectively, our view is very different from the 'Spectator's'; that is to say, we like most of the critical part, but rather mistrust some of the constructive measures, particularly the vision of the Minority Report which seems to see everybody fitted into a cast-iron industrial machine, for the benefit of whom exactly is not plain; and we don't like the creation of more inspectors whose judgements on the poor must necessarily be crude – cruder probably than the judgement of events and the struggle to live."[22]

They read and discussed the issues for a fortnight and then, on 5 March, Reynolds settled down to a couple of days concerted writing. He was extremely slow at composition and worked best in concerted bursts; but these always took their toll. He sent the finished Poor Law article off to Strachey on 7 March with an apology: "Please excuse typewriting. With the exception of an hour or two for sleep, I've been slogging at the article continuously for about 40 hours, so that I simply can't tackle that hateful machine. Bad journalism, isn't it, not to be able to say what one wants quicker than that?"[23]

Such massive effort for little more than 1600 words was fully explained when the article came out in early May; the largest part was written in consecutive dialogue, and in the most difficult of formats – the Devon dialect. Initially we catch a glimpse of how these articles had now come to dominate the life of the Woolley household, which approved wholeheartedly of the report's historical analysis.

> In this house we have one of the summaries which have been issued in pamphlet form, together with the reports of *The Times* and of one or two other newspapers. We have read these and discussed them over meals until the children, with that superb indifference which they learn at school, stared and thought us mazed. Though we can only say, 'Seems so to us from those reports,' we have at any rate seen enough to make us admire the keen and careful spirit of the Commissioners; enough to make us glory in their straight talk about workhouses and relief; enough

> to make us hate many of their proposals, because of the one detestable thing on which their working depends.[24]

Which was, of course, the philosophy of means-testing and the proliferation of even larger numbers of prying inspectors. The Minority Report comes under particular attack for its radical creation of ever-expanding bureaucracies, in an attempt not just to cure the immediate problems but to tackle the disease at root, turning lives upside down in the process.

> 'They propose even, when they relieve anybody, to inquire into his family's circumstances and make *them* contribute....'
> 'An' a pretty parcel o' lies they'll get, an' well they'll deserve it too! How'd 'em like their own families 'spected? You'd think the likes o' us was consignments o' rotten fish.[25]

At the close of this short sketch, Reynolds enters an eloquent plea for social support in an atmosphere of *laissez-faire*, the consistent theme of all his political articles.

> In many details the Commissioners' proposals are more kindly and thoughtful than any that have been made before; but to what end, since the general schemes of both majority and minority are dependent on inspection for their proper working? No sooner does the Commission come to handgrips with poverty itself than out pops an inspector, like a Jack-in-the-box. And not only that; voluntary charity is to be thoroughly reorganized and put on an inquisitorial basis. In the sweat of thy brow, and under the eyes of inspectors, shalt thou eat thy bread! Must no one give without being certain of his money's-worth? Can no one receive without being demoralized? Inspection means the judgment of one class by the standards of another; the teaching of people how to live under circumstances of which the teachers have had no personal experience. If carried through, it means also the forcing of the ideals of one class upon another class, and nothing is so demoralizing as that...... We are not sure – who can be? – and we are far from wishing to cast slurs on the proposals of a Commission which has criticized and spoken with such courage; but our impression is that the twin-sisters who love us so – Destitution and Disease – will in the long run weed out the fit from the unfit, the deserving from the undeserving, the hopeless from the hopeful, more fairly, and more mercifully too, than a blight of inspectors let loose upon the land.
> 'Let 'em gie us our chance,' says Dave, 'an' leave us to fight it out for ourselves.' Give us a fair chance, he means, of floating or sinking; stop pushing us under; and let us go forward on our own lines, in our own time. Mankind in the mass moves very slowly, and cannot be hustled

> with impunity. Sociology and efficiency are right enough in their places, but for actual dealing with human beings, patience and charity are still of more avail; patience, always patience, though it is hard to be patient when poor creatures are brought, or bring themselves, to starvation; and charity that suffereth long and is kind, because it knows that in the end no man's judgment of another is worth much. How can it be?[26]

The concentrated effort of the Poor Law article made him think for the first time of writing a whole series and turning it into a book. Next day he told Pinker: "Have had a tremendous doing with a Poor Law article for the *Spectator*, by the both of us. I should like to be able to do enough of these articles to collect 'em under *both* our names. The Ol' Man would be so proud, and he really does collaborate except in the actual writing down."[27]

On 14 March 1909, the day, as we have seen, on which Reynolds decided to write *Alongshore*, he proposed to Strachey the idea of turning the political articles into a book too. At the front of his mind was the effect it would have upon Bob, still the most important person in his life. "I should like in the course of time to be able to do enough Seems So's to publish as a book, not only because I should be enormously proud of having his name with mine on the title-page, but because I believe it would be the first instance of a practically illiterate man, unrisen in life and not become literary, unfuddled by education and controversy, taking his knowledge entirely from tradition and experience, expressing himself directly and authentically on these matters. The unusualness of it might induce a few besides you to listen."[28]

Strachey responded warmly. "You are quite right to want to make the series into a book and I think it will prove a very brilliant one. My advice to you is to go on writing them on any subject that interests you, quite independent of me or anybody else. Submit any you like to me and if I can find room for them and like them I will take them. If not, not. When you have enough written publish them as a book. If half of them have never appeared before it will be all the better...... I am most interested to know that the views are so distinctly those of Bob. I rather imagined that it was a combine of all sorts of opinions that you had heard expressed. When the book comes out you had better in the preface make it clear that you are simply the conduit pipe through which Bob's views are poured. You had better have a picture of him in the frontispiece to show that he is a real man."[29] Thus was born the idea for the elegant photograph by Melville Mackay, "Arguing the Point", which fronts the book – a three cornered discussion with Bob and Tom in the boat and Reynolds standing on the beach looking up to them.

Strachey's blessing on the enterprise was greeted with joy down in Bedford Square. Collaborating with someone he loved gave a new dimension and a new enthusiasm to writing for Reynolds. He told Pinker: "Strachey has written a most decent letter advising us to write enough 'Seem So's' for a book, which he thinks 'will prove a very brilliant one'. Ol' Man hardly knows what to make o' it. He's always been told all his life: 'Hould thy bloody row!'"[30] To Garnett he emphasised the intention to *épater les bourgeois*. "That'll be a splendid yap from the top of the middle-class citadel, and my second success, which I shall be all the prouder of for sharing with the Ol' Man."[31]

The Poor Law article had been intended to cover the Commission's proposals on education, but in the event there had been neither time nor space. So this was to be the next in the series – a full-blown attack on the inappropriateness of elementary education for working-class children. "We should like to do a 'Seems So' on education, which we hold already ends too late (apart from its inanity), though we should like to see every boy who wants to learn more than the three R's have the chance of going to a good part-time continuation school. Bob says, very beautifully, I think, ' I reckon you learns manlihood and womanlihood after you leaves school and has to fend for yourself. If you got to live your life wi' your nose to the grindstone, as most of the likes o' us has, the sooner you learns to put it there the better. You never won't if you don't start early.' The Commission, I see, assigns a great part of unemployment to education and longer schooling for boys – with a changed curriculum! Changed spirit of the whole thing! They may reform the guardians, but they'll have their work cut out to reform the educationalists. I've done some teaching in my time, and I've watched its effect, its atmosphere, pretty closely here."[32]

With the writing of this, the fourth article, the technique of composition had settled down to a more or less ordered routine. "We are more than a little amused at ourselves. First, now there are a lot of people here, we go out to beach, and row people out for cash and tips (I get more tips than Bob and can't make out why), and then we come in house to discuss an article for the *Spectator*! One feels like traitors in their country and that they are impertinences in ours. Anyhow its muddling things with a vengeance."[33]

The education article was submitted on 10 April: "Though you probably won't go all the way with us, I think you'll like it".[34] It was a trenchant piece, and Strachey could see in his mind's eye the possibility of furious, and perhaps unwelcome, controversy. For a time he hedged his bets. "I cannot quite decide whether the education article will suit me or not but at any rate I will have it put in type for I can judge much better when I see it in print."[35] There was to be three months' more of judicious havering before he eventually took the plunge and published at the end of July.[36] Surprisingly, reaction was fairly muted, except among the educational press. But in the long run it was to prove the most controversial of all the articles once the book was published.

Reynolds' next target was to be the Children Act and the so-called Children's Charter with its petty (as perceived by the Woolley household) prohibitions on keeping children out of pubs and tobacconists, and its supervision of parents for neglect of children. "I want to have a go at this astonishingly sentimentally over-rated Children's Charter. I am fond enough of children; can't go up town without half a dozen racing after me, and I can get the baby to feed when no one else can; but this Children's Charter – what an infernal insult to a class of people who on the whole, in spite of bad cases, treat their children as well as any other class, and have to make much greater sacrifices to feed and boot a family".[37]

But the chance for another onslaught on the "blight of inspectors" had rather gone to his head and he began to contemplate quite seriously turning this preoccupation into a new artistic endeavour. "I am thinking of writing – trying to write – a political comedy 'The Working Man's House/Under Social Reform', showing the house invaded by inspectors and grandmama laws, and all other peace- and morale-destroying devices that are in fashion; it could be made very laughable; but I can't find a collaborator with a knowledge of stage-craft who detests the stuff called Social Reform as much as we, the victims, do."[38]

With Pinker he was even more specific. "What do you say to a comedy, 'The Working Man's House Under Social Reform', showing the house harassed by legislation and inspectors (Act I) – row of children outside a public house in the rain because they can't go in and small boy puffing cigarettes out of a window at a policeman (Act II) – and the house again with young people succeeding in getting married in spite of troubles and impediments arising out of Social Reform (sentiment thickish) (Act III). Old lodger who has seen better days and a curate or social reforming suffragette for chorus on opposite sides. Whole thing at once savage and funny. Producible, election time."[39] It never got beyond this rudimentary skeleton plan, for which we may perhaps be granted a collective sigh of relief.

The Children's Charter article went in on 8 May but Strachey had even more doubts about it than the education one, and eventually decided not to publish.[40] The decision, which led to a sudden drying up of Seems So articles, may have had something to do with a little public spat that Strachey had had with Reynolds over the perennially ill-fated *Holy Mountain*.

Back in April, when sending in the education article, Reynolds had taken pains to assure Strachey that the remarks on religious education were in no way irreverent, and had underlined the point with a reference to the *Mountain*: "In the same way, I think you will see that my satire on religious hocus-pocus in *The Holy Mountain* that is running in the "English Review", though apparently flippant, has underneath it a very serious view of what religion might be made; that is, if you should happen to chance across the thing."[41]

Strachey did not in fact run the serialised *Mountain* to ground until the following month, when he decided, quite out of the blue, to give it a hostile review. He may have been genuinely appalled by its content, but he was also a strong opponent of the editorial policy of the *English Review*, which he regarded as licence, and that may have swayed his decision. But whatever the reason, he did not spare his young protégé.

> The *English Review* contains a portion of a novel by Mr. Stephen Reynolds which, to recall Mr. Galsworthy's image, he would no doubt claim to be

a lantern. However, it throws anything but an undistorting ray, since its preposterous theme is meaningless except for its profanity. A youthful degenerate, son of a shopkeeper, by faith moves a hill from Wiltshire to London. The affair is seized upon by the proprietor of the *Halfpenny Press* and exploited financially. The youth is keenly interested in making money out of his miracle; he also ruins a girl in his father's employment, and then takes up with another. This all goes on to a sordid accompaniment of alcoholic Mayors and Aldermen. We are, as our readers know, sincere admirers of Mr. Reynolds's book, *A Poor Man's House*, and gladly recognise the power of his style, the vividness of his descriptions, and the skill and sound sense of much of his social diagnosis. That he can if he likes do good and useful work makes us regret very deeply the spirit of this new venture.[42]

Reynolds would not normally have responded to an expression of opinion on his work, however damning, and particularly not to that of an influential editor currently giving him free run of his columns. But this was a grossly inaccurate account of the plot of his novel, and he felt he owed it to his characters, if no one else, to set the record straight. He sent in to Strachey a detailed rebuttal for publication, but pretended it was just a matter of form. "Enclosed is a formal letter to you Spectatorially. Please print it or not as you like; 'tisn't a serious matter in question. The underlying intention of the book – not a bad one, I think – is too obscure; the superficial expression free enough. If I wrote it again, I'd expose the one more and prune the other a bit; but the thing has been written three times throughout already, and I can't for the life of me tackle it again."[43]

Strachey felt obliged to take up the rebuttal which was published the following week.

I do not want to contest your criticism any more than I want to contest those of your remarks which were kindly in the extreme; and I readily admit that the book's satire on profanity has sometimes itself the appearance of profanity. But may I point out that there were in one sentence of your notice three errors of fact? (1) So far from being keenly interested in making money out of his miracle, the hero only wants enough to get married on. (2) He does not ruin a girl in his father's employment; he is only suspected of doing so. (3) He does not then take up with another; he is absolutely faithful to his Julia the whole way through. That, I had hoped, was sufficiently plain, and you will, I am sure, want to correct your errors of fact, whether or no such correction causes you to modify your opinion.[44]

Most sensible editors would have left it there, but Strachey was far from sensible when it came to issues of morality, as his later crusade against the *Review* was to show. He did not like being accused quite so baldly of "errors of fact"; so he now added a footnote to Reynolds letter in waspish tones rebutting the rebuttal. It was a ludicrous descent into a wrangle over the *minutiae* of the plot of an obscure novel not yet published.

> The author, of course, understands the unexpressed working of the minds of his characters better than does the reader. With regard to error (1), the young man's desire for money is described without the qualifying reason now given. (2) Three people, Julia, the Magistrate's clerk, and the old nurse, all announce their belief that Alec is the father of the child, and no contrary view is expressed by anyone. The nurse tells the young man of this conviction, and is not contradicted by him; while Julia informs his father. (3) Of course, if Alec is guiltless, there is no reason why he should not be engaged to Julia. The possibility of a mistake is not hinted at by the author.[45]

Reynolds was used to having the last word himself, and cannot have been entertained by this riposte. A frost settled over his relationship with the editor of the *Spectator*. Their correspondence abruptly broke off, as did the regular stream of Seem Sos. But he had taken care to leave the door ajar just a little. "Anyhow, we hope that whatever opinion you may ultimately form of that book won't make you throw us over, because we've got a heap more to say somewhere or other on other subjects, and we aren't in much doubt about the few places we prefer."[46]

There were to be no further Seems So articles for another ten months. Throughout that summer from June to September Reynolds was heavily engaged with the weekly *Longshore Sketches* for Spender, and when they ground to a halt in the autumn he took up the commission for a new and lengthy political article for a periodical even more prestigious than the *Spectator*.

Throughout the spring of 1909 he had been pursuing G.W. Prothero, the editor of the highly respected *Quarterly Review*, to take a definitive article on the poor, and the associated literature on the subject, as a timely follow-up to *A Poor Man's House*, developing at greater length the philosophical views only touched on in the book. Finally in early May he caught up with him and the commission was agreed, with publication set for the October or January edition.[47] As he told Strachey, he saw the planned article as an extension of, or rather commentary on, the *Seems So!* series. "The editor of the 'Quarterly Review' has asked me to see him with a view to contributing; so the long article I was speaking to you about, in which I want to explain the standpoint of these shorter articles, and correlate them into something like a system, may very likely go in there. That's good; and I have very largely to thank the 'Spectator' and you for it; and do. It has surprised me from how many directions I have heard about the 'Seems So's'".[48]

He asked John Lane to send Prothero a copy of *A Poor Man's House* as a taster. He must have been one of the few editors in London who had not already read it. "He has just commissioned me to do an article for the 'Quarterly' and wants to read my book. I'm rather pleased over getting in there, especially as editor people seem rather to be fighting shy of my short stories."[49]

He asked Garnett whether he knew of any books dealing with the poor from the inside other than the obvious recent ones by Mary Loane, Lady Bell, George Bourne and W.H. Davies. "Prothero has asked me to do an article for the *Quarterly* on that sort of book, and I want to make it as complete as can be. I've hopes that when I've set forth the basis of it, some of you people won't disapprove of our attitude towards 'social reform' quite as tilt-nosedly." For a young writer, an invitation from the *Quarterly* was a distinct mark of having "arrived", and he could not, in writing to his old friend, hold back from a note of teasing delight: "Rather fine, getting into the *Quarterly*, isn't it? Shall be able to become an old fogie in double quick time."[50]

Certainly Reynolds' political attitudes had been developing fast enough in recent months, and in a direction that was bound to incline Garnett and his Fabian friends to tilt their noses. In 1907, in the middle of writing *A Poor Man's House*, he had still been relatively open about Socialism and willing to explore further. In August that year he had written to Garnett: "I've been reading very carefully the Fabian book of essays, and, d'you know? I don't feel at all certain that, things being as they are, socialism doesn't open a rapider path to the individualism I stick to as an ideal, than does the *political* individualism. If they'd only avoid grandmotherly legislation, and Mrs Besant wouldn't talk rot about an 8 hours day on farms with cows to be milked at 12 hrs' intervals and crops to be got in in a hurry.... Indeed, I almost, if not quite, think at present, that Fabianism offers the shortest cut to individualism, mental at any rate, if not material. For it doesn't seem to be so anti-individualistic as its only practical opponent, conservatism plus capitalism. Want to discuss the matter with you."[51]

In *A Poor Man's House* itself he had concentrated on a positive portrayal of the virtues of working-class life, which he had characterised as "the courage to live". The criticism of middle-class intellectuals and their programme of social reform with its restraining effect on that natural resilience was present in the book, but in a relatively muted form. In the early months of 1909, the writing of the first Seems So articles and the long discussions with Bob had led to a shift of emphasis. Now all his political weight was thrown against the middle-class proponents of social reform, and as genuine emotion worked itself up within him, fuelled by his own personal experience of poverty and his literary disappointments, so did the tone become increasingly more strident and querulous.

The change of tone becomes apparent in a letter he wrote to Strachey in March 1909 in which he starts to formulate the distinction between economic and social reform which was to become a major plank in his political thought in the coming years. "'Social reform', the vote-catching thing it is, is the last and most dangerous of the cants, if only because it has collared so many generous minds, let alone on account of its insidiousness and tendency to shut up everything bad in whited sepulchres...... I would try to right all of what I call economic disabilities, inequality of chance, character, and so forth being equal; but this social reform stuff, it penalises the poor by taking away from them the strength they have and forcing upon them useless imitations of middle-class virtues in return; by making them collectively a huge hypocrite. It is what I mean by saying that economically I'm socialistic, and socially I'm high Tory. That's not it, but near enough."[52]

Political and social progress was for Reynolds a spiritual process, not a mechanical, materialistic one. "A little history, a little science less out of date than the *Encyclopaedia Britannica*, a glance at your little book *The Wisdom of the Bible* should show them how all progress works outwards from the mind.... But they won't. It makes me passionately savage...... "[53]

It was this hostility to the socialist programme that was slowly to erode the relationship with Garnett, who took his politics very personally and very seriously, and felt Reynolds' approach to be both reactionary and grossly distorted. Reynolds, for his part equally serious about politics, could nevertheless unbend when it came to political discussion with his friends. His response to Garnett's criticism was always relaxed. "No doubt my views – our views – on social reform appear to you one-sided; no doubt they are; and yours too; but I can only say what I think, and out of the clash something good may come, for most good things come out of clashes. I'm going to play on, on my Tory-Democratic lines. It isn't a paradox to say that it is from a democratic point of view that we attack social reform (not economic reform, so far as they can be differentiated) and, from our point of view, it's only an accident that for the moment we chime in rather with the Conservatives. It is because I hope to justify my attitude there, that I am so pleased about the *Quarterly*."[54]

He did not get down to the *Quarterly* article, originally entitled *The Poor as Human Beings* but finally *What the Poor Want*, until September when he was hoping to finish it in time to use as a lecture at Cambridge at the end of October.[55] He had received from Prothero as background material a number of books about the poor and had started reading Sturt's (George Bourne's) Bettesworth books consecutively for the first time. They had given him a new assurance with which to confront the common criticism that *A Poor Man's House* had tackled an unrepresentative slice of working-class life. "It has very much pleased me in reading the books you sent down (Bourne's Bettesworth books are wonderful), to find that so much of what I've said of 'the poor' I know is said, sometimes in almost the same words but in different dialects, by other writers of those they know. One of the criticisms levelled against me was that I didn't know enough poor in sufficiently separate parts of the country. But 'tis apparently the intimacy with which one knows some typical 'poor' that really matters."[56]

The final text of the article was finished by November and Prothero pronounced himself extremely pleased.[57] It was published in January 1910.[58] It is not, perhaps, the most distinguished of Reynolds' political writings from this period, principally because at Prothero's behest it was to be a review of the literature of poverty rather than a free-wheeling development of the pure idiosyncratic Reynolds line. That said, readers were left in no doubt of the author's views right from the first page.

> Social reform has come very largely to mean reform of those inarticulate classes. They are different in their habits and customs; therefore it seems they are probably wrong. Materially they are unsuccessful, else they would have risen in life; and therefore they must be wrong; or at least, in an age which judges success in living by material prosperity, they are fit objects of pity. On that basis the public interest in them has grown apace.[59]

And there is the typical odd barb thrown out to the middle classes – here when Reynolds recounts his own experience of moving between the poor and the well-heeled.

> In moving from the one *milieu* to the other and back again, the change one specially notes is of tradition and atmosphere; almost the only readjustment that has to be made in oneself, is mental. (Not that one's wits have to be polished up on entering the society of educated people; mentally their pace always strikes me as rather slow and restful; they have invented so many certainties to repose upon, and in their conversation the great disturbing problems of human existence are tacitly ruled out.)[60]

We have as well some powerful images to underline his distinctions – here on the difference between the majority and minority reports of the Poor Law Commission.

> Both Majority and Minority treat the poor too much as inferiors. The Majority's proposed poor law reminds me of a home for children where, though there is sometimes scarcely enough to eat, a lump or two of sugar can usually be sneaked for the stomach's delight; whereas that of the Minority reminds me oftener of a barrack where there is always a sufficiency of plain, nourishing food, not over tasty, but never a lump of sugar can be stolen because everything is under lock and key, and is weighed out. The essential difference between these two homes would be in the attitude towards the children, not in the management of the sugar-bags. The Minority's proposals, admirable though some of them are, and highly systematized, waken in me the same sort of horror as a huge piece of machinery which, should one have the misfortune to tumble into it, will go on grinding and will crush one's vitals out.[61]

There is also the best description to date of the mode of working class perception and reasoning, a development of the ideas in *A Poor Man's House* highly influenced by Reynolds' growing attachment to Bergson and the philosophy of intuition.

> The poor are not logical; they neither make any great use of, nor are at home in, logical processes of thought; but in compensation they have an astonishing faculty of allowing for that penumbra of hazy or apparently unrelated facts, thoughts, and minor impressions which, in life and in the human consciousness, always surrounds and modifies every fact, thought, and major impression. Theirs is the impressionistic, the intuitional, method. Instead of trying to proceed from hypothetical premises to logical conclusions, they feel rather than reason their way from a mass of perceptions too large and mixed for logic, to conclusions which are hypothetical in the sense that they cannot be logically proved, but which, probably, are equally sound in their bearing on real life. The educated man attempts to reason a matter out; the poor man – in his own phrase – *to weigh it up*.[62]

The article, perhaps because of its restricted remit, is essentially descriptive and gives too much space to the old hobbyhorse of inspection. It attempts no new solutions but ends with a succinct plea for a new political attitude "founded on respect for the poor; less bent on 'raising them out of their station' than on providing them with justice in that station, and the chance of bettering themselves whenever by their own efforts they can do it."[63]

Despite these deficiencies, its appearance in the *Quarterly* was public recognition that here was a new political voice to be taken seriously. Immediately on publication, Strachey wrote a leading article in the *Spectator* praising it as "of remarkable interest". He gave unequivocal support to Reynolds' views on education, and fully endorsed his critique of social reformers legislating in total ignorance of the needs and attitudes of the poor: "This is a tremendous indictment, and it hits every one of us more or less. We have all erred in one or other of the ways which Mr. Reynolds describes".[64]

If an olive branch were needed to put behind them the disagreement of six months before, this was it. Reynolds responded warmly. "I am naturally immensely pleased with the *Spectator* article; not so much because it's a score for me – though of course it is that, in effect, and I don't see why I shouldn't be glad of it; – as because it helps so much what I'm driving at – drives too, and hard. One feels that with the *Spectator* article one really will be able to get understood and to make some impression. So far, the notices that have appeared simply seem to judge my article according to the reforms that are at present being urged, with no reference at all to its underlying ideas. They pick out a statement, drive it to a logical conclusion that it never would or could be driven to in practice, and exclaim: 'Absurd!' And accordingly on the one hand they have accused me of over-estimating the intelligence of the working classes and on the other hand of underestimating it! Just as I complained; they have no notion of any types of intelligence different from their own."[65]

In addition to this public endorsement by the *Spectator*, the *Quarterly* article had won unexpected praise from some of his literary friends. The month before publication, Reynolds had sent the manuscript proudly off to Conrad for his blessing. Political articles were not exactly up Conrad's street and his reaction was rather hurried and non-committal: "*Quite* all right. Pardon my delay in sending the MS back. It's quite worthy of you. Excuse me saying more just now."[66]

But Conrad had taken the opportunity of sending it on to Galsworthy, the social conscience of Edwardian art, as being more in his line; and Galsworthy had reacted very favourably: "Conrad sent me on your most admirable article on 'The poor'. I'm all at one with the spirit of it."[67] But he was perplexed by Reynolds' distinction between economic and social reform. In the article itself Reynolds had made the most concerted attempt so far to tackle this central aspect of his platform.

> Social reform and economic reform have been much confused; they stand confused in the public mind, except in so far as economic reform suggests robbing the rich, whilst social reform suggests, very unaccountably, mending the manners and customs of the poor only; and, of course, economic and social reform do merge into and react upon one another. It may indeed be that they appear much the same thing from the point of view of those who want to 'raise', and otherwise modify by legal force, the personal lives of the poor; but from the standpoint of the poor themselves they are quite distinct; and the right and reason of the State to interfere is far from the same in both cases. Perhaps the difference may be put thus: a man's economic relations depend closely on the State, and the State should be a sleeping partner with one eye open, ready at all times to ensure not only shilling honesty between parties, but general honesty; whereas a man's social relations and personal conduct are primarily his own affair, and the State should be a partner sound asleep unless violently awakened. For the State, though capable, theoretically at all events, of judging a man's economic transactions and position, is not capable of judging a man's life and self, and ought not to make a pretence of doing so, except where crime, for example, forces its hand. Distinguished thus, economic and social reform appear very different in nature and effect. The first is warrantable and necessary; the second is not, and in practice usually does more harm than good.[68]

Reynolds had gone on to cite illustrations of both concepts: the Factory Acts, Food Adulteration Acts and improved housing came under the economic category, while such benighted programmes as temperance reform fell under the social.[69] This was not enough for Galsworthy, who worried away at the issue like a dog with a bone, perhaps because he feared he might be aligned with "those who want to 'raise' the personal lives of the poor". The lack of a precise boundary seemed to disturb his desire for a neatly packaged order in social and political questions. "I'm only sorry you do not elaborate more the distinction between 'economic' and 'social' reform. It seems to me, and I want to know whether it seems to you, that under the first heading comes the *provision* of machinery by which the 'poor' if so minded can secure themselves e.g. *insurance* versus sickness, unemployment etc. Labour exchanges; Wages Boards with the ultimate aim of no recognized labour under a living wage. Compulsory pulling down of slums. Are these all economic, according to you? I'm also for feeding schoolchildren when they want it in school hours. Is that economic? What do you say, too, to the question of that large and growing class the hopelessly unemployable? Would you let them hang on as they are? I feel that your views are absolutely right with regard to the country poor, and in the main with the town poor; but there are horrible features in connection with the dregs of the town poor, which are right outside the main thesis; and most social reform has its eye mainly on these."[70]

Reynolds must have been a little irritated with this string of questions to which most of the answers were fairly obvious. But he was also a little flattered to be consulted like a new prophet for clarification of the sacred text. He would have been flattered too had he known the extent to which this article had confirmed the hopes of both Conrad and Galsworthy in their protégé; and not a little embarrassed at the sight of them patting each other on the back.

The episode in particular gives us a special insight into the feelings of Conrad. In returning the manuscript to him, Galsworthy had been loud in its praise. Conrad, attempting to draw Reynolds out of his usual pre-Christmas depression, passed the message on in a rather ham-fisted way. "Jack's opinion of your article, as written to me, contains the word admirable. And I don't shy at it tho' I have perhaps the right to reserve that word for things which I am confident shall come from you yet. But Jack is as sincere as myself. You may rest assured of that."[71]

Sometimes an assurance of sincerity was needed from Conrad, the past master of the flattering phrase. But his response to Galsworthy at this time shows decisively that his faith in the young author was still both serious and profound.

> I am very glad of your warm commendation of S. Reynolds. That good fellow is worth encouraging and I know that you are one of the very few men for whom he has a intellectual, moral and artistic respect. He's only 28 and if his health does not give out we may yet have some comfort from that baby. For under many defects of form, there is in him a very sound substance; a lot of service for the ideas you and I have always

shared as the basis of the emotional life, with only superficial differences.[72]

1910 was the year of the two general elections, called to procure a clear mandate for action against the House of Lords but which ended, both in January and December, in virtual stalemate between the two main parties. At the beginning of February, with the Longshore and *Quarterly* articles out of the way and a good relationship with Strachey once more, Reynolds found a breathing space to tackle some more Seems Sos. The January election was the first he had experienced since coming to Sidmouth and since beginning to see the political world through working-class eyes. He suggested to Strachey he might do a piece with Bob on the electoral process as seen through this most recent experience and from his new perspective.[73]

The People and their Vote was completed by mid March, but Strachey was unhappy with it as a *Spectator* article and it eventually found a home in April in the *Fortnightly Review* where Reynolds had recently placed one of his short stories.[74] It did not in the event follow the Seems So format, but was a traditional political article with little in the way of new analysis or original ideas. Its main theme, which may have been too cynical for Strachey's taste, was popular disillusion with the electoral process under which genuine debate about serious issues was obscured by false emotion about trivia generated by the press.

Reynolds' proposed remedy was to conduct, as an experiment in one or two constituencies, a "fair-play" election where both sides would agree a very tight set of rules designed to equalise party effort and resources, exclude so far as possible the influence of national party organisation and the media, and conduct free from emotion and trivia a high-minded debate which would expose the real issues and the electorate's views on them.[75] It is not one of Reynolds' more convincing pieces. For once the real world seems to have passed him by.

When the December election was called, he fired off a proper Seems So to Strachey: "Have you room for the enclosed very topical 'Seems So' article: it is all of a piece, though from a different point of view, with your own frequent protests against election dodgery? The sentiments of it are being loudly expressed down here by working men of all parties – more loudly than ever before. When that long process of translating every-day opinions into political action is finished, we shall see – well, ructions."[76] Again Strachey was unwilling to make room for a further attack on the sacred democratic process and *Electioneering* eventually found a refuge among the more radical pages of the *Nation*.[77]

It works better than the longer, more cerebral, article because it is more human; a little cameo of the Perring family being canvassed in a brow-beating manner by a middle-class woman and her grown up daughter. The lady tries to pat Semaphore on the head and is met with the unequivocal response "Git 'ome an' die, you dirty ning!"[78] Dave Perring is offered a lift on election day and his response neatly underlines the weariness and disillusion with politics brought on by two elections in less than a year.

> 'You needn't send no motor-car, thank you, not unless the young lady there wants to take me for a drive up-country. If I do go to vote, I can walk up. But very likely I shan't. What's the use? What have 'em ever done for me, or the likes of me? Is it any easier to live, an' keep out of debt? That's what I looks at. An' we knows 'tisn't, 'cept for them as got plenty. Yet they kicks up a buzz about an election, as if your life was depending on it; an' whichever side gets in, they don't do nort, 'cepting they makes a few more rules an' regulations, an' fines 'ee or puts 'ee in chokey for not carrying of 'em out; an' then they has another 'lection, an' 'tis all the same all over again, buzzing round 'ee like flies, same as they be now. Hanged if I blame ol' Charlie Whimble for saying anybody can have his vote, which way they like, for five shillings! He'll never get five shill'orth out of it no other way, never, so long as he lives.'[79]

We have in both these articles a unique insight into the psychology of working class voters in 1910. And yet, despite this undoubted disillusion with politics, the two elections recorded massive turn-outs – 86 and 82 per cent. Reynolds perceptively takes account of the role of mass emotion and the concept of the turning-point in electoral psychology.

> Whenever one watches an election carefully, it is possible to discern, shortly before the polling, what men of science would call a critical point – a critical day, on which political argument gives way to election fever, inference to impulse. The psychology of the electorate changes from that of a collection of individuals to a psychology, if not of the crowd, at all events of public excitement. After that day the man whose opinions have been strongly on one side is led into voting for the other side on impulse...... On the critical day the greater portion of the electorate definitely divides into two sets of partisans; doubters draw into line; the sower of irrational inferences begins to reap; the exploiter of impulse and instinct sets to work in earnest.[80]

The article on *The Children's Charter* which Strachey had rejected in May 1909 was still hanging fire. In April 1910 Reynolds came across an article by Belloc in the Socialist magazine, the *New Age*, which castigated over-zealous State interference in the name of the eradication of poverty. He decided as a result to try his children article on the editor, A.R. Orage: "I have been trying to say somewhat the same thing – chiefly in periodicals read by the people I was hitting at. Enclosed is an article on the Children Act that none of them would touch, however. If it is of any use to you, pray use it, with or without pay, with or without my name to it. One would do anything to hinder the increasing penalisation of poverty."[81]

Orage agreed to take the article and Reynolds leapt in immediately to consolidate this new opening. He introduced himself with a brief account of his life and its problems. "If I could get the chance, there's a lot more we should like to say that other journals wouldn't print; but I'm a very poorly-paying business myself besides being a very slow writer, and a great part of my year is taken up with the fishing and boating work I do; so that usually I am compelled by sheer lack of money to write saleable stuff, and leave the unsaleable ideas till my ship comes in! But if you'll give us hospitality, we *will* blow our hooters a bit."[82]

He even had the temerity to offer Orage, highly regarded for his literary discrimination, his 1901 short story, *Turned Out*, which was not, to say the least, the strongest advertisement for Reynolds' contemporary literary skills. "I enclose a short story which no other journal will print. As a matter of fact, it's the first I ever wrote. Perhaps on that account I'm soft over it, perhaps it is some good."[83] Whatever Orage in fact thought, he seems to have been determined to give Reynolds a break, and the story was published on 11 May. Another, and much better, early Devizes story, *With Baby's Help*, followed at the end of the month.[84]

Correspondence between the two men quickly advanced to the level of intimacy. In thanking Orage for taking the children article, Reynolds explained how life at Sidmouth had developed the ideas behind it – his hatred of middle-class condescension.

> I get savage. You see, the working people among whom I live and for whom I work half my time, are my people now: so that I feel a good deal more with them than for most, and I hear what neither they – nor I – would think of saying in front of 'the likes of they', meaning the educated people and so forth. When one has done one's labour which in fishing is pretty hard and has taken people out to sea for a bob an hour and tips, one sees or rather feels a lot that one did not see before, especially in regards to the essential differences in emotional attitude; and I only wish I could express it properly. But I'm wandering on.... Please accept our thanks and, if I may say so, our admiration of the way you don't funk free discussion.[85]

The new relationship with Orage was a significant development in the growing politicisation of Reynolds' thought. Since taking up and reviving the *New Age* in 1907, Orage had built a high reputation for open-minded discussion which avoided the bias and tendentiousness of some of his periodical rivals. Though Socialist in its principles, it was one of those magazines read avidly by non-Socialists for the intellectual rigour of its political discussion. Even Strachey at the *Spectator* had a soft spot for it. Orage was no conventional Socialist – he was eventually to become a leading proponent of Guild Socialism – and had early broken away from the Fabian line. His critique of Fabianism was identical to Reynolds' – that it lacked the dimension of spirit and soul. Through the *New Age* he hoped to draw Britain into the mainstream of contemporary European ideas. He was, for instance, instrumental in bringing Nietzsche and Bergson to the attention of the British public, and it was mostly through the *New Age* that they had become icons for Reynolds too.

But Orage's rigorous intellectual approach did not stop just at politics. He was a great classical scholar and believed that literature, politics and economics were one and indivisible; it may well have been the talk within the Orage circle that gave Reynolds his first inspiration for drawing together psychology and economics. The standard of literary criticism had to be as high as that of the political discussion, and for that purpose he employed for some years Arnold Bennett whose "European" outlook was a mirror image of his own. In a very short time, Bennett's weekly article "Books and Things", under the pseudonym of Jacob Tonson, became the unquestioned arbiter of the upper reaches of Edwardian literary taste. Orage, like Bennett, put strong faith in attention to the craft of good writing and expended much time and patience in counselling, without condescension, his young contributors in their writing technique.

This was the kind of intellectual political and literary environment just made for Reynolds. From May 1910, on his increasingly rare visits to London, he would now make for the *New Age* offices in Cursitor Street off Chancery Lane, which was approached from the back by regular contributors through the side alley known as Took's Court. As befitted his open intellectual approach, Orage ran the magazine on collectivist principles. There was little money and most contributors were unpaid, but they had their say on editorial policy. Every Monday afternoon until six o'clock he would meet the contributors in the basement of the ABC restaurant in Chancery Lane and read over with them the proofs of the next Thursday's edition for discussion and collective decision.

Reynolds became an occasional visitor to these brainstorming sessions, as did H.G. Wells, Katherine Mansfield and Arnold Bennett – the latter, of course, living mainly in France at this period and only in England on the odd visit.[86] Reynolds had long been indebted to Bennett for the very favourable reviews of his books and articles, and now took some pleasure at being a part of the same literary enterprise. The ABC basement in Chancery Lane, where politics, literature and putting the world to rights were all discussed with revolutionary gusto, was a very congenial alternative to the sleepy pretensions of the Mont Blanc back in Gerrard Street.

On 6 May 1910, a few days after Reynolds had joined the Orage circle, Edward VII died. The King, with his surprisingly common touch, had been a man of enormous personal popularity. For Edwardians, on constant watch for the end of the world, the event was seen as defining moment, almost as much as the death of his mother nine years before. In early June, to mark the beginning of the new reign, Orage ran a feature entitled "Some Forecasts of the Coming Dispensation" under which he invited various figures to give their personal forecast of the character of the coming era.

Reynolds took *his* invitation as the opportunity for a formal statement of the recent development of working class consciousness and to underline the insidious threat of Fabian socialism.

> It's a very pretty compliment – makes one feel so comically important – to be asked one's "views and forecast of the character of the era now being begun", and as to the forecast part of it, I can't for the life of me answer otherwise than with the schoolboy's "Don't know, sir!" In this prophesying game, above all, the wish is usually father to the thought. What a man foresees is more or less what he wants to foresee. At one and the same time, I desire change and hate it. The modern art of making forecasts lies, I gather, in detecting causes now at work and tracing out their inevitable effects. But it seems to me that in human affairs the bond between cause and effect is so vague and complex beyond human reckoning that the law of cause and effect is practically about as trustworthy as Old Moore's Almanac. It is a point which Socialists will forget at the peril of their Socialism. Change prepares itself for birth in the *Vie Intime* of people, not in politics. I doubt if the governing classes and those who talk are in any degree aware of the ferments now at work among the governed, who at present have only the illusion of governing themselves. Scepticism as to the party system, as to politics themselves and even the whole theory of democracy, is spreading amazingly. It is not now the rightness of this or that party which is debated at street corners and in the public-house, so much as whether all the parties are not frauds and self-seekers. Scepticism cannot be confined to one thing. Theology has fallen to bits; politics will, I think.

After a discussion of class antagonism, he wound up with his most forceful call to date for the expansion of life and against the socialism which set out to restrict it.

> Society demands more prudence. The good of the race demands less. Society demands a damping down of individual life. Does the race? The race demands more and more life; and it cares nothing whether that lifefulness (to coin a word) dovetails into any industrial or political system whatever. It is no use offering me art, comfort, scope for my inclinations if, as a condition, outlet for my passions is denied me. My passions will bust it all up. It is no use offering me freedom from destitution if, as a condition, I must knuckle under to a scheme of industrial conscription

> like the Webbs' Minority Report. That's the sort of thing I mean; and I do venture to make one prediction: any society whose welfare involves racial harm will go to pieces; and any reform which involves the slowing down of life will be destroyed by life itself.
>
> There or thereabout lies my quarrel with the ordinary forms of Socialism. Useful as a leaven, it carries as a system, I believe, its own destruction within it. Were it practicable it would be unnecessary. I greatly admire your *New Age* for its outspokenness and the hospitality it gives to all sorts of opinions; but I have read in your columns socialistic schemes which give one the shivers and make me savage; for they deal with the life, however imperfect it is, that I and those I care for live. The greatest tyranny to beware of in the next era is that of the intellectuals ordering other people's lives – they are so well-intentioned and so cruel.[87]

It was a powerful cry with which to begin the twentieth century. He was particularly pleased with the characterisation of the Webbs' Minority Report as "industrial conscription", a phrase he had coined in *What the Poor Want*.[88] Never one to miss out on the recycling of good material, he was to use the latter part of this *New Age* article almost verbatim in the introduction to *Seems So!*[89]

On 11 June Strachey gave prominence in the *Spectator* to Reynolds' *New Age* piece and followed up with his own attack on Socialist intellectuals – "amid this hubbub of words it is a pleasure to find Mr Stephen Reynolds's piece of downright good sense".[90] Reynolds was no end grateful. "Thank you very much indeed for it, not so much because it's a biggish lift for me, of course, as because it will do an immense deal to help along our point of view, and to help us to state it where it ought to be stated. That letter to the *New Age* was a quick thing, done in a day; I fancy that if I had had time to express it better you would have agreed with more of it, notably that part about the class feeling. I am astonished at it almost continually. I've worked here with working men long and hard enough; I'm now in business partnership with them; and yet let the slightest thing go wrong, and, as I said, 'Ignorant!' comes to the tip of my tongue, instinctively, and 'Bloody gen'leman!' to theirs. Though nobody would take me for a champion of the middle class, I seem here to spend half my time defending it; and when I go back to it for a time I'm all agog to clear out again; so profoundly do they misunderstand each other and put wrong constructions on each other's actions. It's no joke trying to weigh the thing up fairly."[91]

Down in the fastnesses of Kent, Conrad too had remarked this unexpected love-in between the editor of the *Spectator* and the champion of the working classes. "The doddery old *Spectator* seems to be honouring you with his special predilection. It's the fashion to abuse that publication but I've always had a soft spot for it. And lo and behold! that blind and unaccountable trust stands justified in an unexpected manner. Give Strachey a kiss from me the very first time you and he go 'on the burst' together. I am almost moved to tears."[92]

In 1910 Reynolds took up another vexed issue of Edwardian social reform – the question of divorce. Here his firmly held libertarian views were to be given full rein, but with just a touch of conservatism and male chauvinism peeping out from beneath the skirts.

Typical of Reynolds, his involvement had started from a personal experience. In the summer of 1909, he had heard out on the beach a strange story of two incompatible working-class marriages where, after a series of trials and tribulations, each had swapped partners and achieved thereby domestic stability. He wrote it up as a short story with a touching ending in which one of the men, worried about the spiritual consequences of living with a woman who is not his wife, is greatly reassured by being told by the narrator that he is part of "an unofficial divorce" – the title of the piece.[93]

It was regarded by his friends as one of the best stories he had ever written. Reynolds passed the manuscript to Harold Wright, down on holiday with his friend Norman Keen; and Keen has left us with a charming picture of the first reading.

> As we were getting into bed one night, Harold said that Steve had given him the manuscript of a short story to look over. By the candle-light Harold read it aloud to me. It was "An Unofficial Divorce" which was later published in "How 'Twas" (1912).
> When the story was finished, Harold turned to me – holding the bowl of his pipe and gently shaking the mouthpiece in the way he had when he was thinking – and said:
> "Splendid, isn't it?"
> "Yes" I replied. "Isn't it So-and-so?"
> "That's him right 'nuff, but *isn't* it good?"[94]

In August, he tried to sell it in the States, first to McClure who found it "too English" and then to Paul Reynolds who was a little concerned about the morality.[95] "Confounded cheek, calling the story improper. 'Tisn't. Shall I let him see any of the non-improper ones, or not?"[96] But he had already sold it to the *Fortnightly Review* to come out in January 1910, the same month as his article on the poor for the equally prestigious *Quarterly* – "there ought to be a splash then".[97]

The Royal Commission on Marriage and Divorce had been appointed the previous year and by the spring of 1910 the debate had started to bubble on whether divorce should be made more accessible to ordinary people. When Reynolds joined the fray it seemed natural, as a follow-up to the short story, that he should offer the *Fortnightly* a political article on the same subject. He gave Strachey a pre-publication warning of the article which, for good reason, had not been offered to the *Spectator*. "I'm afraid you'll disagree very heartily with a good deal of it, but not perhaps with quite so much of it when you come to look into it. At all events, it represents the much-deliberated opinions of several of us down here, and at the back of it there is nothing but an intense appreciation of how very very fine working-class marriage can be, and mostly is. It is indeed out of my admiration for the good marriages that I'd like to facilitate ending the bad ones."[98]

Divorce for the Poor is another elegant Reynoldsian analysis of the attitudes of working people from the inside. "For the majority of working people divorce no more exists as a way out of matrimonial difficulties than champagne as a morning pick-me-up or private motor-cars for Sunday outings. It is not borne in mind as a possibility, let alone not within their means. By many of them, indeed, it is looked upon as a vice for the wealthy, more scandalous than adultery, very much worse than simple immorality on the part of the unmarried."[99]

He argues once more from the class divide: the poor are more tolerant of moral irregularity than the middle class and the break-up of a home is for them far more catastrophic in economic terms. If divorce is to embrace the poor, it should not just become more accessible but change its principles from an exercise in deciding fault to a discussion whether the marriage should survive. It is a deft piece of humanitarian good sense, but on the way there are some amusing touches on the class theme.

> Broadly speaking – very broadly speaking, of course – the wife of the well-to-do man is a luxury; as such she is often kept in ornamental idleness, or busy with matters of no importance. She is not necessary to his business or profession. By means of paid servants, his household can be carried on without her. But the working-man's wife is a household necessity. Without her, or if she is a bad wife to him, his home as well as his comfort, his life itself, goes to pieces. She herself cooks the food that keeps him fit to work, and washes his clothes on one steaming day of the week.[100]

In the new grounds of divorce proposed by the article adultery comes way down on the shopping list, and occasional adultery is an absolute ground only if committed by the wife; in the case of the husband, it has to be accompanied by the making of an affiliation order. Reynolds feels moved to justify his case.

> The advisability of putting husband and wife on a legal equality as regards occasional adultery has been much obscured by the present political conflict between the sexes. Admitting that the moral delinquency is the same on either side, the fact still remains that the result is not the same; and by the result only can unfaithfulness be judged in practice. For the act of unfaithfulness in itself is a momentary deed, the outcome of an impulse become uncontrollable, an outward sign of an inward state of mind; and neither the state of the mind, nor the temptation, nor the strength of the impulse can be estimated. But the result, so long as a husband is liable for

> the support of his wife and children, and she is not liable for the support of him and his, is plainly different. The injustice, if injustice there be, lies not in the law which takes that into account, but in the nature of things, whereby women bear the children. In other words, it is what may be called a primary injustice, irremediable by laws.[101]

But even Reynolds can see how this will read in a hundred years time, and adds "Possibly, even probably, this inequality between the sexes will diminish in the future. If so, well and good."[102]

We have also tantalising little insights of sexual morality, designed to tease and shock, but also showing a greater confidence in the writer to tackle such themes in public: "It ought not to need repeating, yet it does need repeating, that love and lust – if a definite line, which in life does not exist, must be drawn between the two – are haphazard and reckless passions, not to be controlled by public law if they cannot be by private and social morality."[103] He was talking of divorce – but here is the unequivocal voice of a homosexual in England in the decade after Oscar Wilde.

That autumn there were two more long articles to flow from his pen – perhaps the most interesting of the *Seems So!* collection because the most personal. They were the start of an intellectual preoccupation that was to last him the rest of his life.

The economic force behind the industrial unrest of the late Edwardian period was a marked slowdown in the growth of real wages compared with the last years of Victoria. Money wages grew by about 1 per cent per annum up to 1914, but commodity prices tended to rise in step leaving real wages more or less stationary. It was not only Bob Woolley who "worked and worked and got no for'arder". Discontent was spread by the growing conspicuous consumption of the middle and upper classes.

1910 was the first in a run of four bad years. In the second half of the year there were strikes on the railways, in shipbuilding and the cotton industry, and finally in the South Wales mines. In the summer a correspondence sprang up in *The Times* on the causes of this new bout of labour disaffection. It was joined on 19 August by a Mr Howard Little of Plumstead who, in a succinctly provocative letter, took a new slant.

> There is but one root cause of labour disaffection. The workers fail to appreciate the logic of things in their normal condition. They ask in effect why they, working the longest hours and being allowed no annual holiday, should receive the least pay.[104]

He went on to pose the crucial question: was brainwork really more fatiguing and of greater value than manual labour? The views of manual workers, temperately expressed, on this issue were never granted publicity, which led to frustration and militancy.

The Times picked the issue up the same day in an editorial which, though basically agnostic, wondered whether the feeling of injustice were more to do with social distinctions than with differentials of pay. It thought, nevertheless, the question a good one and asked those who had had serious experience of both kinds of work to come forward with their views.[105] This was a platform tailor-made for Reynolds, the fisherman-writer, and he wrote straight off to the editor.

> I see by my weekly *Times* – and if I may say so, have been very delighted to see – that you are running some sort of a controversy on Brainwork *v.* Labour. If you have chanced to read my *Poor Man's House* or "What the Poor Want" (*Quarterly Review*, January 10) you will already know that I have combined the two for some years now, in the form of writing one part of the year and working for a fisherman when there's anything doing. Fishing, while it is on, is one of the most violent forms of labour, as, I suppose, writing is of brainwork. For that reason, and because we are always coming into collision on the subject with the people we take out to sea in boats, we argue the question endlessly.
>
> That point in your leader, why don't labourers do brainwork for recreation? is pretty near the crux of the matter. But though we don't see any smashing argument against it, we do think it can be explained and disposed of. And a point I should like to bring out is that many forms of labour do call for much more brainwork than people think...... And the physical effects of brainwork are profoundly interesting...... [106]

Reynolds' own brain had gone into overdrive at the thought of the article in prospect. The editor proved equally eager. Reynolds told Pinker: "They asked for one article of 1500; I sent 'em two of 2500 each, and hanged if they haven't sent a proof of the first, numbered 1.! Meaty articles, but queer stuff for the *Times*".[107] They were written at the end of September in a hectic period – "I have been so desperately busy with the boats and some articles for the *Times*, which gave me the literary equivalent of severe stage-fright" – but he needn't have rushed.[108] He anxiously awaited their publication, but no space was found for them until March 1911, with the original controversy long since dead.[109]

No matter, since they stand alone most successfully as pieces of concerted writing – logical and pungent because they are close to home. As ever, it is Reynolds' personal experience that makes the direct hit – particularly in his explanation of inter-class hostility and the causes of the growing unrest.

> There is, of course, a strong unconscious freemasonry on the other part. I am astonished how often my educated acquaintances expect me to side

> against my working friends, on demand, because I have been through the school and University mill. Quite frequently I am questioned in such a way that I can only reply, 'The man you are talking about is a friend of mine.' And then, an awkward silence.
>
> Disunited on most subjects, easy to set at sixes and sevens, working people are curiously at one within the bounds of their informal freemasonry. It is when a grievance of theirs is brought within its scope that they become what is called dangerous. Then they will fight for an idea or a sentiment, and hold together. Labour unrest, the spontaneity of some recent strikes, are not the only signs that the economic questions of capital and labour and wages are becoming matters of feeling, and, therefore, sooner or later, of action. Trade unions are supposed to represent the most advanced working men; but while the trade unions have been spending their energies in political action, working people generally have advanced a step further. Silently, so far as the reading public is concerned, they have been learning to question the whole of the present system of wages and earnings and social position. They do question it, now, with a growing resentment.[110]

In opening out the idea of 'feeling' at the heart of the unrest, Reynolds poses the possibility of a new dimension to economic relations and rubs the message home.

> For the question of wages and earnings, though capable, in books, of economic treatment, is not in life a purely economic matter. It is nothing so simple. No doubt the reason of the grievance is a stark inequality of reward for different kinds of work, but the driving force behind the grievance is social and personal – a matter of feeling and class-friction. The labourer's self is even more hurt than his pocket. He sees that the brain-worker is paid on a different scale altogether; that the professional man, though he calls himself poor, lives pretty well; that the negotiator is still more highly paid; that the organizer exacts a heavy toll for arranging other people's labour; that the manipulator of money and of the necessities of life stands to make a huge fortune; while he himself is lucky if he merely lives, with few of the comforts and pleasures which the brain-worker takes as of right, and with nothing to look forward to after all his work except a still poorer old age. He sees all that plainly enough, but it is the calm assumption of superior worth on the part of 'the likes o' they', or the more offensive holding of their own on the part of half-bred people, which drives it home.[111]

On the main issue, manual *versus* brain work, it is only direct experience of workmen's labour that can bring understanding – the ultimate justification for Reynolds' own choice of life.

> Unfortunately there is no standard by which to judge the wage value of different sorts of work. The market value and the real value of labour can hardly be distinguished...... Two things stand out plain before the labourer's eyes – a gross inequality in rewards for work and also a mortifying social inequality founded largely upon the first inequality. And of one other thing I am certain: it is not possible to understand the labourer's feeling in the matter without doing his labour, living his life, and knowing his weariness. One cannot feel by proxy.
> ...... The labourer's grievance cannot be fully appreciated without experience of the labourer's life. Upon that point working men insist, and rightly. To take part in their life is nothing short of a revelation. One finds oneself looking out upon the world with other eyes.
> ...... It happens that my own experience does include both brain-work and labour in two of their most fatiguing forms – namely, writing of a creative or fairly solid nature, and fishing, which has to be done in bursts of severe labour and exposure, with intermediate periods of very trying idleness........ But so ingrained are class distinctions, so great the dissympathy between brain-worker and labourer, that most people are simply unable to believe a man can be both with equal thoroughness and equal seriousness. One's manual work they insist on regarding as the hobby of a very eccentric man...... At other times one is supposed to be a madman, or a freak, or a wealthy gentleman of low tastes. Well-meaning acquaintances urge me in all manner of ways, with all kinds of flattering half-truths, to break adrift from my working friends, now I have the 'copy', now I have the health, now I have got what I can out of them; and it should be noted, too, that every one of those misunderstandings casts an implied, if unintentional slur on working people.[112]

Reynolds' conclusion is that of the two forms of labour, brainwork is the more fatiguing, "but not by a great deal".[113] But manual work fatigues both body *and* brain. "I find myself that to make the change from hard bodily labour to full mental work, or *vice versa*, occupies about three days; so that if either sort of work were daily and regular, I could not do both."[114]

There are, however, many forms of manual labour which should command better rewards because their loss to society would be both damaging and irreversible.

> It is said that fishermen must be bred, not made. Probably I know more *concerning* fishing than my mates do, but not more *of* fishing. What I find out by observation and reasoning, they know more surely by an inbred instinct. Where my skill is deliberate, theirs is a part of them. They are in the tradition of fishing. What would we not give to have men alive who were in the tradition of medieval cathedral building? Yet

> we neglect, underpay, and allow to die out the men we have, who are members of great traditions; and because their learning is not mere book-knowledge they are called ignorant.[115]

Labour and Brain Work was arguably the most effective of Reynolds' political articles in explaining to the Edwardian public the reasons for and the feelings behind the disturbing spate of industrial unrest. They read him with attention because they accepted his credentials as a genuine spokesman for the working class. For him personally, it marked the development of a new strand in his thinking – a philosophy of work, born of Bergson out of Nietzsche, which he was to worry away at for the next few years. It emerges in the article itself, printed in italics as if it were indeed a new law – the first law of psycho-economics.

> *Ultimately, of course, work is a giving of life, one way or another, in return for the means of more life than could otherwise be obtained – in return, that is to say, not only for the means of living, but for the means of living more fully.* It is, or ought to be, a putting out of one's life at interest.[116]

One of the major drives of Reynolds' life was to build an intellectual system entirely of his own. It was the ambition that had created the artistic tensions in the format of *A Poor Man's House*, where the philosophical interludes appeared to many a distraction. Now he was more than pleased to find this new framework of ideas given some credence from no less a place than the economics faculty at Cambridge. He told Pinker with some pride that the article "contains a sort of philosophical-economical proposition which Harold Wright, who's an Economics tripos man, says is a discovery. If so, that's good".[117]

By the middle of October 1910, Reynolds had completed the "brainwork" articles for *The Times*, and had seen *Alongshore* safely into print. He was now free to plan his usual November holiday with Bob and went up to town at the end of the month. On the spur of the moment he remembered Hugh Walpole and their contact that summer, and fired off a telegram to suggest a new meeting. Walpole was tied up in Cambridge but the anxious tone in his reply suggested an interest somewhat more than merely friendly.

> Your wire has just reached me – too late alas to do anything – even reply. And yet you would be absurdly surprised how greatly getting it has pleased me. I have often thought of our evening at the Irish Theatre and have even meditated, on occasions, writing. But that was to be up to you, and you have brought anything in the future onto your own head. At any rate, for the present there is this. I am not in London again until

> next Monday. Can you stay until then and see me? Would you let me put you up for a day or two?
> I am engaged and so are you but I shall be delighted on any occasion to offer you a bed.
> I like 'Alongshore' immensely and am reviewing it next week.
> You are one of the few real people I have ever met and I want to be a friend if 'Ships (which is you) and Sealing-Wax' (which is me) allows. Will you write me a line here.[118]

But the French holiday was due to start the following weekend, and the second meeting of the two writers had to be postponed.

For this fourth annual holiday, he and Bob decided on a more ambitious use of their two weeks. They determined to make a dash for the Mediterranean "where there's sunshine and flowers in the autumn".[119] They were greeted once more as long lost friends by the fishermen of Boulogne, and were invited to meet again the skipper of the *Marie-Marthe* with whom they had gone herring drifting the previous autumn. Their inn had changed hands and they could not take their usual places in the small square back room in which they had formerly eaten their meals.

> The little dining-room was occupied by a couple very much in love. At least, when I burst in there to hang up our hats and coats, they were kissing each other most tenderly over their coffee-cups. Indefinably we were given to understand that the privacy of the small dining-room was to be respected. *L'amour,* in France, is treated with such easy-going kindness.[120]

After three days in Boulogne they bade goodbye to their friends and set off for Paris to catch the *rapide* for Marseille *via* Lyon – fifteen hours on the wooden benches of a third-class carriage. Reynolds has left us with a vivid description of that journey – an archetype for all overnight railway journeys – which is worth quoting at some length, if only to show how he might have written had he had the courage to tackle a novel at this time of his literary maturity.

> We found an empty carriage, hired pillows for the night, spread ourselves about the seats, and told the usual lies. But railway lies are useless except where there are English people to believe them. Gradually our third-class horse-box filled up. A plump and haughty German young woman took the other end of Jim's longer seat. A young man travelling to Tarascon sat down in the centre. A very jaunty French girl bounced into the carriage, and flung some small baggage with a hat-box on the other end of my shorter seat. Her dress was smart, but a little worn, as if it had been turned. Her face, though heavy in the bone, was fresh and lively. She spoke in a deep contralto voice that was rich and at the same time hard, even devil-may-care, in tone. After examining us all with a perfectly

> frank bold gaze, she decided to make friends with the young man of Tarascon. She smiled at him, winked towards the German young woman, and remarked carelessly that there were always a lot of foreigners in the Mediterranean trains. They both smiled. A good-fellowship was established between them. She offered him a cigarette from her case, and lighted one herself. Both the match and the cigarette she knew how to handle. She was all there.
>
> The German young woman, who hitherto had made no objection either to cigars or cigarettes, immediately began to sniff. She lowered the window. "Smoke stifles me," she said. For a time she held her head out of the window. Then, very quickly, she drew back. Her face was red and screwed up. A big smut had blown into her eye. She rocked herself with pain. She rubbed her eyelids with hands that were all of a shake. She burst into broken exclamations. She was nearly hysterical.
>
> Thereupon, the French girl said very sweetly: *"Permettez-moi, Mademoiselle!"*
>
> Like a trained nurse, she took command of the German young woman, placed her in the best light, and extracted the smut in several pieces, which she duly exhibited to the unaffected eye. Very neatly she did it. With the aid of the smut she conquered. The German young woman no longer shrank from her company with righteous sniffs. She allowed herself to be laid on the seat, and forthwith fell asleep. We smiled all round.
>
> Through the long black night the train jogged on. Storms rattled against the windows. After passing Lyons (where the German young woman got out) we could hear from time to time the sound of a great torrent, the Rhone in flood. Faces in the carriage had long since lost their freshness. Even in sleep they were curiously lined. Dawn stole like a ghost into the Rhone valley. It showed up gradually the rocks, the dark olives, and the bare little almond trees. It made us all look ghastly. The sensation of a new day failed to make headway against the sensation of a stale unfinished night.[121]

They enjoyed the cosmopolitan atmosphere of Marseille where "all the tribes of the Mediterranean seem to have gathered together...... each in its own dress, with its own speech and habits".[122] They stayed in a hotel recommended by an English painter friend from Paris – possibly Henry Lamb. Inevitably, they made their way down to the Old Harbour, were taken out frighting and given a demonstration of Mediterranean seining. Back in Boulogne once more, after another fifteen-hour journey, they were shocked to learn of the deaths of almost forty fishermen in the recent storms. Much of their mail from England had gone missing which Reynolds, with accustomed paranoia, attributed to interception by the French police, regarding them as German spies.[123]

Back in England, he told Garnett of their southern adventure and Bob's unequal struggle with the language. "Marseilles is the finest city I have ever seen, not excluding Paris, and the most pushing. Its streets are full of buying and selling, and touts and pimps. We didn't get so far as Nice. It was too expensive by any reasonably quick train. Bob says he enjoyed this last holiday best of all, but he is very sick with himself because he can't pick up any French. And I can't teach him any. His ears fail to pick up any of the niceties of sound, and in addition, he has no memory for words. He can seldom catch and remember an English name, let alone a French. I wish he could; but nevertheless my interpretations in his flirtations with French maids are gorgeously comic. And it's a bit of a job tackling three dialects in a fortnight – the Boulogne fishing patois, the Paris cockney and the Italianized Marseillais, where they say 'il capitano' for 'le capitain' and 'un*a* salade' and so forth."[124]

Although he complained of the sparse comfort of the French railway journeys, the greater luxury of the train home to Sidmouth took a more severe toll. He told Frederick Macmillan: "I came home in fine trim for work, but on my way down here, in one of those foul super-heated railway carriages, I caught a cold which has knocked me out altogether. A freezing night to sea wouldn't make me ill at all, but hot carriages nearly always do."[125] In five months of dealing with his hypochondriacal young author, Macmillan had retained his impeccable manner of patient sympathy: "I am sorry to hear that you have been laid up with a cold. There is nothing so bad as those super-heated railway carriages: it is unfortunate that the 'march of civilization' brings so many disagreeable things in its train."[126]

The cold proved the advance guard of his usual pre-Christmas depression. He determined, nevertheless, to go up to London for a few days to see his literary friends and to visit the Macmillan office at Christmas party time.[127] He had replied to Hugh Walpole just before setting off for France but had received no response in return. He wrote again suggesting they meet in London if Walpole were still there. There was a staccato but friendly reply: "Rather! – very much here. Won't you come and make my rooms your centre for a day or two? I have so much to do that that seems to me the only way that I should see you. Will you do that? ......I never had your other letter. Come and see me at once".[128]

Reynolds agreed to come up and stay for a few nights, but there was a warning from Walpole: "I hope you won't think me inhospitable because I have to be out so many evenings next week. It's beastly and they were all engagements fixed long ago but I will trust to your sometimes being awake late-ish. I'll lunch on Monday with pleasure and you shall turn up what time you please".[129] Reynolds came up on 12 December and they lunched together at the Mont Blanc where Walpole found his new friend "pleasant and agreeable". Walpole had gone to see "Salome" that evening – "felt it disgusting and the music's fine but the acting moderate" – but arrived back at his Chelsea flat early enough for the two to sit up late chatting over Reynolds' bottle of whisky.[130]

Walpole was back late the next night, full of excitement over a varsity match which Cambridge had almost won and having enjoyed in the meantime a lively dinner and late supper with friends.[131] Reynolds, drinking alone, was in a deeply depressive mood and Walpole had to listen patiently to his literary and other tribulations. He may have been a little piqued by Walpole's late return and his excitement over the rugby, an additional irritant. In any event, he decided to cut short his visit and return to Sidmouth the following day. Walpole had himself begun to sense the future tensions of this relationship. He noted in his diary: "Stephen Reynolds left – a wild, weird creature and I think I'm too patient – bothered for him".[132]

On 20 December, as a substitute Christmas card, Reynolds sent Frederick Macmillan a photograph of himself sitting in fisherman's jersey and blue serge trousers on the edge of a boat in Bob Woolley's backyard. For the first time, he is sporting a moustache, which he was to keep to the end of his life. The picture reveals very plainly both sides of his personality. Hands thrust in pockets and staring fixedly at the camera, there is a determined truculence in the posture; but also, at the same time, a youthful and nervous vulnerability. It was part of one very fruitful photographic session that winter which produced further highly atmospheric pictures of himself with Margot and with Semaphore, the latter a unique portrayal of the protective, avuncular side of Reynolds when close to children.

He knew the portrait was a powerful image and wrote to Macmillan: "I don't know whether the enclosed photograph will be any use; but in any case, pray keep the original, if you care to, and have any reproductions made for any purpose".[133] Macmillan was equally pleased with it. "Thank you very much for the photograph, which we shall certainly have reproduced and printed at the top of a prospectus of your books which we are preparing for circulation immediately after Christmas."[134] Reynolds was pleased when the leaflets arrived in January – "They are truly elegant , and I hope they'll perform their proper function of selling the book!"[135] The small leaflet, six inches by three, on glossy paper, with just the Reynolds' portrait on the front, achieved a wide circulation. It became the standard image by which Reynolds was to be known to his public.[136]

In the same letter to Macmillan, he could not avoid a reference to his pre-Christmas woes: "All the work I came home to do has had to give way to getting myself tired enough to sleep, in consequence of one of the wretched little breakdowns that I'm always getting just when I've plenty of time to get some writing. However, I don't think it's going to put me out of work for a couple of months this year, as it did last."[137]

On Boxing Day the *Daily News* published an old "Christmas Carol" short story he had dusted off and rewritten in the run-up to Christmas 1908, entitled *Brother Christmas and Mr Bookworm*. It had been commissioned by the *News* in 1908 but then rejected, as later by the *Nation*, for being too long. In the scurry before Christmas that year, he had tried to plug it at the *Mail* as well but had failed to find a home.[138] This year the *News* found room for a much cut-down version.

Though youthful and uneven, it is significant in helping us to understand Reynolds' own view of himself in this crucial time of his year. Withdrawn and low-key in style, it is nevertheless a devastating admission of emotional failure, as the Scrooge-like figure, self-jokingly named Mr Bookworm, confronts the optimistic spirit of Christmas present. It seems to date from the Christmas of 1905, his first at Pans Lane and the last he was to spend entirely alone, when the Wyers had gone off leaving him in the company of Mike, the malevolent cat of the dirty white fur and the doleful countenance.

> Last Christmas, while she was clearing away breakfast, my landlady said: "We are going to spend Christmas at my brother's, Mr Bookworm. Won't you come with us? I don't like leaving you here to cold Christmas dinner alone."
> "Thank you" I replied. "I prefer my books. I am not fond of Christmas."
> In the afternoon, therefore, not a soul remained in the house except the cat and myself. The twilight of a warm, cloudy Christmas Day was deepening into dusk. A yellow lamp flickered, then brightened and stayed bright, in the window opposite. When they pulled down their blinds I had a sense of being shut out, like the murky darkness. My own lamp I did not light, having a headache. I took a book – out of habit – and sat down by the fire. Beside my cold Christmas dinner lay three books. I could just see, not without pride, the gaps in my packed shelves from which the books had been taken.
> At the end of a severe headache there sometimes comes to one a kind of sleep, or trance, when the body slumbers, but the brain is more awake than usual; for with closed eyelids one sees brilliant pictures and hears words spoken in the room, and one knows that it is not altogether a dream because one knows that it partly is.

Into this entranced Ryecroft-like world marches the jolly figure of Brother Christmas, in postman's uniform delivering presents. He immediately hits Reynolds on his rawest spot with a boast that he has kissed 23 girls.

> "How many have you kissed?"
> "I am not," I answered, "much given to kissing."
> "Let's see the books that you prefer to people."
> I pointed towards my well-laden shelves.

Brother Christmas digs out some stuffy volumes which he throws immediately to the ground. Reynolds lays hold of some childhood works, like the *Water Babies* beloved of Aunt Jane. Brother Christmas shows him scenes in a magic lantern – children playing, his landlady celebrating, a drunken couple in mutual enjoyment. He gives him a present of books.

Reynolds wakes up to find the cat has eaten his dinner. "This Christmas I think I shall accept my cousin's invitation. His children are only moderately noisy – merry, Brother Christmas would call it."[139]

The next Christmas of real life, that of 1906, was in the same little house but playing Father Christmas himself to a boisterous and undoubtedly merry little boy. In that year his life had changed beyond recognition. And yet – as he sat in the midst of the Woolleys that Boxing Day of 1910 – he knew that some things would always be the same.

By November 1910 Reynolds had agreed with Macmillans to publish the Seems So articles in book form and in January they decided on publication that autumn.[140] He was anxious to get early proofs to discuss with Bob and Tom whether they would put their names to it, but then held back, wondering whether there might be time to rewrite. "I would send you along most of the Seems So stuff at once, but I want to go through it rather drastically, if possible after I have written the introductory chapter, and in the light of it, in order to make the book as coherent as possible."[141] But by the end of March he had not yet written the introduction and had decided to write some more Seems So's, even though his chief collaborator was acting up the *prima donna*. He wrote to Pinker: "Only five short Seems So's to do and the Introduction. George Macmillan, who has been down here with his family – is here again now – has been trying to buck Bob up. It's very difficult to get him inclined for one of the definite pow-wows which results in an article".[142]

A month later he still had two to do – a short one on the police, which took him nearly a fortnight to write, and then one on magistrates, for which he saved up a few prize images – "they'm bound to be pretty well in the hands of the lawyers and the police. You see how they bends down over for to ask questions o' their clerk, an' how they lets 'en hae his say in everything. You see, when they've a-got a crack lawyer afore 'em, how he'll waggle his finger at 'em an' lay down the law to 'em, what they ought to do – for his side's benefit, o' course – them sitting an' listening like a lot o' owls along a perch."[143]

But in May he decided to write a new article on the current discontent in the Navy, also destined for the book, and it was not until 23 July that he sent the full copy in to George Macmillan who, with his visits to Sidmouth, had become personal friend to all three joint authors and now handled the Reynolds portfolio for the firm.[144] The book now comprised no less than 13 Seems So articles in the first part, and in the second his recent heavyweight political articles, including *Labour and Brain Work*, *The People and their Vote* and one published in the *English Review* that April on the political fall-out from the Tariff Reform debate.[145]

He also made room for lighter personal pieces, like the article he had published in *T.P.'s Magazine* with his views on "the simple life", neatly entitled *Roughing It in Literature and Practice*. Since shooting into the public limelight, he had been blessed with countless letters from city dwellers envying his lifestyle and seeking advice on how to become simple fishermen themselves.[146] He knew that for most of them, as for Edward Garnett, the fantasy would never find its way into action. He therefore sets out to furnish his readers with a few home truths.

> Books about the so-called Simple Life fill a larger and larger space in each year's bookshelf. They rouse an enthusiasm of their own. They do more than express dissatisfaction with whatever is. On the one hand they minister to an ache for peacefulness, for 'the intense tranquillity of silent hills, and more than silent sky'; and, on the other hand, they feed a longing that lurks always in men's minds for a fuller, freer use of their bodies and of their five senses. Roughing it is regarded by the majority as a spectacle, to be enjoyed from afar off in comfort, but by some as a picnic, and by others as a life to be led – if possible. It has become an ideal. It has been idealized. Elaborate clothes and apparatus for roughing it can be bought in and about the Haymarket. The resources of science and of architectural scholarship are brought to bear on cottages in which to live the simple old life. (Cottagers' cottages are not found sanitary enough.) Simplicity urges people, as it turns out, into a yet greater complexity. Roughing it, in literature and in life, is not the same. It is found, in actual practice, to want improving.
>
> Men tell me in London: 'Ah, lucky you! I only wish *I* could throw up all this and come and do fishing among your strong, simple fisherfolk.' The luck that is mine, I don't dispute. But about their cultured, comfortable wish I am left wondering. Says a shrewd old friend of mine, a man nearing seventy: 'Lord, wouldn't I like for to have one o' they sort 'long wi' me, doing what I does for a week! I'll warrant they'd want a softer feather bed an' a better meal than I got. But they takes good care not to come....' For it is not real roughing it that they have in mind; not the roughing it of people who have to, because they can do no other. The Simple Life they envy does not exist out of books. The meal is there, but not the washing up; the open window, but not the sink.[147]

And the better to rub home his point, he describes a typical winter's herring drifting – eleven consecutive nights rowing out ten miles to the fishing grounds, hauling and freezing, rowing home at dawn to spend the morning on the beach in the pouring rain picking fish from the nets and packing them in boxes. In answering the question "why on earth?" with a touching personal anecdote, we catch a glimpse of the old Reynolds of 1906, prouder now because his reputation has gone beyond the beach at Sidmouth to the fishermen from other ports as they meet ten miles out on the fishing grounds. And of the new Reynolds of 1911 with his gospel of work – the true work that is life enhancing.

> Why on earth does one do it, one asks, unless starvation compels? Why does anybody do it who can earn a crust otherwise? While I was tired

the question refused to be answered. But there is an answer, I think. It came to us over the dark water, on a previous night, when there was a thicket of us on the fishing-ground and the sea was dotted with riding-lights. 'Who's got for thy third hand?' asked a distant voice in the sing-song drawl that carries for a mile over calm water. 'Hast got thic chap?'
'Aye!' we replied.
'I reckon,' sing-songed the voice, 'that a chap as 'ould come out here wi'out having to, 'ould go to hell for pleasure!'
Understand by *pleasure* that craving for *more life at any cost,* which lies behind all our instincts, all our pleasures and all our vices – and there the answer is. Literary roughing it is a hankering for rest and ease, a desire to be less painfully alive.

Many a time
I have been half in love with easeful Death,

sighed a literary poet. But real roughing it is a flinging of life to the winds in the hope of gathering more life. It is going to hell for pleasure. It is going to hell for life.[148]

Here we anticipate by a few years the distinctive call of D.H.Lawrence. For Lawrence the means to more life was sex; for Reynolds, yet unliberated, it was work.

The long-postponed introduction to the book finally got itself written at the beginning of July 1911.[149] It is a masterpiece of clear English in full Orwellian mode – what Conrad was to call "first rate literary Reynolds". In it, he makes his most eloquent plea to date for active participation in the class war.

In a country where, being poor, one may not even sleep under the sky without money in one's pocket, the economic difference tells most in the long run. Between master and man, ruler and ruled, top-dog and under-dog; the man who has something to start on and something to fall back on, and the man who has neither; the man who looks forward to a competency at the end of his working days, and the man who can only look forward to a bare subsistence at best; the man to whom failure means bankruptcy and diminished ease, and the man to whom it means starvation for himself and for his wife and children; between the man of one tradition and of another, of one education and of another, of one domestic habit and of another, of one class-feeling and of another class-feeling – that is where the line of cleavage runs through town and country alike. Compared with that wide cleavage, the political cleft is narrow and artificial. It serves to obscure the issue, and is used for that purpose. Whatever else he may be, a working man is first and foremost a working

> man. One recognizes it, feels it, without further inquiry. He betrays it as indefinably and as certainly as a man betrays himself who has been accustomed to authority. It is the common opinion and point of view, the underlying feeling of working men in general, that we have tried to set forth.
>
> Several times we have been asked, 'Why be so down on the likes o' they. Most of them mean very well, and are very decent people. Do you hate the likes o' they?' On the contrary, we have many good friends among the likes o' they, and often great pleasure in their company. But it is impossible to attack a system – the class system or any other – without attacking those who carry it out and are made what they are by it; those who, collectively, are the system. Dives may have been a kindly old boy, and Lazarus a lazy sponger, but the point of the parable remains just the same. Class antagonism is a very powerful force, growing rather than diminishing, acting in all sorts of unsuspected ways, cropping up in all sorts of unexpected places. Let things go wrong, make a false step, and in a moment it flashes out: 'Ignorant fellow!' – 'Bloody gen'leman!' It was there, beneath, all the time.[150]

Reynolds was keen to spell out the highly original process for creating the Seems Sos and to anticipate the criticism that this was only a shadow collaboration.

> More often than not, when I have told people that I was writing a book in collaboration with two fishermen, they have smiled indulgently, as if I were telling an amiable untruth, and have said, 'You mean, of course, that *you* are writing it.' They found it hard to believe that any working men, thumb-fingered with a pen and dubious over spelling, could really have a hand in the writing of a book. They made the very general mistake of supposing that those who lack the means of ready expression have nothing in their minds to express.
>
> Nevertheless, the book is a true collaboration, although one of us has done all the pen-work, and although, for simplicity's sake, the greater part of it has been printed serially under my name only. Even where I have written in the first person – 'I this...' 'I that...' – it is still a collaboration, but those passages represent contributions to the common stock which were more particularly mine; just as we invented the Perring family in order to express naturally, in their proper dialect and atmosphere, the contributions which were more particularly my collaborators'; for opinions out of their atmosphere are like sentences without the context. Every page, however, has been debated and passed by the three of us. Our usual method has been, first to pick up a subject that interested us, perhaps a subject we had been talking about for a long while, then to discuss it and argue over it, ashore and afloat, in company and by ourselves,

> till we came to our joint conclusion. Then on a rough day, in a set-to discussion, I would take down notes, which frequently amounted in length to more than half the finished article. From the notes I would make a rough draft, which, after more discussion, would be re-written, and again, after revision, typewritten. We would go through the printer's proofs together, and finally, after reading the matter in print, we have once more revised it for book publication. Collaboration could not very well be more thorough. In writing books – unless, to be sure, they are copy-books – the mere act of writing with a pen and spelling conventionally is not the chief part. It is the words themselves, the feeling, the ideas, which count. If I had a secretary, and never touched a pen myself nor banged away at a typewriter, I shouldn't be expected to say that my secretary wrote my books. Similarly, my own share in *Seems So!* is precisely this: I am one of three collaborators, and secretary to the three.[151]

And yet, the implication from this passage that the creative process was neatly cut and dried from the beginning was a little disingenuous. It was in reality much more hand to mouth and evolutionary. Although the names of both Bob and Tom were joined equally to the authorship, no doubt to evade family squabbles, the early articles were, as we have seen, collaborations with Bob alone. In describing to Pinker how the three of them would share out the spoils from the work, he gave a more accurate account of the relative contributions. "Either Bob or else Tom has had something to do with most of the articles; but not both together on the same articles; so we shall divide up just the same as a catch, that is to say into three parts, of which I shall take the boat's share and a man's, and they between them will have the other man's share; your share being taken out before the sharing up. Then of their share, Bob will have two-thirds because he has actually sat down to the job, and Tom one-third because he has been more of a consulting collaborator, chiefly coming in on the revise."[152]

But no matter what the precise division of labour, it was the fact of collaboration of which he was so inordinately proud. He boasted it to everybody. He wrote to Arnold Bennett in June: "My two fishermen partners and myself are getting out a book this Autumn, to be called 'Seems So'. If I'm not mistaken, it's the first appearance of the illiterate in literature, as authors!"[153]

In typical fashion, that summer he had a finger in every pie of the publication process. There was a long discussion with Macmillans over the placing of the frontispiece picture "Arguing the Point" which showed Tom and Bob in earnest discussion up in the boat and Reynolds down on the beach, his back to the camera. The figures were so spread out that, to get them all in, the photograph had to be landscaped (turned on the page), which was against house rules for a frontispiece.[154] At length, George Macmillan reluctantly gave way: "my only regret is that Tom was standing quite so far to the left, but the portraits are excellent, especially the back of your head."[155]

In June he sought Strachey's agreement to a brief mention of himself in the introduction as the first inspiration of the book three years before. "You were the original suggestor of the series – a fact I should like to mention in the Introduction to the book, if I may; mentioning also, of course, that there's a good deal in the book you wouldn't wish to act foster-father to...... I'm really very much indebted to you for the watchful eye you have kept on my stuff, and your several appreciations of it. Someday I hope I may be in a position to make my thanks better worth offering".[156]

On 22 July he was delighted to receive a letter from George Sturt (George Bourne of the Bettesworth books and close friend of Arnold Bennett) congratulating him on the political articles he had read in the press and suggesting a meeting. "Very many thanks for your kind letter which does encourage one very much. In the autumn we are going to publish the whole bookfull – Seems So – under our 3 names. Yes; do let us meet. I am hellish far away but I am coming up to town next Wed. pm around about fishery business."[157]

On 1 July Walpole had broken the silence since their dismal meeting the previous December to pass on a message from Edmund Gosse and to tell him of his move to Hallam Street: "Perhaps one day you will write to this, my new, address. Perhaps one day you will come and see me?"[158] Reynolds replied in friendly fashion, inviting him down to Sidmouth that summer if he were prepared to rough it. Walpole was enthusiastic. "I am so very glad that you wrote to me. I will love to come down for a week-end but it will have to be in September when I get back from abroad. I'm not so genteel as you think." And he was on the defensive too about the last meeting: "If you ever come to see me again I will give you a better 'housing' and you shan't have to provide your own whiskey!"[159]

On 26 July Reynolds travelled up to London as planned, calling in on Pinker at 11.30 and George Macmillan at 3.00 to discuss the final arrangements for the book.[160] He stayed up for three nights, apparently bypassing the delights of Walpole's whisky in favour of the Chelsea home of his friend Reginald Page, with whom he had maintained firm links despite the break with Lane. He spent most of the stay bustling around meeting MPs and civil servants at the Board of Agriculture, but it seems to have been on this occasion too that he had his first meeting with George Sturt who was to prove a sterling supporter when *Seems So!* finally hit the bookshelves.

Returning to Sidmouth on the Saturday, he found himself with an hour to spare at Waterloo before the departure of his train. Being Reynolds, he always put waiting time on railway stations to good business use. He told George Macmillan: "in wandering round I couldn't see any of your shilling books on the many bookstalls. Smiths have been withdrawing *Alongshore* from their libraries and lumping the copies on Sidmouth at 2/- each. I'm going to ask everybody I can to go to their libraries and insist on having the book. They seem determined to catalogue my non-fiction under fiction. I trust that some day cheap books will kill those detestable libraries".[161] Home at last, he found he had missed some excitement. "Tornado here yesterday when I got home, and lifeboat out searching for boats! Eye of it passed just outside Sidmouth."[162]

At 3 p.m. on 9 August Pinker called in on St Martin's Street to settle with George Macmillan the business terms for the publication of *Seems So!*[163] There was a disappointment in store for Reynolds. *Alongshore* had as yet sold nowhere near the 2,000 copies needed to pay off the £100 advance he had received. Macmillan now offered, and Pinker accepted, an advance for the new book of only £50. It is a mark of the sea-change in the sensitivity with which Reynolds was now being handled that George Macmillan wrote straight off to forewarn him of the disappointment and explain the reasons. "I have seen Mr. Pinker this afternoon and settled the question of terms. You may, I fear, be a little disappointed about the preliminary payment, but unfortunately, as I told Mr. Pinker, that which we made in the case of 'Alongshore' has not yet been justified, and 'Seems So', though of course it may do much better, is still something of a toss up."[164]

It was a blow to Reynolds, still hoping to buy himself the time to write his next novel. He told Pinker: "That advance is the devil, but anyhow, if the book earns more, one knows one will get it all right".[165] He was even more philosophic in his response to Macmillan: "Of course I *am* very disappointed about the advance, but I don't see any reason to adopt a complaining tone, seeing that I am confident you wouldn't make less than a fair offer. I am only sorry 'Alongshore' hasn't gone better".[166]

The agreement was finally signed on 28 August but Reynolds, as usual, was fretting to get on with publication and catch the current tide of industrial unrest.[167] At the beginning of August new strikes paralysed the docks in London, Manchester and Liverpool. On 16 August, the first national railway strike was about to break out and he wrote to Pinker: "What a pity the book isn't ready for publication while these strikes are on; for in the book there is precisely that psychology of working-class dissatisfaction which all the newspapers are groping for and can't find so long as they use their party politics for a rake".[168]

The timing of publication, in the event, turned out a complicated affair. Late in the day, the *Fortnightly* became worried about the political content of the last article for the book, on discontent in the Navy, and abandoned the planned publication. It was quickly transferred to the October edition of the *English Review* which necessitated a slight delay in publication of the book.[169] This now threatened to mess up Reynolds' annual holiday; he had hoped for a late October publication so that he could be in France for the usual first two weeks in November.[170]

When publication was put back to early November, he decided to make a dash for France for just the last week in October. Bob was unavailable – waiting to take charge of the household when Mam, now expecting a new baby, went into labour – and Reynolds took Tom in his place. Given the past tensions in his relationship with Tom, it was a surprising move. They spent a few days in London, staying in Chelsea with Reginald Page while Reynolds gave last minute instructions to Macmillans on the arrangements for publication.[171] They divided their French week between Boulogne and Paris, a repeat of the first trip with Bob in 1908. He told Katie Powys: "We had an excellent time in London, Boulogne and Paris; saw a hurricane at Boulogne – a tremendous sight."[172] She noted ruefully in her diary "I wish I could have seen it".[173]

Publication was then postponed again until the middle of November, a date which in retrospect had made the holiday rush unnecessary and landed Reynolds in the midst of competing engagements – some fisheries meetings in East Anglia, a weekend at Conrad's, and Mam Woolley on the brink of a new confinement which would turn him out of his rooms once more. "Don't imagine me reproachful over the, no doubt, unavoidable, but.... these two short-notice postponements.... have landed me in an almost comical muddle."[174]

At last on 14 November 1911 *Seems So! – A Working-Class View of Politics* was finally published.[175] The day of publication, Reynolds called in at St Martin's Street and sent off personal copies to his friends, including once again to Colonel Balfour: "In a sense, it's more Sidmouthian than the other two...... In Sidmouth, I know, by the more ignorant of the local politicians, I am dubbed 'socialist' – a piece of mud-chucking the absurdity of which you will see if you read 'Seems So'."[176]

It was accepted at once as the authentic voice of working class opinion and caught the mood of the times. Following the summer of discontent, there was a widespread strike among Lancashire weavers and a national coal strike in preparation. The book provided some of the answers to the big question – Why? The "Seems So" formula, with the perky opinions of the newly created Perring family, was a novel and attractively palatable way of getting across a political point. Here was humour and an unstuffy approach to difficult and important issues. The public was attracted too by the all-pervading libertarian feel of the book, best epitomised by Dave Perring's approach to the Edwardian demon – drink.

> What he drinks he holds to be his own business, so long as he does his work, avoids debt, and harms nobody. He is rather old-fashioned. He believes in personal liberty. He thinks it outweighs its risks.[177]

The early reviews were highly laudatory. Scott-James in the *Daily News*, while reiterating the old reservation as to whether Devon fishermen could represent the views of the industrial working class, was in no doubt about the value of the book. "Mr Stephen Reynolds is exceptional in that he adds to his knowledge of a certain working class community literary and intellectual gifts that are unique. His plain, direct, forcible style assails the mind and the ear instantaneously...... He presents facts from life concretely, vigorously; he grasps their larger bearing, and rounds upon us with a flood of logical arguments...... Mr Reynolds has probed deep. He has made his collaborators articulate. He does not merely generalise. He shows us vividly through conversation and pictures of life what the habits of working people are."[178]

On 2 December there was a surprise conjunction of the journalistic planets. On that day there appeared two lengthy articles, by Massingham in the Socialist *Nation* and by Strachey in the Conservative *Spectator*, both praising the book for introducing the authentic working-class voice into the political debate and pondering what it all meant for future policy. Massingham thought it "a really remarkable book of revelation and interpretation". He found disconcerting the revelation of class antagonism "which we (the well-to-do) do not like to think exists" and of working class resentment of social interference from above: "Only so far as the feelings and opinions of the 'Seems So!' classes can become fully articulate, and can get into the art of government, can this fact and feeling of 'interference' be got rid of".[179]

Strachey was struck by many of the same points, and drew the surprising conclusion that the best way of sounding working class opinion could only be by referendum. "The working man may go on voting for this or that candidate because there is no one else to vote for, but his true feelings are expressed by the chaotic strikes we have lately experienced. He wants a new standard of comfort – a rise in wages which shall be a real, not a fictitious rise – and we heartily sympathize with him."[180]

This support from the arch Conservative periodical caused some confusion down in Sidmouth where Reynolds was regarded by respectable townsfolk as the arch revolutionary Socialist. On the day the *Spectator* article appeared, one of the joint authors received his criticism in the flesh. "Last Saturday, in Veale's bar, Jimmy Skinner, who was standing, knocked Tom down where he was sitting, and Tom, on getting up, laid Jimmy Skinner out 'like a skinned duncow'. Profuse black eyes and chatter."[181]

He explained the background more fully to George Macmillan. "The conservative papers praising the book has produced a truly comic situation down here, and, not being able to understand, some of the up-street people are rather angry. Yesterday, some of the freemason set went for Tom unawares, and downed him. He's got a black eye, but their ringleader has a blacker one, besides a well-bumped head. The beggars are always civil when I'm there. We must be very annoying to them, and, taken together with our several weapons, a little difficult to tackle."[182] Macmillan was unused to his authors being treated in quite this way. "I am sorry for Tom's sake that local criticism should have taken such a material form, but am glad to know that he gave as good as he got."[183]

Reynolds was delighted by such serious attention from the leading political journals. He wrote to Harold Wright on 8 December: "The book has had tremendous reviews, but the circulation isn't furious, yet at all events".[184] For such a polemical work, however, there were bound to be views on the other side. Despite Reynolds' close relationship with Spender, the Liberal *Westminster* gave short shrift to the new book, complaining of its failure to give sufficient weight to the political, social and economic progress of the working class over the past half century, and of the authors' "reckless impatience" and "lack of any constructive ideal".

> They and their kind have become impatient, and are losing reason as a natural result. They argue from the present to some dimly conceived end which they do not know how to attain, instead of arguing from the past to the present, and so on by a logical progression to a soundly constructed and attainable ideal.[185]

Reynolds' new friend, George Sturt, sprang to his, and their, defence with a letter proclaiming that if the workers only had a fair opportunity, they would soon find ideals for themselves. He noted privately in his journal: "isn't it rather an impertinence, this asking the Workers to have and to formulate ideals? Do we do it for any other class? Do we expect it of the shopkeepers, or of farmers, or of country house people, or of manufacturers, or of titled noblemen? It seems to me that we all get along pretty well without any such baggage, and don't require to be asked to exhibit any such thing. Why then should the workers be asked?"[186]

Reynolds, who had a great respect for Sturt's books, was delighted. "I haven't yet thanked you for your gallant defence of us in the unsympathetic *Westminster*. I was, and am, very proud of your intervention. I only wish you'd write a review article on the book; I mean an understanding article such as only you could write. We have had gigantic reviews, but not a single one of them have [*sic*] tackled the real guts of the book – the middlemen paragraph in the introduction, the theory of work in terms of life in 'Labour and Brainwork', and the difference in mentality, into which I dragged your own books. I can't write sermons and homilies on our own book, and how the deuce are people to be made to see that the thing has philosophy in it, as well as politics? In fact, I did set up signposts in the introduction, but they had eyes and saw not, ears and be damn'd if they heard!"[187]

A rather bitter review in *Country Life*, which accused Reynolds of dismissing the social and economic progress of the last forty years, thought the *Spectator* and the *Nation* had been taken in: "These two thoughtful and ably-conducted journals represent extremes of thought, yet the writers had very much the same things to say about this book. They did not subject it to very searching examination".[188] But Reynolds was always first to see the sales potential of strong notices, however pejorative: "Considering the plain speaking in the book, people seem to have stood it wonderfully well. But *Country Life* – an old enemy of mine – is very disgusted, and has been good enough to say so at great length prominently".[189]

His literary friends responded with enthusiasm. Although a book of political articles was not exactly Conrad's cup of tea, he was quick to post his congratulations. "The volume is very emphatically *all right*. In many respects better than I expected. That is it puts the point more clearly than I should have thought it possible in that form. Perhaps I mean more consecutively. On the other hand the form is very dangerous. It does away with a certain amount of force and authority. That is perfectly apparent in contrast with the preface which indeed from every point of view, is a very fine, effective and sympathetic statement of your moral and intellectual position in the face of modern events – or modern manipulations, if you like. Yes. I like the preface immensely. It's first rate literary Reynolds. The ease and point of expression are quite fascinating".[190]

But Conrad had some harsh things to say about the end of the book. As with his previous books, Reynolds had been totally careless with the final chapter. Instead of a purpose-written summary to fit the material, he had taken the lazy way out by tacking on the *Quarterly* article from 1910, *What the Poor Want*, under the new and uninspiring title, *Various Conclusions*. It did not flow relevantly from the preceding text, not least because it had been essentially a critique of previous books on the poor. Conrad may not have recognised it from the text he had seen in 1909, but he certainly knew it was out of place here.

> What I regret are the quotations from other works in the last third of the book. A production of that kind should have been written as if there had been no other book in the world. Your volume is professedly a first hand thing – living words. Then why drag in these dead bits of books? can the opinions of Miss X and Messrs: X Y Z add an atom of authority to what is supposed to come out of the warm lips of men? Their intrusion damages the simplicity and the sincerity of the scheme and in so far is shocking to my sensibilities. You might have said all you wanted to say on the points dealt with in these quotations without disfiguring the book by a single line not coming from the three authors. And it would have been more effective if not so easy to do.[191]

It was a crushing indictment, fully merited. But Conrad was judging essentially from the viewpoint of a work of art, and nothing could have been further from Reynolds mind. He softened the blow with a gentle explanation and more praise.

> I am telling you these things on which I might have honestly held my tongue because I am concerned as to the *integrity* of your work – any of your work – as much as you can possibly be. And that in the merest trifles even. For obviously my remarks, in view of the general quality of the work, are of no particular importance. *Quality* is not the right word. General sentiment of the book, I should have said. It is in what they say,

> you all say, and you say alone, a most right and valuable expression of stark humanity confronted by problems and theories fabricated within four walls of some sort or other.
> I wonder very much what reception you will get. I imagine it can't be but good. What I want is to see it *exceptional*.... [192]

There was enough material in the book, sufficiently variegated, to spawn any number of controversies and thereby keep it alive well beyond the initial reception. The most furious centred on the Seems So on education. In it, Reynolds had repeated his standard critique of the elementary system: that it was positively damaging to working children, attempting to turn them into lower middle class clerks, dispensing snobbery and false expectations when it should have been training them in the disciplines of work. He did not mince his words. "'Twice one are two, twice two are four....' parrot-fashion, and 'Tommy, don't yer wish yer wuz a gen'leman?' are the two characteristics of our present educational system. It offers the neatest possible example of the folly of trying to force upon one class the standards and ideals of another...... We have heard education called the cruellest thing ever forced upon the poor. That may or not be. Many things are forced upon the poor. But it does seem to us that education is the biggest fraud ever forced upon us; and the most dangerous, too; for it has been held forth so persistently and so loudly as a cure-all that even the poor themselves have been very largely deceived."[193]

When the article had first appeared in 1909 it had caused a little buzz in educational circles. Now it led to a much more public furore. Five weeks after publication, it was denounced by Michael Sadler, the leading educational expert of the day. Sadler had been a member of the Bryce Commission in the 1890s and a leading reforming figure in the department of education and the new Board of Education set up in 1900. It was he who had introduced Robert Morant into educational administration to become the founding father of the modern Department. He had recently departed from the Civil Service to take up the post of Vice-Chancellor at Leeds University.

On the evening of 18 December, at a school speech day in Leeds, Sadler set out to defend his past labours against "the most thorough-going denunciation of the spirit and effects of English elementary education which had been published since, in 1867, Ruskin wrote 'Time and Tide'". The defence was distinctly underwhelming. It did not absolutely refute shortcomings in the system, but claimed that "the dawn of a better day had already broken" under which there was a new emphasis on handwork and practical training as indispensable factors in equipping children for the duties of life.[194]

What alerted Reynolds when the speech was reported in *The Times* was less perhaps the weakness of the argument than the attack on his own experience and *bona fides*. He shot a letter off to *The Times* the same day. Sadler had struck a raw nerve by casting doubt on the nature of his collaboration: "Mr.

Reynolds's report of the views of his fishermen friends bore every mark of genuineness. But it was impossible for a literary man, however sincere in his intentions, to avoid imposing on his less instructed friends his own point of view and getting them to assent to cleverly worded statements which were only in an artificial sense the outcome of their own thoughts and lacked the qualifications present in their minds but not within the range of their powers of expression. He doubted, therefore, the value of Mr. Reynolds's book as a true reflection of the complicated feelings of English working men and women."[195]

The response was swift and to the point: "Why, more than half the statements in our book about education *were* theirs, not mine! It's not so easy, I can assure Mr. Sadler, to impose points of view and clever statements upon my collaborators. They have a troublesome habit of cutting the cackle and coming to the hosses. What Mr. Sadler calls 'the elements of a liberal education with wise preparation for the practical duties of life', they call 'knowing how to keep your end up and rear a family of kids fitty on a quid a week'."[196]

Sadler had been at his most patronising on Reynolds' qualification for the debate: "There were many signs in the book that Mr. Reynolds's own experience of elementary education was nearly as limited as that of his unlettered acquaintances. Had he known at first hand the work of a really good elementary school he would have shown more discrimination in his judgment of the question and would not have so blindly generalized about the supposed defects of the whole system".[197]

The reply was crushing. "Certainly I did not go to an elementary school, nor have I taught in one; but I have taught children of school age in my own old preparatory school, and I have taught young men what they ought to have learnt during their years at an elementary school. My experience, moreover, of the *results* of elementary education is pretty extensive and peculiar. For some years I have acted as a sort of general secretary to any working people who liked to come to me. Almost daily I have been doing writing and so forth for them, that they could easily have done for themselves, if only, at school, they had been taught 'to read and write and reckon well'. I do the work with pleasure, but I must confess it makes me savage that youngsters should be compelled to spend – or waste – eight or nine years of their life catching nasal catarrh and snobbery in an elementary school, and come away not able even to write a decent letter for themselves, let alone to know where to look up the bits of information they want."[198]

After pointing out the poverty of Sadler's defence, he ended on a conciliatory note. "We don't wish to attack Mr. Sadler himself, who spoke very kindly and much more reasonably than most educationalists; still less do we wish to attack the elementary school-teachers, who work hard for small pay in carrying out a bad system; but we do wish to repeat that elementary education is a fraud forced upon us: it gives to the children about three years' worth of second-rate education in exchange for eight or nine years of their lives. It's a bad bargain the law compels them to make."[199]

It was a certain boost for sales. George Macmillan wrote to Reynolds: "all this controversy will help the book".[200] Reynolds wrote to Sturt: "On the whole we have had miraculous reviews of *Seems So!*, and Prof. Sadler was good enough to jump on us in a speech reported in the *Times*".[201]

Sturt wrote in his journal: "Stephen Reynolds says, in a letter to hand this morning, that Professor Sadler took occasion to 'jump on' him in a speech reported in the Times, apropos of his book 'Seems So'. Probably this was a reference to something or other not over polite, on the subject of Elementary Education. It seemed to me that Sadler, man of intellect and heart though he is, probably has never seen under the surface of his subject. He knows about theories of Education: knows, and perhaps feels too: but he may easily know nothing at all about the people to be educated. At any rate I am sure that this is so with most of the educationalists of the day. It would surprise me to find that there is even a solitary individual at the Board of Education, from the President downwards, who has any view of the subject from that side. They have the theory, and the tools, for their work; but they don't know the material."[202]

Other newspapers leapt into the fray. Reynolds was stoutly defended by Orage in the *New Age* but attacked as a Neandertal by *The Schoolmaster* in a leader headed *Stephen Stoned*: "Stephen has been rather stoned by reviewers and press correspondents, and that without earning the dignity of a martyr".[203] He wrote to Maurice Macmillan: "We seem to have roused the educationalists to no small, and – in their paper *The Schoolmaster* – a rather vulgar, fury".[204]

By the first week of January 1912, when the education row was at its height, the book had sold nearly 1,500 copies and that week alone sold 180.[205] These were large figures for Reynolds just six weeks into publication. Just before Christmas he had the unaccustomed pleasure of being consulted on a reprint: "By way of a very fine Xmas Card, we had an urgent reprint notice from St Martin's St."[206]

With the disappointing sales of *Alongshore*, Macmillans had reduced the initial print run of the new book from 3,000 to 2,000, and the advance from £100 to £50. Now Reynolds had already almost earned his £100, £30 of which was to go to Bob and Tom. There was a new print of 1,000 immediately, another of 1,000 in January 1913, and in December 1913, a cheap edition of 5,000.[207] It was Reynolds' best selling book after *A Poor Man's House*. For many readers it was the book by which his name was to be remembered. Even after his death, Bob and Tom would still receive their annual royalty cheque from Pinker's office – much diminished in size (11/11d in the year of his death) but nonetheless indubitably theirs.[208]

For Bob and Tom had truly caught the publicity bug. In April 1912, they prepared a surprise for the unsuspecting secretary to their little literary collaboration, out walking the beach one spring morning. "Rather a shock the other morning.... Bob pointed furiously at a little new boat we got last year, as if it had a high explosive with a time-fuse in it, and then I perceived that, unbeknownst to me, they had had the backboard painted –

SEEMS SO!
Pleasure Boat
R & T WOOLLEY

I tell 'em that, while they were about it, they ought to have had on the board too, 'Macmillan & Co. 5s. net.'!"[209]

THIRTEEN

Weekends at Nesscombe 1911

It was in August 1906 that Reynolds had first set Pinker off on the chase to find a *causerie*, that safe journalistic haven that would act as the springboard for his creative literary career. Much as the "simple life" for the London office worker, it had been his ideal. It had become idealised. The monthly slot in the *Mail Supplement* for reviewing country books, which he had wrung from Archibald Marshall in May 1907, had proved a false dawn. Only two articles appeared in the series before the *Supplement* itself collapsed.[1] Two years later, though now an established and well known writer, he was no nearer his goal.

In the summer of 1909 his *Longshore Sketches* in the *Westminster* had proved an undoubted success and he had agreed with Spender to follow them up with a series of *Beachcombings* the following spring. At the end of December that year, as he planned the literary campaign for 1910, it suddenly occurred to him that Spender might now be the man to realise this long-standing ambition.

He wrote to Pinker: "Do you think there would be any chance of my inducing the weekly *Westminster* to let me do a weekly causerie on books and things to be hung on that peg, anonymous and very independent rather on the line of Arnold Bennett's "Jacob Tonson" – not any great finesse of criticism, but rather from the point of view I spoke of literature in the *P. M's H.*? I think I could carry readers on from week to week. That would give me five days a week free from scribbling for cash".[2]

Spender was happy in principle with the idea but unsure when he would have room to start, particularly with Reynolds' new series of longshore articles booked for the spring. He had to wait almost another year before, in the autumn of 1910, it was agreed that the new series of regular articles, to go into the Saturday rather than the weekday edition of the paper, should begin sometime in the New Year.[3] By the beginning of 1911 Reynolds had already started to plan them.

Originally, he was still thinking of a series based on book reviews, like his slot in the *Mail Supplement*, since that would provide a free flow of subject matter without the labour of hunting it down. But as he began to give thought to their development, inevitably the articles started to take on a life of their own. Towards the end of January, he told Frederick Macmillan: "I've got a series of week-end articles on books and things to do for the *Westminster*. They were to have been *causeries* by one John Hannaford, but they seem to be collecting material round them and a somewhat solider frame – a series of essays rather than causeries".[4]

The plan for a simple potboiler which could be tossed off each week without effort had now become a far more serious enterprise – a vehicle for some of

Reynolds' most cherished and difficult intellectual ideas. From a means to an end, they were fast becoming an end in themselves. Hannaford, the central figure, was to be "a Devonian returned home – a man who has managed to miss most of the commonplace things of life". "My idea is to create a character, giving in 1 a sketch of his life and reasons to return into the country to a place like this and simply to let him talk to his weekend guests. He reads books, spots things in the newspapers, hears stories, sees scenes, in fact exists rather keenly as a spectator."[5]

He would be Reynolds in all but name. The articles would form an account of "simple talks at large, his talk being forcible because of his habit of talking from experience". By using a fictional character as mouthpiece, Reynolds could express views that cut diametrically across those of the *Westminster* and "it gives one the chance of putting down a good deal that is too much felt, too *intime*, for writing formally under my own name". And it might provide for a little fun, enabling him, for example, "to chaff literary London".[6]

He told Conrad of his plans and got a warmly encouraging response. "Your letter delights me. I've a great confidence in your future – and indeed I've always had it. But somehow the tone of this last missive has warmed me and cheered me. Your plan of contribution to the West^er^ Gaz. strikes me as most promising."[7]

In April he got the go-ahead from Spender who would start printing at the beginning of June. By now the format was clear and he had a name for the series. He wrote to Garnett: "My *Westminster* causeries, which start in a month or so, have developed into a cross between a novel and a book of essays – the week-end talk, illustrated by his own history and experience, of a man who has savoured all sorts of good things and has made a career, and yet has missed the good common life of men. To be called "Weekends at Nesscombe", I think, and to deal with anything, and to be commonplace to the point of originality".[8]

As he was settling down to start on the first episode, a spectre from the past suddenly bounced back upon the scene to challenge his equilibrium – the long-running battle with the *English Review* over the money for *The Holy Mountain*. The old dispute had already resurfaced a couple of times in the previous eighteen months, but now matters seemed truly to be drawing to a head.

In August 1909 Reynolds had refused to take up Hueffer's challenge to issue a writ over the £100, knowing full well that the magazine was on the verge of bankruptcy and there was no money in the coffers. He was waiting until the enterprise were taken over by someone who could pay.

The previous May, when Hueffer's money had run out, effective control had passed to his brother-in-law, David Soskice, and through the rest of that year it was generally expected that the Soskice group would find the backers to buy the magazine outright. Later in August, Reynolds began pushing Pinker to take action: "can the extraction of the money be hustled on rapidly and without tenderness for them? I don't care how their delicacies are hurt so long as they are compelled to shell out".[9] When in September publication of the *Review* passed along Henrietta Street from Duckworth to Chapman & Hall, his hopes revived. "I see they've changed publishers; there must be money in it now, anyhow; and if the new owners have simply bought shares in the original company, we ought to be able to get ours...... let's erect the machinery to sue whomsoever ought to stump up. Possibly they will when the machinery is before their gates".[10]

But the Soskice group never succeeded in buying out the magazine. Their "revolutionary socialist" politics were hostile to those of Hueffer who, early in 1910, managed to outflank them by persuading the Liberal MP Alfred Mond, a family friend of Hueffer's mistress, Violet Hunt, to take over the venture. But Mond, a renowned chemist and businessman and the eventual founder of ICI, had not bought the business to run it in the haphazard manner of the previous year. He immediately sacked Hueffer and installed Austin Harrison as editor. The literary brilliance of the *Review* evaporated overnight; but its financial future was secured.

In April Pinker drew Reynolds' attention to a notice in *The Author*, the magazine of the Society of Authors, that had been placed at the request of Austin Harrison.[11]

> We understand that Mr. Austin Harrison has been appointed Editor of the 'English Review', which, in future, will be published from Messrs. Chapman and Hall's offices, 11, Henrietta Street, Covent Garden, W.C. We are further informed that the unsatisfied claims of contributors to the Review under the old management will be settled by the new management.
>
> We are very pleased to be able to make this announcement officially, as it is not often that a new proprietor, taking over the assets of an old company, also takes over its liabilities and undertakes to satisfy them.[12]

Reynolds fired off a new letter to the *Review* which responded by protesting complete ignorance of his claim. He sent the reply to Pinker: "Bright, isn't it? But I suppose there is nothing to be done, except that I shall try and get at Mond himself, if I can do so in an informal sort of way".[13] He was, however, a little worried about this direct approach. "It's difficult to do it myself without letting 'those about him' know that I don't quite take their word."[14] By July he had all but given up the struggle: "There seems no chance of getting anything from Mond".[15]

The issue revived once more a month later when he received an invitation to join the Society of Authors, and this decided him to get the Society to do the dirty work and pursue the matter on his behalf. "I'm thinking of letting them take the matter up; not because I think they are very likely to succeed where our joint efforts have failed, but because it is just possible that persistence, and the collective importunity of the A.S., may make them think it advisable to come to some sort of settlement."[16] On 23 August he wrote to Herbert Thring, the dedicated if somewhat bureaucratic Secretary of the Society, who had already held the post for eighteen years and was to continue to do so for another twenty. Thring received the request in a friendly fashion and promised to send the papers on to the Society's solicitors: "I am sorry to say we have one or two other cases against the same review in respect of work submitted during Mr Hueffer's Editorship".[17]

Matters hung fire while the old company was being wound up, but when it became clear in October that no money was to emerge from the liquidation, Thring began to press Austin Harrison on whether the *Review* would honour its voluntary undertaking of the previous spring.[18] In early November Harrison called on Thring at the Society's offices and told him candidly that the offer had been made on the assumption that the debts were insignificant; it would never have been made if he had known that the debts were so numerous.[19] But from the Society there were only two claims – that of Reynolds, and one other of only ten pounds. Thring told Harrison that if he were now about to renege on the offer, he should provide an authorised statement that could be printed in *The Author*.[20]

Thring continued to press by letter and Harrison continued to evade taking a decision. Finally, just before Christmas, Thring determined to bring matters to a head and sent Harrison the draft of a notice he planned to publish which stated the Society's regret that the Mond promise had not been kept despite repeated claims on behalf of the members.[21] A furious row now erupted in which the normally patient Thring gave the *Review* staff as good as he got: "The present difficulty is not of my making at all, nor am I asking for the fulfilment of promises which have never been made...... You further say, that this is not a matter that can be settled without very careful consideration. If that was the case, the promise should never have been made, now, over a year ago. There have been 12 months for the careful consideration to which you refer".[22]

In February 1911 Thring put forward a new claim on behalf of Ernest Rhys.[23] When a month later he had received no reply from the *Review* he threatened to put the whole matter before the Committee of the Society.[24] At last, the threat produced the necessary action. Harrison paid the two outstanding claims for ten pounds and ten guineas, but refused to recognise the Reynolds claim.[25] It fell to Herbert Thring on 4 April to break the bad news to Reynolds in his best bureaucratic English.

> I beg to inform you that as your claim against THE ENGLISH REVIEW has been disputed, the former Editor stating that nothing is due to you, we cannot recover the money under Sir Alfred Mond's promise. You fully understand, of course, that there never was a legal claim against Sir Alfred Mond, and he is meeting the claims of those Members of the

> Society which have been acknowledged as undisputed. I can, therefore, in the circumstances, but refer you to the former Editor. If you can obtain from him a statement that the claim you have put forward is a proper and just one against the old company I think our Committee would be willing again to submit your claim to the present proprietor, but we cannot take the matter any further until the former Editor with whom the contract was made acknowledges your claim as a fair one.[26]

Reynolds had just come back from a lively weekend with Conrad in Kent and was in a good mood. He was immersed in Constance Garnett's translation of *Anna Karenina* he had picked up on a station bookstall and Ford Hueffer could not have been further from his thoughts.[27] For some months he had given up all idea of obtaining satisfaction from the *Review*. The letter thus hit him as a shattering bolt from the blue. Not only did it revive the painful memory of the loss, it made it clear that the refusal had depended entirely on the word of Hueffer. Even more insulting, he was now being asked to go on his knees to Hueffer if he wanted the claim to be taken further.

The following morning found him on the doorstep of the Society of Authors in an uncontrollable rage. In a fiery interview with Thring, he turned all his anger, not on Hueffer, but on the way he had been treated by the Committee of the Society. They had accepted Hueffer's lies when they were equally entitled to have accepted his own statements. Thring tried to calm the situation, stressing there was no legal case, that the Society had done all it could but that if Mond refused to pay because Hueffer disputed the claim, nothing further could be done without a clear statement which would infer that Hueffer was lying.

It emerged in the course of the interview that Hueffer had claimed he had given Reynolds board and lodging for a long time in payment for the serialisation.[28] This could have referred only to the two months in Holland Park Avenue in the spring of 1908 or the two or three weeks he spent there the following winter. In neither case could the notional charge have approached anything near £100, and the claim was in any case refuted by Hueffer's letters of May 1909 offering to pay the acknowledged debt out of his own pocket. In recent years Hueffer's rather original approach to the truth has been defended by his apologists as an aspect of his creative genius and because, at the least, it never caused anyone harm. Here, however, we have a deliberate and malicious lie designed to deprive a former friend of his rightful and much-needed payment.

Thring suggested that Reynolds should lay a full statement of his case before the Committee. Reynolds replied that it was scarcely worth the trouble given the attitude the Committee had already taken, and hinted that he had been sold out for the benefit of the smaller claims. It was now Thring's turn to get angry at this charge of dishonourable conduct. He told Reynolds that if he chose to prepare a statement, he ought at the same time to make these accusations personally to the Committee itself.[29]

But privately, he felt that Reynolds might well be in the right. After he had gone, he reported the interview to the Chairman of the Society and added: "I must say it is quite possible that Hueffer is lying from what I know of the way in which he managed the business while he was Editor of the "ENGLISH REVIEW", but as long as he sticks to his statement I do not see how we can coerce Sir Alfred Mond".[30]

That week Reynolds went off for a short pre-Easter break in Boulogne, and arrived home to find a letter from the Society inviting him positively to put a statement before the Committee.[31] He decided to take up the challenge: "I want to have another go at the Socy. of Authors, who show signs of climbing down, and prove that before the *Holy Mtn.* was published I was in expectation of the money".[32] On 21 April he submitted his case which was formally considered by the Committee of the Society at its meeting on 1 May. The Committee was convinced by the new evidence and charged the Secretary to put it before Sir Alfred Mond.[33]

Thring wrote to Mond on 3 May with a copy of Reynolds' statement, its backing letters and a plea to reconsider: "fresh facts have come before the Committee of the Society which appear to show that Mr Reynolds' claim, though not legally enforceable, is a just one against the old management and ought not to have been passed over upon Mr Hueffer's statements".[34]

It seems to have been the size, rather than the justice, of the claim that eventually decided the outcome. Mond wrote swiftly back, sheltering behind the absence of legal responsibility. It was another week before Thring, in some trepidation, wrote off to tell Reynolds that Mond would not recognise his claim and there was no further hope.[35] It was just two days before Reynolds' thirtieth birthday and he was feeling tired and depressed. There was no repeat of the previous month's histrionics. He was already beginning to weigh up his advance for the forthcoming *Seems So!* and took the news with apparent resignation.[36] But it reconfirmed for him the existence of the evil star that had for years now dogged the progress of his first much-maligned book; and the duplicity of the London literary world which he would shortly be leaving for good.

There was a little compensating cheer for him the following month when the *English Review* came under attack from his new friend, the editor of the *Spectator*. The June number of the *Review* had contained a typically free-speaking article from Frank Harris, entitled *Thoughts on Morals*, in which he had had the temerity to suggest that temporary excesses of the flesh, even for women, were better than abstinence. Strachey attacked the moral tone of the *Review* and announced that he would no longer advertise or notice it.[37]

Reynolds was delighted: "I read your article on the English Review with a lot of glee and a good deal of satisfaction...... I detest vulgarity and rather revel in coarseness, whenever it's a sign of abundance of life". But Harris' brand of vulgar showmanship was too much. "Unfortunately, to be outspoken is to find oneself lumped in with the likes of him, just as your campaign against dishonest insincere indecency associates you, in people's muddled minds, at all events, with the contemptible smellers-out of impurity, who pretend to be frightened at frankness, and with their suppressions do, in my opinion, much more harm than all the racy writers put together."[38]

Strachey was pleased with this distinction; it drew him back to his own particular *bête noire* of the time, H.G. Wells, whom he had taken to task over both *Ann Veronica* and *The New Macchiavelli*. "I have no personal objection to plain speaking, even to coarseness, if it is honestly meant and not used for base purposes, and I quite agree with your illuminating remark that such plain speaking is as much liable to misrepresentation as my kind of plain speaking against indecency. There is a whole world of difference between you and Wells. You want what you believe to be right to win the day. Wells merely wants to make sophistical apologies for self indulgence and want of control. I may think your view wrong in particular cases but I should never think it that of a beast."[39]

There was another public literary diversion that June. The Swindon Branch of the Workers' Educational Association had decided to hold a festival in honour of Richard Jefferies at Coate Farm, the writer's birthplace just outside Swindon. Both Edward Garnett and Edward Thomas had been invited to speak, the latter on account of his recently published book on Jefferies which had become the standard biography. Thomas, who was excessively nervous of public speaking, asked Reynolds, as a Wiltshire author and lover of Jefferies, to take his place.

The last week of May, Reynolds wrote to Garnett to try and co-ordinate their contributions: "Hear you are speaking at the Jefferies affair at Swindon on the tenth of June.... What on precisely? At the suggestion of Edward Thomas, who says he absolutely can't speak, they've asked me to spout. I thought of taking 'Jefferies and the Downs' with particular reference to 'The Story of my Heart', but I haven't time to prepare a set paper. Have a lot of work to do, and an awful tiredness on me almost too great to do anything at all, even fishing".[40]

On the second Saturday in June a crowd of some 400 assembled outside the Swindon Corn Exchange in the Market Square and walked across the fields to take up their places on the lawn in front of Coate Farmhouse. The first of the literary speakers was Alfred Williams, the young Swindon poet and yet another "discovery" of Garnett. He was followed by Reynolds who, in his opening, did nothing to spare the blushes of Edward Thomas. "I ought to acknowledge at once that I am here as a substitute for one who would have discharged the duty much better than I can. I refer to Edward Thomas, the last and most exhaustive biographer of Richard Jefferies. He writes me that he could not possibly make a speech – he never had and never would (*laughter*). He asked me if I would come and do it for him. Accordingly I have come (*more laughter*)."

Although, Reynolds went on, it was a local festival, it was to honour a national figure. Jefferies had extended right throughout the country the spirit and influence of their own Wiltshire Downs until they had entered into the national life. In recent years there had been what was called a return to nature – a delight in bodily health and strength. When he was a boy it was considered an honour and a distinction to be delicate (*laughter*). It was otherwise difficult to be thoroughly appreciated by one's aunts; but today one got more appreciated for being healthy and strong and he considered that the writings of Jefferies and his influence through other writers had had a great deal to do with that change of feeling. It was necessary that people should glory in nature and glory in their own existence. Those were the lessons of "The Story of my Heart" – the religion of nature, the cult of the body, and the hope beyond.

Reynolds ended by quoting his own personal spiritual text, lines 89-112 of *Tintern Abbey*, as the summation of Jefferies' inspiration. Jefferies had brought it down from the Cumberland mountains to the Wiltshire hills and made it accessible to many more people than if it had come from Wordsworth alone.

It was a typical Reynolds off-the-cuff address. By contrast there followed a carefully prepared and erudite speech from Edward Garnett which, among other things, compared Jefferies' way of looking at man and nature with that of the ancient Greeks. The speeches over, the large party went over to Coate Reservoir for tea, followed by a display of Morris dancing, and the day was finally rounded off with a simple service at Chiseldon church.[41]

It was a rare event now, since the publication of the *Mountain*, for Reynolds to appear in Wiltshire and it was a joy to see once more his beloved Downs as well as praise them in public. It was also his first introduction to Alfred Williams, and the following day he walked with his cousin, with whom he was staying in Swindon, over to the poet's home in South Marston. Both of them were much impressed by the Williamses.[42]

Seems So! was not the only Reynolds book to hit the streets in 1911. *A Poor Man's House* was still selling steadily and in January Macmillans decided to bring out a cheap edition as part of a batch of shilling volumes being published that summer. Reynolds offered to provide a new preface to help the publication on its way.[43] Towards the end of April he sent a draft off for George Macmillan to consider, but acknowledged it had given him a lot of trouble. "You know us down here.... therefore I'm sending you this Preface to look at, if you will, before it finally calls itself *sent in*. It has been very difficult to write: I've felt the need of the utmost truthfulness; and, in fact, I have expressed myself with the utmost precision. But unfortunately, precise expression doesn't always enable one to convey one's meaning precisely. Readers seize on one sentence to the exclusion of another equally important. They run away with an idea. For that reason I should be very glad to know your impression of the preface. The note of tiredness I can't get out of it, not if I rewrite it forty times; for I'm incredibly tired. But I don't want the thing to leave in anybody's mind a flavour of complaint. If it doesn't do that, I'll stand by it."[44]

The doubts were misplaced. George Macmillan thought it admirable and sent it straight off for printing.[45] It was, in effect, an eloquent update on Reynolds' life with the Woolley family in the three years since the book was first published and, in particular, on the ambivalence inherent in routine existence once the first glow of revelation had worn off.

> I am still here; more here, more tied, than ever. It is still home. Sometimes, of course, I have said to myself, 'I'll go. I'll break free. Why should I expose myself to endless troubles, rebuffs, and even enmities, when I've no need?' That I have said because very often I have been tired to death with trying to carry on two jobs at once, besides some half-a-dozen related schemes; and it is not exactly easy to do mental work among hand-workers, who neither adapt their daily life to it (why should they?), nor realize fully the conditions under which it has to be done. In the irritation and tiredness of the moment one is apt to forget the kindnesses of yesterday and the sure kindness of to-morrow. Usually one blames somebody else for miseries which have their origin in one's own self. At the back of everything there lies in wait that profound discouragement which arises from the fact that one's dearest projects move slowly – so much more slowly than one's life flits along. It is no holiday to be a buffer between two classes, continually subject on both sides to misunderstandings and suspicions, very cruel, very absurd, very excusable; nor is it sport to be kin to one class in education and one part of one's work, and to another class in feeling and the other part of one's work; though I for one, being troubled in mind, am more heartened by the touch of a friendly hand and the sound of a friendly voice saying, 'What the hell's the matter with 'ee?' than by any amount of intellectual analytical non-creature sympathy. But it means much loneliness and disappointment, towards whichever side one turns.
>
> I mention these things not to complain; far from it; still less to blame; but for the purpose of showing that the opinions herein expressed have been tested and tried almost beyond endurance, and yet have survived the racket of it. One other test there is, even more conclusive. When I say to myself, 'Well, where else would you like to be? Is there anything else you'd like to do, anything else you are keen on?' the reply comes at once, 'Nowhere. Nothing. Nothing at all.' To up-anchor would be to go adrift, to become derelict. I fuss about noise, like most writers, yet write with my door wide open; not to hear what is said, but still to have in my ears the sound of voices which one day I shall never hear any more.[46]

And then, with this thought of mortality at the front of his mind, a nostalgic glance back to the young man of 1906 and his discovery of the lost domain which now has to bear the burden of the compromise of existence.

> Therefore, nothing has been altered in this edition. There is nothing there I wish to unsay. Doubtless after more experience of fishing, writing, and living, I could revise it and touch it up and add to it, but I do not think I could better it as a whole. It was written in the springtime of an experience. The freshness and glow of that springtime I could not retrap, now in the sweats of summer. Outlines have become obscured by detail. Opinions are absorbed in the carrying of them out. It is as if a man should see a fair country that instantly imprinted itself on his mind's eye, and then should settle there to earn his living. Never again can he see it as he did at first. The question of whether the ten-acre field would do with a top-dressing will blot his view of younder hill; the tranquillity of evening will be disturbed by the best cow going dry or the sow overlaying her young; and walking under the open sky he will have in his mind the crops underfoot. Within short compass, he will not be able to give so accurate a picture of the country as he could have done at first. Its beauty will be the same; it will mean as much to him, and more; but with this difference: that instead of lying outside him, to be looked at and described in general, it will have become a part of his own life, not so easy to put into words. So, when I happen to look at *A Poor Man's House*, it reads like another man's work, with which I am almost astonished to find myself in enthusiastic agreement.[47]

The shilling edition, complete with this new confessional preface, was published on 4 July 1911. As ever, Reynolds took especial delight in the design of the little red book: "It's a jolly get-up for it. I couldn't have wished for a better".[48] He was even more delighted by the print-run – 10,000 copies.[49] He was never to see such numbers again.

The over-arching tiredness which Reynolds bemoaned to all his friends in the spring of 1911 was compounded of a number of work and emotional pressures. He was struggling to complete the Seems So articles for the book while fighting down his fury over the battle with the *English Review*. Fishing was poor – the mackerel had been a complete failure – and Bob was getting poorer.[50] At the same time, he had the start of the *Westminster causeries* – the easy potboiler which had developed into a tricky intellectual excursion – hanging over his head.

At last on 8 May he took a deep breath and started off on the new series.[51] By 16 May, his thirtieth birthday, he had completed the first episode, long enough to split into two instalments, introducing his hero, John Hannaford. His thirtieth birthday had for many years been a key milestone in his life – the day on which he aimed to regain full health once and for all. The achieved reality, however, felt somewhat different. He wrote to George Macmillan: "Two instalments of the *Westminster* series are done, but I don't get on very fast. Somehow I can't throw off the dreadful tiredness which has been growing upon me for some time, although on the whole I have been decidedly better physically. That I'm thirty to-day doesn't make me any merrier. It's like a door banging behind one".[52]

Throughout Reynolds' life one can sense the anxious feeling of a race against a limited ration of time – the complaint he had made in his new preface about life flitting by with his projects uncompleted. In part it was the response to permanent neurotic bad health. At a deeper level, it is a kind of foreknowledge, common to many creative people destined to die young. George Macmillan did not understand – why should he have? He took the reference to the door banging shut with a certain detached amusement. "It amuses me to see you speaking of your thirtieth as if it were at least the seventieth, but as time goes on you will realise that at that epoch you were still in your first youth."[53]

Reynolds knew instinctively that this might indeed be the equivalent of a seventieth for others, but he was careful and diplomatic in his response. "You mistook my meaning over the birthday. What I mean is, that do what one will, feel as young as one may, one can't be twenty-something when one isn't, however good the imitation. And when I think of how most of my twenties were wasted in mere study and detailed fighting against illness, I feel very sick. And the latter process hasn't quite come off, for although I set myself the achieving of proper health before I was thirty, I've never felt so fundamentally tired, so up against a wall, so racing hard merely to stand still, not even when I was very ill. However that isn't fair; my books are bother enough to you, without adding the see-saw that produces 'em."[54]

It was in this deeply felt atmosphere of "see-saw", and a sense of the beginning of the end, that *Weekends at Nesscombe* was produced. It was Reynolds' literary swan-song, just as *Ryecroft* had been the swan-song of Gissing. It was in many respects an imitation of Gissing's book, one that perhaps Reynolds may not have wanted to admit, even to himself. John Hannaford is a man who has retired from the literary world of London to take a cottage at Nesscombe, a little hamlet two miles over the cliffs to the west of the fishing town of Salterport (Sidmouth). Though middle class, his parents had been bankrupted financially and had abandoned him emotionally in his youth, when he had taken to sailing and fishing under the eye of Benjie (Uncle Sam). A gentleman had paid to finish his education and he had been reluctantly whisked off to Cambridge, studied art in Florence and published in London a book of essays and "a couple of rather intellectual novels".[55] He had reviewed books and still read for a publisher. There is a dark hint of a period in his life which remains unaccounted for and which creates an atmosphere of mystery to be later resolved.

The scenario is neatly set up for Reynolds to ride his deeply felt hobby horse – the contrast between the false sophistication of London and its literary and bureaucratic worlds and the true reality of the world of Salterport which comprises that very essence of life – the commonplace. "The life he has led, the ideas he plays with, belong to a world very far from here. But the ideas which really move him, the feeling he has towards life, they hark back to the days and nights he spent with Benjie."[56]

The conflict between these two worlds had been implied in Reynolds' own life ever since he first landed on the Woolleys back in 1906. But this attempt to bring it so openly to a head is a true reflection of the compulsive feelings of 1911. Hannaford's stance, the final turning of his back on London and literature, is an idealisation of Reynolds' own hidden desires. *Nesscombe* is, in fact, the sublimation of those desires; the necessary precursor of his own fast growing conviction that he too would soon abandon literature for good.

Nesscombe the place, the narrow coombe running down between high red cliffs to the sea, was another idealisation. It is Ladram Bay, the most cherished of Reynolds' beauty spots around Sidmouth. He had friends in a cottage there, and most days when he was writing he would take the two mile walk along the cliffs up Peak Hill, over High Peak and down through the pinewoods to the open meadows surrounding the little bay. Hannaford settles in Nesscombe Cottage, looked after by an old Devon couple, with his books, piano, painting gear and a couple of dogs, and takes the walk every day in the opposite direction, into Salterport to pick up the newspapers and lounge about with his fishermen friends on the beach or in the public houses.

The Hannaford table-talk is given us by an anonymous and detached narrator, much in the style of Conrad. In the beginning, he is commissioned to write the Hannaford biography, an indication even at this early period that Reynolds too was contemplating the possibility of a record of his own life.

> Shortly afterwards – I am not sure it wasn't the same evening – Hannaford said to me: "You know, my life ought to be written down. 'Twould serve at least as a warning to other young men, not to throw themselves away as I have done. Will you write it – a genuinely truthful biography – if I give you all the particulars?" Knowing we are all of us apt at times to think that our lives are strange and worth writing, I replied half in joke: "Why don't you write your autobiography yourself?" "I can't," he said, with a funny mixture of hopelessness and pride. "I can't do the writing part of it. I've lost the power, the concentration"..........
>
> When, however, I began to get my material from him, I found there was too little of it – too little, at all events, that he was willing to tell in cold blood. Besides, it was not the deeds, not events, which bulked largely in his mind; it was what he had made of them, what he had thought and felt about them. In other words, his life, that he wanted written, had been chiefly mental. One can write a biography of a man, but not his autobiography for him.[57]

Thus is born the compromise of recording the after-dinner talk of a Sunday evening in Nesscombe Cottage between Hannaford, his local friends, and his literary friends from London, some of whom are young authors that he is taking up. The talks are monologues; the friends are there to listen.

The first two scene-setting articles, though a little stilted in style, work reasonably enough because they provide the stimulation of an interesting narrative line. The next seven articles, published up to the end of July, were an unexpected let-down. The intellectual themes are sharp enough – art versus life, the idea of progress, death and tragedy. But both conception and style seem brittle and stilted, creaking in most of their joints. They appear rushed and uncertain, carrying with them all the worst faults of Reynolds' youthful journalism. The voice of Hannaford, in particular, is unsure. Is he a London intellectual or a Devon fisherman? – the ultimate Reynolds question. But his use of either mode of speech appears random and unconvincing.

It is true that in May and June Reynolds was under much pressure of work and the articles were written to tight deadlines. He may have hoped to iron out their inadequacies when rewriting for the book. But the problem goes deeper than that. In these first articles, Reynolds appears at last to be getting off his chest the intellectual baggage of years. All the ideas, however intricate, have been worked out for some time, with supporting arguments and images already constructed. To the new reader, they are not only too dense and compressed to be easily comprehensible, they are at times rather boring. What they lack is freshness and spontaneity. Reynolds has let his intellectual obsessions run away with him without the time or the inclination to give a fresh life to old material.

That said, there are small oases of good writing and little autobiographical insights. One of Hannaford's regular weekenders is a Garnett lookalike. "F.N. Jackson, the critic, comes, who spells art with an enormous A, and rails unceasingly at the poor British Public. He belongs to Hannaford's London days, and if they did not like one another they would hardly tolerate each other's opinions for five minutes."[58] Reynolds makes an open and unrestrained attack on the Garnett habit, from which he had himself suffered, of dropping a young author as soon as he had become famous.

> Jackson provoked it. He brought down with him for the week-end a bundle of novels to review, and instead of reading them, to say nothing of writing about them, he sat all day long on the sunny beach in Nesscombe Cove, picking up pebbles and throwing them one after another into the water. On the Sunday evening, at the end of supper, he was complaining that he found it impossible to work at Nesscombe. "The Cove and the sea are so exquisite," he said, "and English fiction is so horribly commonplace. Serious criticism is useless. Nobody takes any notice of it. I suppose our novelists are bound to write down to the stupidity of the public, unless their ambition is to starve."[59]

It is a convincing recollection of the despondent Garnett who had visited Sidmouth the previous autumn and on return to London dreamed of abandoning his manuscripts for the whitewashed cottage by the shore. But Hannaford takes him to task.

> "You'd think a great deal better of them if they did starve, because you have a theory that if genius doesn't starve – well, it ought to. Otherwise you genius merchants couldn't go on feeling so superior to the poor stupid heedless public. I remember, when I was in London, that so long as a young author had no success whatever, you were all of you most kind to him, and held him to be a budding genius; but directly his luck turned, you began to sneer at him, because you assumed that in so far as his work became popular, it couldn't be good...... You are like the gardeners who take such a pride in the vegetables of their own growing, that they don't like them eaten."[60]

There is a stinging bite in this passage, and an unwelcome home truth, which must have left a mark at the Cearne that Saturday morning.

In *The Conquest of Ugliness*, the eighth and ninth articles, the series seems to hit its nadir, at least as a literary event. Reynolds sets out in his best didactic manner to spell out the role of aesthetics and morality as part of man's drive for more life. It is the gospel of psycho-economics from a spiritual rather than an economic standpoint. As an intellectual exercise, it may have stimulated many readers; but as an aesthetic one it leaves a lot to be desired. As in much of Reynolds' didactic writing, his enthusiasm tends to run away with him and he leaves the audience floundering in his wake.

Predictably, these were the articles of which Reynolds was proudest at the time – a theory of aesthetics which might perhaps have been wasted on such an ephemeral audience. When they came out at the end of July, he wrote to George Macmillan: "Very glad you like the 'Weekends'. Last Saturday's and next Saturday's are likely, I think, to be the chief ones of the lot. I'm not certain I wasn't an idiot to throw the stuff like that into two chapters of a book, for I think it's capable of being worked out in much greater detail".[61]

A certain piquancy was added to these articles by an odd coincidence that occurred on 29 June, the day of their conception. At breakfast that Thursday morning, after roughing out his notes, he opened the week's edition of the *New Age* to find an article by Arnold Bennett on an identical theme. He wrote off at once to his friend in some embarrassment. "This morning, before breakfast, I wrote out notes for an article in my *Westminster* series, to be called 'The Conquest of Ugliness'. After breakfast, the day's papers, 'New Age' included, over a customary pint of cyder shandy! And in the 'New Age' your article largely about Rodin. His 'Il n'y a pas de laideur!' which I met with in Judith Cladel's book years ago, is the chief point in my article to be. I ought to curse you by all the high gods, didn't I, and drop my article? But I shan't do either. On the contrary, I'm glad to see you saying what you do; and I'm going on writing the article of mine, as yet unwritten, just the same. But I thought I'd write and tell you so beforehand, because otherwise the evidence of plagiarism would be very strong. And perhaps if I am jumped on for it, you'll exonerate me!"[62]

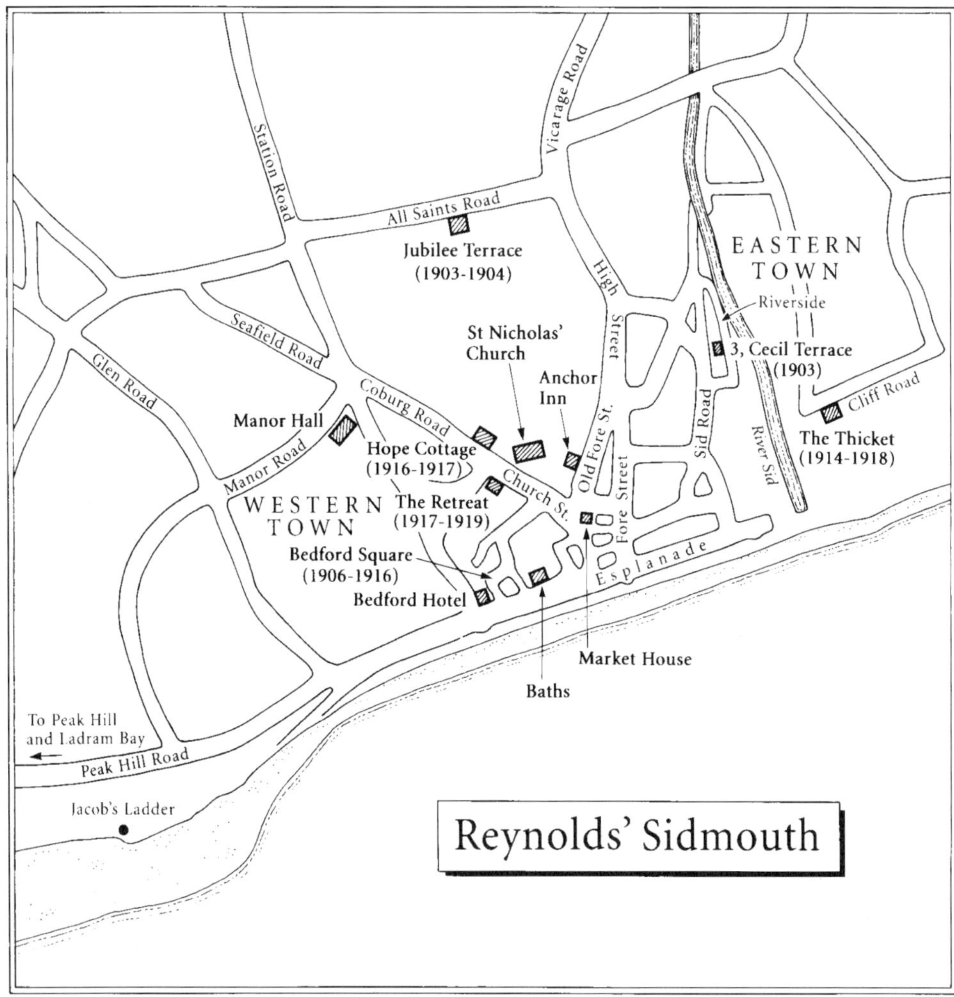

Getting the weight of these predigested opinions off his chest proved, in the event, to be the saviour of the *Nesscombe* series. Just as in Paris in 1903 his articles for the *Cheltenham Examiner* began to improve immediately he started to look around him for material, so this summer when he ran out of prepared copy and turned to daily happenings in Sidmouth the writing took on a new immediacy and the prose a welcome clarity.

On 29 May a certain Percy Deadman from Calne in Wiltshire had arrived on foot in Sidmouth seeking work. Finding none, he set off over Peak Hill for Budleigh Salterton and on the way decided rather optimistically to climb down the cliff to bathe his feet in the sea. Inevitably, he slipped on the edge and fell some 100 feet, coming to rest in a gully 200 feet above the water. He spent an horrendous night there, unable either to climb up or down, until he was spotted by two fishermen from the sea next morning.

Reynolds organised a rescue party of twelve, including Bob Woolley, George Woolley, and their friend Jim Horn; and they eventually hauled the unfortunate Deadman up off the cliff in a state of shock. A few shillings were collected for him and Reynolds with typical generosity paid his railway fare back to Calne.[63] Reynolds later organised a local collection for the rescuers "not as payment – they don't want pay for what they did – but by way of a small acknowledgement for saving life".[64] Later Deadman was reported to have been begging with threats in the neighbourhood, having pocketed all the money, and Reynolds found himself defending his charitable action in the local paper: "I, for one, can see no cause for regret in helping a man, after so terrible an experience, whatever he was".[65]

He wrote the episode up for his next article, *Deadman's Escape*, as a sort of adventure story, emphasising the touch and go of the rescue and the horror of the night on the cliffs: "When we asked him how he had felt, out there all night on the cliff, he couldn't tell us; he shuddered; but he did say that several times, especially after the boats went by without hearing him, he had been in two minds whether or not to throw himself down the rest of the way and chance it. His almost overwhelming impulse had been to go to a certain death rather than drag on through the darkness in uncertainty".[66]

The element of actuality reporting brought a new and personalised dimension to the series of articles. Katie Powys in Somerset had heard of the cliff rescue from her family; but tantalisingly they had determined not to send her a copy of the report in the local paper, for fear of untoward consequences. She noted in her diary: "I have had an excellent letter from Stephen Reynolds and since then he has been saving folks from the Cliff, in fact High Peak. An account of it was in the Western Gazette and both Lucy and Violet dare not lend it to me".[67]

This may have been purely paranoia, but is one intimation of the new intensity of Katie's feelings towards Reynolds since the last day visit to Sidmouth the previous summer. Her reclusive existence in the country and perhaps too her decision to start serious writing in eager imitation of Reynolds was already affecting her heightened sensitivity. On a visit to relatives in London in February 1910 she had had the first in a series of panic attacks. Left on her own one evening "I got rather nervous.... I felt as if some horrible demon was on the point of attacking." It was a major relief to hear the doorbell and her friends return.[68] The family, rather naively, put it down to over-excitement brought on by the story she was writing; but it was an ominous forewarning of things to come.[69]

It was about this time in 1910 that Katie and Lucy had gone to help their brother Will on his farm at Witcombe, near Montacute. There they worked happily tending the cows and learning the hidden secrets of cheesemaking, training for the farm they were planning to run together themselves. The major shock for Katie in the spring of 1911 was Lucy's marriage and the sudden rupture of such a close bond. When Lucy left Montacute to live with her husband in Hampshire, Katie was left stranded with her life plans in ruins.

Scarcely surprising then that she should turn emotionally and with revived energy to her old fantasy. In May she took her courage in both hands and wrote direct to Reynolds in Sidmouth. Ostensibly, it was to ask how everybody was and when his next books were coming out. But she also dropped a tentative invitation, as to a one-time farmer, to come and visit her at Witcombe and see the farm for himself. He was quick to head off the approach. "Thank you for your letter and kind invitation to call. But unfortunately I never seem to get anywhere except full speed up and down the line. I've got a sister and sundry nieces living near Bournemouth whom I haven't succeeded in seeing for three years! Now we have a motor boat which only myself can run I am more tied than ever."[70] But Dot and her children on the farm at Parkstone, and the time-consuming *Puffin* on the beach, were only the flimsiest of excuses.

For Katie, however, the remainder of the letter, chatty though somewhat distant, was the beginning of a correspondence. It was the "excellent" letter recorded in her diary. It provided the excuse to write again. If the family wanted to keep her away from the *Western Gazette*, it can only have been because they sensed the new disturbance to her equilibrium.

Lucy came down to Montacute for August bank holiday and that week the two sisters made their annual day's pilgrimage to Sidmouth, as if life were back to normal again. Katie had alerted Reynolds to their arrival and had brought him a duck from the farm ready for cooking.[71]

Once again, they searched for him on the beach but saw only Bob and Tom. They were told he was up in his study, and Katie set off on her own to find him, for the first time at home in his lair.

> How my knees gave and how with loud beating my heart rose to my ears when they told me my love was still with them and we should see him in the upper room. In a room laden with books, in a room with an opening towards the sea, he stretched forth his right hand. My spirit leapt as a playing deer, leapt with inspired awe, for through the entrance of his sanctuary I had come, into his very presence I was admitted. Before, it was to see him, now it was to know him
> Strange and various were the intimations he threw out to me...... In love I beheld him. I felt his range of vision was boundless. Merciless he could be. Hypocrisy was his abomination and deceit ran from him. He spared no man. To revenge injustice he would face the stake. Men feared him.

> Children knew him as one of themselves, they forsook their games to follow him.[72]

He promised to take her out for a row once again that afternoon. "With intense happiness I left him, with unbounded joy I found my sister."[73] The two sisters went for a swim and talked on the Esplanade with Uncle Sam. They took a stroll a little way up both Peak and Salcombe Hills, returning hungry for lunch in Fore Street.[74] "My heart it would not rest, so tremulous it was within me."[75]

That afternoon she waited for him below the Bedford steps.

> The fishermen steadied the boat, and the oars lay cross-wise as he came lightly running down the steps and down the beach. Their calls rang fresh within my ears as they slid her towards the sea; and more pleasant than a thousand sheep bells was the grating of her keel as she parted the shingle. They signed me to get in, the light waves lifted the bow of the boat. They floated her off, he sprang with his knee upon her side. He caught up the oar. He steered her forth. The aged fisherman smiled, and stepped back from the touch of the waves. He lifted his hand as if he blessed us.
>
> My heart flooded, and the veils of my happiness were loosed. One short moment of time I would now share with him whom I loved. One passing hour we were to be alone in a narrow wooden craft. There to possess him. His eyes searched mine, searched and pinioned me forever. In the wilderness of his sight I was lost.[76]

Reynolds was keen to keep the atmosphere low-key. He told her all his mundane woes, how swamped he was with work, both fishing and writing.[77] Katie missed most of it. "In the midst of so much, words fell to be forgotten. Unmindful were my ears, but my heart it whispered tremulous heeding."[78]

For her, it was another miraculous day – the longed-for row, tea afterwards at the Woolleys and a sudden parting with which she invested her own particular superstitious significance. "Oh I had such a nice time and I was so happy...... I did so enjoy my row. The talk was so good. I was loath to come in. He said they wanted us to have tea with them, so we did. Mrs. Woolley got it ready and I felt so hungry, but in the middle a man came and seized 'Olaf' away...... We never saw Olaf again. Still I did not mind for it made one think that not to say a 'goodbye' perhaps meant the next meeting would come sooner. I wonder."[79]

Reynolds, himself so hypersensitive to those who shared his own brand of vulnerability, was at a loss how to deal with this woman. He was the last person to be able to take her aside and talk straight. Nor was it a situation that could be circumvented by humour. He chose to be as kind and polite as he could on the surface, while maintaining a determined distance.

Soon after this latest visit, Katie wrote to him again under a literary smoke-screen, enclosing some newspaper cuttings and asking how she might get hold of some Nietzsche. He replied in strictly business fashion, kindly but like a schoolmaster addressing a rather naive pupil: "Nietzsche is published in a cheap edition by Foulis of Edinburgh. Book shops can get him. 'Thus Spake Zarathustra' is his celebrated work, but I think 'Beyond Good and Evil' is about the best of his books for a peck at. He's good as an antidote against sloppy sentimentalism, but not good to read as an authority on things, because he is a special pleader for comparatively few philosophical ideas. Therefore, read, mark, learn, but don't inwardly digest too much of him".[80]

This was a lecture designed to keep the relationship at arms length, but the reading plan, with its call to action and involvement, had just the opposite effect. By the same token, the signature to the letter, intended to appear cheery and offhand, might be read quite differently by someone in love: "I hope yourself and the cows and the cheeses are flourishing".[81]

The freshness of the article on the cliff rescue must have been evident to Reynolds too, for the *Nesscombe* series takes on a new atmosphere from that moment. Each article would still make a philosophical point, but it would be grounded on recent, living experience rather than on an accumulation of now dead thoughts.

He had recently taken Bob and another fisherman, probably Tom, to hear a concert given at the Manor Hall by Wilhelm Backhaus. Neither found anything in the music but noise and boredom, which leads Reynolds, as Hannaford, in the next article to reflect on how the middle class have deliberately appropriated high art to themselves. Interestingly, Hannaford's interlocutor on this occasion is a young novelist called Erwin, deeply interested in music, who bears no little resemblance to Hugh Walpole, the rampant Wagnerian.

> Erwin is almost the only man who can stand up to Hannaford successfully – as successfully as some children can stand up to their elders. And I think he gets on with him the better for it. An Oxford man, who worked fairly hard, but took afterwards to the lighter sorts of literature, he has the ease and self-confidence, not to say the flippancy, of a strongish man handling light weights. No doubt he feels behind him the backing of Oxford, and for practical purposes it scarcely matters whether that backing is illusory or not. His novels are not so much serious contributions to thought as graceful reflections of it. Although, like most other people, he has bees in his bonnet, he knows as a rule how to keep them from buzzing unpleasantly. He is lackadaisical and active, indolent and sharp-witted. As he treats life, so he treats Hannaford; lightly, dexterously, amiably, with a spice of condescension.[82]

This is gentle stuff compared with *Cakes and Ale*, but Walpole, who was following the series from London, may not have taken it in a kindly spirit.[83] It gives, however, a strong flavour of Reynolds' sense of inferiority in the face of someone he regarded, nevertheless, as essentially lightweight, a feeling that was to lead to the final break between the two men the following year.

What stands out in this article is Reynolds' description of the concert itself and how the music moved him. It is a timely reminder of the depth of his musical knowledge and how strongly the passion for music of his adolescence was still gripping him in his maturity.

> The second part of the recital consisted mainly of a group of Chopin pieces, including the delicate Berceuse, with its countless grace-notes, like stars in the Milky Way, and the tremendous A-flat Polonaise, which I specially wanted to hear because Backhaus has, or used to have, the reputation of a thumper, and the base strings of his piano were said to be reinforced in order to obtain a purer bass *fortissimo*. He didn't thump: the Berceuse was fairy-like. But it was the Polonaise – wild and elegant at the same time – which set my imagination to work, though I know quite well almost every note in it. They say that the Polonaise was a kind of dance-march with which the nobility of old Poland used to present themselves before their king and queen. Be that as it may, the spirit of a half-barbaric magnificence seized hold of me and stirred my blood, roused the barbarian in me, like the sudden sound of trumpets in a prosaic modern street. And then I pictured Chopin, playing his music in the drawing-rooms of Europe, whilst wars and revolutions were in the air, and Europe was spotted with tide-rips of passion let loose – wars that were life-and-death struggles...... The thoughts that music suggests flash by like waking dreams. I lived for the time being, gloriously, to the tune of that Polonaise.[84]

His three day visit to London at the end of July, primarily on fishery business, stirred in him the idea of writing a new article on the metropolis, picking up where he had left off in 1907 in *A Yokel's Impression of London*. His love-hate relationship with London, the joy of a short visit and the relief of escape home, was a puzzle he had savoured for most of his life.

> London is not home to me; it never was, even while I lived there; and I hope it never will be. It is not included in my patriotism. If a foreign force were to occupy Devon I should be roused at once to bitter hatred and revolt; I should feel 'twas a personal outrage; and no international law, with its twaddle about the amenities of civilised warfare, would prevent me, if I had the chance, from poisoning their streams and killing them off anyhow, as one kills vermin. But if it were to occupy London – well, I should be enormously interested to read about it in such

> newspapers as continued publication, and in time, no doubt, my little investments would suffer, and myself with them. I am part of the country, but only a part-possessor of London. An invasion of London would injure my small possessions; invasion of Devon would hurt me myself.[85]

And yet there remains a permanent fascination, as Reynolds arrives at Waterloo Station, takes the tube to Piccadilly Circus and emerges blinking into the light to catch the first thunderous roar of the London traffic, which he sees as a work of art in itself.

> When I imagine myself in London it is no one picture that always rises to my mind's eye. Sometimes I see the Strand and Fleet-street, sometimes the East End...... Sometimes it is my favourite restaurant in Soho [*the Mont Blanc*] that I seem to smell, and sometimes it is Paddington I picture to myself, but more often, latterly, it is the top of the Haymarket, where one comes out of the Waterloo Tube Station straight upon the hurly-burly of motor-'buses plunging down the hill to Trafalgar-square. Country fashion, I stand upon the pavement and look around for a face I know. Quite frequently I see one. In the country we should hail each other, but in London they flit by, and before I have realised their presence they have gone. I have never once succeeded in stopping anyone at that spot......
>
> The one great native art of London is an art of distribution. I mean its traffic, which *is* an art, not of a static permanent sort, like a piece of painting or a book, but dynamic and transitory, like music. Vehicles of every build and speed crowd from every direction into a central thoroughfare. They drive by hair's breadths, swiftly and continuously, and if but one man fails to do what the collective mind of all the drivers expects of him, then the whole stretch of traffic is instantly in a dangerous disorder. It reminds me of nothing so much as of boat-sailing, where, by skill alone, one uses every puff of wind, which otherwise would capsize the boat, to drive it along. And in a way it is a greater art than boat-sailing, in that it's collective, and depends upon a collective technique, as the medieval builders' art must have done. It's the art of the London folk. From end to end of London there is nothing of London's own more wonderful than the traffic, and more beautifully done.[86]

This visit in July took Reynolds through a number of bureaucratic worlds, some of which were fairly new to him: Pinker, the literary agent, in Arundel Street, George Macmillan, the publisher, in St Martin's Street, fisheries officials of the Board of Agriculture in Parliament Street, MPs and Ministers at the House of Commons. What struck him most this time as he moved from world to world was the illusory nature of their "work". It confirmed for him his essential prejudice against London – its parasitical nature.

> It is as a parasite that London most and most often impresses me. After all, the primary work of man on earth is the preservation of his existence by gaining food from the soil and sea, and by making for himself sufficient shelter from the weather. In varying degrees, all other work is secondary, and at a last pinch can be done without. But food and shelter mankind must have in any case. We are apt to forget it in civilised countries, but labouring people don't forget it, and that is what they mean when they say with their deep resentment: 'Why should 'em all look down on us, an' grudge us the fruits of our labour, when they all, the whole lot of 'em, lives on our labour?'
>
> London is the head and centre of that process of blood-sucking. It struck me especially, the last time I was up there, that practically no primary work was being done in London. Hundreds of thousands were engaged in the secondary work of distributing and elaborating the products of primary labour; thousands made no pretence of doing any work at all, and as a rule seemed proud of the fact; and thousands, again, were occupied in the tertiary work of merely ministering to the comfort and pleasure of the other two sections. Millions, altogether, were living ultimately on the primary labour which was being done humbly and ceaselessly elsewhere. But for that they would find themselves with nothing to do, let alone nothing to eat. Imagine London, always so scornful of the yokel and the savage, trying to grow its own food in flower-pots! When I look at the sleek and well-fed West Enders; when I plunge about among the offices of lawyers, officials, journals, and agents of all sorts; when I meet respected and distinguished people; and when, at the same time, I call to mind my labouring friends at home and the multitude like them all over the earth, who sweat and toil for the support of London, an indignation and contempt that I can't express floods through me. Besides, it wouldn't do to express it. The contempt includes myself.[87]

Again this article, though missing much of the lyrical quality of its 1907 predecessor, works well within the series because it has all the fresh feeling of a recently lived experience. In terms of journalism it is primary work, rather than the reheated philosophical food with which Reynolds had started the series.

His next two articles, the penultimate ones, on *Nakedness* and *Rabelaisianism*, drew again on directly personal experience at Sidmouth that scorching summer. The summer of 1911 was in fact the hottest in England since 1868. At the beginning of August the shade temperature in London was regularly over 90 degrees, and on the ninth it hit 97. While the Government, which should have been on holiday, was struggling to settle the industrial unrest in those sweltering August days, and many Londoners saw the strikes and the heat as an image of the end of the world, Reynolds had rediscovered the joys of bathing naked on the secluded beach of West Bay beyond Jacob's

Ladder. In a lyrical passage, Hannaford describes his first discovery of another beach to the east of the town and of how nakedness can draw one close to nature.

> It was hot, hazily hot; so that the Brixham trawlers, becalmed out in the Channel, looked unreal and ghostly. The combe narrows and deepens near the sea to a small steep gorge, on the sides of which the bushes, whose roots are always watered by the Linnbrook, grow so tall and thick that they meet together overhead. I splashed down the shadowy green tunnel so formed, and in one step, as it were, came out through a break in the cliffs upon the open beach. The sun's rays, the glow of the sun-baked pebbles, seemed actually to hit me. The hot air trembled visibly above the shingle in multitudes of quick-dancing little wavelets. All sounds had at once a perfect clearness and a thin, dreamlike remoteness. I don't know what took hold of me; it wasn't merely a desire for coolness and refreshment. Some old instinct wakened into life, some heightened sense of relationship between myself and nature, some deep-lying impulse to shed off my clothes, the signs of man's detachment from nature, and to go to her just as she made me.... Naked, I was not more ashamed, but less. Clothed, I had felt an intruder; naked, I felt simply myself, unabashed...... After a swim in the sea, I lay out naked upon the beach, like one of the cats
>
> Qui semblent s'endormir dans un rêve sans fin.
>
> It was, I think, the loveliest experience I had had for years. High above me the jutting red cliffs were patched with flowering sea-kale, and higher still the gulls hovered, screaming wild-heartedly because, doubtless, the weather was about to change. The caress of the air was softer than silk. The breath of the wind off land, eddying round beneath the cliff, had in it a faint scent of hay. The purr and rattle of the waves was always growing nearer and at the same time dying away into the distance. And like the sound of the waves, my own thoughts floated through my mind, lazily, tranquilly, melodiously wafted to me from far-off. I held up my own wrist, which was sunburnt and not unflexible, and its beauty struck me with a curious surprise. I was proud of my body, inasmuch as I felt myself, then, to be not a spectator, but a part of nature, and to share in her acknowledged beauty.[88]

It was an article that Katie Powys had at last caught up with. On holiday that September at her brother Theodore's house in East Chaldon, she too went swimming off the Dorset coast watched by Violet, her sister-in-law. She noted her diary: "That same afternoon, Violet, I and Maud went down to the sea. I dipped myself as 'Hannaford' advises. I agree with him, nothing is better and the run afterwards. I chased Violet and she laughed when I caught her and kissed her as I was."[89]

But there were others that were not amused. That August, the Sidmouth Council had put up a notice on Jacob's Ladder prohibiting naked bathing by men and boys in the vicinity because the eastern end of the West Bay beach was frequented by ladies. It was quite common in Edwardian England for men and boys to swim naked from public beaches while propriety demanded that women should bathe almost fully dressed from bathing tents or machines – a double standard which generally went unchallenged. In defending this male right, the fictional Hannaford lays into the Council for its narrow-minded sniffing out of indecencies where none exist, and argues the need for a "breeze of Rabelaisianism" to sweep the country.[90]

On the same day that Hannaford launched his attack on the Council in the *Westminster Gazette*, Reynolds opened up a second front in the *Sidmouth Herald* with a letter complaining that the women were at fault for pitching their bathing tents close to the men's bathing place, whose special status had been recognised for generations. "It is no uncommon thing, moreover, for so many women to be sitting about or paddling in the men's bathing place that it is almost impossible to find any spot from which to bathe except under their eyes. I don't so much mind their coming there, if they very much want to; what I do mind is this, that they should first of all intrude on our bathing place, and then complain because they find us naked there. Such conduct can be only put down either to ignorance of the fact that it is the men's bathing place...... or else to sheer wantonness or an itch for creating trouble – in which two latter cases, let the blame be upon them, not on us."[91]

The response was remarkable. Two weeks later, a poem addressed to Reynolds, signed by a Bessie Kittley, appeared in the local paper claiming that women did indeed enjoy watching the men bathing and might obtain useful swimming instruction from it. It also made a plea for equality.

> Why can't us bathe the same as they?
> Why should us have to cap our tresses?
> Why should us have to shun that road?
> In days of old we wore no dresses,
> And men just stained themselves with woad....
> We're not ashamed to see a dimple.... [92]

Reynolds decided to take this lady correspondent head on.

> Well, dear Bessie Kittley, you are most welcome, so far as I am concerned, to come and bathe "the same as us", without any dress; for then, at any rate, you shouldn't very well complain of us. I wouldn't say you were shocking, if others did. Only, do come stained with woad. It would be so interesting to see what the Ancient British women looked like.

> And if, as your rhyme seems to say, it's myself you wish to watch swimming, I should be delighted to give you an exhibition of "the water art" in any attire whatsoever – from a great coat to a fig-leaf, or without – provided you would let me know in advance the precise degree of nakedness you desire. I won't be ashamed any more than you. I don't see any reason to be ashamed, for, if anything, I am even uglier dressed than I am undressed, and it's pleasant to know you feel likewise. As for dimples, however, if you consider dimples indispensable – I deeply regret to have to say that I have looked over myself, and, hang it all, I can't find a single one! Will vaccination marks do?
>
> But oh, Bessie, Bessie! where is that modesty of yours, that you should know so much about men's bathing drawers? You remind me – forgive me – of the old tale about Dr Johnson, who was congratulated by a young lady on having omitted from his dictionary all improper and objectionable words. "So," said the doctor, "you have been looking to see, my dear!"[93]

Reynolds, who always enjoyed a bit of fun with newspapers, was rather proud of this effort. He told Katie Powys: "I have a most amusing controversy on over the bathing with a woman named Bessie Kittley. She wrote a poem *at* me; and I have written an Open Letter to her, which itself is rather Rabelaisian!"[94]

But the wind was soon taken out of his sails. He received a letter from a Miss Kitley (one t) proclaiming that she had had nothing to do with the verses published in her name.[95] The letter was a complete hoax and an embarrassed Reynolds, whatever his behaviour on the beach, found he had indecently exposed himself in the public prints. Worst of all, the hoax poem was probably written by a man! Reynolds publicly apologised for directing his open letter at the wrong person but, for someone who himself delighted in writing anonymous letters to the press, took a rather holier than thou attitude towards the hoaxer: "The practice of writing anonymous letters to newspapers is dubious enough, and reflects little credit on those who are afraid to back their opinions with their names. To borrow somebody else's name for the purpose is a kind of forgery...... Someone evidently needs to learn the lesson that one can play the fool *in* the Press, but not *with* the Press."[96] Three years later it was a lesson he had still not learned himself.

The sweltering summer of 1911 was somewhat less stifling at Sidmouth where the onshore breezes kept the temperature rarely above 80 degrees. Despite Bessie Kittley, Reynolds went swimming every day without fail and managed to pick up a touch of sunstroke before the weather finally broke half way through September.[97]

His social and civic duties were not confined, however, to rescuing foolhardy visitors from the cliffs and protecting the bathing rights of the weaker sex. On 22 June, the Coronation day of George V, he and Harold Wright organised a "Beach and Lifeboat" lunch for 30 to 40 Sidmouth fishermen at the Marine Hotel.[98] The speeches and discussion delighted him with their intimation of a new desire for close co-operation among the fishermen – an ambition for which he had been battling for the previous five years.[99] A rumour went round that this event had been got up as a rival attraction to the official public luncheon for the older parishioners of Sidmouth, and Reynolds was forced to deny it in the local paper.[100] He wrote a little sourly to Garnett: "We had a beach and lifeboat dinner for the Coronation. It went off very well, except for the unfortunate ass who had the trouble of getting it up and the honour of paying for most of it."[101]

That spring and summer, two new Woolley faces were to be seen taking the air in their white bonnets and double pram along the Esplanade. The previous November, Tom's wife Nellie had given birth to non-identical twins, Sylvia and Gladys – the latter soon becoming "Fay" when Bob commandeered the name of Gladys for his own next offspring.[102] It was a new responsibility for Tom, especially when his wife fell ill. "Tom and his wife have been having rather a bad time. A chill gave her abscesses in the breast, with fever and great pain, so that she had to go to bed. Tom had to do boating, housework, and baby nursing – all three together; – and he ended up by taking the twins out in a perambulator by himself, across the Esplanade! Really, they have been plucky, both of them, over those blessed Twinses."[103]

At the beginning of May, the shingle question raised its ugly head once more. The Council, at the behest of the Board of Trade, made a sample prosecution of a local man for taking shingle from the beach, a practice which was now once again, despite the 1908 Order, becoming widespread. After much legal wrangling, the Otterton magistrates threw the case out on the technical ground that the Council could not act as a common informant.[104] Reynolds was surprised but not despondent: "Last week-end we were all agog with a shingle prosecution, in which the case was dismissed, by a bench that wanted to wash their hands of it, on a technical quibble that has never been raised before – a mere formality in the making out of the summonses. But I think it will do good in that it has set up the back of the Bd. of Trade to fight the thing through itself".[105]

The legal issue drifted on that summer by way of case stated, and landed up in the Divisional Court where in early December the Council and Reynolds were victorious.[106] The Manor and some local residents were up in arms. Some form of *rapprochement* was needed if a long legal battle were to be avoided. At midday on 7 December, Reynolds sat down with Colonel Balfour and Hastings, his agent, to try and work out a compromise with which both sides could live. They reached a preliminary agreement under which the Manor undertook not to take or countenance the taking of any shingle while the fishermen would turn a blind eye to the taking of sand for local purposes.[107]

It fell to Reynolds the following week to gain acceptance of all parties to the deal. "My negotiations with the Manor seem to be within sight of an end if only I can get everybody to stick to the points at issue and forget the past malpractices and insults of the local builders. It has been very tough work, but even if the negotiations break down, I think the Manor people will have a better understanding of my fishery aims here and more disposition to further them."[108] He managed to negotiate a satisfactory *modus vivendi* that was to survive for the next two years.

The shingle issue was a perennial problem that ebbed and flowed like the tide itself. Political gains of one year turned into the losses of the next. But 1911 was a turning point for Reynolds' involvement in a question where long term solutions *were* feasible – the better organisation of the longshore fisheries and the more efficient marketing of their product.

Since the arrival of the *Puffin* and the formation of the firm of Woolley and Reynolds in the summer of 1910, Reynolds involvement in fisheries issues had become both more personal and more professional. Before, he had been merely an extra hand on the boats, trying to prove his worth to his companions on the beach. Now he became the driving force behind the new enterprise, with a determination to maximise its efficiency and its profits. In July 1910 he established the company's records on a sound footing, but as always with Reynolds it was a process of self experiment. He told Pinker: "Last week, knowing no bookkeeping, I had a huge struggle with the firm's bookkeeping, and finally evolved a system that seems satisfactory – by algebra, knowing no other way".[109]

In *Alongshore*, he had argued for businessmen with capital to come forward and assist the longshore fishermen in new marketing schemes to fight the existing fish dealers on their own ground and plough back the profits to the fishermen themselves. He had intended to perform that role himself for Sidmouth, but only once he had built up sufficient capital. January 1911, however, produced the best herring season at Sidmouth for some years – two short, but very profitable bursts of activity, westward off Budleigh Salterton and eastward in Seaton Bay. He was tempted away from the cautious approach and started marketing direct the catches of their two boats using the firm's barrels.[110]

The experiment was an instant success, raising the local price from six to twenty shillings a thousand, and making for their own firm a few shillings a thousand above that.[111] It was a most encouraging start but he was conscious, as he told Frederick Macmillan, of the need to proceed with caution: "I have been rather unwell, and desperately busy day and night, drifting for herrings, taking third oar to Seaton and walking home, picking out fish, and packing them. For many herrings and much dissatisfaction has driven me into starting the fish-buying scheme outlined in *Alongshore* before I was ready, before, in fact, I had earned the capital I wanted. Therefore, I have to be most wary, and am for the present rather a forwarding agent than a buyer, but so far, every time except once I have succeeded in getting them a price better than the local prices which my small operations have considerably driven up".[112]

The first season of the *Puffin* had entirely fulfilled its main object by converting the local fishermen to the feasibility of motors for fishing. A second season would pay off the initial investment. Motors would have made all the difference to the herring season that year: "If we had had a motor in our drifter last January we should have paid it off in a fortnight; instead of which we worked ourselves almost to death catching herrings 12 miles from home with no wind to get there".[113] He planned to instal a motor in the new drifter that Bob and Tom were having built the next autumn, and use the advance from *Seems So!* to pay for it.[114]

Success at Sidmouth was one thing, but he was determined that the message should be spread abroad to help, despite their innate conservatism, longshore fishermen throughout the country. He had been negotiating with the editor of *The Times* to write a series of articles on the subject but had found it impossible to find the time to get started on them.[115]

A new opportunity arose on 20 June when Noel Buxton, the Liberal MP for North Norfolk who had a strong constituency interest in small fisheries, raised the future of longshore fishing in a Consolidated Fund Bill debate in the House of Commons. He castigated the Government for the long delays in publishing the annual fishery reports and in pursuing Development Fund grants for small fishermen. There was altogether too little information on the inshore fishing industry and its needs.[116] Other members pressed the case for special commissioners to inquire into the industry, and for the setting up of co-operative societies and insurance schemes.[117]

Responding to the debate, the junior minister at the Board of Agriculture and Fisheries, Sir Edward Strachey, was more accommodating than anyone had quite expected.

> We desire to have special commissioners appointed – not a permanent commissioner – to inquire into such grievances of the inshore fishermen as have been brought before the House to-day, and at the present time we are asking for a sum of money to be placed at our disposal in order to have a special investigation into the matter and to have a report presented on the various subjects mentioned by the hon. Member.
> It is perfectly impossible for the President of the Board of Agriculture to make up his mind as to what should be done in the matter of co-operation, credit banking, loans to fishermen, and the improvement of shellfish beds unless he has full information before him; and for that purpose the Board propose to ask for a sum of money to be placed at their disposal in order that the whole of the question may be thoroughly gone into, and also that there may be an investigation on the spot as to what may be done for the advantage of fishermen, and especially inshore fishermen.[118]

Reading this somewhat off-the-cuff announcement in the press, Reynolds' eye alighted on the familiar name of Strachey and he wrote straight off to his friend, the editor of the *Spectator*. It was a letter that was to change his life.

> Is not Sir Edward Strachey a brother or relative of yours? I have been wondering if I might go so far as to ask for an introduction to him, witnessing, so to speak, that in fishery matters I'm a worker and not a mere windbag. I see by his answer in the House the other night that they are going to inquire into the small inshore fisheries to see what can be done for them, and naturally, after working here on my own for so long, I am in a position to help them with knowledge not to be picked up by inspection and in inquiries, just as they are in a position to help us with the power they've got in their elbow. It's largely the fishermen themselves who form the difficulty; it is fatally easy to set their backs up; the Fishery Boards, formed to help them, have done little else. It's no earthly use their ladling out money, without ploughing the field to sow it in; and it's no use their sending round commissioners unless the commissioners know how to get the right side of the fishermen. They'll be confused with 'bogey-men' and hear nothing at all of any real utility.
> I should like to send Sir Edward Strachey the fishery chapters of my longshore book, and show him the results of our rather successful fish-forwarding experiment last winter, when we rose the price from 6/- a thousand to 20/-, and kept it there. I've succeeded in convincing the fishermen along this bit of coast of the utility of motors, which, I believe, offer the best chance of survival to small fishermen. That they haven't got them yet is due to want of capital, and even more to want of instruction in the use of them. What every small fishery wants is a man ashore who would see that every motor went to sea all right. To judge by the speeches and talk at our Beach and Lifeboat lunch yesterday, the fishermen here are just about ripe for co-operative methods. It has taken me five years of talking, working with them, and experimenting at my own risk, to bring them to that point. You can judge from that the difficulties lying ahead of a government department approaching the matter from outside, with all the bad reputation of government departments to live down!
> And now, with success in sight, the job has grown too big for me alone, with the limited time and money at my disposal.[119]

St Loe Strachey was only too pleased to pass on the burden of the letter to his brother at the Board of Agriculture. He did so with a notable puff for Reynolds, his experience and his integrity.

> In case you may not know about Mr Reynolds I may say that he is a very able man of letters who has written some of the most remarkable books published in the last ten years in regard to the condition of the working class. Though a University man and possessed of a most remarkable style and liberal perception, Mr. Reynolds has for the last five or six years not only lived in a fisherman's family like a fisherman, but he has worked at

> the fishing trade seriously for his living and not merely in order to try what it was like and to write about it. That is the real difference between him and so many people of the semi-reporter kind, who here and in America go and work for a few weeks or months, and then come out and write of "what it feels like to be a locomotive stoker", and so forth. Mr. Reynolds, by the way, has often written things for me in the "Spectator", and very able things, and I hope that when my paper is less congested he will write more, for he always hits the nail on the head......
> Of course I do not know whether you will be able to help Reynolds, but I do not think he is a man who will let you in [*down*] in fact, and I am sure that you can depend upon him not wanting to let you in at all. He is a straightforward sensible man and not a crank, humbug, or a self-seeker.[120]

The introduction worked wonders. Reynolds was invited up to town for talks at the Board with officials and made his usual strong first impression. In fact, he used his three days in London from 26 to 28 July to spread his net wider and hold discussions with a number of fishery MPs, including Noel Buxton who was in the process of forming a committee of backbenchers to deal with fisheries problems.[121] He invited Noel Buxton down to Sidmouth for a weekend in August and Buxton invited him to join the parliamentary committee as its adviser.[122] He was delighted with the progress – "Things seem at last to be moving a bit".[123] But on his return home, with a Nesscombe article to do, he was reminded more strongly than ever of the emotional conflict between fisheries politics and writing. He told Pinker: "That plunge into fishery affairs has put me off writing, with a weekly article to get done. I groan, à la Conrad!"[124]

His visit to London bore instant fruit. The Board of Agriculture inquired unofficially if he would be prepared, if formally offered appointment, to become one of the special commissioners to look into the inshore fisheries. He was both pleased and flattered, and inclined to accept provided, as always, he could fulfil the function on his own terms. He wrote to Pinker: "I shall probably accept, but only provided I retain freedom to carry on with my writing at my own time. Already I do more work at fisheries than the average government official does, and if I can continue it, backed by government money.... Well and good. But I shan't sell my liberty to them".[125]

He filled up, on a provisional basis, an official form giving his personal particulars. In the space for "Testimonials", he scrawled across it "None"; "and I explained to them carefully that I'm a man who wants to do a job, not a man who wants a job; thinking that if they don't want me as I am, and mean to continue, they had better chuck me first than last".[126] He took the precaution, however, of quoting George Macmillan as a personal referee.[127] Macmillan, who perhaps saw the appointment as a chance to give his young author some greater stability, was all in favour of his acceptance: "If the appointment you speak of is definitely offered you I strongly advise you to accept it, as it can hardly fail to be of advantage to your fishery work and is not likely to interfere seriously with your literary work. And it should help your position generally".[128]

Formal establishment of the Commission was held up to await a Commons debate and vote in the autumn session of Parliament, and Reynolds determined to complete his fishery articles for *The Times* in anticipation of the debate.[129] It was held up further that autumn by internal Government politics – the incursion of the newly formed Development Commission into fisheries issues and the replacement in the October reshuffle of Lord Carrington as President of the Board of Agriculture by the more radical and dynamic Walter Runciman, fresh from his reforms at the Board of Education.

For the last three weeks of November, Reynolds had once more to abandon the security of his two rooms in Sidmouth to make way for Mam Woolley and her latest confinement. The enforced exile in the event coincided neatly with the publication of *Seems So!* and some more fisheries work for the Parliamentary Committee. He stayed the weekend of 11/12 November with Conrad where he indulged, as a change from fisheries, in a little publishing politics.

Macmillan had expressed an interest in the past in taking on Conrad, but an approach through Austin Harrison in June had come to naught, mainly because Conrad was tied to Methuen for three books, with one still to deliver.[130] Conrad, with his natural antipathy towards publishers in general, was now beginning to feel about Methuen what Reynolds had felt about John Lane the year before. On the eve of Reynolds' visit, he wrote to Pinker: "I will be very frank with you in this matter. I don't like my position with Methuen. It's a very modern manufactory of books, no doubt with very up to date methods (or used to be) but without any sort of literary associations or tradition. Methuen's is a shop...... And really they are irritating. They bother one to write pars for their list about one's own work. I told them plainly twice to attend to their own business and try to do it half as well as I do mine...... Their imprint has no particular distinction; their proceedings are queer...... I had the pleasure of seeing Mr. Methuen once. He had the impudence to advise me what to write. I prefer to deal with men who know better than to talk like that to an author who has always stood on his own feet, quite alone both in vision and expression".[131]

Reynolds now saw the opportunity to act as intermediary and took the matter up with George Macmillan. "You will recollect remarking that you would like to have the publication of Conrad's work.... I should be glad enough to see him settled with you, after listening for so many hours at different times to his publishing troubles. If I am at liberty to tell him of your wish, or can say anything in furtherance of it, perhaps you'll let me know."[132] George Macmillan was interested: "If you are going down to see Conrad there is no reason why you should not tell him that if he is thinking of changing his publisher we should be quite willing to consider any proposal for a new book. Of course we know nothing as to his sales, though we do know that he has a good reputation as a writer".[133]

That weekend Conrad responded warmly to the idea, and reported back to Pinker: "I fancy they would be willing to take over all my books if the thing could be negotiated. Perhaps it wouldn't be a bad thing. These people have money. I asked Reynolds who was to call on Sir Frederick to say that I was open to such a proposal. But I haven't heard anything from him or them yet".[134]

Reynolds discussed the matter with Macmillan the following week, whereupon it became clear that the hopes of picking up Conrad might take rather longer to turn into reality. When Reynolds wrote to Conrad to explain the position, the elder writer, with his fairly jaundiced view of publishers, expressed no surprise: "Thanks for the McM. mission. I quite see. It's bound to be a long affair if it ever comes off, which I doubt somewhat. It seems P [*Pinker*] had some sort of conversation with G. McM. lately."[135] Conrad's prediction was right; it never did come off. Two years later, with *Chance*, he became a bestselling author. It was one of Macmillans' rare lost opportunities.

In London, Reynolds spent the weekdays in Chelsea with Reginald Page, his old friend from Lane's.[136] The first weekend he went down with Noel Buxton to the east coast to speak at two meetings on fisheries matters.[137] On Saturday 18 November he addressed the fishermen of Cromer at the town's Lecture Hall on the problems of the three mile limit, trawling, the insurance of boats and gear, the sale of immature fish and, favourite subject of all, the improvement of marketing. After some discussion, Noel Buxton proposed the formation of a local fisheries association, which was established on the spot.[138] Co-operation was at last truly in the air.

The next weekend, he stayed with Harold Wright's parents at Sutton where he heard from Bob of the arrival of the new baby and a winter storm that had wreaked havoc on the beach.[139] He had been absent from Sidmouth for only two weeks and yet he wrote back in a notably homesick tone: "What a time you must have had with the boats! Wish I had been there. Anyhow I'm getting rather sick of being up country but I am more or less bound to go up to the meeting at the House of Commons next Wed. It is no good spoiling the ship over a ha'porth of tar".[140]

On 29 November he attended a most successful meeting of Buxton's Parliamentary Inshore Fisheries Committee and made arrangements to meet the new President of the Board, Walter Runciman, at a later date.[141] He had now been introduced to the very centre of affairs and saw for the first time the very real possibility of projecting his long-meditated policy ideas on a truly national scale.

But he was still sticking fast to the principle of maintaining his independence, in the Board and the Committee's case by refusing to accept any out-of-pocket expenses. He looked anxiously to George Macmillan and the sales of the new book: "I'm afraid, unless I can buck up my earnings, that I shan't be able to pay my own rather heavy expenses; and if I accept the money that has been offered me from three or four quarters, then I shall lose the complete independence of action that I have found so useful. If, for example, I had accepted the Inshore Fisheries Committee's offer of expenses, I should hardly have been able to go into direct communication with Runciman, as I have succeeded in doing, because it would have been going over the heads of my employers, so to speak".[142]

For some, this looked like gross over-sensitivity; but for Reynolds it was essential to maintaining the independence without which he could not operate. He was beginning to realise that the conflict between his political ambition and his poorly paid writing might soon lead to a parting of the ways. The whirl of fisheries discussions at the end of November had caused him to break a planned meeting with George Sturt. In writing to apologise, he indulged in some thinking aloud: "I was so sorry not to see you that day in London. Being furiously busy with fishery affairs, committee at the House of Commons and such-like, it was the only chance I had. It looks as if fishery matters will drag me out of literature altogether soon. They leave me less and less time to write, and cost me so much that I shall be compelled to accept one of the fishery appointments they have been offering me".[143]

It was to come sooner than he could have dreamed. On 9 and 16 September the last of the Nesscombe articles, entitled *Immortality*, was published in two instalments in the *Westminster Gazette*. Reynolds had deliberately broken off the series to make way for his *Times* fishery articles, but he hoped to pick it up the following year and eventually turn *Nesscombe* into a book.[144]

Immortality is the vehicle for a moving account of Reynolds' scepticism, mysticism and belief in the superiority of the intuitive over the intellectual. In it Hannaford, at one of his evening gatherings, tears to shreds the book of a young clergyman attempting to show that immortality can be proved by science. After dinner, Hannaford accompanies the local Catholic priest, the French-born Father Chapuis, back home to Salterport over Steep Head (High Peak). Reynolds succumbs to the special beauty of his favourite walk.

> Steep Head itself – abrupt enough on the landward side, and precipitous over the sea – stood up black into the sky, so that the faint light which filtered through the cloud seemed to be resting upon it. Without so much as a word said, we started climbing up towards the light by a narrow track through the bracken, and presently we came out upon the brow of the Head, where falls of cliff have sliced in half the bare entrenchments of an early British camp. 'Twas the crown of the hill; the crown of the cliff also.
>
> The tilled lands lay below us, all the blacker for being spotted here and there with lamp-lit cottage windows. On the other side, deep down below our feet, the sea was like a misty bottomless pit, but for the waves

> breaking white on the darker shadow of Picket Rock. Across the bay, the occulting light on Berry Head blinked the wordless message, the assurance of fellow-humanity's existence, which lighthouses seem always to throw out across the lonely water. A startled gull roused the colony of sea-birds and jackdaws from the face of the cliff. Very gradually their wild screaming, mewing, and cawing died away, until once more the whole of nature was sunk in that still sleep, through which, nevertheless, one feels all the time the breathing presence of life. The sea, the cliffs, the hills – they, too, seemed only asleep. From our vantage-point, midway between earth and sky, it was as if we were looking out over the dim world.

Looking down across the cliffs, Reynolds makes his declaration of faith.

> He pointed with his hand at the sea, and at the shadowy long-lying range of cliffs, which an invisible moon, risen behind the clouds, had seemingly created out of darkness. "What is it that one feels there? Is it God? or what god? or any other kind of spirit? Is it a stirring of life on the face of the earth? Or is it only a projection of oneself? I don't know; I can't know; and, as I have said, I don't care, so long as I can feel its presence and feel myself in union with it; since it is, for me, a fact which transcends its own nature, whatever that may be. And likewise with immortality. Whether or no I am immortal, and, if so, in what sense or form – I don't know, I don't care. If only I can feel myself an integral, living part of this living, existing world, can I not await with confidence whatever may become of me, even supposing it is but re-absorption into the whole. Am I not already a part of the whole? I put my trust – in I know not whom. I have faith – in I know not what. Before argument, I believe life. The one ultimate fact I know, that I am, I am alive – that is the fact least likely to lie."

In an almost biblical scene, the priest takes Hannaford to the edge of the cliff and shows him the lights of Sidmouth twinkling up the valley far below across the bay. His gentle critique is also a new call.

> Father Chapuis took hold of Hannaford's arm and led him to the side of the hill from which one could see the lights of Salterport. They lay twinkling for a mile or more down the valley; a curved line of them marked the beach; and in their shimmer it was possible to see the town's smoke and the river-mist drifting in the light air far out to sea. ""My dear shild," said the Father, "you are philosophic; but I have even the same fault to find with your philosophy as you have found with the young man's arguments – that it is too clear-cut, as you say. Look down from here at the town, so pretty, so quiet, so tranquil. But it is veritably a hub-

bub of people – love and hate, evil and goodness, birth, begetting, a fluttering, and death, all woven in together, and the fabric which results, it is the town. Can they all see as you see, and if they cannot, must they then see nothing? The blessed saints, by going apart, have they not perceived Truth? Yet I do not think that the Truth can be said to be apprehended, and be possessed, until it is seen without going apart from men. How they are tied the one to the other down there! How entangled! How they cannot be what they would! Ah, do I not know! And yet it is more like flames, they are, with flickering and with smoke mingled, upleaping. If you were more bound to other men, would your philosophy from it emerge so clearly? If, for example, you had a wife and little shildren? Have you regarded the cost of living to yourself, where, perhaps, you can see more clearly with a greater ease? Is it not that you value so greatly life because you do not find yourself in the middle stream of it? I am become old, and my flock it is my shildren; but I could wish to see you with shildren of your own, even if they did tie you down to earth. It is not good to live as you do, with nothing but your vision. It is better to live in the dim light, and the warmth, than to see far away the bright light, but to be oneself in the cold and the darkness. You would say so yourself, is it not?"[145]

Hannaford breaks down, as Reynolds himself might have done. Part of the desperation and loneliness of a man who would never have children was in him too. But the story is much more than that. It reads now as a sort of farewell to the Sidmouth of 1906 and the cosy, self-sufficient world of writing; and as a clarion call to the life of action and of men. It was a kind of prediction.

Apart from one short story, these were the last words of fiction he ever would write.

FOURTEEN

How 'Twas 1912

On Friday 1 December 1911 Stephen Reynolds returned home from his second period of exile from the poor man's house, enforced by the new arrival of yet another of the poor man's babies.[1] It was three and a half years since the last occasion and this time he had spent only three weeks away – hectically rushing round in London and East Anglia, supervising the launch of *Seems So!* and of his new political career in the fisheries.

The baby had been born on 15 November and Mam Woolley had already been downstairs a week when he returned.[2] His first encounter with the new addition to the Woolley household had none of the emotional overtones of his meeting with Semaphore three years before, but he shared equally in the family's delight: "The baby isn't half a bad little animal – the first in the family to have dark hair – a regular fuzz of it."[3] The distaff side of his London literary world rallied round. George Macmillan's wife sent down a large parcel of baby things, and Conrad passed on his good wishes for the birth of *Seems So!* and of the baby: "Give my regards and congratulations to your collaborators and to Bob also on the other kind of authorship, with wishes of all possible luck to the newcomer. Jessie has begun to knit a coat already."[4] There was no fancy nickname this time. The baby was christened simply Gladys Clara. She was the last child to be born to Bob and Mary Woolley and the only one to survive into the next century and the new millennium.

The stormy weather that had marked his absence continued into the following week, when the sea poured over the front and down the Gut no less than three times and the little low-lying square was completely flooded out. On 7 December he was out with the others at three in the morning to save what they could of the boats that were smashing about along the shore road. They took a break in the protection of the shelter on the front and had a narrow escape. Just after they left it, it smashed to pieces in a sudden squall.[5] They spent much of the time wading up to their thighs in water, and Reynolds spent one day wet through to the skin from breakfast till tea-time, proudly boasting that he had taken no harm.[6] As ever, he found the violence and danger exhilarating. He sent George Macmillan a photograph of the *Puffin* floating up the road: "Sidmouth has been quite exciting lately with the sea over the front three times in one week! No such a flood out for twenty years they say".[7]

Macmillan was to spend Christmas and the New Year in Bath in an attempt to cure a sudden onset of lumbago. "My lumbago is no better and I am ordered to Bath next week for waters and other special treatment. I am advised that the plant is better there than at Sidmouth......"[8] Reynolds, who had been for some time a keen customer of the salt water baths on the front, a few doors down from Bedford Square, pretended offence at this snub to the local facilities: "Sorry to hear you are no better and that they've ordered you to a dead-alive place like Bath. Our man at the baths here is exceedingly good, and was trained at Bath".[9] Macmillan agreed to complete his cure at the Victoria Hotel in January with a week of bracing Sidmouth air.[10]

The excitement of the floods and news of the early reprint of *Seems So!* was not enough, however, to stave off the traditional Reynolds Christmas blues, which hit him in an even more aggravated form this year. In the run-up to Christmas, he always shared in the Bedford Square festivities, sending out small gifts of food to his fishermen neighbours, especially those in need, and silver coins to all his children friends.[11] But much as he loved the Woolleys, he could not bear a family Christmas dinner which served only to accentuate his private loss of family and deep sense of isolation. He was also of late becoming increasingly irritated with Bob and with the noisy interruption of his work by both family and outside callers.

This Christmas Day he walked over to Beer on his own and stopped at a pub to take a bread and cheese Christmas dinner with a party of gipsies, social outcasts like himself. A few days later, cheered up a little, he wrote brightly of the experience to George Macmillan: "I had a new sort of dinner. Christmas always upsets my applecart; sleeplessness, the blues, or summat; and this year I simply cleared out, and had a bread and cheese dinner with a horde of horse-dealing gipsies in a wayside tap-room. One of them was very wealthy, and it was most amusing to hear the others getting at him".[12]

But on Christmas night itself, with the feelings of isolation still close, he confided to his journal one of the most deeply felt of his Christmas laments.

> Got up late. 11 A.M. walked out of Town to Three Horseshoes. Dined cheese, bread and beer. On to Beer. Tea at Anchor. Back to Three Horseshoes, and jawed fisheries. Home about 9.... Bloody day, but better than staying at home. Christmas breaks the illusions that outcasts weave about themselves. For those who have no ties, except those they hang on to by force of their wits, it's a dismal festival.[13]

Soon after Christmas his spirits revived with a little malicious teasing of an eminent figure from literary London. Fisher Unwin, Edward Garnett's first boss, was down in Sidmouth for the New Year to take the air and pick up the campaign he had been pursuing for some months – to get Reynolds to write a book for him. He called in at Bedford Square and invited the reluctant author up to his hotel for dinner.

Reynolds recounted the episode to George Macmillan with some relish. "I went; not without a bit of mischief at the back of my mind. The attentions of people who want books, and ain't going to get 'em, is like turtle soup. Anyhow, I told him the rather comic tale of how I first came to St Martin's Street, ending up: 'And there, no doubt, I shall stay, so long as they'll have me.' 'H'm! Ah! Yes! No doubt! Of course!' So striking that I felt I had gone a bit too far in teasing – had led the ferret into an ambush where a dragon was! But I can't resist telling publishers who tie up my friends that you haven't got me tied for a single book."[14]

But this was not the end of Unwin's attentions. Ever since the cheap edition of *A Poor Man's House* had appeared, Reynolds had been toying with a similar edition for *The Holy Mountain* which he would embellish with "a guidebook preface".[15] He now decided to off-load this doubtful publishing prize on the persistent Fisher Unwin. "Fisher Unwin seems to be nibbling at the *Mountain*. I'll take care the hook has a damn good barb!"[16] In January, Unwin finally came forward with a proposal for a shilling edition with which George Macmillan was inclined to acquiesce, only to discover two obstacles. There were no plates in existence, just moulds from which plates could be made; and there was still an outstanding advance of £40 on the book, taken over from Lane, which would need to be set against the sales of the new edition.[17] Even though he would pick up no money, Reynolds was still keen on the project for the publicity it would afford.

Unwin vacillated for some days, but finally buried the project in February with the bold proposition that once he had taken plates from the free moulds he should sell them back to Macmillan. Reynolds was more amused than annoyed. "Unwin is 'havering' as we thought he would. Talks about the book having a small popular appeal, and wants to know, if he made stereos from your mould, whether you wouldn't buy the stereos from him for use in (the numerous, no doubt) future editions. Does he suppose, do you think, that I wheel along the firm of Macmillans in a perambulator?"[18]

Reynolds did not, however, give up entirely. In June he was negotiating a 7d edition with a lower-down publisher, Everetts of Essex Street, but by the middle of that month this too had run into the sand.[19] But with the *Mountain*, hope, as ever, sprang eternal. He told George Macmillan: "Everetts apparently are not going to have the poor old *Mountain*. Someone'll want it somewhen, if I bide my time with my eyes open".[20]

One important literary project did come off that January – a commission he had negotiated with the *Quarterly Review* to write a critical article on Conrad, one of the first comprehensive studies to appear in England. It was, of course, a labour of love, but no less a labour for that. He completed it on 21 January and wrote to Pinker: "I have been grovelling over the Conrad article, and only finished it yesterday. I hope it's all right. Anyhow, it's out of the line of ordinary criticism, and George Macmillan, who has been down here, seems to think well of it. I have tried to relate Conrad to life rather than to literature, and to get at the psychological innards of his stuff".[21]

It came out in the *Quarterly* for April 1912, but not without a battle with Prothero, the editor, who insisted on cutting it down: "Prothero has had to cut 600 out of the Conrad article, and wants me to cut 800 more. One ought to have gas for an operation like that".[22] Even in its reduced form, it is a thorough and quite sensitive appreciation of both the land and the sea novels, emphasising in the latter case the contribution of the positive ideals of the British maritime tradition. "Behind his psychological windings and subtleties, behind his brooding impressionism and keen realism, one comes almost always upon the strong working ideal that belongs to British seafaring tradition. When he judges his characters, that is his final test – the seaman's." Conrad had revolutionised the sea novel: "He has given the novel a reality it lacked; he has, if one may put it so, taken it to sea."[23]

This emphasis upon his position as a sea-writer was unlikely to appeal to Conrad, who was always wary of having his works interpreted by a single formula.[24] But to be fair, this is only one aspect of Reynolds' account. The central theme of the article is Conrad's psychological preoccupations – "his management of mind is far superior to his management of events and narration" – and the land novels are dealt with in equal detail. He praises Conrad's perception of the fragility of man-made civilisation – "They are very fascinating and very terrible, these tales of Conrad's in which he brings civilisation to the judgment of nature, and causes it to shake like a withering tree".[25]

In the beginning, Conrad himself appeared to be flattered. In February, he wrote to an ex-naval admirer with seeming enthusiasm: "I heard only two days ago that an article on me is to appear in the next issue of the Quarterly Review".[26] But when the article eventually came out, there were signs that he was distinctly underwhelmed, perhaps more because of the odd personal revelation than the actual thrust of the criticism. The reference to his foreign accent, for example – "he has never mastered the pronunciation of English" – was a matter of some sensitivity and not one that he welcomed spread abroad among his reading public.

He appears to have acknowledged the article briefly when Reynolds first showed it him, but did not react on publication. Towards the end of August, Reynolds probed him a little and got a friendly but also rather prickly response: "I think my dear fellow that I told you how much I appreciated your article on me long before it appeared. I did not write to you on its appearance because I had nothing more to add; but you must not suspect me of ingratitude".[27]

Conrad's popular reputation was then about to take off with the publication of *Chance*, the book he was still struggling to complete. Even Reynolds' reputation was pushing out its own more modest frontiers. In January 1912, he learned from George Sturt that Oliver Elton, who must have known Reynolds at Owens College when he was lecturer in English there, was about to embark on a series of lectures at the University of the Punjab in Lahore on the works of Sturt and Reynolds, taking the view that both authors shared the same standpoint on the working class and poverty.[28]

Reynolds hurriedly drew the news to his publisher's attention to see what commercial mileage might be made from it. Maurice Macmillan brought him soberly down to earth. "There is already some stock of your books both in our

Calcutta and Bombay depots and we will see that the supply is kept up, although I do not think you can count upon any great results of these lectures. If 'Seems So', or any other book of yours, were prescribed for study by the students that would be a different matter."[29]

He was now also to receive some remarkable new publicity closer to home than the sub-Continent. On 28 January, inspired by the reading of *Seems So!* which "gave me furiously to think", the Rev. John Kingsland, who had been the Congregationalist minister in Devizes since 1909, preached a sermon attacking Reynolds' works for their lack of religious grounding. He was particularly hard on *A Poor Man's House* and the Woolleys.

> Mr Reynolds is describing the life and the thoughts of a working-class home and working-class people where there is love indeed, and not a few redeeming virtues (though hardly any graces); but where there is not a sign of any faith and life in God, not a sign that any member of the family is living for anything except the things which are seen...... It is, in fact, a godless home, and a godless life...... We find that bad language is often used; that drunkenness is occasionally indulged in; that the children are unruly and ill-mannered, and there is no attempt to train them; that at least half of the ten commandments are ignored and the other half only partially recognised...... We find that the adult members of the family and its circle never talk about – apparently never think about – the deeper questions of life, never are awed or even are aroused to interest by the wonders and mysteries of birth and death, sorrow and pain, sin and repentance. Even the sea and the sky – their constant companions – make no appeal to their deeper natures, arouse in them no "thoughts which wander through eternity". Their interest in sea and sky is limited to the relations in which these stand to their occupation as fishermen...... The adult members of the family are (so far as the books represent them) out-and-out materialists.[30]

This was an odd critique of a writer whose central political message was the maintenance of spiritual values in the face of economic advancement. If it were nothing else, *A Poor Man's House* was at the very least a fundamentally spiritual book. The editor of the *Wiltshire Advertiser*, Frederick Gillman, the son of Russell Gillman who had died two years before, was an old school friend of Reynolds from Devizes College days. Spotting here a good journalistic controversy, he wrote up the sermon in detail in his paper and sought a formal response from his friend in Sidmouth. "A Congregational devil-dodger at Devizes has printed in the local paper a sermon of his in which he roundly denounced us as godless and irreligious, deep sunk in trespasses and sin, etc., and the editor, an old schoolfellow of mine, asked for a rejoinder. And he's got it, too. There'll be a jolly little storm in Devizes!"[31]

Reynolds, with Bloxham behind him, was well equipped to trade biblical texts with militant clergymen. He used all his best rhetorical skills in framing the response, but for once it was not just the usual journalistic play-acting. What emerged was a deeply felt apologia of both the life he had lived and the life he had written about.

> It's very kind of you to offer me space for a rejoinder to the Rev. J.P. Kingsland's sermon. But what sort of a rejoinder could be of any use? If he can't understand my books, even after thinking furiously, who can make him understand? For ourselves, we are well content to be denounced as irreligious and godless by so able a modern Pharisee.
>
> Getting up into a pulpit, however, doesn't entitle a man to mis-represent either people or books. It doesn't excuse untruthfulness. I didn't represent the people in my books as "never awed or even roused to interest by the wonders and mysteries of birth and death, sorrow and pain...." Quite the contrary. I didn't represent "the sea and the sky – their constant companions" as making "no appeal to their deeper natures". On the contrary I said that the beauty and wonder of the sea and sky became part of them; not merely something to talk about; and I spoke of their sea-largeness and generosity. "The adult members of the family" are *not* "(so far as the books represent them) out-and-out materialists". On the contrary, they are most concerned to know what a man's feeling is, and what's in his heart...... It's easy enough for people with assured stipends and position to talk glibly about *character*: we want to know what the characters, which they call bad, have had to contend with. All my books (even the much-misunderstood *Holy Mountain*) are one long protest against materialism either in politics, in sociology, or in religion. Mr Kingsland doesn't seem to realise how basely materialistic is the religiousness which occupies itself with running up a sort of profit and loss account in heaven, and thinks to keep itself on the safe side with its God by conforming to the minor rules and regulations of respectability.
>
> He fastens, for instance, on bad language as a test of men. I know an old man (and my readers know him too, though not all the tragedy of his life) who swears, when he's up for it, "summut terrible". But if by night he meets with some poor beggar who is hungry and cold, he doesn't hand him over to the police or tell him to get a workhouse ticket. He takes him into his cottage, gives him warmth and shares with him the little food he has, without so much as making sure first that the beggar isn't lousy. Humanity, he reckons, and pity for those who've fallen on evil days, is above even that consideration. Therefore we more than respect the old man, and as for his cussing – well, it's only his way. Let Mr. Kingsland keep the faith and hope he denounces us for lacking. We think more of the good "irreligious" old man's charity. And so, I fancy, would St. Paul have done, to judge by his first letter (chap. 13) to the Corinthians.

But more than the personal attacks on himself and his books, Reynolds was most riled by the clergyman's easy dismissal of the social and economic problems of the day.

> "I would we all realized, as the Apostle realized," proceeded Mr. Kingsland, "the insignificance of these social problems of which we hear so much to-day, and of the questions concerning wages and the more equitable distribution of wealth and also of the political questions which are the burning questions of the hour – the insignificance of these things compared with the importance of the problem on which the Apostle concentrated his attention, the problem of the spiritual condition of the men and women whom we see around us to-day." *Insignificance* is a strongish word to use. And what on earth does he mean by *spiritual condition*? Church and chapel going? Believing creeds and doctrines? And what, in any case, can be the spiritual condition of a nation where men and women and children are allowed to starve in the midst of plenty, while people with full bellies talk about their hope of eternal life?

And he takes as his illustration the new Woolley baby, perhaps warmer than many, braving the floods and the winter weather.

> How about the small babies, this weather, in homes where there's no fire to wash them by, nor any dry napkins to put on them? I should think their crying and squalling must go up to Mr. Kingsland's heaven like a curse against the professed Christians who can describe our social abominations as insignificant. What would Mr. Kingsland's Sunday sermon have been like if he'd had no breakfast and hadn't known where to get any dinner? How many of his congregation would have sat there listening to him, if they'd had no food and no money to get any? Or even if his chapel hadn't been nicely warmed? Isn't it a question now, in Devizes, of giving the borough scavengers (for whom every rate-payer is responsible) enough wages to live on decently? There are many thousands of poor souls far too hard-pressed to think much about booking their seats in heaven.

Finally, he looks back to the example of the Catholic priest whom in fictional form he had already put before the public in his last *Nesscombe* article.

> Unless religious tolerance forbids, I should recommend Mr. Kingsland to study the life of that saintly man, the late Father Bouvard, who would give away all he had (not a mere percentage) to the needy, and who, instead of dubbing people irreligious, godless, and so forth, called them all, Catholics and sceptics alike, "my children".

> It *is* a new spirit that is chiefly wanted – or wanted in the first place. I quite agree. I wrote from that point of view. But not Mr. Kingsland's sort of spirit. *That has already failed.* His sermon is really a confession of failure. People write books: *If Christ came to* – this or t'other place. If He did come, it would be, as it was before, among the godless, irreligious workers, among the sinners and despised, that He would find His following, and people after His own heart. For His teaching (His original teaching, I mean) had the uncompromising simplicity, the reckless compassion, that appeals to them. He wasn't a bit respectable. He'd pretty soon find Himself in the hands of the police, nowadays. He was considered one of the "bad characters" and blasphemers of His time, and so He'd be again. And how He'd run amuck among the vested religious interests which cry out against the working classes, because they refuse to knuckle under to what they perceive isn't the real thing![32]

Ada Bennett, his old schoolmistress, had been stung by one particular aside in the sermon – "I gather that Mr. Stephen Reynolds is not a religious man himself" – and leapt to his defence. She wrote from the College where she was still teaching after 21 years.

> I think I may claim to know Mr. Stephen Reynolds as well as, if not better than, any other person does.
>
> I must therefore take exception to Mr. Kingsland's description of him as an irreligious man. Unorthodox he is, very; but irreligious, most certainly not. None who know his large heartedness and tenderness for even the least of God's creatures could for a moment call him so.
>
> These qualities are shown in many places in his books, and certainly, also, in his daily life of self-sacrifice for what he thinks right. If in his endeavours to point out the wrongs he sees exist, he treads on our corns, surely we need not cry out too loudly – for after all it is hardly his fault more than our misfortune.
>
> Judged by the standard set in the General Epistle of James, 1-27, Mr. Reynolds is decidedly a religious man.
>
> I also know the fisher-folk, of whom Mr. Reynolds writes, in their home life. I have spent some happy hours amongst them, and hope to spend many more. They are far from being the irreligious lot Mr. Kingsland imagines.[33]

He was proud of and moved by this testimonial which he sent on to George Macmillan at the latter's request. "Of course, you'll understand that my old schoolmistress, Miss Bennett, sees me *couleur de rose*, the more so as she took care of me when I was ill, saving my life undoubtedly, and therefore has, so to speak, a proprietary interest in me. She is a great woman, an educational genius, and runs a splendid school. I got all the best of my education there."[34]

Finding himself up against such personalised arguments, the Devizes minister beat a cautious retreat, lamenting the attacks upon him and reiterating his case more defensively and soberly this time.[35] "He of Devizes is very outraged; most lengthily, laboriously and righteously hurt."[36] With that, Reynolds was content to let him go.

Through January and February he was still planning the completion of the *Nesscombe* series, though he had not yet managed to agree terms for it with Spender and the *Westminster Gazette*. As an alternative, he turned to Austin Harrison and the *English Review* to try and negotiate a formal commission for the rest of the series, now labelled *All-Night Talk*, but Harrison was nervous of committing himself sight unseen and Reynolds refused to start writing again without some security of publication. In typically ironic vein, he appealed to Harrison's sense of realism as a publisher.

> As to the "All-Night Talk".... It would plainly be of the nature of a short serial, possibly for small print. It would, I agree, be an outrage to cause you to break your principles, but equally it would not be wise to write the thing for adults unless the only periodical at present converted to adultism were prepared to consider it as, say, semi-commissioned; for if, afterwards, the adult periodical chucked it out, it would be an adult's labour lost. And there are, you know, some quite capable periodicals which do accept in advance (subject to its being up to scratch) the work of writers of pretty uniform quality. I'll bet half a pint that you've done it with the work of writers less uniform than I am; for it is an adult function to exercise intelligent anticipation.
>
> You won't play to a blind hole, but suggest I should. I should suggest that we might both play at a hole neither blind nor fit only for a budding golfer's first smite. A sporting hole, in other words. Perhaps we might talk the matter over when I get up to London in the near future. You probably saw enough of Part I. of the book in the *Westminster* last summer to know the style and quality of it. This, as I said, becomes practically a little novel in the same style of narration.
>
> As, thirdly, for golf.... Damn golf![37]

He was planning a further twelve chapters of the book which he told George Macmillan would be ready by the autumn. But it was the "adult" nature of the content which seemed to be proving the stumbling block with both Harrison and Spender. "I am going to see Spender when I come to Town over the serialization of the last 12 chapters (the last one-third or quarter) of Hannaford; for the style I do it in rather depends on what he'll do. It's a rather delicate – though really very highly moral subject – namely, the utter failure of a *liaison* which was condoned by the paralysed husband, but could neither proclaim itself to the world, nor dared to carry itself to expression and permanent satisfaction in children. I'm going to be so matter-of-fact that no one will find it risky, but at the same time it's obvious that for the *Westminster* Hannaford must talk more roundabout the central events, and concentrate more on the outcome than on the *liaison* itself."[38]

This then was Hannaford's dark secret, hinted at in the early chapters of the series – a Lady Chatterley scenario sixteen years before its time. It was not, perhaps, too surprising a sexual theme, a reflection of Reynolds' own clandestine sexuality. Macmillan saw it as a problem not just for the *Westminster*: "As to Hannaford, we will see what comes of it when it is complete, but delicate handling will be required not only for the *Westminster* but for us!"[39] Reynolds hastened to reassure him. "I don't think you need be troubled about Hannaford in any case, however I tackle him. I shall not indulge in riskiness for riskiness' sake, nor on the other hand in *suppressio veri* or what I should regard as such. I'm not out for a *succès d'esclandre*. I think my matter-of-fact, rather scientific method of handling delicate subjects, by simply facing them and their consequences, and refusing to dress them in literary tights, must be fairly sound."[40]

But the interview with Spender came to nothing, and it can only have been the subject matter that proved the sticking point. Reynolds allowed the matter to drift, like his novels, until a new, more immediately personal, subject stole his attention and what little remained of his energy for writing. Hannaford was heard of no more.

When he went up to London on 27 February, it was not just to see Spender over the articles, nor to transact fisheries business, though this appears to be the visit at which he had his first interview with Walter Runciman, the new President of the Board of Agriculture and Fisheries. It was primarily to see his doctor.

He had been unwell since Christmas, and for the first two months of the year had not felt strong enough to tackle long stretches of consecutive writing, apart from the article on Conrad which he had managed painfully to drag out of himself. At the beginning of February, he had a recurrence of his old liver complaint but this, as he told George Macmillan, was only part of the problem. "I got a chilled liver almost a week ago, out whiting fishing in the worst of the N.E. wind, and have been trebly worm-like ever since. Ought to get a change, I suppose, but don't feel I could go without having constantly in mind that I ought to be at work. The strain of carrying on so much, and being driven all the time by the necessity of earning the money to do it in, gets simply paralysing when one isn't up to the mark. I feel as if all the resilience is being very slowly sapped out of me, so that there's nothing to do but to hang on tough and run henceforward on solid tyres."[41]

He had always begun a new year badly, with Christmas depression and winter illness combining to intensify the black days of January and February and blot out all hope of work. But the first months of 1912 were worse than usual. For one thing, as he saw the winter cycle repeating itself yet again, he was beginning to give up hope. For another, he was now taking on too many non-writing assignments, the fisheries work both in London and Sidmouth, which would have threatened to put paid to his writing even had he been fully fit.

Matters bubbled up to a crisis in the weekend of 10/11 February on a visit to Brixham to try and breathe new life into a time-honoured project that had played around the Sidmouth foreshore for many years – the idea of constructing a man-made harbour. On 25 January he had attended with Bob at the Anchor the annual Foresters' Dinner, and in his toast to "The Town and Trade of Sidmouth" had had a little fun at the expense of the Manor representatives. "I had great sport at the Foresters' dinner last Thursday, with Hastings, the manor steward in the chair, pulling the Manor's leg affable-fashion. They were so scared, that when I sat down there wasn't a sound; but I hadn't left an opening for them to take anything amiss, and I think they were still more horrified at my drawing (rather like a dentist) an expression of friendliness from the said Chair. I mean to make 'em realize that it's expedient to placate us. There's no sport in playing with tools without edges, as any kid knows."[42]

It was in this speech that he announced his new project, as the local press reported. "During the time he had been in Sidmouth, the town had been in a flourishing condition. The fishermen, however, had had rather rougher times, owing to various causes, and it was to be hoped better days lay in store for them. The question of the desirability of a harbour for Sidmouth was one which he thought required looking into. Personally he was of opinion it would be a good thing. It would enable vessels to bring in various commodities at a cheaper rate than was at present charged, while people on yachting cruises would be able to call, and so additional money would be spent in the town. He hoped the matter would soon receive the attention it deserved. He was glad to say Mr Mildmay and Major Morrison-Bell [*the two local MPs*] were interesting themselves in the question."[43]

Francis Mildmay, the MP for Totnes, whom Reynolds was consulting more and more on local fisheries matters, had found for him a harbour engineer at Brixham prepared to give advice on the potential for a harbour at Sidmouth, asking no payment but out-of-pocket expenses – "Beastly using a man's professional knowledge on those terms, but there's no help for it, if I'm to get the Council to move in the matter".[44]

He went down to Brixham on Saturday 10 February. Apart from the business to transact, there was an element of holiday in the weekend – the change of air he needed – for he was to stay once more with his friends the Tanners, who had recently given up the farming life at Ford House and taken over the Castle Hotel at Dartmouth, a return to their old profession. It was perhaps the motherly attentions of Lizzie Tanner that caused him to succumb completely to his illness, just as five years earlier he had been wont, on abandoning Pans Lane, to collapse into the security of Ford. "The congested liver ended at Dartmouth in one truly infernal night's pain – right away at the top of the hotel where I couldn't call anybody."[45]

He stayed on some extra days and, uncharacteristically, turned to take out his misery and frustration on, of all people, Bob. There is some evidence of a distancing between Reynolds and Bob Woolley at this time, reinforced by a closer relationship with Tom. It was Tom who had gone with him on the short French holiday the previous autumn, and in many of his letters to Macmillan at this period it is Tom, not Bob, who features as his chief literary collaborator – the man who has to be consulted on publicity, for example.[46]

It had been a trying winter for Bob too; the herring season had been a complete failure, little compensated for by the odd catch of whiting. At such times, Bob also was inclined to lie around bemoaning his fate.[47] There had been hints in the preface to the cheap edition of *A Poor Man's House* that life in Bob's cottage had its trying aspects. Now, after five years residence there, it seemed that the noise and bustle and claustrophobia was finally getting to Reynolds' nerves. On the Monday he wrote home to Bob from Dartmouth.

> Mackintosh says that a large part of my ill-health is caused by my being troubled in mind and not having the quietness I need. I knew that before and have told you times enough that the pull dog pull devil time I have had, after the work and noise of the day, for the last 2 years or so had got on my nerves and was breaking me down. You would never let outsiders to get on my nerves and worry me if you had only understood how worried and miserable it made me, and how it harmed me, and how harmed yourselves in harming me.[48]

For once the curtain is lifted on the idyllic family life of 1906 and we catch an untoward glimpse of the tensions generated between the struggling writer, striving to harbour his resources of energy and moments of peace, and the noisy, careless working environment in which he had chosen to live. But it was too much to ask of Bob that he should weave about him the kind of warm cocoon that only the Tanners could provide. There were two ways out of this predicament – to find someone to help with his writing work and protect his peace; or to move to larger premises. Both strategies were to engage a large part of his attention over the coming two years.

He was in no better mood when he arrived home. As he told George Macmillan: "Coming home in one of those foul super-heated corridor carriages, I caught a bad sore throat which has spread into an ear and kept me awake with earache. Lively, altogether! I believe I should have been much better and far happier if I had simply gone on fishing, and had left fishery affairs alone. But what can one do, when there's so much wants doing, and one can at any rate do some of it? I shall probably come up and see a Town doctor soon. It's no good being put off work so much as I have been this winter. Besides, to feel one is really tackling a malady in itself half cures it".[49]

In London on 27 February he had lunch with Frederic Chapman, Edward Thomas and the latter's close friend, the poet W.H. Davies – perhaps their first meeting.[50] He rushed around from his doctor to the Board of Agriculture, from Pinker to George Macmillan in St Martin's Street. But he did manage on 29 February to squeeze in lunch with Hugh Walpole. Walpole had pursued him the previous December from Edinburgh where he always spent Christmas and New Year with his parents and where, on Christmas Eve, he always wrote the first lines of his annual book. "I haven't heard anything of you for ages. When may I come down to Sidmouth? When will you come and see me in Hallam St.? I promise you, on this occasion, whiskey. I'm so glad that 'Seems So' is having such a success. Answer this. I *want* to hear."[51]

It was a greeting that Reynolds needed that dismal Christmas but he declined the offer of accommodation in favour of lunch when next in town. But Walpole seemed fated now to meet with Reynolds only when he was ill, harassed with too much work, and in a deeply self-pitying mood. The lunch proved no exception, with Reynolds full of his illness, the problems with his writing, his new Ministerial contacts at the Board of Agriculture. Walpole recorded tersely in his diary that night "Leap Year day. Stephen Reynolds to lunch. Has become tiresome, self-centred, boring".[52] As he moved away from creative writing into fishery politics, it was an opinion that other of his London literary friends were to come soon to share.

But not Conrad, not yet. On 2 March Reynolds rounded off his London trip with a visit to Capel House, where the welcome was as warm as ever and as usual the two authors sat up late into the night, putting the literary world to rights. A visit from Perceval Gibbon followed straight after, and even for Conrad the pace was beginning to tell. He confided to Pinker: "Reynolds & Gibbon have been here (and I was *really* pleased to see them) one off the other on. But all this is a check. Those young men think nothing of talking till 2 or 3 in the morning and I like it well enough myself – but that does not help me for next day's writing".[53]

Back in Sidmouth in early March Reynolds' concern for his own symptoms gave way to a much more serious anxiety over a much more serious illness. He wrote to George Macmillan: "All are well here; babies very flourishing; but Semaphore's little mate, Violet Cordey (Cordey works for us) is likely to die of consumption, and wherever we try to get her, for expert treatment, we are met by batteries of rules and regulations against taking children. Seems as if children under five aren't supposed to be cured of tuberculosis!"[54]

The Cordeys had been a fixture in Bedford Square for almost as long as the Woolleys. William Cordey was a fisherman, a casual worker for the firm, while his wife Henrietta, the more reliable breadwinner, used to help Mam Woolley on washdays. Back in April 1907, in a highly charged passage in *A Poor Man's House,* Reynolds had graphically depicted her courage (as the fictional Mrs Yarty) as she prepared to give birth to Violet, knowing that, because of her husband's fecklessness, her family might starve during the confinement.[55] The doctors had now advised that little Violet would never get better unless she were taken out of Bedford Square, but all the consumption hospitals in the neighbourhood put a bar on children.

Violet Cordey died on 18 March 1912, just four years old. Reynolds was deeply moved and very angry. It brought keenly back to him the fate of "Rosie", Bob's daughter in that other highly charged passage in *A Poor Man's House*, on whom too the medical establishment had turned its back.

They buried her three days later in the cemetery up on the hill. "We buried poor little Violet Cordey on Thursday with a wonderful lot of flowers, but that magnificent service in a beastly brick rabbit-hutch of a cemetery chapel – such as people have to use who can't afford to be carted into church – and an old clergyman with a big muffler round his neck standing by the graveside in a sort of sentry-box – *une affaire pour rire*, if it hadn't been so miserable and I hadn't been so angry with all that the poor kid's life failed to make headway against. And since, I've had a perfectly devilish time getting the disinfection and so forth carried through to the bitter necessary end. Mam 'Oolley, as usual, came out the big quiet figure in all the affair."[56]

Ever since the publication of *A Poor Man's House* he had had at the back of his mind the idea of writing the individual life of one of the unknown people with whom he lived and worked – an extension of his first book and the ultimate in alternative biography. He had toyed with Uncle Sam as his subject, but had surrendered the idea in favour of *Alongshore*. Now the notion revived. He would write the life of this child to prove she was more than just another tuberculosis statistic. As always, his first resolve was full of hesitation. "I wish I could write the child's life quite truthfully, with all the mesh of complications, extenuating circumstances, and helplessness. I think I could do a book that would carry reality where now there is mainly tuberculosis statistics. But the requisite truthfulness doesn't seem practicable."[57]

A week after the funeral, the idea had taken an unrelenting grip on his mind. George Macmillan suggested an article rather than a book, but Reynolds had a new extension of *A Poor Man's House* in his sights. "I don't think I could do what I want to do in an article; it's a short book that I see in my mind with a singular definiteness and completeness. In fact, it's all so boiling up mentally that I can turn to nothing else, and am doing nothing. If you look at the *P. M's H.*, p.221 (cheap ed.) you'll see the chapter on the Yartys. Well, what I have in mind is to continue that chapter into another book in the same style – the thing as it struck me, with the thoughts it gave rise to. It's only in that way that I can get down all the immense complications of the subject and at the same time keep the main theme – the child's life and death – quite clear and prominent. I think I must try. I feel that I ought to, even at some risk of making the place too hot to hold me."[58] On 31 March he sent a postcard to Macmillan with the cryptic message "Am starting child book today".[59]

The Life of a Child that Died went strongly at first. In the first two weeks of April he completed the first four short chapters, and by 23 April more than

10,000 words were written, a quarter to a third of the whole. But it was agonising writing – not just the competition with his aching liver, but with a general lassitude that was beginning to spell the end of his writing life. Even the stimulation of a new reprise of *A Poor Man's House* was not enough now to carry him through the silt built up by the wear and tear of the past few years – as he explained to George Macmillan.

> Four chapters of the Child book are done, including a description of Sidmouth from the poor-man-having-to-live-in-its-cheap-houses point of view – with a simply ghastly toil in writing. Certainly, I have been rather unwell, and have had to have my ribs nearly skinned with a mustard pack to get my stupid liver to work more and ache less. But that apart, I don't seem to have a bit of spring in me, and can't get down the simplest thing without a labour that makes me gasp, physically as well as metaphysically. It's evident that the last ten years racket of various activities, coupled with a good deal of private trouble, and troublesome health and constant anxiety as to how to pull a bare living out of it all, has permanently damaged, not so much the superficial strength, as the interior energy one ultimately draws on, the core, as it were, of one's life-impulse. I don't suppose you people of an assured foothold can possibly imagine what it's like to produce literature as a by-product of fighting all the time for existence, for the doing of decent work, and, worst of all, for sufficient health to fight at all. It's like being a piece of elastic, continually on the stretch, and losing, bit by bit, therefore, its elasticity. If I can't succeed in easing down fairly soon, I'm sure I shall snap.
>
> You mustn't, of course, read into this any implied reproach. It's a great thing, a very great thing, not to have to fight one's publisher too. So in gratitude, I suppose, one treats him to one's complaints against things in general, as one can't against himself![60]

This was not the usual Reynolds' lament – the quicksilver thrust, over in a flash – but a more controlled, almost resigned, recognition that he was approaching his literary end-game.

A week later he was looking to put the child book on the back-burner. "I think I shall finish as quick as I can and have a couple of copies typed, and then put it away while I finish Hannaford, meanwhile trying to rig up a serialization, if I can see a place I'd like to serialize in. Then, when Hannaford's finished, I'll set to work and rewrite the child book very carefully for actual publication. I want it to be a little thing extra well done, with no squashiness or sloppiness – all the notes quite clear and precise in tone."[61] In London in the middle of May he got a tentative agreement out of J.L.Garvin to run the book through the *Pall Mall Gazette*, which had recently serialised his lengthy account of the Marseille holiday two years before.[62] But the completion both of the *Nesscombe* series and the child book was to become submerged in an effort that summer to begin his psycho-economics articles for *The Times* and by a more topical and urgent concern – the growing discontent in the Navy.

So far as we know, the life of Violet Cordey was never completed. It marks in some ways a symbolic turning point in Reynolds' literary career. It stood to draw him back to the personal, intimate style and preoccupations of *A Poor Man's House* at a time when his writing had reached its full maturity. But in the conditions of 1912 he had no longer the tenacity to see even a short book through, and all creative endeavour became lost to more pressing, more easily assimilable, political concerns.

After May 1912, we lose both sight and sound of the third to a half that had already been written. Was it merely a tract against bad housing and disease, or something potentially much bigger? He may have destroyed it – Harold Wright does not mention it among his papers at his death.[63] Or alternatively, it perished with all his other papers in the 1930s, a prey to the lethal combination of damp and mice. It is one of the more important losses of a writer whose purely literary output was relatively small.

We should not underestimate the strains that were building up on Stephen Reynolds as day followed day, week followed week, throughout the course of 1912. He seems to alternate sharply between a stolid acceptance that his writing life might be drawing to its close and then sudden bursts of frenetic energy, packed with new writing ideas – as if somehow he were making a last desperate effort to escape the inevitable. It was a bruising conflict between hope and reality which seemed likely to end, on his own admission, in another breakdown. The elastic was indeed about to snap.

In a typical letter of the time, he wrote to George Sturt on 20 March with an excited shopping list of new activity but finally coming down to earth with a bump.

> I've got a book in the press now: *How 'Twas; Short Stories and Small Travels*. Thirty pieces and some of my best work, but I suppose 'twon't go. I want to write a book on *Human Economics* – where the shoe pinches, instead of where the so-called laws don't pinch, a theory of work in terms of life; in short, an enlargement of our "Labour and Brainwork" chapter, especially the italicised paragraph. Also I want to write the life of a special little kid of mine who died of general tuberculosis – *i.e.* poverty – a couple of days ago. Also there's a novel to be done. Also the Government may want me to make a survey of the small fisheries. Also my health is very far from satisfactory. Hemmed in all round and buggered up, as we say hereabout.[64]

How 'Twas, the book of short stories and sketches being prepared for publication, had had a long gestation. In Paris in 1903 he had put together a number of his early stories, including the latest French ones, in the hope that some London publisher could make a small volume out of them, but the failure had led to a total despair of his writing career. It was in March 1907, when he was starting *A Poor Man's House* and still nursed hopes of early publication of the *Mountain*, that he returned to the idea of a volume of short stories, but the next two years were fully engaged with the uphill struggle to get those first two books into print.[65] Through the spring and summer of 1909 he was actively planning the volume as a follow-up to the *Mountain*. In March that year he wrote to Pinker: "I ought to have some short stories to send you soon.... Are any of those you have selling? I wish they would hurry up, because after the *Mtn.* I want Lane to publish a collection of my poor people stories – 'Up along and Down along: Tales of Poor Folk' – or something like that".[66] By August the working title had shifted to "The Way O' It" and he was aiming for publication in the spring of 1910, but his battle with Lane over *Alongshore* soon put paid to that.[67]

The idea was still in his mind in June 1910 when he switched publishers, but it was a year later, with *Alongshore* published and *Seems So!* in preparation, that he raised the issue formally with George Macmillan.[68] "As I'm unlikely to be doing many, or any, short stories for some time, I'm thinking of collecting together 'The Way o' It: Short Stories and Small Travels'. Of the two together (and they aren't very different in execution) I've more than enough for a volume, which could be published anywhen that seemed good to you...."[69] Macmillan advised a breathing space after the publication of *Seems So!* "as it would be a mistake to crowd your books too close" and they agreed to aim for the spring of 1912.[70]

In the autumn and winter of 1911, he began the task of putting the volume together, puzzling how many to leave out. He consulted Conrad who, as always, took a bullish line: "I still think that the short stories vol should be a thick one. A severe sifting but everything that will go through the sieve should be given out at once. And soon! I think it important that it should be soon".[71] He took Conrad's enthusiasm at face value and determined that *he* should do the sieving, but he knew it would be politic to hold on until the long awaited *Chance* was out of the way. On the last day of 1911, he wrote to Pinker: "Have you heard whether *Chance* is finished yet? I'm not sending my short stories for Conrad to look at till it is".[72]

He was still waiting in early February for news of the completion of *Chance*, as was George Macmillan for a rather different reason: "We still look forward to having the opportunity of publishing something for him hereafter, if only that opportunity is given."[73] Reynolds thought the wait would not be long. "Conrad is neither to be seen nor heard of while he is finishing *Chance*, which I believe is his last volume due to Methuen, but I'm expecting him to become visible daily now. Then one will hear, and I daresay he will get to Town." But Reynolds had already taken the precaution of priming his personal representative in the Conrad household. "My bundle of short stories and small travels has gone on to Mrs. Conrad – 38 of them, amounting to over 100,000 words.

I expect they'll knock out at least ten of the shorter ones: the longer ones are less doubtful. That ought to make a fattish volume, containing some better work, I think, than either of my long books."[74]

On 8 February Macmillan agreed to publish the volume in the spring with a, now customary, advance of £50, and asked for a snappy title.[75] Reynolds had abandoned "The Way o' It" and offered him a choice of "How 'Tis" or "How 'Twas".[76] Macmillan took the latter – "we are rather inclined to prefer the preterite form".[77] There was a small hint of disappointment in Reynolds' acknowledgement of the advance: "The terms you suggest will do quite well, thank you. I hope to goodness 'twon't do less than earn its £50 advance, and if it earns more – well, the money is just as well in your hands, where I can get at it if necessary, as it would be in my current account, at no interest to me, helping my bank to pay its 25% per annum!"[78]

Though generous to a fault with the money in his pocket, Reynolds always adopted a tight-fisted stance towards a new negotiation or the ups and downs of his bank balance. For in 1912 money was still a problem. In returning the signed agreement for *How 'Twas* to Pinker on 16 March, he underlined the difficulty that still faced them both: "On the Income Tax people trying to get at me, I was forced to reckon out my exact income (net) for the current financial year. £147-10-8½! That's very bad, considering how much I am in the press, and how many read me (in library copies). Evidently we haven't solved the problem of turning reputation into circulation. I wish I could see a way".[79] With George Macmillan he was more succinct. "The Income Tax people have been getting at me, and I've proved with triumph that my net income this, my best, year is £147-10-8½. But, diable! What a sort of triumph. You shall have put on my tombstone: 'He was read in library copies'."[80]

How 'Twas did, however, provide a supplementary form of income because he had made a vow to achieve serial publication of all the stories and sketches that went into it. And he just made it in time. "One thing, I did succeed in serializing every item of *How 'Twas*. I made up my mind I would, but, by Jove, didn't it want some sticking to, and I only did it by the skin of my teeth! Garvin (whom I saw) and the *Throne* came to the rescue of the last two things."[81]

Printing and publication had been held up to await Conrad's final choice. "The book will be unusually long of its kind, I think, although I'm uncertain yet what Conrad will retain or reject. He has a wonderful nose for the real thing, as opposed to the literary thing."[82] News came from Capel House in the second week of March, but in the event an exhausted Conrad, still in the final toils of *Chance*, had taken the easy way out.

> My dear Stephen
> You have given me a very invidious task. A very difficult one too. And very pleasant. It would have been still more pleasant if I had not had behind me that black care which sits behind the horseman and from

which I can not escape – not till I can afford to buy a motor car anyhow. I am driving at my book end......
Well I have read all your copy. And the result of my extreme fastidiousness is enclosed in the envelope. But my dear who am I to pick and choose in the stuff of a man who *can* write, always has something to say and never fails on one side or another to secure my sympathy? It's hopeless! I like it all. And really a writer of your quality ought to do his own sifting. Bless my soul, you know more about it than I shall ever know if I live to a hundred. I am no critic. Now and then I may utter a phrase of value but reasoned judgement I have none. However here it is. The book will be young but interesting and valuable. It's not everybody who can produce such "juvenilia". Print with my blessing – if that's any good to you – and may your shadow never grow less!
No more my dear fellow. I am 1/2 dead. It's hardly a figure of speech.[83]

He had suggested some deletions and Reynolds finally decided on the removal of eight items, to make a round thirty which he packed off to Macmillan on 13 March in a carefully selected order.[84] Some early stories, with very fragile endings, like *Her Immortality* and *A Piano and an Omnibus*, had been wisely left out. But others, like the lively *Pauvre Punaise* and the delicately drawn *With Baby's Help*, could well have replaced some of the weaker items that *had* been selected. In some cases, it may have been a question more of taste than of quality. *With Baby's Help*, the story of a poor widow working the Bear for men, may have been withdrawn for lack of courage.

By the beginning of April the proofs were beginning to filter through from Macmillan's printer, R. & R. Clark Ltd. of Edinburgh, and Reynolds was anxious to dispatch them as quickly as possible. He was hoping for publication on 16 May, both his birthday and the week in which Bob's brother Harry, and his brother-in-law Jack Collier, both Chief Petty Officers, were due to come out of the Navy – "we may as well, if possible, celebrate everything up together, book and all."[85] George Macmillan hastened to press on him the realities of publishing life: "We shall lose no time in getting the book out, but the date you name, May 16, is I fear quite impossible, so you must find some other way of celebrating your birthday."[86]

Though this was just a reprint of old serialised material, Reynolds would not relinquish any of his close personal supervision of the publication process, nor his relentless attention to detail. He treated the book as if it were a new novel, hot from the pen. He had in fact taken the opportunity to edit some of the material, to "improve" the style of some of the early stories, and in consequence the proof-reading was no mere formality. But this was his longest book and the exercise grew into something of a burden. He became impatient and on 19 April snapped off a postcard to the staff at Macmillans: "Could you please buck up the printers? They started sending first proofs on March 29th.; none have come this week till this morning; and now I am only in the 19th

[*Twinses*] out of 30 items in the book! And I have a few of the page-proofs dribbling in in the same manner...... The proofs are extremely good, as usual from Charles', but slow to exasperation."[87]

Somewhat to his embarrassment, George Macmillan stepped in personally to hurry up the printers.[88] Reynolds felt an explanation of his earlier annoyance was due. It shows once again with what anxious care he followed his work to the press, and at the same time the fragility, in these days, of both his concentration and his desire to write. "The printers' way of letting the proofs dribble down south only a page or two at the time makes a sort of daily nuisance of them over a long period of time, for one knocks off the bit of proof before starting work, and then the mood to start it is gone. Besides, it prevents one looking backwards and forwards to regularize doubtful spellings. The proofs, however, are exceedingly good ones, and perhaps they haven't many men they care to put on to my dialect stuff."[89]

At last on 2 May the proofs were finally completed and on 30 May George Macmillan gave the go-ahead for publication on Friday 7 June.[90] In deference to the unexpected success of *Seems So!* the print run was returned to the level of *Alongshore* – a solid 3000.[91] And as always, Reynolds was delighted by the get-up of the specimen volume he received on the last day of May. "That is exceedingly nice – *How 'Twas* – just exactly as I most like a book of mine to look. Many thanks. I greatly appreciate the trouble you must have taken to get out the book so 'just so'."[92] And when his free volumes arrived on publication day, the enthusiasm was no less: "A parcel of half a dozen copies of *How 'Twas* has come safely. They *do* look well, as I said before, and say again because my pleasure in it hasn't in the least abated."[93] In a later letter he wrote to Frederick Macmillan: "I daresay you have heard how delighted I am with the turn-out of *How 'Twas*. I only hope its inside will please other people half so much".[94]

But he himself took some pride in the inside too. He felt that some of his finest writing had gone into it, thinking perhaps of *Twinses, An Unofficial Divorce, A Dog's Life, A Steam Burst Afloat, Dear Papa's Love Story, Puffin Home* and, deliberately placed last in the volume for maximum impact, *A Third Class Journey*. But his own personal selection of favourites from his work was notoriously unpredictable, based often on the emotional circumstances of their writing. Some of his early stories, though failing the most basic test of literary competence, could well have figured on this particular list.

He divided the thirty stories and sketches into three sections – People (17); Kids and Cats (7); Small Travels (6). More interesting, however, is their division into place and time. *How 'Twas*, however uneven its quality, provides the student of Reynolds with some fascinating glimpses of his life in the crucial decade between 20 and 30. He neither spoke nor wrote much about his past, mainly because he wanted to forget; and the sketches, such as *The Citizenry of Cats*, that he wrote on emerging from his breakdown in 1904 are an autobiographical goldmine in an otherwise wasted desert. The book as a whole provides a picture of a life, with its ups and downs, its shifting enthusiasms for places and people. Most phases of his life are there – the one story from Manchester, *Mrs Tripp's Flutter*, three from Paris (if one includes *A Marriage of Learning*, written there), three from the *Coranian* cruise of 1905, and one from his later series of autumn holidays – *A Third Class Journey*.

But the bulk of the book is shared almost equally between nine stories of Devizes before 1906, and 13 of Sidmouth during and after that date. The Devizes stories, particularly the very early ones with their Hardyesque colouring, are patchy in quality. But they are sharpened by the animal sketches, mostly cats, the reminiscences of childhood, and by the inclusion of *Dear Papa's Love Story*, whose atmosphere and sequence of letters is strongly redolent of the early chapters of *Howards End*. The Sidmouth sketches are a real jumble, mostly life on the beach and in the Woolley family, but a few of them, and only a very few, come up to the literary standard of *A Poor Man's House*.

The question naturally arises as to why Reynolds was prepared to allow his best work to sit cheek by jowl with some of his worst. It was a question that some of his reviewers were inevitably to ask. The answer in a word was sentiment. Just as he was never prepared to admit that the *Mountain*, which had suffered such tribulations, was perhaps his weakest long book, so did he set out in this volume to protect and nurture those early pieces of writing whose constant rejection had led to his breakdown and almost to his death. He wanted to pay his debt to them by giving them a share in his life as a well-known writer. There is also a sense that now in 1912, with his writing life fast running out of steam, he wanted to leave his readers with a complete picture of Reynolds – not just the *cliché* of fisherman-writer, but the lover of cats and dogs, of children and down-and-outs, of the countryside, of travel and adventure. It was in some ways, perhaps, a memorial volume – but by no means the best. Years later it was to be soundly eclipsed by the intentionally memorial work that was to follow his death.

Reynolds sent off to Macmillans his usual list of instructions as to the newspapers with which the book should be pushed, and received a prompt assurance: "We will take care that 'How 'Twas' goes to all your pet papers...... In fact, you may depend upon our giving it a good show".[95] Reynolds sensed a hint of irritation in the tone: "I know, of course, that you'll give the book a good show. Don't imagine that any suggestions I may make or more I may propose imply the least lack of confidence. Regard them rather as a species of co-partnership which you render possible, and I hope I on my side do the same, instead of the conventional pull dog pull devil relation. As to my pet papers, to use your phrase.... Well, I do, very naturally, like to get you to pat my pets and make their tails wag. Voilà tout! Il n'y a rien de plus."[96]

That June the reviews of *How 'Twas* were slow in coming through, perhaps the penalty of its length. The sales were also rather disappointing at first but had started to pick up by the end of the month.[97] First reactions came from close at hand. Even a simple book of short stories proved a source of controversy at Sidmouth. "Amusing bother here.... They are saying that the Thos. J. Skinner of *Robbery Robbed* (written and first published in the *Daily News* in 1908) is my revenge on a Jim Skinner of Sidmouth, the man who knocked Tom down over *Seems So!* I shall roast them in the local press if they continue that absurdity over a Wiltshire, not Devon, story."[98]

Reynolds had taken the somewhat casual selection of the items in the book by Joseph and Jessie Conrad as an excuse to make the formal dedication to them. It was an opportunity he had been looking for for some time. Conrad responded with his usual magnanimity.

> I need not tell you, because you know it, that Jessie and I are immensely gratified by the dedication. Indeed my dear fellow I am very proud that you should have chosen to commemorate thus our mental affinities and the friendship which having once sprung between us has become one of these solid things that count in one's life. I am speaking of mine now. You shall have its memory later; and this dedicatory line will help to keep it green long after I and Jessie are gone from this world in which I trust you will find all the honour and success you deserve.
>
> I have told you before, more or less lamely, what I think of this collection. And I shall say nothing more now, because I haven't yet read it in print...... I am going to read your vol tomorrow as one goes with a parched throat for a "rare and refreshing fruit" – to quote a phrase from modern politics.[99]

There were some quietly sympathetic reviews which gave Reynolds a modicum of hope. Massingham in the *Nation* was eager to praise the author's working class credentials.

> Mr Reynolds is, in fact, the one living English writer who shows us working class life from the inside. This is a very different thing to the writing of those who are, indeed, in close touch with working-class life, but, after all, remain outside it. Anyone, so to speak – at least anyone with some power of observation and sympathy – can get into close touch with working people, and then come away and, in an altogether different atmosphere, record his impressions; but Mr Reynolds appears to have merged himself in the life of the working classes. Hence, one looks upon him with the rather uncomfortable veneration with which one regards a mystic. Mr Bourne [*George Sturt*] comes nearest to him; but Mr Bourne lives in a Surrey village, and writes about the people – with admirable discernment and sympathy, no doubt – while Mr Reynolds lives in a Devon village, amid fishermen, and lives the life of the people. He shares their work and food. With an artist's power of expression, and writing an English of extraordinary lucidity, he puts down a fisherman's thoughts......

> "One half of the world doesn't know how the other half lives," says the proverb. But Mr Reynolds does.[100]

His friend, Richard Curle, had some harsh things to say about some items in the book – "he has jumped on me in this month's *Bookman*!" – but understood that it was a compilation put together over time.[101]

> Mr Reynolds' great reputation is hardly likely to be increased by this very unequal book...... The fact is, there must always be a danger in collecting together in one volume work from many different papers and reviews which have appeared over a considerable number of years, and the book before us is a very fair example of what that danger is.

In choosing his own favourite stories, however, Curle was at great pains to accentuate the positive.

> They show Mr Reynolds at that high level of clear and vivid portraiture, of finished and simple writing, that cause his best work to be excellent in so singular a degree. The truth is that he belongs to a very rare class of realist – that is, a realist that does not exaggerate realism in much the same way as the romantics invariably exaggerated romance.[102]

But a number of reviewers, sensing equally the uneven quality of the book, were politely scathing. Though he had received much criticism in the past for his political attitudes, which he could take as part of the rough and tumble of politics, he was not used to such hostility towards his actual writing. He could not see as clearly as some of his readers that it was the juvenile pieces that were giving this unwelcome colour to the book.

The *Athenaeum*, which had upset him so much over the *Mountain* three years before, was unhappy about the depth of the human portrayals.

> If we were asked for a reason for his comparative failure, we should assign it to the fact that his presentments are rather silhouettes than portraits. In his longer work we get his outlines from so many angles that we are at length familiarized with his types, and mistake familiarity for intimacy. The best of his stories here have to do with fishing and fishermen, subjects which he knows as well as any man in England. He is so informative about them and their work that it is the more provoking that we just fail to know the men themselves.[103]

Though gently phrased, it seemed to unsettle him even more than the bruising attack on the *Mountain*. "Did you notice the *Athenaeum* review of *How 'Twas* – a very miserly note, which rather worries me? They say that I familiarize the reader with my characters, but convey no sense of intimacy. Do you get that notion? I can't help thinking it's because such readers aren't *qualified* to be intimate with my people, and therefore don't grasp what *is* in the writing, though [*sic*] they can't see it there; or in a measure, perhaps, because my working class characters do not come up to the literary convention which has been established by previous writers. At all events, I hope so, and console myself with Bob's frequent saying: "They never don't understand, nor never won't, what a fellows feeling is; nor never can't, no matter what you tells 'em!"[104]

This time George Macmillan sprang to reassure him. "I did see, with considerable annoyance, the notice of 'How 'Twas' in the *Athenaeum*, but I think it only showed the writer's want of insight, and fortunately the *Athenaeum* is by no means the power that it once was in the literary world."[105] Conrad reacted in similar fashion. "I am surprised that a man of your absolute (and also relative) worth should concern himself with any newspaper criticism. The Ath: par: simply means that the man can't see. And the beggar *must* write something. But really this is such a characteristic ineptitude that I am almost ashamed both for you and myself to state my contempt for it here."[106]

On 3 July came a very cheeky review in *Punch*.

> In the face of the almost lyrical raptures with which the Press greets MR STEPHEN REYNOLDS' sketches of life among the poor but honest, I feel a certain diffidence in saying what I think of his latest collection, *How 'Twas* (MACMILLAN). According to one critic, Mr REYNOLDS has the passionate observation of a GILBERT WHITE, combined with a style more easy than STEVENSON'S. I found him dull. He has the knowledge, but he seems to me to lack the art of selection.

The review had hit the nail on the head, but by default. The problem with *How 'Twas* was the selection of stories, not (as the reviewer intended) the selection of material within each story. He was jocularly tough on *Puffin Home* and the, now widely accepted, Reynolds use of dialect.

> I have the misfortune to belong to the minority which cannot see why tedious small-talk becomes less tedious when the speeches say "us" and "thic" and "you'm" and "bain't 'ee" in place of their more conventional equivalents.

There was an even more waspish sting in the tail.

> I like Mr REYNOLDS better when he leaves the ocean and treats of cats. On the subject of cats he has many good things to say. "Power of Life and Death" is the gem of the collection, and almost equally good is "A Cat's Tragedy". As a matter of criticism, this choice of mine may be wrong. I admit that I am prejudiced in favour of cats by the fact that they do not talk in dialect. After all those "you'm's" and "thic's", the

> dignified silence of *Tib* was a rare and refreshing fruit.[107]

Reynolds, however, was not amused. "Didn't Punch go out of its way to be nasty! He must have a liver like mine, that man."[108]

Worse was to follow from Hugh Walpole in the *Standard*. On 9 July, in a hectic day of writing at the cottage of his new boyfriend, Percy Anderson, near Basingstoke, Walpole took time out from his current novel, *Fortitude*, to polish off *How 'Twas*.[109] He attacked the book as "journalism of the most ephemeral kind" and refused to make allowances for the age of some of the pieces. Reynolds, he felt, was unfairly exploiting his earlier success.

> We do not know, of course, at what dates the various tales and sketches have been written – some of them go back, in all probability, a considerable distance – but they have all of them been passed in this present year of grace by Mr. Reynolds, and he considers all of them worthy of preservation. If one takes the short stories alone it is almost impossible to find one that would not have been improved by a little care or trouble. Some of them, "The Missioner", "Mrs. Tripp's Flutter", "Robbery Robbed", display no kind of idea as to the art of the short story. Incidents are casually selected, details are flung in helter-skelter, an episode is finished so carelessly that it might have figured roughly in Mr. Reynolds's note book and been then casually transferred to print.... He has so original a talent, is so acute and well balanced a student of life, that it would be a thousand pities if the success of "A Poor Man's House" and "Alongshore" – a success most legitimate and honourable – allowed him to think that he could now give the public anything he pleased in any form that he liked.[110]

The *Standard* article was ample revenge for those personal remarks from Hannaford the previous year. The fault was not, of course, that the book had been put together carelessly – Reynolds had in fact put a lot of work into it – but that the selection process had been hopelessly lacking in discrimination. Reynolds exploded to George Macmillan: "*Punch* was bad. Did you see the *Standard*? What abominable cheek to say I was chucking unrevised notes into covers! An underground stream of opposition somewhere, looks so. I resent being treated as a careless writer, for, anyhow, I'm not that".[111]

Discounting *The Lower Deck* – much more in the nature of a political pamphlet – *How 'Twas* was to be Reynolds' final published book. These stinging criticisms from a handful of reviewers may themselves have contributed in no small way to his self-extinction as a writer.

The summer of 1912 was not the scorching heatwave of the previous year but, along with the worry and the work, it brought with it also its moments of relaxation and of fun. In January, as a by-product of the *Seems So!* controversy on education, he had agreed to give an address to the General Association of Church School Managers and Teachers at their meeting at Wooburn Green, near High Wycombe.[112] He was surprised and delighted to be offered expenses, but the surprise and delight turned to something else when, after successfully fulfilling the engagement in early May and putting in his claim for £4, he received a cheque for 30/- based on a third-class fare and minimal out-of-pocket expenses.[113] The unsuspecting clergyman responsible for this miserly affront was treated to a Reynolds special.

> Thank you for your letter of the 14th inst., and your enclosed cheque for 30/-, which I return herewith.
>
> I speak oftenest for nothing; or otherwise for my expenses on the recognised scale; but I do not undertake to speak on the cheap. The recognised scale of expenses is first-class. Ladies'-maids, butlers, valets, and other personal servants are, I understand, given second-class tickets, where such tickets still exist. Third-class expenses are only allowed by oneself to oneself, not to other people. To a man who is shortly coming here at my expense I should not think of offering less than first-class expenses. How he actually uses the money, or travels, is his business. The return third-class fare, which you say is 25/11d., deducted from 30/-, leaves 4/1d. for incidental expenses. Did you expect me to cart my bags the mile to and from the station in a wheelbarrow; to feed myself on eight-hour journeys out of a bit of newspaper, and to give porters penny tips? As I say, I am not accustomed to doing things on the cheap. What I can't afford to do properly I don't do at all.
>
> Owing to the distance, the roundabout route, and no Sunday train to Sidmouth, I had to start Friday, and I could not, if I had come straight home, have got there earlier than Monday. That is to say, I was bound to lose four days' work. (I always work Sundays.) If you clergy drop four days' work, you are paid your stipends just the same. If I drop four days' work, it is four days' earnings out of my pocket. By travelling third I reckoned on recouping a portion of that expense, which I did not charge you. You say that you felt bound to send my letter on to learn the opinion of your colleagues before replying. Kindly send this letter on, too, so that they may learn my opinion.[114]

He did, however, admit to George Macmillan that he had gilded the note of protest just a little. "In one respect I was not quite accurate. I do do things cheaply for myself, but I try not to make other people suffer for it. His attitude is precisely that which irritates labouring people beyond endurance. They don't do such things themselves. They haggle for wages, but they do know how to pay or give."[115]

It was another six weeks before the organisers re-emerged with their counter bid. "Those educational people – the High Wycombe clergy – instead of sending me the £4 of my bill have risen from the previous 30/- to £2. So I've returned that cheque, too, suggesting that their Committee should devote it to 'some other charitable object'. But I really think they're too dense to appreciate my snarls."[116] It was typical of Reynolds to prefer on principle no money to the receipt of less than his due.

There was another diversion early in June when the firm of Macmillan made a leap – almost – into the twentieth century. They were approached by William Holt White, a recently retired editor and a future novelist in his own right, to mount an experimental campaign for one of their budding authors, not someone completely unknown, by inserting articles and interviews on a concerted basis in a number of newspapers and periodicals.[117]

George Macmillan broke the news rather diffidently, and could not conceal a certain distaste: "His idea was that if a writer's name were to some extent in the public eye, and his writings topical in character, a good deal might be done to increase his popularity by a little judicious wire-pulling etc. among newspaper editors on the look out for attractive 'copy'. The man he had his eye on for the experiment was no less a person than Stephen Reynolds! We did not altogether take to the proposal...... And please understand that we do not in the least press you to lend yourself to the scheme. There are obvious objections to it, and there is something rather 'American' about it which is against the grain with us".

But he was content to let Reynolds have the final say. "Still we thought it only right to let you know of the proposal, and if you feel that you would like to take advantage of the suggested 'boom', and that it would not be likely to injure your position as a writer, we are prepared to regard it as so much extra advertising undertaken in the hope of future results."[118] From this moment on, Holt White became in Reynolds-speak "The Boomster".

The proposition itself was a difficult one for Reynolds. He was torn on the one hand by the fear of cheapening his image and losing a degree of his writer's independence, and on the other by the ever-present need to increase his circulation and improve his income. After discussing it carefully with Tom Woolley – "he has the Devonian's secrecy, and we neither of us act in any affair without the other" – he set out the countervailing pros and cons in a long letter to Frederick Macmillan which developed into a serious stocktaking of his current position, both in writing and in life.

> Well, we feel like you. It goes against the grain, in its extent and its cynicism. Not that we mind advertising and the bunkum it involves. Not that we see any sense in refusing to push by all means possible what one believes in. Not that we turn up our noses at money results. Not that I don't wire-pull myself pretty energetically on occasion. But this scheme, in its expression, at all events, if not in itself, looks rather unscrupulous, although, when one comes to examine it carefully, it only proposes to do on a large scale what one doesn't hesitate to do on a small scale, and in

industrial cases. If it were designed to push what one knew to be a bogus product, it would likewise be a different matter; but naturally I can't take up the view that my own stuff is a sort of intellectual patent medecine. One needs, I take it, to face the situation very frankly, and set out the problem to be solved quite clearly. I have already a fair reputation of good quality (compounded, I am glad to admit, of my reputation and my publishers'), together with some influence in the centres of affairs. But it continues to hang fire in widening itself out among the "mostly fools". Like my literary connexion, it has been built up on very personal and individual lines: Pinker gave up the handling of my work to me. The problem is, therefore, as this man seems to have assumed, not so much one of making reputation, as of widening it without cheapening it (which would, I think, only be done on the same lines as those on which it has been built up so far), and, in fine, of turning it into sales. I fancy it is now getting pretty ripe.

I want that more circulation both for more position and influence in affairs, and also for more money, which I do want very badly:

(1) In all sorts of work I have in hand (fisheries etc.) I am badly hampered for lack of money. Directly one takes any part in affairs, the preservation of one's independence costs a lot, because it so largely precludes one from doing the job on someone else's or the public's money or terms.

(2) If I can't soon procure myself the time, i.e. the money, to write my top best and to tackle the bigger things I have in mind, instead of having to keep the pot boiling on smaller stuff, – it will be too late. It is mainly by the careful serialization of my stuff that I have rubbed along so far.

(3) I don't think I can keep up much longer the racket and strain of the last few years. It is sapping me out, and it is a question of whether things will ease up or I shall break down first. A second breakdown would probably be the finish of me; I shan't be 22 next time. I shall have to get help for my spade-work in any case. Health, too, demands money! On the other hand, I'm determined at all costs to keep my freedom and to write what I want to write. And insofar as this scheme might bring me money by stimulating competition for my work among publishers, it's of no use to me. I happen to have the publishers I want.[119]

He had made marginal comments on the voluminous scheme itself. Where Holt White had written "I trust it is seen that I shall do my best to put myself inside the skin of each individual Editor", he had added "Poor devils". And another annotation summed up his very real doubts. "Is he capable of really understanding the real drift of my work? Otherwise I run the risk of being given a pseudo-reputation and having to write and play the fool up to it."[120]

But in the end he was not prepared to make up his mind, and left the decision firmly to Macmillans, offering a discussion in London. He went up to town on 13 June for a 1.30 lunch with Frederick Macmillan where they chewed the matter over. Holt White was called in after lunch and the three eventually decided to give the scheme a go.[121] Whereupon Holt White, anxious to prove his *bona fides*, rushed like a scalded cat round the London newspaper offices. At the day's close, he sent a rather breathless communication to Frederick Macmillan, with all the hallmarks of the modern management consultant on the first enthusiastic days of an assignment.

> After I left Mr. Reynolds and you I saw Mr. Perris, the News Editor of the Daily Chronicle, who did not in the least mind my knowing that Mr. Reynolds was writing certain articles for him, and he took quite kindly to the suggestion that Philip Gibbs should write an article on Mr. Reynolds and his work. I also saw Mr. Kennedy, the Editor of the Daily Mirror, who is anxious to send down and take a page of photographs of Mr. Reynolds next week. I was seeing Mr. Blumenfeld, the editor of the Daily Express, on other matters, and when I mentioned Mr. Reynolds he promptly asked me to write a special article for him on my return from Sidmouth. I also met Mr. Huskinson, the Editor of the Tatler, quite by accident, and he said that he would like to have some photographs of Mr. Reynolds. I have also asked Mr. Bullock, the Editor of the Graphic, to meet Mr. Reynolds at lunch tomorrow.
>
> I think, therefore, that I have made quite a nice little beginning, and everything has been quite friendly and pleasant, and I am sure that there is no reason for Mr. Reynolds to be alarmed. I thought I would just let you know that I had already put things in train.[122]

Reynolds had lunch next day as planned with the editor of the *Graphic* and dinner in the evening with Holt White, whom he was beginning to find just a little overwhelming. "The Boomster tells me that he proposes to run down here this week on behalf of the Daily Express! I had him to dinner with me on Friday evening, to box his compass for him, and advised him to turn up as a visitor I am acquainted with, the better to carry through his job, and also, partly, so that I can bolt into my burrow till I'm cooler if his exuberance makes me boil." The fertility and ingenuity of the Holt White brain was a source of unending pleasure. "He says he's suggested to a Punch man a series of Henry James and other authors living à la S.R. in order to improve the authenticity of their books. That ought to be rather funny if it comes off.... I should like to do myself Joseph Conrad shoving off a seine-boat in a lop, and Henry James explaining the constitution of our firm to an Insurance Umpire."[123]

Once the initial Macmillan cheque was in the post on 18 June, all suddenly went quiet on the Holt White front.[124] By the end of the month, Reynolds was still looking out anxiously for him from Sidmouth, but the Boomster had already made his excuses to George Macmillan: "He explained that he had been very much occupied with some other publicity scheme, not in connection with books, on which he is engaged".[125] Then out of the blue he suddenly announced his intention of coming down the last weekend in June, a time when Reynolds was already booked for two days in Plymouth on fishery business and to interview a prospective new secretary to help him with his "spadework". After a furious exchange of telegrams in all directions, Holt White postponed his visit but by then Reynolds' weekend in Plymouth was already lost. "The Boomster is now coming Tuesday, and meanwhile has landed several of us in such a hobble that it's a good job, perhaps, he's so weighty, else I should feel inclined when he does come to carry 'en down over baych an' chuck 'en in zay!...... I hope I shall feel more amiable by Tuesday, specially as he seems to be bringing a photographer, and being asked to 'pose' always makes me feel like a conger on a hook."[126]

Macmillans read Holt White the riot act, but still he did not turn up on the Tuesday as planned.[127] Reynolds was growing more complaisant. "It's very kind of you to be so annoyed on my behalf. I really was savage, and felt inclined to write to him and cuss him up in heaps. But I suppose, if he's going to do the job, he'd best be kept in a fairly good heart towards it...... It strikes me he is only wanting to give us the fag end of his time and convenience, when he's got nothing better to do...... Evidently he's one of those people who go pretty slow very quick. Hustlers frequently do."[128]

But, like the modern management consultant, Holt White's special skill was not getting on fast with the assignment in hand but the more creative function of settling down the anxious client. In this new experimental profession, personality was all, and when he *did* arrive the following weekend he soon had both Reynolds and the Woolley family eating out of his hand. "I made quite a nice recovery in temper before he arrived last Saturday with a rather nice little *Mirror* snapshotter. And the Boomster was really very amusing down here, and I think well amused. I've never in my life seen anyone – not even our own kids – put away greasy cake hot from the oven and plastered with scald cream, as he can! Amazing! No wonder he's 18 st. at 33! Anyhow, our people quite took to him, and he talked, and t'other man snapshotted, and I used him as ballast for the motor boat, and all went well. Evidently, from what he said, he has carted away pretty vivid impressions."[129]

With that, Holt White disappeared into oblivion. Six weeks later, Reynolds broached the matter with George Macmillan: "Neither sound nor echo of the Boomster for at least a month! Still does that normal circulation of 10,000 recede into the future!"[130] Macmillan was equally non-plussed. "We have heard nothing at all of Mr. Holt White, but we intend to ask him at once what is really going on for certainly there is nothing to show."[131] At the end of August Macmillans were still trying vainly to call the Boomster in for a meeting to give an account of himself.[132]

There was, however, one substantive result of the "boom". The "nice little snapshotter" from the *Mirror* had at least completed *his* mission. On 10 July there appeared a half page spread of three photographs under the headline "Author who lives the life of an ordinary fisherman". There was a shot of Reynolds with Bob and Tom, posed very stiffly holding a rather aimless net over the side of the boat, high and dry on the beach – a photograph of which Madame Tussaud's might well have been proud. There was an affectionate snap of a shy looking Reynolds posing with Margot at Bob's front door, and a portrait of him in his first floor study, sitting at his desk at the window overlooking the Square, young and intense-looking, as he stares out up the Gut towards the sea – probably the only extant photograph of his writing environment through most of his writing life.

The picture-spread had instant results, of a less than predictable kind. He wrote to George Macmillan for help.

> By the first post next day I received from a young lady, aged 28, of Brighton, a leap-year proposal that I should forthwith proceed to marry her, on the strength of *my* photograph! Diable! If your firm, out of the vastness of its publishing experience has gathered the necessary renseignements for dealing with such-like cases, why, you'd better let me have 'em. I daren't write back, "No go!" for fear of encouraging the young lady to continue the correspondence, and at the same time her letter was really rather pathetic.

But there was more to come. "Then by the next post, we got three very nice knives, wrapped up in literary texts and exhortations, and inscribed "From one fighting the fight". What fight, not explained. I have been fighting cigarettes, and have continued to keep them down to two a day, which I believe has broken their back, the worst of it being now over; and from the "friendly pipe" I have an exceedingly sore and evil-tasting mouth! That serves to remind me that I am being quite extraordinarily virtuous, and if Tom and I throw up beer, as we both threaten to do, we shall undoubtedly become too virtuous to live near!"[133]

George Macmillan pondered the problem of the lady from Brighton for three days and apologised for the delay. "I am afraid however that even after this period for consideration we are still unable to help you in regard to the communication you have received from the young lady at Brighton, such a communication being quite beyond our experience either as publishers or individuals."[134]

Though the Boomster was not going to win for him the coveted 10,000 circulation, Reynolds was nonetheless pleased with the *Mirror* photographs and posted the one of himself and Margot at the front door off to Aunt Jane. He was still enjoying the flattery of the proposal.

> Would you and Aunt Allie care for the enclosed photograph? I think it's the best there is of me and Margot. It's one of the photographs the *Daily Mirror* man took when he came down. About three days after the photos. appeared in the *Mirror* I had a letter from a lady on the E. [*sic*] coast proposing that I should marry her forthwith, she being convinced from the photograph that I was easy-going and good-tempered. I dared not reply to assure her that I was neither, for fear she'd continue the correspondence or descend on us here![135]

The summer too brought its usual trail of waifs and strays, which now seemed an inseparable part of his life. On 4 June William Mitchell, a labourer of Sid Row in Sidmouth, appeared at Ottery Magistrates Court charged with using obscene language. A couple of his neighbours appeared in court to testify how he would suddenly break out with the language like a wild man, and the whole neighbourhood would be forced to run inside and slam their doors. The forty or fifty small children in the Row would rush indoors too, repeating every word he uttered. Mitchell denied using the language, but admitted that when he was out of work "he dared say he felt a bit nasty".

The local paper reported

> Mr Stephen Reynolds, the well-known author, of Sidmouth, appeared to give evidence as to defendant's general character. He said defendant had been invalided out of the Navy, having had sunstroke. Defendant was quite alright until one of these fits came over him. Then he burst out, and could not be regarded as exactly knowing what he was doing. It could not be good for him to live alone, as he was subject to such fits. Witness handed in a letter sent to him (witness) by the Sidmouth Medical Officer of Health. Defendant was fined 10s inclusive.[136]

The incident well illustrates how closely Reynolds regarded the working people around him as his own responsibility. Though quite without any legal training, he prided himself on his ability to gain justice for them when in trouble with the law. It was his own personal social service, not only helping *them* but giving him too the feeling of being wanted and of use.

He gave George Macmillan the inside story.

> Meanwhile, I have landed myself in for a lively responsibility – a madman! He was invalided out for sunstroke in '94; a nice harmless fellow, good workman and as honest as daylight; but when he's out of work he broods, gets imaginary suspicions of people against him, goes wild and flares out into the most unimaginable language. Last Tuesday when he was had up for obscenity, I gave evidence to raise the case from a legal to a medico-legal status, guaranteed his fine to save him from chokey (it would have been a most dangerous thing to send him to brood in prison

for seven days and come out to revenge himself on the witnesses against him) and got his fine reduced to 10/- which he can pay, and which it will probably steady him to have to pay. But it was grimly farcical. They swore him to give evidence on his own behalf, made him read two papers of his extraordinary language, and asked: "Now, Mitchell, did you use that language on those papers?"
"No,sir," he replied with the utmost truthfulness. "I never uses such language!"
He had clean forgotten.
Walking home from Ottery with him, I got inside his cranky mind a bit. He is enormously grateful, and thinks he is under bond to me, or I am for him to the Beak, to hold himself in when he feels inclined towards a wild fit. It has got me into a pretty row with those who wanted him sent to prison, but I am sure that it is no good shoving such a case in and out of prison, and if we can get him along quietly, as there seems a chance of doing, while he earns his living, it is better than taking away his living and charging him to the country. The Medical Officer of Health – we have a splendid little man, one of the Peiles – thinks with me that it's one of those cases that a certain amount of personal attention and control can get to rub along quite well – if the neighbours will only not tease him.[137]

A month later he had an even stranger story for Macmillan. "A queer man picked me up last night, imploring me in an almost tragic manner to talk to him, for the purpose, apparently, of easing his distress of mind. Said he had taken a house here. I thought I had seen him before, and on asking him, he said he was the Dick Cunningham, V.C. who was supposed to have been killed at Ladysmith. Do you know anything of him? he really seemed as if his mind was on the rock – and slightly *in vino veritas*!"

These strange encounters gave him pause for thought. "Funny so many such people seem to make a dead course my way. I wonder do I carry traces of having known what Borrow called the horrors, or of having, temporarily at any rate, achieved a *modus vivendi* for a rocky mind of my own?"[138]

That summer a more deeply personal crisis was to break above his head involving someone who, like the others, was attracted by his sensitivity and vulnerability, but who was seeking the one kind of help he was unable to supply.

Since her day visit to Sidmouth the previous August, Katie Powys had kept up her correspondence with him, her only link, assuming the role of devoted pupil to his all-knowing teacher. Inspired by his example, she was sublimating her feelings in writing. By October 1911 she had completed two short stories, and was planning three more. "One, the biggest and most deep, will be called 'The Thoughts of a Dairymaid' or 'While Milking' in[to] which I hope to bring in some distant time the three great things that affect humanity, that is: the elements, love and religion." Despite the brave front, there was a growing awareness of the unequal nature of the relationship. She confided to her diary: "I go on writing to Sidmouth and at times I have a letter from 'Olaf'; otherwise I have to content myself with different articles that come to my hand".[139]

The short stories were not just sublimation; they were material means of attracting his attention. She sent him one in late October, just as he was setting off with Tom for France. On return on 1 November he sent her a holding reply: "The MS. is getting itself steadily read through. When I'm finished, I'll let you know what I think; and then you'd best disbelieve me entirely! The best criticism, the only ultimate criticism, is one's own."[140]

She was staying with her brother, Theodore, at East Chaldon when his comments on the manuscript finally arrived, the source of much pleasure. But her diary entries show how much she was measuring out her life with his letters. "I have been to the cliffs now four times. Twice before Olaf's letters to me and twice afterward. He wrote me a splendid one on my old story, one which is full of sound advice."[141]

In February she sent him a new manuscript, which he read on his return from London. He noted the power of feeling, always her greatest strength, but also the uneven quality of the expression. "Your letter and sketch came while I was in Town on fishery business – rushing round furiously. The sketch, which I return, is almost grim in parts. Its faults are precisely those which I pointed out before – plenty of feeling, plenty of thought, but inattention to detail. A thing, to be artistic, must be *just so* all the way through."[142]

She was desperate to see him. "Dreams and inward meditations were the grace of the spirit, but the flesh of the body lacked hope. To see and to hear was the repeated wish...... Written messages availed little. Words were mirages, they tempted, but they could not satisfy. My love was my irresistible want. To him I must hasten. Through mud and through heat I must reach him, through cold and through rain I must find him. Athirst with great longing I craved for him."[143]

She had been planning an earlier than usual visit to Sidmouth, but fate was against it. Still at Chaldon in December 1911, she went walking the cliffs at White Nose with her brother Llewelyn and seems to have had some presentiments of the calamity that was about to break.

> That shore, how the spirit thereof has wrapped itself round me. The times Lulu and I went down before Xmas when we climbed back in the deepening darkness. Weird and strange and awe-inspiring, it shook my very soul. I felt that Olaf would have understood it. Then when the wave came towards me on the ledge, the feeling of death was not far and I wished that I could have seen him again.
> ......Curious how full of omens for my visit to Sidmouth [it] has been. Always something happened to prove more and more that I was not going down as I wished, and so it is.[144]

The early visit came to nothing, but the summer one went ahead as usual. In early August, she went down with Llewelyn and her elder sister Gertrude for the few days, so achingly anticipated, that were to lead to the disaster.[145] It was her fifth visit to Sidmouth, and the last she would make while Reynolds was alive.

Afterwards, back home at Witcombe, she made a tersely laconic record in her diary.

> Sidmouth has come and gone.
> Olaf was down there. I first saw him in the kitchen that first night. Bob took us a row the next day and we had tea at Tom's while we saw the Twins. We climbed Salcombe and High Peak. Olaf came down on us once the other side. I would go every morning down to the sea and the black lady would haunt me. Tom I met sometime. Saw Bob the first morning and Olaf never then. He came to tea on Sunday but when he left he bunked like ten thousand Aunt Marthas had been set loose after her calf. It was good to see them again. We had a lovely tea there. Bob really charming – Mrs. Woolley and the New baby. The great thing was Gertrude drawing Bob and the baby. I hated going again. I feel further away every time I go......[146]

The diary breaks off. It was fifteen years before she would write in it again.

And it was in the late 1920's too that she felt strong enough to write *Phoenix*, the prose-poem charting her breakdown – her own version of the *Ex Profundis* book that Reynolds never wrote. In it she brought herself to face what actually had happened that August. It is a disturbing, highly emotional, but also deeply moving, account.

At the beginning there hovers the symbol of the dark lady she recorded in her diary – a woman in black by the seashore mourning another lost love – "Only a woman with garments of mourning paced beside the white-tongued waves, steadfastly turning her eyes away from the long-limbed men".[147]

On arrival, she combs the beach for Reynolds, but in vain. "Where was my love? I continued my search by the high bows of the boats. I expected still to see him by the shores of the receding tides. Instead, over the waters flew the dark birds; for in the knowledge of death, the white birds hide. Lonely and disappointed, the shadow of my dawn fell before me and my spirit drooped even as a broken wing."[148]

The defining moment came on the day she walked over High Peak with Gertrude and down into the green valley below. There they are overtaken by Reynolds on his daily walk to Ladram Bay. For both parties it is a shock encounter. She stands tongue-tied before him. From her demeanour, he can tell even more clearly than before the strength of her feelings. He cannot explain to her in terms the barrier that stands between them. But on the spur of the moment, he determines on a personal declaration that should provide the hint: he is alone, loved only by the natural world around him, and so always will remain. She understands the purpose of this stark confession, but not its hidden reasoning. It is a message of devastation and despair.

> Yet another day we wandered away through the woods where in fancy the sweetest of earth-born violets grow. In heaviness I bore my heart; to see him and to hear him being my sole imperative. Onwards and onwards my sister led me; to the steep rocks where the gulls meet and have their being, to where the high cliffs stand jagged and washed to the colour of blood. Presently we returned to where the grass was greenest, to where the wind was hidden, when quicker than a meteor he appeared. Unconscious of things mortal, unconscious of things immortal, we stood together. In mute diffidence my soul remained. Standing with his eyes searching mine I heard him cry. "No friends but these, I have. Alone I am. None there are who love me."
>
> In a moment the sun turned to darkness, and the grass turned to dust. Then flashed the fiery sword from heaven, until it pierced my side. As a woman I could not speak, emboldened by love I was bound by silence. I suffered from a judgement severe. Henceforth would I know the wail of the seabirds as they gathered in the air; and my cry would follow theirs in the over-shadowed night. "Terrible, terrible, Oh! my God! is the destruction of a woman!"
>
> If ever mute creation desired words to confess, my spirit fast panted within me, but the ways of the world sealed my lips and the manner of man silenced my tongue. Broken and dumb as the sharp cliffs below, and as indifferent as the clouds which raced above, I remained. Passive and wrought I stood before him. I could not show the running wound to the physician himself. I dared not lift my countenance to his face. He spoke, but I could not answer. He mourned, but I could not comfort. He was sorrowful, but I dared not console. With the anguish of an imprisoned bird, my spirit beat itself against the bars of conformity.
>
> He gave; but to give to him I was denied.
>
> Cruel are the ways of the world. Men come and men go, but how wretchedly their hands are held. The hour of their day passeth, but only the shell adorns their dwelling. In the rising of the sun there cometh rain.
>
> Sorely stricken was my heart, and the love cords of my life were twisted in misery. There in sadness I stood apart, and in silent woe I kept his words.[149]

The remaining days were desolation. As the final day approaches, she scours the town for one last sight of him. "By hidden ways and low houses I came forth alone to where I met the sea. I paced the long stretch of the weather-beaten wall. All was deserted. Like the dead bellies of black horses the big boats lay where the waves could not harm them. I looked to the right, I looked to the left, but no man moved."[150]

In desperation, she goes down the Gut to Bob's cottage. In the joy of meeting Reynolds once more, she determines on a new mission for her life.

> I was afraid; unbeckoned, I sought the house where he lived. I hastened between the walls where the children play. In nervous terror I passed by the wrapped sails, where I heeded not the up-turned boat, nor the grey of sea-worn oars. At the doorway I reached out my hand. I faltered. I knocked. It was opened. I was led through the passage into the low kitchen, where before me I saw his fellow-fisherman, and the mother and babe. They rose up to receive me. With the outstretching of hands they welcomed me. When I saw them lean over the little one, the fire lighting with warm colour the figures, the cradle and the infant clothing, I understood. Astonished I could not forget the father, and the mother, and the sleeping child.
>
> They brought to my mind how in the wantonness of a tangled underwood, the delicate primrose and the slender campion bring forth their buds in hidden secret, and their flowers in careless safety. It is there where the berries of the bramble drop sweet and unknown, for the thorns are their protection and the nettles their true defence. Here, I perceived a shelter for the lonely heart and comfort for the troubled in mind.
>
> In response to the maddened beating of my heart, my own friend appeared. My love was before us. In our midst he had come. Yea, to himself he had gathered his own, and with one accent we were glad.
>
> My soul mounted upwards. Much happiness was mine. Great joy rose as the fire before me, stretching in scarlet and gold, transforming all in its piercing heat. Through the light of its glory I beheld the one I adored. In brilliance greater than the day-born sun I found him. I took of his spirit, wherewith never to renounce it. Thanks-giving was the expression of my exaltation, and the magnitude of all worship was in my praise. In silent intensity I knew my affection and in the sight of him I blessed my existence. He spoke; and as at the first sound of distant breakers I caught fast my breath. Thus contentment came by the crooning of a baby and by the side of a deep-sea fisherman I foresaw my destiny. To be near my love was my satisfaction, and to live for him, my ambition.[151]

Another day, she returns to the cottage again, and waits for him in his first floor study, alone with all his books and personal possessions. He comes to her, but this time in imagination only. "At the coming of another day, when, wrapped in my shawl, I lay in sickness of mind and body upon his couch, I was caught as if in a trance. There in the secret of his chamber, he was allowed me. There in dozing and light dreaming he touched me. Among sounds and objects he knew, I found him. He came to my side, and yet he was not. He came to the bed-pillow, and I heard him speak; I roused myself, but he was not. He approached in spirit, but not in flesh."[152]

The obsession, and the knowledge of certain loss, was too much for the delicate balance of her mind. Back at her brother Will's farm at Witcombe, she suffered, like Reynolds in 1903, a total collapse. "Too quickly, in a moment, in a second, the mighty arm of my exaltation felled me. The waters of my want overcame me. A malady of the brain possessed me. I was sick. My passion outreached itself; the flames of my love overpowered me."[153]

She became religiously obsessed with the Cross. Very early one morning, she escaped her bedroom leaving all the pictures, books, jewellery and objects arranged in the shape of crosses. Will thought she had gone out to drown herself, and she was found and rushed back to Montacute Vicarage to the protection of her parents.[154] On 22 August, her brother, John Cowper, travelled up from his home in Sussex to be by her side. He was sure that the stifling atmosphere of the vicarage was the real culprit: "The real cause of all this is our present cursed system which permits no freedom to a child of unhappy and hopeless passions like Katie".[155]

She cried out for her copy of Walt Whitman's *Leaves of Grass* which Gertrude believed was one of the causes of the trouble.[156] She would wake up in the middle of the night when her medication wore off and terrify the trained nurse put to watch over her. "Katie becomes, just as animals do, conscious at once of anyone's fear of her, and rendered by it at once angry and bold."[157] At three o'clock in the morning of 25 August, she got on to the window-sill of her room and threatened to throw herself out.[158] The family's thoughts turned towards institutional care.

In all of this frightening chaos, Reynolds was at the centre of her thoughts. "I was become more and more obsessed with a vehement desire to go to my beloved. It mattered not how, as long as my face was turned to the south-west, to where lay the wide encircling bay upon which the fishermen sailed. With this one fixed idea, I bethought my will-power would suffice to induce all mankind, instantaneously to take me to his side. But in my madness I was mistaken...... I fancied my love himself was come; and that it was his footsteps I heard through the thin partition of the wall. I called, but there came no answer."[159]

So close was the identification, she began to believe that she herself was an incarnation of Reynolds and signed little notes "Katie (S.R.)".[160] On 27 August, John Cowper wisely decided to involve Reynolds himself. "I have got Gertrude to write to Stephen Reynolds asking him for a letter to her commanding her to use her will to be calm. But I fear things are really beyond his power to cure."[161]

The request came at a bad time for Reynolds. Overworked, physically ill, torn in the throes of the final conflict between his moneyless writing and the increasing burden of fisheries business, he was, as he had told George Macmillan, fast heading for his second breakdown himself. The cause of

Katie's violent illness went close to the heart of his own private anxieties, and threatened to expose his own hidden secret. It was a situation on which many would have inclined to turn their backs.

He didn't. On 1 September, he drafted a careful letter, designed to calm her and give her hope for recovery. He drew on his own experience, but not so much as to waken a different kind of hope. It was a difficult tightrope to walk.

> We are all very glad to hear you are better. The great thing is, when an attack comes on, to sit tight, confident that, as it has had a beginning, so it will have an end. That practice makes perfect is even truer as regards controlling nerve-storms than it is of most things. You will find, first that they will cease to surprise you, and then that you can act in quite an ordinary manner even in the middle of them, giving no sign to anyone of your interior distress; and then, almost suddenly, you will wake up to the fact that they have ceased, only to recur at lengthening intervals, if at all. Then is the time to get thoroughly interested in some comparatively commonplace light work, so that one has, as it were, a centre to revolve round and keep one steady.
>
> As I told you before – for the relief of overstrained nature, there is nothing like a long spell of being very ordinary. And, as a matter of fact, the most original thinkers have nearly all led pretty humdrum lives themselves.
>
> Now you have begun to get better, you can go on, with constant watchfulness and care in self-management.[162]

But she was not better. The periods of remission proved something of a chimera. By the time the letter arrived, the family had decided on the safety of institutional care, and she was moved to a psychiatric home – Brislington Hall in Bristol. In one of the most ironically tragic twists of the whole story, when her father accompanied her to Bristol, she believed he was taking her to her wedding.

> My father watched from the entrance of the door. Suddenly, without a word or a prayer, he outstretched his arm to the bush of high myrtle. Heedlessly he plucked sprays of the sweet smelling blossoms. With dignity, he hastened down the stone-steps which divided us. Hastily, without thought, he pushed into my hands those delicate blooms – blooms of the white Myrtle – the flower of the bride.
>
> Oh! Cruel Significance. Oh! gesture fantastical!
>
> The illusion became truth. I imagined they were of a certainty taking me to my dear one. Never to be parted.
>
> The further we went, the more sure I became, and when we reached the journey's end I advanced trembling, but the church and the altar were wanting. The bridegroom was missing. Instead of the joyful pealing of

> bells, it was the moaning of the mad. Instead of the scattering of rice, it was the uncanny dance of the demented....... I cursed my Father and my Mother, and the day of my delivery, for here the day was turned to darkness and the night beheld no moon. I sank into the pit of madness, into the most loathsome of dungeons, there to meet the grinding of teeth and the wild tearing of hair.[163]

Amidst the despair, Reynolds' letter came as a sign of deliverance and salvation. All her personal possessions had been taken from her, but this treasure she secreted away.

> At last, at the time of the many bells, at the time of happiness and the healing of wounds, there came a message into my hands. In the depth of a cess-pool, in the tumult of feeling it was brought to me. Whether borne on the wind, I knew not; nevertheless it came in the likeness of a boat, in the shape of an high hill it appeared before me.... I caught it up in my hand, and in the tight lace of my dress I hid it. By day it revived me, by night it gladdened me. It brought the scent of spring flowers. I was better. I was happy. It revealed the One who remained by the rough waves. It renewed me as the strong smell of seaweed.[164]

It became the precious symbol of their relationship, of his care for her, and as she carried it with her around the hospital, so did she carry it through life. Held fast between the pages of her battered green volume of *Leaves of Grass*, it went wherever she did. Forty years after her death, it lies safe in that volume today.

Then, as she started to recover, a terrible recognition was borne in upon her. She had been mad, and he knew of it. He could not possibly fall in love with her now.

> How could I seek him now that the fiends of madness had hold of me? How could I go to him now that I had lain in the dung of pigs? Therefore I saw the departing of my Sun and instead the darkness of vain longing pressed heavily upon me. In the eagerness to leap the way between us, I had fallen to be seared.... I was cursed, for these arms would never encircle the head of the man I loved.
>
> Who would walk with one who smelt of the mad-house?
> Who would gather among roots blackened by fire?
> None can give birth whose dreams are a furnace,
> Whose wells are poison and whose hopes are perished.
>
> Here in my bed of affliction it was borne to me. In horror it filled my being. I gathered up my covering and wept. My tears watered the pillow even faster than the rain outside. But no one heard for there was no one to hear.[165]

Terrible as was the finality of this realisation, it was nonetheless the beginning of the healing. Here was now a rational justification for his behaviour to which she might at last come to be reconciled. Slowly over time the despair turned to hope in the fulfilment of the new determination she had made in Bob's cottage at their final meeting.

She spent years in the wilderness, working on farms more as a penitential therapy than as the chosen vocation of which she had dreamed.

> They kept my love from me.
> In the breaking of sods, there came no hope. With the care of cows was my separation contrived. Alone I continued my way; each day passed as the other, without mercy and without hope. In constant labour I carried my secret and in strange fields I laid it low. In the rime of winter and in the drought of summer my love haunted me. His presence pursued me, and the days of remembrance clung like burrs to my side. They would not leave me, nor could I shake them off.[166]

It was only years later, with Reynolds' death, that reconciliation finally came and she reaffirmed the determination to live henceforward in the light of his being. She never saw him again, but he was to remain with her for the rest of her life.

> Though I find him not, he is near me; though I walk not with him, he is beside me. In the vapours of mists he beckons me, and in strange cities he holds my hand.[167]

FIFTEEN

The Navy and the Nation 1912

When Stephen Reynolds threw in his lot with the Woolleys in 1906, he was joining not just a fisher family but a Navy one too. It was common for the sons of fishermen, with the sea in their veins, to set their sights on the senior service. For the more outgoing, it was the call of travel and adventure; for the more cautious, it was the security of a regular, if paltry, wage and a pension at the end of it. Fishermen in general regarded the Navy with ambivalence. They were proud of the tradition, even more so if their sons were a part of it, but also somewhat disdainful of the principle of paid employment and of knuckling under to naval discipline, which conflicted with the fishing traditions of rugged independence. What is more, the majority of able seamen, unlike the fisher recruits, were ignorant of sea lore and could not sail a boat.

Bob Woolley's brother, Harry, and his brother-in-law, Jack Collier, spent most of their working lives in the Navy, rising to the rank of Chief Petty Officer. Bob himself would have joined the Navy but for the rheumatic fever of his childhood which had physically disqualified him, but he nonetheless served his time as a member of the Royal Naval Reserve. And he was no end proud of his eldest son, who was a *very* able seaman.

For it was on that emotional evening of September 1904, when he found Bob weeping in Fore Street because his son Bill had gone that day for a sailor, that Reynolds first recognised the closeness of the historic relationship between fishing families and the Navy. His own perceptions changed that night, as he delivered Bob safe home to Bedford Square and made his way back across the town to his lodgings in Jubilee Terrace.

> When Tony went down the narrow roadway, homewards, he had had just the amount of grog to make him sleep: no more, no less. That father's grief – the boy gone to sea, the father left stranded ashore – it was bad to listen to. While going up town, I wondered with how much sorrow the Navy is recruited. We look on our sailors rather less fondly than on the expensive pieces of machinery we send them to sea in. I don't think I shall ever again be able to regard the Navy newspaper-fashion. It seems as if someone of mine belongs to it.... [1]

This dichotomy between the lavish attention given to the building of ships, the Dreadnought mentality, and the poor conditions of the average sailor was at the core of his critique of Admiralty and national policy.

Any new experience in Reynolds' life, any fresh social context in which he happened to find himself, turned quickly to political thought and political action. A few days at sea with the Woolleys had him pondering the commercial organisation of the market for fish. A few nights dragging boats up over the sea wall to the safety of the Esplanade had him planning the next steps in the shingle question. In June 1907, his first full summer with the Woolleys, the appearance of Bill home on leave found him worrying about the lot and the career of the average able seaman.

He wrote to Edward Garnett: "Bill, Bob's eldest boy, has gone back to Plymouth naval barracks to-day, after a tremendous flourish among the maids. When he used to be my skipper he used to be a brown, untidy, rather scraggy boy. Now the Navy has sent him home with a magnificent neck and carriage, but a complexion à l'envie des femmes".

But Bill had also brought home some tales of the cynicism with which short-term men, cooped up in barracks, regarded their naval careers.

> From what I hear – which is a good deal – the present Admiralty manner of keeping many bluejackets in barracks for long periods is bad in every way. How appallingly ignorant the newspapers and politicians are of the men's own feeling. Grumbling one may always hear – the sailor-man's privilege – but these barracks are giving them a contempt for the service, making them regard it as so much time to be done. They are beginning to regard it – as I've never heard older sailors do – as something that so much can be got out of on certain conditions – as a preliminary career, a pension earning affair, preliminary to a real career that's to come after. It doesn't strike me as wise to allow, by short service, barrack-life and other innovations, the sailors to regard the navy as anything other than their *main* career.

This passive, grudging attitude to a career was the antithesis of Reynolds' own developing philosophy of work – the giving of life for an enhancement of life. He was also highly doubtful of the growing dependence of the Navy upon technocrats with their narrow outlook and limited personal qualification. "The navy is the only public service in which men, on the whole, become more men, instead of less men, and it appears to me that reduction, even for the purpose of greater mechanic ability in its personnel, is false economy. Warships are delicate unreliable things. It seems to me that the sea will always require manliness (in all senses) before and above mere ability or brains, in the ordinary stupid educational sense of the words. How this cursed educationalism has infected everything."[2]

From May 1909 onwards, weekends with Bob and their lower deck friends "on the bust" at Devonport became a regular source of relaxation and diversion from the routine grind of fishing and boating. They would take lodgings for a couple of days and meet their naval friends for more than a few pints in the local Navy pubs. For Reynolds, there was the added attraction of a weekend surrounded by young sailors with their "magnificent necks and carriage"; but these were also occasions when he saw the problems of the Navy at first hand and from the inside.

Another frequent point of contact with the Navy was the work it brought to the small fishing boats whenever a battleship dropped anchor off Sidmouth and transport was needed to take the occupants to shore and back again. On one such assignment in May 1911, just a few days before his thirtieth birthday when he was worrying about the circulation of the cheap edition of *A Poor Man's House* and of *Seems So!*, due out that autumn, he was surprised to discover that the Navy was not just a source of political "copy" but also a thriving audience for his work. He wrote to George Macmillan to suggest the exploitation of this welcome discovery.

> I'm wondering if it would be worth while making a special effort to get at the Navy. The other day I went out to a battleship to see the commander and get him to shift anchorage out of our way, and couldn't make out why I was received with rather extra consideration; ship's corporal sent to my boat to take care of it, invitation to wardroom, and so forth; for I had only been out there putting frights and bluejackets aboard with the rest of the boats. Then it turned out that the officers not only knew my work, but recognized the motor boat from it. Young Bobby saw someone reading Alongshore aboard the battleship that was in here before that one. I should think that if the railway bookstalls at the Naval Ports could be induced to give the books a show they would get rid of a good many copies.

The incident gave him the idea of writing up the current political concerns of the Navy, on which he was so well informed, in a final article for the *Seems So!* series. "I think we will do a Navy article, to go into the Seems So book only if it is done in time. What I want to bring out are the impersonal causes of the rather tense personal feeling that exists between aft and for'ard."[3] George Macmillan was encouraging: "I should think it would be a good plan to have a Navy article in 'Seems So'."[4]

In the middle of June, he decided to harness the support of Lionel Yexley, the well-known journalistic champion of the cause of the lower deck. Yexley, twenty years Reynolds' senior, had worked in the Navy from 1877 to 1897, the last six as a coastguard, finally stationed at Weston Mouth, a row of out-of-the-way cottages a mile beyond Salcombe Hill where there was no road, and furniture had to be lowered down the cliff. After contributing articles to the *Coastguard Gazette*, he left the Navy and forfeited his pension to take up editorship of the magazine and become a political propagandist on behalf of the lower ranks. Later with Gerard Meynell he founded the *Fleet*, which became the most noted of the lower deck journals and with which he remained involved right up to his death in 1933.[5] A bull-faced, curly-haired man, he was a most persistent agitator for naval reform, and through his direct acquaintance with Admiral Fisher and Winston Churchill a most effective one.

Reynolds knew him well by reputation. A man who could give up his job and his pension in order to speak out was one after his own heart – "he is known throughout the service as the man who chucked his pension for a free tongue". In December 1908 Reynolds had reviewed in the *Daily News* Yexley's most famous book, *The Inner Life of the Navy*. He had spoken strongly in the author's favour: "He is doing a fine work, and his book will be a revelation to the ordinary civilian who thinks of our Navy in terms of pounds, shillings. pence, glory, and triumphs of engineering." But he was critical too, particularly when it came to casting aspersions on fishermen. "In pouring contempt on fishermen Naval Reservists, he omits to mention that, though indifferent mechanics, and barely at home on a modern battleship, they know how to row, sail, and beach boats better than the Navy has ever done, or is ever likely to do."[6]

He wrote to Yexley in the summer of 1911 for a copy of the *Fleet Annual* as background to his own planned work. "I want to quote and support your article in an article on Lower Deck Discontents, which I am thinking of writing for one of the reviews, and subsequent inclusion in a book called 'Seems So'...... I have a great many Lower Deck friends, and the subject is most interesting, and, except by you, ignored." He reminded Yexley that he had reviewed his book – "My copy of the book went round like hot cakes here and in several ships" – and that even 14 years later he was still well remembered in Sidmouth – "They still recollect here driving you back to Weston one afternoon or evening after you had been down for your letters!"[7]

With Yexley's help, Reynolds was able to complete his research by the middle of July and write the article, which Courtney had agreed to take for the *Fortnightly Review*, working under very high pressure. "I did the Fortnightly article in four days, which is wonderful for me."[8] But when Courtney saw the political tone of the article, he began to have cold feet. Reynolds suspected a political plot. If the Establishment were trying to suppress open discussion, there would soon be as much unrest in the Navy as there was currently throughout industry. He wrote in an exasperated vein on 20 August to George Macmillan.

> The *Fortnightly* has suddenly discovered that our *Navy* article is "an attack on a great Public Department". It isn't; it's a very scrupulously careful study of lower-deck feeling which, whether justified or not, will sooner or later have to be reckoned with; and the sooner the better, if a 'bust-up', regrettable from every point of view, is to be avoided. I strongly suspect that Archibald Hurd, the *Fortnightly* and *D.Telegraph* naval authority, and a friend of McKenna's, has something to do with the totally unnecessary alarm. Surely these strikes might have taught them the uselessness of sitting on working-class safety-valves. When working people

> get ugly is when they feel that they can't speak up for themselves, or aren't listened to, and the lower deck does feel that, deny it as they may. Possibly I shall run up to London this week to discuss the article with Courtney. I could publish it in the *New Age*, but that might make people think it alarmist, whereas that is what it precisely isn't. What do you think? It's psychological. I am far too proud of the Navy, and too keen on it, to wish to see there an explosion of suppressed feeling. But I know they'll get it if they aren't careful as surely as I knew the present labour unrest was brewing. I suppose, barring Yexley, who wrote much more strongly than I have done, and whose articles on the subject were discussed in the *Morning Post*, there is hardly another writing man in the country sufficiently intimate with numbers of lower deck men to hear them speak their mind, and intimate, too, with their people ashore. If they won't hear a forewarning, they'll be compelled to hear worse.[9]

In the event, it was Austin Harrison and the *English Review* who came to his rescue, and the article, *Navy Discontents*, appeared in the October issue and in *Seems So!* a month later. It began with a plea for more open discussion of conditions on the lower deck, and put forward a case for better pay and an overhaul of the insensitive discipline system.

On pay, he gave vent to the argument he had begun to formulate back in 1904 that too much attention was given to the ships and not enough to the men.

> Stinginess in dealing with the men is, indeed, almost inevitable from the economic position of the Navy. It needs vasts sums of money, and in order to get them from Parliament it is bound to bulk largely in the public eye, to keep the country in a state of naval enthusiasm – to advertise itself, in short. And it does advertise itself exceedingly well. But for advertising purposes, huge new ships, even if undermanned, which can be photographed, measured, pitted on paper against those of other navies, and gushed over in the Press – splendid creatures of steel with nerves of electricity, which can be seen with the eye at great, expensive, spectacular naval reviews – they give much better value for the money obtainable than a more or less invisible increase in the welfare of the men. Thus the nation is induced to play the naval game with a generous gusto, and a vicious circle is established – more money wanted, more ships to get it; more money obtained, more ships built with it. What might be called strategic expenses are also mounting up. Contractors don't die poor. Hence the men are the very last to feel the benefit of what money can be screwed out of the Exchequer, and the Navy becomes like a man who just succeeds in maintaining a large household by skimping his servants; only the Navy has the additional advantage that its servants can't leave when they like, are liable to

imprisonment if they kick against it, and dare not openly appeal to public opinion.[10]

The low pay of the lower ratings was exacerbated by the slowness of promotion. He uses Bill Woolley to illustrate the point. "Promotion lags, and men are kept waiting for it long after they have qualified. An A.B. for instance, of seven years' service, a good seaman, belonging to a family of good seamen, whom I coached myself, last year, in arithmetic for his leading seaman's examination, and who passed pretty easily, is still waiting for his leading seaman's rate and pay, although meantime he has been set to do leading seaman's work."[11]

A further source of tension was the higher pay given to the new technocrats, such as engineers and electricians. "The seamen point out with some force that so long as a battleship goes to sea at all, it is the executive branch, that is to say themselves, which navigates it and prevents the whole box of tricks, artificers included, from going to the bottom. They resent not so much the pay and privileges of the artificers as the action of the Admiralty in taking advantage of the labour market to continue paying their seamen badly."[12]

The system of discipline still gave plenty of scope for some officers to use their position to "worry the men out of their lives, and then break them altogether for resenting the treatment. Officers of that sort may not be very numerous; certainly not so numerous as they used to be; but it doesn't take many flies instead of currants to make a cake uneatable."[13] He drew a further illustration from a ship that had anchored off Sidmouth that hot summer.

Whilst a battleship in which there had been considerable trouble over leave-stopping, was lying at anchor off the town in which I write, one of her boats was sent ashore on a day when it was unfit for any boat to be beached, let alone a Navy boat. In shoving off again, a bluejacket fell, damaging the boat and some of her gear. It was an accident which might have happened to the best of surf-men. Notwithstanding which, the unfortunate man was heavily punished. The spiritless, careless bearing of the men aboard that ship, and her general lack of smartness, was plain to see when one rode out around her.[14]

He rounds off his case with a telling, but typical, plea for a return to the old values, to treating the men well for their personal qualities and, above all, their courage.

At present the Admiralty seems to be out of touch with its men, and still more with those seafaring communities which supply the best of them. A tale is often told among Service people of how a high officer went aboard a ship and demanded volunteers for a landing party which expected tough and dangerous work. An order was given for good-con-

> duct men to fall in on deck. 'Who are these?' said the officer. 'Where are your bad characters? Fall *them* in. I want men who can fight!' Strictly true or not, the popularity of the yarn and the approval which always greets it, show that the attempt to force Sunday-school standards upon the Navy, in place of the old standards of action, has not succeeded. A little drunkenness, a little leave-breaking – what about it, they say, if the man can fight? Reckless men for desperate work: always was and always will be!
>
> That is still the popular sentiment, and it tells equally against those men who creep up the Service by means of their ability to pass examinations. Those of us who have passed many examinations know what a gamble they are, and know also the type of man who does best. So do bluejackets. The mere examinees who jump over their heads give rise to much dissatisfaction.
>
> It is useless to say that every man is a free agent either to enter the Navy or not to do so, and having entered into the contract, must make the best of it. Working people are not such shallow psychologists. They face the fact that the Navy calls to all that is best and most high-spirited in a youth, before he has had much experience of life, and that once there, he is bound to it for a term of years. In the old days of hand-to-hand fighting, men would fight for fighting's sake when their blood was up. But modern warfare, carried on in death-traps, with scientific instruments of destruction, is rather a matter of nerve than of animal pluck. Therefore, goodwill is more than ever needful.[15]

When the article came out, Reynolds was not surprised by the conspiracy of silence in the newspapers. No one gave it a notice, although it was the first to open the subject out in the public press, as against the service papers. Likewise, the reviews of *Seems So!* quietly ignored it. A year later, Reynolds put it down to the fact it was then too hot to handle.

> Whilst the article was pretty widely read and was quite good journalistic "copy", it went curiously unnoticed by the London political daily Press, and when, during the month following, it was reprinted in a book very widely and kindly reviewed, still, for the most part, it was strangely ignored by the Press, though several provincial papers did go so far as to remark, in effect, "Startling – if true". Evidently, at that time, only a year ago, lower-deck discontent was a cake too hot to hold, or, anyhow, to do more than nibble at.[16]

But he was genuinely surprised when, in January 1912, a review of *Seems So!* by Yexley in the *Fleet* quietly ignored it too. Reynolds wrote off to his collaborator in some puzzlement. "We had hoped that we were doing at least something to forward your admirable work on behalf of the Lower Deck, and that perhaps we might be the means of extending its influence, introducing it into quarters where at present it is insufficiently known...... The press all round has been quite suspiciously silent over that chapter, but we hardly anticipated it from you."[17]

Yexley was able to satisfy him of the reasons for the omission and assured him of his intention to cover the chapter in a future edition.[18] But there is a hint in this episode that Yexley, who had been toiling in this particular vineyard for some years, was not altogether pleased by the sight of a stranger with a wider public reputation muscling in on his territory.

Reynolds was nevertheless heartened by the response from within the Navy itself, the one audience that really counted. In early November he wrote to George Macmillan: "Have had a letter to-night from a Chief Petty Officer aboard one of the newest battleships about the Navy article: "I am passing it around among my own class of chiefs. They are all delighted and quite agree with what is written there. One would almost fancy you had done time in the Navy". That's more to the point than newspaper cuttings, isn't it?"[19]

And a month before, immediately on publication, he had had an enthusiastic letter from John Masefield whose poem, *The Everlasting Mercy*, which was to make his name, had appeared in the same edition of the *English Review* as the Reynolds article. Masefield had been a friend and correspondent for some five years, and had visited Reynolds at the Woolleys when on holiday in the West Country. It was now some time since their last meeting. Reynolds had written to congratulate him on the poem and received an equally warm response. Masefield promised a copy of *The Everlasting Mercy*, shortly to come out in book form.

> I was going to send you a copy of the book when it appears, which will be in a few days, as I have had so much pleasure from your own books; especially the last one [*Alongshore*]; and when your letter came I was reading your capital paper in the English Review; it's very good that someone's saying this; there is always the danger that a routine will become a machine and dominate the brains of those who run it; and that danger has played the devil in ships too often, as you know. I often feel that Nelson might (judging from his portraits) have turned out just as hard a bargain as St Vincent if he hadn't made a voyage as a fore topman. It's a great pity men qualifying for command aren't put to keep their end up for a year under the routine they hope to apply to others...... You are doing first rate work, and one hears your praise sung everywhere.
> I often think of you and of Mr and Mrs Woolley. I shall never forget their very kind welcome to me. I hope those jolly boys of theirs are well and hearty and that all of you are prospering.[20]

Masefield's comparison of Nelson with St Vincent Reynolds was to incorporate into one of his next series of articles – *The Future of the Lower Deck*.[21]

For the *English Review* article was not to be a one-off. Reynolds now saw himself as the one writer with sufficient reputation as a political journalist to keep the matter in the public eye. It was a cause dear to his heart, but would also provide some extra publicity that would do him no harm at all. In January 1912 he put his name down with Yexley as a regular subscriber to the *Fleet*, determined to keep up to speed with the latest developments in lower deck reform which the Government, with Churchill now at the Admiralty, was at last beginning to take seriously.[22]

Reynolds had been hoping for some time to meet Yexley in the flesh, and finally, in the week of 6 May, after Reynolds had delivered his weekend address to the High Wycombe educationists, they managed to fix up a lunch at the Mont Blanc. Reynolds was waiting for him when Yexley arrived, and the latter has left us with a touching description of how seaman strangers meet.

> Men who have much in common usually manage to meet – "birds of a feather flock together" – and some months ago the present writer met Stephen Reynolds by appointment. It was at an unpretentious restaurant off Wardour Street. We neither knew the other, but there is a freemasonry of the sea which tells, and as I walked in I spotted a man in pilot suit – the garb of the fisherman. He glanced up, held out his hand with the salutation "Yexley!". There was no note of interrogation in the salute: we had mutually recognised each other, though till that moment we had never met. And Reynolds was of the sea-salt. And that is how he is in his book [*How 'Twas*]...... there is no living man who can take us so close to the fisherman or the fisherman's home as Stephen Reynolds.[23]

Over lunch, Reynolds filled Yexley in on the convoluted story of the eventual publication of *Navy Discontents* and received in return the latest inside information in the struggle for reform. It was this conversation that most probably decided him in principle to write some more articles on the subject.

The final decision to do so may well have been influenced by a new injection of naval expertise to the firm of Woolley and Reynolds. For it was in the following week that Harry Woolley and Jack Collier, within a few days of each other, won their discharge from the Navy – the event that Reynolds had hoped to celebrate along with the publication of *How 'Twas* and his 31st birthday.

He had seen a lot of Harry and Jack in the days running up to their discharge. He had visited them in their naval barracks on the weekend of 27/28 April, rather nervous to be there so soon after the appearance of the Navy article. He told George Macmillan: "Last weekend I spent at Devonport with some petty officer friends of mine. It was rather amusing skidding round the Naval Barracks at the risk of being spotted, and their wanting to know what I was there for. One good naval officer of Plymouth threatened to horsewhip Austin Harrison for publishing the Navy article. Me, too, I suppose!"[24]

It seems to have been the first time he had put his nose inside the petty officers' quarters at Devonport, for he wrote up the experience in some detail in the new series of articles, to give the impression of being an habitué there. The barracks themselves brought back memories of Bloxham. "Going into a naval barracks reminds me, each time afresh, of nothing so much as of going in through the school gates at the end of holidays. 'Freedom abandon, ye who enter here!' The high stone gateway, the officers on watch with their aloof routine stare, the chill rectangular grey buildings, all seem to be saying much the same as the school quad, the hourly bell and the bare cleaned-up schoolroom used to say – only much more so. Nominally a ship ashore – Devonport Royal Naval Barracks is HMS *Vivid* – it represents to one's eye the bound, tied, and regulated, the routine, element of naval life, without that softening width that the sea lends to everything afloat on it."[25]

On the Sunday, he relaxed in the mess which had all the trappings of a London club. "In the writing and smoking (and snoozing) room are the deep easy-chairs and springy couches of a club, but over the two long tables, laid out for a meal, are iron frames bearing hooks for hammocks." He shared with his friends the traditional Sunday lunch of pork and apple-sauce, tinned fruit and custard. "Afterwards, the cover was dragged off one of the billiard tables, and we played a scandalously skittish game of snooker, in which each of us scored heavily, much less by our own hits than off each other's misses, whilst the chiefs, most of them solid, not to say portly men, capered round the table as if they'd been kittens. At the other end of the room a political argument was lashing about like a cock-fight...... "[26] This was the kind of environment in which Reynolds received most of his education in naval politics.

When he and Bob left in mid-afternoon, the hand of naval discipline was still hovering in the air. "After dinner in barracks, of a Sunday, one hurries out a few minutes before four o'clock, the time laid down, not so much to avoid getting kicked out or held up at the gates, as to avoid even the risk of getting somebody into trouble. Other big institutions, the House of Commons, say, or a Government Department, fail to make one feel half so careful. They have their rules and penalties, to be brought out and used on occasion. But naval discipline is more like a semi-intelligent guillotine, always poised overhead, waiting to drop."[27]

Fishing had been poor that summer, but in early July the mackerel started to come in to the bay and the extra naval hands were to prove both their worth and the source of some amusement. "Mackerel seining is in full swing, and now these Navy men are home we have a very complete crew of eight of our own, and are working it rather well. It's tremendously exciting quick work getting the net round the schools of fish. Tom and I, at the net, have Harry Woolley and a brother-in-law, also a retired Chief P.O., at the oars, and when we aren't all furious with each other, we have continual merriment over making these solid dignified Chiefs row to our orders as if they were Ordinary Seamen – mere flatfoots!"[28]

Harry Woolley brought back with him from Devonport not just a mine of inside information for any future Navy articles, but also a far more interesting acquisition. At his last posting on Malta station, he had been befriended in hospital there by a 16-year-old stoker, Arthur Dolby, who had cheered him up and given him plenty of moral support. In early April he brought Dolby with him to Sidmouth, and Reynolds' eyes lighted up. The visit ended in farce. "The other day, I had to carry Harry on my back from the top of Mutter's Mow to the bottom of the hill, through the woods, to catch the last possible train for a stoker who was with us, because the said Harry, having sciatica, couldn't walk downhill! And then the beggar was three hours adrift next morning, after travelling most of the night from here to Plymouth!"[29]

It was from this moment that Reynolds began to develop the idea of help for his "spadework". For him, writing an initial draft, painfully slowly in longhand, was often excruciating hard labour. By contrast, he always enjoyed the more relaxing affair of improving a draft on the first revise.[30] The interim stage of typing up the manuscript was an equally tiresome burden. He could never teach himself to compose directly on to the machine.

In May he found himself in the midst of articles and plans for books. "I must certainly get help for the spade-work of all this. One can't forever go on writing from 6 a.m. and spend the evening banging it out on a nerve-racking typewriter."[31] By the middle of June he had fixed upon the secretary he wanted. Dolby came back from Malta on 28 June and Reynolds made arrangements to go down to Plymouth to interview him on the 29th. "Dolby, my prospective secretary, had come back from the Malta station on Thursday, and by pulling sundry wires I got him a short weekend's leave, and having need anyhow to see the fishery people at Plymouth, I got myself digs in Devonport, and arranged to go down."

But this was the weekend ruined by the Boomster, and Reynolds had to cancel the Plymouth trip at the last moment. The telegram telling Dolby of the cancellation did not, however, reach the ship till after he had left. "So here I am, tied up with a knot here, and the unfortunate Dolby is adrift down along; and several bluejackets, who had heard I was coming, will be hunting for me half to-day – get pretty well bottled up, I shouldn't wonder, drawing all the Sidmouthian public houses down there!!"[32]

But on the Monday morning Dolby turned up to perform his most important function – that of calming Reynolds down. "Dolby has got an extension of leave and has strolled up from Devonport to-day – so I shan't be so bad-tempered after all which, doubtless, is for the best."[33] No one thought an extension of leave possible just before mobilization. "It appears, however, that when he asked his commander, and, on being questioned where he wanted to go, said Sidmouth, to see me, the com. said, yes, he'd got some of my books, and Dolby could come. Diable! That's gratifying. I wonder what the com. will say when my *Chronicle* lower deck series starts!"

By the Wednesday, the problem of the spade-work had been sorted. "I think Dolby will come and do secretary's job for me. He seems not likely to get on my nerves, which is the unpardonable sin with me. And he appears to have a handy intelligence to grasp my multifarious affairs. It will be a bit of a pull at first – I think I shall send him for a week or two to a shorthand and typing school, to polish himself up in that, and get hold of a few filing dodges, and so forth – after which he will be worth to me, I don't doubt, more than his share that he'll get, by leaving me more time for the work that must anyhow be done by myself."[34]

A week later he was more than happy with his new acquisition, but a little worried that he might be leading him into a dead-end. "I think Dolby will do. I must try very hard to give him a good time: it's not nothing to ask a man to play second fiddle for mere pay. He was extremely kind to Harry Woolley in Malta Naval Hospital, which, as Harry says, is rather extraordinary from a stoker to a Chief P.O. And as to the work – well, his own pay, above a minimum of a pound a week, is to depend entirely on how much I earn – so that there will be every reason on both sides to work well together."[35]

The arrival of Dolby represented a quiet revolution in the Woolley household. For five years Reynolds had lodged alone in the two rooms on the first floor, sleeping in the back. Now he was to get his full money's worth, as Dolby took over the front as study-cum-bed-sitting-room. The Woolleys themselves were not a little put out that a stranger should now engross the attention of their long-time lodger. They must by this time have had at least an inkling of his sexual preferences and may have smelt a whiff of scandal in the air. Reynolds felt irritated but even more determined. "My people seem a bit inclined to set their backs up, but when they find I shall be able to attend to their affairs better, instead of worse, no doubt they'll revise their opinion. Anyhow, I must have help, and I'm going to have it, and there's an end o' it."[36]

One of Dolby's first tasks was the typing of a new series of articles, an extension of the previous year's *Navy Discontents*. The May meeting with Yexley seems to have sown the seed and by the beginning of June Reynolds had settled a commission for the series with William Maas, the editor of the *Daily Chronicle*.

He completed the introductory article, *The Great Silent Navy*, on 23 June and sent it off to Maas with a skeleton synopsis. Since his big theme was the superior value of the men to the floating machines, most of the articles would be devoted to the variety of humanity who made up the Navy.

> I enclose the introductory lower-deck article, emphasizing what I think the navy people themselves usually overlook, the responsibility of the nation. I should propose to follow on with a sketch of the modern bluejacket himself, compared with the old-fashioned seaman – a general sketch of the type – and then with two or three sketches of particular navy people – 'The Sort of Boy', 'An A.B.', 'A P.O.'s Mess', and 'Invalided

> Out' (a very scandalous subject), rounding up with a plea for better lower-deck treatment, based on the fact that Nelson's brother officers complained that he was too good to his men. One doesn't want, I take it, merely to reiterate the sort of thing that has lately been appearing in plenty of newspapers; therefore, after this introductory article, I propose to state the case by picturing the people.

He had given it the "Seems So" treatment, though this time Harry and Jack had taken the place of Bob and Tom.

> The enclosed article has been carefully checked by some petty officers, friends of mine. This town, indeed, is a sort of annex of the lower deck. You shall have the next by the end of this week, and the others not slower than one a week.[37]

The following day he wrote to Yexley to tell him of the articles and to seek confirmation of naval tuberculosis statistics for his sketch *Invalided Out*, intended as the emotional centrepiece of the series. The subversive nature of running a campaign against Admiralty policy was strengthening Reynolds natural tendency to paranoia and *délusions de grandeur*. As he and his collaborators chewed over the issues in their usual local, the Anchor in Old Fore Street, he had the feeling of being watched; but even Reynolds the spy-watcher could see the funny side. "We've got a queer naval fish hanging about here. A Commander Bolye, I understand. We wondered what the hell he wanted, hanging about our very lower-deckish public house, but he only seems to be consuming unlimited halfs of stout!"[38]

The first article appeared in the *Chronicle* on 10 July and the remaining seven at more or less weekly intervals ending on 7 September. More or less, because they never managed to appear on the same day of the week, much to Reynolds' annoyance. He sent a veiled rebuke to Maas: "The irregularity of appearance of the articles has rather gone against them in lower-deck circles – from the *Chronicle*'s point of view, anyhow. Landsmen might have ordered the paper for every day: bluejackets got rather sick of not knowing which days to get it."[39]

In the early days of publication he was worried that the articles might be overtaken by Government announcements on naval policy – in particular, a Churchill statement on increasing pay due on 22 July.[40]

The statement that afternoon, shorn of its Churchillian rhetoric, might well have been drafted by Reynolds himself.

> It is our duty to see that the seamen and stokers and others, on whose courage and conduct in peace and war the whole fortunes of the State depend, are not left behind, or overlooked, or neglected. It would ill become this House to vote year after year unexampled millions for the

> grim machinery of modern Naval war, and then to grudge the officers and men of the Fleet – without whose devotion these prodigious engines would only be worthless metal – the rewards which are their due, and which are necessary for their comfort and their contentment.

But Churchill was not ready with concrete proposals. He announced the first promotions from the lower deck and a revision of the system of punishments, but postponed the announcement of a scheme for higher pay until the autumn.[41] In the event, it did not arrive until 4 December when ratings were promised an extra threepence a day, which the Government claimed as an effective rise of 15%.[42]

Reynolds kept in close touch with Yexley and other naval contacts who appeared out of the woodwork as soon as the first few articles made their mark. On 24 July, two days after the Churchill statement, he went up to London for a typical town day, Pinker in the morning, George Macmillan in the afternoon, and his second meeting with Yexley at 7.30 that evening.[43] Yexley was still rather wary of this relatively recent convert to the cause, for he was already himself negotiating with the Government on some of the finer points of policy reform and wanted to make sure his new friend understood who was in the driving seat. At the end of July, he wrote rather boastfully to Reynolds: "I may tell you – *this quite confidentially* – that Winston has asked me to 'send me in memorandum form concrete suggestions for dealing with the question of increasing the pay of men serving in the Navy' and I am at work on it now. This is coming into one's own with a vengeance!"[44]

Tensions and potential jealousies were rife among the reformers. Reynolds was approached by the secretary to the Naval Writers Association in Chatham – the general administrators of the ships – to include their own personal grievances in his articles. They themselves were inclined to regard Yexley as a civilian interloper nosing into their professional affairs, though did not appear to have the same objection to Reynolds.[45] The latter sprang to Yexley's defence. "Now, in the first place, Yexley does not become a civilian because he chucked his pension. In the second place, most men understand the grievances of their own branches, but who better than Yexley understands the grievances of all the branches; and what man, fully occupied with active service, could possibly find time to examine the grievances of all branches and ratings...... you, and I, and the whole lower deck owe a great deal not only to his accumulated knowledge but also to the spade work he has been doing for several years. Without him, the attention which is now being given to lower-deck affairs would have been greatly delayed...... The lower deck should make use of all the good it can. Make use of everybody in so far as they can be made useful: that is a lesson which the governing classes have learnt much better than the working classes and the lower deck. I say it because I know it from experience and because I want to see them win."[46]

But he knew that working with Yexley could at times prove very frustrating.

In July, the Government had conceded two of the major demands, agreeing to a scheme of promotion from the ranks and to a right of appeal for petty officers under threat of disrating. In his final *Chronicle* article, Reynolds had questioned whether the right of appeal provisions would work fairly in practice.[47] He was astonished to find Yexley attacking his article in a letter to the *Chronicle*, and was forced to respond in kind: "It is no light matter to find Mr Lionel Yexley 'in entire disagreement' with something one has written on his own subject, the lower deck. But had he read more carefully, perhaps, my article on the new regulations, I rather think he might not have disagreed so entirely."[48]

At the same time, he delivered a private rebuke to Yexley on the naivety of his tactics. "If you'll forgive my saying so, I think you have made a mistake...... It is for us to disagree as much as we like among ourselves or in the Service Press, but we ought not, I think, to carry even the honestest disagreements into the Public Press. We ought to present a solid front before the public. Otherwise, should we enter into public controversy, I may lose, or you may lose, or it may be honours easy: the one thing certain to lose is the cause of the lower deck."[49]

It turned out that Yexley's attack on him had been just a piece of *amour propre* – the new regulations on the right of appeal had been inspired by Yexley himself. "Yes of course you are right from your point of view, but seeing that that Circular letter was largely the work of my hands and that I was called from my holiday to discuss the necessary safeguards to protect the P.O.s and that the whole of those safeguards were accepted as proposed, your article came as a bit of a shock to me because you were without knowing it directly challenging a piece of work I specially prided myself on."[50]

This and a number of other incidents left a sour taste. Reynolds was sickened by much of the backbiting and petty in-fighting. When the immediate campaign was over, he toyed with maintaining his interest in lower deck affairs through a regular column in the national press, but it was the behaviour of his fellow campaigners that finally decided him against.[51] He wrote to Frank Brandt, a naval captain who had become a close friend as a result of the articles, and had offered him some detailed comments on them: "It's such a complex affair, that I'm only too glad to get fresh light, and correct my mistakes, where I find I have been mistaken; though I don't propose to spout publicly on it any more, now I have had my say. Among bluejackets I have many friends; some are almost, as one might say, my relations, since the large naval fisherman's family I live with *is* my family to me; but lower deck *politics* – largely, I think, because of the anonymity – are the dirtiest affair I have ever stuck my nose into".[52]

But while the campaign was on, he was pleased and flattered by the attention it brought him. When the naval writers wrote praising his first articles, he responded with some humility: "I hope my articles will really do some good, and not result, merely, in a big blowing of hooters with nothing done".

And he was scrupulous in his detailed research into the technical issues. For this reason, he was reluctant to take up new angles, like the naval writers' grievances, with only a superficial knowledge. "Whether I shall be able to deal separately and at length with the writers' case is rather another matter. I am not a naval man myself, though I have a great number of friends on the lower deck, and for nearly ten years have lived and worked with a very naval family of fishermen. All that time, being soaked in lower deck talk, I have been sifting and comparing hours upon hours of lower deck conversation, till I think I've pretty well got hold of the right end of the stick."

He agreed to mention the writers briefly as an illustration of "the way in which the Admiralty speeds up and piles on responsibility without betterment of pay and conditions." But to write at greater length would conflict with his professional standards. "Well, it's my habit – I think you'll admit a good one – not to write on points I am not familiar with, and it happens I know almost least of all of the naval writers, except as part and parcel of the lower deck generally. If I were to write at much length about them, I should risk making mistakes to their detriment."[53]

The articles were, indeed, a highly polished and professional performance – well researched and lucidly written. He deliberately eschewed the campaigning rhetoric of the previous year's article, *Navy Discontents*, for a quieter, more impressionistic approach. His decision to concentrate on the people who made up the lower deck, to turn dry technical regulations into human issues, enabled him to avoid the tedium of bureaucratic niceties and create for his readers an emotional atmosphere far more persuasive than the most strident political hectoring.

Thus the main themes of *Navy Discontents* – the shortcomings of pay and discipline, the priority given to ships over men – are treated once again, but this time in a gentler, more human, manner. And as always, anecdotes from Reynolds' own personal experience prove the most telling. Discussing the poverty of naval pensions which force men, after a lifetime's service, to find other work in their retirement, he lightens the atmosphere with a boisterous account of the early trials of Harry Woolley and Jack Collier as they return to fishing.

> A couple of chief petty officers came out of the Navy on pension within a week of one another. As executive chiefs, they had been somebodies on the lower deck – men having authority to give orders; wearers of button-coats and peak-caps, instead of the familiar jumper, wide trousers, and round cap; men of some dignity and sedate, not to say rather genteel – *hommes sérieux*. Anyhow, their pensions were not sufficient to live upon, and they needed to turn their hand to something till they could find suitable regular work. So, since it was about the middle of the mackerel season, and they were both related to fishing people, they put on blue jerseys again, and shipped in a seine-boat which was being skippered by a young fisherman. They each took an oar for'ard, while the

> young fisherman, whose rating in the Reserve had only been more or less equivalent to that of ordinary seaman – he sat on the stern of the boat, the other side of the pile of net, steering, and very much in command. Being tickled by the turning of the tables, and thinking of all the naval seamen whom those two chiefs must have had to chivy and jump on in their time, we shouted from the shore: "Hi, you able seamen! Give way to it! Now then, skipper! Make those bloody flatfoots row!" I'm not quite sure they liked it. But still, they weren't in the Navy any longer; they were fishing.
>
> And they did row. While waiting for the mackerel to play up, they paddled about in great style, Navy stroke. I don't think I have ever seen a seine-boat go faster round the fish or a seine-net shot quicker.[54]

In *Invalided Out*, written towards the end of July when Dolby had gone back to his ship, he boldly announces to the world the acquisition of his new secretary. He could never resist giving life in his writing to those who were close to him.

> It is obvious that the Navy, quite apart from warfare, cannot be carried on without a considerable wastage of life and health, and it is equally obvious that losses of life and health can never be made good by mere money payments. But, at all events, they can be minimised, and unnecessary misery can be prevented. Only this morning, while I have been finishing this, the news has come that the able seaman who shares my writing-room with me, when he is home, has overstrained himself at his work aboard ship, and must either undergo an operation or be invalided out. And that is the sort of thing continually happening. Naval invalidity is not a thing of small importance, because it has to do with men no longer of use to the Navy. It hovers over us in these Navy towns and villages like an evil spirit, flinging sorrow, haphazard, at we never know whom next.[55]

Invalided Out had had a deeply personal inspiration. It was to call attention to the scandal of tuberculosis in the Navy – the "Invalided Outs with Sixpence a Day to Die on. Mostly we get them too late except to ease their unwilling deaths. It makes me very sick and savage."[56] In May, his friend Dr Peile, the local Medical Officer of Health, had drawn his attention to one such recent discharge, "Young Budd", and Reynolds took responsibility for him as visitor, sympathiser, organiser of his pension applications.[57] He was as moved by this young man's plight as he had been by the death of Violet Cordey two months before; and as with Violet, he determined to write about him as an example to the public. Indeed, Budd's case appears to have been instrumental in deciding him to embark on the new naval articles, and may have contributed too to the loss of interest in completing his "child" book.

Budd died in June and his old father, the only person with whom he lived, was immediately evicted from the lodgings. Reynolds wrote to Macmillan on 29 June: "You remember my telling you about the consumptive bluejacket who died.... The landlady of the cottage has evicted his old father, who spent all his savings on the boy, in revenge for the house having to be disinfected. There have been several similar evictions here, so the M.O.H. and myself are plotting a considerable scandal over it. We'll put fear into 'em, if we can't get the law of 'em!"[58]

On 6 August he reported the final dénouement. "You mind the bluejacket who died of phthisis. I think I told you his father was chucked out of his cottage as revenge for its having to be disinfected. Well, last night, in the strange lodging he had found, the old man fell downstairs and broke his neck. So that's the end of that tale – completed according to the best traditions of melodramatic farce. Poor devils!"[59]

Invalided Out makes its point far better than all the tuberculosis statistics in the world by a straight description of the young man in illness and in death, sparing no reader's squeamishness, in the simple, intimate prose in which Reynolds excelled. It takes us back five years to the emotional atmosphere of *A Poor Man's House.*

Reynolds makes his first visit to Budd at home on the day after he has suffered a major haemorrhage which has put paid to his chances of taking up the place he had been promised in the sanatorium.

> Through the open door and windows of the Budds' cottage, in a poor over-crowded part of the town, there came the sound of a hacking cough – the choked-back cough of a man who dares not cough too hard. The downstair kitchen living-room being empty, I went up some stairs that were built through the floor itself of the front bedroom. Budd was lying propped up on his back in the middle of the bed, with an old jacket over his shoulders. He only turned his eyes towards me, not his head. They had cleaned the place up all right. There wasn't any blood about.
>
> It wouldn't have done to make him talk much; he was still exhausted and scared by the haemorrhage; so I tried to cheer him up by telling him how Stevenson had many haemorrhages and died of something else in his forties, and by promising him a motor-car to take him to the sanatorium as soon as ever he should be able to be moved – anything to put some hope and resistance into him. It was all a make-believe. I knew it; I could see he was broken; and he knew it too.
>
> I confess I was afraid, every time he heaved with coughing, that the haemorrhage would start again while I was there alone with him. Neither then nor afterwards was he easy to talk to. With "No, sir," and "Yes,sir," – always, very carefully, the "sir" – he would keep one at arm's length. He seemed to regard all of us who visited him as death's crew, there in advance of death's self, and in that, poor fellow, he was but right. While I was trying to think of fresh encouraging things to say, I had in

my mind's eye the bluejackets home on leave, swinging across the front, laughing, chaffing, smart and full of vigour. Then, to look at the shrunken figure on the bed, the muddy-coloured face, the wisp of sweaty hair down over the forehead, the shifting stare of a hard-hunted animal in his eyes.... Is there anything more pitiful, more wrong, more repulsive even, than to see young people dying of preventable disease before they have had their whack of life?[60]

It was arranged that Budd's sister, a labourer's wife, should come round every day to cook and clean up. He had a few days of remission.

His bed was moved downstairs, where he could look out of window at the flowers in their tiny patch of garden and at the men working cheerfully in a store opposite. He rallied somewhat. When I went to write up his pension papers for him, he was out of bed and dressed. But while he leaned over me to watch what I was writing I could hear the hissing and squelching inside his chest. His invalid pension was not a shilling a day. It was only sixpence a day for a year, or a year and a quarter.

More haemorrhages drove him back to bed. He had to be propped up higher in order to breathe at all. He knew now, not only that he had to die, but that he was, in fact, dying; and though he said nothing, though he showed no outward funk, he was very frightened. A new terror was in his feverish eyes, while he sat in bed and toyed with newspapers or tracts or banana-skins, waiting for death to take grip. After all, he was quite young.[61]

Dr Peile undertakes to give him regular shots of morphine to ensure he dies easy.

I shall never forget how, one evening, outside a fishing village seven or eight miles from home, we struggled with the ignition of the M.O.H.'s motor-car, in order to get back in time to give young Budd his morphine before the horror of death should overtake him again. We treated it all as a sporting joke, young Budd himself included; we were too upset to do otherwise, because we had tried very hard, and had completely failed.

Late that night he died in his sister's arms – the living skeleton, full of a squash of filthy disease, who once had filled out proudly a bluejacket's uniform. He had lived just long enough to draw his next quarter's pension, and he told his father that there was a pound to come for every year he had done in the Navy. But it wasn't so. That fell through when he took the sixpence a day. Not even death can waive an Admiralty regulation.[62]

Not surprisingly, Reynolds took a closely proprietorial interest in the fate of

Invalided Out and was pleased to find it had made a stir. On 19 August he told George Macmillan: "Now, I think, is probably the time to push lower deck reforms right through. My last Tuesday's *Invalided Out* article really does seem to have made a bit of an impression".[63] And in the highest quarters too. Next day he wrote to William Maas: "The *Invalided Out* article has considerably upset Sir Joseph Leese, a friend of Mr. Churchill's, who is down here. I felt I had done the trick in that one".[64]

When the series of articles was launched in July, Austin Harrison asked Reynolds to do a more general article for the September issue of the *English Review*, a kind of follow-up to *Navy Discontents* of the previous year. The deadline was 19 August and he was still in the throes of finishing off his *Chronicle* series.[65] Little wonder, then, that Katie Powys on her final visit found a man harassed and preoccupied. He wrote to George Macmillan on 6 August: "You must have had a wet holiday.... I've had none but have been working within half-an-inch of a breakdown at Lower Deck articles. Three articles in one week! Mon dieu! Parbleu! and all the exclamations of an historical novel! So I'm going to Devonport before I tackle the final article – for the *Eng. Rev.* That's always good holiday".[66]

He just managed to complete the final article in a three day burst before the deadline. "I'm just over what I hope is the hardest burst of working to time I shall ever do; 30 of my big pages in three days' sitting at it from dawn to dark! I doubt I could have done it at all but for the *unfriendly* pipe, instead of fuddling on cigarettes."[67] The article, *Ships versus Men*, proved a more than fitting climax to the series as a whole – a highly intelligent and cogently written critique of the inability of the political establishment to balance the human and the non-human elements of the equation.

He borrowed from Yexley, with his full permission, a Churchill anecdote to sum up the current feeling of the lower deck.[68] It was both flattering and unflattering to the dashing young First Lord of the Admiralty.

> The First Lord, to the great glee of the lower deck, has a habit of going straight to the men, with a disregard of ceremonial and official receptions very scandalous to the old school of officer. Aboard one of the ships he fell in with a stoker, asked him how long he had been in the Service, and was duly informed. Said Mr. Churchill, "D'you like your job?"
> "I can't say I do, sir," replied the stoker.
> "Well, what's wrong with it?" asked Mr. Churchill.
> "What's wrong with it?" repeated the stoker, looking very frankly into his face. "Well, what's right with it?"
> And Mr. Churchill was nonplussed. For once, he had no answer ready. The wrongs so far outweigh the rights.[69]

Churchill was, of course, the architect of the lower deck reforms of 1912. His appointment in October 1911 brought a breath of fresh air to the Admiralty and a greater sense of purpose. And Yexley must be credited with the lion's share of the pressure to which he was forced to respond. But Reynolds too had played a major role in persuading the Government to a more sensitive approach towards the lower ratings. Although *Navy Discontents* had not been noticed in the press, it had been widely read and its message digested by the large numbers of readers of *Seems So!* The *Chronicle* articles of the following summer rammed home the message in a climate more attuned to reform. While Yexley worked on Navy and Admiralty opinion, it was Reynolds who delivered the backbenchers and the public.

From an early stage, he was keen to increase the impact of the articles by turning them into a book. Originally he had hoped to get the *Chronicle* to print them in a cheap pamphlet for circulation round the lower deck, but that paper had already too many pamphlets on its hands.[70] He cautiously sounded out Macmillan: "The subject is, I take it, too topical for book publication and the articles too topical to save for a future book, and on the other hand, should be topical enough to sell if properly distributed where naval interest is highest. You, of course, would be welcome to the stuff if you thought you could do anything with it in a small cheap book, but it is not, I imagine, in your firm's line."[71] Macmillan confirmed that it was not.[72]

So by the end of August he was still looking round, thinking primarily of a naval publisher. He told Pinker: "I think I shall take the stuff off to another publisher's (it's not in Macmillan's line and is too topical to save up for a big book) for publication in 6d. form. With, of course, a hell of a cover!"[73]

In 1912 the publisher J.M. Dent decided to expand on the success of his "Everyman's Library", the shilling series of popular classics now in its sixth year, by founding a weekly literary review, also to be called *Everyman*. He appointed as editor the brilliant academic Charles Sarolea, born in Belgium in 1870, who had come to Edinburgh at the age of 24 as the first lecturer, and later Professor, in French at the University. It was in many ways a surprising choice since, though an excellent linguist, with a knowledge of 18 to 21 languages, and an ardent book-collector, building a private library of over 200,000 volumes, he had absolutely no experience of day-to-day journalism, editing or running a business.[74]

The summer of 1912 was a particularly harassing one for the new editor as he juggled his teaching and academic work with the heavy demands of finding contributors, advertisers and readers for the October launch of the venture. It was not made easier by the attitude of Dent himself, who was clearly losing confidence as he watched an unworldly academic struggling to learn how to run a business. He would blow hot and cold, at times issuing directives mandating the inclusion of particular authors, or dropping hints on subjects he would like to see covered. At others, he would sympathise with Sarolea over the pressures which he himself was largely creating. Just before launch day, when Sarolea was at his wits end, Dent sent him a typical word of encouragement: "Do take care of your health and do not try to do too much. If you take the moon for a green cheese you will tumble in the water and get drowned……"[75]

At the end of July Dent had just been reading *A Poor Man's House*, or possibly *Alongshore*, and he took the opportunity to drop a large hint in Sarolea's direction. "I have been reading one of Stephen Reynolds' books where he goes into the economy of the fisherman and the wonderful life at sea. He is a man I think of standing and really fine purpose, and certainly of very great literary value. Perhaps you know his work…… "[76]

It may be that Dent had been alerted to the book by the first articles in Reynolds' *Chronicle* series, for he had instructed Sarolea to commission a series on the need for a vibrant *merchant* navy and the latter had prevailed on his celebrated brother-in-law, the explorer Ernest Shackleton, to write the launch article. To continue the series with articles, like Reynolds', on the personnel of the merchant navy, Sarolea had approached R.B. Cunninghame Graham, the adventurer, writer and politician, well known to Reynolds as an old Mont Blanc hand.

Cunninghame Graham was a man with a sense of humour and could not avoid a little fun at the rather innocent Sarolea's expense. He declined the commission but suggested Sarolea should approach the one writer in England whom the world knew would not respond to requests for bread and butter articles. With tongue evidently in cheek, he replied to the anxious editor: "On the young sailors I can think of no one better to write to than Joseph Conrad, Capel House, Orlestone, Nr Ashford, Kent. He is possibly the greatest writer in the country and is sure to be in touch with sailors. Personally he is rather conservative. So write gingerly."[77]

It was the perfect set-up. In addition to the article, Sarolea asked Conrad if he would sit for one in a series of literary portraits he was planning for the journal. Conrad may well have recognised the element of provocation behind the request, for instead of anger he treated Sarolea to his coolest vein of courteous irony.

> I thank you very much for your very interesting communication. The Chancellor of the Exchequer has given the suffering humanity ninepence for fourpence [*a reference to the Insurance Act then being implemented*], but I see that Mr Dent means to beat that generous statesman hollow by offering a weekly 'feast of reason and flow of soul' for a penny. The Golden Age is upon us. I had some idea of this before but now there can be no mistake. I am sorry I can't contribute anything to the projected weekly. 'Contributions' are not in my line. They are an interruption to what I look upon as my work. For the same reason I beg to be excused from indicating an artist. 'Sitting' is a most odious experience

> and I wouldn't have the time to go to town for the purpose. And besides I know nothing of them with the exception of Rothenstein who's an old friend. I live a very retired life and see only a few intimates who for the most part belong neither to the literary nor the artistic world. Like some infinitely more choice souls than mine: j'ai le goût de la solitude – and indeed I need it for my work.[78]

But, nothing daunted, Sarolea had an alternative up his sleeve. He had taken Dent's hint and written to Reynolds, asking him to suggest someone to review his books for the magazine, and whether he would contribute himself to the merchant navy series. Reynolds suggested Conrad's new young friend Richard Curle as "a reviewer who takes a pretty competent interest in my books. I know he has them all, and he has jumped on me in this month's *Bookman*!".

But he was doubtful about the merchant navy series and particularly Shackleton's contention, relayed by Sarolea, that both services could do with an injection of experience from other walks of life. "As to the articles on a Merchant Navy.... May I write to you again after Aug. 19th. Till then I'm nearly standing on my head with some Lower Deck articles I have to do. I'm not certain I believe in a Merchant Navy. I am inclined to think that the naval seaman ought to be a well-paid and well-treated specialist who gives his whole career to the profession. The Navy depends on catching men young. Sir Ernest Shackleton doesn't really think – does he? – that mature men are going to stick their noses into the absurdities of naval pay and discipline? If so, it must be in the innocence of his courageous heart!"[79]

Nonetheless, the Sarolea approach was a new potential outlet for pot-boiling and increasing Reynolds' reputation. He passed the letter on to George Macmillan: "He appears, too, to want review copies for his new literary journal. Is it Dent's journal? – I can't read his spider-scrawl".[80]

He saw too an opportunity for picking up one of his lost threads of reviewing. For some time, he had been noticing occasional sea and navy books for the *Daily News*, but was now a little concerned by the recurrent rumours since the paper's amalgamation with the *Morning Leader* that the editor, A.G. Gardiner, was on the move. He wrote to him to clear the matter up. "We hear rumours, via Cambridge, that you are gone from the *News*.... Is that so? If it is, then I hope in a manner satisfactory to yourself. My connexion with it will likewise cease; for I can't stand cocoa without any cyder."[81]

He now smelt a useful substitute in *Everyman* and broached the matter with Sarolea. "Are you set up for your fishery, Navy and general sea-book reviewing? I did it for a good many years for the *Daily News*, but I rather think that the recent changes have done me out of it, and don't want to cease getting the books on these subjects along my way. For a sure thing, I can't afford to buy 'em all!"

He offered the sweetener of a possible contribution to the merchant navy series. "I might be able to get in at the subject either from a naval or a fishery point of view – the need of fostering the fishery recruiting grounds for the best sort of seamen. The ultimate importance of seamanship in everything designed to go to sea is much neglected nowadays, and a while ago we had a big argument with an Admiralty official on the point. I should rather like, somewhen, to hit that in."[82]

Meanwhile, Sarolea had been reading the review copy of *How 'Twas* sent on to him by George Macmillan – and had rather gone overboard in his enthusiasm.[83] "In several stories, especially in 'A Third-Class Journey', in 'Love's Hunger', in 'An Unofficial Divorce', I admired that power of which I felt the grip on first reading a book of yours 'A Poor Man's House', and the best proof of my appreciation is that I am now on the outlook for every paper you write. I have recently subscribed to the 'Daily Chronicle' mainly to read your articles on the Navy. I see that you have a new article in this month's 'English Review' which I am ordering."

It now transpired that Shackleton had got cold feet – to coin a phrase – over his planned "Plea for the Merchant Navy". Sarolea told Reynolds: "He is going to send an article on "Polar Exploration" instead, but perhaps you might feel inclined to take his place?"[84] Dent in London was greatly put out by Sarolea's failure to deliver his brother-in-law. "I am very disappointed that Shackleton will not be able to do the Merchant Navy. It sadly wants doing, and if you could get Stephen Reynolds to do it, why you would score...... "[85]

But Reynolds was not to be so easily flattered and manipulated. He had – to coin another phrase – bigger fish to fry. He would do a sea article if pressed, but did it really have to be about the merchant navy? Far better might be a serialisation of his planned big book on psycho-economics, which he had failed to negotiate satisfactorily with *The Times*. He sent off the rather heavy chapter and verse for Sarolea to consider.[86]

It was now the latter's turn to be distinctly underwhelmed. "Owing to the very importance and complexity of the subject, it may not be suitable for the 200,000 readers we are appealing to. The public we are addressing will be composed mainly of students, educated artisans and clerks and teachers."[87] This was not the kind of excuse to make to Reynolds. "As to its being too stiff for your readers.... If I can't make it plain to anybody of intelligence – well, I must have spent pretty fruitlessly my ten years of talking to uneducated people."[88]

Sarolea had recently taken on the job of General Literary Adviser to Dent and he saw in the psycho-economics proposal a chance to curry favour with his master in London by winning Reynolds over to the Dent fold. He suggested they consider both serialisation and a Dent book, so that the journal would not have to shoulder all of the expense. He was not, after all, totally averse to some demanding fare. "Still, I want to make a determined effort to keep the literary and intellectual level of our paper as high as possible. I do not want to make it another 'T.P.'s Weekly', and I shall not object to giving my readers a few hard nuts to crack."[89]

Reynolds was coming up to town on 11 September for some crucial discussions on his future in fisheries administration; but he was also pursuing further naval business, including separate meetings with Yexley and the Chatham naval writers, and a weekend in Guildford with Sir Joseph Leese, the friend of Churchill who had been so moved by *Invalided Out*. He suggested that he meet with Sarolea to discuss the matter.[90]

He told Macmillan in advance of the Sarolea proposition and gave him a firm assurance: "Of course, Dents can't have the book. It's to be just the sort of book for you. The thing is: can I get Sarolea to serialize it all the same. That would be a fine thing both for me and the book."[91] The answer, as it turned out, was no. When they met, Sarolea made plain once more that there could be no serialisation without the book. Always alert to opportunities, however, Reynolds came up with a counter-proposal. If Dent were so keen on a book, would they publish his Navy articles? Sarolea was very interested.

If this were a coup for Sarolea, it was also one for Reynolds who had never dreamed of *The Lower Deck* being taken by a first level publisher. That Friday he looked in at Dent's offices in Aldine House in Bedford Street and, finding Sarolea out, deposited the manuscript. "Called in. No you. Here's the stuff."[92]

Early the next week, having heard nothing further, he called in on Dent himself. As usual, the first impression worked wonders and Dent asked for a new copy of the manuscript. On 18 September Dent wrote to Sarolea with a touch of petulance but also with a firm decision. "I have had Stephen Reynolds in about his book, and you had carried away the MS. I have got another copy, however, and am going ahead with it."[93]

Dent issued him straightway with a draft agreement which Macmillans combed through to turn "a rather drastic document into a reasonable one".[94] Reynolds set to work at once to write a preface. On 26 September he told Macmillan: "Dent has actually signed the Agreement as amended by Mr Foster and me! I have been furiously busy with the Preface, which needed to be a very judicious effort, and the proofs, which are rather ticklish to get up to date."[95]

Three days later, he completed the preface, designed to reassure the world that, though the book was full of criticism of the Navy, the author was a patriot at heart.

> In order to avoid needless misunderstanding, let me say at once that *The Lower Deck* was not written as an attack on the Navy, as a whole, or even on the Admiralty, let alone on naval officers. It is the nation which must ultimately be held responsible...... But attack the Navy itself, as a whole.... No. I don't pretend to be a patriot of the flag-flourishing sort, though I think that the love I have for my country – its soil, its coasts, its climate even, and the countless familiarities which make it home – is none the less genuine for running fairly deep and quiet, for being intensive rather than extensive; and of all our great public institutions I confess to being proudest by far of the Navy. For it does seem to me that, whatever its faults, the Navy is the outward and visible sign of that which

> is best in the British seafaring spirit......
> Though I have made every effort to be fair, the sympathy of this book with the lower deck will be sufficiently obvious – naturally so, seeing how many of my friends are, or have been, on it. Underlying that, and not perhaps so obvious, is a feeling of injured pride, that in the Navy – *our* Navy, in which I, as an Englishman, am proud to have a share – the lower deck should have just cause for complaint.[96]

The switch to Dent caused some consternation among Reynolds' literary friends which Reynolds, who always revelled in appearing what he was not, much enjoyed. He told George Macmillan: "I find that Dent doing this booklet for me, and not you, has created a sort of mild scandal all round. 'Have you left Macmillans then? Is it that you're an ass, or that they aren't what they seem?' That sort of tone! When they see the booklet, however.... I put a clause in the Agreement that a whole-page adv. of my books with you had either to face title or follow text, in a form approved by me, and yesterday I proceeded to approve it by writing it myself, most elegantly, in a manner chaste, but striking – quite a good imitation of the genuine St. Martin's St. production!"[97]

In the preface, he had talked emotionally of his lower deck friends, but there was one in particular on his mind just at that moment. On 12 October, he went down to Plymouth Naval Hospital to see Dolby before his operation.[98] It went well, and six days later his old secretary was back recuperating in Bedford Square and attending to some light pieces of correspondence.[99] Meanwhile, Reynolds had secured the permanent services of another secretary whom he had been looking out for.[100] Dolby won his discharge from the Navy, but re-enlisted in September 1913. He served in the First War as a steward on HMS *Vanguard* and went down with his ship when it was sunk off Scapa Flow in July 1917.[101]

The Lower Deck came out in the third week of October complete with the colourful pictorial cover that Reynolds had hoped for. Almost immediately, a predictable row blew up over its reviewing. Sarolea had failed to cover it in that week's *Everyman* and received a rocket from Dent. Now the magazine was finally launched, however, he was learning to stand up for himself and responded in kind: "I would have written a strong article on Stephen Reynolds' book: 'Men of the Lower Deck' [*sic*], but I only heard casually, through an advertisement in the 'Daily News' that you had already published the book. They might send review copies of your most important books to 'EVERYMAN'".[102]

Ten days after publication few reviews had trickled through and Reynolds was growing restive at the prospect of yet another conspiracy of silence. Dent's son, Hugh, wrote urgently to Sarolea from Aldine House: "Mr. Stephen Reynolds has been in and is most anxious to get a review of the 'Lower Deck' at the earliest possible moment. Can you review it in 'Everyman' immediately? Unfortunately for the book most of the Daily papers seem to wish not to review it in order to give it as little publicity as possible".[103]

On 31 October Sarolea wrote, rather optimistically, to Ernest Shackleton commissioning a 1200 word review of the book.[104] On the same day, he sent a reassuring letter to Reynolds which was more than economical with the truth. "I wrote *several days ago* to my brother-in-law, Sir Ernest Shackleton, to ask him to undertake the review of your book. I have not yet had an answer." [*my italics*].[105] Shackleton wrote back to confirm that he was so snowed under with worries and business that writing was impossible.[106] In early November telegrams flew in all directions as Reynolds urgently co-opted an officer friend from Portsmouth to write an anonymous full page.[107] It was the only major review the book was to receive.

There remained the little matter of the merchant navy article promised to *Everyman*. That too was destined to end in tears.

When they met in mid-September Reynolds and Dent had done a private deal behind Sarolea's back. Reynolds had recounted his own experience of the merchant marine – the *Coranian* adventure of 1905 – and wondered whether he might make material out of that. Dent was happy so long as the sketch could be seen as a piece of campaigning journalism on the treatment of the men. Reynolds decided to write a story around his role as ship's doctor treating the suspected diphtheria case – a kind of merchant version of *Invalided Out*, but in an altogether lighter vein.

By mid October no copy had appeared in Edinburgh, and Sarolea ventured on a gentle reminder – with a little incentive attached. "May I remind you of your kind promise to send me an article and a Short Story. Both would be very acceptable. I also hope to arrange in one of our early issues for a character sketch of yourself and a full-page portrait. I want to advertise you to a hundred and twenty thousand readers as one of the big young men of tomorrow."[108]

Flattery will get you everywhere. Reynolds stirred into life. "It is most kind of you to arrange for a sketch about me, and I've no doubt it would do a good deal to pull the sale of my books up to the noise they make. At present I seem to be read mainly in library copies, and am continually harried into pot-boiling, which I hate, being naturally a very laborious workman, and finding nearly all my joie d'écrire (to coin a phrase) not in drafting but in polishing. If you carry out the idea, I should suggest sending the sketcher down here, for a day or two. I'm only my proper self at home among my people."

He was able too to report some progress on his contribution. "I have had one of my sort of travel yarns lying on my table for days half written for you, but have been so overwhelmed with a lot of worries coming to a head at once, and consequently have been so unwell, that I simply haven't been able to bully my brains into finishing the thing. And to-morrow, I have to fly off to Town for a week, and I never can write there. But it shall be finished for you all right, and fairly soon. Now I have it half done, I shall start nothing else till it's completed."

But signing off, he remembered that Sarolea was not up with the plot, and added a hasty postscript. "The travel yarn, *Tramping Afloat,* is cast in short story form, loosely and driving at the humorous in telling. It's an account, really, of a diphtheria case I looked after once in the dismal forecastle of a tramp steamer."[109]

Ten days later he was getting on with it. "The sketch is getting itself written at last, or rather rewritten and finished. You shall have it for the issue after next."[110] On 3 November, he completed it and sent it in, emphasising once more the autobiographical truth to life. "Enclosed, at last, is the promised sketch – 'Tramping Afloat'. Hope you'll like it. The chap was me, of course, and so far as the ship's concerned it's a true story. Mr. Dent was insistent on my doing something to 'show up' seamen's condition in the Merchant Service."[111] It was this Dent instruction that was to cause all the problems.

Tramping Afloat came out on 15 November in the fifth number of *Everyman.* It was a jolly, well-written little piece with a good flavour of the *Coranian* atmosphere, but it did not stint on the criticism of lower deck conditions.

> A rusty little cargo-box of a ship.... Her sister-ship foundered with all hands in the Bay while we were coming up through it, and there wasn't any sea to speak of; we only rolled and rolled till we woke up with sore ribs. It might just as well have been us with Davy Jones – a Welshman originally, no doubt.
>
> Whether our old biscuit-box paid her shareholders, I don't know. She paid the shipping people who managed her, insured her against desirable wreck, and rushed her in and out of port so that her officers hardly knew their own children.

When the cook falls seriously ill, the narrator pays a visit to his quarters.

> Outside the fo'c'stle door there was a litter of vegetable garbage that the ship's boys hadn't cleared away, and inside.... Good Lord! To sleep in it! To be ill in it! A sort of dim triangular steel cellar, with wooden bunks, like sacks, up the sides. The rusty iron walls were running with condensed breath and moisture, on which the light made little flickers of rainbow colours, as it does on a sluice. Two or three of the Spanish stokers had turned in, without washing, under their dirty brown blankets, and while they slept the sweat was trickling down the black on their faces. The atmosphere – well, one knows what atmosphere is considered good enough for seamen. They have to get used to it, and they couldn't have opened the ports there, because the sea was beating up the bows of the ship.
>
> The cook's temperature was nearly six above normal. So far as one could see in the light, his throat had greyish patches in it, and next day the greyish scum had spread all over his throat. It was diphtheria right enough.

With the cook out of action, the narrator takes his turn in the galley.

> Then I saw what sort of messes the crew used to fetch away from the galley in the pannikins for food. A sporting dog, fed once a day and well exercised, might have relished it.

This was not Reynolds at his most searing by any manner of means. His contemporary sea journal contained plenty more pungent material. But two weeks after publication, Sarolea received a letter from the *Coranian* shipping firm, Messrs. Owen, Watkins Williams of Cardiff, threatening legal action.[112] Reynolds prepared a draft reply and was inclined at first to be dismissive – but he was no longer emphasising the actuality nature of the material. "This is really very absurd. I did once go a voyage in one of Owen and Watkin Williams's ships, but the story was written as fiction, and never purported to be anything else. I enclose a sketch of a letter to them. If the cap fits them, that should prevent them from being anxious to wear it, though I don't know how they can be prevented if they are bent on doing so."[113]

Reynolds called in on Aldine House on 5 December to show the correspondence to Dent. A letter winged its way to Edinburgh asking what Sarolea was planning to do about it.[114] He had already written in the terms of Reynolds' draft, but the shippers returned straight to the charge.

> We duly received your letter of the 4th. The name of the narrator, the opinion of Mr Reynold's [*sic*] friends, and Mr Reynold's description of his effort are entirely irrelevant to our complaint. We manage the only line of Welsh steamers following the itinerary mentioned in the article, and the reference thereto is so detailed as to establish conclusively its identity, to anyone the least interested in the matter. Further the whole tone of the article reflects grossly on our management, imputing to us motives inhuman and scandalous: it belittles the discipline aboard the steamers, and disparages the boats generally. It relates the loss of a sister ship which is true, but it states "*She foundered with all hands*" which is absolutely untrue.
>
> Our attention was called to the article, and you can well imagine with what feelings we read the allusions therein, which were so uncalled for, and quite unworthy. Apart from our personal feeling, and the prejudice to our line, we cannot help suggesting that Mr Reynold's talents might be better employed in contributing something to the popularizing of the British Mercantile Marine, rather than to depreciating it, by misrepresenting, even in a "story", conditions which, by our favour, he experienced. Unfortunately the class of story which *Tramping Afloat* represents appeals to the morbid taste of a certain class who are ever ready, without thought or investigation, to decry that which is British.

> Before we take any further steps in the matter, we should like to know what reply Mr Reynold's has to our complaint.[115]

Reynolds had spent the previous month rushing round the Devon ports on his first major public fisheries assignment; he was exhausted and building up to his usual pre-Christmas tensions. He was especially racked with anxiety for Tom who had fallen seriously ill back in Sidmouth. To all this could be added resentment with Dent for failing to exploit the naval reform issue that was coming to a head, and even to pay him for his article, the result of bureaucratic indecision between London and Edinburgh. He was hard pressed for money since he was planning to bring down a surgeon from London to take a look at Tom.[116] He was also clearly worried about the outcome of the row with the shipping firm.

In London on 13 December everything came to a head in predictable Reynolds fashion in a friendly letter to his latest publisher.

> I have had no word of acknowledgement of my letter last week to Dr Sarolea, who, so I understand, is, or has been, in Town; nor have I received yet any payment for "Tramping Afloat"; nor do I see that you are taking any steps whatever to utilize the present naval scuffle in giving "The Lower Deck" a jump.
> The first two facts speak for themselves, and the last is surely very contrary to your reputation for knowing how to take the tide in pushing a book.[117]

It was not for nothing that he regarded the Macmillans as gods among publishers.

In the event, he took the wisest course and wrote a conciliatory letter to Sarolea for onward transmission to the Cardiff shippers. He sheltered behind the anonymity of the fictional shipping line about which he had written.

> I made the steamer of my story follow an itinerary among ports I happen to be acquainted with. If I had supposed for a moment that that itinerary could act as a pointer at Messrs. Williams' steamers – well, I should very carefully have altered it. For I neither wanted to single out their steamers, nor should have had any object in doing so. Quite the contrary; for it was aboard one of their steamers that I had, nearly ten years ago, one of the pleasantest times of my life, and in an article about their steamers – as distinguished from a story about nobody's steamers in particular – I should naturally have said so.

This was all pretty disingenuous, but comfortably lawyer-proof. He ended with a lament for creative writers wherever they might be.

> I know, of course, that there are people who concern themselves to make out that fiction is all fact, and treat stories as if they were articles or factual reports. I recollect that once, when I was describing in a lecture how an unfortunate love affair hastened a poet's death, a lady piped up from the back: "Are you speaking from your own experience, Mr. Reynolds?" And again, because I once wrote a story of divorce, I am still sometimes said to have a charming and pathetic young wife, from whom I have been separated, stowed away somewhere!
>
> It is authors themselves who suffer most from people who make caps out of fiction for themselves or others to wear, and if Messrs. Williams have been worried by their unwarrantable operations, I am very sorry.[118]

By the middle of January, London and Edinburgh had still not sorted out the matter of his payment. Dent's office wrote to Sarolea: "I have seen Mr Dent today with regard to Mr Reynolds' payment for the short story, and he says that you yourself arranged for this story and payment when you saw Mr Reynolds in London and when you took him out to lunch. Mr Dent denies that he himself had anything whatever to do with it. Would you be good enough to settle this for us."[119] A weary Sarolea replied. "Will you please send Mr Reynolds £5. (Five pounds) for his story, 'Tramping Afloat'. I certainly did not arrange any terms with Mr Reynolds, as I understood from Mr Dent's previous letters that he had settled with author."[120]

As this was going on, a rather chastened Reynolds now made a polite enquiry. "I take it that the Cardiff excitement over 'Tramping Afloat' has died of malnutrition.... But may I remind you that payment for the story is still outstanding? £3 a page, I think, was what you agreed to pay for that sort of stuff."[121] Sarolea, still smarting from Dent and from troublesome authors, was terse in the extreme. "I had some very unpleasant correspondence with the Cardiff people which was protracted for about six weeks, and which took a great deal of my time and rather worried me, as under my contract with Mr Dent, I am financially responsible for any lawsuit."[122]

Reynolds, who had evidently consulted Charles Wright, had long given up any fears of the Cardiff *démarche*. But he was so astonished by Dent's control over his editor, deciding policy but taking no responsibility for it, he could scarcely maintain his politeness. "I'm sorry those people worried you. According to my information from Lloyd's, it was probably all bluff. Had I known you were personally responsible for lawsuits, I should have taken more of the trouble on myself. But what an ungodly position to let yourself into – with Mr. Dent pressing hard for stuff specifically dealing with Merchant Service abuses!"[123]

Sarolea had not learnt his lesson. At last on 18 January he sent Reynolds the money: "I enclose Cheque for Five Pounds (£5.) for the Story 'Tramping Afloat'. I hope you will be able to send me another one at your early convenience."[124]

But Reynolds was not to be tempted again.

On 17 September 1912, just after his first meeting with Dent, Reynolds had lunch, almost for the last time, at the Mont Blanc. Present were Edward Garnett (in the chair), Edward Thomas, Richard Curle, Norman Douglas and W.H.Davies.[125] It was, almost certainly, the occasion of the celebrated Mont Blanc anecdote at Reynolds' expense.

Let Davies tell it in his own words.

> Edward Garnett had a natural wit, and it had to come out, whether people liked it or not; but, being a kind-hearted man, he was very quick in smoothing matters over if he saw his words taken too seriously. On one occasion Stephen Reynolds came to lunch. It will be remembered that Stephen Reynolds lived with two fishermen down in Devonshire, and wrote several books dealing with their experience as fishermen, and their idea of other matters.
>
> But on this occasion Reynolds launched into a long account of Bob Wooley [*sic*] which bored everybody present, and Garnett had to head him off with the remark:- 'You live with two fishermen, but some day a man will live with *three* fishermen, and what will you do then?'[126]

More malicious than witty. David Garnett thought the remark unkind but that it had a rational explanation: "I suspect that my father became rather disappointed that Reynolds did not develop as a writer more than he did."[127] In fact, it was no surprise. The two men had been drifting apart ever since their earnest differences over socialism and the censorship controversy. In a sense the rift was inevitable once *A Poor Man's House* shot Reynolds to fame. Garnett almost invariably dropped his protégés once they had achieved celebrity. A charitable person might say that his work was then done. But there is perhaps a glimmer of truth in Hannaford's assessment that Garnett wanted to keep his obscure writers to himself. Once a wider public had taken hold of their mystery, there was nothing left on which he might polish his ego.

Howsobeit, the remarkable Reynolds-Garnett correspondence, almost richer than *A Poor Man's House* itself, had begun to falter by 1910 and by 1914 was finally closed. A similar fate was to overtake the contacts with Joseph Conrad and with Edward Thomas. As Reynolds moved out of literature into fisheries administration, there was no longer common ground beneath their feet. Reynolds connived at it. He had turned a major page of his book and was reluctant to look back to chapters that spelled more heartache than anything else. He was moving now in the real world. He felt he had outgrown them.

There was one exception. In September 1912 Hudson had come down for a few weeks' stay in Devon. As he later told his friend, J.R. Harding, he had finally found Uncle Sam's ravens. "I spent some weeks in S. Devon, mostly at Sidmouth, and I met there a native wild naturalist, a gardener named Ernest Selley, who knows a good deal about local bird life and is a perfect enthusiast.

On the Sidmouth cliffs I saw two pairs of ravens on several occasions. Both pairs breed on the cliffs, one near Beere [*sic*], the other pair between Sidmouth and Budleigh."[128]

Reynolds had met Hudson more than once at the Mont Blanc, but this was the first time he had seen him close up in his natural habitat. He reported to George Macmillan: "W H Hudson, the *Nature in Downland* man, is down here. He's a delightful old chap – like a long grey bird himself. But unfortunately his heart wont let him get up our hills much. Not that I could take him far just at present, for I'm supposed to have chipped a bone in my foot, stamping on sticks to break them to a size for lighting the kitchen fire".[129]

With no further manuscripts to deliver, Reynolds said a metaphorical farewell too to his practitioner friends, J.B. Pinker and George Macmillan, who had helped him so much. The close feeling had not faded; it was an occupational parting. But the relationship with Hudson was to blossom and survive right up to Reynolds' death. Not so surprising, for they had Cornwall in common, and love of nature, and love of people less fortunate than themselves. Not many of the Mont Blanc mafia put people above literature, but Reynolds did – and so did Hudson.

As literature gave way to fishery politics, the cast made a speedy change. But Reynolds was not lacking in his new career for mentors to give him strength and boost his confidence. Out went Edward Garnett and Joseph Conrad. In came Henry Maurice and Cecil Harmsworth.

SIXTEEN

The Cornish Committee 1912–13

There is a long tradition in England of writers and journalists going slumming – what the more refined observers have termed "social exploration". It starts in the mid-Victorian period when the growth of the great industrial cities drew attention as never before to the massive gulf between working class poverty and middle class comfort. It ends in the 1930s with George Orwell its most famous practitioner, the last decade before the welfare state put an end to mass poverty and began to merge the boundaries of class.

Most of the social explorers, including the young Orwell, were driven by negative motives – guilt at their position as members of a ruling élite whose fortune had been built on the backs of the poor. Many saw good copy in the process of exploration and the chance of making their names, an opportunity soon rationalised into a missionary belief that the exposure of working-class conditions through publicity would lead to amelioration. This somewhat self-regarding approach meant that those who went so far as to live among the poor did not stay long.

As a member of this tradition Reynolds is unique. He rejected middle-class life, not through feelings of class guilt, but because it had dealt him, habitual outsider that he was, such grievous blows in childhood and adolescence. He embraced the warmth of working-class culture because it gave him for the first time a home, a genuine place by the fire – "this wandering, scratching cat has found a fireside where it can lie down and purr".[1] His approach to working-class life was entirely positive. For him, unlike the other social explorers, it was not working-class, but middle-class, life that was the problem. And unlike the others, he stayed for a lifetime.

When he rode to celebrity on the back of the experiences recorded in *A Poor Man's House*, all his friends expected him to move on shortly to other things. As time went by and he maintained his Western Town address, they were forced to revise their opinions and begin to accept his behaviour as more than just a social gesture. When after 1912 he abandoned literature altogether for fishery politics and administration, it was all of a piece with the rest of his life. He had decided to work for what mattered most to him – the working-class friends with whom he lived. It finally put paid to the old accusations of posturing.

It also put paid to a misunderstanding of Reynolds' political outlook which has gained currency since his death – that he was a nostalgic conservative, dreaming of a return to a golden proletarian past, quite oblivious to, even hostile towards, the economic betterment of working people. In fact, he devoted the rest of his life to a tireless pursuit of the most radical solutions – technological, organisational, managerial – for improving the lot of the working men he knew best, the longshore fishermen. He was determined that the future successors of Bob and Tom should never again approach every winter in the shadow of starvation.

His "conservatism", such as it was, was limited to a desire to preserve the spiritual values that had warmed his place by that fireside. Simple things like solidarity, courage in adversity. A hundred years later, when the guiding spiritual value is ever-expanding material consumption, and a different kind of poverty stalks the land, who is to say he was wrong?

The shift into the world of fishery politics was not the result of any single decision, but a gradual, almost unconscious process, over a period of three or more years. It had started formally with his appointment in the autumn of 1911 as adviser to Noel Buxton's Inshore Fisheries Parliamentary Committee, a warm-up for the projected appointment he had been offered informally that summer to the Commission the Government was planning to set up to look into the state of the fisheries.

In August that year, he had agreed to do a series of fishery articles for *The Times* to set the scene for the Parliamentary debates that autumn.[2] It was the prospect of these that had brought an end – he hoped temporary – to the *Nesscombe* series for the *Westminster Gazette*, but by 21 September he was still struggling to construct the first words. He told Katie Powys: "Hannaford, as you see, is come to an end – for the time, at any rate. I've been trying to get started with some fishing articles for the *Times*, and so far have not succeeded. Trying to start an article makes one feel inclined to go and get blind drunk and then sleep for three days!"[3]

By the beginning of October, however, he was well under way and beginning to surprise himself by the quality of what he was writing. As he told Frederick Macmillan, it might be good enough to make a book. "I am head over heels in my *Times* fishery articles, which are turning out much more comprehensive than I intended they should be; and when I come up to Town I should like to consult you on the possibilities of enlarging them into a more permanent form."[4]

That same month he completed them under the generic title *The Inshore Fisheries*, with separate subtitles for each article – *Decline, Revival* and *Administration*.[5] But *The Times* was too congested to take them at once and by the middle of December, with the Parliamentary Committee in active debate, he feared he might be missing the political boat. "That exasperating *Times* has not yet printed my articles. It's like having one's powder not only dry, but locked away. However, I got some proofs for Runciman and shall probably see him after Christmas."[6] For Walter Runciman, the radical politician who had come to the Board of Agriculture in the same October reshuffle that brought Churchill to the Admiralty, was now the single most important person whose eye he had to catch.

The articles were finally published over a ten-day period in the middle of February 1912 and had an immediate impact in the political and bureaucratic circles at which they were directed.[7] Readers were struck above all by the quality of the expression, so different from that of the usual bread and butter political article. It was the subject closest to Reynolds' heart and found his intellect at its most incisive, his prose its most clinical.

He begins with a scathing attack on the sterility of market economics.

> Certain industries decay because, under modern conditions, their relative value to the community has diminished. Thatching, horse-omnibus driving, horse-breeding, the building of wooden ships, and most kinds of hand-work are cases in point. The community ceases to buy the older industry's products or to hire its particular skill. Economically speaking, the industry dies a natural death. It lacks vitality; it fails to attract fresh capital for new developments; it cannot be bolstered up; and as a rule an easy death is the best that can happen to it. Furthermore, an industry which does succeed in adapting itself to new conditions may yet be as good as dead for those of its workers who cannot learn the new methods – a point by no means unimportant so far as it is the aim of industry in general to provide a living for every one.
>
> But it must not be assumed, as too often it is assumed, that every such decline is inevitable and irremediable, or that every decayed industry has become valueless. The tangled semi-impersonal forces included under the term "modern conditions" are neither very far-seeing, nor very intelligent, nor greatly concerned with national, as opposed to commercial, welfare. They do not care that the nation may have need of an industry if commerce has not. They want profits, and immediate profits at that. Quite frequently they kill the goose that lays the golden eggs in order to sell its carcase at cost price and make a little on its giblets. Middlemen and distributors, for instance, combine to bleed the very industries on which their own existence depends. Capital flows into the easiest channels. Competition degenerates from a stimulus into a knock-out fight, which in the long run benefits nobody and ruins the smaller men. An industry's downfall may be due to its own inherent weakness or to the outside odds against it, or to any combination of the two. It is true that industries decay naturally under modern conditions. It is also true that industries are crushed out by modern conditions, not because they have become valueless, not because they are wanting in usefulness or possibilities, but because – like a man of fine character and abilities who just fails to prosper – in some respect or other they cannot keep pace, have not kept up with the times. Among such industries, the most noteworthy, and the least noticed, is that of the small fisheries. As Mr. R.W. Crowly has remarked in his pamphlet on "State-Aid for Fishermen": "Unfortunately, fishermen have not the organising spirit. The self-

> reliance that the sea breeds in them forbids that. And they have a certain pride that prevents them from airing their troubles." Thereabout lies their weakness, if weakness it really is. Advantage has been taken of it to neglect and crush their industry.[8]

He describes how the small fisheries have been reduced by competition from the new capital-intensive steamers working out of the great ports.

> In the old days each little port supplied its own *hinterland* with fish. Except when gluts occurred, the price of each fish in its own season was well maintained. Railways and steam and ice have altered all that. The smallest fishing village is in competition with the great ports. Worse still, it is not so easy for the small fisherman to send fresh-caught fish to the central markets as it is for the central markets to send iced fish, caught outside home waters, into his own district. Thus the local markets have been spoilt, and the central markets remain comparatively inaccessible.[9]

But the new steamship companies are inefficient in national terms, taking too much wealth unnecessarily out of the industry.

> And it is important to note that although they have had their boom, and although they have ruined the sailing craft, the company-owned steamers have, after the first spurt, done nothing so very great for their shareholders. From a fishery point of view they are enormously wasteful; so great a percentage of their gross earnings has to be paid out of the fish trade in the shape of first cost and running expenses before they begin to pay wages and dividends within the trade. In a measure, the companies have burnt down the house to roast the pig.[10]

But why can't the small fishermen just buck themselves up? Here Reynolds answers from the inside, with five years of fishing behind him.

> "Why don't the small fishermen combine against their competitors and against the middlemen?" is a common enough question. There are many reasons, among them the decisive fact that effective combination demands a backing of capital and a well-organised industry. And again, "Why can't fishermen be more business-like?" A sufficient answer is that they can't be made young and be sent to school again, and if they could, they'd be better learning their trade. Those who ask such questions should try a few nights' work in a fishing-boat, and then, when they come ashore, see how fit they feel to carry through several complicated and urgent pieces of business. They would go to bed, if the fish made not a penny![11]

Both market forces and the education system are combining to contrive the extinction of small fishermen as a class.

> Fishermen are bred, not made; they exercise an ancient traditional craft; even ex-naval men cannot, as a rule, become proper fishermen. Modern education, which wastes 10 years of a boy's life in teaching him no more than he could learn in three, must take its share of the blame. It is increasingly difficult for a fisherman's son to turn straight away from schoolroom and playground to the hardships and hazards of a fisherman's life, in face, too, of his discouraged father's advice. Given sufficient recompense and the chance of independence, no doubt he would do it. But once allowed to die down, the fisherman breed can never be revived at will.[12]

Reynolds' broad solution is the one he had recommended to the Parliamentary Committee the year before – the establishment of credit banks to inject new capital into the industry for modernisation, above all the harnessing of motor power; the institution of co-operative schemes, particularly in marketing, to escape the predatory clutches of the middlemen. But the manner of implementing any such schemes must take account of the fishermen themselves, and is therefore crucial. Here once again Reynolds carries the conviction of the insider.

> A neglected industry, like a neglected child, is difficult to take in hand, and requires, as the schoolmasters say, individual attention. Men who feel that everything has been against them, and that they have been robbed all round of the full fruits of their labour, are not very easy either to convince of one's good intentions or to help. Past neglect of the small fisheries will have to be paid for by extreme care in getting any scheme for their revival under way. The nature of fishermen, the defects of their fine qualities, their prejudices even, form as important a factor as any. Their work, though rough, is highly skilled; they are not to be looked down on, or treated as if they were fish-catching machines. It is useless to blame them for those of their characteristics which will not fit into a cut-and-dried scheme. The better, and in the end the cheaper, course is to make the scheme fit them – fit them comfortably, like a jersey, so that they can move about in it. Above all, they will not be driven.
> ......Like most men whose lives are full of risk, they are intensely conservative, in the sense that they hold very fast to that which is, and will not loose grip till that which might be is thoroughly proved. A premature attempt to spring upon them any full-fledged system of credit banks and co-operative societies – supposing they could run it – would meet with stolid opposition, under the guise of indifference and unprintable language.[13]

It is this psychology of approach that was the key to Reynolds' contribution to and influence upon the revival of the longshore fisheries in the years following 1913. Many members of the committees on which he sat could readily appreciate and advocate the benefits of motor power and co-operative marketing, but Reynolds was unique among them in seeing and pressing home the crucial importance of sensitive and realistic implementation. He drove the policy discussion and invariably got his way. And he too was uniquely fitted to drive the implementation on the ground. His own experimental co-operative schemes in West Cornwall provided the template from which the other schemes throughout the country were to be developed.

In his *Times* articles he trod on a lot of toes by rejecting the existing vested interests – the seaboard local authorities and the local Sea Fisheries Committees – as bodies suitable to run the projected new schemes. Instead he looked to a revitalised Board of Agriculture and Fisheries under Runciman, sufficiently distant from local squabbles, to take the work into its own hands and later decentralise it into the hands of the fishermen themselves. "In other words, run the scheme and allot the credit in the first place from headquarters, meanwhile preparing the fishermen by every means possible for co-operation. Then, wherever the ground is favourable, plant a co-operative society, which would manage the credit banking, alongside of its other affairs and enterprises, under the general supervision of the Board and with the advice of its officers. Afterwards, affiliate the local societies into district societies, with due regard to communication and a constant supply of fish."[14]

On the day of publication of the final article *The Times* produced a full-column leader in support of the longshore fishermen and all of Reynolds' arguments. "At a time when the majority of the labouring classes seem inclined to rest more and more on State assistance, every section of the population which maintains an instinct of obstinate independence is an encouraging phenomenon...... Our Correspondent's suggestions for the best line of action are based on plenty of experience, and are well worth the detailed consideration of the ordinary citizen."

Most important it backed Reynolds' specific suggestions, such as the recommendation that loans for motor engines should come from the Development Fund, and his strategic approach to implementation: "But the Board of Agriculture and Fisheries has, after all, the most obvious fitness to superintend the harvests of the sea as well as of the land; and, although its record up to the present is not one of very vigorous achievement, it may be hoped that the needs of the fisheries will receive their fair share of the energy which Mr Runciman is putting forth."[15]

Runciman indeed had already identified the fisheries debate as a useful means of consolidating his radical reputation, and Reynolds as the man to inject some energy and commonsense experience into the Fisheries Division which, on taking over fishery responsibilities from the Board of Trade in 1903, had inherited something of the sluggardly ethos of its predecessor.

Runciman's long-awaited meeting with Reynolds appears to have taken place in the last week of February 1912, with *The Times* articles still fresh in public memory, and he seems to have determined instantly to sign him up for the Department. That week Reynolds was commissioned to write a policy memorandum on the spot in London to be formally submitted to the Board as the blueprint for future action.[16] There was talk of his following up *The Times* articles with a survey of the small fisheries.[17] It was an unprecedented way for a Government Department to employ an outsider over the heads of its officials.

The next three months were taken up by internal discussion within the Department on the creation of the new fisheries policy. In a Supply debate on 26 June, Runciman at last came out into the open and put the whole of his weight behind the inshore fishermen and the policy of co-operation. His emphasis on their importance to the nation and the Navy, and on the pointlessness of merely throwing money at them, showed just how strongly Reynolds had his ear.

> If there is one class of fishermen in this country who are well worth preserving as a great national asset, it is certainly the inshore men, who, in their intimate acquaintance with the coast of this country and their extraordinary skill in dealing with very difficult ground, have a position second to none in the world. They not only provide us with excellent stock for national purposes, but I might also add with the best of the material from which the manning of our Navy can be organised. The Board of Fisheries is well alive to this fact, and I am taking the problems with which I see any chance of dealing one by one, and, with the assistance of the members of my staff *and those whom I hope will shortly join it*, I hope first of all to deal with the subjects which can be helped by Development Fund moneys, and then by better organisation or by a further extension or dissemination of knowledge, to give the smaller men engaged in the fishing industry a chance of competing with those organised on a larger scale.
>
> ......I am not going to be a party to handing over to fishermen, or to any other class, national moneys on a philanthropic basis. I think it would be bad for them, and it certainly is not desirable for the nation, but we can by national organisation enable them to do collectively what they cannot do singly......
>
> I hope when the Fishery Division is put on a slightly different basis it may be possible for us to set apart one of our officers entirely for the purpose of organising co-operative effort among our fishermen. (*my italics*)[18]

There is little doubt whom the President of the Board had in mind, from among those "shortly to join" the Department, for this very specialised task. Reynolds' was delighted when he read the report of the announcement the next day. He told George Macmillan: "Probably you have seen in to-day's *Times* that Runciman has adopted the fishery policy I urged upon him of not financing the fisheries without a co-operative effort to improve the marketing of fish. That's a score, anyhow."[19]

Part of Runciman's strategy within the Department was to replace the ageing and rather battered Assistant Secretary, Walter Archer, as head of the Fisheries Division with his young, dynamic and rather dashing Private Secretary, Henry Maurice.[20] This he managed finally to achieve during the summer recess of 1912. Reynolds had already met Maurice in Runciman's outer office, but now that they shared the fisheries together the relationship was to become ever closer, ever deepening.

Coincidentally, Maurice came from Reynolds' part of the world. His family had been doctors in Marlborough for 200 years, and he shared with Reynolds a scientific interest in nature and a love for the Wiltshire countryside. He was a pioneering enthusiast of zoos, and in retirement became both President of the London Zoo and a popular writer of children's stories about animals, some of which were broadcast on the BBC.

Here, late in life, he was taking a leaf out of Reynolds' own book. In perhaps the best of the stories he recaptures for children of the 1940s the wonder of exotic animals to a small child in a provincial town of the early 1880s.

> When I was a boy of six or seven years I first heard the roar of a lion as I lay in bed, and I thrilled to the marrow of my bones, for I knew that the voice could be no other than that of the King of the Beasts, of whom I had read in my book of African adventure. The next morning I was taken to visit Wombwell's Menagerie which was camped in the broad High Street of my native town. I remember vividly to this day the glory of the chief lion of the show, whose name was Bruce; of the rest of the animals I only remember clearly the pelicans, whose race to the fish bucket filled me with joy.[21]

The two pelicans that had stuck in his mind were made by their keeper to race the whole length of the enclosure to reach their food. In the 1930s the same menagerie was bought up by London Zoo and Maurice, going down to see it at Whipsnade, was astonished to meet again one of the pelicans that had raced to the bucket fifty years before.[22]

After Marlborough and Oxford, the young Maurice had trained as a lawyer and become assistant to the Director of Education for Wiltshire, at the time that Reynolds himself was drifting at Devizes College, recovering from his breakdown. From there, he graduated to the Legal Branch of the Board of Education and in 1907 became Private Secretary to the reforming Permanent Secretary, Sir Robert Morant. In 1909 he was spotted by Runciman and moved to become his Private Secretary, following with him to the Board of Agriculture in 1911.

When Reynolds first met him he was almost 38 – a slender, rather suave figure, with something of the dandy's interest in clothes. Dark-haired and slightly balding, with a long, strongly expressive face, he was inherently shy, and sometimes a difficult person to engage in conversation. But by contrast he loved social occasions which always brought him to life and where he could deploy to best effect his considerable charm. Though in later life he would complain of the Civil Service and the trials of being forever at the beck and call of ministers, he was something of a workaholic and believed utterly in the job he was doing.[23] As head of the Fisheries Division, he soon became indispensable and remained in the post till his retirement 26 years later.

Reynolds admired his sharp intelligence, his single-minded application to his duties, his seemingly miraculous manipulation of the Whitehall machine. Seven years older than Reynolds, and considerably more sophisticated, he became yet another new father figure. The admiration was mutual. Maurice has left us with a vivid account of Reynolds' personal impact upon the Fisheries Division and one of the best descriptions of the ambivalence and volatility of his personality.

> Author, musician, scientist, man of affairs, Stephen Reynolds was a man of many gifts, but to those who knew him best his most remarkable characteristics were his intense personal devotion to individuals and his consuming zeal for fishermen as such: one he endeavoured vainly to conceal behind a veil of satire or of truculent cynicism, the other he made no effort to conceal, and carried to almost extravagant lengths. It is probably the fact that the latter was largely the outcome of the former – that his zeal for fishermen was a result of his devotion to individuals who came to his aid at a crisis in his life, and to whom he believed he owed a debt greater than life itself. However that may be, it was a happy day for the Fisheries and for the Board when Reynolds decided to devote his genius to the service of the one through the other. He imparted to the councils of the Fisheries Division an infectious enthusiasm, and, in spite of his cherished prejudices, a clarity of thought and a wholly good-natured, if occasionally somewhat acidulated, humour which in the days of difficulty and stress were an invaluable asset. His work among us will never be forgotten, and if with some of us the more vivid recollection is that of his personality – of his moments of depression, of a quivering sensibility which carried an air of truculence before it as a shield, and his quick impulsive response to every indication of understanding and sympathy – it is because the human being leaves always a more vivid impression than the colleague and the official, and Reynolds was utterly human.[24]

Right from the time Maurice took over the Fisheries Division in the summer of 1912 Reynolds began to bombard him with local fisheries problems, and even to seek his help in a more personal matter – the discharge of Dolby from the Navy: "If they won't give it to him, I am afraid I shall be rather badly dropped with arrears of work, horrible to contemplate, on my hands".[25] Maurice, in the midst of planning the strategy for his new job, still found time to take up Dolby's case with the Admiralty.[26]

Maurice was looking for something in return from Reynolds, whom his political masters saw as an essential ingredient in the new fishery reforms. On 7 September he invited him up to Town on a matter of importance. "What I wished to discuss with you was the possibility of your assisting us in a general inquiry into the conditions and needs of inshore fisheries and possible means of assisting them. I have not yet got a plan of operations ready, cut and dried, but, as I expect to be away during a considerable part of this month, I should like to discuss the matter with you before I go."[27]

Reynolds went up to London on 11 September – the visit on which he did the deal with Dent over *The Lower Deck* – and met with Henry Maurice at noon that Wednesday morning in the offices of the Fisheries Division at 43 Parliament Street. The plan was for a tiny three-man Departmental Committee, headed by Sir James Wilson, a retired Indian civil servant and now Superintending Inspector at the Board, Selwyn Fremantle, a Board inspector as secretary, and with Reynolds as the expert member. Reynolds was distinctly unenthusiastic about the personnel of the Committee, but his worst fears were confirmed when he met Sir James Wilson at Whitehall Place and discussed the detail with him over lunch. Wilson, in the cherished tradition of English amateurism, declared himself at the outset completely ignorant of fishery matters, and proposed a softly softly, civil servantish approach to the vested interests Reynolds was out to confront.

By the end of his week in London Reynolds had almost made up his mind to reject the invitation outright, but went home to discuss it with Bob and Tom. Two days later, he sent in a formal refusal to Maurice with a forthright account of his reasons.

> The Commission, as I understand, was to have been composed of Sir James Wilson, as chairman, Mr. Freemantle [*sic*], a department inspector, as secretary, and myself. Sir James Wilson most frankly confesses he knows nothing about fishing, and Mr. Freemantle is, I take it, in a like case. In other words, the one fishing member, myself, would be hopelessly outweighed by a majority of members adequately conversant, no doubt, with small holdings and other land questions, mainly in India, and with certain financial remedies from the financial side thereof, but naturally and pardonably ignorant of English inshore fishing and its working conditions.
>
> It is not in the least likely that, in a three months' rush round the coast, the non-fishing members could become usefully conversant with a trade about which my own knowledge is still imperfect after eight years' close

association with it – doing the job of fishing and marketing as well as investigating so far as my means allowed; – and under the circumstances, it seems to me, if I may say so, somewhat supererogatory for Sir James Wilson (and presumably yourself too) to think that there is a lot of good stuff in my Inshore Fishery Memorandum submitted to the Board last spring, but that I am adrift as regards marketing and middlemen. I suggest, on the contrary, that a closer practical acquaintance with selling fish would be more likely to modify the official view than mine. What I have said on the subject has been from actual experience of marketing fish, and every fisherman I have ever come across is of the same mind. Quite naturally, on the other hand, the people who make money out of fishermen don't agree; and these latter are precisely the people whom your Commission will find so kind and ready to impart their knowledge – *i.e.* back up their own interest. Sir James Wilson showed me a list of the ports he has visited; the sort of ports he proposes to visit; the only ports, in fact, he can visit in the time. They were not inshore fisheries at all; they were what I call "intermediate fisheries"; that is to say, deep-sea fisheries carried on in the old-fashioned way, with sailing boats – Brixham, Mevagissey, and the like; and I cannot see how the more scattered inshore fisheries are to be studied by going to the intermediate ports. The problems and conditions of the two – in both cases urgent enough – differ in kind as well as in degree. An inshore fishery is not merely a small intermediate fishery. Sir James Wilson likewise indicated to me the sort of people from whom he expects to get authentic information – all the old gang, in short, under whose operations and influence the fisheries have been decaying. I am unable to share his optimism, nor would any fisherman do so.

Again, Sir James Wilson insists that no one of influence in connexion with the fisheries must be upset. That they should be upset as little and as warily as possible, I fully agree. Middlemen should only be knocked out *pari passu* with the creation and growth of better machinery to supersede them. But that questions liable to upset them must not be touched or investigated, is a proposal to which I cannot lend myself. I repeat: if the marketing of fish is put in a healthy state, fishermen will hardly need financing, except by a little at first; and unless it is put in a healthy state, it will be practically useless to finance them. You cannot do good to fishermen without, sooner or later, upsetting those who to their own advantage control the fishermen's markets. I am well aware that it is not within the province of Govt. directly to attack or favour one set of tradesmen for the benefit of another, even when the one maintains its position by sharp practices and rings in restraint of trade. I am also aware that Govt., if it wants to, can take indirect measures to maintain an honest balance between the different sections of a trade, or at least, with its resources, can accumulate information for some other body to do so.

> In fine, I cannot join a Commission to the report of which there is no likelihood of my being able to subscribe, and from the report of which it would be futile for me to dissent; and as the expert member – comparatively speaking, at any rate – I cannot allow myself to be swamped in a Commission which will be regarded as one whole.
>
> This is not, of course, to say anything against Sir James Wilson, on the excellence of whose intentions I cast no manner of doubt. It has to be remembered that my position is not that of a Civil Servant, who is sheltered within his department and whose public responsibility is borne by his chief. I have to bear my own responsibility before the public, and, above all, before fishermen, and I cannot, therefore, make myself responsible for a procedure of which I do not approve. For the same reason, I am compelled to reserve to myself, should my name crop up, liberty to make public my reasons for dissent.[28]

This letter was a calculated political act. He knew full well that both Maurice and Runciman were desperate to get him on board and that any figurehead chairman of the proposed committee would be entirely expendable in order to achieve that aim. He was firing a warning shot above the official heads. If they wanted to employ him, they should do so on his terms; if they were attracted to his views and his constituency, they would have to listen. No one was going to silence *him* in the cause of political expediency.

He clearly saw it as a negotiation and was looking out for the response. Three days later, he followed up with a formal letter of refusal to Wilson himself.[29] A few days later still, he wrote to George Macmillan: "Very glad to get your letter and to hear that your more circumspect mind approved my action in the fisheries matter. I've had no reply yet, but fully mean to sit tight".[30]

For the Board it was imperative to get him – the acknowledged leader of the public debate with the best formed set of ideas. With his command of the emotional argument and of the public media, the prospect of leaving him outside the tent was unthinkable. When Maurice got back from his international meeting, he sent off a letter at once, in a low key to defuse the emotion. "I was sorry to receive your letter, which followed me abroad, but on consideration I am inclined to think that you have misunderstood the situation and that a conversation between us may remove your difficulties."[31]

He had business in Plymouth the last weekend of September and had planned in any case to look in at Sidmouth to see Reynolds on the Monday after. Thus, on 1 October, in Bob's cottage that Maurice so far had only read about, he asked Reynolds for his terms. The answer was a different chairman, a *thorough* investigation of the *inshore* ports, and freedom to consider marketing conditions and prices. He also made a unique proposal – that he as a member should be accompanied, "letting me and a fisherman act as a sort of joint committee-man". He had done it in his books, so why not in his public appointments? "I know so well by now the conditions under which I can work my best, and they, for years, have included collaboration with my people."[32]

Maurice had a remarkable day, meeting all the Woolley clan for the first time. "I enjoyed my visit much. I will write you again when I am able to make definite suggestions. PS My regards to the various members of the various Woolley establishments." But even he may have baulked at the prospect of Robert William Woolley as a potential Royal Commissioner.

As a good civil servant, keen to live up to the stereotype, he left without his umbrella. "Would you mind bringing along my umbrella for me when next you are up this way. I forgot it. There is no hurry. I have others up here."[33] Returning it, Reynolds could not resist a mildly wry aside. "Glad you got your umbrella all right. One rather forgets the existence of the things down here."[34]

Some distinguished heads were put together the next fortnight in the Board of Agriculture. One of them came up with a smart idea. If Reynolds were to be captured, why not give him some problem-solving on his own home patch – an offer he could not refuse?

For a particular West Country problem had been boiling up for some months and now was coming rapidly to a head. The setting up of the Development Commission under the Development Act of 1909 had created expectations of financial assistance by bodies all around the country, not least among the fishermen of the west. In the autumn of 1911 the Cornwall and Devon Sea Fisheries Committees had been meeting jointly to agree the making of co-ordinated applications to the Commission for funds to instal motor power in fishing vessels. In November 1911 the Cornwall County Council had taken the first step by putting in a general application for money for the improvement of fisheries around the coast.[35] In December the Commission deferred consideration of the application and asked the Board of Agriculture to prepare an overarching scheme to embrace all such applications.[36]

The Sea Fisheries Committees in the west were pressing the case for grants made direct to individual fishermen, but in the early days of operation of the Act it was thought that help could only legally be given to the infrastructure of an industry in a general way, through such matters as scientific research.[37] Reynolds had taken the matter up in his *Times* articles that spring. "The Development Fund, which at its inception might reasonably have been expected to help develop such industries as fishing, has provided money for scientific work, but refuses it for making 'grants to individual fishermen for the purpose of introducing machinery into their boats'. Meanwhile the small fisheries go on declining, so that it is doubtful who will be left to make practical use of the scientific experiments."[38]

The Times in its leader supported this criticism of the negative stance of the Development Commission. "Our Correspondent declares that at present the Development Fund refuses to make grants for this purpose. But with proper management to ensure that the money was wisely laid out on deserving men who had a reasonable chance of repaying it, this refusal can hardly be permanently justified."[39] This passing remark gave new life to the hopes of the Devon and Cornwall Fisheries Committees who in March put in formal petitions for grants of £10,000 to each Committee for making loans to their fishermen for the installation of motor power.[40]

This put more political pressure on the Board of Agriculture, still in the laborious process of drawing up the definitive scheme for which the Commission had asked. The Cornishmen were becoming particularly vociferous about the delay as autumn approached and their petition still went unanswered. Reynolds told Maurice he was keeping a low profile locally and not attempting to defend the Board. Maurice responded rather archly. "I am grateful to you for not having entered the lists on my behalf; above all things I desire to be saved from apologists. The excitement of the Cornish men and others seems to me to be perfectly natural and if they would express themselves in rather less reckless terms, I should sympathise with them entirely."[41] Reynolds took up the rather sour reference to apologists. "Pray set your mind retrospectively at rest. You didn't stand to be apologised for in any case. Apologies for mistakes.... yes. But I never attempt to apologise for anything I continue to approve of. It's so much more effective to defy – to brazen it out."[42]

Now in October the Board saw the opportunity to kill both Reynolds and the Cornishmen with one stone. They would set up a small committee to advise on the Devon and Cornish applications which, though ostensibly concerned with grants for installing motors in fishing boats, would be allowed to range wide enough to engage the problems of the small western fisheries in general. Maurice wrote to Reynolds on 16 October with the new plan.

Reynolds' first reaction was favourable. "I am afraid I am giving you a lot of trouble, but can't very well help o' it. This small special committee does seem to me, as you evidently anticipated it would, a more promising beginning than the other committee as at first proposed." But now that he was so clearly in the driving seat so far as Government policy was concerned, he wanted copper-bottomed assurances about the terms of reference.

> However, I may take it – may I not? – with regard to this small committee:
> (1) That it will really go to and investigate the smaller inshore fisheries within the two counties of Devon and Cornwall; and
> (2) that marketing conditions and prices would not be excluded from its terms of reference – with a view to finding out if the small fisheries *can* economically be revived, if not with an immediate intention of tackling the middleman question. What I am anxious for is, that the *material* for tackling that question should be gathered together in such a form (comparative tables of local prices, railway charges, etc.) that it can afterwards be tackled by a voluntary organization, if not by Govt.
> Should the terms of reference include those two points, my objections to the committee first proposed would, in effect, be more or less met, and, terms making it possible, I should be pleased to do what I can.

He proposed they settle the matter finally in London the following week. "Probably I shall be in Town next week – on my way to abuse liberalism to the Cambridge Liberal Club! May I call on you then?"

And he held out the promise of a new and highly relevant qualification for the peripatetic enterprise on which he was about to embark. "I have been learning motor-driving in a small car rather tricky to drive, and after nearly running down a retired General and just shaving a big smash into a large car that was road-hogging, I'm really getting on. But driving on our sort of roads isn't exactly a joke to begin with."[43]

Reynolds was appointed to the Devon and Cornwall Committee on 5 November 1912 along with Selwyn Fremantle, the Board of Agriculture inspector. The secretary was G.T. Atkinson, another Board civil servant.

After all the care that had been taken, the terms of reference were entirely to his liking.

> To consider the applications of the Devon and Cornwall Sea Fisheries Committees, respectively, for grants of £10,000 each for the purpose of assisting the fishermen of those counties to instal motor power in their boats, and to advise the Board whether such installation is advisable, and whether for this or other purposes connected with the development of the fisheries of those counties it is necessary to make advances out of public funds, or whether the same can be adequately secured by alternative measures.[44]

The final limb had been carefully constructed to appear in line with the narrow thrust of the inquiry, while at the same time conferring ample scope to enquire into any issues concerned with "the development of the fisheries". Reynolds was well pleased.

He was pleased too by the choice of chairman. In place of the rather opinionated Sir James Wilson, Runciman had called upon another, but much more sensitive, in-house candidate – Cecil Harmsworth, a Liberal politician like himself. Harmsworth came from a family forever in the news. He was the younger brother of the newspaper magnates, Lord Northcliffe and Lord Rothermere-to-be; thus a member of a then unique triumvirate of siblings who were all appointed to the peerage, though Cecil had to wait for his barony till 1939.

He had none of the swagger of his eldest brother, nor the narrow managerial obsession of Rothermere. Unlike them, he was after neither power nor money. He was a shy, gentle man of much more liberal views, who had gone into politics above all to help his fellow men. Northcliffe often referred to him as "the gentleman of our family" and it was said that he would have made an ideal bishop or ambassador.[45]

In the early days, he had made his contribution to the Harmsworth empire – for a time he was a very able editor of *Answers* – but had none of his brothers' mental force or drive to stand the competitive world of newspapers for long. In the Liberal landslide of 1906, he had become MP for Droitwich, and then later South Bedfordshire where he soon became associated with the Garden Cities movement, and with the improvement of working class conditions through smallholdings and cheap model housing. The new committee and his association with Reynolds were soon to add a new political reputation as champion of the fishermen.

Reynolds knew of him already through Runciman, who in November 1911, soon after his arrival at the Board, had invited Harmsworth to join the Department as his Parliamentary Private Secretary and become "an authoritative exponent of our agricultural policy".[46] He was therefore a Board insider who, in addition to being a keen recreational fisherman himself, already knew a little of the twists and turns of fishery politics. There was another, more personal, connection. Working in the same private office, he had become a close friend of Henry Maurice, his Minister's private secretary. In 1912 Maurice had been invited down to Harmsworth's country house – Magdalen House, on the Thames at Henley – where he had met Ruth Spencer, the niece of Harmsworth's wife, Emily, and fallen instantly in love.[47] Ruth and Henry Maurice were married the following year, establishing a lasting bond between the Maurice and Harmsworth families and tieing Cecil in permanently with the world of fishery politics.

The Devon and Cornwall Committee brought Reynolds and Harmsworth very close. It came at a time when Reynolds' worries at home were getting on top of him and he was relieved to get away from Sidmouth and lean on the sympathetic shoulder of the older man. Harmsworth recalled his first reactions to the young author some years later.

> I met him first in connexion with a fisheries inquiry in Devon and Cornwall. For some weeks we were much together, and we visited well-nigh every fishing station from the eastern borders of Devonshire to the north of Cornwall. It was a happy time for both of us. Stephen, who had written so much about fishermen and had lived with the Woolleys at Sidmouth for ten years [*sic*] with the object of perfecting his knowledge of fishermen and fishing conditions, had now an opportunity of exercising influence: he was engaged on a Government inquiry with every prospect of inspiring decisions of much importance to the fisheries. I was quickly infected with his zeal and enthusiasm. Stephen would and could talk high philosophy on occasion, but there was a severely practical side to his character that ensured the success of his schemes when at last they received official sanction.[48]

The appointment of Reynolds was not universally well received. He was surprised to find himself attacked in public as lacking the necessary political experience for the job by none other than Francis Mildmay, the MP for Totnes, with whom he had worked up till now quite closely and amicably on local fisheries issues.[49] Reynolds was inclined to dismiss it as political sour grapes, the price to be paid for all such appointments.

The principal task of the Committee in gathering its evidence was the tour Reynolds had been promised of all the inshore fishing ports in Devon and Cornwall. Atkinson organised the Devon and the Cornwall itineraries in two distinct tranches. In the two and a half weeks from 11 to 28 November 1912 they covered the 27 principal fishing ports in Devon. In a further concerted burst over the first 14 days of 1913, they visited the remaining 24 ports of Cornwall. It was not an itinerary for the faint-hearted, but they managed to turn it, particularly the Cornish tour, into something of a holiday and experience to remember – more and more nostalgically as the years progressed. For Reynolds it was the first experience of concerted administrative work and of political power.

On Monday 11 November, a week after the committee's appointment, Reynolds joined Harmsworth and Atkinson at the offices in Exeter of the secretary to the Devon Sea Fisheries Committee for a general briefing on the situation in the county. With Reynolds as a member of the committee, it was inevitable that they should start close to home. That afternoon, the three drove by car down to Beer for two nights at the Dolphin Hotel, where they dined off cutlets and herring caught fresh the same day. Before dinner, they wandered down to the Anchor Inn by the shore and spent some time in the bar there talking to the fishermen.[50] It was not the usual venue for a Government committee to collect its evidence but, with Reynolds at the helm, it became the normal, and most valuable, procedure for this committee.

And throughout the tour Reynolds was very much at the helm, as Harmsworth recalled.

> Memory dwells with wistful pleasure on visits to the almost Italian fishing villages of South Cornwall and to conversations with fishermen in sanded parlours of quayside inns and in the close forecastles of fishing smacks. The inquiry had to be conducted with rigorous thoroughness: Stephen would brook no slipshod treatment of the affairs of fishermen. So it was that in a visit to any fishing port we discussed their grievances with the fishermen and put ourselves into touch with every man – coastguard, boat builder, fish salesman, fisheries inspector – who knew anything of or had anything to do with sea fishing.[51]

This comprehensive approach was fully tested out on their first full day at Beer. They were joined by Fremantle from London and inspected all the local fishing facilities. They found the beach, like Sidmouth, difficult to work but the fishermen prosperous enough. They walked over to Seaton to interview the few part-time fishermen there and the head of the local coastguard. After lunch, they held a more formal meeting with the Beer fishermen in the shelter on the cliff and found them generally hostile to the idea of motor power. It soon became clear – a common pattern in the smaller beach ports – that their chief priority was the building of a harbour.

Already Reynolds had been doing a bit of stage-management behind the scenes, preparing the way for a Venetian entry into Sidmouth. That evening, Tom and Harry Woolley came over in the *Puffin* to take dinner at the Dolphin, and the Seaton coastguard joined them later for after dinner talks.[52] Wednesday dawned fine and fresh, and the Committee were treated to some motor power in action as they cruised down the coast in the *Puffin*, Tom and Harry in charge, to put in on the hazardous open Sidmouth beach. They were installed at the Bedford Hotel, which Harmsworth found old-fashioned and snug, remarking particularly on the presence of *English* waiters.

A meeting of fishermen was summoned for 6.30 that evening at Reynolds' local, the Anchor in Old Fore Street, where among a fairly small gathering the question of the £10,000 grant and other fishing matters were thoroughly thrashed out. After dinner, Reynolds led the committee down to Bedford Square where the arguments continued over a nightcap in the little back kitchen with Harry, Bob and Dr Peile – and the fisherman best qualified to give evidence to a Government Committee, Uncle Sam himself.[53]

Next day, deliciously warm for November, they took the boat on to Budleigh Salterton where they found the town all agog with a carnival. They managed to gather a handful of fishermen together for an informal meeting on the sea front, and were left in no doubt that Budleigh at least was anxious to reap the benefits of motor power. They visited the coastguard station where Reynolds had been a constant visitor of his old friend and mentor Battershall in the early years at Sidmouth. In the evening they took the train to Exmouth, putting up in the Imperial Hotel.[54]

Friday was another fine sunny day, and they wandered down to the quay in the morning to look at the boats and meet one of the local members of the Devon Committee. After lunch, they made their way to Lympstone, which they found a rather sad little place on the muddy Exe estuary, and where they chatted with a knot of fisherman, most of whom were highly sceptical of the idea of motor power.[55] They began to realise that, so far as their core remit went, there was little hope of building a consensus. This was the last day of their first outing. On the Saturday morning, Reynolds returned to Sidmouth and Harmsworth and Fremantle made tracks for London, leaving the hapless Atkinson alone in Exeter to write up his notes and concert the next week's arrangements.

On 11 November, when Harmsworth had been dining in the comfort of the Dolphin Hotel at Beer, the Government had been defeated by 22 votes on the financial clause of the Home Rule Bill. His local Conservative newspaper, the *Luton Reporter*, wrote a few lines of doggerel to celebrate his "expedition" that summer to the family's paper-mill estate in Newfoundland and his absence from the vote.

He was not in the wreck of the Party machine –
He had other fish to fry!
Piscatorial exploits in his late expedition
Have gained him a seat on a Fishery Commission![56]

The party managers were not to be caught out again, and his second week in Devon was conducted cautiously on the edge of a three-line whip.

On 18 November Harmsworth set off leisurely for Devon, taking the mid-day train from London to Brixham, where the committee was to meet with one of its most intractable problems. The leading citizens of the town were anxious that the large sailing trawlers operating from there should instal motor power, while the fishermen themselves were generally hostile to the proposal.[57] Tuesday was a very beautiful, but very full, day. They were down on the quay before breakfast to inspect the night's catches – turbot, soles, red mullet and plaice. They took a short trip in a boat from Looe fitted with an engine, and then proceeded to a meeting in the Harbourmaster's office. The afternoon was spent in a visit to a boat-building yard and further informal discussions. After dinner, they had a long discussion until midnight with local worthies in the Town Clerk's office on the principles and practice of fishermen's co-operation.[58]

Next day they took a motor boat on to Torquay where the fishing was almost negligible. Then on to Paignton where they sat on up-turned boats in a public conference with the local coastguard officer. Harmsworth rushed off to Town for a Commons' division, leaving Reynolds and the others to follow up the smaller south Devon ports round to Plymouth.[59]

Reynolds was not with them when Fremantle and Atkinson went on to Hallsands and Beesands, but met by chance a Hallsands fisherman over a pint in Kingsbridge and was persuaded to double back there for some further committee investigations of his own. He became convinced from this encounter that the Start Bay men, whose beaches were unsuitable for motors, would be driven off their fishing grounds by the introduction of motors elsewhere. He was beginning to sense the interlocking complexities of the apparently simple remit on which they had embarked.[60]

Harmsworth did not surface again until the following Tuesday. He was delayed in Town that day for one of Asquith's little luncheon parties at No. 10, but managed to emerge in time for the afternoon train to Plymouth where he found Reynolds, Fremantle and Atkinson waiting for him at the Central Hotel.[61]

The following morning, 27 November, they went down to the Barbican before breakfast, but found the fish market already over. At the hotel that morning they held a round-up meeting with members of the Devon Sea Fisheries Committee and others to discuss the whole range of the county's fishing problems. That afternoon they toured the laboratory of the Marine Biological Association on the Hoe, and had a short discussion after dinner with a few local fishermen. By now, Harmsworth had begun to recognise Reynolds not only as the key to the Committee's thinking and its ultimate recommendations, but also as the most congenial and stimulating of its members. They had become firm friends. Late that evening, in a sharp frost, Reynolds took him off alone by tram to show him his familial haunts in Devonport.[62] It was the beginning of the Reynolds-Harmsworth axis which was to set the course of British fisheries policy for the next ten years.

The following day, the last of their Devon tour all together, the Committee got up in time to catch the fish market before breakfast and wonder at the large catch of dog-fish, now the pride of the Plymouth industry. Harmsworth rushed off for the Commons debate on the Welsh Disestablishment Bill, leaving the others once more to clean up the schedule with visits to the small north Devon ports around Bideford.[63]

Reynolds got back to Sidmouth that weekend to find awaiting him the furore over *Tramping Afloat* and the Cardiff shipping firm. He went up to Town on 3 December on more fisheries and publishing business.[64] On 6 December he spent all day with Harmsworth and the others in Runciman's room in the House of Commons discussing the shape of the interim report of the Devon leg of their investigations.[65]

He was in London again, staying as usual at Horrex's Hotel in Norfolk Street, for much of the next two weeks, the last before Christmas. He had been exhausted by the frantic running round the ports, the botherations of Dent and Sarolea, the necessity of being so much in London. To cap it all, Tom was taken dangerously ill in Sidmouth and had to be rushed off to hospital for an operation before Reynolds' plans to have him looked at by a London surgeon (he never trusted local doctors) could be realised.

The worry over Tom turned his usual pre-Christmas malaise into a bitingly virulent hostility to the world in general. On 13 December, as we have seen, he blasted off an uncompromising rebuke to Dent for the shortcomings of his firm. A week later, a dinner party he had arranged in London for a friend had been ruined because the sensitivities of the host had not been taken account of by the principal guest. Straight after the dinner, Reynolds sent his unsuspecting friend a full list of the charges. Harold Wright later published the letter to this anonymous recipient as "characteristic" of Reynolds' short fuse; but special allowances have to be made. In these days, he was more than usually exhausted, worried and anxious.

> I invited Mrs. H. and yourself to dinner with me to-night at the place most convenient to you. It was open to you to decline the invitation had you wished, and your re-arrangement of my dinner party would have been unpardonable in any one less pressed than yourself.
>
> And your jostling me into your paying for my dinner when I wished to

> do so, and when, under the circumstances, a hint from me should have been sufficient, was an insult masquerading as hospitality. You may have a legacy: I don't wish to sponge on it. Moreover, your referring to me, before two newspaper men, as the author of news about a proposed snap-division, was indiscreet in the highest degree, and a breach of the trust under which my own information has always been open to you.
>
> Add to that your carelessness in neglecting to let me know you were not coming up in the week, and therefore could not dine with me as arranged, – and I think you will acknowledge that, if not an apology, at any rate some kind of assurance is due to me that I shall not be exposed to that sort of thing in the future.
>
> No friendliness, in fact, however enjoyable, nor any amount of admiration, could be expected so to expose itself twice.[66]

But at the same anxious time, he had managed to make peace with Francis Mildmay, who had written to apologise for his public attack on Reynolds' appointment to the Committee. Reynolds took the apology lightly, stressing the unexpected influence the affair had had in pulling Tom through. "As to the more personal matter between you and me – as you suggest, let it swing. You did me, unintentionally, a very good turn, by making a very close friend of mine, a fisherman, who was dangerously ill, so angry that he bucked up forthwith, and pulled round out of danger – came to life, as it were, to swear heartily at you. And in the happy relief from the black and almost hopeless anxiety of his illness, I feel anything but ready to wrangle fruitlessly, for the sake of merely putting myself straight."[67]

For Tom's operation had, in fact, been a touch and go affair – as Reynolds told Harold Wright: "Needless to say we are all very broken over it, but Nellie Tom is keeping going well. Bob was pretty bad; they kept him up at the hos: all the time it was on; and he got no sleep afterwards as before, for two or three nights till Peile dosed [him] with bromide. He is better now".[68]

As Tom was recovering on Christmas Eve, Reynolds sent him a present of five pounds and an even more substantial declaration.

> Please accept the enclosed Christmas card with all the good wishes that you'll know without my putting them down. You'd do as much for me, I'm damn well sure, without any bones about it; and, after all, it is only by a bad chance that you'm crocked up while I'm earning more than usual, – instead of me crocking up first.
>
> Or, if you don't like it that way – well, reckon it's from the Government. For the fact is, you've given them all the worth of it through me. As I have told them – only they are too stupid to believe it – they can't employ me on a fishery job without employing you too; because I should never have been able to do the job without you.
>
> Besides, what the hell is it – five quid – compared with thee pulling

> through? We'd have given all we bloody well had for thy life, and been glad to do it; for I don't think we hardly realised – until thy illness gave us such a shock – how much the partnership meant, that we've taken half in joke. All thee's got to do is to get well again.[69]

And in spite of all the turmoil at home, he found time too for a comforting Christmas Eve word for Katie Powys, still marooned in the desert of Brislington Hall. "All here very glad to hear you are so much better. Tom has been ill, and has had a rather bad operation, but is now getting along all right. The rest, including Margot, are well."[70]

New Year's Eve marked the return of the Committee to its business. Harmsworth and Walter Runciman escaped from the Report Stage of the Home Rule Bill for a night on the tiles – dinner at Brooks's and a play at Wyndham's – before Harmsworth joined Atkinson a little breathlessly at Paddington to take the midnight train for Cornwall. As the train drew out of the station, the two men clapped each other metaphorically upon the back and uttered a stream of Happy New Years.[71]

They arrived rather bleary-eyed next morning at Liskeard where they took an early breakfast and changed trains. They got to Looe at 10 o'clock, to be greeted by Fremantle, but no Reynolds, before starting a day of individual interviews – with the coastguard officer, the clerk to the harbour commissioners, a local boat and yacht builder and Jonathan Barron, the fishery officer of the Cornwall Sea Fisheries Committee who had been put at their disposal for most of their tour and was to prove indispensable. Reynolds joined them at the Looe Hotel that evening from Sidmouth.[72]

The next day they inspected the fish quay before breakfast and then took a car over the hill and down through the narrow, high-banked lanes to Polperro, where they went through the same string of interviews, with the coastguard, the clerk to the harbour commissioners, and the harbour master himself. They toured a pilchard packing establishment where Harmsworth noted the "comely fish-wives" as they packed the fish neatly into barrels for the Italian market.[73]

The next morning, a Friday, they found nothing doing on the fish quay at Looe because bad weather had prevented the boats going out, but visited a couple of building yards before setting off by car for Fowey. There they took lunch but noted there was really little fishing to speak of. They motored on through a fine bright day to the more substantial port of Mevagissey where they were lucky enough to find room at Treloen, a white-fronted boarding house run by a Mrs Blight, right at the top of Polkirt Hill with breathtaking views across the bay below.[74]

On Saturday the weather changed abruptly to rain. They visited the factory of the Cornish Sardine Company to see the process of canning in oil. They motored to the tiny coves of Gorran and Portloe to talk to the fishermen there, who specialised mainly in lobsters and crabs.[75]

Sunday 5 January, which turned out fine and sunny, they spent quietly in Mevagissey. In the morning, they visited Jonathan Barron's sail and net loft at the end of the harbour, and chatted for some time with him and the harbour master. They relaxed in the cliff-top garden at Treloen where the jonquils were already in full bloom. In the evening after dinner, Reynolds strolled with Harmsworth under a starlit sky down to the little sandy cove at Portmellon and up the hill beyond.[76]

On Monday morning, they looked in at the netting factory on the quay before taking Barron's fishing smack, along with Henry Hill of Gorran Haven, through grey windy seas to Falmouth. Next day they took the ferry round St Anthony's Head to Portscatho, where they had a conference with the local people in the long room of the Feathers Inn, followed by a lunch of bread and cheese and beer. Later in the day, Reynolds and Harmsworth together crossed in the ferry to Flushing for a long interview with Mr Solomon, a huge man reputed to be the most skilful and successful fisherman in all Falmouth Harbour.[77]

On 8 January they motored on to Penzance, stopping on the way at Porthleven, the first place they had come to in Cornwall showing evident signs of distress, with all the large mackerel-drifters gone and the fishing in a bad way. They held a meeting with the fishermen there in one of the net lofts. They put up at the Queen's Hotel in Penzance where, in the evening, they had a meeting with Mr Bazeley, the Vice-Chairman of the Cornish Sea Fisheries Committee.[78]

9 January was a day to remember, as the stormy weather was matched by equally stormy meetings with the local fishing interests. They visited Newlyn and Mousehole, going aboard one motor drifter in the harbour of the former and two in the latter, holding long discussions in the forecastles of each. Afterwards, in the harbourmaster's office at Mousehole, there was a violent argument with 20 fishermen, led by Matthias Dunn, the most pugnacious member of the Cornish Fisheries Committee who for months had been leading the charge in favour of motor power. He roundly accused Harmsworth and his committee, and the Board of Agriculture, of mounting a cynical operation designed to spike the pressure for grants for the installation of motors and sweep the whole matter under the carpet. There was much harsh talking and indignation on both sides.[79] Even for Reynolds, who enjoyed a dose of verbal pyrotechnics, it was an encounter he couldn't put out of his mind.

From this moment on the Committee, which had enjoyed a fairly gentle stroll up to now, began to ponder anxiously the evident decay of the Mounts Bay ports they could see all around them. Still a little shaken from the confrontation of the previous day, they spent a quiet Friday morning at Newlyn in a long discussion with the Board's local Collector of Statistics. They took lunch in the refreshment room at Penzance Station before making the short train journey on to St Ives.

There they put up at the Western Hotel in the centre of the town and went down to the quay for a talk with the Board's Collector, Mr Warren. After dinner they had a meeting with old Colonel Williams, the Chairman of the Cornish Fisheries Committee, whom they found friendly and amiable but rather woolly on the subject of his Committee's scheme. His father, a St Ives fisherman, had been taken prisoner in the Napoleonic wars and Colonel Williams proudly showed them his father's release, signed by the Emperor himself. Saturday was dismally wet, and they did little more than hold a further discussion with the Collector and go aboard two fishing boats in the harbour to inspect their motors.[80]

If the encounter with Matthias Dunn at Mousehole – the day they had been openly challenged to show their mettle – had been one defining moment for the Committee, so was the walk they took on Sunday 12 January another. It was as full of emotion, but of a rather more productive kind. The weather had improved, and in the afternoon Reynolds, Harmsworth and Atkinson walked over to Lelant where most of the large St Ives boats were traditionally laid up between seasons. There at dusk on the sand flats of Hayle harbour they met a mournful spectacle – some 80 sail of the once proud St Ives fleet, many of whom would never leave their moorings again.[81]

It was a sight that had stirred all three of them, and Reynolds wrote it up in deliberately colourful vein for the report – the so-called "purple patch" – designed to catch the eye and achieve the maximum of publicity. No Government report has seen such prose, before or since.

> On a grey Sunday afternoon, near about sundown, we walked to Lelant, where the St. Ives boats are laid up. There, on one side of the broad sand and mud flats of Hayle Harbour, we saw a fleet of seventy or eighty boats, mostly luggers, moored up with old chains and rotting ropes to rusty railway lines of the old broad-gauge along a grass-grown quay. In local phrase, they were the St. Ives boats that have died. The unpainted hulls of many were ripe and rotten. On their still standing masts, the running gear, left as it returned from sea for another season that never came, had flapped in the wind till it parted. Only one boat of all the laid-up fleet was being repaired, perhaps not for the St. Ives fishing. The picture of that silent dead boats' graveyard remains vividly in our minds. It impressed upon us, more than all the sometimes contradictory representations we had heard, far more than angry protests, the decline of the West Cornish fisheries. In no light spirit we began our investigations. With a deep sense of the tragedy of the present situation we ended them.[82]

This was the start of Reynolds' special relationship with St Ives, and accounts for his particular joy at the revival of the industry there in the early years of the War, much of it due to his own efforts. But by that time, his special emotion had taken on a human face.

Next day, alternating between rain and fine weather, they took the train to Penzance, and then motored round the southern coves of the Penwith peninsula. They called in at Penberth and Porthgwarra, finding flourishing little communities in both, given over to crabbing and pilchard and grey-mullet seining, despite the lack of harbourage and anchorage. As still today, all boats had to be drawn up the steep and narrow slipways by massive capstans. They ended the day at Sennen where they found the fishermen equally thriving, and lunched at the hotel on the cliff off bread and cheese, pickled onions, walnuts and beer, rounded off in a seasonal manner by cold Christmas pudding and Cornish cream.[83]

At Penzance came the parting of the ways before the final day of the tour – Fremantle and Atkinson made for the Lizard, while Harmsworth and Reynolds headed for Padstow, putting up at the South Western Hotel. There the next day, they interviewed the stationmaster and the Board's Collector, before driving off to Port Isaac where they were surprised by the exposed nature of the beach, the boats being drawn up into the village streets in stormy weather, very much like Sidmouth. It was the last day of the evidence gathering stage. Harmsworth had the night train for London stopped for him at Bodmin Road, leaving Reynolds to find his way home to Sidmouth.[84]

The committee had agreed to leave the writing of the report to Reynolds, not just out of deference to his role as professional writer.[85] They knew that he would demand the largest say as to its contents, and a draft from any other hand would soon find itself in shreds upon the floor. His literary laments now took on a new and unaccustomed flavour: "For the present, being on a Govt. Fishery Committee, I am writing absolutely nothing – except an eternal Report".[86] Harmsworth spent the next Sunday in London at work on the draft and discussed it in the evening over dinner with Henry Maurice. On 24 January he had another long talk over it with Vaughan Nash of the Development Commission, for it was Commission money that was at stake.[87]

There were further meetings of the Committee in London at the end of January. All three members were united in acceding to both the Devon and Cornwall applications, and agreed to recommend a Government loan of £3,000 in each case to establish a system of credit banking. But Harmsworth and Fremantle had been so struck by the urgency of the needs of West Cornwall that they favoured an allocation of an additional £4,000 to St Ives and the Mounts Bay ports in order to make money available more quickly there. Reynolds was totally opposed to this additional recommendation; he saw it as a hopeless gesture – merely throwing money at the problem without any sense or direction. He feared that a naive approach of this kind would undermine the necessarily slow process of building co-operation and a viable system of credit banking.

He failed to argue the other members round, but expressed his determination to hold out for a minority report. Not getting Reynolds fully in line would be a certain source of embarrassment to the Government. At the same time he was resisting other efforts to get him to join a wider Departmental Committee just set up by the Board to look at the problem of the inshore fisheries on a national canvas. At the end of January, a harassed but determined Reynolds wrote from London to a rather sickly Bob in Sidmouth:

> I'm so sorry to hear from Tom that you are bad. He says you look worse than he does. We don't seem to have had any luck at all since I've been on this damn'd Fishery job, do we? I've had a feeling for a long time that our luck stops short when we work separately, and not all together. There 'tis, however. I expect I shall soon get shot out of this job now, and it doesn't look like doing much more for them, as I am now fighting them for all I'm worth, both over that bloody silly Departmental Committee and over our report. I am to see Runciman, the Minister for Agriculture and Fisheries, at the House of Commons on Monday, and I suppose he, too, will try to win me over from sending in a minority report of my own. But he won't. They don't want a minority report, but they'll have to have one, whether or no.[88]

On 17 February the Committee met in London for the last time to take the final decisions on their recommendations, and Reynolds finally won his minority report.[89] In the rush for trains at the end of the meeting, he failed to thank Harmsworth as he would have wished; but made up for it the next day.

> In our hurry yesterday, we ended up all of a straggle, so to speak.... I've got to thank you – and do, very much – for making our Inquiry pleasant for me. Indeed, you made it possible to go through with it, when every damn thing everywhere was going wrong, and I felt like a bottleful of sour worry. Likewise, your hospitalities – which I'm afraid I accepted shamelessly, without hope of returning them – were like hot grogs of a frosty night, picking herrings out of the nets, in the boredom of London.[90]

Harmsworth had helped him through his lowest moments that winter, from Tom's illness downwards, and another father-son relationship was now pretty firmly in the making.

It was another couple of months before the final report was finally put to bed, and Reynolds placed himself voluntarily in charge of production. He could never keep his fingers out of the publishing process and was never short of advice for his colleagues. He had words for the drafter who let his text run away with him: "Forgive me saying this. If I were an editor and you a prospective contributor, I should say 'Rewrite in one page' and you would too!"[91] He had words for Harmsworth's attempts to sanitise his most expressive passages: "Discretion is, no doubt, the better part of valour, but it's death to style, as Government reports without exception testify."[92]

He had also taken on himself the burdensome task of detailing the harbourage problems of all the beach ports they had visited, a sort of potted itinerary which became Appendix V to the report. By 6 April, even that was almost complete and he was able to sign off the report with Henry Maurice. "The Devon and Cornish *Itinerary* is nearly done – ass that I was to suggest so huge a piece of work, though I think it will prove useful! And the whole of the publishable Report is finished and proof-corrected so far as I am concerned."[93]

It was published in the middle of April, a relatively short report of 16 foolscap pages but with numerous appendices to back up the arguments. The applications of both the Devon and Cornish Fisheries Committees were recommended for approval, with extra money suggested for experiments in installing motor power in the various classes of Brixham trawler (a problem the Committee had still not quite got its head round) and in providing urgent assistance to the West Cornwall ports. Reynolds' minority note rejected the idea of parachuting in a full system of credit banking before there had been time to prepare the ground – "by no advisable means can its pace be forced. To press it to failure would be disastrous" – but held out for a time-limited experiment which would supply urgent loans direct to the fishermen most in need.[94]

On the wider issues, the Committee had performed a valuable service in drawing attention to the need for new and improved harbour construction in many ports – every bit as urgent as the installation of motor power. But on the broader terms of reference which Reynolds had fought so hard to achieve at the outset, it confined itself disappointingly to a very short summary made up of a few general suggestions.[95] It argued that the urgency of the Devon and Cornwall applications forbad delaying the report for a long dissertation on issues such as co-operation, but in reality the appointment of the Departmental Committee two months before to look at the national issues had effectively taken the matters out of its hands.

But it did, nevertheless, make three suggestions that were to have a far-reaching influence on future longshore policy: the creation of an inshore fisheries section within the Fisheries Division; the establishment of an Inshore Fisheries Association, on the lines of the Agricultural Organisation Society, to oversee effective co-operation; and the need for further Development Commission aid for promoting co-operation and practical experimental work.[96]

In addition to the minority note and the "purple patch", Reynolds' thumbprint is everywhere apparent. This, on the rivalry between East and West Cornwall: "The Western Cornishmen, with their pride in their big deep-sea boats, describe the East Cornishmen as 'fishers in their own puddle'. At all events, the East Cornishmen have succeeded in fishing a living out of their puddle, and it is possible that the Western Cornishmen will sooner or later be driven to withdraw from competition with steam, and to develop in smaller boats the mixed and shell fishing resources of *their* puddles."[97] This, on the incidental causes of fisheries decline which human hand cannot remedy: "Shoals of fish, for example, cannot be brought back to a coast they have forsaken, though they may come back of themselves, and sometimes it is possible, in suitable boats, to track them to their new grounds. Fish, in any case, are not amenable to State aid."[98]

But, much to his pleasure, it was the purple patch that caught the public eye. Almost every paper quoted it, some in full. It had been a deliberate piece of media manipulation, as Reynolds explained to Cecil Harmsworth. "We are getting a devil of a big 'press', and practically every paper quotes the patch. And observe the power of the patch.... They seized on it, as I calculated they would; but they naturally couldn't quote only that, and needed, if they used it, to give it a setting of weightier stuff (the *Mail* had another half-column that same day further on in the paper); so accordingly the Report and the subject have got a publicity of columns where they would only have got paragraphs otherwise. The *Express* was very funny the same day. 'Most tragic passage ever in a Blue Book....' and so forth!"[99]

Reynolds had milked the publicity with some aplomb. Now he was doing it from an unaccustomed position with the organs of state on his side. The Committee had been for him a smooth introduction to his new role close to the seats of power. It had broadened his appreciation of tactical political in-fighting and the enigmatic process of decision making. It had also, through the intensive tours of Devon and Cornwall, given him a deeper understanding of the complexity of inshore fishery issues than he could ever have gleaned from his little corner of south-east Devon. The western fisheries expert of the Great War was now truly in the making. He would look back with nostalgia on these happy days of his apprenticeship.

On 20 June 1913 Reynolds went down for the first time to Magdalen House at Henley as Harmsworth's weekend guest. It was an idyllic spot for relaxation after a weary week of work. On the Sunday Reynolds was up early for a swim in the river with Cecil and the children. Afterwards it was all hands to the strawberry bed in the back garden. They played in and on the edge of the river for most of the day, finishing with a row up to Hambleden in the skiff to see the weir and the miller's garden.[100]

The day before had been another perfect fresh June day. Harmsworth took Reynolds and a fellow guest, Herbert Craig, by car to Newbury on a fishing expedition. He had his own special spot on the River Lambourn, where he often went with Henry Maurice, amidst meadows tangled with ragged robin, yellow iris and purple orchis, and hedges bursting with dog roses. Craig and Harmsworth fished vigorously until the rise failed early in the afternoon and caught a mere one-and-a-half brace.

Reynolds had graduated from the rod and line of his youth, and now liked to pretend he was above such things. He elected to doze stretched out on a little plank bridge which crossed the stream, and in the intervals of wakefulness composed a nostalgic midsummer sonnet in honour of his host.[101] He reported this unexpected re-emergence of the Muse enthusiastically to George Macmillan. "Didn't get home till yesterday after a most delightfully restful weekend with Cecil Harmsworth fishing near Newbury and lounging about the river at Henley. Only I didn't fish; the Kennet valley was altogether too lovely to kill trout in. So I snoozed full-length on a plank bridge across the river (the only dry place) and wrote a sonnet!"[102]

To CECIL HARMSWORTH
21: VI: 13

'TWAS strenuous days we spent on Devon's coast,
 Hearing of fish gone, strayed to other seas,
 And humbugs begging with half-bended knees
For aid – the fishers' poverty their boast!
And down along the Cornish coves where most
 They fight the waves with land-sharks on their lee,
 And Mathias* with "gross impropriety"
Did snarl untruths, and cuss us, tho' our host.
To-day you've brought me to a lush-grown river field,
 Where yellow-flags and orchis strew the grass,
And while upon the banks your rod you wield,
 I'm full content to let the minutes pass;
Happy – I thank you – in earth's happiness,
I will not try to make your trout the less.[103]

Harmsworth queried the length of line nine. Reynolds pleaded a noble precedent. Shakespeare had often done the same.[104]

*Mathias Dunn, member of the Cornish Sea Fisheries Committee, who took us to Mousehole, and was very disagreeable there.

SEVENTEEN

Development Commission 1913–14

On 27 January 1913, Runciman set up a new Departmental Committee, under the chairmanship of Sir Stafford Howard, a junior minister in Gladstone's third Government whose political career had ended there, to pick up where the Devon and Cornwall Inquiry had left off and address the problem on a national scale. It was given the all-embracing terms of reference that Reynolds had fought so hard for for the Cornish Committee: "to inquire into the present condition of the Inshore Fisheries, and to advise the Board as to the steps which could with advantage be taken for their preservation and development".[1] At this stage eleven members had been appointed from among the great and the good, including, crucially, Cecil Harmsworth.

From the outset, Reynolds seems to have taken against "that bloody silly Departmental Committee" and the whole proceeding.[2] He refused outright the invitation from Runciman to join it. The reservations were probably an assorted mixture. He was still in the process of drafting the report of the Cornish Committee, and he saw that as the vehicle for driving future policy. Moreover, a further committee might hold up the urgent action that was needed in West Cornwall. Above all, an unwieldy committee a dozen strong, consisting of four knights of the realm and four Members of Parliament – the usual sprinkling of amateurs – would not be easy to manipulate, and all the good work of the previous four months might now start to unravel.

On 3 February, Reynolds met Runciman in his room in the House of Commons to discuss his minority contribution to the Cornish report and his attitude to the new Committee.[3] He held his ground on both issues, but this was the start of the softening up process. The Board of Agriculture knew that without Reynolds the new Committee could carry no conviction. A little further arm-twisting by Henry Maurice did the trick and on 7 February his appointment was formally made. He left open a personal escape route. If the Committee consumed all his time and his earnings, he would have to resign.[4]

Just as his appointment to the Cornish Committee had led to a protest from Francis Mildmay, so did this new appointment arouse some unpleasantness – this time in the *Evening Standard*. On 24 February, it furnished its readers with this rather snide piece of work.

> The numerous admirers of Mr Stephen Reynolds will congratulate him on his appointment to the Departmental Fisheries Committee. The committee is also to be congratulated, for the author of "The Poor Man's House" [*sic*], "How 'Twas" and other books is an authority on the life of

> the fisherman. Mr Reynolds has been living with the fisher-folk of Sidmouth for six or seven years. He and the brothers Woolley formed a little company; when the company wrote a book, Mr Reynolds was the senior partner. When it fished, he was the junior. Now he is dissolving partnership, and in time, we fear, he will come to forget the point of view he so nearly made his own. Has he tired of the simple life of fisher-folk, or did he always regard it as but a stepping-stone to administrative work? That is what makes us fearful of taking "simple life" advocates seriously; they always come round to our way of thinking before we have time to come round to theirs.[5]

Not just the reference to the "simple life", the whole piece touched a raw nerve. His administrative work was entirely in tune with the life he had lived at Sidmouth – it was to pay back his fisher friends for all their help to him. But at the same time, he was only too well aware that it was taking him physically further and further away from the old life with Bob and Tom.

But he managed to suppress his irritation and, with a little more dignity and less emotion than usual, he sent a simple refutation to the Editor. "That is what the writer of your note surmised. Allow me, therefore, to say that it is wrong, both as a statement of fact and inferentially. Such partnership as has existed is not dissolved because it extends or otherwise modifies its activities, nor, I trust, am I likely to forget the point of view of the people with whom I continue to live. And as to coming round to your way of thinking – why, Heaven forbid!"[6]

The Inshore Fisheries Committee met for the first time on 14 February at Winchester House in St James' Square, which had formed the palace of the Bishops of Winchester in the middle years of the nineteenth century until taken over by the War Office in 1876.[7] This first meeting was taken up with plotting the plan of campaign – who to call to give evidence, where to visit, the division into sub-committees to specialise on particular geographical areas. Harmsworth was appointed chairman of the south and south-east sub-committee, ranging from north Norfolk to west Dorset. Reynolds steered clear of the sub-committees altogether. He had learnt from the Devon and Cornwall Inquiry how much time touring could consume.

The Committee met again from 11 to 4 on 12 March at Winchester House, its first session for taking evidence, and then on most Wednesdays thereafter. For Reynolds, not the most patient observer of bureaucratic nit-picking, it got off to a bad start The whole of the first morning was given over to a discussion of how to define "inshore" fisheries, whether by distance from the coast, depth of the sea, characteristics of fishermen, size of boat. As lunch was approaching, Reynolds could restrain himself no longer: "I think we are literally trying to define the indefinable, instead of merely cutting the line somewhere where we think it should be".[8] The Committee came speedily to the decision to abandon the search for a watertight definition.

Reynolds attended the first five evidence days and took a very active part in proceedings, drawing out from witnesses support for his pet theses – the advantages of co-operation, the failure of the fisheries committees to represent the local fishermen, the pointlessness of the local bye-laws, especially as regards prohibition of undersize catches.

Throughout he was relatively tolerant and well-behaved. But Cecil Harmsworth knew he could be otherwise: "Stephen possessed a fine temper of his own; and many times I have known his wrath blaze out uncontrollably against people who presumed to patronize fishermen or, having some sort of authority over them, exercised it without knowledge or sympathy."[9] Thus when a witness was so foolish as to talk the fishermen down, a furious Reynolds was soon biting at his ankles.

As happened to the unsuspecting Mr St Barbe, the solicitor Clerk to the Southern Local Fisheries Committee, under cross-examination by Mr Bostock.

> Bostock: Are the fishermen able to know the market price of fish, and, if not, would the extension of the telephone do any good to them; are they able to use any telephones to check the market price?
> St Barbe: It might be so. The fisherman you know, as a class, is a very difficult man to help, if you understand me.
> Bostock: I know.
> St Barbe: He is the most conservative creature under the sun. A fisherman does as his grandfather did before him; he likes going on as his people did before him; he has got no idea of improving his lot or having it improved for him.
> Bostock: He would have to have a good deal of education before he combined with his fellows?
> St Barbe: I think so. And, curiously enough, they are marvellously suspicious. It is very difficult, indeed, to get any particulars at all as to the values of catches anywhere. If the fishermen are making a particularly good thing in any one corner, and our Fishery Officer gets hold of it, he is always enjoined not to make use of it.
> SR: Can you suggest any reason why he should not want the information given away? If you found a hundred law cases in one corner you would not like an announcement made of it, which might bring down a dozen solicitors from London to share the corner with you. There would be local objections if London solicitors were hired to come down for all these legal and official jobs which are going in the provinces.
> St Barbe: If I had a £100 job I have not the least objection to 40 London solicitors coming after it, if I have got it.
> SR: Because you are going to keep it, but then, you cannot keep the fishing in that way.
> St Barbe: Certainly.[10]

Following the second evidence meeting there was a two-week Easter break in which he had hoped to catch up on his writing – his book on psycho-economics was still awaiting its first sentence. But he found that, as in the previous winter, the committee work had entirely disabled him for writing. He went up to London on 1 April for the third session next day wondering how much longer he could go on.

The main witness over the first three evidence days of the Committee was Richard Martyr, the 55-year old Principal and Head of Branch in the Fisheries Division. He had joined the Board of Trade as a Clerk in 1873, and had moved with the five other members of the Fisheries Division to the Board of Agriculture during the 1903 take-over. His knowledge of fisheries administration stretched well back into the nineteenth century and Maurice had thankfully left it to him, as the best equipped, to give evidence on behalf of the Board.

Reynolds knew him well as a colleague, respected his erudition on past Acts and policies, but could not resist on occasion a little teasing of the civil servant in him. On this third day, there was an undeniable note of pleasure as he put him to the test. First, on the composition of the fisheries committees.

> SR: Is it not the case that what you might call the practical fishing people on the present Sea Fisheries Committees are very largely fish-buyers themselves. On looking through the lists of counties one knows, it seems to occur to me, that they are sea fishermen who no longer go to sea, and have taken to fish-buying – people like that?
> Martyr: I do not think the majority of the members of the local Fisheries Committee are fish dealers or fish merchants.
> SR: I do not mean the majority. I mean the people who represent what you might call the practical fishing interest, because one knows the majority does not represent fishing at all.

Martyr decides to kill him with statistics.

> Martyr: Of the 162 Fishery Members appointed by the Board of Agriculture and Fisheries on the local committees, 57 are representatives of fishermen; 41 are fishermen, and fishermen who are also boat-owners; 26 are smack and trawl owners; 14 fish merchants, curers etc.; 7 representatives of oyster fisheries; 17 representatives of owners of fisheries.

Reynolds is more than a match for him.

> SR: Then you are not aware, officially, that a considerable number of the men in those lists who come as fishermen are in reality fish-buyers who have been fishermen?
> Martyr: No.

SR: But you would agree that a fish-buying man would have a much better chance of attending the meetings of the Committee than a sea-going fisherman?
Martyr: Quite so.
SR: Would you anticipate that the Sea Fisheries Committees would be a proper body to work a co-operative scheme, having for one of its purposes the reduction of middleman's profits?
Martyr: Not under their present organisation.
SR: You would not?
Martyr: No.[11]

His technique of cross-examination had come a long way since the full day he had spent in the first shingle inquiry of 1908.

They then locked horns over the effectiveness of the inshore bye-laws for protecting undersized fish when large trawlers could sweep up as much as they liked outside the three mile limit.

SR: Do you agree that this question of policing is much more complicated than it appears to be to the merely prohibitory person? For example, the word "policing" sounds to be an easy affair, but is this a question of policing the inshore waters, or of policing the inshore waters as against the extra-territorial waters?
Martyr: Efficient enforcement of Bye-laws, perhaps, would be a happier term.
SR: Then, in the case of the efficient enforcement of Bye-laws, which only applies now to territorial waters, I take it that the intention of this policing is to preserve the fish, to add to the fish supply, the main intention of it?
Martyr: To protect the stock of fish.
SR: That is to say, to add to the fish supply. For what other reason would the fish be protected but to add to the fish supply, or to prevent it decreasing?
Martyr: That is so.
SR: Then, in the case of the two sorts of policing, the policing of the inshore waters as against the extra territorial vessels – the deep-sea vessels – and the policing of the inshore waters themselves, you would agree that, if the policing of the inshore waters as against the deep-sea boats were properly efficient, it would do more to preserve the fish than all the policing of the inshore waters which would take place, if that were efficient?
Martyr: Yes, as regards large trawlers, but I do not mean to infer that if districts were efficiently policed against large deep-sea boats there would be no necessity for policing or enforcing the other Bye-laws.
SR: The effect of my question really is that in enforcing the Bye-laws – with all this talk about policing in the purely inshore waters, and not

enforcing it outside the inshore waters, because you cannot – are you not rather straining at a gnat and swallowing a camel? For instance, I see in a *précis* we have got here to-day of another witness a complaint about the landing of crabs caught by people who fish outside, and not by inshore people, and one hears complaints on the East Coast of the steamers catching a tremendous lot of crabs that ought not to be caught and taking them in. There is no policing against that?
Martyr: No; it may be found desirable to have regulations with regard to methods of taking fish outside territorial waters, but that can only be done by International agreement.
SR: Yes, exactly. Then, my inference is that you are slapping the small boy because he is not a big one, so to speak?
Martyr: No, I think your point arises in connection with big boats and the mesh of trawl nets, for instance. I do not think, if you will allow me to say so, that your point arises with regard to the other Bye-laws. You would still want some regulations for the inshore fisheries.
SR: Yes, I am not trying to get the admission that one wants absolutely no regulations.
Martyr: I understood you in that sense.
SR: I am trying to get the admission that the regulation is not in point of fact effective.
Martyr: No, I cannot admit that.[12]

They had a little brush on the Board's statistics of catches.

SR: Does the Board regard these statistics as moderately accurate?
Martyr: Yes.
SR: Kicking about the coast one finds that one gets to accept their accuracy in the widest manner possible...... The provisions for collecting the figures in the smaller ports being worse than they are in those big ports, the statistics will under-estimate the importance of the inshore fisheries rather than over-estimate it. They will give a wrong impression; they will give an impression that the inshore fisheries are less important than they are, I take it?
Martyr: I do not say that.
SR: I mean you have those big ports where they have means of getting at the number of fish landed, and you have small ports where they have not. It is all very well, of course, for the Board to send round inspectors, and statistical collectors; one does not tell an inspector or collector how many one has caught, and I think that rule will be followed by inshore fishermen on every possible occasion. In that case, the statistics for the inshore fisheries will appear to be less than they really were, and their importance lessened?
Martyr: No; take the case of a small fishing station, the collector may be

the Coastguard officer. When he sees the boat come in he goes down and takes a note of the fish landed.
SR: What he actually says is, "They pay me £2 or £3 a year for doing this work; they are always piling papers on me, and I am not going to do the job for them". He goes down, has a drink, asks how many herrings came in to-day, they tell him 2 tons, and he goes and puts that down, and that is the Board's statistics.[13]

Towards the end of this witness's evidence, Reynolds raised the most delicate question of all – the experience and competence of the staff of the Fisheries Division. Were they fit to take on the extra, more constructive, work that was now needed of them? Though the Division had expanded since 1903 from 6 to 32, the combination of a new and dynamic Minister and a new and dynamic Assistant Secretary was now putting the staff under more pressure than ever. After almost three days of gruelling questioning, Martyr now took the chance to live up to his name.

SR: You would advocate powers to do more constructive work?
Martyr: Quite so.
SR: Is the division short-handed?
Martyr: Yes, short-handed and over-worked; I am here against the advice of my doctor.
SR: I am sorry to bother you so much then. There is another question arising out of that. I want you to understand before I ask you, that it implies absolutely nothing derogatory to the staff. How many of the staff are conversant with the working details of inshore fishing? I do not mean by making inspections, because I should like to point out that in dealing with these small fisheries, I take it it is more important to be conversant with the working details than it is with the big fishings, in order to judge the situations in various ports. How many of the staff would be described as conversant with the working details of inshore fishing?
Martyr: It is hardly a fair question to ask me. I must get your exact meaning; do you mean how many of the technical staff, the Inspector's staff, including clerks?
SR: Including the clerks; the scientific staff. One knows they are acquainted with the details of deep-sea fishing, some of them.
Martyr: We are short-handed with regard to Inspectors; we have vacancies for two Assistant Inspectors.
SR: I asked that question because in reports of the Board, which I have been privileged to read in the course of fishery work, I have found that gentlemen who have been round have had their legs very badly pulled at times. If they had been acquainted with the details of inshore fishing, I think they would not have had their legs pulled. In that sense it strikes me as rather important.

> Martyr: They are conversant with the work. There is this that may be said: we have been so short-handed in the past, and there has been such a pressure of work, that the Inspectors have not been able to visit the small fishing stations so frequently.
> SR: The point of my question is, in fact, that they have not had the chance of becoming conversant with these details.
> Martyr: You must not take my answer as admitting that; we have not a full staff, and the existing officers have been so pressed with work that they have not been round the coast as much as their duties require.[14]

Reynolds revelled in this kind of exchange, particularly when his interlocutor was capable of standing up to him. He reported afterwards to Henry Maurice: "Mr. Martyr and I had some diverting passes o' pate, but not, as I trust he understands, in cross-examinational enmity".[15]

But three days of taking evidence in London, and particularly the barren Easter break when he could get no writing done, had convinced him that he could not continue with the Committee and survive. Not for the first time in his life, he had taken on a job he was unable to carry through for more than a few weeks.

When he got home to Sidmouth after the meeting of 2 April and tried once again to start the first chapter of his psycho-economics book, the gathering doubts all came to a head and he decided definitely to quit. That weekend he wrote a formal letter to Runciman to explain that his writing and the Committee could not comfortably co-habit.

> A meeting in London takes three days out of the week, and what I hoped was, that by literary work on the other four days, I might earn enough to live along on.
> Unfortunately, I find it absolutely impossible to throw fishery affairs straight out of my mind and to get into the stride of writing within four days, between two journeys to London, and I am able to do no writing whatever; nor for that matter, have been able to do any during the last six months. Fishery communications, all requiring attention, all calculated to divert and unconcentrate one's mind, come tumbling on my head by every other post. Nevertheless, I have to get started somehow a book which is designed to be (in publisher's phrase) my most important, and which will require very concentrated work. I had hoped, as I say, to get it done in the intervals of fishery business, but I can't even get it begun, let alone done. Moreover, I have been now on the Departmental Committee long enough to see that the work of it, to be done properly, would need much more than three days' attention a week, and I would rather not do it at all than scamp it.
> You will, I am afraid, regard me as a sort of conger eel that gets hauled into the boat on one side and wriggles out over the other; and I do blame

> myself for my error of judgment in thinking I could do more than, in fact, I can do. I might have known, but the wish was father to the thought. Obviously, however, if I let myself go broke, I can be of no use to myself or anybody else.[16]

He wrote to Maurice an even more explicit letter of apology for having to break his personal undertaking to join the Committee.

> Anyhow, I'm very sorry; I would have liked to have done much more. But it can't be helped. When I saw you, I meant to *compel* myself to write in the intervals, and I trust it's not a deadly sin to be willing to do more than one can. However, it's no go; I can't sandwich writing in with official fishery business; my brains go on strike against more than one thing at a time. Brains can be coerced to affairs, but not into the peculiar state in which they will write – write stuff worth writing, I mean. Which means I can't earn. Which means, if I can't earn, that soon I should be powerless to do anything at all for anything I'm keen on.
> During the Easter fortnight, I tried my hardest to force myself, but succeeded in doing nothing except make myself miserable and ill – and smoke-fuddled. It was like trying to start a motor speed test in, say, Oxford Street at noon: one could not see one's mental course for the traffic in the way, buzzing about one. Better, therefore, to face the fact promptly than late; particularly as the Committee is visibly dividing itself into two essentially antagonistic camps. Better to drop it altogether than to fail for lack of time to keep what I regard as the fishermen's end up properly.

He ended, in typical Reynolds fashion, with the simple personal disclaimer that even the most hostile correspondent found irresistible.

> This is a letter to you personally, and is not meant for the Board's entertaining files. If you wish, you can have a corresponding highly proper letter for them. I am under the impression that you have, as they say, borne rather well with me and my botherations, and I'm sure I thank you for it. A man with half a dozen irons to keep hot, and short of coals for the fire into the bargain, is not, I know, very easy to deal with compared with men whose sole business is the matter in hand. Nor, I suppose, is the notorious literary temperament easy to deal with; but it's worse to live with, and I'm damn'd if 'tisn't worse still to possess.

But he wanted too to assure Maurice that this was not the end of his involvement in central fisheries policy. "Not, you understand, that I mean to throw up Inshore Fisheries. I shall continue to do what I can do, and I hope I shall call on you and discuss things from time to time. We hope, too, that we shall see you down here again." Nor was it quite the end of his interest in the Committee. "I am proposing to come up Tuesday (Horrex's Hotel as usual) for next Wednesday's meeting; there are one or two points I want to leave behind me on the Committee's records."[17]

He did, in fact, attend the next two meetings on 9 and 16 April. The point he wanted especially to rub home was the lack of competition among the fish-buyers which condemned fishermen to starvation prices. Typical is this exchange on 16 April with Edward Page, the Chief Fishery Officer of the Sussex Committee.

> SR: In these places where you have fish buyers, is there much competition between them?
> Page: As far as I know, it is all open competition.
> SR: I know it is always open competition so far as anybody can see looking from the outside of it; I was asking you a question about the inside of it.
> Page: It is impossible for me to deal with that.[18]

He attended no more meetings of the Committee that spring and summer, but his position on it remained unresolved. Remembering the way they had managed to cajole him on to the Harmsworth Committee the previous autumn after his earlier point-blank refusal, Maurice and the Board now played a waiting game. While refusing formally to accept his resignation, they tried at the same time to contrive some official source of income for him which would overcome the financial problem.

Even Aunt Jane now came forward with an offer of money which once more he felt bound to refuse. He told her of the machinations at the Board.

> I am having some amusing negotiations with Runciman and the Board of Fisheries. They don't want me to go, and have suggested I should take an inspectorship. I've told them that I don't want a salary and won't undertake to work like a civil servant; but would consider a commissionership paid by the days given up to it and leaving me free to work at my own time. So there the matter stands – pull dog, pull devil – me being the devil, I'm afraid.
> Your offer at the end of your letter – if you and Auntie Allie could be of any use – is more than kind, and I don't the less appreciate it because I hope I shall never be ground down to taking advantage of it. As a matter of fact, I could more or less have lived on other people for the past several years, but I feel in the matter rather like fishermen: that if I ceased to live on my own, or what I earned, I should soon become totally demoralised. Writing stuff that's any good is such a labour and pain that I don't believe I should ever do it if I hadn't got to.[19]

Here he hit the nail on the head. The issue was not whether he would swallow his pride and take the money, from the Board or anybody else; nor was it, in any case, merely a matter of money. His writing was still, even in these days, at the emotional centre of his life, and any paid job which did not give him the time and intellectual space to keep writing was out of the question. But it had also to be a job of influence; he was not prepared to take a routine post in the bowels of the Whitehall machine – the administrative equivalent of potboiling. "What I'm always after is a hand on the inshore fishery steering wheel. For that, I'm prepared in some measure to spoil my literary career – to hang it up even for a time is to risk it – but not to spoil for garbage work."[20]

The "steering wheel" was firmly in the hands of the Board of Agriculture and Fisheries. But there was a new administrative power boat coming up fast on its stern – the Development Commission with Vaughan Nash at the wheel – which might in the end prove faster and easier to board.

The Development Commission had been established under the Development and Road Improvement Funds Act of 1909 to provide development aid to the rural economy. Originally its emphasis was on scientific research in agriculture, but its terms of reference also included the promotion of fisheries and the improvement of road transport and harbours. It came into working operation in 1910 but was still an infant body, finding its feet and investigating its powers, when in February 1912 Vaughan Nash was appointed Vice-Chairman at the head of its administration. He was to prove instrumental in creating the powerful body it was to become.

It was in many ways a chance appointment, but one which stuck. Nash, who was then 50, had started his career in journalism. In 1893 he joined the editorial staff of the *Daily Chronicle* where he remained under Massingham until 1899 when both resigned over their pro-Boer views. In 1900 he was sent to India to cover the great famine for the *Manchester Guardian*, and on return in 1901 moved to the *Daily News* under A.G. Gardiner. An established London journalist, his special talents were well known in the political world and, with the Liberal landslide of 1906, he became private secretary to the next two Prime Ministers, Campbell-Bannerman and Asquith.

Six years at No 10 had given him unparalleled experience of politicians and the workings of Government. As Assistant Private Secretary, and then as Principal Private Secretary in succession to Ponsonby, he had carried much of the personal burden of looking after Campbell-Bannerman during the recurring heart-attacks of his last few months in office, and had played no small part in the delicate undertaking of persuading him to resign.

He had also walked, or rather sat, with Kings – to wit, the cheery and informal monarch that was Edward VII. In April 1908 he reported to his old boss Ponsonby a typical encounter with the King at No.10, on his return from Biarritz after Campbell-Bannerman's resignation.

> The monarch came without a word of warning and sat in your old chair, nearly knocking the bottom out of it (it was already beginning to go) and I talked to him as fearlessly as I could, remembering your maxim. He was extremely jolly though I had to fend him off from going upstairs to see Sir H. [*Campbell-Bannerman*]. He congratulated me with his own Royal lips and laughed very much at Robertson being made a peer. I expect you will be hearing what he really thinks about the way the resignation took place. One thing I told him was that if it had been put off till now it wouldn't have been done at all, which seemed to impress him. I know you like hearing all the talk of crowned heads...... [21]

It was something of a leap from these dizzy heights to the administrative chair of the Development Commission. Originally, a career in the Civil Service could not have been further from Nash's thoughts. When in 1906 Ponsonby had offered to find him a permanent post outside No.10, the response was plain: "Thanks for what you say about finding me something; but if the worst comes to the worst, I can always fall back on scribbling, and I don't believe any official work would be possible for me or I for it".[22]

But the six years at No.10 had either seduced him or unfitted him for anything else. When in early 1912 he had at last to move, he was eyeing with interest another job about to fall vacant and was rather shocked by his interim posting to the Development Commission. "As you may have seen from the papers, things have gone rather differently from what I expected, and I am to go to the Development Commission for the time being. They couldn't do a shuffle for Elliott at the moment but I hope they may later on, as 'Develing' will be rather too tranquil for me."[23]

Even more than he had anticipated. He was not the first bright star from a Private Office to find himself on promotion brought very much down to earth. From behind the unaccustomed desk in the quiet of the Commission's offices in Queen Anne's Chambers, he bemoaned his new fate to Arthur Ponsonby. "Behold my new address. Come and see me. No messengers or other formalities to frighten you. I am quite accessible...... I can't tell you how queer it feels here. There is precious little to do that I can find but I suppose one will be able to make something. I am browsing on reports at present...... "[24]

And make something of it he did, for the next seventeen years. Soon after his appointment he became entangled in the problems posed by the fishery applications to the Commission and many days of 1912 found him holed up in meetings with Henry Maurice trying to concert a Government line – often of procrastination.[25] The Devon and Cornwall Inquiry brought him for the first time within the purview of Reynolds, for it was the task of that Committee, though formally reporting to Runciman, in essence to tender advice to the Commission. Personally, Reynolds got on well with him. They had writing and journalism in common, and in their approach to the task in hand brought none of the impeding official baggage of the career civil servants.

On 7 May 1913, with Nash sitting as Vice-Chairman, the Commission met to discuss the report of the Devon and Cornwall Inquiry forwarded by the Board of Agriculture. Most of the discussion turned on the urgency of the problem in West Cornwall which had received so much public attention, and on the conclusions Reynolds had reached in his minority note – the desirability of making direct loans to fishermen pending the more careful establishment of a system of mutual credit. The Commission was impressed by Reynolds' arguments and appointed Nash to confer with him on the best way of implementing his provisional scheme and organising, as an experiment, societies based on a mutual credit system.[26]

This decision to ignore the majority recommendations of the Harmsworth report fully vindicated Reynolds in his struggle that winter to hold out against the Board of Agriculture for his minority views, and he now found himself, like it or not, fully drawn into the creation of Commission policy. He was delighted, after the grudging attitude of the Board, by this sudden and unexpected endorsement. He told Harold Wright: "Apparently they've gone all the bundle on me, which so far is admirable, because what I'm playing for, of course, is virtual control of the Inshore Fisheries. For that, *and only for that,* I am prepared to sink to some degree my literary work".[27]

On 26 May Reynolds went up to Town to confer with Nash, and an official from the Board (almost certainly Henry Maurice) before the Commission's next meeting two days later. Discussion ranged not just over Reynolds' scheme for provisional assistance, but also Reynolds' own part in the scheme. Inevitably Nash wanted him to play the guiding role at the Commission, but since it was the Board that held executive responsibility for implementing fisheries policy, Maurice insisted that he should be employed by the Board, and only act or give advice within the parameters of Board policy. This was no mere constitutional nicety. Maurice clearly had visions, well justified on past experience, of an unrestrained Reynolds rushing off to create *de facto* policy on the ground on behalf of a body that had no executive responsibility in the matter whatsoever.

For Reynolds this was just a senseless and irritating Whitehall turf war, hours of argument and nothing done. He was particularly galled by the Board's attitude that he, although not a Board employee as such, should toe the party line in public. Back in Sidmouth, he penned a hurried letter to Nash, threatening initially to take the ball away, but finally coming round to a concrete proposition for by-passing the Board of Agriculture.

> I wanted to write between yesterday's three-cornered discussion and your meeting of to-morrow. I can't help saying that the discussion left rather a mixed flavour in my mind – such that I felt not disinclined to kick the whole thing overboard and continue to act purely on my own in the press and elsewhere. I am, in fact, and at least, rather inclined to think

> that if your D.C. is at all likely to go off on its own to some extent, and does want to use me as its representative, that it might in the end be better for it to employ me on its own. Then I should at any rate be more free. For, if there is really any intention to improve the Inshore Fisheries, it would, it seems to me, be very false economy to shut me up on the subject in print. For my own part, I haven't the slightest intention of confining my speech to "the Board's declared policy" unless my status with regard to it was such that I had a good deal to do with the framing of the said policy. And that doesn't seem very probable. Put very baldly, the price of shutting me up is a good dose of my own way. Why not? I was on the subject long before they noticed its existence; and if I am to continue putting my knowledge at the disposal of *their* way, I don't propose to be shut up too.
>
> I imagine, on the other hand, that the D.C. requires no such strict reticence, seeing it has on it, in the person of Sidney Webb, a man responsible for a journal which is bound to express opinions on Development Commission subjects.
>
> Isn't it possible, since you are framing committees, that by acting as your representative upon them, I might, indirectly, but effectively, exercise the executive powers which your Commission is unable directly to confer, without need of obtaining executive powers from the Board?[28]

He had promised Nash a rough outline of his proposed West Cornwall scheme to take to the Commission meeting the following day, but immediately on his return from London Sidmouth life, with its inescapable realities, had intervened. There had been no time to sketch out the scheme. Reading his explanation, Nash caught a glimpse for the first time inside the strange domestic life of this extraordinary new colleague.

> 'Tis a life o' it! I got stopped in my cab on the way down from station to pack a catch of mackerel; rushed into my dirtiest fishing rig; and have been counting, carrying, icing, mailing, tallying, and generally on the furious rush ever since; sweating in streams for mackerel that will probably bust this thundery night on their way to Portsmouth! One day's absence, and all my packing gear, etc., is God knows where. One has simply to curse order and organisation into existence each time there is fish to send.
>
> Needless to say, I've had no time to jot down a scheme for West Cornwall, nor with every nerve buzzing can I write very coherently. If you could combine business with what I hope would be pleasure, and run down for a week-end, instead of a mere night, I think it would be greatly to the advantage of a feasible scheme. Thrashed-out schemes are so much sounder than study-concocted ones.[29]

On 28 May Nash attended the next meeting of the Commission without a draft of the projected Cornish scheme but tabled a full report on his meeting with Reynolds. After some discussion, the Commission decided in principle to provide loans for the installation of motor power in the West Cornwall ports and to invite the Cornish Fisheries Committee to convene a new committee to administer the advances (the Administration Committee) consisting of two members of the Fisheries Committee, two local men nominated by the Commission, and Stephen Reynolds – to be nominated by the Board of Agriculture. It was agreed that the Board should be invited formally to make this nomination. At the same meeting, the Commission agreed in principle an advance for experiments on the types of boat suitable for motor power in Devon, the remaining piece of unfinished business from the Devon and Cornwall Inquiry.[30]

Nash reported to Reynolds the outcome of the meeting. Reynolds sent Nash in return his outline scheme for West Cornwall. He continued to be pleased by the faith the Commission had placed in him, but was highly sceptical of these endless meetings and setting up of new committees while his own livelihood was all the time drifting steadily down the drain.

> When is anything, whatever it is, likely to start? It is pleasant to be put on committees, to have one's advice asked, and to frame schemes, but over and above the actual work involved, it means continual disturbance of one's mind, together with a large amount of correspondence; and the net result of my last year's fishery work is that I am becoming seriously impoverished, and in addition more tired than I can tell you with the effort and worry of trying ineffectually to keep everything going at once. During the whole of the last eight months, apart from some payments made for literary work previously done, and apart from the Board's £30, not paid yet, I have earned only my fee of £100. No more. Well, one can't go on like that, no matter how willing, and as an ex-journalist you will understand, without being told, how risky it is to let one's name lapse for a period from the public eye. The unpleasant fact is that, being without unearned income, I cannot continue much longer to hold myself at the service of the Government without having some means of living to fall back upon. If I let myself go on the rocks, I'm finished, sure enough, and then can do no more at all for the Fisheries.
>
> Forgive me for calling attention to these damn'd hard facts, which naturally would not occur so quickly to those fortunate enough not to have to live from pen to mouth and able to take their time over things.[31]

It was the first time Nash had received this standard wail to which Reynolds' past friends had long become inured. He reacted predictably with a profusion of thanks for all the effort that must have gone into the drafting of the West Cornwall scheme. It was now for Reynolds, equally predictably, to feel a little guilty that he might have said too much.

> As to that very sketchy scheme.... I hope it may be of some use. But you've no need to thank me much for the thing. I wasn't hinting in my letter that it was a nuisance to do, for which you ought to be highly grateful, and so forth. Far from it. All I meant was, simply to indicate the damnable necessities with which an entire willingness on my part is unfortunately circumscribed. I'm glad of course to have opportunities of pushing what I want to push. But doing it without means of one's own is tough work. The rich man mayn't get through the eye of the needle, but the poor man sits on the point thereof.[32]

It was, however, a productive exchange, for it determined Nash to get Reynolds' position sorted out as quickly as he could. Reynolds for his part had reacted rather truculently to the Commission's proposal that the sluggard Board of Agriculture should nominate him to the committee to oversee the Cornish experiment. He was still hankering after a free-lance role with the Commission itself.

> As to the other matter, the position and so forth of me.... What I mean is, if the Board – "not liking the whole thing" – is going to hang back all the time, and exercise its famous inertia, and if I am to be its nominee, then it will be through me that they will retard you! I am not disposed to be shut up, as a Board's official, simply to be used as a brake. Nor, in any case, unless they are willing to give me a more or less independent footing all to myself – as Commissioner of Inshore Fisheries, or something of that sort – am I keen on entering their service, even nominally; I have, in fact, already refused to be one of their inspectors. Why should I? It would be well, I think, to see if your non-executive constitution cannot be dodged – in case. Can you not employ advisers, or sub-commissioners, so to speak? To be adviser to the money-bags is, in effect, to possess executive powers.[33]

It was a new idea – with immediate appeal for Nash. He discussed it with Maurice. Since the inception of the Commission, the Board had been wrestling with the difficulty of getting their policy advice into Commission deliberations, since they were precluded constitutionally from placing representatives on Commission committees. The idea of a Reynolds with a foot in both camps carried some attraction.

A scheme was worked out under which Reynolds would be paid when acting for the Commission but not when representative of the Board – for example, on the planned Administration Committee in Cornwall. When Reynolds came up to London at midsummer – the weekend of the Lambourn sonnet – Nash had a fully worked out proposition for him.

Back in Sidmouth, he reported the good news to George Macmillan. "While I was in Town, I saw the various fishery people, including Vaughan Nash, and it looks as if I am to get my way as to the conditions under which I may do that Development work. That is to say, they think it a good idea that I should be attached to and paid directly by the Development Commission, and if nominated to committees by the Board of A. and F. should be honorary so far as they are concerned. In that way I should share in the far greater freedom of the Development Commission, should be able to write as I like, and should be able to take part in propaganda that the Board could not directly countenance."[34]

At the next meeting of the Commission on 26 June, Nash reported on discussions with the Cornish Sea Fisheries Committee on the planned experiment in West Cornwall. At the same meeting, the Commission resolved to seek authority from the Treasury to appoint Reynolds as adviser for a three year period at the princely salary of £250 a year. He had never seen such money in his life.[35]

The wheels of the Treasury ground extremely slow, particularly through the summer leave season, and it was not until the middle of October that Reynolds was able to report progress in one of his now rare letters to Garnett. Even now, he was keen to show his old mentor there were new ones who had taken his place. He pressed home the irony of his new relationship with Harmsworth in the light of the anti-Northcliffe propaganda of the *Mountain*. "I've been made Fisheries Adviser to the Development Commission, a half-time job mainly created to enable me to whisk round the fisheries. It's rather amusing that after the *Holy Mountain* one of the Harmsworths – Cecil – should through the fisheries, have become one of my more intimate friends. Damn good chap – with a remarkable flair for fishermen's point of view."[36]

It was not quite true that he had been appointed, for he was still arguing the toss with Nash over one small aspect of his contract. He told Cecil Harmsworth three days later: "No reply yet from the Development Commission to my protest against being asked to sign half of a contract. It's no use disguising the fact that psycho-economics lifts its battered head and smiles at the idea that the appointment might fall through at the last moment".[37]

But he was not to escape that easily. On 25 October, *The Times* announced his appointment, wrongly describing him as "the son of Mr Stephen Reynolds of Devizes". He was inundated with congratulations from all and sundry, including a kind letter from Harmsworth which referred, without exaggeration, to his indispensability. Though secretly he enjoyed the fuss, he enjoyed even more to present a churlish countenance to the world. He told Harmsworth: "I've got the written assurance I wanted out of Nash, though I don't think he much liked committing his Commission to it. However, there has been no quarrel, and the thing, as you probably saw, was announced to-day. How telegrams of congratulation do turn up when one has got through the rough of things – afterwards, not during, when such encouragement would make all the difference! It's nice of you to describe me as 'indispensable'.... I wonder – and I doubt. Anyhow, doesn't do to act on such an assumption".[38]

Amongst the congratulations came a letter from Jonathan Barron, the fishery officer for the Cornish Fisheries Committee who had helped them so much on the tour of the previous winter – "a charming letter, too, of kindliness jammed into the cracked old bottle of official phrasing".[39] In replying, he was at pains to point out that the new job and the scheme was not for him, but for the fishermen, particularly those of Mounts Bay and St Ives. "I hope, too, that all hands will help me to try and make the thing as good as ever possible for the fishermen concerned. Nobody else matters: this is, and has got to be, for their benefit."[40]

Adviser on Inshore Fisheries to the Development Commission was a strange concoction of a post that only a Reynolds could have contrived. He recognised it for the anomaly it was. When in May 1914 Edward Garnett approached him to ask whether he knew of any jobs going, possibly with David in mind, he set out his constitutional position in detail: "The Development Commission, you know, is not an executive body or employer. I get my screw from them, it is true, as their Adviser, but I have to get my executive powers from the Board, as their representative, and I don't much expect there will be any more such highly anomalous persons!"[41]

The very fact of employment, part-time though it was, had a major impact on his personal life. After a few months he struggled yet again to be released from it, but this time without success. He was paid initially £250 a year. A year later, in November 1914, the Commission raised it to £400, an acknowledgement of his then increased duties for the Board.[42] There would be no more moans about money. For the first time in his life he was financially secure. As he approached his middle thirties, the acceptance world was hovering into view. The possibility of a return to writing – and voluntary impoverishment – grew more and more remote.

Through the summer and autumn of 1913 the Inshore Fisheries Committee, of which Reynolds was still ostensibly a member, ground on with its meetings. Reynolds attended no more of them, but he kept in touch by receiving the papers and through Harmsworth's reports. From time to time, he indulged in a little manipulation from the touch line. In July he dragged in, of all people, Pinker – his now almost redundant literary agent.

> You were telling me that your waiter at Sweeting's, I think, is well acquainted with the abuses of Billingsgate market.... Do you think he would consent to give evidence before the Departmental Committee on Inshore Fisheries, expenses paid, and privately if he wished it? I should be no end obliged if you could let me know, together with his name and address, if he will.

> I haven't been myself to the Committee since I sent in my unaccepted resignation, but I see from the papers sent me that they are calling evidence to prove that Billingsgate is the best of possible markets in the best of possible worlds, and I should dearly like to upset it a bit.[43]

His appointment to the Development Commission reopened his lines to the Board of Agriculture just at the time the Departmental Committee was beginning to ponder the contents of its draft report. Both Minister and Superintending Inspector were keen to welcome him back into the fold. "Had a very kind letter from Runciman and one from Sir James Wilson asking me to call and have a talk at 4 Whitehall Place."[44]

As his business in London increased, so were his contacts with Harmsworth renewed. Now that he was reimbursed for his business trips to London, he had developed the habit of staying in Horrex's Hotel in Norfolk Street, just next door to Pinker in Arundel Street. On 25 September he had dinner with Harmsworth at his home in Montagu Square and his host suggested that on his future trips to London he might abandon the delights of Horrex's and come and stay with him.[45] He was up and down to Town throughout that October, engaged with the Commission and the Board in the preparation of the West Cornwall scheme, in the plans for the projected Fisheries Organisation Society recommended by the Devon and Cornwall Committee and, horror of horrors, a resurgence of the dreaded shingle question.

In a snatched weekend at Sidmouth, where he was caught up in plans to build his own house on Salcombe Hill, he found time to unburden himself to Aunt Jane. "At present I am up to my ears in working, fishery affairs, building plans, legal contracts, a Board of Trade Con: on our shingle dispute and goodness knows what besides. I only returned from London last Sat. and shall have to go up again next Tuesday.... I must get out for some exercise – which means walking over to Ladram Bay and feeding a very friendly donkey, who won't bray for any one else but me."[46]

From now on his London base was Montagu Square, and in the discussions with Cecil Harmsworth over dinner and breakfast he was sucked back into the work of the Departmental Committee.[47] Now that the Committee's report and final recommendations were up for grabs, he did not need much persuading.

By the end of October, Harmsworth was concerting the ground with him over the coming debates in the Committee, on matters such as the future of the Fisheries Division, which the Devon and Cornwall Committee had already recommended beefing up. Reynolds was of a like mind, though his own personal scheme for the future of the Division showed an understanding of the British constitution that still left much to be desired.

> Yes; it struck me at once; what is to become of the Fisheries? I hope to God not a re-absorption into the Bd. of Trade, which is still a stick-in-the-

mud Dept. on strictly official lines, whereas the Bd. of A. and F., since Runciman's advent, has anyhow had some ideas, and indeed, considering its income, has been pretty active. I think with you that we ought to aim at a separate Dept. of Fisheries with its own minister, not necessarily in the cabinet, and *therefore* not necessarily changing with a change of Govt. If you think there is anything in that idea, why not suggest it straight to L.G. He has a flair for novelties!

You know very well whom I personally should like to see holding that portfolio.

But anyhow we need at all costs to avoid being swamped in Land or stultified by Trade, and in any protest you make, *if I can be useful*, I should like to be associated with you.[48]

He attended the last two evidence-gathering days of the Committee on 12 and 18 November but kept a relatively low profile throughout, perhaps in recognition of his long absence. But after the first of these meetings, he accompanied Harmsworth and his southern sub-committee to King's Lynn and Boston to inspect the shell-fisheries of the Wash.[49] On 18 November, he also attended an informal meeting with Harmsworth at the Fisheries Division to consider the draft report of the Committee.[50]

Tempers were rising in the Committee and drafts and counter-drafts were flying around in all directions – "the report of the Departmental Committee seems, from what I hear, to be an awful mess; a pretty scuffle brewing".[51] The turgid, non-committal official draft produced by the secretary – the "lumpy skilly" in Reynolds' phrase – was neither to his nor Harmsworth's liking. Both had circulated their own memoranda, and Reynolds had already signed up three other members of the Committee to his.

After Harmsworth had reported back on a particularly difficult drafting meeting, Reynolds suggested they combine forces. To express his sympathy and solidarity, he began his letter with the catchphrase of Grannie Pratt, the tough old stick, long since passed into his own working vocabulary.

Aw! my dear saoul! it must have been a rotten meeting to make even you testy – and a most irregular procedure! (I keep that in reserve.)

Seeing you say you'd plump for my memorandum, I enclose a copy of it, in case, out of mine and yours, you are driven to compose a draft Report to substitute for the lumpy skilly. Then that of yours would incorporate mine, and have more chance of acceptance than mine.

I've been walking on the matter since I've been home, and though I don't want to add to your conciliatory difficulties, I've made up my mind to produce my best brand of longshore obstinacy; and on those points where you are in agreement, I'm not going to budge an inch, even if I have to stand alone. Why, damn it! if I've disagreed with you and not given way – the last thing in the world I like doing – I'm jolly sure I'm

> not going to agree with you and give way.
> If the worst comes to the worst, we'll divide the House, and if beaten, go to the country! Et puis alors, nous verrons où se place la confiance du monde qui lit.
> Beastly shame it is you should be troubled like this. But the last word on this august committee rests so obviously with you. I commend once more to your consideration the question of a brief umbrella Report as the most practicable alternative to the 2½ gallons of skilly.[52]

For the next few weeks Harmsworth spent many weary days at 43, Parliament Street trying to hammer out an acceptable report with the Chairman, secretary and another influential member, Reynolds' old sparring partner, Thomas Pelham, recently retired as head of the Harbours Department at the Board of Trade. On 10 and 11 December he took two days off to go with Reynolds and the secretary to Brightlingsea to interview fishermen and survey the Colchester oyster beds.[53]

Reynolds spent much of December in London on Commission business and on hand to help Harmsworth with the report. Just before Christmas, in Sidmouth once more, he drafted a long section on marketing, his expert subject, which was to form the most coherent part of the final report. "I enclose for you the section on fish marketing, re-written in one explosion. I think I have steered a fairly good course between what we are sure certain of and what we can actually prove."

His new life with its financial security was not enough to dispatch the usual Christmas blues. He was, as he now told Harmsworth, already contemplating throwing it up.

> I rather suspect – though I don't know yet – that my mind is making itself up at the back of itself to kick out of fishery affairs. I can't stand this drive much longer, and as you know I live in a perpetual terror of falling back into my illness of ten or twelve years ago. Besides, if I have a gift for writing – and certainly what gift I have, I have trained carefully – I'm not sure I oughtn't to look after it better. In any case, one ought to live before one dies.
> I lump this down to you because but for you I know I shouldn't have kept going so long as I have. You, so to speak, a lien on me it would be untruthful to ignore. But one wants to have time to live – in Bergsonian phrase – in the presence of myself. However, don't take too much notice of what I say.
> ......End of the postal day, and about half I intended to do done. Can't help o' it. Hope you'll have a good Xmas. I may clear off somewhere, but if I do I will let you have my address in case there arise any urgent interim fishery matters.[54]

He sent an equivalent greeting to Pinker. "Pleasant 'Xmas to you! I'm, as usual about this time, clean knocked up."[55]

He was bad all through Christmas and immediately after told Nash he would have to resign. But both Nash and Maurice had learned by now that the best way to handle a Reynolds resignation was quietly to ignore it. Half way through January he told George Macmillan: "Still more or less on the sick list, skating over a breakdown, seems so. I've told the Dev. Comm. that they'd better give me the shove-off – but they won't. Indeed, they are exceedingly kind – couldn't be nicer to me. I'm going on as long as I can, but I daren't risk a smash-up, and I think I shall end by falling back again on writing exclusively – which is much like retiring on starvation by the present look o' it!".[56]

It was not just the usual hypochondria. He had pushed himself too hard that autumn and winter, and fear of breakdown was real. He put it all in context for Pinker who had first met him in his breakdown days.

> I'm afraid I'm not really very much better. Fact is, although I know how to hang on fairly tough, the last twelve years' racket has pretty well battered me to pieces, and I have been for some time skating over the rather thin ice of the illness that I had not long before I first came to you. However, if I bust you can agentize my remains, and that, I'd bet you 100 to 1 in pounds, will be my first really successful book.[57]

Hang on tough he did with the controversy over the Departmental Committee's report, which drifted on from month to month. At the end of February, he reported to Harmsworth from Truro where he had a meeting of the Administration Committee: "shall not be able to come and gnaw the bones of the Report this week, but I shall get up next".[58]

For some days, he did not hear from Harmsworth, who was busy too, and he went through the typical little charade, dating from the days of the battles with his father, when silence told him he had given offence and signalled the possibility of more wrath to come. He had tried to explain it to George Macmillan two years before after a similar imaginary stand-off with Mrs Macmillan.

> Probably it is a legacy of my teens, when continuous rows used to break over my head for I never knew what reasons next, that directly I don't hear from people I can't help imagining they are angry with me, and something or other is brewing. People talk about their young days.... I never cease being thankful that I shall never have mine to go through again.[59]

He had gone through this experience with all his friends – with Pinker, Garnett, Conrad and the Macmillans – and now he found a name for it. He wrote to Harmsworth on 8 March.

> After a very fast rush in London yesterday and the long last-train journey down, I was more than delighted to get your letter of the third. Fact is, I had been imagining that some way or other I had upset you; had made up my mind to tackle you on the subject; and if it was so, to clear clean out of the work in which your backing has been a great deal more indispensable than probably you realize.
> However, if 'tisn't so, I don't mind waiting till you are more at leisure, on the same principle as I always tell the doctor: that I don't mind how long the pain goes on, so long as I know it's going to end somewhen. But it doesn't make for serenity, having a very smoky chimney to one's imagination![60]

Like most neurotic people, his restless, creative imagination tended to overcompensate for future fears by imagining the worst. The chimney was destined to smoke for a few years yet.

There were two more two-day marathon sessions on 11/12 and 26/27 March as the Committee continued to thrash out the final details of its report. Reynolds attended both, determined to preserve as much as he could of the clarity he had endeavoured to weave into the report: "we *must* not let them haggle the shop-window summary: it is the only place in the Report where the *policy* has the least chance of emerging from the mash of pious and timid opinions".[61] But it was an exhausting fight. As Harmsworth came wearily away from Winchester House on 27 March, he prayed that the next meeting would be the signing ceremony.[62]

And so it proved, but he was not there to celebrate it. The meeting on 8 April coincided with the debate on the Easter adjournment and an interminable string of blocking motions from the Liberal benches kept him in the House all day. Reynolds had a field day – for he had got his way on most of the policy issues for which he had stood out. There was no minority report this time.

Government departments were as pressed then as they are today, but people still found time to celebrate in a human way the completion of a major piece of work. Reynolds entered into the ceremonies of the signature meeting with gusto. He handed round a dramatic representation of the event, and sent it on to Harmsworth afterwards, regretting the latter's enforced absence. "Was sorry you weren't able to be present at the signature meeting – 'twas the day of blocking motions in the House, wasn't it? Part I of the enclosed was handed round. The Chairman thought it 'Rather severe, isn't it?' but presently saw the spoofery of it, and took it in good part."

It is a clever but gentle satire on the whole Civil Service ethos – from the committee system to the convoluted prose.

THE BREAKING-UP PARTY

The Chairman

Now Gentlemen, this is the end....
(*Omnes*) Hooray!
I had almost said "Hooray!" myself, but that
It seemed too poor a compliment to all your labours....
(*Omnes*) And yours, sir!
Where were we? Oh, yes, – labours
Conducted with such amiability;
And also sometimes often furthermore,
As it has seemed, forgive me, to appear,
Brains slightly muddled by our arduous tongues,
Tho' gingered up at lunch.

Mr. Bostock

Co-operation, Sir, that's what it was....

Mr. Reynolds

Not registered!

Mr. Pelham

Unregistered? But wait
A moment, pray – one little moment wait!
By a Treasury minute of forty years ago....

Mr. Reynolds

Damn the Treasury!

The Secretary (*sotto voce*)

The Treasury.... Yes, damn!

Omnes

The Treasury we all unite to damn,
Except for what we want....

The Chairman

Order, gentlemen, please. Mar not our labours
By saying what you mean....
Circumlocutions we have oft-times sought
For the avoidance of that perilous course.
Our young Olympus born his talent has applied,
Not to the chasing of elusive rhymes,[63]
But to the softening of the official style;
And like the Israelites at Jericho
We have walked round the facts full seven times,
Blowing our muted trumpets;
And, having avoided shouting what we meant,
To our Report a growl we have appended,
Saying we mean it; and what we meant to mean
Have duly signed.
Thanks, gentlemen, farewell!

The Committee starts ponderously....

Remote from the shores where the fisherman hauls up the catches
of fish that he sells at low price,
Immured in this old bishop's palace we've wrangled....

A few days later, on a train journey up to London from Cornwall, he added a Greek chorus of fishermen, congratulating the Committee on its foresight and its support for voluntary co-operation.

You've see'd some sense.
An' put it down:
You poops up there
To Lon'on town.

Come an' help us
Where we lack,
An us'll pay
Your kindness back.

But keep compulsion
For the fools
As takes yer pay
An' is yer tools.

For us is freemen
Of the sea,
And though us dies out,
Free will be.

He titivated it a little and, to gain more publicity for the Committee's report, got his friend R.A.Scott-James to publish it in his new magazine, the *New Weekly*.[64]

In the final Report of the Committee, Reynolds had successfully managed to preserve the shop-window summary at the end, and all the policy. The Committee recommended a revolution in fisheries administration: the strengthening of the Fisheries Division to equal status with Agriculture, with new law-making and enforcement powers, the whole to be funded centrally; division of the country into four or five fishery districts, each headed by a resident local inspector "in constant personal touch with the fishermen and their difficulties" – a recommendation which was to revolutionise Reynolds' life also;[65] the reconstitution of the local fisheries committees into purely advisory bodies; prohibition of the sale of undersized fish; funding of motor installation in line with the Reynolds' schemes; a survey of all inshore fishing stations to prepare for the funding of harbour works to improve the landing accommodation of fishing boats; the immediate formation of a Fisheries Organisation Society, on the lines of the Agricultural Organisation Society, to spread the principles of co-operation for credit, for better business in fishing and marketing, and to give general support to the local co-operative societies.

The "growl" at the end could not have been clearer. "We trust that the foregoing recommendations will be carried into effect without delay. Former Committees on Fisheries have made important recommendations in the interests of the inshore and general sea fisheries which have been ignored. Our considered judgment is that our recommendations represent the minimum of what is necessary to be done, and to be done quickly, if the Inshore Fisheries are to be preserved and developed."[66]

It was a total triumph for Reynolds. Apart from the sections that he wrote himself, like the forthright passages on marketing and exploitation by middlemen, the Report contained all the policy proposals for which he had been fighting since his arrival in Sidmouth. If one compares the final text with the memoranda and summary of recommendations he had drafted for Harmsworth in those final months of wrangling, the match is remarkable.[67] The Committee in the end had deferred entirely to the one member who knew the subject far better than all of them, notwithstanding the fact he had attended less than a quarter of their meetings.

When the Report was published that May, he wrote proudly to Aunt Jane. "The Inshore Fisheries report has had a great success, and is pretty generally attributed to me – quite rightly, for I drove through the whole of my policy, by dint of arguing and hanging on tough."[68]

For the last six months of the Committee's deliberations, he had been wrestling with another piece of public business – on a smaller scale, but no less fraught with difficulty. In the summer of 1913, Hastings, the Sidmouth Manor agent, had approached the Board of Trade to propose a temporary working resolution of the shingle dispute: Colonel Balfour would undertake not to remove any shingle from the beach, but would reserve the right to take 200 tons of sand a year. The Board of Trade, seeing this as a possible practical resolution of their legal dispute with the Manor over rights to the foreshore, decided to send down an inspector to discuss the proposal with all of the parties, including Reynolds as spokesman for the fishermen.[69]

The proposed "working arrangement" suggested by the Manor followed closely the deal that Reynolds had attempted to broker informally at the end of 1911, and which had ultimately failed. He was quick to point out the technical difficulty at the heart of the proposition.

> In point of fact, on my own initiative, I had considerable discussion two years ago with Mr. Hastings and Col. Balfour with a view to seeing if a compromise could be effected along the lines now described as those of

> Mr. Hastings, but negotiations (which were, of course, entirely provisional) broke down because he wanted settlement and beach material too. He has, no doubt, informed you that there are here two kinds of sand, locally termed sharp-sand and mud-sand, and that the former kind is an integral part of the beach, subject to the same wave-action as the shingle, whereas the latter is not. It is the sharp-sand he wants, but it is only the mud-sand which my fishermen are willing in any case to see taken.[70]

The proposed conference at Sidmouth had to be postponed because of Reynolds' busy schedule of fishery engagements in London, but he called in on Whitehall Gardens on the morning of 9 October for a full legal briefing from the Board of Trade Solicitor.[71] He wanted to ensure that Hastings should have no informational advantage. He prepared a careful case, disputing the need for the sand either for building or for the local golf course, and predicting that any lifting of the 1908 Order would lead to a free-for-all.[72]

On the evening of 24 October, he convened a meeting of the fishermen, most probably in the bar of the Anchor, to approve his instructions. It was a predictably angry affair, but the result showed how far he had now come in winning the local confidence.

> Last night I had a rather stormy meeting of my people – had to be in my own chair – and they are so furious they won't throw out a sprat to catch a mackerel. Lord! how they argued and cussed! They'd fight 'em; they wouldn't let 'em have so much as a grain o' mud-sand. I had continually to remind them that we hadn't the money to fight anybody in the courts. 'Twas the devil to get them to vote my instructions for the conference, but I made them do it, and finally, fisherman fashion, after much language, they passed a unanimous vote of confidence in whatever course I thought best to take. Heard afterwards that my most troublesome man said outside: "I meant to tell 'en what I thought, but don't thee trouble, Steve Reynolds'll go so straight as a line for what he thinks best". So I'm not downhearted. And I've got a most niggardly legal twister up my sleeve for the Manor agent.[73]

His "legal twister" was the creative contention that if the Order were lifted, neither the local council nor the Board would have power to prosecute other removers of material. Such enforcement would have to be left to the Manor, and the Crown would *de facto* concede its own claim to the foreshore.

When the Conference was held in the Council offices on 28 October, before Captain Monro, the Board's inspector, Reynolds was too ill with a cold to do adequate oral justice to his case. He had only voice enough to underline the fishermen's total opposition to the removal of sharp-sand, and handed in his memorandum of the rest of the case. Hastings had brought along as his assistant the secretary to the golf club, and argued that sharp-sand was needed for dressing the grass on the course, for building works and for the filter beds of the water works. Monro went down to inspect the beach and found it at a level some five to eight feet below the top of the wall. He chatted to some of the fishermen who assured him to a man that the beach never replenished itself naturally and any removal would form a net loss.[74]

Three years later Reynolds remembered how vitriolic the conference had been. "If we would concede the Manor's disputed right to the foreshore, and to take what they wanted, they, on their part, would let us try to prevent everyone else taking any. At a somewhat acrimonious B.T. conference, I refused flatly so to give the beach away on behalf of the fishermen."[75]

At the time, he was more inclined to see the funny side of the drama.

> The Bd. of Trade Shingle Conference was a diverting affair. His manorial lordship turned up in a very bad temper, as well as his agent and estate pupil. I had such a bad cold for the occasion that I had to half stupefy myself with quinine to get my voice at all! Luckily I had our case entirely in writing and slammed in a copy to go with the Inspector's report. T'other side were visibly furious, especially at my legal twister, and refusal to discuss terms till the legal effect of the suggested agreement was cleared up. They lost their tempers and became most insulting – blathered on about "Mr. Reynolds is not the only friend the fishermen have got. The Lord of the Manor – the L. of the M. – the L. of the M...." till I wonder the beggar didn't blush. It was truly the virtues of landlordism in excelsis! Apparently they think they've lost, and I'm not so certain, though the Inspector frankly admitted the Bd. of Trade was disposed to grant them their compromise – in effect, had shifted the burden of proof on to our shoulders.
>
> I'm rather anxious as to reprisals against our people.[76]

His anxiety over the Inspector was well justified. Monro submitted his report on 31 October. In principle, he was opposed to removal. "Were it possible, with or without considerable expense and legal difficulty, to insure the entire stoppage of removal from this part of the beach, I should certainly advocate it...... I should be inclined to advise that it should be entirely stopped." But he knew that this was not the answer for which the Department was waiting, and fell back on the lame argument that the baby was only a small one. "At the same time I do not think, at least as a temporary measure, that the removal of so small a quantity as 200 tons from the area proposed and under the conditions proposed, provided, of course, that the amount be limited to that, would materially affect the beach so far as navigation is concerned."[77]

Despite the intimations of a foregone conclusion, it took the Department a further six months to come to a decision on the report. No doubt the spectre of an angry Reynolds was lurking somewhere at the back of their minds. Reynolds used the space to continue to lobby at the highest level. When in

February 1914 his old friend John Burns was appointed President of the Board of Trade, he saw his chance.

At the beginning of March, he collared Cecil Harmsworth. "Do you know anyone in the House who would ask J.B. a question for me on the Sidmouth Shingle Order? I know you can't: nor can our own member very well, as the shingle thieves are his supporters. First, however, I propose to look in on J.B. when I'm up this week, and ask him to look through the file on the subject, with a view to the Bd. of Trade putting an end to the way it is being flouted."[78]

On 7 March he did call in at the Board of Trade and reported back to Harmsworth.

> I went and saw John Burns yesterday about the shingle and asked him to look into the matter himself, which he promised to do – and made a remembrancer note which he read out!: "Stealing shingle at Sidmouth." If you should get a chance to put in a good word, please do. You saw the beach when 'twas bad: it's much worse now; and the man who is arranging to put a motor in a drifter for the time being is scared off it. After all, we are now only asking the Bd. of Trade to enforce the Order they saw fit to make after a long and exhaustive Inquiry.[79]

This going behind their backs to Ministers did not endear him to the Board's officials. The lobbying had no success. Out of the blue on 30 April came the decision letter. The limited removal was to be permitted over a prescribed area of the foreshore and the 1908 Order would be adjusted accordingly.[80] It later became clear that, to avoid Reynolds' "legal twister", the Board was to do a deal under which it would lease the relevant part of the foreshore to the Manor while the latter would use its influence to prevent anyone else from removing material there.

On 4 May a furious Reynolds called in on Richard Martyr at the Fisheries Division, having already bombarded the Board of Trade with a barrage of questions.[81] He demanded that, because of the impact of the decision on the local fishery and the installation of motor power, the Board of Agriculture should seek a suspension of action until it had carried out its own investigation. Martyr told him to put the request in writing.[82]

On 5 May he bearded John Burns once more with a new string of points. When Martyr went over to the Board of Trade two days later to request a deferment of action, he reported back: "Mr Reynolds is sharply criticised in that Department".[83] On 6 May Maurice requested the Superintending Fisheries Inspector, Charles Fryer, to go down to Sidmouth and take a look.[84]

Reynolds met Fryer on 18 May and took him out in the *Puffin* to show him the disputed portion of the shore. He pressed upon him the dangers of lifting the Order which would open the beach to depredations from all and sundry. Hastings, when interviewed, was equally adamant that the erosion by nature was far greater than that by any human agency and that 200 tons would make no impact whatsoever. Fryer was of the same opinion. "Altogether it does not appear that there are any very strong reasons for regarding the present proposal as detrimental to fishery interests. The state of the beach is bad, but the taking of 200 tons of sand a year is not going to make it much worse."[85]

Despite this acquiescence by the Board of Agriculture, the Board of Trade did not move. In July the papers were still lying on the desk of John Burns, paralysed to move.[86] Finally, at a further meeting with Reynolds to try and put his own doubts to rest, Burns asked for a formal statement of his views on the proposal to lease the foreshore to the Manor.

Back home, Reynolds in typical fashion began to worry he had not done adequate oral justice to his case. He followed up with a memorandum of it, together with an impassioned statement of his actions in defence of the fishermen.

> It was rather staggering to be asked to produce our objections to the proposed lease suddenly and without notice; I'm afraid I did it pretty badly, and I am venturing to enclose a memorandum of them. At the same time, I am not, or ought not to be, placed in the position of the defendant in the matter. I am only asking the Board of Trade to stick to its guns – to hold to its own Inquiry and Prohibitory Order.
>
> You pointed out that the fishermen can't expect to own the town. They don't want to. They only want their livelihood intact. And, anyhow, whether from the fishery or visitors' point of view, their value as an asset to the town is far greater than the value of what they want. It is simply a case – too frequent around the coast, as the Departmental Committee found – of "wealthy and influential interests which have not scrupled to jeopardise or destroy fishermen's livelihoods for a paltry extra profit, or even for the profitless satisfaction of their *amour propre*". Therefore I have fought it for years, and at no gain to myself except in worry and expense, the enmity of the Manor set – and a certain amount of rather acid experience.
>
> When we had got the Order, Mr. Hastings told me that I had put a thousand a year into the Lord of the Manor's pocket from his flint quarries. Doubtless an exaggeration, and I don't care if it's forty thousand. But if, as I suspect, it's their prestige they conceive to be at stake – I am quite willing publicly to accept the shingle and sand, not as a win, but as a gift, and let them take the credit. It's not the prestige of a won case that I'm out after, but merely a good beach that the fishermen can work from. I worked on it myself too many years not to know the hauling and straining, the broken nights, the risk to men's small capital, and the general discouragement to the fishery, of a bad beach.
>
> I am sorry to trouble you so much over this small – but very typical affair. But if I left any stone unturned, how could I do my general fishery work? My people would say that, having got a paid job, I'd forsaken them. And they'd be right. If I have been able to be of any public service in fishery

> affairs – and I suppose I have, some – it is to these fishermen here that the public owes it at least as much as to me. It would be a strange irony if their fishery were crushed out while I was flying round country resurrecting other people's.[87]

With this personal plea ringing in his ears, Burns continued to haver and by the time of his resignation on the outbreak of war had still not come to a decision. Nor did his successor either. The matter was allowed to moulder away under the weight of more pressing wartime business.

The file came up regularly in the Board of Agriculture until, in November, Fryer decided to put it away. "As the B.T. have promised to inform us of any action on their part, and as we are sure to hear from Mr Reynolds if they move, perhaps these papers might be p.a. for the present."[88] Stephen Reynolds, as everyone knew, was the most effective BF system that any Government Department could contrive.

When the issue raised its head again, it was an act of God, not man, that was the cause.

Much of the ground for the recommendations of the Inshore Fisheries Committee had been well prepared long before its report was published in May 1914. Reynolds, Harmsworth and the Development Commission were waiting on no man.

Work had already started on the setting up of a Fisheries Organisation Society, predicated as essential by the Devon and Cornwall Inquiry report. On 9 October 1913, Reynolds and Harmsworth attended a meeting at the offices of the Agricultural Organisation Society at which a provisional committee was formed and a decision taken in principle that the F.O.S. should be set up. Harmsworth was elected to the chair.[89] Reynolds attended two further meetings of the provisional committee on 6 and 24 March at which the educational and support programme of the projected Society was hammered out.[90]

Once the Departmental Committee had reported, more substantive progress could be made. On 9 July the provisional committee met once more to draw up a memorandum on the establishment of the Society which a deputation, including Reynolds, presented to Runciman on 22 July.[91] The following day Reynolds presented the memorandum to a meeting of the Development Commission, reporting that Runciman had approved the scheme in principle and had urged quick action. Subject to the legal and financial detail the Commission also approved the scheme.[92] The Society was finally established that August with a Commission grant of £2,000, with Harmsworth in the chair and Reynolds as one of the Governors.[93] There was now a formal body to oversee and support his long awaited schemes for co-operation.

The West Cornwall scheme that was the precursor of them all was by this time already well in place. In August 1913 the Commission had authorised a loan of £4,000 to the Cornwall Sea Fisheries Committee.[94] Most of the organisation fell to Reynolds himself. On 29 October all was prepared for the first meeting of the Administration Committee which was to oversee the scheme. "All day yesterday I spent slamming out letters on a typewriter to convene the first meeting of the W. Cornish ad hoc Ctee. I'm trying to get it for Nov. 13 or 14, and there is a probability of Nash being able to run down and start the ball rolling."[95]

The meeting at Truro was held successfully a week later than planned, but he found the unaccustomed role of chairing a formal committee, particularly in the presence of an old hand like Nash, somewhat daunting. Here were new skills to be learned. "The meeting at Truro went off pretty well on the whole. I was voted to the chair forthwith, and came away with a feeling that I had handled the meeting very amateurishly, nor did Nash's satisfaction make me feel it any the less. I must set to work and learn the way of doing that job well."[96]

The nervous energy of the experience had totally exhausted him, as he told Nash on his return to Sidmouth. "Hope you had a pleasant journey on. I got home scarcely earlier than you, and as Tom put it, "the tiredest most lonesome looking bugger he ever see'd wander into anywhere." I was done, too, and still feel as if the finest thing on earth would be to sleep for a week. Anti-climax!"[97]

It was decided that the local administration of the loans should be entrusted to fishermen's societies in each of the four ports – Mousehole, Newlyn, Porthleven and St Ives. The Administration Committee would charge the local societies 3% interest, while the societies in turn would charge the fishermen 3½% to allow for administration.[98] It fell naturally to Reynolds to call the fishermen together and facilitate the setting up of the new co-operative societies. Now all the talk was over, here at last was co-operation on the ground.

He spent the early weeks of 1914 rushing round the four ports in an effort to pull the fishermen together. He was given sterling support from Jonathan Barron and from Matthias Dunn, who had made the terrible *démarche* at Mousehole exactly a year before but now was completely won over by Reynolds' undoubted zeal.

By the last week of February all was ready for the launch. On 24 February he was in Truro again for another meeting of the Administration Committee to set the ball rolling. He wrote to Edward Carpenter with a qualified optimism. "In point of fact, I'm writing in a damn'd dismal smoking room at Truro, but it's best to write to me via Sidmouth, as I'm usually much on the move in Cornwall, trying to start our fishermen's co-operative societies. Looks as if we're going to succeed, too; though whether they'll progress when our shove is removed – Lord knows!"[99]

The launch itself brought back nostalgic memories of the Cornish Committee, as he confided to Cecil Harmsworth: "This week, however, I suppose I shall have to whisk round the W. Cornish ports as we did last year. Wish you were down along this, too".[100]

All went off in perfect order; the societies were formed and duly registered. "Last week, we formed the four co-operative societies, and we are going immediately to found a Cornish County Co-operative Boat Insurance Club. Things, in fact, are going rather well, and I'm hoping now that our Cornish system will soon stand to the English F.O.S. as the I.A.O.S. does to the more laggard A.O.S. Matthias Dunn has thrown himself into the matter, and is pushing it on hard. He is very valuable, and I'm glad I took a good deal of trouble to placate him."[101] The societies and the loan they administered were quickly to put the west Cornish fisheries back on their feet, aided fortuitously by the war that was looming just on the horizon.

He spent Easter at St Ives and found that the St Ives and Mousehole societies were already hard at work and flourishing. He went out for the day with Colonel Williams, the elderly and kindly Chairman of the Cornwall Sea Fisheries Committee.

> The weather was splendid at St. Ives, and the place more lovely than ever. The old Colonel – who's kindness itself to me nowadays – took me for a gorgeous drive to Gurnard's Head, over hills and moors covered with rocks and a blaze of gorse blossom. Makes me feel torn in two pieces between a desire to write down the beauties of it, and to do a little towards making its people prosperous enough to stay there instead of clearing out to America. At each of the many stops up the line yesterday, fine lads were getting into the train with emigration agents' red labels on their bags. Mostly they had a cheery send off, but in nearly every group was some woman crying or choking back tears.[102]

Though his work for the Commission rushed from success to success, there were still moments that spring when nervous exhaustion was counselling him to throw the whole thing up. He was in an argument with the Commission over an allowance for secretarial help – and the frustration of it all pointed up the conflict between his ambition to do good on a national scale and the longing to go back to the smaller stage of Sidmouth and his friends. He spelled it out for Bob.

> I had something of a dispute with the Development Commission, or rather the Treasury, before I left London, over an allowance I asked for to get help with the work. Anyhow, I told them I shouldn't come to any decision till I'd talked it over with you. You know, I feel more and more inclined to chuck this Government work, only I don't see who there is to take it on and plug out for fishermen. After all I was a lot happier, and could write better stuff, when I was working for thee than I am working for the Government. But what the devil would become of all I've got under way, if I were to chuck my hand in? – that, I don't know. Well, 'tis only for a lifetime, I suppose.[103]

It was true that his single-handed efforts had made him indispensable, both in the west country and nationally. He was gradually being sucked into a situation from which it was impossible to escape. He told the same tale to Nash, and came to the same resigned conclusion. "What I most *wish* is to shove through fishery affairs, but what I most *want* is to go back to my own people entirely and be my own man again with time to realize I am alive.... It's the irony of my buffer existence that [what] I try to do for my people tends to separate me from them, but it has the advantage of rendering either upshot satisfactory one way or the other."[104]

By July 1914 he was feeling more positive about his work for the Commission as the West Cornwall scheme and the motor installation experiments in Devon were settling down and encouraging results coming on stream. He had completed reports on both and from his base at the Porthminster Hotel in St Ives warned Vaughan Nash of their imminent despatch. "The Reports on the two West Country schemes are home being typed, and I follow home today. I hope the reports will do all right. I have tried to give the Commissioners some idea of the moving complexities their so simple stipulations result in; the Cornish scheme swims, as it were, on the surface of the human element involved in it, to such a degree that impressions give a truer idea of it than statistics or official dead talk could."[105] The writer was still in charge over the civil servant.

As his long-held policy ideas now fructified on the ground, they brought with them a new and inevitable sense of commitment. A month later, the declaration of war was to cut off his line of retreat for good and all.

The brilliant summer of 1914 he spent much time at work in St Ives, the largest and most destitute of the West Cornwall ports. There he made a chance encounter which was for an instant to bring back the rapidly fading images of his life in literature and London.

In June Hilaire Belloc put in at St Ives in his nine-ton cutter the *Nona*, travelling west from Bideford – and bumped into Reynolds. His wife had died four months before and he was entering on the period of indefatigable mourning that was to last the rest of his long life. This cruise from Holyhead to Shoreham, broken by halts for business in London, was the initiation into a new and solitary existence.

He and Chesterton had been Mont Blanc regulars in the early days of Garnett and Hudson. There, most probably, he had first met Reynolds some years later. The chance meeting now with Reynolds, who too was a lonely man and an outsider, seemed to chime with the melancholy of his own situation. Called away to London soon after, he asked Reynolds if he would take the boat round Lands End for him to a south Cornish port, Fowey or beyond. A novel way to make the part journey back to Sidmouth, Reynolds was happy to agree.

Eleven years later, in elegiac mood, Belloc wrote of the encounter and of his feelings for this exceptional man. It is an obituary coloured by thoughts of all the many other exceptional friends that Belloc had now lost in the war. Yet, at the same time, it throws a new sidelight on Reynolds – and the emotional impact of his words and actions on others who felt, like him, a personal sense of responsibility towards their fellow men.

> From that Cornish town I had the next morning to make my way back to London; and Stephen Reynolds, whom I met, got her round the land safely to the ports upon the southern side, whence later I resumed this cruise: Stephen Reynolds, that strongest-souled and most sincere of men, who desired and did good all his life. It is the meeting with such men, and the comparison of their public label with their true function, of their false renown or lack of renown with their certain standing in the eyes of their Maker, which lead all wise men to a perfect contempt for the modern world.
>
> Does any one remember him now of those who are reading this? Perhaps one or two, perhaps no one. He loved the poor: he understood the sea. He was a brother and a support to sailing-men, and he had charity, humility, and justice in equal poise. But the truth is, I take it, that our world is no longer fitted for governance by, nor even for advice from, its rare great men. It is fitted for governance by those who boast so exact an admixture of folly and of vice as makes them reasonably consonant with the stuff they have to govern. As to those who are too good for us, or too wise for us, why, the sooner they are out of it the better for them. And so it is the better with Reynolds....
>
> But I wish that I could come across him again in this world, somewhere at the meeting of sea and land, and talk with him again about the schools of fishes, and the labours of those who seek them along our shores, and the souls of sailormen.[106]

51 Edward Thomas about the time he first met Reynolds.

52 Berryfield Cottage where Reynolds visited Edward Thomas in April 1907.

53 Ford Hueffer, with whom Reynolds lived in the spring of 1908, an episode that ended in bitterness.

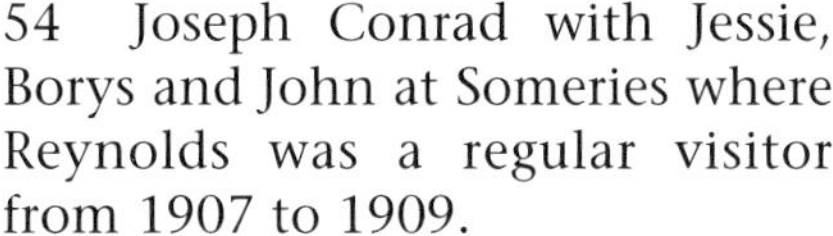

54 Joseph Conrad with Jessie, Borys and John at Someries where Reynolds was a regular visitor from 1907 to 1909.

55 M.P. Willcocks, the other chronicler of the Woolley household.

56 Harold Wright in 1933.

57 W.H. Hudson, the most devoted of the Mont Blanc friends - "a delightful old chap, like a long grey bird himself".

58 The firm of Woolley and Reynolds lined up on Western Beach, 2 July 1908. *Left to right* George (Punch), Uncle Sam, Chip (Tom's son), Tom, SR and Bob, with Margot like a beached whale at Bob's feet. Bobby and Semaphore, in pram, look on from the Promenade (*see page 222*).

59 Grannie Pratt, "the tough old stick".

60 A contemporary cartoon.

61 John Galsworthy at Wingstone, his Devon retreat.

62 Charles Masterman, the solver of the shingle question.

63 Hugh Walpole, an ambivalent friend.

64 George Macmillan, Reynolds' second publisher.

65 The new tourist attraction on Sidmouth beach, August 1909. "'Twas taken for the 'Bookman'. It's 'frighting' rig. Observe the sunburn!" (*see page 288*).

66 The Woolley family take the sun outside their home in Bedford Square in the summer of 1909. *Left to right* Bob, Mam with Semaphore on her lap, Lulu, Gertie and Bobby.

67 With Semaphore in Bob's back-yard around December 1910 (*see page 373*).

68 With Margot in the same photo shoot.

69 *Puffin*, the first motorboat on Sidmouth beach, two years after she first came home – Bob, Tom and SR aboard.

70 Katie Powys, with her sister Lucy behind, in the garden of Montacute Vicarage about the time she first met Reynolds.

71 Tom and Nellie's twins, Fay and Sylvia, take the air in the summer of 1911, watched by the proud parents and Bob (*left*), and guarded by Margot.

72 The author at his desk overlooking Bedford Square, 6 July 1912 (*see page 455*).

73 Reynolds and Margot at the front door, taken the same day by the "rather nice little *Mirror* snapshotter".

74 Semaphore and her little sister Gladys about 1915.

75 Frank and Leonie Reynolds by the ornamental urn at Nether Velly, long after the break with their son.

76 Henry Maurice, head of the Fisheries Division, about the time he met Reynolds.

77 Cecil Harmsworth, Reynolds' chief political ally.

78 Bob in his London gear, complete with RNVR medal.

79 The be-suited civil servant.

80 Vaughan Nash (*right*) with Lloyd George and Megan about 1911.

81 Edward Carpenter at Millthorpe, 1905.

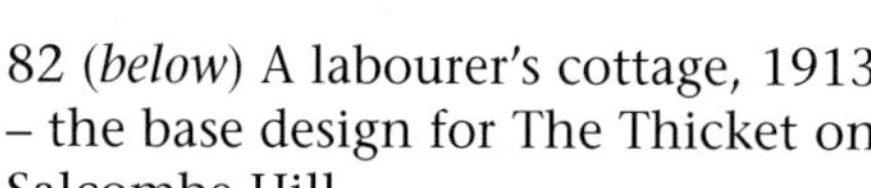

82 (*below*) A labourer's cottage, 1913 – the base design for The Thicket on Salcombe Hill.

83 (*inset*) The Thicket today, greatly extended.
Photo: Sara Hannant.

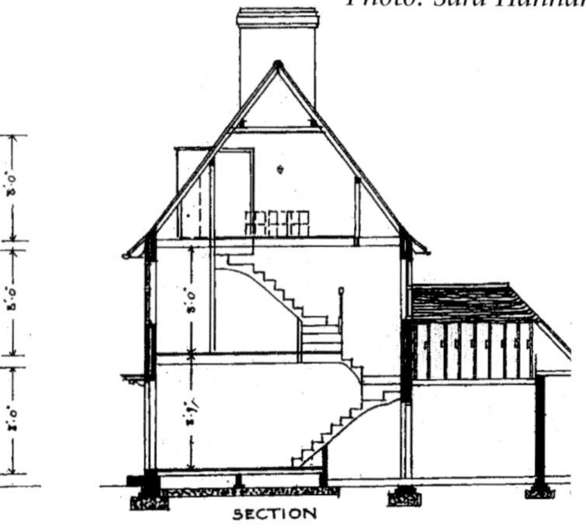

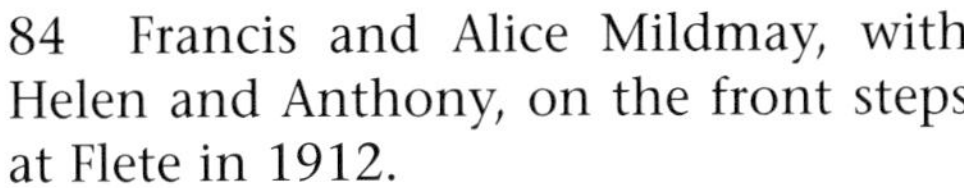
84 Francis and Alice Mildmay, with Helen and Anthony, on the front steps at Flete in 1912.

85 (*above right*) Harry Paynter, the young Cornish fisherman and Reynolds' only long-term partner.

86 (*right*) Mary Paynter, Harry's mother, in old age. "Rare old woman, she is – worth a novel all to herself."

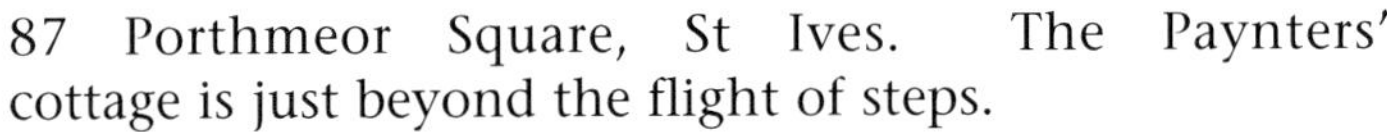
87 Porthmeor Square, St Ives. The Paynters' cottage is just beyond the flight of steps.

88 Lulu's wedding group in Bedford Square, 5 August 1915. *Standing left to right* Tom and Florence Pratt, Florrie Collier with Bobby (*in trilby*) behind, Mrs Counter, Jack and Lizzie Collier, Granfer, Alf Parsons, Lulu, Bob, Mam, Bertha Verschelely, Henrietta Cordey, Grannie Pratt, SR. *Seated* Miss Cordey, Gertie, Dorothy Woolley, Ethel, Lizzie Woolley, Miss Pratt. *On the ground* Ella Pratt, Semaphore, Gladys, Reggie (*see page 613*).

89 Hope Cottage, where Reynolds lived and worked from 1916 to 1917.

90 The Retreat, Reynolds' last home.

91 The burial of Stephen Reynolds, 15 February 1919. *Second row from right* Bob and Mam (*furthest from camera*), Frank and Leonie Reynolds (*nearest camera*). Bill, in sailor's uniform, stands behind.

92 The grave.

93 Harry Paynter's wedding in Buxton, Derbyshire, 1 June 1925.

94 Old friends. Katie Powys and Bob at Sidmouth, 8 October 1929.

95 Bob and Mam in later days outside Sea View Terrace.

96 The last picture of Bob, April 1947, five months before his death.

97 Bedford Square today, the epitome of modern "improvement"

Photo: Sara Hannant.

98 Semaphore, now Mrs Doris Reed, *right*, at the unveiling of the plaque to Reynolds on Hope Cottage, 26 June 1980.

99 He still looks out to Salcombe Hill.

Photo: Sara Hannant.

100 A weary Inspector of Fisheries approaches the endgame.

EIGHTEEN

Psycho-economics 1913-14

We know very little about Reynolds' sexual life – rightly so, for it belonged to him rather than to the world. Nor is it surprising, for in the early years of the twentieth century it was a dangerous thing to be a homosexual and many concealed it by careful reticence or by formal social devices, such as heterosexual marriage. Reynolds was one of the more reticent about his personal inner life.

Yet there is little doubt that he was strongly interested in sex, that his sexual impulses were not wholly suppressed, nor entirely sublimated by his creative work. We catch strong glimpses of it in his writing. Those rare diary entries of the autumn of 1906, when he had first encountered Bob and the family at Sidmouth, are bursting with fairly raw sexual emotion, at times disguised in a mystical religious cloak. It is there in the loving descriptions of male bodies in *A Poor Man's House*. It can be seen in the personal theory of aesthetics he was trying to build at the end of 1906, marshalling sex along with art, religion and society among the main ingredients. This led him on, in the summer of 1908, to an intensive reading of Weininger and Havelock Ellis and a new scientific interest in the mainsprings of "inversion".[1]

He was a man of considerable personal charm and never lacking for admirers. It was not only women like Elizabeth von Arnim and Katie Powys, or the young sailors down in Devonport, who fell for him; a whole bevy of London editors, as we have seen, were bowled over by him on first encounter. Despite his initial diffidence when meeting strangers, he was well aware of his powers in this regard. It was no coincidence that he had once planned to write a book entitled *Charm*.

It is in the spring of 1913 that we catch the first objective evidence of the pressures and tensions that went with being a homosexual in the shadow of Oscar Wilde. There is a hint that the violent explosions of anger in the run-up to Christmas 1912 may have had some more deep-seated cause than the pressures of work on the Cornish Committee and the life-threatening illness of Tom.

We cannot know whether there was such a hidden cause. He seems to have employed a new secretary at this time, a successor to Dolby, and someone of whom we know nothing. Later he took off for a stenographer's job in Canada and the parting appears to have been quite amicable – they kept in touch and there were later plans for him to return to work for Reynolds again.[2] But it would not be surprising if the cramped first floor of the poor man's house did not generate some domestic tensions from time to time.

Whatever the cause, the inner crisis was sufficiently great that spring for Reynolds to cast around for professional help. He made contact with

Havelock Ellis, the writer, doctor and sexologist, and fixed an appointment to see him at his surgery flat in Dover Mansions in Brixton. Ellis had a standard procedure with his patients: he just let them talk freely about themselves and their sex lives. The purpose of his therapy was to get them to accept themselves.

When male homosexuals came to him, he would advise them of books to read and, if he thought them safe, write off to Edward Carpenter or some other homosexual friend inviting them to make contact with the patient if they thought they could be of help. It was a proceeding not without its dangers. There was always the possibility that the homosexual in distress might turn out to be a policeman in disguise.[3]

In the case of Reynolds, an established writer, it was inevitable that Ellis should pass him on to another writer, Edward Carpenter, the socialist whose alternative vegetarian lifestyle in his farmhouse outside Sheffield and quiet campaigning on behalf of homosexuals were matters of public notoriety. It was now almost 40 years since Carpenter had broken with the middle-class world of priest and Cambridge don to turn to the working classes and eventually to manual labour for his salvation – a career profile that had a lot in common with Reynolds' own.

In March, Ellis made the approach to Carpenter under cover of a gentle introduction to Reynolds' book: "I am just reading with much enjoyment Stephen Reynolds's "A Poor Man's House", now issued in a cheap edition. Doubtless you know it. It would certainly appeal to you, and is a record of fact. The author, also, who came to see me lately, is an attractive person. He still lives with his fishes and friends".[4]

Carpenter took the hint, read the book and wrote to Reynolds praising it. In friendly fashion, he invited the young author to make the trek to Millthorpe and share a pint at his local pub. Reynolds, himself an avid reader of Carpenter in the past, was more than a little flattered.

> It's many years I've been hoping to make your acquaintance more directly than through your books, nearly all of which I have read. I was glad when Havelock Ellis wrote to me that you were reading my book and intended to write; and delighted when I got your letter. Havelock Ellis remarked that he had given you no hint of what he calls "the inwardness" of the book, but I daresay you detected the homogenic basis of it. For most people it is by the frankness of its expression that it is hidden. Funny thing is, I am still here in the same house. The events and feelings related in the P. M's H. so mashed me up, that I can't go away, though often I want to do so for I've had to give up most of the fishing and plunge into fishery affairs just because others can be got to man a boat, but not others to do the business. One is not so happy on Govt. committees and the like as one was in the boats for one's paltry "share" of the catch's proceeds.

> I should like to see your wayside pub; I should like you to see ours, which acts to us as our club. Perhaps I may get so far, or nearabout, on Govt. business. I remain too poor to undertake many long journeys solely on my own account. It's the price of knuckling under to nobody – not regularly paid![5]

He was soon to meet Carpenter in London, the prelude to a continuing correspondence; but it was more than five years before he was able to taste the delights of Millthorpe.

The Havelock Ellis therapy seems, however, to have done the trick of opening him up, and in both writing and behaviour the next few years seem to mark a greater relaxation in his sexual life. The greatest benefit of all was that with Carpenter he could be himself, even to the point of making sexual jokes in letters. A year later he wrote to him: "Have been reading your "Toward Democracy" [*sic*] again with renewed appreciation. It reminds me of watching gangs of fine navvys from a railway train that one can't get out of!"[6]

It seems also to have opened up a new area of creativity – the Lambourn sonnet of the summer of 1913 and a poem in the spring of 1914 entitled *Prisoners*. When the latter was published that April, he drew it to Cecil Harmsworth's attention with an apparent note of apology: "Did you happen to see my poem in last week's *New Weekly*? Should like you to see it – a thing called "Prisoners" – but haven't by me a copy to send on. Don't know why official work is making me write more bad poetry than I've done for ten years. Must be the train journeys."[7]

It is a poem full of homosexual angst, revealing the depth of the emotional disturbance he had himself been passing through. It seems also to have had a symbolic significance for him, marking perhaps the beginning of his own release from the psychological burdens it depicts. In 1915 he sent it to his first and only long-term partner shortly after their first meeting, acknowledging both its importance and its sensitivity: "It's a funny thing that though one doesn't mind publishing things like that in print, one doesn't like showing them to people one knows, unless one knows them very well. The poem hasn't got any rhymes in it; it's in imitation of an old sort of verse that didn't have rhymes. But if you read it once, and then again, sailing free, so to speak, you'll find it's got a regular measure in it. You want to look out for the stops".[8]

It describes an incident on the long platform at Salisbury station that he witnessed from the train as he travelled down to Sidmouth the Saturday morning after the last working day of the Inshore Fisheries Committee. The shame is that of a man whose special sexuality prevents him in public from performing the charitable act his soul demands; but its power comes also from the evident overtones of Oscar Wilde on Reading station.

Prisoners
(*Salisbury Long Platform*, 28.3.14.)

Slim, upright, fresh-faced, no more than a full-grown boy,
Clad in a bluejacket's rig – blue trousers and jumper
Stripped bare of its badges and braid, silk scarf and lanyard;
With a blue convict's cap on his head – all navy blue –
And handcuffed:
In charge of a warder, he walked down the platform's length
Of the Plymouth express, with a splendid lissom stride,
And a gait the more taut for its handcuffed lack of balance;
Looking the world in the face, neither subdued nor defiant,
Nor broken by prison.
A chap I'd have trusted on sight, a figure apart
From the scurrying crowd, and by far the most dignified there.
"What the hell have you done, poor devil?" I wondered at first,
And then the thought spoke itself, like a voice in my ear:
"Who's wronged you? What man or what ironbound system
Have you hit your head against?"
And the tears started into my eyes, just as they will for sick pity
On seeing a beautiful animal maimed or dying,
Or a horse fallen down in a greasy London street,
Helpless, mud-smeared, and dumb.
What was his crime? What does it matter? I didn't know – don't care!
For a shame is on me that, while lounging at ease
In a comfortable carriage, with tea and tobacco, and gold in my pocket,
Rattling West towards home and its welcome,
I never went through the train to light him a cigarette,
Or order some scran or a drink from the restaurant car,
And give him west-country cheer, to ease his journey
From prison to prison.
I very much doubt whether what had landed him
In chokey was half so wrong as that I, wishing, failed
To go and speak him friendly;
And I more than doubt whether the prison he's gone to
Is any more shameful than that which barred me back
From following the kindlier impulse of the moment,
To grip his handcuffed hand and wish him luck.[9]

By 1913 Reynolds had not entirely given up his career in prose for occasional verse from railway carriages. He was about to embark on his big book – the *magnum opus* that had been building in his mind for the past three years.

Since the critical failure of the *Mountain*, Reynolds appears to have recognised instinctively that his essential creativity lay in the intellect, not the imagination. He was much happier manipulating concepts on paper than human characters. Though he prepared the skeletons of at least three more novels, he could never bring himself to write the first sentence. At the same time, his intellectual energy was developing an ambition to make his mark on the world not, as Conrad had hoped, with *the* definitive novel but with the creation of his own personal system of thought. The model had turned from Flaubert into Bergson.

As we have seen, he wrestled for a time in 1906-8 with a new system of aesthetics, but its central thesis that art, religion and love were all aspects of a desire to communicate was not so earth-shattering as to maintain his interest for very long. These ideas had sprung from deep inside himself, his own creative, religious and sexual feelings. But, good scientist that he was, it was when he turned to observation of the external world that his ideas began to draw some power and originality.

His new system of the psychology of work started, like all important things in his life, with Bob and Tom and the Sidmouth of 1906. At first, it was the emotions of the new experience that overwhelmed him, but as life settled down to a routine in the summer of 1907 he began to ponder the differences between the two types of work on which he was engaged – the manual and the intellectual, the fishing and the writing. Which was the harder? How much brain-power went into manual work, and how much physical effort into the intellectual? Which was of greatest value to society? Which deserved the highest remuneration?

This last was the crucial question. For the inequality of reward for varying degrees of effort stood out for him as the greatest scandal in the relationship between the working class and the rest of Edwardian society. The manual worker worked incomparably harder than the average office clerk, let alone the average *rentier*, but was paid incomparably lower. This was one injustice he shared with Bob and Tom. He worked as long and hard at his writing as they did at their fishing, but all of them were permanently on the borderline of economic survival.

The fault lay in the philosophy of remuneration which was based not on a rational system of objective values – paying the worker according to the worth of his product, but on an irrational system of subjective values – paying him according to his status in society. Manual work was of such low status that the value of what it produced hardly entered into the equation at all.

Reynolds set out to expose these scandalous inequalities by drawing up his own philosophy of work which would hold within it a generalised and implied system of remuneration. Like many Englishmen of this period, he had come under the spell of the writings of Henri Bergson, reinforced by Bergson's first appearance at the lectern in this country in May 1911.[10] It was no surprise then that he should couch his new philosophy in terms of the Bergsonian concept of "the will to life".

The *Labour v. Brainwork* controversy run by *The Times* in the summer of 1910 had proved fortuitously the perfect vehicle for developing these ideas and getting them into print. In his two articles, republished in *Seems So!*, he had formulated the basic law that work was a giving of life in return for more life – "the putting out of one's life at interest" – but had not thought this the context in which to spell out the logical system on which these ideas were predicated. Instead, he had spelled out the consequence of his system that was most relevant to an understanding of the current industrial unrest. The workers were giving of their life through work, but were not receiving in return the interest due to them. The cause of unrest was not so much a material monetary one, but one based on feeling – frustration at the failure of society to honour its side of the bargain.

The continuance of the strikes into 1912 and the assumption of his ideas by other journalists, but without attribution, determined him to write a book in which the ideas would appear as incontestably his own. He told George Sturt in March: "I want to write a book on *Human Economics* – where the shoe pinches, instead of where the so-called laws don't pinch, a theory of work in terms of life."[11]

The emergence of syndicalism for the first time in England at the heart of this period of unrest seemed further justification of his theory; for he saw it as more a psychological than a purely economic development. When *The Times* that spring produced a background feature article, entitled *Syndicalism: what it means*, he wrote privately to Buckle, the editor, to set him straight.[12] "I pointed out that though the article explained what it does, or rather how it acts, it just doesn't explain what it means. And it doesn't, I'm absolutely sure. Syndicalism is only the present outward form – tentative, and therefore rather violent – of all that is finest, and noblest too, in the awakening of the working classes. It's a psychologic, and not really an economic product, and it's as rife among the best men here as it is near the influence of the trades unions. This labour unrest is more a psychological than an economic problem – as we have said, but few will listen. So syndicalism – if the people 'up topsides' (as Tom calls them) will only help guide it to good ends, instead of opposing it blindly in toto."[13]

He saw the current journalistic interest in plumbing the causes of the industrial unrest as the opportunity to launch his new system of ideas. In May the *Daily Mail* invited him to contribute to its series on the strikes, but he was not going to waste his intellectual brilliance on the semi-educated readers of a popular Conservative daily. He had already agreed with Buckle to set the *Times* readers straight on what Syndicalism *actually* meant.

> The *Mail* asked me to do 1000 words in this series of theirs on the labour unrest. I didn't feel inclined to try and cram my weightier ideas into 1000 words, for people with public names to peck at and use, as they have done with *Seems So!*, so I asked the *Times* if they'd take a series of three articles, and they consented. Accordingly, I've written for the *Mail*

> a splash-article which should appear to-morrow, and which may give *Seems So!* a good flood tide for us to take. It's a roundabout-the-mulberry-bush kind of article, but it goes off like a volley of pop-guns; and the 13.5-ers are saved for the *Times*, where they'll do more real service.[14]

He waited two weeks for the article to appear, all the time wrestling with the start of his more definitive articles for *The Times*. At the end of May he told George Macmillan: "The *Mail*, according to a telegram therefrom, will be printing my article early next week. I have been a fortnight, now, trying unsuccessfully to start my *Times* articles on the psychological side, and almost fear I shall have to give up the attempt. I want a whole book, and to try to get what I want to say into articles is maddening. The antagonistic *attitudes*, which I regard as at the bottom of the antagonistic actions, require so much making plain to people unconscious of their existence and power".[15]

George Macmillan was rather less than enthusiastic about a book on such a subject and tried to keep his author to the task in hand. "I hope, however, that you will persist with the "Times" articles. There you are certain to reach an important audience, and I think it is politic for you to keep in with them. Moreover, there is such a thing as writing too many books, and the art of compression is in itself useful discipline!"[16]

The contribution to the *Mail* appeared on 1 June under the title *The Blindness of the Ruling Class* and had been so cut about as to be almost unintelligible. It managed to preserve the basic statement of psycho-economics, quoted verbatim from *Seems So!*, and at least one or two clear statements of Reynolds' faith in the strikers.

> It is noteworthy that most of the recent strikes have been provoked less by extreme poverty, still less by grab, than by a desire for the general betterment of working-class life. The working classes have been raising their ideals on a falling purchasing power, and the fulfilment of ideals usually costs money in practice. The labour unrest, it seems to me, has much more good than bad in it, and it is much easier to over-estimate its alarming nature than to over-estimate the boundless possibilities of the voluntarily co-operating spirit and the growth of a corporate sense. In that direction, I believe, the solution lies.

What incensed Reynolds even more than the cutting was that the paper had turned his article into a letter. He told George Macmillan: "The *Daily Mail* cut my article very unscrupulously, and, what made me really savage, printed it as a letter. I'm not accustomed to writing letters to the Editor of the *Mail*, and resent the appearance of it."[17] With Pinker, as always, he was more explicit: "That *Daily Mail* letter was commissioned as an article and damnably cut. Printing it as a letter made me savage: I don't write letters to the *Mail* like schoolmasters and bishops".[18]

Meanwhile, on 6 June he managed to complete the first of his syndicalism articles for *The Times* and had coined for the first time the new English word "psycho-economics". "The first *Times* article was finished this morning after a fortnight's very hard slogging and is sent in for approval before I go on. Largely it's a condensation of that proposed book on "Human Economics" – psycho-economics, so to say, which is extremely hard to expound, but I think firmly is on the right track. Perhaps if they don't see what I'm driving at they won't print, but I hope they will."[19]

His fears were partially justified. *The Times* would print, but could not give him all the space he wanted. "The *Times* wants the *English Syndicalism* condensed into two articles, and it can't possibly be done anyhow, so I'm rather in a fix whether to print somewhere else or keep until I can get at the 'Human Economics' book."[20] As before, George Macmillan tried to steer him clear of the latter. "I am sorry that you cannot cut down your articles on Syndicalism to the space that the *Times* can give you, as it is a pity for you to lose your hold on their audience; but I suppose you know your own business best."[21]

But, as with all those projects closest to his heart, Reynolds "business" was perfectionism. "I, too, am more than sorry over the *Times* articles, but I don't see how I can *say effectively* what I want to say in only two instalments, though the temptation to try is considerable, especially as I have already given three weeks to the first and have very full notes for the lot. But it wouldn't do to fail to explain myself for lack of space. I should do harm rather than good. I mean that book on 'Human Economics' (of which they form part) to be a bit of an intellectual bomb, when it does get done."[22]

While he was still contemplating what to do, the commission in the middle of June 1912 by the *Daily Chronicle* of the series on naval discontent decided the matter for him. He could not possibly handle both sets of articles at the same time. So it was not until after the last Navy article had gone in on 19 August that he returned once more to the psycho-economics charge.

Rather surprisingly, in view of the *débâcle* over the labour unrest article in June, it was to the *Daily Mail* that he now turned. A chance encounter with Lindsay Bashford of the *Mail* had produced a new expression of interest in the subject. Reynolds quickly followed up this unexpected opening with a letter in the middle of the August holiday season.

> Are you up there, or away on holiday? If you are there, I will prepare and send you sufficient synopsis and notes for you to see the trend of those articles I spoke to you about.
>
> Only I must ask you to regard the stuff as strictly confidential till ready for publication; for I don't want my pitch queered by some facile personage who'd pick up the skin without the guts o' it. All the stuff, as I told you, belongs to my projected book on psycho-economics, which will be, I hope, my magnum opus, in the sense that it will contain an exposition of the thought that underlies all my books. Either I've got

> hold of a big thing, or else I'm all wrong; and my friends qualified to judge give me a fair amount of confidence that the latter is not the case. I want to carry the advance made in metaphysics by Bergson into economics and social affairs, restating them, not in terms of money, the counters of life, but in terms of conscious volitional life itself.
> What I should propose to do, would be to sketch out the book as it will be, then pick up the striking portions, and on them write a series of articles, under the title 'Wealth and Life', making statements as lucidly as possible rather than shoving into the articles all the prop-arguments which will have to come into the book. You will find the nucleus of it all in that paragraph which I quoted in my article for your recent Labour symposium.
> I take it you wouldn't mind copyrighting the articles. To be quite frank, I shouldn't serialise the stuff but for the damnable necessity I'm under of carrying on meanwhile.
> Seeing I do succeed in explaining my ideas to my friends here, I ought to be able to succeed in making myself plain to your readers, though the majority of them, of course, being semi-educated middle class, are denser than my uneducated friends.[23]

As he told Pinker, he was looking for serialisation in the States as well. "Am negotiating with the *Mail* for serialization of the more striking chapters – or drafts of them – of my projected book, 'Wealth and Life', on psycho-economics, a new cross-bred science of my own invention; and I intend to try very hard for Yankee publication and copyright. I *must* try and touch their damn'd barbarian market!"[24]

He had hoped to put his serialisation strategy to George Macmillan in person, but the latter's plans for running down to Sidmouth for a few days at the start of his summer holiday fell through. So at the beginning of September, Reynolds set it out in a letter.

> You will, I suppose, soon be going north, if you are not already potting at the unfortunate little partridges. I wish cat-shooting were a proper diversion for you sportsmen: I'd invite you here for three days sport ten times annually.
> However, seriously. I do wish you had been able to run down. I'd have liked to discuss with you the question of getting written the projected book on psycho-economics. I'm not very given to thinking my books mark epochs, but I do really believe that in this case I have got hold of quite a big thing – if I can only get it down properly, – and in a sense I feel the more responsible over it because if my own life and experiences haven't fitted me to handle the subject – well, whose have? Bergson's metaphysic is acknowledged to have given a new twist to philosophy. Psycho-economics is, precisely, the carrying of the Bergsonian meta-

> physic, and *mode of thought*, into sociology, economics and politics – into active, as distinct from contemplative, human affairs. That has been implicit in all my work, and the job now is to disentangle it as an ordered scheme. Then, I believe, people will say, "Why, of course; we've known that all along, only nobody said so." What, in fact, I want to do, is to bring down out of the air what is already in the air – a work, not of punditry, but of real solidity – the sort of book your house is already famous for.
>
> Anyhow, it's already on the books that the *Mail* might serialize, in nine or ten longish articles, the more striking chapters in draft form. That would provide the money to write the book on, or a good deal of it, and would give it a big advance advertisement, so that, if they consent to the arrangement, I suppose I shall. But time would have to elapse between the draft form and the publication of the book proper, and I'm not very keen on leaving my ideas at the mercy of London's very prehensile intellects – with their horrid metropolitan facility in seizing the superficies of a thing and leaving its real meaning twice-buried.
>
> What do you think about such an arrangement – from your point of view, too, as the probable future publishers of the book itself? Please understand.... This is not an attempt to sub. you in advance. I've got to work out ways and means of getting the book done, and that's why I wanted your opinion, etc., – not your coin.[25]

The negotiations with the *Mail* achieved only partial success. The newspaper agreed to take nine articles, but only as separate items, not in the serial form that Reynolds regarded as essential. It was then that he turned to his new editorial friend, Charles Sarolea, with the plan to publish in *Everyman*, but, as we have seen, those negotiations foundered too on Sarolea's insistence that the resultant book would have to be offered to Dent.

In October, he was still wondering whether to accept the *Mail* offer as the best of a bad job, but his appointment to the Cornish Committee put paid to any immediate hope of writing and once again psycho-economics was relegated to the back-burner.[26]

But through that heavy winter of physical and emotional exhaustion, he had not lost sight of his next literary objective. In January 1913, when he was still entangled in the fisheries committee, he was interviewed by a journalist from the *Christian Commonwealth*. Reynolds' personality was still a source of some intrigue to those meeting him for the first time, as this journalist admitted.

> Mr. Reynolds's personality is more of a challenge and a puzzle than his books. They, indeed, react stimulatingly upon the reader, and leave him with quickened pulses, but they are less provocative than he; he cannot be easily classified, and his directness and strength, his candour, his fresh

> and bracing moral judgments, his ruthlessness and disdain of convention, whether of dress and habit or of opinion, are emanations of large and dignified personality. In appearance he belongs to the class among whom he lives. His dress, as he himself describes it in "Alongshore" (one of the five books published by Messrs. Macmillan), is "something between a tramp steamer's second mate ashore and a Wild West scoundrel". I do not myself endorse the second part of the description, but perhaps he was slightly differently attired when we met. He exhibits the characteristics of both the callings he has embraced – of the fisherman and the man of letters. His hands are firm and strong, his frame well knit, and his face, though the skin is slightly tanned and roughened by exposure to all sorts of weather, has the fine lines and the alert expression that reveal an active and educated brain behind. The combination of youth with an unusually wide and deep experience of life in its starkest and most elemental form endows him with a peculiarly tonic and invigorating quality, and for a city dweller, at least, contact with him has the same fresh and bracing effect as a holiday by the changeful sea he loves and writes about so graphically and intimately.

To this journalist Reynolds was now prepared to unload the most intimate secrets of his writing life. "We talked for some time of his methods and aims in writing. He explained that he wrote slowly, not more than five hundred words a day, and there are many days when he writes nothing at all." But he was keen to emphasise that his writing life was far from over, and that psycho-economics was to be the next milestone.

> At the present moment he is travelling in the West-country on a fishery commission, but he has other books in hand which, if I understood their scope and aim aright, will strike out a new line of thought. "Psycho-Economics" is the title given to the provisional draft, but it will probably be published first serially under the title, "Wealth and Life". My glance at the draft was necessarily hurried and cursory. It seemed to me, however, that if Mr. Reynolds succeeds in working out his thesis he will do for economics what Mr. Norman Angell has done for international peace. I could not help feeling that notwithstanding the number of books already placed to his credit in the publisher's lists Mr. Reynolds is only at the beginning of his real literary work. His best books are not yet written.[27]

With the Cornish Committee out of the way, he settled down that spring to the real work on his *magnum opus*. But all his efforts over Easter to put pen to paper were thwarted by the fresh distractions of the Inshore Fisheries Committee he had been persuaded against his better judgment to join. His resignation from the Committee, though unaccepted, gave him the psychological freedom he needed to get down to work. With much effort, he wrestled for some weeks with the first article. On 11 June he reported jubilantly to Harold Wright: "Today, I have finished the "Wealth and Life" groundwork article of my psycho-economics book, and am rather pleased, because I think after an atrocious labour something has really got itself born".[28]

The sight of the first instalment finally decided the *Mail* that this abstruse philosophising was not for them. As he had done when the more controversial *Seems So!* articles had been rejected, he now fell back on Massingham and the *Nation* where he was always assured of a warm welcome. On 13 July he reported to Pinker: "I am getting on with my psycho-economics book, very slowly, but I think to some effect. The *Mail* couldn't stomach it, when it came to the point; I couldn't help getting rather metaphysical; but Massingham has taken the English serial rights with considerable enthusiasm for the *Nation*".[29]

Though the focus of what literary energy remained to him that summer and autumn was on this new book, he nevertheless took every opportunity to nurture the books he had already written. In June, he received permission from Macmillans to negotiate with Nelsons and his old friend John Buchan for a shilling edition of *Alongshore*. He felt some guilt about the necessity of turning to another publisher. "I think it's a judicious step. All the same, I can't say I entirely like it."[30]

In August, the assistant editor of the *English Review*, Chalmers Dixon, on holiday in Sidmouth, asked Reynolds for permission to produce a small anthology from his works. Reynolds was enthusiastic, but when Dixon approached Macmillans he got short shrift: "We do not think...... that Mr. Reynolds' work has been before the public long enough to make such an anthology advisable." Nor were they prepared for Dixon to approach another publisher.[31] Reynolds was full of sympathy for Dixon's efforts: "Lord knows that, as a writer, I need hauling out of the stagnation into which I seem to have fallen".[32]

He took the matter up himself with Frederick Macmillan, manning the bridge at St Martin's Street at the height of the holiday season. "I understand from Chalmers Dixon, of the English Review, who has been staying down here, and mooted the idea then, that he wants to compile a sort of anthology or tit-bit book from my work, and that you aren't very keen on its being done. Nor am I in some ways, but I do feel that anything deserves the benefit of the doubt (if there is one) which might tend to lift me, as a literary concern, out of the depressing stagnation into which I seem to have fallen while I have been attending to fishery things; and which, moreover – for it has come to that – might produce any hard cash. You will understand, of course, that I'm not wanting to press; I leave, and in any case should leave, the matter entirely to you."[33]

Macmillans stuck to their view that Reynolds had not yet written enough to be anthologised; in any case, anthologies didn't sell and would make him no money.[34] Reynolds felt there had been a misunderstanding. "As for the anthology.... I believe we've been talking about two different sorts of anthology. I didn't imagine from what Dixon said that he contemplated a *serious* anthology, suitable to a long-established author of weight; but rather one of those gimcrack little anthologies *de luxe*, which sell, if they do, merely because they're pretty and handy for presents!"[35]

Macmillans were at last prepared to concede. "We think that if it really is one of the tiny booklets of the kind you refer to it cannot do any harm; but we could really only judge of this if Mr. Dixon were to send a complete list of the passages which he proposes to use."[36] Reynolds had had enough experience of drafting Ministerial submissions to recognise this treatment. "Poor Dixon! Surely only Govt. could ask him to do all his selecting with the chance of having it sat on at the end of his work! For I understand it isn't long passages he wants to use, but sayings rather, and aphorisms. If you refer to my letter to Danby, you will see, I think, that I did not describe the thing as a "tiny booklet"; it might, indeed, for all I know, be wadded out with blue ribbons and such-like, to a considerable adiposity!"

Reynolds was at pains to offer reassurance. "You can be quite certain that I should hasten to put my own foot down on anything calculated to harm my books or our joint, not, alack! very profitable interest in them."[37] With that, Frederick Macmillan was happy to agree. "We are quite willing to withdraw our objection to his Anthology, and he is at liberty to get it issued if he can find a publisher for it. The only thing that we do not want to do is to publish it ourselves."[38] But no other publisher came forward, and the free publicity which Reynolds had hoped for from the book had to be foregone.

But while all this niggling had been going on over the anthology, Macmillans had been positively statesmanlike in their generosity over another literary project. In August Reynolds' negotiations with Nelsons over the cheap edition of *Alongshore* broke down. "I had hopes that a cheap edition of *Alongshore* would rouse things up, but Nelsons, to whom you kindly allowed me to take it, say that it is too much a collection, though I told them it was conceived and written as one book. Yet they ask for *Seems So*, which they can't have, though that is frankly in the second half of it a collection!"[39]

Reynolds was still two months away from his permanent appointment with the Development Commission and desperately short of money. Macmillans were fully aware of this, but aware also of the commercial possibilities of a cheap edition of *Seems So!* George Macmillan wrote back without prompting: "As Nelson's will not do a shilling edition of "Alongshore" but would like to do "Seems So", which, as you say, they can't have, we will do "Seems So" ourselves upon the same terms, namely, a royalty of ten per cent, as in the case of "A Poor Man's House". Only let us know if you wish to make any alterations and the book can then be put in hand whenever you like. We have some hundreds of copies of the six shilling edition, but there seems to be no particular object in waiting for these to sell out as the book is now going rather slowly".[40]

Reynolds was a little sheepish and embarrassed at such generosity out of the blue. "Your proposal about a cheap edition of *Seems So* is very kind and I thank you. But I don't want you to do it against the grain and your better judgement because I'm in a worrit. Those several hundred copies of the 5/- [*sic*] edition don't sound nice."[41] But he buckled to and by 4 September had got together the slightly revised copy for the cheap edition and written a new preface.[42]

The chapter on *Navy Discontents*, now overtaken by the enlarged version in *The Lower Deck*, was to go out and be replaced by his *Times* fishery articles from the previous February, "which are pretty lively reading, and will soon be pretty topical".[43] He had made some small amendments to the articles for reasons explained in the preface: "Some of the more controversial matter I have cut out, not because we think it was wrong, but because it is no use shaking the tree when the apples are down".[44] And, as ever, more keen on propaganda than on art, he had piled in at the end an appendix consisting of his 1912 letter to the *Times* on Share Fishermen and the Insurance Act.

Five thousand copies were printed that November, half the cheap edition of *A Poor Man's House*.[45] On return from fisheries business in London in the middle of January 1914, Reynolds found his newly published copies waiting for him. "It looks very nice, and I only hope it will go."[46]

Although in July 1913 he had found an English home for his psycho-economics articles, he was still looking out for the profitable American serialisation. On 23 July, he went up to London on fisheries and publishing business, seeing Vaughan Nash, Pinker, Massingham and Buckle.[47] He spent the weekend with Harmsworth at Henley, and once again they meandered through Saturday on the banks of the Lambourn. The mimulus and meadow sweet were in full bloom though the weather this time was cool and dull. As before, Reynolds slumbered most of the day by the side of the stream while Harmsworth fished. The next day they took the car to Nettlebed and walked the five miles back through the woods to Henley. They rounded off a perfect weekend playing cricket with the children on the lawn after Sunday tea.[48]

But Reynolds had failed in his main aim that visit of seeing George Brett, Macmillans' American counterpart. Returned home, he sought George Macmillan's support. "I have just missed Mr Brett twice.... Do you think I might send him the first half-dozen psycho-economics articles in case he may know anyone who would take to them over there? Massingham will not start printing at any rate till Sept. and it is very necessary for me – both from a copyright and a pecuniary point of view – to get them settled somehow in America. The *Nation* pays £5-5 each, and they average three weeks each to write!"[49]

As July passed into August, the writing got slower still and his money worries more pressing. Then in the middle of the month came a devastating personal blow.

Life had changed much for Margot since she had first joined him permanently in Sidmouth in the spring of 1907. Gone were the twenty-mile-a-day tramps across Dartmoor and the misbehaviour in butchers shops. Most of her exercise now was leaping about on the beach or playing up to the children on the Esplanade. As she grew older, she spent more time sleeping in her kennel in the back garden, seeing less of her master as business took him increasingly away from home. Like him, she had never been wholly well – bad pregnancies, severe rheumatism even as a young dog. Now she fell ill for the last time and, at the age of eight and a half, Reynolds had to have her put down.

She had long been the substitute for the intimate friend he had still not yet found. She was all that was left from the days of his youthful struggles. His friends had changed, but she had remained the same. It was a loss he found difficult to communicate, in the midst of all his other worries, to Frederick Macmillan: "The new book is going with great labour and slowness, and I haven't yet succeeded in serializing in America. What with that and half a dozen other worries – worst of all, last week, I had to have my poor old dog, Margot, killed – I feel distracted from work and all to bits; sapped out with getting no for'arder".[50]

At home, he had to keep the grief and the loss to himself, but he was quick to unleash his feelings of frustration on his friends up-country. "Work has been going badly amid noises that have been getting more and more on my nerves; finances slack and troublesome, – and worst of all, I have had to have poor old Margot killed. Makes one feel very damn'd lonely, for I find that one gets precious little sympathy from anyone here, except one is engaged in promoting their affairs and not always there".[51]

Two years later, commiserating with Aunt Jane over the loss of Aunt Allie's dog Toby, he was more generous in recalling the reaction of the Woolleys.

> I am so sorry to hear that Toby has gone. The inevitability of it was often in my mind. One can't say – what could one say? When Margot went, nobody said anything to me for weeks about her. All my people knew, with the delicacy they've got, times like that, that there was nothing at all to say.
>
> Nothing that I know can make up for the loss of a dog, – in the same department of one's existence, so to speak – and there it is. The pain of such things does get less, though one thinks it never will. It becomes a watermark in the tissue of one's life, instead of an ink-mark on the surface: that's all.[52]

Three months later, at the beginning of December, it was the turn of the family cat – but this time it was entirely his own doing. For a few years now, he had been in the habit of taking a friendly pot-shot at the local cats to stifle their caterwauling beneath his window. In his frustration with the noise, he was reverting to the wildness and violence of his youth out on the Wiltshire

Downs. The invitation to George Macmillan to come on an autumn cat-shoot was not quite a joke. In the latest incident, he had gone too far and was now full of guilt and remorse.

> Another job too.... Have just had to drown the household cat – a nasty beast, but a contemporary here of mine. The heller had taken to mewing at the back door under my window very early in the morning, and yesterday, furious with unending struggle against noise, I took up my air rifle, intending to tickle her rump – and hit her more vitally. Put her in the linhay to die, and first thing Bob did when he came down was to poke her about with a broom, up there, to make her get out of the way. Had to tell him then, at risk of all the kids gathering round and howling. Mam 'Oolley was rather glad, having meant to make an end of her. I was sorry and upset in the extreme, for I hate hurting animals unless I'm mad with them.
>
> However, to-day, the thing having revived, came down mewing again all through dinner, turning round and round, round and round, and as I'd started the job, I had to end it, and did so, with old Mother Cordey at the washing tub close by prophesying bad luck to all who kill cats.
>
> Margot gone, the cat gone – it's like links breaking all round the circle.[53]

This violent episode was the latest admission of the personal hell which living cooped up in Bob's cottage had now at times become. But he was already in process of breaking the final link.

In 1913, Salcombe Hill was a green-field site with scarcely a house or a road to its name. There were potential building plots on it, mostly owned by wealthy middle-class Sidmouthians with a view eventually to building for themselves. The sites were not intended to furnish the solution to the working class housing problem of the town, as represented by the overcrowded and crumbling Bedford Square.

In mid-July Reynolds had found, through his friend and solicitor, Philip Michelmore, a site on the edge of the cliff, the second plot on what is now Cliff Road, with only the cliff footpath between it and the drop to the sea. It stood in the parish of Salcombe; technically, he would be leaving Sidmouth altogether. A long narrow plot, 350 foot by 50, it was large enough to build a roomy house for Reynolds and the Woolleys to share; he would take the front with the Woolleys spaciously housed at the back. But neither Bob nor Mam were prepared to play ball. Mam was afraid that the children would fall over the cliff. Bob was even less enthusiastic at losing his independent property rights: "if he has the front and we're pushed to the back, we'll end up treated like bloody servants".[54]

So a new plan was devised under which Reynolds would build for himself alone, with room for a secretary and arrangements for a woman to come in daily, while Tom would set himself up in a cottage at the other end of the plot. It was many years since he had first promised the upwardly-mobile Tom to help find a place of his own.

It was a perfect site, light and airy, looking right down to the sea and with commanding views across the town to High Peak on the other side of the bay. For Reynolds, it was not escape from the dirt and disease of Bedford Square that held out most promise; it was escape from noise. As he returned to the slow laborious work on his psycho-economics articles, he told Pinker: "I found it devilish difficult to settle down properly to writing again, and have been so maddened by noises by day and night that Tom and myself are trying to get a patch of land on the cliff, whereon to build ourselves a couple of cottages".[55]

It was a complex acquisition, for the land was tied up in a tangle of earlier mortgages and outright purchase could not be made at once.[56] But by October, arrangements had been made to assign the site to Reynolds and he told Garnett with some relief: "Tom and I have got a bit of land on the eastern cliff and are going to build ourselves a couple of cottages. Not that I want to leave Bob's, but I am simply crowded out, can't have more room, and have been tormented to death with greatly increased noise".[57] Three days later he gave Cecil Harmsworth a graphic example of his trials. "All the confounded kids are howling together with bellyache upstairs. I'm off. Fly-blown food, I believe."[58]

When he finally made the purchase the plot was to cost him £150. But his new salary for the Development Commission, also agreed that October, now offered him the possibility of expanding the landholding to embrace the two plots on either side and give more space to Tom. For Reynolds, the unaccustomed security of a salary meant not an enhancement of his own lifestyle, but the chance to do good by stealth. He swore Aunt Jane to secrecy.

> But it will enable me, with my always small personal expenditure, to do sundry things I want. I think I shall get a chance of rounding up the 'estate' to the cliff on both sides for £175. In that case, as I don't approve of land being kept for building I shall give Tom a plot for a cottage behind the building line and add the field apart to mine. I have a bigger financial project of buying Bob an annuity on his own and his wife's life of about £1 a week to come down to 5/- or 10/- as they arrive at old age pensions. After all, if I am going to prosper (financially), there's no knowing how much of it I owe to them, but it is a very great deal, and I think the Ol' man – Bob – has slaved years enough. Also I have had a project of running a consumptive hut for open air treatment up either on the cottage verandah or in an open shelter on the ground. A few pounds a year would just make that possible, and it makes me sick to watch the young chaps die of it as I have done lately.... Don't pass on these projects of mine. I want to work at them quietly without cackle.[59]

But first priority was the design of his new cottage. He wanted it to be in some way exemplary, and tapped all of Harmsworth's specialist knowledge of designs for model working-class housing. He finally decided upon one of the plans, slightly adapted, set out in the recent report of the Departmental Committee on Buildings for Small Holdings on which Harmsworth himself had sat. He gave most attention to the design of his study on the first floor, which would look down the back garden straight out to sea, with a window on the left giving on to the top of Salcombe Hill and on the right a spectacular view across to High Peak.

In negotiating the plans with the local authorities, he chanced upon an old friend of Harmsworth's. "I sent for the Sanitary Inspector of the Honiton R.D.C. to discuss the plans of our cottages, and when I happened to mention you in connexion with concrete structures, he burst out: "Why, Cecil, I worked like the devil for him in Worcestershire!" Evidently you've left faithful behind you there! His name is Redfern, and he is reputed hereabout to be much too smart at his job for the skimping local builders. He told me the builder we have chosen is the only honest one in the whole lot."[60]

By 1 December, the dismal day on which he had drowned the cat, most of the legal consultations had been completed and he was partially cheered to receive the final drafts of the plans. But there was another cloud on the horizon; Tom was not sure that he was getting value for money. Reynolds wrote to Cecil Harmsworth.

> Got the complete draft plans of the cottages to-day. But I'm afraid I shall have to lump the agreement and plans down before Tom with a "take it so, or leave it; which you like."! He doesn't understand, nor take part in, the amount of work it has been to wriggle through a mass of legal rottery, building instructions, price limitations, planning and bye-laws, and in consequence continually harks back to the supreme desirability of impossibilities, and does not see how he has got what he could not have got otherwise all along the line. 'Tisn't his fault – but it's my misfortune; and having done my best for him, my temper (at present) is scarcely reliable enough to stand being treated as if, like a builder, I were out to make something. So, for the avoidance of explosions, I think I must take up the position of offering so much for so much – "Yes, or no?" 'Tisn't co-operation, that, but I can't help o' it. There is no doubt that all working people – though I'd like to think otherwise – are the devil's own job to do business with on level terms, otherwise than as vendor and buyer, mainly because, while refusing or unable to go into the intricacies of the matter, they reserve full rights of criticism both reasonable and the reverse.[61]

Presented with the choice of take it or leave it, Tom decided on the latter option. Reynolds decided to plough on with the plans. Three days later he told Harold Wright

> Had to write and tell your father this morning that my joint housing scheme has gone bust. Having got the plans – extremely good ones, in my opinion – Tom thinks he is not getting his money's worth! So I have told him that he can have that plot, if he likes, and I'll go higher up, and that he had better go and do better for himself, and let off the part corresponding with mine. Had he not carefully refused to be worried with the mass of difficulties I have had to worm my way through, I think he would have seen that he was being done rather better than well; but he hasn't; and it's no good persuading him (if it were possible) to take over a cottage he doesn't like, and I'm damn sure nothing better can be produced for what he wants to pay.
>
> I shall go on and build (if I can) according to the plan, which, as I say, is ingeniously good, and shall let what would have been Tom's to a caretaking tenant. Mam 'Oolley will have the refusal; I have redeemed my old promise to Tom that if ever I could get hold of suitable land, he should have the chance of a place of his own.
>
> Now I'm free.[62]

The decision to go it alone increased the tension in his relationship with both Woolley families and heightened his usual December depression. "Things very depressing here. On account of the collapse of the house scheme. They are all up against me, and Tom has a face like a pile of herring nets without a fish in 'em. One would have thought my many years' efforts would at least have been kept to my credit.... But I suppose one mustn't expect too much. And I daresay I'm over-sensitive to atmospheres...."[63]

But the troubles did not deflect him from his usual generosity. Bob and Tom had earned £2 each that year on the royalties of *Seems So!* but the money was not due to filter out of Macmillans until the New Year. He sent Pinker a cheque for £4 so that both could be sent official cheques in time for Christmas.[64]

The legal preliminaries to the building of his cottage had brought him into touch with the general development plan for Sidmouth, which filled him with disgust. It provided that the prime sites near the sea, like those on Salcombe Hill, should be limited to two houses per acre, putting the land prices well beyond the pockets of the working classes who were to be shoved on to housing estates much further inland. In typical Reynolds fashion, his private dealings were now to lead him into public controversy.

On 15 January, at the Foresters' Dinner at the Anchor, when the select of the town played host to the working men, he was called upon as usual to second the toast of "The Town and Trade of Sidmouth". He was in a particularly bolshy mood. He expressed surprise at being invited to second the toast since, so far as he personally was concerned, the increased prosperity of the town meant that he had to pay more for his bacon and other commodities. He then picked up the theme of the toast's proponent, who had praised the local working men's dwelling scheme, by haranguing his audience at length on the iniquities of the development plan, demanding that the Council should display the planning map in a shop window in the town rather than hide it away in the Council offices.[65]

He followed up this plea in a letter to the local paper. "What chance have working people or people with small incomes of ever being able to live in houses built two, or four, or six to the acre on the unbuilt land of Sidmouth anywhere near the sea. Such land would be too expensive...... The impression I gained from the above mentioned coloured map in the Council chamber was that, except on one or two patches near the river, new houses for working people or people of small means were to be shoved off to Landpart, Woolbrook, or thereabout. So far as the much-needed working men's houses are concerned, it amounts to turning the working classes out of the town, right away from the sea."[66]

Next week came a stinging response from one of Reynolds' neighbours, Mr Clements, a lodging-house keeper in Marine Place, on the seaward side of Bedford Square: "This self-appointed 'Champion of the Working Man' displays much of the qualities of imagination that has made him successful in fiction." Clements argued that if working-class dwellings, rather than lodging-houses, were built by the sea, that would be the end of the visitors. "We all would like to see it made possible for the working classes to live by, and enjoy to the full, the health-giving breezes and the glorious scenery that the esplanade affords; but would anyone seriously propose this?"[67]

Typically, Reynolds saw this as his chance to treble the publicity. He concocted an anonymous letter, subscribed "Sidmouth Resident", supporting the previous correspondent and attacking himself. "As Mr Clements so truly remarks, how can anyone seriously propose that the working classes should 'live by, and enjoy to the full, the health-giving breezes and the glorious scenery that the Esplanade affords' if they cannot pay for it. They cannot expect to enjoy what they cannot pay for. We none of us can. It is my belief that the working classes know their place better than to listen to the mischief-making of Mr S Reynolds. I have always found them most respectful, though apt at times to overcharge for their services."

He attacked the mischief-maker with undisguised relish. "And who, sir, may I ask, is Mr S Reynolds that he should thus intervene in local affairs? He is not a Sidmouthian, nor yet a resident, though for some years, I understand, he has been an inhabitant of the town. He is not, I am told, without a certain talent for writing, and it is greatly to be regretted that an educated man should allow his notorious partiality for low-class company to lead him into speaking and writing with that bluntness, that coarseness, that lamentable want of tone, which we are accustomed to expect only from the uneducated. It is also a great pity he should be invited to those dinners and suppers at which the local gentry are accustomed to enter into friendly intercourse with working men, and to instruct them for their own good. I suggest, therefore, that in future he be not invited. The local gentry cannot be expected to sit and listen to his nonsense."[68]

The letter was taken at face value by most of the working people of the town, and it is some measure of their feelings for Reynolds at this time that it caused an angry explosion. He himself was delighted with this "rare bit of sport" and sent a copy of his letter proudly on to Harmsworth.

> A lodging-house keeper, related to the Manor people, wrote to the mid-week paper complaining of the lack of tone and the "slashing attacks" of the "self-appointed champion of the working classes". So it occurred to me that I could bring my protest into still greater publicity if I didn't wait for anyone else to slang me, but wrote and slanged myself in the best style of the Sidmouth selectitudinous. The enclosed letter, therefore, signed "Sidmouth Resident" is by myself. But the secret has been well kept; the Town has swallowed it; and the working people are simply raging, and threatening to smash every window in "Sidmouth Resident's" house.
>
> Best of it is, the letter contains nothing that is not said by the select; it's a piece of true fiction. And 'twill dish utterly their nice little scheme for pushing all working-class houses into the background.[69]

In fact, the letter had caused more stir than Reynolds had ever expected, and the whole enterprise was in danger of backfiring into violence. Word went round that it had been written by William Hastings, the Manor agent, who accused Reynolds to his face of fabricating the rumour. It was then that Reynolds admitted his authorship, which he had always intended to make public. The next edition of the paper carried a vitriolic attack by Hastings on Reynolds for his "duplicity", cheek by jowl with Reynolds' letter confessing his responsibility.[70]

He was unrepentant over the furore he had caused. "There is a sort of highly select people still in existence in places like Sidmouth, though a good deal behind the times, who don't mind the working people being alive, so long as they keep off the grass, and who, as I once told them at a meeting, would rather have a pigsty up against their wall, than a working man's house within sight. It struck me that what such people say and work for privately had far better be said openly. So I said it for them." The resultant publicity given to the local development plan had fully justified the unorthodox means. "The Plan I saw needed bringing to the notice of everybody. The town needed waking up to what was afoot. And I think I've succeeded in doing it, haven't I?"[71]

The reverberations rumbled on in the local press for another four weeks, until Reynolds was forced to admit: "Had I imagined it possible my spoof letter could have been taken so seriously, and have roused so much feeling, I would certainly have made its spoofery much plainer than it was."[72]

And he did a little to defuse the violence of that feeling with another spoof letter, this time purporting to come from the pen of Bob. "Oh, Mr Stephen

Reynolds, what a naughty man you are! How could you be so wicked as to write a letter to the Press, abusing yourself in the way you did, deceiving and causing us so much indignation that we nearly rose up and stoned perfectly innocent folks...... to delude us into the belief that the letter expressed the genuine bona-fide opinion of a 'Sidmouth Resident' was really too bad. It 'Seems So' to me, at least. I cannot find words (and I have searched the dictionary nearly through) to suitably tell you how angry I am. You had better get up into 'The Holy Mountain' for a time, and not stay 'Alongshore', occupying 'The Lower Deck' of 'A Poor Man's House', until you have fittingly and becomingly expressed your regret for your 'spoof' letter."[73]

But Reynolds himself took the issue with the utmost seriousness, and went to the lengths of sending the correspondence on to John Burns at the Board of Trade as demonstrating a potential weakness in the Housing and Town Planning Act, which Burns had personally driven through the Commons in 1909 and which was already proving a dead letter.

> You may remember my telling you one day that we were on the point of adopting the H. and T.P. Acts here. But I find, actually, that there is a grave risk of the Act being perverted in the interests of the selectitudinous people here, and of its being used to prevent any working-class or even small middle-class houses from ever being built on any of the good open land anywhere near the sea. Not that the owners will sell or lease land for that purpose now; but one objects to your act being used to confirm in perpetuity a policy which doesn't care twopence what happens to the working-classes so long as they are kept out of sight. The letter, two copies of which are enclosed, and the speech to which it refers, were an attempt to expose the little game which was being played, before the town should be committed to a plan which schedules practically all the unbuilt land near the sea for two houses to an acre. At the dinner at which I spoke, not one of the seventy or eighty working men to whom I was speaking could say he had seen the map, but the faces of the "local gentry" above the salt – well, they were my reward!
>
> For this is a place where the select buy up fields at building prices, and keep a cow or two on them, in order to prevent what they call low-class houses from ever being built near them. As I once told them at a housing meeting, they'd rather have pigstyes up against their houses than a working-man's cottage within sight. I believe myself that working people are undesirable as neighbours merely because of the ugly hutches they are compelled to live in, and that some groups of working-men's cottages, near the sea where they are so badly wanted, and properly laid out, as your Act allows, would no more spoil the place than the gimcrack expensive villas that they put up here, about two to an acre.
>
> By using great circumspection, I succeeded last year in collaring rather more than 1/4 acre of land on the cliff near the sea, before the selecti-

> tudinous got wind of it to overbid me. Now I'm having a cottage put up there...... and I'm indulging myself in a certain amount of hope that when the place is up you will redeem your promise to run down this way.[74]

For all the time he was exploiting to the full this foray into the new field of housing politics, his own practical demonstration of what a working-class house should be was steadily gathering momentum. He had finally decided to build just the one cottage, and on 20 January 1914 the first work began on the cliff-top site. There was a thrill of anticipation in his letter to Aunt Jane. "We pegged out the four – or rather the six – corners of the house last Tuesday and I think they are now digging off the top spit for the foundations. Sudweeks [*the current landlord of the Bear*] is going to give me back my mother's blue china, and I think, some of her pictures. I am curiously looking forward to seeing that china laid out again and on my own table. I have cut a corner off the landing outside my study, which will be a fine room looking E., S., and W., so as to make sure of getting up the long waited for grand piano."[75]

Building took off quite rapidly. A month later he reported to Edward Carpenter "my cottage on the cliff is now climbing up"; and to Harmsworth on 2 March: "My cottage is up to the first floor! And the controversy has fizzled out: conclusive evidence of the truth of my statements come forward in the local press, and the Manor clique suddenly went mum."[76] A month later, he told Carpenter: "The cottage has nearly got its roof on, spite of the continuous rain, and gives promise of being quite pretty."[77]

It was an imaginatively designed small house, built of brick to the first floor with plaster facings above and gently curving ends to the gables. The windows, particularly those of the first floor study, were carefully designed to maximise the effect of the spectacular sea views. Altogether, house and land, it had cost him £350.[78] Apart from the Coastguard station a little higher up, and an old country house nearby, his was the only building on the green open pastures that covered the whole of the hill. Next to it was a small landmark – a clump of tangled trees and bushes. Taking his cue from this, he named his house The Thicket.

By the middle of May, it was ready for furnishing and Aunt Jane was still offering her financial support. But he was now getting cold feet at the thought of leaving Bob. "As to the house.... It's very kind of you to say the P.O. money is still waiting and to offer me furnishing items. I don't see why I should denude you of your household goods, and as to their not being good enough for my shanty – well, it's very uncertain whether I'm going there. The nearer we come to it, the less Bob and I like parting, and though where I am is in many respects very bad for me and my present brain-work, I'm by no means certain that living elsewhere wouldn't be worse. We have become more dependent on each other than perhaps we realise when things are going all right, and so far as I can tell, my mind is making itself up not to move up the hill till he can go too, plus all the family."[79]

It was not until the middle of July that he could grab the necessary few days to complete the furnishing, but now all the heart had gone out of the project. He told Carpenter: "The cottage I have been building is finished now, but I have not gone up there yet – and, indeed, haven't any great enthusiasm for doing so now it comes to the point. I have been here so long."[80]

This was to be the greatest change to his life since 1906 and now, as he confided to Aunt Jane, the nostalgic memories began to come flooding back.

> The cottage is furnished, but even now I have not started to go up there. Bob and I neither of us like separating; we have been each other's most intimate friend for so many years; and I have a feeling that just as my health resurrected itself with him, so without him it may go to bits again. The point at issue is, whether, if I build on a couple of rooms, he will come up. I'm content to go in front, as it were, but not if he isn't coming. Funny a chance visit to Sidmouth should have settled my whole life.... [81]

At the end of July, with some finishing touches yet to make, there was still no resolution of the main issue. "I'm supposed to be furnishing my cottage and I dread going there – and I can't continue my work here for lack of facilities. Result – complete deadlock!"[82] But the threatening war was, in the end, to unlock the problem. Immediately, he was rushed away on a tour of the fishery ports and where he touched base in Sidmouth soon became of purely academic importance. In the early days of August, he offered his cottage on the hill to the Admiralty as a convalescent hospital, if needed, and its immediate future was effectively frozen.[83]

In July 1913, as Reynolds was taking these first tentative steps in property ownership, he was starting too to make progress with his newly commissioned psycho-economics articles for the *Nation*. It was slow and wearisome progress at first, for he was taking considerable pains. On 14 July, he reported to Cecil Harmsworth: "I am grinding on with my book. Am just starting today to do all over again my last fortnight's work, which isn't pleasant, but the writing of the thing must be as good as ever possible".[84]

He laboured slowly on through August and September, but by the middle of October, with nine instalments complete, he was beginning to pick up confidence. His main enemy was the combined distraction of his fisheries work and the cottage on the hill. "I'm getting along with the book slowly – have sat, today, on Insurance Co.'s, and Sidney Webb – and I think I'm grinding out fairly good stuff. But, Lord, how I'm swamped in speeches, conferences, committees, sanitary inspectors, lawyers, fisheries, estate agents, builder, mortgagee, income tax man.... Makes a fellow whirl in the head if one dares to think of it instead of tackle one thing at a time."[85]

Five days later, he sent Harmsworth proofs of the first two articles, due out in November, and was worrying how much writing time was now left to him following his appointment to the Development Commission. "Enclosed – since you are to be somewhat identified with it – are duplicate proofs of the first two chaps. of the book, for you to glance at if you've time and 'tisn't too much trouble. They indicate the line to be taken. At present it's going rather well; I'm in the X chap. with several ahead bubbling well in my brain; so that I'm praying all the Gods Nash won't rake me out of it for a couple of weeks. Heard to-day, however, from U.S.A. that it's not, after all, to be serialized there. That's a clear hundred pounds I was licking my lips up for (for furniture!) gone pop. But so long as I'm in the vein to write I don't much care."[86]

The first article came out on 8 November, while he was up to his eyes in fisheries business, but raised scarcely a ripple in the press. He wrote to Pinker on 21 November: "I've been nearly run off my head with several fishery matters arriving at the critical stage all to once, but now I think I've snatched two or three weeks at home to get on with the serial. Vaughan Nash tells me he has heard it well spoken of in elevated political quarters, but I didn't get one single news cutting out of the publication of the first article".[87]

On 1 December he was still ploughing on. "Have succeeded by dint of working morning, noon and night in getting another chapter and a half (on *Labour*) of my book done, and hope to have three done by the time I have to stir again for Brightlingsea and Cornwall."[88] But this eleventh article turned out to be the last. Massingham himself was getting cold feet. "Massingham has sent my literary spirits down to zero by writing to say that my articles are still on the side of over-abstraction, and asking me to make them as concrete and illustrative of actual life as possible. They're such a grind to write at all that I can't see how on earth I am to make them other than as they come; besides I'm out, not only to put the working-class point of view, but to show that it is philosophically righter than t'other people's. He wants another *Seems So* and I want to write a *'Tis So!*".[89]

The first ten articles of *Wealth and Life* were published in the *Nation* at fortnightly intervals from 8 November 1913 to 21 March 1914. The final one, *The Attitude of Labor*, was held back until 23 May after Massingham had already pulled the plug on the series. It is some of the best of Reynolds' politico-philosophical writing.

Reynolds sets out to discover the fundamental reason for the current industrial unrest, against the premise that "all political and social questions, all human problems, are at bottom psychological".[90] The question what do the workers want – better wages – raises the prior question, is life for wealth, or wealth for life? – which Reynolds answers in terms of the Bergsonian concept of *élan vital*. "Ultimately, of course, wealth is for life, else useless; and in turn is a product of life. For what is the driving force of humanity, its evolution, civilization, and infinitely complex affairs – of more than humanity, indeed – if not that impulse towards more life, which is inherent in life itself, and without which life would come to an end? Self-interest, self-preservation, reproduction, will to live, will to power, all human motives, do they not find themselves summed up in an *élan de vie*, or impulse towards life and ever more life – life more in quantity or more intense in quality?"[91]

The central thesis of the articles can be stated simply. Wealth is man interacting with matter to produce more life, both quantitively and qualitatively. Civilisation is man interacting with himself to produce more life. In both cases, that interaction is, in its widest sense, work. The fundamental problem of current society is that work is valued in terms of class, not of life. A revaluation in terms of life, while not providing a precise scale of remuneration, could produce a general guide that would redress the massive inequalities.

The existing party political system is redundant, unable to address the rifts in society.

> As the basis of dispute has shifted from Conservatism *versus* Radicalism to Capital *versus* Labor, the old party system has been left stranded, remote from the living realities of national life, endlessly debating outworn quarrels, endlessly tinkering with the details of men's lives instead of plumbing the main currents; and only under extreme pressure does it give up an evening to the discussion, say, of a strike which threatens to bring the country to a standstill, besides entailing misery on helpless thousands of non-combatants. Government, inevitably, has fallen more and more into the hands of lawyers, the profession whose business it is not to create new standards, but to judge new situations by old standards – to cram the new wine of life into the old bottles of precedent. Cloistered behind its protective cordons of police, Parliament fiddles and quibbles, whilst the nation smoulders with a discontent that here and there bursts into flame like beacons at night upon the dark hills.[92]

When he comes to difficult concepts – the relationship between wealth and life – his prose maintains an admirable clarity and simplicity.

> Plainly, wealth and life are bound up together, more intimately, indeed, than is suspected by those who look upon wealth as an end in itself, or upon living men as so much labor. Wealth is nothing without life to use it, any more than foodstuffs could be food with nobody to eat them. If the human race were to cease, wealth, as such, would likewise cease. The "untold wealth" of a newly-discovered country literally cannot be told, because it is not, till men go there and work it. Otherwise, it will forever remain potential, and never come into actual existence – like a piece of music never played; for it is life which brings wealth into actual being, as a player does music by playing it......
>
> For, consider the origin of wealth. The whole fabric of it is reared on the necessity of food. All else might conceivably be dispensed with – shelter,

> clothing, every amenity of life – but mankind must feed to live. Unlike vegetables, however, we cannot directly assimilate inorganic matter. Whether we eat animal or vegetable food, it has to have lived. If, moreover, we plant a grain to harvest it manifold; if our flocks and herds multiply; if we fish the self-replenishing sea – we owe the increase to life. It is life's reproductive power, aided in most cases by our living selves, that maintains or increases the stock of food on the earth, so maintaining us, or enabling us to increase.[93]

By the sixth article, Reynolds has arrived at his favourite subject – work. "Everyone knows what work is, and, as is usually the case with what everybody knows, no one can tell exactly. By a vice of mind which escapes notice only because it is so common, we fasten on that which is tangible or calculable about work, neglecting the rest, and treating the part as if it were the whole." He notes that the four economic textbooks he has consulted contain no discussion of work. "Yet the nature of work, and the intrinsic as well as the extrinsic value of different sorts of it, must obviously be a most important factor in any political economy which deals with living reality, rather than with arbitrary abstractions from it...... As we shall see, the science of political economy has some very hollow bricks at its foundation."[94]

When it comes to the prestige valuation of work, we find Reynolds once more at his most sardonic, and at the same time, most serious.

> "The price of petrol," said a cynical financier, "is what it will fetch." So is the price of work, the price of a man. But the rule applies in its fulness only to those kinds of work, chiefly manual, which go through the so-called labor market. The price of the brain-worker does, with many anomalies, include the factors of repute, esteem, prestige, effort, in addition to that of result, which is sometimes worse than valueless; else long ago, no doubt, they would have used their brains to upset a state of things which they are fairly content should exist in regard to the hand-worker. Bishops, for instance – to take an extreme and ironical case of prestige-valuation – are paid by the thousand a year to follow the footsteps of the Son of Man. (Suffragan bishops, as such, for doing the same spiritual work, nothing.) And although they have mostly told us how extremely poor they are, still it is observable that their dinners and general comforts are distinctly better than the curate's egg. Suppose the official, clerical, and political work, of which their pastorate mainly consists, were delegated to competent assistants, and for their purely spiritual work they were paid the average trades union rate of their diocese, and had to pay away about a quarter of that for an insanitary brick box to live in....
>
> It is not unlikely their spiritual force would gain. It is scarcely likely they would go on talking about the state of the working classes so academi-

> cally, as from on high, stooping. Imagine the Athenaeum decorated in honor of a rise of a penny-ha'penny an hour, with jubilant old gentlemen in aprons and gaiters running out to shake the oily hands of the motor-bus drivers because they can see their way clear to a new pair of boots (on tick) for each and all of the episcopal children. An absurd picture, you say, unworthy of serious discussion. No. The absurdity of it lies in the current social and pecuniary valuations of work. Bishops are, first of all, men, or should be.
>
> For, observe that the valuation of work by what it will fetch – that is to say, by a shifting combination of result and market price, with scant attention to effort, and no cognizance of the intrinsic nature or purpose of work itself – though a rough and ready method, leads inevitably to those social inequalities which, by adding insult to injury, embitter the grievances of the under-paid. It hardens the class system, and bars the attainment of anything much better than our bogus democracy, under which the mass of the people has but fallen out of the frying-pan of feudalism into the hell-fire of capitalism. A man's price is taken to be his worth. He is cheap – and held cheap; expensive – and held in honor. Thus the vicious circle is perpetuated, under which the worker's price is gauged by his social position, and, in turn, his social position by his price; and neither the violence of strikes nor the ineffectitudes of Labor parties have succeeded in breaking it down......
>
> The valuation of work is all at sixes and sevens; its price even more so; and both are further complicated by considerations of time, liberty, fatigue, rest, and the like. There should be no need to labor here the enormous inequalities of payment for work (or for not working) in a nation whose income goes up by leaps and bounds while real wages fall; where the wealth of the few flaunts itself in the face of millions condemned to live in a shameful poverty and hopelessness. But a juster valuation of work must necessarily precede a juster price for it.[95]

How, then, to evaluate work? Well, not this way.

> If human beings were simply machines, absorbing a certain amount of latent energy in the form of fuel, food, or what not, and giving forth again a corresponding amount (less mechanical loss) of active energy, reducible to foot-pounds, both a definition and a valuation of work could readily be arrived at. It would only be a question of refining sufficiently one's methods of measurement. But human work is more than that, though interested parties and pseudo-scientific thinkers of the efficiency school insist on regarding men – especially working-men – as rather troublesome machines, requiring so much protein and carbohydrate, so much air and the like, together with lubricants in the form of enough hygiene to keep them healthy, enough education to render them

> more profitable, a dose of morality and propriety to prevent them from being needlessly offensive, and a modicum of religion to make them contented by promising them in heaven, if they are good, that is to say obedient, under a kind of deferred Workmen's Compensation Act, what is grudged them on earth.[96]

In the final article, Reynolds comes close to a philosophical explanation of his distinction between economic reform (good) and social reform (bad) which had so perplexed readers like Galsworthy five years before. He argues that the two sides of industry approach social problems from two different perspectives – one from wealth, the other from life.

> The worker assumes that life is the primary consideration; the masters, wealth. In the workers' view, wealth should subserve life. But the masters take it for granted that life – especially other people's – must subserve wealth. And the actual situation is further complicated by the fact that we possess, in a state of considerable development, an economics of wealth, while an economics of life – such as I have been trying to adumbrate in these studies – has yet to be evolved as a branch of knowledge. Not that there has been no movement at all towards an economics of life.... Humanitarianism assumes the precedence of life itself over every other consideration. Its political outgrowth, social reform, is founded on the same basis, but because social reformers have never troubled to work out their root principle, and have sought their justification where it is not to be found, namely, in the economics of wealth, they have made egregious blunders in dealing with the *lives* of the poor – as if such lives were mere economic propositions – and by trying to run with the hares of life and hunt with the hounds of wealth, they have time after time succeeded in offending and oppressing precisely those whom they set out to benefit.[97]

In his analysis of the relative position of the classes, he returns to an old theme – while the upper and middle class have the economic advantage, it is the working class that has the *psycho*-economic advantage.

> From the figures alone, it might be concluded that the rich were wallowing in happiness, that the middle class were just about right, and that the poor were sunk in misery and unhappiness. It would not be true. By one of the miracles of human adaptation, the poor, if tolerably free from sheer physical want, are not nearly so unhappy as they might be, or as others would be in their place; nor are the rich nearly so happy as the poor think they ought to be; while the middle classes – they possess an unparalleled aptitude for being dull, worried, and unhappy. What partial process, then, of compensation is at work?[98]

He goes on to explain it is the ability of the poor to develop more life.

> Just as it is possible to use up much more wealth without achieving more life, without, in effect, raising one's standard of life, so it is possible – by changing and improving one's habitual method of getting life out of life, and by that means only – to use up less wealth, and still not to lower one's standard of life, or even to increase it. The change is psychological, not economic. For that reason, every marked advance in the civilization of mankind and in economic progress must necessarily have its spiritual side, and in history always has had.
>
> Here we see how it is that the young can stand better than their elders a decrease in wealth, and a lowering of their standard of life. They have more resistance, more strength and lifetime to earn back the wealth; they have, in addition, more adaptability to find life somehow else. Here, too, we see why the poor are not unhappy in proportion to their poverty, nor the rich happy in proportion to their wealth. The poor, perforce, know better how to extract life from wealth; they hold closer to those means of life-intensification which all men share and which are less dependent on wealth. If the rich have the economic advantage, the psycho-economic advantage rests with the poor.[99]

This raises all manner of questions, not least the delicate one as to how far to redistribute wealth in the new system of wage rates without losing altogether that psycho-economic advantage. Is it possible, in any case, to restrict man's economic appetite, which is also a means to more life, to Reynolds' prescription of "tolerably free from sheer physical want"?

But it would be wrong to expect this stimulating series of articles to deliver a complete system, with all the answers. It was still developing in Reynolds' own mind, and even as a series of articles is incomplete. The early instalments represent a closely argued development of the basic thesis. The later ones – the working of the thesis in social practice – are more diffuse and come to an abrupt halt *in medias res*. Had the series been completed, it would no doubt have returned to a proper summing up and conclusion.

We cannot, therefore, judge from these articles the likely quality of the potential book. All we can say is that they introduce a novel and sweeping critique of the then very new science of economics, attempting as no one had done before to develop a psychological scheme which would fit with the basic lines of economic thought. For Reynolds, it was not just some intellectual flight of fancy, developed for its own sake, or in order to be thought clever. It was, as he was keen to stress, fundamental to the thought and action of his whole life – the intellectual expression of how he had lived and sought to live. It attempted to explain the spiritual vibrancy he had found in the working class, and prescribe a method of preserving it.

But as a critique of economic behaviour, its significance goes much wider. Reynolds developed his thesis in face of the grinding working class poverty of western Europe consequent on the industrial revolution. In his time the overarching dominance of economic greed in western society, whether of multinationals or of lone consumers, had not quite taken hold. The threat of the extinction of man and the destruction of his planet by such forces lay still in the future. Even today, the message that the economy should subserve man and nature, and not *vice versa*, is still, sadly, some hundred years before its time.

As the articles came out that winter of 1913-14, they went almost completely unnoticed. They would, inevitably, have been difficult to review; but Massingham began to think they were becoming difficult to read as well. When he decided to pull them in early March 1914, Reynolds was disappointed, but saw it as only a temporary set-back. His faith in the system he had developed was in no way broken. "Massingham is closing down my 'Wealth and Life' articles in the *Nation*. Journalistic'ly they've been a failure: they cut too much across the rut of recent economic thought. Were I not so dead certain they represent (though feebly) an advance on it, I should be very sick. As 'tis, I hug my psychoeconomic theory the closer."[100]

This was the final disappointment of his writing life. But he continued to hug the ideas closely for the remainder of his physical one. They, and the great book he would one day make out of them, became the symbol both of his past life as a writer and of the continuity of his writing instincts and ambition into the future. They retained an immense importance for him, even though, when boring his friends with them, he affected to treat them with irony.

On the last day of 1916, with the war crisis and the new government threatening a radical overhaul of fisheries policy, perhaps nationalisation, Reynolds invited Henry Maurice down to Sidmouth for a couple of days brainstorming to develop a "far-reaching politico-economic" strategy to stem the administrative drift.

> I only wish I had succeeded in getting out my *Wealth and Life* book. That would have made me one of the people to be consulted by the politicians, because the psycho-economics hypothesis, even if it isn't complete, does clear up and range a whole heap of uncorrelated ideas amongst which people are feeling their way. I know it's "the goods" – as the Yankees say......
>
> It is up to us to make of the fisheries a nation within a nation; a part to lead the whole towards something better in economic and social conditions. For just because the fisheries have held tight to primitive conditions and valuations, as against the dominance of industrialism in everything else, so, I think, they may easily be the jumping-off point towards

a better condition of things under which wealth will subserve life, instead of life subserving wealth.

You may smile.... It wouldn't be the first time.[101]

NINETEEN

District Inspector 1914-16

The War that broke over Europe in the first week of August 1914 came as the apparent salvation of a United Kingdom that was falling apart at the seams. With industrial unrest still grinding on, constitutional disturbance at home over women's rights, and the threatened breakdown in the rule of law in Ulster, a quite different kind of Armageddon was in prospect. The declaration of war against Germany on 4 August relegated all these domestic disputes to the petty category, and united the nation as nothing else could have done.

For many individuals, particularly working men unemployed or on low wages, war came too as a new opportunity. For Reynolds, by contrast, it could not have come at a worse time. The careful plans and hard work of the previous two years in reconstruction of the inshore fisheries were bedding down successfully in the west and poised to deliver their first fruits. The devastating upheaval of war now threatened to extinguish those efforts almost overnight. In addition to the dislocation of markets, war spelled two dire consequences for the fishing industry: the disruption and closure of fishing grounds by naval action, and the wholesale depletion of manpower through call-up to the Navy. On the other hand, it laid out a challenge: fish as a "free" food for a blockaded island was of priceless importance.

In the run-up to the war, Reynolds had toyed with the ideas of the peace movement propagated by Norman Angell, the friend of Harold Wright with whom Angell had founded the War and Peace Society at Cambridge. In the spring of 1913, along with Charles and Harold Wright, Reynolds had attended one of Angell's conferences at Le Touquet which he had found "very funny but interesting".[1] As war loomed in the last days of July, the madness of it all filled him with deep depression. But he was no pacifist. Once war was declared, he accepted the inevitable necessity of seeing it through.

The personal impact of impending hostilities came to him rather earlier than most. On 26 July, Churchill ordered the Navy, already on manoeuvres, not to disperse, and two days later to war-stations. Though full mobilisation was not decreed until 2 August, a silent mobilisation was already going on behind the scenes. On 27 July, a Monday morning before breakfast, Reynolds stood on Sidmouth station to wave goodbye to all the naval Woolleys and Woolley in-laws, including Bob's son Bill, who had joined up on that never-to-be-forgotten day in 1904.[2]

On 1 August, the Saturday of that fateful weekend, he wrote to Aunt Jane, who had known no European war since the Crimea: "I expect you are very startled and worried over these threatenings of war. It has hit us very hard here, for the British mobilisation – newspapers to the contrary – is undoubtedly very complete; all our Navy people are at sea, and we don't know where. The suspense is sickening". But like many others, he was striving to convince himself that it wasn't going to happen. "All the same, though one can't tell what will have happened by the time you get this, I am under the impression that the crisis will blow over, leaving Europe all the better for this glimpse into her own mad idiocy of armaments."[3]

On 4 August, with Bank Holiday celebrations still in full swing in Sidmouth, but declaration of war only hours away, he wrote again.

> War seems almost inevitable, but I gather that when the scare settles down to business the financial situation will improve. I am more or less resigned to losing my scrapings of years, if need be. It is my people gone who are an almost unbearable loss. Four Woolley brothers, Bob's son, two of Mam 'Oolley's brothers, one brother-in-law of hers, and two of Bob's. We three crocks, Bob, Tom and myself, remain.
>
> Possibly I may clear off to London soon, to help up there with the fisheries administration; for I fear it is going to prove a terrible job to keep the country running in any case. Here there is an infernal roundabout etc. concern in a field in the town, taking away the people's pence. I have had a shot at getting it shunted, and am at present trying to get a Public Aid Society in train to look after the reservists' families and the poor generally. It was the last thing I promised our navy chaps when, Monday morning, before breakfast, we saw them off at the station. We were the saddest – Lord, how sad we are. And when I think of my fishery work of years smashed, probably, by this accursed international insanity.... They are lucky now who have not the faculty of seeing too far in front. They get the war fever, see red, and are happy.
>
> One hope I have – and that is that afterwards the common sense of the peoples will declare against these bloated armaments that bring it all about.[4]

With death at the forefront of every mind, there were many wills drawn up that first week of the war. Reynolds made his on 7 August. He chose to divide his small estate equally between Bob and the children of his sister Dot, who had died just six weeks before at the age of 29, four years younger than his mother had been. Bob's portion was to include a free life tenancy in the cottage on Salcombe Hill should he and Mam decide after all to go and live there. The plot next door, which he was still hoping to purchase, would go to Tom to build the promised house of his own. He chose as his executors his solicitor, Philip Michelmore, and his old friends, Harold Wright and Lizzie Tanner.

He went straight up to London to offer his services at Parliament Street. In the chaos of the early days of the war emergency, the first priority of the Fisheries Division was to establish how much unemployment had been created by the disturbance of markets – the closure of the profitable German and

Russian markets was thought likely to hit the herring industry severely – and the naval restrictions on fishing movement.

There was now no time for constitutional debates as to whether Reynolds should be employed directly by the Board or not. He was signed up immediately to carry out one of the local surveys. At first, they proposed to give him the east coast, but he managed to persuade Maurice that west, and familiarity, was best. In the middle of August he wrote a breathless letter to Aunt Jane from Penzance.

> How are you getting on? I am flying round the country with a portable typewriter, holding meetings in the fishing ports, to find out what amount of distress is probable in the fishing ports, and how it can be dealt with. At first they wanted me to go right up the east coast to the north of Scotland; then they switched me off to the west – my own country, where I know most of the ports and a good many of the people. I was rather glad. It's nicer to plunge in on people who are glad to see one. So far the distress is not so great as one might have expected, and as the Government is sanctioning local schemes which will provide employment almost by return of post, I am hopeful that it won't be so very bad when people have succeeded in sorting themselves out into work of some sort.

The atmosphere of emergency was creating something of a buzz. "It's pretty fast travelling. Last Saturday, Sidmouth to Gwinear Road, and on to Porthleven and St Ives by car. Sunday, St Ives to Porthleven, to Penzance, to Pendeen, to St Ives. Monday to Sidmouth. Tuesday to London. Wednesday to Sidmouth. Thursday to St Ives. Friday, by car, to Sennen Cove, Mousehole, Newlyn and Penzance. To-day I work on to Falmouth, so as to have to-morrow for writing up reports and interviewing pilchard curers. I have to work right on up the coast so far as Poole!"[5]

For this the first of many such peripatetic reviews, the sensible decision to allot the west country to Reynolds was to set the pattern for the rest of the war. While his main eye remained firmly fixed on the development of national policy, it was in his own backyard that he tested out the first experiments – in motor installation, co-operative schemes, boat insurance, harbour administration. St Ives and Mevagissey were almost to take over from Sidmouth as his home base. And in those early months, the geographical distance from London created for him his own personal sense of phoney war. "It seems incredible that war can be on at all in this peaceful and beautiful Cornwall."[6]

On this first tour of the war, he made a new friend – at the very opposite end of the social spectrum from Bob and Tom – his first real brush with gentility. He had known and worked with Francis Mildmay, the MP for Totnes, for some years on fisheries questions. Now he was to get to know his wife Alice, who became for the next 18 months or so yet another of his substitute mothers.

The main Mildmay country estate had originally been in Samuel Palmer country, Shoreham in Kent, but Francis' mother, Georgiana, was a Devon woman who fretted at exile from her native county. In 1873, she had persuaded her husband to purchase Mothecombe, an old Queen Anne House in a beautiful wooded setting at the mouth of the river Erme. In 1876, he consolidated his holding by buying the adjoining and extensive Flete estate, four miles to the north, with its magnificent Elizabethan house high on a hill overlooking the river. The house at Flete was in a dilapidated condition, and he called in Norman Shaw to design the rebuild on the original ground plan, incorporating part of the Elizabethan structure and considerably heightening the tower above the front porch, so that the building now completely dominated the local landscape.

Francis Mildmay had succeeded to the Flete estate on the death of his father in 1905. He had been the local MP for 20 years, but was now 44 and still a bachelor. Something had to be done, and quickly, to consolidate the dynasty. The following year he married Alice Grenfell, a sensitive, intelligent woman, from an old Cornish family now based in Buckinghamshire. The couple had two children: Helen in 1907 and Anthony in 1909, who was to make his mark on the world of English steeple-chasing.

The Mildmays lived a luxurious life by modern standards, but nothing exceptional for an Edwardian country landowner. In fact Mildmay's father, a partner in Barings, had had to surrender most of his personal fortune, old masters and polo ponies, in 1892 to prevent a potential first Barings crash. They stayed at Flete each year from the beginning of August to the middle of October, returning to their house in Berkeley Square when Parliament reassembled. They came down to Flete for the big shooting parties and for the Christmas break which lasted till the end of January. They usually went to Shoreham for Easter and for weekends from May to July.[7]

This annual cycle, which involved a major logistical deployment of servants and possessions, like a medieval baggage train or the European Parliament, was broken by the war. Colonel Mildmay went off to the front in October 1914 as a French interpreter, with a cheery farewell from Reynolds: "Wishing you the best of good luck at the Front, and a speedy safe return, with the whole abominable anachronism ended...."[8] Alice was left on her own as mistress of Flete, performing the usual country social round. The appearance on the scene of Reynolds, with his quirky imitation of a working man and his dashing enthusiasm for the local fisheries, was a welcome distraction from a safe and predictable existence.

Reynolds had visited Flete before the war in his peregrinations on behalf of the Development Commission, and though he pretended to be put off by the luxury and Alice Mildmay's loquacious manner, there is evidence of a sneaking attraction for the grand style of living. In the spring of 1914 he reported to

Bob: "I had tea at Mildmay's in Ermington, and they want me to put up at their cottage when next I'm that way, instead of at the hotel. But I'm damn'd if I dare. The furniture is more terrifying than ever, and instead of the blue satin chairs, there are green spangled ones, and silk bedspreads, and winged looking-glasses for admiring oneself all the way round – and Lord knows what. Mrs. Mildmay very kind and hospitable, but.... O my dear soul! I feel sure I should end up by telling her to hould her bloody chawl!"[9]

On Saturday 29 August, Reynolds drove down to Beesands to interview the fishermen there as part of his Board of Agriculture inquiry. He was accompanied by Ashley Froude, a magistrate from Kingsbridge with whom he was staying the weekend. There he met Alice Mildmay herself talking to the crabbers whose livelihood was being undermined by the large trawlers encroaching illegally into the bay. The two parties joined up and motored on to Torcross where Reynolds held a further meeting in the hotel. Here the fishermen complained that the loss of flatfish to the trawlers had cut their income from six shillings to six pence a day.[10] As the meeting broke up, Alice Mildmay invited Reynolds to stay the Monday night at Flete on the way to his next meeting at Newton Ferrers.

That first night at Flete was a new and somewhat intimidating experience for Reynolds. Despite the war, the Mildmays still maintained a full retinue of servants. At the pinnacle, there was a butler who gave direction to all the menservants, and looked after the silver, the wines and everything to do with the dining-room. Under him, there were two footmen who cleaned the silver and boots and shoes, and waited on table. They were over six foot in height, but not taller than the six foot two of the butler, who could not bear to be over-topped. The butler and one footman were on duty every afternoon to greet unwary visitors like Reynolds.[11]

He arrived at about five on the Monday evening, to be greeted by Alice Mildmay, just back from a game of tennis with friends. He reported the burdensome formalities of his arrival to Bob. "I stayed...... last night with Mrs. Mildmay. She was very kind, and is as keen as mustard on the inshore fisheries, but it was rather a trial in some ways. They have a great big house, like a castle on a hill, with wonderful furniture, and a whole taddick of men-servants. When you get there a butler and a couple of footmen show you in, and take you to a bedroom like a big sitting-room, with a silk bed in one corner and a bathroom in a sort of big cupboard – and all the rest of it sitting-room. Then they unpack your bag, and solemnly lay out all your clothes for you to put on. God knows what they made of my damn'd rags!"[12]

It was a far cry from the informal welcome given to visitors "down the Gut" but Alice Mildmay did her best to make the impoverished stranger feel at home. They talked for a couple of hours and she showed him round the magnificent Flete gardens with their stunning hydrangeas and fuchsia hedges. She was anxiously awaiting her other dinner guests, the newspaper proprietor Waldorf Astor and his wife Nancy. When they finally arrived at 8, she rushed to warn them of her visitor and not to dress for dinner.[13]

They had dinner in the main dining room looking out over the front courtyard. Though every care was taken not to intimidate him, the rituals left their mark on Reynolds. "At dinner, a butler and a couple of footmen walk in, in solemn procession, with each course, and help you to everything, even bringing the mustard round on a silver tray! I told Mrs. Mildmay that I was more used to blacking my own boots and botching my own socks, when I didn't leave 'em in holes – which was most times!"[14]

He was much taken with Nancy Astor who talked garrulously all evening about the war and the reported German atrocities, the herding of men and women along the roads in front of them, the firing on doctors and Red Cross wagons. Alice Mildmay noticed Reynolds' reluctance to talk about the war. "Mr Reynolds has all his Woolley friends in ships, and so is very anxious, but you can see he hates the whole subject."[15] But, as he told Bob, the lively Nancy Astor was keen to meet all the Woolleys. "I reckon she'd be a fair match for Uncle Sam, and told her she'd better come up and see him. So she asked if she could come and stay with us, and when I told her 'No', because we are already crowded enough, she didn't at all like it."[16]

It was a strange introduction to the world of the rich, against whom he had inveighed for years in his books and articles. At 10.30 he climbed the broad staircase to his palatial bedroom with some mixed feelings. "I like to see how those people live, same as they like to see how us people live, but on the whole, same as they prefer their ways, so I prefer our own."[17]

But he stuck with the Mildmays because of their local influence on which he came greatly to rely when wrestling with the fishery problems of the neighbourhood. And Alice Mildmay was not the first nor last woman to catch the infectious Reynolds enthusiasm for protecting the rights and livelihood of the fishermen. Next morning they breakfasted at 8.30 before the Astors' early departure, and she then took Reynolds on by car to his meeting at Newton Ferrers. They arrived very early and went for a walk along the cliffs together, Reynolds talking all the time about the Woolleys and life in Bedford Square – and politics: "He is a Syndicalist, and has very peculiar views, but is most amusing and very original on every subject."

The meeting with about ten fishermen was held at 11.30 in the local Reading Room and she watched quietly as Reynolds directed the proceedings. Afterwards, she drove him back to Flete *via* Mothecombe and along the beautiful wooded track that runs along the banks of the Erme. She was a little put out that her short-sighted companion, chattering on about the fishery problems they had just encountered, did not appear to take in all the glories of nature around them: "I am not sure his appreciation of scenery is very keen."

They took lunch alone together in the vastnesses of Flete, the children away for a day at the sea. She then drove him on to Ivybridge to catch the train for his next meeting that evening at Teignmouth.[18] The two days had cemented a surprising new relationship, and a genuine fellow-feeling. That night, 1 September, he wrote her a thank you letter from his less palatial hotel bedroom.

> We neither of us realized, did we, when we were talking of game, that partridges begin to-day?
>
> Anyhow, here I am on my game, and had a horrid meeting to-night with a lodging-housey set of "fishermen" and a worser set of local leading lights. Mrs. Astor lets drive at Paris: I believe the English visitor is a more corrupting influence.
>
> May I thank you again for your kindness? A little of it goes a long way, times like this, and when one is so much on the hustle; and much kindness, like yours.... Well, one is more grateful than one can say. I'm very glad, too, to have seen those fishing villages with you. When I'm down there again, it will help me a lot then also.
>
> I only hope you will manage to get to Sidmouth one day and make the acquaintance of my people. Maybe I think too much of them – more than I do of anybody at all – but I feel certain you will like them too.[19]

Alice Mildmay was suitably touched. "Got a charming letter early from Mr. Stephen Reynolds, the first of very many. He certainly is quite unlike other people, and proportionately refreshing."[20] At their meeting, she had set him off on an important mission. The pressing problem in Start Bay was one of enforcement. Since the local policeman had been called off to the war, there was no-one left to protect the crabbers and others from the incursions of the marauding trawlers.[21] She wanted to act as unofficial policewoman herself and enforce the fishery bye-laws single handed; but would it be legal?

On 6 September, after another hard day, Reynolds reported progress.

> All the week's reports have been banged out on the typewriter, and to-morrow I'm off to Weymouth – London – Cornwall. The questions you have wanted answering, I have inquired about, particularly as to the competence of unauthorized persons (I hope you don't mind being so described!) to enforce fishery byelaws or take proceedings. You see, technically speaking, it's worse still you want to be, namely, what the law calls "a common informer". But perhaps that's how the law protects itself, by calling every layman who uses it opprobrious names.... When I get any answer, I'll let you know. You realize, of course, that if you can, and do, take active part in enforcing the bye-laws, there'll be a terrible scuffle with your opponents!
>
> Do, please, come up along when you have the opportunity. And I'm going to take advantage of your invitation to return down along – though I'm bound to confess that what Mrs. Astor dubs your luxury would terrify me but for your kindness and keenness on fishing. I've been more used to blacking my own boots, etc., and making shift in every conceivable way. But on the other side, you will know from your own experience what it has been like fighting the cause of small fisher-

> men without any resources, and until latterly, with no status or standing whatsoever. Only, don't understand me as complaining in the least. I don't: wouldn't have had any of it otherwise. But, like a stable cat, when I'm smoothed, I do enjoy it and purr very loudly.
> I wonder how soon the Admiralty will be taking over my cottage, if you are preparing Flete.... As it's only the Admiralty it was offered to, perhaps it will be later.
> Never at all, I hope, in one way.
> I hope, indeed, Mr. Mildmay will soon be home, with the war at an end. My people too. One long procession of wives seems to come into this house, all saying, how can they sleep. Poor things! they who sleep so well, ordinary times, seem so little able to compel themselves to sleep when the odds are against it.[22]

After a lightning visit to Weymouth, he spent the rest of the week in London in discussions at the Development Commission, and managed to snatch a rare weekend at Devizes, to check that Aunt Jane was all right.[23] He also snatched time for another letter to Alice Mildmay who had written to thank him for his visit.

> Don't call it kindness, my going round your fisheries. It was my job; and in so far as it was done rather enthusiastically – well, we each had an oar in the same boat......
> Meanwhile, we are all considering means to make people eat fish this winter, included pickled herrings! and I am going to try and "get at" the *Daily Mail*, with an article and daily recipes. I recollect once frying herrings and reviewing a book on Italian art after coming in from drifting at 1 a.m.; and I know a first class way of cooking mackerel; but otherwise am rather weak on the recipe side. We fry fish badly at home, and make 'em go down with copious anchovy sauce!
> As to your legal competence to be a fisheries policewoman.... I haven't yet got the problem solved. Your general competence I doubt so little that if I were a bye-law breaking fisherman, I think I should try to run you down and drown you out of hand.[24]

That weekend in Devizes he set to work on a memorandum outlining the management arrangements needed to fill the vacuum at those small ports where no harbour authority existed – the preliminary instructions for the Fishery Harbours Act which became law the following year.[25] He travelled up to London on the Monday morning to discuss at the Development Commission arrangements for his next lightning tour of the coast – this time to make an inventory of urgently needed harbour works.[26]

Since the Inshore Fisheries Committee the previous spring had thrown its weight behind the structural improvement of small harbours, the Development Commission had received a string of applications, filtered through the Board of Agriculture, for grants for port improvements. As before, it was Devon and Cornwall, the heart of the country's inshore fishing industry, that had been first off the mark. Back in July 1913, the Commission had discussed an application for harbour works at Mousehole and a report from the Board recommending a general survey of the Cornish coast, but had deferred any action to await the report of the Departmental Committee.[27]

On 22 April 1914, Reynolds had attended a Commission meeting to discuss a new memorandum from the Board pressing the urgency of harbour works at a number of Cornish ports. The Commission took fright at the extent of the Cornish requirement and determined to take no action until the demand for the rest of the country had been properly assessed. For the time being, it proposed that the Cornwall County Council should draw up a scheme for securing more finance and resolving the knotty problem of how to administer grants in the absence of local harbour authorities.[28]

At a meeting at Falmouth on 3 July of the Commission sub-committee charged with implementing the Harmsworth report (Nash, Reynolds and the secretary) it had been agreed that a new Harbour Commission might be set up to take control of those harbours that lacked an authority of their own. At the Commission meeting of 23 July, the one at which Reynolds had submitted his memorandum on the establishment of the FOS, the sub-committee's proposal had been approved. At that meeting too, the Commission considered individual applications for harbour works grants from Portloe, Newlyn and Mousehole, and decided to call for a report from an independent engineer on the last two applications.[29]

By September, the harbour engineer for Ramsgate, E.W. Hollingworth, had been commissioned to carry out the survey, which had been extended to embrace 16 ports in Cornwall, Devon and Dorset, only half of which had made formal applications for grant. Reynolds was appointed to accompany him to provide the necessary fisheries perspective.

It was an exhausting and whirlwind tour. They began on Tuesday 22 September with visits to Penberth, Porthgwarra and Sennen; on the Thursday to Porthallow, Coverack and Cadgwith; Friday, Gorran Haven, Portloe and Portscatho; Saturday, Portwrinkle, Polperro and Looe. The next week was a little more gentle: Monday, Port Isaac; Tuesday, Hope Cove and Prawle in Devon; finishing on the Wednesday at Durdle Pier on Portland.

There was only time for the briefest of visits to each port, but long enough to talk to the local authorities concerned and for Reynolds to call together ad hoc meetings of the fishermen.[30] It was in many respects a rapid re-run of the Cornish Committee of 1913, but this time round Reynolds was already a well-known and accepted figure at most of the ports. It provided the factual basis on which the Commission was able to make grants over the next few years, working through harbour authorities newly constituted under the 1915 Act.

Curiously, whereas in his writing days such an undertaking would have ended in exhaustion and depression, now the excitement of frenetic and committed activity seemed to give new buoyancy to his health and mental outlook. In mid-October he tried to snatch a week's holiday with Bob in Mevagissey, but seemed not the least put out when urgent work intervened. He wrote to Aunt Jane on a train from St Ives to Paddington, his only opportunity to catch up on letter-writing. "Seems some time since I had your last letter, which I haven't answered yet, I believe. Most of the time I have been rushing up and down country, with occasional rushes home. Last week I went to Mevagissey, with the intention of having a week's holiday with Bob down there as well, and writing a fishery article for the *Times*. But, alack! letters followed me and then the news of a harbour row at Sennen Cove. So there wasn't any holiday. However, I don't mind so long as I can keep well, and carry on snapping, as they say at home."[31]

It was only when the pressure eased that the old tiredness caught up with him. He wrote to Harold Wright in November: "I should be very glad to run down though I'm afraid I'm a very dull person at present, for I'm almost unendurably tired with work, and not working is more tiring than keeping at it. ....Bob is all right but very anxious, and can't keep still anyhow".[32]

The Woolleys at sea were still all safe and it was only the early loss of the *Monmouth* that had cast a shadow over Sidmouth. With it, Reynolds had lost Frank Brandt, the captain who had become a friend after reading *The Lower Deck*. This death revived in him thoughts of the wider war he had been trying so hard to forget. "I can't get out of my head that this war, so ghastly, so absurd, and leading people to talk and write such unmitigated tosh, will appear to future generations as a huge abominable joke – as the Napoleonic combats do to the Spirits in Hardy's *Dynasts*. Truly they die for the honour of their nations, on both sides, but it seems to me, at the same time, that they are sacrifices to the dishonour of the race as a whole".[33]

The end of November found him rushing round in the vicinity of Brixham trying to sort out the contentions over the Commission's Devon Motor Grant, the one recommendation of the Harmsworth Committee that had not gone smoothly. Work at Brixham, however, gave him the chance to see the Tanners once more and use their Dartmouth hotel as his base.[34] He was also working on an assignment from Henry Maurice and rapidly becoming the *de facto* representative of the Board of Agriculture in the western fisheries. He told Aunt Jane: "The West-Country fisheries, which I am practically in charge of now, while I am working for the Board of Fisheries as well as the Dev. Comm., are going along very well, all things considered, so I'm far from complaining, though I wish I had time to write down some of the many things that crop up to write about."

For the Cornish rescue grant, that other limb of the Harmsworth report, was bearing rapid fruit. Fortuitously, for the first time in years, large shoals of herring had appeared that November in St Ives Bay and, combined with the wartime rise in fish prices, had produced for the little town a dramatic bonanza. Reynolds was excited and delighted. All the hard work on the local fishermen's co-operative was now paying off. "At St. Ives they have had their turn of luck after 7 years' failure in the fishing. Now, hundreds of thousands of herrings and record prices. You should have seen the gladness in that town, after the grey despair one had been used to meeting there."[35] He wrote in similar vein to Henry Maurice: "St Ives, with great catches of herring, high prices, and great joy in the town was like a dead place coming to life; very wonderful."[36]

His Development Commission salary had increased that November to £400, probably in recognition of the extra work he was now carrying out for the Board.[37] The prospect of more money turned his thoughts immediately to the good he might do with it. Although he touched base at Sidmouth only two or three days a fortnight, he had not forgotten the social needs of his adopted town. He had given up the old plans to establish a little sanatorium up at his cottage. "I'm arranging to let the cottage when the Admiralty has done with its option on it. When it came to the point, Bob and I didn't feel inclined to part, and I don't suppose I shall go up there till we all do."

His new social project was designed once again to *épater les bourgeois*. He told Aunt Jane: "I am going to scandalise the unco guid of Sidmouth this week. Perhaps 'twill scandalise you, though I don't think so. The vicar has been kicking up a moralistic dust, and making a fuss over maidens and soldiers, and things hard for girls who get into trouble. So I have authorised the Excise Officer, who acts as my paymaster over a private fund of mine, to give a couple of guineas to the mother of every illegitimate child, and generally look after their welfare, in order that such children as arrive do so under not the worst circumstances possible, but under the best practicable. I have been waiting for years till I should be in a position to do that; the war will provide opportunity enough; and now I hope to be able to go on doing it so long as I live here."[38]

Even when he spent the money on himself, there was a hidden motive – the greater efficiency of his fisheries work. The last few months of racing round, on trains as far as they would take him and then by car with the likes of Alice Mildmay, had demonstrated the overriding need for a motor car of his own. His driving was still a little shaky but practice would make perfect. In early January 1915, he went up to London for a fisheries debate in the House of Lords and, more important, to collect his first car.

But his new unaccustomed riches proved psychologically too much for him, who all his life had been used to the security of living only from hand to mouth. As he told Vaughan Nash, the expedition soon degenerated into farce.

> The car has resolved itself into a horrid comedy. I got up to London, had it registered, paid my £50 deposit, and had a Sidmouth driver up there to help me down with it, if it had been possible to get across the Hampshire floods. Then a bad night.... All my small financial commitments danced about on the foot of the bed. Taxes, my one or two small debts, mort-

> gage, interest and repayment of principal £50 yearly, Tom's dubious appendix, every damn thing I could think of, actual and contingent; and I foresaw that if the mileage was not done, I should be able to pay for the thing, but with considerable tightness in the financial department. And – well, even in my poorest days, I've always been able to put my hand in my pocket for a few pounds, and I've never owed what I couldn't pay down, if I wanted to. It was financial D.T.'s – the spirit of Sennen Cove – financial funk, indeed, and ignominious. I can only offer as an excuse that I was depressed by a bad cold, the chilly fifth floor of Horrex's, and my only half-finished lecture. Either it was a sound business proposition, or else it wasn't; but I'm afraid I myself am the only business proposition I'm always unable to tackle successfully. I combine with considerable reliability, such a damn'd unreliability to myself.
>
> Anyhow, knowing that, I carried on; signed the contracts and examined the car, which really is a little beauty.
>
> Then came the H. of Lords speeches and a wet Saturday morning. I gained the impression that the fisheries might fade away; that I might find myself doing stay-still Government work pro tem. We started off to the garage, the chauffeur and me, plus luggage; but by the time I got there I had decided not to accept delivery. Where was the manager? Northampton for a trade dinner! Rang up Trunk, and waited, walking up and down between long rows of new-varnished cars that looked at one with dull road-hoggish eyes. Got on. Made a fair offer of withdrawal, for the time, at all events. But the manager man very kindly said, leave it over till you're next in town and then can see better what's likely to happen. So there it stands – and the chauffeur and myself came home by the midday express, to Bob's no small indignation, for he had been picturing us up to our necks in floods, and felt himself cheated of it!
>
> I suppose I shall come to a decision later. Meanwhile I've a house that I ought to live in, and can't, and a car that I am well assured I ought to have, and.... But the fact is, I'm altogether too tired to face alternatives containing such a slippery factor as myself.[39]

Though Reynolds' contact with Pinker was now only fragmentary, confined mainly to the end of the year when the meagre royalties rolled in, he still kept his eye on the literary ball. The hectic rushing round the ports in the early months of the war was packed with good copy. He repeated to Harold Wright what he had told Aunt Jane: "I am rather sick that I have had no time during the last three weeks to get down any notes for literary notes. I could have written A BOOK".[40]

He still had three books on the stocks, partially written – *Weekends at Nesscombe*, his psycho-economics work *Wealth and Life*, and the little life of Violet Cordey he had put away in 1912. As he totted up the annual accounts with Pinker in December 1914, amidst the gloom of the miserable figures there still lurked thoughts of a future in writing. "Strikes me we shall have to bring some shove-genius to bear on my magna opera! Else they'll die of not being followed up. And, damn it, I've got three books half done, and no chance to get on wi' 'em!"[41]

He was also fretting over his loss of contact with Conrad who had been in Poland when war broke out and had a narrow escape in getting back to England. Since 1912 there had been something of a distance between the two men. Conrad had lost faith in the protégé who had given up novel writing, and turned his attention to other young writers. Recalling Conrad's apparent irritation in his acknowledgement of Reynolds' *Quarterly* article on his work, Reynolds had concluded that the article itself was to blame.

Doing up the accounts with Pinker at the end of 1913, he had sent his agent a copy of the article. "You should have received by now a copy of the *Quarterly* with the Conrad article in it. When you see him, you might suggest that wicked and inArtistic as I am, I am scarcely worthy of being cast into permanent outer darkness. Your turn next, no doubt!"[42] The following January he made a further plea to Pinker. "I see Conrad is getting a very good show with "Chance", and I'm glad of it. D'you think 'twill mellow him enough to forgive me my imaginary wickedness?!"[43] Later that year, at Pinker's office in Arundel Street, he had bumped into Conrad's eldest son, Borys, who had greeted him as friendly as ever. "That was funny, running into Boris Conrad in your outer office. Conrad himself doesn't seem to have forgiven me yet! But evidently Boris had not been enjoined to be disagreeable."[44]

Just before Christmas 1914, he took his life in his hands and sent Conrad a cheerful seasonal greeting. "I risked another scorching letter and wrote to Conrad a week or two ago – and received an entirely amiable reply from Mrs. Conrad, pending Conrad's being well enough to write. Well, I'm glad o' it. Quarrels about nothing are a waste of time and energy, though tonic enough when about something."[45] But although his mind was put at rest, the friendship which had been so inspirational seven years before was now finally at an end.

But the writing bug was still in him, even though it served only to produce propaganda to boost his administrative work. Already in 1914 he had written three fisheries articles for the *Daily Mail*, one for the *Daily News*, and the one for *The Times* he had been struggling to start during the failed holiday in Mevagissey. He wanted, however, to produce a more concerted, thoughtful piece to record the current developments in the fishery landscape he was now overseeing; and so he turned once more to the prestigious *Quarterly* for the commission. On New Year's Day 1915 he wrote to Pinker: "I am having the devil of a time, trying to write a Quarterly article when I ought to be being lazy against getting on the rush again next week"[46]

He had been asked to give a lecture in Birmingham that month, and planned to test out the article on that audience. It was still only half written, and an added source of anxiety, during his abortive car mission to London the second weekend in January. But back home in Sidmouth, it began to go well again. "The fishery article for the lecture has now got to its 5000 words, and I think is pretty decent stuff."[47] By the end of the week, with the lecture deadline looming, he managed to complete it, at the cost of some days of concentrated effort.

On the Saturday evening, as he was just surfacing again, he received what must be counted the most curious of all the numerous visits spawned by the celebrity of *A Poor Man's House*.

> Had just signed my name to the thing last night, and was up to neck in papers and the general disorder that marks the end of a tough bit of writing, when in marched the Archbishop of Canterbury, Mrs. Davidson, and the chaplain. I had been breakfasting with them earlier in the week, and it was their return call. No chance of the kitchen: the kids were having their baths.
>
> Nothing to offer 'em, except whiskey and soda – which was no good! So they trapsed upstairs. However, after chattering, they went down and talked to the kids in their nightshirts, and seemed to be well amused, for Mrs. Davidson asked if she could come to see Mam 'Oolley, and they want me to go and see them at Lambeth, which I think I shall do: it would be rather sport, for the Archbishop is rather a nice old man, and as keen in argument as our people.[48]

Had Randall Davidson chanced to read *The Holy Mountain* and the death of the Archbishop of All the Empire, his enthusiasm for the young author might have cooled a shade.

On 18 January, Reynolds took the train to Birmingham to deliver his lecture. His host, a man who also rejoiced in the name of Reynolds, turned out to be one of those middle-class sticklers for social form that he most detested. He was worried about Reynolds' unorthodox dress.

> "Of course, you will wear evening clothes?"
> "No. I haven't got any."
> "But won't it be very disagreeable?"
> "Do you mean disagreeable for those I am going to meet?"
> "No, disagreeable for you."
> "Oh, please don't trouble about me, if that's all. I wore out my only evening suit last summer, and I don't intend to give myself another till the end of the War."

Despite his host's valiant efforts to press his own clothes on him, Reynolds stuck stubbornly to his best suit of fisherman's serge.[49]

The sartorial deficiency was fully made up by the elegance of the lecture. It was another cool piece of Reynolds' prose, a clear exposition of the past and present context of the inshore fisheries, the problems, the findings of the two Government committees on which he had sat, and his own recent efforts to implement their reports. It was a *tour de force* of fishery expertise which no one then alive could have bettered.

He did not spare his middle-class urban audience his strictures on their attitude to the working class, revolutionised since war had come.

> War, with its sudden disruption of civilian values, furnishes a peculiarly striking example. Bill Wage-earner, workman, malcontent, striker – what not that can be deprecated and patronized – becomes the admired Tommy Atkins, heroic and irrepressibly cheerful. His physique, which had to be protected by a network of Factory Acts, and not very adequately at that, becomes now a tender consideration. The fact is, of course, that he was a splendid fellow all the time, though unrecognized as such till he was doubly wanted and his normal heroism was provided with a spectacular setting.[50]

He produces a telling illustration of how middle class attitudes to working men can change when they actually come up against them in the flesh.

> That inshore fishermen are so much "a set to themselves" is part of their fascination for those who come to know them. In sitting on two Committees of Inquiry into Inshore Fisheries, it has been my amusement and satisfaction to see my colleagues – officials and men of affairs – approach the subject with a mind detached and highly judicial, and then, as they went about among fishermen, to watch their gradually growing admiration and enthusiasm, and their open indignation over the manner in which the inshore fisheries have too often been treated.[51]

The carefully crafted peroration to the lecture shows that he had lost none of his creative touch. He read to his audience verbatim the purple patch from the Harmsworth report, detailing the woes of St Ives in the winter of 1912/13. Then followed it immediately with the latest report of the recent joyful revival, equally, and designedly, purple in its colouring.

> Last autumn, however, the herrings came properly into the bay, the first time for years, and prices were high. They went as high, some days, as thirteen to fifteen shillings a long hundred. Boats returned laden from sea. Men staggered up the beach inside the harbour under the weight of the hand-barrows, or "gurries", of fine full herrings. The women were out counting the fish, or standing by their menfolk's catches. Salesmen and merchants shouted prices; half the town, it seemed, was down along chackling. Ponies strained into their collars, and went at it with a run,

> to drag the packed barrels up over the steep hill to the station. The gulls shrieked joyously overhead, over the masts, over the beach and town. People whom one did not know one knew greeted one in the street with news of the latest big catch, the latest price. One motor fisherman came home with £170 worth, and long enough he had waited for such luck. Money was coming into the town, good fish money, and long years, too, the town had waited. Men would be back from the mines, and if it went on, sons and brothers from America and South Africa. It was as if the most brilliant sunshine imaginable had suddenly come out over the grey little town in its wonderful bay, and over the grey people, who had been hanging on tough, grimly, patiently, with waning hope, and only determined not themselves to expose their poverty.... [52]

The lecture appeared five months later, slightly adapted for the readership of the *Quarterly* – "I have cut some of it out – the flub-dup parts, put in to amuse an audience!"[53] He was pleased by the political influence promised by its prominent position. "The *Quarterly* did us a good turn by printing my inshore fisheries article first in the July number."[54]

His journalism was still the source of widespread discussion. His *Times* article *Fishermen in War* of December 1914 spawned many letters, including supportive ones from Cecil Harmsworth and Francis Mildmay.[55] Reynolds was impressed to receive the latter's support almost as it were from the trenches. He told Alice Mildmay: "He not only wrote from the Front, but had written a fishery letter to the *Times* from the Front, backing up our propaganda. Besides feeling very grateful, I can't say how much I admire such a sticking to the matter even at the Front, where most men would regard their civilian life as being behind them, and not to be troubled about, for the time being. It strikes me, indeed, as a thing to do scarcely less heroic than the fighting part. Proper West-country!"[56]

Reynolds himself was supporting tenaciously the Mildmays' local fishery interests. On 13 January 1915 he was at Dartmouth to attend the Start Bay inquiry, set up to adjudicate the continuing war between the great trawlers and the little crabbers for supremacy in the bay.[57] On 30 January, he stayed again at the Mildmays, this time at the smaller house at Mothecombe because the drains were up at Flete.[58] He had at last taken the plunge for independence and invested in his own means of transport. When at a quarter to three that afternoon Alice Mildmay came out of the front doors of Mothecombe on her way to pay some village visits, a novel sight met her eyes: "I saw a little grey motor arriving, and my friend in it, and as I saw by his tiny luggage he had come to stay. I flew up and lit his fire...."

They went for a long walk together that afternoon along the Battisborough cliffs, talking all the time of fishery questions. After tea with some local friends, they played patience with the children, Helen and Anthony, Reynolds joining in with his usual infectious enthusiasm.

There were three who sat down to dinner that evening – Reynolds, Alice Mildmay and her mother, who was staying for a few days. Afterwards, he entertained the small company to his well-honed stories of life with the Woolleys, always the source of middle-class wonderment, as the hostess, unused to entertaining in Mothecombe, shuffled the party between the drawing-room and the little smoking-room next door in search of warmth on a stormy night of high winds.

> We had a delightful dinner, and later on he gave us a description of life at Sidmouth, and of his breakfast beside the kitchen range when all appetite was taken away by seeing "Mamouli" [*sic*] washing the baby near him, and another child's hair being brushed! He said the coffee was unspeakable, made out of tins with a Union Jack on them! His simplicity is delightful, and Mother fell as complete a victim to him as I always do, and the evening, spent half in the drawing-room and half in the smoking room, which I thought warmer, felt quite sadly short, as he is so light in hand. He told us all about "Uncle Sam", who lives on 5/- a week, and whose wife died a short time ago. When I asked him whether he was devoted to her: "I really don't quite know how much she was an Institution and how much she was a Habit!" which we both thought an excellent description of many people we know!

Like the organiser of the Birmingham lecture, Alice and her mother were both deeply conscious of the odd sartorial behaviour of their fascinating guest, but now they had to dress up to him, rather than dress down. "He scrupulously changes into another suit of dark blue serge for dinner, and we both very carefully put on the highest up clothes we could find to keep him company, but I don't think he would care or notice what one did. He is much too independent for that."[59]

Next morning the storms had abated, it was fine but windy, and Alice Mildmay bicycled early over to the little church at Holbeton. Cruising down the hill to Mothecombe on her return, she found Reynolds in the driveway with his nose under the bonnet of his car. They had a quiet breakfast alone together, with Reynolds in the same lively form as the night before, even regaling her with tales of his assignations with the "Merry Widow" in Sidmouth. "He told me a delightful story of Archdeacon Peel's brother being taken at Worcester to have his meals in a kitchen, 'being rather a "miscellaneous" looking person like me', and then from that he went on to enlarge on the amusing amount of fat tips he had been given, which he had divided with the other Woolleys, who felt quite envious of his luck. He said one American widow used to ply him with champagne suppers, which at first amused him, but finally he could not stand them any more."

But Reynolds had always an eye to the main chance of progressing his fishery business. "He then asked me whether in Frank's absence, I would let myself be made Governor of the Fisheries Organization Society, and when I demurred, and said: 'But shouldn't I be the only woman at your Meetings', he said: 'Yes, but then you are, so far as I know, the only woman in England who has worked to help the Fisherman's cause!'"

Reynolds left just before half past ten to motor home to Sidmouth. There then occurred a strange little incident which illustrates how very much Alice Mildmay, like many women before her, had been smitten by her new friend. As he left, she suddenly had qualms that she had not said goodbye to him properly, and raced after him up the hill of the driveway to make amends. "I flew after him as my good-bye in the house had not been warm enough, and I caught him up on the hill."[60]

It was an incident that puzzled Reynolds too, taking the guilt for the abridged farewell upon himself. Once home, he sent her a warm thank you letter, in contemporary parlance a "Collins", after the obsequious clergyman in *Pride and Prejudice* whose thanks were always too profuse.

> Here begins my "Collins"
>
> . . . .
>
> . . . . .
>
> . . . . .
>
> And here it ends.
>
> Because if one was to put down in solemn black and white how keenly one enjoys your kindness it would either be a literary exercise – which I know you'll excuse – or else would read like – well, like the Rev. Mr. Collins – too mellifluously! And how on earth I caused you to race after the car.... Surely I did say goodbye in house, didn't I – or else was mazed with whether the car would go or not![61]

The friendship, with its occasional little mock flirtations, continued strongly for the rest of the year, Reynolds dropping regularly off at Flete on his way home after a heavy working week. On 4 August 1915, a year to the day since the war broke out, he wrote to Francis Mildmay: "This week I finish a whole year without a single whole day's leave, Sundays or any other day; an occasional half-day underneath the car, to keep her going well; that's all. And I'm lots better than when I started – mainly, I think, owing to travelling by road in the fresh air...... Cornwall is having rather a good time with high fish prices and less restrictions than any other county. Sometimes, in the way up or down, I go by the Totnes road to Plymouth, and give myself the pleasure of a call on Mrs. Mildmay. It is wonderful to me how she keeps up her spirit and interests with so many losses and anxieties".[62]

But after the first flush of enthusiasm, Alice Mildmay, like many others before her, grew slightly tired of Reynolds' persistent one-track mind. Though he continued to see her throughout the war, after 1915 the visits became noticeably less frequent.

The second year of the war began on 5 August 1915 with great celebrations in Bedford Square. That Thursday Lulu, just 23, was married at St Nicholas' Church to Alfred Parsons from Sidcup in Kent. The two official witnesses were Robert Woolley and Stephen Reynolds.

After the service, the massed ranks of the Woolley family assembled in the corner of Bedford Square nearest the hotel for the official photograph. Reynolds stands on the right of the group with Grannie Pratt – the tough old stick – on his arm. He has noticeably put on weight since those seagoing pictures of three years earlier, and looks a little embarrassed and out of place in his crumpled Sunday suit. It is the last public photograph that has survived.

War had brought with it a whole new tranche of unofficial duties for the hard-pressed staff of the Fisheries Division of the Board of Agriculture. Most crucial among them was liaison with the Board of Admiralty. Under wartime arrangements, the Admiralty made regulations specifying those areas around the coast reserved for naval purposes and prohibited to fishermen. At first, it had appeared bent on sweeping the fishermen from the seas altogether, but a system of prohibited areas was soon developed with permits issued to approved fishermen to fish within them.

Since Admiralty knowledge of fishery practice and needs was rudimentary, Fisheries Division staff had to scrutinise the Navy regulations in the light of conditions on the coast, and help with their enforcement. There were other areas too where fisheries expertise was crucial. The commandeering of fishing vessels – *Puffin* herself was commandeered[63] – was the source of considerable tension between Naval authorities and ship owners, in which the Fisheries Division had to play the role of peacemaker. The call-up of fishermen from the Royal Naval Reserve caused similar personal tensions, but also threatened serious manpower problems for the fishing industry. While the Board of Agriculture strove to put the demands of the Navy first, it had to prevent the wholesale break-up of the industry. Board officials advised the Admiralty on the distribution of the monthly levies to help balance the demands as between one port and the next.

In the past, the Board had taken care to distance itself from local fishery concerns, leaving the making and enforcement of local byelaws and untangling of local problems exclusively to the largely dormant and ineffective sea fisheries committees. Now it needed an active organisation on the coast for day-to-day liaison with the Naval authorities, since local issues could not all be sorted out from London. But the problem was it had no presence on the coast. The part-time and ill-paid Collectors were there only to gather the rather dubious statistics of catches. Its corps of seven fishery inspectors were all based in London and only appeared on the coast to inspect the collection of statistics or for special inquiries, like the dispute over the Sidmouth shingle.

In the summer of 1915 the Board finally grasped this nettle and instituted a new class of appointment – a district inspector whose first role was to liaise with the authorities of the local naval command. It was, in effect, a belated implementation of the Inshore Fisheries Committee's recommendation of the previous year, though the emphasis of the Committee had been on liaison with the fishermen to sort out the whole range of their peacetime problems. The new system was provided on a shoestring. The Inspectors and Assistant Inspectors numbered only twelve for the whole of England and Wales, and were supported by some fragmented quasi-volunteer labour, local correspondents, permit-issuers and port fishery officers.[64]

Reynolds was formally appointed the District Inspector for the South West Naval Command to liaise with the authorities at Mount Wise in Plymouth. As he told Francis Mildmay, it was a job he had already been filling for a year. "Latterly, I've become the Inspector of the Bd. of Fisheries accredited to the S.W. Naval Command; so that the abeyance in ladling out the Dev. Fund doesn't make much difference. Nor, in fact, does that nominal appointment; for I've been doing the work of it all along. Owing to the fishing restrictions, and the various concessions we have been fortunate enough to get, negotiations with Mount Wise have become an all-the-time affair. I haven't happened to see the Admiral yet; but the rest, considering how busy they are, are very good in giving attention to fishery questions."[65]

His fisheries district ran initially from the Severn to Portland, but for the purpose of naval liaison there was added the whole of the coast of Wales. With its coastline of 750 miles, it was by far the biggest and busiest of all the inspectorates. By the middle of 1917, it had issued about 2,500 wartime fishing permits out of an England and Wales total of 3,000.[66] And yet, because he had run it so effectively on an unofficial basis since the outbreak of war, no thought was given to building a proper system of administration. He was still paid his old salary by the Development Commission, for whom he had less and less time to work, and nothing by the Board. He ran the machine single-handed from the two small first floor rooms in Bob Woolley's cottage he had now inhabited for the past eight years.

But the formal appointment to inspector did mean something, if only psychologically. From being an "outside" adviser to a Government body, he had now become a fully fledged civil servant – and the difference in status meant a lot to him. In 1916 he told Edward Carpenter: "Have been conscious for a long time that I have neglected to write to you. But all my private correspondence has gone fut during the war; for I have had just the job I wanted – Fisheries Inspector on the S.W. Naval Command."[67]

There had in the past been many professional writers who had started their careers in the Civil Service, but these had been almost invariably in the Richard Church mould, content to while away their life in a quiet backwater of the official machine to earn the bread and the time that would allow them to write.

For Church it was almost a philosophy. "My conception of the Civil Service was Trollopian. I had entered it naively, partly under compulsion from my father, partly because I knew of no other way of earning a living without having to give my whole attention to the matter.... I proposed to myself (and thought myself shrewd and worldly-wise in doing so) that I would be content with the humblest rank so long as it was permanent and guaranteed to give me the opportunity to practise my life-work, as a poet. I saw nothing immoral in this purpose...." But when he assigned this set of attitudes to a character in his early novel *The Porch*, he was taken severely to task in a review by George Orwell.[68]

Reynolds' sympathies were all with Orwell. He was almost unique in coming to the Civil Service as an already established writer, and with a strong sense of purpose, in keeping with his cry of 1911 "I'm a man who wants to do a job, not a man who wants a job".[69] Full engagement was at the heart of his psycho-economical philosophy of work, and throughout his time in the Civil Service he looked to apply its laws to the working environment around him.

Towards the end of the war, with "reconstruction" on everyone's lips, he saw that the reconstruction of Government departments depended above all on a change in personnel policy.

> It interests me on another ground, because it involves the whole big policy of whether public servants should be paid small safe salaries, and be expected to do merely their duty, or whether they should be paid and otherwise treated generously, and be expected to give themselves generously to their work. In psycho-economics, work is a giving of life in return for the means of more life: on the material plane, the means of living; and on the mental plane because the exercise of the functions of life is in itself an intensification of life, is in itself creative. Do we not speak of creative work, working with a will, giving oneself to one's work? All psycho-economics is implicit in colloquial language. If reconstruction is to be recreative, as it must needs be to achieve success, and if the Government is to have a heavy hand in it, it is of the utmost importance that the conditions of Government work shall be such that generous treatment shall evoke generous work, and that mean, saving workers, who grudge life to their work, shall be scrapped.[70]

There was never any question as to where he stood personally on the psycho-economics scale. He gave the equivalent of a dozen lives and more to his work.

But however integrated into the administrative machine, however constantly his waking life was devoted to the solution of the next policy problem, however accomplished a civil servant he became, he still retained the writer's power to stand aside, as he had done in the Woolley household, and observe the curious, slightly alien, world that was going on around him.

The literary clarity of his prose shone through in his routine minutes, interspersed with the quirky jokes and interjections – that special voice that the reading public knew so well. He was intrigued by the drama of the most mundane meetings, the poetry of human personality transcending the dead dust of conference rooms. This in March 1917 on a typical deputation to the Board led by Francis Mildmay, which he and Maurice had attended.

> I wish I could draw a picture of that deputation: Sir R.W. endeavouring to understand what it's all about; the old stub-bearded Plymouth fisherman with the shaky jaw, dragged up, heaven knows why, before the seats of the mighty; Col. Mildmay looking slightly fishy-eyed and too, too, patrician, "knowing all about these constituents of mine, of course"; H.G.M. [*Maurice*] chucking bombs about; and Bl—— very nearly startled back into being a fisherman again, instead of an owner. But not quite – which was one up to him. The government of a country is unconsciously, also, the embodiment of its comedy.[71]

And three months later he commiserated with Henry Maurice after a particularly wearisome meeting on the fringes of the newly formed Fish Food Committee, when a typically thorough Scotsman had made a meal of questions to Howard Dunn, Reynolds' Mevagissey friend, representing the fish merchant interest. Reynolds had learnt the civil service technique of stoic endurance and pouncing when the guard is down.

> T——— is a juicy bore; press him and he exudes a juice slightly rancid. But J——— is a dusty bore; one daren't touch him for fear of the dust blowing.
>
> I thought as much at lunch from his mixture of vacuity as to facts and platitudes to crown them with. And, by all the gods, he started off on Howard Dunn and the pilchard trade au fond, de novo, ab initio.... anything you like! After a couple of hours – Howard Dunn marvellously patient – his worship comically in the witness box – I grabbed paper and wrote letters; while J——— yackled his questions, made page after page of compendious notes; and "what we do with the Scotch herrings"; until finally he got into such details that I mildly protested that we were not there to count the meshes in a pilchard net. It was nearly seven; we'd been at it since lunch; while outside P.Z. sunned itself; and poor S——- looked as if he'd soon finish shrinking into the middle of his uniform, and be no more seen. And suddenly, on points of principle and policy, on the generalisations of the subject, J——— revealed himself as slow of understanding. He's what you might call quick in the grab-take, but slow in the uptake. He'd noticed with mild protest that your District Inspector had been going to sleep, and he positively hopped when the said D.I. woke up and grabbed the steering wheel, with a "Here's the road we're going!" Said D.I. hasn't worked with H.G.M. without learning a thing or two, though not all.
>
> As R. said afterwards: "Ah thot it best to let him talk himself out." No

longer do I wonder at your always returning from Scottish meetings in a state of exacerbated straffishness.[72]

He could laugh at the whole system, not just these excrescences. One sure-fire target was the deep fixation with procedure. He was puzzled by the perplexing rules on the transmission of classified documents. "You will probably like to see the enclosed orders for S.S. motor smacks, but as they are marked secret, and have been sent to me in double-registered envelopes, and as, I suppose, it is an extremity of naughtiness for me to have a copy made, I had better send the copy on to you *avec une cérémonie pareille*!.... "[73]

In March 1916 he received a note from Richard Martyr in Head Office setting out the correct procedure for sending official telegrams, designed no doubt to prevent the waste of Government money. This was too good for Reynolds to let pass. "Many thanks for your note with the telegraphic adjurations. Would it not be more departmental, when one sends a wire from anywhere to anywhere, first to send it up to London by letter post to have it certified? After all, whether a wire goes swiftly or otherwise, is of no great importance from a truly philosophical standpoint; nor is bothering you unnecessarily, for that matter; 'twill be all the same when we'm a-grinning up at the daisy-roots."[74]

The spring of 1915 marked a watershed in his personal life, a lightening of the emotional load that made even the absurdities of official bureaucracy bearable. For he found at last the special friend he had been seeking unconsciously for most of his life.

Harry Paynter was a young fisherman from an ancient St Ives fishing family. He had been born there in Carn Crows Street in August 1894, the third of the four sons of Harry Paynter senior, two of whom remained fishermen all their lives. Harry was good-looking, with close-cropped wavy hair, a broad forehead, bright blue eyes and a disarming smile. He dressed well, with a keen eye for clothes. He was lively and intelligent, but also non-conformist and with a will of his own – in Cornish phrase "never in the right place".

A childhood anecdote encapsulates the stubborn streak. Early one morning, young Harry accompanied the fishermen out in the punt to take his father off the boat returned from the fishing grounds. He carried with him a "carken bobber", the little home-made boat of Cornish fishing children – hull fashioned from the cork float of a net, keel from the hoop iron of a fish barrel, sails of wood shavings.[75] On the return journey, he set the carken afloat. A tired father had to fish it out of the water. When it happened once more, his father warned him that next time he would have to fetch it himself. Harry, being Harry, did it again – and was dropped overboard in the shallow waters of the harbour.

He left school at the age of 14 and like his brothers went straight into fishing. He was particularly good at the domestic side of the fishing routine –

a wizard with the needle out on the quay mending nets. In October 1915, age 21, he joined the Royal Naval Reserve in Penzance and served on a patrol boat, the converted trawler *Sardius*. His short naval career provided one living illustration of Reynolds' lifelong contention that fishermen were far better sailors than bluejackets. One night early in his service, on watch from the bridge of the *Sardius* rounding Lands End, he warned his captain that they were far too close to the shore. The captain argued but Harry got his way. When he finally snatched the wheel and took evasive action, they were within a hair's breadth of foundering on the rocks.

Since 1913 Reynolds had spent much time in St Ives directing the revival of the fisheries. It was probably through Harry's father, one of the town's leading fishermen, that he had first come in touch with Harry himself. The Paynters lived right in the heart of the old town, in a tiny whitewashed terraced cottage in the south-east corner of Porthmeor Square, which Harry senior had bought from his own father at the turn of the century. From 1915 onwards the little downstairs kitchen became Reynolds' second home, a worthy rival to its counterpart in Bedford Square.

At the close of a busy day, having knocked out the last report, despatched the last file, he would wander down the hill from his base at the Porthminster Hotel, turn left up the Digey to the welcoming bustle of Porthmeor Square, and settle down in the warmth and comfort of Mrs Paynter's kitchen. He had "gone to hut".

In the corner by the window, Harry's mother, born Mary Noall, presided over the great black range, and waited at table while the ravenous menfolk ate. She was a remarkable woman, then in her mid-fifties, with a strong and determined personality. On the far wall, standing under a picture of the Good Samaritan and taking up much of the living space, was a high backed sofa, in brown studded leather with scrolled ends, under a loose cover. This in Paynter parlance was the "hutch" which Reynolds, less strong on Cornish accents than on Devon ones, transcribed as "hut". In the early morning, the father and sons back from the sea could not disappear straight to bed for fear of being called out again. They kicked off their boots in the cellar next door and settled down for a nap on the sofa, which could hold at least two people fully stretched out. This was the true meaning of gone to hutch.[76]

In the early days, Harry and Reynolds could meet only at St Ives where Harry was still fishing, and then only infrequently. They had to rely upon letters, and an exchange of photographs. In March 1915, as we have seen, Reynolds sent his new friend a copy of his emotive poem, *Prisoners*. A letter from Harry always took his mind off the latest botheration at work.

> Got your letter just this morning. I was expecting it, and jolly glad I was to get a letter that was neither work nor annoyance. I've been having a hell of a row over my expenses, with bloody fools that don't and couldn't understand my work, nosing into it, and asking questions – damn

fool questions that waste my time and make me furious. Last night I went to bed so mad that I had to get out again about midnight to take a sleeping draught to get to sleep. What wouldn't I have given to have been able to "go to Hut" and have a stroll afterwards!
As for the photograph.... well, I'll wait, as you say. And then you'll see me in an infernal temper; for I hate cocking a mug in front of a camera. When the newspapers used to send men down to take my photograph I used to slang 'em till they didn't know what to make o' it. Finally I used to say: "Look here, if you can get a snapshot of me without my knowing it, you can; but I'm damned if I'll stand up on the beach in front of your camera." And in the end they used to do that – take me when I wasn't looking. I enclose another later one, but you must keep that yourself, because it's got a poem of mine on the same page......

They were waiting for Reynolds' leave to come through so they could meet once again. We catch an unaccustomed glimpse of an apprehensive Reynolds declaring himself at the start of an important relationship, and acknowledging the possibility of inequality of feeling. "I'm going to start west next Monday, and if that leave doesn't come along – well, I shall be sick – sicker than you, I expect."[77]

By the autumn, all such anxieties had disappeared – and, despite Harry's absence on war service, he felt secure. When his old illness threatened, he had Howard Dunn in Mevagissey for moral support, but nothing could compete with the recuperative breezes of Porthmeor Square. In October he wrote to Henry Maurice from St Ives.

Nobody could have been kinder to me than Howard Dunn while I was at Mevagissey last week, feeling – well, rather near busting point. For a person robust throughout, he has a singular understanding of maggoty-apple people like me. However, here I've bucked up a good deal, partly I think because the north-coast climate gives better quality sleep, and partly because I can spend my evenings down at the Paynters – "gone to hut" as old Mrs. Paynter says of her big kitchen couch. Rare old woman, she is – worth a novel all to herself.[78]

But the fact that he was feeling emotionally secure did not in any way diminish his feeling for those whose sexual lives were in a mess. In fact, it made him more angry than ever at the intolerance of the age. In the autumn of 1915, Jim Horn, a 57-year-old fisherman from Sidmouth and a good friend of the Woolley firm, was indicted on four counts of incest with two of his daughters. On 30 October, in a closed trial at Exeter Assizes, he was found guilty and sentenced to three years penal servitude.[79] Reynolds went down at once to see what legal or other support he could give. It was a chilling occasion, as he told Harold Wright.

> I got down to Exeter – beastly cold – and went and saw Horn. Seems to me he's determined to give me a power of attorney, in effect, if not in fact; and I suppose I'll have to carry through for him. No one else will, and he must have a chance when he comes out – at least a chance. The picture of him talking through the bars – paddling with his hands in explanation through the bars, like a subdued logical ape, seems to be simply branded in my eyesight. I took his notes; wrote 'em somehow; but when he began to protest his innocence, etc., etc., – well, I fled. For I couldn't believe it; anyhow, in face of his own letter; and, in my case, what could one do, even if one believed it true.
> Great mistake, such cases. The law's revenge; incited by those filthy Christian clergy; one man punished; no good at all to anybody; and no deterrent to anybody else. Farce![80]

Soon after meeting Harry, he had plans to try and consolidate their relationship through his work. Since his appointment to the Development Commission, he had been trying to find a new secretary to assist with the "spadework". His last secretary, the successor to Dolby, had gone to Canada to work for a businessman and Reynolds had soldiered on for a period without secretarial support. By early 1914, he was beginning to give up all hope of luring him back, and sought help from Edward Carpenter. "It looks, too, as if I shall have to find another secretary-handy-man, as my old one seems to be jammed up in Canada (though he wants to come home) with half his relations living on him. If you happen to hear of a suitable chap, you might let me know."[81]

Carpenter seems to have got the wrong end of the stick, thinking the requirement was more social than business. He drew on his worldwide web to come up with a strange assortment of nationalities. Reynolds baulked at the offer of a Japanese. "I'm afraid the Japanese chap would scarcely do for secretary handy-man, with indifferent English, as what I want badly is someone who can pretty nearly, being given an indication, run off my routine letters for me, and so save me from having my writing hours so infernally interrupted by mere spade work."[82]

He was tempted by the next offer – a Sicilian – but the needs of the job, regretfully, came first. "One couldn't recall the Sicilian from Messina on the chance of liking him and finding him of use. You see, I am bound to have rather good shorthand and typewriting: my clerical allowance is for that purpose."[83]

In June 1914, he had found a temporary man to fill in, but his social class was wrong. Reynolds was quite open about the prejudice. "I must confess I like either working people – them best of all – or else a gentleman. And this tweeny man, who is neither, irritates me. Why is it that the lower middle class seem to taint one's brain by their presence?"[84] A few weeks later, the tensions were getting to such a pitch that even Reynolds felt guilty. "The trouble is that efficient clerical assistants are usually lower-middle class. I get on with working people; I can put up with 'gentlemen'; but the tweeny people I simply can't stand roundabout me. Their presence, even if they're silent, worries me; and if they try to talk to me.... Well, I lash out. And then I'm sorry, if they're well meaning; and the savager, because sorry."[85]

He took the opportunity of the outbreak of war to pack the "tweeny" man off home – "I don't want the responsibility of him, should there be difficulty in looking after our people and the kids".[86] And as his work for the Fisheries Division grew in size and complexity, the requirement changed from a shorthand typist to a full blown assistant who could handle the paperwork and take initiatives, play a full part in the clerical machine.

From the end of 1915 he worked on his contacts at Devonport to obtain Harry's release for this more important war work. It was little different in principle from his regular negotiations, saving young fishermen from call up where their presence was essential in the fisheries. At last in the spring of 1916, both the Admiralty and the Board of Agriculture succumbed to the pressure, and on 20 April Harry was discharged to join him in the little office-cum-flat in Bedford Square as a fully fledged official of the Fisheries Division at a salary of 50 shillings a week plus expenses.[87]

This was business as well as pleasure. Reynolds took enormous pains to train Harry to maximum effectiveness, and was proud of the Pygmalion aspect of the experiment. Nine months later, he explained its success to Philip Hartog, his former teacher from Manchester and now a well-known educationist.

> I've been putting into effect some of the educational theories we used to talk about. Needing an assistant, I decided that it would be easier to teach a fisherman clerking, filing, etc., than to teach a clerk fishing. So I got the Admiralty to let me have a young St. Ives fisherman from a patrol boat. And he has proved a great success; has learnt typewriting etc., and is capable of being left in charge of all the business not involving special decisions when I am up in town. Not very sure of punctuation yet – but not worse than most business men – he writes a good letter or minute; says what he wants to say, and conveys shades of meaning very well.
>
> His only trouble is writing how he thinks he ought to write, instead of how he does think: in elementary schools they seem to think that composition is to be taught by giving the pupils a lucky-bag of clichés, and teaching them more or less which ones to pull out![88]

Bedford Square now took on a new atmosphere. While most of the time Reynolds and Harry travelled the Devon and Cornwall circuit in the little grey car, it remained the centre of business for at least a few days a fortnight. And a warmer place to come home to.... But its days as the most unlikely outpost of a Government department were drawing to a close.

Back in 1915, with Harry still at sea, Reynolds' working life for the Commission and the Board had taken on more of a pattern of regularity. Much of his time was spent west of Sidmouth, in Dartmouth (with the Tanners), Plymouth, Mevagissey and St Ives. The car he had finally bought that January had brought with it new health as well as efficiency. But the roads were the biggest bugbear. "I have done nearly 2000 miles in the little car in under two months, so you can imagine I haven't been exactly lethargic! She's going well; saves me a lot of time, and driving in the open air, with one's mind switched off from work to mechanism, seems to be doing me an enormous lot of good. But the roads in some places.... Mon dieu! For a sure thing the question of heavy traction-engine traffic will have to be tackled, else the road communications of the country will be destroyed. I had to go for miles into Salisbury the other day on 2nd gear at a crawl, and the main road from the West was frankly labelled "Impossible".[89]

At least once a month, he would appear on the doorstep of Flete on his journey back upalong. Alice Mildmay looked after him well. On a flying visit in May, he was treated to a working lunch of cider, sandwiches and cake. Alice's sister-in-law, meeting him for the first time, found him very attractive, but Alice herself noted rather archly that "he is terribly inconsistent on the subject of War".[90] She made him work as well as sing for his supper. In early July, "Mr Reynolds came in to tea, and was as delightful as ever, and afterwards we made him help to weed the front drive and kept him quite busy till nearly 11".[91] In August, on another visit, he asked if she would launch the new experimental motor boat he had organised for the Beesands fishermen, and demonstrated his French credentials to the Mildmays' governess: "He was very nice, and talked beautiful French to Mademoiselle, and seemed so at his ease with her".[92]

But life was not all cider, cakes and admiration. His liaison with Devonport was serving his fishermen well. Early in 1916, he proudly told Cecil Harmsworth: "I am still, in addition, flying round as buffer between the Naval Authorities and the fisheries. We have almost free fishing now in my district".[93] But in those few places, like Start Bay, where the fishing was still controlled by a permit regime, the unaccustomed role of official enforcer, and the unpopularity it brought in its train, gave him more sleepless nights than usual.

> Saturday, I touched at Looe; warned seven fishermen for being in Start Bay a little bit after time, a little bit inside; and endorsed the permits of three more "compound offenders". It was something of a town sensation, tracking them home over it; and I certainly never expected the men whose permits were endorsed to be so staggered over it. Upset me, too; lost me a night's sleep and the next day's work, confound 'em. I'm no

good at inflicting penalties on fishermen in cold blood, when they're so squashed and nice over it that one can't lose one's temper.[94]

When he did lose the celebrated temper, it was more likely to be with Admiralty officials whose injudicious call-up of fishermen was threatening the viability of the local fleets. But guilt always followed a typical "busting off", and apologies – in his own special vein of truculence.

Hope I didn't shock you badly last week on the feeling of the W. Country fishing communities.... 'Tisn't perhaps disadvantageous for you people up topsides to sniff between-whiles what smoulders down along, and I've lived with fishing people so many years that when I start busting off – well, I do bust off, I'm afraid! Anyhow, whoso lays up the fishing fleets for anything short of real naval needs – may they be fed on dogfish at dinner till the end of their lives![95]

Against the enmity that naturally came with the job, he took careful steps to protect his back. Discussing the drafting of a naval order with the Flag-Captain at Plymouth, he asked for a subtle change – the substitution of "The Inspector" for his own name wherever it occurred. "Heaven knows, the designation 'Inspector' isn't a particularly pleasant one, with its detestable connotations, specially after the way I have slatted at it in books! On the other hand, there aren't lacking some excellent people who feel there's too much "Stephen Reynolds" sculling about, and not altogether groundlessly either; and it's as well not to be an offence to them on points of form. The scuffle over points of substance comes all too inevitably soon."[96]

His philosophy for handling the enemies was to keep out of their way, especially after the day's work was done and the temper was at its most volatile. "As to the making of enemies – I doubt the necessary ones matter half so much as the unnecessary ones. Those who queer my pitch worst, I find, are the people I've stuck a fish-hook of a retort into, not for anything that matters, but merely because they've grated on me when I was tired. For that reason, when I get to a place towards the end of a day, I generally slop about, do typewriting, drink whiskey, anything, rather than tackle people it's best not to risk offending."[97]

In September 1916, he faced his worst crisis to date – one which would have made enemies of most of the fishermen on his patch. The process of saving individual fishermen from call-up while others went to war was itself a highly invidious one, with great potential for ill-feeling and recrimination. When fishermen asked for his advice on call-up, he had told them to join the naval reserve, then if rejected for service they would be certain to remain in fishing.

Now he learnt that the War Office was planning to turn such naval rejects over to the Army. Apart from the absurd loss of sailing skills, the new policy would mark a massive breach of faith. He wrote urgently to Maurice at home in Leatherhead, snatching a well-earned holiday among his cabbages and potatoes. "What are people on the coast, with feelings, prejudices if you like, and memories, are only names and figures in London. I do not, therefore, wish to blame anybody at all; it's as things are. But if this affair goes through, then, I am certain, for a gain to the Army not balanced by diminished food, our relations with the fishermen will receive the severest set-back. Constructive work isn't to be done on a breach of faith."[98]

Maurice dropped his spade and rushed to the rescue. The new policy was quietly shelved. It is an instance of the incomparable value to the Fisheries Division and to the cause of food production of such a sensitive nose as Reynolds' out on the coast. His total dedication to the success of the fisheries, his 24 hour a day vigilance, ensured that major crises were defused long before their presence could be felt in London.

And in spite of the special problems created by the war, the south-west fisheries were thriving economically under the new policy of co-operation, aided by wartime prices. He could savour with nostalgia the start of it all in the Cornish Committee of four years before. Cecil Harmsworth had reminded him of it at lunch in November 1916.

> That lunch was an extraordinary unanticipated pleasure; you were speaking of the Devon and Cornwall Committee days, and you can scarcely imagine how pleasant it was, after so much grinding detail work, to hark back to our old long discussions of fishery ideas. And as one goes on, one sees the more plainly how, unbeknownst to us then, those discussions were like a bursting seed-pod. New things crop up, war comes; and still I find things going back to that tour. It was much more critical than we knew.[99]

The last days of 1916 were to bring not just a change of Government, with new headaches for fisheries administrators, but the change of abode that Reynolds had been planning unsuccessfully for years.

Not the long-awaited move to the cottage on the hill. That was still empty – and the source of both suspicion and amusement. The year before it had produced a very good rumour. As with D.H. Lawrence at Zennor, it was the writing of books that merited the most suspicion.

> My newsagent's niece came back from Cullompton – of all places – with the "fact" that the man who lives to Sidmouth and writes books (*i.e.* myself) is a German spy, who has built a house on the cliff (I built one there last year), and goes up there signalling by night!
> The cottage has stood empty since it was built, and I've been there only three times since the war started, so I can't guarantee that no one has been there, although if they had I should probably have heard of it......

> but, as I say, such absurd reports, seriously passed along, can only hinder the detection of real spy work, and help play the enemy's game.[100]

The events of 27 October 1916 brought a move to the cottage back into contention once more. In the small hours the most violent storm within living memory (that of Uncle Sam!) brought water in sheets over the Esplanade, and in struggling with the boats, Reynolds was carried away on the side of one and almost crushed. Bedford Square was waist deep in water; Bob took tea round to the women in a boat, passing it through the bedroom windows. The sea filled the town again the next night, and a third time a week later.[101]

It had brought the shingle question back with a vengeance. Reynolds wrote a long official minute, inviting his colleagues in the Fisheries Division to take up the urgent need for new works with the Local Government Board.

> The gale a week ago flooded the town twice in one day to a depth of several feet; did extensive damage on the front; carried away part of the eastern pier and the roadway; swept away the beach by the river mouth...... and did such considerable damage to the sea wall as to make it imperative, now, to put the whole of it in sound condition.
> In short, what the local fishermen have long foreseen, came to pass. The shingle beach has almost entirely disappeared, and the sea now runs against the wall at every tide.[102]

But the domestic position down at Bob's cottage was equally critical, as he told Aunt Jane. "As the tide ebbed, the water ran away, and people spent all day cleaning the filth out of their houses. And in the evening exactly the same thing happened again...... The stink and the flies afterwards were abominable. In my room here, where I seldom have flies, I filled two big fly-papers in twenty-four hours! The water did not come into our house; the tide started ebbing just as it was flowing into the passage. But Mam 'Oolley is pretty sick of the mud and mess round about."

On 5 November, the day of the final flood, he caught wind of a property to let – Hope Cottage, the large white house at the top of Church Street, owned by the Town Clerk, his friend and solicitor Philip Michelmore, and used in part as his office. It held out the prospect of more space even than the cottage on Salcombe Hill, about which Bob was still adamant, and was only a couple of hundred yards inland from Bedford Square. The following day, with Reynolds away on business, Harry showed Bob and Mam round the premises, and by the evening it was all decided.

For Reynolds, it was the chance for the better environment he had long been seeking – the possibility of creating a proper office, and more space and privacy for Harry and himself. He told the news to Aunt Jane with some excitement. "The place is up near the church, looking over the cricket field to Peak Hill, and detached, except for the Town Clerk's offices. (It used to be the dwelling-house of the old Town Clerk.) I am to have the first floor – three rooms, unfurnished, and a bathroom, while the Woolleys will have the ground floor (kitchen, etc., and dining-room) and the three bedrooms on the top floor. Then if my work takes me away for any time, they will be able to lock up my study, and let the dining-room with my two bedrooms."

For himself and the Woolleys it seemed to hold out the promise of salvation, but each personal vision of domestic paradise had a distinctive character of its own. "What specially appeals to Mam 'Oolley is a back door, to avoid muddy boots, etc., right through the house; to Bob, the bathroom, I think; and to me, the chance of quietness. I usually get home so fagged nowadays that there's nothing for it but to do the same as a dog, and sleep it off. And one can't do that with a lot of noise over, and under, and around. In fact, for a long time I've been telling them that I go to London for quietness."[103]

They quickly moved in, abandoning the tall house in the little square to the mud and the flies, and a new generation of inhabitants. For Reynolds, it was the final physical break between his home and his most famous book.

TWENTY

The Book's Written 1917-19

The Lloyd George coup of December 1916 ushered in a revolution in Whitehall, both of policy and administration. There had been growing a recognition that the country might lose the war, on the battlefield and in the blockaded homeland, unless there were a new direction. To maximise the war effort, the new Government was determined to take a firm control of the economy and direct the main industries itself. New departments were set up almost overnight – shipping, labour, food, national service and food production – to administer the new policies and to ginger up their counterparts in the *ancien régime*, the old departments who were left to run their established "peacetime" functions relatively undisturbed. The new departments were to be headed at ministerial and official level by successful businessmen who would show the ancient administrators how whelk-stalls should be run.

Whether one called the new direction "War Socialism" or "Prussianism" – that is, borrowing the methods of totalitarian bureaucracy from the enemy – either slogan was opposed to most of what Reynolds had always stood for in social policy – minimal interference by the State. In his fisheries field, the creative tensions were to be developed at the interface of the Board of Agriculture with the new Ministry of Food, under the Food Controller, Lord Devonport. The newly-recruited Ministry of Food official, charged with increasing the supply of fish food, was Arthur Towle, who with his brother ran the successful Midland Hotel chain. As the new Ministry began to challenge the Board for supremacy over fish once landed, Towle soon became the *bête noire* of Parliament Street.

In the early days, perhaps surprisingly, Reynolds was prepared to welcome the new approach. Like Lloyd George, he was perpetually frustrated by the old Whitehall bureaucracy. In January 1917, he groaned to Cecil Harmsworth about the Board of Trade: "It's curious how the B.T. slows down everything that comes under it. I am at present swearing very hard over their puerile oversight of fishing harbours. They seem to do simply nothing to keep their administration on the rails of financial soundness; let them live from hand to mouth...... What makes most trouble is that infernal official disposition (Maurice apart) to 'wait till moved'. It means, as Maurice and myself both complain, that one spends 75% of one's time not in getting for'arder, not in doing things, but merely in picking up the pieces of things not attended to until too late. People wait for pressure, when they ought to press; and then when the thing's got to be dealt with, they've nothing ready".[1]

So even Prussianism, if effective, might be a tolerable alternative in war conditions. In the middle of November 1916, just moved in to Hope Cottage, he wrote to Cecil Harmsworth: "I see a Food Dictator has been appointed – or rather I am told so – and that he is going to commandeer spuds. I am wondering whether we shall also have to commandeer the produce of what Maurice now aptly terms 'the Sea Fishing Service'. Some flap, if that's the case, but on the whole I have rather favoured such a step for some time".[2]

What attracted him most about the new régime, however, was the challenge and personal stimulus of upheaval. "I resent the new ministry; yet inconsistently hope for some flap out of it. The fact is I want the stimulus. My unstable equilibrium must have that to keep going. I like the initiatory work; I delight in the technical details, but where stable men would congratulate themselves on organisation completed, and an easy time, is precisely where I begin to deliquesce. The stimulus becomes insufficient."[3]

But what he could not stomach was the possibility of being overrun by smart businessmen, totally ignorant of the fishing industry but backed by new money and the paraphernalia of state socialism. It was urgent that the Board should now develop its own strategy to take advantage of the new opportunity. After Christmas, he invited Maurice down to Sidmouth to thrash out the new strategy, appealing to his Tory fear of socialism. "You recollect I once told you that Maurice the Tory would be a socialist administrator. That's proving true to this extent, that if you don't command events by knocking out a far-reaching politico-economic, as well as administrative, policy, they'll command you, and we shall assuredly see a reluctant, though still efficient Maurice, continually forced along the State socialism, nationalisation of fisheries path."[4]

Maurice, inevitably, was too busy to grasp the invitation or heed the warning. Though the Ministry of Food recognised immediately the significance to the domestic economy of maintaining or increasing the fish supply, it was content to leave the implementation of that policy in Board hands. Throughout the war the annual catches had rapidly declined as naval requirements eroded both manpower and fishing grounds. Of the 45,000 fishermen in England and Wales at the start of the war, almost half were called up to the Navy. The 16 million cwts of fish caught in 1913 fell to just over 4 million in the last three years of the war. As a result prices rocketed. The catch in 1918, though a quarter of that of 1913, was worth half as much again in value.[5]

The contribution made by the new ministry was to set the maximisation of fish supplies as an overt political priority. Since Reynolds' West Cornwall experiment of 1914, the installation of motor power in fishing vessels, which could treble the catch, had been seen as the most effective short cut to increased production. The Government wanted a new motor scheme, which the Board of Agriculture was charged with drawing up and implementing. In January 1917, the Development Commission, on an application from the Board, set the ball rolling with a grant of £50,000 for a new programme of motor installation throughout England and Wales.[6]

Reynolds began planning at once the contribution that could be made from his ports. On 14 January, he wrote to Cecil Harmsworth from St Ives, having abandoned a planned visit to London the day before. "I'm afraid I didn't turn up in Town on Saturday morning, and hope you had made no arrangements for a motor scheme talk. I wasn't very well, and when the D.C. wired there was no need to come up for their business, I came on down here. But we must have a good pow-wow; and I expect you will like to see some of the stuff that went towards making the B.A.F. report on the scheme – in particular the rough estimate of boats feasible for motors around my district. As soon as the scheme is anything like decided upon, we shall have to tackle the motor supply question with the makers and the M.M.[*Ministry of Munitions*]"[7]

On 22 January Harmsworth called in at Parliament Street for more discussions with Maurice and was invited to become chairman of the Motor Loan Committee being set up to administer the scheme. A week later, Reynolds came up to Town to concert plans for the new committee with Maurice and Harmsworth. The discussions continued over lunch with Harmsworth at the Reform Club the following day.[8]

The Committee met for the first time on Tuesday 6 February at Parliament Street – Harmsworth, Maurice, Reynolds, and Moss Blundell of the Admiralty, with Collingwood from the Board as secretary. They met again on the Thursday, another day of great frost in this the hardest winter of the war, but Reynolds had departed west before the third meeting the following day.[9]

This was a major new executive commitment for the Fisheries Division, and Reynolds' prime concern was how it could be adequately staffed without damage to the rest of the central machine. For war had depleted the Division almost as successfully as it had the catches of fish. Maurice had started the war with 34 male staff, of which 21 had left to fight in the forces and a further four had departed on special services.[10] On this visit, Reynolds had pressed on Maurice the crucial importance of finding more staff.

He had at least one name to suggest himself. In February 1915, Reynolds had been instrumental in securing Harold Wright, whose illness still precluded him from full-time employment, as a Governor of the Fisheries Organisation Society, in the hope of securing from him some additional voluntary labour. He told Harmsworth at the time: "I'm hoping that Harold Wright, whom I rather jockeyed on to the Governors for that purpose, and who has heaps of savvy, will get into a habit of calling at the office. He will save both you and me such constant reference as to trifles, and act the F.O.S. pilot a bit".[11]

In 1916 Wright had had a bad recurrence of illness, but now was fit again and looking round for some light work. Reynolds proposed him to Maurice, and the latter gratefully accepted. On 10 February, stopping off at the Chough Hotel in Yeovil on his journey back home, Reynolds broke the news to Wright. "I have spoken to Maurice, and he would like you to call as soon as may be. Do your best for us as regards your time: Maurice is top-hole to work with, and I think in a very short time you'd feel aboard a ship with a skipper you'd do your damnedest for. Good ship, too. The best going. For we are steering through the war, but getting to wind'ard all the time for after the war."[12]

Maurice was impressed from the start with the ability of his new recruit, but Wright did not fit in easily at Parliament Street where, in the atmosphere of war fervour, his pacifism made him something of an outsider.[13] By an inspired decision, he was shortly transferred to work for the District Inspector of the South West at his favourite holiday haunt. Thus he became the anchor-man of the little office in Hope Cottage, running the show while Reynolds and Harry were off on the road.

When later that year, Maurice did a motor tour with Reynolds of the south west district and stopped off at Sidmouth, he was delighted to see how well Wright was coping with his ebullient boss. "He was, admittedly, thrown into the shadow by the vivid, electrical personality of Reynolds, but he worked better in the shadow." And Maurice saw too the great benefit to Reynolds of this constant stabilising influence. "To no-one, I think, was he more indebted for guidance as well as support, and for the provision of that ballast which at times he sadly lacked."[14]

When Reynolds got back to Sidmouth after the first two meetings of the Motor Loan Committee, the staffing at Parliament Street was still at the forefront of his mind. The peacetime pressures about which Richard Martyr had complained to the Inshore Fisheries Committee four years before had now increased tenfold. But, as Reynolds told Cecil Harmsworth, he felt he had at last made an impression on Maurice.

> Seems I have scarcely seen you, though we have sat on two committees. I had to rush off. I think I have finally convinced Maurice that he *must* demand more staff. I do not think he realises to what an extent his personal influence has made a sort of sink-or-swim ship of the Fisheries. He is so good to work with that any decent chap would over-work for him to keep his ship going. Consequence is: if any accession of business crops up – as it may well do – we shall be compelled to leave him in the lurch, for the simple reason that we are working on no margin now, and then shall crock.
>
> We tease Martyr and tell him that Maurice may look in any day when he is surrounded by files as high as his head, and say: "Oh by the way, Martyr, you might draft a new Fisheries Act; I want to send it forward to-morrow morning!"
>
> And if Maurice should go bust, the Fisheries go bust: as I say, the Department is being run on any amount of devotion to Maurice, but devil a bit of margin at all.[15]

Two days later, he wrote to Maurice himself repeating what he had said in London. It was not just the lack of staff, but Maurice's lack of interest in organisation – the more efficient use of staff – that was the problem. "In the higher qualities of organisation – the capacity to make the crew go all the bundle on the skipper – I don't know any one to come near you, or any one into whose hands I'd put my people's affairs with half the confidence. But you aren't so interested in what I may call the technique, the machine part, of an organisation; it always seems to me when I'm in town that you people, up there, should be saving yourselves a lot more labour than you do, and at times I simply itch to overhaul the machinery part. When, too, I think of the work you, and Martyr, and Collingwood have had to do because the machine rests on a clay bed of coastal collectors, instead of concrete – well, I simply get angry and start strafing someone who least deserves it."

But beneath all this anxiety lay a growing recognition that the new Government's efforts towards a "Prussian" industrialisation of the industry stood, after all, in direct opposition to the fisheries policy he had been espousing all these years, which placed the fisherman himself in the driving seat. "Finally, in opposition to the kultur which has conquered Govt. Depts., with its get-results-quick methods, and be hang'd to the victims, I'm at all times out for the policy you, Harmsworth and myself stand for, the anti-Prussian policy of earning and eliciting an industry's response, of making it grow, instead of banging it into an artificial shape; of regarding its people as aggregations of individuals, not aggregations of units. It's the alternative between building with bricks for to-morrow, or creating with life for time."[16]

In the end, Maurice did get more staff to administer the motor scheme. A new section of 16 people was set up in makeshift offices – "three dingy rooms in the attics of a dingy tumble-down house". Unlike the Cornish experiment of three years before, the main problem now was finding the engines and engineers to instal them rather than persuading the fishermen to use them. Engines and parts had to be begged from other Government departments. Whereas before, out on the coast, a loan would be given to the individual fisherman who arranged his own installation, now the whole installation process had to be organised by the authorities. It was a painfully slow process; by the end of the war, only a further 207 engines had been installed.[17]

The Committee soon recognised that it was not going to do much to maximise catches by means of the motor scheme alone. At its sixth meeting on 15 February, Maurice announced that he would seek to have the terms of reference enlarged to take general responsibility for fish food supply as long as the war continued.[18] In part, it may have been intended to dish the Ministry of Food, but when the Cabinet endorsed the proposition it took care that the reconstituted committee should have a representative from the Ministry, in the shape of Arthur Towle.[19]

The Fish Food Committee was quickly established that February and for a time its meetings alternated almost daily with those of the separate Motor Loan Committee. In March, the two committees were amalgamated to become the Fish Food and Motor Loan Committee, the same personnel as the original committee, with the addition of Towle and a new secretary, G.K. Hext, borrowed from the London & North Western Railway Company.

The terms of reference of the new committee were "to consider practical means for increasing the supplies of sea fish for the home markets and for encouraging the consumption of such fish, whether cured or fresh, in substitution for other foods".[20] In broad terms, its role was to stimulate fishing activity, and keep a close watch on the fishing industry, supplying its needs and resolving its difficulties. It was set up not to enquire and report, but to supervise an executive function. Another new section was established within the Board to carry out the fish food remit.

For Cecil Harmsworth, the chairman, the greatest challenge was not increasing the supply of fish but persuading the Great British Public to eat it.

> We are charged with duty of advising the Food Controller as to the best use to be made of the vast quantities of pickled herrings and pilchards and dried cod that are usually sent abroad and are so heavily salted as to be unacceptable in the home market.
> Pilchards, for instance, are not eaten fresh in this country. The bulk of the catch is salted down and exported to Italy in times of peace. Of the British herring catch 85 per cent is normally salted down and sold to Germany, Russia, etc. In addition to our own heavy stocks the Govt. has been buying large quantities of these pickled herrings in Norway, Holland, etc. in order to prevent the Germans getting them and has now in hand or in sight 150,000 tons of them.
> How best to desalt and render these pickled herrings more palatable is an important object of our enquiry and we are getting all sorts of people to make experiments. Further, we must try to arrange things so that the herrings etc, of this season's harvest are not put into brine but are either marketed fresh or are kippered, "redded" or bloatered. All this means in effect the upheaving of a great and complicated trade.
> The tantalising circumstance is that here we have a huge supply of nutritious food that our people won't eat in its present condition unless indeed they are driven by severe privation to doing so.[21]

But despite all the best efforts of the Committee, and the shortage and dearness of meat, the public could not be brought to eat this brined fish. One could only conclude that, in extreme privation, they would have preferred the taste of rats. The Committee soldiered on through the war and was finally wound up at the end of 1919. But its executive functions were slowly absorbed by the Ministry of Food, especially after the food panic of early 1918 and the introduction of price control on fish, which greatly altered the balance of power between the Ministry and the Board of Agriculture.

In these early months, March to May 1917, the Committee met almost daily and Harmsworth was heard to lament "This Fish Food and Motor Boat Committee is the most exacting I have had to do with so far".[22] He would walk each morning, sometimes with his eldest son, from his home in Montagu

Square to the office in Parliament Street until soon there was little to distinguish him from the full-time administrators. "The duties and hours of an (unpaid) Civil Servant are hardly compatible with those of a Member of Parliament."[23]

Reynolds, as the Development Commission representative on the Committee, and with more than a full-time job in the west, got off more lightly. He would look in on it occasionally when he was up on Commission business or needed to consult Maurice in person. He went up for a committee meeting on 12 March, but two days before sent an anxious letter to Harmsworth. He had heard nothing from Maurice since his February *démarche* over staff, and his "smoky chimney" nerves were beginning to worry how much offence he had caused.

> I'm afraid my query about Maurice is more a matter of nerves than of reason. I'm almost always outrunning the rather limited amount of confidence I have in myself (far less than I allow myself to show), and directly I cease to hear from London, I begin to be tormented by a fear that I have put my foot in it – or, still worse, Maurice's. And my desire to see Maurice top-dog is equal to my confidence in him, which is enormous.
> I shall be up on Monday, as I have wired, and I hear confidentially that staffing is to be discussed. That is good. I cannot keep up this racket myself – a perpetual struggle to overwork on the cheap – it is sapping not only my physique, which isn't up to much, but my working morale. And in piling stuff on Maurice we are like a boat in squalls with the sheet made fast. If he crocks, we may as well shut up the fisheries shop. It is all profoundly unsatisfactory. I need something approaching an organization for getting the work done, and the Board needs it. The times more.
> Excuse writing. I've been slamming off files, after a cold day in the rain.[24]

Here was the first sign of the crack in his own personal armour that by the end of the year was to develop into a full-blown crisis – to match any of those of his writing days.

For the winter and spring of 1917 had been particularly hard – more snow than rain, with heavy falls right into April. Harder still for those whose working lives were spent touring the country in an open top car. On 8 March Reynolds and Harry turned up once more at Flete. Alice Mildmay noted in her diary: "Mr Stephen Reynolds and his under-study, whose name I never know, came by appointment at 10, and were so perished with cold that I had to revive them with hot coffee".[25]

And there were some very personal blows. On 15 February, news came through that his sister Dot's fourth child and only boy, Robert, had died at the farm at Parkstone at the age of four, just three years after his mother herself had died, aged 29, in her next childbirth. The curse of illness and early death now seemed to be visited on a third generation. "Heard today at dinner time that my sister's youngest child, the boy, died of pneumonia, poor little chap; though indeed, one does wonder, for the kids, whether the future is going to be worth living in at all."[26]

In April he was cheered a little by renewed contact with M.P. Willcocks, his one-time novelist friend from Exeter. There had been a distancing of their relationship in recent years, brought on apparently by her move in 1914 from Powderham Crescent to Pennsylvania Road in that city. It is a puzzling episode that even she could not fathom. In her obituary of him, she later wrote: "He was a man of eccentricities of manner and character, and had curious prejudices. For example, for several years he declined to visit a friend because she moved into a new house."[27]

It seems likely, however, there was a little imaginative paranoia on her side too. With the weight of his work, he had had during the war to let many personal relationships slide. He knew she had been complaining of him to his old schoolmistress, Ada Bennett, with whom she was now just as close as him, and he was still not above a little teasing of her persecution complexes. "Now, why didn't you come over to see us, instead of complaining to Miss Ada that I was often in Exeter, but had not been up to see you? So I am, often in Exeter, but never otherwise than on the rush. Whereas, though I'm not at home most times, Mam 'Oolley always is, likewise Bob. Still, I suppose you reckon you've been coming over in spirit – and expect carcasses to Exeter in return."[28]

Her visits "in spirit" were to compile her new novel, *The Eyes of the Blind,* written round a Reynolds character, Dr Rudd, who lodges with his fisherman friend, Sam Cornish. Both Bob and Reynolds come off badly in the book – Bob for his whining and childlike behaviour, Reynolds for his working-class posturing. It would not have been surprising if Reynolds had taken some offence at the copy he had been sent.

But the physical portraits are painted with some endearment, and give us a grasp of Reynolds in the flesh that can be found nowhere else. "For at the open piano, with a cigarette drooping from his lips, sat Dr Rudd. He was running his hands lightly across the keys, like a tuner who would test the tone of the instrument before him...... He reached the final chord and got up to fling away his cigarette end." "She noticed with a sort of awe the nicotine stains on thumb and forefinger...... She was glad he was ugly, glad at the curious pale face with the slim neck and great head." "He ate, she discovered, with great vigour, pushing up his glasses at intervals." "Dr Dan was telling the story of the three little pigs; and never before had she realized what a pleasant voice was his, strong and sonorous, gentle and deep."[29]

And Mary Willcocks is also rather good with the paradoxes of the Reynolds personality. "He opened his mouth to speak and closed it with a snap. When he did speak at last, it was as though he had lost all his boyishness and was a responsible man. His freakishness usually evaporated when other people fluttered." "He's a young man with a kink in his brain and a deuced sulky temper. No compromise with the average, says he, and straightway stirs up a more than average hotch-potch of folly and ill will." "Still, the doctor seemed harassed and hardly left the house for half an hour. In the thick of things, he put a fierce determination into his energies, and the thing he did worst was to wait." "'That's what Dad says you are', she exclaimed. 'A damn-your-eyes-get-out-of-my-light sort of man to all the world and inside as sensitive as if you hadn't any skin.'"[30]

And she excels most in her minute description of life in the tight little cottage in Bedford Square. Here is what it was like to visit Reynolds late in the evening – sharp observation right down to the Henry Lamb portrait hanging on the wall of his writing room.

> The passage into the house was dark, but voices came from a room at the far end and a light from under the door. Sam Cornish, who opened it in answer to her knock, had apparently been preparing for bed, for his jersey was off and he in shirt and trousers. Mrs Cornish hurried forward, as she always did when Sam's mouth opened in an ineffective grin. The smell of lamp-oil and of a family living with tight-closed windows filled the little place......... Presently in his stockinged feet Dr Rudd appeared, tumbling down the steep staircase like a sailor down a companion way...... While he hesitated, Mrs Sam laughed; her broad mouth seemed extraordinarily full of teeth.
> "Oh, take her upstairs, Dan," said she, "or Sam and me'll clear out, if that's what you want."
> With a quick gesture he seized the lamp from the table and led the way upstairs. The flaming signals flying in her face, Dorothy followed him. With a glance round at the littered room, its bed half hidden under books, the doctor turned into his den and pulled forward a beehive chair for his visitor. Leaning his arm on the narrow bedroom mantelpiece, he stood looking down on her.
> ......He stared at her a second and then laughed. She noticed how the whole surface of his face broke out into innumerable wrinkles. On the wall beside him hung a pencil sketch drawn in bold detail; she recognized it, as she had not done before, for a picture of the doctor laughing.

But she is treading on dangerous ground when she, who had long-term female rather than male friends, begins to explore Reynolds' sexuality.

> To Sam, in fact, whose humour was distinctly Chaucerian, finding its most vitalizing food in the sex-war, the doctor's own abstention from women was an incessant cause of raillery. Yet he never ceased to press the claims of this woman or that on Dan, and when they travelled

> together, found it a keen disappointment that the doctor refused to seize the opportunities offered by stray females of coming-on dispositions.
> To Sam the chances offered by civilization for stray amours formed the keenest joy; he himself might be tied, by Dan's orders, to fidelity, but for a man to refuse who had no such home-keeping restraint upon him was next door to being incomprehensible, a sign of the half-man.
> Dan's attitude to all this was queer: it reminded him, like a perpetual death's-head, of his own want of charm, especially of sex-charm; where Sam could get on with any woman, his mate hovered round like an uneasy, but solid, spirit, looking on at amusements to which he possessed no open sesame. This Dr Rudd ascribed, along with other disabilities, to the finicky weakness due to his breeding, from which Sam, as the natural man, was free, as well as from the other queasy habits of gentility. It was like Sam's capacity for comfortably going unwashed, this ability to love, and kiss, and go light-heartedly. Yet, for all the doctor's theories of the advisability of these practices, he was quite unable to follow them. To slip an arm round any girl's waist, or to wash in a bucket with perfect satisfaction, were freedoms denied to him by both nature and art.[32]

Reynolds, in his new-found sexual security, may well have been prepared to look good naturedly on all of this. For, as in all good romances, Dr Rudd manages in the end to overcome his qualms, marry the heroine and whisk her off to a honeymoon in Paris. Just six months after the move to the new house, he may also have been touched a little nostalgically by the old images of Bedford Square. The criticism he had to offer was gentle and relaxed; he was careful to laugh off the sexual dénouement, and quick to reassure her about the apparent invasion of his private life.

> We all bow before you 15½ miles away. Mam Cornish is the best portrait; there's something dynamically immobile in Mam, that lends itself to portraiture. Sam Cornish isn't adequate to the original: there's more in the original than that. As for Dr. Rudd.... I've always suspected that marriage was a damn'd troublesome affair o' it, and am confirmed in my ways by the awful spectacle of what might happen.
> Anyhow, I hope your book will do you well, and you're all welcome to any hints for it you've got at Sidmouth. Heaven knows, 'tis hard enough to write a live book at all, without being grudged living originals! For pay for the privilege, you can come over and add the light of your countenance to that of your ink.

He brought her up to date with the latest events, including the farewell to Bedford Square. "We are all moved to Hope Cottage – under the very shadow of the church. My office work became so great – two assistants going now, and devil knows what to come – that we simply grew out of the old house, and, not wishing to break up the crew, we all came up here. Where we've got a barf-room and a telephone, and, Lord love us, the vicar has threatened to call!"

The family was growing up. "Everybody is very well. Bill is to be married his next leave from the N. Sea. Bobby is courting; Reg goes to the barber's to get shaved. Semaphore hath a devil, curiously resembling her aunt, Lil Brixham; and Pooh-bah [*Gladys, now 6*] has fallen deeply in love with my Cornish fisherman assistant. We were all alive; and remain so."

And yet, the contact with a live author who had just given birth to a book, brought with it nostalgia of a different kind. "As a liter'ary gent. I don't know whether I am deceased or merely in a state of suspended animation – with my magnum opus, as was to be, half written."[33]

Throughout 1917 his already heavy workload for the Board increased further under the weight of the new Government initiatives. At the same time, the work for which he was being paid by the Commission, and which was not being done, served to heighten the pressure. He spent the second half of the year worrying intensively about a memorandum on the definitive harbour needs of the west which he had undertaken to draw up for the Commission and could not find a spare minute to get started.[34] It was without doubt his worst year of the war.

In the midst of the heavy routine came individual battles, often of his own making, which tautened the nerves even more. From the beginning of 1916, he had been worried by a clique on the Fisheries Organisation Society from its sister institution, the Agricultural Organisation Society, which was trying to railroad its own agenda through the Executive.[35] A year later he had become alarmed by F.O.S. plans to make war on the fish merchants and itself market fish direct from the fishermen to obtain better prices. He knew there was no organisation in place to carry through this foolhardy aim, and that in war conditions stability was required above all.

In January 1917 he set out his concerns to Jonathan Barron, his sterling support in Mevagissey.

> You know already what I think about fish trade conditions in Mevagissey and elsewhere. They need a lot of improvement. The weekly settlement system is thoroughly bad. At present, however, we are not so much fighting for the improvement of the fisheries in that respect, as for their very existence. Such as the conditions are, we have to make the best of them; and for that, we need the confidence and help of all parties, fish merchants as well as fishermen. We can't, under war conditions, reform the fish trade; we've got to make the best of what we've got. This is not the time, as I see it, to bring about a quarrel between the fishermen and the merchants, provided the latter do not, at all events, worsen the con-

> ditions which existed before the war; and if the F.O.S. is bent on doing it, then we can't afford to be mixed up with it, or associated with it in people's minds. I have already told the Chairman of the F.O.S. Executive that if they are bent on making now a breach between different sections of the industry as a whole, I shall go into opposition to them, and shall have nothing to do with them in Cornwall.
> ......Cornwall, so far as we are concerned, is rather a case to itself; we are not merely involved in the administrative side of the work; we are already involved in co-operative development schemes, which start, as I think, at the right end – the financial. We don't want their pitch queered by ill-calculated action on the part of the F.O.S.[36]

At a meeting of the Development Commission on 11 May, he struck. He announced that he was thoroughly dissatisfied with the policy of the F.O.S. which was causing great uneasiness in the fish trade in Cornwall. He felt bound to protest against it and had therefore resigned his position as Governor. Then he played his trump card. As the Commission's fishery adviser, he considered that the work of the Society was so unsatisfactory that no further grant should be made to it from the Development Fund.[37]

Though members of the Commission were well aware of Reynolds' temperamental volatility, they still had complete trust in his judgment on fisheries matters. After consultation with B.A.F., they decided to withhold the current year's grant, which would have effectively wound up the Society. There were immediate changes in policy and personnel, and in September the grant was renewed under very strict conditions.[38] It had been a most successful Reynolds coup, but one which had gained him no friends at the F.O.S.

That summer he was to lose friends close to home in an initiative that was to turn the tourist industry of Sidmouth into a flat spin. Since the day he had given up "frighting" and had ridiculed the frights themselves in the pages of *Alongshore*, he had loathed on principle the distraction of fishermen from their main task by pleasure boating. It was not just the servility involved; he saw this "easy" money as turning many men away from the rigours of fishing for good.

These concerns were magnified in his mind by the conditions of war, when every hour lost to fishing was a loss to food stocks and a gain to the enemy. He was now drafting single-handed most of the naval regulations controlling fishing, and persuaded the local naval authorities to apply the permit controls to pleasure boating. At the back of his mind was "the difficulty of keeping up the ring fence around fishermen, as workers in a national service only less important than the Naval Service, if they will crawl under the fence to waste fishing time on seaside visitors."[39]

The regulations caused an instant outcry in Sidmouth, as much among the townsfolk and visitors as the fishermen themselves. Tom Woolley was loud in his protest. As the war progressed, he had begun to feel that Reynolds' enthusiasm for exercising his powers, even over his erstwhile friends, had rather run away with him.[40] He openly defied the regulations to create a test case which might lead to their annulment and thus, as he claimed, get Reynolds off the hook of the local fury.

But Reynolds was quick to divert him from an appearance before the magistrates at Ottery and took him down to lay his case before the naval authorities at Mount Wise. "I'm not willing that anything in which I have had a hand shall be the means of dragging one of the biggest and honestest men I know before a bench of damn fools, armed with Acts of worse fools."[41] At Mount Wise, the immediate position was defused by a decision to issue Tom with a permit but defer it for 15 days. Tom came home still bent on breaking the embargo, but soon after the offending policy was rescinded.

For Reynolds, it was a more than usually draining period. "I shan't be sorry to get over to Wales; I've had these infernal regulations for every meal here for nearly three weeks, and feel that with much more of it I shall suddenly give and run amok, and begin smashing up the 'appy 'ome, or go for somebody blind. Which would be stupid. Every Government official ought to live among the people he deals with. Then Prussianism would be impossible."[42]

The affair had a lasting impact on his view of how the fisheries should be governed, confirming long-held prejudice. "Are we going to succumb to Prussianism as a cheap and easy, a *proximately* efficient method of attaining, or rather of failing to attain, the end desired. Those Pleasure Regulations – my one experiment in Prussianism – have brought me more sharply to my intellectual bearings than certainly anything else in my official life. I got a dose of infection, betrayed myself and my people; the end was good; the method Prussian; and not till the end of my life shall I get clear of the consequences."[43]

One continuing source of anxiety, and criticism, was the unending process of recruitment to the Navy. Although he deliberately stood aside from the decisions on individual fishermen, his status as the single most powerful person in the fisheries of the west put him in the firing line of the inevitable resentment as if he had been the recruiting master himself. A complaint to Maurice late in 1917 that he had been responsible for recruiting unfairness brought the whole matter bubbling to the surface. Though stoically resigned to the situation, the criticism clearly hurt.

He wrote to Henry Maurice in his own defence.

> I gave you months ago my reasons for taking no active part in this calling up, and why I considered it neither expedient nor effectively fair for me, in my huge district, to decide who should stay and who should go. I thought my reasons conclusive; I believe you regarded them as adequate. You know what a misery it has been to me, to have my fishing fleets whittled away from below; you know how I have intervened to ease the trouble down, and how I have fought for men to man the West Country boats. I have done what I thought right. Cheap gibes have

been flung at me at the London end, with its invincible ignorance of what things mean to country people's and family's lives. By carrying out the instructions of the Government only too effectively, I have earned the enmity of the provincial patriots whose patriotism, while they are on the safe side of military age, consists in superintending the patriotism of those who aren't. And I have not escaped the opprobrium of the people in whose interests I was acting. They have not been able to see the rationale of the calling up. I confess that I have often myself been able to find no rationale. At best, it was bound to be a clumsy process. What more easy for those who bore us a grudge than to say that we got back on people by calling them up? What more easy to believe, when people are cornered and must scratch, that I am the *diabolus ex machina* of the matter? It is a fact that in Devonport Barracks the called-up Cornishmen are dubbed "Reynolds's Men". I cannot help it, and I see nothing to regret in the line I have taken. I don't blame them; in their distress they seize on anything that suggests itself or is suggested to them; but it hurts, damnably.[44]

These persistent psychological pressures, to which he was more susceptible than most, both sapped his strength and increased manifold the weight of the everyday burden of work. For the workload was relentless, made worse by his own perfectionism and unwillingness to cut corners. At times he could treat it with typical irony. Late in 1917, he wrote to Collingwood, his colleague back in London: "I daresay you have heard that the Admiral, Devonport, has issued a thunderstorm sort of order, practically closing all the water for 20 miles out from the Start to Land's End. He ain't going to keep it so closed, I think, but there's a deuce of a flap on over it, and it looks like a good deal of work over it. Still, we wanted something in the nature of work to fill in the hours between 9 P.M. and say 5 A.M."[45]

His laments to Maurice were directed, at least superficially, to a more constructive end.

I read your letter, and wrote, in the midst of the biggest day I have ever had – thirteen hours solid at blotting pad or typewriter, with three ten-minute intervals for bath and a couple of meals. When I've half an hour to sort the stuff, I'm going to send you last week's diary and correspondence, not to prove that I didn't spend my time playing bridge, still less by way of grousing, but because I think you may be interested in it as a picture of what is involved on the coast by what is decided in London. And it may strengthen your hand in reorganising the coast side.

When Sunday evening's post was gone, I felt like the day one ends writing a book, and, in a curiously similar way, looked back over, and wondered how the devil I'd got through it![46]

For despite the advent of Harry Paynter and Harold Wright, the administration of his vast district was still being run on a shoestring. As 1917 progressed, his initial preoccupation with the inadequate staffing and organisation of the Fisheries Division in London gradually transmuted into a pressing concern for the staffing of Hope Cottage and others like him on the coast. In September, he sent Maurice a mammoth letter of some 7,000 words setting out the case for more resources and better organisation.

It was another Reynolds' literary *tour de force*. Though dealing at some length with the principles of district inspecting, a function he could fairly claim to have invented himself, its greatest eloquence is reserved for the description of the workload and methods of his little office, and the burning frustration of getting "no for'arder".

> One never knows what more one can get out of oneself, if the incentive and excitement are only strong enough, but it does seem to me that I am up against the physical limits of work. My staff is visibly wilting under the strain. I rush around, by railway or car, seeing to things where only they can be properly seen to – on the spot. This week, for example, between Tuesday noon and Thursday midnight, I have started from Sidmouth, have picked up the threads in London, done a day's business in Glasgow, a day's work in London, and returned to Sidmouth again. Back at Sidmouth I ought to be able to think out the results of my journeys, settle my course of action, write my memoranda. Yet, though my working hours are from 7 A.M. to 9 P.M., with ten-minute intervals for meals; though I seldom show my nose out of doors, except to make sure that my car will carry me over my next official journey – still I never get within sight of catching up the work waiting to be done. The morning post comes in, with a grunt from the postman at its bulk; the evening post goes out; both are mostly composed of those urgent small matters which always, in virtue of their urgency, set aside bigger matters which can be postponed. And which go on being postponed! My Development Commission work is scamped or let slide. The map of my district is strewn with matters I have not been able to tackle. My way to hell is carpeted with memoranda I have promised to write.
>
> Don't think for a moment that I am complaining for myself, or of overwork. I am doing in all respects what I want to do: overwork is nothing; everybody who is any good is overworked. But not to make headway with fishery business is to make leeway. I do complain of having to make leeway. Not to keep the many bits of fishery business spinning in the air is to let them come down smash. I can't acquiesce in doing that. It seems to me that we have squeezed the uttermost limit of effectiveness out of makeshift; that unless our fisheries edifice is to crumble; unless the prestige of the Board, that we have been so laboriously building up, is to be changed into a thing *pour rire*; unless our long-reached policies are to

> go fut; unless the ground we have ploughed in advance is to grow charlick, in place of the not bad grass it grew before – unless, in a word, the fisheries are to be the worse instead of the better, for all our efforts, makeshift has to come to an end.
> Organisation is no substitute for brains. But it's the cart that gives them a lift. It's the speedway for initiative to travel on. It is, anyhow, the only substitute for makeshift.[47]

He acknowledges fully the debt to his underpaid staff.

> Paynter is a fisherman, born and bred, with a fisherman's knowledge of working, daily-bread-earning, motor fishing. He has become quite a good typist, and is rapidly making up what education he went short of. He has worked with me now for a year and a half, under the most trying conditions of cramped hustle, and I think more and more of him and his work. Permits used to be his special care, but both for his health's sake, and because his aptitudes lie that way, I am getting him out and about the district as much as possible on his motor bicycle, on motor loan negotiations and special bits of enquiry – fully one man's job. He can jump into a boat and put an engine right; takes a great interest in teaching fishermen new ways of fishing or handling gear; makes friends wherever he goes; and is first-rate as an intelligence scout. Wright, an honours man in economics and ex-President of the Union at Cambridge, had made his mark before he came here, and I suppose, when his health permits, that he will plunge back into London work. He keeps the office going in the absence of Paynter and myself; does practically all the heavy recruiting correspondence, and most matters involving the interpretation of regulations, or the handling of forms, tend to fall into his hands. Unless he be regarded in some sort as an apprentice, the salary I am able to give Paynter is very inadequate for the work he does; Wright is unpaid.[48]

After a full description of the regular workload under thirteen heads, and the *ad hoc* problem solving, he adds: "It will not, I think, be found difficult to realise why I am cornered; why my work beats about my head like a flock of screaming birds with sharp beaks".[49] The possibility of dividing the district is unthinkable. He is determined to soldier on.

> When I go round my district; most of all when I perch myself above a harbour; when I watch the far-reaching consequences of even a single official act – right and well-timed, or wrong and ill-timed, as the case may be – I confess it gives me a powerful shake-up. And I won't bate a jot of my two district mottoes: "What needs doing has got to be done", and "No fisherman's trouble but is worth attention".

> You, in your kindness, say: "Why can't you let some things slide, and take a rest?" It can't be done without letting somebody down; you at one end or fishermen at the other. A district is a huge contraption, that can't be safely driven with nuts missing, any more than a car can. It has got to be kept all taut. It is a far-thrown fabric of stitches-in-time stretched always to breaking-point. Let a tear start in it, and heaven knows where 'twill end!
>
> My large district might, of course, be divided up. But I don't think that is the solution. It may sound conceited, but I don't feel in the least incompetent to run it. I want to sow, tend, and reap all the acreage I've ploughed. What neither time nor strength will allow me to continue is the directive work and the donkey-work too. Not that I think the donkey-work beneath me. On the contrary, I am rather a good clerk and typist, and thoroughly enjoy the craftsmanship of it. But it can now only be done at the expense of the directive work, just as the latter can only be done at the expense of the donkey-work – just as this letter (only written in sheer desperation as to how to carry on) has been done at the expense of piles of stuff waiting to be dealt with.
>
> Furthermore, if crocking myself is mainly my own business, it does not entitle me to go on overdriving my present staff.[50]

Getting all this off his chest provided, perhaps, a psychological relief which the Fisheries Division in London was unable to match with money or hard action. The immediate result appears to have been a tour of the south west district by Maurice with Reynolds at the wheel.[51] But the only, rather fragile, resources available to Henry Maurice were honours and promotion. In early November, Harry was promoted to Assistant Inspector which, in addition to the status, brought with it a small increase in salary. Reynolds was delighted with Maurice's letter when the news came through.

> Literary training may be useful for certain purposes, but I don't think all the literary training in the world could make your nice letters nicer (or your snorty official letters snortier!) when you set out to write them. Harry is delighted. His mother will be "high up". She hasn't yet fully realised that he has been doing much more than looking after me. As for him, you and Thomson are the only two he has met in official life on whom he goes "all the bundle"; the only two on whom he doesn't inflict that inconvenient question of fishermen: "What their feeling is", and about whom he doesn't weigh up in what directions they can be trusted, and in what directions they can't. So that, as you can imagine, a letter like yours could have pleased him from no one so much as from you (me,too). His work has all along been keen and ungrudging – with a free heart, as Devon fishermen put it – but in hitting on the Assistant Inspector idea, you have certainly hit on a thing which has most notice-

> ably improved his bearing towards his work – made him at the same time more confident and more cautious. Once more, undoubtedly, you've done the trick.[52]

Promotion was not available to Reynolds; there were no higher grades within the district inspectorate. But honours were now being used most liberally to reward civil servants working their legs off in wartime. Maurice himself had been made a Companion of the Bath in the New Year Honours of 1916, the standard award for a civil servant at his level. He now made a very tentative approach to Reynolds about the possibility of an award of the newly-minted OBE, guarding his back against a possible burst of fury by assuring him that the feeling in London was that he was certain to refuse.

Indeed, one would have expected the champion of the working classes to have some coruscating words for these vacuous trinkets of the Establishment. But Reynolds was touched by the proposition – "your letter from Leatherhead...... gave me the buck yesterday to work like the very devil". He was quick to see the human side, and the scientist in him moved straight into analytical mode.

> What you told Hall is quite right, though I appreciate intensely what you and he said. Speaking flippantly, I don't think I should quite deserve the fourth class of the O.B.E. After all, I was a bit of a gun among the intellectually alert, and you will all of you some day be taking count of my psycho-economics, though whether the general and inevitable movement of thought will forestall my being able to complete my book on it, is another matter. I don't regret my choice to turn to what seemed to want doing most, but to have myself signed and sealed, so to speak, as an author deceased, a minor official alive, would be a bit of a blow to me. Again, a premature minor honour would expose me to the accusation of having ratted to "the likes o' they", without giving me prestige and power to counterbalance the effect of the accusation. For, what is there in any honour? I conceive that your C.B. had three aspects for you more important than the C.B. itself, namely, (1) the appreciation that led to conferring it, (2) the pleasure we all had in our H.G.M. being recognised, and (3) on a lower plane, an added prestige with which you could more easily bring fools and snobs to heel, and get on with the main job. (1) I have; it is that which gives me a working capacity which really surprises myself. (2) I should have, and shouldn't have: it would be mixed. While for (3), the O.B.E. ain't good enough.

It was the most gracious of letters of decline. It ended, as always, with a typical image to lighten the load. "When I'm too old to be active, I shall come along to you, with a gift of seven salt herrings in my hand, for a peerage, in order to introduce in a serener atmosphere the bills of the Permanent Secretary of the Imperial Fisheries Department, and for a Civil List pension of £75 per annum, 'in consideration of his literary merits and of his reduced circumstances'!"[53]

There is no doubt that Reynolds was more than a handful as subordinate. His immense and irreplaceable contribution as national policymaker and local executor made it no easier to cope with the wayward volatility of his temperament. For he soon began to treat Henry Maurice, as in younger days he had treated Seccombe, Pinker and Garnett, as the trusted father-figure he could praise or berate as the mood took him. But Maurice was not a publisher or literary agent whose regular duty was to soak up the emotional outbursts of young protégés and coax them gently into the path of creativity.

Like many people unused to handling neurotics, he was inclined to assume that "knocking some sense" into people, urging them "to get a grip on themselves", was the most productive strategy. Reynolds was only too adept at countering banal exhortations of this kind. "But don't descend to nonsense about my heart governing my head. The only difference is, that, as a result of the philosophy on which I try to base my work, the so-called heart is ostensible, an admitted factor, whereas, according to your outworn philosophy, it's a sideshow. But the result's much the same. The only difference is that your practice is better than your theory, and mine, I'm sorry to say, is worse. If I could teach you philosophy, and you could teach me equilibrium, what bloody angels we should be! Meanwhile, if you think we work for your *head*, you much deceive yourself. It's H.G.M. *in toto* we work for."[54]

When Reynolds hit rock bottom once more, as he did at the end of 1917, Maurice was singled out as father-confessor because none of the old ones were still around. The accusation Reynolds had received from Mevagissey of recruiting unfairness had included also the taunt that he was now afraid to walk out on the quay. The actual truth was that when in residence there he sat in his lodgings and did the directive work while Barron and Paynter rushed round to deal with the individual problems. He could not do both.

But the accusation had stung him because it had hit upon a wider truth which brought him back face-to-face with his breakdown of 1903.

> And, also, there is this further truth in the matter. I don't shirk unpleasantness in the way of work; you've had evidence enough of that! But as my nerves are progressively giving way under this present strain, I find that, apart from a few friends, I do shrink more and more from meeting people, except in the way of work and with a definite object. All work and no play is making Jack a damn'd dull boy outside of work. Years ago, when I was ill, I couldn't bring myself to meet anybody, and if I went out to a meal, I used to have to get up half-way through, and go home. I couldn't help it, and I trained myself out of it. In those days I had no

> object in life to steady me. Nowadays I have, and I do not find my tenacity diminishing. But outside that object, I find the same thing growing on me again. And that is where your friend has heedlessly stung me: I was trying to hide it from myself till I had finished what I set out to do.[55]

Since meeting Harry early in 1915, the last two Christmases had passed comparatively peacefully – a novel experience for Reynolds. Now, in December 1917, the old Christmas demons returned. In London, he was growing anxious about the fate of the Fisheries Division, under pressure from Towle and the Ministry of Food, plotting to take over much of its responsibilities. He was worrying too about his own future, whether to revitalise his work for the Development Commission which had been falling slowly into abeyance, or seek a more responsible position at the heart of fisheries policy with the Board in London.

At least one thing was clear. He had come to the despondent conclusion that his writing life was definitely over.

> I can go back to writing, and, if I can only get my Psycho-economics done, I think I can achieve my fill of distinction. Also those friends do rather cut me, who say: "You, who can hatch ideas, and, what's more, can express them, what the devil are you doing with forms and the like?" I think the best I could have done for my generation would have been with a pen. "Would" and "could".... For I feel inwardly too battered about, too tired. Creative work is the extremest concentration of all: I doubt my morale would any longer stand up to it. The cancer of war eats away at all, subconsciously, if not consciously. It is not my disappointment or sense of tragic futility that a new generation will want after the war; they will want re-creation, not reconstruction, which latter is only an effort of the old gang to get back top-dog. I don't now feel that I have the world before me, as one needs to do to write; I want to finish what I've begun, conscious, even while doing it, that there isn't time left. When one's creative climacteric is gone past, the best one can do is to help and encourage the next, younger batch. I am, I fear, a deceased author.[56]

It appears to be at about this time, just before Christmas 1917, that he broke his domestic links with the Woolleys – the meals round the kitchen table – and moved with Harry across the top of Church Street to The Retreat, the large white-washed cottage which in the 1850s had been home to the curates of the parish and which later became a war memorial in the shape of the Servicemen's Club. There the two of them lodged with Ernest Gibbs and his wife (Gibbs had played rugby for Sidmouth with Tom) and their daughter, Dorothy.[57] Mrs Gibbs, who saw to all their domestic needs, was a wizard at making the food rations go round.[58] Hope Cottage remained the office, but no longer home.

We do not know the nature of the rows which led to the break, but we can guess – no doubt the old enemy of children's noise and the inability of the Woolley family to fit in with his working hours and working temper. In Hope Cottage he was, in any case, no longer their dependent lodger, and the relationship with Harry had inevitably created a distance not present in the old days. Though recognising the necessity, he was nonetheless devastated by this breach after so many years with the Woolleys "because they cannot live up to my needs".[59]

It had one other longer term consequence. The Thicket, his cottage on Salcombe Hill, had not been taken up by the Admiralty as a nursing home after all. In April 1915, to release the large sum tied up in it, he had taken out a mortgage of £375 with the ever obliging Charles Wright. Having broken with the Woolleys, the house he had built purposely to share with them now seemed no longer to have any point. He put it on the market and sold it the following April for £600.[60] His will still gave Bob the first option to live there, but this was an option that was no longer his to confer.

Christmas Day found him alone in the office, Harry having collapsed with exhaustion and been packed off home to St Ives. He was worried that Harry's persistent cough might be the onset of T.B. In defence, he immersed himself unwillingly in work. In June the Development Commission had set up a small harbours committee, including Nash and himself, and he had been asked to contribute a memorandum on harbours, coves and landing places in the south west area. The task had been hanging guiltily over his head for the rest of the year, with no time to begin it. Now, on a more than usually blank Christmas Day, he forced himself to complete the first half.

On Boxing Day, after a sleepless night and furious with the world, he slammed the memorandum off to Stagg, Nash's private secretary at the Commission with an uncompromising statement of his feelings.

> I worked straight away yesterday from 6 A.M. to 10 P.M. (with not more than fifteen minutes for tough cow Christmas dinner) in the effort to get done what I have got done. (I have no staff here; they are all left, or ill, or overworked and on leave; and therefore am having to tackle everything myself.) In any case, being fool enough to work like that for anybody, I spent, in spite of bromide, a nearly sleepless night, nearer a breakdown, certainly, than I have been for many years.
>
> That, you will say, is not the sort of thing the D.C. wants. Perhaps, then, you will investigate and explain how it is to be avoided. It is the direct result of holding oneself responsible for one's work, instead of responsible, merely, for doing enough to satisfy.
>
> If, as you frequently remind me, I am primarily the servant of the D.C., is it not up to the D.C., in the interests of efficient service, to look after me a bit, as well as desiderate less pressure, and at the same time bring amiably insidious pressure to bear upon me to make me do what it is well

known I cannot get done except under worse pressure still?
This is not a friendly letter. I don't feel friendly to anybody. I have been hard put to it lately to keep my head above water at all; everybody has been willing to discuss my difficulties, and to act to me in an advisory capacity as to what, of course, I ought to do. But nobody, Maurice and Paynter excepted, has really stirred a finger to see me through; and of those two, the former is overwhelmed with heaps else to do, and the latter has made himself ill in the process.
No, I don't feel pleasant over it; and I'm not going to pretend I do.[61]

On the same day, he wrote to Maurice to exculpate himself, the same letter he would have sent to Garnett Christmases ago. "I'm afraid you are tired, and fed up. So am I. Oh! I am so damn tired, so tired in the innards of my being. Indeed, but for your encouragement, and Harry's caretaking of me, and Thomson's solid good faith, I think I must have gone to the devil long ago."

He sent to Maurice, a little shame-facedly, a copy of the outburst to Stagg. What now became obvious was that Stagg was just the scapegoat, the real disturbance was the thoughts of Harry. Just as Christmas 1912 had been ruined by anxiety over the physical welfare of Tom, now Christmas 1917 had gone the same way. The absence of Harry brought flooding back childhood memories of the Bear with Peter, the black and white cat, snuggling down on the end of his bed.

I enclose copy of a letter I have sent to Stagg with half the Harbours Memo. It isn't good tempered, I'm afraid. And I'm glad that that accursed memo. should be more the last straw than all the work I've done for you. And, indeed, I have never felt more done. I worked all day yesterday with the strength and energy of bad temper and resentment, and I spent nearly all last night hanging on tough, so to say, to my equilibrium, and my imagination, which was darting in every direction I know not to be safe; and wishing Harry were here, as a sort of focus of stability, or even that, as when I was a child, I could so much as hear a cat purring on my feet – anything solid and stable, in that infernal turmoil of thinking, to hang on to. If it comes again to-night I shall pack and drive to Plymouth. It seems like a bad dream now, but it didn't, and won't, at 2.0 or 3.0 A.M.
As to the administrative machine – or its mechanics, that I was talking about. I know it goes for little, really, but I'm sure it's like warmth and meals to men who have to work. What has hardened my thinking on the subject is not the strain on myself – that's my business: I growl, and accept it – but watching my people wilting under the strain reflected from me. It has, for one thing, broken up what has been my home for fifteen [*sic*] years, because they cannot live up to my needs. Worse than that, I have watched its effects on Harry, the brightest, keenest, sweetest-

> natured young thing I have come across. (His mother is a great old woman.) I can't stand that; his coughing, though I hope there's no T.B., goes through me, till I wish I had the T.B. myself, and could say, "So many months, and have done with it".
> Well, all this isn't very cheerful. But there's little cheerfulness anywhere. The most one can hope for these days is comrades in trouble. You have that. So have I.[62]

This was driven, above all, by the usual post-Christmas depression, and by next day he was ready to recognise it, especially when Maurice, talking of his own battles, reminded him of his fatal propensity to quarrel with people over nothing.

> What you say about quarrelling with people so chimes with a lot I have been thinking. So have I been quarrelling with people. Partly, with me, but not with you, I think it's my own fault, or misfortune. I get, mixed up with depressions, moods of savage anger; and who I lash out on depends more on the chance of their being in the way than anything else; and I don't think I can entirely help it. My father was just the same – and is now, for all I know – only he took it out on his family. And Christmas is the worst time, because it's when one most wants to have one's cake and eat it; when one most envies the family life one would not on any account go back to, and the conventional religious twaddle, with its naive beauties, that one wouldn't be again tied up to at any price.[63]

It was the final Christmas lament. This was the last bad Christmas of his life.

The crisis past, he entered 1918 in an altogether more optimistic frame of mind, which he managed to maintain throughout most of the year. The new home, alone with Harry at last, seems to have brought a measure of psychological relief. Though he still worried from time to time about the status and future reconstruction of the Fisheries Division, even the strongest assaults of the Ministry of Food, with price control of fish, introduced along with food rationing in the spring, did not seem to fill him with the same despair as before.

In January the widespread discussion of Northcliffe's ambitions as the most likely candidate to head the planned Ministry of Information brought back memories of his first and only novel – still his favourite child. He wrote to Pinker: "I wish Macmillans could be induced to overcome their repugnance to my poking fun at bishops sufficiently to give *The Holy Mountain* a chance of demonstrating its topicality at the present time. I forget the precise words, but my anticipation of the ambition of the Director of the Ha'penny Press was very near the mark: 'One God, one King, one Empire, one Church, one nation, one

Press, and one Director of the lot'". Even now, when addressing his erstwhile agent, a writing life still held out possibilities. "No writing getting done at present. I suppose I shall start again some day."[64]

His discussions with Maurice of the shortcomings of their respective machines took on a much lighter, less insistent, note. His former critical approach he now defended as merely the routine work of a creative observer.

> I do wish you'd get out of your head the notion you seem to have – you've alluded to it so many times lately – that I criticise you. There, you are quite wrong – entirely on the wrong track. Consider for a moment that all my training is that of an observer of people who happens to have the power to make them live again in books. For that portrait of them which has to exist in my mind before I can put it into words, it is a *sine qua non* that I should never stop observing material. And I never do stop. I must see them as I see them, so to speak; else they won't live. They'd be only corpses in print – like the subject of the average official biography. It is that continuous and scarcely conscious process of observation, that building of you alive in my own mind, that you mistake for criticism.
>
> Not altogether pleasant, perhaps, to be so observed. But I could make you walk and talk and have a second being in the pages of a book and make people feel they knew you, who never met you; and keep you alive after you're dead and gone in the portrait of an English official in a transition period.[65]

He was already stepping back a few feet from his own work and imagining its continuation in other hands. "I myself love organising a thing, but when it's organised, I don't a bit want to go on running it. It's a book that's written then; I don't want to write it again. And I'm trying really very hard to knock my district into such a shape that it would run itself without me, in order to guard against that propensity. I'm hugely interested in working out a district filing and communications system, but when I've got it right – heaven defend me from having to *do* the filing!"[66]

He could now talk of the office with more humour than anxiety. "I've watched you handling people with the heye of an 'awk, and owe much more to that than is probably evident to you. One thing I simply can't achieve. You, at your desk, receive patiently an endless stream of interrupters. But they look round my door; I look round out of the corner of my eye – and they fade out again! I suppose it's partly due to having always worked for so many years in complete solitude. It's one of the office laughs at my expense."[67]

With the spring of 1918 came a new relaxed carelessness about work, allied to a heightened sensitivity to the wonders of nature about him – a conjunction that had not been seen in him for many years. Harry was well again, that may have been half the story. But there is a kind of reckless gate fever about it all, which seems to hint at an unconscious presentiment that the sands were running out.

Invitations went flying up to Maurice in London to make a spring visit. Here, at the end of April, is an especially boyish one.

> I'm sending this to Leatherhead, because wiseacres agree that next week end (*i.e.* the first in May) will be apple-blossom in the S.W. Looks so at present: the weather has been hot; we had a big thunderstorm Thursday night, and the blackbirds are in full song. So it is urged that you come on leave, if you consider that the S.W. sees too much of you officially. And if you get tired of leave.... Why, here's your Reconstruction Memo. down here, that you came down to talk about 11 months and three weeks ago!!
>
> We've got some grub, too. Heaven knows how Mrs. Gibbs gets joints and frying-fat on $(15 - [10 + 5])^3$ coupons! She does.
>
> In short, us wants our Maurice; that's the long and short of it. If you will come we're going to have much pleasure. And if you won't come, and inspect us and our dispositions, we're going to have a grievance.
>
> { Government }
Another { Georgian } Blunder.
District Office not Inspected.
Allowed to carry on without Discouragement.
SEND FOR FRYER
>
> ......Gardening weather this! We have planted half of the little waiter's garlic. I tried the other day the experiment of putting a sliced rootlet into a bottle of olive oil, with the idea of the oil dissolving out the oil of garlic, and then using it for salads. And, by Jove! it does dissolve it out! The oil becomes stronger than the garlic root itself. 'Sauce à baiser' I propose to call it in my salad recipes![68]

And, wonder of wonders, on 4 May, with the weather still holding up, he suggested himself an unscheduled day off for everyone – that powerful management technique of Civil Service summers long gone by.

> We all got more strained and tatchy all the week – until yesterday I said I meant to say, Hell about the office, and go to Beer, the mackerel coast and Bridport. Harold said: "Maurice's Memo., you know". Harry said he'd got *x* licences, *y* priorities, *z* motor applications, matches, paraffin to tackle, and all the rest of the Fisheries general store that he looks after. But I said: "Very well, the Donkey-Cart starts at 11.0, and if you people don't choose to tip into it...."
>
> A most perfect day! You should have been there. Sunshine, brilliantly clear air, one of those days, with huge woolpacks in a clear blue sky, so rare in the S.W. The gorse was like yellow fire, and the bluebells like a

> rich blue haze, on the Dorset hills. Cherries in full bloom; your apple-blossom coming out, still in the pink bud stage, except in the combes. Donkey-Cart, after a fortnight's puzzle with the ignition, went so well that I felt myself as if out for the first time after an illness. We went to the "Greyhound" at Bridport, and were told we couldn't have meat lunch without cards. So they gave us crab and lobster, and we told the landlord we were glad we had no meat cards. At Beer we found some of the fishermen out of fuel oil – transport from the depôt broken down. Off goes Harry up the village, and, how he did it I don't quite know: he seems to have commandeered the domestic oil in the village for the boats, as and when the fishermen want it. Thus we all came home in good spirits.[69]

And that summer, in this more relaxed mood, he seemed to find time to write the long policy memoranda while still keeping abreast of the routine office work. In July, he wrote a most effective one in the old Reynolds style – a close analysis of the overmanning of the distributive fish trade by salesmen and merchants, and a warning of the harmful consequences for reconstruction and development.[70]

With sure signs that the war was coming to an end, reconstruction was on everybody's lips. In September and October, he went with Maurice on a final exploratory tour of the ports to assess the major post-war needs. It took them from the Thames up the east coast as far as Cullercoats, and then from Carlisle down the west and Welsh coasts as far as the Severn, Maurice leaving him at Barmouth Junction to return for business in London. They left out the well-explored south-east, and Reynolds' south west district which both had toured the previous year. For at least part of the journey, Ruth Maurice accompanied them, and it took on some aspects of the old autumn holidays he had taken so regularly before the war.

From an official standpoint, it was a depressing exercise. Reynolds noted a marked contrast between the activity and enthusiasm of his own South West, where on the road he was never given a moment's peace, and the apparent lethargy of much of the rest of the country, harking back to the St Ives of 1913.

> Outside the steam ports, I did not find anywhere that chain of liveliness in the fisheries which runs along the S. Devon and Cornwall coasts. In certain places there was considerable activity – e.g., Sheringham, Bridlington, Flamborough – but they were too scattered; they seemed, so to speak, to be islands of activity on comparatively unworked stretches of coast.
>
> Word that the Head of the Fisheries Division was out around did not go along the coast as it should have done, had the fishing places been thoroughly alert and in organized communication with each other; there

were no fishermen and others waiting at the hotel front door before the bags could be unpacked or a meal taken, wanting something, objecting to something, or protesting against the preposterous anomalies of the fisheries.[71]

His natural prejudices soon emerged when they made their inspection of the large steam ports. "Personally, I was most struck by the filth of the wooden fish market at Grimsby, and the enormous waste of power and energy involved in its lack of arrangement and of transport, other than by a horde of men and boys with barrows. A trade that will put up with such conditions at the largest fish port in the world cannot be said to have much notion of cleanliness and power-economy."[72] Whereas just fifty miles up the coast, the smaller scale produced signs of hope. "At Filey, we came across a fishing village which has a genuine breed of fishermen, good fishing grounds, and is badly in need of harbourage."[73]

Coming down the west coast, the picture in the larger ports was much the same. "The deadness of many ports was evident enough – most of all, perhaps, in the famous old port of Whitehaven, where, in a good roomy harbour, the few boats were badly kept up, and the only show of business was two groups of men and lads playing chuck ha'penny."[74]

But there were hopes of new and profitable developments too. At Conway they inspected the Board's experiments in mussel purification, one of the war measures inspired by the Fish Food Committee for the rapid production of cheap wholesome food. "It was most impressive to see in the one tank at Conway about £80 worth of fine mussels, which, without the purification process there applied, would have been worse than worthless as human food; and to watch also the working precision with which a highly scientific process is carried out by the staff. Just as one can tell at a glance whether a piece of writing has literary style and grip, so it was easy to see that the scientific research and control experiments at Conway are being done with scientific style and grip."[75]

After the visit to Grimsby on 12 September, he took a day off and drove over that evening to Millthorpe to keep his five-year-old promise of a visit to Edward Carpenter.[76] He was feeling the physical and psychological exhaustion of the tour, made worse by the constant tyre trouble he was having with his little car. The Carpenter farmhouse, with its simplicity of living, its sexual openness, was like a haven of peace in the midst of his anxiety – a sense of homecoming to rival that first visit down the Gut in the August of 1906.

He took immediately to George Merrill, Carpenter's long-time partner who, since the publication of *My Days and Dreams* two years before, had become almost as much a public figure as Carpenter himself. On the Friday morning, he drove off with George to Totley to send a telegram; but for the rest of that day, he was able to relax in the peace of the garden and forget about work altogether.

In the evening, they sat down to one of George's sumptuous meals and talked way into the night. Carpenter got out his collection of Taormina prints, the notorious photographs of pubescent youths which made Sicily such a great Edwardian tourist attraction.[77] It was an unforgettable evening in such an atmosphere of freedom. Reynolds did not forget the photographs either. Two months later he was to write to Carpenter: "Somewhen when you are down country, could I get a chance of looking through the Soames collection of Taormina prints? Yours were so fine, I should like to see the lot".[78]

The break from responsibility lasted only one full day. He set off at 9 that rainy Saturday morning to pick up Ruth and Henry Maurice and drive them to Scarborough *via* York.[79] It was another disastrous day. He hurt his back early on and the little car with its troublesome tyres had to be abandoned halfway through the journey. On the Sunday evening before dinner, he wrote to Carpenter from his Scarborough hotel.

> We got here in the dark last night in a hired Neddy Ford car driven by a nice boy who was as blind as a bat. I had had more tyre trouble between York and New Malton, and had left my car at the latter.
> I don't know how to thank you for the day's peacefulness you gave me at Millthorpe – or George for his efforts to make me overeat myself with his nice cookeries. Without it, I think I should have broken down altogether. As it was, in Chesterfield, I was suddenly seized with lumbago, and had no small trouble, the rest of the day, to stoop at all about anything!......
> Must go down to grub. I am going to try to get you some fish and send it along, for George to try his fine arts on.[80]

But the continuous troubles of the tour prevented him from keeping the promise. Back in London a month later, he wrote to explain. "On the rest of the tour – after that blessed rest at Millthorpe – I had no chance of sending any fish.... The tyre trouble, and all the other troubles, went on, so that even on the rare occasions when I had time to go rooting round a harbour, I hadn't the inclination. And, in fact, didn't go." But the memory of George lingered on. "How is George? In many a hotel afterwards, when they put up swank insufficiency, I reminded me of his efforts to make me overeat – and weigh 18 stone!"[81]

The complete break provided by the tour had wrought a change in him. A month after, he was still feeling its effects. "I am really feeling incredibly slack; keen on a few things and fed up with several. It's not the fatigue of the tour. I think it is that the break in routine broke, as it were, the surface tension, and allowed a lot of old previous staleness to flood to the top."[82]

It was not until 10 November in Sidmouth that he started to write up a report of the tour, which took him three days. The message for reconstruction policy was still much the same, with psycho-economics at its heart.

> It is thought by many who still put the economic cart before the horse, and reckon men in terms of money, instead of wealth in terms of life, that the permanent welfare of the fisheries is to be achieved by completing their industrialization – by squeezing them into that industrial system from which other trades are now trying to extricate themselves. The co-operatism which other trades are trying to find again, the smaller fisheries have never lost, nor even have the steam fisheries lost it entirely. In short, the circle has met; the old-fashioned syndicalism (in the better sense of the word) of the fisheries finds itself, in principle, to be what the formerly advanced industries are now aiming at!"[83]

His conclusion after four years of war was that the pre-war prescriptions were still entirely valid.

> So far as general policy goes, the report of the Departmental Committee on Inshore Fisheries has withstood completely the harder test of war conditions, and such of its recommendations as have been acted upon have more than proved their value. It is not, therefore, another generalized consideration which is needed, so much as the application of the Inshore Committee's recommendations to the varied needs of individual fishing ports. In any case, rapidity of action is essential. When meat becomes less scarce, and fish cheap again, this unique opportunity of re-capitalizing and re-instating the smaller fisheries will be gone.[84]

The end of the war, reinforcing the futility of it all, fed his feelings of pessimism for the future post-war world. The mood was established when at Prospect Rise on 3 November Aunt Allie died. She was 61 and had been completely bedridden for the past seven years. The little cortège of family mourners which on 6 November followed the coffin from Prospect Rise the hundred yards over to the church was led by Aunt Jane, followed by Reynolds' father and stepmother, and then Reynolds himself walking with his stepsister Frances.[85] In grief, the family quarrels were temporarily silenced. It had been the first such family gathering for many years. The next was just around the corner.

Three days later, Reynolds wrote to Carpenter in sombre mood. "It looks now, doesn't it, as if the nightmare is pretty well over.... Now, I suppose, there will be twice as much work as ever to do, trying futilely to reconstruct along lines dictated by the capitalists and governing classes...."[86]

On Armistice Day itself, he took time from his memorandum on the recent tour to send a word to Henry Maurice.

> One doesn't feel one can let to-day's post go out without dropping a line to you. We turned the office out this morning; obviously no work was going to be done. But somehow or other, the intense relief of to-day's

> news seems to be swamped for me in a kind of backwash – the thought of who and what will never be any more – the inadequacy of the end compared with the horror of getting there. So that the festivity in the streets gives one the feeling of witnessing an orgie in a graveyard.[87]

Peace gave a fresh dimension to the thoughts he had been giving over the past year to his personal future. He felt in no doubt that his inspector's job was at an end, that his district could run its peacetime duties perfectly well without him. But he would not give up on the fisheries themselves, and offered himself to Maurice in any capacity in which he might maximise his contribution – perhaps a senior policy post in London.

For Maurice the problems of handling Reynolds at a distance of 200 miles were still fresh in the memory. The prospect of working with him just a few feet away in the same office was not enticing; and he hid behind the administrative difficulties of fitting his inspector into the Whitehall policy machine. Reynolds was hurt by the rebuff, but understood the reason behind the excuses. "When I asked you what you personally wanted of me, with full intent to sink all my own aims in yours if of advantage to you; and asked you again; you fobbed me off with a recital of administrative snags which I knew quite well already."[88]

Then, on 24 November, an ideal new opportunity seemed suddenly to offer. In March 1918 Harold Wright, with his strong political nose, had hinted to Reynolds that a Labour constituency was his for the asking.[89] It had given him pause for thought – how much more loudly his fisheries voice might sound from the House of Commons.

Now, with an election in the offing, the idea re-emerged from a most unlikely source. Reynolds wrote to Maurice in an air of excitement.

> You recollect my telling you once that I was playing with the idea of standing for Parliament, and trying to become the specialist fishery member. Well, last night, Paynter sprung on Wright and myself the idea of putting up for the St. Ives Division of Cornwall, as a fishermen's candidate in particular, and Labour in general. To-night, things have so far advanced that it looks as if it is coming off – provided, that is, I can retain my advisorship to the Development Commission.
>
> In allowing the matter to go so far, so quickly, I have assumed that you meant all you said, when I asked you what, if anything, you wanted of me after the war, and you told me, in effect, that for your purposes I was a hoss too given to kicking the stable about. In any case, the Army and Navy people get leave for election purposes, and I presume, therefore, that you would have no objection to my taking leave for the official period of an election – a leave which would, I suppose, have to become permanent if I happened to get in.[90]

But the little would-be political team had not done its homework quite thoroughly enough. Two days later it emerged that the party officially had quite another candidate up its sleeve. A ciphered message winged up to Parliament Street from Mevagissey.

> *Re* last two letters cloud capped fabric vision all this dissolved another man caught early tide and already footing it featly these yellow sands stop.[91]

He knew that Maurice would be disappointed. "You, I think, may well be sorry I didn't contest the seat. Had I won it, you'd have had the advantage without the nuisance of me. My entourage, as you like to call them, are pretty sick over it; it seems almost certain I should have got in." And despite immediate feelings of relief, he was kicking himself at the opportunity lost. "Personally I feel relieved not to have to face the hurly-burly of an election; and at the same time, rather savage that I have so egregiously missed the train – once and for all, I rather think. For I believe I could have made myself heard on fishery subjects better than by writing memos. that no one has time to read."

But this false start brought home to him more assuredly than all the thinking of the previous year that his life was on the verge of major change.

> I don't know that contesting a seat was a "vision splendid". It was a road of escape from the blind alley in which I find myself, and in which, if I can't find a road leading to somewhere, I shall either run amok or go fut. What I mean is, I am feeling acutely that I have carried my coastal organising work for the Board as far as – even further than – the Board will stand; that, even with you, I am depending on your indulgence rather than your full concurrence. Meanwhile, the world positively heaves with the hope of a better life for itself, and I – am travelling at a hell of a pace – to nowhere. To use the old metaphor: the book's written, and I shall be in my customary fret till I've got a new one started.[92]

His failed candidature gave him an especial interest in the December election and in disturbing the equilibrium of the Sidmouth voters. There was no Labour candidate in the constituency and the workers of Hope Cottage made their own protest.

> On polling day we hung out of Hope Cottage the Labour Flag, but with a Union Jack pinned on it. Sidmouth saw the red flag in a jiffey – but not the Union Jack – and they're no end excited – half the town cursing like mad, and t'other half laughing at 'em. We are telling them that the combination was intended to denote "Revolutionary measures by Constitutional means", in defiance of the Coalition's "Stick-in-the-mud

measures by Revolutionary means".
One local eminence got at Bob:
"Do you know what that red flag outside your house means, Mr. Woolley?"
"I haven't rightly taken much notice o' it: I been too busy wi' the herrings."
"It means the first step to REVOLUTION!"
"Oh," said Bob, "that's it, is it? And a bloody good job too!"[93]

Though exhausted, he spent Christmas 1918 at St. Ives, "doing the invalid" in the human warmth of Porthmeor Square.[94] For once, there were no complaints of the festive season – a sure sign that he had enjoyed himself. Three days after Christmas, he wrote in a teasing mood to Cecil Harmsworth, waiting for his election result held up by the overseas service vote.

> I suppose you will be up at Luton to-day, waiting to see whether you are in, or whether, politically:
>
> Man that is born of woman
> Hath a very little time to live;
> He goeth up like a foretopmast staysail,
> And down like a small flying jib!
>
> After the so kind letter you wrote me about my abortive project, I haven't the heart to hope your Labour man has done you in, though politically.... Well, I don't concur in the Coalition's existence!"[95]

He was still pledged to continue his work for Maurice and the Board of Agriculture, even if only for a matter of a few weeks more. "I'll drive ahead for you, as long as you need it; without that incentive, the work now is sheer slavery, without even a war on to justify it; but – and the cat may as well be let out of the bag – I am not going to be slave-driven by the Board."[96]

His November memorandum of the autumn fishery tour had been discussed at a meeting of the Development Commission he had attended on 11 December. He spelled out a seven-point plan for the reconstruction and development of the fisheries, and the meeting invited him to elaborate it in a further memorandum concentrating on the future Commission policy towards small harbour development.[97] He spent the post-Christmas period working on the new memorandum, which he completed on 6 January. It advocated a new and coherent approach for the Commission in distributing grants and loans, in contrast to the piecemeal operation it had followed from the beginning. It called for a major reconstruction conference on the fisheries bringing together all interested parties. It was his last major think-piece, the final summing up of his own contribution over the previous seven years.[98]

He was still actively on the road in pursuit of Board business. On 4 January he motored through sleet and fog down to Plymouth with Harry to discuss with the naval authorities the problems arising from the recent reopening of the fishing grounds. On the way back, they ran into a blizzard and picked up a couple whose car had broken down. Reynolds powers of observation and description were still firing on all cylinders.

> Picked up a courting or honeymooning couple from one of Dagworthy's cars that had broken down on the hill, and drove into Exeter in driving snow that blew in blobs off the windscreen into one's eyes. Arrived there, the excellent couple – a huge, tall, slightly deaf young woman in many furs, who looked as if she'd been exported from a drawing-room couch, and an undistinguished little man whose grey overcoat had too much waist to it – Birmingham courting Kensington, I should think – they were quite ratty because I wouldn't drive on to Sidmouth, and risk leaving the car in a ditch all night. They'd have liked to pay me, and tell me to do as I was damn well told. Arrived at Sidmouth, and finding at the station only one taxi for the lot of us, the huge young woman remarked to the small young man: "Do you mind, Fatty?" But Fatty was not in furs, and minded not, so long as he got home quick.[99]

The next lift that he and Harry were destined to offer would not give rise to the same hilarity.

One pressing post-war need was to decide what form the makeshift District Inspectorate should take now that its wartime regulatory and liaison duties had disappeared. Reynolds offered, as his swansong assignment, to come up to London for three months and prepare the new scheme. "The attraction of the idea to me is twofold: I don't know what better help I could give you, and I don't like leaving a job of work unfinished."[100]

In mid-January, Maurice rejected the offer. He was thinking of keeping the inspectorate system fluid for the present to see how it developed, rather than setting the powers, duties and organisation in concrete. He was planning an extended Inspectors' Conference in London to thrash the matter out. Reynolds was disappointed, but understanding. But he did not want to contribute to a discussion that was not his.

> The assumption now is – isn't it? – that I shall come up to the extended Inspectors' Conference, brimful of ideas on district inspecting, and shall force or wangle through as many of them as is good for me – getting beneficially pruned in the process! But, no. That does not come within the terms of my offer to you. It is expecting me to start afresh the same old game that I am sick to death of. All good workmen claim their own way of doing things; you do, and I do. The way you propose in this matter isn't my way; but you are entitled to have your way; let me, therefore, I beg you, drop out......
>
> If you tell me to come up, I must, of course. But, once more, I hope you

> won't. I should come without hope of getting any forrarder, and I am sure you will agree that in that mood I am best away.[101]

He did not go. Nor did he take part in the Commission meeting on 29 January at which his memorandum of 6 January was discussed and fully endorsed. At the meeting the Commission decided to call the general Fisheries Conference that Reynolds had suggested.[102] He was to be one of the major participants, but he did not go to that either.

On 29 January he had a much more pressing commitment at home. Edward Carpenter was staying in Budleigh Salterton on a West Country holiday and drove over in a cart to Sidmouth. He was warmly welcomed by Reynolds and Harry in their little *ménage* – a full return for the visit to Millthorpe the previous autumn.[103]

On the afternoon of Tuesday 4 February Reynolds set off in foul weather from Sidmouth to drive to London for a discussion with Maurice on his immediate future. He was not feeling well enough to tackle the journey alone and decided to take Harry with him. They got as far as Devizes, where they called a halt and put up at the Bear for the night.[104]

They drove over to Prospect Rise to take tea with Aunt Jane, still adjusting to her solitary life since the death of Aunt Allie three months before. Later that evening Reynolds drove over again from the Bear, this time alone, for a private chat with her. She noticed he had a bad cough.[105]

Next morning, snow was everywhere and driving conditions at their worst. They made it as far as Marlborough where they wandered around for some time to find some chains for the back wheels to get them up the hill to the Forest. There they picked up a penniless demobilised soldier in search of a lift to London, but it was so deadly cold and snow-wet, he decided to get out at Newbury. It was an encounter that may have decided both their fates. The Services were awash with the third wave of the influenza pandemic which people feared but few talked about.

In London on 6 February Reynolds failed to catch Maurice at his office in Parliament Street; and in the afternoon Harry collapsed with the onset of flu. Abandoning the car, Reynolds rushed him home by train that evening *via* Exeter "in a state of semi-collapse and he has now subsided into bed for some days with the flue. But no pneumonia, luckily".[106]

Pneumonia was the danger sign. When the first wave hit England in June and July 1918, it took the form of a three day fever and there were few deaths. What was remarkable, however, was its age incidence; it attacked disproportionately the young able-bodied, between 20 and 40, rather than the usual pattern of children and old men. The second and third waves, in October/November 1918 and February 1919, produced a much more virulent form of the disease. Of every thousand attacked, 200 would develop pulmonary complications, and of those 60 to 80 would die – a total of 150,000 deaths in England and Wales over the nine months of the outbreak.[107]

The odds were in favour of Harry's survival, but Reynolds was not to know that. He was at the end of his physical tether himself and wrote to Maurice in the evening of 7 February with the message he had gone to London to convey.

> I was looking for you at the Board in order to tell you quite definitely that neither of us can go on as we have been going, and to ask you immediately to arrange for us to get leave. My idea was, that as Paynter, who has been going back in health for some time, wanted leave even more than I do, I would hang on for three weeks, while he got his leave – and then, on his return, would chuck the office myself. But the flue has quite sweepingly settled that; I must finish nursing him first, and then without question he must have leave.
>
> I am sorry to give you this trouble, but I can't help it. I am prepared to work *ad lib.*, but I am not prepared to collapse, and many bad nights have made me realise that I am not far off it. As I have not hidden from you, the squashy uncertainty since the Armistice has been far more trying to me than all the work of the war.
>
> At the same time, I wanted to ask you to drop me off the Yorkshire harbours committee. I don't feel up to a rush-round of that sort, nor do I feel that I should do much good on the committee. If I go at all, it must be quietly on my own, for the Dev. Comm., so that, if I have to see a lot of people, it can be at times I feel more up to it than I do at present......
>
> Some of the above, being written on post time, seems to have a tinge of asperity, perhaps; but none the less, I cannot hide the fact that the two things which are most appealing to me, and cropping up into my mind at the present, are the "Lotus Eaters" and the picture of a fisherman chucking his dunnage ashore – and following it. I have for so long, and so unavailingly, been saying what was bound to happen, but this I will not admit – that it is work which has reduced me to saying that I shall ride off on a doctor's certificate unless matters quickly arrange themselves to reduce the strain on me.[108]

Next day he sent a telegram.

> Reference my letter of last night. Have got influenza myself now. Stop. Pretty sure unable to come to London next week.[109]

They took him with Harry, whom he could no longer look after, to the nursing home a couple of hundred yards away in Seafield Road, where he was tended by Sister Atkinson.[110] The course of his disease followed the deadliest pattern. Four days later, on the Wednesday, pulmonary complications set in with acute inflammation of the lungs.[111] As the body fought back, a white liquid flooded the throat and lungs. It was a kind of drowning, the fisherman's death.

> I find, somewhat to my surprise and satisfaction, that there isn't in me any fear of death itself. I seem to have a pretty complete faith, beyond reason, that it would only mean, at the worst, an absorption into the spirit of things; more perfect union with what one is always reaching out towards.

On Friday 14 February 1919, St Valentine's Day, he found the perfect union he had struggled to find in life. He was 37, with all the world still before him.

His father rushed down from Nether Velly, thinking to take charge of the arrangements. But his son had outflanked him even in death. His will proclaimed: "My funeral is to be simple and cheap and to be carried out by my executors not by my relations."

They buried him the following afternoon up on the sloping hillside cemetery – in Landpart, the working class end of the town. John Thomson attended from the Board and Vaughan Nash from the Commission. Harry crawled from his sickbed to be there.[112] As the coffin was lowered into the ground, Mam Woolley stood in the second row from the graveside and laid her head on her husband's shoulder.

His grave, with its crusty headstone of Cornish granite, looks out today across the river valley to the slopes of Salcombe Hill and the cottage he built but never lived in. He lies just a stone's throw away from Jubilee Terrace, his first much-despised lodgings in the town.

But I can hear the sea-gulls screaming, even here.

TWENTY ONE

The Letters 1923

The voice – that unique voice – was finally stilled. All his friends, both past and present, were deafened by the silence.

The news came through fast. Cecil Harmsworth heard it the same day and wrote unemotionally in his diary "I learn with deep regret of the death of Stephen Reynolds today".[1] He was saving the emotion for the obituary letter he now began to write.

On the Saturday morning, Alice Mildmay, who had not seen Reynolds since the previous July, was sitting with her husband at Flete reading as usual the *Western Morning News* when their eyes alighted on the obituary report by Mary Willcocks.[2] "When we were reading the newspaper in Francis' room, we suddenly realized the death of our friend, Mr Stephen Reynolds, and I feel really sad, as it is a loss not only to us and the Woolleys, but to every fisherman in England. I recall such interesting talks with him, and wish I had not been so terribly hurried the last times he came....."

She placed in her diary her own idiosyncratic personal obituary.

> He was an extraordinary character, and though we differed on nearly every point, I delighted in him as he was so original. He called himself a syndicalist and was very wrong-headed about the poor, I think, but he had such wide interests, once tearing himself away from translating an Italian sonnet [*sic*] to cook herrings for his fishermen. He lived in a regular cottage with the fisher folk sharing their kitchen for the only sitting room, etc. and yet was cultured to his fingertips.
> When he stayed with us, he was always fearfully fussy about changing for dinner, but always into another suit of dark blue serge.[3]

She made the mistake of sending her letter of condolence to Mam Woolley, with whom Reynolds on his death was no longer living. Many others may have done the same. But not Edward Carpenter. His first thoughts were for Reynolds' young partner he had met only two weeks before and who, recovering himself in the same nursing home, had now been told the shocking news. On the Saturday he sent Harry a letter with all the words of comfort he could muster. It was not until the following Thursday that the patient, whose English had been learnt at the office, was well enough to reply.

> I was very pleased indeed to receive your kind and consoling letter of the 15th inst. I'm still in bed at the Nursing Home, but hope to get out about within the next few days, and shall feel more myself then. As you can

> well imagine I'm not feeling well enough to reply in full to your kind letter, but I feel I cannot let it pass unacknowledged. The death of Stephen is a very serious blow to me and also to the Fisheries we have seen through the war. When I get well enough to travel I'm going home for two or three months to recuperate for I'm completely run down and this hour of bitterness and sorrow is very trying. Stephen was always next to my heart and I feel a gap in my life that can never be filled.[4]

In the headlong rush of war work, Reynolds had not given a thought to altering the will of 1914 which left all his estate to his sister's children and to Bob. Had death not come so suddenly, there is little doubt that the lion's share would have gone to Harry. There was, however, one stipulation of the will that brought Harry in: "I ask my Executors...... within their sole discretion to give of my personal effects with generosity to Miss Ada M. Bennett now of Weymouth High School, Mrs. L. Tanner, Harry Woolley and others of my known close friends".

His three executors, with admirable sensitivity, left this melancholy task to Harry Paynter. By the end of March he was fit enough to come up from St Ives and help them with the sharing out. On 21 April he wrote to Cecil Harmsworth in London from the shelter of Porthmeor Square.

> I should have written to you before, but during my first visit to St. Ives, I was fully occupied guarding against the complications that follow an attack of flu! I am glad to say that I am much stronger and less nervy; and if I can continue to make such good progress, I hope to start work again in [*sic*] 1st June.
>
> While I was at Sidmouth about three weeks ago, we allocated all the little things that Stephen treasured, as mementoes, to his most intimate friends. And I am sending you one of Stephen's pocket wallets with his name inscribed on it. I know you will appreciate, and cherish it, for you were such intimate friends.[5]

There was one long-forgotten friend who was not a beneficiary of this share-out. Katie Powys, toiling on her little farm in Montacute where she had been throughout the war, had that cold February felt a sense of foreboding. She waited until confirmation came, and the deep wounds of seven years broke out in blood again.

> On the land I was estranged. In the dairy I heard no tidings. Nevertheless, when the snow lay cold upon the ground, I betook myself, and hid myself, for an obscure reason, among the dry grain of the linhay. There no one came; and there to myself I outpoured the depression which had fallen across me. "Why was this renewed trouble come upon me?"

> "Why this abundance of tears?"
> In this lowness of spirit I recked not; nor was the meaning made clear to my sight.
> In ignorance I continued to labour on my farm and serve the cattle with their fodder. The snow melted, and green sprouted the grass. The sun broke out in beauty upon new life, and the songs of the birds were united......
> My sister came; when the milking was over she broke to me the most terrible of news.... My love was dead.... Never, never would I see him.... Never, never would he come as a fisherman. All, all was over.... This was the end. He breathed no more.
> Broken, I turned away; broken, I searched for comfort.... The boats would lie unwanted; and friendless would remain the fishermen. The waves would hurl themselves upon the shore. They would pound the great cliffs. My love was dead.
> I could not weep. I could not tell. I was as if among strangers. Darkness deeper than night spread across me; all movement was paralyzed. I roamed from field to field; I hid as one confused. I slept at night, only to wake with a cry of pain; my dreams were torture and my thoughts were anguish. The cows dropped their still-born in the stall, and much rain fell to blight the young corn. Pleasure was barrenness, and all virtue was departed. My spirit closed as the petals of an anemone when devoid of light.[6]

Most of the obituaries were written by his friends. Cecil Harmsworth, in a letter to the *Times Literary Supplement*, wrote chiefly from the perspective of his administrative and political achievements.

> In a way Stephen Reynolds was one of the most fortunate men I have ever known. He set out to perform a certain task and, lamentably brief as was his life, he succeeded in accomplishing a great part of it. ......he desired above all things to help the class to which he had allied himself: and before he died he laid the foundations of a policy that is now being carried out and has already done much for the welfare and prosperity of one of the most valuable elements in our community...... I know of few cases where a man of ideas has found the way open so quickly and so directly to their acceptance.

But he also remembered, with some nostalgic emotion, the days of the Cornish tour when their friendship had first blossomed and that memorable summer day of the Lambourn sonnet. He did not gloss over the Reynolds' temper or "difficult" personality, but paid a warm tribute to his formidable loyalty as a friend.

> I have heard Stephen Reynolds described as a "rough diamond", but never by anyone who really knew him. True it is that he was wont to bear himself gruffly to strangers, and that he was perhaps too quick to take offence, to form unfavourable impressions, and to show himself a little careless at times of the susceptibilities of others. In fact, however, he had a heart of gold and was capable of an absolute fidelity to his friends.[7]

The "fisheries" part of *The Times* obituary seemed to spring from a Board "insider", most probably Henry Maurice.

> Reynolds might be said to have lived for the fisheries; he brought the system of district inspection to a high pitch of organisation; he maintained the closest touch with every fishing port and cove; he was known from end to end of his district. He was constantly on the alert to promote the interests of the fishermen and to remedy grievances. Driving his own car, he maintained a continuous tour of his district, with intervals of absence in London to attend committees and conferences at the Board's office. In the process he consistently overworked himself; protests were unavailing; he worked weekdays and Sundays; and all through the war he was in harness. His fatal illness was undoubtedly contracted after a journey from Sidmouth to London, when he was already unwell, but from which he would not be deterred.[8]

In a letter to the *Spectator*, George Macmillan testified as a publisher that in *A Poor Man's House* Reynolds had broken new ground. "Stephen Reynolds had struck a new note in literature. Not only had he something new to say, in describing from the inside the life and point of view of a fisherman family, but he had handled his characters with true insight and sympathy and in a fresh and attractive literary form."

He recalled their first meeting.

> My own acquaintance dates from the time when, in 1910, he approached our firm in regard to the publication of his second study of fisherfolk – *Alongshore* – and as I had already delighted in *A Poor Man's House* (transferred to us in the same year) we soon became intimate friends. His personality was singularly attractive, and his talk vigorous and racy. One might not always agree with his views on social questions, but one felt that they were genuinely held, and inspired by an earnest desire to promote better relations between the classes.[9]

Many tributes were paid too by his local West Country friends. On the day of his death, Mary Willcocks lamented the loss of his writing career to fisheries administration: "By his death the nation has lost a most promising literary man, for, although of late years his genius as a writer was obscured by his work as a Government inspector of fisheries in the South-West, into which he threw himself with astonishing zeal, it was the hope of his friends that he would return to the development of his great literary gifts." She praised his personal sincerity. "He had a violent detestation of 'side'. For a person to put on 'airs' of manner or conversation was a signal to Stephen Reynolds to lapse into his broadest dialect, and even to the least polite vocabulary of the fishermen."

She gave a generous appraisal of his most famous book, and of his writing career.

> It is undoubtedy one of the treasures of English literature, full of tenderness, grace and humour...... His death is a loss to the world; but at least his work, "Poor Man's House", will live. His work was of too fine a strain and too exquisite to make a wide popular appeal, and it was with the knowledge of this that he somewhat bitterly suggested on one occasion that over his grave might be written "Here lies one read in library copies only". But those with the gift of understanding will appreciate the worth of his life's work and the quality of his genius.[10]

For the readers of Devizes, Aunt Jane supplied some childhood anecdotes for the official obituary of the *Wiltshire Gazette*. His old friend, George Simpson, who had long since left the editorial chair, emerged from his Sussex retirement to write it. He recalled the thoroughness and enthusiasm of his one-time next door neighbour in the Market Place when approaching his first commission for the *Mail Literary Supplement* in October 1906.

> Mr Reynolds was an original, distinctive "personality", and it is not exaggerating to say that his talents in some directions approached to genius. His literary tastes early manifested themselves. The writer of this notice well remembers young Stephen coming into his room from The College (next door) to look at the literary page of a London daily newspaper; he had just received a commission to do book reviewing and he wished to see its "style". Perhaps that was his earliest responsible work as a litterateur, and it was refreshing to see the pleasure he so ingenuously manifested.[11]

The literary world that Reynolds had inhabited so many years before had changed beyond recognition. Edward Thomas had been killed at the Front. Conrad was ailing and had written himself out. He, Pinker, Seccombe and W.H. Hudson would all die in the next five years. The death of Reynolds, now long forgotten as a writer, sent a frisson of anxiety through all the old Mont Blanc group, as they looked back on the past and contemplated their own mortality.

Three weeks after Reynolds' death, Thomas Seccombe, his earliest mentor, wrote to Edward Garnett in nostalgic mood.

> The death of Reynolds rather strongly evoked our old gatherings at the Mont Blanc, and about two weeks ago I revisited it to take part in a farewell supper to Mrs. Cecil Chesterton. Another thing was the reading of Hudson's "Far Away and Long Ago". It seems to me, between ourselves, to be a good bit below his great books. I know how apt one is to say this of the latest one. Finally, I have had "The Twilight of the Gods" lent me, so that I have many opportunities of remembering your wicked smile! I expect you are still disinterring creations of genius. How many have been déterré owing to your endeavours! I suppose the two successes of the year, "Eminent Victorians" and "Married Life", are not due to your efforts, but after those! The old familiar faces seem strangely absent![12]

Hudson was the only one of those old faces with whom Reynolds had kept in regular touch. Throughout the war he had wintered in Cornwall for the sake of his health – tended by the Ranee at Lelant, gazing from Flushing across Falmouth Harbour, or closeted in the homely warmth of North Parade, Penzance with the treasures of the Morrab Library just a short walk away. In his constant tours of the Mounts Bay ports, Reynolds would look in on him whenever he could. Two weeks after Reynolds' death, Hudson wrote to Garnett with his own personal assessment.

> I felt very bad about Stephen Reynolds' premature death. For some years past I have always met him once or twice each winter down here, Penzance, Falmouth, St Ives, somewhere, and I was just looking out for him constantly expecting to see him when the news of his death came. He had done good work, but it was nothing to what he had it in him to do. His books are not great: he had no imagination – his one attempt at a work of imagination [*The Mountain*] was a ghastly thing. But he had a tremendous reasoning brain and he was too big to stand forever on that narrow plot of ground when the end came to him.[13]

While Reynolds talked often of giving his subjects an extended life in books, he had taken careful steps to preserve for himself a share of literary immortality. He had kept his letters and later manuscripts in good order for those who came after. In his will he appointed Harold Wright as his literary executor and enjoined him to exploit his copyrights to the full. He had also laid upon him the task of arranging his little corner of posterity, but not as the subject of the average official biography, one of the "corpses in print".[14] "I desire Harold Wright...... to have possession of all my letters and papers for writing a biography of me or compiling a volume of letters both to be truthful and not mealy-mouthed."

Early on, Wright decided on the softer option of producing the volume of letters. He was still involved in fisheries work and, more important, still subject to recurring bouts of illness. He had neither the time nor strength to contemplate the years of work a full biography would entail. Furthermore, his knowledge of Reynolds' early life before meeting him in Sidmouth was sketchy in the extreme. Much research would have been required.

In going through the papers, Wright found, in addition to a large number of letters, the psycho-economics book (not much more material than the articles already published) and the manuscript of *Weekends at Nesscombe*, both items which Reynolds had clearly still hoped to see published in book form. Because Reynolds had attached so much importance to the psycho-economics book, Wright decided to give priority to that over everything else and took the manuscript along to George Macmillan, not just Reynolds' publisher, but also his personal friend.

Macmillan's reaction was positive, but he wanted to see the text in final form before definitely deciding it would make a book. A little later someone suggested to Wright that it might be wiser to publish first the volume of letters to reawaken public interest in Reynolds' personality and pave the way for the more indigestible *Wealth and Life*.[15] Wright put this revised plan to Macmillan who showed a considerable interest.[16]

Thus it was in the late autumn of 1919 that Wright circulated Reynolds' major friends to elicit their support – Garnett, Maurice, Harmsworth, Vaughan Nash – and other minor contacts. He sent a letter to the *Spectator* seeking any letters in private hands, and received an encouraging response from Stanley Unwin, of Allen and Unwin, saying the firm would be deeply interested in the book.[17] The Unwin desire to get hold of Reynolds was still every bit as strong as in the winter of 1911.

Wright seems to have been unsure of his bearings in Reynolds' literary world; either he failed to contact the likes of Seccombe, Conrad, Hueffer or Galsworthy, or else they were able to offer few letters of significance. He did not think of an approach to Pinker until April 1920, and received a bumper batch of letters in return the following month.[18] But he did pick up the most important relative; Aunt Jane came forward to offer a substantial leavening of personal correspondence.

On 8 November 1919 he wrote to Cecil Harmsworth.

> Our friend, Stephen Reynolds, expressed the wish in his will that I should write his biography or compile a volume of his letters. In view of his very early death, I have decided that the latter course will be the better one to adopt; and I am writing to you in the hope that you may have kept some of Stephen's letters to you, and that you will let me see them to select for publication.[19]

Harmsworth burrowed among his papers, but came up with very little. He did, however, lay hands on a copy of the mammoth letter of September 1917 to Henry Maurice on the South West area organisation. He sent it off to Maurice so as not to usurp his contributions.

> You will be aware that Harold Wright is preparing a book on Stephen Reynolds. He has asked me for letter [*sic*] from Stephen, but unhappily I seem to have destroyed almost every one I received from him, excepting a few relating to departmental affairs. In the course of my search I came across the enclosed copy of a letter to you. It is of course generally unsuited for Harold Wright's purpose, but incidentally it gives a life like account of Stephen's only too strenuous activities during the last two months [*sic*] of his life. You may perhaps think it worthwhile sending it to Harold Wright who will I suppose preface his volume with some general statement as to Stephen's official work...... It is a perfect example of his unique way of treating official matters in his own incomparable style.[20]

Maurice, however, had been more successful in preserving the store of Reynolds' letters with which he had been bombarded throughout the war, including this one. He wrote back to Harmsworth: "I find that Harold Wright has, as I expected, a copy of it – for I gave him all the Reynolds correspondence I possessed, which was fairly considerable – and he tells me that he proposes to make quotations from it."[21]

In the middle of December, Harmsworth sent his small offering rather apologetically off to Wright. "I have made diligent search and am sorry to say that I have preserved very few of Stephen's letters and those I have as you will see are not of much interest." He had, however, marked up one letter of November 1916 referring nostalgically to the Cornish Committee, equally dear to Harmsworth's heart: "Stephen refers, as indeed he was very fond of doing, to the Devon and Cornwall enquiry and to the settled policy that he always believed sprang directly from it".

But he had also found the Lambourn sonnet in its two versions, the original one castigating Matthias Dunn by name, and the bowdlerised version that Wright was eventually to publish. "Probably you will not think the sonnet worth reproducing..... Stephen dashed it off in the course of a visit of ours to the Lambourn, a little chalk stream in Berkshire. There are two versions of the sonnet and in the one I send you Stephen made some alterations which I have marked in pencil."

Harmsworth took care to flag up the organisation letter. "I found among my papers a copy of a long letter addressed by Stephen to Henry Maurice. In this Stephen gave a most vivid account of his war-time activities – those activities that as we must fear led directly to his untimely end. I had intended to send it to you but Maurice tells me you have a copy."[22]

Wright had every intention of using both the organisation letter and the sonnet. He wrote back to Harmsworth: "I came across the rough draft of the sonnet to you among Stephen's papers, and am much interested to see the later version. Yes, I have a copy of Stephen's letter to Maurice about S.W. organisation, which is valuable, both for its vivid account of his many activities at that time, and also because of the characteristic energy with which it is written."[23]

That winter and spring Wright worked on the text of the planned book. He would select and transcribe the liveliest and most representative passages of the letters offered him before returning them to their owners. He had a clear strategy. "In selecting the letters for publication, I tried to make them reveal something of the man and his interests and to keep a fair balance between the writer and the official."[24] In this way, he built up a text of well over 300,000 words; and began to have misgivings about its length.

But the progress of his work was dogged by ill health. When in October 1920 Cecil Harmsworth came forward with a few more letters he had rustled up, including some on the abortive election project of 1918, he was surprised to find he had not missed the boat. Harold Wright explained the reason. "Illness and absence from home have delayed my work which has consequently not yet reach [*sic*] the stage at which further material is unwelcome."

Wright had his own reminiscence of the election venture. "I was with Stephen when the idea occurred to him (or rather to Harry Paynter) to stand as Labour candidate for the St.Ives Division. He entertained the idea quite seriously for two days when it was absolutely squashed by the discovery simultaneously (1) that another Labour candidate was already in the field, and (2) that he would have to resign his position as Fisheries Adviser to the Development Commission."[25]

Wright returned this, the final, batch of letters on 18 October. "I found in them several passages which I am glad to incorporate in the book; and those referring to the Sidmouth Beach controversy have a topical interest for me at the moment, for when I left Sidmouth at the beginning of this month, the sea-wall was being rapidly demolished!"[26]

By the week before Christmas 1920 Wright's book was ready for the publisher. In it he demonstrated his considerable editorial skills, first learned in his work as editor of *Granta* ten years before. He had selected the best material with assurance and with a facility for making the narrative flow. The only criticism that might be levelled at the text, apart from its unwieldy length, was the occasional failure to clarify the context of a particular episode. It could have done with more heavy footnoting than Wright had either time or energy to research.

Though the balance between Reynolds the writer and Reynolds the official was well maintained, slightly greater weight being given to the former in line with the likely public interest, there is an unfortunate vacuum at the start of the book. In its final version, it leaps straight into the Garnett letters of August 1906, though ample material was available to the editor from before that date.

It is clear, however, that Wright was unsure of the precise narrative of Reynolds' earlier life. In his preface, for example, he implies, but is careful not to assert, that the crucial breakdown of 1903 took place after the *Coranian* adventure of 1905, a misunderstanding which has muddied the waters for writers on Reynolds who followed after.[27]

The greatest achievement of the book is that it allows the authentic Reynolds voice – from the intellectual and lyrical at one end to the humorous, quirky and obsessive at the other – to breathe and sing just as Reynolds himself had wanted. It gives to Reynolds the man the same accession of life that he himself had given to the Woolleys in *A Poor Man's House*.

And Wright fully lives up to the strict injunction that the book should not be "mealy-mouthed". Though for reasons of personal sensitivity or of libel he disguises some individual names, he does not conceal the more awkward material necessary to a full picture of the man. The homosexuality is handled with great sensitivity, implied rather than stated, by inclusion of the lovesick diary entries of 1906, the poem *Prisoners*, and the delicate introduction of Harry Paynter.[28] He is assiduous also in providing examples of Reynolds' explosive temper even when, as in the letter of December 1912 to the anonymous recipient, it seems to break the narrative. With so much material to handle, this externally imposed requirement must have cost much soul-searching and many sleepless nights.

By December 1920 he was confident he had sufficient high quality material both to do justice to the memory of his friend and to satisfy the interest George Macmillan had already shown in the project. If the book could not find a home with Macmillans, its prospects were surely bleak. In sending up the manuscript on 18 December, Wright confessed to the problem of its length and suggested the possibility of two volumes.[29] George Macmillan promised an early decision but was not at all taken with Wright's suggestion. "I note what you say as to a possible reduction of the book, but we should not be at all favourably inclined to breaking it up into two volumes."[30]

Macmillans' reader worked quickly and the Board took its decision even quicker. On 10 January 1921 George Macmillan sent Wright an official response.

> We only on Thursday received the report of our principal adviser on the Letters of Stephen Reynolds, and I am sorry to say it is not at all favourable. He says, to begin with, that the book is far too long and that there are countless repetitions, but further that even if it were drastically cut down it is a question whether there is very much more about Reynolds which is likely to be of interest to the public at large than he has already put into his books. We know unfortunately that the demand for his books has considerably fallen off and we therefore feel that in face of this report, and in view of the present very difficult conditions of publishing, we could not undertake the book with any confident hope of success.

It was the letter Reynolds himself had received through that summer of 1907 in response to *The Mountain* – "inopportune owing to the price of strawberries". It was clear that Macmillan had been personally torn by the decision and may have had some rugged words with his colleagues. But, in the official letter at least, he made a show of overcoming his doubts.

> Since the report came in, as I was shut up last week with an attack of influenza, I have been able to go through most of the letters myself, and I am bound to say that, although of course to me as his friend there is a great deal of matter which I am glad to have seen, on the whole I am inclined to concur in our reader's judgment. Scattered up and down in the letters there are some admirable things, and the series of letters to Edward Garnett is of particular interest. On the other hand, one sees in this case particularly that he actually used the letters as part of his material for "A Poor Man's House".
> You will realise that it is a personal disappointment to myself that we do not see our way to a favourable decision, but I have no doubt you will find a publisher, though I think that in any case you will be called upon to reduce the bulk very considerably.[31]

This seemed a poor outcome given the faith the company had been prepared to invest in Reynolds when he was alive, but Wright, a seasoned journalist, could understand the arguments from the bottom line. He called in to see Macmillan and offered to halve the size of the book and alter its form, but the publisher could not hold out any hope of publication even with these changes.[32]

What annoyed Wright most of all was Macmillan's attempts to distance himself personally from the judgment of his colleagues and that conveyed in his own official letter.[33] Wright told Pinker: "Mr George Macmillan said that personally he would like to publish the book, but that some of his partners were unwilling to do so; an attitude that reminded me of Spenlow and Jorkins! He also advised me to cut it down a great deal before submitting it to another publisher. I am very much inclined to think that this is good advice, but I should very much like to have your opinion first, partly on the ground that one likes a second opinion before having one's leg amputated, but mainly because I have already spent a great deal of time over the book and do not want to rearrange it unless it is likely to be published".[34]

Pinker with customary loyalty reassumed his ancient role as Reynolds' literary agent, but with little more success than when his client had been alive. It was the story of the *Mountain* all over again. For the next two years Wright traipsed from publishing house to publishing house but could find no one prepared to take the risk. Even the enthusiasm of Unwin evaporated on the air when he had the bulky manuscript actually in his hands. To improve its prospects, Wright whittled it down and down until it had reached 120,000 words, about a third of its original size.[35] Most of the publishers he approached wanted him to cut out the letters on fishery affairs altogether, but this he refused point blank to do.[36] His final selection consisted of 221 letters, the majority addressed to just five people. On a quick head count, 27% were to Henry Maurice, 19% to Edward Garnett, with Harmsworth, Pinker and Aunt Jane contributing a further 17% between them.

By the end of 1922 Wright's desperation was coming close to that of Reynolds in 1907. He decided to turn to a personal friend. He had known Leonard Woolf from their work for the *Nation*, of which Woolf was then political editor and Wright shortly to become assistant editor. The Woolfs had bought a printing press in 1917 and had published a few small volumes under the insignia of the Hogarth Press, notable as much for their high quality finish as artefacts as for their contents. The enterprise had started essentially as a hobby, but since 1921 had begun to turn into a small business. There were sufficient profits now for the Woolfs to contemplate appointing a manager, but not enough to take any major risks.[37]

It was not until the end of November 1922 that Wright suddenly thought of Woolf. "For two years I have been trying to find a publisher for a selection of the Letters of Stephen Reynolds, and it has suddenly occurred to me that you might be the man. I am willing to put up part of the cost, but do not want to get into the hands of the publishing sharks who live on fools like me."[38]

Woolf read the letters and the critical response was favourable. "Personally I have found them extremely interesting and I think that they are well worth publishing. I think however that the publication of them as they stand would very probably result in a financial loss which unfortunately..... I do not think the Press ought to risk." He was keen to publish if Wright would stand the printing and financial costs, and allow the Press 15% of the receipts. Wright was happy to agree; on a rough estimate, if he managed to sell 500 at a cover price of 16 shillings, he would recoup his costs.[39]

Woolf had thought the text was still "on the side of being overlong", but a weary Wright was happy to leave any further cutting to him.[40] "If you feel inclined to make some moderate cuts in the book yourself, I am perfectly willing to trust to your judgement. I have made so many cuts myself – pruning the book over and over again – that I do not think I can make any more. I am stale in that matter. So do not even ask me to consider your suggestions on this point."[41] In the event, Woolf could not face the task either, so the manuscript was printed as it stood.[42]

Wright put together a number of photographs, including the celebrated one of Uncle Sam from *Alongshore*. He hoped he might shame George Macmillan to release them cheaply. "I rather think that Macmillan, who was fond of Reynolds and is conscious that it is rather shabby of him not to publish the Letters, would lend us the blocks of these for a small fee."[43] George Macmillan waived the fee.[44]

On 22 February 1923 Wright returned the completed proofs to Woolf. He now realised that there were no photographs to represent the second half of the book and suggested one of Henry Maurice; but by this time it was too late to disturb the run.[45] One thousand copies were printed and 500 bound at a cost to Wright of just over £200.[46] His parents agreed to bear a part.[47] Cecil Harmsworth chipped in on the distribution arrangements by promising to present copies to the library of every fishing port in the country.[48]

Publication was delayed because the Woolfs were in Spain at Gerald Brenan's, but the bound copies finally arrived on 19 April and the book was published in May.[49] It was a great critical success which more than justified Harold Wright's stubborn perseverance.

Cecil Harmsworth set the ball rolling in Harold Wright's *Nation* with predictable praise of the editor and the letters which constituted "some of the best English that has been written in our time".[50] But the more independent assessments were equally favourable. The *Daily Telegraph*, while objecting typically to the bad language, thought them "some of the breeziest letters ever published...... there is in them a Swiftian humour which scarifies, an ever-present passion against injustice, and a keen sense of the fun, as well as of the tears, of mortal things".[51]

Osbert Burdett thought the book "contains the real thing" and that the letters might come to be regarded as the best of Reynolds' writing. He sensed one aspect of the draw of the Reynolds' story: "Between literature, politics and administration, he remained undetermined, and his figure has the charm and the pathos of all unfinished things".[52]

The Times made much the same point, but saw the letters as a major new revelation on the man.

> In his short life, which ended in 1919 at the age of 38 [*sic*], Stephen Reynolds gained fame as a man of letters, a social theorist, a working inshore fisherman, and a fisheries administrator. What he would have come to had his unceasing labour during the war not sapped a delicate constitution and left him a ready prey to a sudden attack of influenza no one can tell, but the extracts from his outspoken diary and frank letters now brought together complete the picture of a very remarkable personality, only partly revealed by his well-known books......
> His life was a desperate effort to feel and act with a class which was not his own, and out of the conflict there came not only a fruitful knowledge which was of great service to his country, but a dynamic vitality which informed all that he wrote with a spirit more like that of the great Russians than of evenly-balanced Englishmen. It is the revelation of a sincere but amazingly self-centred personality, a human document of more than usual value.[53]

The book brought out some new assessments from some of his oldest friends. H.J. Massingham, who had long been his publisher of last resort at the *Nation*, was also bowled over by the letters which "fairly dance with life". But in a deeply reflective piece, he put his finger on a crucial point that few had understood or been able to express so well: that both Reynolds' writing and political activity sprang directly out of his emotional relationships, in which his homosexuality was a key ingredient.

> The human contact with fishermen was what was responsible for the art of his work and the art of his life, and all art, all living, was personal to him or it was nothing. Reynolds did not take up the fishermen's cause out of a disinterested passion for abstract justice – not he – but because he loved Bob and Tom. He always called himself an individualist, but that was because he was an individual. And this is, I am sure, the whole secret of Stephen Reynolds – that he was Stephen Reynolds. It is curious that in this respect, which was all respects, Reynolds, who was absolutely untouched by women, should have been so like a woman, who mercifully keeps alive for a world soggy with generalities the personal aspect of things.
> The same attitude was at the bottom of his feeling about "social reform". He abominated it, not altogether for the reasons he gives, but, I fancy, because he had in his mind's eye a superior, wealthy person patronizing Bob and Tom.[54]

The reception of the book was remarkable, but perhaps predictable for an author who was now safely dead. As Reynolds had told Pinker nine years before: "if I bust you can agentize my remains, and that, I'd bet you 100 to 1 in pounds, will be my first really successful book".[55] But needless to say, the success was critical, not financial. By 1932, the demand for the book had practically dried up, with sufficient copies still in hand for future orders. The remaining unbound stock was destroyed.[56] It had sold less than 400 copies and Harold Wright had made a small loss. But it was a price worth paying. He had kept faith with his friend and the flame still burning.

Ironically, it was the first substantial work undertaken by the Hogarth Press and gave to the business a new credibility. Woolf was keen to quote it by way of advertisement. A year after publication, he wrote to Norman Leys, a future Hogarth Press author: "We have published ourselves novels and poetry and one 'serious' work – Stephen Reynolds' *Letters* which was published at 16/-".[57]

Wright himself survived just a further year beyond the final demise of the book. Worn out by continuing bad health, he suffered a bad attack of influenza which led to complications. He died on 21 February 1934 at the age of 50. His ashes were buried in Sidmouth up on the hill in the grave plot just behind his friend.

By the 1930s, when the Edwardian generation got round to writing its memoirs, Reynolds' name was just a distant memory. It was still potent enough, however, for those who had known him to want to declare their allegiance.

Hueffer, now transmogrified into Ford Madox Ford, had left behind him the financial rows and meannesses of the past. In 1931, with accustomed hyperbole, he passed his final judgment. "Reynolds was a most original figure. He lived with a fisherman somewhere in the West and appeared in London usually in the garb of the trade of Peter. He wrote a book called *The Poor Man's House* [*sic*] which was a success, and died much too young...... He would have been a very great writer could Fate have seen her way to spare him. His books are full of faults and arrogances. But a young writer's future work will deteriorate if his first books are not full of faults and arrogance. I have found that an invariable rule. On the whole I should say that his death was the greatest loss that has befallen English literature for many years."[58]

Jessie Conrad, who still had a soft spot for Reynolds long after her husband had given up on him, remembered him in 1935, but for the wrong book. "The Someries also saw the first meeting with Stephen Reynolds, whose book *The Holy Mountain* is firmly established in the world of letters."[59] Reynolds *would* have been pleased.

Other judgments, from lesser literary friends, were more down to earth. Archibald Marshall, the erstwhile *Mail Supplementarian*, tied his achievement very closely to the insights of his main book: "I never thought of him as a first class writer, but he was going through an experience which made him a very interesting one."[60] Douglas Goldring, who had known him well at the time of the *English Review*, looked to a wider canvas for his judgment: "I still think that Reynolds was that rather rare thing among writers, a greater man than his works".[61]

Edward Garnett stood by him after his death, the coolness of the later years completely forgotten. In 1928, now working for Jonathan Cape, he selected *A Poor Man's House* for the new Travellers' Library series. It was the first republication of a Reynolds work since his death and did more than anything else to keep the book alive through the twentieth century. It is still to be found on the shelves of public libraries and second-hand bookshops today.

Garnett also continued to recruit new readers from among his friends. In the twenties he fed Reynolds to T.E. Lawrence who quickly became a fan. In May 1928 Lawrence wrote to Garnett: "I'm so glad the *Poor Man's House* has got into the Travellers Library: Cape must add *Alongshore*, and *The Holy Mountain*...... "[62] But, sadly for Reynolds' reputation, it was not to be.

Whatever the survival rate of Reynolds' books, his influence still lived on in the hearts and minds of his closest friends.

During the war, the annual sea fisheries reports from the Board of Agriculture had dried up, for lack of paper and time to compile them. In 1920 Henry Maurice produced a compendium report for the years 1915 to 1918 in which he paid one of the most perceptive and generous tributes to Reynolds.[63] But Reynolds had pervaded the work in other ways. Its title was not to be the usual "Report of...... " but a more eye-catching and literary *Fisheries in the Great War*. In his prefatory letter to the new Minister of Agriculture, Maurice explained the sea-change in style and approach.

> The recognition of the fishing industry as one of the vital industries of the nation is so important that no apology is offered or should be needed for any departure in the present volume from the old traditions of official reserve, for the endeavour which has been made to impart here and there into the narrative something of the independent spirit of the fisherman, something of his ironic humour and something of our own enthusiasm, nor for veiling the official title of the volume with one less suggestive of the Blue Book, in the hope that the British citizen may be induced to acquire it instead of passing it by as dull and unreadable.[64]

Someone was guiding the pen from on high!

On 27 May 1920 Cecil Harmsworth and his wife, on a holiday tour of the West Country, arrived in Sidmouth to stay the night. They called in at the Post Office to enquire for Bob Woolley's address. At Hope Cottage, Mam Woolley was in and they had a long chat. She directed them down to the beach where they found Bob and Harry hard at work on the propeller of the *Puffin*. They were all pleased to see each other, and talked at length of Steve and of the trip with him in the *Puffin* from Beer seven years before. Out of the corner of his eye, Harmsworth spotted something familiar. "His little old green-painted row-boat, his "Moon Daisy", is lying on the beach close at hand". It was, indeed, the little *Ivy*. No longer abandoned up on the Esplanade, but one of Tom's proudest possessions, still going strong after seventeen years.[65]

Next day, after a morning bathe, Harmsworth bumped into Tom on the Esplanade. He congratulated Harmsworth for his letter to *The Times*. "He dwells, as Bob had done the night before, on Stephen's prescience in agitating against the removal of shingle from the beach. At the Western end of the Parade the big breakwater is now partly undermined and there are great holes in the path."

As they left, the Harmsworths looked in on Mam Woolley once more, and then a final pilgrimage up to the cemetery where they read the inscription on the headstone

IN MEMORY OF
STEPHEN REYNOLDS
WRITER AND FISHERMAN
1881 – 1919.

When he read the dates, Harmsworth took a step backwards. "I had not realised that he was so young."[66]

In November 1924 Harmsworth, still with the F.O.S., went on a new tour of the West Country ports, retracing much of the ground of the Cornish Committee. He found that the fishermen's memories were long. At a gathering on the beach at Hope Cove, he paid a glowing tribute to Reynolds' work, and a strong murmur of approval went round his fisherman audience.[67] It was a scene repeated wherever he went.

But like the Sidmouth beach, Reynolds' drive for co-operative marketing was fast eroding. Bobby Woolley, Reynolds' favourite in the early days, had followed in the footsteps of his mentor and was now full-time Secretary of the Sidmouth Fishermen's Co-operative Society. Harmsworth met him in Sidmouth on this tour, together with Bob and Harry once again. "Alas, some of them, including Bob and Harry Woolley, are falling away from the Society and selling their fish through the old channels. They say that with our 10% charge for expenses they do better under the former system."[68]

Like Bobby Woolley, Harry Paynter could not escape the influence of the master in his choice of long term career. He stayed on with the Fisheries Division and in the early 1920s was promoted Inspector of the North East district, based at Tynemouth. He kept his links with Reynolds' friends, holidaying with Harold Wright and his family and, less frequently, with Edward Carpenter.

The emotional legacy of Reynolds was massive and distinctive. In June 1924 Harry wrote to Edward Carpenter inviting himself for the Whitsun holiday. Office life was now very different from working under Steve: "It would be nice to be called 'Harry' again...... a warmer feeling to the heart, so to speak, than one gets in official circles these days". The expressive style of this letter, along with many others, is self-consciously ersatz Reynolds; but the handwriting takes one's breath away. It has altered completely since 1919 and is now facsimile Reynolds, indistinguishable in every respect from the model it has set out to copy.[69]

Harry spent the whole of his working life with the Department – Inspector for the North West at Fleetwood in the 1920s and 30s and ending his career at Colwyn Bay, back on the Reynolds' patch once more. He was married twice, the second time to a long-term friend, the local postmistress at St Ives. He retired there in the 1950s and in his spare time conducted, in the style he had been taught, a campaign for improving the harbour and strengthening the breakwater. *Plus ça change.*[70]

It was some time before Katie Powys could bring herself to visit Sidmouth again, and to look for his grave.

> Long, long it was before I could bring myself to the coast where he had been; or return to the beach where he had learnt his craft.
> "Oh! God, Oh! God! Where have they lain him?"
> Over the mounds of green and gold I faltered. Over the turned turf and beside faded flowers I stumbled. Another pointed me the way, and alone I found the grave. There in tribulation and in great sorrow I dared not

own him. What right had I to mourn? I was neither sister nor brother. Only a wanderer to whom he had turned.[71]

The flood of memories that accompanied this sorrowful return sent her back to the old grieving. As she walked the hills on either side of the town, up High Peak and down Salcombe Hill, the despair returned.

> The terraced valleys gave forth their flowers, and the dividing hills their splendour. In despair, I wandered between them; lonely, I clambered their heights. I was overcome with sorrow and in great tribulation; and my days were as a cold fog. Instead of the music of life, I heard the loud barking of curs. I was forlorn, for knowledge was bitterness. My love was my tragedy, I could not accept his death.
>
> By the meshes of the fishing-nets I remembered my affection; by the rounded sides of the boats I renewed my longings. In the hearing of the gulls I wept. By the incoming tides I tarried. The fishermen who had known him held out their hands towards me; they gave of their hearts, and together we mourned.[72]

Bob, the other Woolleys, and the rest of the beach took her in. She became an honorary citizen of the fishing community – out trawling with them occasionally by night, sitting next them on the beach in the sunshine as they mended their nets. Later she took a small cottage just off the sea front from where in the small hours of the morning she would dispense cups of tea to the fishermen returning from their all night labours. At other times, she stayed with Bob and Mam and, after their deaths, with Semaphore and her family in Lawn Vista. On every visit she would carry flowers to Reynolds' grave. On one occasion, she brought an offering of mackerel and bay leaves.[73]

Her relationship with Bob was close, despite occasional fallings-out. She wrote a novel, *Further West*, following a fleeting infatuation with Bill Woolley, Bob's son now returned from the Navy. Set in Sidmouth, it depicts a heroine in love with the fishermen's life in general and a fisherman's son in particular. It was never published.[74]

She befriended Ada Bennett and loved to listen to his old schoolmistress with the early anecdotes of her "Sydney".[75] Miss Bennett and her friend, Frances Lapham, had started their own school in Weymouth but retired in the 1920s to a small bungalow in Wyke Regis, quite close to Katie's main home in East Chaldon. Ada Bennett died there in December 1945 at the age of 84.

Just before Christmas 1930, Katie made the pilgrimage to Prospect Rise to meet for the first time Aunt Jane and the daughters of Reynolds' sister, Dot. "Wonderful to sit by her side and be shown the old albums and to see and hear the various little incidents of Steve's childhood. My love! My love! It seemed for one precious second I had broken through the thickset hedge of early experiences all combining to make the character of the man, what he was."[76]

Aunt Jane lived on at the house until her death in March 1938, tirelessly devoted to keeping the flame of her famous nephew alive. When her great great nephew was born in 1928 to Dot's daughter, Gretchen Wiltshire, she insisted he should be christened "Stephen Reynolds", although his father wanted the name "James".

Katie too kept the flame alive – but much longer than all the rest. When she died at Buckland Newton in January 1963, at the age of 76, she still had by her bedside the copy of *Leaves of Grass* with Reynolds' last letter safe inside, and the little round frame with the photograph of her love, sitting in the sun on the Bedford steps, grinning sheepishly from under his flop-brimmed hat, as battered as the photograph itself. That little picture had gone with her all her life, a symbol of the love that could not die.

Uncle Sam was not granted his thousand years after all. He outlived his mate of the nocturnal expeditions by a mere matter of nine months. In November 1919, also worn out by the deprivations of war, he died of bronchitis at the age of 75. Tom was there at his bedside that Monday morning in the little cottage in West Lane.

Tom himself continued to fish right up to the second war. As late as 1937, he had invested in a brand new herring drifter and that December made another "catch of the season".[77] After retirement, he lived on in the terraced house in Riverside and, following in the footsteps of Uncle Sam, would walk out early each morning to Chit Rocks to comb the shore for driftwood. On 21 January 1953, before he could set out on his morning walk, he died in the house by the river where he had lived continuously since his marriage in 1898. He was 76. Nellie, his wife, survived him another twelve years.[78]

Bob and Mam no longer had the chance to move to the cottage on Salcombe Hill, though the memory of what might have been still lingered on in the family.[79] They stayed on in Hope Cottage where Bobby had made his office as Secretary to the Sidmouth Fishermen's Co-operative Society. In October 1927 they moved, together with Reggie and Gladys, to 3 Sea View Terrace, off Peaslands Road at the back of the town. Whereupon Bob had a heart attack and was whisked off to Weston super Mare to recover.[80]

The household at Peaslands Road became once more a haven for the next generation of Woolleys, Mam supervising from there the confinements of her daughter, Semaphore, to whom she felt closest. The life and laughter of Bedford Square lived on. When Semaphore's own daughter, Frances, visited from round the corner in Lawn Vista, Mam would teach her the polka, whirling her round the kitchen till, collapsing in exhaustion, she would proffer her the kitchen chair as substitute partner. Bob, now retired from active fishing, was still up to his tricks. Most days he would go down to the front to pick up some fish. He would come back with live crabs and set them to crawl across the kitchen floor towards his petrified granddaughter.[81]

On 18 September 1944 at Lawn Vista, Semaphore gave birth to her third child, Geoffrey, and Mam, as ever, took charge of the arrangements. This time, she may have overdone it. Shortly after, she caught pneumonia and was herself confined to bed at Lawn Vista. She died there on 7 October, at the age of 73.

Bob lived on without her, cared for by his daughters, for another three years. On 13 September 1947, he died at the old house off Peaslands Road, where he had lived for the last 20 years. Though racked with rheumatism for most of his life, he had survived to the good age of 82. With him died most of the memories of those early days in Bedford Square and the household that had made a book.

The Poor Man's House was pulled down in 1938, along with the rest of Bedford Square and Uncle Sam's cottage in West Lane – it was a slum, after all – to make room eventually for the anonymous mock-Mediterranean flats that stand there today.[82]

There are few great books in English literature in which a house plays a starring role along with the leading characters – where readers can go back to look around and re-live the experience in so-called "real" time. They make museums out of such places today, attracting money and tourism. Sidmouth Council toyed with the idea of purchasing the clearance area in Bedford Square but soon broke off negotiations with the owner.[83] At war with Reynolds for much of his life, it had at last succeeded in wiping him off the town map. In doing so, it had inadvertently shot itself in the foot. He would have allowed himself a quiet smile.

In the 1970s, a new generation of modern Councillors, now bent on preserving the history and culture of the town, looked round for a suitable building on which to plant a blue plaque to commemorate the vaguely remembered fisherman author.[84] They lighted on Hope Cottage where everyone knew he had had his office; but where few seemed to remember that he had actually lived through most of 1917.[85] Hence the strange plaque that adorns the wall today, commemorating an office rather than a home.

STEPHEN REYNOLDS
1881 – 1919
Fisherman's Friend,
Social Reformer
and author,
worked here

He would have flinched at those two dire words, social and reform. He would have preferred the gravestone, which at least put his writing first.

The plaque was unveiled by Semaphore, now Mrs Doris Reed – an inspired choice – on 26 June 1980. Public occasions had not been her life and she was nervous before the event. But she carried it off with aplomb.

She died a year later on 17 May 1981. The day before was Reynolds' hundredth birthday.

Epilogue
June 1927

I reached Sidmouth before dinner but had such a job to find a field for Josephine and it was expensive at that, but Bob's cousin called Spenser at last obtained me a field. It was above the cottage Stephen built and I even am allowed to keep my saddle in one of his out-houses, which is extraordinarily pleasing. It is wonderful to see Bob going out to sea at night in the full wealth of the setting sun, but I do not seem to see nearly so much of him. I took Mam Woolley a trip up as far as Sidford. They like Josephine.

Oh! I wish my mind would only revive so that I could write. I seem so heavy and dull.... I seem only happy if I am with Bob and Mam....

Thank heaven Whitsun is over. It is not the same here when the place is crowded out with the boys from Bristol, and Bob gone to sea at night. Nevertheless, Saturday Bob and Bill and I went as far as Bowd where I sat in Steve's favourite chimney corner, and listened to Old Bob singing, not to say Bill, his son, singing in turn. He has a very full voice, very pleasant to listen unto. I was happy there until Bill sang one and I could no more bear it and left to see Josephine. It was dark under the Station trees coming home.

I had a happy day Saturday helping with the nets and the winding up the big boats. To see them about the Beach is fascinating: certainly I get flashes of extreme feeling at certain moments, but otherwise my despondency gets worse rather than better, except such moments as when on Sunday morning I lay under the bows of the drifter while Bob was mending his nets above me even though it was raining.

I rode off for the day on Josephine Tuesday, for I could not stand the Bristol boys. They swarm over everything. While riding I found at last toward Ladram a wonderful lane which dipped right in between high banks and was arched all through upwards of half a mile with the growth of the hedges above.... I wondered if Stephen had ever been there.

I was in the "old house" one night. It seemed strange to stand and to know between those narrow walls of the kitchen was the last scene of our meeting. More and more I think of it, more and more I resent the present day system of propriety. Why should my fate have been to have seen so little of him, and then at the last only to have a memory – a memory which brings tears, for longing of what cannot be.

Some say the spirit is more powerful when dead: so it may be, but while the flesh is warm it is not sufficient unto life – of those whom you love with passion. This I know, I shall be haunted until I am also dead.

While at Sidmouth I had three unforgettable nights out with Bob and Reg in the drifter upon the sea. To understand the craft of it is almost beyond me, but this I know, that to lie down at rest in boats after the nets are shot and between waking and sleeping to realize that Bob is then watching so near me, to know that I then realize what he had realized brings me nearer to a real peace than I have ever experienced since I have known he was dead. It is an experience which is excruciated by the nearness of the sea and the wonder of night.

I took Tom's two girls for a drive one day. We came back just below Core Hill and saw a magnificent view of the westward hills. Then also I took Gran Pratt as far as Cecil's home. I like Bill more and more I see him; his wife is also a nice woman, but her children are almost too much for her.

Bill took me out for a row once, but my trip to Ladram with old Jack Collier was most pleasurable. We just followed on slowly, along by the rocks which Uncle Sam used to haunt and where the seagulls breed. In fact, we saw several pairs of their young, crouched on the different ledges while the old birds guarded them. I bathed in Sandy Cove, and then round the very next bend we came on a crowd in Ladram Bay. It pleased my fancy to walk in the lanes with J.C. even as Steve might have done.

Mam left us Sunday dinner time. We felt quite sad to see her go. After tea Bob and I wandered up to the flag staff and into the cottage nearby. I liked the last evening when we all gathered in the little pub not far from the Post Office; there is something peculiarly congenial in it. While Bob was wondering if it was "fitty" or not to go out, I slipped up and spent my last moments in the room he built for himself.

I knelt at the open window where I could see and hear the sea....

Notes and References

Note on sources

When Stephen Reynolds died in February 1919 he left his letters and papers to his literary executor, Harold Wright, from which Wright compiled the volume of *Letters* of 1923. When Wright died in February 1934, the papers were left in the keeping of his wife, Florence.

In July 1934 Commander Harry Pursey, then planning some work on Lionel Yexley, borrowed two files of Reynolds' letters from Mrs Wright. The first was his own selection of 62 incoming and outgoing letters relating to Reynolds' involvement in the naval reforms of 1912. Most are from that year, though one is from 1911 and eight from 1913. The second file appears to have been the whole of Reynolds' preserved correspondence for 1909, containing according to Pursey 460 incoming and outgoing letters. It indicates that Reynolds had taken considerable care to file and preserve his correspondence.

Pursey failed to return these two files, which turned out a blessing in disguise. When Mrs Wright died in the 1940s, the remaining Reynolds papers were found to have suffered destruction by damp and mice. Her daughters managed to rescue 59 of the most significant letters still decipherable, including 28 from Conrad and six from Galsworthy.

These letters, then in the possession of Harold Wright's elder daughter, Margaret Wallace, were rediscovered in the 1970s by John Osborne when working on his unpublished thesis on Reynolds. The minor letters, except for 13 from Harold Wright retained by Mrs Wallace, were deposited in the National Maritime Museum in Greenwich in 1978. The 28 Conrad letters were a major find for the late twentieth century and eventually found their way, *via* the Conrad family, to the Berg Collection in the New York Public Library. They were first published in 1990 and 1996 in volumes 4 and 5 of Frederick Karl's collected edition of Conrad letters.

The 1909 file, and the abbreviated file of 1912, of Reynolds' letters, borrowed by Commander Pursey, were likewise rediscovered by John Osborne in the 1970s. They were purchased by the National Maritime Museum in 1977 along with the rest of Commander Pursey's papers and should have been deposited there on Pursey's death in 1980. A search through the 215 boxes of Pursey's uncatalogued papers in April 1997 failed to locate them. In August 1997 the 1912 file came to light in Manchester University, having been borrowed for research in the late 1970s, and was repatriated to Greenwich. Nothing has been seen of the 1909 file. The originals of some of the outgoing letters it contained are present in other holdings; a few of the incoming letters, for example from Arthur Marwood and Dr Mackintosh, are quoted in the Osborne thesis.

Harold Wright's initial text of the 1923 *Letters* was three times as long as the published version, and was probably lost with the rest of the Wright holding. It was seen, however, in the 1920s by Philippa Powys, who copied extracts, including from some of the unpublished letters, into her farm accounts book, now in the possession of Gerard Casey in Mappowder.

The main holdings of Reynolds' letters are to be found in the Edward Garnett and John Lane papers in the University of Texas; in the Pinker papers at Northwestern University; in the Macmillan papers in the British Library; and in the Pursey papers at the National Maritime Museum. Minor holdings are to be found in the Carpenter papers at Sheffield Archives; the Harmsworth papers at Lime Lodge, Egham; the Mildmay papers at Mothecombe; the Philippa Powys and Jane Reynolds papers in the University of Texas; the Sarolea papers at Edinburgh University; and the Strachey papers in the House of Lords Record Office.

Abbreviations

Add.Mss.	British Library Additional Manuscripts, St.Pancras.
AS	*Alongshore, Where Man and the Sea Face One Another*, Macmillan 1910.
Edinburgh	Edinburgh University Library.
HL	Strachey papers, House of Lords Record Office.
HM	*The Holy Mountain, A Satire on Tendencies*, John Lane 1909.
HT	*How 'Twas, Short Stories and Small Travels*, Macmillan 1912.
Illinois	University of Illinois Library at Urbana-Champaign.
Karl	Frederick R. Karl and Laurence Davies (edited) *The Collected Letters of Joseph Conrad*, Volume 1 (1861-1897), CUP 1983; Volume 3 (1903-1907), CUP 1988; Volume 4 (1908-1911), CUP 1990; Volume 5 (1912-1916), CUP 1996.
LD	*The Lower Deck, The Navy and The Nation*, Dent 1912.
Mappowder	Diaries and papers of Philippa Powys in possession of Gerard Casey, Mappowder, Dorset.
Mothecombe	Diaries and papers of Alice Mildmay in possession of Anthony Mildmay-White, Mothecombe, Devon.
NLW	National Library of Wales, Aberystwyth.
Northwestern	Charles Deering McCormick Library of Special

	Collections, Northwestern University Library, Evanston, Illinois.
Osborne	J.D.Osborne "Stephen Reynolds: a biographical and critical study", unpublished thesis 1977.
PMH	*A Poor Man's House*, London Magazine Editions 1980.
PRO	Public Record Office, Kew.
Pursey	Papers, uncatalogued, of Commander Harry Pursey R.N., MS/80/098 National Maritime Museum, Greenwich.
Reading	University of Reading Library, Whiteknights.
Rylands	The John Rylands University Library, University of Manchester.
Sheffield	Papers of Edward Carpenter, MSS 386, Sheffield Archives.
SS	*Seems So! A Working-Class View of Politics* (with Bob and Tom Woolley), Macmillan 1911.
Texas	Harry Ransom Humanities Research Center, University of Texas at Austin.
Wallace	Papers of Margaret Wallace, MS/78/162, National Maritime Museum, Greenwich.
Wright	*Letters of Stephen Reynolds*, edited by Harold Wright, Hogarth Press 1923.

Prologue 15 August 1906

The date of Reynolds' arrival at Sidmouth in August 1906 cannot be established with certainty. The parameters are set by two letters. On Friday 10 August he wrote to Pinker from Pans Lane: "To-morrow we start for Sidmouth and Dartmoor. If our feet hold out and the weather's kind, I reckon to make Prince Town in about eight days." (Northwestern). On Monday 20 August he wrote to Garnett from Bedford Square: "I've been living the last week with one of my fishermen......" (Wright 27, original Texas). The reference here to a "week" cannot be taken literally; Reynolds was notoriously vague in dating past events.

The walking distance from Devizes to Sidmouth is between 90 and 100 miles depending on the route. To put it at 95 would be a conservative estimate; it could have been longer as Reynolds deviated from his path to find a pub for the night. Margot was the limiting factor on speed; when he bought her in 1905, it was with the aim of walking 20 miles a day (HT 300). Counting the last day as one half, since he arrived in mid-afternoon, the average daily mileage would have been 27 for a Tuesday arrival, 21 for Wednesday, and 17 for Thursday. It is likely that 27 miles would have been beyond Margot, especially with more walking planned after Sidmouth. 17 miles was rather too leisurely for Reynolds, with his aim of reaching Princetown in eight days. Neither is arrival on Thursday afternoon consonant with a week's stay by Monday morning, however vague Reynolds' description of time. In any case, Thursday was the annual Sidmouth regatta and Bob was out racing in *Old Cockbird* (*Sidmouth Herald*, 18 August 1906). 20 miles a day was Reynolds' usual average and a stay of six days inclusive fits well with his description of a week. There is an outside chance that he arrived on the Tuesday, but a very high probability must be placed on a Wednesday arrival.

Part of the physical description in the Prologue is based on *Another Prodigal*, HT 51. Since August 1906 was the only occasion on which Reynolds arrived at Sidmouth with Margot on foot, the first paragraphs of this story appear to be drawn from that experience.

Chapter 1 Trowbury 1881–92

1 *The Citizenry of Cats*, HT 274.

2 The original slab from the Market House with the inscription on Ruth Pierce was discovered in the Bear in 1892 and deposited by Frank Reynolds in the Museum, *Wiltshire Archaeological Magazine*, 1892, xxvi 172.
Reynolds himself records that her "tombstone" was found under a doorstep when the billiard room was built in the Bear Hotel garden – *Devizes and Roundabout*, Mates Illustrated Guides 1906 [24].
The present inscription on the market cross reads: "The Mayor and Corporation of Devizes avail themselves of the stability of this building to transmit to future times the record of an awful event which occurred in this market place in the year 1753, hoping that such record may serve as a salutary warning against the danger of impiously invoking divine vengeance or of calling on the holy name of God to conceal the devices of falsehood and fraud. On Thursday the 25th of January 1753, Ruth Pierce of Potterne in this county agreed with three other women to buy a sack of wheat in the market, each paying her due proportion towards the same. One of these women in collecting the several quotas of money discovered a deficiency, and demanded of Ruth Pierce the sum which was wanting to make good the amount. Ruth Pierce protested that she had paid her share and said she wished she might drop down dead if she had not. She rashly repeated this awful wish when, to the consternation and terror of the surrounding multitude, she instantly fell down and expired, having the money concealed in her hand.

3 HM 5.

4 Edward Kite, *The Bear Hotel Devizes, Some Notes on its History*, Mendip Press 1931 17.

5 Kite *op.cit.*

6 *Devizes and Roundabout,* Mates Illustrated Guides 1906 [26].
7 *ibid.*
8 *ibid.*
9 On the other hand, Frank may have had literary leanings that were to be fulfilled in his son. In Jane Reynolds' autograph album, now in possession of Stephen Wiltshire, is a pretty excruciating 64-line doggerel poem written by Frank Reynolds to record a fishing trip at Nether Velly. He may, however, have just been taking a leaf out of his son's book.
10 PMH 114.
11 Brother Christmas and Mr Bookworm, *Daily News,* 26 December 1910.
12 1891 census. The billiard marker, the 18 year old William Offer, born in Devizes, also performed odd jobs about the hotel. In *The Holy Mountain* (page 12) he becomes "Robert".
13 Reynolds to Henry Maurice, 17 October 1915, Wright 209.
14 Weekends at Nesscombe XVI, Immortality, *Westminster Gazette,* 16 September 1911. London Road, Devizes was the site of his first school.
15 *Wiltshire Gazette,* 20 February 1919. Forty years later, Jane Reynolds was still pressing *The Water Babies* on her latest great-great-nephew – interview with Stephen Wiltshire, 22 May 1997.
16 Reynolds to Henry Maurice, 17 October 1915, Wright 209. Frank Buckland, *Log-book of a Fisherman and Zoologist,* Chapman & Hall 1875. The whale story appeared in a talk given to Home Office staff by Sir Edward Troup, the Permanent Secretary, some time before his retirement in 1922. It has never been documented further. More generally on Buckland, see G.H.O. Burgess, *The Curious World of Frank Buckland,* John Baker 1967.
17 *Devizes and Roundabout op.cit.*[54].
18 The Simple Cat, *English Review,* 21 October 1905.
19 *The Citizenry of Cats,* HT 271.
20 *ibid.* 272.
21 *ibid.* 272.
22 *ibid.* 273.
23 *ibid.* 273.
24 *ibid.* 274.
25 Reynolds to Edward Carpenter, 28 July 1914, Sheffield.
26 Will of Jane Reynolds, 24 March 1934. This account of Reynolds' genealogy is based largely on an article in the *Wiltshire Gazette,* 16 April 1925, compiled from information supplied by Jane Reynolds. For a more extensive discussion of the family history, see Andrew Sewell "The Reynolds of Devizes" 1985, unpublished monograph, copy in Devizes Museum. There is a further genealogy compiled by Herbert Reynolds, 26 August 1898, now in the possession of Stephen Wiltshire.
27 There is a little confusion as to when precisely Robert arrived in Devizes. In the article of April 1925 (*see note above*), Jane Reynolds says 1799. But

in the only extant advertisement for the Reynolds' currier firm (*Gillman's Directory* 1887 152) Frank Reynolds refers to it as established in 1787. The Reynolds family bible, in possession of Stephen Wiltshire, records "Family at St Mary's Church from 1779 to 1887". It is likely therefore that "1799" in the 1925 article is a misprint for "1779". This is further confirmed by the departing presentation to Frank Reynolds in 1902 which refers to the family's arrival 120 years before. If so, Robert arrived as a seven-year-old child, and his uncle Robert, the Wiltshire tanner, who appears to have had no children, may well have looked after him and had a hand in the setting up of the firm eight years later.

28 It is now the general store *Age of Elegance*.

29 *Devizes Advertiser*, 13 November 1873.

30 Sidmouth had a country house at Upottery. He also toyed in 1805 with the additional title of Baron Raleigh of Combe Raleigh until he discovered it would cost him a further £300 – see Philip Ziegler *Addington: A Life of Henry Addington, First Viscount Sidmouth*, Collins 1965 233 and 412.

31 Edward Bradby *The Book of Devizes*, Barracuda Books 1985 79.

32 HM 21. Reynolds, like his sister, was often ill as a child. The main problems may well have been Alec's – croup, bronchitis and a weak stomach.

33 By contrast, Dot was christened on 12 October 1884, just four weeks after her birth.

34 Sydney, 1845-68, was the fourth son of Stephen senior's elder brother Joseph, who later settled in Gloucester – Andrew Sewell *op.cit.* In August 1868, his younger sister Emma wrote *The Sailor's Grave* to his memory into Jane Reynolds' autograph album, now in possession of Stephen Wiltshire.

35 It seems that they were caught between houses and for a few months in 1883 lived in one of the firm's cottages – 28 Monday Market Street. The valuation list for St Mary's parish, signed off on 24 March 1884 but compiled over the previous year, shows Frank Reynolds there (G20 500/3 Entry No.231, Wiltshire Record Office). He must have moved on before the end of the year because *Gillman's Directory* for 1884, compiled by November the previous year, shows him already arrived in Long Street.

36 *Devizes and Wiltshire Gazette*, 30 July 1885.

37 *Wiltshire Gazette*, 7 November 1918.

38 *Gillman's Directory* 1887. The directory was compiled by November each year, so the family move was made between November 1885 and November 1886, probably sooner rather than later.

39 It is now named Langenhoe to distinguish it from Prospect House next door.

40 Elizabeth Gould to Stephen Wiltshire, 12 December 1974, in possession of Stephen Wiltshire.

41 *Wiltshire Gazette*, 20 February 1919.

42 *Dear Papa's Love Story*, HT 195. Miss Vegg is almost certainly Mary Harrison.
43 *The Pictorial Record* Vol III No.24, London June 1900, copy in Devizes Museum. Devizes College is now *The Stationery Cupboard.* For an account of its founding, see Elizabeth Crittall (edited) *A History of Wiltshire*, OUP 1975 307.
44 *Devizes and Roundabout op.cit.* [38].
45 Reynolds to George Macmillan, 9 February 1912, Add.Mss.54965.
46 Weekends at Nesscombe XVI, Immortality, *Westminster Gazette*, 16 September 1911.
47 *Gillman's Directory* 1888 69. *Devizes and Wiltshire Gazette*, 30 June 1887.
48 *Devizes and Wiltshire Gazette*, 27 April 1893.
49 Pencil manuscript in possession of Stephen Wiltshire.
50 *Devizes and Wiltshire Gazette*, 25 May 1893.
51 *Devizes and Wiltshire Gazette*, 25 June 1891.
52 In his will of 18 August 1873, her father George Cox had made elaborate provision for both children and grandchildren out of a modest estate of under £2000. Two hundred pounds had come to her on her marriage in 1880 and the remainder on her 25th birthday three years later, perhaps about £150, half as capital and half held in trust to provide a small annual income. Under her father's will, the annual income continued in trust after her death for the benefit of her children, or only one of them if she so specified, on reaching 21. The capital sum Reynolds inherited from her in 1902 was from £200 to £300 (Wright xiii). In a letter of 1912, probably to Henry Maurice, Reynolds wrote: "my sort of life on an unearned income of £30 a year has been at times an almost unbearable strain" (transcribed Philippa Powys, Mappowder). Since by this time he had realised all his capital investments, the bulk of this was almost certainly the income inherited from his grandfather.
53 *A Love's Hunger*, HT 190.

Chapter 2 Bloxham 1893–8

1 Speech by Rev. P.R. Egerton at Old Bloxhamist annual dinner at the Criterion, 10 January 1898, reported in *The Bloxhamist* No. 230, February 1898, and quoted Brian S. Smith *A History of Bloxham School*, Bloxham School 1978 ix.
2 Brian Smith *op.cit.*18.
3 Bloxham prospectus, August 1896.
4 Osborne 27.
5 Bloxham prospectus *op.cit.* Schedule D assessments 1890, Wiltshire Record Office 1090/81.
6 *The Bloxhamist* No.188, October 1893.

7 Log book of Rev. F.S. Boissier, Bloxham School, 16 September 1893.
8 Pupil card index, Bloxham School.
9 This account of the routine at Bloxham is based on the reminiscences of a 93-year-old former pupil, Edward Lancelot Roberts, *The Bloxhamist* Nos. 526-529, September 1984 to September 1987. Although Colonel Roberts attended Bloxham from 1903-7, a school generation after Reynolds left, the pace of change at this period was such that most of the detail remains valid for the 1890s.
10 Boissier log book, December 1893.
11 *ibid.* 7 May 1894. Brian Smith *op.cit.*56.
12 Boissier log book, December 1893; 28 March and 7 May 1894. Rev. S. Boulter *History of All Saints' School, Bloxham 1860-1910*, Bloxham School 1910 51. *The Bloxhamist* No.193, April 1894.
13 Boissier log book, 7 and 19 July 1895; 28 July and 19 December 1896.
14 Interview with Stephen Wiltshire, 22 May 1997.
15 Bloxham prospectus *op.cit.*
16 *All Saints' School, Bloxham, Centenary 1860-1960*, Bloxham School 1960 12. Brian Smith *op.cit.*106.
17 E.L. Roberts *Reminiscence, The Bloxhamist* No. 528, September 1986. *Two Fishers Abroad*, AS 272.
18 E.L. Roberts *op.cit.*
19 Boulter *op.cit.*62.
20 *The Bloxhamist* No. 203, April 1895; No. 213 April 1896; No. 223, April 1897; No. 231, March 1898.
21 *ibid.* No. 198, October 1894; No. 209, November 1895; No. 218, October 1896; No. 227, October 1897; No. 235, August 1898; No. 236, October 1898. Boissier log book 1895.
22 Boulter *op.cit.* 51. Brian Smith *op.cit.*65.
23 Brian Smith *op.cit.*62. Reynolds to J.O.Borley, 16 August 1918, Wright 331.
24 HM 134.
25 Weekends at Nesscombe XVI, Immortality, *Westminster Gazette*, 16 September 1911.
26 *The Bloxhamist* No.204, May 1895.
27 *ibid.* No.198, October 1894; No.209, November 1895; No.218, October 1896; No.227, October 1897.
28 *The Bodleian*, March 1909.
29 Reynolds to Editor, *Christian Commonwealth*, 10 December 1913, Wright 176.
30 Wright x.
31 Boulter *op.cit.*79.
32 *ibid.*71.
33 Brian Smith *op.cit.*48. E.L. Roberts *Reminiscence, The Bloxhamist* No.529, September 1987.

34 *The Bloxhamist* No.234, July 1898.
35 Brian Smith *op.cit.*45.
36 *The Bloxhamist* No.210, December 1895.
37 *ibid.* No.214, May 1896; No.219, November 1896; No.234, July 1898.
38 *ibid.* No.224, May and June 1897.
39 *ibid.* No.229, December 1897.
40 *ibid.* No.219, November 1896; No.230, February 1898.
41 Bloxham prospectus *op.cit.*
42 Brian Smith *op.cit.*58.
43 Boissier log book, 28 July 1896. *The Bloxhamist* No.236, October 1898.
44 *The Bloxhamist* No. 229, December 1897. Brian Smith *op.cit.*62.
45 William Suter *The Test of Truth* or *It's a long lane that has no turning,* Dramas, Serious and Serio-comic, Thomas Hailes Lacy, no date.
46 Quoted *The Bloxhamist* No.229, December 1897.
47 Boissier log book, 1 November 1897.
48 *The Bloxhamist* No.231, March 1898.
49 Boissier log book, 8 November 1894; 14 December 1894.
50 PMH 162.
51 *The Citizenry of Cats,* HT 275.
52 *Dear Papa's Love Story,* HT 192.
53 Entry in Jane Reynolds' autograph album, in possession of Stephen Wiltshire.
54 After leaving the Bear in 1893, Ellen Blencowe ran a pork butcher's shop at 24 Brittox, right next door to the Tanners. It may have been on Lizzie's visits to her friend there that she first caught George's eye.
55 O'Reilly became later a china and glass merchant – see David Buxton (collected) *Around Devizes in Old Photographs,* Alan Sutton 1990 9.
56 Now in possession of Stephen Wiltshire.
57 *The Bloxhamist* No.218, October 1896; No.221, February 1897.
58 *ibid.* No.233, May and June 1898.
59 *ibid.* No.234, July 1898.
60 Brian Smith *op.cit.*67.
61 Boissier log book, 14 December 1898.
62 Wright xii. HM 93.

Chapter 3 Manchester 1899–1902

1 Frank Reynolds to E. Giddings, 1 February 1897; George Smith to Frank Reynolds, 9 February 1897, Wiltshire Record Office 2816/155/29.
2 Minutes of Devizes Town Council, 16 September 1898, Wiltshire Record Office G20 100/7.
3 The conflict between father and son continued for most of the latter's life and looms large in any Reynolds' biography, but with very little detail to

support it. The most recent commentary, inspired by Wright, talks of Reynolds as the "son of a landowner with whom he later quarrelled bitterly" (Sandra Kemp, Charlotte Mitchell, David Trotter *Edwardian Fiction: An Oxford Companion*, OUP 1997 339). J.D.Osborne (PMH viii) relates that "a permanent quarrel smouldered between them", but this was Reynolds' description not of the father–son battle in *The Holy Mountain* but rather of that between James Trotman and Edith Starkey (HM 46).

4 HM 9 and 11.

5 Osborne 29.

6 Harry Pursey, unpublished note on Reynolds, Pursey.

7 The top 45 successful candidates were placed in Division I. Reynolds fell in Division II with 91 others. Board of Studies minutes 1899, Rylands RA/2/1.

8 *The Bloxhamist* No.246, October 1899.

9 No.5 was demolished in 1977 when 10 four-bedroomed houses were built on the northern side of the street. The two storey bay-fronted houses which still stand on the southern side are identical to No.5.

10 1891 census. Reynolds entered her name in his 1894 Birthday Book, now in possession of Stephen Wiltshire.

11 *The Citizenry of Cats*, HT 275.

12 509 new students were admitted that session, 67 signing on on the same day as Reynolds. Declaration Book 1896-1904, Rylands RA/1/5.

13 *Handbook for the Owen College Students, Session 1899-1900*, Rylands UA/1/130.

14 Alfred Hopkinson in *Owens College Jubilee*, Sherratt & Hughes, Manchester, 1901 1, Rylands UA/5/23. For a contemporary history, see P.J.Hartog (edited) *The Owens College Manchester. A Brief History of the College and Description of its various Departments*, J.E.Cornish, Manchester 1900.

15 G.N.Burkhardt *The School of Chemistry in the University of Manchester (Faculty of Science)*, Journal of Royal Institute of Chemistry, September 1954 451, Rylands UA/78/5. The general description of the faculty in Reynolds' day is taken from this work.

16 Mabel Hartog *P.J. Hartog, A Memoir by his wife*, Constable 1949.

17 Regulations, Honours School of Chemistry 1899. Class Registers 1899-1902, Rylands RA/1/6. Board of Studies minutes, 25 May 1899, Rylands RA/2/1.

18 *Owens College Union Magazine*, No.66 January 1901.

19 *ibid.* No.67 February 1901. Owens College Council Minutes, 16 January 1901, Rylands RA/1/1.

20 *Dictionary of National Biography* 1922-30, OUP 1937 755.

21 Seccombe to Richard Garnett, 21 November 1891 and 27 August 1901, Texas.

22 *Owens College Union Magazine*, Nos. 68 and 69 March and April 1901.

23 Seccombe to Aitken, 19 April 1901, Texas.
24 *Owens College Union Magazine*, Nos. 67-9, 71-2 February, March, April, June and November 1901.
25 *ibid.* No.68 March 1901.
26 *ibid.* No.68 March 1901.
27 *ibid.* No.72 November 1901.
28 Owens College Council Minutes, 3 and 31 July 1901, Rylands RA/1/1. *Owens College Union Magazine*, No.71 June 1901.
29 Seccombe to Richard Garnett, 27 August 1901 and 13 February 1902, Texas.
30 How I began, *T.P.'s Weekly*, 18 October 1912, quoted Wright xiv.
31 Reynolds to Edward Garnett, 1 March 1907, Texas.
32 *Owens College Union Magazine*, No.77 April 1902.
33 *Owens College Jubilee*, Sherratt & Hughes, Manchester, 1901 77, Rylands UA/5/23. *Record of the Jubilee Celebrations at Owens College, Manchester*, Sherratt & Hughes, 1902, Rylands UA/5/26.
34 HT 163. It was not published until May 1910.
35 The tuberculosis Reynolds suffered in Manchester, Paris and the early days in Sidmouth is well attested by family tradition (interview with Stephen Wiltshire, 22 May 1997). It is corroborated by R.A. Scott-James *Fifty Years of English Literature 1900-1950*, Longmans 1951 82.
36 *Owens College Union Magazine*, Nos.72-4 November and December 1901, January 1902.
37 *ibid.* Nos.78-9 May and June 1902. HT 144.
38 *Owens College Union Magazine*, No.72 November 1901. Reynolds to Pinker, 20 July 1905, Northwestern.
39 *Owens College Union Magazine*, No.75 February 1902.
40 Class Register 1901-2, Rylands RA/1/6. Withington electoral register, 1900.
41 She died of chronic bronchitis at 11.30 on 30 September 1904 at 65, St Stephen's Green (General Register Office, Scotland).
42 *Owens College Union Magazine*, No.76 March 1902.
43 *The Citizenry of Cats*, HT 275.
44 Papers in the Honours School of Chemistry, 1902 clxvi. Board of Studies minutes, 1 July 1902, Rylands RA/2/1.
45 Reynolds' diary, 28 October 1906, Wright 54.
46 *The Bodleian*, March 1909.
47 Reynolds to Pinker, 12 July 1904, Northwestern.

Chapter 4 Paris 1902–3

1 Osborne 34.
2 Though Nether Velly remained his principal home, from 1908 to 1911 he

rented Ashville in Avon Road, Devizes, just behind the bacon factory. This was the setting for *A Cat's Tragedy* (HT 260) in which the pet cat of Frances, Reynolds' stepsister, is killed on the railway line that runs along the back of the house. On the way back to her boarding school at Bideford, she buries the cat at Nether Velly. In 1911 Frank resided for a time at 9 Monday Market Street (a remnant of the old currier firm's estate) and then moved to 19, High Street (L752 Poll Book, Devizes 1911, copy in Devizes Museum). Frank was still managing director of the bacon factory when Reynolds died. The edition of the local paper following Reynolds' obituary included an advertisement over Frank's signature proclaiming the virtues of his "prime well-fed bacon pigs" (*Wiltshire Gazette*, 27 February 1919).

3 *Cheltenham Examiner*, 18 March 1903. *Devizes and Wiltshire Gazette*, 27 March 1902.

4 W.Burnett Tracy *Manchester and Salford Contemporary Biographies*, 1899 102. Louis M. Hayes *Reminiscences of Manchester*, 1905 289. David Garforth-Bles, unpublished history of the Bles family.

5 Arthur Bles, The Need of a Minister of Shipping (4), *Weekly Critical Review*, 4 March 1904.

6 Arthur Bles, The British Merchant Marine, *Weekly Critical Review*, 2 July 1903.

7 Arthur Bles to the Secretary of State for War, 20 March 1935, PRO, WO 339/16605.

8 *Owens College Register of Graduates up to July 1st 1908*, Manchester University Press 1908, Rylands UA/7/2. Abraham Bles, the father of Edward and Charles, maintained close links with the College. In July 1902 he presented four volumes of Huxley's Scientific Memoirs to the Zoological Laboratory (Owen College Council Minutes, Vol.9 338, Rylands RA/1/1).

9 A Letter from Paris, *Cheltenham Examiner*, 31 December 1902. We do not know precisely when Reynolds agreed to assist Bles with the setting up of the *Weekly Critical Review*, but it seems likely to have been before he left Cheltenham for Paris. He must have started work on the magazine immediately he arrived there, for in December 1902 the *Owens College Union Magazine* reported: "One of our former contributors, we hear, is at present taking part in the foundation of a new magazine, which will appear for the first time early next year" (No.81 December 1902 34). This notification would have to have come from Reynolds in November or earlier.

10 Reynolds to Pinker, 24 May 1904, Northwestern.

11 Thomas Seccombe and W. Robertson Nicoll *The Bookman Illustrated History of English Literature*, Hodder & Stoughton 1906, Vol.2 354.

12 J.A. Spender *Life, Journalism and Politics*, Cassell 1927 6.

13 Reynolds to John Lane, 26 February 1908, Texas.

14 Osborne 36. Reynolds' address is on the fly-leaf of his copy of Pierre Louÿs' *Aphrodite*, now in possession of John Osborne. When later he moved to No 66, the 36 was excised and replaced by the new address.
15 Pauvre Punaise, *Owens College Union Magazine* No.82 January 1903 75. We do not know for certain that the anonymous friend that appears in this and other accounts of the Paris adventure, and with whom he ate almost every day, *was* Arthur Bles; but since his other close friends of this period – Hartog, Skemp, Lamb – were all working in Manchester or elsewhere, and the violence of the break-up with Bles indicates an emotional closeness, it is safe to assume that Bles was the friend with whom he spent most of his time.
16 *ibid.*74.
17 Osborne 36.
18 Louis Aguillon *L'École des Mines de Paris. Notre Historique*, Paris 1889. *Supplément*, Paris 1900. Gabriel Chesnau *Notre École. Histoire de l'École des Mines*, Paris 1931.
19 The gap is from 1880 to 1907. Ironically, the *École* has the most elaborate historical records of its student intake, making possible very detailed analyses of the social make-up of the mining industry in the 19th century. *See*, for example, Claire Baucher, Arielle Moore *La Formation et la Recrutement de l'Ingénieur Civil des Mines 1817–1939*, typescript thesis 1972-3.
20 *Association Amicale de Élèves de l'École Nationale Supérieure des Mines. 38 Annuaire* 1902-3.
21 Gabriel Chesnau *op.cit.*
22 Weekends at Nesscombe IV, The Commonplace, *Westminster Gazette*, 24 June 1911.
23 Wright xiii.
24 *An Old Woman* HT 282.
25 *ibid.* 284.
26 *A Dog's Life* HT 302.
27 A Letter from Paris, *Cheltenham Examiner*, 19 November 1901.
28 *ibid.* 3 December 1902.
29 *ibid.* 31 December 1902.
30 A Piano and an Omnibus, *Weekly Critical Review*, 4 June 1903.
31 *ibid.* 28 May 1903.
32 Reynolds to Pinker, 10 November 1904, Northwestern.
33 *A Marriage of Learning* HT 205.
34 *ibid.* 208.
35 *ibid.* 219.
36 Reynolds to Edward Garnett, 28 September 1906, Wright 40.
37 A Letter from Paris, *Cheltenham Examiner*, 3 December 1902 and 4 March 1903.
38 *An Old Woman* HT 285.

39 *Self-Exiled* HT 294.
40 Reynolds to Jane Reynolds, April 1903, Texas. The sudden interest in Conrad was probably stimulated by an article on him by Ernest Newman in the *Weekly Critical Review*, 26 March 1903.
41 *The Bodleian*, March 1909.
42 Reynolds to Jane Reynolds, [April] 1903, Texas.
43 Wright x.
44 *Weekly Critical Review*, 9 July 1903.
45 David Garforth-Bles *op.cit.* PRO, WO 339/16605. Three months before his death, he offered himself to the War Office as British Provost Marshal in New York should war break out. The War Office was suitably cool in its response.
46 Will of Jane Reynolds, 24 March 1934.
47 Osborne 45. Volume now in possession of John Osborne. It was the 1901 edition in the Collection Nymphée of the Librairie L. Borel, liberally plastered with highly erotic, and rather beautiful, engravings of naked women by A. Calbet. They would not have been permitted in the average English book of the period, but may not, in any case, have done much for the book's owner, whose primary interest lay in the text.
48 Wright x.

Chapter 5 Into the Abyss 1903–4

1 Sheila Ellis *Down a Cobbled Street*, Badger Books 1997 53.
2 Rosemary Anne Lauder and Michael Williams *Strange Stories from Devon*, Bossiney Books 1994 86. Rosemary Anne Lauder, Unknown & Haunted, *North Devon Magazine* Spring 1986 65.
3 *Cheltenham Examiner*, 18 March 1903. Frank Reynolds henceforth split his life between Nether Velly and his manager's job at the Central Wiltshire Bacon Company to which he now returned.
4 Osborne 44.
5 Interview with Roger Elliott, 10 July 1999. *Sidmouth Herald*, 23 December 1977 and 17 April 1992. Tom lived all his married life in 3, Cecil Terrace, now Redcliffs, the street forming an extension of Riverside. Reynolds' friend, Harold Wright, used often to stay there on holiday. There is a tradition on Tom's side of the family that Reynolds returned to the downstairs front room on occasion in later years to do some of his writing there. It is certainly possible that he might have done so in the period around 1912 when the noise in Bedford Square was getting to him and for a time he was closer to Tom than to Bob.
6 Fishing on this side of the Woolley family at least went back only two generations. Bob's father George, born 18 January 1843, and grandfather Robert, bap. 7 November 1819, were both fishermen, but his great grand-

father, another Robert, was a Sidmouth tailor.

7 Uncle Sam had always been something of a loner in the family. He married much later than the others and after the death of his father, Robert Woolley, lived as a young fisherman in his twenties alone with his widowed mother Caroline, who went out charring. After he married Elizabeth, his mother lived on with the couple until her death.

8 *Weekly Critical Review*, 23 July 1903.

9 PMH 6. The identification of Jubilee Terrace derives from a note, now in possession of Nigel Chanter, drawn up by Bobby Woolley in March 1919, a month after Reynolds' death. It must therefore be regarded as authoritative. Harry Daniell, a Reynolds' enthusiast, in his article "Out to Beach" (*Sidmouth Herald*, 18 September 1982), identifies Egremont Villas with Elysian Villas, the row of six redbrick houses on the corner of Vicarage Road and Lawn Vista. But Daniell is unreliable – in the same article he places Beavis Terrace in Bedford Square – and seems to have deduced that the real Egremont Villas must have begun with an "E". Reynolds probably went through the same mental process and had Elysian Villas in mind when creating the fictional Egremont Villas, just as his choice of Alexandra Square for Bedford Square was probably influenced by Sidmouth's Alexandria Road.
Jubilee Terrace was awash with lodging house keepers at this time, so we cannot pinpoint with any accuracy where Reynolds stayed. The three principal contenders for the role of his landlady, in business both in 1903 *and* 1906 (PMH 13), appear to be Elizabeth Hart at No.6, Emma Salter at No.8 and Caroline Richards at No.14.

10 *Sidmouth Herald*, 9 May 1903.

11 *Frights*, AS 90.

12 Reynolds to Jane Reynolds, 1903, transcribed Philippa Powys, Mappowder.

13 *Seining*, AS 161.

14 Reynolds to Edward Garnett, 19 October 1906, Wright 52.

15 *Fogs*, AS 41.

16 Reynolds to Edward Garnett, 17 September 1906, Wright 33. The identification of Reynolds' crew springs also from the note of March 1919 by Bobby Woolley, now in possession of Nigel Chanter. The cause of Freddie Ware's death the following year was certified as "*tabes dorsalis* [in modern parlance *locomotor ataxia*] 14 years, cardiac disease 12 months". No-one with congenital syphilis that had reached the tertiary stage could expect to live longer than 20 or 30.

17 PMH 107.

18 *Fogs*, AS 41.

19 *ibid*. 42.

20 Reynolds to Pinker, 10 November 1904, Northwestern.

21 Wright xiv.

22 Reynolds to Edward Garnett, 19 October 1906, Wright 52.
23 E.L. Grant Watson *But To What Purpose*, Cresset Press 1946 152. For a short time Grant Watson was, like Reynolds, a protégé of Conrad.
24 Wright xiv. PMH 46.
25 Reynolds to George Macmillan, 9 February 1912, Add.Mss.54965.
26 *The Bodleian*, March 1909. From 27 February 1902 to 18 August 1905 Savill treated 103 cases of neurasthenia which he wrote up in detail for his lectures. Reynolds was among a sub-group of 55 males and another of 20 patients of both sexes aged 20 to 29. Many of the cases Savill assigned to digestive problems. See Thomas Savill *Clinical Lectures on Neurasthenia, 4th edition* 1908 164.
27 Wright xiv.
28 Oliver Wilkinson (edited) *The Letters of John Cowper Powys to Frances Gregg*, Cecil Woolf 1994 252. Although there are inaccuracies in this potted biography of Reynolds, the story about relearning the alphabet appears too strange to have been concocted. Oliver Wilkinson was unsure of its provenance, but it seems most likely it originated with Katie Powys and was passed on by Alyse Gregory (Oliver Wilkinson to the author, 30 November and 3 December 1997).
29 Reynolds to Will Goodchild, 8 November 1907, Wright 100. Wright gave anonymity to the recipient, whose identity is disclosed by Katie Powys' transcription, Mappowder.
30 *ibid.*
31 See *The Pictorial Record*, Vol.III No.24, London June 1900, copy in Devizes Museum, whose interior photographs of the College at this time are reproduced in the present volume. The view of the College from the back garden was used in contemporary advertisements, one of which was included in Reynolds' *Devizes and Roundabout*.
32 Poll Book, Devizes 1904, copy in Devizes Museum.
33 A few years later the *Gazette* moved to larger premises at No.14 which remains its office today.
34 *Wiltshire Gazette*, 20 February 1919.
35 Reynolds to Edward Garnett, 14 June 1907, Texas, partially quoted Wright 82.
36 *The Citizenry of Cats*, HT 270. Reynolds to Henry Maurice, 8 December 1917, Wright 290.
37 PMH 276.
38 Reynolds to an unrecorded correspondent, 23 February 1904, transcribed Philippa Powys, Mappowder.
39 Reynolds to Jane Reynolds, 1904, Texas.
40 Quoted James Hepburn *The Author's Empty Purse and The Rise of the Literary Agent*, OUP 1968 57.
41 Arthur Waugh *A Hundred Years of Publishing, Being the Story of Chapman & Hall, Ltd*, Chapman & Hall 1930 204.

42 Reynolds to Pinker, 24 May 1904, Northwestern.
43 Reynolds to Pinker, 8 June 1904, Berg Collection, New York Public Library.
44 Reynolds to Pinker, 11 June 1904, Northwestern. They met at 3.30 pm.
45 Reynolds to Pinker, 29 June 1904, Northwestern.
46 Reynolds to Pinker, 6 July 1904, Northwestern.
47 Reynolds to Pinker, 12 July 1904, Northwestern.
48 Reynolds to Pinker, 29 June 1904, Northwestern.
49 Reynolds to Pinker, 12 July 1904, Northwestern. The 19 manuscripts were: *They know not what they do*, *Her Immortality* (already published at Owens College), *Astarte the Unconquerable*, *A Changeling Art*, *With Baby's Help**, *The Flutter and Fall of Mrs. Tripp**, *The Land of Dreams*, *The Conjugal Segregation Experiment**, *Salterport's Longshoreman*, *On Nakedness*, *A Love's Hunger**, *Our Old Woman**, *Artistical Toothache*, *Variance*, *Jane Mary's Dot*, *Thus Spake the Popular Author*, *His Home-Coming*, *Types of the Trade I*, *A kitten: That's all** (those published later are asterisked).
50 Ministry of Defence leaflet on Ford House. The Tanners remained there as tenants of the Blake family until about 1912, and the house was taken over informally by the Air Ministry in 1917, perhaps being used to accommodate the Station Commander of the nearby Old Sarum Airfield. It was compulsorily purchased on 15 March 1921 and has remained in Ministry of Defence hands ever since.
51 *The Citizenry of Cats*, HT 277.
52 A Kitten: That's All, *Week's Survey*, 3 December 1904. I have used here the original version rather than the one slightly amended for *How 'Twas* (page 266) where some of the emotional impact is softened.
53 Reynolds to Pinker, 3 August 1904, Northwestern.
54 Reynolds to Pinker, 13 August 1904, Northwestern.
55 Reynolds to Pinker, 6 July 1904, Northwestern.
56 PMH 1.
57 Service record of William Thomas Woolley, Boy 2nd Class, No.232122, Ministry of Defence.
58 PMH 3.
59 *ibid.* 6.
60 Reynolds to Pinker, 4 December 1904, Northwestern. Sheila Ellis *op.cit.*6.
61 *A Legend*, AS 259, 260.
62 *ibid.* 265.

Chapter 6 The Holy Mountain 1904–6

1 Seccombe to Edward Garnett, 12 March 1907, Texas.
2 David Garnett *The Golden Echo*, Chatto & Windus 1953 3.
3 Wright xiv.

4 *ibid.*
5 *ibid.* xv.
6 Halkett to Pinker, 3 November 1904, Northwestern.
7 Reynolds to Pinker, 10 November and 4 December 1904, Northwestern.
8 Reynolds to Pinker, 4 December 1904, Northwestern.
9 Reynolds to Pinker, 27 December 1904, Northwestern.
10 Reynolds to Pinker, 1 January 1905, Northwestern.
11 Reynolds to Pinker, 23 January [1905], Northwestern. The letter is misdated "1904", a typical Reynolds turn-of-year slip.
12 Reynolds to Pinker, 2 February 1905, Northwestern. It was a question that the next two Prime Ministers were to ask nine months later when they met to share out the future spoils of office – see Roy Jenkins *Asquith*, Papermac 1994 147. Reynolds to Pinker, 9 March 1905, Northwestern.
13 Morley to Pinker, 6 March 1905, Northwestern.
14 Tramping Afloat, *Everyman*, 15 November 1912.
15 *ibid.*
16 Coranian Journal 3, Texas. This typescript journal, the only consecutive one Reynolds was to keep, runs from 17 May to 20 June 1905. Since the amendments are in his hand, it seems likely he typed it up himself.
17 Tramping Afloat *op.cit.*
18 Coranian Journal *op.cit.* 5 and 7.
19 *ibid.* 13.
20 *A Steam-Burst Afloat*, HT 311.
21 *The Engineer's Kiss*, HT 107.
22 Coranian Journal *op.cit.* 27.
23 *ibid.* 12.
24 *ibid.* 25c.
25 *ibid.* 21.
26 *ibid.* 25c.
27 Seamen and the Sea, *Country Life*, 16 May 1908.
28 *A Steam-Burst Afloat*, HT 311.
29 *ibid.* 313.
30 Coranian Journal *op.cit.* 30.
31 *ibid.* 32.
32 Tramping Afloat *op.cit.* Coranian Journal *op.cit.* 33 and 34.
33 Coranian Journal *op.cit.* 33.
34 *ibid.* 16.
35 *ibid.* unnumbered and headed "missed out".
36 *ibid.* unnumbered and headed "extra page".
37 *ibid.* 34.
38 *ibid.* 36.
39 *ibid.* 38.
40 *ibid.* 43.
41 *ibid.*

42 *ibid.* 44.
43 The portrait was drawn in June 1905. A photograph of it, signed by Reynolds in August 1908, is now in the possession of Margaret Wallace.
44 Reynolds to Pinker, 20 July 1905, Northwestern.
45 Reynolds to Pinker, 29 June 1905, Northwestern.
46 L1394, Poll Book, Devizes 1907, copy in Devizes Museum.
47 PMH 13.
48 Reynolds to Edward Garnett, 14 June 1907, Wright 84, original Texas.
49 *A Dog's Life*, HT 299.
50 *ibid.* 300.
51 For the classic description of the role of a dog in the life of a lonely homosexual, see Appendix to J.R. Ackerley *My Father and Myself*, Penguin 1971 184.
52 *A Dog's Life*, HT 303.
53 *ibid.* 305.
54 Reynolds to Pinker, 20 July 1905, Northwestern.
55 *A Dog's Life*, HT 305.
56 *ibid.* 307.
57 *ibid.*
58 Reynolds to Pinker, 8 December 1905, Northwestern; 16 December 1905, Berg Collection, New York Public Library.
59 Reynolds to Pinker, 16 December 1905, Berg Collection, New York Public Library.
60 Reynolds to Pinker, 29 June and 8 December 1905, Northwestern.
61 The loss was a serious one – £2.12.6. Reynolds to Pinker, 31 December 1905, 18 February and 4 April 1906, Northwestern.
62 Reynolds to Pinker, 23 and 26 November 1905, Berg Collection, New York Public Library; 11 January 1906, Northwestern.
63 Brother Christmas and Mr Bookworm, *Daily News*, 26 December 1910.
64 Reynolds to Pinker, 16 January 1906, Northwestern. *A Dog's Life*, HT 307.
65 Reynolds to Pinker, 19 January 1906, Northwestern.
66 Reynolds to Pinker, 6 February 1906, Northwestern.
67 Joseph Conrad and Ford Hueffer, *The Inheritors*, New York, Doubleday, Page & Co. 1920 71, quoted Carolyn G. Heilbrun, *The Garnett Family*, Allen & Unwin 1961 78.
68 *Letters from W.H. Hudson to Edward Garnett*, Dent 1925 1.
69 This list of the shifting clientele has been compiled from the diaries of Edward Thomas, NLW, the best source for the Mont Blanc lunches. Both Conrad and Scott-James appeared there as late as 1914 (R.A.Scott-James, Ford Madox Ford When He Was Hueffer, *South Atlantic Quarterly* 57, Spring 1958 237).
70 Edward Garnett to Galsworthy, 5 June 1922, Eton College Library.
71 R.H. Mottram, *For Some We Loved: An Intimate Portrait of Ada and John Galsworthy*, Hutchinson 1956 30. Mottram's first account has slightly

different detail – see R.H. Mottram, *John Galsworthy: Writers and their Work No.38*, NBL 1953 8.
72 Arthur Mizener *The Saddest Story: A Biography of Ford Madox Ford*, Bodley Head 1972 107.
73 Reynolds to Pinker, 18 February 1906, Northwestern.
74 *ibid.*
75 Edward Garnett to Galsworthy, 8 March 1906, Edward Garnett (edited) *Letters from John Galsworthy 1900-1932*, Jonathan Cape 1934 111.
76 "March 9 1906 E.G. and S.S.R. here to supper J.R." – annotation by Jane Reynolds on page 41 of her edition of Wright, now in possession of Stephen Wiltshire.
77 How I began, *T.P.'s Weekly*, 18 October 1912, quoted Wright xiv.
78 Reynolds to Pinker, 3 July 1906, Northwestern – the first of two letters written to Pinker that day.
79 Reynolds to Pinker, 10 August 1906, Northwestern.
80 How I began *op.cit.*, quoted Wright xiv.
81 *Bookman*, October 1909.
82 HM 33.
83 *ibid.* 62.
84 How I began *op.cit.*, quoted Wright xvi.
85 HM 154.
86 *ibid.* 157.
87 *ibid.* 229.
88 Reynolds to Pinker, 10 March 1909, Northwestern.
89 There are two notable mistakes of continuity. Julia Jepp, referred to by Alec's father as "that yellow girl" (page 263), is mistakenly described as "that yellow girl at Turner's" (page 12) when she actually works at Clinch's. Julia and Miss Starkey first think of going to London *after* Mrs Parfitt's departure for church (page 219) and tell her on her return that evening; whereas Mrs Parfitt tells Alec of the London plan, of which she could not then be aware, *during* the church service (page 216).
90 HM 49.
91 *ibid.* 73.
92 *ibid.* 267.
93 W.H. Hudson to Edward Garnett, 2 March 1919, *Letters from W.H. Hudson to Edward Garnett*, Dent 1925 190. Enclosure to letter from Edward Garnett to Pinker, 16 July 1907, Northwestern.
94 How I began *op.cit.*, quoted Wright xv.
95 *ibid.*, quoted Wright xvi.

Chapter 7 Revelation at Seacombe 1906–7

1 *Wiltshire Archaeological Magazine*, June 1910, xxxvi 492

2 R.D.Gillman to the Editor of the Devizes and Wiltshire Advertiser, *Wiltshire Advertiser*, 26 April 1906. This was Gillman writing in his personal capacity to himself in his official capacity
3 Butcher was best known as a local political agent, but he was also interested in local history and an authority on the Norman Castle in Devizes. In the episode of the Guide, however, his antiquarian leanings were overwhelmed by another great interest – the water supply of the town, he being chairman of the gas and water committee. He died two days before Reynolds (*Wiltshire Gazette*, 20 February 1919).
4 R.D.Gillman to the Editor of the Devizes and Wiltshire Advertiser *op.cit.*
5 *ibid.*
6 *ibid.*
7 *Wiltshire Advertiser*, 3 May 1906.
8 *ibid.*
9 *Wiltshire Advertiser*, 3 and 10 May 1906.
10 *Wiltshire Advertiser*, 10 May 1906.
11 *ibid.* Reynolds to Pinker, 7 May 1906, Northwestern.
12 R.D. Gillman *Popular Guide to Devizes and Its District*, Devizes and Wiltshire Advertiser Office, Devizes 1906 v. It was well reviewed by the rival *Gazette – Devizes and Wiltshire Gazette*, 10 May 1906.
13 Reynolds to Pinker, 7 May 1906, Northwestern.
14 Reynolds to Pinker, 12 May 1906, Northwestern.
15 Reynolds to Pinker, 23 May 1906, Northwestern.
16 Reynolds to W. Mate & Sons, 28 May 1906, Northwestern.
17 Reynolds to Pinker, 3 July 1906, Northwestern.
18 *Devizes and Roundabout*, Mate's Illustrated Guides, Bournemouth 1906 [1]. There was a second edition the following year. The pages are not numbered; the references given here start with the preface as a notional page [1].
19 *ibid.* [3].
20 *ibid.* [10,22,24,26,28,30,38].
21 *ibid.* [54].
22 *ibid.* [32]
23 *ibid.* [46].
24 *ibid.* [46].
25 *ibid.* [62].
26 *ibid.* [64].
27 *Wiltshire Advertiser*, 12 July 1906.
28 B. Howard Cunnington to the Editor, *Wiltshire Advertiser*, 19 July 1906.
29 *Devizes and Wiltshire Gazette*, 19 July 1906.
30 *Devizes and Roundabout op.cit.* [10].
31 *Devizes and Wiltshire Gazette*, 19 July 1906.
32 Reynolds to Pinker, 26 July 1906, Northwestern.
33 *Wiltshire Advertiser*, 2 August 1906.

34 W. Mate & Sons to Reynolds, 11 July 1906, Northwestern.
35 Reynolds to Pinker, 3 July 1906, Northwestern. This was the last visit paid to London before Reynolds set off west on holiday. He had apparently been there in mid-April (Reynolds to Pinker, 4 April 1906, Northwestern) but not with a view to visiting Garnett since he planned to remain up on Thursday. On 17 September he refers to the discussions with Garnett at the Cearne as a relatively recent event (Wright 35); and placing the first visit to the Cearne in mid-July explains why the extant Reynolds-Garnett correspondence begins a month later.
36 Richard Garnett *Constance Garnett: A Heroic Life*, Sinclair-Stevenson 1991 75.
37 The image comes from D.H. Lawrence in an interview with Kyle S. Crichton, *The World* (New York), 11 October 1925, section 3, page 4m, quoted Richard Garnett *op.cit.*133
38 Reynolds to Edward Garnett, 12 September 1906, Texas, partially quoted Wright 29.
39 Reynolds to Edward Garnett, undated, Wright 89.
40 David Garnett to the author, 11 May 1980.
41 Reynolds to Edward Garnett, 29 June 1907, Texas, partially quoted Wright 89.
42 Reynolds to Edward Garnett, 17 September 1906, Wright 35.
43 Reynolds to Pinker, 10 August 1906, Northwestern.
44 Reynolds to Pinker, 26 July 1906, Northwestern.
45 Reynolds to Pinker, 12 May 1906, Northwestern.
46 Reynolds to Pinker, 10 August 1906, Northwestern.
47 PMH 6.
48 PMH 8.
49 PMH 14.
50 Henry Pinn arrived in Bedford Square in the late 1840s and brought up his family of three sons and two daughters there. Some time in the 1870s, when his family had grown up and left home, he moved just round the corner and up the steps to a smaller cottage, 1 Silver Terrace, where he remained into the 1890s. For a working-class area, Western Town appears to have had more than its fair share of lawyers. Another one, Henry Merrifield, moved into 6, Western Row in the 1870s where he too stayed into the 1890s. His son, Charles, grew up as a fisherman but in his thirties switched to his father's profession of lawyer. He was still living in Western Town at the time of *A Poor Man's House* and features in the book as "the Little Russian" who comes out of fishing retirement to capitalise on temporary high prices (PMH 294).
51 PMH 14.
52 PMH 9.
53 PMH 12.
54 PMH 20.

55 *ibid.*
56 Reynolds to Edward Garnett, 20 August 1906, Wright 27, original Texas.
57 PMH 23.
58 *ibid.*
59 Extract from notebook, undated, Texas. Wright places the second of these extracts, also undated, between 12 and 17 September 1906 (Wright 32), but the reference to the pine-belt in this one firmly fixes the location as Nether Velly and therefore the date between about 25 August and 6 September when he set off again down south. The style and content (he is talking of the Sidmouth experience as one in exile from it) of the second extract makes it almost certainly contemporaneous with this one.
60 Reynolds to Edward Garnett, 4 September 1906, Texas.
61 Reynolds to Pinker, 2 September 1906, Northwestern.
62 Reynolds to Edward Garnett, 4 September 1906, Texas.
63 Reynolds to Edward Garnett, 20 August 1906, Wright 28.
64 Extract from notebook, undated, Texas (*see note 59 above*).
65 Reynolds to Edward Garnett, 12 September 1906, Wright 30. The original of this letter, Texas, is incomplete; Wright omits the first paragraph and last eleven words.
66 Reynolds claimed to have returned in the evening of Monday 10th, but it is possible that he meant Sunday 9th since two sentences later he talks of fishing on the Monday before breakfast (Reynolds to Edward Garnett, 12 September 1906, Wright 29). What is more likely, however, is that the letter dated 12 September was actually written on the 13th, in which case he did return on Monday 10th.
67 PMH 26.
68 Reynolds to Edward Garnett, 12 September 1906, annotation to address, Texas. Reynolds to Edward Garnett, 17 September 1906, Wright 36. Reynolds to Pinker, 23 September 1906, Northwestern.
69 PMH 35.
70 Reynolds to Edward Garnett, 25 September 1906, Wright 37.
71 *ibid.* 39.
72 Reynolds to Pinker, 23 September 1906, Northwestern.
73 The metaphor was not lost on his literary friends. Hueffer wrote of him appearing in London dressed "in the garb of the trade of Peter" (Ford Madox Ford *Return to Yesterday*, Carcanet 1999 290). Conrad once made the point in his usual elaborate fashion in a joking response to a gift of prawns. "I have devoured the prawns with infinite thankfulness and a great appreciation of their goodness and intense admiration for your benevolence which prompted you to send them to us. I don't know whether you will take it as a compliment but there is something Christianlike in it – a touch of love and charity (I don't mean it in the eleemosynary sense) and a picturesquely evangelistic aspect – distribution of fishes (*not* in the scientific sense) almost as unexpected as a

miracle. (The loaf I have managed to provide). In my state of dreamy repletion (the miracle was curried for my lunch) your figure acquires – what with your remoteness in space and time and your occupations of fishing and preaching – an Apostolic and en-haloed aspect. Is it possible that without knowing it I have been, I am, in communion with the Peter of a new dispensation in whom our future creed shall be founded as on a rock? (Conrad to Reynolds, [30 September 1911], Karl 4, 483). Karl inserts a redundant "on" in the fifth sentence.

74 Reynolds to Edward Garnett, 12 September 1906, Wright 29. Reynolds to Pinker, 23 September 1906, Northwestern.

75 Reynolds to Edward Garnett, 17 September 1906, Wright 33.

76 Readers of *A Poor Man's House* need a key to translate the Woolley children into the fictional Widgers: Bill = George; Lulu = Jenny; Gertie = Bessie; Ethel = Mabel; Bobby = Jimmy; Reggie = Tommy; Lilian = Rosie.

77 The Pratts later lived in a cottage in Chapel Street behind the Masons Arms which may have been the earlier home of the Woolleys (interview with Frances Woodward, 7 October 1999).

78 PMH 44.

79 PMH 30.

80 PMH 28, 71. Neither birth nor death appear to have been registered – they may have been still-born.

81 Reynolds disguises both date and cause of death, giving Rosie the teething convulsions that had killed Henry in June 1896 (PMH 73). Similarly he slightly alters the history of the other dead children, perhaps to save the Woolleys' feelings (PMH 28).

82 PMH 71.

83 PMH 68.

84 Reynolds to Edward Garnett, 17 September 1906, Wright 33.

85 PMH 15. I am indebted to John Osborne for the suggestion of the death of Falstaff.

86 Reynolds to Edward Garnett, 17 September 1906, Wright 33.

87 Reynolds to Edward Garnett, 12 September 1906, Wright 29.

88 Reynolds to Edward Garnett, 7 January 1907, Wright 66. PMH 289.

89 Reynolds' diary, 16 October 1906, Wright 48.

90 Reynolds to Edward Garnett, 17 September 1906, Wright 32.

91 Reynolds to Edward Garnett, 25 September 1906, Wright 36.

92 Reynolds to Edward Garnett, 28 September 1906, Wright 39.

93 *ibid.* 40.

94 Reynolds to Edward Garnett, 12 September 1906, Wright 30.

95 Reynolds to Pinker, 23 September 1906, Northwestern.

96 W. Mate & Sons to Dodd, Longstaffe Sons and Fenwick, 26 September 1906, Northwestern.

97 Reynolds to Pinker, 26 September, 19 and 24 October 1906, Northwestern. Reynolds to Edward Garnett, 25 September 1906, Wright

43; 24 October 1906, Texas.
98 Reynolds to Edward Garnett, 12 September 1906, Wright 31.
99 Reynolds to Edward Garnett, 25 September 1906, Wright 39.
100 Reynolds to Edward Garnett, 28 September 1906, Wright 42. The source of the invitation is not mentioned, but it is clearly the Tanners who instead took him for a day out in Hampshire the following Thursday.
101 Reynolds to Edward Garnett, 2 October 1906, Wright 43.
102 PMH 161.
103 Reynolds to Edward Garnett, 3 October 1906, Wright 47.
104 *ibid.* 46.
105 Reynolds to Pinker, 26 September 1906, Northwestern.
106 On 3 October he was anticipating the first lecture the following day (Reynolds to Edward Garnett, 3 October 1906, Wright 47) but it was actually given on 18 October (*Wiltshire Advertiser*, 25 October 1906; Reynolds to Edward Garnett, 19 October 1906, Wright 52). Either the lecture was postponed or he was badly confused as to the dates.
107 Reynolds to Edward Garnett, 17 September 1906, Wright 36.
108 Reynolds to Pinker, 7 October 1906, Northwestern.
109 Autobiografiction, *Speaker*, 6 October 1906.
110 *ibid.* For an academic discussion of this genre and Reynolds' contribution to its theory, see Peter Keating *The Haunted Study: A Social History of the English Novel 1875-1914*, Secker & Warburg, 1989 308-11.
111 Reynolds to Edward Garnett, 3 October 1906, Wright 47.
112 Reynolds to Edward Garnett, 12 October 1906, Wright 48.
113 *ibid.*
114 Reynolds to Edward Garnett, 7 January 1907, Wright 68.
115 Reynolds' diary, 16 October 1906, Wright 48.
116 *ibid.* 49.
117 *ibid.* 50.
118 Reynolds to Edward Garnett, 19 October 1906, Wright 53.
119 Reynolds' diary, 17 October 1906, Wright 51.
120 Reynolds' diary, 18 October 1906, Wright 51.
121 Reynolds' diary, [mid October 1906], transcribed Philippa Powys, Mappowder. This could be from 18 October, but since sun was in short supply that day, it may come from a few days earlier.
122 *Wiltshire Advertiser*, 25 October 1906.
123 Reynolds to Edward Garnett, [19 November 1906], Texas. Reynolds to Pinker, 16 January 1907, Northwestern. His fee was later increased to six shillings (Reynolds to Edward Garnett, 12 January 1907, Wright 70).
124 Reynolds to Edward Garnett, 19 October 1906, Wright 51.
125 Reynolds to Edward Garnett, 24 October 1906, Texas.
126 *ibid.*
127 Reynolds' diary, 28 October 1906, Wright 53. Skemp was now studying

at Berlin University.

128 Gosse to Maurice Baring, 21 March 1907, Evan Charteris *The Life and Letters of Sir Edmund Gosse*, Heinemann 1931 303.

129 See, for example, his delightful *Simple Stories: For Children and Grown-ups*, Harrap 1927.

130 Reynolds to Pinker, 19 October 1906, Northwestern.

131 Reynolds to Pinker, 24 October 1906, Northwestern.

132 Reynolds to Edward Garnett, [19 November 1906], Texas.

133 Archibald Marshall *Out and About*, John Murray 1933 141.

134 Reynolds to Pinker, 30 October and 30 November 1906; 30 January 1907, Northwestern; Reynolds to Edward Garnett, 18 December 1906, Wright 58.

135 Reynolds to Pinker, 30 October 1906, Northwestern.

136 Reynolds to Edward Garnett, 3 November 1906, Wright 55.

137 Reynolds to Pinker, 4 November 1906, Northwestern. The meeting with Pinker clearly took place between 12 and 1 on 6 November, since Reynolds had to tell him later of the offer from Hueffer (Reynolds to Pinker, 13 November 1906, Northwestern).

138 Divers Country Books, *Speaker*, 25 August 1906.

139 Reynolds to Edward Garnett, 9 November 1906, Texas. Reynolds to Pinker, 13 November 1906, Northwestern.

140 Reynolds to Pinker, 13 and 30 November 1906, Northwestern. Reynolds to Edward Garnett, [19 November 1906], Texas.

141 Reynolds to Edward Garnett, [19 November 1906], Texas.

142 Reynolds to Edward Garnett, 27 November 1906, Texas.

143 Reynolds to Edward Garnett, [19 November 1906], Texas. Reynolds to Charles Sarolea, [17 December 1912], Edinburgh. It is only the Keats lecture that seems to fit this particular anecdote.

144 Reynolds to Edward Garnett, 27 November 1906, Texas. The baby, christened Clara Thirza after Reynolds' mother, was born on the same day as Aunt Jane. She was drowned on 1 January 1934. Reynolds reported the birth in similar vein to Pinker: "My sister has been terribly ill four miles from here, and has made me uncle of a shrimpish little animal" (Reynolds to Pinker, 30 November 1906, Northwestern). But three weeks later Dot had fully recovered: "My sister is downstairs again, so funny with her baby, which, following her husband's example, she talks to as if it were a horse!" (Reynolds to Edward Garnett, 18 December 1906, Wright 56).

145 Reynolds to Edward Garnett, 9 November 1906, Texas.

146 Reynolds to Edward Garnett, 27 November 1906, Texas. *Wiltshire Advertiser*, 29 November 1906.

147 Reynolds to Pinker, 30 November 1906, Northwestern.

148 Reynolds to Pinker, 18 December 1906, Northwestern.

149 *ibid.*

150 Reynolds to Edward Garnett, 18 December 1906, Wright 56.
151 Reynolds to Edward Garnett, 27 December 1906, Wright 59.
152 PMH 294.
153 Reynolds to Edward Garnett, 27 December 1906, Wright 59.
154 *ibid.* 61.
155 *ibid.* 60.
156 *ibid.* 58.
157 Reynolds to Edward Garnett, 2 January 1907, Wright 63.
158 Monumental Art, *Daily Mail*, 19 January 1907.
159 Reynolds to Edward Garnett, 2 January 1907, Wright 63.
160 *ibid.* 65.
161 PMH 313.
162 Reynolds to Edward Garnett, 2 January 1907, Wright 64.
163 *ibid.* 65.
164 Reynolds' diary, 16 October 1906, Wright 49.
165 Reynolds to Pinker, 18 December 1906, Northwestern.
166 Reynolds to Edward Garnett, 2 January 1907, Wright 64.
167 Reynolds to Edward Garnett, 7 January 1907, Wright 68.
168 *ibid.*
169 Reynolds to Edward Garnett, 12 January 1907, Wright 69.
170 Reynolds to Edward Garnett, 13 January 1907, Wright 72.

Chapter 8 Marketing the Mountain 1907

1 Reynolds to Pinker, 16 January 1907, Northwestern.
2 *ibid.*
3 Reynolds to Pinker, 18 January 1907, Northwestern.
4 Reynolds to unrecorded recipient, January 1907, transcribed Philippa Powys, Mappowder. The recipient is almost certainly Garnett and the date 20 January.
5 Reynolds to Pinker, 30 January 1907, Northwestern.
6 Reynolds to Pinker, 14 February 1907, Northwestern.
7 Reynolds to Edward Garnett, 27 February 1907, Texas
8 *ibid.*
9 *ibid.*
10 Reynolds to Edward Garnett, 1 March 1907, Texas.
11 Reynolds to Pinker, 10 March 1907, Northwestern.
12 *ibid.* Reynolds to Edward Garnett, 8 March 1907, Texas, partially quoted Wright 72.
13 Reynolds to Edward Garnett, 8 March 1907, Texas.
14 Reynolds to Edward Garnett, 27 February and 8 March 1907, Texas. Reynolds to Pinker, 10 March 1907, Northwestern. The two returned works appear to be "Ghosts of Old Sarum", now lost, and "The Engineer's

Kiss", later published in HT (Reynolds to Pinker, 18 and 30 January 1907, Northwestern).

15 Reynolds to Pinker, 25 March 1907, Northwestern.

16 Reynolds to Edward Garnett, 4 April 1907, Texas; 25 June 1907, Wright 87. Reynolds to Pinker, 16 June 1907, Northwestern.

17 Reynolds to Pinker, 10 March 1907, Northwestern.

18 Reynolds to Edward Garnett, 8 March 1907, Texas. Edward Thomas diary, 12 March 1907, NLW. Seccombe to Edward Garnett, 12 March 1907, Texas.

19 Edward Thomas diary, 18 and 19 March 1907, NLW. Edward Thomas to Walter de la Mare, [19 March 1907], Bodleian Library.

20 Edward Thomas diary, 20 March 1907, NLW.

21 PMH 181.

22 Reynolds to Edward Garnett, 29 March 1907, Texas, partially quoted Wright 74.

23 PMH 183.

24 Reynolds to Edward Garnett, 29 March 1907, Wright 74.

25 *ibid.* 73.

26 Reynolds to Edward Garnett, 4 April 1907, Texas, partially quoted Wright 74.

27 Reynolds to Edward Garnett, 29 March 1907, Texas.

28 Reynolds to Edward Garnett, 4 April 1907, Texas.

29 Reynolds to Edward Garnett, 10 April 1907, Texas.

30 *ibid.*

31 *ibid.*

32 Reynolds to Edward Garnett, [12 April 1907], Texas.

33 Reynolds to Edward Garnett, 15 April 1907, Texas, partially quoted Wright 76.

34 Reynolds to Edward Garnett, 20 April 1907, Texas, partially quoted Wright 78.

35 Reynolds to Edward Garnett, 15 April 1907, Wright 77.

36 Reynolds to Edward Garnett, 15 April 1907, Texas.

37 Reynolds to Edward Garnett, 20 April 1907, Wright 78.

38 Reynolds to Edward Garnett, 20 April 1907, Texas.

39 Edward Thomas diary, 25 April 1907, NLW.

40 Edward Thomas to Gordon Bottomley, quoted John Moore *The Life and Letters of Edward Thomas*, Heinemann 1939 145.

41 Edward Thomas diary, 27 and 29 April 1907, NLW.

42 Edward Thomas to Walter de la Mare, [19 March 1907], Bodleian Library. Edward Thomas diary, 20 March 1907, NLW.

43 Edward Thomas diary, 30 April 1907, NLW.

44 Reynolds to Pinker, 2 May 1907, Northwestern.

45 Reynolds to Edward Garnett, 20 April 1907, Texas.

46 Reynolds to Pinker, 10 May 1907, Northwestern.

47 Reynolds to Pinker, 2 May 1907, Northwestern.
48 *ibid.*
49 Reynolds to Pinker, 23 June 1907, Northwestern. Reynolds to Edward Garnett, 25 June 1907, Wright 88.
50 Reynolds to Edward Garnett, 2 June 1907, Texas, partially quoted Wright 81.
51 Reynolds to Edward Garnett, 20 May 1907, Texas.
52 PMH 276.
53 Reynolds to Edward Garnett, 20 May 1907, Texas.
54 *ibid.*
55 Reynolds to Pinker, 26 May 1907, Northwestern.
56 Reynolds to Edward Garnett, 25 May 1907, Texas.
57 Reynolds to Edward Garnett, 1 June 1907, Wright 79, original Texas.
58 Reynolds to Edward Garnett, 29 May 1907, Texas, partially quoted Wright 79.
59 *ibid.*
60 Reynolds to Pinker, telegram, 29 May 1907, Northwestern.
61 Reynolds to Pinker, 29 May 1907, Northwestern.
62 Reynolds to Pinker, 2 June 1907, Northwestern.
63 Reynolds to Edward Garnett, 1 June 1907, Wright 79.
64 *ibid.* 80.
65 Reynolds to Edward Garnett, 29 May 1907, Texas.
66 Reynolds to Edward Garnett, 1 June 1907, Wright 80.
67 Reynolds to Edward Garnett, 25 August 1907, Texas, partially quoted Wright 95.
68 Reynolds to Edward Garnett, 2 June 1907, Wright 80.
69 Reynolds to Edward Garnett, 14 June 1907, Texas, partially quoted Wright 82.
70 *ibid.*
71 Reynolds to Edward Garnett, 2 June 1907, Wright 81.
72 Reynolds to Edward Garnett, 2 June 1907, Texas.
73 Reynolds to Edward Garnett, 14 June 1907, Wright 83.
74 Reynolds to Pinker, 16 June 1907, Northwestern.
75 Reynolds to Edward Garnett, 25 June 1907, Wright 87.
76 Reynolds to Edward Garnett, 29 June 1907, Texas, partially quoted Wright 89.
77 Reynolds to Edward Garnett, undated, Wright 88.
78 Reynolds to Edward Garnett, 3 June 1907, Texas.
79 Reynolds to Edward Garnett, 14 June 1907, Wright 84.
80 Reynolds to Pinker, 23 June 1907, Northwestern.
81 Reynolds to Edward Garnett, 25 June 1907, Wright 85.
82 PMH 149.
83 Reynolds to Edward Garnett, 25 June 1907, Wright 85.
84 *ibid.* 86.

85 Reynolds to Edward Garnett, 29 June 1907, Wright 89.
86 Reynolds to Edward Garnett, 29 June 1907, Texas.
87 Reynolds to Edward Garnett, 2 July 1907, Texas.
88 PRO, MT 10/1131.
89 Reynolds to Edward Garnett, [19 November 1906], Texas.
90 Reynolds to Edward Garnett, 15 April 1907, Wright 77.
91 Reynolds to Edward Garnett, 20 April 1907, Texas.
92 Reynolds to Edward Garnett, 14 June 1907, Wright 83.
93 Reynolds to Edward Garnett, 29 June 1907, Texas.
94 C. Ernest Fayle *Harold Wright: A Memoir*, Allen & Unwin, 1934 94.
95 Reynolds to Edward Garnett, 14 June 1907, Wright 81; 25 June 1907, Wright 88. Reynolds to Pinker, 16 June 1907, Northwestern.
96 Reynolds to Edward Garnett, 29 June 1907, Texas.
97 There is no independent evidence that Reynolds first met Hudson on this day, but the first letter he wrote to him was on 21 July (Reynolds to Edward Garnett, 21 July 1907, Texas) and that must carry the strong presumption of a recent meeting. 9 July was Reynolds' first appearance at the Mont Blanc since Hudson had returned from Cornwall.
98 Reynolds to Rose Wright, 12 July 1907, Wright 90.
99 Reynolds to Edward Garnett, 12 July 1907, Texas, partially quoted Wright 90.
100 Pinker to Grant Richards, 11 July 1907, Illinois.
101 How I began, *T.P.'s Weekly*, 18 October 1912, quoted Wright xv. This was the only occasion that Reynolds was in London that summer when the manuscript passed to a new publisher.
102 Reynolds to Edward Garnett, 12 July 1907, Texas.
103 *ibid.*
104 *ibid.*, partially quoted Wright 90.
105 Reynolds to Edward Garnett, 12 July 1907, Texas.
106 Reynolds to Edward Garnett, 15 July 1907, Texas.
107 *ibid.*
108 Enclosure to Edward Garnett to Pinker, 16 July 1907, Northwestern.
109 Edward Garnett to Pinker, 16 July 1907, Northwestern.
110 Grant Richards to Pinker, 15 July 1907, Illinois.
111 Reynolds to Pinker, 17 July 1907, Northwestern.
112 *ibid.*
113 Reynolds to Pinker, 18 July 1907, Northwestern.
114 *ibid.*
115 Reynolds to Edward Garnett, 21 July 1907, Texas, partially quoted Wright 91.
116 Reynolds to Edward Garnett, 24 July 1907, Wright 93, original Texas.
117 Reynolds to Pinker, 25 July 1907, Northwestern.
118 Reynolds to Pinker, 26 July 1907, Northwestern.
119 Reynolds to Edward Garnett, 26 July 1907, Wright 93, original Texas.

120 Reynolds to Edward Garnett, 21 July 1907, Wright 91.
121 Reynolds to Pinker, 11 August 1907, Northwestern.
122 Reynolds to Edward Garnett, 25 August 1907, Texas, partially quoted Wright 94.
123 Reynolds to Edward Garnett, 21 July 1907, Texas.
124 Field Club Devastation, *Daily Mail*, 9 January 1907.
125 Reynolds to W.H. Hudson, 3 August 1907, RSPB Library, Sandy, Bedfordshire.
126 Pawling to Edward Garnett, 14 August 1907, Wright 97 footnote.
127 Reynolds to Edward Garnett, 25 August 1907, Texas.
128 How I began *op.cit.*, quoted Wright xiv.
129 Reynolds to Pinker, 28 August 1907, Northwestern, partially quoted Wright 97.
130 Nature and the Country, *Daily Mail*, 6 July 1907.
131 Reynolds to Edward Garnett, 25 August 1907, Wright 95.
132 *ibid.*
133 Reynolds to Pinker, 25 July 1907, Northwestern.
134 Reynolds to Edward Garnett, 25 August 1907, Wright 94.
135 *ibid.* 95.
136 PMH 314.
137 Reynolds to Edward Garnett, 25 August 1907, Wright 96.
138 Reynolds to Pinker, 28 August 1907, Wright 97.
139 Reynolds to Edward Garnett, 26 October 1907, Texas.
140 A Yokel's Impression of London, *Daily Mail*, 31 August 1907.
141 Reynolds to Edward Garnett, 21 July 1907, Texas. For the preface itself, see Edward Garnett *The Breaking Point: A Censured Play*, Duckworth 1907 ix.
142 Nash to Ponsonby, 18 February 1908, MS Eng.Lett.c.656/47, Bodleian Library.
143 Granville Barker to Ponsonby, 4 March 1908, MS Eng.Lett.c.656/60 Bodleian Library.
144 Constance Garnett to Edward Garnett, [11 September 1907], Eton College Library. The envelope is addressed c/o Mr Bob Wooley [*sic*], Western Town, which indicates that Garnett had not put up at an hotel.
145 Reynolds to Pinker, 19 September 1907, Northwestern.
146 Reynolds to Pinker, 24 September 1907, Northwestern.
147 Reynolds to Pinker, 19 September 1907, Northwestern.
148 Reynolds to Edward Garnett, 9 October 1907, Texas.
149 Free Libraries and Novel Censorship, *T.P.'s Weekly*, 12 September 1913.
150 Reynolds to Edward Garnett, undated, Texas.
151 Reynolds to Pinker, 24 September 1907, Northwestern.
152 Reynolds to Pinker, 25 September 1907, Northwestern.
153 Reynolds to Pinker, 27 September 1907, Northwestern.
154 *ibid.*

155 Reynolds to Pinker, 11 October 1907, Northwestern. Reynolds to Edward Garnett, 9 October 1907, Texas.
156 Reynolds to Pinker, 11 October 1907, Northwestern.
157 Edward Thomas diary, 15 October 1907, NLW.
158 Reynolds to Pinker, 8 November 1907, Northwestern. Conrad had hoped to meet up with Hueffer that day, but had been too exhausted to hunt him down. He wrote to him after: "I was in town yesterday and at about 12.30 telephoned to the Club asking if you were there. The reply being 'No' I went on then to the Mont Blanc where I found the usual crowd. I was too damnably done up to do anything except going home early in the afternoon." (Conrad to Hueffer, [16] October 1907, Karl 3, 501).
159 Edward Garnett to Galsworthy, [?18 October 1907], Eton College Library.
160 Edward Thomas diary, 16 October 1907, NLW.
161 Edward Thomas diary, 17 October 1907, NLW.
162 Edward Thomas diary, 18 October 1907, NLW.
163 Conrad to Pinker, [22 October 1907], Karl 3, 496. They discussed the performance of *Joy* that Reynolds and Thomas had seen that week and Reynolds told Conrad the play had made a deep impression on Pinker too.
164 Reynolds to Edward Garnett, 26 October 1907, Texas.
165 Reynolds to Pinker, 8 November, 11 and 29 December 1907, Northwestern.
166 *ibid.*
167 *ibid.* Reynolds to Edward Garnett, 26 October 1907, Texas.
168 Edward Thomas diary, 12 November 1907, NLW.
169 PMH 281.
170 Reynolds to Pinker, 11 December 1907, Northwestern.
171 Edward Thomas diary, 3 and 6 December 1907, NLW.
172 Reynolds to Pinker, [6 December 1907], Northwestern. This note describing the encounter with Lane poses some problems of dating. It was written hurriedly on Pinker's notepaper and left in his office in Arundel Street. Below the address is written "4.15. Sat." but the 4 appears to be superimposed on what was originally 12.

The Saturday dateline must have been a typical Reynolds dating slip since we know from Edward Thomas' diary that the two travelled down to Devizes that Friday evening and were walking the Wiltshire Downs on the Saturday. Reynolds does not confirm his note with Pinker until the following Wednesday (Reynolds to Pinker, 11 December 1907, Northwestern). If the meeting with Lane had taken place on the Wednesday or Thursday, there would have been time before Friday evening to confirm it in person. Thomas went up to the Mont Blanc lunch from Devizes the following Tuesday, but Reynolds was not present which he almost certainly would have been had he gone to meet Lane in London that day. In any event, even Reynolds is unlikely to have mistaken a Tuesday, Wednesday or Thursday for a Saturday. It seems most likely, therefore, that Reynolds met Lane soon after 11 on Friday 6 December, rushed straight over to Arundel Street to tell Pinker, found him out and scribbled a hurried note at 12.15 before heading off for lunch with Thomas. In his haste he wrote Saturday instead of Friday – most firms worked Saturdays then. He looked in again on Pinker's office after 4, found him still out, and merely changed the time on the note from 12 to 4 before rushing off to catch the 5 o'clock train at Paddington.

173 Edward Thomas diary, 6 December 1907, NLW.

Chapter 9 A Poor Man's House 1907–8

1 Edward Thomas diary, 7 December 1907, NLW.
2 Reynolds to Pinker, 25 July 1907, Northwestern.
3 Reynolds to Pinker, 8 November 1907, Northwestern. It is not clear precisely how much of the second half he had now completed. Two months later he was still telling Pinker "Am hoping this month to get along fast with the second half of the Poor Man's House." (Reynolds to Pinker, 2 January 1908, Northwestern).
4 Reynolds to Pinker, 11 December 1907, Northwestern.
5 Edward Thomas diary, 8 December 1907, NLW.
6 Grant Richards to Edward Thomas, 2 September 1907, Illinois.
7 Reynolds to Pinker, 11 December 1907, Northwestern.
8 Edward Thomas to Grant Richards, 11 September 1907, transcripts from the collection of Robert P. Eckert, Bodleian Library.
9 Edward Thomas to Grant Richards, 8 and 11 October 1907, Eckert transcripts, Bodleian Library. Grant Richards to Edward Thomas, 10 October 1907, Illinois.
10 Edward Thomas to Grant Richards, 8 December 1907, Eckert transcripts, Bodleian Library. In this document 'Speaker' is recorded as 'Spectator', but this is most likely a transcription error rather than one by Thomas.
11 Edward Thomas diary, 9 and 10 December 1907, NLW.
12 Reynolds to Pinker, 11 December 1907, Northwestern.
13 Reynolds to Pinker, 17 December 1907, Northwestern, partially quoted Wright 101.
14 *ibid.*
15 Reynolds to Pinker, 11 December 1907, Northwestern.
16 Reynolds to Pinker, 17 December 1907, Northwestern.
17 Conrad to Pinker, 30 December 1907, Karl 3, 516.
18 Reynolds to Pinker, 29 December 1907, Northwestern.

19 Reynolds to Lane, 18 January 1908, Texas.
20 Conrad to Wells, 1 January 1908, Karl 4, 7.
21 Conrad to Pinker, 30 December 1907, Karl 3, 516. Conrad to Galsworthy, 6 January 1908, Karl 4, 8.
22 Edward Thomas diary, 27 December 1907, NLW.
23 Reynolds to Pinker, 29 December 1907, Northwestern.
24 "I am living, you know, in touch with the genuine land-fishery, if it isn't quite so salt – t'as got a bare flavour tu 'en." (Galsworthy to Reynolds, 11 February 1909, Wallace).
25 Reynolds to Pinker, 2 January 1908, Northwestern.
26 Reynolds to Pinker, 29 December 1907, Northwestern.
27 Reynolds to Pinker, 2 and 26 January 1907, Northwestern.
28 Grant Richards to Reynolds, 6 January and 11 April 1908, Illinois. Reynolds to Lane, 18 January 1908, Texas.
29 Reynolds to Lane, 18 January 1908, Texas. Reynolds to Pinker, 26 January 1908, Northwestern.
30 Reynolds to Lane, 18 January 1908, Texas.
31 Reynolds to Pinker, 26 January 1908, Northwestern.
32 *ibid.*
33 Douglas Goldring *South Lodge: Reminiscences of Violet Hunt, Ford Madox Ford and the English Review Circle*, Constable 1943 16.
34 R.A. Scott-James, Ford Madox Ford When He Was Hueffer, *South Atlantic Quarterly* 57, Spring 1958 241. A little of the detail of Reynolds' life with Hueffer at this period has been taken from this article.
35 Grant Richards to Reynolds, 11 April 1908, Illinois.
36 Edward Thomas diary, 17 March 1908, NLW.
37 Reynolds to Lane, 26 February 1908, Texas.
38 Harold Wright to Reynolds, 29 January and 9 April 1908, in possession of Margaret Wallace. Reynolds appears to have stopped off at Wright's on the weekend of 1/2 February on his way up to Holland Park. On a visit to Holland Park on 3 April, Wright met Hueffer for the first time: "I was interested in meeting Hueffer, he seemed a nice chap but frightfully nervous and worried".
39 Conrad to Galsworthy, 17 and 20 February 1908, Karl 4, 43 and 48. Galsworthy was then working on *Fraternity*, a very London novel.
40 Reynolds to Lane, 26 February 1908, Texas.
41 *ibid.*
42 *Devizes and Wiltshire Gazette*, 1 October 1908. We do not know who the first reader was, but this extract from his report was widely quoted in publicity material for the book.
43 Reader's report by Frederic Chapman, undated, Lane papers, Texas.
44 Wright x. C. Ernest Fayle *Harold Wright: A Memoir*, Allen & Unwin 1934 94.
45 Reynolds to Edward Garnett, 27 March 1908, Texas, partially quoted

Wright 101.
46 *ibid.*
47 *ibid.*
48 Reynolds to Pinker, 26 January 1908, Northwestern.
49 David Garnett *The Golden Echo*, Chatto & Windus 1953 130.
50 Ford Madox Ford *Return to Yesterday*, Carcanet 1999 270.
51 Reynolds to Lane, 14 April 1908, Texas.
52 *Semaphore*, AS 71.
53 *ibid.* 72.
54 *ibid.* 73.
55 Reynolds to Edward Garnett, 14 October 1908, Texas.
56 Reynolds to Pinker, 12 June 1908, Northwestern.
57 Reynolds to Lane, 9 April 1908, Texas.
58 *ibid.*
59 Reynolds to Lane, 14 April 1908, Texas.
60 Annotation by John Lane on Reynolds to Lane, 7 May 1908, Texas.
61 Conrad to Reynolds, [6 May 1908], Karl 4, 84. Reynolds told Lane of this letter on 7 May (Texas), which makes the dating certain. Karl has inadvertently omitted the postscript to it.
62 Reynolds to Pinker, 10 January 1909, Northwestern. Reynolds to Lane, 4 February 1909, Texas.
63 Reynolds to Lane, 7 May 1908, Texas.
64 Masefield to Reynolds, 16 April 1908, Wallace.
65 Reynolds to Lane, 1 May 1908, Texas.
66 Reynolds to Lane, 7 and 18 May 1908, Texas.
67 Reynolds to Lane, 7 May 1908, Texas.
68 Reynolds to John Lane Ltd, 20 May 1908, Texas.
69 Edward Thomas diary, 26 and 27 May 1908, NLW. Reynolds to Lane, 18 May 1908, Texas.
70 Frederic Chapman to Lane, [early June 1908], Texas.
71 Grant Richards to Reynolds, 6 January and 11 April 1908, Illinois.
72 Reynolds to Lane, 14 April 1908, Texas.
73 Grant Richards to Pinker, 4 June 1908, Illinois.
74 Grant Richards to Reynolds, 11 June 1908, Illinois.
75 Reynolds to Pinker, 12 June 1908, Northwestern.
76 Grant Richards to Pinker, 16 June 1908, Illinois.
77 Reynolds to Conrad, 3 July 1908, Texas.
78 Reynolds to Pinker, 19 June 1908, Northwestern.
79 Frederic Chapman to Lane, [early June 1908], Texas.
80 Reynolds to Pinker, 19 June and 1 July 1908, Northwestern.
81 Reynolds to Conrad, 3 July 1908, Texas.
82 Reynolds to Edward Garnett, 18 December 1906, Wright 57.
83 Reynolds to Edward Garnett, 8 July 1908, Texas, partially quoted Wright 103. To the same end he was also studying Weininger, borrowed from

Harold Wright who wrote to him on 30 June: "I am making enquiries about Weininger's "Sex and Character" which I lent to a man who has lent it to someone else. As soon as I recover it I will send it on to you." (letter in possession of Margaret Wallace). See also Reynolds to Edward Garnett, 18 July 1908, Texas, partially quoted Wright 104.

84 Reynolds to Pinker, 12 June 1908, Northwestern.

85 A West Country Novel, *Daily News*, 11 June 1908.

86 Reynolds to Lane, 12 June 1908, Texas.

87 *ibid.*

88 M.P. Willcocks *The Eyes of the Blind*, Hutchinson 1917 20.

89 *ibid.* 31.

90 *ibid.* 30.

91 *ibid.* 29.

92 *ibid.* 29.

93 *ibid.* 30.

94 Reynolds to Pinker, 1 July 1908, Northwestern.

95 Miss Willcocks at Large, *Bodleian*, January 1910.

96 Reynolds to Lane, 12 June 1908, Texas.

97 Reynolds to Pinker, 19 June 1908, Northwestern.

98 Reynolds to Conrad, 3 July 1908, Texas.

99 *Sidmouth Herald*, 25 April 1908.

100 Reynolds to Lane, 1 May 1908, Texas, partially quoted Wright 102.

101 Reynolds to Edward Garnett, 8 July 1908, Texas, partially quoted Wright 103.

102 *ibid.* This was a postscript written on 9 July.

103 *Sidmouth Herald*, 11 July 1908.

104 Reynolds to Edward Garnett, 18 July 1908, Texas, partially quoted Wright 104.

105 Reynolds to Pinker, 23 August 1908, Northwestern.

106 Reynolds to Edward Garnett, 1 September 1908, Texas.

107 Reynolds to Pinker, 12 June 1908, Northwestern.

108 Reynolds to Edward Garnett, 1 September 1908, Texas.

109 *ibid.*

110 Reynolds to Pinker, 1 July, 23 August and 7 September 1908, Northwestern.

111 Reynolds to Conrad, 3 July 1908, Texas.

112 *ibid.*

113 Reynolds to Pinker, 1 July 1908, Northwestern. On 3 July he told Conrad the photographing had taken place the day before (Reynolds to Conrad, 3 July 1908, Texas). Even allowing for Reynolds' problem with dates, recall of a past event must be assumed more accurate than anticipation of a future.

114 Reynolds to Pinker, 15 July 1908, Northwestern.

115 Reynolds to Edward Garnett, 1 September 1908, Texas. Harold Wright

to Reynolds, 30 June 1908, in possession of Margaret Wallace.
116 Reynolds to Pinker, 23 August 1908, Northwestern.
117 Reynolds to Edward Garnett, 1 September 1908, Texas.
118 Reynolds to Edward Garnett, 7 September 1908, Wright 106, original Texas.
119 *ibid.*
120 *ibid.*
121 Reynolds to Edward Garnett, 20 October 1908, Texas, partially quoted Wright 107.
122 Reynolds to Edward Garnett, 1 September 1908, Texas. The page proofs, which Reynolds later had bound up for his personal use after losing so many copies of the book to "borrowers", are now in the possession of Nigel Chanter.
123 Reynolds to Edward Garnett, 1 September 1908, Texas.
124 Edward Thomas diary, 22, 29 and 30 September 1908, NLW. It was probably Reynolds who brought Burns along to the Mont Blanc after his meeting with him. Constance Garnett to Edward Garnett, [12 September 1908], Eton College Library.
125 Reynolds to Lane, 5 and 13 October 1908, Texas.
126 Reynolds to Pinker, 15 October 1908, Northwestern.
127 Reynolds to Lane, 5 October 1908, Texas. *Devizes and Wiltshire Gazette*, 1 October 1908.
128 Reynolds to Edward Garnett, 14 October 1908, Texas. Reynolds to Pinker, 15 October 1908, Northwestern. Volume now in possession of Nigel Chanter.
129 PMH 68.
130 PMH 238.
131 PMH 315.
132 PMH 89.
133 PMH 257.
134 PMH 219.
135 PMH 120.
136 PMH 205.
137 PMH 142. On the eastern side of the Bedford Hotel, there is still the same feeling today.
138 PMH 277.
139 PMH 83.
140 *A Third-Class Journey*, HT 349.
141 PMH 83.
142 What the Poor Man Thinks, *Christian Commonwealth*, 22 January 1913.
143 Roy Hattersley *Introduction* to *A Poor Man's House*, OUP 1982 x.
144 PMH 7.
145 Reynolds to Edward Carpenter, 25 May 1913, Sheffield.
146 Paul Barker, review of *Into Unknown England, The Times*, 28 June 1976.

Zdzislaw Najder, in his *Joseph Conrad: A Chronicle*, CUP 1983 415, appears to be the first writer publicly to identify Reynolds unequivocally as homosexual. Dr Najder cannot recall the precise source but believes he may have picked up the point from discussions with David Garnett in the 1960s (Zdzislaw Najder to the author, 24 September 1997). Jeffrey Meyers in *Joseph Conrad: A Biography*, Charles Scribner's Sons 1991 225, repeats the information but was only following Najder's lead (Jeffrey Meyers to the author, 24 May 1997).

147 PMH 214.

148 PMH 250.

149 PMH 51.

150 Arnold Bennett (Jacob Tonson), *New Age*, 1 April 1909.

151 Reynolds to Tom Woolley, 25 October 1908, Wright 110.

Chapter 10 The English Review 1908-9

1 Reynolds to Edward Garnett, 14 October 1908, Texas.

2 Reynolds to Edward Garnett, 20 October 1908, Wright 107.

3 Reynolds to R.A. Scott-James, 18 November 1908, Texas.

4 R.A. Scott-James, The Other Side, *Daily News*, 25 November 1908.

5 Reynolds to Tom Woolley, 25 October 1908, Wright 110.

6 Reynolds to Edward Garnett, 1 September 1908, Texas.

7 *Daily Mail*, 24 October 1908.

8 Reynolds to Frederic Chapman, 21 October 1908, Wright 108.

9 Reynolds to Lane, 22 October 1908, Texas.

10 Reynolds to Lane, 25 October 1908, Texas.

11 *Daily Telegraph*, 23 October 1908.

12 Reynolds to Lane, 25 October 1908, Texas.

13 Reynolds to Lane, 27 October 1908, Texas.

14 *ibid.*

15 See, for example, his letter to Edward Garnett of 15 March 1895 on arriving home at his lodgings in Gillingham Street: "I arrived from Brussels about an hour ago and found your letter. I've read it with my hat on, rug over the arm, and umbrella hanging by its tassel-string to my finger. Then I undressed, unpacked and before breaking bread read once more. I could not have had a more charming welcome." (Karl 1, 205).

16 Conrad to Reynolds, [24 October 1908], Karl 4, 134. Reynolds report to Lane on 27 October (Texas) "I have had a fine letter from Conrad" makes this dating certain. Karl has omitted a "that" from the first line; and has misread "that torch" as "thy torch" in the last.

17 Galsworthy to Reynolds, 11 February 1909, Wallace.

18 *Daily Mail*, 24 October 1908.

19 Thomas Seccombe, From a Poor Man's House, *Readers' Review*, November

1908.
20 Reynolds to Lane, 25 October 1908, Texas.
21 M.P.Willcocks, The Wayfaring Man, *Literary World and Reader*, 15 November 1908.
22 David Garnett to Edward Garnett, undated, Eton College Library.
23 Edward Thomas diary, 21 October 1908, NLW. He must have been reading from a borrowed copy since two days later he asked St John Adcock of the *Bookman* for a review copy of his own (Edward Thomas to St John Adcock, 23 October 1908, Bodleian Library).
24 Edward Thomas diary, 23-25 October 1908, NLW.
25 Edward Thomas diary, 3 and 8 November 1908, NLW. The 1800 words he wrote for the *Bookman* on 8 November is the only writing for that periodical he recorded around that period and is almost certainly his review of Reynolds' book.
26 Edward Thomas, A Poor Man's House, *Bookman*, December 1908.
27 John Buchan, A Poor Man's House, *Westminster Gazette*, 21 November 1908.
28 *ibid.*
29 Reynolds to Spender, 11 March 1909, under cover of Reynolds to Pinker, 14 March 1909, Northwestern.
30 Arnold Bennett (Jacob Tonson), *New Age*, 19 November 1908.
31 Edward Thomas, A Poor Man's House, *Bookman*, December 1908.
32 M.P.Willcocks, The Wayfaring Man, *Literary World and Reader*, 15 November 1908.
33 *ibid.*
34 *Spectator*, 14 November 1908. The review may have been written by the editor, St Loe Strachey, shortly to become Reynolds' friend.
35 Galsworthy to Reynolds, 13 April 1909, Wallace.
36 Charles Wright to Reynolds, 22 November 1908, Wright 111 footnote.
37 Reynolds to Charles Wright, 26 November 1908, Wright 112.
38 C.F.G. Masterman, The Thoughts of the Poor, *Nation*, 14 November 1908. Masterman repeated much of this article in *The Condition of England*, Methuen 1909 115.
39 Ford Madox Ford *Return to Yesterday*, Carcanet 1999 243.
40 Samuel Hynes *The Edwardian Turn of Mind*, Pimlico 1991 68.
41 *ibid.* 71.
42 PMH 320. It was a problem he was to address more scientifically in his psycho-economics articles, *Wealth and Life*.
43 Reynolds to Lane, 9 September 1909, Texas.
44 Macmillans to Pinker, 4 August 1910, Add.Mss.55499.
45 Reynolds to Edward Garnett, 14 October 1908, Texas.
46 Reynolds to Pinker, 15 October 1908, Northwestern.
47 Reynolds to Pinker, 19 October 1908, Northwestern. Reynolds to Lane, 25 October 1908, Texas.

48 Reynolds to Edward Garnett, 14 October 1908, Texas.
49 Reynolds to Edward Garnett, 20 October 1908, Texas, partially quoted Wright 107.
50 Reynolds to Lane, 27 October 1908, Texas. Reynolds to Herbert Jenkins, 30 October 1908, Texas.
51 Reynolds to Edward Garnett, 20 October 1908, Texas. His mother in fact died of tuberculosis and a deteriorating *liver.*
52 Reynolds to Lane, 27 October 1908, Texas. Edward Thomas diary, 3 November 1908, NLW.
53 C.F.G. Masterman, Stephen Reynolds, *Nation*, 22 February 1919.
54 *London Gazette*, 18 December 1908, copy in PRO, MAF 41/443.
55 Reynolds to Masterman, 16 December 1908, Wright 114.
56 C.F.G. Masterman, Stephen Reynolds, *Nation*, 22 February 1919.
57 In a letter the following month, Conrad wrote "Remember me in real friendly terms to Bob" (Conrad to Reynolds, 18 December 1908, Karl 4, 173). Alternatively, it is possible that they visited Conrad the weekend of 14/15 November on their return from France.
58 *Two Fishers Abroad*, AS 269.
59 *ibid.* 272.
60 *ibid.* 273.
61 "I shall demand a detailed account of the first journey to Paris and the second to Boulogne when I come down" – Harold Wright to Reynolds, 20 November 1908, in possession of Margaret Wallace. They appear to have spent at least a week abroad and were back home in Sidmouth by 16 November.
62 *Two Fishers Abroad*, AS 285.
63 Conrad to Ford Madox Ford, 23 October 1923, G. Jean-Aubry, *Joseph Conrad: Life and Letters*, Heinemann 1927 vol.2 323.
64 Hueffer to R.A. Scott-James, undated but spring 1910, R.A. Scott-James, Ford Madox Ford When He Was Hueffer, *South Atlantic Quarterly* 57, Spring 1958 245.
65 Arthur Mizener, *The Saddest Story: A Biography of Ford Madox Ford,* Carroll & Graf 1985 161.
66 Enclosure to Seccombe to Hueffer, undated, Cornell University Library, Ithaca, New York.
67 Douglas Goldring *South Lodge: Reminiscences of Violet Hunt, Ford Madox Ford and the English Review Circle*, Constable 1943 24.
68 Reynolds to Herbert Jenkins, 17 November 1908, Texas.
69 Edward Thomas diary, 24 November 1908, NLW.
70 Marwood to Reynolds, 26 January 1909, quoted Osborne 139. Reynolds to Marwood, 29 January 1909, transcribed Philippa Powys, Mappowder.
71 Edward Thomas diary, 25 November 1908, NLW.
72 Reynolds to Edward Garnett, 29 November 1908, Texas, partially quoted Wright 113.

73 Reynolds to St John Adcock, 14 December 1908, MS Eng lett d 470 fol 11, Bodleian Library.
74 Reynolds to Edward Garnett, 7 September 1908, Wright 106.
75 *English Review*, December 1908 162.
76 Wells to Bennett, [December 1908], Harris Wilson (edited) *Arnold Bennett and H.G. Wells: A Record of a Personal and Literary Friendship*, Hart-Davis 1960 160.
77 Wells to Bennett, December 1897, *ibid.* 40.
78 Bennett to Wells, 7 January 1909, *ibid.* 160.
79 Edward Thomas diary, 1 December 1908, NLW.
80 Reynolds to Pinker, 3 December 1908 (first letter), Northwestern.
81 Reynolds to Pinker, 7 December 1908, Northwestern.
82 Reynolds to Pinker, 3 December 1908 (second letter), Northwestern.
83 Miss Thomas (Hueffer's secretary) to Wells, 31 March 1909, Illinois. For a detailed discussion of the Huefferian economics of the *Review*, *see* Mizener *op.cit.*157-161.
84 Reynolds to Pinker, 7 December 1908, Northwestern.
85 Reynolds to Pinker, 7,9 and 11 December 1908, Northwestern.
86 Conrad to Hueffer, [7 December 1908], Karl 4, 158.
87 Reynolds to Pinker, 7 December 1908, Northwestern. Reynolds to Hueffer, 10 January 1909, Wright 115. We do not know with whom he stayed on these later visits to Devizes – possibly with Ada Bennett at the College or, more likely, with Aunt Jane at Prospect Rise. Much later, when he had a regular income, and a boy-friend, he would stay at the Bear.
88 Reynolds to Lane, 11 December 1908, Texas.
89 Reynolds to Pinker, 18 December 1908, Northwestern.
90 Conrad to Reynolds, 18 December 1908, Karl 4, 172.
91 Reynolds to Lane, 1 January 1909, Texas.
92 Sandra Kemp, Charlotte Mitchell, David Trotter *Edwardian Fiction: An Oxford Companion*, OUP 1997 340.
93 Reynolds to Edward Garnett, 29 November 1908, Wright 113. Wright had written to Reynolds the week before: "By the way, the undergraduates, whom you hate, are very enthusiastic about the book. One friend of mine, Ramsey, is reading a paper upon it to a select society; another is advertising it in all directions and making it his standing Christmas present". (Harold Wright to Reynolds, 20 November 1908, in possession of Margaret Wallace).
94 J.C.Squire (Solomon Eagle), *Books in General*, Third Series, Hodder & Stoughton 1921 154.
95 *Western Morning News*, 15 February 1919.
96 Reynolds to Henry Maurice, 13 February 1917, Wright 237.
97 SS 279.
98 *See*, for example, his unpublished manuscript "Over the Bar: A Story of

the Devon Fisher Folk by Ambrose Seabert", Pursey, 1926, which makes Philippa Powys' "Further West", Texas, look like a work of art.

99 Note on envelope 1978, Box 26, Pursey.

100 *A Poor Man's House*, OUP 1982 xiv. And in later years he was at pains to point out the inevitably restricted success of *A Poor Man's House* in portraying the minds of the poor: "The educated man, howsoever he plunge into the life of the uneducated, is almost bound, as a condition of making himself plain, to climb out on the bank, to relapse into his education, to express with more or less falsity the one life in terms of another." (The Dead End, *New Weekly*, 21 March 1914).

101 C.F.G. Masterman, Stephen Reynolds, *Nation*, 22 February 1919.

102 Stephen Reynolds at Seacombe, *Bodleian*, March 1909.

103 Reynolds to Lane, 28 February 1909, Texas.

104 Douglas Goldring *op.cit.* 35.

105 *ibid.* 32.

106 Reynolds had written to Lane on 1 January 1909 from Holland Park Avenue just before setting off for Conrad's: "It's rather an ironic comment on all my good reviews that the P.M.'s H. doesn't seem to have helped me one bit in getting rid of my short stories, even those on same subject" (Texas).

107 Conrad to Pinker, [5 January 1909], Karl 4, 182. Karl is tentative about the dating, but this is clearly written just after Reynolds' weekend visit. Conrad softened the asperity of all the preachifying by arranging to send Reynolds a signed copy of *The Nigger of the Narcissus* (Conrad to Pinker, [early January 1909], Karl 4, 183). When George Macmillan borrowed it three years later, he remarked: "The author's inscription in this copy is a thing to be proud of" (George Macmillan to Reynolds, 1 February 1912, Add.Mss.55505), to which Reynolds replied: "My copy of the Nigger is my chiefest treasure of all my books, most of which I don't mind chucking about the room; for I haven't any sense of a book qua book." (Reynolds to George Macmillan, 7 February 1912, Add.Mss.54965).

108 Harold Wright to Reynolds, 11 January 1909, in possession of Margaret Wallace.

109 Reynolds to Hueffer, 10 January 1909, Wright 115.

110 Reynolds to Pinker, 10 January 1909, Northwestern, partially quoted Wright 114. The reference to "reversion of the editorship" is indication that Hueffer was grooming Reynolds to succeed him in the longer term.

111 Reynolds to Strachey, 17 January 1909, HL.

112 Ford Madox Ford *Return to Yesterday*, Carcanet 1999 290.

113 Marwood to Reynolds, 26 January 1909, quoted Osborne 139.

114 Reynolds to Marwood, 29 January 1909, transcribed Philippa Powys, Mappowder.

115 Conrad to Reynolds, 30 January 1909, Karl 4, 191. Karl has misread

"horrid" as "harried", and duplicated the error on page xxxiii.
116 Reynolds to Herbert Jenkins, 31 January 1909, Texas.
117 Reynolds to Pinker, 8 February 1909, Northwestern.
118 Reynolds to Edward Garnett, 8 February 1909, Texas.
119 Conrad to Pinker, [?19 March 1908], Karl 4, 60.
120 Reynolds to Pinker, 8 February 1909, Northwestern
121 Conrad to Reynolds, [14 February 1909], Karl 4, 96. Karl misreads "bigger" as "better".
122 *ibid.* Karl places this undated letter in the previous year but it clearly follows Reynolds letter of 8 February 1909 to Pinker with the McClure news. The reference to one volume published is, of course, to *A Poor Man's House*. Karl omits "quite" from the tenth sentence.
123 Reynolds to Lane, 12 February 1909, Texas. Reynolds to Herbert Jenkins, 16 and 31 January, 14 February 1909, Texas.
124 Reynolds to Pinker, 5 March 1909, Northwestern.
125 Reynolds to Pinker, 10 March 1909, Northwestern.
126 Reynolds to Pinker, 5 March 1909, Northwestern.
127 Reynolds to Pinker, 16 February 1909, Northwestern.
128 Ford Madox Ford *op.cit.*290.
129 Arnold Bennett (Jacob Tonson), *New Age*, 14 January 1909.
130 Reynolds to Pinker, 16 February 1909, Northwestern. *Wiltshire Gazette*, 18 February 1909.
131 Reynolds to Lane, 28 February 1909, Texas.
132 Conrad to Reynolds, 6 March 1909, Karl 4, 199.
133 Reynolds to Herbert Jenkins, 9 March 1909, Texas.
134 Reynolds to Pinker, 10 March 1909, Northwestern.
135 Conrad to Reynolds, [12/19 March 1909], Karl 4, 204.
136 Reynolds to Pinker, 31 March 1909, Northwestern.
137 Douglas Goldring *Reputations: Essays in Criticism*, Chapman & Hall 1920 224.
138 Galsworthy to Reynolds, 13 April 1909, Wallace.
139 Conrad to Reynolds, 14 April 1909, Karl 4, 215.
140 Savill was declining himself; he died on 10 January 1910, aged 53. Conrad had only met Mackintosh, a friend of Perceval Gibbon, during the move on 14 February from Someries to Aldington when Mackintosh had driven him in his car.
141 Reynolds to Edward Garnett, 30 March 1909, Texas, partially quoted Wright 120.
142 Reynolds to Pinker, 8 March 1909, Northwestern.
143 Reynolds to Marwood, 17 May 1909, quoted Osborne 142.
144 Reynolds to Hueffer, 29 April 1909, Cornell University Library, Ithaca, New York.
145 Reynolds to Marwood, 17 May 1909, quoted Osborne 142. Reynolds to Pinker, 10 May 1909, Northwestern.

146 Reynolds to Pinker, 10 May 1909, Northwestern.
147 Reynolds to Lane, 10 May 1909, Texas.
148 Reynolds to Strachey, 8 May 1909, HL.
149 Reynolds to Pinker, 10 May 1909, Northwestern, partially quoted Wright 121.
150 *ibid.*
151 Reynolds to Edward Garnett, 17 May 1909, Texas, partially quoted Wright 123.
152 Reynolds to Edward Garnett, 11 May 1909, Texas, partially quoted Wright 122.
153 Reynolds to Edward Garnett, 17 May 1909, Texas, partially quoted Wright 123.
154 Reynolds to Edward Garnett, 18 June 1909, Texas.
155 Hueffer to Pinker, 21 May 1909, Huntington Library, San Marino, California.
156 Reynolds to Marwood, 24 May 1909, quoted Osborne 142.
157 Reynolds to Pinker, 24 May 1909, quoted Osborne 143.
158 Reynolds to Pinker, 26 May 1909, Northwestern.
159 Pinker to Reynolds, 27 May 1909, quoted Osborne 143.
160 Reynolds to Pinker, 28 May 1909, Northwestern.
161 Reynolds to Herbert Jenkins, 5 June 1909, Texas. See also Reynolds to Herbert Jenkins, 28 and 30 May, 4,8 and 24 June 1909, Texas.
162 Reynolds to Herbert Jenkins, 30 May 1909, Texas.
163 Darley, Cumberland & Co. to Pinker, 13 July 1909, Northwestern. Reynolds to Pinker, 17 July 1909, Northwestern.
164 Darley, Cumberland & Co. to Pinker, 26 July 1909, Northwestern.
165 Conrad to Reynolds, [?31 May 1909], Karl 4, 225.
166 Conrad to Reynolds, 31 July 1909, Karl 4, 264.
167 Conrad to Reynolds, 7 August 1909, Karl 4, 268. In the ninth sentence Karl has misread "with our" as "without".
168 Reynolds to Edward Garnett, 17 May 1909, Wright 123.
169 Philippa Powys diary, 18 and 25 June 1909, Mappowder.
170 Louis Marlow *Welsh Ambassadors: Powys Lives and Letters*, Village Press 1975 2. Kenneth Hopkins in *The Powys Brothers* (Warren House Press, 1972 147) attributes this quotation to Llewelyn. For the best brief biography of Katie, see Alyse Gregory, Notes on C.E.P.P., *Powys Review* No.20 1987 66.
171 Philippa Powys diary, 20-29 February 1908, Mappowder.
172 Philippa Powys diary, 5 July 1909, Mappowder.
173 Philippa Powys "Phoenix *or* Driven Passion", third version, unpublished typescript, Texas 8. This version was probably completed in 1927 or 1928, since the second is dated 1927. A fragment was published in *The Dial*, New York, LXXXV No.2, August 1928.
174 Philippa Powys diary, 5 July 1909, Mappowder.

175 "Phoenix" *op.cit.*12.
176 Philippa Powys diary, 5 July 1909, Mappowder.
177 Philippa Powys diary, 9 July 1909, Mappowder.
178 "Phoenix" *op.cit.*12a and 14b.
179 Philippa Powys diary, 9 July 1909, Mappowder.
180 Reynolds to Edward Garnett, 18 June 1909, Texas. Reynolds to Lane, 15 July 1909, Texas.
181 Philippa Powys diary, 10 July 1909, Mappowder.
182 Philippa Powys diary, 13-17 July 1909, Mappowder.
183 Reynolds to Edward Garnett, 18 June 1909, Texas.
184 Reynolds to Lane, 15 July 1909, Texas.
185 Arnold Bennett (Jacob Tonson), *New Age*, 19 November 1908.
186 Reynolds to Herbert Jenkins, 25 May 1909, Texas.
187 Reynolds to Herbert Jenkins, 8 June 1909, Texas.
188 Reynolds to Herbert Jenkins, 10 June 1909, Texas.
189 Reynolds to Herbert Jenkins, 10 and 24 June 1909, Texas.
190 Wright xv.
191 Reynolds to Lane, 4 August 1909, Texas.
192 Reynolds to Herbert Jenkins, 18 August 1909, Texas.
193 Enclosure to Reynolds to Reginald Page, 9 September 1909, quoted Osborne 150.
194 Reynolds to Lane, 9 September 1909, Texas.
195 Reynolds to Lane, 25 September 1909, Texas.
196 Reynolds to Lane, 6 September 1909, Texas.
197 Reynolds to Pinker, 18 August 1909, Northwestern.
198 Reynolds to Pinker, 10 September 1909, Northwestern.
199 Reynolds to Lane, 12 September 1909, Texas.
200 Volume in possession of Nigel Chanter.
201 Reynolds to Pinker, 8 August 1909, Northwestern, partially quoted Wright 124.
202 Reynolds to Lane, 8 August 1909, Texas.
203 Elizabeth von Arnim to Reynolds, [9 August 1909], Wallace.
204 Reynolds to Lane, 9 September 1909, Texas.
205 Elizabeth von Arnim to Reynolds, 18 September 1909, Wallace.
206 Conrad to Reynolds, [17 September 1909], Karl 4, 274. Conrad would have received his copy of the *Mountain* on 16 September and this is a preliminary thank you after a first quick browse through.
207 *Athenaeum*, 16 October 1909.
208 Edward Garnett, Satire and Realism, *Nation*, 25 September 1909.
209 Reynolds to Edward Garnett, [26 September 1909], Texas.
210 Advertisement in *Spectator*, 16 October 1909. Reynolds told Lane (25 September 1909, Texas): "I should suggest printing damnatory as well as laudatory quotes in the advertisements". Lane took care that the latter should greatly outnumber the former.

211 *Times Literary Supplement*, 30 September 1909.
212 *Westminster Gazette*, 2 October 1909.
213 *Devizes and Wiltshire Gazette*, 7 October 1909.
214 *Daily News*, 21 September 1909.
215 Reynolds to A.G. Gardiner, 26 September 1909, transcribed Philippa Powys, Mappowder.
216 Arnold Bennett (Jacob Tonson), *New Age*, 19 November 1908.
217 Arnold Bennett diary, 8 April 1909, Berg Collection, New York Public Library.
218 Arnold Bennett diary,12 May 1911, Berg Collection, New York Public Library.
219 Arnold Bennett diary, 20 April 1909, Berg Collection, New York Public Library.
220 Arnold Bennett (Jacob Tonson), *New Age*, 23 September 1909.
221 Reynolds to Pinker, 18 August 1909, Northwestern.
222 *Bookman*, October 1909.
223 Reynolds to Perceval Gibbon, 8 October 1909, Wright 127.
224 Reynolds to J.F. Drew, 3 September 1909, Wright 126.
225 *Devizes and Wiltshire Gazette*, 7 October 1909.
226 Interview with Stephen Wiltshire, 22 May 1997.
227 HM 309.
228 Reynolds to Herbert Jenkins, 24 June 1909, Texas.
229 Reynolds to George Macmillan, 1 July 1912, Add.Mss.54965.
230 George Macmillan to Reynolds, 2 July 1912, Add.Mss.55507.

Chapter 11 Alongshore 1909–10

1 Reynolds to William Blackwood, 10 March 1910, Wright 129.
2 Reynolds to Pinker, 19 June 1908, Northwestern.
3 Reynolds to Conrad, 3 July 1908, Texas. Reynolds to Edward Garnett, 14 October 1908, Texas.
4 Reynolds to Pinker, 16 February 1909, Northwestern.
5 *A Poor Man's House*, OUP 1982 xiii.
6 Reynolds to Edward Garnett, 4 April 1907, Wright 76.
7 Reynolds to Edward Garnett, 11 May 1909, Texas, partially quoted Wright 122.
8 Reynolds to Edward Garnett, 18 June 1909, Texas. Reynolds to Lane, 12 September 1909, Texas. Harold Wright saw the synopsis in July and declared it "rouses one's interest" (Harold Wright to Reynolds, [July 1909], in possession of Margaret Wallace).
9 Reynolds to Pinker, 6 September 1909, Northwestern.
10 Frederic Chapman to Lane, [early June 1908], Texas.
11 Reynolds to William Blackwood, 10 March 1910, Wright 129.

12 Reynolds to Pinker, 30 December 1909, Northwestern.
13 Reynolds to Edward Garnett, 23 November 1910, Texas.
14 Reynolds to Pinker, 21 November 1909, Northwestern.
15 Reynolds to Pinker, 5 June 1910, Northwestern.
16 Conrad to Reynolds, 27 November 1909, Karl 4, 293.
17 Reynolds to Pinker, 28 August and 16 October 1910, Northwestern. But as late as March 1911, he still had the novel firmly in his sights. He wrote to Pinker: "I see the *Times Weekly Ed.* has not dropped its serial after all. When I can see the serialization of that novel clear, I expect I shall start it, and I doubt if I shall before. It wants just that stimulus to overcome the initial funk of a long tough piece of work, and set one's mind easy to do it." (Reynolds to Pinker, 25 March 1911, Northwestern).
18 Reynolds to Edward Garnett, 29 March 1907, Texas.
19 Coranian Journal 43, Texas.
20 Reynolds to Edward Garnett, 20 May and 1 June 1907, Texas.
21 Reynolds to Pinker, 19 and 24 September 1907, Northwestern. PMH 228.
22 *Country Life*, 19 September 1908.
23 Reynolds to Pinker, 14 March 1909, Northwestern. This sketch seems never to have appeared in magazine form.
24 Reynolds to Hueffer, 10 January 1909, Wright 116
25 Reynolds to Pinker, 8 February 1909, Northwestern.
26 Reynolds to Strachey, 23 February 1909, HL. Reynolds to Pinker, 14 March 1909, Northwestern.
27 Reynolds to Spender, 11 March 1909, under cover of Reynolds to Pinker, 14 March 1909, Northwestern.
28 Spender to Reynolds, 13 March 1909, under cover of Reynolds to Pinker, 14 March 1909, Northwestern.
29 Reynolds to Pinker, 14 March 1909, Northwestern.
30 Pinker to Reynolds, 16 March 1909, quoted Osborne 145.
31 Reynolds to Pinker, 18 March 1909, Northwestern.
32 Reynolds to Pinker, 14 March 1909, Northwestern. Reynolds to Strachey, 14 March 1909, Wright 119.
33 Reynolds to Pinker, 14 March 1909, Northwestern.
34 *ibid.*
35 AS 7. Reynolds to Herbert Jenkins, 5 June 1909, Texas.
36 Reynolds to Pinker, 8 August 1909, Northwestern.
37 Reynolds to Pinker, 18 August 1909, Northwestern.
38 Reynolds to Lane, 25 September 1909, Texas.
39 Reynolds to Pinker, 28 September 1909, Northwestern.
40 Reynolds to Pinker, 30 December 1909, Northwestern.
41 Reynolds to Conrad, 27 November 1909, Karl 4, 293.
42 Edward Thomas diary, 9 November 1909, NLW. Reynolds to Lane, 11 November 1909, quoted Osborne 153. Reynolds to Pinker, 21 November 1909, Northwestern.

43 AS 293.
44 A Herring Haul in a French Steam Drifter, *Blackwoods Magazine*, May 1910.
45 Reynolds to Lane, 6, 9 and 12 September 1909, Texas.
46 Reynolds to Lane, 12 September 1909, Texas.
47 Reynolds to Lane, 25 September 1909, Texas.
48 Reynolds to Pinker, 21 November 1909, Northwestern.
49 Reynolds to Lane, 11 November 1909, quoted Osborne 153.
50 Reynolds to Pinker, 21 November 1909, Northwestern.
51 Pinker to Reynolds, 23 November 1909, quoted Osborne 154.
52 Reynolds to Pinker, 21 November 1909, Northwestern. Lane to Reynolds, 24 November 1909, quoted Osborne 154.
53 Reynolds to Lane, 7 December 1909, quoted Osborne 155.
54 Lane to Reynolds, 24 November 1909, quoted Osborne 154. Reynolds to Pinker, 7 December 1909, Northwestern.
55 Reynolds to Pinker, 7 December 1909, Northwestern.
56 Galsworthy to Reynolds, 8 December 1909, Wallace.
57 Conrad to Reynolds, 14 December 1909, Karl 4, 296.
58 Reynolds to Lane, 16 December 1909, Texas.
59 Reynolds to R.D.Mackintosh, 8 December 1909, Osborne 144. R.D. Mackintosh to Reynolds, 12 December 1909, Osborne 145.
60 Reynolds to Lane, 16 December 1909, Texas.
61 Reynolds to Edward Garnett, 23 December 1909, Texas.
62 Reynolds to Pinker, 30 December 1909, Northwestern.
63 Edward Thomas diary, 11 January 1910, NLW. Reynolds to Strachey, 2 February 1910, HL. Reynolds to Lane, 25 February 1910, Texas.
64 Reynolds to Lane, 25 February 1910, Texas.
65 Reynolds to Lane, 10 April 1910, Texas.
66 Reynolds to Pinker, 12 April 1910, Northwestern.
67 By Land and Sea, *Daily Chronicle*, 13 April 1910.
68 Reynolds to Lane, 15 April 1910, Texas.
69 Reynolds to Lane, 18 April 1910, Texas.
70 Reynolds to Edward Garnett, 27 May 1910, Texas, partially quoted Wright 131.
71 Reynolds to Pinker, 2 June 1910, Northwestern.
72 Reynolds to Lane, 2 June 1910, Texas. The letter was intentionally provocative with a tactical aim, as Reynolds told Pinker: "It was meant precisely to *border* upon the indiscreet. I had tried such suavity as I'm capable of, and thought it might be well to blow off and see what happened" (Reynolds to Pinker, 5 June 1910, Northwestern).
73 Reynolds to Pinker, 5 June 1910, Northwestern.
74 Reynolds to Pinker, 10 June 1910, Northwestern.
75 Reynolds to Lane, 10 June 1910, Texas.
76 Reynolds to Pinker, 5 June 1910, Northwestern.

77 *ibid.*
78 Hugh Walpole to Reynolds, [31 October 1910], Wallace.
79 Hugh Walpole diary, 20 June 1910, Texas.
80 Reynolds to Lane, 22 June 1910, Texas.
81 Conrad to Reynolds, 26 June 1910, Karl 4, 342.
82 Reynolds to Frederick Macmillan, 2 July 1910, Add.Mss.54965, partially quoted Wright 136.
83 Reynolds to Pinker, 8 August 1909, Northwestern, partially quoted Wright 124. Reynolds to J.F. Drew, 3 September 1909, Wright 125.
84 *Puffin Home*, HT 320.
85 *ibid.*
86 J.F. Drew to Reynolds, 29 November 1909, quoted Osborne 164. AS 323.
87 AS 324.
88 Reynolds to Edward Garnett, 27 May 1910, Texas. Reynolds to Pinker, 2 June 1910, Northwestern. *Puffin Home*, HT 339.
89 Reynolds to Edward Garnett, 27 May 1910, Texas.
90 Puffin Home, *Blackwoods Magazine*, October 1910. Fisherman and Motorboat, *Daily News*, 5 July 1910.
91 Osborne 167.
92 Share Fishermen and the Insurance Act, *The Times*, 27 May 1912.
93 Reynolds to J.F. Drew, 21 October 1909, quoted Osborne 164.
94 Reynolds to J.F. Drew, 3 September 1909, Wright 126.
95 Reynolds to Pinker, 2 June 1910, Northwestern.
96 Philippa Powys diary, 3 June 1910, Mappowder.
97 *ibid.*
98 *ibid.*
99 *ibid.*
100 Edward Garnett to Galsworthy, 21 September 1910 and [23 September 1910], H.V. Marrot *The Life and Letters of John Galsworthy*, Heinemann 1935 298 and 301.
101 He told Hudson of it and asked what he thought of that stretch of coast. Hudson replied: "I really can't remember all that cliff between Sidmouth and Beer; 'tis a long way and though I've walked from one to the other I went by the road I imagine, and only saw all the cliff from Branscombe to Beer and Seton [sic]" (W.H. Hudson to Edward Garnett, 11 October 1910, *Letters from W.H. Hudson to Edward Garnett*, Dent 1925 113).
102 Edward Garnett to Galsworthy, 16 November 1910, H.V. Marrot *The Life and Letters of John Galsworthy*, Heinemann 1935 305.
103 Reynolds to Pinker, 20 October 1910, Northwestern.
104 Reynolds to Pinker, 23 October 1910, Northwestern.
105 Proceedings of the Thirty-Third Annual Meeting of the Library Association, *Library Association Record*, October 1910 595.
106 Reynolds to Frederick Macmillan, 11 September 1910, Add.Mss.54965

107 Reynolds to Frederick Macmillan, 27 June 1910, Reading 55/198. Reynolds to Frederick Macmillan, 11 July 1910, Add.Mss.54965. Harold Wright, on a fortnight's holiday in Sidmouth, read the proofs for him and returned them *via* Tom with whom he was staying. He thought it "a gorgeous book" (Harold Wright to Reynolds, [July 1909], in possession of Margaret Wallace).
108 Macmillans to Pinker, 4 August 1910, Add.Mss.55499.
109 Macmillans to Pinker, 12 July 1910, Add.Mss.55499.
110 Reynolds to Pinker, 6 July 1910, Northwestern.
111 Reynolds to Pinker, 16 July 1910, Northwestern.
112 Memorandum of Agreement Reynolds/Macmillan, 24 August 1910, Macmillan Archive, Basingstoke.
113 *ibid.* clause 5. Macmillans to Pinker, 4 August 1910, Add.Mss.55499.
114 Reynolds to Pinker, 28 August 1910, Northwestern.
115 Reynolds to Frederick Macmillan, 28 August 1910, Add.Mss.54965.
116 Reynolds to Pinker, 13 August 1910, Northwestern.
117 Reynolds to Frederick Macmillan, 2 July 1910, Add.Mss.54965. Frederick Macmillan to Reynolds, 4 July 1910, Add.Mss.55499.
118 Reynolds to Frederick Macmillan, 27 July 1910, Add.Mss.54965.
119 Reynolds to Frederick Macmillan, 3 October 1910, Add.Mss.54965.
120 Reynolds to Macmillans, 3 August 1910, Add.Mss.54965.
121 Frederick Macmillan to Reynolds, 4 August 1910, Add.Mss.55499.
122 Reynolds to Frederick Macmillan, 12 October 1910, Add.Mss.54965. Frederick Macmillan to Reynolds, 13 October 1910, Add.Mss.55500.
123 Reynolds to Frederick Macmillan, 12 October 1910, Add.Mss.54965.
124 Frederick Macmillan to Reynolds, 13 October 1910, Add.Mss.55500.
125 Reynolds to Frederick Macmillan, 17 October 1910, Add.Mss.54965. He meant he didn't begin to live until after his breakdown of 1903 – the watershed of his life.
126 See Reynolds to J.F. Drew, 3 September 1909, Wright 126.
127 AS v.
128 Reynolds to Frederick Macmillan, 2 July 1910, Add.Mss.54965.
129 AS xiv.
130 Reynolds to Lane, 12 September 1909, Texas.
131 AS 12.
132 AS 126.
133 AS 27.
134 AS 251.
135 AS 195.
136 AS 202.
137 AS 150.
138 AS 75.
139 AS 76.
140 AS 81.

141 AS 83.
142 AS 90.
143 AS 92
144 AS 95.
145 AS 218.
146 Reynolds to Frederick Macmillan, 17 October 1910, Add.Mss.54965.
147 *ibid.*
148 Arnold Bennett (Jacob Tonson), *New Age*, 27 October 1910.
149 *Daily News*, 24 October 1910.
150 *Spectator*, 19 November 1910.
151 *Nation*, 19 November 1910.
152 Reynolds to Edward Garnett, 23 November 1910, Texas.
153 Reynolds to John Burns, 20 October 1910, Add.Mss.46301. Burns drafted his reply on the letter sheet.
154 Reynolds to J.E.H. Balfour, 24 November 1910, Sidmouth Museum.
155 Reynolds to Frederick Macmillan, 26 November 1910, Add.Mss.54965.
156 Frederick Macmillan to Reynolds, 28 November 1910, Add.Mss.55501.
157 Hugh Walpole to Reynolds, [31 October 1910], Wallace.
158 *Standard*, 18 November 1910.
159 Conrad to Reynolds, 27 October 1910, Karl 4, 382.
160 *ibid.*
161 D.H. Lawrence to Edward Garnett, 17 December 1912, James T. Boulton (edited), *The Letters of D.H. Lawrence, Vol 1 Sept 1901 – May 1913*, CUP 1979 488. Aldous Huxley, editing the first Lawrence letters (Heinemann, 1932 84), incorrectly assigns this one to 19 December.

Chapter 12 Seems So! 1909-11

1 Conrad to Galsworthy, [15 November 1909], Karl 4, 289. He was speaking, in fact, of the Liberal Government, which was revolutionary enough for him.
2 SS xvi
3 *Spectator*, 14 November 1908. Reynolds was particularly proud of the *Spectator*'s attention. He told Herbert Jenkins: "The *Spectator* is going to give the book a 2-col. article. That will add power to your elbow, won't it? If the elbow wants it, that is . . . ." (Reynolds to Herbert Jenkins, 30 October 1908, Texas). See also Reynolds to Herbert Jenkins, 17 November 1908, Texas.
4 Reynolds to Strachey, 21 December 1908, HL.
5 *ibid.*
6 Strachey to Reynolds, 23 December 1908, HL.
7 Strachey to Reynolds, 20 January 1909, HL.
8 *ibid.*

9 Reynolds to Strachey, 14 February 1909, HL.
10 What Workmen Think of Conscription, *Nation*, 13 February 1909.
11 SS 13.
12 SS xiii.
13 SS 14.
14 SS 15.
15 SS 17.
16 *ibid.*
17 SS 15.
18 SS 16.
19 SS 20.
20 Reynolds to Strachey, 23 February 1909, HL.
21 Reynolds to Strachey, 7 March 1909, HL.
22 Reynolds to Strachey, 23 February 1909, HL.
23 Reynolds to Strachey, 7 March 1909, HL.
24 SS 22.
25 SS 24.
26 SS 26.
27 Reynolds to Pinker, 8 March 1909, Northwestern.
28 Reynolds to Strachey, 14 March 1909, Wright 119.
29 Strachey to Reynolds, 16 March 1909, HL.
30 Reynolds to Pinker, 18 March 1909, Northwestern.
31 Reynolds to Edward Garnett, 30 March 1909, Texas, partially quoted Wright 120.
32 Reynolds to Strachey, 14 March 1909, Wright 119; and 7 March 1909, HL. Apart from his evening lectures in Devizes, Reynolds' teaching experience was, of course, confined to his time at Devizes College 1904-5.
33 Reynolds to Strachey, 10 April 1909, HL, partially quoted Wright 121.
34 *ibid.*
35 Strachey to Reynolds, 13 April 1909, HL.
36 Seems So! Education, *Spectator*, 24 July 1909.
37 Reynolds to Strachey, 10 April 1909, HL.
38 *ibid.*
39 Reynolds to Pinker, 31 March 1909, Northwestern.
40 Reynolds to Strachey, 8 May 1909, HL.
41 Reynolds to Strachey, 10 April 1909, HL.
42 *Spectator*, 5 June 1909.
43 Reynolds to Strachey, 5 June 1909, HL.
44 *Spectator*, 12 June 1909.
45 *ibid.*
46 Reynolds to Strachey, 5 June 1909, HL.
47 Reynolds to Pinker, 10 May 1909, Northwestern.
48 Reynolds to Strachey, 8 May 1909, HL.
49 Reynolds to Lane, 10 May 1909, Texas.

50 Reynolds to Edward Garnett, 11 May 1909, Texas, partially quoted Wright 122.
51 Reynolds to Edward Garnett, 25 August 1907, partially quoted Wright 96.
52 Reynolds to Strachey, 14 March 1909, Wright 119.
53 *ibid.*
54 Reynolds to Edward Garnett, 17 May 1909, Texas, partially quoted Wright 123.
55 The original title appears in the pre-publication manuscript of *Seems So!*, Westcountry Studies Library, Exeter, MSX 820.2/REY. Reynolds presented the manuscript to Exeter Public Library a month before publication as part of a campaign to preserve such documents – see *Devon and Exeter Gazette*, 3 October 1911. Reynolds to Lane, 25 September 1909, Texas.
56 Reynolds to G.W.Prothero, 5 October 1909, Wright 126.
57 Reynolds to Pinker, 21 November 1909, Northwestern.
58 What the Poor Want, *Quarterly Review*, January 1910.
59 SS 268.
60 SS 288.
61 SS 284.
62 SS 297.
63 SS 320.
64 The Poor and Education, *Spectator*, 22 January 1910.
65 Reynolds to Strachey, 23 January [1910] but mistakenly dated 1909, HL.
66 Conrad to Reynolds, 14 December 1909, Karl 4, 296.
67 Galsworthy to Reynolds, 2 December 1909, Wallace.
68 SS 314.
69 SS 316.
70 Galsworthy to Reynolds, 2 December 1909, Wallace.
71 Conrad to Reynolds, 14 December 1909, Karl 4, 297.
72 Conrad to Galsworthy, [10 December 1909], Karl 4, 294.
73 Reynolds to Strachey, 2 February 1910, HL.
74 The People and their Vote, *Fortnightly Review*, April 1910. The story taken earlier was *An Unofficial Divorce*.
75 SS 153.
76 Reynolds to Strachey, 4 December 1910, HL.
77 Where it was simply entitled "Seems So", *Nation*, 24 December 1910.
78 SS 4.
79 SS 6. The Woolley cynicism was sufficiently outrageous to catch the eye of a modern commentator; see Paul Thompson *The Edwardians: The Remaking of British Society*, Routledge 1992 215.
80 SS 151
81 Reynolds to Orage, 16 April 1910, Wright 130.
82 Reynolds to Orage, 22 April 1910, Wright 131.
83 *ibid.*
84 With Baby's Help, *New Age*, 30 June 1910.

85 Reynolds to Orage, 30 April 1910, transcribed Philippa Powys, Mappowder.
86 Paul Selver *Orage and the New Age Circle*, Allen & Unwin 1959 23.
87 *New Age*, 2 June 1910, reproduced Wright 132.
88 Reynolds to Orage, 22 April 1910, Wright 131.
89 SS xxiii.
90 Political Vivisection, *Spectator*, 11 June 1910.
91 Reynolds to Strachey, 11 June 1910, Wright 135.
92 Conrad to Reynolds, 26 June 1910, Karl 4, 342.
93 HT 106.
94 Norman Keen in C. Ernest Fayle *Harold Wright: A Memoir*, Allen & Unwin 1934 94.
95 Reynolds to Pinker, 18 August 1909, Northwestern.
96 Reynolds to Pinker, 6 September 1909, Northwestern.
97 Reynolds to Lane, 9 September 1909, Texas.
98 Reynolds to Strachey, 11 June 1910, Wright 135.
99 SS 247.
100 SS 255.
101 SS 263.
102 SS 264.
103 SS 266.
104 Labour Disaffection, *The Times*, 19 August 1910.
105 Mental and Manual Work, *The Times*, 19 August 1910.
106 Reynolds to Editor, *The Times*, 28 August 1910, Wright 138.
107 Reynolds to Pinker, 16 October 1910, Northwestern.
108 Reynolds to Frederick Macmillan, 3 October 1910, Add.Mss.54965.
109 Reynolds to Frederick Macmillan, 20 January and 15 February 1911, Add. Mss.54965. Frederick Macmillan to Reynolds, 26 January 1911, Add.Mss.55501.
110 SS 182.
111 SS 186.
112 SS 189 *et seq.*
113 SS 197.
114 SS 198.
115 SS 199.
116 SS 193.
117 Reynolds to Pinker, 16 October 1910, Northwestern, partially quoted Wright 139.
118 Hugh Walpole to Reynolds, [31 October 1910], Wallace.
119 HT 340.
120 HT 349.
121 HT 355.
122 HT 361.
123 SS 381.

124 Reynolds to Edward Garnett, 23 November 1910, Texas.
125 Reynolds to Frederick Macmillan, 26 November 1910, Add.Mss.54965.
126 Frederick Macmillan to Reynolds, 28 November 1910, Add.Mss.55501.
127 Reynolds to Frederick Macmillan, 20 December 1910, Add.Mss.54965.
128 Hugh Walpole to Reynolds, 3 December 1910, Wallace.
129 Hugh Walpole to Reynolds, [*c* 7 December 1910], Wallace.
130 Hugh Walpole diary, 12 December 1910, Texas.
131 Hugh Walpole diary, 13 December 1910, Texas.
132 Hugh Walpole diary, 14 December 1910, Texas.
133 Reynolds to Frederick Macmillan, 20 December 1910, Add.Mss.54965. In this photo session, he had boldly experimented with an identical pose with spectacles on, but the result was even more forbidding.
134 Frederick Macmillan to Reynolds, 21 December 1910, Add.Mss.55501.
135 Reynolds to Frederick Macmillan, 17 January 1911, Add.Mss.54965.
136 There is a copy of a later 1911 version, probably the only one extant, among the Harmsworth papers at Lime Lodge.
137 Reynolds to Frederick Macmillan, 20 December 1910, Add.Mss.54965.
138 Reynolds to Pinker, 18 December 1908, Northwestern. It was then called "*Father* Christmas and Mr Bookworm" and 1750 words in length.
139 Brother Christmas and Mr Bookworm, *Daily News*, 26 December 1910.
140 Reynolds to Edward Garnett, 23 November 1910, Texas. Frederick Macmillan to Reynolds, 19 January 1911, Add.Mss.55501.
141 Reynolds to Frederick Macmillan, 20 January and 15 February 1911, Add.Mss.54965.
142 Reynolds to Pinker, 25 March 1911, Northwestern.
143 Reynolds to George Macmillan, 26 April and 5 May 1911, Add.Mss.54965. SS 98.
144 Reynolds to George Macmillan, 28 May and 23 July 1911, Add.Mss.54965.
145 The By-Products of Tariff Reform, *English Review*, April 1911.
146 For examples of Reynolds' patient but practical response to such enquiries, see Wright 179 and 313.
147 SS 210.
148 SS 217.
149 Reynolds to George Macmillan, 6 July 1911, Add.Mss.54965.
150 SS xviii.
151 SS ix.
152 Reynolds to Pinker, 25 March 1911, Northwestern.
153 Reynolds to Arnold Bennett, 29 June 1911, Keele University Library.
154 Reynolds to George Macmillan, 25 and 29 August 1911, and to Frederick Macmillan, 19 September 1911, Add.Mss.54965. George Macmillan to Reynolds, 28 August 1911, Add.Mss.55504.
155 George Macmillan to Reynolds, 18 May 1911, Add.Mss.55503. The original frontispiece, rejected at first proof stage, is included in the manu-

script in the Westcountry Studies Library, Exeter, MSX 820.2/REY.
156 Reynolds to Strachey, 4 June 1911, HL.
157 Reynolds to George Sturt, 22 July 1911, transcribed Philippa Powys, Mappowder.
158 Hugh Walpole to Reynolds, 1 July 1911, Wallace.
159 Hugh Walpole to Reynolds, [mid-July 1911], Wallace.
160 Reynolds to Pinker, 25 July 1911, Northwestern. George Macmillan to Reynolds, 25 July 1911, Add.Mss.55503.
161 Reynolds to George Macmillan, 30 July 1911, Add.Mss.54965.
162 Reynolds to Pinker, 30 July 1911, Northwestern.
163 Macmillans to Pinker, 8 August 1911, Add.Mss.55503.
164 George Macmillan to Reynolds, 9 August 1911, Add.Mss.55503.
165 Reynolds to Pinker, 14 August 1911, Northwestern.
166 Reynolds to George Macmillan, 14 August 1911, Add.Mss.54965.
167 Memorandum of Agreement Reynolds/Macmillan, 28 August 1911, Macmillan Archive, Basingstoke.
168 Reynolds to Pinker, 16 August 1911, Northwestern.
169 Reynolds to George Macmillan, 20 August 1911, and to Frederick Macmillan, 19 September 1911, Add.Mss.54965.
170 Reynolds to Frederick Macmillan, 21 September 1911, Add.Mss.54965.
171 Reynolds to Macmillans, 20 October 1911, Add.Mss.54965.
172 Reynolds to Philippa Powys, 1 November 1911, Texas.
173 Philippa Powys diary, November 1911, Mappowder.
174 Reynolds to George Macmillan, 6 November 1911, Add.Mss.54965.
175 It was originally sub-titled *A Working*-Man *View of Politics* – see the manuscript in the Westcountry Studies Library, Exeter, MSX 820.2/REY.
176 Reynolds to J.E.H. Balfour, 14 November 1911, Sidmouth Museum. Reynolds to George Macmillan, 6 November 1911, Add.Mss.54965.
177 SS 60.
178 A Fisherman's Politics, *Daily News*, 30 November 1911.
179 The Likes O' Us, *Nation*, 2 December 1911.
180 *Spectator*, 2 December 1911.
181 Reynolds to Harold Wright, 8 December 1911, Texas.
182 Reynolds to George Macmillan, 3 December 1911, Add.Mss.54965.
183 George Macmillan to Reynolds, 4 December 1911, Add.Mss.55505.
184 Reynolds to Harold Wright, 8 December 1911, Texas.
185 Mr Reynolds as Spokesman, *Westminster Gazette*, 25 November 1911.
186 George Sturt journal, 25 December 1911, Add.Mss.43366.
187 Reynolds to George Sturt, 17 December 1911, Wright 141.
188 *Country Life*, 23 December 1911.
189 Reynolds to George Sturt, 23 December 1911, Wright 146.
190 Conrad to Reynolds, [30 November 1911], Karl 4, 516. As the last sentence indicates, this was posted to coincide with Reynolds' return to Sidmouth on 1 December, and thus makes a firm dating possible.

191 *ibid.* In the fourth sentence Karl has misread "bits" as "lists".
192 *ibid.*
193 SS 47.
194 Mr Sadler on Modern Education, *The Times*, 19 December 1911.
195 *ibid.*
196 Reynolds to Editor, *The Times*, 19 December 1911, Wright 142.
197 Mr Sadler on Modern Education, *The Times*, 19 December 1911.
198 Reynolds to Editor, *The Times*, 19 December 1911, Wright 143.
199 *ibid.*, Wright 145.
200 George Macmillan to Reynolds, 19 December 1911, Add.Mss.55505.
201 Reynolds to George Sturt, 23 December 1911, Wright 146.
202 George Sturt journal, 24 December 1911, Add.Mss.43366.
203 *New Age*, 4 January 1912. *The Schoolmaster*, 6 January 1912.
204 Reynolds to Maurice Macmillan, 10 January 1912, Add.Mss.54965.
205 Maurice Macmillan to Reynolds, 11 January 1912, Add.Mss.55505.
206 Reynolds to George Macmillan, 31 December 1911, Add.Mss.54965.
207 Macmillan edition books, Add.Mss.55919.
208 Harold Wright to Pinker, 28 April and 7 May 1920, Northwestern. This was the account to 30 June 1919.
209 Reynolds to George Macmillan, 14 April 1912, Add.Mss.54965.

Chapter 13 Weekends at Nesscombe 1911

1 Nature and the Country, *Daily Mail*, 6 July 1907 was Reynolds' first contribution. By Australasian Seas, *Daily Mail*, 13 July 1907, seems likely, despite the subject matter, to have been the second.
2 Reynolds to Pinker, 30 December 1909, Northwestern.
3 Reynolds to Frederick Macmillan, 17 October 1910, Add.Mss.54965.
4 Reynolds to Frederick Macmillan, 20 January 1911, Add.Mss.54965.
5 Reynolds to an unrecorded correspondent, 28 January 1911, transcribed Philippa Powys, Mappowder.
6 *ibid.*
7 Conrad to Reynolds, 14 February 1911, Karl 4, 412.
8 Reynolds to Edward Garnett, 23 April 1911, Texas.
9 Reynolds to Pinker, 8 August 1909, Northwestern.
10 Reynolds to Pinker, 6 and 10 September 1909, Northwestern.
11 Reynolds to Pinker, 12 April 1910, Northwestern.
12 *The Author*, March 1910. Enclosure to Herbert Thring to General Manager, *English Review*, 24 December 1910, Add.Mss.57139.
13 Reynolds to Pinker, 2 June 1910, Northwestern.
14 Reynolds to Pinker, 5 June 1910, Northwestern.
15 Reynolds to Pinker, 6 July 1910, Northwestern.
16 Reynolds to Pinker, 28 August 1910, Northwestern.

17 Herbert Thring to Reynolds, 27 August 1910, Add.Mss.57137.
18 Herbert Thring to Austin Harrison, 18, 20 and 22 October 1910, Add.Mss.57138.
19 Herbert Thring to Austin Harrison, 15 November 1910 and 21 February 1911, Add.Mss.57138 and 57141.
20 Herbert Thring to Austin Harrison, 14 December 1910, Add.Mss.57139.
21 Herbert Thring to Austin Harrison, 21 December 1910, Add.Mss.57139.
22 Herbert Thring to General Manager, *English Review*, 24 December 1910, Add.Mss.57139.
23 Herbert Thring to Austin Harrison, 21 February 1911, Add.Mss.57141.
24 Herbert Thring to Austin Harrison, 15 March 1911, Add.Mss.57141.
25 Herbert Thring to Austin Harrison, 28 March, 4 and 5 April 1911, Add.Mss.57141.
26 Herbert Thring to Reynolds, 4 April 1911, Add.Mss.57141.
27 Reynolds to Pinker, 25 March 1911, Northwestern. Conrad to Reynolds, 28 March 1911, Karl 4, 433. Reynolds to Garnett, 23 April 1911, Texas.
28 Herbert Thring to Squire Sprigge, 5 April 1911, Add.Mss.57141. It is clear that Hueffer was highly selective as to which past contributors he helped. A year earlier, when Mond took over, he told Scott-James: "The fact is that I stand here to be shot at and meekly ready to pay such contributors as Mond does not pay and I am perfectly ready to pay for your partly written article if you will send in a claim." (R.A.Scott-James, Ford Madox Ford When He Was Hueffer, *South Atlantic Quarterly* 57, Spring 1958 245).
29 *ibid.*
30 *ibid.*
31 Reynolds to Pinker, Easter Monday 1911, Northwestern. Herbert Thring to Reynolds, 7 April 1911, Add.Mss.57141.
32 Reynolds to Pinker, Easter Monday 1911, Northwestern.
33 Herbert Thring to Reynolds, 22 April and 2 May 1911, Add.Mss.57142.
34 Herbert Thring to Sir Alfred Mond, 3 May 1911, Add.Mss.57142.
35 Herbert Thring to Sir Alfred Mond, 6 May 1911; to Squire Sprigge, 9 May 1911; and to Reynolds, 13 May 1911; Add.Mss.57142.
36 Reynolds to George Macmillan, 16 May 1911, Add.Mss.54965.
37 The Great Adult Review, *Spectator*, 10 June 1911.
38 Reynolds to Strachey, 15 June 1911, HL.
39 Strachey to Reynolds, 16 June 1911, HL.
40 Reynolds to Edward Garnett, 24 May 1911, Texas.
41 *Swindon Advertiser*, 16 June 1911.
42 Reynolds to Edward Garnett, 26 June 1911, Texas.
43 Reynolds to Frederick Macmillan, 17 and 20 January 1911, Add.Mss.54965. Frederick Macmillan to Reynolds, 19 and 26 January 1911, Add.Mss.55501.
44 Reynolds to George Macmillan, 26 April 1911, Add.Mss.54965.

45 George Macmillan to Reynolds, 28 April 1911, Add.Mss.55502.
46 *A Poor Man's House*, OUP 1982 xvi.
47 *ibid.* xvii.
48 Reynolds to George Macmillan, 6 July 1911, Add.Mss.54965.
49 Macmillan edition books, Add.Mss.55919.
50 Reynolds to George Macmillan, 28 May 1911, Add.Mss.54965.
51 Reynolds to Philippa Powys, 7 May 1911, Texas.
52 Reynolds to George Macmillan, 16 May 1911, Add.Mss.54965.
53 George Macmillan to Reynolds, 18 May 1911, Add.Mss.55503.
54 Reynolds to George Macmillan, 28 May 1911, Add.Mss.54965.
55 Hannaford Himself, *Westminster Gazette*, 3 June 1911.
56 *ibid.*
57 Hannaford Himself, *Westminster Gazette*, 10 June 1911.
58 *ibid.*
59 The Commonplace, *Westminster Gazette*, 17 June 1911.
60 *ibid.*
61 Reynolds to George Macmillan, 23 July 1911, Add.Mss.54965.
62 Reynolds to Arnold Bennett, 29 June 1911, Keele University Library.
63 Sensational Occurrence, *Sidmouth Herald*, 3 June 1911.
64 Reynolds to Editor, *Sidmouth Herald*, 3 June 1911.
65 Reynolds to Editor, *Sidmouth Herald*, 17 June 1911.
66 Deadman's Escape, *Westminster Gazette*, 5 August 1911.
67 Philippa Powys diary, July 1911, Mappowder.
68 Philippa Powys diary, 24 February 1910, Mappowder.
69 Philippa Powys diary, 3 March 1910, Mappowder. It appears from Llewelyn's diaries that following her first meeting with Reynolds in 1909 she had decided to write a novel. Certainly by the end of 1910 Llewelyn was reading and enjoying it so much that he copied large chunks into his diary. On 1 December he wrote in his diary: "All the evening I read Katie's novel and was immensely impressed, so that for a long time I couldn't sleep. Nelly Lovelas, Dick Upton, Sally Rockets, Lilian and Fred Wooley [*sic*] with his polished crook, crossed and re-crossed my mental vision. She has power and genius, power and genius, and with all the faults and immaturities the story is admirable". It may have been this novel that allegedly contributed to her nervous attacks in the spring of 1910. I am grateful to Dr Peter Foss, who is currently editing Llewelyn's diaries, for drawing this work to my attention.
70 Reynolds to Philippa Powys, 7 May 1911, Texas.
71 Philippa Powys diary, August 1911, Mappowder.
72 Philippa Powys, "Phoenix", third version, unpublished typescript, Texas 15.
73 *ibid.*16.
74 Philippa Powys diary, August 1911, Mappowder.
75 "Phoenix" *op.cit.*16.

76 *ibid.*17.
77 Philippa Powys diary, August 1911, Mappowder.
78 "Phoenix" *op.cit.*18.
79 Philippa Powys diary, August 1911, Mappowder.
80 Reynolds to Philippa Powys, 29 August 1911, Texas. Reynolds' hold on Nietzsche was not quite so profound as this implies. When the *Sunday Sun* commented on the Nietzschean quality of *A Poor Man's House* he reacted with some embarrassment: "Never knew I was an exponent of the Nietzschian philosophy before!" (Reynolds to Lane, 1 January 1909, Texas). When borrowing Nietzsche from Garnett as background reading for "Yesterday and Tomorrow", he underlined the point: "I should like to borrow any Nietzsches that would do for the young man to have read. *Zarathustra* if you have it.... Though one good critic was pleased to call me the foremost exponent of Nietzschianism in English, I don't know much about him" (Reynolds to Edward Garnett, 18 June 1909, Texas).
81 *ibid.*
82 The Concert, *Westminster Gazette,* 12 August 1911. This is art anticipating life. At the time Reynolds wrote this article in July, he had just invited Walpole to come down to Sidmouth, an invitation which, despite Walpole's good intentions, never seems to have been taken up.
83 "I have been enjoying your 'Westminster' things immensely." (Hugh Walpole to Reynolds, [mid-July 1911], Wallace). After the Concert article, he may not have enjoyed them quite so much.
84 The Concert, *Westminster Gazette,* 12 August 1911.
85 London, *Westminster Gazette,* 19 August 1911.
86 *ibid.*
87 *ibid.*
88 Nakedness, *Westminster Gazette,* 26 August 1911.
89 Philippa Powys diary, 28 September 1911, Mappowder.
90 Rabelaisianism, *Westminster Gazette,* 2 September 1911.
91 Reynolds to Editor, *Sidmouth Herald,* 2 September 1911.
92 *Sidmouth Herald,* 16 September 1911.
93 An Open Letter to Mrs or Miss Bessie Kittley, *Sidmouth Herald,* 23 September 1911.
94 Reynolds to Philippa Powys, 21 September 1911, Texas.
95 *Sidmouth Herald,* 30 September 1911.
96 *ibid.*
97 Reynolds to Frederick Macmillan, 19 September 1911, Add.Mss.54965.
98 *Sidmouth Herald,* 24 June 1911. This lunch was not an isolated instance of Reynolds' generosity. Each Christmas he and Harold Wright gave a dinner of roast beef and Christmas pudding to about 50 fishermen, which similarly ended in speeches about co-operation and a general singsong (C. Ernest Fayle *Harold Wright: A Memoir,* Allen & Unwin 1934 96).
99 Reynolds to Strachey, 23 June 1911, HL.

100 Reynolds to Editor, *Sidmouth Herald*, 24 June 1911.
101 Reynolds to Edward Garnett, 26 June 1911, Texas.
102 Interview with Roger Elliott, 10 July 1999.
103 Reynolds to George Macmillan, 26 April 1911, Add.Mss.54965.
104 The Shingle Question, *Sidmouth Herald*, 6 May 1911.
105 Reynolds to George Macmillan, 5 May 1911, Add.Mss.54965.
106 Reynolds to George Macmillan, 3 December 1911, Add.Mss.54965.
107 Reynolds to Harold Wright, 8 December 1911, Texas.
108 Reynolds to George Macmillan, 13 December 1911, Add.Mss.54965.
109 Reynolds to Pinker, 16 July 1910, Northwestern.
110 Reynolds to Edward Garnett, 4 February 1911, Texas.
111 Reynolds to Strachey, 23 June 1911, HL. Reynolds to Edward Garnett, 4 February 1911, Texas.
112 Reynolds to Frederick Macmillan, 17 January 1911, Add.Mss.54965.
113 Reynolds to Pinker, 25 March 1911, Northwestern.
114 Reynolds to George Macmillan, 16 May 1911, Add.Mss.54965.
115 Reynolds to Strachey, 23 June 1911, HL.
116 House of Commons Report, 20 June 1911, Col.187.
117 House of Commons Report, 20 June 1911, Col.190.
118 House of Commons Report, 20 June 1911, Col.193.
119 Reynolds to Strachey, 23 June 1911, HL.
120 St Loe Strachey to Sir Edward Strachey, 26 June 1911, HL.
121 Reynolds to George Macmillan, 23 and 30 July 1911, Add.Mss.54965.
122 Reynolds to George Macmillan, 8 August 1911, Add.Mss.54965.
123 Reynolds to Pinker, 25 July 1911, Northwestern.
124 Reynolds to Pinker, 1 August 1911, Northwestern.
125 Reynolds to Pinker, 14 August 1911, Northwestern.
126 Reynolds to George Sturt, 23 December 1911, Wright 146.
127 Reynolds to George Macmillan, 14 August 1911, Add.Mss.54965.
128 George Macmillan to Reynolds, 15 August 1911, enclosure to Reynolds to Pinker, 16 August 1911, Northwestern. At this time Reynolds invited Harold Wright to join him in the new enterprise, presumably as his research and secretarial assistant, but Wright's course at Cambridge had another year to run (Harold Wright to Reynolds, 14 August 1911, in possession of Margaret Wallace).
129 Reynolds to George Macmillan, 20 August 1911, Add.Mss.54965.
130 Conrad to Austin Harrison, 7 June 1911, Karl 4, 448. Conrad to Pinker, 19 June 1911, Karl 4, 450.
131 Conrad to Pinker, [10 November 1911], Karl 4, 502.
132 Reynolds to George Macmillan, 6 November 1911, Add.Mss.54965.
133 George Macmillan to Reynolds, 7 November 1911, Add.Mss.55504
134 Conrad to Pinker, 21 November 1911, Karl 4, 508. Reynolds was also that weekend acting as intermediary between William Blackwood and the author, further confirmation of his intense devotion to the

Conradian cause.

135 Conrad to Reynolds, [30 November 1911], Karl 4, 517.

136 Reynolds to J.E.H. Balfour, 14 November 1911, Sidmouth Museum. Reynolds to George Macmillan, 1 December 1911, Add.Mss.54965.

137 Reynolds to Harold Wright, 8 December 1911, Texas.

138 *Cromer and North Walsham Post*, 24 November 1911. The same evening there was a large meeting of Scottish fishermen at Yarmouth to demand State aid for putting motors into their drifters, which may have been the second meeting Reynolds attended.

139 Reynolds to Harold Wright, 8 December 1911, Texas.

140 Reynolds to Bob Woolley, 25 November 1911, transcribed Philippa Powys, Mappowder.

141 Reynolds to Harold Wright, 8 December 1911, Texas.

142 Reynolds to George Macmillan, 11 December 1911, Add.Mss.54965.

143 Reynolds to George Sturt, 17 December 1911, Wright 140.

144 Reynolds to George Macmillan, 20 August 1911, Add.Mss.54965. Reynolds to Pinker, 25 July 1911, Northwestern. Reynolds to Austin Harrison, 22 January 1912, Wright 147.

145 Immortality, *Westminster Gazette*, 16 September 1911.

Chapter 14 How 'Twas 1912

1 Reynolds to George Macmillan, 1 December 1911, Add.Mss.54965.

2 Reynolds to Harold Wright, 8 December 1911, Texas.

3 Reynolds to George Macmillan, 3 December 1911, Add.Mss.54965.

4 *ibid.* Conrad to Reynolds, [30 November 1911], Karl 4, 517.

5 Reynolds to George Macmillan, 11 December 1911, Add.Mss.54965.

6 Reynolds to George Macmillan, 22 December 1911, Add.Mss.54965.

7 Reynolds to George Macmillan, 13 December 1911, Add.Mss.54965.

8 George Macmillan to Reynolds, 12 December 1911, Add.Mss.55505.

9 Reynolds to George Macmillan, 13 December 1911, Add.Mss.54965.

10 Reynolds to George Macmillan, 20 December 1911, Add.Mss.54965.

11 Osborne 193.

12 Reynolds to George Macmillan, 31 December 1911, Add.Mss.54965.

13 Reynolds' diary, 25 December 1911, Wright 146.

14 Reynolds to George Macmillan, 31 December 1911, Add.Mss.54965.

15 Reynolds to Pinker, 31 December 1911, Northwestern. Reynolds to Pinker, 16 and 21 August 1911, Northwestern.

16 Reynolds to Pinker, 22 January 1912, Northwestern.

17 Reynolds to George Macmillan, 24 and 29 January 1912, Add.Mss.54965. George Macmillan to Reynolds, 26 January and 1 February 1912, Add.Mss.55505.

18 Reynolds to George Macmillan, 9 February 1912, Add.Mss.54965.

19 Reynolds to Pinker, 6 June 1912, Northwestern.
20 Reynolds to George Macmillan, 18 June 1912, Add.Mss.54965.
21 Reynolds to Pinker, 22 January 1912, Northwestern.
22 Reynolds to George Macmillan, 9 February 1912, Add.Mss.54965.
23 Joseph Conrad and Sea Fiction, *Quarterly Review*, July 1912.
24 Zdzislaw Najder, *Joseph Conrad: A Chronicle*, CUP 1983 381.
25 Joseph Conrad and Sea Fiction, *Quarterly Review*, July 1912.
26 Conrad to an unknown correspondent, 25 February 1912, Karl 5, 25.
27 Conrad to Reynolds, 31 August 1912, Karl 5, 104. Karl misreads the date as 30 August.
28 Reynolds to Maurice Macmillan, 10 January 1912, Add.Mss.54965. Although the "Professor of English Literature" is not identified, it is almost certainly Elton, then Professor of English Literature at Liverpool University, who had lectured in English at Owens from 1890 to 1900 and had ties with the University of the Punjab. He was special lecturer there in the winter of 1917-18 and at other times. See J.F. Bruce *A History of the University of the Punjab*, Lahore 1933 136.
29 Maurice Macmillan to Reynolds, 11 January 1912, Add.Mss.55505.
30 Pulpit Criticism of Mr Stephen Reynolds' Books, *Wiltshire Advertiser*, 1 February 1912.
31 Reynolds to George Macmillan, 7 February 1912, Add.Mss.54965.
32 Stephen Reynolds Replies, *Wiltshire Advertiser*, 8 February 1912.
33 Ada Bennett to Editor, *Wiltshire Advertiser*, 8 February 1912.
34 Reynolds to George Macmillan, 9 February 1912, Add.Mss.54965.
35 Rev. John Kingsland to Editor, *Wiltshire Advertiser*, 15 February 1912.
36 Reynolds to George Macmillan, 17 February 1912, Add.Mss.54965.
37 Reynolds to Austin Harrison, 22 January 1912, Wright 147.
38 Reynolds to George Macmillan, 9 February 1912, Add.Mss.54695.
39 George Macmillan to Reynolds, 12 February 1912, Add.Mss.55506.
40 Reynolds to George Macmillan, 17 February 1912, Add.Mss.54965.
41 Reynolds to George Macmillan, 7 February 1912, Add.Mss.54965.
42 Reynolds to George Macmillan, 29 January 1912, Add.Mss.54965.
43 *Sidmouth Herald*, 3 February 1912.
44 Reynolds to George Macmillan, 7 February 1912, Add.Mss.54965.
45 Reynolds to George Macmillan, 17 February 1912, Add.Mss.54965.
46 "Tom Woolley and myself discussed it pretty fully yesterday afternoon: it cannot affect me without affecting them; he has the Devonian's secrecy; and we neither of us ever act in any affair without the other." (Reynolds to Frederick Macmillan, 9 June 1912, Add.Mss.54965).
47 "The herring season has been a total failure, and Bob is very miserable about it – like a stray cat that wants its feet buttering." (Reynolds to Pinker, 22 January 1912, Northwestern).
48 Reynolds to Bob Woolley, 12 February 1912, transcribed Philippa Powys, Mappowder.

49 Reynolds to George Macmillan, 17 February 1912, Add.Mss.54965.
50 Edward Thomas diary, 27 February 1912, NLW.
51 Hugh Walpole to Reynolds, [23/30 December 1911], Wallace.
52 Hugh Walpole diary, 29 February 1912, Texas.
53 Conrad to Pinker, [8 March 1912], Karl 5, 29.
54 Reynolds to George Macmillan, 13 March 1912, Add.Mss.54965.
55 PMH 221.
56 Reynolds to George Macmillan, 23 March 1912, Add.Mss.54965.
57 *ibid.*
58 Reynolds to George Macmillan, 28 March 1912, Add.Mss.54965.
59 Reynolds to George Macmillan, 31 March 1912, Add.Mss.54965.
60 Reynolds to George Macmillan, 14 April 1912, Add.Mss.54965.
61 Reynolds to George Macmillan, 23 April 1912, Add.Mss.54965.
62 Reynolds to George Macmillan, 20 May 1912, Add.Mss.54965.
63 Harold Wright to Pinker, 2 February 1921, Northwestern.
64 Reynolds to George Sturt, 20 March 1912, Wright 149.
65 Reynolds to Edward Garnett, 29 March 1907, Texas.
66 Reynolds to Pinker, 5 March 1909, Northwestern.
67 Reynolds to Herbert Jenkins, 18 August 1909, Texas.
68 Reynolds to Pinker, 5 June 1910, Northwestern.
69 Reynolds to George Macmillan, 28 May 1911, Add.Mss.54965.
70 George Macmillan to Reynolds, 1 June 1911, Add.Mss.55503. Reynolds to George Macmillan, 6 July 1911, Add.Mss.54965.
71 Conrad to Reynolds, [30 November 1911], Karl 4, 517.
72 Reynolds to Pinker, 31 December 1911, Northwestern.
73 George Macmillan to Reynolds, 1 February 1912, Add.Mss.55505.
74 Reynolds to George Macmillan, 7 February 1912, Add.Mss.54965.
75 George Macmillan to Reynolds, 8 February 1912, Add.Mss.55506.
76 Reynolds to George Macmillan, 9 February 1912, Add.Mss.54965.
77 George Macmillan to Reynolds, 12 February 1912, Add.Mss.55506.
78 Reynolds to George Macmillan, 9 February 1912, Add.Mss.54965.
79 Reynolds to Pinker, 16 March 1912, Northwestern, partially quoted Wright 147.
80 Reynolds to George Macmillan, 16 March 1912, Add.Mss.54965.
81 Reynolds to Pinker, 16 March 1912, Northwestern. The last two things were A Third Class Journey, published in April and May 1912 as A Fisherman's Holiday in Garvin's *Pall Mall Gazette*; and Sillie Saltie, *Throne*, 11 November 1911.
82 Reynolds to George Macmillan, 9 February 1912, Add.Mss.54965.
83 Conrad to Reynolds, [?12 March 1912], Karl 5, 33. Reynolds would have lost no time in sending the proofs off to Macmillan (13 March) immediately on receipt of the text from Conrad; but a date of 11 March for this letter is possible.
84 Reynolds to George Macmillan, 13 March 1912, Add.Mss.54965.

85 Reynolds to George Macmillan, 14 April 1912, Add.Mss.54965.
86 George Macmillan to Reynolds, 3 May 1912, Add.Mss.55507.
87 Reynolds to Macmillans, 19 April 1912, Add.Mss.54965.
88 George Macmillan to Reynolds, 22 April 1912, Add.Mss.55506.
89 Reynolds to George Macmillan, 23 April 1912, Add.Mss.54965.
90 Reynolds to George Macmillan, 2 May 1912, Add.Mss.54965. George Macmillan to Reynolds, 30 May 1912, Add.Mss.55507.
91 Macmillan edition books, Add.Mss.55919.
92 Reynolds to George Macmillan, 31 May 1912, Add.Mss.54965.
93 Reynolds to George Macmillan, 7 June 1912, Add.Mss.54965.
94 Reynolds to Frederick Macmillan, 9 June 1912, Add.Mss.54965.
95 George Macmillan to Reynolds, 4 June 1912, Add.Mss.55507.
96 Reynolds to George Macmillan, 6 June 1912, Add.Mss.54965.
97 Reynolds to George Macmillan, 29 June 1912, Add.Mss.54965. George Macmillan to Reynolds, 1 July 1912, Add.Mss.55507.
98 Reynolds to George Macmillan, 16 June 1912, Add.Mss.54965.
99 Conrad to Reynolds, 18 June 1912, Karl 5, 74.
100 Lobster-Catchers and Lobster-Eaters, *Nation*, 13 July 1912.
101 Reynolds to Charles Sarolea, 6 August 1912, Edinburgh.
102 *Bookman*, August 1912.
103 *Athenaeum*, 29 June 1912.
104 Reynolds to George Macmillan, 3 July 1912, Add.Mss.54965.
105 George Macmillan to Reynolds, 5 July 1912, Add.Mss.55507.
106 Conrad to Reynolds, [10 July 1912], Karl 5, 82.
107 *Punch*, 3 July 1912.
108 Reynolds to George Macmillan, 9 July 1912, Add.Mss.54965.
109 Hugh Walpole diary, 9 July 1912, Texas.
110 *Standard*, 12 July 1912.
111 Reynolds to George Macmillan, 14 July 1912, Add.Mss.54965.
112 Reynolds to George Macmillan, 29 January 1912, Add.Mss.54965.
113 Reynolds to George Macmillan, 20 May 1912, Add.Mss.54965.
114 Reynolds to the Rev. – , 16 May 1912, Wright 149.
115 Reynolds to George Macmillan, 20 May 1912, Add.Mss.54965.
116 Reynolds to George Macmillan, 1 July 1912, Add.Mss.54965.
117 Holt White to F.J. Ratcliffe, 8 June 1912, Add.Mss.55268.
118 George Macmillan to Reynolds, 7 June 1912, Add.Mss.55507.
119 Reynolds to Frederick Macmillan, 9 June 1912, Add.Mss.54965.
120 Enclosure to Reynolds to Frederick Macmillan, 9 June 1912, Add.Mss.54965.
121 Frederick Macmillan to Reynolds, 10 June 1912, Add.Mss.55507.
122 Holt White to Frederick Macmillan, 13 June 1912, Add.Mss.55268.
123 Reynolds to George Macmillan, 16 June 1912, Add.Mss.54965.
124 F.J. Ratcliffe to Holt White, 18 June 1912, Add.Mss.55507.
125 George Macmillan to Reynolds, 28 June 1912, Add.Mss.55507.

126 Reynolds to George Macmillan, 29 June 1912, Add.Mss.54965.
127 F.J. Ratcliffe to Holt White, 1 July 1912, Add.Mss.55507.
128 Reynolds to George Macmillan, 3 and 9 July 1912, Add.Mss.54965.
129 Reynolds to George Macmillan, 9 July 1912, Add.Mss.54965.
130 Reynolds to George Macmillan, 19 August 1912, Add.Mss.54965.
131 George Macmillan to Reynolds, 20 August 1912, Add.Mss.55508.
132 F.J. Ratcliffe to Holt White, 31 August 1912, Add.Mss.55508.
133 Reynolds to George Macmillan, 14 July 1912, Add.Mss.54965.
134 George Macmillan to Reynolds, 17 July 1912, Add.Mss.55508.
135 Reynolds to Jane Reynolds, 7 August 1912, Wright 150.
136 *Sidmouth Herald*, 8 June 1912.
137 Reynolds to George Macmillan, 6 June 1912, Add.Mss.54965.
138 Reynolds to George Macmillan, 3 July 1912, Add.Mss.54965.
139 Philippa Powys diary, October 1911, Mappowder.
140 Reynolds to Philippa Powys, 1 November 1911, Texas.
141 Philippa Powys diary, November 1911, Mappowder.
142 Reynolds to Philippa Powys, 13 March 1912, Texas.
143 Philippa Powys "Phoenix", third version, unpublished typescript, Texas 24.
144 Philippa Powys diary, January 1912, Mappowder.
145 In her diary, she refers to Gertrude's presence. In "Phoenix" *op.cit.* 31, she talks of walking the sea wall with her brother, most probably Llewelyn who was staying at Montacute at the time.
146 Philippa Powys diary, undated but August 1912, Mappowder.
147 "Phoenix" *op.cit.*24.
148 *ibid.* 25.
149 *ibid.* 25. Judith Stinton in *Chaldon Herring: The Powys Circle in a Dorset Village*, Boydell Press 1988 124 gives the perhaps unintended impression that Reynolds' declaration "No friends but these, I have" took place when rowing Katie out in his boat, the episode of the previous year. From Ms Stinton's notes, which she very kindly showed me, it is clear that this is not the case.
150 *ibid.* 27.
151 *ibid.* 28.
152 *ibid.* 31.
153 *ibid.* 32a.
154 John Cowper Powys to Frances Gregg, 24 August 1912, Oliver Wilkinson (edited) *The Letters of John Cowper Powys to Frances Gregg*, Cecil Woolf 1994 30.
155 John Cowper Powys to Frances Gregg, 22 August 1912, Oliver Wilkinson *op.cit.*29.
156 John Cowper Powys to Frances Gregg, 24 August 1912, Oliver Wilkinson *op.cit.*30.
157 John Cowper Powys to Frances Gregg, [27 August 1912], Oliver

Wilkinson *op.cit.*32.
158 John Cowper Powys to Frances Gregg, 25 August 1912, Oliver Wilkinson *op.cit.*32.
159 "Phoenix" *op.cit.*32a.
160 She wrote a note on 25 August: "By *willing* we can walk upon the sea. I have broken the cross Christ is freed and returned to the deserts a child. The moon and the owls are our sisters. The seagulls and ravens help us. Fear thou not much but hope thou not at all. Nietzsche's madness has not been in vain – love from Katie (S.R.)" (John Cowper Powys to Frances Gregg, 25 August 1912, Oliver Wilkinson *op.cit.*31).
161 John Cowper Powys to Frances Gregg, [27 August 1912], Oliver Wilkinson *op.cit.*33.
162 Reynolds to Philippa Powys, 1 September 1912, Mappowder.
163 "Phoenix" *op.cit.*32B.
164 *ibid.* 33.
165 *ibid.* 37.
166 *ibid.* 40.
167 *ibid.* 47.

Chapter 15 The Navy and the Nation 1912

1 PMH 5.
2 Reynolds to Edward Garnett, 3 June 1907, Texas.
3 Reynolds to George Macmillan, 28 May 1911, Add.Mss.54965.
4 George Macmillan to Reynolds, 1 June 1911, Add.Mss.55503.
5 The Lower Deck, *Daily News*, 17 December 1908.
6 *ibid.*
7 Reynolds to Lionel Yexley, 18 June 1911, Pursey.
8 Reynolds to George Macmillan, 23 July 1911, Add.Mss.54965.
9 Reynolds to George Macmillan, 20 August 1911, Add.Mss.54965.
10 SS 227.
11 SS 230.
12 SS 235.
13 SS 239.
14 SS 240.
15 SS 242.
16 LD 85.
17 Reynolds to Yexley, 14 January 1912, Pursey.
18 Reynolds to Yexley, 22 January 1912, Pursey.
19 Reynolds to George Macmillan, 6 November 1911, Add.Mss.54965.
20 John Masefield to Reynolds, 7 October 1911, Wallace.
21 LD 68.
22 Reynolds to Yexley, 22 January 1912, Pursey.

23 *Fleet*, August 1912.
24 Reynolds to George Macmillan, 2 May 1912, Add.Mss.54965.
25 LD 44.
26 LD 46.
27 LD 45.
28 Reynolds to George Macmillan, 9 July 1912, Add.Mss.54965.
29 Reynolds to George Macmillan, 14 April 1912, Add.Mss.54965. The stoker is not identified, but it is almost certainly Dolby who was then Harry Woolley's friend.
30 Reynolds to Charles Sarolea, 22 October 1912, Edinburgh.
31 Reynolds to George Macmillan, 20 May 1912, Add.Mss.54965.
32 Reynolds to George Macmillan, 29 June 1912, Add.Mss.54965.
33 Reynolds to George Macmillan, 1 July 1912, Add.Mss.54965.
34 Reynolds to George Macmillan, 3 July 1912, Add.Mss.54965.
35 Reynolds to George Macmillan, 9 July 1912, Add.Mss.54965. Arthur Dolby was Reynolds' first secretary. Born in Windsor on 28 June 1895, after leaving Reynolds he served in HMS *Pembroke* from September 1913 to March 1914 when he transferred to HMS *Vanguard*. When the *Vanguard*, at anchor off Scapa Flow on 9 July 1917, blew up as the result of faulty ammunition, Dolby went down with 803 of his shipmates (PRO, L4774).
36 *ibid.*
37 Reynolds to William Maas, 23 June 1912, Pursey.
38 Reynolds to Yexley, 24 June 1912, Pursey.
39 Reynolds to William Maas, 20 August 1912, Pursey.
40 Reynolds to William Maas, 16 July 1912, Pursey.
41 House of Commons Report, 22 July 1912, Cols.851-2.
42 House of Commons Report, 4 December 1912, Col.2272.
43 Reynolds to Pinker, [22 July 1912], Northwestern. George Macmillan to Reynolds, 23 July 1912, Add.Mss.55508. Yexley to Reynolds, 23 July 1912, Pursey.
44 Yexley to Reynolds, 29 July 1912, Pursey.
45 J.G.Attersoll to Reynolds, 22 July and 3 September 1912, Pursey.
46 Reynolds to J.G.Attersoll, 4 September 1912, Pursey.
47 LD 102.
48 *Daily Chronicle*, 2 October 1912. Reynolds to Editor, *Daily Chronicle*, 2 October 1912.
49 Reynolds to Yexley, 3 October 1912, Pursey.
50 Yexley to Reynolds, 8 October 1912, Pursey.
51 Reynolds to Robert Goldsack, 19 October 1912, Pursey. Robert Goldsack to Reynolds, 6 November 1912, Pursey.
52 Reynolds to Frank Brandt, 15 January 1913, Pursey.
53 Reynolds to J.G.Attersoll, 30 July 1912, Pursey.
54 LD 53.

55 LD 41.
56 Reynolds to Yexley, 24 June 1912, Pursey.
57 Reynolds to George Macmillan, 6 June 1912, Add.Mss.54965.
58 Reynolds to George Macmillan, 29 June 1912, Add.Mss.54965.
59 Reynolds to George Macmillan, 6 August 1912, Add.Mss.54965.
60 LD 34.
61 LD 36.
62 LD 37.
63 Reynolds to George Macmillan, 19 August 1912, Add.Mss.54965.
64 Reynolds to William Maas, 20 August 1912, Pursey. Leese, the lawyer and ex-Liberal MP for Accrington, owned the Red House in Sidmouth. Reynolds stayed with him at his home in Guildford on 13 September (Reynolds to Charles Sarolea, [13 September 1912], Edinburgh).
65 Reynolds to Yexley, 30 July 1912, Pursey.
66 Reynolds to George Macmillan, 6 August 1912, Add.Mss.54965.
67 Reynolds to George Macmillan, 19 August 1912, Add.Mss.54965.
68 Reynolds to Yexley, 30 July 1912, Pursey. Yexley to Reynolds, 29 July 1912, Pursey. Yexley's letter is a reply to Reynolds', so someone, most probably Reynolds, has got his date wrong.
69 LD 82.
70 Reynolds to Yexley, 30 July 1912, Pursey. Reynolds to William Maas, 20 August 1912, Pursey. Reynolds to Pinker, 1 September 1912, Northwestern.
71 Reynolds to George Macmillan, 19 August 1912, Add.Mss.54965.
72 George Macmillan to Reynolds, 20 August 1912, Add.Mss.55508.
73 Reynolds to Pinker, 28 August 1912, Northwestern.
74 Introduction to catalogue of Sarolea papers, Edinburgh.
75 J.M. Dent to Charles Sarolea, 18 September 1912, Edinburgh.
76 J.M. Dent to Charles Sarolea, 29 July 1912, Edinburgh.
77 R.B. Cunninghame Graham to Charles Sarolea, 3 August 1912, Edinburgh.
78 Conrad to Charles Sarolea, 6 August 1912, Karl 5, 94.
79 Reynolds to Charles Sarolea, 6 August 1912, Edinburgh.
80 Reynolds to George Macmillan, 6 August 1911, Add.Mss.54965.
81 Reynolds to A.G.Gardiner, 25 August 1912, British Library of Political and Economic Science.
82 Reynolds to Charles Sarolea, 20 August 1912, Edinburgh.
83 George Macmillan to Reynolds, 9 August 1912, Add.Mss.55508.
84 Charles Sarolea to Reynolds, 2 September 1912, Edinburgh.
85 J.M. Dent to Charles Sarolea, 6 September 1912, Edinburgh.
86 Reynolds to Charles Sarolea, 7 September 1912, Edinburgh.
87 Charles Sarolea to Reynolds, 9 September 1912, Edinburgh.
88 Reynolds to Charles Sarolea, 10 September 1912, Edinburgh.
89 Charles Sarolea to Reynolds, 9 September 1912, Edinburgh.

90 Reynolds to Henry Maurice, 6 September 1912, Pursey. Reynolds to George Macmillan, 10 September 1912, Add.Mss.54965. Yexley to Reynolds, 15 September 1912, Pursey. J.G.Attersoll to Reynolds, 20 September 1912, Pursey. Reynolds to Charles Sarolea, 10 September 1912 and [13 September 1912], Edinburgh.
91 Reynolds to George Macmillan, 10 September 1912, Add.Mss.54965.
92 Reynolds to Charles Sarolea, [13 September 1912], Edinburgh.
93 J.M. Dent to Charles Sarolea, 18 September 1912, Edinburgh.
94 James Foster to Reynolds, 18 September 1912, Add.Mss.55508.
95 Reynolds to George Macmillan, 26 September 1912, Add.Mss.54965.
96 LD vi.
97 Reynolds to George Macmillan, 26 September 1912, Add.Mss.54965.
98 C. Marsh Beadnell to Reynolds, 11 and 17 October 1912, Pursey.
99 A.R. Dolby to Pinker, 17 October 1912, Northwestern.
100 Reynolds to Henry Maurice, 6 September 1912, Pursey.
101 PRO, L4774.
102 Charles Sarolea to J.M. Dent, 21 October 1912, Edinburgh.
103 Hugh Dent to Charles Sarolea, 30 October 1912, Edinburgh.
104 Charles Sarolea to Ernest Shackleton, 31 October 1912, Edinburgh.
105 Charles Sarolea to Reynolds, 31 October 1912, Edinburgh.
106 Ernest Shackleton to Charles Sarolea, 5 November 1912, Edinburgh.
107 Reynolds to Charles Sarolea, 1, 2 and 3 November 1912, Edinburgh. Naval Officer to Charles Sarolea, 3 November 1912, Edinburgh. Charles Sarolea to J.M. Dent, 4 November 1912, Edinburgh.
108 Charles Sarolea to Reynolds, 19 October 1912, Edinburgh.
109 Reynolds to Charles Sarolea, 22 October 1912, Edinburgh.
110 Reynolds to Charles Sarolea, 1 November 1912, Edinburgh.
111 Reynolds to Charles Sarolea, 3 November 1912, Edinburgh.
112 Charles Sarolea to Reynolds, 29 November 1912, Edinburgh.
113 Reynolds to Charles Sarolea, 2 December 1912, Edinburgh.
114 Hugh Dent to Charles Sarolea, 5 December 1912, Edinburgh.
115 Owen, Watkins Williams to Charles Sarolea, 12 December 1912, Edinburgh.
116 Reynolds to Charles Sarolea, 20 January 1913, Edinburgh.
117 Reynolds to J.M. Dent, 13 December 1912, Edinburgh.
118 Reynolds to Charles Sarolea, [17 December 1912], Edinburgh. Reynolds was in fact exploiting the story of the young wife some nine months before *An Unofficial Divorce* came out. The edition of the *Bodleian* for April 1909 carried a follow-up report to the interview with Reynolds the previous month, from a local correspondent that can only have been Reynolds himself. "The latest, according to the gospel of the Seacombe tea-table, is that Stephen Reynolds lives in a fisherman's house and flouts the middle-class would-be patronisers because he's been so cruel to his young wife that he's had to separate and hide his head. The lady

who tells it knows it's true, because it was told her by a lady who visits much among the poor. Stephen Reynolds, however, denies it and authorises the lady who told him to state that the real reason is bigamy."

119 William Reddeford to Charles Sarolea, 10 January 1913, Edinburgh.
120 Charles Sarolea to William Reddeford, 11 January 1913, Edinburgh.
121 Reynolds to Charles Sarolea, 16 January 1913, Edinburgh.
122 Charles Sarolea to Reynolds, 18 January 1913, Edinburgh.
123 Reynolds to Charles Sarolea, 20 January 1913, Edinburgh.
124 Charles Sarolea to Reynolds, 18 January 1912, Edinburgh.
125 Edward Thomas diary, 17 September 1912, NLW.
126 W.H. Davies *Later Days*, Jonathan Cape 1927 37.
127 David Garnett to the author, 11 May 1980. See also David Garnett *The Golden Echo*, Chatto & Windus 1953 130.
128 W.H. Hudson to J.R.Harding, 9 November 1912, RSPB Library, Sandy.
129 Reynolds to George Macmillan, 26 September 1912, Add.Mss.54965.

Chapter 16 The Cornish Committee 1912–13

1 Reynolds to Edward Garnett, 2 January 1907, Wright 65.
2 Reynolds to George Macmillan, 20 August 1911, Add.Mss.54965.
3 Reynolds to Philippa Powys, 21 September 1911, Texas.
4 Reynolds to Frederick Macmillan, 1 October 1911, Add.Mss.54965.
5 Preface to *The Inshore Fisheries*, 23 February 1913, PRO, MAF/41 1500. The articles were gathered together and reprinted in February 1913 as preliminary background reading for the Departmental Committee on Inshore Fisheries, giving Reynolds a firm platform even before the Committee had started its work. They reappeared, slightly amended, later in 1913 in the cheap edition of *Seems So!* under the title *Small Holdings of the Sea*.
6 Reynolds to George Macmillan, 13 December 1911, Add.Mss.54965.
7 *The Times*, 7, 10 and 17 February 1912.
8 *Seems So!*, cheap edition 1913 219.
9 *ibid*. 228.
10 *ibid*. 230.
11 *ibid*. 227.
12 *ibid*. 231.
13 *ibid*. 245.
14 *The Times*, 17 February 1912. In the cheap edition of *Seems So!*, page 251, he adjusted this passage to allow for the possible alternative of a central organisation at *county* level.
15 *The Times*, 17 February 1912.
16 Reynolds to Henry Maurice, 20 September 1912, Wright 153.

17 Reynolds to George Sturt, 20 March 1912, Wright 149.
18 House of Commons Report, 26 June 1912, Col.378.
19 Reynolds to George Macmillan, 27 June 1912, Add.Mss.54965.
20 The Eton-educated Archer, born in 1855, was more of an academic expert than a hands-on administrator. He had spent eight years in Norway engaged in salmon research and had been an Inspector of Salmon Fisheries from 1892-8. He clearly failed to win the confidence of Runciman who, in January 1912, treated him rather cruelly by directing at the last minute that an inspector, W.O.Borley, should give evidence to the Development Commission in his place. Runciman was patently concerned that Archer would give a less than dynamic public impression (Minutes Walter Runciman, 24 January and 15 February 1912, PRO, MAF/41 1229). It was in the same Supply debate that Runciman announced Archer's retirement on health grounds with a fulsome tribute, and hinted at his successor (House of Commons Report, 26 June 1912, Col. 382). Archer died five years later in August 1917.
21 "Farewell to the Road", transcript in possession of Grizelda Maurice.
22 "An Aged Pelican", transcript in possession of Grizelda Maurice.
23 Interview with Grizelda Maurice, 20 October 1997.
24 Henry Maurice, prefatory letter to Minister of Agriculture in *Fisheries in the Great War, being the Report on Sea Fisheries for the years 1915, 1916, 1917 and 1918 of the Board of Agriculture and Fisheries. Parts I and II.* Cmd.585. 1920. Quoted Wright xxiii.
25 Reynolds to Henry Maurice, 20 August 1912, Pursey.
26 Henry Maurice to Reynolds, 5 September 1912, Pursey.
27 Henry Maurice to Reynolds, 7 September 1912, Pursey.
28 Reynolds to Henry Maurice, 20 September 1912, Wright 152. Wright had rather cautiously disguised Wilson's identity.
29 Reynolds to Sir James Wilson, 23 September 1912, Pursey.
30 Reynolds to George Macmillan, 26 September 1912, Add.Mss.54965.
31 Henry Maurice to Reynolds, 26 September 1912, Pursey.
32 Reynolds to Henry Maurice, 19 October 1912, Pursey. He may have been thinking of Tom, rather than Bob, as his accompanying collaborator – *see* page 519.
33 Henry Maurice to Reynolds, 3 October 1912, Pursey.
34 Reynolds to Henry Maurice, 19 October 1912, Pursey.
35 Report of the Committee appointed to consider applications of the Devon and Cornwall Local Fisheries Committees for grants from the Development Fund for assisting fishermen to instal motor power in their boats and for other purposes (the Harmsworth Committee), Cd.6752, 1913 para. 3.
36 Meeting of Development Commission, 19 December 1911. The Commission wrote to the Board of Agriculture and Fisheries on 22 December requesting the preparation of an overall national scheme to

enable them to decide the Cornish application in the wider context (PRO, MAF/41 1230).

37 At its meeting on 6 October 1911, the Commission had specifically rejected the idea of making loans to fund policy developments (PRO, MAF/41 1229).

38 *The Times*, 10 February 1912. This restriction on the use of Development Fund money was later reversed by the Law Officers in England (see *The Inshore Fisheries* 7 footnote, PRO, MAF/41 1500). Accordingly, Reynolds omitted this passage from the cheap edition of *Seems So!* (page 237).

39 *The Times*, 17 February 1912.

40 Harmsworth Committee Report *op.cit.* 22.

41 Henry Maurice to Reynolds, 5 September 1912, Pursey.

42 Reynolds to Henry Maurice, 6 September 1912, Pursey.

43 Reynolds to Henry Maurice, 19 October 1912, Pursey.

44 Minute of Appointment by Walter Runciman, 5 November 1912, Harmsworth Committee Report *op.cit.* 3.

45 Reginald Pound and Geoffrey Harmsworth *Northcliffe*, Cassell 1959 228.

46 Walter Runciman to Cecil Harmsworth, 15 November 1911, Lime Lodge. Runciman's previous PPS, Harold Cawley, was bored with agriculture and had been stolen by McKenna for the Home Office.

47 Interview with Grizelda Maurice, 20 October 1997.

48 *Times Literary Supplement*, 20 February 1919.

49 Reynolds to Francis Mildmay, 27 December 1912, Wright 157.

50 Cecil Harmsworth diary, 11 November 1912, Lime Lodge.

51 *Times Literary Supplement*, 20 February 1919.

52 Cecil Harmsworth diary, 12 November 1912, Lime Lodge.

53 *ibid.* 13 November 1912.

54 *ibid.* 14 November 1912.

55 *ibid.* 15 November 1912.

56 *ibid.* 16 November 1912.

57 *ibid.* 18 November 1912.

58 *ibid.* 19 November 1912.

59 *ibid.* 20 November 1912.

60 Reynolds to Francis Mildmay, 27 December 1912, Wright 157.

61 Cecil Harmsworth diary, 26 November 1912, Lime Lodge.

62 *ibid.* 27 November 1912.

63 *ibid.* 28 November 1912.

64 Reynolds to Charles Sarolea, 2 December 1912, Edinburgh.

65 Cecil Harmsworth diary, 6 December 1912, Lime Lodge.

66 Reynolds to an unknown correspondent, 20 December 1912, Wright 155.

67 Reynolds to Francis Mildmay, 27 December 1912, Wright 157.

68 Reynolds to Harold Wright, [December 1912], transcribed Philippa Powys, Mappowder.

69 Reynolds to Tom Woolley, 24 December 1912, Wright 156.

70 Reynolds to Philippa Powys, undated but postmarked 24 December 1912, Texas.
71 Cecil Harmsworth diary, 31 December 1912, Lime Lodge.
72 *ibid.* 1 January 1913.
73 *ibid.* 2 January 1913.
74 *ibid.* 3 and 4 January 1913. Treloen is now a set of modern holiday apartments, next door to Mrs Blight's house which is privately owned. In his diary Harmsworth anglicised the spelling to "Trelawn".
75 *ibid.* 4 January 1913.
76 *ibid.* 5 January 1913.
77 *ibid.* 6 and 7 January 1913.
78 *ibid.* 8 January 1913.
79 *ibid.* 9 January 1913.
80 *ibid.* 10 and 11 January 1913.
81 *ibid.* 12 January 1913.
82 Harmsworth Committee Report *op.cit.* para. 38, quoted Wright 164.
83 Cecil Harmsworth diary, 13 January 1913, Lime Lodge. Harmsworth misheard Porthgwarra as "Porthwarren".
84 *ibid.* 14 January 1913.
85 *Times Literary Supplement*, 20 February 1919.
86 Reynolds to Charles Sarolea, 20 January 1913, Edinburgh.
87 Cecil Harmsworth diary, 19 and 24 January 1913, Lime Lodge.
88 Reynolds to Bob Woolley, 31 January 1913, Wright 158.
89 Cecil Harmsworth diary, 17 February 1913, Lime Lodge.
90 Reynolds to Cecil Harmsworth, 18 February 1913, Wright 159.
91 Reynolds to an unrecorded correspondent, 6 March 1913, transcribed Philippa Powys, Mappowder. It may have been to Atkinson, the Secretary to the Committee, who collaborated with Reynolds on Appendix IV to the Report on the technical details of motors for fishing boats.
92 Reynolds to Cecil Harmsworth, 26 March 1913, Wright 160.
93 Reynolds to Henry Maurice, 6 April 1913, Wright 163.
94 Harmsworth Committee Report *op.cit.* Minority Note, para 2 (10).
95 *ibid.* paras.53-5.
96 *ibid.* para.54.
97 *ibid.* para.39.
98 *ibid.* para.40.
99 Reynolds to Cecil Harmsworth, 23 April 1913, Wright 164.
100 Cecil Harmsworth diary, 22 June 1913, Lime Lodge.
101 *ibid.* 21 June 1913.
102 Reynolds to George Macmillan, 24 June 1913, Add.Mss.54965, partially quoted Wright 171.
103 Manuscript version, possibly the original, in Harmsworth papers, Lime Lodge. In addition to the footnote reproduced here, Reynolds had sug-

gested an alternative bowdlerised reading for lines 7 and 8: "And buyers with 'gross impropriety' / Did snarl untruths to brown us well on toast". This much weakened version was used by Wright (page 171) with his eye on the libel laws.

104 Cecil Harmsworth diary, 21 June 1913, Lime Lodge.

Chapter 17 Development Commission 1913–14

1 Report of the Departmental Committee on Inshore Fisheries 1914 Cd.7373 iii.
2 Reynolds to Bob Woolley, 31 January 1913, Wright 158.
3 *ibid.*
4 Reynolds to Walter Runciman, 6 April 1913, Wright 160.
5 *Evening Standard*, 24 February 1913.
6 Reynolds to Editor, *Evening Standard*, 28 February 1913, Wright 159.
7 Cecil Harmsworth diary, 14 February 1913, Lime Lodge.
8 Report of the Departmental Committee on Inshore Fisheries, Minutes of Evidence 1914 Cd.7374, 12 March 1913, 53.
9 *Times Literary Supplement*, 20 February 1919.
10 Minutes of Evidence *op.cit.*, 2 April 1913, 1443-47.
11 *ibid.* 921-6.
12 *ibid.* 1028-35.
13 *ibid.* 1060-69.
14 *ibid.* 1135-40.
15 Reynolds to Henry Maurice, 6 April 1913, Wright 163.
16 Reynolds to Walter Runciman, 6 April 1913, Wright 161.
17 Reynolds to Henry Maurice, 6 April 1913, Wright 162.
18 Minutes of Evidence *op.cit.*, 16 April 1913, 2423-4.
19 Reynolds to Jane Reynolds, 10 April 1913, Wright 163.
20 Reynolds to an unrecorded correspondent [?April] 1913, transcribed Philippa Powys, Mappowder.
21 Vaughan Nash to Ponsonby, 19 April 1908, MS Eng.Lett.c.656 Bodleian Library.
22 Vaughan Nash to Ponsonby, 10 October 1906, MS Eng.Lett.c.653 Bodleian Library.
23 Vaughan Nash to Ponsonby, 6 February 1912, MS Eng.Lett.c.659/53 Bodleian Library.
24 Vaughan Nash to Ponsonby, 6 March 1912, MS Eng.Lett.c.659/59 Bodleian Library.
25 *See*, for example, Maurice's minute of 4 May 1912 on their meeting of 2 May to discuss Noel Buxton's PQ of 7 May, which produced the all-time stonewalling reply (PRO, MAF/41 1230).
26 Minutes of 37th meeting, 7 May 1913, PRO, D 1/1.

27 Reynolds to Harold Wright, 17 May 1913, transcribed Philippa Powys, Mappowder.
28 Reynolds to Vaughan Nash, 27 May 1913, Wright 166.
29 Reynolds to Vaughan Nash, 27 May 1913, Wright 165.
30 Minutes of 38th meeting, 28 May 1913, PRO, D 1/1.
31 Reynolds to Vaughan Nash, 3 June 1913, Wright 169.
32 Reynolds to Vaughan Nash, 5 June 1913, Wright 170.
33 Reynolds to Vaughan Nash, 3 June 1913, Wright 169.
34 Reynolds to George Macmillan, 24 June 1913, Add.Mss.54965.
35 Minutes of 39th meeting, 26 June 1913, PRO, D 1/1.
36 Reynolds to Edward Garnett, 17 October 1913, Texas.
37 Reynolds to Cecil Harmsworth, 20 October 1913, Wright 172.
38 Reynolds to Cecil Harmsworth, 25 October 1913, Lime Lodge.
39 Reynolds to Cecil Harmsworth, 30 October 1913, Lime Lodge.
40 Reynolds to Jonathan Barron, [?30 October 1913], transcribed Philippa Powys, Mappowder.
41 Reynolds to Edward Garnett, 21 May 1914, Texas.
42 Minutes of 55th meeting, 25 November 1914, PRO, D 1/1.
43 Reynolds to Pinker, 13 July 1913, Northwestern.
44 Reynolds to Cecil Harmsworth, 30 October 1913, Lime Lodge.
45 Cecil Harmsworth diary, 25 September 1913, Lime Lodge.
46 Reynolds to Jane Reynolds, 2 October 1913, transcribed Philippa Powys, Mappowder.
47 He stayed there, for example, from 7 to 10 October, and was back for supper on the 12th (Cecil Harmsworth diary, Lime Lodge).
48 Reynolds to Cecil Harmsworth, 25 October 1913, Lime Lodge.
49 Cecil Harmsworth diary, 11-14 November 1913, Lime Lodge.
50 Cecil Harmsworth diary, 17-18 November 1913, Lime Lodge.
51 Reynolds to Vaughan Nash, 24 November 1913, Wright 173.
52 Reynolds to Cecil Harmsworth, 22 November 1913, Lime Lodge.
53 Cecil Harmsworth diary, 10-11 December 1913, Lime Lodge.
54 Reynolds to Cecil Harmsworth, 21 December 1913, Lime Lodge.
55 Reynolds to Pinker, 22 December 1913, Northwestern.
56 Reynolds to George Macmillan, 13 January 1914, Add.Mss.54965.
57 Reynolds to Pinker, 15 January 1914, Northwestern.
58 Reynolds to Cecil Harmsworth (two PCs), 24 February 1914, Lime Lodge.
59 Reynolds to George Macmillan, 21 August 1912, Add.Mss.54965. Reynolds had written on the 19th: "Is Mrs. Macmillan, do you know, angry with me? I very much hope not, for the last thing I'd want to do would be to upset her, because, after all, kindness is much more important than opinions" (Add.Mss.54965). Macmillan was reassuring: "I will give your message to Mrs. Macmillan, but I know that she was much pleased at the last letter she had from you and it can only have been the extreme pressure that is always upon her during the first weeks up at

Danby which has prevented her writing to say so" (George Macmillan to Reynolds, 20 August 1912, Add.Mss. 55508).

60 Reynolds to Cecil Harmsworth, 8 March 1913, Lime Lodge.

61 *ibid.*

62 "During the day I attend at Winchester House what I fervently trust will prove the penultimate meeting of the Inshore Fisheries Committee." (Cecil Harmsworth diary, 27 March 1914, Lime Lodge).

63 The secretary was A.T.A. Dobson, son of Austin Dobson, the poet Reynolds had parodied at Owens College. He was later to succeed Maurice as head of the Fisheries Division.

64 Reynolds to Cecil Harmsworth, 15 April 1914, Wright 180. A Fishermen's Song, *New Weekly*, 16 May 1914. The *New Weekly* lasted only seven months, folding with the outbreak of war.

65 Cd.7373 *op.cit.*, Recommendation I (b).

66 *ibid.* xxxvii.

67 Now at Lime Lodge.

68 Reynolds to Jane Reynolds, 15 May 1914, Wright 186.

69 Farnham Roper, Assistant Secretary, Harbour Department, Board of Trade, to Reynolds, 30 September 1913, copy at Lime Lodge.

70 Reynolds to Farnham Roper, 1 October 1913, copy at Lime Lodge.

71 R.Ellis Cunliffe, Solicitor, Board of Trade, to Reynolds, 7 October 1913, copy at Lime Lodge.

72 Board of Trade Conference, 28 October 1913, The Fishermen's Case, PRO, MAF 41/443.

73 Reynolds to Cecil Harmsworth, 25 October 1913, Lime Lodge.

74 Removal of sand and shingle at Sidmouth, Report of Captain C.E. Monro, 31 October 1913, PRO, MAF 41/443.

75 Minute Reynolds, 3 November 1916, PRO, MAF 41/443.

76 Reynolds to Cecil Harmsworth, 30 October 1913, Lime Lodge.

77 Report of Captain Monro *op.cit.*

78 Reynolds to Cecil Harmsworth, 2 March 1914, Lime Lodge.

79 Reynolds to Cecil Harmsworth, 8 March 1914, Lime Lodge, partially quoted Wright 178.

80 Farnham Roper to Reynolds, 30 April 1914, copy at Lime Lodge.

81 The Sidmouth Foreshore. Prohibitionary Order and the proposed revocation of it over a certain area, under an arrangement with the Sidmouth Manor, memorandum by Reynolds, 4 May 1913. The Harbour Department, in very defensive mood, drew up a list of answers to Reynolds' ten points, classified Confidential, which Roper handed over to Martyr on 7 May (PRO, MAF 41/443).

82 Minute Richard Martyr, 5 May 1914; Reynolds to Board of Agriculture and Fisheries, 5 May 1914, PRO, MAF 41/443.

83 Minute Richard Martyr, 7 May 1914, PRO, MAF 41/443.

84 Minute Henry Maurice, 6 May 1914, PRO, MAF 41/443.

85 Report of an inspection of the foreshore at Sidmouth, Charles Fryer, 21 May 1914, PRO, MAF 41/443.

86 "Mr Reynolds came in at the end of last week on another matter, and mentioned incidentally that he had heard nothing further from the B.T. I telephoned them today to ascertain the position of the matter, and am informed that the papers are now before the President, and that *nothing definite has been done in the matter of the granting of the lease.* As soon as definite action is taken, we shall be advised. (Minute Charles Fryer, 14 July 1914, PRO, MAF 41/443).

87 Reynolds to John Burns, 25 July 1914, Wright 189.

88 Minute Charles Fryer, 12 November 1914, PRO, MAF 41/443.

89 Cecil Harmsworth diary, 9 October 1913, Lime Lodge.

90 Cecil Harmsworth diary, 6 March 1914; Reynolds to Cecil Harmsworth, 23 March 1914, Lime Lodge.

91 Cecil Harmsworth diary, 9 July 1914, Lime Lodge.

92 Minutes of 51st meeting, 23 July 1914, PRO, D 1/1.

93 Cecil Harmsworth diary, 26 August 1914, Lime Lodge. Minutes of 53rd meeting of Development Commission, 25 September 1914, PRO, D 1/1.

94 Report of the Development Commissioners for the year ended 31 March 1920, 216. The decision must have been cleared in correspondence since there was no meeting of the Commission between 31 July and 1 October.

95 Reynolds to Cecil Harmsworth, 30 October 1913, Lime Lodge.

96 Reynolds to Cecil Harmsworth, 22 November 1913, Lime Lodge.

97 Reynolds to Vaughan Nash, 24 November 1913, Wright 172.

98 Report of the Development Commissioners for the year ended 31 March 1920, 217.

99 Reynolds to Edward Carpenter, 23 February 1914, Sheffield.

100 Reynolds to Cecil Harmsworth (two PCs), 24 February 1914, Lime Lodge.

101 Reynolds to Cecil Harmsworth, 2 March 1914, Lime Lodge. The establishment of the boat insurance scheme was another single-handed Reynolds success. None of the co-operative insurance concerns would touch boat insurance (Reynolds to Cecil Harmsworth, 22 November 1912, Lime Lodge), but he fought on against all the odds until his "Cornish Fishing Vessels Insurance Society Limited" was finally set up in 1915, and by the end of its first year had 63 vessels insured. So successful did it become that in 1917, at the behest of the Government, it took over boat insurance for the whole of England and Wales. For a discussion of this remarkable achievement, see *Fisheries in the Great War,* Cmd.585 *op.cit.* 78.

102 Reynolds to Cecil Harmsworth, 15 April 1914, Wright 181.

103 Reynolds to Bob Woolley, [?May 1914], Wright 185.

104 Reynolds to Vaughan Nash, 6 May 1914, transcribed Philippa Powys, Mappowder.

105 Reynolds to Vaughan Nash, 14 July 1914, Wright 187.
106 Hilaire Belloc *The Cruise of the "Nona"*, Constable 1925 129.

Chapter 18 Psycho-economics 1913–14

1 Reynolds to Edward Garnett, 18 July 1908, Wright 104.
2 Reynolds to Edward Carpenter, 2 April 1914, Sheffield.
3 Arthur Calder-Marshall *Havelock Ellis*, Hart-Davis 1959 174. There is a remote possibility that one of the case studies in Ellis' revised and enlarged third edition of *Sexual Inversion* could have been Reynolds.
4 Havelock Ellis to Edward Carpenter, 25 March 1913, Sheffield.
5 Reynolds to Edward Carpenter, 25 May 1913, Sheffield.
6 Reynolds to Edward Carpenter, 23 February 1914, Sheffield.
7 Reynolds to Cecil Harmsworth, 15 April 1914, Wright 180.
8 Reynolds to Harry Paynter, 16 March 1915, Wright 205.
9 *New Weekly*, 11 April 1914, reproduced Wright 206.
10 The Huxley Lecture "Life and Consciousness", delivered at the University of Birmingham on 24 May 1911 – see Henri Bergson *Mind-Energy*, Macmillan 1920 1. The lecture was linked in popular imagination with the first post-impressionist exhibition in London six months before as heralding a revolution in thought and culture.
11 Reynolds to George Sturt, 20 March 1912, Wright 149.
12 *The Times*, 25 March 1912.
13 Reynolds to George Macmillan, 28 March 1912, Add.Mss.54965.
14 Reynolds to George Macmillan, 20 May 1912, Add.Mss.54965.
15 Reynolds to George Macmillan, 31 May 1912, Add.Mss.54965.
16 George Macmillan to Reynolds, 4 June 1912, Add.Mss.55507.
17 Reynolds to George Macmillan, 6 June 1912, Add.Mss.54965.
18 Reynolds to Pinker, 6 June 1912, Northwestern.
19 Reynolds to George Macmillan, 6 June 1912, Add.Mss.54965.
20 Reynolds to George Macmillan, 16 June 1912, Add.Mss.54965.
21 George Macmillan to Reynolds, 17 June 1912, Add.Mss.55507.
22 Reynolds to George Macmillan, 18 June 1912, Add.Mss.54965.
23 Reynolds to Lindsay Bashford, 26 August 1912, Wright 151.
24 Reynolds to Pinker, 1 September 1912, Northwestern.
25 Reynolds to George Macmillan, 4 September 1912, Add.Mss.54965.
26 Reynolds to Frederick Macmillan, 10 October 1912, Add.Mss.54965.
27 What the Poor Man Thinks, *Christian Commonwealth*, 22 January 1913.
28 Reynolds to Harold Wright, 11 June 1913, transcribed Philippa Powys, Mappowder.
29 Reynolds to Pinker, 13 July 1913, Northwestern.
30 George Macmillan to Reynolds, 20 June 1913, Add.Mss.55514. Reynolds to George Macmillan, 24 June 1913, Add.Mss.54965.
31 Macmillans to F. Chalmers Dixon, 20 and 22 August 1913,

Add.Mss.55516.
32 Reynolds to F. Chalmers Dixon, 24 August 1913, transcribed Philippa Powys, Mappowder.
33 Reynolds to Frederick Macmillan, 24 August 1913, Reading.
34 George Macmillan to Reynolds, 26 August 1913, Add.Mss.55516.
35 Reynolds to George Macmillan, 29 August 1913, Add.Mss.54965.
36 Will Macmillan to Reynolds, 3 September 1913, Add.Mss.55517.
37 Reynolds to Will Macmillan, 4 September 1913, Add.Mss.54965.
38 Frederick Macmillan to Reynolds, 5 September 1913, Add.Mss.55517.
39 Reynolds to Frederick Macmillan, 24 August 1913, Reading.
40 George Macmillan to Reynolds, 26 August 1913, Add.Mss.55516.
41 Reynolds to George Macmillan, 29 August 1913, Add.Mss.54965.
42 Reynolds to Will Macmillan, 4 September 1913, Add.Mss.54965.
43 Reynolds to George Macmillan, 29 August 1913, Add.Mss.54965.
44 *Seems So!*, cheap edition, Macmillan 1913 vii.
45 Macmillan edition books, Add.Mss.55919.
46 Reynolds to George Macmillan, 13 January 1914, Add.Mss.54965.
47 Reynolds to George Macmillan, 30 July 1913, Add.Mss.54965.
48 Cecil Harmsworth diary, 26 and 27 July 1913, Lime Lodge.
49 Reynolds to George Macmillan, 30 July 1913, Add.Mss.54965.
50 Reynolds to Frederick Macmillan, 24 August 1913, Reading.
51 Reynolds to an unrecorded correspondent, 25 August 1913, transcribed Philippa Powys, Mappowder.
52 Reynolds to Jane Reynolds, 30 September 1915, Wright 209.
53 Reynolds to Cecil Harmsworth, 1 December 1913, Wright 174, original Lime Lodge.
54 Tradition in the Woolley family, interview with Frances Woodward, 30 April and 1 May 1999.
55 Reynolds to Pinker, 13 July 1913, Northwestern.
56 Conveyance Philip H. Payn and his mortgagees to S.S. Reynolds, 3 November 1914, in possession of Peter Hand.
57 Reynolds to Edward Garnett, 17 October 1913, Texas.
58 Reynolds to Cecil Harmsworth, 20 October 1913, Wright 172.
59 Reynolds to Jane Reynolds, [?October 1913], transcribed Philippa Powys, Mappowder.
60 Reynolds to Cecil Harmsworth, 25 October 1913, Lime Lodge.
61 Reynolds to Cecil Harmsworth, 1 December 1913, Wright 173.
62 Reynolds to Harold Wright, 4 December 1913, Wright 175.
63 Reynolds to Cecil Harmsworth, 21 December 1913, Lime Lodge.
64 Reynolds to Pinker, 22 December 1913, Northwestern.
65 *Sidmouth Herald*, 17 January 1914.
66 Reynolds to Editor, *Sidmouth Herald*, 17 January 1914.
67 H.F. Clements to Editor, *Sidmouth Observer*, 21 January 1914.
68 "Sidmouth Resident" to Editor, *Sidmouth Herald*, 24 January 1914.

69 Reynolds to Cecil Harmsworth, 25 January 1914, Lime Lodge.
70 William Hastings to Editor, *Sidmouth Herald*, 29 January 1914.
71 Reynolds to Editor, *Sidmouth Herald*, 26 January 1914.
72 Reynolds to Editor, *Sidmouth Herald*, 19 February 1914.
73 An Open Letter to Mr Stephen Reynolds, *Sidmouth Herald*, 4 February 1914.
74 Reynolds to John Burns, 21 January 1914, Wright 177.
75 Reynolds to Jane Reynolds, 24 January 1914, transcribed Philippa Powys, Mappowder.
76 Reynolds to Edward Carpenter, 23 February 1914, Sheffield. Reynolds to Cecil Harmsworth, 2 March 1914, Lime Lodge.
77 Reynolds to Edward Carpenter, 2 April 1914, Sheffield.
78 Conveyance Philip H. Payn and his mortgagees to S.S. Reynolds, 3 November 1914, in possession of Peter Hand. Reynolds to Jane Reynolds, 1 August 1914, Wright 191.
79 Reynolds to Jane Reynolds, 15 May 1914, Wright 186.
80 Reynolds to Edward Carpenter, 17 July 1914, Sheffield.
81 Reynolds to Jane Reynolds, 17 July 1914, Wright 189.
82 Reynolds to Edward Carpenter, 28 July 1914, Sheffield.
83 Reynolds to Jane Reynolds, 15 August 1914, Wright 193.
84 Reynolds to Cecil Harmsworth, 14 July 1913, transcribed Philippa Powys, Mappowder.
85 Reynolds to Cecil Harmsworth, 20 October 1913, Wright 172.
86 Reynolds to Cecil Harmsworth, 25 October 1913, Lime Lodge.
87 Reynolds to Pinker, 21 November 1913, Northwestern.
88 Reynolds to Cecil Harmsworth, 1 December 1913, Wright 173.
89 Reynolds to Vaughan Nash, 24 November 1913, Wright 173.
90 Wealth and Life, I Politics, *Nation*, 8 November 1913 247.
91 Wealth and Life, II Unrest, *Nation*, 22 November 1913 355.
92 Wealth and Life, I Politics, *Nation*, 8 November 1913 247.
93 Wealth and Life, III Wealth Itself, *Nation*, 6 December 1913 425.
94 Wealth and Life, VI Work (i), *Nation*, 17 January 1914 669.
95 *ibid.*
96 Wealth and Life, VII Work (ii), *Nation*, 31 January 1914 741.
97 Wealth and Life, XI The Attitude of Labor, *Nation*, 23 May 1914 300.
98 Wealth and Life, IX Class (i), *Nation*, 28 February 1914 898.
99 Wealth and Life, X Class (ii), *Nation*, 21 March 1914 1038.
100 Reynolds to Cecil Harmsworth, 8 March 1914, Lime Lodge, partially quoted Wright 179.
101 Reynolds to Henry Maurice, 31 December 1916, Wright 228.

Chapter 19 District Inspector 1914–16

1 C. Ernest Fayle *Charles Wright: A Memoir*, Allen & Unwin 1943 94.

Reynolds to Cecil Harmsworth, undated PC, Lime Lodge.
2 Reynolds to Jane Reynolds, 4 August 1914, Wright 192.
3 Reynolds to Jane Reynolds, 1 August 1914, Wright 191.
4 Reynolds to Jane Reynolds, 4 August 1914, Wright 192.
5 Reynolds to Jane Reynolds, 15 August 1914, Wright 193.
6 Reynolds to Jane Reynolds, 27 October 1914, Wright 199.
7 Helen Mildmay *Flete*, local pamphlet.
8 Reynolds to Francis Mildmay, 21 October 1914, Wright 197.
9 Reynolds to Bob Woolley, undated, Wright 185.
10 Alice Mildmay diary, 29 August 1914, Mothecombe.
11 Helen Mildmay *Flete*.
12 Reynolds to Bob Woolley, 1 September 1914, Wright 194. Wright gives the origin of this letter as Mevagissey, but it was in fact Teignmouth.
13 Alice Mildmay diary, 31 August 1914, Mothecombe.
14 Reynolds to Bob Woolley, 1 September 1914, Wright 194.
15 Alice Mildmay diary, 31 August 1914, Mothecombe.
16 Reynolds to Bob Woolley, 1 September 1914, Wright 194.
17 *ibid*.
18 Alice Mildmay diary, 1 September 1914, Mothecombe.
19 Reynolds to Alice Mildmay, 1 September 1914, Mothecombe.
20 Alice Mildmay diary, 2 September 1914, Mothecombe.
21 Alice Mildmay diary, 29 August 1914, Mothecombe.
22 Reynolds to Alice Mildmay, 6 September 1914, Mothecombe.
23 Reynolds to Harold Wright, 7 September 1914, Wright 195. Reynolds to Bob Woolley, 8 September 1914, Wright 196.
24 Reynolds to Alice Mildmay, 12 September 1914, Mothecombe. The letter was written from Devizes.
25 Memorandum on Small Harbours Commissions, 15 September 1914, Lime Lodge.
26 Reynolds to Alice Mildmay, 12 September 1914, Mothecombe.
27 Minutes of 40th meeting, 31 July 1913, PRO, D1/1.
28 Minutes of 48th meeting, 22 April 1914, PRO, D1/1.
29 Minutes of 51st meeting, 23 July 1914, PRO, D1/1.
30 E.W. Hollingworth to Secretary, Development Commission, covering individual harbour reports, 13 October 1914, PRO, D4/73.
31 Reynolds to Jane Reynolds, 27 October 1914, Wright 197.
32 Reynolds to Harold Wright, 10 November 1914, transcribed Philippa Powys, Mappowder.
33 Reynolds to Harold Wright, 6 November 1914, Wright 199.
34 He wrote to Pinker on 30 November from the Bolton Hotel, Brixham: "Hope you are fit and flourishing. I am fittish, but more druv than ever" (Northwestern). He wrote to Cecil Harmsworth on 2 December from the Tanners' hotel: "At present, I am racing round over the Devon Motor Grant, and a job for Maurice" (Lime Lodge).

35 Reynolds to Jane Reynolds, 29 November 1914, Wright 199.
36 Reynolds to Henry Maurice, [November 1914], transcribed Philippa Powys, Mappowder.
37 Minutes of 55th meeting of Development Commission, 25 November 1914, PRO, D1/1.
38 Reynolds to Jane Reynolds, 29 November 1914, Wright 199.
39 Reynolds to Vaughan Nash, 11 January 1915, Wright 201.
40 Reynolds to Harold Wright, [November 1914], transcribed Philippa Powys, Mappowder.
41 Reynolds to Pinker, 16 December 1914, Northwestern.
42 Reynolds to Pinker, 21 November 1913, Northwestern.
43 Reynolds to Pinker, 15 January 1914, Northwestern.
44 Reynolds to Pinker, 30 November 1914, Northwestern.
45 Reynolds to Pinker, 1 January 1915, Northwestern.
46 *ibid.*
47 Reynolds to Vaughan Nash, 11 January 1915, Wright 202.
48 Reynolds to Jane Reynolds, 17 January 1915, Wright 203.
49 Alice Mildmay diary, 30 January 1915, Mothecombe.
50 Lecture "Inshore Fisheries", 18 January 1915, Lime Lodge 2.
51 *ibid.*16.
52 *ibid.*50.
53 Reynolds to Cecil Harmsworth, 4 February 1915, Lime Lodge.
54 Reynolds to Francis Mildmay, 4 August 1915, Mothecombe.
55 Fishermen in War, *The Times*, 11 December 1914. F.B. Mildmay to Editor, *The Times*, 13 and 26 January 1915. Cecil Harmsworth to Editor, *The Times*, 15 January 1915.
56 Reynolds to Alice Mildmay, 10 January 1915, Mothecombe.
57 Reynolds to Vaughan Nash, 11 January 1915, Wright 202.
58 Alice Mildmay diary, 17 November 1914, Mothecombe.
59 Alice Mildmay diary, 30 January 1915, Mothecombe.
60 Alice Mildmay diary, 31 January 1915, Mothecombe.
61 Reynolds to Alice Mildmay, 31 January 1915, Mothecombe.
62 Reynolds to Francis Mildmay, 4 August 1915, Mothecombe.
63 Interview with Frances Woodward, 30 April 1999. *Puffin* never came home again.
64 For a full account of the fisheries problems of the war, see *Fisheries in the Great War* Cmd.585 *op.cit.*
65 Reynolds to Francis Mildmay, 4 August 1915, Mothecombe.
66 Reynolds to Henry Maurice, 18 September 1917, Wright 251.
67 Reynolds to Edward Carpenter, 14 April 1916, Sheffield.
68 Richard Church *The Voyage Home*, Heinemann 1964 95. The review has not been traced. When *The Porch* was published in February 1937, Orwell was up to his neck in the trenches of the Aragon front, so either Church's memory was at fault, or this was a much later review. Church

had already paid an indirect tribute to Reynolds in *Over the Bridge*: "Dramatic critics, black-and-white artists, *longshore writers*, roosted in the Government departments, pretending to ignore the larger reputations which they were making in the outside world" (Heinemann 1957 108) [*my italics*].

69 Reynolds to George Sturt, 23 December 1911, Wright 146.
70 Reynolds to Henry Maurice, 11 June 1918, Wright 329.
71 Reynolds to Henry Maurice, 19 March 1917, Wright 238.
72 Reynolds to Henry Maurice, 18 June 1917, Wright 240.
73 Reynolds to Henry Maurice, 18 November 1917, Wright 283.
74 Reynolds to Richard Martyr, 23 March 1916, Wright 216. Wright mistakenly gives Martyr the first initial C.
75 They were not the preserve of just *Cornish* fisher children; back in Sidmouth, Bobby had a fleet of them too (PMH 18).
76 Interview with Annie Allen and Mary Paynter, 10 March 1999.
77 Reynolds to Harry Paynter, 16 March 1915, Wright 205.
78 Reynolds to Henry Maurice, 17 October 1915, Wright 209.
79 *Western Times*, 1 November 1915. PRO, ASSI/21/83.
80 Reynolds to Harold Wright, 7 November 1915, Wright 210.
81 Reynolds to Edward Carpenter, 23 February 1914, Sheffield.
82 Reynolds to Edward Carpenter, 2 April 1914, Sheffield.
83 Reynolds to Edward Carpenter, 28 July 1914, Sheffield.
84 Reynolds to Edward Carpenter, 17 July 1914, Sheffield.
85 Reynolds to Edward Carpenter, 28 July 1914, Sheffield. It was not uncommon for middle-class homosexuals to choose working-class partners – the social unacceptability of transcending the class barrier in a way relieving the sexual stigma. For a useful discussion of the relationship of homosexuality to art, see Jeffrey Meyers *Homosexuality and Literature 1890-1930*, Athlone Press 1977.
86 Reynolds to Jane Reynolds, 1 August 1914, Wright 191.
87 Reynolds to Henry Maurice, 18 September 1917, Wright 256.
88 Reynolds to Philip Hartog, 7 January 1917, Wright 231.
89 Reynolds to Cecil Harmsworth, 16 March 1915, Lime Lodge, partially quoted Wright 204.
90 Alice Mildmay diary, 29 May 1915, Mothecombe.
91 Alice Mildmay diary, 3 July 1915, Mothecombe.
92 Alice Mildmay diary, 8 August 1915, Mothecombe.
93 Reynolds to Cecil Harmsworth, 26 January 1916, Lime Lodge.
94 Reynolds to Henry Maurice, 26 January 1916, Wright 213.
95 Reynolds to R. Skinner, 7 May 1916, Wright 216.
96 Reynolds to Charles Thorp, 31 January 1916, Wright 213.
97 Reynolds to Henry Maurice, 7 September 1916, Wright 218.
98 Reynolds to Henry Maurice, 27 September 1916, Wright 219.
99 Reynolds to Cecil Harmsworth, 17 November 1916, Lime Lodge, partially

quoted Wright 223.
100 Reynolds to H. Ford, 27 January 1915, Wright 203.
101 Reynolds to Henry Maurice, 27 October 1916, Wright 221. Reynolds to Jane Reynolds, 12 November 1916, Wright 222.
102 Minute, 3 November 1916, PRO, MAF 41/443.
103 Reynolds to Jane Reynolds, 12 November 1916, Wright 222.

Chapter 20 The Book's Written 1917–19

1 Reynolds to Cecil Harmsworth, 14 January 1917, Lime Lodge.
2 Reynolds to Cecil Harmsworth, 17 November 1916, Wright 224.
3 Reynolds to Henry Maurice, 20 December 1916, Wright 228.
4 Reynolds to Henry Maurice, 31 December 1916, Wright 228.
5 *Fisheries in the Great War* Cmd.585 *op.cit.* Chapters I and IX.
6 Ninth report of Development Commission, PRO, D3.
7 Reynolds to Cecil Harmsworth, 14 January 1917, Lime Lodge.
8 Cecil Harmsworth diary, 22, 29 and 30 January 1917, Lime Lodge.
9 Cecil Harmsworth diary, 6, 8 and 9 February 1917, Lime Lodge. I have taken the reference in Reynolds to Cecil Harmsworth, 11 February 1917, to having "sat on two committees" as indicating his attendance at only the first two *meetings* of the Motor Loans Committee. There is no indication, in Harmsworth's diary or elsewhere, of a *separate* committee they both attended that week.
10 *Fisheries in the Great War* Cmd.585 *op.cit.* Chapter VII.
11 Reynolds to Cecil Harmsworth, 16 March 1915, Lime Lodge.
12 Reynolds to Harold Wright, 10 February 1917, Wright 234. Katie Powys in her transcription, Mappowder, added in the name of the hotel.
13 Henry Maurice in C. Ernest Fayle *Harold Wright: A Memoir,* Allen & Unwin 1934.
14 *ibid.*100.
15 Reynolds to Cecil Harmsworth, 11 February 1917, Lime Lodge, partially quoted Wright 235.
16 Reynolds to Henry Maurice, 13 February 1917, Wright 235.
17 *Fisheries in the Great War* Cmd.585 *op.cit.* Chapter VI.
18 Cecil Harmsworth diary, 15 February 1917, Lime Lodge.
19 *Fisheries in the Great War* Cmd.585 *op.cit.* Chapter VI.
20 *Morning Post*, 27 March 1917.
21 Cecil Harmsworth diary, 28 March 1917, Lime Lodge.
22 Cecil Harmsworth diary, 22 March 1917, Lime Lodge.
23 Cecil Harmsworth diary, 19 April 1917, Lime Lodge.
24 Reynolds to Cecil Harmsworth, 10 March 1917, Lime Lodge.
25 Alice Mildmay diary, 8 March 1917, Mothecombe.
26 Reynolds to an unrecorded correspondent, 15 February 1917, transcribed

Philippa Powys, Mappowder
27 *Western Morning News*, 15 February 1919.
28 Reynolds to M.P. Willcocks, 9 April 1917, Devon Record Office, partially quoted Wright 238.
29 M.P. Willcocks *The Eyes of the Blind*, Hutchinson 1917 131, 147, 248 and 289.
30 *ibid.* 133, 245, 149 and 249.
31 *ibid.* 105.
32 *ibid.* 178.
33 Reynolds to M.P. Willcocks, 9 April 1917, Wright 238.
34 On 26 June the Development Commission set up a four man committee, including Reynolds and Nash, to consider the management and finance of fishery harbours (72nd meeting minutes, PRO, D1/2). At the meeting of this committee on 13 July (PRO, D4/73) it was agreed to draw up a list of current projects and of harbours requiring work. It appears to have been the completion of this paper that hung guiltily over Reynolds' head for the rest of the year.
35 Reynolds to Cecil Harmsworth, 26 January 1916, Lime Lodge.
36 Reynolds to Jonathan Barron, 27 January 1917, Lime Lodge.
37 71st meeting minutes, 11 May 1917, PRO, D1/2.
38 72nd meeting minutes, 26 June 1917; 73rd meeting minutes, 25 September 1917, PRO, D1/2.
39 Reynolds to Cecil Fox, 27 July 1917, Wright 242.
40 Interview with Roger Elliott, 10 July 1999.
41 Reynolds to Henry Maurice, 29 July 1917, Wright 243.
42 Reynolds to Henry Maurice, 31 July 1917, Wright 244.
43 Reynolds to Henry Maurice, 21 August 1917, Wright 248.
44 Reynolds to Henry Maurice, 8 December 1917, Wright 290.
45 Reynolds to E.H. Collingwood, 23 September 1917, Wright 272.
46 Reynolds to Henry Maurice, 28 November 1916, Wright 225.
47 Reynolds to Henry Maurice, 18 September 1917, Wright 252.
48 *ibid.* 260.
49 *ibid.* 265.
50 *ibid.* 270.
51 *see* note 13 above.
52 Reynolds to Henry Maurice, 11 November 1917, Wright 282.
53 Reynolds to Henry Maurice, 5 December 1917, Wright 284.
54 Reynolds to Henry Maurice, 18 November 1917, Wright 284.
55 Reynolds to Henry Maurice, 8 December 1917, Wright 290.
56 Reynolds to Henry Maurice, 16 December 1917, Wright 297.
57 "Those two old warriors Tom Woolley and E. Gibbs again turned out and there is a good deal of football in both yet" – *Sidmouth Herald*, 30 October 1908.
58 Reynolds to Henry Maurice, 26 April 1918, Wright 326.

59 Reynolds to Henry Maurice, 26 December 1917, Wright 302.
60 Indenture Stephen Reynolds, Charles Wright and Martha Lole, 19 April 1918, in possession of Peter Hand.
61 Reynolds to S. Stagg, 26 December 1917, Wright 299.
62 Reynolds to Henry Maurice, 26 December 1917, Wright 300.
63 Reynolds to Henry Maurice, 27 December 1917, Wright 303.
64 Reynolds to Pinker, 20 January 1918, Wright 309.
65 Reynolds to Henry Maurice, 23 March 1918, Wright 312.
66 Reynolds to Henry Maurice, 7 April 1918, Wright 320.
67 Reynolds to Henry Maurice, 8 August 1918, Wright 330.
68 Reynolds to Henry Maurice, 26 April 1918, Wright 326.
69 Reynolds to Henry Maurice, 5 May 1918, Wright 327.
70 "The Fish Trade. Note on the superfluity of middlemen, and on the official tendency to grant them a vested interest in their position", 15 July 1918, Lime Lodge.
71 "Notes arising out of recent fishery tour", 10-12 November 1918, Lime Lodge 1.
72 *ibid.* 7.
73 *ibid.* 6.
74 *ibid.* 2.
75 *ibid.* 5.
76 Edward Carpenter diary, 12 September 1918, Sheffield.
77 Edward Carpenter diary, 13 September 1918, Sheffield. For the decline of the Taormina print, see Jocelyn Brooke *The Dog at Clambercrown*, Bodley Head 1955 77.
78 Reynolds to Edward Carpenter, 9 November 1918, Sheffield.
79 Edward Carpenter diary, 14 September 1918, Sheffield.
80 Reynolds to Edward Carpenter and George Merrill, 15 September 1918, Sheffield.
81 Reynolds to Edward Carpenter, 11 October 1918, Sheffield. The letter was written from the 1917 Club, next door to the Mont Blanc.
82 Reynolds to an unrecorded correspondent, 22 October 1918, transcribed Philippa Powys, Mappowder.
83 "Notes arising out of recent fishery tour" *op.cit.* 9.
84 *ibid.*12.
85 *Wiltshire Gazette*, 7 November 1918.
86 Reynolds to Edward Carpenter, 9 November 1918, Sheffield.
87 Reynolds to Henry Maurice, 11 November 1918, Wright 333.
88 Reynolds to Henry Maurice, 1 December 1918, Wright 335.
89 Reynolds to Henry Maurice, 30 March 1918, Wright 318.
90 Reynolds to Henry Maurice, 25 November 1918, Wright 334.
91 Reynolds to Henry Maurice, 27 November 1918, Wright 334.
92 Reynolds to Henry Maurice, 1 December 1918, Wright 335.
93 Reynolds to Henry Maurice, 17 December 1918, 337.

94 Reynolds to Cecil Harmsworth, 28 December 1918, Lime Lodge, partially quoted Wright 338.
95 *ibid.*
96 Reynolds to Henry Maurice, 1 December 1918, Wright 335.
97 Minutes of 81st meeting, 11 December 1918, PRO, D1/2.
98 "Development Commission and Fisheries", 6 January 1919, PRO, D4/50. Nash had already suggested the idea of a conference at the meeting of 11 December.
99 Reynolds to Henry Maurice, 5 January 1919, Wright 339. William Albert Dagworthy, popularly known as WAD, was the chief Sidmouth entrepreneur of the early days of motoring who ran a garage, first established in 1911, next to the Bedford Hotel and backing on to Bedford Square (*see* Reginald Lane *Old Sidmouth*, Devon Books 1995 120 and 122-3). He was to play an important part in the pulling down of the poor man's house 20 years later.
100 Reynolds to Henry Maurice, 17 December 1918, Wright 337.
101 Reynolds to Henry Maurice, 20 January 1919, Wright 342.
102 Minutes of 82nd meeting, 29 January 1919, PRO, D4/50. See also Lyster Jameson to Vaughan Nash, 4 March 1919, with his comments on Reynolds' last memorandum (PRO, D4/50).
103 Edward Carpenter diary, 29 January 1919, Sheffield.
104 Reynolds to Henry Maurice, 7 February 1919, Wright 344.
105 Annotation by Jane Reynolds in her edition of Wright, in possession of Stephen Wiltshire.
106 Reynolds to Henry Maurice, 7 February 1919, Wright 344.
107 *Reports on Public Health and Medical Subjects No.4: Report on the Pandemic of Influenza 1918-1919*, Ministry of Health 1920. One explanation of the unusual age incidence was that the adolescent and adult populations were suffering disproportionately from the debilitating influences of war. Another theory which carries more weight today is that the physical reaction of young adults to the virus was so swift and intense that they were killed by the general inflammation and swamping of the lungs that it produced. By contrast, the body of those under 20 had not yet learned the reaction; in those over 40, the reaction had slowed (*see* Alfred W. Crosby *America's Forgotten Pandemic: The Influenza of 1918*, CUP 1989 221).
108 Reynolds to Henry Maurice, 7 February 1919, Wright 344.
109 Reynolds to Henry Maurice, 8 February 1919, Wright 346.
110 She attended his funeral – *Sidmouth Herald*, 22 February 1919.
111 His death certificate, which records the onset of acute inflammation of the lungs after four days, shows that his illness followed the classic pattern. It is described in detail in Ministry of Health Report No.4 *op.cit.*: "Some cases became pulmonary at the outset, others in a few hours or days. The pulmonary involvement was an acute infective inflamma-

tion, sometimes progressing as a broncho-pneumonia, at other times it swept through the body like a virulent toxaemia or septicaemia. In some cases there were few or no physical signs, in others dullness, bronchial breathing, crackling rales, broncophony, and pectoriloquy; in others signs of coagulative oedema, haemorrhage, abscess and collapse. The normal progress of a pneumonia case was rare. There was pain, headache 'behind the eyes', ear-ache, cough, a high respiration rate ('polypnoea'), variable fever, followed by a toxaemic or pulmonary complication on the third or fourth day. The toxaemia was heralded by early cyanosis, delirium, a rapid pulse and epistaxis. The heliotrope cyanosis indicated a bad prognosis; it was evidently not cardiac in origin, but an intoxication, recalling the 'purulent bronchitis' experienced in 1916-17 in Aldershot (expectoration of enormous quantities of purulent sputum, heliotrope cyanosis, and high fatality), itself an infection due in part to *B. Influenzae* and in part to the *Micrococcus catarrhalis*, streptococcus, or associated organisms. There are grounds for believing that both forms of cyanosis were caused by an albuminous exudate [*the white liquid of my text*] in the alveoli and interstitial tissue of the lung. The pulmonary complications which arose were various, and included oedema, broncho-pneumonia, haemorrhage, effusions, and sometimes abscess. The onset of the lung changes was indicated by alteration in the character of the sputum, increased respiration rate, pain, and diminished respiratory movements and air entry".

112 *Sidmouth Herald*, 22 February 1919. It was a remarkable turn-out at such short notice: Leonie Reynolds, Ada Bennett, Robert Harraway (his brother-in-law), Nellie Woolley and Chip (Tom was away on mine-sweeping duty), Harry Woolley, Bill Woolley and Bobby, Granfer and Grannie Pratt. Frances, his step-sister, now 22, was desolate at being unable to get down in time (Osborne 244). Two of the floral tributes placed on the grave tell the whole story of his two families: "In *affectionate* memory from his father, mother and sister". "In *loving* memory from 'Mam' and Bob Woolley and family" [*my italics*].

Chapter 21 The Letters 1923

1 Cecil Harmsworth diary, 14 February 1919, Lime Lodge.
2 Alice Mildmay diary, 31 July 1918, Mothecombe. She had met him at Newton Abbot where both were attending a public meeting on Hallsands.
3 Alice Mildmay diary, 15 February 1919, Mothecombe.
4 Harry Paynter to Edward Carpenter, 20 February 1919, Sheffield.
5 Harry Paynter to Cecil Harmsworth, 21 April 1919, Lime Lodge.
6 Philippa Powys "Phoenix" third version, Texas 41.

7 *Times Literary Supplement*, 20 February 1919.
8 *The Times*, 15 February 1919.
9 *Spectator*, 22 March 1919.
10 *Western Morning News*, 15 February 1919.
11 *Wiltshire Gazette*, 20 February 1919.
12 Seccombe to Edward Garnett, 8 March 1919, in possession of Richard Garnett, Hilton Hall.
13 W.H. Hudson to Edward Garnett, 2 March 1919, *Letters from W.H. Hudson to Edward Garnett*, Dent 1925 190.
14 Reynolds to Henry Maurice, 23 March 1918, Wright 313.
15 Harold Wright to Pinker, 2 February 1921, Northwestern.
16 Harold Wright to Pinker, 28 April 1920, Northwestern.
17 Harold Wright to Pinker, 2 February 1921, Northwestern.
18 Harold Wright to Pinker, 17 May 1920, Northwestern.
19 Harold Wright to Cecil Harmsworth, 8 November 1919, Lime Lodge.
20 Cecil Harmsworth to Henry Maurice, 3 December 1919, Lime Lodge.
21 Henry Maurice to Cecil Harmsworth, 10 December 1919, Lime Lodge.
22 Cecil Harmsworth to Harold Wright, 15 December 1919, Lime Lodge.
23 Harold Wright to Cecil Harmsworth, 16 December 1919, Lime Lodge.
24 Harold Wright to Leonard Woolf, 27 December 1922, Reading.
25 Harold Wright to Cecil Harmsworth, 6 October 1920, Lime Lodge.
26 Harold Wright to Cecil Harmsworth, 18 October 1920, Lime Lodge.
27 Wright xiii. Osborne 52.
28 He compares the relationship with Harry to that of father and son (Wright xxiii).
29 Harold Wright to Pinker, 2 February 1921, Northwestern.
30 George Macmillan to Harold Wright, 20 December 1920, Add.Mss.55567.
31 George Macmillan to Harold Wright, 10 January 1921, Add.Mss.55567.
32 Harold Wright to Pinker, 2 February 1921, Northwestern.
33 Macmillan sent two letters to Wright on 10 January, of which only the official one has survived (Harold Wright to Pinker, 2 February 1921, Northwestern). It seems likely that the personal one was designed to distance himself even further from the official decision.
34 Harold Wright to Pinker, 2 February 1921, Northwestern.
35 Wright vi. Harold Wright to Leonard Woolf, 27 December 1922, Reading.
36 Harold Wright to Leonard Woolf, 27 December 1922, Reading.
37 Leonard Woolf to Harold Wright, 20 December 1922, Reading.
38 Harold Wright to Leonard Woolf, 30 November 1922, Reading.
39 Leonard Woolf to Harold Wright, 20 December 1922; Harold Wright to Leonard Woolf, 27 December 1922, Reading.
40 Leonard Woolf to Harold Wright, 28 December 1922, Reading.
41 Harold Wright to Leonard Woolf, 29 December 1922, Reading.
42 Leonard Woolf to Harold Wright, 12 January 1923, Reading.

43 Harold Wright to Leonard Woolf, 29 December 1922, Reading.
44 George Macmillan to Harold Wright, 26 January 1923, Reading.
45 Harold Wright to Leonard Woolf, 22 February 1923, Reading.
46 Leonard Woolf to Harold Wright, 12 January 1923, Reading. Wright signed the contract on 5 March and paid £100 on account on 8 June.
47 Harold Wright to Leonard Woolf, 14 January 1923, Reading.
48 Harold Wright to Leonard Woolf, 5 March 1923; Cecil Harmsworth to Harold Wright, 22 May 1923, Reading. Wright drew up a list of 38 ports with libraries, now in the Hogarth Press papers, Reading.
49 Leonard Woolf to Clara Walker, 11 March 1923, Reading. Despatch note R. and R. Clark to Hogarth Press, 13 April 1923, Reading.
50 *Nation and Athenaeum*, 19 May 1923.
51 *Daily Telegraph*, 19 June 1923.
52 *Challenge*, 25 May 1923.
53 *Times*, 15 May 1923.
54 *Cassell's Weekly*, 8 August 1923.
55 Reynolds to Pinker, 15 January 1914, Northwestern.
56 Hogarth Press to Harold Wright, 7 November 1932; Harold Wright to Hogarth Press, 12 November 1932, Reading.
57 Leonard Woolf to Norman Leys, 18 July 1924, Frederic Spotts (edited) *Letters of Leonard Woolf*, Harcourt, Brace, Jovanovich 1989 286.
58 Ford Madox Ford *Return to Yesterday*, Carcanet 1999 290.
59 Jessie Conrad *Joseph Conrad and his Circle*, Jarrolds 1935 132. She remembered the *Mountain*, no doubt, because Reynolds had sent a personal copy to her, rather than her husband.
60 Archibald Marshall *Out and About*, John Murray 1933 141.
61 Douglas Goldring *Reputations: Essays in Criticism*, Chapman & Hall 1920 224.
62 T.E. Lawrence to Edward Garnett, 2 May 1928, David Garnett (edited) *The Letters of T.E. Lawrence*, Spring Books 1964 603. Lawrence placed Reynolds with D.H. Lawrence and Stephen Crane among the writers "who excited me in my youth", despite his "irritating sense of the difference between a complicated man and a worker". In September 1933, he was overjoyed to run across in Salisbury a copy of *A Poor Man's House* and the *Mountain* going cheap (*ibid.* 779, 846 and 777).
63 Prefatory letter to *Fisheries in the Great War* Cmd.585 *op.cit.*
64 *ibid.* iv.
65 Cecil Harmsworth diary, 27 May 1920, Lime Lodge.
66 Cecil Harmsworth diary, 28 May 1920, Lime Lodge.
67 Sir Herbert Russell *Friend of the Fisherman. Mr Cecil Harmsworth's Tour of the West. Cooperation the Remedy against Extinction.* Reprinted from the *Western Morning News* November 1924 4. There is a copy at Lime Lodge.
68 Cecil Harmsworth diary, 1 December 1924, Lime Lodge.
69 Harry Paynter to Edward Carpenter, 2 June 1924, Sheffield.

70 Interview with Annie Allen and Mary Paynter, 10 March 1999. At a meeting of St Ives fishermen he organised on 6 June 1955, a resolution was passed "that the St Ives Fishermen's Protection Association be formed as a memorial to Lord Harmsworth, Vaughan Nash, Stephen Reynolds and Harold Wright for their love of seamen and fishermen." Harry became the very active Chairman and Secretary, cajoling the local MP – see his letters of 21, 24 and 31 May 1955 in the *Western Echo*, quoting, among other things, the old purple patch of 1913.
71 "Phoenix" *op.cit.* 42.
72 *ibid.* 45.
73 Philippa Powys diary, June-July 1928, Mappowder.
74 The manuscript is at Texas.
75 Philippa Powys diary, 23 May 1927, Mappowder.
76 Philippa Powys diary, 6 December 1930, Mappowder.
77 *Sidmouth Herald*, 11 December 1937.
78 Anna Sutton *A Story of Sidmouth*, 1959 128.
79 When Semaphore took her children on cliff walks in the early 1940s, she pointed to the house and told them "That could have been ours" – interview with Frances Woodward, 30 April 1999.
80 Interview with Frances Woodward, 30 April 1999. Philippa Powys diary, March 1928, Mappowder. The Woolleys moved in to 3, Sea View Terrace on 14 October 1927.
81 Interview with Frances Woodward, 30 April 1999.
82 The area had been made the subject of Ministry of Health clearance orders early in 1937 (*see*, for example, *Sidmouth Herald*, 3 April 1937). On 13 December 1937 the Town Planning Committee considered an application from William Dagworthy to expand his garage into the clearance area, building a garage and flats (Minutes of Sidmouth Town Planning Committee, Devon Record Office 6730). It was approved by the full Council on 4 January 1938 (*Sidmouth Herald*, 8 January 1938). A revised version of the scheme was passed by the Planning Committee on 14 March 1938 and approved by the full Council on 29 March (*Sidmouth Herald*, 2 April 1938). A similar application by Burgoyne Brothers to build a garage and flats on the south-eastern side of the Square did not go through so smoothly, but was finally passed by the Committee on 24 January 1939 and the Council on 31 January (*Sidmouth Herald*, 4 February 1939).

There is evidence that the Council felt a modicum of guilt at this wholesale clearance of the oldest part of the town. At a Council meeting on 19 April 1938, the Chairman, Mr Fitzgerald, referred somewhat defensively "to the demolition of some of the old cottages, and said he believed anyone who had seen for himself the actual conditions existing in such areas could not help but feeling the Council had done the right thing" (*Sidmouth Herald*, 23 April 1938).

In April 1978 the Council gave approval to the building of the present Western Court – 12 flats in two blocks with 18 car spaces (*Sidmouth Herald*, 29 April 1978). By March the following year, the first phase of building was complete (*Sidmouth Herald*, 24 March 1979).

83 *Sidmouth Herald*, 2 October 1937.

84 The original suggestion for a plaque came in a letter to the local paper from the Reynolds enthusiast Harry Daniell, a local headmaster, who had been banging away at the Council for years: "My then sixth form was amazed to learn that Sidmouth had not sufficient pride and interest to provide a memorial plaque in appreciation of the one literary masterpiece created in our town: Stephen Reynolds "A Poor Man's House". Alas! No one in the Council cared then. But could they not now provide such an acknowledgement with the last oozings of their coffers? The original house is no longer in situ, due to a local speculator's ideas of progress, but Hope Cottage, where Steve Reynolds also lived with the Woolleys until his untimely death, would provide an apt location" (*Sidmouth Herald*, 16 March 1974). A distant relative, Walter Reynolds from Essex, came forward with an offer to put up the money (*Sidmouth Herald*, 1 June 1974).

85 In fact, Harry Daniell had made the point that he had lived there (*see* note 84 above) but this was unaccountably contradicted by the *Sidmouth Herald* article of 1 June 1974: "One snag is that Reynolds never actually lived at Hope Cottage. The building was used for a time as a local fisheries office when Reynolds was championing the fishermen's cause and opposing Whitehall bureaucrats. No doubt research will be made to find if there is a more suitable building to bear a memorial plaque".

Six years later, by the week of the plaque unveiling, the paper had at last caught up with the truth, even revealing the little-known information that Reynolds had lived in The Retreat as well: "The plaque cannot be mounted on the Poor Man's House in Bedford Square, for the Woolley family's old home has long vanished. So Mrs. Reed will unveil it at 11.30 next Thursday morning on a wall at Sidmouth Museum, where Stephen Reynolds *also lived* and worked at an important time of his life, when it was Hope Cottage [*my italics*]. ......when he returned to Hope Cottage for rest, he found stacks of paper, so he moved over the road to Mrs. Gibbs for peace in the house where Sidmouth War Memorial Ex-Servicemen's Club is now" (*Sidmouth Herald*, 21 June 1980). The message came too late for the Museum Committee of the Sid Vale Association who had authorised the design of the plaque.

Epilogue June 1927

The epilogue is made up of verbatim extracts from Philippa Powys' diary of

June 1927, Mappowder, with some material excised. The Bowd Inn on the A3052, just a mile up the road from Sidmouth station, seems to have been Reynolds' second "local" after the Anchor in Old Fore Street. It was no doubt a useful retreat when political and domestic pressures in the town centre became too hot.

Bibliography of Stephen Reynolds

Harold Wright was the first to compile a bibliography, comprising over a hundred items and published in the *Wiltshire Archaeological Magazine* in June 1920 (xli 74-8). J.D. Osborne in his 1977 thesis extended this list and corrected some of Wright's inaccuracies. This bibliography now adds a few further items to that of Osborne, but is by no means exhaustive. There is, in particular, one major gap still to be filled. In 1920 Wright left a list of 140 book reviews with the Wiltshire bibliographical collections in Devizes Museum, but this has since gone missing. I have been able to trace only a limited number of Reynolds' reviews, all of which are included in the present list.

BOOKS

Devizes and Roundabout.	Mate's Illustrated Guides. 1906.
A Poor Man's House.	John Lane. 1908.
The Holy Mountain.	John Lane. 1909.
Alongshore.	Macmillan. 1910.
Seems So!	Macmillan. 1911.
How 'Twas.	Macmillan. 1912.
The Lower Deck.	Dent. 1912.
Letters.	Hogarth Press. 1923.

Devizes and Roundabout was given a second edition in 1907. There was a second edition of *A Poor Man's House* in 1909 and a cheap edition, with a new preface, from Macmillan in 1911. It was republished by Jonathan Cape in 1928 in the Travellers' Library, and there were further editions from London Magazine Editions in 1980 and OUP in 1982. A cheap edition of *Seems So!* appeared in 1913. *A Poor Man's House, The Holy Mountain* and *Alongshore* were all published in separate editions in the United States.

SHORT STORIES AND ARTICLES

Edmund Spenser. The Poet's Poet, *Owen's College Union Magazine,* May 1900.

The Great English Elegies, *Owen's College Union Magazine,* February 1901.

John Keats, *Owen's College Union Magazine,* March 1901.

Funeral Marches, *Owen's College Union Magazine,* April 1901.

Izaak Walton. His Life and 'Lives', *Owen's College Union Magazine,* June 1901.

Izaak Walton. The Compleat Angler, *Owen's College Union Magazine,* November 1901.

The Career and Opinions of Dr. Ahazuerus Tims, B.Sc., Ph.D., *Owen's College Union Magazine,* November and December 1901; January 1902.

Her Immortality, *Owen's College Union Magazine*, March 1902.
The Narratives of a Laboratory Liar, *Owen's College Union Magazine*, May and June 1902.
A Letter from Paris, *Cheltenham Examiner*, 19 November, 3, 17 and 31 December 1902; 14, 28 January, 18 February, 4 and 25 March 1903.
Pauvre Punaise, *Owen's College Union Magazine*, January 1903.
Tema con Variazione, *Weekly Critical Review*, 30 April and 7 May, 1903. (HT as *Self-Exiled*)
A Piano and an Omnibus, *Weekly Critical Review*, 28 May, 4 and 11 June, 1903.
A Kitten: That's All, *Week's Survey*, 3 December 1904. (HT)
The Simple Cat, *English Review*, 21 October 1905. (HT as *The Citizenry of Cats*)
The Bookman Illustrated History of English Literature (contributions on Blake, De Quincey and Keats), 1905-6.
A Love's Hunger, *Pall Mall Magazine*, March 1906. (HT)
The Blue-Stocking, *Pall Mall Magazine*, April 1906. (HT as *A Marriage of Learning*)
Twinses, *Speaker*, 30 June 1906. (HT)
Dear Papa's Love Story, *Tribune*, 2 and 3 July, 1906. (HT)
Autobiografiction, *Speaker*, 6 October 1906.
Another Prodigal, *Speaker*, 22 December 1906. (HT)
Field Club Devastation, *Daily Mail*, 9 January 1907.
A Yokel's Impression of London, *Daily Mail*, 31 August 1907.
Fun o' the Fair, *Daily News*, 6 December 1907.
Touch and Go with the Sea, *Country Life*, 4 April 1908.
Seamen and the Sea, *Country Life*, 16 May 1908.
A Poor Man's House (extracts), *Albany Review*, May, July and August 1908.
The Prawner, *Daily News*, 6 July 1908.
Robbery Robbed, *Daily News*, 23 July 1908. (HT)
Literary Green Pastures, *Readers' Review*, August 1908.
A Steam-Burst Afloat, *Daily News*, 31 August 1908. (HT)
The Beachcomber, *Albany Review*, September 1908. (HT)
Squalls, *Country Life*, 19 September 1908. (AS)
The Marketing of Small Produce, *English Review*, January 1909. (AS as *Longshore Fisheries*)
What Workmen Think of Conscription, *Nation*, 13 February 1909. (SS as *Conscription*)
Seems So! The Suffragettes, *Spectator*, 20 February 1909. (SS)
The Holy Mountain (extracts), *English Review*, April, May, June and July 1909.
Four Mothers, *Daily News*, 23 April 1909. (HT as Mothers All)
Poor Law Report, *Spectator*, 1 May 1909. (SS)
Lame Duck Hunting, *Westminster Gazette*, 5 June 1909. (AS)
Longshore Sketches - The Longshore, *Westminster Gazette*, 19 June 1909. (AS)
Longshore Sketches - Tides and the Beach, *Westminster Gazette*, 26 June 1909. (AS)

Longshore Sketches - Old Boats, *Westminster Gazette*, 3 July 1909. (AS)
Longshore Sketches - Winds and Waves, *Westminster Gazette*, 10 July 1909. (AS)
Longshore Sketches - Semaphore, *Westminster Gazette*, 17 July 1909. (AS)
Seems So! Education, *Spectator*, 24 July 1909. (SS)
Longshore Sketches - Fogs, *Westminster Gazette*, 24 and 31 July 1909. (AS)
Longshore Sketches - An Old Man's Tale, *Westminster Gazette*, 7 August 1909. (AS)
Longshore Sketches - Frights, *Westminster Gazette*, 14 August 1909. (AS)
Longshore Sketches - A Sort of a kind of Wreck, *Westminster Gazette*, 21 August 1909. (AS)
Longshore Sketches - A Fleet of Nets, *Westminster Gazette*, 28 August 1909. (AS)
Longshore Sketches - Two Fishers in Boulogne, *Westminster Gazette*, 4 and 11 September 1909. (AS as *Two Fishers Abroad*)
Longshore Sketches - Seining, *Westminster Gazette*, 18 September 1909. (AS)
Longshore Sketches - A Glut of Mackerel, *Westminster Gazette*, 25 September 1909. (AS)
Longshore Sketches - They There Kids, *Westminster Gazette*, 2 October 1909. (AS)
The Coastguard, *Daily Mail*, 16 December 1909.
An Unofficial Divorce, *Fortnightly Review*, January 1910. (HT)
What the Poor Want, *Quarterly Review*, January 1910. (SS as *Various Conclusions*)
Miss Willcocks at Large, *Bodleian*, January 1910.
The People and their Vote, *Fortnightly Review*, April 1910. (SS)
Beachcombings, *Westminster Gazette*, 16 April 1910. (AS)
Beachcombings - Flotsam and Jetsam, *Westminster Gazette*, 23 and 30 April 1910. (AS)
A Herring Haul in a French Steam Drifter, *Blackwoods Magazine*, May 1910. (AS)
Beachcombings - Beautiful Onionhead, *Westminster Gazette*, 7 May 1910. (AS)
The Children's Charter at Home, *New Age*, 5 May 1910. (SS as *The Children's Charter*).
Turned Out, *New Age*, 12 May 1910. (HT)
Beachcombings - The Bare-Kneed Mate, *Westminster Gazette*, 14 May 1910. (AS)
Beachcombings - A Legend, *Westminster Gazette*, 21 May 1910. (AS)
Beachcombings - A Drownded Corpse, *Westminster Gazette*, 28 May 1910. (AS)
Beachcombings - Navy Chaps, *Westminster Gazette*, 4 June 1910. (AS)
With Baby's Help, *New Age*, 30 June 1910.
Fisherman and Motorboat, *Daily News*, 5 July 1910. (AS as *Small Holdings on the Sea*)
His Majesty's Medal, *Westminster Gazette*, 31 August 1910. (HT)
Divorce for the Poor, *Fortnightly Review*, September 1910. (SS)
Puffin Home, *Blackwoods Magazine*, October 1910. (HT)
Log of the Bristol Beauty, *T.P.'s Christmas Magazine*, November 1910. (HT)
Seems So, *Nation*, 24 December 1910. (SS as *Electioneering*)
Brother Christmas and Mr Bookworm, *Daily News*, 26 December 1910.

Benjie and the Bogeyman, *Blackwoods Magazine*, February 1911. (HT)
Jasper Braund's Boat, *T.P.'s Magazine*, March 1911. (HT)
Labour versus Brainwork, *The Times*, 27 and 31 March 1911. (SS)
The By-Products of Tariff Reform, *English Review*, April 1911. (SS)
Public Houses, *New Age*, 4 and 11 May 1911. (SS)
Policemen, *Nation*, 27 May 1911. (SS)
A Dog's Life Told To It, *Open Window*, June 1911. (HT)
Weekends at Nesscombe - Hannaford Himself, *Westminster Gazette*, 3 and 10 June 1911.
Weekends at Nesscombe - The Commonplace, *Westminster Gazette*, 17 and 24 June 1911.
Weekends at Nesscombe - Age against Youth, *Westminster Gazette*, 1 July 1911.
Weekends at Nesscombe - Sweet William, *Westminster Gazette*, 8 July 1911.
Weekends at Nesscombe - Tragedy, *Westminster Gazette*, 15 July 1911.
Magistrates, *Nation*, 15 July 1911. (SS)
Weekends at Nesscombe - The Conquest of Ugliness, *Westminster Gazette*, 22 and 29 July 1911.
Poor Class Houses, *New Age*, 27 July 1911. (SS)
Weekends at Nesscombe - Deadman's Escape, *Westminster Gazette*, 5 August 1911.
Weekends at Nesscombe - The Concert, *Westminster Gazette*, 12 August 1911.
Money, *New Age*, 17 August 1911. (SS)
Weekends at Nesscombe - London, *Westminster Gazette*, 19 August 1911.
Weekends at Nesscombe - Nakedness, *Westminster Gazette*, 26 August 1911.
Weekends at Nesscombe - Rabelaisianism, *Westminster Gazette*, 2 September 1911.
Weekends at Nesscombe - Immortality, *Westminster Gazette*, 9 and 16 September 1911.
Navy Discontents, *English Review*, October 1911. (SS. 1st edition)
An Introduction to Seems So, *New Age*, 5 October 1911. (SS)
Sillie Saltie, *Throne*, 11 November 1911. (HT)
Inshore Fisheries (i) Decline, *The Times*, 7 February 1912. (SS. Cheap edition as *Small Holdings of the Sea*)
Inshore Fisheries (ii) Revival, *The Times*, 10 February 1912. (SS. Cheap edition as *Small Holdings of the Sea*)
Inshore Fisheries (iii) Administration, *The Times*, 17 February 1912. (SS. Cheap edition as *Small Holdings of the Sea*)
A Fisherman's Holiday, *Pall Mall Gazette*, 2,9,11,16,23,30 April and 9 May 1912. (HT as *A Third-Class Journey*)
Mrs Tripp's Flutter, *Bristol Times*, 5 June 1912 (HT)
Joseph Conrad and Sea Fiction, *Quarterly Review*, July 1912.
The Great Silent Navy, *Daily Chronicle*, 10 July 1912. (LD)
Men of the Lower Deck, *Daily Chronicle*, 17 July 1912. (LD)
The Lower Deck - Why the A.B. is Discontented, *Daily Chronicle*, 22 July 1912. (LD)

The Sort of Boy, *Daily Chronicle*, 3 August 1912. (LD)
Invalided Out, *Daily Chronicle*, 13 August 1912. (LD)
A Chief's Mess, *Daily Chronicle*, 24 August 1912. (LD)
Pensioners, *Daily Chronicle*, 29 August 1912. (LD)
Some Questions of its Future, *Daily Chronicle*, 7 September 1912. (LD)
Ships versus Men, *English Review*, September 1912. (LD)
How I began, *T.P.'s Weekly*, 18 October 1912. (Letters)
Tramping Afloat, *Everyman*, 15 November 1912.
Free Libraries and Novel Censorship, *T.P.'s Weekly*, 12 September 1913.
£9,000,000 worth of Fish, *Daily Mail*, 13 September 1913.
The Peacemaker, *Daily Mail*, 20 September 1913.
Wealth and Life - Politics, *Nation*, 8 November 1913.
Wealth and Life - Unrest, *Nation*, 22 November 1913.
Wealth and Life - Wealth Itself, *Nation*, 6 December 1913.
The Faith I Live By, *Christian Commonwealth*, 10 December 1913. (Letters)
Wealth and Life - Civilisation, *Nation*, 20 December 1913.
Wealth and Life - Society, *Nation*, 3 January 1914.
Wealth and Life - Work (i), *Nation*, 17 January 1914.
Wealth and Life - Work (ii), *Nation*, 31 January 1914.
Wealth and Life - Industry, *Nation*, 14 February 1914.
Wealth and Life - Class (i), *Nation*, 28 February 1914.
Wealth and Life - Class (ii), *Nation*, 21 March 1914.
Labour and Religion, *Challenge*, 1 May 1914.
Our Unconquerable Fishermen, *Daily Mail*, 18 May 1914.
Wealth and Life - The Attitude of Labor, *Nation*, 23 May 1914.
Fish, Prices and Profits, *Daily Mail*, 23 June 1914.
Sea Fish at Home, *Daily News*, 25 July 1914.
Fish Food in War Time, *Daily Mail*, 18 September 1914.
Fishermen in War, *The Times*, 11 December 1914.
Frank Brandt R.N., *Asiatic Review*, 15 February 1915.
The One Food that is Cheaper, *Daily Mail*, 20 February 1915.
Our Fishermen and Our Fish, *The Times*, 2 June 1915.
Inshore Fisheries and Naval Needs, *Quarterly Review*, July 1915.
Inshore Fisheries Development, *Country Life*, 22 April and 20 May 1915.
Fish as Food, *The Times Trade Supplement*, January 1917.

POEMS

This Year's Prize Poem, *Owen's College Union Magazine*, February 1901.
From Caen Hill, *Owen's College Union Magazine*, March 1901.
Pecunia Fugit, *Owen's College Union Magazine*, November 1901.
Song, *Owen's College Union Magazine*, December 1901.
A Correspondence: from Chopin's Nocturne Op. 48 no. 2, *Owen's College Union Magazine*, January 1902.
Looking towards Cyprus, *Owen's College Union Magazine*, March 1902.

Prisoners, *New Weekly*, 11 April 1914.
A Fishermen's Song, *New Weekly*, 16 May 1914.

BOOK REVIEWS
Ideas of Good and Evil, *Weekly Critical Review*, 16 and 23 July 1903.
A Guide to Blake, *Speaker*, 27 May 1905.
The Life of Sir Aglovale de Galis, *Bookman*, November 1905.
Gallienne-cum-Hafiz, *Bookman*, March 1906.
Pure and Applied Topography, *Speaker*, 28 April 1906.
The Synthetic Philosophy in Slippers, *Bookman*, May 1906.
The Church's Dilemma, *Speaker*, 7 July 1906.
Baudelaire, *Bookman*, August 1906.
And Other Papers, *Speaker*, 18 August 1906.
Divers Country Books, *Speaker*, 25 August 1906.
Old Wiltshire, *Speaker*, 20 October 1906.
Literary Rambles in the West of England, *Speaker*, 20 October 1906.
The Gate of Death, *Bookman*, November 1906.
The Moods of Nature, *Daily Mail*, 3 November 1906.
Notes on Novels, *Speaker*, 3 November 1906.
The Beloved Vagabond, *Bookman*, December 1906.
William Blake, *Speaker*, 1 December 1906.
Lachrymae Joculatoris, *Bookman*, January 1907.
The Countryside. Nature with the Camera, *Daily Mail*, 5 January 1907.
Old Wiltshire, *Daily Mail*, 12 January 1907.
Monumental Art, *Daily Mail*, 19 January 1907.
The Poor. As They Really Are, *Daily Mail*, 2 March 1907.
Too Much of a Good Thing, *Bookman*, April 1907.
The Ironworkers, *Daily Mail*, 13 April 1907.
The County of Good Earth, *Daily Mail*, 11 May 1907.
A Voice from the Weald, *Bookman*, June 1907.
The Glen O'Weeping, *Bookman*, June 1907.
A Rael Manxman, *Bookman*, July 1907.
Nature and the Country, *Daily Mail*, 6 July 1907.
By Australasian Seas, *Daily Mail*, 13 July 1907.
Two Old Salts, *Daily Mail*, 13 July 1907.
Our National Literary Debt, *Bookman*, August 1907.
The Gentleman, *Bookman*, September 1907.
The Sport of Speleology, *Bookman*, October 1907.
A Literary History of the Arabs, *Scottish Review*, 7 November 1907.
A Novel of Cruelty, *Bookman*, December 1907.
Mr A.C. Benson Self-Criticised, *Bookman*, December 1907.
The Beliefs of an Agnostic, *Bookman*, March 1908.
An Adventure in Criticism, *Bookman*, June 1908.
Highways and Byways in Hampshire, *Bookman*, June 1908.

A West Country Novel, *Daily News*, 11 June 1908.
Dartmoor Fiction, *Bookman*, August 1908.
Beyond the Pale, *Daily News*, 29 October 1908.
The Life Force, *Daily News*, 5 November 1908.
The Lower Deck, *Daily News*, 17 December 1908.
Mr Wells's Confession, *Bookman*, January 1909.
The Growth of Man and of Nature, *Bookman*, February 1909.
The Life of an Admiral, *Daily News*, 3 March 1909.
Off the Track, *Daily News*, 9 March 1909.
100 Years of the Navy, *Daily News*, 27 April 1909.
Gatling-Gun Philosophy, *Bookman*, May 1909.
Essays and Impressions, *Daily News*, 5 May 1909.
Progress by Panic, *Daily News*, 24 May 1909.
The Defence of England, *Daily News*, 4 June 1909.
Chronicles of Inefficiency, *Daily News*, 24 June 1909.
Seafaring Novels, *Daily News*, 28 July 1909.
Novels of the Sea, *Daily News*, 25 August 1909.
The Nature of Freedom, *Bookman*, January 1911.
Bergson and About Bergson, *Bookman*, January 1912.
The Dead End, *New Weekly*, 21 March 1914.

CONCERT REVIEW
The Colonne Concert, *Weekly Critical Review*, 22 January 1903.

LETTERS TO THE NATIONAL PRESS
The Coastguard and the Longshore Fisheries, *The Times*, 27 March 1908.
The Poor and Education, *Spectator*, 5 February 1910.
A Forecast of the Character of the Coming Era, *New Age*, 2 June 1910. (Letters)
Inshore Fisheries, *The Times*, 5 April 1912.
Share Fishermen and the Insurance Act, *The Times*, 27 May 1912. (SS. Cheap edition)
The Lower Deck, *Daily Chronicle*, 2 October 1912.
Harvest Bugs, *Daily Mail*, 1 September 1912.
Wealth and Life, *New Age*, 26 February 1914.
Inshore Fisheries, *The Times*, 10 June 1914.

ARTICLES ETC. ABOUT STEPHEN REYNOLDS

H.W.	Stephen Reynolds at Seacombe, *Bodleian*, March 1909.
Anon.	What the Poor Man Thinks, *Christian Commonwealth*, 22 January 1913.
W. Crabb	Stephen Reynolds, *Manchester Quarterly*, 1926.
E.W. Martin	Writers and Places: 6. Stephen Reynolds and Sidmouth, broadcast in the BBC West of England Home Service at 7.00 p.m. on 17 August 1947.

J.D. Osborne Stephen Reynolds, a biographical and critical study. Unpublished thesis, 1977.
You Might Be The Man, *London Magazine,* October 1979.
Stephen Reynolds, *Report and Transactions of the Devonshire Association* Vol.111, 1979.
Introduction to *A Poor Man's House,* London Magazine Editions 1980.
Conrad and Stephen Reynolds, *Conradiana* 13, 1981.

Roy Hattersley Introduction to *A Poor Man's House,* Oxford University Press, 1982.

Tim Laycock *A Poor Man's House,* a play with music, performed at the Manor Pavilion, Sidmouth 5 and 6 August 1992.

Anne Born Stephen Reynolds, Sidmouth's Adopted Son, *Report and Transactions of the Devonshire Association* Vol.125, 1993.

There are entries for Stephen Reynolds in *Books in General* by Solomon Eagle (J.C. Squire), Third Series, Hodder & Stoughton, 1921; *The New Cambridge Bibliography of English Literature,* Volume 4, 1900-1950, Cambridge University Press, 1972; *Writers on the South-West Coast* by Eric Bird and Lilian Modlock, Ex Libris Press, 1994; *Edwardian Fiction, An Oxford Companion* by Sandra Kemp, Charlotte Mitchell and David Trotter, Oxford University Press, 1997 (including a separate entry for *The Holy Mountain*).

General Bibliography

Ackerley, J.R., *My Father and Myself*, Pimlico, 1992.

Aflalo, F.G., *The Sea-Fishing Industry of England and Wales*, Edward Stanford 1904.

Aguillon, Louis, *L'École des Mines de Paris: Notre Historique*, Paris, 1889.

Anson, Peter F., *Fishermen and Fishing Ways*, EP Publishing, 1975.

Arnim, Elizabeth von, *Elizabeth and her German Garden*, Virago, 1985.

Babington Smith, Constance, *John Masefield: A Life*, Oxford University Press, 1978

Baines, Jocelyn, *Joseph Conrad: A Critical Biography*, Weidenfeld & Nicolson, 1959.

Bates, H.E., *Edward Garnett*, Max Parrish, 1950.

Bell, Florence, Lady, *At the Works: A Study of a Manufacturing Town*, Edward Arnold, 1907.

Belloc, Hilaire, *The Cruise of the "Nona"*, Constable, 1925.

Bennett, Arnold, *The Journals*, Penguin, 1971.

Benson, Arthur Christopher, *The House of Quiet: An Autobiography*, John Murray, 1904.

Bergson, Henri, *Mind-Energy: Lectures & Essays*, Macmillan, 1920.
L'évolution créatrice, Quadrige, 1996.

Berry, Les, and Gerald Gosling, *Around Sidmouth*, Chalford, 1994.

Bird, Eric, and Lilian Modlock, *Writers on the South-West Coast*, Ex Libris Press, 1994.

Bolitho, Hector, *Alfred Mond, First Lord Melchett*, Martin Secker, 1933.

Bompas, George C., *Life of Frank Buckland*, Smith, Elder, 1888.

Boulter, S., *History of All Saints' School, Bloxham, 1860-1910*, Bloxham, 1910.

Boulton, James T., (edited), *The Letters of D.H.Lawrence, Vol 1 Sept.1901 – May 1913*, Cambridge University Press, 1979.

Bradby, Edward, *The Book of Devizes: The Life Story of an Ancient Borough*, Barracuda Books, 1985.

Bray, Rising, *I Give You Sidmouth*, Market Press, no date.

Buckland, Frank, *Log-book of a Fisherman and Zoologist*, Chapman & Hall, 1875.

Burgess, G.H.O., *The Curious World of Frank Buckland*, John Baker, 1967.

Burkhardt, G.N., The School of Chemistry in the University of Manchester (Faculty of Science), *Journal of Royal Institute of Chemistry*, September 1954.

Buxton, David, *Around Devizes in Old Photographs*, Alan Sutton, 1990.

Calder-Marshall, Arthur, *Havelock Ellis*, Hart-Davis, 1959.

Carew, Anthony, *The lower deck of the Royal Navy, 1900-1939: The Invergordon mutiny in perspective*, Manchester University Press, 1981.

Carpenter, Edward, *My Days And Dreams*, Allen & Unwin, 1916.
Charteris, Evan, *The Life and Letters of Sir Edmund Gosse*, Heinemann, 1931.
Chesnau, Gabriel, *Notre École: Histoire de l'École des Mines*, Paris, 1931.
Clark, Leonard, *Alfred Williams: his life and work*, William George, 1945.
Clements, Keith, *Henry Lamb: the artist and his friends*, Redcliffe Press, 1985.
Collier, Richard, *The Plague of the Spanish Lady: The Influenza Pandemic of 1918–1919*, Allison & Busby, 1974.
Conrad, Boris, *My Father: Joseph Conrad*, Calder & Boyars, 1970.
Conrad, Jessie, *Joseph Conrad and his Circle*, Jarrolds, 1935.
Conrad, John, *Joseph Conrad: times remembered*, Cambridge University Press, 1981.
Crosby, Alfred W., *America's Forgotten Pandemic: The Influenza of 1918*, Cambridge University Press, 1989.
Curle, Richard, *Caravansary and Conversation: Memories of Places and Persons*, Jonathan Cape, 1937.
Dangerfield, George, *The Strange Death of Liberal England*, Serif, 1997.
Davies, W.H., *Later Days*, Jonathan Cape, 1927.
Delavenay, Émile, *D.H. Lawrence and Edward Carpenter: A Study in Edwardian Transition*, Heinemann, 1971.
Douglas, Norman, *Looking Back: An Autobiographical Excursion*, Chatto & Windus, 1934.
Drabble, Margaret, *Arnold Bennett: A Biography*, Weidenfeld & Nicolson, 1974.
Dupré, Catherine, *John Galsworthy: A Biography*, Collins, 1976.
Eckert, Robert P., *Edward Thomas: A Biography and a Bibliography*, Dent, 1937.
Ellis, Havelock, *My Life*, Heinemann, 1940.
Ellis, Sheila, *Down a Cobbled Street: The story of Clovelly*, Badger Books, 1997.
Ellmann, Richard, *Oscar Wilde*, Hamish Hamilton, 1987.
Elwin, Malcolm, (edited), *J.C.Powys: Letters to his brother Llewelyn 1902-25*, Village Press, 1975.
Ensor, R.C.K., *England 1870–1914*, Oxford University Press, 1936.
Farjeon, Eleanor, *Edward Thomas: The Last Four Years*, Sutton, 1997.
Farr, Diana, *Gilbert Cannan: A Georgian Prodigy*, Chatto & Windus, 1978.
Fayle, C. Ernest, *Harold Wright: A Memoir*, Allen & Unwin, 1934.
Charles Wright: A Memoir, Allen & Unwin, 1943.
Fisheries in the Great War, being the Report on Sea Fisheries for the years 1915,1916,1917 and 1918 of the Board of Agriculture and Fisheries, Cmd.585, HMSO, 1920.
Ford, Ford Madox, *Return to Yesterday*, Carcanet, 1999.
Garnett, David, *The Golden Echo*, Chatto & Windus, 1953.
(edited), *The Letters of T.E. Lawrence*, Spring Books, 1964.
Great Friends: Portraits of seventeen writers, Macmillan, 1979.
Garnett, Edward, *The Breaking Point: A Censured Play*, Duckworth, 1907.
(edited), *Letters from John Galsworthy 1900-1932*, Jonathan Cape, 1934.
Garnett, Richard, *Constance Garnett: A Heroic Life*, Sinclair-Stevenson, 1991.

Gillman, R.D., *Popular Guide to Devizes and Its District*, Devizes, 1906.
Girvan, John, *Devizes in Focus*, Picton Publishing, 1989.
Gissing, George, *The Private Papers of Henry Ryecroft*, edited Mark Storey, Oxford University Press, 1987.
Goldring, Douglas, *Reputations: Essays in Criticism*, Chapman & Hall, 1920.
South Lodge: Reminiscences of Violet Hunt, Ford Madox Ford and the English Review Circle, Constable, 1943.
Grant Watson, E.L., *But To What Purpose*, Cresset Press, 1946.
Green, Henry, Edward Garnett, *New Statesman*, 30 December 1950.
Halévy, Elie, (translated E.I.Watkin), *The Rule of Democracy 1905–1914*, Ernest Benn, 1961.
Harris, Wilson, *J.A. Spender*, Cassell, 1946.
Hart-Davis, Rupert, *Hugh Walpole: A Biography*, Sutton, 1997.
Hartog, Mabel, *P.J. Hartog: A Memoir by his wife*, Constable 1949.
Hartog, P.J., (edited), *The Owens College Manchester: A Brief History of the College and Description of its various Departments*, Manchester, J.E.Cornish, 1900.
Havighurst, Alfred F., *Radical Journalist: H.W.Massingham* (1860-1924), Cambridge University Press, 1974.
Head, Anthony, (edited), *The Letters of John Cowper Powys to Philippa Powys*, Cecil Woolf, 1996.
Heilbrun, Carolyn G., *The Garnett Family*, Allen & Unwin, 1961.
Hepburn, James, (edited), *Letters of Arnold Bennett: Vol.1. Letters to J.B.Pinker*, Oxford University Press, 1966. *Vol.2. 1889–1915*, Oxford University Press, 1968.
The Author's Empty Purse and The Rise of the Literary Agent, Oxford University Press, 1968.
(edited), *Arnold Bennett: The Critical Heritage*, Routledge & Kegan Paul, 1981.
Hérubel, M.A., (translated B.Miall), *Sea Fisheries, their treasures and toilers*, T. Fisher Unwin, 1912.
Hopkins, Eric, *Charles Masterman (1873-1927), politician and journalist: the splendid failure*, Edwin Mellen Press, 1999.
Hueffer, Ford Madox, *The Soul of London*, Alston Rivers, 1905.
Hunt, Violet, *The Flurried Years*, Hurst & Blackett, 1926.
Hynes, Samuel, *The Edwardian Turn of Mind*, Pimlico, 1991.
Jefferson, George, *Edward Garnett: A Life in Literature*, Jonathan Cape, 1982.
Jenkins, Roy, *Asquith*, Papermac, 1994.
Karl, Frederick R., and Laurence Davies, (edited), *The Collected Letters of Joseph Conrad, Vol.3 1903–1907, Vol.4 1908–1911, Vol.5 1912–1916*, Cambridge University Press, 1988, 1990 and 1996.
Keating, Peter, (edited), *Into Unknown England 1866–1913: Selections from the Social Explorers*, Fontana, 1976.
The Haunted Study: A Social History of the English Novel 1875–1914, Secker & Warburg, 1989.
Kite, Edward, *The Bear Hotel Devizes: Some Notes on its History*, Mendip Press,

1931.
Koss, S.E., *Fleet Street Radical: A.G.Gardiner and the Daily News*, Allen Lane, 1973.
Kemp, Sandra, Charlotte Mitchell, David Trotter, *Edwardian Fiction: An Oxford Companion*, Oxford University Press, 1997.
Lane, Reginald, *Old Sidmouth*, Devon Books, 1995.
Lauder, Rosemary Anne, and Michael Williams, *Strange Stories From Devon*, Bossiney Books, 1982.
Leslie, Robert C., *A Waterbiography*, Ashford Press, 1985.
Letters from W.H. Hudson to Edward Garnett, Dent, 1925.
Loane, M.E., *The Next Street but One*, Edward Arnold, 1907.
Lownie, Andrew, *John Buchan: The Presbyterian Cavalier*, Canongate, 1995.
Louÿs, Pierre, *Aphrodite*, Éditions Gallimard, 1992.
Mackerness, E.D., (edited), *The Journals of George Sturt*, Cambridge University Press, 1967.
MacShane, Frank, *The Life and Work of Ford Madox Ford*, New York, Horizon Press, 1965.
Marrot, H.V., *The Life and Letters of John Galsworthy*, Heinemann, 1935.
Marshall, Archibald, *Out and About*, John Murray, 1933.
Martin, E.W., *A Wanderer in the West Country*, Phoenix House, 1951.
Martin, Wallace, *The New Age under Orage*, Manchester University Press, 1967.
Masterman, C.F.G., *The Condition of England*, Methuen 1909.
Masterman, Lucy, *C.F.G. Masterman: A Biography*, Nicholson & Watson, 1939.
Meyers, Jeffrey, *Joseph Conrad: A Biography*, New York, Scribner's, 1991.
Homosexuality and Literature 1890–1930, Athlone Press, 1977.
Mizener, Arthur, *The Saddest Story: A Biography of Ford Madox Ford*, Bodley Head, 1972.
Moore, John, *The Life and Letters of Edward Thomas*, Heinemann, 1939.
Morton, J.B., *Hilaire Belloc: A Memoir*, Hollis & Carter, 1955.
Morgan, Charles, *The House of Macmillan*, Macmillan, 1944.
Mottram, R.H., *For Some We Loved: An Intimate Portrait of Ada and John Galsworthy*, Hutchinson, 1956.
Najder, Zdzislaw, *Joseph Conrad: A Chronicle*, Cambridge University Press, 1983.
Nelson, James G., *The Early Nineties: A View from the Bodley Head*, Harvard University Press, 1971.
Nowell Smith, S., (edited), *Edwardian England*, Oxford University Press, 1964.
Owens College Jubilee, Manchester, Sherratt & Hughes, 1901.
Pelling, H., *Popular Politics and Society in Late Victorian Britain*, Macmillan, 1968.
Plumptre, George, *Edward VII*, Pavilion, 1995.
Pound, Reginald and Geoffrey Harmsworth, *Northcliffe*, Cassell, 1959.
Powell, Anthony, *Under Review: Further Writings on Writers 1946–1989*, Heinemann, 1991.
Powys, Philippa, "Phoenix *or* Driven Passion", unpublished typescript, 1928.
Read, Donald, *Edwardian England 1901-15: Society and Politics*, Harrap, 1972.
Documents from Edwardian England, Harrap, 1973.

Reconstruction Problems 29, British Fishermen and the Nation, Ministry of Reconstruction, HMSO 1919.
Report of the Committee appointed to consider applications of the Devon and Cornwall Local Fisheries Committees for grants from the Development Fund for assisting fishermen to instal motor power in their boats and for other purposes, Cd.6752, HMSO, 1913.
Report of the Departmental Committee on Inshore Fisheries, Cd.7373, HMSO, 1914.
Report of the Development Commissioners for the year ended 31 March 1920, HMSO, 1920, especially Chapter XIV, The Inshore Fisheries.
Reports on Public Health and Medical Subjects No.4, Report on the Pandemic of Influenza 1918–19, Ministry of Health, HMSO, 1920.
Retinger, J.H., *Conrad and his Contemporaries,* Minerva, 1941.
Roberts, Morley, *W.H. Hudson: A Portrait,* Eveleigh Nash & Grayson, 1926.
Saunders, Max, *Ford Madox Ford: A Dual Life,* Oxford University Press, 1996.
Savill, Thomas, *Clinical Lectures on Neurasthenia,* 4th edition, London, 1908.
Schumann, Maurice, *Bergson ou Le retour de Dieu,* Flammarion, 1995.
Scott-James, R.A., Edward Garnett, *Spectator,* 26 February 1937.
Fifty Years of English Literature 1900–1950, Longmans, 1951.
Ford Madox Ford When He Was Hueffer, *South Atlantic Quarterly* 57, Spring 1958.
Selver, Paul, *Orage and the New Age Circle,* Allen & Unwin, 1959.
Sewell, Andrew, "The Reynolds of Devizes", unpublished monograph, 1985.
Shelden, Michael, *Orwell: The Authorised Biography,* Heinemann, 1991.
Smith, Brian S., *A History of Bloxham School,* Bloxham, 1978.
Spender, J.A., *Life, Journalism and Politics,* Cassell, 1927.
Stern, J.P., *Nietzsche,* Fontana, 1978.
Stinton, Judith, *Chaldon Herring: The Powys Circle in a Dorset Village,* Boydell Press, 1988.
Strachey, J. St Loe, *The Adventure of Living,* Hodder & Stoughton, 1922.
Sturt, George, *Memoirs of a Surrey Labourer,* Breslich & Foss, 1983.
The Bettesworth Book, Caliban Books, 1978.
Sutton, Anna, *A Story of Sidmouth,* Exeter, 1959.
Taylor, A.J.P., *English History 1914–1945,* Oxford University Press, 1965.
Taylor, S.J., *The Great Outsiders: Northcliffe, Rothermere and the Daily Mail,* Weidenfeld & Nicolson, 1996.
Thatcher, David S., *Nietzsche in England 1890–1914: the Growth of a Reputation,* University of Toronto Press, 1970.
Thomas, Edward, *Richard Jefferies: His Life and Work,* Hutchinson, 1908.
Thomas, Helen, *Time & Again: memoirs and letters,* Carcanet, 1978.
(with Myfanwy Thomas), *Under Storm's Wing,* Carcanet, 1997.
Thomas, R.George, *Edward Thomas: A Portrait,* Oxford University Press, 1985.
(edited), *Edward Thomas: Selected Letters,* Oxford University Press, 1995.
Thompson, Paul, *The Edwardians: The Remaking of British Society,* Routledge, 1992.

Tomalin, Ruth, *W.H. Hudson*, New York, Philosophical Library, 1954.
Tressell, Robert, *The Ragged Trousered Philanthropists*, Flamingo, 1993.
Ward, G.H., *Supplement to the History of All Saints' School, Bloxham, 1910–1925*, Bloxham, 1925.
Whitman, Walt, *Leaves of Grass*, Siegle, Hill, 1907.
Wilkinson, Oliver, and Christopher Wilkinson, (edited), *The Letters of John Cowper Powys to Frances Gregg*, Cecil Woolf, 1994.
Willcocks, M.P., *The Eyes of the Blind*, Hutchinson, 1917.
Wilson, A.N., *Hilaire Belloc*, Hamish Hamilton, 1984.
Wilson, Harris, (edited), *Arnold Bennett and H.G.Wells: A Record of a Personal and Literary Friendship*, Hart-Davis, 1960.
Yexley, Lionel, *The Inner Life of the Navy*, Pitman, 1908.
Zweig, Paul, *Walt Whitman: The Making of the Poet*, New York, Basic Books, 1984.

Index

The Index covers the text from Prologue to Epilogue, and the notes and references. The most significant entries are highlighted in **bold**. Numbers in square brackets relate to the numbered photographic plates. Numbers in *italic* relate to the page numbers of the maps.

Abbreviations SR Stephen Reynolds; PMH *A Poor Man's House*; HM *The Holy Mountain.*